2.1.5 Advance human rights and social and economic justice: 1–3, 8–10

   a. Understand the forms and mechanisms of oppression and discrimination 2–4, 6, 8–11, 15

   b. Advocate for human rights and social and economic justice 1–3, 6–11, 13, 15, 16

   c. Engage in practices that advance social and economic justice 2, 3, 5, 8, 11, 13, 16

2.1.6 Engage in research-informed practice and practice-informed research: 1

   a. Use practice experience to inform scientific inquiry 2, 13

   b. Use research evidence to inform practice 2, 4, 7, 8, 13, 15

2.1.7 Apply knowledge of human behavior and the social environment: 1, 5

   a. Utilize conceptual frameworks to guide the processes of assessment, intervention, and evaluati 1, 3, 5, 7–9, 13–16

   b. Critique and apply knowledge to understand person and environment 1–6, 8, 9, 12–16

2.1.8 Engage in policy practice to advance social and economic well-being and to deliver effective social work services: 1, 7

   a. Analyze, formulate, and advocate for policies that advance social well-being 2, 4–13, 15, 16

   b. Collaborate with colleagues and clients for effective policy action 2, 4, 5, 7, 8, 10–13, 15

2.1.9 Respond to contexts that shape practice: 1

   a. Continuously discover, appraise, and attend to changing locales, populations, scientific and technological developments, and emerging societal trends to provide relevant services 2–13, 15, 16

   b. Provide leadership in promoting sustainable changes in service delivery and practice to improve the quality of social services 1, 2, 4, 6–8, 11–13, 15

2.1.10 Engage, assess, intervene, and evaluate with individuals, families, groups, organizations and communities: 1, 2, 4, 13–15

   a. Substantively and affectively prepare for action with individuals, families, groups, organizations, and communities 3–5, 14

   b. Use empathy and other interpersonal skills 4, 5, 8 ,12–14

   c. Develop a mutually agreed-on focus of work and desired outcomes 4, 5, 11, 14

   d. Collect, organize, and interpret client data 3–6, 9, 13–16

   e. Assess client strengths and limitations 3, 4, 9, 10, 12–15

   f. Develop mutually agreed-on intervention goals and objectives 1, 4, 10, 11, 14–16

   g. Select appropriate intervention strategies 3–5, 8 –16

   h. Initiate actions to achieve organizational goals 2, 4, 10, 13, 15

   i. Implement prevention interventions that enhance client capacities 3–5, 8, 9, 12, 13, 15, 16

   j. Help clients resolve problems 3, 4, 8–16

   k. Negotiate, mediate, and advocate for clients 1–5, 7, 9–13, 15, 16

   l. Facilitate transitions and endings 4, 10, 12, 15

   m. Critically analyze, monitor, and evaluate interventions 4, 13, 14, 16

For more information about the standards themselves, and for a complete policy statement, visit the Council on Social Work Education website at www.cswe.org.

Adapted with permission from the Council on Social Work Education

Introduction to Social Work & Social Welfare

CRITICAL THINKING PERSPECTIVES

Introduction to Social Work & Social Welfare

CRITICAL THINKING PERSPECTIVES

Brooks/Cole Empowerment Series

FOURTH EDITION

KAREN K. KIRST-ASHMAN

University of Wisconsin–Whitewater

BROOKS/COLE
CENGAGE Learning™

Australia • Brazil • Japan • Korea • Mexico • Singapore • Spain • United Kingdom • United States

Brooks/Cole Empowerment Series:
Introduction to Social Work and Social Welfare: Critical Thinking Perspectives,
Fourth Edition

Karen K. Kirst-Ashman

Publisher: Linda Schreiber-Ganster

Acquisitions Editor: Seth Dobrin

Developmental Editor: Alicia McLaughlin

Editorial Assistant: Suzanna Kincaid

Media Editor: Elizabeth Momb

Marketing Program Manager: Tami Strang

Content Project Manager: Michelle Clark

Art Director: Caryl Gorska

Manufacturing Planner: Judy Inouye

Rights Acquisitions Specialist: Dean Dauphinais

Production and Composition: S4Carlisle Publishing Services

Photo Researcher: PreMedia Global

Text Researcher: PreMedia Global

Copy Editor: Kirsten Balayti

Text Designer: Diane Beasley

Cover Designer: Gia Giasullo

Cover Image: EschCollection Prime/Alamy

For product information and technology assistance, contact us at **Cengage Learning Customer & Sales Support, 1-800-354-9706.**

For permission to use material from this text or product, submit all requests online at **www.cengage.com/permissions.** Further permissions questions can be e-mailed to **permissionrequest@cengage.com.**

Library of Congress Control Number: 2011943251

Student Edition:
ISBN-13: 978-0-8400-2866-2
ISBN-10: 0-8400-2866-0

Loose-leaf Edition:
ISBN-13: 978-1-133-37203-5
ISBN-10: 1-133-37203-1

Brooks/Cole
20 Davis Drive
Belmont, CA 94002-3098
USA

Cengage Learning is a leading provider of customized learning solutions with office locations around the globe, including Singapore, the United Kingdom, Australia, Mexico, Brazil, and Japan. Locate your local office at **www.cengage.com/global.**

Cengage Learning products are represented in Canada by Nelson Education, Ltd.

To learn more about Brooks/Cole, visit **www.cengage.com/brookscole** Purchase any of our products at your local college store or at our preferred online store **www.CengageBrain.com.**

Printed in Canada
1 2 3 4 5 6 7 16 15 14 13 12

To my dear friends Leon and Camille Radomski

About the Author

Karen K. Kirst-Ashman, BSW, MSSW, PhD, has been a full professor and was a former chairperson in the Social Work Department at the University of Wisconsin-Whitewater, where she has taught for 28 years. She is certified as a Licensed Clinical Social Worker in the State of Wisconsin. She earned her BSW degree in 1972 and MSSW in 1973 at the University of Wisconsin—Madison, and her Ph.D. in Social Work at the University of Illinois at Urbana—Champaign. She has worked as a practitioner and administrator in child welfare and mental health agencies. She received the University of Wisconsin-Whitewater's Excellence in Teaching Award in 1986 and the University Outstanding Teaching Award in 2007. She has been a member of the board of directors of the Council on Social Work Education (CSWE) in addition to being an accreditation site visitor. She is also a current member of CSWE, BPD and NASW. She has served on the Editorial Board of *Affilia: Journal of Women and Social Work,* and as a consulting editor for many social work journals including the *Journal of Social Work Education.* She is the author of numerous publications, articles, and reviews concerning social work and women's issues. Other books she has authored or coauthored include *Understanding Human Behavior and the Social Environment* (9th ed.); *Understanding Generalist Practice* (6th ed.); *Human Behavior in the Macro Social Environment: An Empowerment Approach to Understanding Communities, Organization, and Groups* (3rd ed.); *The Macro Skills Workbook* (2nd ed.); and *Generalist Practice with Organizations and Communities* (5th ed.).

Brief Contents

Contents

CHAPTER 7

Policy, Policy Analysis, Policy Practice, and Policy Advocacy: Foundations for Service Provision 211

CHAPTER 8

Policies and Programs to Combat Poverty 235

PART IV
Client Populations and Contexts

CHAPTER 9

Social Work and Services for Children and Families   275

CHAPTER 10

Social Work and Services for Older Adults   311

Preface

Given limited time and massive volumes of content, what vital information should be conveyed to students in an introductory course about social welfare and social work? What student learning outcomes should instructors strive to attain? This text focuses on the most significant elements of social work. Content complies with the new Council on Social Work Education's Educational Policy and Accreditation Standards (EPAS) (CSWE, 2008b). The text's style is intended to be clear, readable, interesting, and engaging. The goal is to enhance students' ability to grasp the essence and spirit of generalist social work and the issues in social welfare that social workers address every day.

Themes integrated throughout the text include these:

- The advancement of human rights and social and economic justice.
- Client empowerment.
- Dimensions of human diversity ("including age, class, color, culture, disability, ethnicity, gender, gender identity and expression, immigration status, political ideology, race, religion, sex, and sexual orientation").[1]
- The significance of professional values and ethics.
- A generalist approach interrelating social work practice with individuals, families, groups, organizations, and communities.

- Numerous case examples dramatizing various aspects of social work.
- Various global and international perspectives.
- Identification of the relationship between the text's content and EPAS competencies and practice behaviors.

A key word describing this text is *integration*: These themes are infused throughout the book instead of being isolated in independent chapters. For example, values, ethics, aspects of diversity, and client empowerment are defined early on and then addressed throughout the text in various contexts including fields of practice. Boxed features appear regularly to emphasize important concepts and cases, to spark students' interest, and to stimulate critical thinking.

The Fundamental Need for Critical Thinking

Critical thinking perspectives provide an underlying foundation for the text. They are stressed throughout by encouraging identification of values and evaluation of serious issues. Critical thinking involves three facets. First, it focuses on the questioning of beliefs, statements, assumptions, lines of reasoning, actions, and experiences. Second, it involves the assessment of the established facts and issues involved by seeking relevant information. This complies with the Council on Social Work Education's (CSWE) current emphasis on "research-informed practice" and "evidence-based interventions" (CSWE, 2008b, p. 5). Third, it concerns asserting an opinion about the validity of the fact or process being considered.

Critical thinking is essential in social work because social workers address a vast range of issues and problems. New accreditation standards require that social workers demonstrate competency in applying "critical thinking to inform and communicate professional judgments" (CSWE, 2008b, EP 2.1.3). Each chapter stresses the use of critical thinking by integrating a basic "Triple A" formula that students can readily comprehend and apply: (1) *ask* questions, (2) *assess* the established facts and issues involved, and (3) *assert* a concluding opinion. Issues addressed range from client rights to social policy to social work roles in a wide array of contexts. Case studies for critical thinking are presented at the end of each of the book's four main sections.

Organization

The book is organized into four major parts: (1) the profession, (2) social work practice, (3) social welfare policy, and (4) client populations and contexts. A fifth section, the epilogue, focuses on personal values and consideration of a social work career. The intent is to give students a broad look at what social work is all about. Social welfare policy is stressed as the foundation of social welfare programs and social work practice. New accreditation standards require that students demonstrate competency in "policy practice," including being able to "analyze, formulate, and advocate for policies that advance social well-being" (CSWE, 2008b, EP 2.1.8). Students are encouraged to explore issues based on theoretical orientations to social welfare policy development and the resulting program implementation.

Students are provided with thought-provoking information about social welfare and social work within a broad range of circumstances and fields of practice. Settings range from those focusing on child maltreatment, to health care, to work with older adults, to corrections. Social issues are raised in a way that encourages new insights and examination of personal values. This book stresses *what* social workers do, not *how* they do it. Abundant case examples give insights into who clients are and what issues they face in the macro social environment.

Concepts incorporated in the new Council on Social Work Education Educational Policy and Accreditation Standards (EPAS), including the concepts of human rights, marginalization, alienation, evidence-based intervention, and policy practice, in addition to the newly articulated aspects of diversity —gender identity and expression, immigration status, and political ideology—are discussed (CSWE, 2008b). Macro aspects of generalist practice, in addition to micro and mezzo aspects, are frequently highlighted.

This book gives students contemplating a social work major a solid orientation to the profession. The text should help students determine whether social work is really the field for them. For nonmajors, the text is designed to provide a sound introduction to social welfare, social work, available services, social welfare policy development and implementation, and social workers' involvement in the helping process. The emphasis is on those issues and fields of practice in which social workers are most likely to be employed. For example, significant attention is given to child and family services, mental health, and health care.

Part 1, "The Profession of Social Work," includes three chapters. Chapter 1 defines social welfare and social work, discusses political values and views about social welfare, reviews content areas in the social work curriculum, introduces the various fields of practice, and reviews the social work career continuum. Critical thinking is defined, and its importance throughout the text is stressed. Chapter 2 focuses on the importance of social work values and ethics, thus providing a framework for remaining chapters. This chapter introduces the concept of ethical dilemmas, summarizes the NASW *Code of Ethics*, gives examples of practice applications, and helps students explore personal values. Chapter 3 defines and discusses various dimensions of human diversity, empowerment, resiliency, and cultural competence, paving the way for integration of this content throughout the book.

Part 2, "Social Work Practice," includes two chapters that focus on what social workers *do*. Chapter 4 defines generalist social work practice, introduces the wide range of social work roles, and describes the planned-change process. Emphases include the importance of client empowerment, appreciation of cultural differences, and intervention with macro systems. Chapter 5 focuses on the settings in which social workers practice, including rural and urban communities. It describes what micro, mezzo, and macro practice involve in terms of social workers' functions and practice settings. Finally, it explores social work licensure, employment, and salaries.

Part 3, "Social Welfare Policy," includes three chapters. Chapter 6 explains the historical development of social welfare and social work, thereby providing a context for the next chapter, which focuses on social welfare policy and policy practice. Chapter 7 defines policy, discusses its significance, and describes how it is developed and structured. The significance of social welfare policy as the basis upon which social programs are developed is stressed. Chapter 8 discusses the infrastructure of policies and programs designed to combat poverty and provide financial assistance to those in need. It also describes social insurance (including the Medicare Prescription Drug Program) and public assistance programs, and explores students' values about various aspects of social welfare.

Part 4, "Client Populations and Contexts," includes eight chapters that focus on specific social work settings. Chapter 9 introduces service provision for children and families. It describes supportive services for children and families, including those involving child maltreatment, intensive family preservation, and child day care. It stresses the importance of addressing macro issues. This chapter also reviews substitute services for children and families, including kinship care, foster family care, residential settings, and adoption.

Chapter 10 discusses social work with older adults. Issues include common problems facing older adults, critical thinking about Social Security, the global context for aging, contexts of social work practice with older adults, and empowerment for diverse populations of older adults.

Chapter 11 explores social work with people who have disabilities. Ethical implications for social work practice are discussed. Empowerment through policy practice and advocacy, legislative advocacy, and community support are stressed.

Chapter 12 explains social work roles in health care, health-care problems in the macro environment, issues involving health-care policy, managed care, and international perspectives on the global crisis of AIDS. Sensitivity to populations-at-risk and macro issues in practice are emphasized.

Chapter 13 addresses social work and mental health. Employment settings in mental health for social workers are identified, social work functions are explained, and clients' conditions are described. Managed care in mental health is critiqued, and cultural competence in the field is examined.

Chapter 14 explores alcohol and other drug abuse (AODA). It describes AODA terms, methods of ingestion, types of substances, the development and personal dynamics of abuse, the family dynamics

involved, the treatment process, treatment approaches, two treatment models, and available resources for treatment.

Chapter 15 focuses on social work with youths and in the schools. Positive social programming in macro practice, violence in the schools, bullying, and teenage sexual activity and pregnancy are examined. Social work roles with respect to each are discussed.

Chapter 16 explores social work and corrections. Questions requiring critical thinking are posed regarding the complexity of the crime rate, the issue of punishment versus empowerment, and health care for prisoners. Practice settings and gang membership are also discussed.

The epilogue, "Your Values and Your Future: Applying Critical Thinking Skills," serves as a capstone for the book. Students are urged to come to conclusions about various issues in social welfare policy and programming. Finally, they are encouraged to evaluate their personal characteristics and values and their potential for a career in social work, responding to many questions initiated in Chapter 1.

Relationship Between Content and the Educational Policy and Accreditation Standards [EPAS], and Professional Competencies

This book addresses accreditation standards established by the Council on Social Work Education (CSWE).[2] Our intent is to facilitate programs' ability to link content provided in this textbook with expectations for student learning and accomplishment. As is true in almost all learning, students must acquire knowledge before they are expected to apply it to practice situations.

CSWE has identified 41 practice behaviors that operationalize 10 core competencies that are critical for professional practice (CSWE, 2008b). For clarity, we have alphabetized in lowercase the practice behaviors under each competency. **"Helping Hands" icons** located within paragraphs clearly show the linkage between content in the textbook and specific practice behaviors and competencies. Each icon is labeled with

---

[2]Please note that this content addresses standards posed in the EPAS. In no way does it claim to verify compliance with standards. Only the Council on Social Work Education Commission on Accreditation can make those determinations.

the specific practice behavior or competency that relates directly to the content conveyed in the paragraph. For example, an icon might be labeled EP [Educational Policy] 2.1.2, which is the competency, "apply social work ethical principles to guide professional practice" (CSWE, 2008b). Accredited social work programs are required to prove that students have mastered all practice behaviors for competence as specified in the EPAS. (Please refer to http://www.cswe.org for the EPAS document.)

For all icons "**Competency Notes**" are provided at the end of each chapter. These Competency Notes explain the relationship between chapter content and CSWE's practice behaviors and competencies. They also list page numbers where icons are located and this content is discussed. A summary chart of the icons' locations in all chapters and their respective competency or practice behavior is placed in the inside front covers of the book.

A new **Practice Behaviors Workbook** has replaced the Student Manual for this edition. The experiential exercises provided here give students opportunities to develop the practice behaviors in class or as part of their homework, facilitating their mastery over practical aspects of social work and minimizing the need for programs to develop additional assessments.

New to This Edition

In addition to updating subject matter throughout, other new and expanded content in this edition includes the following:

Chapter 1
- Introduction of the concept of sustainability on a global level

Chapter 2
- An example of a strategy of ethical reasoning to arrive at principled decisions
- Discussion of ethical conflicts for military social workers during combat

Chapter 3
- A highlight summarizing the definitions of terms characterizing diversity
- Examination of the concept of intersectionality
- Updated statistics on the economic status of African Americans and women
- Description of Klinefelter's syndrome

- Discussion of terms often used in connection with the word *Muslim*, including Arab American and Middle Eastern

Chapter 4
- Discussion of the use of consultation
- Explanation of the negotiator role
- Discussion of professional identity and conduct
- Examination of the concept of sustainability and the process and practice of social work

Chapter 5
- A case example of a dual relationship in a rural community where a strategy is applied to arrive at ethical decisions
- New content on practice with individuals involving interviewing
- Additional content on treatment groups
- New content on task groups, including staff development groups, cabinets, boards of directors, and coalitions
- New content on practice with organizations and communities including "social advocacy," "planning and policy practice," and "community capacity development" (Rothman, 2007, p. 12)
- Updated categories for NASW professional Social Work Credentials and Advanced Practice Specialty Credentials

Chapter 6
- Discussion of the Voting Rights Act of 1965
- New content on the "housing bubble" and the Great Recession
- Discussion of people living in poverty and their problems with credit
- Coverage of Barack Obama's presidency

Chapter 7
- New case example demonstrating innovative policy practice

Chapter 8
- New and revised content on Temporary Assistance to Needy Families (TANF)
- New content on the Children's Health Insurance Program (CHIP)

Chapter 9
- Update on gay marriage, including new content on the international picture

- New content on psychological maltreatment
- Discussion of assessment of family strength and resiliency in child maltreatment cases
- New content on cultural competence, including questions that investigate the cultural perspectives of children and their families

Chapter 10
- Presentation of an empowerment perspective for working with older adults that incorporates values and goals, in addition to exploring and providing case examples of active aging
- An example of adult day care for Chinese Americans
- A new case example portraying social work roles

Chapter 11
- Updated discussion of the use of language for people with intellectual disabilities
- New and expanded content on autistism spectrum disorders
- Coverage of the Individuals with Disabilities Education Improvement Act

Chapter 12
- Discussion of the relationship between social class and health care
- Discussion of the Patient Protection and Affordable Care Act of 2010
- Coverage of new HIV testing and treatment approaches

Chapter 13
- Significant expansion of coverage concerning veterans with posttraumatic stress disorder
- Updated and new content on anorexia and bulimia
- Summaries of existential, person-centered, and behavioral therapy

Chapter 14
- Description of GHB, a "date rape drug"
- A summary of AA's 12 steps

Chapter 15
- Discussion of advocacy for culturally competent policies and practices in schools
- Discussion of advocacy on the behalf of refugee and immigrant students

- Discussion of the advantages of establishing groups in schools
- Coverage of protective factors that decrease the risk of school violence
- New statistics on youth violence
- Coverage of bullying and cyberbullying
- Updated statistics on teen sexual activity

Chapter 16
- Updated crime statistics
- Additional content on domestic violence, including emotional abuse
- New content on working with gangs

Ancillaries

Additional resources are available, including a Practice Behaviors Workbook filled with classroom exercises and assignments. These are designed to coincide directly with text content and can be used to help students integrate reading material. The intent is to help students organize the material and take notes if they so choose.

Also available is Cengage Learning's Social Work CourseMate that includes interactive learning, study, and exam preparation tools that support the textbook. CourseMate includes an integrated eBook, videos, quizzes, flashcards, and more, and EngagementTracker, a tool that monitors student engagement in the course. The accompanying instructor website offers access to password-protected resources such as an electronic version of the instructor's manual, test bank, and PowerPoint® slides. Students can access CourseMate through www.cengagebrain.com and instructors can access the accompanying instructor site through login.cengage.com.

My sincere hope is that students will find this text interesting and informative, and that instructors will find it an easy one from which to teach. The intent is to provide a sound foundation on which to build professional expertise and commitment.

Acknowledgments

This book is possible due to the dedication and hard work of many people. I express my sincere appreciation to Seth Dobrin, Acquisitions Editor, for his consistent enthusiastic encouragement and conscientious help. I wish to thank Alicia McLaughlin, Developmental Editor, and Suzanna Kincaid, Editorial Assistant, for their wholehearted help and support.

Many thanks go to Tami Stang, Marketing Program Manager, who provided imaginative ideas and innovative approaches for marketing the book. Heartfelt appreciation is extended to Vicki Vogel, who creatively developed all the ancillary materials and provided me with help and constructive feedback whenever I requested it (which was often). Thanks also to Karen Thomson, who did an excellent job assisting her. Many thanks are extended to Christian Holdener, Project Editor, who did an amazing job of coordinating the day-to-day editing and production process. Much gratitude goes to Michelle Clark, Content Project Manager, who oversaw the production process and made certain it progressed smoothly and efficiently. I also want to thank the following reviewers of this book for their help and input:

Ivette Barbosa, Indiana University—Purdue;
Barbara Horcha, Mott Community College;
Samuel Gioia, Portland State University;
Carlene Quinn, Indiana Univeristy;
Barbara Barton, Western Michigan University.

My most sincere thanks go to Gary A. Kirst, MSW, and Ruth Kirst, who provided me with ongoing support and encouragement. I also want to thank Gary S. Kirst for his input concerning the Turkana Tribe in Northern Kenya. Thankful recognition is also extended to my delightful nieces and nephews, who bring so much joy and inspiration to my life. Finally, I express my sincere gratitude and appreciation to Nick Ashman, who provided incredible support and encouragement throughout the 28-year process since this book's inception.

PART ONE

THE PROFESSION OF SOCIAL WORK

What is social work? How does it differ from sociology, psychology, or other types of counseling? What types of people choose it as a career? This book answers these and many other questions you might have about what social workers do, what rules and policies they must follow, and whom they serve.

This book has four parts:

1. The Profession of Social Work
2. Social Work Practice
3. Social Welfare Policy
4. Client Populations and Contexts

Part 1 contains three chapters that emphasize key aspects of social work and provide a general introduction to the field. Chapter 1 defines social work and social welfare and discusses various theoretical perspectives you can use to think about how to help people. It introduces you to the concept of critical thinking, which will be emphasized throughout the book. It also describes the content areas in the social work curriculum.

Chapter 2 focuses on social work values and ethics. It summarizes social work's ethical principles and practitioners' ethical responsibilities to clients. It also challenges you to examine your own personal values and how they relate to social work values. Finally, it examines a range of ethical dilemmas potentially facing social workers.

Chapter 3 explores human diversity and the ways in which people might be empowered to enhance their well-being and reach their full potential. It stresses social work's quest for social and economic justice, especially for populations-at-risk of deprivation and oppression. Populations-at-risk include groups characterized by diverse aspects of race, ethnicity, color, culture, class, immigration status, political ideology, gender, gender identity and expression, sexual orientation, age, disability, and religion.

I hope you will enjoy this book and gain a much better understanding of social work and social welfare. Let's begin.

CHAPTER 1

Introduction to Social Work and Social Welfare

Ariel Skelley/Blend Images/Getty Images

Case A: *The couple is ecstatic. In their early 30s, they have been struggling with infertility for almost a decade and have been languishing on a waiting list to adopt a baby for almost five years. The moment has finally almost come: They will soon meet their new baby, Juliette. Alani, their social worker in the adoptions unit at a family services agency, is assisting them in completing the paperwork and helping them launch their new family life.*

Case B: *Cassius, a social worker at a community mental health center, is about to start the weekly support group session. His seven clients all are dealing with spouses who have Lou Gehrig's disease, which is characterized by deterioration of neurons in the brainstem and spinal cord. It involves loss of muscle function, paralysis, and finally death. The purpose of the group is to provide mutual emotional support and share information about coping with the disease. Cassius facilitates the group to* *keep things moving along and, when necessary, gives information about the disease. He notices that Erica, one of his clients, seems to be struggling to hold back a flood of tears. He knows that her husband, Tom, is deteriorating rapidly, so she must have had a rough week. This may be a difficult session.*

Case C: Lolita is exhilarated. Several hundred people have shown up for and are eagerly participating in this "Take Back the Night" march against sexual assault. Lolita, a social worker at a rape crisis center, was one of the primary organizers of the event. The march's intent is to raise people's consciousness about this serious issue, promote education about sexual assault, and increase funding for crisis centers.

These vignettes portray brief moments in the actual lives of social workers. Some moments may be tremendously difficult, and others enormously satisfying.

When you think of social work, what comes to mind? Helping people? Being on welfare? Facing bureaucratic red tape? Solving problems? Saving children? What do social workers actually do?

I once visited a quaint little crafts shop in Bar Harbor, Maine. It had little shadow boxes, about five inches square, filled with tacks. On these tacks, someone had painted little symbols to reflect the tools, tasks, and people involved in various professions. For example, one shadow box reflecting dentistry had tacks painted with tiny teeth, big toothy smiles, and toothbrushes (which is probably no surprise). I managed to find a box for social work. What do you think was painted on those tacks?

There were tiny images of the following: a Kleenex® box, a pencil, a compact car, a smiling face, a watch, and a heart. What do you think each of these are supposed to mean?

Here are some ideas. The Kleenex box reflects how social workers help people deal with tough, and frequently very sad, issues. Sometimes clients are hurting badly, and sometimes they cry. The pencil signifies record keeping and paperwork, a mainstay of what social workers do. It probably should have been a computer, but the artist most likely couldn't fit one on that little tack. The compact car symbolizes travel because social workers often must visit clients' homes and other agencies. The smiling face signifies how social workers aim to help people solve their problems, to seek social justice on their behalf, and to make their lives a little bit better. (Social justice involves the concept that all citizens should be treated equally and have equal access to resources.) The watch reflects scheduling—there's always a lot to do and limited time in which to do it. Finally, the heart symbolizes caring about the welfare of others: That's the core of what the social work profession is all about.

Learning Objectives

A Define social work and social welfare.
B Explain critical thinking and provide a framework for examining a wide range of concepts and issues.

C Discuss residual, institutional, and developmental perspectives on social welfare, as well as the concept of sustainability.

D Explain the conservative–liberal continuum with respect to viewing the social welfare system.

E Examine your personal attitudes about some social welfare issues.

F Explain social work's fields of practice.

G Explore the process of choosing a career.

H Address how social work builds on other disciplines.

I Discuss the uniqueness of social work.

J Identify some basic concepts in systems theories and the ecological perspective that are important for understanding social work.

K Describe social work education's goals, curriculum, and competencies.

[Note that **"helping hands" icons** of two hands embracing a sun are located next to the learning objectives just cited and other content throughout the book. Accredited social work programs must demonstrate that they're teaching students to be proficient in 10 core competencies that are operationalized by 41 practice behaviors designated by the Council on Social Work Education (CSWE) Educational Policy and Accreditation Standards (EPAS). Students require knowledge in order to develop skills and become competent. Our intent here is to specify what chapter content and knowledge coincides with the development of specific competencies and practice behaviors. (This ultimately is intended to assist in a social work program's accreditation process.)

Throughout each chapter, icons such as those located on this page call attention to the location of EPAS-related content. Each icon identifies what competency or practice behavior is relevant by specifying the designated Educational Policy (EP) reference number beneath it. "Competency Notes" are provided at the end of each chapter that describe how EPAS competencies and practice behaviors are related to designated content in the chapter. EPAS competencies and practice behaviors are cited in the inside covers of this book. A summary chart indicating where icons are located throughout the book along with their respective competencies and practice behaviors is placed after the Table of Contents in the front of the book.

The EPAS document lists practice behaviors under each of the 10 core competencies as bulleted items. To clarify the "Competency Notes" at the end of each chapter, the bulleted practice behaviors have been alphabetized under each competency. Please observe that for EP 2.1.10, only the bulleted practice behaviors are labeled "a" through "m" (not the "engagement," "assessment," "intervention," and "evaluation" subcategories identified in EP 2.1.10). Practice behaviors are alphabetized both under the icons placed throughout the book and in the "competency notes" cited in each chapter.]

What Is Social Work?

The National Association of Social Work (NASW) defines *social work* as follows:

Social work is the professional activity of helping individuals, groups, or communities enhance or restore their capacity for social functioning and creating societal conditions favorable to this goal. Social work practice consists of the professional application of social work values, principles, and techniques to one or more of the following ends:

- *Helping people obtain tangible services (e.g., those involving provision of food, housing, or income).*
- *Providing counseling and psychotherapy with individuals, families, and groups.*
- *Helping communities or groups provide or improve social and health services.*
- *Participating in relevant legislative processes. (NASW, 1973, pp. 4–5)*

What does this really mean? Imagine the vast range of human problems and issues. Because social workers can be in positions to help people deal with almost anything, it is difficult to define the field adequately in a few words. Highlighted here are some of the important concepts inherent in the definition just cited. Because of its breadth, the foundation of social work practice is referred to as *generalist practice,* described more thoroughly in Chapter 4.

Five themes permeate social work practice in virtually any setting (e.g., child welfare agencies, nursing homes, schools, or corrections facilities). First, social work concerns helping individuals, groups, or communities. Social workers provide counseling when necessary to help clients address problems. In addition to counseling an individual or family, much social work involves collaborating with organizations and communities to improve social and health services. Second, social work entails a solid foundation of values and principles that guide what practitioners should and should not do. Third, a firm basis of techniques and skills provides directions for *how* social workers should provide treatment and accomplish goals. Fourth, social workers help people get the services they need by linking them to available

resources. If the right resources are not available, social workers may advocate for service development on their clients' behalf. Fifth, social workers participate in legislative processes to promote positive social change. Such participation might include urging lawmakers to pass laws that improve social services and conditions. Social workers can also serve as expert witnesses to educate legislators about social issues and client needs, write or phone legislators to share socially responsible opinions, and run for elected office themselves.

NASW reports how Representative Bob Etheridge (D–N.C.) paid homage to social workers during Social Work Month (March 2001). He shared with the speaker of the U.S. House of Representatives the following remarks:

Social workers affect our lives in so many ways.... Their work touches all of us as individuals and as whole communities. They are educated, highly trained, and committed professionals. They work in family service and community mental health agencies, schools, hospitals, nursing homes, and many other private and public agencies. They listen, they care. And most importantly, they help those in need.

(Vallianatos, 2001, May, p. 1)

What Is Social Welfare?

What does the term *social welfare* mean? And exactly whose welfare are we talking about? Answers to these questions require critical thinking because, as a citizen and voter, your opinions are vital. You have the opportunity to help determine and shape how you and others are treated, how your own and their welfare is respected and nurtured.

A central theme of this book is encouraging you to think critically about problems, issues, and policies affecting people's lives and welfare. Highlight 1.1 defines critical thinking and provides a basic framework for analysis.

Social welfare is "a nation's system of programs, benefits, and services that help people meet those social, economic, educational, and health needs that are fundamental to the maintenance of society" (Barker, 2003, p. 408). Social welfare, then, is a broad concept related to the general well-being of all people in a society. Inherent in the definition are two basic dimensions: (1) what people get from society (in terms of programs, benefits, and services) and (2) how well their needs (including social, economic, educational, and health) are being met.

Reid (1995) describes social welfare as "an idea, that idea being one of a decent society that provides opportunities for work and human meaning, provides reasonable security from want and assault, promotes fairness and evaluation based on individual merit, and is economically productive and stable" (p. 2206).

How are social welfare and social work related? Simply put, *social work* serves to improve people's social and economic welfare. It does so in the many fields or settings discussed in this book, including health, mental health, and financial assistance, among many others. Populations served include older adults, children and families, people with disabilities, and people involved with the legal system.

Note that social work is not the only field concerned with people's social welfare. Others include those providing health, educational, recreational, and public safety services. Physicians, nurses, other health-care personnel, teachers, park recreational counselors, police, firefighters, and many others work to enhance people's well-being and quality of life.

Social welfare can be quite controversial on two counts. One involves individuals' responsibility to take care of themselves independently of government, which reflects the old saying "You get what you deserve." The other concerns society's responsibility to take care of all its members, especially those belonging to oppressed groups. There is constant political debate about what social services should and should not provide, and about who should receive them and who should not.

The following section explores various perspectives that structure how you might think about social welfare. Each addresses the following questions: What should be the most important focus and goals of social welfare? Who should assume responsibility for people's social welfare?

Residual, Institutional, and Developmental Perspectives on Social Welfare

We can look at social welfare and the ways its programs are developed from three different perspectives—residual, institutional, and developmental

(Dobelstein, 2003; Gilbert & Terrell, 2010; Herrick, 2008; E.A. Segal, 2010; Wilensky & Lebeaux, 1965). The *residual perspective* conceives of social welfare as focusing on problems and gaps. Social welfare benefits and services should be supplied

**EP 2.1.7a,
2.1.7b**

only when people fail to provide adequately for themselves and problems arise. The implication is that it's people's own fault if they require outside help. Society, then, must aid them until they can once again assume responsibility for meeting their own needs. Blaming women and children for being "on welfare," for example, reflects a residual view. The focus is on their supposed failures and faults; they are viewed in a demeaning and critical manner.

The *institutional* perspective of social welfare, in contrast, views people's needs as a normal part of life. Society has a responsibility to support its members and provide needed benefits and services. It's not people's fault that they require such services, but rather it is an expected part of the human condition. People have a right to receive benefits and services on an ongoing basis. In many ways, this is a more humane and supportive approach to helping people. Public education available to all is an example of an institutional form of social welfare; similarly, fire and police protection are available to all (McInnis-Dittrich, 1994).

Prior to the Great Depression in the 1930s, the residual approach to social welfare dominated. Since then, however, both approaches have been apparent, depending on the program at issue. Temporary Assistance to Needy Families (TANF), described in a later chapter, is an example of a residually oriented program. Families in need receive temporary, limited financial assistance until they can get back on their feet.

A newer view on social welfare is the *developmental* perspective. This approach "seeks to identify social interventions that have a positive impact on economic development" (Midgley & Livermore, 1997, p. 574). It originated after World War II in Third World countries seeking to design social welfare programs that would also enhance their economic development. This perspective gained impetus in the United States in the 1970s because "it justifies social programs in terms of economic efficiency criteria" (Lowe, 1995; Midgley & Livermore, 1997, p. 575).

HIGHLIGHT 1.1

What Is Critical Thinking?

EP 2.1.3

Critical thinking is (1) the careful scrutiny of what is stated as true or what appears to be true and the resulting expression of an opinion or conclusion based on that scrutiny, and (2) the creative formulation of an opinion or conclusion when presented with a question, problem, or issue. Critical thinking concentrates on "the process of reasoning" (Gambrill & Gibbs, 2009, p. 4). It stresses *how* individuals think about the truth inherent in a statement or *how* they analyze an issue to formulate their own conclusions. As Gambrill and Gibbs (2009) so aptly state, "Critical thinkers question what others take for granted" (p. 9).

Two dimensions in the definition of critical thinking are significant. First, critical thinking focuses on the questioning of beliefs, statements, assumptions, lines of reasoning, actions, and experiences. Suppose you read a "fact" in a book or hear about it from a friend or an instructor. Critical thinking focuses on *not* taking this "fact" at face value. Rather, it entails the following "Triple-A" approach to examining and evaluating its validity:

1. *Ask* questions.
2. *Assess* the established facts and issues involved.
3. *Assert* a concluding opinion.

For example, a friend and fellow student might tell you, "It's impossible to get financial aid at our school." To what extent is this statement really true? To find out, you first *ask* questions about what the statement is really saying. What does "impossible" mean? Some people must be eligible for financial aid. What are the criteria for receiving aid? What experiences has your friend had to come to such a conclusion?

Second, you *assess* the established facts and issues involved by seeking relevant information. What does the financial aid policy state? To what extent does eligibility depend on students' and their parents' earnings? To what extent is grade point average or full-time student status involved? How many students are actually receiving aid at any time? What percentage of the student population does this number reflect?

Third, you *assert* a concluding opinion. To what extent do you agree with your friend's statement? If you find out that only two people on your campus are receiving aid, you might agree that such aid is almost impossible to get. However, if you find out that

about a third of the student population is receiving aid, you might heartily conclude that your friend's statement is false.

Critical thinking can be applied to virtually any belief, statement, assumption, line of reasoning, action, or experience claimed as true. Consider the following statements of proposed "facts":

- Rich people are selfish.
- Taxes are unfair.
- A crocodile cannot stick its tongue out.
- Most lipstick contains fish scales.
- It is physically impossible for a person to lick his or her elbow.
- Over 75% of people who read this will try to lick their elbow.

These statements may seem silly (although some may also be true), but the point is that critical thinking can be applied to an infinite array of thoughts and ideas. For each of the statements, (1) what questions would you *ask*, (2) how would you *assess* the established facts and issues involved, and (3) what concluding opinion would you finally *assert*?

The second facet of the definition of critical thinking is the creative formulation of an opinion or conclusion when presented with a question, problem, or issue. Instead of being told a proposed "fact" to be scrutinized for its validity, you are asked your *opinion* about an issue, assumption, or action. Examples include the following:

- Should prisoners who commit violent crimes be ineligible for parole? (In other words, should they be required to serve their full sentences?)
- Should all interstate highways have toll booths to finance them and their repairs, so that only the people who use them pay for them (instead of general tax revenues paying for highway construction and repair)?
- What is the best way to eliminate poverty in this nation?

Consider answering the last question, which could be posed as a term paper or exam topic in one of your courses. First, what questions about it would you ask? What are the reasons for poverty in a rich industrialized country? What social welfare programs are currently available to address poverty? What innovative ideas for programs might be tried? Where might

(continued)

HIGHLIGHT 1.1 (continued)

funding for such programs be found? How much money would it take to eliminate poverty, and who would pay for this?

Second, what facts and issues would you seek to address and assess? You probably would first try to define poverty—what income level or lack of income makes a person or family "poor"? You then might research statistics, costs, and studies concerning the effectiveness of various programs intending to reduce poverty. You might also investigate innovative ideas. Perhaps there are proposals for programs that look promising. You might explore what various programs cost and how they are funded. Note that these suggestions only scratch the surface of how you might examine the issue.

Third, what opinion or conclusion would you assert? To what extent do you think it is possible to eliminate poverty? What kinds of resources and programs do you think it would take? What do you feel citizens and their government should do about poverty?

Gambrill and Gibbs (2009) stress that critical thinking enhances self-awareness and the ability to detect various modes of distorted thinking that can trick people into assuming truth. Critical thinking can help you do the following:

1. *Identify propaganda* ("ideas, facts, or allegations spread deliberately to further one's cause or to damage an opposing cause" [Mish, 2008, p. 996]). Propaganda may be true or untrue. It often sensationalizes a point of view by blowing it out of proportion. For example, a law firm with the slogan "Our Way Is the Only and Best Way" emphasizes its own prowess while demeaning the effectiveness of other firms. Critical thinking

would prompt you to assess upon what basis this law firm is making its claim of superiority.

2. *Distinguish intentionally deceptive claims.* For instance, an advertiser might boast, "This miracle drug has been scientifically proven to make you lose a pound a day—without exercising or changing your eating habits!" when, in actuality, little or no meticulous research has been done. Critical thinking would lead you to question how the drug has been scientifically proven to be effective.

3. *Focus on and choose words carefully.* Critical thinking helps you focus your attention on the meaning of each word used to convey an idea or concept. For example, consider the statement "Schools produce a bunch of real losers these days." What does each word really mean or imply? Which schools produce "losers"? What is a "loser"? What does "a bunch" mean? To what are "these days" compared?

4. *Be wary of emotional ploys and appeals.* They play on your emotions and urge you to concur with their intent by using as little logical thinking as possible. For instance, a sales representative on a televised marketing program might urge you to "buy this genuine fake leather jacket now and we'll send a pair of matching gloves—and a pair of matching boots. This is the only time you'll get this additional value. Aren't they lovely? But you have to act now—we have only two jackets left!" The intent here is to pressure you to make a decision quickly based on desire rather than on logical thinking about what the jacket costs and how you will make the payments.

Midgley and Livermore (1997) cite three major ways that economic development can occur in a developmental context. First, "investments in [services to people such as] education, nutrition, and health care" can be evaluated so that people get the most for their money (p. 577). For example, investments in education may result in a more skilled labor force that, in turn, generates a stronger economy. Second, investment in physical facilities involving "the creation of economic and social infrastructure, such as roads, bridges, irrigation and drinking water systems, clinics, [and] schools . . .

provide[s] the economic and social bases on which development efforts depend" (pp. 577–578). Workers must have a transportation system to get to work and a building in which to work to get anything done. Therefore, resources expended on developing such things are economically productive. Third, developing "programs that help needy people engage in productive employment and self-employment" is more economically viable than giving people public assistance payments over years and even decades (p. 578). It is an efficient economic investment to educate and train people in need

HIGHLIGHT 1.2

Sustainability on a Global Level

The developmental perspective emphasizes the importance of economic development. Such progress can affect communities of any size, ranging from small local communities to nations as communities at the global level. The well-being of the global community has become a pressing concern. Mary (2008) reflects:

> The world is changing. Our human activities are clearly becoming global in nature. Our understanding of nature—the infrastructure upon which all humankind rests—is changing as well. . . . We have reached a point in our understanding of systems at which social welfare must be considered part of a larger global imperative of planetary survival. There is a profound connection between the micro problems that individuals and families manifest (e.g., environmental pollution, the lack of sustaining and meaningful work, addiction, domestic violence) and the macro problems that local and global communities experience [e.g., rampant poverty, lack of educational infrastructure, widespread unemployment, inadequate food production, political unrest]. (p. 1)

EP 2.1.5b, 2.1.9b

A concept related to global and international development is the concept of sustainability. *Sustainability* involves "development that meets the current needs of the present generations without jeopardizing the ability of future generations to meet their needs" (Mary, 2008, p. 32; Pace, 2011). This concept encompasses much more than just economic development. In view of concerns about overpopulation and overcrowding, insufficient food and fresh water, global warming, and a host of other issues, sustainability involves the need for citizens of the earth to work together to save themselves and their world (Gamble & Weil, 2008; Healy, 2008; Mary, 2008).

An internationally supported document entitled the *Earth Charter* has been developed to define and stress the importance of sustainability on a global basis (Earth Charter Initiative, 2011). After many years of planning, cooperation, and compromise, socially concerned organizations around the world met to create a document with the following intent:

> We must join together to bring forth a sustainable global society founded on respect for nature, universal human rights, economic justice, and a culture of peace. Towards this end, it is imperative that we, the peoples of Earth, declare our responsibility to one another, to the greater community of life, and to future generations. *(Earth Charter Initiative, 2011)*

The Charter emphasizes four categories of principles necessary to promote "a sustainable way of life by which the conduct of all individuals, organizations, businesses, governments, and transnational institutions is to be guided and assessed": "respect and care for the community of life [with all its diversity]," "ecological integrity," "social and economic justice," and "democracy, nonviolence and peace" (Earth Charter Initiative, 2011).

The Charter calls for "a new sense of global interdependence and universal responsibility" where all the citizens of earth "imaginatively develop and apply the vision of a sustainable way of life locally, nationally, regionally, and globally" (Earth Charter Initiative, 2011). It has been endorsed by thousands of organizations around the globe and has significantly influenced the United Nations Educational, Scientific, and Cultural Organization (UNESCO) (Healy, 2008). It is "now increasingly recognized as a global consensus statement on the meaning of sustainability, the challenge and vision of sustainable development, and the principles by which sustainable development is to be achieved" (Earth Charter Initiative, 2011).

To achieve sustainability, Mary (2008) calls for major shifts in our economic system. For example, she suggests that some military spending could be shifted to the following earth-preserving goals:

Basic Social Goals

- Universal primary education
- Adult literacy
- School lunch programs for the world's forty-four poorest countries
- Assistance to preschool children and pregnant women in the world's forty-four poorest countries
- Universal basic health care
- Reproductive health and family planning
- Closing the condom gap

Earth Restoration Goals

- Reforesting the earth
- Protecting topsoil on cropland
- Restoring rangelands
- Stabilizing water tables
- Restoring fisheries
- Protecting biological diversity (pp. 188–189)

The application of sustainability to social work practice will be discussed further in Chapter 4.

so that they can get jobs and eventually support themselves.

The developmental perspective is relatively new and requires a more extensive grasp of social welfare issues and policies than can be described in an introductory book such as this. It involves both in-depth analysis of current social programs and the ability to creatively propose new ones. Therefore, it will not be a primary focus in this book.

What are your views about social welfare? Focus on Critical Thinking 1.1 poses some questions.

Highlight 1.2 explores a concept related to the developmental perspective on social welfare—the notion of sustainability on a global basis.

The Conservative–Liberal Continuum

Political ideology is the "relatively coherent system of ideas (beliefs, traditions, principles, and myths) about human nature, institutional arrangements, and social processes" that indicate how a government should be run and what principles that government should support (Abramovitz, 2007, p. 126). A person's political ideology will frame the way that person views the world. It affects what that person feels is valuable and what is not; it influences how an individual believes things should be and how they should not be.

Another way of thinking about how people should be served by social welfare programs involves political ideology and the conservative–liberal continuum (Dolgoff & Feldstein, 2009; Jansson, 2011; McInnis-Dittrich, 1994). In some ways, this continuum reflects concepts similar to those of the residual and institutional perspectives of social welfare program development. However, the continuum focuses more on values related to social responsibility for human welfare.

Conservatism

Conservatism is the philosophy that individuals are responsible for themselves, government should provide minimal interference in people's lives, and change is generally unnecessary.

At least three concepts tend to characterize conservatives. First, conservatives usually oppose change and thrive on tradition (Chapin, 2011; Gilbert & Terrell, 2010). They generally feel that change results in more trouble than it's worth, so it's best to leave things the way they are. In other words, if it ain't broke, don't fix it.

Second, conservatives generally assume a negative view of human nature, stressing that it is sinful and prone to corruption (Abramovitz, 2008). If people can get "welfare," they'll take it, and society is foolish for giving it to them. Conservatives also feel that

---

FOCUS ON CRITICAL THINKING 1.1

What Are Your Views About Social Welfare?

EP 2.1.1b, 2.1.2a

We have established that a consistent theme in social work is the importance of thinking critically and formulating opinions about what is right and wrong. A key question here concerns your own views about social welfare. What ensuing questions might you ask? What facts would you need to seek out and assess? What opinions and conclusions would you finally assert?

A related question concerns the extent to which your opinions reflect residual or institutional views about social welfare programs, benefits, and services. What are your opinions about the following concerns posed? (The issues are more complicated than you might think.) Does your thinking lean more toward a residual or institutional perspective?

- Should single mothers of young children be required to work, or should they be entitled to public assistance while they care for their children at home?
- Should public housing be routinely provided to homeless people at public expense?
- Should national health insurance automatically be provided to all Americans, or should they be expected to obtain health insurance through employment or by purchasing it themselves?
- Should homeless people who have mental illnesses be institutionalized, or should they be allowed to roam at will in the community?
- Should children in families suspected of child abuse be placed elsewhere, or should treatment focus on strengthening the family so that children remain in their own homes?

society has the responsibility of regulating people's behavior so that it's in compliance with the laws of God and a patriarchal society (Abramovitz, 2008). Areas requiring strict regulation include maintaining bans on gay marriage and abortion, in addition to the provision of strict consequences for deviant behavior such as illegal drug use and other crimes.

Third, conservatives usually conceive of people as perfectly capable of taking care of themselves (Abramovitz, 2008). This implies that if people would work hard and take responsibility for their actions, they wouldn't need any help. People "on welfare" don't deserve such resources, but rather should make their own way. People have only themselves to blame if they don't succeed. Government should provide minimal interference in people's lives and assistance only when it's absolutely necessary to help the very needy.

Liberalism

Liberalism is the philosophy that government should be involved in the social, political, and economic structure so that all people's rights and privileges are protected in the name of social justice.

Poverty is a social welfare issue. Depending on their political orientation, people view the causes of poverty and the potential solutions very differently

At least three concepts tend to characterize liberals, more or less reflecting the opposite of a conservative perspective. First, liberals like change and tend to think there's always a better way to get things done (Chapin, 2011; Gilbert & Terrell, 2010). They are always looking for different approaches to improve policies and provide services.

Second, liberals have a much more positive perspective on human nature (Abramovitz, 2008). They view people as rational beings fully capable of making their own choices and decisions about what is right and wrong. Each individual deserves the right to compete and be provided with equal opportunities to blossom and prosper.

Third, liberals view government as the best entity to provide a structure and an environment where adequate services and opportunities can be made available (Abramovitz, 2008). Therefore, it is government's responsibility to make certain that citizens' needs are met, public participation is maximized, and people's equal rights are preserved. Liberals believe that it's the government's job to protect people from such impediments as racism, sexism, various other forms of discrimination, and poverty.

Radicalism

A more extreme approach is *radicalism,* the philosophy that the social and political system as it stands is not structurally capable of truly providing social justice. Rather, drastic, fundamental changes are necessary in the basic social and political structure to achieve truly fair and equal treatment.

According to a radical philosophy, for example, poverty, defined as "the result of exploitation by the ruling or dominant class," exists for at least two reasons (Karger & Stoesz, 2010, p. 111). First, having a multitude of poor people as workers enables higher classes to keep wages low because of the numerous replacement workers. If low-paid workers complain, they can simply be fired, with someone else eagerly waiting to take their place to avoid poverty. The working class thus serves to labor for the wealthy and keep them rich. Second, keeping a class of people in poverty enhances the "prestige" and status of the middle and upper classes. To remedy this state of affairs, an entirely new social structure would have to be developed.

A radical perspective requires the ability to propose a new social structure. It is far beyond the scope of this book to discuss how to plan new policies and promote broad social change. Therefore, from here on, when the term *radical* is used, it will be in the context of soliciting any *very general* ideas you might have about changing social welfare service provision.

How Do You Fare on the Conservative–Liberal Continuum?

Return to Focus on Critical Thinking 1.1 and review the answers you gave to those questions. Do they lean toward a liberal or conservative point of view? Focus on Critical Thinking 1.2 contains a series of statements geared to assessing further your liberal or conservative views.

Note that this discussion of conservatism and liberalism is overly simplified. Many people, and perhaps most, have a complex mixture of views depending on their perceptions and personal experiences. (That last sentence probably reflects a liberal perspective.)

Social Work and Social Welfare History

EP 2.1.1

Social work has been a developing field since the late 19th century. The profession is intimately intertwined with historical events and trends in social welfare. Social work emphasizes the importance of the social environment as it affects the quality of people's lives. Therefore, the way people are treated by laws that govern them and the services and resources provided to them are integral parts of the social work perspective.

Chapter 6 reviews the history of social welfare beginning in European medieval times, continuing throughout U.S. history, and culminating with today's programs and services. It elaborates on the effects of history on the social work profession's development. The chapter is placed immediately before Chapter 7 (which addresses policy, policy analysis, and policy advocacy) because today's programs, all based on current social welfare policies, are products of historical events concerning social welfare. Chapter 8 then discusses the policies and programs developed to combat poverty.

Fields of Practice in Social Work

The remainder of the book focuses on *fields of practice* in social work. These are the various practice contexts that address certain types of populations and needs and require a special knowledge and skill base for effective work. Each field of practice involves a labyrinth of typical human problems and the services attempting to address them. Current fields of practice include children and families, aging, disabilities, health, mental health, substance abuse, schools, and corrections. Other contexts for practice are occupational social work (focusing on work in employee assistance programs or directed toward organizational change), rural social work (addressing the unique problems of people living in rural areas), police social work (emphasizing work in police, courthouse, and jail settings with crime victims, alleged offenders, and their families), and forensic social work (dealing with the law, educating lawyers, and serving as expert witnesses) (Barker, 2003).

Social workers require information about people who need help in each of these areas. They also must be knowledgeable about the services available to meet needs and the major issues related to each area. A social worker may be called upon to work with a problem that clearly falls within one field of practice or a problem that involves several of these fields.

For example, the Wullbinkle family comes to a social worker's attention when a neighbor reports that Rocky, their 5-year-old son, is frequently seen with odd-looking bruises on his arms and legs. The neighbor suspects child abuse. Upon investigation, the social worker finds that the parents are indeed abusive. They often grab the child violently by a limb and throw him against the wall. This problem initially falls under the umbrella of family and children's services.

However, the social worker also finds a number of other problems operating within the family. The mother, Natasia, is seriously depressed and frequently suicidal, so she needs mental health services. And the father, Boris, is struggling with a drinking problem that is beginning to affect his performance at work. A program is available at his place of employment, where an occupational social worker helps employees deal with such problems. Thus occupational social work may also be involved.

FOCUS ON CRITICAL THINKING 1.2

Where Do You Stand on the Conservative–Liberal Continuum?

**EP 2.1.1b,
2.1.2a**

Rate how much you agree with statements 1–6 by assigning a number for each. The scale is as follows:

Strongly agree	Somewhat agree	Somewhat disagree	Strongly disagree
1	2	3	4

1. I don't like change very much.
2. The old tried-and-true way of getting things done is usually the best way.
3. People will do whatever they can to get things for themselves.
4. If they're sure they can get away with it, students will inevitably cheat on exams.
5. People should be independent, take care of themselves, and not rely on the charity of others.
6. People who commit crimes should be punished with severity to match the severity of their crimes.

Now rate how much you agree with statements 7–12 by assigning a number for each. The scale is as follows:

Strongly agree	Somewhat agree	Somewhat disagree	Strongly disagree
4	3	2	1

7. I like to see and do new things because it makes life more interesting.
8. Trying some new way to get things done often results in a better, more effective approach.
9. People are generally good at heart.

10. It's often the bad things that happen to people that make them "go wrong."
11. With a little help and support, people who are less privileged than the rest can usually pull themselves together and do pretty well.
12. It's better to try to rehabilitate people who commit crimes than to throw them in jail.

Now add up your total score for all 12 items and divide by 12. A score of 1 means that you probably are quite conservative, a 2 that you're somewhat conservative, a 3 that you're somewhat liberal, and a 4 that you're quite liberal.

This little exercise in no way defines your political orientation or labels you as a conservative or liberal for life. Its intent is to give you some food for thought about your own values.

Social work values tend to be more liberal than conservative, as is demonstrated by the NASW *Code of Ethics* and NASW's usual support of Democratic political candidates, who traditionally are more liberal than Republicans.

However, people's values and belief systems often are much more complex than that. For example, you may be conservative in that you don't want to pay a high percentage of taxes for social welfare programs. But you may also be liberal in that you believe in a woman's right to choice when it comes to having an abortion. Or you might feel just the opposite.

Social workers must continuously examine their personal values, on the one hand, and respect the values of their clients, on the other. They must constantly strive not to impose personal values on clients. It's a difficult but interesting task.

In addition, the maternal grandmother, Emma, is living with the Wullbinkle family. Emma's physical health is failing. Although her daughter dreads the idea of nursing home placement, the issue must be addressed. Emma, who is also overweight, finds it increasingly difficult to move around by herself. She is demanding more and more physical help and support from Natasia. Natasia, who has back problems, is finding it increasingly burdensome to help her mother. Finally, Vernite, Boris and Natasia's 12-year-old daughter, is falling behind in school, and truancy is becoming a problem. This last issue falls under the school's umbrella.

Most of the problems that social workers face are complex. They may involve a variety of practice fields all at one time. To understand clients' needs, social workers must know something about a wide range of problems and services.

The Continuum of Social Work Careers

There are various ways to look at advancement through a social work career. Some workers progress through a series of levels, while others

EP 2.1.1c

remain at an earlier point of entry. Degrees in social work include the baccalaureate, master's, and doctorate.

Baccalaureate Social Workers (BSWs)

Baccalaureate social workers (BSWs) complete an accredited course of study, with required content described later in the chapter, to prepare for entry-level social work. They are also required to complete at least 400 hours of field experience supervised by a social work practitioner. Job settings involve many fields of practice and include child welfare agencies (e.g., those involving protective services, foster care, or adoption), residential treatment centers (e.g., serving adolescents with behavioral or emotional problems), services for people with various disabilities (including intellectual [mental retardation]), settings serving older adults, correctional institutions, public welfare agencies, schools, health centers and hospitals, substance abuse treatment centers, shelters for the homeless, shelters for domestic violence survivors, and family planning organizations.

At the preprofessional or paraprofessional level involving people who assist social workers in their practice are social service technicians and social service aides (Hopps & Lowe, 2008). _Social service technicians_ typically hold an associate's degree (e.g., in human services) or a baccalaureate degree in a non–social work discipline and serve as a paraprofessional (a person trained to assist the social worker under the social worker's supervision in designated tasks such as conducting basic interviews, making referrals, and completing paperwork). _Social service aides_ are people with a high school degree, often with relevant life experience or strong connections to the community, who perform clerical and scheduling tasks. Aides may or may not have an associate's degree.

Master's Social Workers (MSWs)

Master's social workers (MSWs) receive more specialized training built on the same foundation as the BSW curriculum and integrated with field internships. Most master's programs require two years of study. However, many give _advanced standing_ to BSWs (as opposed to people entering the program with non–social work undergraduate majors) where up to one year of study is waived because they've already completed the foundation curriculum.

Both BSWs and MSWs can find employment in a wide range of settings. However, there are some differences in the types of jobs for which each is qualified. MSWs are considered more specialized than BSWs. The implication is that MSWs are competent to address more difficult problems than BSWs and have the potential to assume greater responsibility. In reality, this distinction is not always so clear-cut. Performance expectations and job availability vary significantly depending on the area of the country and state.

The realm of psychotherapy is generally limited to MSWs instead of BSWs. _Psychotherapy,_ sometimes referred to simply as _therapy,_ is a skilled treatment process whereby a therapist works with an individual, couple, family, or group to address a mental disorder or alleviate other problems the client(s) may be having in the social environment. Another difference between MSWs and BSWs is that higher-level supervisory and administrative positions in any field of practice often require an MSW or other master's-level degree. Such positions usually offer higher salaries. MSWs generally earn significantly more than BSWs, although years of experience enhance salaries for both groups.

Licensure or certification of some level of social work practice exists in all 50 states. Chapter 5 discusses this more thoroughly. Chapter 5 also discusses social work salaries and employment prospects at the BSW and MSW levels.

Doctorates in Social Work

A small percentage of social workers hold doctorate degrees, either a Ph.D. (Doctor of Philosophy) or DSW (Doctor of Social Work). Either degree qualifies the holder to teach at the college level or conduct research. (Note that some social workers without a doctorate but with an MSW get jobs teaching at community colleges, in universities as part-time instructors, or, sometimes, in non-tenure-track faculty positions.) Some Ph.D.s or DSWs assume administrative positions or enter private practice in psychotherapy. These degrees involve advanced and specialized study, a focus on research, and completion of a dissertation.

This section has reviewed the continuum of social work careers according to the college and university degrees attained. Focus on Critical Thinking 1.3 suggests how you might start thinking about the career that's right for you in whatever field you choose.

FOCUS ON CRITICAL THINKING 1.3

Thinking About Your Career

EP 2.1.1b

As a student, you may have some career goals clearly in mind. Or you may still be wondering what the best career path is. The following is a discussion of how you might think about determining a career course. You might be a student of traditional age or an older student returning to school. Note that not all career ideas and possibilities are mentioned because they are countless. Although this career consideration process is oriented toward social work, the purpose here is to stimulate your thinking, not to tell you what to do. Each person must decide for herself or himself how to spend time and life.

1. General orientation toward the future (conducting a self-assessment)

What values are important to you? Achieving personal satisfaction? Becoming famous? Earning money? Being respected? Building a family life? Finding security? Having adventures? Leading others? Finding excitement? Developing personal relationships? Having fun? Being loved? Helping others? Getting ahead? Being successful? Being happy? Being popular? Fitting into a work environment? Feeling important? Having free time? Traveling? Having a good reputation?

What work have you done or thought about doing in life?

What dimensions of work appeal to you most? Liking the people you work with? Communicating with others? Working alone? Working with others? Giving attention to detail? Solving problems creatively? Using specific skills? Being successful? Having flexibility? Having structured work expectations? Maintaining predictability? Helping others? Having opportunities to get ahead? Being productive? Making lots of money? Being a leader? Fitting in? Being challenged?

What jobs or careers come to mind? Which, if any, have you given any thought to?

Your answers may be vague or specific at this point, depending on where you are in your decision-making process. You may know more about what jobs you don't want (e.g., fast-food restaurant worker, waitress/waiter, pizza delivery person, factory worker, or cashier) because of prior experience in minimum-wage or close to minimum-wage jobs that you know you don't want to do for the rest of your working life.

Why are you taking the course that requires this book? Is it to fulfill some general education requirement? Is it because you're mildly interested in the topic? Or is it because you think this might be the major for you?

2. People-oriented versus non-people-oriented careers (exploring your options)

What types of things tend to interest you?

Do you enjoy being with others? Or do you prefer being by yourself?

Are you interested in human relationships, issues such as mental health, health, and women's concerns, and problems such as substance abuse, child maltreatment, and crime?

Do people tend to come to you to talk about their problems? Do you enjoy "helping" people?

If you say yes to these questions, then you might consider occupations that deal with people and continue the career consideration process addressed here. Non-people-oriented career courses might include those such as engineering, accounting, biology, chemistry, or computer science. Of course, it's not that you don't have to work with people in those jobs. Relating to and communicating with others in the work environment is always important. However, in non-people-oriented careers, the focus and goal are accomplishing specific tasks using specific skills, not interpersonal interaction and problem solving.

3. Ways of working with people

In what capacities do you think you'd like to work with people? Are you more interested in physical, business, legal, educational, spiritual, or psychosocial aspects?

Examples of hands-on work with people include being a medical doctor, nursing, *occupational therapy* (treatment that uses creative activity to improve psychological or physical rehabilitation), and *physical therapy* "the treatment of disease, injury, or deformity by physical methods such as massage, heat treatment, and exercise rather than by drugs or surgery" (Lindberg, 2007, p. 1034). These fields also have varying requirements in science, so you probably should have some interest in this area.

Many business careers also focus on developing relationships, but, of course, with the ultimate goal of making a monetary profit instead of helping people improve their life conditions. To what extent is your

(continued)

FOCUS ON CRITICAL THINKING 1.3 *(continued)*

ultimate goal to earn large amounts of money instead of having impacts on the human condition? This is a significant issue. One family comes to mind in which almost all members have various types of business degrees. They can't understand why I might be interested in how to address human problems such as child maltreatment, sexual assault, or mental illness. They cringe when I talk about watching movies about such issues. They think of these issues as someone else's problem and focus their energies on their own families, finances, and lives. Social work would not be their preferred field. Each of us must follow our own calling.

Law or teaching provides other career options. Law, of course, requires a serious interest in the legal process and more years of study beyond the bachelor's degree. In my school we see many students deciding between social work and teaching. They must determine whether they're more interested in helping children learn information and skills, or in working with clients and their families to help them deal with psychological, behavioral, and economic issues. Students more interested in pursuing a spiritual career such as rabbi, priest, or minister might seek education preparing them for such religious callings. One person comes to mind who, after receiving his master's degree in meteorology, decided that he really wanted to be a minister and attained a degree in divinity four years later.

If you're primarily interested in psychosocial aspects of human functioning and improving the human condition, continue reading the next section.

4. Selection of a major

To what extent do you understand the differences among fields addressing psychosocial issues such as social work, psychology, sociology, psychiatry, criminal justice, or counseling? How can you determine which field is for you?

If you decide you want to work with people concerning psychosocial issues, it's best to talk with advisers in the various majors available to you at your school. Think about what aspects of a major appeal to you most. Find out what kind of jobs its graduates tend to get. Explore what courses make up the curriculum, and determine the extent to which the major will give you the values, knowledge, and skills necessary for you to "hit the ground running" when you get your first job after graduating. Does it prepare you with skills such as interviewing, running groups and meetings, and working within organizations? Does the major provide a significant field internship to help pre-

pare you for work with clients? To what extent does each major you're considering match your values, interests, and goals?

Understanding the primary focus of various majors can be confusing. Just a few alternatives will be mentioned here. Generally speaking, *psychology* emphasizes the study of behavior and cognitive processing (Barker, 2003). Work is often associated with treatment of mental disorders or testing people for intelligence or aptitude. A master's or Ph.D. degree is required to provide psychotherapy. *Sociology* is the study of human society, how various groups interact with each other, and how social institutions structure the social environment in which we live. *Social work* uses a significant amount of the knowledge produced both by sociology and psychology, and applies it to helping situations. Figure 1.1 illustrates the broad range of foundation knowledge contributing to social work practice. *Psychiatry* is the branch of medicine that specializes in the diagnosis and treatment of mental disorders. Psychiatrists must have advanced training beyond a medical degree and assume responsibility for diagnosing mental illness and prescribing psychotropic drugs. *Criminal justice* is the configuration of programs, policies, and agencies dealing with crime, incarceration, legal processes, and the rehabilitation of criminal offenders. Social workers can assume a wide range of positions in the criminal justice system. *Counseling* is a field overlapping various other fields, including social work, which focuses on problem solving and providing help to individuals, families, or groups. Often it involves additional education and expertise such as that in marriage and family therapy. Many social workers in clinical practice also are licensed marriage and family therapists. Generally, counseling focuses on providing some kind of psychotherapy, whereas social work also emphasizes the importance of the social environment concerning human behavior and advocacy to improve people's quality of life.

An issue related to choice of major involves the extent to which you're interested in attending graduate school. Some career paths require graduate education. Graduate school raises more questions. To what extent do you think you'll be tired of school by the time you graduate? So many seniors tell me they can't wait "to get out" and "work to make money" instead of doing schoolwork and spending money on tuition. To what extent is graduate school financially feasible? Do you have access to funding or loans? To what extent are you already financially burdened? What, if any, is

(continued)

your motivation to attend graduate school? Is your grade point average sufficient to be accepted?

If you decide to consider social work as a major or have already declared this major, the next section addresses some choices within the realm of social work.

5. Considering or choosing a social work major

Because social workers practice in so many different settings and work with so many kinds of people, it can be daunting trying to decide what field of practice is right for you. Such a struggle makes sense when you still know little about all the types of social work settings available. How can you make an informed choice without adequate information? Many students, even as they complete their major, have difficulty deciding what they prefer even as they enter a supervised field practicum within an agency setting. Usually, however, by that time students have narrowed their preferences considerably. It takes time to think things through as you acquire more information about the field and gain broader experiences.

The following list should at least give you an idea of the social work career options available. At this point, what interests you the most? What settings are most attractive to you? What client populations, problems, and issues concern you most? What are your reactions to considering work in the following settings, which are just a sampling of those available?

- Mental health settings such as inpatient hospitals, where people experience and seek treatment for various mental health problems.
- Health settings such as hospitals, where people need help understanding complex information and getting the appropriate resources.
- Settings aimed at enhancing the welfare of children, including protective services, adoption, foster care, school social work, and treatment for behavioral and emotional difficulties in outpatient, group home, or residential facilities.
- Settings for older adults, such as health care facilities where older adults who require physical and medical support live, or supportive services aimed at keeping people in their own homes as long as possible.
- Agencies providing services to people with physical disabilities, including linking them to appropriate services and advocating for services when necessary.

- Correctional settings for adults or juvenile delinquents, such as prisons where social workers help inmates by providing counseling and assisting in inmates' adjustment to the correctional environment or preparation for release, and probation or parole offices where they monitor the behavior of people released into the community.
- Domestic violence hotlines and programs addressing the needs of women who have been physically and emotionally abused.
- Counseling programs for alcohol and other substance abuse.
- Services for people with intellectual disabilities, such as those aimed at linking them to needed services, supervising noninstitutional living settings such as group homes, helping them gain employment, and advocating for resources that are unavailable.
- Crisis hotlines, where a wide range of crises, including threats of suicide or violence toward others, mental health and substance abuse, issues, or physical abuse are addressed and referrals to appropriate services made.
- Family planning agencies that help people make choices about contraception.
- Homeless shelters that provide temporary shelter, counseling, and training for people on the street.

Another facet of thinking about your career involves the types of responsibilities characterizing a work setting and the skills needed to practice effectively in it. What are your thoughts about undertaking the following?

- Counseling
- Running groups
- Working with families
- Linking people with needed resources
- Coordinating service provision for people receiving multiple services through case management
- Supervising staff or administering agencies
- Supervising volunteers
- Undertaking community organization
- Running meetings
- Writing grants
- Developing policy
- Promoting
- Lobbying

There are lots of things to consider. Choosing a career is not easy.

Social Work Builds on Many Disciplines

The foundation of professional social work is a body of knowledge, skills, and values. Knowledge originates not only from social workers but also from a range of disciplines that focus on understanding people's needs and behavior. These include psychology, sociology, political science, economics, biology, psychiatry, counseling, and cultural anthropology. Figure 1.1, on page 20, illustrates how social work knowledge builds on both other disciplines and its own firm and growing body of research. It summarizes the primary focus and core concepts involved in each discipline. Social workers use knowledge drawn from each field, in conjunction with social work skills and values, to help individuals, families, groups, organizations, and communities solve problems and improve their quality of life.

The Uniqueness of Social Work

We have established that social work builds on the knowledge base of other professions in addition to its own. Other fields perform some of the same functions as social work. For instance, mental health clinicians in psychology, psychiatry, and counseling use interviewing skills, and some also use a planned-change approach. Figure 1.2, on page 21, illustrates how social work overlaps, to some extent, with other helping professions. All, for example, have a common core of interviewing and counseling skills.

However, social work involves much more than simply sitting down with an individual, group, or family and solving some problem. (This is not to imply that this is all other helping professions do. Their own unique thrusts and emphases are beyond the scope of what can be included here.) Social work has at least five major dimensions that make it unique.

EP 2.1.10

First, social workers may focus on any problems or clusters of problems that are complex and difficult. Social workers don't refuse to work with clients or refer them elsewhere because those clients have unappealing characteristics. For instance, there may be a family in which sexual abuse is occurring, and that abuse must be stopped. Likewise, there may be a community in which the juvenile crime rate is skyrocketing, and something must be done.

Not every problem can be solved, but some can be—or at least alleviated. Social work practitioners are equipped with a repertoire of skills to help them identify and examine problems. They then make choices about where their efforts can be best directed.

The second dimension that makes social work unique is that it often targets the environment encompassing clients, and not the clients themselves, for change. Sometimes services are unavailable or difficult to obtain, policies are unfair, or people are oppressed by other people. Administrators and people in power don't always have the motivation or insight to initiate needed change. Social workers must look at where change is essential outside the individual and work with the environment to effect that change. Highlight 1.3 on page 22 discusses some of the theoretical concepts underlying social work practice.

EP 2.1.7, 2.1.8a

Consider an example of targeting the environment for change involving a midwestern city of about half a million people. Several dozen teenagers in the city had been expelled from various schools. They all had lengthy delinquency records and serious emotional problems. These young people had been attending a private day treatment program that provided them with special education and counseling at the individual, group, and family levels. The day treatment approach allowed them to remain living at home in the community but still receive special treatment. The program had been paid for by public funds, with the county department of social services purchasing treatment services from the private agency.[1] The public schools had no special resources to help these teens. Therefore, purchasing such services from a private agency was more cost-effective for the county than developing its own program from scratch. Suddenly, however, money became scarce, and community leaders decided they could no longer afford a day treatment program. Now these teenagers had nowhere to go.

This problem involved many children and their families, and the social environment was no longer

---

[1]Public agencies are those run by a designated unit of government and are usually regulated by laws that directly affect policy. The county department of social services is a public agency. Private agencies, of course, are privately owned and run by people not employed by government. Chapter 5 describes social service agencies in greater detail.

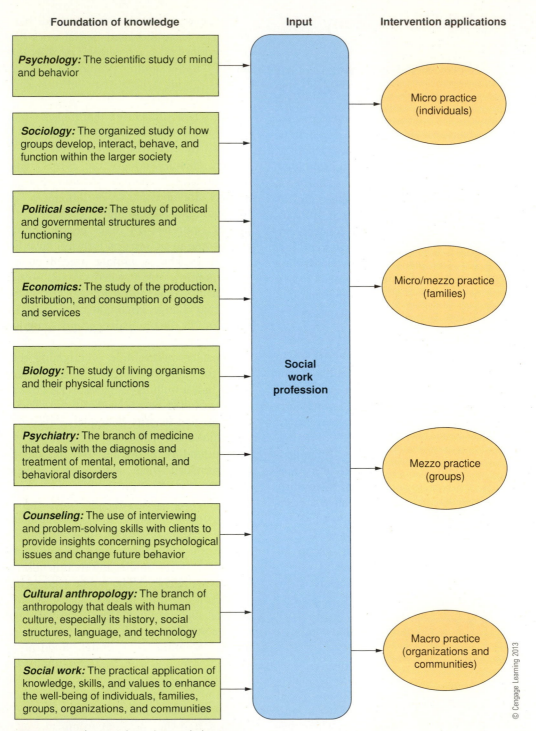

Figure 1.1 The Social Work Knowledge Base

responding to their desperate needs. A social worker addressing this problem might look at it from several perspectives. First, the city's various communities might need to be made acutely aware both of the existence of these teens and of the sudden cuts in funding. The media may need to be contacted as well. Second, the public school system may need to develop its own program to meet these children's

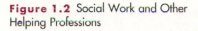

Figure 1.2 Social Work and Other Helping Professions

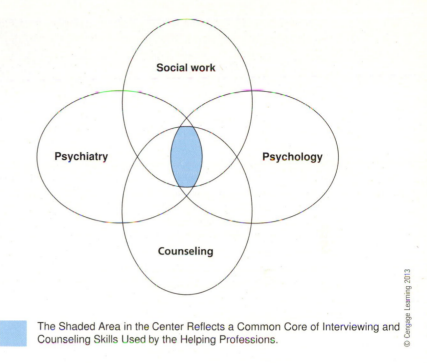

Social work

Psychiatry

Psychology

Counseling

The Shaded Area in the Center Reflects a Common Core of Interviewing and Counseling Skills Used by the Helping Professions.

and their families' needs. Third, the parents of these children may need to band together and lobby for attention and services.

In this case, social workers involved in the agency whose funding had been cut off mobilized immediately. They contacted the parents of their clients and told them about the situation. Outraged, the parents demanded that the community provide education for their children as it did for all the other children. Several parents became outspoken leaders of the group. Assisted by social workers, they filed a class-action suit. The court determined that until the situation had been evaluated, funding for services must continue. Eventually, the public school system (also with the help of social workers) developed its own programs to meet the needs of such teenagers, and the private program was phased out.

EP 2.1.10k

The third dimension that makes social work unique is related to targeting the environment: namely, social workers often find it necessary to advocate for their clients. *Advocacy* involves actively intervening to help clients get what they need. Most frequently, this intervention focuses on "the relationship between the client and an unresponsive 'system'" (Epstein, 1981, p. 8). Clients have specified needs, and social

agencies, organizations, or communities may not be meeting these needs. These unresponsive systems must be pressured to make changes so needs can be met.

The fourth dimension that makes social work unique is its emphasis on and adherence to a core of professional values. The NASW *Code of Ethics* focuses on the right of the individual to make free choices and have a quality life (NASW, 1999).

EP 2.1.2, 2.1.2b

Social workers do not force people into specific ways of thinking or acting. Rather, they help people make their own decisions about how to think or act.

The fifth dimension making social work unique is related to the core of social work values and how important it is for clients to make their own decisions. Social workers do not track people into specific ways of thinking or acting. Rather, they practice in a *partnership* with clients, making and implementing plans together. Most other professions emphasize the authority and expertise of the professional, on the one hand, and the subordinate status of the client as recipient of services, on the other.

EP 2.1.10f

Theoretical Ways of Viewing Social Work: A Focus on Systems in the Environment

EP 2.1.3a, 2.1.7a

Theoretical approaches provide ways of organizing information and looking at the world. For example, the *medical model* is a theoretical approach characterized by four major features (Barker, 2003). First, the focus of attention is the individual, who is seen as having something wrong, such as an illness. Therefore, treatment focuses on curing or helping the individual. Second, little attention is paid to factors outside the individual in his or her environment. The individual, not the environment, is the target of change. Third, the problem or illness is identified or diagnosed and categorized by placing a label on it. Fourth, the individual is the target of treatment that usually involves a series of clinical treatments.

In contrast, a common theoretical approach to social work focuses on the interactions between individuals and various systems in the environment. The focus on the individual and the environment is important because the latter is where social workers direct their efforts at change.

This system- and environment-oriented approach, called *ecosystems theory,* is particularly relevant to social work (Beckett & Johnson, 1995; McNutt, 2008). It combines some of the major concepts from two different theoretical perspectives: the ecological approach and systems theories.

Important Concepts in Systems Theories

Systems theories focus on the dynamics among and interactions of people in their environment. A *system* is a set of elements that are orderly and interrelated to make a functional whole. Social work refers primarily to social systems composed of people (as opposed to, say, an industrial manufacturing system or an ant colony system). An individual, a family, a social services agency, and a neighborhood are all examples of systems.

Social workers work with and on the behalf of various sized systems. A *micro system* is an individual, and a *mezzo system* a group. Families, because of their intimate nature, arbitrarily lie somewhere between micro and mezzo systems. A *macro system* includes organizations and communities. This terminology is important because it's used throughout social work and this book.

Target Systems and Client Systems

It's helpful to conceptualize social workers and clients in terms of systems. A *target system* or *target of change*

is the system that social workers need "to change or influence in order to accomplish [their] goals" (Pincus & Minahan, 1973, p. 58). Targets of change may be individual clients, families, formal groups, administrators, or policymakers. At the micro level, a 5-year-old child with behavioral problems might be the target of change, the goal being to improve behavior. At the mezzo level, a support group of people with eating disorders might be the target of change in an attempt to control their eating behavior.[2] Finally, at the macro level, an agency director might be the target of change when the social worker's aim is to improve some agency policy and the director is the primary decision maker capable of implementing that change.

Another system critical to the planned-change process is the *client system*—any individual, family, group, organization, or community that will ultimately benefit from social work intervention (CSWE, 2008b; Pincus & Minahan, 1973; Resnick, 1980a; Resnick, 1980b). For example, individual clients are client systems when the social worker's goal is to get them needed resources. Families are client systems when the practitioner is working on behalf of the entire family. Similarly, a community is the client system when a social worker is trying to help residents open a new community center to improve their quality of life.

Important Ecological Concepts

Two important concepts taken from the ecological approach are the social environment and coping. The *social environment* includes the conditions, circumstances, and interactions that encompass human beings. Individuals must have effective interactions with their environment to survive and thrive. The social environment involves the type of home a person lives in, the type of work a person does, the amount of money that is available, and the laws and social rules people live by. The social environment also includes the individuals, groups, organizations, and systems with which a person comes into contact, such as family, friends, work groups, and governments.

Coping is the struggle to adjust to environmental conditions and overcome problems. This is significant because social workers often help people cope with problems in their environments.

---

[2]Eating disorders, extremely serious disturbances in eating patterns, are considered mental disorders by the American Psychiatric Association (APA) (APA, 2000). Examples include anorexia and bulimia.

Social Work Education's Goals, Curricula, and Competencies

EP 2.1.1, 2.1.1c, 2.1.1d

One way of understanding social work is to review the content and expectations evident in the curricula of accredited social work programs. The Council on Social Work Education (CSWE) is the organization that accredits social work programs throughout the United States. *Accreditation* is the official designation by an authorized body (in this case, CSWE) that an educational program meets specified standards. This is usually required in becoming licensed as a social worker (described more thoroughly in Chapter 5).

To begin with, CSWE's Educational Policy and Accreditation Standards (EPAS) emphasize that social work programs must reflect certain values throughout their curricula. EPAS states that "service, social justice, the dignity and worth of the person, the importance of human relationships, integrity, competence, human rights, and scientific inquiry are among the core values of social work" (CSWE, 2008b, p. 2). EPAS also specifies the 10 areas in which graduates of social work programs must display competency. These are discussed in the following section. Subsequently, the core social work concepts of generalist practice, advanced practice, and field education will be introduced.

Social Workers Demonstrate Competencies

Competencies are "measurable practice behaviors that are comprised of sufficient knowledge, skills, and values" and have the goal of practicing effective social work. Highlight 1.4 summarizes the 10 required competencies for accredited social work programs. The following sections describe each competency and identify content areas in the traditional social work curriculum. The first five competencies involve knowledge, skills, and values that are evident throughout social work curricula. The last five competencies relate to traditional content areas or courses in social work programs—social work research, human behavior and the social environment, social welfare policy, and social work practice (competencies 9 and 10).

Competency 1: Identification as a Professional Social Worker

Social workers should "serve as representatives of the profession, its mission, and its core values" (CSWE, 2008b, p. 3). They should be knowledgeable about social work's development and history

EP 2.1.1

HIGHLIGHT 1.4

Social Workers Demonstrate Competencies

CSWE (2008b) requires that social work graduates demonstrate competency in the following 10 major areas.

Educational Policy Competencies

Social workers must:

2.1.1   Identify as a professional social worker and conduct oneself accordingly.

2.1.2   Apply social work ethical principles to guide professional practice.

2.1.3   Apply critical thinking to inform and communicate professional judgments.

2.1.4   Engage diversity and difference in practice.

2.1.5   Advance human rights and social and economic justice.

2.1.6   Engage in research-informed practice and practice-informed research.

2.1.7   Apply knowledge of human behavior and the social environment.

2.1.8   Engage in policy practice to advance social and economic well-being and to deliver effective social work services.

2.1.9   Respond to contexts that shape practice.

2.1.10 Engage, assess, intervene, and evaluate with individuals, families, groups, organizations, and communities. (pp. 3–7)

(discussed in Chapter 6). They should conduct themselves in an ethical, professional manner, providing effective service to clients and respecting clients' right to self-determination.

In practice, social workers should advocate on their clients' behalf when services or improved policies governing service provision are necessary. They should continue developing their skills and acquiring new knowledge throughout their careers to better serve clients. Finally, they should seek help from supervisors and consultants when needed.

Competency 2: The Application of Social Work Ethical Principles to Guide Practice

EP 2.1.2

From the many times they've been mentioned already, you probably have noticed that social work values and ethics are critical to social work practice. They help practitioners assess what's important or right in any situation and provide guidelines for making ethical decisions and good judgment calls. Professional social workers should demonstrate competency in recognizing personal values and in employing "principles of ethical reasoning to arrive at principled decisions" (CSWE, 2008b, p. 4).

The NASW *Code of Ethics* mentioned earlier provides some basic guidelines for social work practitioners, as does the International Federation of Social Workers/International Association of Schools of Social Work *Ethics in Social Work, Statement of Principles*. Chapter 2 reviews values, ethics, and some of the issues involved more thoroughly.

Competency 3: The Application of Critical Thinking to Inform Professional Judgments

EP 2.1.3

We have already stressed the importance of critical thinking. It is defined as (1) the careful scrutiny of what is stated as true or what appears to be true and the resulting expression of an opinion or conclusion based on that scrutiny, and (2) the creative formulation of an opinion or conclusion when presented with a question, problem, or issue. It involves not taking at face value what you are told to believe. Rather, critical thinking entails using creative analysis of suppositions to determine for yourself what is really true or what is the best choice among alternatives. It also concerns the ability to communicate clearly and effectively, both orally and in writing.

Competency 4: Engagement of Diversity in Practice

Diversity refers to the wide variety of differences characterizing people. People meriting special attention from the social work profession include, but are not limited to, groups distinguished by "age, class, color,

EP 2.1.4

culture, disability, ethnicity, gender, gender identity and expression, immigration status, political ideology, race, religion, sex, and sexual orientation" (CSWE, 2008b, p. 5). Any time a person can be identified as belonging to a group that differs in some respect from the majority of others in society, that person is subject to the effects of human diversity.

Because social workers have a wide variety of clients, demonstrating almost every type of need and problem, they must be integrally familiar with the concept of human diversity. Four facets are especially significant. First, social workers must appreciate differences and focus on strengths. Second, they must be sensitive to and address any hardships and negative treatment clients may face because they belong to some diverse group. Third, they must introspectively assess their own attitudes and strive to eliminate any prejudices they might have. Fourth, social workers must see themselves as lifelong learners about the many facets of human diversity, especially those characterizing their clients. Chapter 3 examines various aspects of human diversity in more depth.

Competency 5: The Advancement of Human Rights and Social and Economic Justice

The concepts of human rights and social and economic justice are related to the concept of human diversity. *Human rights* involve the premise that all people, regardless of race, culture, or national origin,

EP 2.1.5

are entitled to basic rights and treatment. *Social justice* is the idea that in a perfect world all citizens would have identical "rights, protection, opportunities, obligations, and social benefits" (Barker, 2003, p. 405). Similarly, *economic justice* involves the distribution of resources in a fair and equitable manner. Social work graduates must demonstrate competency in understanding these concepts and their theoretical bases; social workers must advocate on the behalf of these principles and incorporate the principles into their practice (CSWE, 2008b, p. 5).

Another important concept in social work is *populations-at-risk,* groups of people with some identified characteristics that are at greater risk of social and economic deprivation than those in the mainstream. Because social work practice involves getting people resources and helping them solve problems, social workers frequently work with populations-at-risk of such deprivations. It follows that social workers need information and insight concerning these people's special issues and needs. Therefore, social workers require both theoretical and practice content concerning the dynamics and results of differential, unfair treatment.

One especially important social work value is *empowerment*—the "process of increasing personal, interpersonal, or political power so that individuals can take action to improve their life situations" (Gutierrez, 2001, p. 210). Some groups of people suffer from stereotypes, discrimination, and oppression. It is social work's task to empower clients in general and members of oppressed groups in particular.

Competency 6: Engagement in Research-Informed Practice

EP 2.1.6

Social work students must demonstrate competency in *research-informed practice.* This means social workers should use the approaches and interventions in their practice that research has determined are effective. Social workers should employ "research findings to improve practice, policy, and social service delivery" (CSWE, 2008b, p. 5). Social workers might also have opportunities to participate in *practice-based research.* This research, which closely involves the everyday work of practitioners, focuses on collecting data and providing results directly related to the processes of social work practice (Tripodi & Lalayants, 2008, p. 518). Social work programs have traditionally included a "Social Work Research" course or sequence of courses in their curricula.

Knowledge of social work research is important for two basic reasons. First, it can help social workers become more effective in their direct practice by choosing interventions that have been proven successful, thereby getting better and clearer results. Framing social work interventions so they can be evaluated through research provides information about which specific techniques work best with which problems. Evaluation of practice throughout

the intervention process can help determine whether a worker is really helping a client.

Second, accumulated research helps build a foundation for planning effective interventions. Knowledge of what has worked best in the past provides guidelines for approaches and techniques to be used in the present and in the future. Research establishes the basis for the development of programs and policies that affect many people. Such knowledge can also be used to generate new theories and ideas to further enhance the effectiveness of social work practice.

Evidence-Based Practice   Another term frequently used in social work, which has a meaning similar to research-informed practice, is *evidence-based practice.* This is "the conscientious, explicit, and judicious use of current best evidence in making decisions about the care of clients" (Gambrill, 2000, p. 46; Race, 2008; Rubin, 2008). Gambrill (2000) explains:

> It involves integrating individual practice expertise with the best available external evidence from systematic research as well as considering the values and expectations of clients. External research findings related to problems are drawn on if they are available and they apply to a particular client. Involving clients as informed participants in a collaborative helping relationship is a hallmark of evidence-based practice. Clients are fully informed about the risks and benefits of recommended services as well as alternatives (including the alternative of doing nothing).... The term evidence-based practice *is preferable to the term* empirical practice. *The latter term now seems to be applied to material that has been published, whether or not it is evidence-based. Such use represents an appeal to authority (not evidence). (pp. 46–47)*

Content of Social Work Research   The content of social work research tends to fall within four major categories (Reid, 1995; Tripodi & Lalayants, 2008). First, many studies involve the behavior of individual clients and their interactions with others close to them, including families and small groups. Second, much research focuses on how services are provided to clients, what such services involve, and how successfully they accomplish their goals. Third, some studies address social workers' attitudes and educational backgrounds, in addition to major trends in the profession. Fourth, some research involves the study of "organizations, communities, and social policy" (Reid, 1995, p. 2044). This latter category emphasizes the importance of the larger social environment and its effects on clients' behavior and conditions.

Competency 7: Application of Knowledge of Human Behavior and the Social Environment

EP 2.1.7

Social workers must be knowledgeable about human behavior and the social environment. We have established that focusing on people's functioning within the environmental context is an important thrust of social work. Only after assessing and understanding that functioning can social workers proceed with an intervention plan. Social workers should have knowledge of "biological, social, cultural, psychological, and spiritual development" as this occurs over the lifespan (CSWE, 2008b, p. 6). "Human Behavior and the Social Environment" is the basis for another course or sequence of courses traditionally included in the social work curriculum.

People are constantly and dynamically involved in ongoing activity and communication with others in the environment. *Assessment* is the identification of the "nature and extent of client needs and concerns, as well as critical information about client resources and supports and other environmental factors" so that a helping plan can be devised and implemented (Blythe & Reithoffer, 2000, p. 551). Social work assessment seeks to discover what in any particular situation causes a problem to continue despite the client's expressed wish to change it. Focusing on the environment means looking not only at individuals themselves but also at their involvement with family members, neighbors, work colleagues, the political system, and agencies providing services within the community. This means that clients' problems are not viewed solely as their own fault. The forces surrounding the client frequently cause or contribute to problems, so social workers must focus their assessment on many levels. How the client and the problem fit into the larger scheme of things is critical. Poverty, discrimination, social pressures, and the effects of social welfare policies are all aspects of people's lives that can fall under scrutiny. Focus on Critical Thinking 1.4 provides an example of how social workers might focus on the environmental context of a problem.

Competency 8: Engagement in Policy Practice to Advance Social and Economic Well-Being

EP 2.1.8

Social workers must understand social welfare policies, their history, and how they affect work with clients. Policy, in its simplest form, can be thought of as *rules*. Our lives and those of social workers' clients are governed by rules—about how we drive our cars, when we go to school, how we talk or write sentences, and so on. (Note that Chapter 6 explores the history of social welfare policy development.)

Policies, in essence, are rules that tell us which actions among a multitude of actions we may take and which we may not. Policies guide our work and our decisions. For the purpose of understanding social welfare and the provision of social welfare services, policy might be divided into two major categories: social welfare policy and agency policy. *Social welfare policies* are the laws and regulations that govern which social welfare programs exist, what categories of clients are served, and who qualifies for a given program. They also set standards regarding the type of services to be provided and the qualifications of the service provider.

In addition to the broader realm of social welfare policies, *agency policies* are standards adopted by individual organizations and programs that provide services (e.g., a family service agency, a Department of Human Services, or a nursing home). Such standards may specify the agency's structure, the qualifications of supervisors and workers, the rules governing what workers can do, and the proper procedures for completing a family assessment.

Knowledge of policy is vital for social workers. An organization's policy can dictate how much vacation an employee can have and how raises are earned. An adoption agency's policy can determine who is eligible to adopt a child. A social program's policies determine who gets needed services and resources.

Social workers must become actively involved in establishing and changing social welfare policies for the benefit of their clients; policies determine how money is budgeted and spent, and where resources are made available for clients. Practitioners must be competent in undertaking policy practice to enhance people's well-being and deliver effective social work services. *Policy practice* involves "efforts to change policies in legislative, agency, and community settings, whether by establishing new policies, improving

FOCUS ON CRITICAL THINKING 1.4

Focusing on the Environmental Context of Problems

EP 2.1.7b

Trevor is a 15-year-old gang member in an inner city. The gang is involved in drug dealing, which, of course, is illegal. However, when assessing the situation and potential actions, a broader perspective is necessary. Looking at how the environment encourages and even supports the illegal activity is critical in understanding how to solve the problem. Trevor's father is no longer involved with Trevor's family. Now it's only Trevor, his mother, and three younger brothers. Trevor's mother works a six-day-per-week, nine-hour-per-day second-shift job at Harry's Hole, a local all-night diner, where she slings burgers. Although she loves her children dearly, she can barely make ends meet and has little time to supervise them.

All of the neighborhood kids belong to one gang or another. It gives them a sense of identity and importance, and it provides social support that often is lacking in their families. Easy access to drugs offers an opportunity to escape from impoverished, depressing, and apparently hopeless conditions. Finally, gang membership gives these young people a source of income. In fact, they can get relatively large amounts of money in a hurry.

The gang members' alternatives appear grim. There are few, if any, positive role models to show them other ways of existence. They don't see their peers or adults close to them becoming corporate lawyers, surgeons, or nuclear physicists. They don't even see anyone who is going or has gone to college. In fact, finishing high school is considered quite a feat. Neighborhood unemployment runs at more than 50%. A few part-time, minimum-wage jobs are available—cleaning washrooms at Bugger's Burger Bungalow or unloading freight at Shirley's Shop-Right. But these are unappealing alternatives to the immediate sources of gratification and income provided by gang membership and drug dealing. Even if another minimal source of income could be found, the other rewarding aspects of gang membership would be lost. Also, there's the all-consuming problem of having no positive future to look forward to, so the excitement of the present remains seductive.

This is not to say that it's right for people like Trevor to join vicious gangs and participate in illegal activities. Nor does it mean that Trevor's plight is hopeless. Going beyond a focus on the individual to assess the many environmental impacts and interactions gives the social worker a better understanding of the whole situation. The answer might not be to send Trevor to the state juvenile correctional facility for a year or two and then return him to the same community with the same friends and same problems. Such a "remedy" focuses on the individual in a very limited manner.

A social work perspective views Trevor as a person who's acting as part of a family and a community. Trevor is affected, influenced, supported, and limited by his immediate environment. Continuing along this line of thought, other questions can be raised: How might Trevor's environment be changed? What other alternatives could be made available to him?

Many alternatives would involve major changes in the larger systems around him. Neighborhood youth centers with staff serving as positive role models could be developed as an alternative to gang membership. Trevor's school system could be evaluated. Does it have enough resources to give him a good education? Is there a teacher who could serve as his mentor and enthusiastic supporter? Can a mentorship system be established within the school? Are scholarships and loans available to offer him a viable alternative of college or trade school? Can positive role models demonstrate to Trevor and his peers that other ways of life may be open to them? Where might the resources for implementation of any of these ideas come from?

Concerning Trevor's family environment, can additional resources be provided? These might include food and housing assistance, quality day care for his younger brothers, and even educational opportunities for Trevor's mother so that she, too, could see a brighter future. Is there a Big Brother organization to provide support for Trevor and his siblings? Can the neighborhood be made a better place to live? Can crime be curbed and housing conditions improved?

There obviously are no easy answers. Scarcity of resources remains a fundamental problem. However, this illustration is intended to show how a social worker would look at a variety of options and targets of change, and not just at Trevor.

existing ones, or defeating the policy initiatives of other people" (Jansson, 2011, p. 15).

Sometimes, for whatever reason, social welfare policies are unfair or oppressive to clients. Ironically, although such policies are intended to enhance people's welfare, sometimes they do not. A social worker may decide that a policy is ethically or morally intolerable and advocate on the behalf of clients to try to change it. Practitioners can work to change policy to advance social and economic justice and provide fair treatment to a wide range of people. Traditional social work curricula typically include a course or sequence of courses on "Social Welfare Policy and Services."

Social welfare policy sets the stage for what social workers can do in practice; Chapter 7 explores the topic more thoroughly. Other chapters discuss many types of social welfare policies that affect various client populations and social work practices.

Competency 9: Responsiveness to Contexts That Shape Practice

EP 2.1.9

Social workers must demonstrate competency in functioning within a wide variety of contexts and settings. They must understand the dynamics involved in macro environments like organizations, communities, and legislative bodies that establish social welfare policies. Practitioners must function with and within these systems, serving as leaders to advocate on the behalf of clients. They must keep abreast of new technology, demographic changes, and social trends in order to respond to current issues.

Competency 9 reflects an aspect of social work practice that is closely related to Competency 10, which is described next.

Competency 10: Engagement, Assessment, Intervention, and Evaluation with Individuals, Families, Groups, Organizations, and Communities

EP 2.1.10

Social workers must be competent in employing engagement, assessment, intervention, and evaluation when working with individuals, families, groups, organizations, and communities. All of these terms are prominent in social work practice, which involves the *doing* of social work.

There are two main dimensions inherent in Competency 10. First, the process of social work includes engagement, assessment, intervention, and evaluation (CSWE, 2008b; Kirst-Ashman & Hull, 2012b). *Engagement* is the initial period when practitioners orient themselves to the problem at hand and begin to establish communication and relationships with others also addressing the problem. We have established that *assessment* involves the investigation and determination of variables affecting an identified problem including the client's needs and strengths. *Intervention* is the planning and implementation of the plan to solve the problem and achieve goals. *Evaluation* is "the process of determining whether a given change effort was worthwhile" (Kirst-Ashman & Hull, 2012a, p. 34). Other skills involved in social work practice include "providing leadership for policies and services" and "promoting social and economic justice" (CSWE, 2008b, p. 7).

The second important dimension inherent in Competency 10 is that practice involves working with individuals, families, groups, organizations (large and small), and communities. The acquisition of practice skills for use in all of these contexts is what makes social work useful and practical. Skills provide the muscle to make social work practice effective. Traditional social work curricula typically incorporate a sequence of "Social Work Practice" courses that address the content described in Competencies 9 and 10.

The social work knowledge base includes information about skills in addition to data concerning problems and services. A social worker must know what skills will be most effective in what situations.

Consider a family whose home suddenly burns to the ground. Its members need immediate shelter. The social worker decides it's necessary to use brokering skills—that is, skills for seeking out and linking people with the resources they need. In this situation, brokering skills take precedence over other skills. For instance, using less directive counseling techniques to explore the relationship between the spouses is inappropriate at this time because there is no current evidence of need. Such intervention may be necessary in the future, but only after the immediate crisis of a lack of shelter has been resolved.

Social workers can choose from a multitude of practice techniques and theories about these techniques. Knowledge of the effectiveness of various techniques is critical to selecting those that can accomplish the most in a given situation and to implementing research-informed practice (Competency 6). Regardless of techniques chosen and used, emphasis is placed on client strengths and empowerment, ongoing client collaboration at all stages of the change process, and appreciation of diversity (Pinderhughes, 1995). The foundation of social work practice is generalist practice, discussed next.

Generalist Practice

Generalist practice incorporates all 10 competencies and forms the heart of work education and social work practice. It distinguishes social work from other professions. *Generalist practice* is the application of an eclectic knowledge base,[3] professional values, and a wide range of skills to target any size system for change within the context of four primary processes (Kirst-Ashman & Hull, 2012b). First, generalist practice emphasizes client empowerment. Second, it involves working effectively within an organizational structure and doing so under supervision. Third, it requires the assumption of a wide range of professional roles. Fourth, it involves the application of critical thinking skills to the planned-change (intervention) process. Chapter 4 elaborates further on generalist practice. Note that BSW programs prepare graduates for generalist practice by providing curricula that integrate all 10 competencies (CSWE, 2008b).

Advanced Practice

Advanced practice, which characterizes MSW curricula, provides a specialized concentration that builds upon a generalist practice foundation. For instance, concentrations might include a specialization in mental health, school social work, work with children and families, corrections, health, social services administration, or community organization.

Field Education

Field education is considered the "signature pedagogy" of social work education by CSWE; "signature pedagogy represents the central form of instruction and learning in which a profession socializes its students to perform the role of practitioner" (CSWE, 2008b, p. 8). Field education provides a real-life experience in a social work setting where

student social workers are placed and can practice their skills under supervision. Placement settings may vary. They include social service agencies, hospitals, schools, correctional facilities, organizational placements such as a state NASW branch office, policy-related placements such as legislative offices, or placements in community organizations. Any of these settings must provide appropriate social work supervision. BSW placements require a minimum of 400 hours and MSW placements a minimum of 900 hours. Many social work students find their field education to be the high point of their educational experience.

Chapter Summary

The following summarizes this chapter's content as it relates to the chapter objectives presented at the beginning of the chapter. Objectives include the following:

A Define social work and social welfare.

Social work is the professional activity of helping individuals, groups, or communities enhance or restore their capacity for social functioning and creating societal conditions favorable to this goal. Social welfare is a nation's system of programs, benefits, and services that help people meet those social, economic, educational, and health needs that are fundamental to the maintenance of society.

B Explain critical thinking and provide a framework for examining a wide range of concepts and issues.

Critical thinking is (1) the careful scrutiny of what is stated as true or what appears to be true and the resulting expression of an opinion or conclusion based on that scrutiny, and (2) the creative formulation of an opinion or conclusion when presented with a question, problem, or issue. Examining and evaluating facts and issues involve three steps: (1) ask questions, (2) assess the established facts and issues involved, and (3) assert a concluding opinion.

C Discuss residual, institutional, and developmental perspectives on social welfare, as well as the concept of sustainability.

The residual perspective conceives of social welfare as focusing on problems and gaps. The institutional perspective of social welfare views people's needs as

---

[3]The term *eclectic* refers to "selecting what appears to be best in various doctrines, methods, or styles" (Mish, 2008, p. 394).

a normal part of life. Society has a responsibility to support its members and provide needed benefits and services. The developmental perspective seeks to identify social interventions that have a positive impact on economic development. Sustainability involves "development that meets the current needs of the present generations without jeopardizing the ability of future generations to meet their needs" (Mary, 2008, p. 32).

D Explain the conservative–liberal continuum with respect to viewing the social welfare system.

Conservatism is the philosophy that individuals are responsible for themselves, government should provide minimal interference in people's lives, and change is generally unnecessary. Liberalism is the philosophy that government should be involved in the social, political, and economic structure so that all people's rights and privileges are protected in the name of social justice. Radicalism is the philosophy that the social and political systems as they stand are not structurally capable of truly providing social justice, so fundamental changes in those systems are necessary.

E Examine your personal attitudes about some social welfare issues.

Responding to issues and questions regarding the importance of change and the responsibility of government can help an individual determine his or her personal stance on the conservative–liberal continuum.

F Explain social work's fields of practice.

Fields of practice in social work include children and families, aging, disabilities, health, mental health, substance abuse, schools, and corrections. Other contexts for practice are occupational social work, rural social work, police social work, and forensic social work.

G Explore the process of choosing a career.

The continuum of social work careers includes baccalaureate social workers (BSWs), master's social workers (MSWs), and social workers who have doctorates in social work (Ph.D. or DSW). When considering a career, it's important to think about your general orientation toward the future, the extent to which you are people-oriented versus non-people-oriented, the ways in which you would like to work with people, what majors are available, and, if appropriate, what type of social work you would like to practice.

H Address how social work builds on other disciplines.

Social work builds on many disciplines, including psychology, sociology, political science, economics, biology, psychiatry, counseling, and cultural anthropology.

I Discuss the uniqueness of social work.

Social work is unique in that it focuses on people's most difficult problems, often targets the environment for change, stresses the need for advocacy on a client's behalf, stems from a core of professional values, and emphasizes the importance of working in a partnership with clients.

J Identify some basic concepts in systems theories and the ecological perspective that are important for understanding social work.

Important concepts in systems theories and the ecological perspective relevant to social work practice include system (micro, mezzo, and macro), client system, social environment, and coping.

K Describe social work education's goals, curriculum, and competencies.

The Council on Social Work Education's Educational Policy and Accreditation Standards require that accredited social work programs prove that students demonstrate 10 competencies. These competencies are stated and explained. Courses offered in traditional social work curricula are identified. The core social work concepts of general practice, advanced practice, and field education are introduced.

LOOKING AHEAD

This chapter introduced the basic concept of social welfare and the foundations of the social work profession. The next chapter focuses on social work values and ethics, a primary content area that underlies and guides the social work profession.

COMPETENCY NOTES

This section relates chapter content to the Council on Social Work Education's (CSWE) Educational

Policy and Accreditation Standards (EPAS) (CSWE, 2008b). One major goal of social work education is to facilitate students' attainment of the EPAS-designated 10 core competencies and their 41 related practice behaviors so that students develop into competent practitioners.

Students require knowledge in order to develop skills and become competent. Our intent here is to specify what chapter content and knowledge coincides with the development of specific competencies and practice behaviors. (This ultimately is intended to assist in the accreditation process.) Therefore, the listing presented here first cites the various Educational Policy (EP) core competencies and their related practice behaviors that are relevant to chapter content. Note that the listing follows the order that competencies and practice behaviors are cited in the EPAS.

The EPAS document lists practice behaviors under each of the 10 core competencies as bulleted items. To clarify the "Competency Notes" here, the bulleted practice behaviors have been alphabetized under each competency. Please observe that for EP 2.1.10, only the bulleted practice behaviors are labeled "a" through "m" (not the "engagement," "assessment," "intervention," and "evaluation" subcategories identified in EP 2.1.10). Practice behaviors are alphabetized both under the icons placed throughout the book and in the "Competency Notes" cited at the end of each chapter.

You have observed that "helping hands" icons are interspersed throughout the chapter to indicate where relevant accompanying content is located. Page numbers noted below indicate where icons are placed in the chapter. Following the icon's page number is a brief explanation of how the content accompanying the icon relates to the specified competency or practice behavior.

The following identifies where Educational Policy (EP) competencies and practice behaviors are discussed in the chapter.

EP 2.1.1 Identify as a professional social worker and conduct oneself accordingly. *(p. 13):* Establishing a professional identity includes having knowledge about the history of the social work profession and social welfare. *(p. 23):* Professional social workers must attain competency in the 10 areas identified here. *(p. 23):* EP 2.1.1 is introduced and described.

EP 2.1.1b Practice personal reflection and self-correction to assure continual professional development. *(p. 11):* It's important for social workers to use personal reflection to understand their own views and values in order to practice objectively and not impose personal views on clients. *(p. 14):* Social workers should practice self-reflection regarding their own attitudes and values so that personal views don't interfere with the development of professional values and ethics. *(p. 16):* It's important to practice personal reflection to determine one's most appropriate career path.

EP 2.1.1c Attend to professional roles and boundaries. *(p. 14):* Professional social work roles at the BSW and MSW levels are introduced. *(p. 23):* Attending to professional roles and practices as demonstrated by achieving competency in these defined areas is part of becoming a professional social worker.

EP 2.1.1d Demonstrate professional demeanor in behavior, appearance, and communication. *(p. 23):* Attaining competency in the areas identified by the EPAS involves demonstrating professional behavior, appearance, and communication.

EP 2.1.2 Apply social work ethical principles to guide professional practice. *(p. 21):* Social workers adhere to a core of professional values that guide practice. *(p. 24):* EP 2.1.2 is introduced and described.

EP 2.1.2a Recognize and manage personal values in a way that allows professional values to guide practice. *(p. 11):* Identifying personal values allows practitioners to manage these values so that they don't interfere with professional values and ethics. *(p. 14):* Social workers should recognize and manage their own personal values so that professional values, not personal values, may guide practice.

**EP 2.1.2b Make ethical decisions by applying standards of the National Association of Social Workers (NASW) *Code of Ethics* and, as applicable, of the International Federation of Social Workers/International Association of Schools of Social Work *Ethics in Social Work, Statement of Principles.* *(p. 21):* Social workers should follow the NASW *Code of Ethics*, which emphasizes client self-determination.

EP 2.1.3 Apply critical thinking to inform and communicate professional judgments. *(p. 8):* Social workers should think critically about what is true and what is only thought or said to be true. *(p. 24):* EP 2.1.3 is introduced and described.

EP 2.1.3a Distinguish, appraise, and integrate multiple sources of knowledge, including research-based knowledge, and practice wisdom. *(p. 22):* Systems theories and ecological concepts provide useful sources of knowledge for understanding social work practice.

EP 2.1.4 Engage diversity and difference in practice. *(p. 24):* EP 2.1.4 is introduced and described.

EP 2.1.5 Advance human rights social and economic justice. *(p. 24):* EP 2.1.5 is introduced and described.

EP 2.1.5b Advocate for human rights and social and economic justice. *(p. 10):* The concept of sustainability is related to the pursuit of human rights.

EP 2.1.6 Engage in research-informed practice and practice-informed research. *(p. 25):* EP 2.1.6 is introduced and described.

EP 2.1.7 Apply knowledge of human behavior and the social environment. *(p. 19):* Social workers apply knowledge about human behavior and the social environment to target the environment for change. *(p. 26):* EP 2.1.7 is introduced and described.

EP 2.1.7a Utilize conceptual frameworks to guide the processes of assessment, intervention, and evaluation. *(p. 7):* Residual, institutional, and developmental perspectives provide conceptual frameworks for understanding and assessing the concept of social welfare. *(p. 22):* Systems theories and ecological concepts provide useful conceptual frameworks to guide social work assessment and intervention.

EP 2.1.7b Critique and apply knowledge to understand person and environment. *(p. 7):* Critiquing residual, institutional, and developmental perspectives on social welfare can help social workers understand people's functioning in their environment. *(p. 27):* This case example reflects the need to critique and apply a wide range of knowledge to understand Trevor's functioning within his environment.

EP 2.1.8 Engage in policy practice to advance social and economic well-being and to deliver effective social work services. *(p. 26):* EP 2.1.8 is introduced and described.

EP 2.1.8a Analyze, formulate, and advocate for policies that advance social well-being. *(p. 19):* Social work is unique in that practitioners are charged with changing policies and the environment on people's behalf.

EP 2.1.9 Respond to contexts that shape practice. *(p. 28):* EP 2.1.9 is introduced and described.

EP 2.1.9b Provide leadership in promoting sustainable changes in service delivery and practice to improve the quality of social services. *(p. 10):* Social workers should provide leadership in promoting sustainable changes to benefit the human condition.

EP 2.1.10 Engage, assess, intervene, and evaluate with individuals, families, groups, organizations, and communities. *(p. 19):* Social work is unique in that practitioners work with individuals, families, groups, organizations, and communities on a wide range of problems and issues. *(p. 28):* EP 2.1.10 is introduced and described.

EP 2.1.10f Develop mutually agreed-on intervention goals and objectives. *(p. 21):* The social work profession stresses the importance of working together with clients to develop mutually agreed-on goals.

EP 2.1.10k Negotiate, mediate, and advocate for clients. *(p. 21):* Advocacy on clients' behalf is a major focus of social work and a dimension of it that makes it unique.

FOR FURTHER EXPLORATION ON THE INTERNET

See this text's Social Work CourseMate website at *www.cengagebrain.com* for learning tools such as chapter quizzing, videos, glossary flashcards, and more.

CHAPTER 2

Social Work Values and Ethics

John Lund/Nevada Wier/Blend Images/Getty Images

How might you answer these questions?

- *How do you determine what is right and what is wrong?*
- *Have you ever run into situations in which it's difficult to decide what is the right thing to do? If so, what were the circumstances?*
- *What personal values do you have about controversial issues such as the death penalty? Abortion? School prayer? Gun control? Affirmative action? Assisted suicide?*

Social work is a values-based profession; that is, everything social workers do must be with professional values in mind. Values involve what you do and do not consider important and worthwhile. They also involve judgments and decisions about relative worth—that is, about what is more valuable and what is less valuable.

The Council on Social Work Education (CSWE), the organization that accredits social work programs throughout the United States, establishes standards guiding social work education. CSWE (2008b) cites social work's purpose, which is based on its professional values:

The purpose of the social work profession is to promote human and community well-being. Guided by a person and environment construct, a global perspective, respect for human diversity, and knowledge based on scientific inquiry, social work's purpose is actualized through its quest for social and economic justice, the prevention of conditions that limit human rights, the elimination of poverty, and the enhancement of the quality of life for all persons. (p. 1)

Ethics *involve principles that specify what is good and what is bad. They clarify what should and should not be done. The National Association of Social Workers (NASW) Code of Ethics is based on professional values (NASW, 2008). CSWE requires that social work programs educate students to achieve competence in applying "social work ethical principles to guide professional practice" (CSWE, 2008b, p. 4).*

Dolgoff, Harrington, & Loewenberg (2012) explain, "Ethics are deduced from values and must be in consonance with them. The difference between them is that values are concerned with what is good *and desirable, while ethics deal with what is* right *and correct" (p. 25). Values determine what beliefs are appropriate. Ethics address what to do* with *or how to* apply *those beliefs to do the "right" thing.*

Cournoyer (2011) clearly summarizes the importance of social work ethics:

We must consider every aspect of practice, every decision, every assessment, every intervention, and virtually every action we undertake as social workers from the perspective of your professional ethics and obligations. This dimension supersedes all others. Ethical responsibilities take precedence over theoretical knowledge, research findings, practice wisdom, agency policies, and, of course, our own personal values, preferences, and beliefs. (p. 126)

Professional judgments may seem to be a simple matter of common sense. However, in real-life decisions, values and ethical principles conflict constantly. This can result in ethical dilemmas—problematic situations in which one must make a difficult choice among two or more alternatives. A dilemma occurs when no one answer can conform to all the ethical principles involved.

For example, a client might inform her social worker that she plans to murder her mother-in-law because she can't take the condescending nagging anymore. On the one hand, is the social worker required to report to the authorities that this client has threatened to harm another person? On the other, how can this worker maintain confidentiality and report the threats at the same time? (Confidentiality is the ethical principle that workers should not share information provided by or about a client unless that worker has the client's explicit permission to do so.)

Social workers have established guidelines to ethical decision making that can help them get through the difficult decision-making process when solving an ethical dilemma (Kirst-Ashman & Hull, 2012b; Dolgoff et al., 2012; Reamer, 1998). The NASW Code of Ethics offers a good starting point for discussing professional values and ethics. It highlights some of the field's primary values and provides suggestions for working in an ethical manner. However, it's only a beginning. The potential value conflicts and ethical dilemmas social workers may face are infinite.

It should be clear to you by now that the social work profession has a strong set of values. Some of you reading this are embracing these values and deciding whether to become a social worker. Others take this course out of some level of interest in people's welfare or simply for the credits. You may have personal opinions strongly opposed to some of the value stances. Regardless, the content of this book will provide some provocative food for thought. It seeks to challenge some of your views about the world and enhance your understanding of people and their environments, and ways they can work together to improve the welfare of all.

Learning Objectives

A   Review the general categories in the NASW *Code of Ethics*.

EP 2.1.2

B   Provide case examples of compliance and noncompliance concerning some of the major ethical issues involved, including self-determination, privacy and confidentiality, conflict of interest and dual relationships, sexual relationships, respect for colleagues, and referral for services.

C   Introduce critical thinking about ethical dilemmas.

D   Discuss ethical issues concerning the Internet.

E   Examine ethical conflicts faced by military social workers during combat.

F   Recognize ethical obligations at the macro level.

G   Introduce the importance of social work in a global context, including international social work and international social work organizations.

H   Define and discuss human rights and examine the human rights violation of human trafficking.

I   Discuss the difference between personal and professional values.

The NASW *Code of Ethics*

EP 2.1.2b

We have established the importance of ethics in guiding professional behavior. Because of its significance, we will examine various aspects of the NASW *Code of Ethics*, which has four primary facets (2008). First, the preamble summarizes social work's general goals or mission and identifies its core values. The mission "is to enhance human well-being and help meet the basic human needs of all people, with particular attention to the needs and empowerment of people who are vulnerable, oppressed, and living in poverty" (NASW, 2008). The six core values include these:

1. *Service*: Providing help, resources, and benefits so people can achieve their maximum potential.
2. *Social justice*: Upholding the condition that in a perfect world all citizens would have identical

"rights, protection, opportunities, obligations, and social benefits," regardless of their backgrounds and membership in diverse groups (Barker, 2003, pp. 404–405).

3. *Dignity and worth of the person*: Holding in high esteem and appreciating individual value.
4. *Importance of human relationships*: Valuing the dynamic reciprocal interactions between social workers and clients, including how they communicate, think and feel about each other, and behave toward each other.
5. *Integrity*: Maintaining trustworthiness and sound adherence to moral ideals.
6. *Competence*: Having the necessary skills and abilities to work effectively with clients.

The second major facet in the *Code*, "Purpose of the NASW Code of Ethics," identifies its six major aims:

1. Identifying primary social work values.
2. Summarizing broad ethical principles as guidelines for practice.
3. Helping determine relevant considerations when addressing an ethical dilemma.
4. Providing broad ethical standards to which the public in general may hold the profession accountable.
5. Socializing new practitioners to the mission, goals, and ethics inherent in the profession.
6. Articulating specific standards that the profession may use to judge its members' conduct.

Of particular note is the *Code's* emphasis on the complexity of ethical dilemmas. The *Code* provides no simple formula for resolution; rather, it stresses that ethical dilemmas may be viewed from a range of perspectives. Therefore, social workers must use critical thinking to resolve ethical issues with the *Code* as a springboard. Focus on Critical Thinking 2.1 provides examples of ethical dilemmas social workers may experience.

The *Code's* third facet, "Ethical Principles," is based on the six core values described previously and sets forth standards to which all practitioners should strive. For example, the ethical principle relating to the value of *social justice* states that "social workers challenge social injustice." Likewise, the principle based on *integrity* states that "social workers [should] behave in a trustworthy manner."

The final facet of the *Code*, the "Ethical Standards," is by far the most extensive. It encompasses

155 specific principles clustered under six major categories. These include social workers' ethical responsibilities to clients, to colleagues, in practice settings, as professionals, to the social work profession, and to the broader society. Highlight 2.1 lists the concepts involved in each, and subsequent sections discuss the major categories, providing some specific examples for each.

Social Workers' Ethical Responsibilities to Clients

The first category of ethical standards addresses how practitioners should behave with respect to clients and what aspects of worker–client interaction are most significant within an ethical context. It is beyond the scope of this book to cover all 16 areas within this category, so we will focus on only a few arbitrarily selected ones. These are self-determination, privacy and confidentiality, conflict of interest and dual relationships, and sexual relationships with clients. After each, examples of compliance and of violation are provided.

Self-Determination

Practitioners should nurture and support client *self-determination*—each individual's right to make his or her own decisions. Applied to social work, this means that practitioners are responsible for (1) informing clients about available resources, (2) helping them define and articulate their alternatives, and (3) assisting them in evaluating the consequences of each option. The goal is to assist clients in making the best, most informed choices possible.

Example of Compliance   Gilda is a social worker in a protective services unit for older adults in a large urban county's Department of Social Services. Her job is to visit older adults who may be at risk of some harm (e.g., being unable to care for themselves or suffering physical abuse by others), assess the situation, and help them in whatever ways possible. Sometimes Gilda connects clients with appropriate resources like Meals-on-Wheels, an agency that delivers daily hot meals to older adults' homes for minimal cost. Other times, Gilda helps place older adults in more structured settings, such as nursing homes, to meet their increasingly dependent needs.

One of Gilda's clients, Desiree, age 89, tripped on a crack in the sidewalk outside her home and severely sprained her ankle. Desiree is adamant that she will not leave her home, no matter what. She feels that

FOCUS ON CRITICAL THINKING 2.1

What Should a Social Worker Do?

**EP 2.1.2c,
2.1.3**

The following are examples of ethical dilemmas confronting social workers. Answers are difficult because there are no perfect solutions. What would you do if you were a social worker in each of the following situations?

Scenario A[1]

Evita was a hospital social worker called in to talk with parents who had just brought their 6-week-old infant Eric, the youngest of their three children, to the emergency room. Eric, whose skin had turned blue and who was not breathing, was placed on a respirator in intensive care for three days. After that time, the medical staff determined that he was brain-dead, and the parents, Bill and Brenda, sorrowfully gave their permission to "pull the plug."

Evita had the opportunity to speak with Bill and Brenda as they waited steadfastly by Eric's bedside hoping he would revive. She discovered that Bill had been babysitting Eric while Brenda ran some errands. Eric had been sleeping on the bed when Bill lay down to take a nap next to him. Apparently Bill had fallen asleep and rolled over on Eric, accidentally smothering him. Evita thought it was odd that Bill had not awakened when Eric, an active baby who was large for his age, must have been struggling desperately for breath. Bill admitted that he had had a couple of beers prior to his nap but insisted that he was not drunk.

Tests revealed that Eric displayed no sign of injuries or other suspicious symptoms. The physician in charge of Eric was unaware of the story's details. Therefore, she determined that Eric must have died of sudden infant death syndrome (SIDS), which she planned to cite as the cause of death. *SIDS* is "the death of a seemingly healthy baby in its sleep, due to an apparent spontaneous cessation of breathing" (Lindberg, 2007, p. 1370).

Evita knew Eric's death was not due to SIDS. Yet informing the overseeing physician about what really happened would probably do little good. Bill and Brenda were filled with sorrow and blamed themselves for the tragedy.

Critical Thinking Questions

What good would it do to raise suspicions about the cause of death and parental competence? Might it only put the parents through an agonizing investigation and potentially cause removal of the other two children? If you were Evita, what would you do?

Scenario B

Harry is a county Department of Social Services worker whose clients consist primarily of poor, female-headed families receiving public assistance. During one of his meetings with Dora, a single mother of three small children, she happily reveals that she is babysitting for several neighborhood children. She is thrilled to earn the extra income and is proud to share her news with Harry. Regulations state that people receiving public assistance must report any additional income, with benefits then decreased proportionally. But reporting her extra income would probably undermine Dora's trust and destroy Harry's relationship with her. And Dora would probably stop babysitting because it would no longer get her ahead. She is barely making ends meet as it is with her meager public assistance payments. Dora already is participating in a compulsory job-training program, preparing her for full-time employment.

Critical Thinking Questions

What good would it do to report this scanty income despite the fact that regulations require such reporting? Dora likely will get a full-time job soon, at which time public assistance payments will no longer be an issue. What should Harry do?

Scenario C

Ping is a social worker at a mental health center that provides individual and group counseling for a wide range of problems and issues. One of Ping's clients is Cheyenne, age 14, who is depressed and potentially suicidal. During one of their individual counseling sessions, Cheyenne tells Ping that she is sexually active. She states that if she gets pregnant with her current boyfriend she will surely kill herself. Cheyenne asks Ping to help her get some form of contraception, possibly from Planned Parenthood. Cheyenne indicates that her boyfriend refuses to use condoms because he says he doesn't like to feel restricted. Ping knows Cheyenne's parents are very religious and are fervently against premarital sex. They would never consent to Cheyenne using contraception and would vehemently oppose Ping's interference in this matter.

Critical Thinking Questions

What about Cheyenne's life and well-being? What should Ping do?

(continued)

FOCUS ON CRITICAL THINKING 2.1 *(continued)*

EP 2.1.2d

Commentary

When confronting an ethical dilemma, it's important to use ethical reasoning to determine the right thing to do. By definition a dilemma has no perfect answer or it wouldn't be a dilemma. There would simply be a more obvious solution. Strom-Gottfried (2007) proposes a strategy of asking and answering six questions to help make such a decision:

- Who will be helpful?
- What are my choices?
- When have I faced a similar dilemma?
- Where do ethical and clinical guidelines lead me?
- Why am I selecting a particular course of action?
- How should I enact my decision?" (p. 27)

---

[1]This case is based on one presented in Robison and Reeser (2000, pp. 2–3).

HIGHLIGHT 2.1

Ethical Standards in the NASW Code of Ethics

EP 2.1.2b

1. Social Workers' Ethical Responsibilities to Clients
   1.01 Commitment to Clients
   1.02 Self-Determination
   1.03 Informed Consent
   1.04 Competence
   1.05 Cultural Competence and Social Diversity
   1.06 Conflicts of Interest
   1.07 Privacy and Confidentiality
   1.08 Access to Records
   1.09 Sexual Relationships
   1.10 Physical Contact
   1.11 Sexual Harassment
   1.12 Derogatory Language
   1.13 Payment for Services
   1.14 Clients Who Lack Decision-Making Capacity
   1.15 Interruption of Services
   1.16 Termination of Services

2. Social Workers' Ethical Responsibilities to Colleagues
   2.01 Respect
   2.02 Confidentiality
   2.03 Interdisciplinary Collaboration
   2.04 Disputes Involving Colleagues
   2.05 Consultation
   2.06 Referral for Services
   2.07 Sexual Relationships
   2.08 Sexual Harassment
   2.09 Impairment of Colleagues
   2.10 Incompetence of Colleagues
   2.11 Unethical Conduct of Colleagues

3. Social Workers' Ethical Responsibilities in Practice Settings
   3.01 Supervision and Consultation
   3.02 Education and Training
   3.03 Performance Evaluation
   3.04 Client Records
   3.05 Billing
   3.06 Client Transfer
   3.07 Administration
   3.08 Continuing Education and Staff Development
   3.09 Commitments to Employers
   3.10 Labor–Management Disputes

4. Social Workers' Ethical Responsibilities as Professionals
   4.01 Competence
   4.02 Discrimination
   4.03 Private Conduct
   4.04 Dishonesty, Fraud, and Deception
   4.05 Impairment
   4.06 Misrepresentation
   4.07 Solicitations
   4.08 Acknowledging Credit

5. Social Workers' Ethical Responsibilities to the Social Work Profession
   5.01 Integrity of the Profession
   5.02 Evaluation and Research

6. Social Workers' Ethical Responsibilities to the Broader Society
   6.01 Social Welfare
   6.02 Public Participation
   6.03 Public Emergencies
   6.04 Social and Political Action

would destroy her independence and effectively be the first step into the grave. However, Desiree is having a terrible time getting around in her own home. She can barely walk and usually has to crawl to the bathroom when no one is around to help her.

Gilda thinks Desiree would probably be better off in a more structured setting where she could get the help she needs. However, Gilda respects Desiree's right to self-determination. So she works out a plan with Desiree that's satisfactory to the client. Desiree will temporarily reside in a nearby health-care facility for older adults until she can once again put pressure on her ankle and walk. Gilda makes arrangements with the facility for Desiree to stay there. Gilda also helps Desiree arrange for someone to watch her home and forward her mail to her temporarily.

Example of a Violation   Jorge is a job coach for a county social services department. His job involves evaluating people's strengths, skills, and interests; linking them with appropriate employment; and helping them adjust to their work environments. Daisy, age 19, is one of Jorge's clients. Daisy emphasizes that she would like to get a job as a secretary or administrative assistant. Daisy says that she's generally shy with people and would like a job in which she could work in a more solitary manner. She also says that she has always been good at typing. Jorge knows that Daisy never graduated from high school, and he doesn't believe that her typing or writing skills are anywhere near adequate for such a position. Therefore, he decides not to inform Daisy about available clerical positions. Rather, he steers her to think about becoming a sales clerk.

Privacy and Confidentiality

Social workers must uphold client privacy and confidentiality. *Privacy* is the condition of being free from unauthorized observation or intrusion. We have established that *confidentiality* is the ethical principle that workers should not share information provided by a client or about a client unless they have the client's explicit permission to do so.

There is more to confidentiality than may be immediately apparent. Confidentiality means more than not revealing information about clients to others. It also involves not asking for more information than is necessary, as well as informing clients about the limitations of confidentiality within the agency setting. For example, will supervisors, researchers, or students have access to private information? Must statistics and other data about clients' personal lives be submitted to public regulatory agencies or funding sources for *accountability* (a profession's responsibility to clients and the community that workers are effectively doing what they say they are going to do)? Highlight 2.2 explores some issues involving confidentiality and the Internet.

Example of Compliance   Mackenzie is a school social worker who is just beginning a support group for sixth-grade children coping with their parents' recent divorces. Early in the first session, she explains to the children the limits of confidentiality. For example, if they share anything about wanting to hurt someone or themselves, committing a crime, or participating in sexual activity, it's her responsibility to report it. This way, group members know where they stand. If they share this kind of information, they know Mackenzie has no choice but to report it.

Example of a Violation   Peter and Piper are social work counselors at a group home for adolescent boys with emotional and behavioral problems. They and their significant others occasionally have dinner with a mutual friend, Jack, a county social services worker, along with his significant other. The three social workers regularly compare "battle stories" about their most difficult cases. This occurs despite the fact that they have very different caseloads and their significant others are present to hear their discussion. Sometimes, after a few cocktails, voices elevate, and other diners can overhear.

Conflict of Interest and Dual Relationships

The *Code of Ethics* warns practitioners to be acutely aware and steer clear of any possible conflicts of interest that might obstruct professional judgment. In the social work context, a *conflict of interest* is a clash between the responsibilities of the professional role and the potential for personal gain. An example is a hospital social worker who encourages clients to purchase health insurance policies from her spouse, who is an insurance salesman. To what extent might this practice not be in the clients' best interest? To what extent will this worker be biased to experience personal income gain? Another example involves a practitioner running for office who pressures clients to vote for her. To what extent does this interfere with her ability to work with and help these clients? What if the clients don't agree with the worker's political views? How will this alter the clients' perception of the worker–client relationship? "Similarly, a practitioner who invests money in a client's business is embedded in a conflict of interest; the professional's financial interests may clash with her duty to the client (for example, if the professional's relationship with the client becomes strained because they disagree about some aspect of their shared business venture)" (Reamer, 2001, p. 5). A client who is a used car salesman may even "offer to sell ... [a worker] a car at a discount"; Dolgoff, Lewenberg, and Harrington (2005) emphasize to workers, "Don't accept his offer, no matter how good it is!" (p. 142). Such a scenario may result in the client expecting something from the worker in return, such as special treatment or personal closeness.

The *Code* emphasizes that clients' best interests must be protected to the maximum extent possible. If these interests are jeopardized, termination of the worker–client relationship and appropriate referral elsewhere may be necessary.

One type of conflict of interest involves dual or multiple relationships. Corey, Corey, and Callanan (2011) explain:

[Dual *or*] multiple relationships *occur when professionals assume two or more roles at the same time or sequentially with a client. This may involve assuming more than one professional role (such as instructor and [counselor]...) or blending a professional and nonprofessional relationship (such as counselor and friend or counselor and business partner). Multiple relationships also include providing [counseling] ... to a relative or a friend's relative, socializing with clients, becoming emotionally or sexually involved with a client or former client, combining the roles of supervisor and [counselor,] ... having a business relationship with a client, borrowing money from a client, or loaning money to a client. (p. 268)*

HIGHLIGHT 2.2

Social Work, Confidentiality, and the Internet

EP 2.1.3c, 2.1.9a

The Internet has become a primary and essential means for communicating information among social work professionals. Internet etiquette (or "netiquette") in some ways corresponds with ethics in person-to-person or "hardcopy" situations, but in other ways it does not (Guffey, 2010, p.110). "Cyberspace remains a new culture and has unique social forces and social sanctions that have no functional equivalent in the real world" (Marson, 2000, p. 20). For example, client confidentiality is important in virtually all situations, yet the means of maintaining it electronically are unique. At least three issues are significant (Marson, 2000).

First, social workers and their agencies must be well versed in any Internet functions they undertake. It must be clear who has access to client information and how. In the real world, workers lock their offices and, sometimes, their filing cabinets when they go home. They must know how to do the same thing in the electronic environment if that's where client communications and records are kept. Some simple rules apply:

1. Keep passwords confidential.
2. Avoid calling up a password on the screen when others are in the room (this is akin to talking loudly about clients in a crowded lunchroom).
3. Avoid writing the password down or making it readily available on some database.
4. Alter passwords every few months.

Second, any language used should be professional and socially appropriate. Many people seem to feel more comfortable using derogatory language on the Internet. Perhaps it's the anonymity or lack of physical interpersonal contact that makes people using the Internet feel more informal and, possibly, freer. Guffey (2010) reflects:

[Many] writers sometimes send sensitive, confidential, inflammatory, or potentially embarrassing messages. Beware! E-mail creates a permanent record that does not go away even when deleted. Every message is a ... communication that can be used against you or your employer. Don't write anything that you wouldn't want your boss, your family, or a judge to read. (p. 110)

Professional ethics can provide guidelines for proper behavior. The NASW *Code of Ethics* states that "[s]ocial workers should not use derogatory language in their written or verbal communications to or about clients" (NASW, 2008, 1.12).

A third issue involving confidentiality concerns the ease with which information can be shared with large numbers of people such as those on a *listserv*—"a computerized system by which subscribers are able to

(continued)

HIGHLIGHT 2.2 (continued)

communicate to all other subscribers by sending a transmission to one address" (Marson, 1998, p. 21). It is easy to reply to all listserv members, instead of only the person who initiated a contact or raised a question. Information conveyed in chatroom conversations (in which a number of people can communicate concurrently at a Website) should also be carefully monitored.

Social workers use the Internet for many reasons, including the following (Marson, 1998):

- *Networking.* This involves the establishment of communication and interpersonal interaction among people to provide support, exchange information, or achieve some designated goal. For example, social workers in one state network with each other to share information about pending social legislation and advocate for positive changes.
- *Sharing resource material to improve practice and agency service.* However, note that not all resource material is of equal value or even of any value. For example, one brief Internet search revealed Websites entitled Captain Ozone, Cheesy-wotsits, Evil Fluffy Bunnies of Doom, and Puppet Terrors. It's important to evaluate the validity of any Website

concerning its currency, the reliability of who developed or sponsors the site, the content's purpose and intended audience, and accuracy (Guffey, 2008).

- *Identifying referral services for specific client needs.* Marson (1998) cites a case in which "an anonymous social worker had a client who was suffering from terminal lung cancer and was receiving hospice services at her home. [A *hospice* is a place of rest or a system of services providing care for people who are terminally ill. The idea is to make people as comfortable as possible in the little time they have before they die.] The client's physical isolation made a dreadful situation worse. In an effort to assist with her last months, the social worker linked the client to UseNet's cancer support group [on the Internet], which provided her with the support vital for her morale" (p. 24).
- *Seeking out or conducting research.* It's easy to consult with colleagues and to exchange documents regarding effective practice techniques and research projects.
- *Communicating efficiently.* Sometimes it's difficult to reach people, especially when they're busy and unavailable. When information must be conveyed quickly, e-mail provides a good alternative.

The *Code of Ethics* states that "[s]ocial workers should not engage in dual or multiple relationships with clients or former clients" where such people have any risk of being harmed (NASW, 2008, 1.06c). As in other potential conflicts of interest, social workers should always give top priority to clients' best interests. Dolgoff and his colleagues (2012) reflect:

Must dual-role relationships necessarily interfere with professional relationships? Do they always result in conflict? In modern society where everyone fills multiple roles, there are many situations where social workers and clients participate in dual or multiple relationships. Both may be members of the same political party, church, mosque, or synagogue, or their children may attend the same school or be classmates. There is no reason for a social worker to withdraw from these activities simply because the client also engages in them. The issue is to separate the professional relationship from other relationships [in order to avoid ethical dilemmas]. (p. 126)

However, it remains important for the worker to remember that "there is always the potential for a conflict of interest and of exploitation of the person seeking help. This makes it critical that whenever there is a possibility of a dual relationship the . . . [practitioner], who is the person who knows the difficulties that could arise in such relationships, must think about and perhaps discuss with a supervisor the potential conflicts of interest and exploitation before entering into such a relationship" (Syme, 2003, p. 8).

Example of Compliance[2]   Javon is a social worker at a substance abuse counseling center. He has just received a referral of a client, Laura Hedgehog, whose name is not familiar to him. When she arrives at his office, he is surprised to find out he knows her. He used to work with her at another social services agency several years ago and had even formed a

[2]This example is loosely based on one presented in *Ethical Decisions for Social Work Practice* (7th ed.) by Dolgoff et al. (2005, p. 247).

mild friendship with her. She apparently had since married and changed her last name. Laura greets Javon enthusiastically and emphasizes how happy she is that he will be her counselor. She stresses how much she trusts his competence and knows he can help her. Javon feels uncomfortable about this dual relationship, knowing Laura both as a client and a former colleague. Javon gently thanks her for her confidence and then explains how he feels such a dual relationship would create a serious ethical dilemma for him. He feels he cannot be objective and offer her the best help possible. He refers her to one of his colleagues, whom he candidly describes as an excellent counselor.

Example of a Violation Huda is a protective services worker whose primary job is to investigate alleged cases of child maltreatment and make recommendations for treatment, sometimes involving children's removal from the home. Huda attends the first session of a yoga class where she is startled to see that the instructor, Hope, is the mother in one of the families with whom Huda is currently working. Huda participates in the whole class, after which Hope approaches her. Hope enthusiastically welcomes her and says she'd be happy to give Huda a discount in registration fees. Huda thinks to herself, "What would it hurt? I'm pretty strapped for cash this month. It certainly won't influence my decision about her family or anything like that." *Will it?*

Sexual Relationships

Another type of dual relationship involves sexual relationships, which the *Code* emphasizes by addressing it as a separate topic. Simply put, social workers should not have sexual relationships with current clients, clients' relatives, or others personally involved with clients. The *Code of Ethics* also discourages social workers from having sexual relationships with former clients. If a social worker pursues this under "extraordinary circumstances, it is social workers—not their clients—who assume the full burden of demonstrating that the former client has not been exploited, coerced, or manipulated, intentionally or unintentionally" (NASW, 2008, 1.09c). Additionally, social workers should not provide clinical services to clients with whom they were formerly sexual partners.

The *Code* uses powerful language to emphasize that workers should not have sex with clients under any circumstances. Parsons (2001) explains that the "inappropriateness of [a] sexual relationship between helper and client rests in the fact that the helping relationship is unbalanced in power ... Thus, the reciprocal nature characteristic of a healthy intimate relationship is not possible" (p. 146). Corey and his colleagues (2011) indicate that harmful effects can range "from mistrust of opposite sex relationships to hospitalization and, in some cases, suicide. Other effects of sexual intimacies on clients' emotional, social, and sexual adjustment" include "negative feelings about the experience, a negative impact on their personality, and a deterioration of their sexual relationship with their primary partner" (p. 310).

Example of Compliance Tyrone is a social worker with a caseload of families, mostly young women, receiving public assistance. Diana, one of his clients, has worked quite hard to get through a job-training program and find stable employment. They had hit it off since the beginning and respected each other's efforts. One day, Diana casually asks Tyrone if he'd be interested in dinner and a movie the following weekend. He politely declines. They continue working together until Diana gets back on her feet and leaves Tyrone's program.

Example of a Violation Alyssa, age 24, is a counselor at a community-based halfway house for men on parole who are also substance abusers. *Halfway houses* are transitional dwellings that provide structure, support, and guidance for persons unable to function independently in the community. They are transitional because they provide a middle ground between a full-time residential setting (e.g., an institution or prison) and the relative freedom of living in the community.[3] *Parole* is the "conditional release of a prisoner serving an indeterminate or unexpired sentence," usually for good behavior or the promise of good behavior, under the supervision of a designated parole officer (Mish, 2008, p. 902).

Most of the clients residing in the halfway house are in their 20s and early 30s. Alyssa finds herself physically attracted to Butch, a good-looking, charming 26-year-old parolee who resides in the house. She fights her feelings but finally gives in. When he asks her for a date, she assents and begins an intimate relationship with Butch "on the sly." Agency policy clearly forbids any such relationships with current clients or anyone who has been a client within the past six months.

---

[3]Clients using halfway houses may also include people with a history of mental illness.

Social Workers' Ethical Responsibilities to Colleagues

The NASW *Code of Ethics* specifies 11 areas in which practitioners have ethical responsibilities to colleagues. The focus is on maintaining respect for colleagues even when differences of opinion arise and on working cooperatively for clients' benefit. Social workers should make referrals to professionals with other areas of expertise when necessary. In addition, they should address situations in which colleagues are functioning ineffectively due to personal problems or unethical conduct. They should either approach the colleague directly or go through appropriate channels (such as in the agency or through professional associations) to help alleviate the problem. Arbitrarily, two areas involving social workers' ethical responsibilities to colleagues are discussed here—respect and referral for services.

Respect

Social workers should respect and work cooperatively with colleagues. They should avoid unfounded criticism of colleagues, including that directed at personal characteristics unrelated to professional performance.

Example of Compliance   Bo, a social worker at a diagnostic and treatment center for children with multiple disabilities, has a different professional orientation than many of her colleagues in the other disciplines there. For example, she feels that the family environment is important and so often works with families to discuss issues and link them with needed services. She sees the entire family as the client system. However, Darwin, the agency's psychologist, does not see such family work as important. Rather, he views the child as the client and focuses on changing the child's behavior by using structured behavior modification techniques. He primarily does individual therapy with children and offers consultation to other therapists (including speech, occupational therapy,[4] and physical therapy[5]) regarding how to control and improve children's behavior.

Bo respects Darwin and strives to work together with him in a cooperative effort. Although she does

not always agree with his treatment focus, she appreciates how they both bring their professional strengths to the process.

Example of a Violation   Simon, a foster care worker, intensely dislikes his colleague Joellen, a worker in the same unit. He feels that she is lazy, knows little, and fails to take her job seriously. Simon takes every opportunity to criticize Joellen behind her back to other workers by focusing on the fact that she has a high-pitched, screechy voice and a grating, cackling laugh.

Referral for Services

Social workers should refer clients to other professionals when these others have the knowledge and skills necessary for making progress with clients. Practitioners should make such referrals as smoothly as possible, conveying vital information to the new service provider. Workers should receive no personal payment or gain from such referrals.

Example of Compliance   Jacob is a housing worker for a county social services department who helps "disadvantaged populations who need assistance in obtaining quality and affordable housing in the housing market" (Gibelman, 1995, pp. 298–299). One of Jacob's clients, Kendra, has significant physical disabilities, including advancing arthritis and declining eyesight. Jacob determines that housing is only one of Kendra's needs. Her health requirements are also critical. Jacob acknowledges that he knows little about the health services that Kendra needs and so refers her to another agency worker with expertise in that area. Meanwhile, Jacob continues working to fulfill her housing needs.

Example of a Violation   Olivia is a case manager for people with intellectual disabilities (formerly referred to as mental retardation). Tyler, age 20, has just begun living in a group home for people with intellectual disabilities and working in *sheltered employment,* a program involving work in a safe, closely supervised environment for people who have trouble functioning more independently. Clients usually receive at most minimum and usually significantly less than minimum wage. Because of his relatively high level of functioning, Olivia thinks Tyler could actually do well in regular employment (e.g., doing maintenance work or stocking shelves at a grocery store). He has good job skills, such as

---

[4]*Occupational therapy* is "therapy for those recuperating from illness that encourages rehabilitation by performing the activities of daily life" (Lindberg, 2007, p. 949).

[5]*Physical therapy* is "the treatment of disease, injury, or deformity by physical methods such as massage, heat treatment, and exercise rather than by drugs or surgery" (Lindberg, 2007, p. 1034).

readily complying with supervisors' instructions, being punctual, and taking his work seriously.

The problem is that Olivia has a large caseload of clients and can barely keep up with her most critical work. Referring Tyler to a job specialist, filling out all the required paperwork, and arranging whatever transportation is necessary would take a huge amount of time. On the one hand, referring Tyler would help him better live up to his potential, enhance his self-esteem because he could hold a regular job, and, frankly, earn him more money. On the other, it's not really hurting him to remain where he is, despite the fact that it's not the best work setting for him. Olivia decides that Tyler will stay working in sheltered employment. Her time is too valuable, and she simply doesn't have enough of it.

Social Workers' Ethical Responsibilities in Practice Settings

This section of the *Code of Ethics* focuses on appropriate behavior in practice settings. Social workers who supervise others should be competent and evaluate supervisees fairly. Any information or data social workers record should be accurate. They should advocate for increased funding both inside and outside their agencies when resources are needed for clients. They also should "act to prevent and eliminate discrimination in the employing organization's work assignments and in its employment policies and practices" (NASW, 2008, 3.9e). Finally, practitioners should make sure their employers are aware of unethical practices. The following is an example of a dilemma faced by a social worker in an agency setting. Highlight 2.3 discusses some of the special ethical conflicts experienced by social workers serving in the military practice setting during active combat.

Case Example Lakeisha got a job as a social worker at a nursing home three weeks ago. She is just beginning to feel comfortable there and is gradually learning the agency's policies and practices. Unfortunately, twice she's observed a disturbing scenario. Papers such as wills or insurance statements must be signed by witnesses. On two occasions, Lakeisha saw the nursing supervisor, who is really quite powerful within the agency, ask a resident with Alzheimer's disease[6] to sign the paper for

another patient with the same disease. Witnesses who sign legal papers are supposed to be of sound mind, and these residents obviously were not. No one was safeguarding either of the patients' best interests. Lakeisha was new at the agency and did not want to come across as a troublemaker, yet this signing practice was clearly wrong. The *Code of Ethics* instructs social workers to "act on behalf of clients who lack the capacity to make informed decisions" and to "take reasonable steps to safeguard the interests and rights of those clients" (NASW, 2008, 1.14). Lakiesha was also responsible for making sure the agency was aware of unethical practices (NASW, 2008, 3.09c). What should Lakeisha do?

Example of Compliance Lakeisha decides that she cannot overlook this unethical practice despite the fact that speaking up might endanger her job. She has over five months of probation to go. She resolves to speak with the nursing supervisor. If that doesn't work, she will go over the nursing supervisor's head and speak with the home's director, who is also her immediate supervisor.[7] If worst comes to worst, she'll report this to the state agency that licenses and regulates nursing homes. She knows that will make almost everyone at the home angry because it will make the entire agency and all its employees look bad to the outside world.

Example of a Violation Lakeisha determines that she doesn't want to make waves. After all, she thinks to herself, the practice really isn't hurting anybody, is it? The papers being signed aren't all that important anyway. She decides to forget that she ever saw the signings happen and look the other way if she ever sees it again.

Social Workers' Ethical Responsibilities as Professionals

Social workers' ethical responsibilities as professionals include eight broad dimensions by which they should judge their behavior and responsibility.

---

[6] *Alzheimer's disease* is a common disease of unknown origin that is characterized by mental decline and numerous cognitive problems.

[7] Note that when a worker has a complaint it's often most useful to go directly to the people the complaint involves and give them feedback. Subsequently, if that doesn't work, it's usually best to go to a supervisor and, as needed, gradually go up the chain of command. Going over supervisors' and administrators' heads without first approaching them with complaints generally makes them mad. It implies that they can't handle the problem at their level and may make them look incompetent to those above them in the agency's power structure.

HIGHLIGHT 2.3

Ethical Conflicts for Military Social Workers During Combat

**EP 2.1.6a,
2.1.6b**

Practitioners who serve as professional social workers in the military experience exceptional ethical dilemmas. Military social workers now participate in virtually all levels of practice and assume a wide range of positions, including program manager, consultant to military leaders, researcher, client advocate, officer, and direct service provider; their arenas of involvement include "military family policy, child welfare, health care, substance abuse, mental health, hostage repatriation, combat stress, and humanitarian relief" (Harris & Pehrson, 2008, p. 270).

Simmons and Rycraft (2010) conducted an in-depth *qualitative* study "of the ethical challenges faced by 24 military social workers who were deployed during Operation Iraqi Freedom, and Operation Enduring Freedom (combat operations in Afghanistan)" (p. 9). (*Qualitative research methods* are those "that emphasize depth of understanding and the deeper meanings of human experience, and that aim to generate theoretically richer, albeit more tentative, observations"; frequently used qualitative methods include "intensive interviewing" and "direct observation" [Rubin & Babbie, 2011, p. 627].) All participants in the study had a master's degree in social work and a clinical license. (The latter is described more thoroughly in Chapter 5.) Simmons and Rycraft (2010) maintain that "the ethical challenges faced in combat areas by social workers serving as active duty components of the military can teach all social workers about dealing with challenges in extremely stressful environments" (p. 11). Although military social workers do not take part in the actual fighting, they are often deployed in combat areas where fighting is taking place. There they provide "mental health prevention and treatment services" to service men and women who are fighting the war.

Issues military social workers face include "serving during controversial wars, meeting the needs of the individual client while simultaneously meeting the needs of the military unit, the military's particular expectations regarding confidentiality, and personal fears inherent to the specific deployment" (Simmons & Rycraft, 2010, p. 10). A key concern for these social workers in their practice is the basic ethical concept of self-determination on the part of individual soldiers versus the needs of fellow soldiers and the military operation itself.

The study focused on the answers to two primary questions. The first question asked participants, "How do you deal with situations where a patient/client with mild trauma symptoms wants to go home (needs of the client) and his/her unit needs them to continue fighting (needs of the unit)?" (p. 12). Social workers' answers came together to cluster in three areas. First, military social workers "would analytically work through a problem before taking action" (p. 12). This required careful assessment of the client, the client's strengths and weaknesses, and the client's ability to handle the trauma.

The second cluster of answers involved "problem-focused intervention" (p. 13). Practitioners "would work with the clients, focusing on the problem, helping them to deal with their concerns" while keeping them in the combat context (p. 13). Some social workers indicated that keeping clients on the job was better for their mental health in the long run. It would prevent them from experiencing failure, long-term regret, and even potential suicide.

The third cluster of the social workers' answers were "mission oriented" (p. 13). Here workers indicated that they "would focus on the mission, reminding clients that they voluntarily signed up for military service" (pp. 13–14). Practitioners might also emphasize how important the client was to the military and the mission, and discuss the client's "good prognosis for recovery" (p. 14).

The second major question posed in the study was, "While deployed, what other ethical dilemmas did you face? How did you deal with them?" (p. 14). Four clusters of social workers' answers merit discussion. The first cluster involved "confidentiality and privacy" (p. 14). Military social workers indicated that maintaining these values was very difficult while being in such close contact and having very little privacy in any aspect of combat-zone life.

A second cluster of answers concerned "conflicts with commanders" (p. 14). Issues included military leaders ignoring social work recommendations and some leaders having little regard for the importance and relevance of mental health problems. (Mental health is discussed more thoroughly in Chapter 13.)

(continued)

HIGHLIGHT 2.3 (continued)

A third cluster of answers focused on "relationships and boundaries" (p. 15). Social workers found it quite difficult to keep distinct boundaries between themselves and their clients while living in such close quarters. "A military social worker on deployment eats, sleeps, [and] showers with people they will see professionally as well" (p. 15).

Finally, a fourth cluster of answers involved "diagnosis and treatment" (p. 15). At times it was hard to determine what really was in a client's best interest. Who was just pretending to have a problem and who was in real agony? In such instances, when possible, it was good to seek out a second opinion.

Simmons and Rycraft (2010) reflect that the ethical issues identified here are not so far removed from those faced by social workers in other contexts. Granted, the military environment is more extreme in terms of structure, rigidity, and purpose.

Answers to the first question posed by the study involved the needs of the individual (self-determination) versus the requirements of the military unit and mission. The researchers determined that the military social workers participating in the study based decisions primarily on clinical criteria and judgments, rather than on what might be right or wrong.

Answers to the second question concerning other ethical dilemmas focused on confidentiality and privacy, conflicts with commanders, relationships and boundaries, and diagnosis and treatment. How different are these (although much more intense in the military) from those dilemmas faced by practitioners in other fields of social work practice? The answer is that they reflect similar issues. For example, many a social worker has approached his or her supervisor or agency director with "an amazingly brilliant idea," only to be turned down or ignored. That's simply part of working life.

Simmons and Rycraft (2010) conclude that we should respectfully hold military social workers and their work in high regard. "[F]urther analysis and dialogue about the ethical and practical concerns of military social workers is important"; only then can we aim to ensure "that the integrity of the social work profession and the care provided to those individuals served by military social workers is optimal" (p. 17).

First and foremost, they should be competent to do their jobs. If they are not, they should either seek education and learn the skills they need to become competent or get another job. Next, they should not "practice, condone, facilitate, or collaborate with any form of discrimination on the basis of race, ethnicity, national origin, color, sex, sexual orientation, age, marital status, political belief, religion, or mental or physical disability" (NASW, 2008, 4.02). "Social workers should not permit their private conduct to interfere with their ability to fulfill their professional responsibilities" (NASW, 2008, 4.03). Some types of conduct interfere with a practitioner's ability to function. For instance, one agency administrator actively supported a racist candidate running for public office (Reamer, 2006). As a result, several agency staff resigned in protest and the administrator's supervisor and other personnel were "concerned that the social worker's private conduct was harming the hospital's reputation and interfering with her ability to perform her duties" (Reamer, 2006, p. 199).

Social workers should also be honest, avoid fraud, and seek help when personal problems begin to interfere with their professional effectiveness. They should represent themselves and their qualifications accurately. They should never take credit for someone else's work.

Finally, social workers should not solicit clients for purposes of personal gain. Reamer (2006) provides an example:

A social worker at a public child welfare agency provided [social] . . . services to families whose children had been placed in foster care after allegations of abuse and neglect. She also maintained a small private practice [where she billed clients for counseling on a private basis]. The social worker told a couple she worked with at the child welfare agency that they would need to obtain long-term counseling if they hoped to regain custody of their child. She mentioned that she had a private practice outside the agency, gave the couple her business card, and said, "It might be in your best interest to see me regularly for counseling." The couple felt coerced but nonetheless agreed to see the social worker privately to increase their chances of regaining custody of their child. (pp. 208–209)

Social Workers' Ethical Responsibilities to the Social Work Profession

**EP 2.1.6a,
2.1.6b**

Ethical responsibilities to the social work profession focus on two dimensions—integrity, and evaluation and research. *Integrity* refers to social workers' promotion of high practice standards. Social workers should strive to maintain and enhance professional knowledge, values, and ethics. They should participate in activities aimed at professional contributions such as "teaching, research, consultation, service, legislative testimony, presentations in the community, and participation in their professional organizations" (NASW, 2008, 5.01c). In addition, they should contribute to the social work knowledge base.

Similarly, social workers should encourage research and evaluation of practice effectiveness, monitor practice policies and interventions to ensure effectiveness, and maintain current knowledge of evaluation approaches. Research should be done in an ethical manner. Social workers should be honest with all involved regarding what they plan to do while conducting the research, who will have access to any information and findings gained, and who deserves credit for any findings obtained.

HIGHLIGHT 2.4

Social Workers' Ethical Obligations to Help People at the Macro Level

The following two scenarios reflect situations in which social workers might confront an ethical dilemma that goes beyond their own practice with individuals, families, and groups.

Scenario A

EP 2.1.10

The private social service agency Jack works for does not have a formalized affirmative action policy for hiring personnel. He has overheard the agency director make several crude racial remarks and jokes about people of color. He cannot believe that a person with such authority has gotten away with that. The agency has no people of color on staff despite having numerous clients who are. Jack feels that recruiting staff members who are people of color is essential to the agency's ability to perform the way it's supposed to. He also believes that current staff members, including the agency director, need feedback to work on changing their prejudicial and discriminatory behavior.

Jack determines that he must confront this ethical issue despite possible negative consequences, including being fired. He decides to talk with his colleagues to see if he can muster more support. He knows that often a cohesive group can have a greater impact on making changes in organizations and communities than can one person alone. He finds out that several other agency workers feel the same way he does. Together, they develop a plan to talk to the agency director and provide some suggestions.

Scenario B

L'Toya is a worker at a rural county social services agency. She, her colleagues, and agency administrators have identified a significant lesbian and gay population within the area. She and the other professionals would like to implement a new program providing support groups for lesbian and gay people dealing with several issues, including single parenthood and legal difficulties such as housing discrimination. Two relatively powerful members of the County Board get wind of the idea and react in an angry, negative fashion. They consider people with a sexual orientation other than heterosexuality sinful. They also contend that there are no gay or lesbian people in the area—they surely would know about it if there were.

L'Toya works with the other interested professionals to devise a plan. First, these two board members need to be educated regarding the issues and needs of lesbian and gay people. Perhaps other board members are more knowledgeable and enlightened, and would be more supportive. Maybe some advocates of a gay rights organization in another part of the state can help; perhaps they can assess gay and lesbian people's needs by conducting some research in the area. L'Toya and the others are on their way to developing a plan.

Social Workers' Ethical Responsibilities to the Broader Society

EP 2.1.5a, 2.1.5b, 2.1.5c

Ethical responsibilities to the broader society include four areas that reflect the core of social work —namely, to advocate and work for people's general welfare. This responsibility surpasses those listed in most job descriptions. Social workers should promote people's general welfare on all levels, from the local to the global. They should become actively involved in the formulation of public policy and flock to provide help during emergencies (e.g., floods, tornadoes, or earthquakes).

As part of their professional responsibilities, social workers should pursue social and political action to ensure fair and equal access to resources and opportunities. They should actively support policies to improve the human condition and promote social justice for all. They should especially work to enhance opportunities for "vulnerable, disadvantaged, oppressed, and exploited people and groups" (NASW, 2008, 6.04b). They should support conditions and policies that respect cultural diversity. Similarly, they should work to prevent and eliminate conditions and policies discriminating against or exploiting people, especially vulnerable populations. Highlight 2.4 presents two situations in which social workers are ethically responsible for helping people and go beyond their job of providing direct services to clients.

Social workers have the ethical responsibility to promote people's general welfare. One issue is health care for older adults. Here, older adults rally on the behalf of Medicare benefits.

International Social Welfare in a Global Context

Even beyond a macro focus at the national level, international issues are of concern to social workers. *Globalization* is the "process of global integration in which diverse peoples, economies, cultures, and political processes are increasingly subjected to international influences" (Khinduka, 2008; Midgley, 1997, p. xi). The world is indeed getting smaller. I recently traveled to Southeast Asia, including Ho Chi Minh City in Vietnam. As we motored along a main roadway after dusk, it was amazing to see family members huddled around 12-inch television sets in tiny home after tiny home. I thought of the millions of American homes in which essentially the same thing was happening, although the television sets and homes were much bigger.

We also stayed in a huge new hotel in the cosmopolitan, modern city–state of Singapore. My roommate was going to a grocery store in a shopping center next door to pick up some deli items for an informal supper in our room. I jokingly told her to pick up some Merkt's cheese spread, a brand found all over the Midwest, including Wisconsin, where we live. When she returned and showed me her bounty, she held up a plastic container of Kaukauna cheese spread, amazingly made in Wisconsin only a few miles from my home. I was astonished. We were on the other side of the world.

The world is also getting more interdependent. In a global economy, what social and economic forces impact one nation may well result in repercussions in many other nations. Hokenstad and Midgley (1997) explain:

Social work is one of many players in the response to these realities of global interdependence. The scope of global poverty and the intensity of ethnic conflict require first political and economic responses by nations and international organizations. Global challenges require action on many levels by many actors. Nevertheless, these are problems that are directly related to social work commitment and expertise. Social workers at the local level are directly involved with the implications of international realities by working with refugees or helping displaced workers. At the national level in many countries, the profession is active in promoting economic and social justice policy. Internationally, social work organizations are increasingly active in combating human rights violations. Thus, it is essential for social workers to have an international perspective and understanding to be effective practitioners in today's world. (pp. 3–4)

Note that the distinction will be made between the terms "international" and "global." *International* concerns relationships and issues between two or more nations. *Global* involves relationships and issues concerning all nations around the globe.

Global Human Rights

**EP 2.1.5,
2.1.5a,
2.1.5b,
2.1.5c,
2.1.9a**

In response to the atrocities of World War II, the General Assembly of the United Nations adopted a Universal Declaration of Human Rights (UNDR) in December 1948 (UN, 1948). *Human rights* involve the premise that all people, regardless of race, culture, or national origin, are entitled to basic rights and treatment. Mapp (2008) elaborates:

Within the UNDR, there are three areas of rights: [1] political and civil rights, [2] social, economic, and cultural rights, and [3] collective rights. Political and civil rights are often referred to as "negative freedoms" as they require a government to refrain from an overuse of its power against individuals. Included in this are rights such as freedom of speech and the right to a fair trial. The second groups of rights—social, economic, and cultural rights—are referred to as "positive freedoms" as they require a government to take action for them to be realized for individuals. They include such rights as medical care, the right to an education, and the right to a fair wage. The last group, collective rights, are rights for groups of people and include the rights to religion, peace, and development. (pp. 17–18)

A Global Human Rights Violation: Human Trafficking

An atrocious violation of human rights is human trafficking. *Human trafficking* is the transfer of people across international boundaries to enslave them in some way, usually involving forced labor or sexual exploitation; human trafficking may also include infants and children who are purchased for adoption on the black market (Potocky, 2008).

Another aspect of human trafficking concerns the harvesting of human organs (Childress, 2006; Hodge, 2008).

Three conditions commonly characterize trafficking (Mapp, 2008). The first involves movement of the victim from one place to another. Internationally, victims are usually targeted in countries experiencing economic hardship or serious political unrest and sent to "wealthy, industrialized nations" (Hodge, 2008, p. 145; Mapp, 2008). Second,

deception or coercion is involved. Although the migration might be voluntary, the person is not truly aware of what lies ahead. Many people migrate willingly for better-paying work, but it may become trafficking when they arrive at their destination and realize the work is not what they were promised. They may have been promised a good wage for domestic labor but find that they are imprisoned in a house and paid nothing. They may have signed a contract for factory labor only to arrive and find they have been sold into prostitution.

(Mapp, 2008, p. 32)

The third element of trafficking involves being forced into some form of physical labor or sexual activity against the victim's will.

A Case Example of Human Trafficking

People targeted as victims are often exceptionally vulnerable, poor, or socially isolated. Consider, for example, Safah, a 14-year-old Iraqi girl who was placed in an orphanage after her father's death (Bennett, 2006). There she was befriended by a seemingly kind nurse who said she wanted to adopt Safah. Because the nurse indicated the formal adoption process would take too long, she developed a plan to get Safah out of the orphanage. The nurse instructed Safah to pretend she had appendicitis and scream out in pain so that Safah would be taken to the hospital. Once there "the nurse whisked Safah into a waiting car. The next three weeks were the worst in Safah's life. 'I was tortured and beaten and insulted a lot in that house,' Safah says. She wouldn't provide many details about what happened in the whiskey-soaked den" of a house in a middle-class district of Baghdad; she became "desperate" when she understood she was to be sold to Sa'ad, a man in Dubai, for $10,000 (Bennett, 2006). Safah confided her situation to a neighborhood boy who reported the situation to the police. Both Safah and the nurse were placed in the same prison for the next six months until bureaucratic red tape could be untangled and Safah sent back to the orphanage.

The Extent of Human Trafficking

Although it is difficult to obtain accurate numbers because of the secrecy and shame involved, it is estimated that 600,000 to 800,000 people are trafficked annually across international borders (Hodge, 2008). These numbers include people transported to the United States, which is, after Italy, and followed by Germany and the Netherlands, the most common destination for victims (Monzini, 2004). In the United States most "victims in FBI [Federal Bureau of Investigation] human trafficking cases are women and young girls from Central American and Asian countries"; however, increasing numbers of young males and American citizens (e.g., teenage runaways) are also becoming victims (FBI, 2008). The problem continues to escalate (de Silva, 2007).

Controlling Victims

A number of factors are used to keep victims under control once they have been seized (Fred). First, they may be coerced into labor to pay back the "debt" they accrued by being transported into the new country. Second, captors may threaten to physically injure the victims or report them to immigration authorities for deportation if they don't obey. Third, captors may threaten to harm the victims' families at home or inform their families about the victims' status to shame them. Fourth, captors may disorient victims by moving them frequently from one location (e.g., brothel) to another.

Consequences for Victims

Consequences of trafficking for victims are very serious.

> [M]any trafficking victims will have permanent physical damage from being brutally beaten or raped by their traffickers. Those who've been used as prostitutes may have sexually transmitted [infections] …, while those who've slaved as laborers may have back problems, hearing loss and respiratory or cardiovascular diseases. A number of victims, especially children, also show signs of malnourishment.
>
> (Fred, 2004, p. 4)

The NASW Policy Statement on Human Rights

The National Association of Social Workers (NASW) Policy Statement on human rights indicates that social workers must:

EP 2.1.2b, 2.1.5a, 2.1.5b, 2.1.5c, 2.1.8b

- "advocate for the rights of vulnerable people";
- "be especially vigilant about human rights violations related to children's rights and exploitation such as child labor, child prostitution, and other crimes of abuse and take leadership in developing public and professional awareness regarding these issues";
- "work in collaboration with nongovernmental organizations and community groups when entitlements are nonexistent or inadequately implemented and … becoming a leading force for the health and welfare of all people, including the world's most vulnerable";
- Maintain the "struggle for human rights as "a vital priority for the social work profession in the 21st century." (NASW, 2009, pp. 205–206)

Social Workers' Responsibility to Empower Victims

What can social workers do about this critical global human rights issue? There are a number of suggestions:

EP 2.1.5a, 2.1.5b, 2.1.5c, 2.1.8a, 2.1.8b

1. Social workers should "look below the surface" when working with clients and seek to identify victims of human trafficking so that they can be helped (Fred, 2004, p. 4).

2. Social workers should advocate for the development of programs and provision of services to help victims of human trafficking to escape bondage and get what they need. Such services may include "legal assistance, financial assistance, and help with food and housing" (Mapp, 2008, p. 46). Social workers can also link victims to existing resources.

3. Social workers can strive to formulate and implement "policies that punish those who exploit others into forced labor. In addition, these efforts can be focused on those who commit their crimes

within our borders, as well as extraditing citizens who commit crimes in other countries" (Mapp, 2008, p. 46). For example, social workers can encourage state and national legislators "to pass [strong] anti-trafficking legislation" (Mapp, 2008, p. 48).

They can also support the passage and implementation of legislation helping victims, such as the federal

> *Victims Trafficking and Violence Protection Act of 2000 (P.L. 106-386), which was amended in 2003 by the Trafficking Victims Protection Reauthorization Act (P.L. 108-193). This statute explicitly recognizes that existing laws often fail to protect victims of trafficking and, paradoxically, often punish victims more severely than they do traffickers. Accordingly, the law stipulates that victims of severe trafficking should not be inappropriately penalized for unlawful acts committed as a result of being trafficked, such as using false documents, entering the country without documentation, or working without documentation (P.L. 106-386). This provision, at least in principle, removes one of the key threats that traffickers use to coerce young women and children into the sex industry [i.e., deportation or incarceration].*

> *(Hodge, 2008, p. 148)*

Additionally, this legislation created a unique type of visa for people who experience extreme forms of trafficking, including forced sexual acts, and for victims less than age 18 (Hodge, 2008). The visa allows victims to remain in the United States while they help in the prosecution of perpetrators. It also allows victims to receive a range of services, including those provided by the Witness Protection Program. "After three years, permanent residency may be granted (Aronowitz, 2004)" (Hodge, 2008, p. 148).

4. Social workers can educate others about the issue and what might be done to address it (Mapp, 2008).

5. On a global level, social workers can work together with other practitioners, groups, and international organizations in this and other countries to address the core variables that allow for and encourage human trafficking. Goals may include community development to tackle such issues as "poverty and gender discrimination" (Healy, 2008b; Mapp, 2008, p. 46). (*Community development* is "a planned approach to improving the standard of living and general well-being of people" [Butterfield & Chisanga, 2008, p. 381]. It emphasizes identification, enhancement, and linkage of communities' strengths to generate "self-reliant, self-sustaining communities that mobilize resources for the benefit of their members" [Homan, 2011, p. 61]). Mapp (2008) explains:

> *An example of empowering oppressed people, thus reducing their vulnerability to forced labor, can be found in the case of the Self-Employed Women's Association (SEWA) of India.... Its goal is to assist self-employed women in South and Southeast Asia who face personal barriers such as high rates of illiteracy, having to care for multiple children, and living in slum conditions, as well as macro barriers such as exploitation by moneylenders and harassment by employers and officials. Today, SEWA is the largest single union in India and has founded a bank with 70,000 accounts in order to provide micro-finance loans to its members. The bank also provides insurance for its members, while the union assists with child care and legal aid. Through methods such as these, the women are able to provide for themselves and their families without resorting to forced labor. (pp. 47–48)*

International Social Work

International social work is "international professional action and the capacity for international action by the social work profession and its members. International action has four dimensions: internationally related domestic practice and advocacy, professional exchange, international practice, and international policy development and advocacy" (Healy, 2008, p. 10).

An important concept inherent in this definition is *action,* namely, planning and getting things done. Social workers work together on an international basis to establish goals to enhance human well-being.

EP 2.1.1e,
2.1.4a,
2.1.4d,
2.1.5b,
2.1.5c,
2.1.7b,
2.1.8a,
2.1.8b,
2.1.9a,
2.1.9b,
2.1.10h,
2.1.10k

The first dimension in international action concerns *internationally related domestic practice and advocacy.* Healy (2008) explains:

> Social workers are increasingly called on to deal with problems that have an international dimension, meaning that two or more countries are involved in some way in the case or policy issue. There are many examples of internationally related domestic practice problems, including refugee resettlement, work with other international populations, international adoption work, and social work in border areas. (p. 10)

"Domestic" responsibilities for social workers include, on the one hand, knowledge about people of other national origins in order to conduct culturally competent, effective practice with these people. Learning about various cultures from the people they work with is an ongoing, career-long process. Link, Ramanathan, and Asamoah (1999) assert that an international perspective allows social workers to have expanded "insights about the human condition and more adequately understand, analyze, and predict human behavior" (p. 31). They provide an example of "the 18th Street Gang members in Los Angeles," whose families originated in El Salvador and who maintain an ongoing cultural connection with that country. An international perspective helps social workers "recognize how artificial it is to see national borders as separations between micro or macro systems…. These disenfranchised young people are frequently rounded up and deported to El Salvador, where they pick up with another branch of their gang so that their interactions are seamless despite the structural efforts of immigration and law enforcement to disband or break them" (Link, et al., 1999, p. 31; DeCesare, 1993).

Another aspect of internationally related "domestic" responsibility involves the support of legislation both nationally and internationally that provides fair and humane treatment to people. An example is immigration legislation. "It is logical that as part of accepted advocacy responsibilities of the profession, social workers have an obligation to monitor such legislation as it is being proposed, to follow impending votes at the UN and foreign policy directives and to ensure that social work's voice is heard on relevant issues" (Healy, 2008, pp. 11–12).

Healy (2008) continues:

> The second dimension in the definition of international action is the capacity to exchange social work information and experiences [professional exchange] internationally and to use the knowledge and experience to improve social work practice and social welfare policy at home. This includes a range of actions, such as reading foreign periodicals and books in one's field, corresponding with professionals in other countries or hosting visitors, participating in professional interchange at international meetings, and identifying and adapting social welfare innovations in other countries to one's own setting. Increasingly, professional exchange is facilitated by technological advances in computer-assisted communications and teleconferencing …
>
> The third dimension of international action is the preparation of some professional social workers to contribute directly to international development work [international practice] through employment or volunteer work in international [community] development agencies. (pp. 12–15)

The fourth dimension of international action is "the capacity of the social work profession as a worldwide movement" to publicly support values and legislation concerning "important social issues" (Healy, 2008, p. 15). International social work organizations such as those described in the next section provide mechanisms to accomplish this.

International Social Work Organizations

International social work organizations that actively engage social workers around the globe include the International Federation of Social Workers (IFSW) and the International Association of Schools of Social Work (IASSW). Established in 1956, IFSW "is a global federation of national organizations of social workers…. It is striving for social justice, human rights and social development through the development of social work, best practices and international cooperation between social workers and their professional organizations" (IFSW, 2011). It focuses on improving "the quality of life," "achievement of social justice," and development "of human potential" for people around the globe (IFSW, 2011). It is especially involved in "protesting human rights violations" (Hokenstad & Midgley, 1997, pp. 4–5). It has also developed an International Policy on Human Rights to provide guidance concerning human rights issues to social workers and organizations around the world. (IFSW's home Website is **http://www.ifsw.org**.)

EP 2.1.8b, 2.1.10h

IASSW is a "worldwide association of schools of social work," related "social work educational programmes, and social work educators"; it "promotes the development of social work education throughout the world, develops standards to enhance [the] quality of social work education, encourages international exchange, provides forums for sharing social work research and scholarship, and promotes human rights and social development through policy and advocacy activities" (IASSW, 2011). IASSW is based on humanitarian values and the quest for social justice on the behalf of oppressed populations. It also serves as a consultant to the United Nations. (IASSW's home Website is **http://www.iassw.aiets.org/**)

International Social Work: Codes of Ethics

EP 2.1.2b

Although the NASW *Code of Ethics* is the primary code followed by social workers in the United States, note that other ethical codes also are available in other nations and on an international basis (CSWE, 2008b). Consider, for example, the Association of Canadian Social Workers (CASW) Code of Ethics, accessible at its home Website, **http://www.casw-acts.ca**.

IFSW and IASSW have developed an *Ethics in Social Work, Statement of Principles* that may be applied when addressing *international* (involving two or more nations) or *global* (involving the entire world) ethical issues (CSWE, 2008b). Often, these issues concern human rights. The document, concurrently supported by both organizations, consists of the following five parts:

1. Preface
2. Definition of social work
3. International conventions (that refer to various organizations' specific statements of human rights)
4. Principles
5. Professional conduct (IFSW, 2005).

The "principles" in the *Ethics in Social Work, Statement of Principles* include "human rights and human dignity" and "social justice." The former indicates how "social work is based on respect for the inherent worth and dignity of all people, and the rights that follow from this. Social Workers should uphold and defend each person's physical, psychological, emotional and spiritual integrity and

well-being." It continues that "social workers have a responsibility to promote social justice, in relation to society generally, and in relation to the people with whom they work"; this involves "challenging negative discrimination," "recognizing diversity," "distributing resources equitably," "challenging unjust policies and practices," and "working in solidarity" (i.e., social workers as a group have the responsibility to confront social injustice).

Personal and Professional Values

EP 2.1.1b, 2.1.2a

We have established that values involve what is considered important and what is not. They concern making judgments about right and wrong. We all have the right to our personal values; we all have our own ideas about how things should be. It's a wonderful thing to be able to enjoy our own opinions and have the freedom to express them. An ongoing task for social workers is to identify their own values and distinguish between those and their professional values. As you now know, clients' right to self-determination is a key principle in social work. Therefore, social workers must be careful not to impose their personal values on clients. How difficult do you think this might be?

For example, consider a social worker who strongly supports women's rights. She may work with a Hispanic family that rigidly adheres to patriarchal values. In this family, the wife and daughters are expected to be obedient and follow the rules imposed by the father. Female family members are given much less respect, are allowed less input, and generally have significantly less power than male members. In this case the social worker must work hard to respect the family's values, but she must also focus on the right of self-determination for the family's females. It is the worker's responsibility to help such women articulate their feelings and identify their alternatives as they see them within their own cultural frame of reference. Clients must evaluate the potential positive and negative consequences for each alternative within their own cultural environment. The worker must do all this and still keep her own values in check throughout the intervention process.

Another example concerns a social worker whose adult client has a life-threatening disease and

Identifying Personal Values

EP 2.1.3

Social workers must identify their own personal values so that they are careful not to impose them on clients. What are your personal values and opinions concerning the following issues? How easy or difficult would it be for you to work with people having the opposite opinions?

- Should there be a death penalty for extreme crimes? If so, for what types of crimes (e.g., terrorism, murder, or armed robbery)?
- Should women be allowed the freedom of choice regarding abortion? If not, are there any circumstances under which an abortion could be performed (e.g., rape, incest, or a threat to the life of the mother)?
- Should women change their names to those of their spouses when they marry? Why or why not?

- Should people who are critically ill and in intense pain be able to "pull their own plug"—that is, put themselves to death?
- Should teachers in elementary and secondary school be able to use corporal punishment (i.e., inflicting punishment by causing physical pain)?
- Should prayers be allowed in public schools? What if there are children of various faiths involved (e.g., Buddhist, Muslim, Roman Catholic, Methodist, Unitarian, Hindu, or atheists)?
- Should schools provide sex education to children? If so, what should be taught?
- Should oil companies be allowed to develop untouched lands in the Arctic to keep domestic gas prices down? Or should lumber companies be allowed to cut down old-growth trees such as the giant redwoods in California?

desperately needs surgery to ensure survival. However, the client refuses such medical help because it conflicts with his strong religious beliefs. The social worker personally feels that this perspective is ridiculous, yet he still must respect the client's right to make his own decisions. Focus on Critical Thinking 2.2 identifies a number of potentially controversial issues involving personal values.

Chapter Summary

The following summarizes this chapter's content as it relates to the chapter objectives presented at the beginning of the chapter. Objectives include the following:

A Review the general categories in the NASW Code of Ethics.

The six core values of the NASW *Code of Ethics* are service, social justice, dignity and worth of the person, the importance of human relationships, integrity, and competence. Social workers have ethical responsibilities to clients, to colleagues, in practice settings, as professionals, to the social work profession, and to the broader society.

B Provide case examples of compliance and noncompliance concerning some of the major ethical issues involved, including self-determination, privacy and confidentiality, conflict of interest and dual relationships, sexual relationships, respect for colleagues, and referral for services.

Examples of both compliance and a violation were provided for cases concerning self-determination, privacy and confidentiality, conflict of interest and dual relationships, sexual relationships, respect for colleagues, and referral for services.

C Introduce critical thinking about ethical dilemmas.

Case examples were provided and critical thinking questions posed concerning issues in a hospital setting, a county Department of Social Services, and a mental health center.

D Discuss ethical issues concerning the Internet.

Suggestions for maintaining electronic confidentiality should be followed. Language used should be professional. Various reasons exist for social workers to use the Internet.

E Examine ethical conflicts faced by military social workers during combat.

Ethical conflicts faced by military social workers during combat often focus on self-determination on the part of the individual versus the needs of the military operation. Other ethical conflicts include confidentiality and privacy, conflicts with commanders, relationships and boundaries, and diagnosis and treatment.

F Recognize ethical obligations at the macro level.

Macro examples were provided concerning establishing a formalized affirmative action policy in an agency and initiating a program serving lesbian and gay people.

G Introduce the importance of social work in a global context, including international social work and international social work organizations.

International social work is "international professional action and the capacity for international action by the social work profession and its members" (Healy, 2008, p. 10). International social work organizations include the International Federation of Social Workers (IFSW) and the International Association of Schools of Social Work (IASSW).

H Define and discuss human rights and examine the human rights violation of human trafficking.

Human rights involve the premise that all people regardless of race, culture, or national origin are entitled to basic rights and treatment. Human trafficking is the transfer of people across international boundaries to enslave them in some way, usually involving forced labor or sexual exploitation. Social workers have the responsibility to help human trafficking victims and advocate on their behalf.

I Discuss the difference between personal and professional values.

Social workers should distinguish between their personal and professional values. They should not impose personal values on clients.

LOOKING AHEAD

This chapter established the significance of social work values in all aspects of practice. Primary values include an appreciation of human diversity and respect for people's rights to self-determination, optimal health, and enhanced well-being. The next chapter will focus on these and related values issues in the context of human diversity.

COMPETENCY NOTES

The following identifies where Educational Policy (EP) competencies and practice behaviors are discussed in the chapter.

EP 2.1.1b Practice personal reflection and self-correction to assure continual professional development. *(p. 53):* Practitioners must practice personal reflection about their personal values to make certain that these don't conflict with professional values and ethical practice.

EP 2.1.1e Engage in career-long learning. *(p. 51):* Assuming an international perspective and learning about other cultures is an ongoing, career-long process.

EP 2.1.2 Apply social work ethical principles to guide professional practice. *(p. 35):* This entire chapter addresses this competency.

EP 2.1.2a Recognize and manage personal values in a way that allows professional values to guide practice. *(p. 53):* Reflection about personal values allows practitioners to manage these values so that they don't interfere with professional values and ethics.

**EP 2.1.2b Make ethical decisions by applying standards of the National Association of Social Workers (NASW) *Code of Ethics* and, as applicable, of the International Federation of Social Workers/International Association of Schools of Social Work *Ethics in Social Work, Statement of Principles.* *(p. 35):* Social workers should use the NASW *Code of Ethics* as a guide for ethical practice. Subsequent sections explore various principles championed by the *Code.* *(p. 38):* This highlight summarizes ethical standards identified by the NASW *Code of Ethics.* *(p. 50):* The NASW Policy Statement on human rights reflects the application of NASW ethical standards. *(p. 53):* The IFSW/IASSW *Ethics in Social Work, Statement of Principles* is described.

EP 2.1.2c Tolerate ambiguity in resolving ethical conflicts. *(p. 37):* The controversial issues this highlight describes may be ambiguous and difficult in terms of finding the best solution. Social workers must learn to tolerate such ambiguity as they seek to resolve ethical conflicts.

EP 2.1.2d Apply strategies of ethical reasoning to arrive at principled decisions. *(p. 38):* A strategy involving six questions is proposed to address an ethical dilemma and arrive at an ethical decision.

EP 2.1.3 Apply critical thinking to inform and communicate professional judgments. *(p. 37):* Critical thinking is necessary to synthesize relevant information and make informed ethical decisions. Various critical thinking questions are posed to address the ethical dilemmas described. *(p. 54):* Questions are posed to encourage critical thinking about personal values.

EP 2.1.3c Demonstrate effective oral and written communication in working with individuals, families, groups, organizations, communities, and colleagues. *(p. 40):* Social workers should be careful to communicate professionally and ethically when using the Internet.

EP 2.1.4a Recognize the extent to which culture's structures and values may oppress, marginalize, alienate, or create or enhance privilege and power. *(p. 51):* Social workers should recognize the extent to which a culture's structures and values affect people.

EP 2.1.4d View themselves as learners and engage those with whom they work as informants. *(p. 51):* Social workers should view themselves as learners and engage the people from various cultures with whom they work as importance sources of information.

EP 2.1.5 Advance human rights social and economic justice. *(p. 49):* It's important for social workers to understand the global interconnections of oppression and the significance of global human rights.

EP 2.1.5a Understand the forms and mechanisms of oppression and discrimination. *(p. 48):* Social workers should be aware of their ethical responsibilities to the broader society in terms of fighting oppression and discrimination. *(p. 49):* Practitioners should strive to understand the oppressed circumstances imposed on people globally. Human trafficking poses a major example of global oppression. *(p. 50):* Social workers should be especially vigilant about human rights violations. *(p. 50):* Social workers should actively search out clues that human trafficking is occurring.

EP 2.1.5b Advocate for human rights and social and economic justice. *(p. 48):* Practitioners should advocate for human rights and social and economic justice. *(p. 49):* Social workers should advocate for human rights on a global basis. *(p. 50):* Practitioners should advocate for the rights of vulnerable people. *(p. 50):* Social workers should advocate for the development of programs and services to help human trafficking victims. They should support strong anti-trafficking policies and legislation. *(p. 51):* Advocacy for human rights and justice is a major goal of international social work.

EP 2.1.5c Engage in practices that advance social and economic justice. *(p. 48):* Social workers should engage in practices that advance social and economic justice for oppressed and vulnerable people. *(p. 49):* Practitioners should engage in practices that advance human rights and social and economic justice on a global basis. *(p. 50):* Social workers should engage in practices that advance social justice and enhance the health and welfare of all people. *(p. 50):* Practitioners should engage in practices that advance social and economic justice for victims of human trafficking. *(p. 51):* International social work involves engaging in practices that advance social and economic justice.

EP 2.1.6a Use practice experience to inform scientific inquiry. *(p. 45):* The research discussed here is based on practice experience. *(p. 47):* Social workers should contribute to social work research through their practice experience whenever possible.

EP 2.1.6b Use research evidence to inform practice. *(p. 45):* The results of the research presented here can be used to inform practice. *(p. 47):* Social workers should use research evidence to guide their practice.

EP 2.1.7b Critique and apply knowledge to understand person and environment. *(p. 51):* Practitioners must understand and apply knowledge about various cultures to understand the human behavior of people from these cultures both domestically and abroad.

EP 2.1.8a Analyze, formulate, and advocate for policies that advance social well-being. *(p. 50):* Social workers should strive to establish strong anti-trafficking laws and support the passage of legislation to help victims. *(p. 51):* An international social work perspective maintains that practitioners should advocate for policies and services that advance social well-being for people from various cultures both domestically and internationally.

EP 2.1.8b Collaborate with colleagues and clients for effective policy action. *(p. 50):* Social workers can collaborate with public and private organizations and groups to provide for the health and welfare of all people. *(p. 50):* Practitioners should work together with colleagues and organizations on a global basis to address the variables that encourage human trafficking. They should work together for community development to empower oppressed people. *(p. 51):* A core dimension of international social work involves professional exchange and working together. *(p. 52):* International organizations such as IFSW and IASSW emphasize collaboration with colleagues.

EP 2.1.9a Continuously discover, appraise, and attend to changing locales, populations, scientific and technological developments, and emerging societal trends to provide relevant services. *(p. 40):* Practitioners should continuously respond to the changing issues and conditions involved in using the Internet. *(p. 49):* It's important for social workers to appraise continuously the changing oppressive conditions and troublesome issues confronting the world. *(p. 51):* Social workers must continuously appraise the changing conditions and trends in the international environment in order to provide relevant services.

EP 2.1.9b Provide leadership in promoting sustainable changes in service delivery and practice to improve the quality of social services. *(p. 51):* Social workers can provide leadership in the development of policies, services, and programs at the international level to enhance people's well-being.

EP 2.1.10 Engage, assess, intervene, and evaluate with individuals, families, groups, organizations, and communities. *(p. 47):* Social workers practice by working with systems of all sizes including macro systems.

EP 2.1.10h Initiate actions to achieve organizational goals. *(p. 51):* Practitioners involved in IFSW and IASSW initiate actions to achieve organizational goals. *(p. 52):* Social workers can initiate actions to achieve the organizational goals of international organizations. Action is a keystone of international social work.

EP 2.1.10k Negotiate, mediate, and advocate for clients. *(p. 51):* Social workers should advocate for positive legislation and services at the domestic and international levels.

FOR FURTHER EXPLORATION ON THE INTERNET

See this text's Social Work CourseMate website at *www.cengagebrain.com* for learning tools such as chapter quizzing, videos, glossary flashcards, and more.

CHAPTER 3

Empowerment and Human Diversity

George Rose/Contributor/Getty Images

How many of the following sound familiar to you?

Stereotype: *White males are second-rate basketball players.*

Stereotype: *Women are too emotional to make good supervisors.*

Stereotype: *All Hispanic people speak Spanish as their primary language.*

Stereotype: *Elderly people can't think well.*

Stereotype: *Gay and lesbian people really want to be the opposite gender.*

Stereotype: *People with physical disabilities are unemployable.*

Do you have stereotypes about people from other ethnic groups, races, religions, or age groups? How about people of the other gender or those with disabilities? If so, what are these stereotypes? To what extent do you think that they really characterize every person belonging to that group?

Some people are short, and others are tall. Some are pinkish white, others ebony black, and still others various shades of golden brown. Some have astonishing IQs, and others struggle to make it through early elementary grades. Some are very young, and others are very old. Some are agile athletes; others can barely hit a *volleyball over a net let alone get a basketball through a hoop; and still others can't walk at all. Our society is a vast, surging concoction of many types of diversity.*

This chapter explores various aspects of human diversity, with a focus on the importance of equality, justice, and empowerment, especially for people at risk of discrimination and oppression.

Learning Objectives

A Define discrimination, oppression, marginalization, alienation, power, privilege, acclaim, stereotypes, and prejudice, and examine their relevance to social work practice.

B Explore the concepts of populations-at-risk and social and economic justice.

C Define empowerment and introduce a strengths perspective to social work practice.

D Examine empowerment for women in groups.

E Describe the concept of resiliency.

F Recognize various aspects of human diversity including age, class, color, culture, disability, ethnicity, gender, gender identity and expression, immigration status, political ideology, race, religion, sex, and sexual orientation.

G Examine the social construction of gender.

H Employ critical thinking skills to appraise racial self-awareness, cultural self-awareness, the treatment of intersex people and people with various forms of gender expression, and the feminist perspective.

I Discuss some of the major values characterizing Hispanic, Native American, African American, and Asian American families.

J Define cultural competence and explain its application to social work.

K Identify some of the basic tenets of Islam and discuss Muslims as a population-at-risk of prejudice and discrimination.

Discrimination, Oppression, Marginalization, and Alienation

EP 2.1.4a, 2.1.4c, 2.1.5, 2.1.5a

A major social work value involves the importance of people being treated fairly and equally. Unjust treatment impairs people's ability to determine their own life paths and achieve their optimal well-being. Membership in groups that differ from the mainstream can place people at increased risk of inequitable treatment in the forms of discrimination, oppression, marginalization, alienation, economic deprivation, and poverty. *Discrimination* is the act of treating people differently based on the fact that they belong to some group rather than on merit. *Oppression* involves putting extreme limitations and constraints on some person, group, or larger system. *Marginalization* is the condition of having less power and being viewed as less important than others in the society because of belonging to some group or having some characteristic (e.g., racial, economic, ethnic, or political) (Barker, 2003). *Alienation*, related to marginalization, is the feeling that you don't fit in or aren't treated as well as others in the mainstream of society (Barker, 2003).

Economic deprivation is the condition of having inadequate or unjust access to financial resources. The latter can result from a number of circumstances, including unemployment, job discrimination, insufficient work benefits, and unsatisfactory public fiscal policies (e.g., unfair tax rates or eligibility standards for financial benefits and services that make them inaccessible to those in need). Related to economic deprivation is *poverty*, a concept that has been defined in many ways. One definition of poverty is the condition "of not having enough money to buy things that are considered necessary and desirable" (Kornblum & Julian, 2009, p. 193). One way of looking at this involves not having enough resources to exist. Another view concerns having enough to live, but significantly less than what others around you possess.

It is social workers' responsibility to appreciate diversity and recognize that differences may expose people to "oppression, poverty, marginalization, and alienation as well as privilege, power, and acclaim" (CSWE, 2008b, EP 2.1.4). People with many resources have advantages. They may have *power,* the ability to move people on a chosen course to produce an effect or achieve some goal (Homan, 2011). Related to power are privilege and acclaim. *Privilege* entails special rights or benefits enjoyed because of elevated social, political, or economic status. *Acclaim* is "enthusiastic and public praise" (Lindberg, 2007, p. 7).

Stereotypes and Prejudice

EP 2.1.1b, 2.1.1e, 2.1.2a, 2.1.4b

Stereotypes often contribute to discrimination, oppression, marginalization, alienation, economic deprivation, and poverty. A *stereotype* is a fixed mental picture of a member of some specified group based on some attribute or attributes that reflect an overly simplified view of that group, without consideration or appreciation of individual differences. Stereotypes are related to *prejudice*—a negative opinion or prejudgment about an individual, group, or issue that is not based on fact.

Stereotypes and prejudice can involve preconceived ideas based on a person's skin color, gender, age, ethnic heritage, or external appearance. What mental images and assumed expectations come to mind when you picture a 77-year-old woman, a person using a wheelchair, or a gay man? To what extent do these images reflect stereotypes instead of unique characteristics and strengths?

It's easy to envision a number of scenarios concerning potential discrimination and oppression based on stereotypes. For instance, think of an African American family moving into a small, virtually all-white midwestern town. Picture a 58-year-old woman applying for a job in a software production center where all the employees are under age 30. Or consider a gay couple expressing affection in a primarily heterosexual bar.

Membership in any diverse group provides a different set of environmental circumstances. A wealthy, middle-aged Asian American man who just immigrated to Los Angeles from Tokyo experiences a very different world from an older adult woman of Scandinavian heritage living in Michigan's economically depressed Upper Peninsula.

Becoming aware of any stereotypes and prejudices they hold is an ongoing, career-long process for social workers. They must not allow such personal feelings to interfere with fair, effective practice that is guided by professional values and ethics.

What stereotypes do you harbor about various groups? Focus on Critical Thinking 3.1 provides a self-awareness exercise that might give you some insights.

Populations-at-Risk and Social and Economic Justice

EP 2.1.4, 2.1.5b, 2.1.5c

"*Diversity* emphasizes the similarity and dissimilarity between numerous groups in society that have distinguishing characteristics" (Lum, 2011, p. 129). We have established that factors involved in diversity shape life experiences and may result in oppression or privilege. *Populations-at-risk* are people at greater risk of deprivation and unfair treatment because they share some identifiable characteristic that places them in a diverse group. Multiple factors characterize diversity, including "age, class, color, culture, disability, ethnicity, gender, gender identity and expression, immigration status, political ideology, race, religion, sex, and sexual orientation" (CSWE, 2008b, EP 2.1.4).

FOCUS ON CRITICAL THINKING 3.1

Racial Self-Awareness

EP 2.1.1b, 2.1.2a, 2.1.3, 2.1.4b

Self-awareness is a key quality for people entering social work and other helping professions. To assess your own level of self-awareness, ask yourself these questions:

- What adjectives and concepts automatically come to mind when you think of Hispanics? Native Americans/American Indians? African Americans? Asian Americans? Caucasians?
- Do all of the adjectives for each group apply to every single person in that group?
- In what group or groups do you include yourself? Do all the adjectives and concepts you identified for that group characterize you accurately?

- When did you first become aware of your race? Did you think of yourself as being different from people of other races? If so, in what ways?
- In what ways, if any, have you noticed people of different races being treated differently? What do you think are the reasons for such treatment?
- What experiences have you had with people of races different from your own? To what extent were they positive or negative, and why?
- While you were growing up, was your school integrated with people from other racial backgrounds? How about your neighborhood?
- Did you or your parents have friends of different races? Why or why not?
- Did you ever question why all our presidents have been males? (Schram & Mandell, 2000)

To reemphasize, a major responsibility of social work practitioners is to pursue social and economic justice for populations-at-risk and people in need. Recall from Chapter 1 that *social justice* involves the idea that in a perfect world all citizens would have identical "rights, protection, opportunities, obligations, and social benefits," regardless of their backgrounds and membership in diverse groups (Barker, 2003, p. 405). Similarly, *economic justice* concerns the distribution of resources in a fair and equitable manner.

In real life, social and economic justice are hard goals to attain. Rarely are rights and resources fairly and equitably distributed. Even the definitions of *fair* and *equitable* are widely debated. Do they mean that all people should receive the same income regardless of what work they do, or even whether they have jobs? As you now know, social workers must constantly be on the lookout for injustice because it is their ethical responsibility to combat it whenever necessary and possible to do so.

Empowerment and a Strengths Perspective

Simply put, social workers help people solve problems. However, to do this, practitioners must focus on clients' strengths. Concentrating on the problem at hand tells workers what is wrong, but not what

EP 2.1.4d, 2.1.10e, 2.1.10j

to do about it. Focusing on clients' strengths provides social workers with clues about how to proceed by building on these strengths. Practitioners should view themselves as learners and consider their clients as important providers of information.

Saleebey (2006b, p. 85) provides an example of emphasizing client strengths with Michael, a middle-aged man who has moderate intellectual (cognitive) disabilities. A social work student working with Michael visited him in his apartment one day. Michael was capable of living alone if he had some supportive supervision, including help with getting groceries, paying bills, and organizing other necessary activities. The student noticed that Michael's walls were covered with intricately drawn maps of his town, state, and country, and was awestruck at the careful detail and attractive colors. Taking the initiative, the student worked with Michael to make the local newspaper and museum aware of his talent and his output. The paper published articles about Michael, and a local museum exhibited his work. Subsequently, a greeting card company with national distribution approached Michael and other amateur artists with intellectual or physical disabilities about initiating a whole new card line.

We have established that *empowerment* is the "process of increasing personal, interpersonal, or political power so that individuals can take action to improve their life situations" (Gutierrez, 2001, p. 210). Empowerment means increasing, emphasizing, developing, and nurturing strengths and positive attributes. It aims at enhancing individuals', groups', families', and communities' power and control over their destinies.

Cowger (1994) maintains that social work historically has focused on dysfunction, pathology, and "individual inadequacies" (p. 262). He states that "if assessment focuses on deficits, it is likely that deficits will remain the focus of both the worker and the client during remaining contacts. Concentrating on deficits or strengths can lead to self-fulfilling prophecies" (p. 264). He continues that a strengths perspective can provide "structure and content for an examination of realizable alternatives, for the mobilization of competencies that can make things different, and for the building of self-confidence that stimulates hope" (p. 265).

Saleebey (2009a) articulates a *strengths perspective* that is essentially based on empowerment. He cites at least five primary underlying principles (pp. 15–18):

1. "Every individual, group, family and community has strengths."
2. "Trauma and abuse, illness and struggle may be injurious but they may also be sources of challenge and opportunity."
3. Social workers should assume that they "do not know the upper limits of the capacity to grow and change and take individual, group, and community aspirations seriously."
4. Social workers "best serve clients by collaborating with them."
5. "Every environment is full of resources."

As noted previously, empowerment implies that people lack power and thereby need it increased. Several designated groups of people suffer from stereotypes, discrimination, and oppression. It is social work's task to empower clients in general and members of oppressed groups in particular. Highlight 3.1 discusses some research concerning effective empowerment approaches with women.

Resiliency: Seeking Strength amid Adversity

A concept related to the strengths perspective and empowerment is *resiliency*: the ability of an individual,

family, group, community, or organization to recover from adversity and resume functioning even when suffering serious trouble, confusion, or hardship (CSWE, 2008b, EP B2.2; Greene, 2007). For example, Norman (2000) provides an illustration of this notion:

> When a pitched baseball hits a window, the glass usually shatters. When that same ball meets a baseball bat, the bat is rarely damaged. When a hammer strikes a ceramic vase, it too usually shatters. But when that same hammer hits a rubber automobile tire, the tire quickly returns to its original shape. The baseball bat and the automobile tire both demonstrate resiliency. (p. 3)

Resiliency involves two dimensions—"risk factors" and "protective factors" (Norman, 2000, p. 3). In this context, *risk factors* involve "stressful life events or adverse environmental conditions that increase the *vulnerability* [defenselessness or helplessness] of individuals" or other systems (p. 3). *Protective factors*, on the other hand, "buffer, moderate, and protect against those vulnerabilities" (p. 3).

For example, Watkins (2002) studied six urban girls between ages 11 and 14 who were at risk of negative influences including poverty, "poor parental education, tenuous family structure, . . . history of abuse or neglect, and the influence of negative home environments" (p. 117). The study investigated how these girls were able to survive and even thrive in the midst of adversity, demonstrating their capacity for resiliency. Two of the girls are described as follows (Watkins, 2002):

> **Shatika**: This 12-year-old African American girl was tall and thin. She described herself as "I'm what you call light-skinned." Adolescent acne (which she called "skin bumps") was noticeable on her forehead, nose, and cheeks. Shatika's brown hair with red highlights was pulled behind her ears with a rubber band. She explained that her hair "needed to be done," but her mother was unable to afford the cost of a permanent. Shatika was very soft-spoken and hesitatingly made eye contact as the interview process was explained. . . .
>
> **Daisy**: This 13-year-old Caucasian girl was petite with symmetrical fullness of hips and breasts. Her heavily permed dark blond hair was shoulder length and she wore a ribbon to keep her hair out

Empowerment for Women in Groups

**EP 2.1.10a,
2.1.10g,
2.1.10i,
2.1.10j,
2.1.10k**

Parsons (2001) conducted a qualitative study of effective empowerment strategies for women. There is substantial support for the use of consciousness-raising as a strategy to empower women (GlenMaye, 1998). *Consciousness-raising* is the process of facilitating people's understanding of a social issue, with personal implications when there was little grasp of that issue before. Women often don't realize the relationship between their troubles and the world around them, thereby unjustly assuming all the blame themselves (Barnett, et al., 2011). For example, a woman in a relationship in which she is regularly battered will frequently blame herself, and not the batterer, for her problems. She might think that she shouldn't have yelled back at him because that was only asking to be punched. Or she might think that she should have ironed his collar the correct way and then he wouldn't have had to hit her in retribution.

Parsons (2001) studied two women's groups and evaluated the conditions conducive to women's empowerment. The Domestic Violence Survivors (DVS) was made up of women coping with battery who were trying to regain control of their lives. The All Families Deserve a Chance group was made up of women receiving public assistance who wished to advocate for improved policies and conditions for themselves and other women receiving aid. The two groups were chosen because they reflected two very different objectives. One involved improving the lives of individuals by gaining personal control, a micro goal. The other concentrated on advocating for change in social policy, a macro goal.

The following themes emerged as providing successful conditions for women's empowerment within a group setting:

- *Safety:* Knowing nothing horrible will happen makes group members feel more comfortable about participating and having control.
- *Mutual interaction:* Having the ability to interact and communicate with other group members without feeling threatened is reassuring.
- *Commonality:* Finding out that they are not the only ones having these problems is empowering.

- *Acceptance:* Feeling that they belong, regardless of their problems, self-criticism, or mistakes, gives group members increased self-confidence and a sense of power.
- *Validation:* Having what they say about their experiences be "confirmed" and "heard" by others helps them learn "that they [are] ... not crazy" (Parsons, 2001, p. 168).
- *Interdependence:* Feeling that they can rely on each other for help and support bolsters their confidence and ability to take action.

Strategies used by the social workers running the groups were also found to enhance feelings of empowerment. First, social workers provided support by encouraging group members to speak, listening to what they had to say, and believing them. Group members thus felt they had the right to be listened to and to think through their issues. One group member explained:

"[The group leader] is like a mentor. She challenges you. She won't let me get away with being afraid. She isn't going to let me get in the way of me. Her instincts for people have made me aware of my own feelings. She taught me that even though I am not always strong, I am not a weak person. I have high expectations, push myself. She says you are doing a good job even though you are not doing everything you want to be doing. She has more faith in me than I do in myself sometimes. I say, if she has this kind of faith in me, why can't I have it myself?" (Parsons, 2001, p. 170)

Providing support for survivors of violence is vital (Barnett, et al., 2011). Breton and Nosko (1997) cite an interaction demonstrating worker support that occurred in another group for women who had suffered domestic violence:

Woman: I have no self-esteem.
Worker: What does self-esteem mean to you?
Woman: I don't know, really.
Worker: Well, then, maybe you have some. (p. 137)

A second effective social work strategy for empowerment involved educating group members about relevant issues (Barnett et al., 2011). For the DVS, such education entailed talking about the cycle of violence (i.e., building up of tension, explosive battering

(continued)

incident, making up)—how difficult it is to break it and how perpetrators do all they can to maintain their control through violence. For All Families Deserve a Chance, the social worker taught women the steps for advocacy. Group members learned how to clarify their position, formulate recommendations for changing public assistance policy, and effectively communicate with decision makers.

Third, the social workers actively advocated on the group members' behalf. Workers demonstrated that they were ardently on their clients' side by encouraging them, spurring them on, and readily bestowing positive feedback for their achievements.

Fourth, the social workers helped group members learn how to express, deal with, and resolve conflict without anger or violence. Fifth, the social workers encouraged the women to take risks by trusting others and allowing themselves to hope that things could actually get better. Sixth, the social workers provided a role model for group members, thereby affording guidance for more effective communication and appropriate assertiveness in addition to conflict management. Finally, group members learned that taking small steps could enhance empowerment. Small successes slowly led to increased confidence and achievement of bigger goals.

of her small and closely set gray eyes. Daisy was dressed in "daisy dukes"—short shorts with matching gingham shirt. As she spoke in soft, hushed tones, Daisy made it clear that she was willing to help with the project only if she could be assured that no one would "find out my secrets." She said, "I ain't never got to talk about me before and it could help me. It's good to talk with someone sometimes to hear yourself." (p. 119)

The study found that these girls exhibited resiliency when they actively sought means to enhance their own well-being and protect them from harm in at least two ways (Watkins, 2002). First, the girls used their own positive relationship-building skills to seek positive, close connections with people who were or became central in their lives. Such people might include a parent or parents, members of their extended family (several girls mentioned their close relationships with their aunts), other adults such as "youth workers, coaches, clergy, neighbors, [or] teachers," and peers with whom they were "sharing activities, hanging out together, keeping secrets, and 'keeping . . . out of trouble' " (Watkins, 2002, pp. 121–122).

A second way these girls used resiliency was in developing strategies to protect themselves in an unsafe urban environment. "The girls would deliberately prearrange travel companions when walking to the corner store. To avoid danger, they would map out the route they would take through the streets. They developed other physical resistance strategies, such as personal safety plans or not 'hanging on the streets'" (Watkins, 2002, p. 125).

Resiliency can also characterize larger systems. An example at the organizational level is a public university experiencing budget cuts of several million dollars. That university is resilient to the extent that it responds to the risk of loss, protects its most important functions, makes plans to adapt to the shortfall of resources, and continues providing students with a quality education. Resiliency involves focusing on the university's strengths to maintain basic functioning.

Resiliency in a community is illustrated by a group of urban neighborhoods that addresses an increasing crime and drug use problem. These troubles put the community at risk of disorganization and destruction. Community strengths include availability of organizations that provide resources; residents' expectations for appropriate, positive behavior; and opportunities for "neighborhood youths to constructively participate in the community" (Greene & Livingston, 2002, p. 78). A resilient community might use its concerned citizens to form neighborhood organizations that oversee community conditions and upkeep, work with public services to improve conditions, and advocate for increased resources (Homan, 2011). Neighborhood Watch programs may be formed, where neighborhood residents volunteer to carefully watch each other's premises to prevent and combat crime. Community residents might work with local police and schools to establish drug education and prevention programs for young people. They might also advocate for more police to increase surveillance and apprehension of drug dealers. Many communities have successfully driven out drug vendors, reclaiming and securing their neighborhoods and parks so children can feel safe in these places. A resilient community uses its strengths to address the risks threatening it and protect its residents.

Human Diversity

We have established that human diversity is the vast range of differences among groups, including those related to "age, class, color, culture, disability, ethnicity, gender, gender identity and expression, immigration status, political ideology, race, religion, sex, and sexual orientation" (CSWE, 2008b, EP 2.1.4). Highlight 3.2 provides a summary of definitions for each of these concepts.

EP 2.1.1e, 2.1.2a, 2.1.4, 2.1.4a, 2.1.4c, 2.1.4d, 2.1.10e

HIGHLIGHT 3.2

Dimensions of Diversity

Age: Some period of time during a person's life span. Age is often considered an important aspect of human diversity for older adults as they experience *ageism,* discrimination based on preconceived notions about older people, regardless of their individual qualities and capabilities.

Class (or **social class**): People's status or ranking in society with respect to such standards as "relative wealth, power, prestige, educational level, or family background" (Barker, 2003, p. 402).

Race: The category of people who share a common descent and genetic origin that may be distinguished by "certain physical traits," or "interests, habits, or characteristics" (Mish, 2008, p. 1024).

Ethnicity: The affiliation with a large group of people who have "common racial, national, tribal, religious, linguistic, or cultural origin or background" (Mish, 2008, p. 429).

People of Color: "A collective term that refers to the major groups of African, Latino and Asian Americans, and First Nations Peoples [Native Americans] who have been distinguished from the dominant society by color" (Lum, 2011, p. 129).

Culture: "A way of life including widespread values (about what is good and bad), beliefs (about what is true), and behavior (what people do every day)" (italics deleted) (Macionis, 2010, p. 2).

Disability: "Any physical or mental impairment [or ongoing health or mental health condition] that substantially limits one or more major life activities"; these activities include "seeing, hearing, speaking, walking, breathing, performing manual tasks, learning, caring for oneself, and working" (Equal Employment Opportunity Commission, 1997, p. 1).

Gender: "The social and psychological characteristics associated with being female or male" (McCammon & Knox, 2007, p. 112).

Gender identity: A person's internal psychological self-concept of being either a male or a female, or, possibly, some combination of both (Gilbert, 2008).

Gender expression: The manner in which we express ourselves to others in ways related to gender that include both behavior and personality.

Sex: "The biological distinction between being female and being male, usually categorized on the basis of the reproductive organs and genetic makeup" (McCammon & Knox, 2007, p. 606).

Sexual orientation: Sexual and romantic attraction to persons of one or both genders.

Immigration status: A person's position in terms of legal rights and residency when entering and residing in a country that is not that person's legal country of origin.

Political ideology: The "relatively coherent system of ideas (beliefs, traditions, principles, and myths) about human nature, institutional arrangements, and social processes" that indicate how a government should be run and what principles that government should support (Abramovitz, 2010, p. 131).

Religion: People's spiritual beliefs concerning the origin, character, and reason for being, usually based on the existence of some higher power or powers, that often involves designated rituals and provides direction for what is considered moral or right.

Social workers must understand human diversity for two reasons. First, many members of diverse groups are populations-at-risk of discrimination, oppression, marginalization, and alienation. Second, it's necessary to recognize the values and issues of diverse groups to appreciate differences and build on strengths.

Social work by nature addresses virtually any type of problem posed by any type of person from any type of background. To help people, practitioners must be open-minded, nonjudgmental, knowledgeable, and skilled. Because the range of human diversity is endless, learning about it is a continuous process.

Intersectionality of Diverse Factors

EP 2.1.4

The concept of *intersectionality* involves the idea that people are complex and can belong to multiple, overlapping diverse groups. "The intersectional perspective acknowledges the breadth of human experiences, instead of conceptualizing social relations and identities separately in terms of either race *or* class *or* gender *or* age *or* sexual orientation"; rather, an intersectional approach focuses on the "interactional affects" of belonging to multiple groups (Murphy, Hunt, Zajicek, Norris, & Hamilton, 2009, p. 2). People may experience injustice from a combination of reasons. The concept of intersectionality "underscores the complex nature of cultural and personal identities and human experiences that cannot be defined simply by one dimension of inequality or difference—either race or gender or sexual orientation or ability. The social worker, who is involved in working with individuals, families, groups, and communities belonging to diverse groups, must develop the cultural competence to work with people at the intersections of the multiple dimensions of diversity" (Murphy et al., 2009, p. 42).

Murphy and her colleagues (2009) provide the following case example demonstrating the complexity of intersectionality:

The Vue family emigrated from Laos six months ago. They were happy to find a small apartment that is convenient to a grocery store and meatpacking plant where Mr. Vue works long hours. They have three daughters, aged five years, four years, and six months. Shortly after they moved in, a neighbor called the local Department of

Human Services (DHS). The neighbor, Mrs. Smith, had spotted one of the girls sitting alone in front of the apartment door one afternoon. Mrs. Smith was surprised to see the front door open, the younger girl on the couch, and the infant sleeping. The police arrived on the scene about the same time Mrs. Vue returned home, carrying grocery bags. She was taken aback to see the police in her apartment. Mrs. Vue said she had left the children for thirty minutes to buy milk. The children were taken into DHS custody, and Mr. and Mrs. Vue were told that they would have to appear in court three days later.

The Vue family will be assigned a case worker who is responsible for understanding how race, ethnicity, and class affect this family. Moving from a small village in Laos, could this family have understood the new dangers and expectations that come with parenting in the United States? How does their economic position affect their ability to find appropriate child care? What other factors affect their needs as a family? (p. 42)

Race and Ethnicity

Race and ethnicity are related concepts that reflect primary dimensions of human diversity. *Race* refers to the category of people who share a common descent and genetic origin that may be distinguished by "certain

EP 2.1.4

physical traits," or "interests, habits, or characteristics" (Mish, 2008, p. 1024). *Ethnicity* refers to the affiliation with a large group of people who have "common racial, national, tribal, religious, linguistic, or cultural origin or background" (Mish, 2008, p. 429). Race implies a greater genetic determinant, whereas ethnicity often relates to cultural or national heritage.

Other terms often used are minorities and people of color. *People of color* "is a collective term that refers to the major groups of African, Latino, and Asian Americans, and First Nations Peoples [Native Americans] who have been distinguished from the dominant society by color" (Lum, 2011, p. 129).[1] *Minorities* are members of "a group of people who, because of physical or cultural characteristics, are

---

[1]Note that not all Hispanic people are people of color. Consider, for example, a white woman born in Argentina who speaks Spanish, the national language, and whose ancestors originated in Spain.

HIGHLIGHT 3.3

Terms Used to Describe Latino/Latina/Hispanic People

EP 2.1.3c

The U.S. government's Office of Management and Budget originally coined the term *Hispanic* in 1978 for use in the census (Green, 1999). According to the original definition, a Hispanic was "a person of Mexican, Puerto Rican, Cuban, Central or South American or other Spanish culture or origin, regardless of race" (Green, 1999, p. 256). However, the concept is much more complex than this. For example, does this umbrella term include Brazilians who speak Portuguese, South American Indians whose original language is not Spanish, Filipinos who speak Spanish, or immigrants from Spain (Green, 1999)?

An alternative term is *Latino/Latina,* which makes reference both to the Latin American languages, including Spanish, and to Latin America itself. However, this term omits South Americans who speak English, such as those from Belize or the Guyanas, and "people whose family roots extend to Italy, Germany, and some areas of the Mediterranean" (Green, 1999, p. 256).

Still another term often used is *Chicano/Chicana*, which refers to U.S. citizens with a Mexican heritage. The obvious disadvantage of this term is that it focuses only on Mexico and excludes people with origins in other countries, including those that are primarily Spanish speaking.

Longres and Aisenberg (2008, p. 31) summarize several points. Some people prefer not to refer to themselves as Hispanic because it's not rooted in Spanish but "imposed by American society." The word *Latino/Latina* is probably the most widely accepted. Additionally, this term allows one to distinguish between men and women, giving women greater "visibility." In general, it's best to use whatever terms people and communities prefer. This book will use the terms *Hispanic* and *Latino/Latina* interchangeably unless a specific group (e.g., Puerto Rican Americans or Chicanos/Chicanas [Mexican Americans]) is discussed.

singled out from the others in the society in which they live for differential and unequal treatment, and who therefore regard themselves as objects of collective discrimination" (Lum, 2011; Sue et al., 1998, p. 11; Wirth, 1945, p. 347). It is interesting that in the past many minorities did indeed make up a smaller proportion of the total population than did Anglos (i.e., U.S. citizens of European heritage, also referred to as Caucasians or whites). However, some minority populations such as Latinos/Latinas/Hispanics are making substantial gains and within several decades may surpass Anglos in actual numbers. Highlight 3.3 discusses the terms used to describe the Latino/Latina/Hispanic population in the United States.

Culture and Cultural Competence

EP 2.1.4

Culture, another dimension of diversity, is "the sum total of life patterns passed on from generation to generation within a group of people and includes institutions, language, religious ideals, habits of thinking, artistic expressions, and patterns of social and interpersonal relationships" (Hodge, Struckmann, & Trost, 1975; Lum, 2007, p. 4). Aspects of culture are often related to people's ethnic, racial, and spiritual heritage.

Social workers need to attain *cultural competence*— "mastery of a particular set of knowledge, skills, policies, and programs used by the social worker that address the cultural needs of individuals, families, groups, and communities" (Lum, 2005, p. 4). Cultural competence, strongly supported by the NASW *Code of Ethics*, involves the following six tasks for social workers (Arredondo et al., 1996; Lum, 2011; NASW, 2008, 1.05):

1. Develop an awareness of personal values, assumptions, and biases.
2. Establish an appreciation of other cultures and nurture attitudes that respect differences.
3. Understand how one's own cultural heritage and belief system differ from and may influence interaction with clients who have a different cultural background.

4. Recognize the existence of stereotypes about, discrimination against, and oppression of various diverse groups.
5. Commit to learning about clients' cultures.
6. Acquire effective skills for working with people from other cultures.

Focus on Critical Thinking 3.2 stresses how important it is for social workers to be aware of their clients' values, traditions, and customs.

Ethnic and Cultural Differences

EP 2.1.4d

We've established that understanding and appreciating diversity are essential for social workers to practice effectively with clients. Because families provide a primary arena for conveying values, much of the following discussion will focus on them.

Three points are helpful when we think about multicultural diversity. The first is that certain values tend to characterize each major racial and ethnic group. However, the second point concerns how critical it is not to overly generalize. Various individuals may embrace such cultural values to different degrees. The third point involves the importance of respect for and appreciation of the differences within large groups. For example, American Indians have been referred to as "Indians" only for the past 500 years. In reality, they make up more than 500 nations, including Tsististas, Lakota, Dine, Muscogee, and Ojibway that "maintain 300 separate languages and dialects" (Harjo, 1993, p. 199; Weaver, 2008).

The following section discusses some of the values, beliefs, and perspectives assumed by several cultural groups in our society: Hispanics, Native Americans, African Americans, and Asian Americans. Figure 3.1 summarizes the primary concepts.

Hispanics

We have established that the terms *Hispanic* and *Latino/Latina* have generally been used to refer to people originating in countries in which Spanish is spoken. However, we have also established that the terms refer to people originating in a wide range of places. Essentially, no one term is acceptable to all groups of people. The three primary Hispanic groups in the United States in terms of size are Mexican Americans (over 66% of all Hispanics), Puerto Ricans (almost 9%), and Cuban Americans

(almost 3.5%) (U.S. Census Bureau, 2010). Other groups include those from the Dominican Republic and from other countries in Central and South America (Santiago-Rivera, Arredondo, & Gallardo-Cooper, 2002). However, for any particular family, Goldenberg and Goldenberg (2002) caution, "Socioeconomic, regional, and demographic characteristics vary among Hispanic American groups, making cultural generalizations risky" (p. 326). Santiago-Rivera, and colleagues (2002) reflect:

Perhaps no other ethnic group in the United States is as heterogeneous in its ethnicity, physical appearance, cultural practices and traditions, and Spanish language dialects as the Latino population. Latinos in the United States are a diverse group of multigenerational [people] ... from different Spanish-speaking countries as well as long-term residents in the southwest United States. All have unique social, economic, and political histories. Latino groups vary in their ancestry, blending indigenous [people originating in an area] (e.g., Aztec and Mayan) and Spanish cultural traditions and, for some Latino groups, African traditions.

It's important not to make stereotyped assumptions about such a diverse group. Santiago-Rivera and her colleagues (2002) continue:

Although it is not often reported, Latinos may also be of Asian heritage. The Philippine islands, conquered by Spain, were populated by people of Asian heritage. Whereas the native language of the island is Tagalog, Spanish surnames are commonplace, and in the United States, Filipinos may claim either Asian or Latino heritage. In South America and Mexico, there are settlements of Chinese families as well. Peru is one such example. (p. 23)

Keeping in mind that more specific variations exist within the many subgroups, we will discuss some cultural themes important to Hispanic families in general. Hispanic heritage is rich and diverse, but the groups tend to share similarities in terms of values, beliefs, attitudes, culture, and self-perception. These include the significance of a common language; the importance of family relationships, including extended family and other support systems; spirituality; and the traditional strictness of gender roles.

Cultural Issues to Address

**EP 2.1.3,
2.1.3a,
2.1.4c,
2.1.7b,
2.1.10e**

The U.S. Census Bureau (2010) indicates that over 65% of the total U.S. population of 307,007 million is non-Hispanic white; over 12.9% is African American; about 1% is American Indian and Alaskan Native; 4.6% is Asian; and almost .2% is Native Hawaiian and other Pacific Islander. Over 1.7% reported being a member of more than one race. Almost 16% are Hispanic, who may be of any race.

Two facts stand out from these figures: (1) There is significant diversity in the population, and (2) a person's race is not always clear-cut. A person's family line and genetic heritage may be quite complex.

The racial mix of the United States is rapidly changing. Currently, about 30% of U.S. residents are people of color, and it's predicted that almost half will be by the middle of the century (Neukrug, 2008). Given such a diverse world, social workers and other helping professionals must be prepared to work with people having cultural backgrounds quite different from their own.

Social workers and other helping professionals must address at least four issues to work effectively with multicultural clients. First, they should rebuff the *melting pot myth*, which implies that we're all blended together into one big pot of creamed soup, that we all become essentially the same (Neukrug, 2008, p. 202). In reality, we're more like a salad bowl filled with various types of vegetables and croutons. Although we're all in there together, we maintain our individual and cultural distinctiveness.

The second issue that social workers must address is how people from various cultures have different ideas and expectations about what should happen during the intervention process (Neukrug, 2008, p. 202). For example, an Anglo approach "assumes that the counseling process should emphasize the individual; stress the expression of feelings; [and] encourage self-disclosure, open-mindedness, and insight" (Neukrug, 2008, p. 202). However, people from other cultures may assume very different perspectives. For example, a Hispanic man might emphasize the importance of family over what's best for himself as an individual. Similarly, he may find the blatant expression of emotions inappropriate and distasteful.

The third issue concerns *worldviews*—one's perception of how the world functions (in terms of relationships

with other people, social and economic activity, spirituality, values, and nature) in addition to how one fits into that context. With an *ethnocentric worldview,* people perceive their own race, ethnic background, or cultural values as being better than that of others (Neukrug, 2008, p. 204). Essentially, it's similar to the view "My way is not only the best way, it's the only way."

Sue (1992) provides an interesting example:

A white female elementary school teacher in the United States posed a math problem to her class one day. "Suppose there are four blackbirds sitting in a tree. You take a slingshot and shoot one of them. How many are left?" A white student answered quickly, "That's easy. One subtracted from four is three." An African immigrant youth then answered with equal confidence, "Zero." The teacher chuckled at the latter response and stated that the first student was right and that, perhaps, the second student should study more math. From that day forth, the African student seemed to withdraw from class activities and seldom spoke to other students or the teacher. (pp. 7–8)

What the teacher didn't know was that the African boy viewed the problem from an entirely different perspective. He looked at the whole picture of what shooting a bird with a slingshot meant. If the teacher had sought clarification of his answer instead of making fun of him, she might have better understood. The student's answer made perfect sense to him: If you shoot a slingshot at four birds sitting in a tree and hit one, the other three will fly away immediately, of course, and none will be left. Nigerian educators frequently use this anecdote to portray how differently people in the United States and Africa view the world. The African perspective takes into account how all the parts involved in a problem work together. In contrast, an Anglo perspective tends to focus on individuals searching for isolated, specific, technical aspects of a problem to determine the one correct answer.

The fourth issue concerns the importance of family. Anglos tend to focus on the *nuclear family*—the immediate family group composed of parent[s] and children—and give less credence to the *extended family*—relatives beyond the nuclear family, including at least grandparents, aunts, uncles, and cousins (Stewart & Goldfarb, 2007). A related concept is *kinship,* which refers to the state of being related through a common ancestry.

(continued)

FOCUS ON CRITICAL THINKING 3.2 *(continued)*

For example, I once worked as a social worker at a day treatment center for children and adolescents with emotional and behavioral problems. They attended the center during the day to receive special education and therapy, and then returned to their homes in the community at night and on weekends. A number of African American clients seemed to be staying at a different relative's home each week. This was a problem because clients were bused in from all over the city, so scheduling the bus route was a nightmare. The treatment center's administration, all of whom were Anglos, identified multiple residences as a problem. However, it really was a strength and should have been viewed as such. These adolescents had a strong kinship system with their extended families. Many relatives were ready and willing to take care of these children when their nuclear family (in this case, their mothers) did not always have the resources and capabilities to do so.

Another example of the strengths demonstrated by extended families involves Navajo who live on a reservation stretching from the south central Colorado plateau to parts of Arizona, New Mexico, and Utah. The tribe opened and ran its own nursing home for tribal members (Mercer, 1996). The home's staff had to be very sensitive to the fact that residents had numerous visitors from their extended family, many of whom were quite distant from the nuclear family and some of whom would travel great distances at significant cost. This was in stark contrast to many Anglo nursing homes, in which staff are accustomed to receiving few visitors for residents, and often only immediate family. Staff there frequently view visits as cumbersome and unmanageable. Chapter 10 elaborates further on the Navajo's empowering treatment of older adult family members.

Critical Thinking Questions

How would you describe your racial and cultural background? How would you explain your worldview? How would you describe the dynamics, closeness, and strengths of your own nuclear and extended families?

Figure 3.1 Common Cultural Values for Four Diverse Groups

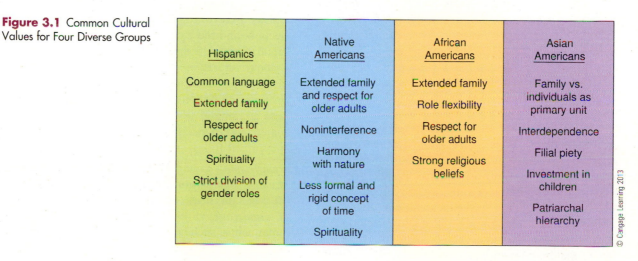

Hispanics	Native Americans	African Americans	Asian Americans
Common language	Extended family and respect for older adults	Extended family	Family vs. individuals as primary unit
Extended family	Noninterference	Role flexibility	Interdependence
Respect for older adults	Harmony with nature	Respect for older adults	Filial piety
Spirituality	Less formal and rigid concept of time	Strong religious beliefs	Investment in children
Strict division of gender roles	Spirituality		Patriarchal hierarchy

© Cengage Learning 2013

The first theme important in understanding the environment for children growing up in Hispanic families is the significance of a common language. Almost 60% of Latinos/Latinas indicate they speak English only or speak it fluently; however, almost 80% of Latinos/Latinas indicate they speak Spanish fluently (Longres & Aisenberg, 2008). Therefore, social workers should "know that there is a growing population of bilingual Latinos who have varying degrees of language proficiencies in English and Spanish" (Santiago-Rivera et al., 2002, p. 121). For instance, recent immigrants may use little if any English, whereas people whose families have been here for centuries may be bilingual or lack any knowledge of Spanish. One strong implication of such diversity is the need for social workers to assess Latino clients' language history and use on an individual basis.

Another important note is the fact that so many cultural activities and aspects of cultural pride are associated with Spanish. Consider the events and holidays (e.g., Cinco de Mayo for Mexican Americans, which refers to the glorious day a small Mexican army defeated a French army battalion), culture, history, and foods, all associated with Spanish origins, that are so meaningful in daily cultural life (Longres, 1995).

A second theme reflecting a major strength in many Hispanic families is the significance placed on relationships with nuclear and extended family, including "aunts, uncles, cousins, and grandparents, as well as close friends," referred to as *familismo* (Brammer, 2012; Diller, 2011; Santiago-Rivera et al., 2002, pp. 42–43; Weaver, 2005).

> *Latino families are typically large, intergenerational, and interdependent, and offer an important source of support to their members.... Extended family ties are highly valued and serve as a source of pride and security.... This emphasis on respect and responsibility to family members often leads to [older] ... adults both being cared for and taking on caregiving responsibilities within the family.... [Older adults] are often cared for within the family rather than through formal social services. When nursing homes are used, family members often continue to fulfill supportive caregiving responsibilities.*

> *(Kolb, 1999; Weaver, 2005, p. 148)*

Another important related concept reflecting a cultural strength is *compadrazco* (godparentage). *Compadres* (godparents) often serve as "substitute parents" who "may be prominent leaders or older people who hold some position of authority and respect within the Latino community. Such individuals play an important role in the Latino family's life and are included in all traditional celebrations. The practice of godparentage formalizes relationships between the child's parents and the *compadres* and promotes a sense of community" (Santiago-Rivera et al., 2002, p. 44).

Other vital sources of strength involve the community support systems often available to Hispanic families. These include the following:

Botanicas: "[S]hops that sell herbs as well as records and novels in Spanish."

Bodegas: "[G]rocery stores" that "also serve as information centers for the Hispanic community,

providing such information as where folk healers can be found ..." (Mexican, Puerto Rican, and Cuban Hispanic cultures espouse folk healers who help people deal with physical, emotional, and spiritual difficulties).

Clubes sociales: Settings that "provide recreation as well as links to community resources, including employment and housing." (Chilman, 1993, p. 160)

A third theme characterizing many Hispanic families is the importance of spirituality and religion (Longres & Aisenberg, 2008). "Spirituality has a fundamental shaping influence on the lives of many Latinos. Catholicism is a defining force of family and gender roles for Latino people.... Latino Catholicism revolves around the concepts of life and death. This fatalistic belief system emphasizes that God will provide. There is a pervading sense that much of what happens is beyond an individual's personal control. Most Latinos are Roman Catholic, but many espouse beliefs and practices influenced by indigenous and African belief systems" (Santiago-Rivera et al., 2002; Weaver, 2005, p. 147). Examples of such folk beliefs are the following:

Espiritismo (among Puerto Ricans): "The belief in spirits. Everyone is believed to have spirits of protection, and these can be increased by performing good deeds and decreasing evil. Latinos who ascribe to *espiritismo* believe that loved ones can be around in spirit after death and can lead one's life in times of difficulties. *Espiritistas* (spiritist healers) communicate with spirits and can be incarnated by them. Healing can take place with prescribed folk healing treatment."

Curanderismo (among Mexican Americans and other Central and South Americans): The practice of curing "physical, emotional, and folk illnesses. *Curanderos/as* are healers who use a range of treatments, such as herbal remedies, inhalation, sweating, massage, incantations, and *limpieza* (a ritual cleansing)."

Santeria (among Cuban Americans): Practices that combine "African deities with Catholic saints. The *santeros/as* are priests who function as healers, diviners, and directors of rituals" (Negroni-Rodriguez & Morales, 2001, p. 135; Santiago-Rivera et al., 2002; Weaver, 2005)

A fourth theme often characterizing Hispanic families involves a strict division of gender roles

(Diller, 2011; Longres & Aisenberg, 2008). This is reflected in two major concepts (Weaver, 2005). *Machismo* is the idea of male "superiority" that "defines the man as provider, protector, and head of the household"; *marianismo,* on the other hand, is the idea that, "after the Virgin Mary," females are valued for their "female spiritual sensitivity and self-sacrifice for the good of husband and children.... The mother and wife roles offer power to exercise authority in the home. However, women are also expected to be dependent on men" (Negroni-Rodriguez & Morales, 2001, p. 135).

Santiago-Rivera and her colleagues (2002) note that these beliefs may give mothers an important yet challenging role in the family. If a woman is self-effacing and giving at all times, she may appear to outsiders to be more like a submissive doormat. However, those who know Latinas, especially mothers, often note that women are the silent power in the family.

Weaver (2005) indicates that "[a]lthough distinct gender roles exist, it is important to recognize that not all Latinas fit these roles to the same extent. For example, Latinas are often stereotyped as passive and submissive, but many changes have taken place in marriages and families in the last decade. Many Latinas now work outside the home and may wield decision-making power about family finances. It is important to understand evolving gender roles within Latino families" (p. 146). Today over 56.5% of Hispanic women are in the work-force compared to over 60% of African American women and over 59% of white women (U.S. Census Bureau, 2010). From a strengths perspective, Hispanic women function as socializers, educators, and promoters of values and beliefs within family systems. Hispanic couples vary widely in terms of who assumes decision-making power and responsibility for family support, as do couples in any other ethnic or racial group. Other factors to consider that influence gender roles include educational level, income, location, history in this country, verbal communication, and family structure (Santiago-Rivera et al., 2002).

American Indians/Native Americans/ First Nations Peoples

We have stressed that there are more than 500 separate American Indian nations with hundreds of dialects (Weaver, 2008). Weaver (2008) comments on the terms used to refer to these indigenous peoples (that is, people who originally populated these geographic areas):

> *There are many terms for the indigenous people of North America including* American Indian, Native American, *and* First Nations Peoples. *There is no consensus about which term is best, yet some Native people have strong preferences for one term over the others. These terms all include many different groups of distinct people. (p. 254)*

Some people feel that the term *First Nations Peoples* emphasizes the true status of these population groups as the first inhabitants of North America who populated intact nations before Europeans arrived. There is also some evidence that many people in these groups prefer the term *American Indian* over *Native American* (Barker, 2003). Additionally, the term *Native American* is "a broader designation" than that referring to North American peoples because it may include Hawaiians and Samoans (American Psychological Association, 2010, p. 75). This book will arbitrarily use the terms *American Indian* and *First Nations Peoples* interchangeably when referring to these population groups. When quoting other sources, sometimes the term *Native American* is used.

Whenever possible, it's best to identify the participants' specific group (American Psychological Association, 2010; Brave Heart & Chase, 2005). Although some nations consist of fewer than 100 people (Weaver, 2007), others including the Cherokee, Chippewa, Choctaw, Navajo, and Sioux have more than 100,000 members (U.S. Census Bureau, 2009). Weaver (2007) further describes the picture:

> *Extensive diversity also exists among people within nations. Some people are very knowledgeable about and grounded in their indigenous culture, while others are not. Sometimes this is based on choices an individual has made; however, it is more often the result of decades of damaging U.S. policies that tried to assimilate Native people. These policies were deliberate in their attempts to eradicate indigenous cultures. Many people lost their ability to speak their language and lost touch with their cultural traditions when they were forcibly taken away from their community and sent to government or church-run boarding schools. This sort of cultural loss impaired their ability to pass on cultural traditions to their children, and left many Native people with limited knowledge of their indigenous heritage. (p. 257)*

Sensitivity to differences among American Indian nations and to individuals within nations, along with appreciation of these differences, is vital to effective social work practice. However, as with Hispanic people, several themes characterize many First Nations Peoples. These include the importance of extended family, noninterference, harmony with nature, the concept of time, and spirituality.

As with Hispanic people, *family ties* including those with extended family are very important (Bearse, 2008; Brammer, 2012; Ho, 1987; Paniagua, 2005). The sense of self is secondary compared to that of the family and of the tribe (Paniagua, 2005). Baruth and Manning (1999) explain:

Family extends well beyond one's immediate relatives to extended family relatives through the second cousin, members of one's clan, members of the community, all other living creatures in this world, nature as a whole, and the universe itself. The entire universe is thought of as a family, with every one of its members serving a useful and necessary function. Native American children develop a heightened level of sensitivity for everything of which they are a part, for the cyclical motion of life, and for the customs and traditions of their people. (p. 325)

Edwards and Edwards (2002) comment:

It is not unusual for large numbers of extended family members to participate in healing ceremonies for cousins, aunts, uncles, parents, and grandparents. It is sometimes confusing to accurately identify family members, as cousins may be affectionately referred to as brothers and sisters, and respected aunts and uncles (sometimes several times removed) may be addressed as mothers, fathers, and grandparents are. Elders are often referred to as "Grandmother" or "Grandfather" when there are no kinship ties to these people. (p. 247)

Elders typically are turned to for advice and consultation on important matters. Paniagua (2005) explains:

American Indians emphasize the "administration" of the family by the father and older relatives. Thus, mutual respect between wife and husband, between parents and children, between immediate family members and other relatives, and between family members and the tribe is highly valued. . . .

An important part of the American Indian cultural value of familism [the well-being of the family is most important and the interests of the individual secondary] is the tradition of consulting tribal leaders, elders, and medicine men or women when marital conflicts emerge. (p. 100)

Children receive supervision and instruction not only from their parents but also from relatives of several generations; thus biological parents have "greater opportunity to engage in more fun-oriented activities with their children" and often are able to establish relationships with their children that are "less pressured and more egalitarian than that of the dominant culture" (Brammer, 2012; Ho, 1992, p. 76).

A second significant concept in American Indian culture involves the emphasis on *noninterference,* "the deep respect for the rights and dignity of individuals [to make their own decisions]. . . . The highest form of respect for another person is respecting his or her natural right to self-determination. This means not interfering with another person's ability to choose, even when it means keeping a person from doing something foolish or dangerous" (Baruth & Manning, 1999, p. 328; Diller, 2011; Sue, 2006; Sue & Sue, 2008). Although First Nations life emphasizes collective work and common goals, it also stresses the individual's right to have opinions (Paniagua, 2005). Therefore, "American Indian children are rarely told directly what to do and are often encouraged to make their own decisions" (Paniagua, 2005, p. 100). Locke (1998) explains:

Many Native American Indians use noncoercive parenting styles that encourage the child's self-determination. . . . Child-rearing practices are characterized by early training in self-sufficiency, and psychological development is in harmony with knowledge gained from the natural world. . . . [American] Indian parents are generally quite permissive in their training, and children have no fixed schedules for eating or sleeping. (pp. 68–69)

Another facet of noninterference involves how fathers or older male adults in a family do not control families. Rather, they administer or organize the family so that it may arrive at a decision regarding how to proceed (Paniagua, 2005).

A third conceptual theme that characterizes American Indian culture is that of *harmony with nature* (Baruth & Manning, 1999; Dhooper &

Moore, 2001; Diller, 2011; Ho, 1987). Ho (1987) reflects:

> *American Indians hold nature as extremely important for they realize that they are but one part of a greater whole. There are many rituals and ceremonies among the tribes that express both their reverence for nature's forces and their observance of the balance that must be maintained between them and all other living and nonliving things. (p. 71)*

A fourth concept basic to First Nations life and related to harmony with nature is the *concept of time* (Bearse, 2008; Diller, 2011; Sue, 2006; Sue & Sue, 2008; Weaver, 2005). Time is considered an aspect of nature. Time flows along with life. It is not something that should take precedence over how you relate to others in your life. Therefore, time should not control or dictate how you live and spend your time. Hence other aspects of life, including interaction with other people, become more important than punctuality.

One other theme reflecting the perspective of many First Nations Peoples is that of *spirituality* (Bearse, 2008; Brammer, 2012; Weaver, 2005). Dhooper and Moore (2001) explain:

> *It was not until the passage of the American Indians Religious Freedom Act of 1978 that Native Americans were permitted religious freedom in the United States. Prior to that time, they were considered heathens and were often arrested and imprisoned for practicing their religion. Religion is a universal concept among Native Americans. When they refer to the universe they include the world, god, the self, and others. Their religion embraces many gods or spirits, but there is usually one great god or Great Spirit to whom reference is made. Faith, an outgrowth of their religiosity, is a harmonizing force that gives purpose and significance to their culture, life, and land (Kasee, 1995). They believe in the reincarnation and infinite existences of their spirits and consider the elements and forces of nature such as the rain, sun, lightning, water, and fire as objects of worship. They believe that the natural world is controlled by the supernatural through spirits. From their perspective, every sphere of life is governed by religion. God and nature are inseparable, and being in disharmony with God will cause disharmony with nature, which will have a negative impact upon the self. (pp. 178–179)*

Note that the extent to which these five themes characterize any individual Native American person or family varies tremendously (Bearse, 2008). Sue and Sue (2008) reflect:

> *Although some of the value differences between [American] Indians and non-[American] Indians have been presented, many Indians are acculturated and hold the values of the larger society. [Acculturation is "the adaptation of language, identity, behavior patterns, and preferences to those of the host/majority society" (Lum, 2004, p. 229).] ... Five cultural orientation types were formulated by M. T. Garrett and Pichette (2000):*

1. Traditional. *The individual may speak little English, thinks in the native language, and practices traditional tribal customs and methods of worship.*
2. Marginal. *The individual may speak both languages but has lost touch with his or her cultural heritage and is not fully accepted in mainstream society.*
3. Bicultural. *The person is conversant with both sets of values and can communicate in a variety of contexts.*
4. Assimilated. *The individual embraces only the mainstream culture's values, behavior, and expectations.*
5. Pantraditional. *Although the individual has only been exposed to or adopted mainstream values, he or she has made a conscious effort to return to the "old ways." (p. 353)*

African Americans

There are 41.8 million African Americans in the United States (U.S. Census Bureau, 2010). Fifty-five percent live in the South, 18.1% in the Midwest, 17.6% in the Northeast, and 9.4% in the West (McRoy & Lombe, 2011). McRoy and Lombe (2011) cite the following facts:

- Between 80% and 89% of African Americans ages 25 and older have at least a high school degree. Eighteen percent of African American women and 16% of African American men have at least a bachelor's degree.
- African Americans tend "to be disproportionately poor." Twenty-three percent of African Americans are poor compared with 8% of whites.

- "The highest poverty rates are among families headed by women. Thirty-five percent of Black families and 19% of White families headed by women with no spouse present are in poverty."
- "The poverty rate of African Americans aged 65 or older is 23.9%, which is more than twice the rate of [older adults] . . . in general."
- African American unemployment rates are twice that of non-Hispanic Whites.
- The median[2] income for African American households is $33,916 versus $54,920 for non-Hispanic Whites. This is less than 62% of white median income.
- "Despite income gains, the racial-wealth gap has widened considerably during the last 20 years . . . The average net worth for Blacks is $6,166 compared with $67,000 for Whites . . . The root of the wealth inequality lies in a past in which African Americans were denied opportunities to accumulate assets. The discrepancies in wealth mean that many African Americans do not benefit from the cushion that assets provide in poverty reduction and social mobility across generations" (pp. 278–280).

African Americans, like other racial, cultural, and ethnic groups, reflect great diversity. "The term *African American* subsumes a diverse array of peoples including African Americans born in this country, Africans, and individuals from the West Indies and Central and South Americas" (Diller, 2011, p. 256).

Despite this diversity, however, four dynamics have "shaped African American experience and culture" (Black, 1996; cited in Diller, 2011, p. 257):

African legacy—rich in culture, custom, and achievement.

History of slavery and deliberate attempt to destroy the core and soul of the people.

Racism and discrimination and ongoing efforts to continue the psychological and economic subjugation started during slavery.

Victim system and process by which individuals and communities are denied access to the instruments of development and advancement.

(Black, 1996, p. 59)

---

[2]The *median* is "a value or quantity lying at the midpoint of a frequency distribution of observed values or quantities," so that one-half of the values fall above it and one-half below it (Lindberg, 2007, p. 847).

Devore (2001) cautions that, on the one hand, we should "begin with the understanding that African American families are not homogeneous. One cannot point to the [typical] African American family. No composite exists. Therefore, social workers must understand that African American [families] will differ in style and composition, but will experience persistent racism" (p. 34).

On the other hand, Solomon (2002) maintains that although many groups have been effectively integrated into the dominant culture (e.g., "Dutch, German, Scandinavian, and Irish"), this has not been the case with African Americans (p. 299). She continues that "the result has been the maintenance of a distinctive culture that possesses elements of the dominant culture, elements of other subcultural groups who have been oppressed, and elements that are a consequence of the unique African American experience. This cultural distinctiveness may be observed" in a variety of ways (Solomon, 2002, p. 299). These include four general commonalities that tend to characterize African American families.

First, extended family ties are very important for African American families (Diller, 2011; Moore, 2008; Sue & Sue, 2008). Often children are raised not only by the nuclear family consisting of parents and children but also by extended family members, including grandparents, aunts and uncles, cousins, and others even further removed. This reflects a significant strength in that children often receive nurturance and support from multiple caring family members, who also provide each other with mutual aid.

A second, related dimension characterizing African American families is role flexibility (Diller, 2011; Moore, 2008; Weaver, 2005). Winkelman (1999) explains that traditional gender roles

tend to be less rigid, with few uniquely male or female characteristics. . . . Both male and female African American children are taught to be assertive and nurturing. The emphasis on interdependence, cooperation, flexibility, adaptation, and mutual respect has required an abandonment of traditional definitions of sex roles. (p. 297)

Paniagua (2005) continues:

Sometimes the mother plays the role of the father as well as the mother, and thus functions as the head of the family, and older children sometimes function as parents, caring for younger children.

In fact, it is not uncommon for older African American children to drop out of school so that they can go to work and help their younger siblings secure a good education. (p. 32)

A third characteristic of African American families is respect for older adults (Usita, 2007). Dhooper and Moore (2001) report:

[Older adults] ... are held in high regard in the African American family and community. This results from (a) the acknowledgment of their having a collective history of lifelong discrimination; (b) the belief that offspring should provide in-home care when the need for assistance arises; and (c) the habit of allowing relatives and nonrelatives to live with them in times of family crises. (p. 103)

A fourth theme in African American life involves strong religious beliefs and a close relationship with the church, especially an African American church (Diller, 2011; Dhooper & Moore, 2001; Moore, 2008). Many African American families consider the church to be a part of the extended family, providing similar nurturance and support (Paniagua, 2005). Dhooper and Moore (2001) explain:

The African American church continues to address not only the religious and spiritual needs of the individual, family, and community, but also their social needs. It serves as a coping and survival mechanism against the effects of racial discrimination and oppression and as a place where African Americans are able to experience unconditional positive regard. (p. 101)

Frame (2003) reflects that for many African Americans,

Spirituality and identity are inseparable. Religion is not compartmentalized into a set of beliefs, doctrine, or dogma. Instead, it is in the life and breath of most African Americans, whether or not they are involved in organized religion. ... Some African Americans believe that spirit may be found in everything. Religion and spirituality are considered major strengths for African Americans, which contributed to their resilience, their survival of slavery, and their ability to overcome present struggles. For many African Americans, spirituality dominates their thinking and is integrally related to their sense of security, adjustment, identity development, behavior, and problem-solving ability. ... When they find themselves in a crisis or particularly

stressed, many African Americans seek solace and strength in their religious and spiritual practices. ...

The focus of worship in most African American churches is on God, who through Jesus Christ, enters into a personal relationship with believers, reconciles, liberates, heals, and guides. ... There is an emphasis on God's "healing presence in life despite suffering and pain" (Wimberly, 1991, p. 16). Worship in African American churches is spirited, emotional, expressive. It often includes "involuntary acts of praise" (Mitchell & Mitchell, 1989, p. 105). In addition, clapping, dancing, and shouting are common in African American worship, which results in spiritual uplifting and an indwelling sense of hope in the worshiper. ... There is the expectation that upon leaving a worship service, participants are empowered to manage the demands of daily life. (pp. 132–133)

Asian Americans

Asian Americans are composed of three basic groups that, in turn, consist of numerous subgroups. These include, but are not limited to, "Asian Americans (Japanese, Chinese, Filipinos, Asian Indians, and Koreans); Pacific Islanders (Hawaiians, Samoans, and Guamanians); and Southeast Asians (Vietnamese, Cambodians, and Laotians)" (Fong, 2008; Paniagua, 2005, p. 73). Obviously, there is huge variation among these groups despite the fact that they are clustered under the umbrella term *Asian Americans.*

Diller (2011) explains that "unlike African Americans, Latinos/as, and Native Americans, Asian Americans have been quite successful economically and educationally, even in comparison with the White population"; this includes median income levels, rate of small business ownership, and attainment of educational degrees (p. 273). However, he maintains that this provides an overly simplistic view and urges us to consider the following facts:

High median income doesn't take into consideration the number of wage earners, the level of poverty among certain Asian subgroups, or the discrepancy between education and income for Asian workers. Education in the Asian community is bimodal; that is, there are both highly educated and uneducated subpopulations. Asian towns in large urban areas represent ghettos with high unemployment, poverty, and widespread social problems. Underutilization of services does not necessarily mean a lack of problems, but may in fact have alternative explanations such as face-saving, shame, or the family's cultural tendency to keep personal information hidden from the outside world. In short, the belief in Asian success does not mean that there is any less racism or discrimination directed toward Asian Americans or that there are not serious problems within crowded urban enclaves.

(Diller, 2011, p. 274; Sue & Sue, 2008)

Discussed here are five themes that tend to characterize many Asian American families. These include the significance of family, interdependence, filial piety, investment made in children, and patriarchal hierarchy.

First, like Hispanics, Asian Americans tend to consider the family as the primary unit and individual family members as secondary in importance (Balgopal, 2008; Diller, 2011; Slattery, 2004). Phillips (1996) describes a key concept:

The welfare and the integrity of the family are of great importance. The individual is expected to submerge or to repress emotions, desires, behaviors, and individual goals to further the welfare of family and maintain its reputation. The individual is obligated to save face, so as to not bring shame onto the family. Therefore, there is incentive to keep problems within the family so that the family will not "lose face." (p. 1)

A second theme, related to the significance of the family, that is common among Asian American families involves interdependence (Green, 1999; Sue & Sue, 2008). For example, Chinese culture emphasizes "kinship from birth to death, and it is expected that the family will serve as a major resource in providing stability, a sense of self-esteem, and satisfaction" (Goldenberg & Goldenberg, 2002, p. 341). Such respect and maintenance of responsibility is expected even when family members move to some other country and never or rarely see the rest of the family again (Goldenberg & Goldenberg, 2002).

A third theme concerns *filial piety*—"a devotion to and compliance with parental and familial authority, to the point of sacrificing individual desires and ambitions" (Brammer, 2012; Kirst-Ashman & Hull, 2012b, p. 459). It is expected, for instance, that children will care for aging parents (Balgopal,

2008; Green, 1999). Goldenberg and Goldenberg (2002) comment:

Elders are afforded unquestioned respect. In Filipino families, for example, elders are greeted in culturally defined ceremonial ways and with kinship terms that denote their special rank; failure either to carry out the ritualized greeting or to use these terms would be considered disrespectful. (p. 345)

A fourth theme characterizing many Asian American families involves the high priority of and tremendous investment in children (Balgopal, 2008; Goldenberg & Goldenberg, 2002; Green, 1999). Goldenberg and Goldenberg (2002) explain:

Young children are indulged long beyond what is considered standard among traditional American families. Toilet training is often delayed, according to Berg and Jaya (1993), until the child insists on it, and older children, even up to the age of 10 or 11, frequently sleep with their parents. Adolescents are not encouraged to learn self-care skills (cleaning their rooms, doing their own laundry, cooking their own meals) and are permitted to maintain a dependent position as long as they wish. What they are expected to do, however, is to be well behaved and obedient and, above all, to bring honor to the family. School achievement is a particularly visible way to do so, but so is earning praise from others in the community for being respectful, knowing good manners, and eventually marrying into a good family. (pp. 341–342)

A fifth related theme distinguishing many Asian American families involves their patriarchal hierarchy (Diller, 2011; Goldenberg & Goldenberg, 2002; Green, 1999). Balgopal (2008) explains:

Asian families are generally patriarchal, and in traditional Asian families, age, sex, and generational status determine the roles that members play. The father is the head of the family, and his authority is unquestioned; he is the main disciplinarian and is usually less approachable and more distant than the mother; the mother is the nurturer and caretaker. (p. 156)

A Note on Difference

Of course, any discussion of these general cultural themes of values and behaviors is just that—general. Actual practices vary dramatically from one ethnic group to another and from one family to another. It's important not to make mistaken assumptions about an individual's values and expectations simply because that person is a member of some group.

National Origin and Immigration Status

EP 2.1.4

National origin, another dimension of diversity, involves individuals', their parents', or their ancestors' country of birth. National origin often is an important factor in people's cultural values and expectations. How individuals are raised, what they're taught, and how they learn to perceive the world around them vary dramatically from one corner of the world to another. Understanding values and customs derived from national origin helps social workers better understand their clients' perspectives and needs.

An important related concept to national origin is immigration status. *Immigration* involves the permanent movement from one country to another. *Immigration status* is a person's position in terms of legal rights and residency when entering and residing in a country that is not that person's legal country of origin. Social workers are often called upon to work with immigrants, so it's important to understand the terms and issues involved. Potocky-Tripodi (2002) defines many of the important concepts:

> *The fundamental distinction between immigrants and refugees is that* immigrants *leave their countries voluntarily (usually in search of better economic opportunities) whereas* refugees *are forced out of their countries because of human rights violations against them. Therefore, immigrants are also sometimes referred to as* voluntary migrants *or* economic migrants, *and refugees may be referred to as* involuntary migrants *or* forced migrants. *Refugees are also sometimes referred to, or refer to themselves, as* exiles *or* émigrés. . . .
>
> *Legally, anyone who is not a citizen of the United States is termed an* alien. *Aliens are further classified as immigrants and nonimmigrants, and as documented or undocumented (Loue, 1998). In this classification, an* immigrant *is a person who has been legally admitted into the United States and granted the privilege to be a permanent resident (a "green card" holder). A* nonimmigrant *is a foreign-born person who is in the United States temporarily, such as a tourist, a student or a journalist. Nonimmigrants also include temporary, or seasonal, workers, who come to the United States to work during certain periods of the year and*

> *return to their countries during the rest of the year. This typically refers to agricultural laborers.*
>
> *A* documented alien *is one who has been granted a legal right to be in the United States. This legal right is determined by admissions policy. The admissions policy details many categories of people who are eligible to be legally admitted. It also specifies how many people from each country may be legally admitted into the U.S. each year. . . .*
>
> *An* undocumented alien *is one who does not have a legal right to be in the United States. These people are also sometimes referred to as* illegal immigrants. *They are also referred to as* deportable aliens, *because if discovered by immigration authorities, they are subject to deportation, or forcible return to their countries of origin. There are two ways in which people become undocumented aliens. One is by entering the U.S. illegally. This means that the person has not received authorization to enter the United States. For example, people who cross the border from Mexico without going through the immigration authorities are undocumented aliens. The second way that people become undocumented aliens is by entering the U.S. legally, but then violating the terms of the visa (the authorization to stay in the U.S.). For example, a tourist may be granted a visa to stay in the United States for a limited period of time. If the person stays after that time period has expired, then that person becomes an undocumented alien. (pp. 4–5)*

Many people from other countries may receive or need social services. Immigrants represent an important portion of the U.S. population. In 2008 almost 38 million people, 12.5% of the total population, were foreign-born (U.S. Census Bureau, 2010). U. A. Segal (2010) reports:

> *Individuals and families from around the globe form a continuous stream of immigrants to the United States. The backlog of visa applications and waiting lists to enter the nation stretches to several years. Undocumented immigrants, both those who arrive without legal papers and those who overstay their visits, abound. Record numbers of refugees and asylees are admitted from countries in political turmoil. Disproportionately large numbers of entrants into the United States in recent years have been people of color from Asia, Africa, and Central and South America, and despite encountering a series of barriers, an overwhelming majority remains applying for permanent residence. (p. 29)*

People with different national origins often find it difficult to integrate themselves into the mainstream culture, especially when language barriers exist (Garcia, 2009; Gushue & Sciarra, 1995). Finding employment and adequate housing and "fitting into" the social fabric of neighborhoods and communities can be difficult. Kamya (1999) cites "social isolation, cultural shock, cultural change, and goal-striving stress as four significant experiences" newcomers often face (p. 607). They may have difficulties understanding new behavioral expectations imposed on them, interacting effectively with others in the new culture, and achieving the goals they had hoped for. Highlight 3.4 identifies some of the differences between cultural expectations in the United States and those adopted by the Turkana tribe in northern Kenya.

Increasing cultural competence is helpful in working with a population having a different national origin. Consider the following example. Thanh, a counselor at a homeless shelter, is seeing an increasing number of Haitian immigrants enter the shelter. He determines that he must enhance his knowledge of their cultural values to work with them more effectively. As he does this, he begins to understand that "the plight of Haitian immigrants is noteworthy because of its complexity and because of their flight from political and economic oppression" (Allen, 1995, p. 125). Thanh discovers that a local organization exists primarily to assist immigrants of Caribbean origin socially, economically, and politically. The organization's goals include "contributing to the economic welfare of the community through the stimulation of businesses, promoting the housing needs of their constituents, and assisting their members in securing employment" (Allen, 1995, p. 125). Obtaining this information about Haitian immigrants

---

HIGHLIGHT 3.4

Appreciating Cultural Differences in National Origin

EP 2.1.4c, 2.1.4d

Imagine a family of the Turkana tribe in northern Kenya immigrating to the United States.[3] What difficulties would members face in terms of cultural differences and expectations? Primarily nomadic goatherds, these people are not accustomed to handling currency, as their subsistence is based on *bartering* (exchanging goods for other goods). Even if they enter a store, have currency, and want to make a purchase, it is unthinkable to pay the asking price without trying to negotiate a lower cost.

Another difference is the common practice of polygamy. The number of a man's wives reflects his wealth, with each wife being purchased with some negotiated number of goats. A wealthy man is one with many wives and many goats.

The Turkana tribe's conception of time reflects yet another difference. Many tribal members have never seen watches. Their time is not split into precise units such as minutes and hours. Rather, they depend on the position of the sun in the sky to determine what should be done at that time of day. They value relationships and mutual respect more than rigorous scheduling and strict punctuality. For example, the person providing this information was two days late for a meeting due to international and internal transportation difficulties. Instead of being angry, tribal members were unconcerned about the lateness and cheerfully welcomed their visitor when he finally arrived. A two-day delay most likely would not be accepted so tranquilly in the United States.

One aspect of U.S. culture Turkana tribe members would probably appreciate is the ready access to public education, as education is highly valued there. Four years of primary school and another four years of secondary are available to children, but it still costs each family an additional $100 for elementary and $300 for secondary school per year. In the United States, this may not seem like much, but in northern Kenya, a professional person holding an exceptionally good job might earn $1,000 in an entire year.

The point of this is not to make judgments about which cultural values are better or worse, but rather to emphasize that significant differences do exist based on ethnicity and national origin. Social workers, then, must listen carefully to such clients regarding their needs, work with them as they adjust to new conditions, and provide the best services possible to meet their needs.

[3]This information was gathered from a personal communication with Gary S. Kirst, who had visited the Turkana tribe.

enhances both Thanh's understanding of their culture and his ability to communicate with his clients. It also makes him aware of a whole new set of resources potentially available to clients.

Note that when we speak about any racial, ethnic, or cultural group, it is important not to overgeneralize. Persons with other national origins may embrace traditional cultural norms to various degrees. They may also experience *acculturation*, already defined as "the adaptation of language, identity, behavior patterns, and preferences to those of the host/-majority society" (Lum, 2004, p. 229). In other words, people from another country may gradually blend into the larger society and adopt its values and customs. Therefore, for a given racial, ethnic, or cultural group, it is important that social workers not assume that all members comply with all cultural values or conform to the same extent. Being of German ethnic heritage does not automatically mean a person loves sauerkraut, liver sausage, and raw ground beef with onions on rye bread simply because these are traditional ethnic foods.

Gushue and Sciarra (1995) address the difference in acculturation between first-generation and later-generation immigrants:

> *As family members differentiate according to ability levels of the language of the dominant culture, distinct forms and levels of acculturation begin to emerge. Children, having gained a knowledge of the language and wanting to be accepted by their peers, take on the ways of the dominant culture. Parents, more isolated because of language and perhaps suspicious of the ways of the dominant culture, enter into conflict with their children. Issues of racial/cultural identity also emerge because children and parents feel differently about their cultural heritage. (p. 597)*

Class

Class or *social class,* another aspect of diversity, refers to people's status or ranking in society

**EP 2.1.4,
2.1.4b,
2.1.5a,
2.1.9a**

with respect to such standards as "relative wealth, power, prestige, educational level, or family background" (Barker, 2003, p. 402). What comes to mind when you think of social class? Whom do you picture when you think of people in higher classes? In lower classes? How would you characterize yourself in terms of class membership? How do you relate to people of other classes?

Social workers must carefully scrutinize their own answers to these questions. They must strive to avoid imposing stereotypes and prejudgments. Rather, they must continue to expand their knowledge base about the environmental circumstances characterizing people's lives in other social classes.

Political Ideology

Political ideology is another aspect of diversity. *Political ideology* is the "relatively coherent system of ideas (beliefs, traditions, principles, and myths) about human nature, institutional arrangements, and social processes" that indicates how a government should

EP 2.1.4

be run and what principles that government should support (Abramovitz, 2010, p. 131). Chapter 1 introduced the "standard" political ideologies concerning social welfare and government policies to address it—conservatism, liberalism, and radicalism (Abramovitz, 2008, p. 368). Your political ideology forms your views on how the government should be run, what responsibilities the government should assume, and what laws and policies should be established and implemented. Abramovitz (2010) explains:

> *The debate on the proper role of government often centers on which of three sites for resource distribution—the family, the market, or the government— should bear the heaviest burden in ensuring the well-being of people. We don't usually think of it this way, but all three systems play this role. The family distributes resources to its members by supporting those who do not work or otherwise cannot care for themselves. The breadwinners supply the wages needed to buy the food, clothing, shelter, medical care, and a host of other goods and services needed by family members. In exchange, adult women and other unpaid family members shop, cook, clean, care for children, and maintain the household. Conservatives believe the families can and should be self-sustaining. Liberals argue that from the start many families, especially those with limited income, have needed some kind of outside help to sustain themselves. Radicals hold that because low wages and high unemployment can raise profits, the operation of the system of production deprives families of resources needed for successful family maintenance. (pp. 147–148)*

Gender, Gender Identity, and Gender Expression

EP 2.1.4, 2.1.4c

Gender is another aspect of diversity that is really much more complex than it may initially seem. "*Gender* refers to the social and psychological characteristics associated with being female or male. Characteristics typically associated with the female gender include being gentle, emotional, and cooperative; characteristics typically associated with the male gender include being aggressive, rational, and competitive. In popular usage, gender is dichotomized as an either/or concept (feminine or masculine), but gender may also be viewed as existing along a continuum of femininity and masculinity" (as Focus on Critical Thinking 3.3 will explore) (McCammon & Knox, 2007, p. 112).

Other important concepts related to gender are gender identity, gender expression, gender roles, and gender-role socialization. *Gender identity* is a person's internal psychological self-concept of being either a male or a female, or, possibly, some combination of both (Gilbert, 2008). *Gender expression* concerns how we express ourselves to others in ways related to gender that include both behavior and personality. *Gender roles* are the "attitudes, behaviors, rights, and responsibilities that society associates with" being male or being female (Yarber, Sayad, & Strong, 2010, p. 127). *Gender role socialization* is the process of conveying what is considered appropriate behavior and perspectives for males and females in a particular culture.

We will differentiate the concepts of gender and sex. *Sex* "refers to the biological distinction between being female and being male, usually categorized on the basis of the reproductive organs and genetic makeup" (McCammon & Knox, 2007, p. 606). Gender, then, emphasizes social and psychological aspects of femaleness or maleness; sex, on the other hand, focuses on the biological qualities of being male or female.

Women as Victims of Oppression

EP 2.1.4a, 2.1.5a

Despite the fact that a wide range of gender expression exists, the mainstream culture is primarily segregated by gender in terms of women and men. As racial, ethnic, and cultural backgrounds affect you, so does your gender affect how you

are treated and what worldview you assume. Women experience many issues, expectations, and life situations that men do not, and they perceive the world in a different way. The following reviews women's plight in the United States:

> *Domestic violence is rapidly increasing: Reports of wife abuse, child abuse, and incest have never been higher. We see an aging society with limited resources for employment opportunity and health care, especially for frail [older adults] ... Women of color and other vulnerable groups are more represented in the changing face of acquired immune deficiency syndrome (AIDS). Increased immigration from Third World countries results in populations at risk for poverty, poor health care, and lack of educational opportunity.... Women are overworked, underpaid, and undersupported by our social programs.... [Rapidly growing] pressures on family life, ... [for women] include fewer resources for children; greater caregiving responsibilities for aging, ill, and disabled family members; and consequent role overload and stress.*
>
> (Brandwein, 2008; Land, 1995, p. 3)

Some disturbing facts reflect the different life contexts of women and men in this country. Consider the following:

- Women are significantly more likely to be poor than men (Brandwein, 2008; Kirk & Okazawa-Rey, 2010).
- "The two poorest groups in the United States are women raising children alone and women over 65 living alone" (Kirk & Okazawa-Rey, 2010, p. 314).
- Non-Asian women of color are significantly more likely to be poor than white women (Brandwein, 2008; Kirk & Okazawa-Rey, 2010).
- The median income of women who work full-time is 78.7% of what men earn (U.S. Census Bureau, 2010).
- For all races, women earn significantly less than men do at every educational level. The median income for women with a bachelor's degree or more is 64% of what men with a college education or more earn; similarly, the average annual income for women with a high school education is less than 73% of what correspondingly educated men earn (U.S. Census Bureau, 2010).

FOCUS ON CRITICAL THINKING 3.3

What Does *Gender* Really Mean?

**EP 2.1.3a,
2.1.4,
2.1.5c,
2.1.10d**

In an overly simplistic, naïve view of the world, one might think, "You're either a male or you're a female. Period." However, in reality neither gender nor sexual orientation are such simple concepts. Money (1987) proposes eight factors of gender that more fully portray some of its complexity. The first six are physical variables that include chromosomal predisposition to gender; the presence of either ovaries or testes; exposure to male or female hormones prior to birth and brain differentiation resulting from hormones prior to birth; the presence of female or male internal reproductive organs; exterior genital appearance; and the production of either male or female hormones during puberty. The two psychological variables are the gender assigned at birth ("It's a boy" or "It's a girl") and the person's *gender identity* (the perception of oneself as being either "female" or "male").

It is estimated that 1 out of every 1,500 to 2,000 babies born has some combination of physical characteristics demonstrated by both sexes (Crooks & Baur, 2011; Intersex Society of North America [ISNA], 2008a). Reasons include having "an atypical combination of sex chromosomes or as a result of prenatal hormonal irregularities" (Crooks & Baur, 2011, p. 120). For example, Klinefelter's syndrome is a sex chromosome disorder where males are born with an extra X chromosome, resulting in an XXY designation; "the Y chromosome triggers the development of male genitalia, but the extra X prevents them from developing fully" (Carroll, 2010, p. 88). Results include a feminized body appearance, low testosterone levels, small testicles, and, possibly, infertility (Lee, Cheng, Ahmed, Shaw, & Hughes, 2007). Treatment may involve testosterone therapy.

Another example of contradiction in physical gender is a genetic female who as a fetus is exposed to excessive androgens (a class of male hormones); as a result she develops external genitals that resemble a male's (Crooks & Baur, 2011). Her clitoris is enlarged enough to resemble a penis, and the labia (folds of tissue around the vaginal entrance) may converge and resemble a scrotum (the pouch that holds the male testes) (Carroll, 2007). When diagnosed at birth, cosmetic surgery can often be performed to "feminize" the person's genitalia.

There are many other examples of people who have some mixture of male and female predisposition and configuration of reproductive structures. Such a person is referred to as *pseudohermaphrodite* or *intersex*. A true *hermaphrodite* is a person "born with fully formed ovaries and fully formed testes, which is exceptionally rare" (Carroll, 2010, p. 89).

Many times parents and/or medical staff make the arbitrary decision to surgically alter infants with ambiguous sexual characteristics soon after birth to make them conform more closely to one gender or another. The Intersex Society of North America (ISNA) (2008c) raises serious questions regarding the right of parents and physicians to physically alter a child without that child's knowledge and consent. Such procedures apparently are undertaken theoretically in the best interests of the child, possibly without parental consent (ISNA, 2008b). The ISNA (2008c) makes several recommendations regarding how intersex children and their families should be treated. First, these children and their parents should be treated with respect; physicians and medical staff should address the condition and issues openly and honestly without shame. Second, families with intersex children should be referred to social workers or other mental health professionals to address issues and potential decisions. Third, these families should also be connected with other families who have intersex children for peer support and deeper insight in the issues involved. Fourth, after careful consideration, an intersex child should be assigned a gender "as boy or girl, depending on which of those genders the child is more likely to feel as she or he grows up." Such gender assignment should not involve surgery because surgery may destroy tissue that the child may want later on in life. Fifth, the child should receive medical treatment "to sustain physical health" (e.g., "surgery to provide a urinary drainage opening when a child is born without one"). Sixth, surgeries to make the child "look 'more normal'" should be avoided until the child is old enough to decide for him- or herself.

Critical Thinking Questions

When infants are born with an ambiguous or unclear gender, should they be assigned to one gender or the other? At that time, should they be physically altered to more closely resemble the assigned gender? If so, who should be responsible for making this decision?

EP 2.1.3

(continued)

FOCUS ON CRITICAL THINKING 3.3 *(continued)*

To what extent might children with ambiguous genitals (even after being given an assigned gender as the ISNA suggests) fit in with their peers and be able to function well socially? Would it be better to wait until children reach adulthood to determine gender and/or to do any relevant surgery? Why or why not? Should society become more open-minded and expand its views of sex and gender to include more variations of male and female (a proposal that the ISNA does not support)?

Other Forms of Gender Expression

Another variation in the expression of gender involves *transgenderism,* including "people whose appearance and/or behaviors do not conform to traditional gender roles" (Crooks & Baur, 2011, p. 129), "living full- or part-time in the other gender's role"—that is, their nonbiological gender—and get psychological satisfaction from doing so (Carroll, 2010, p.101). Among these people are *transsexuals,* people who feel they are imprisoned in the physical body of the wrong gender. Because their gender identity and sense of self are at odds with their biological inclination, they often seek to adjust their physical appearance to that of their gender identity through surgery and hormonal treatment. Many transsexual people prefer to be referred to as transgender people. The word *transsexual* emphasizes *sexual,* whereas *transgender* emphasizes *gender,* which they say is the real issue.

Several other groups of people are also often included under the transgender umbrella. *Transvestites* are people who derive sexual gratification from dressing in the clothing of the opposite gender. In our society, almost all transvestites are heterosexual males (Carroll, 2010; Wheeler, Newring, & Draper, 2008). This might be due to the fact that women experience much greater freedom and flexibility in how they dress. *Drag queens* are gay men who dress up as women. Lesbians who dress up in traditionally masculine clothing may be referred to as *drag kings. Female impersonators* are men who dress up as women, usually for the purpose of providing entertainment. They may be heterosexual or gay. A common performance involves mimicking the dress and style of famous female performers, often lip-synching (moving their lips to a song and music without producing any sound) their greatest hits.

The Social Construction of Gender

Considering these diversities of gender expression, the concept of gender doesn't appear to be quite so clear. One theoretical approach to understanding how we view and interpret gender as a society refers to the social construction of gender. *Social construction* refers to the perspective where the social world is considered "a social creation, originating and evolving through our everyday thoughts and actions. Most of the time, we assume and act as though the world is a given, objectively predetermined outside of our existence. However, ... we also apply subjective meanings to our existence and experience. In other words, our experiences don't just happen to us. Good, bad, positive, or negative—we also attach meanings to our reality" (Leon-Guerrero, 2009, p. 8).

EP 2.1.7a

The *social construction of gender* "looks at the structure of the gendered social order as a whole and at the processes that construct and maintain it" (Lorber, 2010, p. 244). It assumes that traditional gender expectations are not facts carved in stone, but rather perceptions and expectations that can be changed. Lorber (2010) reflects:

> Gender and sexuality are performances, and ... individuals modify their displays of masculinity and femininity to suit their own purposes. Males can masquerade as women, and females can pass for men. ... [One might argue] that, like clothing, sexuality and gender can be put on, taken off, and transformed. Transgendered people especially display the fluidities of gender and sexuality, challenging normals to prove that they aren't also creating their gendered identities through their appearance and behavior. ... [A] focus of gay, lesbian, and transgender studies ... turns the [two categories of male and female] ... sex, sexuality, and gender inside out with "third terms"—intersexuality, bisexuality, transgendering. (p. 195)

Critical Thinking Questions

To what extent do you think people should be given freedom in gender expression? Which aspects of gender expression do you find acceptable? What could society do to make such practices more acceptable and appreciated?

EP 2.1.3

- Women earn significantly less than men even when they're in the same occupation. This gap appears one year after graduation and widens after a 10-year period (Dey & Hill, 2007). For example, women earn 95% as much as men in the field of education, which is female-dominated; they earn only 76% as much as men in fields involving mathematics (which is male-dominated), and 73% in the humanities (a mixed-gender field) (Dey & Hill, 2007). Census data reinforce the gender gap in earnings (U.S. Census Bureau, 2010). Women in management, business, and financial occupations earn a median full-time, year-round salary of 72% of what their male counterparts earn. Similarly, women in professional and related occupations earn less than 70% of what men earn.
- Women tend to be clustered in lower-paying occupations than men. For example, men are more likely to become doctors, dentists, or lawyers (U.S. Census Bureau, 2010). Men also dominate professions involving science, technology, engineering, and math (Hill, Corbin, & St. Rose, 2010). Women are frequently in supportive occupations such as kindergarten teacher, secretary, dental hygienist, child-care worker, and word processor (U.S. Census Bureau, 2010).
- Research conducted since 1961 reflects a significant, consistent wage differential between men and women in social work (Gibelman, 2003). Some recent research focusing on people with master's degrees in social work found that women earned an average of $12,000 less than men; even when various factors were controlled, women social workers earned 14% less than men (Brandwein, 2008; Center for Workforce Studies, 2006). Another recent national survey by the National Association of Social Workers found that median salaries for female social workers were $11,000, or 17.2%, less than those for male social workers (Pace, 2010).
- "Even with a college education ... and equivalent work experience and skills, professional women are far less likely than men to get to the top of their professions or corporations. They are halted by unseen structural barriers, such as men's negative attitudes to senior women and perceptions of their leadership abilities and styles, their motivation, training, and skills. This barrier has been called a *glass ceiling*" (Kirk & Okazawa-Rey, 2010, p. 311; Padavic & Reskin, 2004).
- Almost 68% of single women and 61.6% of married women with children under age 6 work outside the home (U.S. Census Bureau, 2010).

Women, therefore, often are victims of oppression manifested in many ways. They are more likely than men to be poor and are more likely to be primary caregivers for children and older adults. They are victimized by specific kinds of violence, including sexual assault and domestic violence, rarely experienced by men.

Important concepts related to these issues are sexism and sex discrimination. *Sexism* is "prejudice or discrimination based on sex, especially discrimination against women" that involves "behavior, conditions, or attitudes that foster stereotypes of social roles based on sex" (Mish, 2008, p. 1141). *Sex discrimination* is the differential and potentially unfair treatment of people based solely on their gender. Examples include paying males more than females for the same or comparable jobs, or hiring only one gender for certain jobs.

Many people are initially turned off by the concepts of sexism and sex discrimination. They find it difficult consciously to recognize and accept the possibility that this is an imperfect, sexist world. They think that things are supposed to be fair and that they shouldn't have to waste their time and energy battling such problems as sexism. For many women, it's easier to adopt an "out of sight, out of mind" philosophy. In other words, if one doesn't think about a problem, then it doesn't really exist. Why dwell on problems that are nonexistent or insignificant?

To what extent do you think sexism and sex discrimination exist today? How much do they account for the discrepancies between women and men in terms of their life circumstances and treatment? How might you begin to think about these concerns so that you could figure out the reasons for their existence? What theoretical perspective might help you organize information and your view of the world to increase your understanding?

One such theoretical framework is the *feminist perspective,*

one in which women's experiences, ideas, and needs are valued in their own right. Put another way ...

[the perspective that views] man as the norm ceases to be the only recognized frame of reference for human beings. Women's experiences are seen as constituting a different view of "reality"—an entirely different ... way of making sense of the world.

(Cummerton, 1986, p. 85)

Focus on Critical Thinking 3.4 explores the meaning of feminism for women and men and raises some provocative questions.

The Special Issues and Needs of Men

EP 2.1.4a,
2.1.4c,
2.1.5a
2.1.10e

We've discussed how women are a population-at-risk that experiences disadvantages and discrimination based on gender. Men, however, also have disadvantages based on their gender that should be addressed. Kosberg and Adams (2008) cite the following as special issues experienced by men:

1. Society attempts to socialize men to conform to male gender-role stereotypes. Men should be tough, strong, vital, definitive, and unemotional. They should be as unfeminine as possible. These demands place great pressure on men to refrain from expressing emotion. This, in turn, negatively affects their ability to gain insight into their emotions and behavior. It also hampers their ability to communicate freely even in their most intimate and important relationships. Such pressures may prevent them from seeking the human support and love they need.

2. Men risk greater health problems than women. They don't live as long. They have higher death rates than women in all of the 15 leading categories of death with the exception of Alzheimer's disease (Courtenay, 2003). They are more likely than females to be murdered, to successfully complete suicide attempts, to be homeless, to die in car accidents, to abuse mind-altering substances, and to experience injuries related to their work.

3. Men who experience major disturbances or losses in their lives such as divorce or death of a loved one may have difficulty turning to others for emotional support and help. They may experience difficulties in undertaking domestic tasks for which they've never learned the skills. Inability to cope may have harmful effects on their

self-concepts. Providing care to children or aging partners may be exceptionally difficult when they were not socialized into those roles.

4. Men of color experience even greater difficulty. They are more likely to be poor, uneducated, and incarcerated. They are also more likely to experience health problems and die earlier than white men.

5. Men are more likely to use detrimental coping mechanisms such as turning to substance abuse and denial. Because of the pressures on them to be strong and independent, they often underuse community services, especially those involving mental health.

Blundo (2008) makes a number of recommendations regarding social work practice with men. Note that the majority of social workers are women. First, practitioners should strive to be aware of any gender-role stereotypes and expectations they harbor toward men just as with any other diverse group. Biases might affect practitioners' objectivity and effective practice. Second, it's important to be aware of the wide range of diversity among men. It's essential to understand how gender-role stereotypes and expectations affect men's behavior and emotions in order to develop appropriate goals when working with men. It's also crucial to be aware of and attend to the special issues faced by men of color. Third, as traditional treatment has focused on repairing the deficits inherent in masculinity (e.g., helping a man to become better at expressing emotion and seeking help when needed), it's important to focus on strengths. The extent to which a man is an active problem solver and doer should be used to his advantage instead of disadvantage.

Sexual Orientation

Sexual orientation, another significant aspect of diversity, involves sexual and romantic attraction to persons of one or both genders. People having a sexual orientation toward the same gender are generally

EP 2.1.4

referred to as *gay* if they are male or *lesbian* if they are female. However, many people use the term *gay* to refer to both lesbians and gay men. The older term referring to same-gender sexual orientation is *homosexual.* People having a sexual orientation toward persons of the opposite gender are *heterosexual,* or

FOCUS ON CRITICAL THINKING 3.4

What Is Feminism?

**EP 2.1.3,
2.1.5b,
2.1.7a,
2.1.7b**

How do you respond to these questions?

- What words and images come to mind when you hear the word *feminism*?
- What does feminism represent and suggest to you?
- How would you define feminism?
- To what extent do you feel the concept is significant or meaningless in your life?

Some people have extremely negative reactions simply to the word *feminism*. The emotional barriers they forge and the resulting resistance they foster make it difficult even to think about the concept. Others consider feminism a radical ideology that emphasizes separatism and fanaticism. In other words, they think feminism involves the philosophy adopted by women who spurn men, resent past inequities, and strive violently to overthrow male supremacists. Still others think of feminism in terms of an outmoded tradition of women seeking equality with men. They feel it is no longer relevant in contemporary times, nor does it merit their attention.

What Is a Feminist?

Both men and women can be feminists. The definition of feminism proposed here is designed to relate to basic concepts involving the daily lives of people like you. It entails readily understandable concepts. Many people have failed to develop a sensitivity to the sexist barriers surrounding them. For one thing, it's painful to acknowledge such unfairness. For another, it's easy to assume "that's the way things are" simply because people haven't thought about other, better ways of doing things.

For our purposes, *feminism* is the philosophy of equality between women and men that involves both beliefs and actions, that infiltrates virtually all aspects of life, that often necessitates providing education and advocacy on behalf of women, and that appreciates the existence of individual differences and personal accomplishments regardless of gender (Kirst-Ashman, 1992). Five major components within this definition relate directly to the values and goals of professional social work.

First, equality is the core of feminism. *Equality* does not mean identicalness or sameness. It does not mean

that women are trying to shed their female identities and become clones of men. Nor does it mean that women should seek to adopt behaviors that are typically "masculine." Feminism does promote equal or identical rights to opportunities and choices. It relates to women's and men's rights not to be discriminated against and not to be denied opportunities and choices on the basis of gender.

The second major component inherent in feminism is the fact that it embodies *both beliefs and actions*. Beliefs concern how we look at the world and perceive other people; actions reflect expression of the beliefs. Feminism espouses a belief system that views other people objectively and fairly. It means avoiding both stereotypes and assumptions about people on the basis of gender. A person who fails to behave in accordance with expressed feminist beliefs is not a true feminist according to our definition. For example, one of your instructors might say he supports feminist principles yet frequently emphasize how women are too emotional and make sexist jokes that fixate on breast size. Feminism involves acting on one's beliefs on behalf of gender equality and fair, respectful treatment.

The third critical aspect in the definition of feminism is the idea that *all aspects of life* are involved. The concept of equality does not apply only to an equal chance of getting a specific job or promotion. It also involves having the rights to hold personal opinions about political issues and to make decisions within personal relationships. It entails a woman's right to make a decision about what to do on a Friday night date or whether to have a sexual encounter. Essentially, this aspect includes the acknowledgment that our social, legal, and political structure is oriented toward men, not women.

The fourth important aspect of feminism is the frequent necessity of providing *education and advocacy* on the behalf of women, a dimension coinciding with major social work roles. This might involve giving feedback to a person behaving in a sexist fashion or speaking out on the behalf of others being treated unfairly. For example, I once went to a travel agency for vacation information. While the lone travel agent worked with another customer, I waited patiently for about 15 minutes. At that point, two men in business suits walked in. As soon as the agent was finished

(continued)

FOCUS ON CRITICAL THINKING 3.4 *(continued)*

with her customer, she looked directly at the men—as if I were invisible—and asked them if she could help them. If I had behaved more compatibly with feminist principles, I might have assertively stated that I had been waiting for quite a while and that men should not be given precedence simply because of gender. As it was, I was furious and stomped out. I missed an opportunity to educate the agent regarding her sexist behavior so that she might treat women more equitably in the future.

The fifth major concept involved in the definition of feminism is the *appreciation of individual differences*. The feminist perspective lauds the concept of empowering women by emphasizing individual strengths and qualities. Feminism stresses freedom and the right to make choices about one's own life. Note that this concept applies to both women and men.

A feminist perspective refutes and challenges the idea that the potential of women and men is limited by their gender. Rather, it proposes that women should be empowered to develop their abilities and pursue activities to achieve optimal well-being.

Van Den Bergh and Cooper (1987) stress that in many ways a feminist perspective conforms with the core of traditional social work practice in terms of principles and values. Both emphasize the significance of being concerned with "human dignity and the rights of self-determination" (Van Den Bergh & Cooper, 1986, p. 3). Both stress the importance of individuals' interactions with their environments and communities.

Critical Thinking Questions

In light of the preceding discussion, do you think that you are a feminist? Respond to the following questions to help come to a conclusion:

- Do you believe that women and men should have the same rights?
- Do you believe that women and men should have the same access to jobs and social status?
- Do you believe that women and men should not be discriminated against or denied opportunities and choices on the basis of their gender?
- Do you think that employers should treat women and men equally in work settings?
- Do you believe that ideally people's attitudes and behavior should reflect the equal treatment of women and men?
- Do you think that many people need to become more educated about women's issues?
- Would you be willing to advocate on behalf of women (e.g., for poor women or women who have been raped)?
- Do you believe that both women and men have the right to their own individual differences (of course, differences that don't harm other people)?
- Do you think that our society is generally structured legally, socially, and economically by and for men instead of women? (This last question is probably the most difficult, and perhaps the most painful, to answer.)

If you answered "yes" to all or most of these questions, according to our definition, there's a good chance that you are a feminist.

straight. People sexually oriented toward both genders are referred to as *bisexual*. Because lesbian, gay, and bisexual people face some of the same problems, when referring to them as a group, we will use the term *LGB* (i.e., lesbian, gay, or bisexual). Note that sometimes the term *LGBT* (i.e., lesbian, gay, bisexual, and transgender [as described in Focus on Critical Thinking 3.3]) is used to describe this population when addressing issues experienced by all of the groups included.

It's difficult, if not impossible, to state exactly how many people are lesbian or gay. The issue

remains complex. "Homosexuality is stigmatized. Gay men and lesbian women are often reluctant to reveal their identities in random or anonymous surveys for reasons of personal hesitancy as well as conceptual problems surrounding what constitutes sexual orientation (Ellis, Robb, & Burke, 2005)" (Yarber, Sayad, & Strong, 2010, p. 190). Carroll (2010) reports that "estimates for homosexuality range from 2 to 4% to greater than 10% in males and 1 to 3% in females . . . , whereas estimates for bisexuality are approximately 3%" (p. 282). Based on Alfred Kinsey's work in the 1940s and 1950s, "many authors have used 10% as the proportion of men who are gay" (Berger & Kelly, 1995, p. 1066). And many lesbian and gay organizations maintain that they make up 10% of the population. One major lesbian and gay organization is called "The Ten Percent Society." The controversy regarding the actual number of lesbian and gay people continues. Regardless of whether lesbian and gay people make up 1% or 10% of the population, they are a sizable minority group.

Focus on Critical Thinking 3.3 explored the complexity of sexual orientation and gender.

Homophobia

**EP 2.1.4a,
2.1.4c,
2.1.5a**

A major problem gay people face is *homophobia*—an extreme and irrational fear of lesbian and gay people simply because they are lesbian and gay. LGB people are one of the primary groups at risk of discrimination and oppression. Highlight 3.5 reflects the feelings of one person who faces homophobia every day.

Although not all LGB people suffer every day from homophobia in all its forms, all LGB people endure some forms at some times (Tully, 2001). To help LGB people cope with the results of homophobia, social workers must understand their life situations and environmental issues.

LGB people may suffer from the effects of homophobia in at least three ways, one of which is *overt victimization.* Dworkin (2000) remarks,

Anti-LGB violence is more common than most people realize. . . . All the symptoms commonly associated with posttraumatic stress[4] are likely to follow a physical or verbal attack, in varying degrees of intensity, depending on the circumstances of the attack and the vulnerability of the victim. In a four-year study of hate crimes against LGB people, Herek et al. [1997] found that stress, depression, and anger lingered for as long as five years after the attack. In addition to posttraumatic symptoms, an LGB client can experience anxiety about his or her sexual identification. . . . Often

Sexual orientation is an important facet of human diversity. Here, two partners marry at City Hall in San Francisco on Tuesday, June 17, 2008, the first full day same-sex marriages had been legalized throughout California.

there is regression to earlier stages of the coming out process. (p. 170)

A second way LGB people encounter homophobia involves *covert victimization*—discrimination that is not obvious. For instance, Jay, a 21-year-old gay man and college student, applies for a part-time job at Hilda's Humongous Hamburgers, a local fast-food restaurant. Daryl, the manager, somehow finds out that Jay is gay. He then hires another applicant who is heterosexual (or so Daryl thinks) because that applicant is more "appropriate."

A third way LGB people suffer from homophobia involves *internalizing* it (Dworkin, 2000; Miller, 2008; Tully, 2001). If the majority of those around LGB people are homophobic, making fun of and severely criticizing them, it's fairly easy for LGB people to start believing it themselves. Results may include "low self-esteem, depression, suicidal ideation, substance abuse, isolation, self-loathing, . . . or acting out" (Tully, 2001, p. 610).

---

[4]*Posttraumatic stress disorder* is a condition in which a person continues to reexperience some traumatic event like a bloody battle or a sexual assault.

Age

EP 2.1.4

At each age people have different needs and require different services to optimize their well-being. This book introduces social work with people of various ages. There are chapters on children and youth, and content on families with members who represent a range of ages. Because 13% of the U.S. population is age 65 or older, it is important for social workers to understand the strengths, needs, and issues of this group (U.S. Census Bureau, 2010). This will be even more evident as the baby boomer population reaches retirement age. As people age, they are more likely to experience increasing health problems and to require more health and other support services. Kropf and Hutchinson (2000) explain:

Social workers are serving more [older adult] ... clients than ever before. [Older] ... adults are a diverse population, presenting a wide range of practice needs and social issues. Social workers encounter two general types of [older adult] ... clients. One group, older people with developmental disabilities, have used social services at earlier life stages and continue to use services into their later life. The second type of [older adult] ... client seeks a practitioner's help for conditions associated with the aging process. An example is the older person who requires assistance with household maintenance because of physical disabilities associated

with aging. Both types of clients have similarities to younger clients. However, the unique aspects of aging must be understood if social work practice with older clients is to be effective. (p. 3)

Chapter 10 explores in much greater depth the misconceptions about older adults, their needs, resources available to them, and the social work services involved.

Disability

It is estimated that 600 million people in the world today live with some kind of disability, another aspect of diversity (Mackelprang, 2008). Disabilities differ dramatically concerning how they affect people; they may

EP 2.1.4

involve cognitive, physical, and psychiatric conditions (Clute, 2008; Patchner & DeWeaver, 2008; Sullivan, 2008).

Many mistaken beliefs and misunderstandings exist concerning the abilities and prospects of people who have various types of disabilities, often minimizing these people's potential. Myths include, for example, that people with paraplegia (paralysis of both legs due to a spinal cord injury or disease) or intellectual (cognitive) disabilities are unable to work.

Because people with disabilities have unique strengths and needs, social workers can provide a range of services to help them improve their quality

---

HIGHLIGHT 3.5

Reflections About Being a Lesbian in a Homophobic Society

Jackquelyn is a doctoral student in a counseling program at a prestigious Eastern university. She reflects on what it's like to live as a lesbian in a homophobic world:

I am a European American upper-middle-class student. ... I am thoroughly embedded in a Eurocentric, achievement-oriented, individualistic way of life that I am finding to be increasingly maladaptive. ... I seek to unify various parts of me. I am female, lesbian-identified, white, athletic, academic, emotional, and other things that my culture insists be compartmentalized from one another, from

other people, and from myself as a whole person. ... Politically, I am a lesbian, but I am also a white person who confronts racism and ethnocentrism. My labels do not describe me fully, of course; the word lesbian does not account for my full range of emotional, behavioral, and cognitive ways of being. ... I have been told overtly and covertly that I don't belong. Professors, supervisors, and peers ... [treat me like an object] in offices, ... [make offensive gestures] in the hallways, [and] use sexualized language in professional conversations with me.

(Lowe & Mascher, 2001, pp. 773–774)

of life. Chapter 11 addresses types of disabilities, special needs, the issues involved, an emphasis on people's strengths, and social workers' involvement in service provision. Chapter 13 explores social work in mental health.

Religion and Spirituality

EP 2.1.4

Religion and spirituality reflect yet another aspect of human diversity. *Religion* involves people's spiritual beliefs concerning the origin, character, and reason for being, usually based on the existence of some higher power or powers, that often involves designated rituals and provides direction for what is considered moral or right. *Spirituality,* a related concept, "includes one's values, beliefs, mission, awareness, subjectivity, experience, sense of purpose and direction, and a kind of striving toward something greater than oneself. It may or may not include a deity" (Frame, 2003, p. 3). Religion implies membership in a spiritual organization with customs, traditions, and structure. Spirituality may involve religion, or it may reflect a personal, internalized view of existence.

Social workers help people cope with very difficult issues. Consider the following:

> An [older adult] ... hospice patient spends his last days overwhelmed by depression. A young woman, estranged from family and friends, numbs her loneliness with one-night stands and alcohol. A grieving couple drift apart after the death of their child.
>
> (Miller, 2001, p. A12)

Gotterer (2001) maintains that spirituality can be "a bastion of strength" for clients, offering "emotional consolation, inspiration, guidance, structure and security. It can foster personal responsibility, identity, respect for ethical codes, meaningful ritual, and community building" (p. 188). Gotterer (2001) suggests that

> social workers, typically involved with vulnerable people in situations of pain or crisis, need a greater awareness of spiritual and religious issues. Tragedies such as the untimely death of a loved one force a person to confront the inexplicable. People nearing death often wonder whether there is an afterlife. Trying times may cause a person to question the meaning and purpose of life. Those subjected to

> serious disease or long-term oppression need some way to make sense of their experience. Spiritual concerns such as hope, meaning, inner strength, and doubt are relevant in many clients' lives. (p. 187)

O'Neill (1999) warns, however, that the social work community concurs that

> one overriding principle is that of self-determination: social workers should never try to impose their own beliefs on clients. "There are many people who really do need faith and we need to honor it," said [Leona] Furman [associate professor at the University of North Dakota, who undertook the first major national survey of social workers' spirituality]. "We also need to honor those who don't have" the need to seek spiritual help and guidance. (p. 3)

As already indicated, spirituality can also be expressed in ways other than those determined by formal religions. Highlight 3.6 describes Kwanzaa, which "emphasizes spiritual grounding" for many African Americans (Karenga, 2000, p. 62).

Islam and Muslims: A Population-at-Risk of Prejudice and Discrimination

Alavi (2001) cites the following scenario:

> During an annual meeting for the Catholic Archdiocese of Cincinnati, a primary agenda item concerned anti-Muslim furor in the United States during the 1979 Iranian hostage crisis. "Particular attention went to a young boy in Wilmington, Ohio, a small, closely knit farming community that was proud of its Quaker college, considered a beacon of tolerance and intellectualism. The fifth-grade boy on the meeting's agenda had an American mother and an Iranian father working at the college. Being the lone child in town with an Iranian connection made him the only target of abuse in the entire school system. The first sign of trouble, a large rock, flew through his bedroom window, shattering glass on him and landing in the crib of his baby sister. By the end of the week, things were so bad that school administrators decided to dismiss the boy 15 minutes early every day. This would enable him to run home and lock the door before the other children caught up with him and beat him up, as they had done from the beginning of the hostage crisis.

Kwanzaa: A Spiritual Celebration of Life, Culture, and History

Kwanzaa, meaning "first fruits of the harvest" in Swahili, is a week-long celebration of life, culture, and history for many African Americans (Woodward & Johnson, 1995, p. 88). Developed by African American Maulana Karenga in 1966, it is celebrated annually from December 26 through January 1. It was created as a means of reaffirming community and heritage, strengthening the bonds among "African people both nationally and internationally" (Kanda & Furman, 2010; Karenga, 2000, p. 57). Karenga explains:

> It was conceived as a cultural project, as a way to speak a special African truth to the world by recovering lost models and memory, reviving suppressed principles and practices of African culture, and putting them in the service of the struggle for liberation and ever higher levels of human life.

Kwanzaa is based on the following seven principles, called the Nguzo Saba (Canda & Furman, 2010; Karenga, 2000, pp. 58–59; Woodward & Johnson, 1995, p. 88). They each focus on concepts in Swahili because that is the most extensively spoken language in Africa.

1. *Unity (Umoja):* African Americans strive for harmony and a feeling of community in their families, neighborhoods, and nations.
2. *Self-determination (Kujichagulia):* African Americans "define" themselves, "name" themselves, "create" for themselves, and "speak for" themselves "instead of being defined, named for, and spoken for by others" (Karenga, 2000, p. 58).
3. *Collective work and responsibility (Ujima):* African Americans work together in their communities and help each other solve their problems.
4. *Cooperative economics (Ujamaa):* African Americans work together to establish their own economic base, taking responsibility for each other, developing businesses, and sharing wealth.
5. *Purpose (Nia):* African Americans adopt a guiding principle that they will build a world community restoring them "to their historical greatness" (Karenga, 2000, p. 58).
6. *Creativity (Kuumba):* African Americans do as much as possible to make their communities "more beautiful and beneficial" than before they inherited them (Karenga, 2000, p. 58).
7. *Faith (Imani):* African Americans believe strongly in themselves, focus on their strengths, and have faith that in the future they will blossom and stand out as a "free, proud, and productive people" (Karenga, 2000, p. 59).

Kwanzaa is a time when African Americans gather together to celebrate their culture, reach out to old friends, and forge commitments to a bright future. Each day, family members light a candle and focus on one of the Nguzo Saba's seven principles. At the end of the celebration, they exchange gifts usually having cultural significance (Woodward & Johnson, 1995). Kwanzaa is a celebration of African heritage and culture that serves as an avenue of empowerment for African American communities.

That child was my son, Jason. Although he had always been a confident and popular boy, he was never again able to fit into the social scene of his school. He carried the stigma of being "Iran Man" until graduation, and as an adult he feels little desire to see any of his school colleagues again.

Similar pictures exist today after the September 11, 2001 (9/11), terrorist attacks. Ahluwalia and Zaman (2010) reflect that since 9/11:

There has been an increase in attention to and awareness of the experiences of Muslims . . . in America. Less favorable public opinion . . . and media portrayal . . . of Muslims in America have contributed to an increasingly hostile sociopolitical climate. The media have consistently and repeatedly displayed images of suspected terrorists—people with "Islamic-sounding names," those who "appear" Muslim, and men who wear turbans. . . . Alongside this growing interest, the post-9/11 era has witnessed a dramatic backlash against U.S. Muslims . . . with a sharp increase in and record high rates of discrimination, hate crimes, and religious profiling. . . . As a result, Muslim . . . Americans are currently in a precarious situation, left vulnerable to poor physical and psychological outcomes resulting from increased stress and challenges. (p. 467)

HIGHLIGHT 3.7

Terms Often Associated with Muslims

The first thing to understand is the meaning of the terms often involved when referring to people who are Muslims. Many of the associations are erroneous (Schaefer, 2011).

The religion of *Islam* is "derived from the Arabic word meaning peace, the inference being that one who willingly submits to the will of God is a person who has found peace" (Alavi, 2001). *Muslims* are followers of Islam (Pickett, 2002).

The term *Arab American* is a relatively new term. It refers to a diverse group of people who are descendants of people from 22 Arab-speaking nations in North Africa and West Asia (Ajrouch, 2008; Schaefer, 2011). Religious affiliations include Muslim and Christian (Ajrouch, 2008). "Arabs are an ethnic group and Muslims are a religious group" (Schaefer, 2011, p. 263).

Schaefer (2011) explains the term *Middle Eastern:*

Further complicating the use of collective terms of identity such as Arab and Muslim is evoking the term *Middle Eastern* (Middle Eastern American) Although it is also frequently used, the Middle East is an ambiguous geographic designation that includes large numbers of people who are neither Muslim nor Arab (such as Israeli Jews). Collectively, ... Middle Easterners are lumped together and ... subjected to prejudice and discrimination but are not eligible for supportive efforts such as affirmative action. (p. 264)

It is estimated that there are 1.9 to 3 million Muslims in the United States; two-thirds of them were born here (Schaefer, 2011). This is a population-at-risk of prejudice and discrimination. Because of the fear, the unfair condemnation, and the misperceived relationship between Muslims and the terrorist extremists, it is critically important for social workers to develop understanding of Muslim religion and culture. Highlight 3.7 explains some of the terms often used in association with the word Muslim.

The following describes the foundation of Islam:

Islam embraces the monotheism [the belief in one god] of Christianity and Judaism, accepts the Hebrew Bible, and ... [reveres] Jesus as a prophet. It is centered on the Koran—the Islamic scriptures [or Qur'an], which Muslims believe were revealed to the prophet Muhammad—which command five basic devotional duties, called the "Five Pillars":

1. *A declaration of belief that "there is no God but Allah [Arabic for 'the God'] and Mohammad is his prophet."*
2. *Prayers offered five times a day.*
3. *Daytime fasting during the month of Ramadan.*
4. *Charitable giving.*
5. *At least one pilgrimage to Mecca [an Arabian city near the Red Sea that is the birthplace of Muhammad].*

(Ahluwalia & Zaman, 2010; Sheler, 2001, p. 50)

Frame (2003) explains that "Muslims believe that they are called by God (Allah) to be grateful for their blessings and to choose to serve God. For Muslims, both faith and good works are required, but faith is also considered a gift from God. ... Muslims believe that people are essentially created good. Although they may make poor choices, persons can be forgiven if they repent and follow their repentance with ethical living" (pp. 68–69).

Many people have leapt to the conclusion that Islam encourages terrorist attacks. Alavi (2001) stresses that Muslims worldwide have reviled the 9/11 assault and that Islam forbids murdering innocent victims. "In fact, American Muslim and Arab-American organizations and leaders were among the first to react in an organized fashion to condemn the terrorist attacks on that very same day, long before it became clear that individuals calling themselves Muslims were involved in the attacks" (Abdelkarim, 2002).

Robert S. Mueller III, Director of the Federal Bureau of Investigation (FBI), reported that numerous American Muslim

leaders have generously sent educational materials to our [FBI] field offices and to our headquarters. They have taken the time to talk with our agents and support professionals to help them better understand Muslim perspectives and Muslim beliefs. Muslim Americans have cooperated with our interviews and supported our investigations. ... The active work of many in the American Muslim community in cities nationwide has merited public thanks and praise. But perhaps the greatest act of support has been the way Muslim and Arab Americans have responded to our urgent need for translators. Six days after September 11, I announced that the FBI was seeking Arabic and Farsi language experts. The response was extraordinary. Within hours, our switchboard was overwhelmed with calls. Those who came forward included doctors, lawyers, engineers, academics—Muslim and Arab Americans from all walks of life who were willing to quit their jobs, come to work for the FBI, and give something back to their country in the fight against terrorism.

(Mueller III, 2002)

It is estimated that there are 1.3 billion Muslims worldwide, and, as we've established, 1.9 to 3 million in the United States (Schaefer, 2011). It is also estimated that Muslim Americans are members of the following ethnic and racial groups:

- "20–42 percent African American,
- 24–33 percent South Asian (Afghan, Bangladishi, Indian, and Pakistani),
- 12–32 percent Arab, and
- 15–22 percent 'other' (Bosnian, Iranian, Turk, and White and Hispanic converts)"

(Schaefer, 2011, p. 266).

The degree to which individuals practice Muslim beliefs and traditions also varies radically from "traditional—strongly practicing" to "assimilated [into the mainstream culture]—marginally practicing" or "nonpracticing" (Nadir & Dziegielewski, 2001, p. 159).

Although there is great diversity, several values tend to characterize the life of Muslims; these include conception of family, selection of marriage partners, diet, and dress (Nadir & Dziegielewski, 2001). Note that traditional values often conflict with current practices and expectations in the United States. "Family is considered to be the cornerstone of Muslim society, and parents are expected to raise children who will work for social justice. Obedience to parents is a divinely ordained value" (p. 152). Muslims face the dilemma of raising children in a non-Muslim environment. For example, "Muslim children in the public schools, in general, receive negative messages about Islam from their textbooks and their teachers" (p. 154).

Western-style dating (i.e., spending time alone together doing various activities in the process of getting to know each other) is prohibited to avoid risking sexual relationships prior to marriage. Instead, "arranged, not forced, marriage is the tradition in Islam. Chaperoned courtship provides opportunities to meet one's future spouse and discuss concerns and plans for the future. As individuals become more identified with mainstream U.S. culture and less religious, traditional practices meet with resistance from young people, who participate in mixed-gender activities and live in isolated communities far from other Muslims" (pp. 152–153).

Diet restrictions include being forbidden to eat pork or pork by-products. Islam also prohibits the consumption of alcohol or other mind-altering substances. "During the month of Ramadan in which the receipt of the Koran is celebrated, Muslims may not eat, drink, smoke, or have sexual intercourse between sunup and sundown" (Frame, 2003, p. 69).

Islam provides guidelines for both men's and women's dress, emphasizing modesty. "Traditionally, Muslim women show nothing but their face, hands, and feet when they are in the company of those not part of their *mahram* (close family members, those who are not eligible to marry the woman, including her father, grandfather, brothers, sons, uncles, nephews, sons-in-law, and father-in-law). The women's clothing is opaque, loose-fitting, long-sleeved, and ankle-length" (Nadir & Dziegielewski, 2001, p. 151). They also wear a veil, a *khimar,* over their head, neck, and breasts, although dress requirements become less formal when women are with close family.

Nadir and Dziegielewski (2001) reflect:

Because of media stereotypes and sensationalism, many non-Muslims perceive Islam as oppressive to women. Many Muslim women, however, do not agree, as they see Islam as a way of life that provides them with a sense of purpose, peace, and freedom not common in Western society.... It is important to recognize that many of the inequities Muslim women face are the result of cultural or political traditions that have nothing to do with and are not sanctioned by the teachings of Islam. (p. 154)

Muslim men must also adhere to a dress code. They are required to cover from their navel to their knees. Their garments must be loose-fitting. Traditionally Muslim men wear a shirt, which covers their private area, and loose-fitting slacks.... [In addition, they] are forbidden to wear gold or silk. (p. 152)

Chapter Summary

The following summarizes this chapter's content as it relates to the chapter objectives presented at the beginning of the chapter. Objectives include the following statements:

A Define discrimination, oppression, marginalization, alienation, power, privilege, acclaim, stereotypes, and prejudice, and examine their relevance to social work practice.

Discrimination is the act of treating people differently based on the fact that they belong to some group rather than on merit. Oppression involves putting extreme limitations and constraints on some person, group, or larger system. Marginalization is the condition of having less power and being viewed as less important than others in the society because of belonging to some group or having some characteristic (e.g., racial, economic, ethnic, or political). Alienation, related to marginalization, is the feeling that you don't fit in or aren't treated as well as others in the mainstream of society. Power is the ability to move people on a chosen course to produce an effect or achieve some goal. Privilege entails special rights or benefits enjoyed because of elevated social, political, or economic status. Acclaim is "enthusiastic and public praise" (Lindberg, 2007, p. 7).

A stereotype is a fixed mental picture of a member of some specified group based on some attribute or attributes that reflect an overly simplified view of that group, without consideration or appreciation of individual differences. Prejudice is a negative opinion or prejudgment about an individual, group, or issue that is not based on fact. Social workers must address these issues with diverse populations.

B Explore the concepts of populations-at-risk, and social and economic justice.

Populations-at-risk are people at greater risk of deprivation and unfair treatment because they share some identifiable characteristic that places them in a diverse group. Dimensions of diversity include age, class, color, culture, disability, ethnicity, gender, gender identity and expression, immigration status, political ideology, race, religion, sex, and sexual orientation. Social justice involves the idea that in a perfect world all citizens would have identical "rights, protection, opportunities, obligations, and social benefits," regardless of their backgrounds and membership in diverse groups" (Barker, 2003, p. 405). Economic justice concerns the distribution of resources in a fair and equitable manner. Being a member of various diverse groups places people at risk of unfair and unequal treatment.

C Define empowerment and introduce a strengths perspective to social work practice.

Empowerment is the "process of increasing personal, interpersonal, or political power so that individuals can take action to improve their life situations" (Gutierrez, 2001, p. 210). A strengths perspective emphasizes people's strengths in order to pursue their empowerment.

D Examine empowerment for women in groups.

Themes emerging as providing successful conditions for women's empowerment within a group setting include safety, mutual interaction, commonality, acceptance, validation, and interdependence.

E Describe the concept of resiliency.

Resiliency is the ability of an individual, family, group, community, or organization to recover from adversity and resume functioning even when suffering serious trouble, confusion, or hardship. Resiliency can characterize individuals and larger systems.

F Recognize various aspects of human diversity, including age, class, color, culture, disability, ethnicity, gender, gender identity and expression, immigration status, political ideology, race, religion, sex, and sexual orientation.

Race refers to a category of people who share a common descent and genetic origin that may be distinguished by "certain physical traits," or "interests, habits, or characteristics" (Mish, 2008, p. 1024). Ethnicity refers to the affiliation with a large group of people who have "common racial, national, tribal, religious, linguistic, or cultural origin or background" (Mish, 2008, p. 429). Race implies a greater genetic determinant, whereas ethnicity often relates to cultural or national heritage. Other terms such as minorities and people of color are also commonly used to refer to people of different racial and ethnic heritage. People of color "is a collective term that refers to the major groups of African, Latino, and Asian Americans, and First Nations Peoples [Native Americans] who have been distinguished from the dominant society by color" (Lum, 2011, p. 129).

Culture, another dimension of diversity, is "a way of life including widespread values (about what is good and bad), beliefs (about what is true), and behavior (what people do every day)" (italics deleted) (Macionis, 2010, p. 2). Aspects of culture are often related to people's ethnic, racial, and spiritual heritage.

Immigration involves the permanent movement from one country to another. Immigration status is a person's position in terms of legal rights and residency when entering and residing in a country that is not that person's legal country of origin. People may have legal or illegal immigration status. Class refers to people's status or ranking in society with respect to such standards as "relative wealth, power, prestige, educational level, or family background" (Barker, 2003, p. 402). Political ideology is the "relatively coherent system of ideas (beliefs, traditions, principles, and myths) about human nature, institutional arrangements, and social processes" that indicate how a government should be run and what principles that government should support (Abramovitz, 2007, p. 126).

Sex "refers to the biological distinction between being female and being male, usually categorized on the basis of the reproductive organs and genetic makeup" (McCammon & Knox, 2007, p. 606). "Gender refers to the social and psychological characteristics associated with being female or male" (McCammon & Knox, 2007, p. 112). Gender identity is a person's internal psychological self-concept of being either a male or a female, or, possibly, some combination of both. Gender expression concerns how we express ourselves to others in ways related to gender that include both behavior and personality. Sexual orientation involves the sexual and romantic attraction to persons of one or both genders.

At each age people have different needs and require different services to optimize their well-being. Because there is a growing percentage of people in the U.S. population age 65 or older, it is important for social workers to understand the strengths, needs, and issues of this group.

Disabilities affect millions of people globally. Disabilities vary dramatically and include cognitive, physical, and psychiatric conditions.

Religion involves people's spiritual beliefs concerning the origin, character, and reason for being, usually based on the existence of some higher power or powers, that often involves designated rituals and provides direction for what is considered moral or right. Spirituality concerns "one's values, beliefs, mission, awareness, subjectivity, experience, sense of purpose and direction, and a king of striving toward something greater than oneself. It may or may not include a deity" (Frame, 2003, p. 3). Religion implies membership in a spiritual organization with customs, traditions, and structure. Spirituality may involve religion, or it may reflect a personal, internalized view of existence.

G Examine the social construction of gender.

There are many types of gender expression, including intersex, transgenderism, transsexuals, and transvestites. The concept of gender is socially constructed according to social values and beliefs. Women are often victims of oppression on the basis of gender. Men address special issues and have special needs due to their gender.

H Employ critical thinking skills to appraise racial self-awareness, cultural self-awareness, the treatment of intersex people and people with various forms of gender expression, and the feminist perspective.

Questions were posed concerning personal attitudes about race, culture, worldview, family structure, treatment of intersex people, freedom of gender expression, the meaning of gender, fair treatment on the basis of gender, and the feminist perspective.

I Discuss some of the major values characterizing Hispanic, Native American, African American, and Asian American families.

Themes characterizing Hispanic families include the significance of a common language and cultural pride, extended family, respect for older adults, spirituality, and strict division of gender roles. Values reflected in Native American families include the importance of extended family and respect for elders, noninterference, harmony with nature, a less rigid concept of time, and spirituality. Themes evident in many African American families include the importance of extended family, gender-role flexibility, respect for older adults, and strong religious beliefs. Values characterizing Asian American families include the importance of the family versus individual members as the primary unit, interdependence, filial piety, investment in children, and a patriarchal hierarchy.

J Define cultural competence and explain its application to social work.

Social workers need to attain cultural competence—the "mastery of a particular set of knowledge, skills, policies, and programs used by the social worker that address the cultural needs of individuals, families, groups, and communities" (Lum, 2005, p. 4). NASW identifies six tasks necessary to achieve cultural competence.

K Identify some of the basic tenets of Islam and discuss Muslims as a population-at-risk of prejudice and discrimination.

Islam involves a belief in one god and is centered on the Koran, the Islamic Scriptures. Values characterizing Muslim life include conception of family, selection of marriage partners, diet, and dress. Because of the fear, the unfair condemnation, and the misperceived relationship between Muslims and terrorist extremists, it is important for social workers to develop understanding of the Muslim religion and culture.

LOOKING AHEAD

This chapter described various aspects of human diversity and emphasized the importance of social workers being knowledgeable about these dimensions. The significance ascribed to diversity is based on the social work values discussed in Chapter 2. Part 1 of this book has established a foundation for understanding social welfare and social work. The two chapters in Part 2 will explain the process of and settings for generalist social work practice.

COMPETENCY NOTES

The following identifies where Educational Policy (EP) competencies and practice behaviors are discussed in the chapter.

EP 2.1.1b Practice personal reflection and self-correction to assure continual professional development. *(p. 61):* Practitioners must practice personal reflection and self-correction about any prejudices or stereotypes they harbor to prevent these biases from interfering with effective, ethical practice. *(p. 62):* Social workers should practice self-reflection to gain racial self-awareness.

EP 2.1.1e Engage in career-long learning. *(p. 61):* Exploring personal prejudices and stereotypes is a career-long learning process. *(p. 66):* Learning about diverse groups is an ongoing, career-long process.

EP 2.1.2a Recognize and manage personal values in a way that allows professional values to guide practice. *(p. 61):* Social workers should strive to become aware of any stereotypes and prejudices they harbor so that such ideas do not interfere with adherence to professional values to guide practice. *(p. 62):* Social workers should recognize and manage their own values and perceptions concerning race so that professional values may guide practice. *(p. 66):* Social workers should strive to remain open-minded and nonjudgmental.

EP 2.1.3 Apply critical thinking to inform and communicate professional judgments. *(p. 62):* Practitioners should think critically about their personal perceptions of racial differences so that these perceptions don't interfere with ethical practice. *(p. 70):* Social workers should use critical thinking when addressing cultural issues. Critical thinking questions are posed. *(pp. 83, 84):* Critical thinking questions are posed concerning gender expression and intersex people. *(p. 87):* Feminism is discussed and critical thinking questions are posed. *(p. 102):* A case example is presented and critical thinking questions are posed.

EP 2.1.3a Distinguish, appraise, and integrate multiple sources of knowledge, including research-based knowledge, and practice wisdom. *(p. 70):* Social workers should appraise and integrate multiple sources of knowledge when dealing with people having various cultural values. *(p. 83):* Gender expression is reviewed from multiple perspectives. *(p. 102):* A case example is presented and questions are asked to appraise and integrate multiple sources of knowledge in order to come to conclusions.

EP 2.1.3c Demonstrate effective oral and written communication in working with individuals, families, groups, organizations, communities, and colleagues. *(p. 68):* Social workers should be knowledgeable about and use sensitivity when communicating with and about various racial, ethnic, and cultural groups. *(p. 102):* Questions are posed to encourage the articulation and communication of practice decisions.

EP 2.1.4 Engage diversity and difference in practice. *(p. 61):* Dimensions of diversity are identified here. *(p. 66):* Subsequent sections explore each aspect of diversity. *(p. 67):* The significance of the intersectionality of multiple factors involved in diversity is discussed. *(p. 68):* Culture is a dimension of diversity. *(p. 67):* Ethnicity and race are dimensions of diversity. *(p. 79):* Immigration status is an aspect of diversity. *(p. 81):* Class is a dimension of diversity. *(p. 81):* Political ideology is an aspect of diversity. *(p. 82):* Gender, gender identity, and gender expression are dimensions of diversity. *(p. 83):* Various aspects of gender expression and sex, both dimensions of human diversity, are explored. *(p. 86):* Sexual orientation is a dimension of diversity. *(p. 90):* Age is an aspect of diversity. *(p. 90):* Disability is a dimension of diversity. *(p. 91):* Religion and the related concept of spirituality are aspects of diversity.

EP 2.1.4a Recognize the extent to which culture's structures and values may oppress, marginalize, alienate, or create or enhance privilege and power. *(p. 60):* Oppression and the other concepts are defined and explained. *(p. 66):* Aspects of diversity can be related to oppression. *(p. 82):* Women are discussed as victims of oppression. *(p. 86):* Men experience disadvantages based on their gender. *(p. 89):* Cultural values involving homophobia negatively affect LGB people.

EP 2.1.4b Gain sufficient self-awareness to eliminate the influence of personal biases and values in working with diverse groups. *(p. 61):* Practitioners must work hard at developing self-awareness regarding any prejudices and stereotypes they may harbor toward any diverse group. *(p. 62):* Questions posed here should help raise racial self-awareness. *(p. 81):* Social workers must gain sufficient self-awareness to avoid imposing stereotypes and prejudgments on people.

EP 2.1.4c Recognize and communicate their understanding of the importance of difference in shaping life experiences. *(p. 60):* Social workers must recognize how discrimination, economic deprivation, and the other concepts explained here shape life experiences. *(p. 66):* Practitioners should recognize the extent to which aspects of diversity shape life experiences. *(p. 70):* Social workers should recognize how cultural values and expectations shape life experiences. *(p. 80):* The lack of resources available to the Turkana tribe shapes their life experiences. *(p. 82):* Gender is an important factor in shaping life experiences. *(p. 86):* Gender contributes to shaping life experiences for men. *(p. 89):* Having a sexual orientation that is not heterosexual shapes life experiences.

EP 2.1.4d View themselves as learners and engage those with whom they work as informants. *(p. 62):* Practitioners should view themselves as learners and their clients as informants concerning client strengths. *(p. 66):* Learning about human diversity from clients is an ongoing process for social workers. *(p. 60):* Difference shapes life experiences. *(p. 80):* Social workers should learn from their clients about their needs and conditions.

EP 2.1.5 Advance human rights social and economic justice. *(p. 60):* Professional values emphasize fair and equal treatment, and social and economic justice.

EP 2.1.5a Understand the forms and mechanisms of oppression and discrimination. *(p. 60):* Oppression, discrimination, and other related terms are defined and explored. *(p. 81):* Social workers should strive to understand the mechanisms of oppression imposed by social class. *(p. 82):* The oppression of women is discussed. *(p. 86):* Men experience disadvantages that serve to oppress them. *(p. 89):* Homophobia oppresses LGB people and often exposes them to discrimination.

EP 2.1.5b Advocate for human rights and social and economic justice. *(p. 61):* Social workers should advocate for social and economic justice. *(p. 87):* A feminist perspective advocates for human rights and social and economic justice.

EP 2.1.5c Engage in practices that advance social and economic justice. *(p. 61):* Social workers should engage in practices that advance social and economic justice. *(p. 83):* Recommendations are made for advancing social justice for intersex children.

EP 2.1.7a Utilize conceptual frameworks to guide the processes of assessment, intervention, and evaluation. *(p. 84):* Social workers may use the conceptual framework of the social construction of gender to understand gender expression. This may help guide the processes of assessment and intervention. *(p. 87):* Practitioners can use conceptual frameworks such as the feminist perspective to help guide their practice.

EP 2.1.7b Critique and apply knowledge to understand person and environment. *(p. 70):* Practitioners must understand and apply knowledge about cultural issues to understand people's functioning in their environment. *(p. 87):* Social workers can critique the feminist perspective and apply knowledge to understand person and environment where appropriate.

EP 2.1.9a Continuously discover, appraise, and attend to changing locales, populations, scientific and technological developments, and emerging societal trends to provide relevant services. *(p. 81):* Practitioners should continuously respond to the changing environmental circumstances characterizing people's lives depending upon their social class.

EP 2.1.10a Substantively and affectively prepare for action with individuals, families, groups, organizations, and communities *(p. 64):* Exploring the use of consciousness-raising in groups helps prepare social workers for group intervention with female survivors of domestic violence.

EP 2.1.10d Collect, organize, and interpret client data. *(p. 83):* Data regarding gender and gender expression should be collected and interpreted. *(p. 102):* Critical thinking questions are posed to

collect, organize, and interpret client data concerning this case example.

EP 2.1.10e Assess clients' strengths and limitations *(p. 62):* Practitioners should assess clients' strengths. *(p. 66):* Social workers should assess their clients' strengths to build on these strengths. *(p. 70):* Practitioners should assess and emphasize the strengths involved in various cultures. *(p. 86):* Social workers should assess and emphasize the strengths demonstrated by men.

EP 2.1.10g Select appropriate intervention strategies. *(p. 64):* Social workers should select the appropriate intervention strategies when working with domestic violence survivors in groups. Counseling approaches are described.

EP 2.1.20i Implement prevention interventions that enhance client capacities. *(p. 64):* Implementation of consciousness-raising interventions is intended to empower women and to prevent further violence from occurring.

EP 2.1.10j Help clients resolve problems. *(p. 62):* Assessing client strengths provides practitioners with clues regarding how to help clients resolve problems. *(p. 64):* Groups focusing on consciousness-raising can help female survivors of domestic violence resolve their problems.

EP 2.1.10k Negotiate, mediate, and advocate for clients. *(p. 64):* One strategy for working with domestic violence survivors in groups is to advocate on their behalf.

FOR FURTHER EXPLORATION ON THE INTERNET

See this text's Social Work CourseMate website at *www.cengagebrain.com* for learning tools such as chapter quizzing, videos, glossary flashcards, and more.

CASE STUDY FOR CRITICAL THINKING

An Agency Providing Foster Family Care

Consider the following ethical dilemma involving an agency providing foster family care for children (Robison & Reeser, 2000). (*Foster family care* is the provision of substitute care with a family for a planned temporary or extended period when parents or legal guardians are unable to care for a child.) This case study illustrates how the social work profession must continuously address the issue of quality of care versus cost of care. The more intensive and extensive the services provided, the greater the cost. Similarly, social workers must frequently struggle with the issue of providing quality service to clients at minimal cost. The case study also shows how important the agency context is for how social workers can provide services.

Case Study: Jose directs an agency that places children in foster family care. The state mandates that no more than six children may be placed with any one family. The intent is to make certain that the family's ability to care for the children is not overextended.

Jose's agency must make enough money to cover its own costs and pay its workers' salaries. Any "money the agency makes from the placement that is not used for the placement itself or for training the foster parents is used to support other agency activities," such as various programs serving poor people. The state pays an annual administrative fee of $8,933 per child placed in a foster home by the agency (Robison & Reeser, 2000, p. 238).

Being a foster parent is not always easy. Sometimes, when needed, the agency's social workers provide training in such skills as effective parenting, communication, behavior management, and anger control:

> *The problems that the foster parents face with the children can be remedied if they are the result of lack of proper training, and in the worst cases, children are taken from the home. But there are always going to be marginal cases, "gray areas" [where training won't help].... The agency has solved the problem of what to do with cases that fall into the "gray areas" through "benign neglect," preferring to assume that the problems are not serious enough for the child to be taken out of the home.*

> *(Robison & Reeser, 2000, p. 238)*

A problem is that the agency is receiving for placement increasingly difficult children who have more extreme problems. Workers report that provision of training for the foster parents is not working because the children's behavioral and emotional problems are so extreme. All the workers can do is tell foster parents they must "deal with" the problems "somehow" (p. 238).

Jose decides to cut down the number of children placed in a foster home from six to four. This would alleviate some of the stress placed on the parents and allow them to give each child more time and attention. However, this means that both the agency and the foster parents (who are also paid by the state) make significantly less money. In fact, Jose's agency is starting to lose money instead of make it. If that doesn't stop, the agency will have to close.

**EP 2.1.3,
2.1.3a,
2.1.3c,
2.1.10d[5]**

Critical Thinking: How would you use the three-step Triple-A critical thinking process to establish what might be done in this case?

First, *ask* questions like these:

- What options are possible other than the one Jose chose?
- Can children somehow be screened to determine which ones are the most difficult to handle?
- Could these more difficult children be placed in special homes run by the most effective foster parents, with less difficult children placed in homes having six foster children?
- Does decreasing the number of foster children from six to four really make sense? Will this actually solve the problem of better managing difficult behavior? (Workers feel that training still will not help.)
- How possible and effective might it be to decrease the number of children per foster home to five instead of four? Would this be more financially feasible?
- Could other areas of the agency's budget be cut to make up for the decreased number of children in each home?
- What other questions could you ask when thinking about possible solutions in this case?

Second, *assess* the established facts and issues involved. How would you seek answers to the questions just posed and to others you might think up? What information do you need? Where might you find this information? Who could help you get it?

Third, *assert* a concluding opinion. The case poses a difficult problem. After carefully considering the facts, what final conclusion might you reach?

---

[5]Competency Notes explaining this icon are located at the end of Chapter 3.

SOCIAL WORK PRACTICE

Part 2 includes two chapters that introduce you to the *doing* of social work practice. Chapter 4 discusses the process of social work practice. It defines generalist practice and explains the various roles social workers can assume. It also examines the planned-change process social workers follow as they work with clients.

Chapter 5 describes the various practice settings in which social workers do their work. It explains how practitioners work with individuals, families, groups, organizations, and communities. It also introduces you to the professional organizations in social work and discusses career options.

CHAPTER 4

The Process of Generalist Practice

Barros & Barros/The Image Bank/Getty Images

Working with individuals (micro systems), a social worker can

- Help a homeless person get medical help from a community clinic and find a place to stay at a local shelter.
- Counsel a young woman regarding what type of contraception is best for her.
- Assist an older adult in a hospice in making his end-of-life decisions and help him rest as comfortably as possible during his final days.

Working with families (micro/mezzo systems), a social worker can

- Help strengthen families and teach parenting skills to stop or prevent child abuse.
- Link homeless families with needed resources.
- Teach conflict resolution strategies to families besieged with contention.

Working with groups (mezzo systems), a social worker can

- Run a social skills group for adolescents with intellectual (cognitive) disabilities.
- Lead a support group for parents of children diagnosed with cancer.

- *Be in charge of an agency meeting in which various agency staff discuss a client's progress.*

Working with organizations and communities (macro systems), a social worker can

- *Initiate cooperation among social service agencies to sponsor a holiday gift collection program for needy families.*
- *Contact legislators and advocate for increased funding for low-income housing for poor people.*
- *Work with residents in a neighborhood with a high crime rate to start a Neighborhood Watch program in which neighbors, working together, watch each other's homes and report suspicious behavior to reduce crime.*

These scenarios provide examples of what generalist social workers can do at various levels of practice. There are many ways to describe what social workers do. We have established that they work with individuals, families, groups, organizations, and communities to enhance people's well-being. They are prepared to help individuals with highly personal issues and with broad problems that affect whole communities. Social workers identify problems, even difficult ones, and try to help people solve them.

The foundation of social work practice is generalist practice (CSWE, 2008b, EP B2.2). There are many specific definitions of generalist practice. However, all of these definitions appear to involve some common ideas; these include "the concepts of systems, multiple methods, problem solving, and partnership with client. The definitions emphasize the purpose and values of social work, the various roles or capacities in which social workers serve, and the use of the planned-change process to address social problems and restore social functioning" (Hernandez, 2008, p. 264).

Some dimensions are exceptionally important in conceptualizing the definition of generalist social work practice (Association of Baccalaureate Program Directors [BPD], 2008). First, the importance of multiple level interventions (including those with individuals, families, groups, organizations, and communities) should be emphasized. Intervention *is the process of planning and implementing steps to make positive changes and attain goals that solve clients' problems or improve clients' quality of life. Second, generalist practice should emphasize evaluation of practice effectiveness. Interventions should be chosen based on a history of successful application for specific situations, referred to as evidence-based practice. Third, generalist practice should focus both on issues concerning individuals, families, and groups, and those concerning social justice and human rights. Generalist social workers, then, must have infinite flexibility, a solid knowledge base about many things, and a wide range of skills at their disposal.*

Micro practice *is intervention involving an individual client (a micro system).* Mezzo practice *involves work with small groups (mezzo systems). Social work with families combines micro and mezzo practice because it involves a small group (i.e., the family) but one with intimate ties.* Macro practice *is intervention involving organizations and communities (macro systems).*

Integral links exist among micro, mezzo, and macro practice. Generalist practice skills build on each other in a progression from micro to mezzo to macro levels. Relating to individuals in groups (mezzo practice) requires basic micro skills. Likewise, macro practice requires mastery of both micro and mezzo skills for relating to and working with individuals and groups in organizational and community (macro) settings.

Note that throughout this book the terms social worker, generalist social worker, *and* generalist practitioner *are used interchangeably. Specialized aspects of social work practice, usually referring to social workers with master's degrees, will be specified as such.*

Learning Objectives

A Define generalist practice and explain each concept that is involved.

B Discuss some aspects of professional identity.

C Explain how to use critical thinking to review a number of fallacies that can cause people to miss the truth.

D Describe the six steps involved in the planned-change process, the procedure used to undertake social work intervention.

E Discuss some cross-cultural differences in nonverbal and verbal communication.

F Examine how the assessment process should emphasize strengths and empowerment.

G Provide examples of intervention with macro client systems.

Defining Generalist Practice

Generalist social work practice may involve almost any helping situation you can think of. A generalist practitioner may be called on to help a homeless family, a child unable to get along with peers, a pregnant teenager, a sick older adult unable to care for herself any longer, an alcoholic parent, a community that's trying to address its drug abuse problem, or a public assistance agency struggling to amend its policies to conform to new federal regulations. Therefore, as has been established, generalist practitioners must be well prepared to address many kinds of difficult situations.

The social work profession has struggled with the concept of generalist practice for many years. In the past, new practitioners were educated in only one skill area (e.g., work with individuals, groups, or communities) or one area of practice (e.g., children and families, or policy and administration). A generalist practitioner needs competence in a wide variety of areas instead of being limited to a single track.

For our purposes, we will define *generalist practice*[1] as the application of an eclectic knowledge base,[2] professional values, and a wide range of skills to target individual, family, group, organizational, or community systems for change within the context of five primary processes. First, generalist practice

---

[1]Most of the concepts involved in the definition are taken directly from or based on those required by the Educational Policy and Accreditation Standards (CSWE, 2008b).

[2]The term *eclectic* refers to "selecting what appears to be best in various doctrines, methods, or styles" (Mish, 2008, p. 394).

HIGHLIGHT 4.1

Concepts in the Definition of Generalist Practice

1. Acquiring an eclectic knowledge base
   A. Systems theory
   B. Ecological perspective
   C. Curriculum content areas
      1) Values and ethics
      2) Diversity
      3) Populations-at-risk and social and economic justice
      4) Human behavior and the social environment
      5) Social welfare policy and services
      6) Social work practice
      7) Research
      8) Field education
   D. Fields of practice
2. Emphasizing client empowerment
3. Using professional values
   A. National Association of Social Workers (NASW) *Code of Ethics* and, as applicable, the International Federation of Social Workers (IFSW)/International Association of Schools of Social Work (IASSW) *Ethics in Social Work, Statement of Principles.*
   B. Recognition and management of personal values
   C. Application of professional values and strategies of ethical reasoning to make ethical decisions and solve ethical dilemmas.

4. Applying a wide range of skills
   A. Micro
   B. Mezzo
   C. Macro
5. Targeting systems at any size
   A. Individual
   B. Family
   C. Group
   D. Organization
   E. Community
6. Working in an organizational structure
7. Using supervision appropriately
8. Assuming a wide range of professional roles
9. Following the principles of evidence-based practice
10. Employing critical thinking skills
11. Using a planned-change process
    A. Engagement
    B. Assessment
    C. Planning
    D. Implementation
    E. Evaluation
    F. Termination
    G. Follow-up

emphasizes client empowerment. Second, it involves working effectively within an organizational structure and doing so under supervision. Third, it requires the assumption of a wide range of professional roles. Fourth, it concerns following the principles of evidence-based practice (choosing intervention plans based on evidence of past effectiveness and evaluating the outcomes of intervention to improve future service provision). Fifth, it involves the application of critical thinking skills to the planned-change process. Highlight 4.1 outlines the basic concepts involved in this definition.

Figure 4.1 illustrates how the various concepts involved in the definition of generalist practice fit together. The large square in the top half of the figure portrays the organizational structure. An organization (or agency) employs social workers and provides the context for them to do their jobs. *Organizational structure* involves how lines of authority and communication operate within an agency, how the administration runs the organization, and what the agency environment is like. Social workers practice within this environment with all its constraints, requirements, and rules, similar to any other place of employment. Thus, in Figure 4.1, a social worker is represented as a smaller rectangle within this large square.

That same rectangle contains the terms *knowledge*, *skills*, and *values*. These illustrate how social workers bring to their job a broad knowledge base, professional values, and a wide range of skills so they can do their work effectively. Also in the large upper square is another rectangle representing supervision. A downward-pointing arrow links the supervision rectangle to the social worker rectangle,

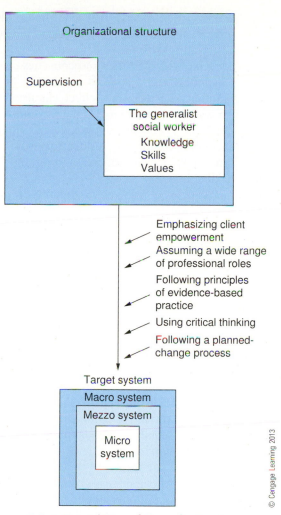

Figure 4.1 A Pictorial View of Generalist Practice

© Cengage Learning 2013

application arrow into the application process. This depicts how social workers use client empowerment, a wide range of professional roles, evidence-based practice, critical thinking, and the planned-change process to solve a problem or help a system improve its functioning.

Chapter 1 discussed the eclectic knowledge base supporting social work; Chapter 2, social work values and ethics; and Chapter 3, client empowerment. The following sections review the other concepts involved in the definition of generalist practice.

Working in an Organizational Structure Under Supervision

Social workers most likely work within an organizational structure (or agency context) under supervision. As mentioned previously, *organizational structure* is the formal and informal manner in which tasks and responsibilities, lines of authority, channels of communication, and dimensions of power are established and coordinated within an organization. Understanding the organizational structure involves knowing how decisions are made, what chain of command is followed, what procedures regulate service provision to clients, and how the social work job expectations fit into the larger scheme of things.

EP 2.1.1f

Supervision is the process by which a designated supervisor watches over a worker's performance, directs activities, and provides feedback. A good supervisor can be valuable in helping social workers perform effectively within an agency setting.

The next section introduces another important aspect of professional agency life—consultation.

The Use of Consultation

Another important facet of effective work within an organizational structure concerns the appropriate use of consultation. *Consultation* is the act of seeking help from someone with expertise in a subject to devise a plan or solve a problem. It usually involves a colleague, administrator, expert, or other who has the appropriate competence or experience.

Consultation differs from supervision. Supervision is generally an ongoing process within an organization. It is undertaken by someone designated as a supervisor who has responsibility for overseeing a

indicating that part of working as a generalist practitioner involves receiving and using supervisory input appropriately.

The large square at the bottom of Figure 4.1 illustrates social workers' potential target system. We have established that generalist practitioners may choose to work with a micro, mezzo, or macro system as the target of their change efforts. These three systems are arbitrarily portrayed in concentric squares to reflect their respective sizes.

An arrow flows from the organizational structure square down to the target system square. This depicts how social workers apply their knowledge, skills, and values to help change a micro, mezzo, or macro system. Likewise, five smaller arrows lead from concepts listed to the right of the supervisee's work. Consultation, on the other hand, is sought out when needed from someone who has specific experience or expertise. It is usually a time-limited process and is oriented toward some specific issue (Harkness, 2008). Consultation may be provided informally among colleagues when help is needed and sought out. It may also be imparted on a formal contractual basis when one party seeks out the established expertise of another. Consultation can occur internally within an agency or expert help can be sought outside of the agency, depending on the assistance needed. It is a generalist practitioner's professional responsibility to use both supervision and consultation appropriately.

A Wide Range of Roles

EP 2.1.1c, 2.1.10k

Assuming a wide range of professional roles is a key concept in the definition of generalist practice. We have emphasized that generalist practitioners can tackle a wide range of problems using many different methods; that is, they assume many roles. We have established that a professional role consists of the behaviors and activities involved in performing some designated function. Roles characterizing generalist practitioners include the following:

- *Counselor*: One who provides guidance to clients and assists them in a planned-change or problem-solving process. For example, a worker might help a troubled teenager make decisions about friendships and sexual activity by identifying alternatives and evaluating their potential consequences.
- *Educator*: One who gives information and teaches skills to others (Kirst-Ashman & Hull, 2012a; Yessian & Broskowski, 1983). For instance, a practitioner might teach child management skills to parents.
- *Broker*: One who links client systems to needed resources (Connaway & Gentry, 1988; Kirst-Ashman & Hull, 2012a). For example, a worker might refer a client to a substance abuse treatment center for inpatient treatment.
- *Case manager* (or *case coordinator*): A practitioner who, on the behalf of a specific client, coordinates needed services provided by any number of agencies, organizations, or facilities.

For instance, a worker might coordinate the many services needed by a cerebral palsy[3] patient living in a group home.

- *Mobilizer*: One who identifies and convenes community members and resources to identify "unmet community needs" and "effect changes for the better in their community" (Halley, Kopp, & Austin, 1998, p. 179). For example, a practitioner might encourage community residents to band together and start a drug education program for residents' children.
- *Mediator*: One who resolves arguments or disagreements among individual, family, group, organizational, or community systems in conflict (Kirst-Ashman & Hull, 2012a; Yessian & Broskowski, 1983). For instance, a worker might serve as a go-between to reach an agreement between an agency that wants to start a group home for people with intellectual disabilities and neighborhood residents who oppose having the facility in their neighborhood.
- *Negotiator:* One who is "an intermediary who acts to settle disputes and/or resolve disagreements. However, unlike mediators, negotiators clearly take the side of one of the parties involved" (Kirst-Ashman & Hull, 2012a, p. 27). For example, a social worker in public welfare might act on behalf of her clients to negotiate for better benefits for them.
- *Facilitator*: One who guides a group experience. For instance, a practitioner might run a support group for young women with bulimia.[4]
- *Advocate*: One who speaks out on behalf of clients to promote fair and equitable treatment or gain needed resources. For example, a worker might meet with an administrator on behalf of a client to change an agency policy to benefit the client.

Regardless of the role assumed by a practitioner, a social worker should identify as a professional social worker and conduct himself or herself accordingly (CSWE, 2008b, EP 2.1.1). Highlight 4.2 addresses several aspects of professional identity.

---

[3]*Cerebral palsy* is a disability involving problems in muscular control and coordination resulting from damage to the brain before it has matured—that is, before or during birth.

[4]*Bulimia* is an eating disorder occurring primarily in females and characterized by uncontrolled overeating followed by purging activities such as self-initiated vomiting and the use of diuretics, as well as excessive guilt and shame over the compulsive behavior.

HIGHLIGHT 4.2

Professional Identity and Conduct

**EP 2.1.1a,
2.1.1b,
2.1.1d,
2.1.1e**

Social workers should identify with the profession. It is an honorable, meaningful field, which seeks at its core to improve people's lives and pursue social and economic justice. Social workers' practice and behavior should represent the field's mission and primary values (the latter of which were discussed in Chapter 2). Workers should manifest a commitment both to the development and growth of the profession and to their own professional growth.

Four dimensions of professionalism are described here (CSWE, 2008b):

1. Social workers should "practice personal reflection and self-correction to assure continual professional development" (EP 2.1.1b). Evaluation of your perceptions means taking time to look deeply at your attitudes, values, and opinions. One theme inherent in this book is the importance of evaluating and critically thinking about any stereotypes and prejudgments you harbor. Such assumptions can conflict with professional values and interfere with objective, effective, professional practice. It's a continual process of reflecting about such assumptions and correcting them.

2. Professional practitioners should "engage in career-long learning" (EP 2.1.1e). Learning about new research results, intervention approaches, cultural differences, aspects of oppression, and the dynamically changing social environment is an ongoing process. When I was very young and had just zipped through school to get my MSW degree, I thought I had worked hard enough and could stop learning. Boy, was I wrong. Learning had just begun. If anything, it accelerates exponentially over a career.

There are many ways to enhance learning. Listen to and learn from your clients. Consult with supervisors and colleagues. Ask questions. Creatively think about what practice alternatives might be available to you and your clients. Watch what's going on around you in agency life—everything from treatment techniques to how management treats you and your clients. Seek out knowledge from professional books, journals, and newspapers. Attend professional training sessions; these can address virtually any area of practice ranging from cognitive-behavioral treatment approaches to legislative advocacy to running task groups. Join professional organizations and be an active member. This is a way to network, keep in touch, and simply learn about what's up in the field.

3. Social workers should "demonstrate professional demeanor in behavior, appearance and communication" (EP 2.1.1d). Part of professional demeanor entails using empathy and other interpersonal skills. Another aspect is following ethical principles. Communication should be straightforward, relevant, purposeful, and clear. I always say that anything you write should be good and appropriate enough to place before a judge in court.

Professional demeanor also involves personal appearance. Sheafor and Horejsi (2008) talk about developing a personal "style" They reflect:

[Social workers'] uniqueness is expressed in their clothing, hairstyle, posture, speech, and in a hundred other choices and behaviors that send out messages about who they are and what they believe about themselves and others.

One's professional style must be appropriate to the situation, the clients served, and the agency setting. For example, a social worker dressed in a three-piece suit will surely have difficulty establishing rapport with a group of street people yet may be highly effective in persuading a city council to create needed services for people living on the street. Similarly, a worker might dress casually when working with children and families but should dress more formally when making a court appearance in their behalf.

"Know thyself" is an important admonition for the social worker.... It is helpful for the social worker to step back periodically and examine how others perceive his or her style. Clues from clients, family, friends, colleagues, and supervisors are helpful in making these assessments. (p. 41)

4. Practitioners should "advocate for client access to the services of social work" (EP 2.1.1a). The social work profession stresses the use of evidence-based practice. Practitioners should choose intervention approaches that have been proven most effective. When people need help in resolving problems, social workers should step forward and advocate that their services be made accessible to clients.

Social Workers as Supervisors and Managers

Note that many social workers advance in the hierarchy of organizations to become supervisors or managers. Even when primary job responsibilities involve administrative capacities instead of direct work with clients, it's imperative that social workers maintain a generalist perspective. This means that they should continue to focus on the potential for targeting positive change at any level of practice—including work with individuals, families, groups, organizations, and communities (Gibelman, 2005). Additionally, social work concerns providing ongoing advocacy for client systems, whether these systems are individuals, families, or large groups of clients.

A social work *supervisor* is a person given authority within an organization to "direct, coordinate, enhance, and evaluate the on-the-job performance" of designated employees (Kadushin & Harkness, 2002, p. 23). The supervisor is then held accountable for the employees' work. Gibelman and Furman (2008) elaborate upon the supervisory role:

> *The supervisor is expected to be qualified for this role by virtue of experience and education. Relevant skills include the ability to motivate employees, coordinate work and workload, set goals and limits, provide corrective feedback, monitor and improve work processes, and educate and consult with employees (Kurland & Salmon, 1992; Menefee, 2000; Rauktis & Koeske, 1994; Walsh, 1990). Typically, a social worker assumes the role of supervisor after working in the field for several years (Gibelman & Schervish, 1997). Ideally, specialized training is provided before the supervisor assumes this position. Supervisors may, and often do, maintain a small active caseload as well. (p. 91)*

Managers generally assume greater responsibility for more aspects of agency functioning than supervisors. Typically, they still provide supervision for designated employees below them in the agency's power structure who, in turn, supervise employees below them, and so on. The terms "manager" and "administrator" are usually used interchangeably (Gibelman, 2005, p. 13). Kirst-Ashman and Hull (2012a) describe the role of manager in generalist practice:

> *A manager in social work is one who assumes some level of administrative responsibility for a social services agency or other organizational system ([Brody, 2005;] Yessian & Broskowsky, 1983).*

Administrators utilize three levels of skills—technical, people, and conceptual (Lewis, Lewis, Packard, & Souflee, 2001, p. 8). Technical skills *include those used to direct an agency's basic activities such as overseeing counseling techniques, developing programs, or evaluating the agency's effectiveness.* People skills *concern "interpersonal effectiveness such as oral communication, listening, conflict management, leading, and motivating" (p. 8).* Conceptual skills *are those oriented toward assessing and understanding the overall operation of the agency and how it fits into its larger macro environment. These also concern being able to solve complex problems and develop creative solutions. The term* management *refers to all "the tasks and activities involved in directing an organization or one of its units: planning, organizing, leading, and controlling" (Hellriegel, Jackson, & Slocum, 2002, p. 7). (p. 25)*

Social workers may assume a wide range of administrative roles. These include lower-level management positions with administrative responsibility for a small agency unit or department. They also may include "upper-level managers," including the chief executive officer (CEO) or executive director who has the primary responsibility for running a large social services organization (Gibelman, 2005, p. 13; Gibelman & Furman, 2008).

Evidence-Based Practice

Chapter 1 introduced the importance of social work research and the increasing focus on evidence-based practice. Rubin and Babbie (2011) explain:

EP 2.1.6b

> *Evidence-based practice (EVP) is a process in which practitioners make practice decisions in light of the best research evidence available. But rather than rigidly constrict practitioner options, the EVP model encourages practitioners to integrate scientific evidence with their practice expertise and knowledge of the idiosyncratic circumstances bearing on specific practice decisions. . . .*
>
> *Evidence-based practice also involves evaluating the outcomes of their decisions. Although evidence-based practice is most commonly discussed in regard to decisions about what interventions to provide clients, it also applies to decisions about*

how best to assess the practice problems and decisions practitioners make at other levels of practice—such as decisions about social policies, communities, and so on.

For example, a clinical practitioner following the EVP model with a newly referred client will attempt to find and use the most scientifically validated diagnostic tools in assessing client problems and treatment needs and then develop a treatment plan in light of the best research evidence available as to what interventions are most likely to be effective in light of that assessment, the practitioner's clinical expertise regarding the client, and the client's idiosyncratic attributes and circumstances. At the level of social policy, evidence-based practitioners will attempt to formulate and advocate policies that the best research available suggests are most likely to achieve their desired aims. Likewise, evidence-based practitioners working at the community level will make practice decisions at that level in light of community-level practice research. Moreover, evidence-based practitioners at each level will utilize research methods to evaluate the outcomes of their practice decisions to see if the chosen course of action is achieving its desired aim. If it is not, then the evidence-based practitioner will choose an alternative course of action— again in light of the best research evidence available and again evaluating its outcome. (p. 26)

Critical Thinking Skills

EP 2.1.3, 2.1.3a, 2.1.3b, 2.1.3c

Chapter 1 defined *critical thinking* as (1) the careful scrutiny of what is stated as true or what appears to be true and the resulting expression of an opinion or conclusion based on that scrutiny, and (2) the creative formulation of an opinion or conclusion when presented with a question, problem, or issue. The process of critical thinking involves asking questions, assessing facts, and asserting a conclusion (the Triple A approach).

Social workers must have the ability to think critically as they work with clients to achieve goals. Critical thinking in social work practice usually involves four dimensions (Gibbs et al., 1994). First, practitioners should be predisposed to ask questions about how their clients are served and treated. Second, they should investigate how interventions are supposed to work and whether they are really

effective. Third, they should carefully examine any assertions presented as facts by evaluating arguments on both sides of an issue. Fourth, they should use "scientific reasoning" to analyze arguments, keeping their eyes open for inconsistencies and deviations from the truth.

In other words, don't believe everything you hear. Rather, critically evaluate for yourself whether it's true. Focus on Critical Thinking 4.1 identifies some common fallacies to watch out for.

The Planned-Change Process

Planned change involves the development and implementation of a strategy for improving or altering "some specified condition, pattern of behavior, or set of circumstances in an effort to improve a client's social functioning or well-being" (Sheafor &

EP 2.1.10, 2.1.10a

Horejsi, 2012, p. 88). Planned change is a process whereby social workers engage a client, assess issues, identify strengths and problems, establish a plan of action, implement the plan, evaluate its effects, and finally terminate the process.

Another term often used to describe what generalist practitioners do is *problem solving,* initially introduced by social work pioneer Helen Harris Perlman in 1957. Essentially, problem solving refers to the same process as planned change, although many debate the nuances of difference. Social work's more recent emphasis on client strengths may be at odds with the more negative connotations of the word *problem.* The term *change* may have more positive implications despite the fact that most social work intervention deals with problem situations. Thus, the term *planned change* will arbitrarily be used here.

Social workers help people deal with problems ranging from personal relationships to lack of resources to blatant discrimination. For instance, a social worker may need to address the problem of a battered woman who is economically and emotionally dependent on her abusive husband and who also has three children to protect. Another social worker might have an adolescent client who has committed a number of serious crimes and who is heavily involved with drugs. Still another social worker may need to advocate for change in a public assistance policy that discriminates against people who don't speak English well and are unable to follow an intricate, exasperating application process to receive

FOCUS ON CRITICAL THINKING 4.1

Avoiding the Fallacy Trap

EP 2.1.3a, 2.1.3b

A number of fallacies can trick people into false beliefs (Gambrill, 2005; Gambrill & Gibbs, 2009, pp. 107–119). A *fallacy* is a false or erroneous idea, often hidden behind what appears to be a sound argument or presentation. A fallacy or mistaken assumption can trick you into believing what is not true. Fallacies often appear to be true, but really are not. They include the following.

Relying on Case Examples

Just because something worked for one person doesn't mean it will work for everyone. It's important to identify what other variables might have been operating.

Example in everyday life

Ernestine lost 20 pounds in two weeks on the baked bean diet. That baked bean diet is the best thing and it really works. I think I'll try it.

Critical Thinking Questions

What proof is there that this baked bean diet really works? How nutritious is it? Does it endanger a person's health if practiced for long? Can other people readily maintain the same willpower as Ernestine, or is she exceptional? How many baked beans can other people really tolerate over that same time? What else was going on in Ernestine's life (e.g., excessive exercise) that could have contributed to her weight loss?

Example in social work practice

Harvey stopped drinking completely after seeing an alcohol and drug abuse counselor for six weeks who used guilt therapy. If you have a drinking problem, you should go to a counselor who uses guilt therapy. It's great.

Critical Thinking Questions

What is guilt therapy anyway? Did the therapy really help Harvey stop drinking, or was it something else (e.g., his wife threatened to leave him, or he joined Alcoholics Anonymous)? How long will Harvey stay "on the wagon"?

Relying on Testimonials

This is similar to relying on case examples. However, here a person swears that something is effective based on personal experience.

Example in everyday life

Gambrill and Gibbs (2009) provide an interesting example:

> "After taking so many other medicines without being helped, you can imagine how happy and surprised I felt when I discovered that Natex was doing me a lot of good. Natex seemed to go right to the root of my trouble, helped my appetite and put an end to the indigestion, gas and shortness of breath." (Local lady took Natex year ago—had good health ever since, 1935, May 27, p. 7).
>
> This woman's testimonial appeared on the same page of a newspaper as her obituary. (p. 109)

Critical Thinking Questions

What proof is there that Natex helped? What else might have affected this woman's condition? What caused her death?

Example in social work practice

Georgia, an agency worker, insists that the most effective child management technique is to bonk the misbehaving child on the nose with a flyswatter. She swears it immediately and permanently curbs obnoxious behaviors such as swearing, hitting other children, and sticking fingers into various facial orifices.

Critical Thinking Questions

What are the theoretical underpinnings of the flyswatter approach to behavior management? How has it been proved effective, with whom, and under what conditions? What are some potential negative consequences of this technique? To what extent can it cause children physical injury?

Being Vague

Making a generalized, imprecise statement about occurrences or conditions may give false impressions. Vagueness can lead to inaccuracies and potentially bogus assumptions.

(continued)

Example in everyday life
Life in Salt Lake City is better.

Critical Thinking Questions
Does this mean life there is good or bad? Does "better" refer to housing conditions, social life, employment opportunities, quality of restaurants, climate, or access to the mountains for good skiing?

Example in social work practice
Working with the neighborhood group improved community conditions.

Critical Thinking Questions
What conditions? Specifically, how were they improved? What proof exists that the neighborhood group, and not some other factors, "improved" conditions?

Being Biased or Unobjective

When a person is so committed to one side of an issue that the other side hardly seems to exist, beware. One sidedness works against objective evaluation of an idea, practice, or issue. As Gambrill and Gibbs (2009) observe, one sidedness reflects this attitude: "In matters controversial, my perception's rather fine. I always see both points of view: the one that's wrong and mine" (p. 111).

Example in everyday life
All politicians are crooks. They don't know anything, and all they do is steal your money.

Critical Thinking Questions
How many politicians do I know? What has led me to believe they're all crooks? What exactly is a political crook? Don't politicians differ regarding their stands on issues? How logical is it to clump them all into one bunch? How do they get away with stealing your money? Aren't most politicians monitored by the public? If there weren't any politicians, who would run the government, and how? If I don't like politicians, why don't I run for office myself and fix the system?

Example in social work practice
The social services agency I work for is the only one in the state that's any good.

Critical Thinking Questions
To what extent am I biased in claiming that my organization's the best one? What proof do I have that mine is better than the others? How do I know that other agencies don't have similar strengths? How many agencies am I familiar with anyway?

Believing That It's Written Down It Must Be Right

Stating something as a fact in a book, article, newspaper, or other medium such as radio or television doesn't mean it's accurate or true.

Example in everyday life
The book said that there have been thousands of alien sightings and abductions, so it must be true. There are even some photos of flying saucers in there.

Critical Thinking Questions
What concrete evidence is there that flying saucers have been here? Who has said they've been abducted, and what do they say about it? Are those really saucers in the pictures or some doctored-up hoax?

Example in social work practice
This textbook says that critical thinking is a necessity in social work practice.

Critical Thinking Questions
What does critical thinking mean? Does it make sense to scrutinize so carefully the things you're told? Is your ability to think as good as that of the people who write textbooks? What have you agreed with and disagreed with so far in this book? Do you tend to agree with everything you read or hear on television or the Internet?

The point is that critical thinking concerns not necessarily accepting situations or stories at face value. Rather, it entails using your own judgment to seriously consider their worth and relevance.

Romilly Lockyer/Stone/Getty Images

Planned change includes micro-, mezzo-, and macro-level practice. Social workers often work with other agency and community members in groups to solve problems and achieve positive change.

benefits. Regardless of the problem being addressed, the planned-change effort follows the same course of action, described shortly.

EP 2.1.10,
2.1.10a,
2.1.10b,
2.1.10d,
2.1.10e,
2.1.10g,
2.1.10h,
2.1.10i,
2.1.10j,
2.1.10k

Case Example We have established that a key feature of a generalist social work approach is that virtually any problem may be analyzed and addressed from multiple levels of intervention (i.e., involving individual, family, group, organizational, or community level). An example of the application of a generalist approach involves DeRon, a school social worker in a large, urban community that serves primarily a low-income population. In his role he may be called upon to work with students with behavioral problems, "to help collect data on the students' behaviors, to recommend behavioral intervention strategies, to teach social skills and strategies to the student, and/or to provide support for the student as part of

the behavior intervention plan" (Atkins-Burnett, 2010, p. 180). He participates with other professionals (e.g., speech therapists, psychologists, teachers) on multidisciplinary teams to determine treatment and educational plans. Often, he serves as a case manager who coordinates the treatment efforts. The school is legally responsible for providing supportive and remedial services to students who experience difficulties in their learning environment.

DeRon receives a new case referral, Peyton, a 5-year-old boy who has severe speech and behavioral problems. He stutters and has difficulty enunciating words and formulating sentences. He frequently refuses to obey his parents at home, often lashing out in violent temper tantrums. At school he has poor communication and relationship-building skills with his peers. He is unable to play with peers without acting out aggressively, such as hitting them in the stomach or poking them in the eye. Such behavior causes serious problems for him with his kindergarten teacher.

As a generalist practitioner, DeRon can assess the situation and proceed with this case at the individual, family, group, organizational, and community levels. First, on an individual level, Peyton requires speech and behavioral assessments to determine a treatment plan. To what extent are his speech difficulties physiologically based? What speech therapy goals might be established? How do Peyton's speech problems affect his ability to interact with others? Peyton is having difficulty interacting with family members, peers, and other adults. How are his parents and other family members reacting to and handling his speech and behavior problems? DeRon may assess Peyton's behavior and work with parents, teachers, and Peyton to improve his behavior and interpersonal relationships.

On the level targeting family intervention, Peyton's parents may require family counseling and education about behavior management techniques. Before DeRon gives the family any help he must first use empathy and other interpersonal skills to engage family members in the planned-change process. DeRon may provide some short-term help, but his job is to focus on Peyton's school performance. Therefore, he may want to help link Peyton's parents with resources and services outside the school, which would involve other organizations in the community.

Intervention at the group level may address Peyton's peer relationships. His teacher may need consultation regarding behavioral control in the classroom. Peyton might benefit from membership in a treatment group with other children experiencing similar difficulties. Group involvement might include discussing feelings and behavior, providing role models for improved behavior, and encouraging positive interaction among group members.

In the school's organizational setting, DeRon may serve as Peyton's case manager, leading multidisciplinary teams and coordinating the involved staff's treatment and educational approaches. As already noted, he may serve as a consultant to teachers and other school staff about how to deal with Peyton's behavior. DeRon might also organize and "lead parent education and informational groups" within the school context for Peyton's parents and other parents whose children demonstrate similar behavioral difficulties (Atkins-Burnett, 2010, p. 187). Also as noted, DeRon may refer Peyton's family to services and resources provided by other organizations in the community as needed.

Intervention at the community level attends to and promotes changes in the broader macro environment. A school social worker may "facilitate the development of relationships that link the services of the school with those found in the community.... [T]o function in the public school ... a social worker must stay informed about legislation and litigation that affect the school and other service providers' responsibility to this group as well as their roles and those of others. Social workers will need to be advocates for many of the children and their families" (Atkins-Burnett, 2010, pp. 187–188). Thus, for example, if needed services are not provided in the community, DeRon may advocate for their development on the behalf of Peyton's family and other families with similar needs. DeRon may also advocate for policies and legislation that enhance resource provision and availability.

Note that intervention involving the various levels of practice (individual, family, group, organizational, and community) is often not clearly delineated. For example, DeRon may assess and work with Peyton on an individual level, but at the same time work with family and school staff to address the same issues. The important point is that generalist practitioners may involve systems of various sizes in the planned-change process.

Figure 4.2 illustrates the generalist approach to assessing this situation and planning intervention at the individual, family, group, organizational, and community levels.

Figure 4.3 illustrates the six primary steps involved in planned change: engagement, assessment, planning, implementation, evaluation, and termination.

Step 1: Engagement

Engagement is the initial period when practitioners orient themselves to the problem at hand and begin to establish communication and a relationship with others also addressing the problem. Regardless of whether workers pursue change

EP 2.1.10a, 2.1.10b

with individuals, families, groups, organizations, or communities, they must establish rapport with clients and target systems in order to communicate and get things done. Engagement is based on the acquisition of a range of micro skills. Both the words social workers speak (verbal communication) and

Figure 4.2 Initiating Micro-, Mezzo-, or Macro-level Change During Assessment

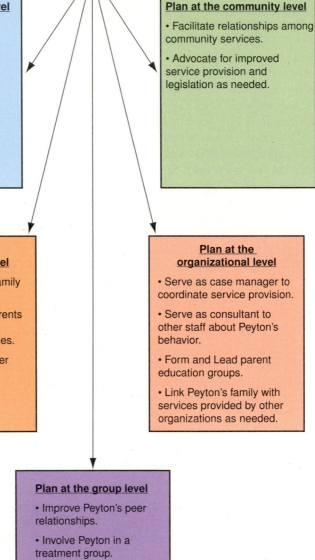

ASSESSMENT

Plan at the individual level

• Arrange for Peyton's speech and behavioral assessments.

• Examine how Peyton's problems affect his interactions with parents and peers.

Plan at the community level

• Facilitate relationships among community services.

• Advocate for improved service provision and legislation as needed.

Plan at the family level

• Provide short-term family counseling.

• Educate Peyton's parents about child behavior management techniques.

• Make referrals to other resources as needed.

Plan at the organizational level

• Serve as case manager to coordinate service provision.

• Serve as consultant to other staff about Peyton's behavior.

• Form and Lead parent education groups.

• Link Peyton's family with services provided by other organizations as needed.

Plan at the group level

• Improve Peyton's peer relationships.

• Involve Peyton in a treatment group.

their coinciding actions and expressions (nonverbal communication) can engage others in the helping process.

Nonverbal communication is body language and sounds that convey information about how a person feels without saying so in words. It includes body positions, facial expressions, vocal tone and expression (e.g., raising your voice or speaking very quietly

and meekly), and vocal noises other than words (e.g., grunts, snorts, chortles, hums). Patterson and Welfel (2000) explain:

You have been with people whose body language invites communication, and you have been with others whose body language indicates disinterest and perhaps even anxiety about communicating. The active,

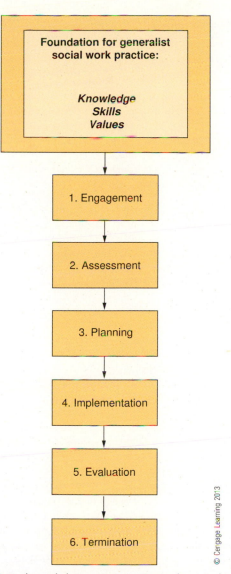

Figure 4.3 Planned-change Steps in Generalist Social Work Practice

interested listener faces and leans toward the speaker in a posture of interest and even excitement. Eyes are focused in the general direction of the person's face. Arms are in an open mode in relation to the trunk, as if to say, "I am very interested in receiving, with all my sensory processes, what it is you want to say to me." The attentive listener maintains an interested facial expression and makes encouraging gestures (nods, smiles, hand gestures, and so forth). (pp. 41–42)

Social workers also need to pay attention to cultural variations in people's nonverbal and verbal behavior. Highlight 4.3 discusses some of the differences among cultures.

Many other dimensions are involved in engagement. Social workers' overall demeanor—including their ability to convey warmth, empathy, and genuineness, concepts related to nonverbal behavior—can enhance engagement. Conveying *warmth* involves enhancing workers' positive feelings toward another person by promoting a sense of comfort and well-being in that person. *Empathy* involves not only being in tune with how clients feel but also conveying to them in a sincere and open manner that workers understand how they feel. *Genuineness* simply means that workers continue to be themselves while working to accomplish goals in their professional role.

Likewise, how social workers introduce themselves and arrange an initial meeting's setting affects the engagement process. Other engagement skills include alleviating initial client anxiety and introducing the worker's purpose and role.

HIGHLIGHT 4.3 *(continued)*

contact while listening and less while talking. Some research indicates that African Americans may reverse this pattern by looking more when talking and slightly less when listening. Among some Native American and Latino groups, eye contact by the young is a sign of disrespect. Some cultural groups generally avoid eye contact when talking about serious subjects. (p. 198)

In Chinese culture, when two people "talk to one another," they "use much less eye contact, especially when it is with the opposite sex"; this implies, for instance, that a male social worker's extended gaze at a female Chinese client could "be considered rude or seductive" (Zhang, 2010, p. 76).

Other expectations regarding facial expressions, including smiling, also differ. The following provides an example:

In general, the value that is placed on control of emotional expressions contributes to a demeanor among selected Asian groups that is often interpreted by Eurocentric individuals as "flat," "stoic," "enigmatic," or even "inscrutable." Koreans, for example, in keeping with the national character of the "Land of the Morning Calm," may present with a demeanor referred to as my-po-jung (lack of facial expression). Casual smiling and direct eye contact when greeting or interacting with strangers is considered inappropriate.

(Chan & Lee, 2004, p. 273; cited in Murphy & Dillon, 2011, p. 105)

A difference between Japanese people and Anglos involves how Anglos typically nod their heads to indicate that they concur with what the speaker is saying. Japanese people, on the other hand, may nod their heads to indicate they are paying close attention to what's being said. However, this behavior has nothing to do with agreement (Lum, 2004, p. 175).

An additional aspect of nonverbal behavior involves the amount of space people allow among themselves as they interact. Ivey, Ivey, and Zalaquett, (2010) explain:

A comfortable conversational distance for many North Americans is slightly more than arm's length, and the English prefer even greater distances. Many Latin people often prefer half that

distance, and those from the Middle East may talk practically eyeball to eyeball. As a result, the slightly forward leaning we recommend for attending behavior is not going to be appropriate all the time. A natural, relaxed body style that is your own is most likely to be effective, but be prepared to adapt and flex according to the individual with whom you are talking. (p. 75)

The way clients from various cultural backgrounds respond verbally also differs considerably. "Many cultures of the world do not place as much premium on talking as do the cultures in the Western Hemisphere." Consider the following case example cited by a counselor about his client (Berg-Cross, Craig, & Wessel, 2001):

Ms. B. was an undergraduate student from Asia. She had failed in one of her clinical rotations in an allied health field. Her failure was attributed not to her knowledge or her ability in her field but to poor judgment in her interpersonal relations. She came to see me in total frustration. One of her negative evaluations by her field supervisor had to do with her insufficient verbal participation in case conferences. Essentially her supervisors were saying that she didn't talk much and interpreted that as a lack of interest and involvement. When this . . . [counselor] explored further her lack of participation in classroom and group discussions, the client uttered in frustration, "I only speak if I have anything to say. In this country people talk even if they have nothing to say." She told me she just doesn't engage in superficial conversation. (p. 862)

How things are said also varies from culture to culture (Brave Heart & Chase, 2005):

First Nations clients may manifest a more indirect communication style, and the social worker must listen closely for disguised requests. Content is often veiled in stories and . . . [symbolic comparisons]. First Nations clients often respond indirectly to questions, and the worker must listen closely; the response may initially appear unrelated, but the answer is usually given in a disguised manner, in a story or through recounting a personal experience or that of another individual. (p. 39)

Step 2: Assessment

**EP 2.1.7b,
2.1.10a,
2.1.10c,
2.1.10d,
2.1.10e**

According to Hepworth, Rooney, Rooney, Strom-Gottfried, and Larsen, (2010), *assessment* is "a process occurring between practitioner and client, in which information is gathered, analyzed, and synthesized to provide a concise picture of the client and his or her needs and strengths" (p. 172). Meyer (1995) defines *assessment* simply as "knowing, understanding, evaluating, individualizing, or figuring out" (p. 260). For our purposes, *assessment* is the investigation and determination of variables affecting an identified problem or issue as viewed from micro, mezzo, or macro perspectives. It refers to gathering relevant information about a problem so decisions can be made about potential solutions. It's also important to work with the client to develop a mutually agreed-on focus of work and desired outcomes.

The crucial task of generalist practice is to look beyond the individual and examine other impinging factors within the client's environment. In a given case, the emphases on different assessment categories may vary. However, each category must still be reviewed and considered for its potential contribution to the problem.

For instance, a couple may come to a social worker for help in their marital relationship. Thus assessment of the mezzo aspects, or relationship issues of the situation, would be emphasized. However, a generalist practitioner would also consider both the micro aspects, such as the strengths, needs, and issues of each partner, and the macro aspects impinging upon their situation. Macro aspects might involve the fact that both spouses have been laid off from their jobs at the local bowling pin manufacturing plant. They had both held these jobs for over 10 years. The layoffs were probably due to a serious economic downturn and a decrease in the growth of recreational facilities such as bowling alleys. The social worker might not be able to do much about the economy's current condition. However, the economic impact on the couple is vital to the assessment of the couple's current conflictual situation.

In addition to limitations, the social worker also must assess the client's strengths. Highlight 4.4 discusses how a social worker assesses an individual's mental health problems and needs by emphasizing strengths. Chapter 13 elaborates on mental health issues and practice.

Human Diversity and Assessment

**EP 2.1.4,
2.1.4a,
2.1.5a**

Social workers must also take aspects of diversity into consideration when conducting assessments. Chapter 3 discussed various facets of human diversity including "age, class, color, culture, disability, ethnicity, gender, gender identity and expression, immigration status, political ideology, race, religion, sex, and sexual orientation" (CSWE, 2008b, EP 2.1.4). For each case, social workers should ask themselves whether any aspects of diversity may be significant.

Case Example   Consider Andrew, a hospital social worker whose client, Florence, age 78, was temporarily hospitalized for complications from diabetes.[5] Andrew is now helping Florence arrange to stay with relatives until she is well enough to return home. In the process of helping Florence, Andrew must identify aspects of diversity that might affect the assessment process or Florence's treatment.

Andrew discovers that Florence is of Italian heritage, a relevant aspect of ethnic and cultural diversity. Florence also feels strongly about her membership in a local Roman Catholic church that many other older adults of similar heritage also attend. For several reasons, Florence's church involvement is very important to her. Therefore, Andrew must take this into consideration when developing Florence's treatment plan with her. She needs a means of maintaining contact with her church.

Another aspect of diversity to consider is Florence's age. Is Florence being treated differently or in a discriminatory manner because of ageism? *Ageism* refers to discrimination based on preconceived notions about older people, regardless of their individual qualities and capabilities. Andrew closely evaluates his own attitudes here. For instance, is he tempted to make assumptions about Florence's mental capability because of the stereotype that older people don't think as well as when they were younger?

---

[5]*Diabetes* is a disease of the pancreas in which the body doesn't manufacture enough insulin to process sugars adequately.

HIGHLIGHT 4.4

HIGHLIGHT 4.4

Assessment: Emphasizing Strengths and Empowerment

Traditional Versus Strengths-Based Assessments

**EP 2.1.10a,
2.1.10d,
2.1.10e**

A traditional social work assessment model for an individual seeking mental health services involves seven dimensions: (1) presenting problem, (2) problem history, (3) personal history, (4) substance abuse history, (5) family history, (6) employment and education, and (7) summary and treatment recommendations (Graybeal, 2001, p. 235).
The traditional medical model described in Chapter 1 focuses on identifying what's wrong with the individual and then trying to fix it. Each dimension emphasizes the negative because the eventual goal is to cure the problem. A strengths-based perspective maintains that "individuals will do better in the long run when they are helped to identify, recognize, and use the strengths and resources available in themselves and their environment" (Graybeal, 2001, p. 234).

Graybeal (2001, p. 238) emphasizes the importance of identifying and using a client's strengths in addition to focusing on problems. For example, when assessing the presenting problem (i.e., the stated reason the client seeks treatment), traditional information solicited includes "detailed descriptions of problem(s)" and a "list of symptoms" (p. 238). A strengths-based assessment also explores personal strengths and available resources, and emphasizes potential solutions to the problem.

Similarly, the problem, personal, substance abuse, and family histories focus on more than all the bad things that have occurred. In addition, the social worker conducting a strengths-based assessment seeks information about what happened during the good times when the problem was not evident. What variables kept the client functioning well and staying healthy? What coping strategies were used? Who provided needed support during crises?

Traditional assessment of employment and education focuses on the facts concerning what occurred and on identification of gaps and problems. Strengths-based assessment of problems emphasizes the individual's skills, interests, and connections with other people in the community, including "spiritual and church involvement."

Finally, the traditional assessment summary and treatment recommendations focus on making a diagnosis and recommending a treatment plan.

A strengths-based assessment downplays labeling the problem and instead stresses a summary of "resources, options, possibilities, exceptions, and solutions" (p. 240).

Graybeal (2001) indicates that significant differences exist between a traditional problem oriented and a strengths-based assessment in cases concerning depression and suicidal thoughts. Consider Sara, who seeks help for her depression.

Traditional Assessment

Presenting problem: Sara, age 24, looking tired, haggard, and older than her years, reports a history of lethargy, depression, lack of self-confidence, low self-esteem, feelings of disheartenment, and thoughts of suicide. She also reports significant weight loss and difficulty sleeping.

Problem history: Sara indicates that these feelings of depression originated at age 16 when she was in a serious car accident in which some of her facial bones were crushed. She experienced 10 difficult and painful plastic surgeries that restored her face nearly to its original condition. She indicates that she has been helped by therapy and medication twice beginning at the time of the accident, although she has not been involved with a therapist for over a year.

Strengths-Based Assessment

Presenting problem: Sara, age 24, reports feelings of depression, uselessness, and loneliness. She also reports significant weight loss and difficulty sleeping. She indicates that these feelings began when her sister moved two states away. Although she has had thoughts of suicide, she is not seriously considering that now. She states that she feels best when at work and when telephoned by her sister.

Problem history: Sara indicates that her depression began at age 16 when she was in a serious car accident resulting in a series of painful facial surgeries. She indicates that members of her family and friends were very supportive of her throughout her physical and emotional trauma. She reports that her depression lifted when she first started this job but gradually crept back over the past few months. She has been involved in therapy twice in the past that she found very helpful. She is hopeful that therapy will result in improving her mood, energy level, and social life. Eventually, she

(continued)

HIGHLIGHT 4.4 (continued)

hopes to have friends instead of a therapist provide her with the support she needs.

Differences Between Traditional and Strengths-Based Approaches in Sara's Assessment

Note that the traditional assessment of the presenting problem stresses the bad things about Sara's problem—how she looks, feels, and experiences difficulties. The strengths-based assessment identifies the problems but also recognizes strengths. Sara has a strong support system in her sister; although her sister has moved away, they still maintain phone contact. It's also a strength that Sara is currently not considering suicide, although she has in the past.

The traditional problem history assessment goes into more detail about Sara's car accident at age 16. It also states that Sara has not been involved in therapy for a year. In contrast, the strengths-based assessment notes the supportiveness of relatives, a significant strength, during Sara's years of surgery and recovery. It also reports that Sara's mood lifted when she first started her job, so there were some positive variables involved there. The strengths-based approach indicates that Sara has found therapy helpful in the past, that she is hopeful it will be helpful again, and that eventually she hopes to develop a

social support system so she will no longer need therapy. In summary, focusing on strengths provides some clues for how to proceed in helping Sara fight her depression.

Aspects of Assessment Focusing on Families, Groups, Organizations, and Communities

When scrutinizing a problem, generalist social workers also look at potential aspects of assessment involving families and groups. When assessing Sara's personal, substance abuse, and family histories, the social worker works with her to examine her relationships with family members and others. Might she need to resolve some issues with her family members? Should they be involved in treatment? Might a support group be appropriate in which she could talk with others also suffering from depression? Or might a socialization group be useful in which members strive to improve their interpersonal behavior and social skills? This may be fitting because Sara has expressed a desire to improve her social life.

Aspects of assessment focusing on organizations and communities might involve how accessible treatment is to Sara. Is agency policy such that she can receive affordable treatment? If she can't afford it, is advocacy to change policy needed on her behalf?

Likewise, Andrew must be aware of any sexist biases he might harbor. *Sexism* refers to any preconceived notions about a person based solely on gender. For instance, does Andrew feel that Florence is a dependent person who needs to be taken care of simply because she's a woman? Such a bias fails to take into account the client as a unique individual with her own strengths and weaknesses.

Step 3: Planning

EP 2.1.6b, 2.1.10e, 2.1.10f, 2.1.10g

Assessment sets the stage for the intervention by identifying problems and strengths. *Planning* specifies what should be done. The following aspects of planning are important:

- The social worker should work *with* the client, not dictate *to* the client, to create the treatment plan.

- The social worker, together with the client, should prioritize the problems so that the most critical ones are addressed first.
- The social worker should identify the client's strengths to provide some guidance for the planned-change process.
- The social worker should identify alternative interventions. Should individual, family, group, organizational, or community systems be targets of change?
- Any course of action considered should be evidence-based. That is, it should be included among those established as the most effective interventions for that particular practice scenario based on scientific research.
- The social worker should help the client evaluate the pros and cons of each course of action to choose the best approach. Figure 4.4 depicts this process.

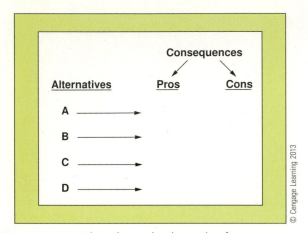

Figure 4.4 Social Workers Help Clients Identify Alternatives and Evaluate the Pros and Cons of Each

- With the client, the social worker should develop *goals*—the results that the client and worker seek to accomplish.
- The social worker should establish a *contract* with the client—that is, an agreement between a client and worker about the goals, time frames, and responsibilities of people involved in the intervention process.

Step 4: Implementation

EP 2.1.10j

Implementation is the process whereby client and worker follow their plan to achieve their goals. It is the actual *doing* of the plan. As you know, social work intervention can involve virtually any size system. Highlight 4.5 describes a series of potential social work interventions involving macro client systems.

Step 5: Evaluation

EP 2.1.10m

Evaluation is the process of analyzing, monitoring, and determining "the effectiveness of the intervention in relationship to the goal" (Hepworth, Rooney, Rooney, Strom-Gottfried, & Larsen, 2010, p. 331). After engagement and assessment, a social worker makes a plan with the client, implements the plan, and then evaluates the extent to which the plan was successful. It boils down to the social worker asking, "Does it work?" and "How do we know?"

(Kirst-Ashman & Hull, 2006, p. 311). Social workers need to be accountable; that is, they must prove that their interventions have been effective. Each goal must be evaluated in terms of the extent to which it has been achieved.

For example, consider Yvonne, a parole[6] officer for adults. George had been imprisoned for six years for armed robbery. He had been drunk when he committed the offenses. As a result, George's goals include attending biweekly Alcoholics Anonymous meetings, avoiding drinking altogether, seeking work from at least four sources weekly, checking in to the halfway house[7] where he resides by 8:00 pm every evening, and faithfully attending his weekly meetings with Yvonne on time. If George goes out drinking and gets a ticket for driving under the influence, he and Yvonne must evaluate the extent to which his rehabilitation plan is working. Does George require more intensive inpatient treatment instead? Is his parole unsuccessful, and so he should return to prison? What appropriate research-based knowledge is available for Yvonne and George to reconsider these goals and develop alternative ones?

Note that evaluation is also essential in mezzo and macro practice. For example, social workers must determine whether intervention involving agency functioning and service provision is successful. *Program evaluation* is the systematic examination of the success, effectiveness, and efficiency of an ongoing program (i.e., a structured plan and procedures for providing designated services to a sizable number of clients or a community).

Step 6: Termination

Termination is "the end of the professional social worker–client relationship" (Kirst-Ashman & Hull, 2012b, p. 311). The worker–client relationship eventually must come to an end. It is not a good ending for

EP 2.1.10l

---

[6] *Parole* is "the conditional release of a person from prison prior to the end of the sentence imposed" (Nichols, 1999, p. 961).

[7] *Halfway houses* are transitional dwellings that provide structure, support, and guidance for persons unable to function independently in the community. They are transitional because they provide a middle ground between a full-time residential setting (e.g., an institution or prison) and the relative freedom of living in the community. Persons requiring halfway houses include those on probation, substance abusers, and those with a history of mental illness.

HIGHLIGHT 4.5

Implementation with Macro Client Systems

**EP 2.1.8a,
2.1.8b,
2.1.9a,
2.1.9b,
2.1.10h,
2.1.10k**

"A *client system* is any individual, family, group, organization, or community that will ultimately benefit from generalist social work intervention. A *macro client system* involves larger numbers of clients, families, or groups of clients with similar characteristics or qualifications for receiving resources or services, or an agency or community that will be the beneficiary of the macro intervention process" (Kirst-Ashman & Hull, 2012a, p. 9). The concept of macro intervention concerns agency or social change that affects larger numbers of people than an individual, family, or small group. The following are examples of interventions involving communities and organizations on the behalf of macro client systems. Social workers might initiate any of these for the benefit of their clientele, community, or organization.

Fundraisers

Social workers can initiate, advocate for, help organize, and implement fundraising events for a wide range of purposes. Fundraising might involve a door-to-door campaign. It might also entail sponsoring special events and charging fees for admission to activities such as bingo nights, turkey dinners, or community dances. Similarly, it might involve selling donated things such as baked goods, crafts, or rummage items to finance some event or activity. Sponsored activities might include a bus trip to Washington, D.C., to march in favor of gay and lesbian rights, a Thanksgiving dinner for the local homeless, or renovations for a community recreational center.

Advocacy for Agency Policy Changes

Social workers can advocate to change internal agency policies when they're inefficient, ineffective, or discriminatory. Although an agency's administration is supposed to institute such changes, it often doesn't. Sometimes administrators are too far removed in the administrative structure from direct service provision to clients to know what's really going on. Other times, they are resistant to change because it requires greater effort or more money.

You may not have any experience in social work, but think of the jobs you've had. Were supervisors always aware of and sensitive to the issues you faced daily? Were the employers' rules and requirements always sensible and fair? Were employees and customers always treated in the most effective, efficient, and considerate way possible? Were you never disgusted with or angry at how you or others were treated? If you can answer "yes" to these four questions, you're lucky. In some ways, agencies, businesses, and other organizations can have similar problems. For whatever reason, agency social workers might be in the position of having to advocate with their own agency on the behalf of clients.

For instance, one worker advocated to initiate a policy to reserve the agency's best parking spaces for clients. Historically, staff would park in the best spots in the parking lot each morning because they always got there first. Clients thus regularly got the very worst parking spots—if there were any spots left at all.

Social workers can also advocate for change when an agency policy gets in the way of their doing their jobs. The policy might state that social workers should visit their clients' homes only when absolutely necessary to hold down transportation costs. The workers might strongly feel that it's essential to visit clients in their home environments to assess accurately what's going on in the family. Therefore, it's their responsibility to advocate for positive policy change and try to negotiate results.

A Volunteer Dental Program

Social workers can initiate and help organize programs for dentists to volunteer to help people with chronic illnesses, developmental disabilities, or other problems prohibiting them from working and having dental insurance. The program can also be made available to people working in low-paying jobs that don't provide dental insurance. Social workers can contact potential volunteers, help coordinate efforts, work with social service agencies to publicize the service, and link clients with the resource when they need dental help.

For instance, Harry, age 60, has severe heart disease and serious, painful gum disease. Because of numerous health expenses, he is financially strapped. He did have upper dentures made several years earlier. His coverage as a veteran at a Veteran's hospital helped as it allowed him to have his lower teeth removed, but prohibited coverage for any further work. Harry's mouth was in appalling shape, and he had extreme difficulty eating

(continued)

and talking. A social worker helped initiate and organize a Tri-County Troubled Teeth Treatment program in which dentists were systematically recruited to volunteer some of their time. One dentist in the program worked carefully with Harry during a half dozen appointments. At the end of the process, Harry couldn't believe he had brand-new porcelain lower dentures. He beamed at the dentist in appreciation.

Murals

Large pictures painted or drawn on walls or ceilings, known as murals, can provide an important means of self-expression and cultural pride. For example, concerning Chicanos and their pride in their history, Treguer (1992) comments about murals:

> Pre-Columbian themes, intended to remind Chicanos of their noble origins, are common. There are motifs from the [ancient] Aztec [manuscripts,] ... gods from the Aztec [temples,] ... allusions to the Spanish conquest and images of the Virgin of Guadalupe, a cherished Mexican icon. (p. 23)

Additionally, such murals can reflect religious and spiritual symbols, and issues related to social justice. Delgado and Barton (1999) remark,

> In some Latino communities, scenes of police brutality, arson, alcohol and other drug abuse, prison, U.S. imperialism (particularly related to government sponsored terrorism in the Caribbean and Latin America), and infant mortality are commonplace.... In essence, mural scenes are based on historical events and are a daily reminder of the trials and tribulations of being Latino in this country and of the search for social justice. (p. 233)

Delgado and Barton (1999) describe a case in Holyoke, Massachusetts, where a large Puerto Rican population lives. They note how "El Arco Iris (the Rainbow), an after school program" under the auspices of "a local community based organization, received funds to create a mural" (p. 241). Having obtained authorization from the owner of a deserted building, 20 Puerto Rican young people painted a mural of a nature panorama on one of the building's large, blank walls. The youths incorporated the U.S. and Puerto Rican flags into the landscape. They positioned the Puerto Rican flag above the U.S. flag, with the latter depicted upside down. Although the youths' intent was to demonstrate the harmony between the two countries, several other community residents were offended by the upside down U.S. flag. The incident caused serious debate among community residents with different cultural heritages. On the positive side, it stimulated discussion and consciousness raising among groups throughout the community. It also brought together Puerto Rican community members, including adults and young people, "to fight for their beliefs and to strengthen their voice within the community" (Delgado & Barton, 1999, p. 241). Eventually, the Puerto Rican youths decided to end the controversy by enlarging the Puerto Rican flag to cover the U.S. flag.

Delgado and Barton (1999) conclude,

> Social workers can play an instrumental role in helping communities negotiate with government authorities and private parties for the painting of murals using their spaces. Murals in prime locations can serve to empower communities to organize to seek services and other resources to help them develop their capacities to help themselves. (p. 236)

a worker to get up one day and, out of the blue, say, "Well, good-bye." Termination in generalist practice involves specific skills and techniques, regardless of the level of intervention.

Appropriate timing of the termination is important. At least three basic types of termination exist (Hellenbrand, 1987, p. 765). First, some terminations are "natural"; that is, goals have been achieved, and it is time for clients to take what they have learned and go out on their own. Other

terminations are "forced." For example, a worker might leave the agency, or a client might leave an institution for some reason or lose eligibility to receive services. Finally, there are "unplanned" terminations. Perhaps the client simply fails to come back, or the family moves, or the client is no longer motivated to return. Or maybe other aspects of the client's life take precedence over the problem he or she originally came to the social worker to help solve.

HIGHLIGHT 4.6

The Concept of Sustainability and the Process of Social Work

EP 2.1.9b

Chapter 1 established that *sustainability* involves "development that meets the current needs of the present generations without jeopardizing the ability of future generations to meet their needs" (Mary, 2008, p. 32). It refers to establishing policies, practices, and behaviors that will sustain the environment and people's quality of life instead of harming it. How does all this apply to social workers and their practice? At the level of working directly with clients, Healy (2008) emphasizes the importance of adopting helping strategies that are more self-supporting and likely to continue after the immediate intervention. For instance, social workers should consider the extent to which clients would continue to use any skills taught on an ongoing basis in view of their "time, financial resources, energy, literacy, and cultural acceptability" (p. 366). One illustration is a "program for teen mothers in May Pen, Jamaica, [that] teaches teen mothers how to use educational toys with their children and how to make the toys from scraps—milk carton blocks decorated with cut-outs from old magazines, for example; these homemade and resource-efficient toys are used in the program, although its grant would pay for expensive developmental toys from abroad. Through this simple strategy, the likelihood of sustainability is increased" (Healy, 2008, p. 366). When the grant runs out and

external funding dries up, the mothers are more likely to continue the practices they learned because they have simple resources readily available.

On a macro level, social workers can advocate for policies supporting sustainability and serve as leaders in implementing them (Gamble & Weil, 2008). Examples of movements promoting sustainability include those emphasizing environmental, green, antiwar, women's, and human rights issues (Gamble & Weil, 2008). Running for office provides one avenue of doing so. Mary (2008) stresses that becoming involved in politics and influencing politicians is critical; she suggests "writing to or meeting with local representatives around fiscal priorities and restructuring tax systems, and educating ourselves on the issues to present them in our own professional, civic, and personal arenas of power" (p. 189).

Also on a macro level, when social programs are developed to help communities, the communities' potential to continue them on an ongoing basis should be considered. "In planning and administering social programs, social workers can also use the concept of sustainability to assess program dependence on material and human resources, including available leadership talent and human energy. Many programs do not survive past the term of outside grants, as they fail to consider availability of ongoing resources" (Healy, 2008, p. 366).

The most effective terminations follow a thoughtful, planned process so that clients are prepared for the relationship to end. Social workers need to acknowledge that endings are near before they abruptly occur. They need to encourage clients to share feelings about the termination and, in turn, to share their own. Additionally, practitioners need to identify clearly whatever progress has been made. This increases the chance that the client will use what has been learned during this intervention to help solve other problems in the future.

The client may be an individual, group, or large agency. Regardless, each needs help in the transition from depending on the worker for support or guidance to making decisions and functioning independently.

Highlight 4.6 discusses how the concept of sustainability (introduced in Chapter 1) might be applied to the process and practice of social work on both micro and macro levels.

Chapter Summary

The following summarizes this chapter's content as it relates to the chapter objectives presented at the beginning of the chapter. Objectives include the following statements:

A Define generalist practice and explain each concept that is involved.

Generalist practice is the application of an eclectic knowledge base, professional values, and a wide range of skills to target individual, family, group, organizational, or community systems for change within the context of five primary processes. First, generalist practice emphasizes client empowerment. Second, it involves working effectively within an organizational structure and doing so under supervision. Third, it requires the assumption of a wide range of professional roles. Fourth, it concerns following the principles of evidence-based practice. Fifth, it involves the application of critical thinking skills to the planned-change process.

B Discuss some aspects of professional identity.

Social workers should identify with the profession. Some aspects of such identification include continual personal reflection and professional development, career-long learning, professional demeanor, and advocacy for client access to social work services.

C Explain how to use critical thinking to review a number of fallacies that can cause people to miss the truth.

Critical thinking questions were posed to address the common fallacies of relying on case examples, relying on testimonials, being vague, being biased or unobjective, and believing that if it's written down it must be right.

D Describe the six steps involved in the planned-change process, the procedure used to undertake social work intervention.

The planned-change process involves engagement, assessment, planning, implementation, evaluation, and termination.

E Discuss some cross-cultural differences in nonverbal and verbal communication.

Cross-cultural differences in nonverbal and verbal communication include amount of eye contact, emotional expression, personal space, verbal responses implying agreement, and the value of talk.

F Examine how the assessment process should emphasize strengths and empowerment.

Traditional assessment approaches emphasize the negative because the eventual goal is to cure the problem. A strengths-based assessment emphasizes

identifying and using a client's strengths in addition to focusing on the problem. Strengths can be used to identify resources to solve problems.

G Provide examples of intervention with macro client systems.

Examples of intervention work with macro systems include fundraisers, advocacy for agency policy changes, volunteer dental programs, and community murals.

LOOKING AHEAD

This chapter discussed the process of generalist social work practice. The next chapter will explain the various practice settings in which this process is implemented.

COMPETENCY NOTES

The following identifies where Educational Policy (EP) competencies and practice behaviors are discussed in the chapter.

EP 2.1.1a Advocate for client access to the services of social work. *(p. 111):* Social workers should advocate that their services be accessible to clients to help clients solve their problems.

EP 2.1.1b Practice personal reflection and self-correction to assure continual professional development. *(p. 111):* Practitioners must practice ongoing personal reflection about their personal values and prejudgments so that these don't interfere with objective, effective practice.

EP 2.1.1c Attend to professional roles and boundaries. *(p. 110):* Various professional social work roles are described.

EP 2.1.1d Demonstrate professional demeanor in behavior, appearance, and communication. *(p. 111):* Demonstration of professional demeanor in behavior, communication, and appearance is discussed.

EP 2.1.1e Engage in career-long learning. *(p. 111):* Learning about practice effectiveness, cultural differences, the constantly shifting social environment, and infinite other aspects of social work practice is a career-long process.

EP 2.1.1f Use supervision and consultation. *(p. 109):* Working under supervision in an organizational setting and using consultation are discussed as important aspects of generalist practice.

EP 2.1.3 Apply critical thinking to inform and communicate professional judgments. *(p. 113):* Social workers should consistently apply critical thinking in practice.

EP 2.1.3a Distinguish, appraise, and integrate multiple sources of knowledge, including research-based knowledge, and practice wisdom. *(p. 113):* Critical thinking involves asking questions and assessing facts from multiple sources of knowledge. *(p. 114):* Practitioners should evaluate and integrate multiple sources of knowledge to dispense with fallacies.

EP 2.1.3b Analyze models of assessment, prevention, intervention, and evaluation. *(p. 113):* Social workers should think critically about what practice approaches are proven effective. *(p. 114):* Readers are asked to evaluate various social work practice scenarios.

EP 2.1.3c Demonstrate effective oral and written communication in working with individuals, families, groups, organizations, communities, and colleagues. *(p. 113):* The Triple-A critical thinking approach emphasizes reaching a conclusion that can be clearly articulated. *(p. 119):* Social workers should attend to cultural differences in verbal and nonverbal communication so that they might communicate effectively with people from other cultures.

EP 2.1.4 Engage diversity and difference in practice. *(p. 119):* Practitioners should be sensitive to cultural differences in nonverbal and verbal communication. *(p. 121):* It's vital for social workers to be concerned about aspects of diversity during assessment.

EP 2.1.4a Recognize the extent to which culture's structures and values may oppress, marginalize, alienate, or create or enhance privilege and power. *(p. 121):* During assessment, social workers should investigate how aspects of diversity may expose clients to oppression.

EP 2.1.5a Understand the forms and mechanisms of oppression and discrimination. *(p. 121):* The following case example described includes consideration of ageism and sexism, both forms of oppression.

EP 2.1.6b Use research evidence to inform practice. *(p. 112):* Social workers should undertake evidence-based practice, which emphasizes using approaches research has shown to be most effective in specific practice situations. *(p. 123):* When planning, social workers and their clients should choose from among evidence-based interventions.

EP 2.1.7b Critique and apply knowledge to understand person and environment. *(p. 121):* Assessment involves looking beyond the individual and examining other impinging factors within the client's environment.

EP 2.1.8a Analyze, formulate, and advocate for policies that advance social well-being. *(p. 125):* Social workers should analyze, formulate, and advocate for policies that advance social well-being on the behalf of macro client systems.

EP 2.1.8b Collaborate with colleagues and clients for effective policy action. *(p. 125):* Several projects are discussed where social workers collaborate with colleagues and clients for effective policy action.

EP 2.1.9a Continuously discover, appraise, and attend to changing locales, populations, scientific and technological developments, and emerging societal trends to provide relevant services. *(p. 125):* Practitioners should continuously respond to the changing issues and conditions affecting macro client systems in the macro environment.

EP 2.1.9b Provide leadership in promoting sustainable changes in service delivery and practice to improve the quality of social services. *(p. 125):* Social workers can be leaders in ventures involving advocacy, and project and program development. *(p. 127):* Social workers should provide leadership in promoting sustainable service delivery.

EP 2.1.10 Engage, assess, intervene, and evaluate with individuals, families, groups, organizations, and communities. *(p. 113):* This section discusses the entire planned-change process, which includes engagement, assessment, intervention, and evaluation with systems of all these sizes. *(p. 116):* This case example portrays the planned-change process that involves intervention with individuals, families, groups, organizations, and communities.

EP 2.1.10a Substantively and affectively prepare for action with individuals, families, groups, organizations, and communities. *(p. 113):* Reviewing the planned-change process will help prepare for practice with systems of all sizes. *(p. 116):* The social worker in this case example may involve systems of various sizes in the planned-change process. *(p. 117):* Step 1 of planned change, engagement, is discussed. *(p. 121):* Engagement with clients helps prepare for action with them. *(p. 122):* Emphasizing strengths and client empowerment during assessment helps prepare for action.

EP 2.1.10b Use empathy and other interpersonal skills. *(p. 116):* Social workers use empathy and other interpersonal skills when undertaking the planned-change process with families. *(p. 117):* Engagement involves using empathy and other interpersonal skills.

EP 2.1.10c Develop a mutually agreed-on focus of work and desired outcomes. *(p. 121):* During assessment, social workers should work together with clients to develop a mutually agreed-on focus of work and desired outcomes.

EP 2.1.10d Collect, organize, and interpret client data. *(p. 116):* Social workers must collect, organize, and interpret client data to undertake the planned-change process. *(p. 121):* Assessment involves the collection, organization, and interpretation of client data. *(p. 122):* Assessment emphasizing strengths involves collecting, organizing, and interpreting client data.

EP 2.1.10e Assess clients' strengths and limitations: *(p. 116):* The school social worker in this case example assesses his client's behavioral limitations. *(p. 121):* Social workers should assess clients' strengths and limitations. *(p. 122):* This highlight and case example stress how workers should focus on clients' strengths. *(p. 123):* A social worker should identify and assess client strengths to incorporate them in the planned-change process.

EP 2.1.10f Develop mutually agreed-on intervention goals and objectives. *(p. 123):* It's vital that social workers develop mutually agreed-on intervention goals and objectives with clients.

EP 2.1.10g Select appropriate intervention strategies. *(p. 116):* This case example involves selecting appropriate intervention strategies that target systems of various sizes. *(p. 123):* Practitioners should work with the client system to plan the most appropriate intervention strategies.

EP 2.1.10h Initiate actions to achieve organizational goals. *(p. 116):* The school social worker in this example helps school staff achieve their educational goals with the client. He may also work with other services in the community to improve relationships with the school and thereby achieve the school's goals (as an organization) more effectively. *(p. 125):* Several ventures are described that can be initiated by social workers to achieve organizational goals and serve clients more effectively.

EP 2.1.10i Implement prevention interventions that enhance client capacities. *(p. 116):* Interventions are designed to help prevent the client from having speech and behavioral problems in the future.

EP 2.1.10j Help clients resolve problems. *(p. 116):* This case example portrays a worker helping clients resolve problems. *(p. 124):* Implementation during planned change concerns helping clients solve problems by putting the plan into action.

EP 2.1.10k Negotiate, mediate, and advocate for clients. *(p. 110):* Mediator, negotiator, and advocate roles are defined and examples of each provided. *(p. 116):* The school social worker in this case example may advocate to improve resource provision and legislation when necessary. *(p. 125):* Various scenarios are described where social workers advocate and negotiate on the behalf of clients.

EP 2.1.10l Facilitate transitions and endings. *(p. 124):* Suggestions are provided for facilitating the termination process.

EP 2.1.10m Critically analyze, monitor, and evaluate interventions. *(p. 124):* Step 5 in the planned-change process is evaluation, where practitioners analyze, monitor, and determine the effectiveness of an intervention.

FOR FURTHER EXPLORATION ON THE INTERNET

See this text's Social Work CourseMate website at *www.cengagebrain.com* for learning tools such as chapter quizzing, videos, glossary flashcards, and more.

CHAPTER **5**

Practice Settings

Bruce Ayres/stones/Getty Images

Consider these questions:

- *Why are social welfare programs the way they are today?*
- *What social welfare problems and issues do we foresee in the future?*
- *What kinds of treatment groups do social workers run?*
- *What fields of practice do most social workers go into?*

This chapter addresses these and many other questions and issues concerning social welfare and social work in the past, present, and future. Chapter 4 discussed generalist social work practice. This chapter focuses on the contexts in which social work has been, is, and will be practiced.

Learning Objectives

A Identify the context of social work practice today in organizations and communities.

B Explain the core treatment approaches in practice with individuals, families, groups, organizations, and communities.

C Explore the special contexts of social work in rural and urban communities.

D Identify some of the major professional associations in social work.

E Describe social work licensure.

F Propose questions to stimulate critical thinking about participation in various systems.

G Discuss employment settings for social workers in terms of fields of practice and compare earnings.

Social Work Practice Today

Chapter 4 discussed the process of generalist social work practice. The following sections continue the exploration of the current context of practice, including social work's organizational and community settings; primary treatment approaches used in practice with individuals, families, groups, organizations and communities; key professional social work organizations; and social workers' most common employment settings according to fields of practice.

Settings in Social Work Practice: Organizations and Communities

EP 2.1.7

Social work practice generally takes place within the context of organizations and communities. *Organizations* are entities made up of people that have rules and structure to achieve specified goals. Social workers practice under the auspices of organizations providing social services.

EP 2.1.7b

Social Services in the Context of Social Agencies

Social services include the tasks that social work practitioners and other helping professionals perform with the goal of improving people's health, enhancing their quality of life, increasing autonomy and independence, supporting families, and helping people and larger systems improve their functioning in the social environment (Barker, 2003). That is quite a mouthful. In essence, social services include the wide range of activities that social workers perform to help people solve problems and improve their personal well-being.

A *social agency* or *social services agency* is an organization providing social services that typically employs a range of helping professionals including social workers in addition to office staff, paraprofessionals (persons trained to assist professionals), and sometimes volunteers (Barker, 2003). Social agencies generally serve some designated client population experiencing some defined need. Services are provided according to a prescribed set of policies regarding how the agency staff should accomplish their service provision goals.

Social agencies come in many forms. For example, they can be either public or private. *Public* social agencies are run by some designated unit of government and are usually regulated by laws impacting policy. For instance, a county board committee oversees a public welfare department and is responsible for establishing its major policies. (Of course, such a committee must function in accordance with the wishes of the state or federal governments that often provide at least some of the money for the agency's programs.)

Private social agencies, in contrast, are privately owned and run by people not employed by government. The services they provide include individual and group counseling, family planning, and other services for children and older adults (Barker, 2003). Note that services sometimes resemble those furnished by public social agencies such as corrections, protective services for children, and job preparation and training for public assistance recipients.

Private social agencies may be either nonprofit or proprietary. *Nonprofit* social agencies seek to accomplish some service provision goal, not to make a profit for private owners. Sources of funding for services can include taxes, private donations, grants, and service fees. A board of directors presides over a private nonprofit agency, formulating policy and making certain that agency staff run the agency appropriately.

Proprietary or *for-profit* private social agencies also provide some designated social services, often quite similar to those provided by nonprofit private social agencies. However, a primary purpose for the existence of a proprietary social agency is to earn a profit for its owners.

Sometimes public agencies buy services from private agencies through a *purchase-of-service contract* or agreement. In a typical scenario, a public agency needs specialized services that it does not normally provide. It may be more cost-effective for the public agency to purchase the service from a private agency. The private agency then assumes responsibility for developing and overseeing service provision.

Social Work Practice in the Context of Communities

EP 2.1.7b

A *community* is "a number of people who have something in common with one another that connects them in some way and that distinguishes them from others" (Homan, 2011, p. 8). A key feature of a community is the fact that participants share some mutual characteristic, such as "location, interest, identification, culture, and/or activities" (Fellin, 1995, p. 3).

Thus communities can be of two primary types— those based on geographic proximity and those based on common ideas, interests, loyalty, and a feeling of membership (Martinez-Brawley, 1995). Locality-based communities include smaller towns such as Crouch, Idaho; Eggemoggin, Maine; and Necessity, Louisiana. Larger communities include mammoth urban environments such as the greater Los Angeles Metropolitan Area or New York City. Still other locality-based communities include smaller portions of larger cities such as a struggling inner-city ghetto or a posh suburban neighborhood.

Nongeographic communities are based on some commonality other than location. For example, African Americans might form a community based on racial identification and a shared history and culture. Similarly, a community of professional social workers shares common values, beliefs, and generalist practice skills. Additionally, gay communities and military communities exist that have distinct compositions, configurations, and purposes. Members of such communities exhibit many common values, expectations, and beliefs. Even scuba divers make up a community based on common interests, activities, and experiences.

In the social work perspective, communities are entities in which citizens can organize or be organized to address mutual concerns and improve their overall quality of life. Social workers have the responsibility to examine the community environment in which their clients reside. Although social workers are surely focused on how specific clients function as individuals, they are also concerned about the environment in which clients live and whether adequate resources are available.

The following sections discuss the special circumstances concerning social work practice in rural and urban communities and those involved in urban and rural social work.

The Special Circumstances of Social Work Practice in Rural Communities

Social work practice in rural communities merits special attention. What do you picture when you think of a rural environment? A farmer wearing a straw hat and chewing on a blade of grass? Cows grazing? Endless, lonesome prairie? Barren desert?

EP 2.1.1e, 2.1.9a

Some things you probably *don't* think of are skyscrapers, chaotic traffic jams, and thousands of people swarming on crowded streets.

Defining the concept of a rural community is not an easy task. An increasing population, spreading suburban sprawl, and decreasing numbers of farmers complicate the issue of what rural means. Yet you may have a sense that life in rural America is quite different than that in urban enclaves.

The U.S. Census Bureau (2010) defines a rural community as one that is not an "urbanized area" (a "densely settled territory that contains 50,000 or more people") or an "urban cluster" (a "densely settled territory with at least 2,500 people but fewer than 50,000 people") (pp. 3–4). But this definition allows for vast discrepancies in economic and social status. Consider the difference between a well-to-do bedroom community 35 miles outside of Chicago where corporate commuters reside in huge mansions versus a farming community in South Dakota where farmers are just managing to get by (Davenport & Davenport, 2008).

One definition of a rural community involves three major facets—having a low population density (i.e., number of residents per square mile), being located a significant distance from large urban hubs, and concentrating its activity in some specialized area like lumbering, farming, ranching, or mining (Davenport & Davenport, 2008). Some definitions indicate that to be "rural," a community must be unincorporated and have fewer than 2,500 inhabitants (Carlton-LaNey, Edwards, & Reid, 1999).

Carlton-LaNey and her colleagues (1999) comment on the special problems of rural communities:

Rural communities experience many of the same social problems as their urban counterparts. Nevertheless, some problems are specific to rural communities. Although the problems themselves may not differ greatly from those in urban centers, they are magnified by the rural communities' inability to target the needed resources in ways that alleviate suffering and ultimately eliminate the problems.

The list of problems with which rural and small town residents must cope includes poverty, lack of transportation, inadequate child care, unemployment, substandard housing, and insufficient health care. Problems of access and adequacy, for example, remain critical issues that must be addressed in rural social work practice. Krout (1994) noted that access problems add time and expense to service delivery efforts, ultimately discouraging both the development of new services and the expansion of existing services into rural areas. For example,

rural homebound individuals who could benefit from home-delivered meals and thereby maintain independence are denied this service because it is too expensive. The cost of delivering meals to remote areas can significantly limit the amount of money available for the service itself.

Health care is another significant problem. Rural areas, particularly low-income areas, are underserved because of a lack of physicians and other health care providers. The South especially suffers from a maldistribution of health care professionals and facilities. (p. 7)

Social workers practicing in rural communities must address at least four special issues. First, they must be true generalists who are prepared to work with individuals, families, groups, local organizations, and the community, using a wide range of skills to meet clients' diverse needs (Daley & Avant, 2004; Davenport & Davenport, 2008; Lohmann, 2005). Urban areas with large populations and a larger tax base can better afford to specialize in service provision. For example, public and private social service agencies might provide specific services such as substance abuse counseling, older adult protective services, services for people with intellectual disabilities, crisis counseling for victims of sexual assault, shelter for victims of domestic violence, and so on. A rural community, on the other hand, probably does not have the resources or enough population to support such specific services (Davenport & Davenport, 2008). Therefore, rural practitioners typically must be more flexible and willing to address a broader range of people with a varied assortment of problems.

A second special issue involves interagency cooperation (Carlton-LeNay et al., 1999, p. 10). Because fewer, more general services are usually provided by public agencies, it's critical for agencies and their staffs to work more closely together than in many urban communities. It's common for practitioners and agency administrations "to know each other and to reach out to each other regularly" to meet clients' diverse needs (Carlton-LeNay et al., 1999, p. 10). In urban areas with hundreds of available services, this may not be the case.

A third issue involving rural social work is the importance placed on understanding the community, knowing its values, and developing relationships with rural residents (Daley & Avant, 2004). People living in rural communities have different

HIGHLIGHT 5.1

Case Example of a Dual Relationship in a Rural Community

**EP 2.1.2c,
2.1.2d**

Corey and his colleagues (2011) relate the following example of a dual relationship in a small rural community setting:

Millie, a [social work] therapist in a small community, experienced heart pain one day. The fire department was called, and the medic on the team turned out to be her client, Fred. To administer proper medical care, Fred had to remove Millie's upper clothing. During subsequent sessions, neither Fred nor Millie discussed the incident, but both exhibited a degree of discomfort with each other. After a few more sessions, Fred discontinued his therapy with Millie.

- Can this case be considered an unavoidable dual relationship? Why or why not?
- What might Millie have done to prevent this outcome?
- Should Millie have discussed her discomfort in the therapy session following the incident? Why or why not?
- If you were in Millie's situation, what would you have done?

Commentary: This case illustrates how some roles can shift and how some multiple relationships are unavoidable, especially in small communities. In small communities, therapists must anticipate frequent, and sometimes uncomfortable, boundary crossings with clients. In our view, Millie should have discussed with Fred how he would like to handle chance encounters in the community during the informed consent process. [Very early in the worker/client relationship, the worker should provide the client with information about the parameters of their relationship. For example, this may include limits of confidentiality and the worker's responsibility to report any criminal behavior to the authorities. In small communities this may also include how informal meetings should be handled because they are so likely to occur.] Even so, we doubt that Millie could have predicted this awkward boundary crossing with Fred. Clinically, Millie might have salvaged the therapy relationship by processing [that is, talking about and dealing with] her own discomfort with a colleague, and then processing the event with Fred. By allowing the discomfort to remain hidden, Millie failed to practice with the best interests of her client in mind. In this instance, neither Millie's nor Fred's needs were being met in the therapeutic relationship. (pp. 285–286)

---

life experiences than those living in bustling cities. Because there are fewer people, social interactions and relationships tend to be much more informal. Rural social workers and their family members might attend the same church or school, participate in the same civic clubs and organizations, and shop at the same grocery store as clients. Therefore, a rural practitioner must be careful to portray an image that reflects positively on his or her agency (Daley & Avant, 2004). Private lives might be more public—some say it's like "life in a goldfish bowl" (Davenport & Davenport, 2008, p. 538). For example, it would not be impressive for a social worker counseling a client with an alcohol problem to be cited in the local newspaper for driving under the influence (DUI).

Because of the close interpersonal nature of rural communities, there is a strong likelihood that dual relationships exist (Daley & Hickman, 2011). As described in Chapter 2, dual or "multiple relationships occur when professionals assume two or more roles at the same time or sequentially with a client" (e.g., both social worker and neighbor or member of the same church, temple, mosque, or synagogue) (Corey Callaman, 2011, p. 268). Especially in rural communities, dual and multiple relationships may be unavoidable. Watkins (2004) suggests that rural social workers in such situations "above all, do no harm; practice only with competence; do not exploit; treat people with respect for their dignity as human beings; protect confidentiality; act, except in the more extreme instances, only after obtaining informal consent; [and] practice, insofar as possible, within the framework of social equity and justice" (p. 70).

Highlight 5.1 provides an example of a dual relationship occurring in a small community.

The fourth issue important for rural social work practice involves emphasizing the strengths inherent in rural communities (Tice, 2005). Because of the informal nature of relationships, rural clients are often integrally involved with informal social support systems of other people willing to help them out—sometimes referred to as *natural helping networks* (Tracy, 2002; Watkins, 2004). Such networks can include family members, neighbors, coworkers, fellow church members, community benefactors, and others not providing formal agency services who are willing to volunteer assistance. (Social support systems are discussed in more detail later in the chapter with respect to working with families.)

Urban Social Work

EP 2.1.9a

Urban social work is practice within the context of large cities, with their vast array of social problems, exceptional diversity, and potential range of resources (Delgad & Staples, 2008). Phillips and Straussner (2002) stress how urban social workers "need to be sensitive to the situations commonly found in the cities and to be knowledgeable about the nature of urban life and the range of impact that the urban environment can have on people" (p. 20). Work in the urban context is important in view of how both the national and global population has been shifting from rural to urban settings. People often flock to cities in search of new opportunities, higher-paying jobs, and greater access to activities and services. Many times, although hopes are high, actual opportunities are scarce or nonexistent, which results in a "disproportionate number of the poor" in the "country's largest cities" (p. 107).

Urban areas are characterized by a number of conditions (Marsella, 1998). First, population is denser and often contains diverse population subgroups (for example, ethnic, racial, cultural, age, sexual orientation). Second, urban economic conditions involve a range of industries, businesses, rent levels, and transportation availability and costs. Third, the urban environment is often a bustling tangle of concrete, traffic, noise, and questions about air quality—in sharp contrast to the more natural rural environment. Fourth, an urban lifestyle entails more condensed interaction and contact with many people. Fifth, the political situation may be intense with many layers of bureaucracy and numerous people in "the system" who have various amounts of power. Sometimes crime, corruption, and social injustice are evident. Conditions in urban environments are often very different than those addressed by rural social workers.

Watkins (2004) explains:

> Urbanization brought dramatic changes in the way people interacted with each other. Individuals moved away from extended family and other primary relationships to cities where primary relationships were replaced by more role-based interactions [for example, employee, renter, customer, student]. Population density and crowding were accompanied by emotional distancing to preserve a sense of privacy and individuality. In low-income neighborhoods, needs overwhelmed the resources of neighbors. Many persons in need were new to the cities and had no support networks. Formalized or institutionalized social services were a rational response to the peculiar social patterns and needs of these urban residents.... However, when federal, state, and local governments increased their role in providing services, the programs were no longer tailored to a specific community. In efforts to increase efficiency and fairness, services became more bureaucratic and standardized. The new model of service delivery that developed preferred secondary, "professional" relationships and interactions that were rule- and role-based rather than more personal. Needy individuals were depersonalized into "clients." ... Personal relationships between client and social workers were not only unlikely in the urban environment, they were actively discouraged. (p. 67)

At least five problems tend to characterize urban areas more than rural areas (Phillips & Straussner, 2002). For one thing, "problems such as poverty, discrimination, overcrowded housing, crime and violence, homelessness, high rates of school dropouts, substance abuse, and HIV/AIDS exist in communities of all sizes. However, they occur with greater frequency and therefore are more visible in the cities" (p. 25).

A second problem is the widespread occurrence of discriminatory behavior because of the wide variety of ethnic, racial, religious, and cultural groups living in cities. Groups may be in conflict and fighting for power and resources. Often public schools are disadvantaged because of inadequate funding, resulting in poorer buildings, libraries, laboratory equipment, and technology, as well as underpaid staff.

Migration of people ill-equipped for the pressures and demands of urban living is a third problem characterizing cities. Phillips and Straussner (2002) explain:

> With their promise of freedom and opportunity, the cities have always been magnets for both the adventurous and the desperate. Most people move to urban areas in search of better opportunities for work or for education, either for themselves or their families, and for many, the cities have served and continue to serve as gateways to success.
>
> However, some who migrate to urban areas, whether from other parts of the United States or from other countries, are faced with unemployment, underemployment, discrimination, poor housing, and language barriers. Those without families or social supports to help them make the transition to the new culture and to city life are at greater risk for poverty, social isolation, and personal and family problems. (p. 27)

Financial shortfalls or unavailability of resources make up a fourth problem characterizing urban areas. "Some cities do not have the financial resources to provide services that would assist people in maximizing their potential, while other cities may have the resources, but do not choose to provide services, particularly for the poor. Consequently, there may be a lack of affordable, good-quality housing, or a lack of adequate police protection, schools, or recreational facilities. For example, preschool children and their parents are underserved in many urban communities" (Phillips & Straussner, 2002, p. 28). Because of cities' dense population, service gaps can affect huge numbers of people.

The fifth problem characterizing cities involves greater amounts of psychological stress. Stressors including "noise, dirty streets," "abandoned buildings," overcrowded housing, lack of geographic mobility, and substance abuse can impose psychological pressure and increase general anxieties (Phillips & Straussner, 2002, p. 29).

As in other types of social work, urban social workers use micro-practice skills in their work with clients, including establishing and working toward goals, using effective communication and interviewing techniques, respecting client values and perspectives, emphasizing strengths, expressing empathy, and "developing self-awareness" to combat biases and effectively understand clients' perspectives (Phillips & Straussner, 2002, p. 201).

Highlight 5.2 discusses skills urban social workers must develop and use. Focus on Critical Thinking 5.1 raises questions to help you think about and understand your home community regardless of whether it's urban, rural, or something that's not quite either.

Social Work Practice with Individuals

Social work practice with individuals involves many dimensions of communication, interaction, sensitivity, and decision making as the practitioner follows the planned-change process. Two important aspects arbitrarily selected for discussion here are interviewing skills and professional roles.

EP 2.1.1c, 2.1.10a

Interviewing Skills in Practice with Individuals

One essential aspect of social work practice with an individual (a micro system) involves interviewing skills. Hepworth Rooney, Rooney, Strom-Gottfried, and Larsen (2010) explain:

EP 2.1.10b

> Interviews in social work have a purpose, structure, direction, and focus. The purpose is to exchange information systematically with a view toward illuminating and solving problems, promoting growth, or planning strategies or actions aimed at improving the quality of life for people. The structure of interviews varies somewhat from setting to setting, from client to client, and from one phase of the helping process to another. Indeed, skillful interviewers adapt flexibly both to different contexts and to the ebb and flow of each individual session. (p. 44)

Ivey, Ivey, and Zalaquett (2010) state that several facets are important in the development of interviewing and other micro-practice skills; one is *"attending behavior,"* the use of "culturally and individually appropriate visuals (eye contact), vocal qualities, verbal tracking skills, and body language" (p. 15). They explain further:

1. *Visual/eye contact.* If you are going to talk to people, look at them. [But as discussed in an earlier chapter, be very sensitive to cultural differences concerning what kind of eye contact and when is considered appropriate.]

HIGHLIGHT 5.2

Skills Necessary for Urban Social Work

**EP 2.1.1e,
2.1.4c,
2.1.4d,
2.1.8a,
2.1.10k**

Urban social workers must focus on using skills in at least four major arenas (Phillips & Straussner, 2002):

1. *Paying close attention to human diversity:* Because urban environments more likely have a wider variety of ethnic, racial, and religious backgrounds, urban social workers must be sensitive to the wide range of cultural differences, become knowledgeable about their various clients' cultures, and focus on the identification and use of clients' respective cultural and personal strengths. Urban practitioners must also be attuned to the potential discrimination experienced by people "based on race, ethnicity, culture, age, gender, religion, sexual orientation, disability, poverty, or language spoken. While historically various immigrant groups such as the Irish, the Jews, the Italians, the Chinese, and the Japanese have experienced discrimination in the United States, the most persistent discrimination today is experienced by Native Americans; blacks, including African Americans, people from the Caribbean, and people from Africa; Latinos; Asians; and people of Middle Eastern backgrounds" (Phillips & Straussner, 2002, p. 26).

2. *Understanding their agency environment:* Urban agencies may be large and complex, or may serve large client populations. Urban workers must understand the intricacy of their agency's power structure, who has decision-making power about what they can and can't do, and where resources are located. Large bureaucracies are often highly impersonal. They tend to emphasize the following rules and regulations to coordinate their complex maze of service provision. Often workers are called on to work with other personnel they don't know. Workers must

then be sensitive to other staff's roles and use good communication skills to work effectively in collaboration with other service providers. Even smaller agencies in urban settings must work within a complex interplay of numerous organizations also addressing client needs. Urban social workers must understand the functioning of other agencies serving the same clients and work carefully with other staff to coordinate service provision.

3. *Seeking resources in the external urban environment:* Urban social workers often function in a complex labyrinth of many public and private agencies, each providing specialized services in one of a broad range of areas (for example, mental health counseling, administration of public assistance, domestic violence shelter, sexual assault hotline, or adolescent pregnancy prevention). This differs from rural agencies that often provide a broader range of services to a smaller population; in other words, they are less likely to specialize to the degree that urban agencies can. In their broker role, urban social workers must often seek resources in a confusing tangle of red tape and available services.

4. *Using advocacy:* Note that just because urban areas tend to have larger and more services, this does not mean that there are no significant gaps in service due to limited or lacking resources. Such gaps may involve massive numbers of people. At the agency level, an urban practitioner may need to develop a coalition with colleagues and approach decision-making administrators with suggestions for positive changes. On another level, public policy may not serve clients' best interests. Therefore, strategies to change legislation may include the use of letter-writing or e-mail campaigns to lawmakers, lobbying (seeking direct contact with legislators to influence their opinions), or using the mass media to publicize clients' needs and issues to gain public support for positive change.

2. *Vocal qualities.* Your vocal tone and speech rate also indicate clearly how you feel about another person. Think of how many ways you can say "I am really interested in what you have to say" just by altering your vocal tone and speech rate.

3. *Verbal tracking.* The client has come to you with a topic of concern. Don't change the subject; stick with the client's story.

4. *Body language: attentive.* Clients know you are interested if you face them squarely and lean

slightly forward, have an expressive face, and use facilitative, encouraging gestures. In short, allow yourself to be yourself—authenticity is essential. (p. 65)

A second aspect basic to the development of interviewing skills involves the use of open and closed questions. Ivey and his colleagues (2010) describe the concepts:

Open questions *are those that can't be answered in a few words. They encourage others to talk and provide you with maximum information. Typically, open questions begin with* what, how, why, *or* could: *For example, "Could you tell me what brings you here today?" You will find these helpful as they can facilitate deeper exploration of client issues.*

Closed questions *can be answered in a few words or sentences. They have the advantage of focusing the interview and obtaining information, but the burden of guiding the talk remains on the interviewer. Closed questions often begin with* is, are, *or* do: *For example, "Are you living with your family?" Used judiciously, they enable you to obtain important specifics [emphasis added]. (p. 95)*

A third facet important in interviewing is the use of client observation skills; Ivey and Ivey (2008) reflect:

Jiggling legs, making complete body shifts, or suddenly closing one's arms most often indicates discomfort. Hand and arm gestures may give you an indication of how you and the client are organizing things. Random, discrepant gestures may indicate confusion, whereas a person seeking to control or organize things may move hands and arms in straight lines and point fingers authoritatively. Smooth, flowing gestures . . . may suggest openness. (p. 53)

Professional Roles in Practice with Individuals

Another dimension important in practice with individuals involves the professional roles a worker can assume. Micro-practice roles include counseling, educating, brokering, and case management, all roles described in Chapter 4. In a *counselor* role, social workers follow the planned-change process described in Chapter 4 and help clients develop solutions to problems. For example, a social worker in corrections might work out with a client on parole a plan for finding housing and employment. Or a social worker who does alcohol abuse counseling might explore with a client her reasons for using alcohol and establish plans to maintain sobriety.

In an *educator* role, a social worker might teach an abusive parent effective child management techniques. Similarly, a hospital social worker might inform a person receiving kidney dialysis about the disease's progression and the dialysis process. (*Kidney dialysis* is a process by which a machine removes uric acid and urea from the blood, thereby substituting for the function of normal kidneys.)

Social workers in the *broker* role link clients to needed resources and services. For instance, a social worker might refer a homeless person to a shelter and to agencies providing financial assistance and job training. Social workers performing *case management* functions coordinate services provided by a number of agencies or services on a client's behalf. For example, a client with quadriplegia (i.e., paralysis of all four limbs due to spinal cord injury or disease) might be receiving resources from a variety of agencies including housing, transportation, financial assistance, personal care, and job training. A *case manager* or *case coordinator* synchronizes and oversees services to make sure the client gets what he or she needs.

Note that frequently a social worker may assume a range of roles with the same clients. For example, consider a family including two parents and children ages 2, 4, and 7 that has been referred to a Protective Services worker to assess possible child maltreatment and develop a service plan if necessary. After conducting the assessment, the worker may serve as counselor to help the parents learn to control their anger and behavior more effectively. The educator role might include teaching them child behavior management skills. The worker might serve as broker in linking the family to resources where they receive resources such as rental vouchers (that subsidize rent for eligible families) to ease their economic stress. The practitioner might also take on the facilitator role if these parents participate in a group she's leading of parents that have maltreated their children. Finally, the worker might become an advocate for the family to receive needed services that are not readily available.

Social Work Practice with Families

EP 2.1.7, 2.1.10g

As noted previously, social work with families combines micro and mezzo practice because it involves a small group (i.e., the family) linked by ties of an intimate nature. Working with families is a very

important aspect of social work as later chapters will emphasize (Rasheed & Rasheed, 2008). Collins, Jordan, and Coleman (2010) explain:

> *The primary purpose of family social work is to help families learn to function more competently while meeting the developmental and emotional needs of all members.... There are many ways in which a family social worker can provide on-the-spot, and concrete assistance. For example, when a teenager and a parent become involved in a conflict, the family social worker can work with the conflict to identify the problem and intervene.... A family social worker can help the parent and child to discover what led up to the argument by identifying problematic and repetitive interactions.... The family social worker can assist the parent and teenager to replace problem behavior with more healthy and satisfying interactions. When a young child throws a temper tantrum, the family social worker can teach the parent more effective methods of dealing with problematic behavior on the spot. (p. 3)*

Maluccio, Pine, and Tracy (2002) stress that when working with families, social workers should:

EP 2.1.10b

- *Be responsive to the styles and values of families from communities of color, immigrants, and other special populations [e.g., leaning forward toward the client and maintaining eye contact to demonstrate attentiveness are considered rude and intrusive by many First Nations Peoples].*
- *Break complex tasks into smaller specific steps [e.g., how to look for housing; how to talk with your child's teacher].*
- *Assess the key skills needed for less stressful family interactions [e.g., accepting "no," giving direct commands, handling anger].*
- *Explain and model appropriate skills, using techniques such as role play, modeling, or videotaped practice.*
- *Assess individual learning styles and ways to teach adults and children [e.g., children learn differently as they age with increasing ability for complex thought; an adult may learn more effectively by observing a modeled behavior than being given verbal instructions or vice versa].*

- *Establish homework and other means of ensuring generalization of skills from one setting to another [e.g., asking family members to practice new communication techniques when in their own home setting].*
- *Promote and reward skill acquisition [e.g., praise family members when they follow through on homework or reach goals].*
- *Emphasize strategies that help develop the strengths of family members [e.g., high motivation to improve or exceptional aptitude at coping with family crises].*
- *Motivate the family to stay involved even when faced with challenges and setbacks [e.g., an alcoholic family member falls off the wagon or a teenager runs away]. (pp. 149–150)*

Social workers can also help families deal with crises and problems they encounter in the external environment. For example, if a breadwinner is laid off, a social worker can help the family cope with these new conditions, link the family with available resources, and assist in the search for new employment. Sometimes it's necessary to advocate for resources that aren't readily available or to change social policies that are not in families' best interests.

The Importance of Social Support Systems for Families

Social workers can help families get connected with social support systems that provide four types of support (Ragg, 2006, p. 382). First, *emotional support* involves people "who can listen to the client, understand his situation, provide encouragement, and celebrate his successes." Second, *instrumental support* includes others "who can offer concrete types of help, such as money, rides, shelter, and so forth." Third, *informational support* embraces people "who can provide important information to the client so that she can make the right connections and actions." Fourth, *appraisal support* involves those "who can give honest feedback to the client on how he is performing and acting."

Maluccio and his colleagues (2002) explain:

Social support [including emotional, informational, and concrete] can occur spontaneously, as in one neighbor bringing meals to another, or it can occur in professionally arranged helping networks, such as Meals on Wheels. Formal social services staffed by paid human service professionals...

often provide social support as either the sole or partial focus of their service; for example, a social worker facilitating a parent education group may provide information, resource referrals, skills training, and emotional support for the participants. Informal support... can be delivered by kinship networks, volunteers, or local community groups.... In many cases social workers can be the catalysts that mobilize and enhance various forms of informal helping to benefit individual clients, family members, and communities. (p. 175)

A social worker can identify potential participants in a social support system that might be available to provide various types of support to a family, link the family with participants in the social support system, and facilitate how the system can help the family. For example, a worker could link a family with needed child care resources, including relatives, friends, neighbors, or a day care center. Another example of enhancing social support involves more formal family support programs that "address family self-sufficiency by offering services such as job training, English as a second language, and literacy classes" (Maluccio et al., 2002, p. 151). Still another example concerns "support groups for children experiencing life transitions or losses as in children of divorce, teenage parents, or children of battered women" (Maluccio et al., 2002, p. 184). Community programs such as neighborhood or cultural centers can also provide programming (e.g., recreational or educational) to help once struggling families prosper.

An example of how social support systems can serve a family involves Gene Yuss, age 13, who lived with his mother and younger brother Perry, age 8, in a federal low-income housing project for people whose family incomes are not high enough to pay for regular housing (adapted from Maluccio et al., 2002). Gene, a husky young 5'5" young man with bright red hair, already had a long history of truancy and delinquent behavior including illegal drug use and petty shoplifting. His problematic behavior and connections with delinquent peers were linked to inadequate parental support and supervision.

The family's social worker, Bertha Day, helped Gene's mother, Ms. Yuss, identify more effective means of addressing Gene's behavior. One idea involved having Gene, who was athletically inclined, join the school's football team. Gene, a relatively popular student, already had some mildly positive relationships with other team players who were

Working with families is a very important aspect of social work.

doing well in school and had no problems with the law. Ms. Yuss agreed that joining the team might be a good idea, so she encouraged this plan of action, to which Gene agreed. Meanwhile, Bertha linked Gene with the football coach, who became part of Gene's supportive social network. Bertha and Ms. Yuss contacted Gene's uncle, who lived only a few blocks from the Yuss family, and asked whether he would transport Gene home from practice. The uncle, Ms. Yuss's brother, readily agreed because he had been quite concerned about Gene's downward spiral into trouble. Bertha and Ms. Yuss then asked the Yuss's church to contribute funding needed for required team equipment and transportation costs, which it did.

Another concern was what Gene would do on days when there was no practice. With Ms. Yuss's approval, Bertha worked with Gene to involve him in a number of other after-school activities in which he expressed some interest. Bertha also arranged for a tutor to help him in subjects with which he was having difficulty.

In addition, Bertha worked with Ms. Yuss to link both herself and Gene's younger brother Perry to a broader social support system. Ms. Yuss joined a group for Parents Without Partners (who meet to provide support, discuss mutual concerns about raising children, and offer opportunities for social interaction) and became more actively involved in her church. She signed Perry up both for recreational activities at the local YMCA[1] and as a participant in a Big Brothers program so Perry could have the opportunity to form a special relationship with a supportive adult role model.

In this case, Gene's football team involvement, his linkage with the coach, the uncle's help with transportation, the church's funding contribution, other after-school activities, tutoring, Ms. Yuss's Parents Without Partners group, her church activities, and Perry's YMCA and Big Brothers program involvement all helped to expand and strengthen the Yuss family's social support system.

[1]The YMCA (Young Men's Christian Association) is a global group of organizations that serves to enhance young men's and others' physical, mental, emotional, and interpersonal well-being, and offers a range of recreational and other services (Barker, 2003).

FOCUS ON CRITICAL THINKING 5.2

You, Your Family, and Social Support Systems

We have established that social support systems are very important for individuals and families.

EP 2.1.1b, 2.1.3

Critical Thinking Questions

With what social support systems have you and your family been involved during your lifetime? What kinds of support were provided? In what ways did they help you and your family?

Thus, there is a wide range of social support systems in which people and their families can be involved. Focus on Critical Thinking 5.2 raises questions regarding your own social support systems.

Social Work Practice with Groups

As with other levels of treatment, social work practice with groups can involve any number of problems, goals, and types of people. The two primary types of groups in social work practice are treatment and task.

EP 2.1.7

Treatment Groups

Treatment groups help individuals solve personal problems, change unwanted behaviors, cope with stress, and improve quality of life. Efforts focus on clients solving their personal problems, enhancing personal qualities, or providing each other with support. Highlight 5.3 identifies and defines five primary types of treatment groups—therapy, support, educational, growth, and socialization—and provides examples of each (Toseland & Horton, 2008; Toseland & Rivas, 2012, p. 20). Corey (2012) provides an overview of many treatment groups:

Group counseling has preventive as well as remedial aims. Generally, the [treatment] . . . group has a specific focus, which may be educational, career, social, or personal. Group work emphasizes

interpersonal communication of conscious thoughts, feelings, and behavior within a here-and-now time frame. [Treatment] . . . groups are often problem oriented, and the members largely determine their content and aims. . . . Group counseling tends to be growth oriented in that the emphasis is on

EP 2.1.10b, 2.1.10c, 2.1.10g, 2.1.10i

discovering internal resources of strength. The participants may be facing situational crises and temporary conflicts, struggling with personal or interpersonal problems of living, experiencing difficulties with life transitions, or trying to change self-defeating behaviors. The group provides the empathy and support necessary to create the atmosphere of trust that leads to sharing and exploring these concerns. Group members are assisted in developing their existing skills in dealing with interpersonal problems so that they will be better able to handle future problems of a similar nature.

The group [leader] . . . uses verbal and nonverbal techniques as well as structured exercises. Basically, the role of the group [leader] . . . is to facilitate interaction among the members, help them learn from one another, assist them in establishing personal goals, and encourage them to translate their insights into concrete plans that involve taking action outside of the group. . . . Group [leaders] . . . perform their role largely by teaching members to focus on the here-and-now and to identify the concerns they wish to explore in the group. (p. 4)

HIGHLIGHT 5.3

Treatment Groups in Social Work

There are five major types of treatment groups in social work practice.

1. *Therapy:* Groups that help members with serious psychological and emotional problems change their behavior. Corey (2012) explains:

   "Some therapy groups are primarily designed to correct emotional and behavioral disorders that impede one's functioning or to remediate in-depth psychological problems. The goal may be either a minor or a major transformation of personality structure.... The people who make up the group may be suffering from severe emotional problems, deep personal conflict, effects of trauma, or psychotic states. Many of these individuals are in need of remedial treatment rather than developmental and preventive work" (p. 7).

   Examples: Groups formed to treat "depression, sexual difficulties, anxiety, and psychosomatic disorders"[2] (Corey, Corey, & Corey, 2010, p. 16).

2. *Support:* Groups whose members share common issues or problems and meet on an ongoing basis to cope with stress, give each other suggestions, provide encouragement, convey information, and furnish emotional support (Jacobs, Masson, & Harvill, 2009; Kurtz, 2004). "Strong emotional bonds often develop quickly in support groups because of members' shared experiences. Emotional bonding may also occur because members are stigmatized by the larger community and find comfort and power in their association with each other. Frequently, there is a high level of self-disclosure of emotionally charged material in support groups" (Toseland & Rivas, 2012, p. 23). Note that support groups differ from therapy groups in two main ways. First, support groups place greater emphasis on members supporting and helping each other—in contrast to therapy groups, in which the focus is on the leader assisting members in solving serious personal problems. Second, support groups differ from therapy groups in stressing ongoing coping and support instead of alleviating psychological difficulties.

   Examples: A group of persons living with AIDS, recovering alcoholics, adult survivors of sexual abuse, and veterans experiencing posttraumatic stress disorder.[3]

3. *Educational:* Groups that provide some type of information to participants. "Educational groups are used in a variety of settings, including treatment agencies, schools, nursing homes, correctional institutions, and hospitals. . . . All educational groups are aimed at increasing members' information or skills. Most groups routinely involve presentation of information and knowledge by experts. They also often include opportunities for group discussion to foster learning" (Toseland & Rivas, 2012, pp. 23–24).

   Examples: A group of parents learning child behavior management techniques, teens receiving sex education, a group of older adults interested in finding jobs, and a group of older adults in a nursing home requesting information about their prescribed drugs.

4. *Growth:* Groups aimed at expanding self-awareness, increasing potential, and maximizing health and well-being, "especially through improved relationships with others. They provide a supportive atmosphere in which individuals can gain insights, experiment with new behaviors, get feedback, and grow as human beings. The bond in growth groups stems from members' commitment to help one another develop and maximize their potential" (Toseland & Rivas, 2012, p. 24).

   Examples: A group of heterosexual singles exploring their attitudes about the opposite gender, "a values clarification group for adolescents," and a group of gay men focusing on gay pride issues (Toseland & Rivas, 2012, p. 24).

5. *Socialization:* Groups that help participants improve interpersonal behavior, communication, and social skills so they might better fit into their social environment. "The personal needs of members and the goals of the group are often met through program activities rather than exclusively through group discussion. Thus, socialization groups feature a learning-through-doing approach in which members improve their interpersonal skills by participating in program activities" (Toseland & Rivas, 2012, p. 26).

   Examples: An urban neighborhood's youth activities group, a school-based group of shy teens working to improve interpersonal skills, and a Parents Without Partners group sponsoring various social activities such as parties and outings (Toseland & Rivas, 2012).

(continued)

HIGHLIGHT 5.3 (continued)

Commentary

Sometimes it's difficult to put a particular group in a specific category. What transpires in treatment groups is as complex as the people who make them up. For instance, Fiske (Nov. 11, 2002) describes an exceptionally creative treatment group program with adolescent residents from several group homes developed by Susan Ciardiello, a clinical social worker. Adolescents typically are placed in residential treatment (including group homes and larger institutions) because of behavioral and emotional problems (discussed more thoroughly in later chapters). For many reasons ranging from their normal quest for independence to having had severely negative experiences with the adults in their lives, it's difficult for these young people to trust adults. Fiske emphasizes that "adolescents in groups can provide an environment where they learn from each other and benefit from the wisdom and experience of those traveling the same path" (p. 16).

Ciardiello first surveyed the adolescents to determine their primary interests—not surprisingly, "hip-hop music and basketball" (p. 17). She then pursued a three-faceted group treatment program. First, she divided participants into two co-ed basketball teams that played each other twice a week. However, instead of just playing neighborhood ball, the difference was that she "arranged it so that the players would get points when they demonstrated teamwork and self-control" (p. 17).

The program's second facet involved a biweekly disc jockey program, for which Ciardiello sought funds from a major recording company and purchased equipment. The program consisted of two parts. During the first hour, the group listened to various carefully chosen hip-hop songs that addressed issues significant in the teens' lives such as drugs, poverty, child abuse, romantic relationship concerns, hope for the future, and racial pride. Participants then discussed how the lyrics affected them and related the songs to their own lives. It allowed them to share stories, empathize with each other, provide support, suggest means of coping, and develop trust. During the second hour, participants were rewarded by taking turns being the DJ and even making their own music.

The program achieved such success that a third empowering facet was added. The group members started their own magazine titled *The Real Deal: Kids Keeping It Real.* Through it they could express themselves and their opinions and talk about things that interested them. Ciardiello indicated that this three-pronged approach to a treatment group incorporating sports, music, and writing "decreased unexcused absences from the [group] homes and improved relations among residents" (p. 18).

What type of treatment group would you label this? *Therapeutically,* throughout the three facets of the program, participants worked on identifying feelings and controlling angry outbursts. One potential result was to help them better understand themselves, improve self-esteem, and make more effective decisions to control behavior that caused them problems. Group members also provided *support* to each other by listening to each other's opinions and making suggestions about coping. *Educationally,* participants learned how to be a DJ, a potentially viable job skill, and worked on writing skills through the magazine. As a *growth* group, they worked on expanding awareness of social issues and interpersonal dynamics. Finally, the entire process involved *socialization,* through which they learned how to get along better with their peers. Hence this treatment group appears to be a combination of approaches. It provides a good illustration of how social workers can be ingeniously resourceful and imaginative in their interventions.

---

[2]*Psychosomatic disorders* are physical symptoms (e.g., stomachaches, numbness, pain) caused by emotional problems.
[3]*Posttraumatic stress disorder* is the psychological and emotional reaction to an extremely stressful and disturbing experience such as a battle, rape, fire, or earthquake.

Corey (2012) continues by identifying potential goals sought by treatment group members, including those:

- *To increase awareness and self-knowledge; to develop a sense of one's unique identity*
- *To recognize the commonality of members' needs and problems and to develop a sense of connectedness*
- *To help members learn how to establish meaningful and intimate relationships*
- *To assist members in discovering resources within their extended family and community as ways of addressing their concerns*
- *To increase self-acceptance, self-confidence, self-respect, and to achieve a new view of oneself and others*

- *To learn how to express one's emotions in a healthy way*
- *To develop concern and compassion for the needs and feelings of others*
- *To find alternative ways of dealing with … conflicts*
- *To become aware of one's choices and to make choices wisely*
- *To make specific plans for changing certain behaviors*
- *To learn more effective social skills*
- *To learn how to challenge others with care, concern, honesty, and directness*
- *To clarify one's values and decide whether and how to modify them. (pp. 4–5)*

Task Groups

Task or *work groups* are those applying the principles of group dynamics to solve problems, develop ideas, formulate plans, make decision, and achieve goals. Task groups in the macro social environment are formed to meet the needs of individuals, families, groups, organizations, or communities. For example, an agency task group might focus on developing treatment strategies to meet the needs of Eastern European immigrants seeking agency resources. This targets both individuals and families. Another task group might include social services personnel and representatives from community groups coordinating a neighborhood watch program aimed at preventing crime. This task group works on behalf of various neighborhood groups and the entire community. Still another organizational task group might consist of representatives from various departments to review the agency's policy manual and recommend changes. This task group serves the organization.

The main difference between task and treatment groups is that the task group's aim is to achieve a desired goal or to implement a change in the group's external environment. In contrast, a treatment group's purpose is to alter group members' behaviors or attitudes in the internal group environment (Toseland & Horton, 2008). Highlight 5.4 discusses task groups, which fall into three categories, those meeting client, organizational, and community needs (Toseland & Rivas, 2012).

Focus on Critical Thinking 5.3 on page 149 urges you to consider the types of groups with which you've been involved. They may include task or treatment groups.

Social Work Practice with Organizations and Communities

Macro practice is intervention involving organizations and communities (macro systems). Historically, *community organization* has been the term used to refer to macro practice in social work that is a specific area of practice in its own right. The methods and directions of social work practice have changed and evolved, just as the economic and social realities

EP 2.1.7, 2.1.7a, 2.1.8a, 2.1.8b, 2.1.10g

of the times have drastically changed. However, reviewing the historical perspective on community practice will help us to understand the significance of community assessment and work today.

Traditional methods of community organization engaged in by social workers included social action, social planning, and locality development (Rothman, 2001). *Social action* is coordinated effort to advocate for change in a social institution to benefit a specific population (e.g., homeless people), solve a social problem, correct unfairness (e.g., racism),[4] or enhance people's well-being. Social action applies macro-practice skills to advocate for people in local, state, national, and global communities. Frequently social action can be used to remedy imbalances of power.

Social planning involves "a technical process of problem-solving regarding substantive social problems, such as delinquency, housing, and mental health" (Rothman, 2001, p. 31). Experts or consultants work, usually with designated community leaders, to solve specific problems. People in the general community have little, if any, participation in or input into the problem-solving process. For example, a city might call in an urban renewal expert to recommend what should be done with a deteriorating area in the community.

Locality development emphasizes "community change … pursued through broad participation by a wide spectrum of people at the local community level in determining goals and taking civic action" (Rothman, 2001, p. 29). The idea is to involve as

---

[4]*Racism* is "a belief that race is the primary determinant of human traits and capacities and that racial differences produce an inherent superiority of a particular race," most often resulting in prejudice or discrimination (Mish, 2008, p. 1024).

HIGHLIGHT 5.4

Task Groups in Social Work

Task groups are often found in organizations and communities. They serve the needs of clients, organizations, or communities. Toseland and Rivas (2012) identify the various types:

> Task groups with the primary purpose of serving client needs include teams, treatment conferences, and staff development groups. Task groups with the primary purpose of serving organizational needs include committees, cabinets, and boards of directors. Task groups with a primary purpose of serving community needs include social action groups, coalitions, and delegate councils. (p. 29)

Task Groups Serving Client Needs

1. *Team:* A group of two or more people gathered together to work collaboratively and interdependently to achieve a designated purpose (Daft, 2012; Toseland & Rivas, 2012).

   Example: A team of social workers in a Veteran's Health Administration (VHA) hospital[5] where social workers assigned to the temporary housing unit for homeless vets, a substance abuse counseling unit, and the hospital surgical unit work together on behalf of a homeless vet who is an alcoholic and has serious kidney malfunctioning.

2. *Treatment conference:* A group that meets to establish, monitor, and coordinate service plans on behalf of a client system (Fatout & Rose, 1995; Toseland & Rivas, 2012).

   Example: A group of professionals (including a social worker, psychologist, psychiatrist, physician, teacher, and unit counselor) at a residential treatment center[6] for children with severe behavioral and emotional problems meeting to discuss the progress of a client residing there and to make recommendations for future treatment.

3. *Staff-development groups:* A group that comes together "to improve services to clients by developing, updating, and refreshing workers' skills. Staff development groups provide workers with an opportunity to learn about new treatment approaches, resources, and community services; to practice new skills; and to review and learn from their previous work with clients" (Toseland & Rivas, 2012, p. 34).

   Example: A group of social workers and other counseling professionals who work at a mental health clinic attend a series of seminars about the use and effects of various psychotropic drugs (drugs that affect the mind and behavior).

Task Groups Serving Organizational Needs

4. *Committee:* A group of persons "delegated to consider, investigate, take action on, or report on some matter" (Daft, 2012; Mish, 2008, p. 250).

   Example: A group of staff representatives appointed to investigate, assess, and make recommendations about the quality of food served in a nursing home.

5. *Cabinet:* A group formed "to provide advice and expertise about policy issues to chief executive officers or other high-level administrators. Policies, procedures, and practices that affect the entire organization are discussed, developed, or modified in cabinets before being announced by a senior administrative officer" (Toseland & Rivas, 2012, pp. 36–37).

   Example: "A weekly meeting of supervisory social work staff and the director of social services in a large municipal hospital" (Toseland & Rivas, 2012, p. 37).

6. *Board of directors:* "A group of people authorized to formulate the organization's mission, objectives, and policies, in addition to overseeing the organization's ongoing activities. A board of directors also has ultimate control over the agency's higher administration, including its executive director or chief executive officer" (Kirst-Ashman, 2011, pp. 123–124).

   Example: "Members of the governing board of a family service agency" (Toseland & Rivas, 2012, p. 37).

Task Groups Serving Community Needs

7. *Social action group:* A group formed to engage in some planned-change effort to modify or improve aspects of their macro social or physical environment (Staples, 2004; Toseland & Rivas, 2012).

   Example: A group of agency workers and clients who join forces to conduct a letter-writing campaign to legislators to place stoplights at a dangerous intersection.

8. *Coalition:* An alliance "of individuals, groups, and organizations with similar goals that become more

(continued)

HIGHLIGHT 5.4 (continued)

influential and powerful when united" (Kirst-Ashman, 2011, p. 148). "Coalition members agree to pursue common goals, which they believe cannot be achieved by any of the members acting alone" (Toseland & Rivas, 2012, p. 40).

Example: "A group of family planning and community health-care clinics who have formed a prochoice coalition to influence state and federal legislation on abortion" (Toseland & Rivas, 2012, p. 40).

9. *Delegate council:* A group of representatives from a series of agencies or units within a single agency that meet to discuss issues of mutual concern. Representatives may be elected by their constituencies or appointed by agency decision makers; goals may include "facilitating interagency communication and cooperation, studying communitywide social issues or social problems, engaging in collective social action, and governing large organizations" (Toseland & Rivas, 2012, p. 41).

Example: A group of professionals working in rape crisis centers throughout a state, with each agency designating a representative to meet in the council to discuss education and treatment issues.

---

[5]The Veterans Health Administration offers veterans an extensive array of health and mental health services. These include inpatient hospital care; outpatient health care; in-home care; nursing home care; medication; reproductive health care for women; and inpatient and outpatient (intensive or regular) mental health counseling to meet many needs including readjustment after return from active duty, mental disorders, substance use disorders, and suicide prevention (U.S. Department of Veterans Affairs, 2011b).

[6]Discussed more thoroughly in a later chapter, a *residential treatment center* is an agency that provides children with serious emotional and behavioral problems with residential round-the-clock care; education (often with an emphasis on special education); interpersonal skills training; and individual, group, and sometimes family therapy.

---

many people as possible within the community in a democratic manner to define their goals and help themselves. Locality development fits extremely well with social work values because individual dignity, participation, and free choice are emphasized.

Macro Practice Today

EP 2.1.5c, 2.1.8a, 2.1.10k

Today macro practice remains a major thrust of generalist social work. The basic concept of community is just as important as ever. However, Rothman (2007) proposes a new outlook more appropriate to current macro practice that calls for "multi modes of intervention" (p. 11). Two new ideas predominate.

One major initiative is that the traditional three community organization methods should be updated to reflect a modification in focus. First, "social advocacy" should replace social action (Rothman, 2007, p. 12). "*Social advocacy* deems the application of pressure as the best course of action to take against people or institutions that may have [brought about]...the problem or that stand in the way of its solution—which frequently involves promoting equity or social justice. When interests clash in this way, conflict is a given" (p. 12). Advocacy becomes the focus of attention.

"Planning and policy practice" then replace the traditional social planning approach (Rothman, 2007, p. 12). Planning continues to involve "proposing and enacting particular solutions" (p. 12). *Policy practice* entails "efforts to change policies in legislative, agency, and community settings, whether by establishing new policies, improving existing ones, or defeating the policy initiatives of other people" (Jansson, 2011, p. 15). Establishing policy becomes the objective.

"Community capacity development" is substituted for community development (Rothman, 2007, p. 12). "*Community capacity development* assumes that change is best accomplished when the people affected by problems are empowered with the knowledge and skills needed to understand their problems, and then work cooperatively together to overcome them. Thus there is a premium on consensus as a tactic and on social solidarity [unity including diverse community groups that is based on mutual interests, support, and goals] as [a means]...and outcome" (p. 12). Here community *capacity* (the potential use of the community's inherent strengths, resources, citizen participation, and leadership) is stressed.

The second primary initiative posed for contemporary macro practice involves the flexibility of mixing various aspects of these three approaches to get things done. Rothman (2007) reflects that macro practice is often a complex process that requires emphasizing various aspects of these three approaches depending on the situation. For example, planning and policy practice may require varying degrees of social advocacy. *Advocacy*, of course, involves stepping forward on the behalf of the client system in order to promote fair and equitable treatment or gain needed resources. *Policy advocacy* is "policy practice that aims to help powerless groups, such as women, children, poor people, persons of color, gay men and lesbians, and people with disabilities to improve their resources and opportunities" (Jansson, 2011, p. 15).

Rothman (2007) provides several examples of people undertaking policy advocacy to improve policies that affect groups at risk of harm; these policy advocates include:

> *Dr. David Kessler, who as head of the Federal Drug Administration clashed with the pharmaceutical companies on behalf of safe and affordable medications for patients; Dr. Everett Koop, who as Surgeon General, stood up to the cigarette companies in the first major effort to warn the public about the serious health dangers in smoking; and Peter Edelman, who faced off with the Clinton administration over sizable service cuts affecting welfare recipients (p. 21).*

Another example of a more flexible combination of methods involves community capacity development with an emphasis on planning. Rothman (2007) explains:

> *Classic [community] capacity development typically has the practitioner starting with a blank page and encouraging residents to decide what situations within their community bother them the most and then what changes they want to initiate....*

> *Community economic [capacity] development [that emphasizes planning], on the other hand, starts with a concrete agenda and organizing mechanisms. It believes that what distressed communities need most is an upgrade of economic conditions. Residents are called on to mount programs and actions that will accomplish that. According to Soifer (2002), this means concentrating on housing development, land development, job creation, and setting up more relevant financial institutions—primarily banks. (p. 25)*

Skills in Macro Practice

Necessary macro skills involve at least three facets (Kirst-Ashman & Hull, 2012a). First, agency or public social policies may require change. For example, social workers may advocate to change a policy that requires all persons receiving public assistance to undergo mandatory drug testing—a practice that is expensive, condescending, and invasive.

A second important macro skill entails initiating and conducting projects within agency or community contexts. An example of a project is fundraising for homeless families in need of food and clothing. Another is initiating an in-service training program to teach agency staff a new treatment technique. (*In-service training programs* are educational sessions provided by an agency for its staff to develop their skills or improve their effectiveness.)

A third significant macro skill concerns planning and implementing new social service programs within an agency or community. An example is development of a program to educate students on a college campus about date rape. Another is developing a new recreation and field trip program for residents in a nursing home.

FOCUS ON CRITICAL THINKING 5.3

Participation in Groups

EP 2.1.1b, 2.1.3

Think of a task or treatment group in which you've participated and consider the following.

Critical Thinking Questions

What kind of group was it? What was the group's purpose? To what extent was the group effective (i.e., did it achieve its goals)? Why or why not? How would you describe the group's functioning? Who led the group and how well was it directed? How could the group's functioning have been improved?

Generalist Practice: A Multi-Level Process

EP 2.1.10g

The point of generalist social work practice is to seek change at all levels of practice, depending on what the client system needs. Many times, a social worker will simultaneously pursue a combination of goals involving change at the individual, family, group, organizational, or community level.

For example, a teacher refers Ralph, age 8, to Juanita, the school social worker. The teacher reports that Ralph is consistently mounting fellow students on the playground in a manner resembling sexual intercourse (more vulgarly referred to as "humping"). Ralph also makes frequent sexual comments and uses sexual language quite inappropriate for his age. Juanita suspects the possibility of sexual abuse. (A later chapter on child welfare discusses child sexual abuse in more depth.)

At the individual (micro) level, Juanita talks with Ralph about what's occurring in his life at home. She informs the school principal, Adolf, that she intends to report the situation to Child Protective Services, which would initiate a more thorough investigation. Adolf forbids Juanita to make the referral on the basis that there is not enough evidence. Why cause trouble when you don't have to? But in her state, Juanita is required to report any *suspected* child abuse (which includes sexual abuse). Juanita knows that it is her ethical responsibility to report Ralph's behavior.

At the organizational and community (macro) levels, Juanita must address the issue with Adolf and possibly the School Board, which supervises Adolf. The school (a macro system) must change so that it becomes responsive to instances of possible abuse instead of simply ignoring them. In the event that Ralph's victimization is proved, family counseling may be called for at the micro/mezzo level and possibly group therapy for Ralph at the mezzo level.

Professional Organizations in Social Work

The National Association of Social Workers

The National Association of Social Workers (NASW) has already been mentioned several times, especially with respect to its *Code of Ethics*. Established in 1955, NASW is the major social work organization with the largest and broadest membership in the profession. Persons holding bachelor's or master's degrees in social work and students in accredited social work programs can join.

EP 2.1.1, 2.1.8a, 2.1.8b

NASW fulfills at least five purposes. First, membership in a professional organization lends credibility. Most, if not all, established professions have an organization to which members can belong. Such membership bolsters members' professional identity, helps them identify with other members, and enhances the visibility of a profession.

NASW's second purpose is to provide opportunities for networking. State, regional, and national conferences and meetings enable members to talk with each other and share news and ideas. Such meetings also provide a means for finding out about new career and job opportunities.

NASW's third purpose is to provide membership services. These include *Social Work,* a quarterly journal that addresses various aspects of practice; *NASW News,* a national newspaper published almost monthly that focuses on relevant research, social welfare policy and service issues, and social workers' accomplishments around the country and the world; and newsletters published by some state chapters.

NASW's fourth purpose is to sponsor organized efforts for lobbying on behalf of socially responsible social welfare policies and services. NASW exerts influence in support of causes and political agendas concurrent with professional social work values. It has also helped states establish licensing or certification regulations for social workers. Highlight 5.5 discusses the importance of licensing for social workers and identifies the common levels of practice.

NASW's fifth purpose is to publish policy statements on various issues (e.g., youth suicide, health care, people with disabilities, affirmative action, and environmental policy) to help guide members in their practice (NASW, 2009).

Numerous other organizations reflect more specific facets or subsets of social work. Examples include the Association of Community Organization and Social Administration (ACOSA) and the National Association of Black Social Workers (NABSW).

The Council on Social Work Education

The Council on Social Work Education (CSWE) is the body that accredits bachelor's and master's programs in social work education. A doctorate of

HIGHLIGHT 5.5

Social Work Licensure and Categories of Social Work Practice

**EP 2.1.1,
2.1.1c**

Every state, the District of Columbia, Puerto Rico, the Virgin Islands, and every Canadian province have laws that define and regulate social work practice, involving some form of licensure or certification (Association of Social Works Boards [ASWB], 2008).

Social work licensure means that one has fulfilled designated requirements to practice social work in a particular state. Certification is used instead of licensure in a number of states. Some feel that *licensure* is a stronger word, implying more advanced skills than *certification*. For example, a social worker with a bachelor's degree might be certified, and one with a master's degree licensed.

Many states have several levels of licensing or certification and require an examination and possibly some work experience (at least for higher levels) to qualify for each level (Ginsberg, 2001).

Typically, there are four categories of practice that jurisdictions may legally regulate.

1. *Bachelors:* Baccalaureate social work degree upon graduation.
2. *Masters:* Master's degree in social work (MSW) with no post-degree experience.
3. *Advanced Generalist:* MSW with two years of post-master's supervised experience.
4. *Clinical:* MSW with two years of post-master's direct clinical social work experience. (ASWB, 2011)

The Association of Social Work Boards (ASWB), initiated in 1979, established and sustains licensing examinations for social workers in 48 states, the District of Columbia, the U.S. Virgin Islands, and Alberta, Canada (ASWB, 2008).[7] Although some states offer licenses or certification for only one level of practice, most offer such validation at two or more levels of practice. The structure of examinations and specific requirements for each level vary from state to state, so people interested in becoming a social worker should explore the regulations in their own state, province, or jurisdiction. ASWB examinations for each level include 170 multiple-choice questions that are administered electronically and provide four hours for test completion (ASWB, 2011). Because of the differences from one jurisdiction to another, certification or licensure does not automatically transfer from one locale to another (ASWB, 2011). Social workers with licensure

or certification in one state who want similar recognition in some other state must complete the application process in that other state.

Note that 37 states, the District of Columbia, the Virgin Islands, and nine Canadian provinces require some form of licensure or certification for BSWs (ASWB, 2008). For each social work program, the ASWB can report the percentages of people taking the ASWB basic examination who pass the first time and who pass when they repeat the test.

A major purpose of licensing is to protect clients from unqualified service providers and maintain the legitimacy of the profession (Licensure, October 2004). Ginsberg (2001) comments on the significance of a social work degree with respect to licensing and getting jobs:

> Although there are many professions engaged in human services work, it is becoming the law in most states that persons may not refer to themselves as social workers or hold a position designated as a social work job unless they have a social work degree. State licensing and regulation laws . . . provide legal protection for the title of social worker. But even without legal regulation, many social work employers want employees with social work preparation because they understand the social services system and have developed some of the skills needed to practice social work. (p. 44)

Additional Credentials

Whereas licensing and certification represent minimal standards to protect clients as consumers of services, the National Association of Social Workers (NASW) credentials represent an even "higher level of competence" (Licensure, October 2004, p. 12). NASW "establishes and promotes additional standards and credentials required for excellence in the practice of social work. A credential certifies that a social worker has achieved competence and professionalism beyond a college degree or state license. Credentials generally require a degree, supervised experience, and a standard examination" (NASW, 2004).[8] Such advanced credentials include these (NASW, 2011):

- Academy of Certified Social Workers (ACSW), the first credential established for the profession that "served to designate the credential holder as competent for independent practice."
- Diplomate in Clinical Social Work (DCSW), "the highest distinction bestowed on clinical social

(continued)

HIGHLIGHT 5.5 (continued)

workers" (work in settings addressing mental health issues or private practice).
- Advanced practice specialty certifications for the MSW in the following areas:
  - Qualified Clinical Social Worker (QCSW), recognizing social workers "who have met *national* standards of knowledge, skill, and experience in clinical social work."
  - Clinical (CSW-G) and Advanced (ASW-G) Social Worker in Gerontology
  - Certified Clinical Alcohol, Tobacco, and Other Drugs Social Workers (C-CATODSW)
  - Advanced Certified Hospice and Palliative Care Social Worker (ACHP-SW)
  - Certified Advanced Children, Youth, and Family Social Worker (C-ACYFSW)
  - Certified Social Worker in Health Care (C-SWHC)

- Certified Advanced Social Work Case Manager (C-ASWCM)
- Certified School Social Work Specialist (C-SSWS)
- Practice specialty certifications for the BSW in the following areas:
  - Social Worker in Gerontology (SW-G)
  - Certified Hospice and Palliative Care Social Worker (CHP-SW)
  - Certified Children, Youth, and Family Social Worker (C-CYFSW)
  - Certified Social Work Case Manager (C-SWCM)

---

[7]More information can be obtained at **http://www.aswb.org**.
[8]For more information on specific requirements for advanced credentials, see **http://www.naswdc.org/credentials/default.asp.**

---

social work and doctorate of philosophy in social work are also available, but CSWE has determined that they need not be accredited. CSWE's membership is composed primarily of social work educators but also includes practitioners. CSWE develops guidelines for the social work curriculum as explained in Chapter 1. In social work, *accreditation* is the official confirmation that a school, college, or program fulfills the necessary requirements in curricular development, program structure, resources, and academic achievement to assume that status.

It is important to make sure a social work program is accredited. To be eligible for licensure or certification, many states require graduation from an accredited program. In the United States there are currently 473 accredited baccalaureate (BSW) programs with 23 more in candidacy for accreditation, and 209 master's (MSW) programs with 19 more in candidacy (CSWE, 2011). According to the Group for the Advancement of Doctoral Education (GADE), there were 74 doctoral (Ph.D. or DSW) programs in the United States as of June 2009 (U.S. Department of Labor, 2008).

Careers in Social Work

Because social workers are employed in such varied areas of human life, it is difficult to gather accurate

data on what members of the entire profession are doing. The Bureau of Labor Statistics predicts that between 2008 and 2018 the number of social workers will increase by 16%, "which is *faster than the average* for all occupations" (U.S. Department of Labor, 2009).

Highlight 5.6 summarizes the findings of two surveys addressing the fields of practice in which social workers are employed. Ongoing research by a group involved with the Association of Baccalaureate Social Work Program Directors (BPD) regularly collects information about BSW graduates that reflects BSW employment both at graduation and two years thereafter (hereafter referred to as *alumni*) (G. H. Hull, personal communication, November 22, 2004; Buchan, Hull, Rogers, Rodenhiser, & Smith, 2004).[9] Another survey, sponsored by the National Association of Social Workers (NASW), reviews the major fields of practice in which MSWs (full-time) tend to be employed (O'Neill, 2003). Respondents in this study were all NASW members, the vast majority of whom have MSWs (versus BSWs as their highest degree or degrees in

---

[9]Information is gathered by a BPD team using the Baccalaureate Educational Assessment Package BEAP. Current members are Vicky Buchan, Brian Christenson, Ruth Gerritsen-McKane, Tobi Delong Hamilton, Roy Rodenhiser, and Marshall Smith.

HIGHLIGHT 5.6

Employment Settings for Social Workers by Fields of Practice

	BSWs (Employment at Graduation)	BSWs (2 Years Postgraduation)	MSWs
Corrections/criminal justice	34.5%	3.0%	–%
Child welfare/child protective services	12.6	18.7	–
Child welfare/family	–	–	7
Youth services	7.1	–	–
Mental/behavioral health	6.1	14.9	37
Aging/geriatrics	5.4	11.1	4
Family services	5.3	7.9	–
Mental retardation/developmental disabilities	5.0	6.0	–
Alcohol, drug, or substance abuse	4.4	3.9	3
Crisis intervention	2.9	4.3	–
School social work	2.6	5.5	5
Health/medical care	2.5	7.3	8
Violence/victim services	2.2	2.0	1
Education/training	1.7	2.1	–
Housing	1.2	1.3	–
Public assistance/public welfare	1.0	1.5	–
Adult protective services	.7	.7	
Community planning	.7	1.5	<1
Group services	.6	.9	–
Rehabilitation	.5	1.0	–
Grief/bereavement	.3	.7	–
Income maintenance	.2	.3	–
Occupational/EAP[10]	.1	.4	1
Adolescents	–	–	3
Disabilities	–	–	1

[10]EAP stands for Employee Assistance Programs, which are services provided by organizations that focus on the prevention and treatment of workers' mental health and adjustment problems that interfere with their work performance. Chapter 13 describes them more fully.

other fields). Note that dashes in the chart reflect lack of data due to different data-gathering techniques.

Be cautious when interpreting this information, however, because a major difference between the two surveys involves social workers' years of experience. For example, BSW respondents have only 2 years of experience at the time of the survey, whereas MSWs have a median (midpoint) of 16 years (Survey Data, 2004). There's no way to tell how results might differ if both groups had identical lengths of experience.

Note that the two surveys reflect some different categories because data were not gathered in identical ways. The categories listed here for MSWs reflect only those in which the most social workers were employed. Because of this and because some responses didn't fit clearly into defined categories, none of the columns add up to 100%.

It's interesting to note that few social workers (of BSWs, 1.2% at graduation and 1.8% two years after) are employed in public welfare and income maintenance. This refutes the stereotype of a social worker sitting in a drab office reviewing applications for welfare checks. Rather, the BSW survey reflects the wide range of practice contexts where social workers find employment.

Let's focus for a moment on the differences in employment settings experienced by BSWs who have jobs at graduation and what they're doing as alumni two years later. Figure 5.1 highlights the differences in practice areas where most BSWs find jobs. Whereas over a third of people at graduation find jobs in corrections, for two-year alumni this drops to only 3%. What are the implications? Might it be that it's relatively easy to find jobs in corrections, but most people discover they don't like it and leave quickly?

The second most common job placement for BSWs at graduation is child welfare and protective services: 12.6% of BSWs start out there. Two years later this figure jumps to 18.7% of BSWs surveyed. BSW alumni also shift in greater numbers to the fields of mental health, aging, and health care. Smaller increases occur in family services, school social work, developmental disabilities, and crisis intervention.

Figure 5.2 compares BSW alumni with MSWs concerning their fields of practice. Three major trends immediately surface. First, the largest proportion of MSWs (37%) work in mental health. Second, most BSWs work in the child welfare/family arena (26.6%).[11] Third, BSWs are also somewhat more likely to work in the areas of aging and disabilities than their MSW counterparts.[12] Note that although fewer than 1% of MSWs cited "community development" as their major practice field, 4% indicated that they were engaged in this area to some extent.

An alternative approach to examining where social workers are employed involves the structure and funding sources of the agency. An earlier part of this chapter discussed public and private organizational settings. Figure 5.3 depicts where BSWs (at their first social work job) and MSWs are employed in the public and private sectors (G. H. Hull, personal communication, November 22, 2004; O'Neill, 2003). This can provide clues regarding where to seek jobs.

Most social workers at both the BSW and MSW level are employed in private social service agencies, with the rest (more than a third) working in public agencies. Over one-third of BSWs get their first

social work job in private *nonprofit* nonreligious settings (e.g., family service agencies, Planned Parenthood, United Way). In contrast, over one-third of MSWs work in private *for-profit* agencies. This probably reflects the significant number of MSWs providing private therapy in agencies where a major goal is to make a profit. Note that BSWs are also more likely than MSWs to work in public *state* agencies. The smaller percentages of practitioners working for the federal government include both military and nonmilitary jobs, with military jobs being less common.

Services provided to clients by BSWs and MSWs also vary somewhat, as illustrated in Figures 5.4 and 5.5, respectively. Data were gathered differently in the two surveys, so the charts use different formats to illustrate results. BSW alumni were asked to cite their four prioritized major roles; Figure 5.4 summarizes what they felt their first major role was (G. H. Hull, personal communication, November 22, 2004). Over 38% identified case management (the coordination of needed services provided by any number of agencies, organizations, or facilities) as their primary role. Advocacy (speaking out on behalf of clients to promote fair and equitable treatment or gain needed resources) was cited by more than one-quarter of respondents. Other roles mentioned were counseling, identified by almost 12%; administration, almost 8%; coordination, almost 5%; brokering (linking client systems to needed resources), almost 2%; and providing education and training, almost 2%. Other roles (consultant, mediator, facilitator, and so on) were identified by fewer than 1% each.

The NASW survey asked MSWs what services they typically provided to their clients without prioritizing them (Survey Data, 2004). As Figure 5.5 illustrates, 81% identified counseling, 23% information and referral, 22% screening and assessment, 20% case management, 14% crisis management, and 7% medication adherence assistance services. It's notable that "social workers in organizational settings provided more information/referral, screening/assessment, case management, and crisis interventions than those in private practice settings" (p. 8). Private practice focuses on providing some type of counseling or therapy, usually within an office context, to address some psychological issue or problem for a specified fee. Twenty-three percent of MSWs surveyed work only in private practice, 18% work both in private practice and organizational

---

[11]Note that the categories in the BSW study of *child welfare/protective services* and *family services* were combined to reflect this result. The intent is to compare this figure with the MSW study's category of *child welfare/family*.

[12]Note that the BSW study uses the term *mental retardation/developmental disabilities*, whereas the MSW study simply uses the word *disabilities*.

Figure 5.1 Employment of BSW Graduates

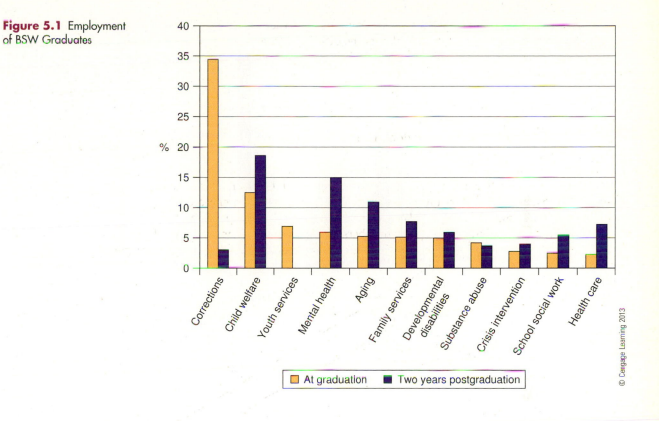

At graduation   Two years postgraduation

© Cengage Learning 2013

Figure 5.2 BSW and MSW Fields of Practice

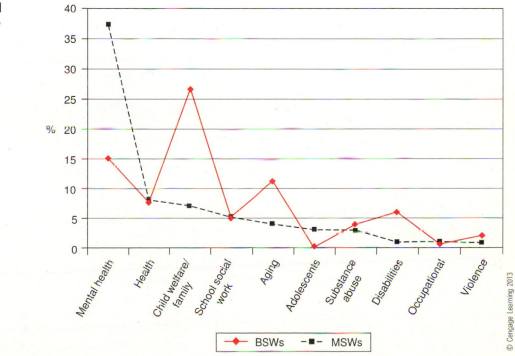

BSWs   MSWs

© Cengage Learning 2013

Figure 5.3 Public- and Private-sector Employment

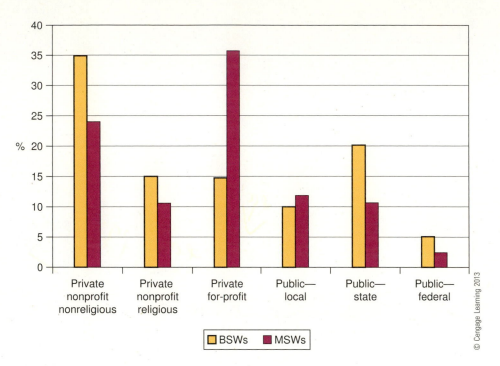

Figure 5.4 BSWs' Major Roles

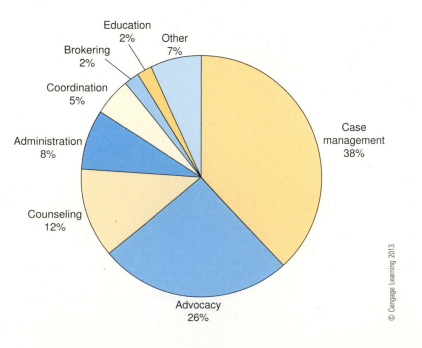

settings, and 45% work only in organizational settings (Survey Data, 2004, p. 8).

When we compare Figures 5.4 and Figure 5.5, at least two implications are evident. Both BSWs and MSWs provide counseling and case management. However, BSWs are much more likely to view case management as a major role, whereas MSWs tend to focus on counseling. Second, over one-quarter of BSWs identify advocacy as a major function, which we have established as a critical basis of the profession.

Figure 5.5 MSW Services to Clients

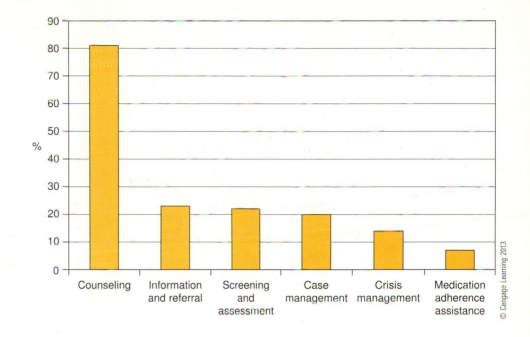

© Cengage Learning 2013

Social Work Salaries

When looking at salary data, remember that there is tremendous variation in salary from one geographic location, field of practice, and type of job (e.g., direct service versus administration) to another. Standards of living (including rent, utilities, and taxes) vary dramatically between parts of the country. Take this into consideration when reading the salary data discussed here. The idea is to give you a general picture of what to expect as a BSW entering the field and as a seasoned MSW who has been in the field many years.

It makes sense that more education usually provides greater opportunities and potentially higher salaries. BSWs tend to work at the foundation level of practice with skills that apply to social work fields of practice across the board, whereas MSWs tend to specialize. People with MSW degrees earn significantly more than those with BSWs (G. H. Hull, personal communication, April 4, 2011; O'Neill, 2003; Pace, 2010).

The Bureau of Labor Statistics[13] cites annual earning information for social workers (U.S. Department of Labor, 2008). However, please note that it does not distinguish between BSWs and MSWs. It also divides the fields of practice differently than the other surveys, structuring information within the following three major dimensions (U.S. Department of Labor, 2009):

1. *"Child, family, and school social workers"* (45.6% of the total) who "provide social services and assistance to improve the social and psychological functioning of children and their families." Subcategories in this practice area include work in elementary and secondary schools, local government, state government, individual and family services, and other residential care facilities.

2. *"Medical and public health social workers"* (21.6% of the total) who "provide psychosocial support to people, families, or vulnerable populations so they can cope with chronic, acute, or terminal illnesses, such as Alzheimer's disease, cancer, or AIDS." Subcategories in this practice include work in general medical and surgical hospitals, home health care services, local government, nursing care facilities, and individual and family services.

3. *"Mental health and substance abuse social workers"* (21.4% of the total) who "assess and treat individuals with mental illness or substance abuse problems, including abuse of alcohol, tobacco, or other drugs." Subcategories in this practice area include local government; psychiatric and substance abuse hospitals; individual and family services; residential mental retardation, mental

---

[13]For further information, you may access the Bureau of Labor Statistics' Website at **http://www.bls.gov/oco/pdf/ocos060.pdf.**

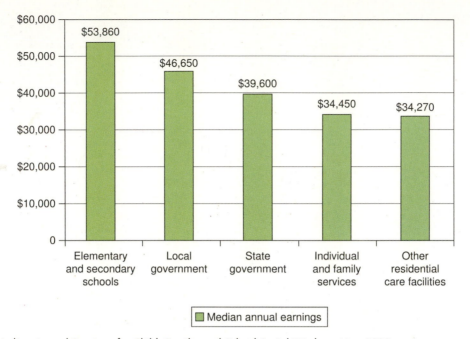

Figure 5.6 Median Annual Earnings for Child, Family, and School Social Workers, May 2008

Source: U.S. Department of Labor. (2009). *Occupational outlook handbook 2010–2011: Social workers.* Retrieved May 7, 2011, from http://www.bls.gov/oco/ocos060.htm

health and substance abuse facilities; and outpatient mental health, and substance abuse centers.

Figure 5.6 through Figure 5.8 report the median annual earnings for the various subcategories in these three general dimensions.[14] Figure 5.9 summarizes median annual earnings for the remaining 11.4% of social workers who do not fit into these three practice dimensions; these jobs include other social work positions in local government, state government, and individual and family services.

Figure 5.10 compares median annual earnings in all four categories reflected in Figure 5.6 through Figure 5.9 (U.S. Department of Labor, 2009). Social workers who work in mental health and substance abuse had median annual earnings of $37,210. "The middle 50 percent [in this category] earned between $28,910 and $48,560." Child, family, and school social workers had median annual earnings of $39,550. "The middle 50 percent [in this category] earned between $31,040 and $52,080." Medical and public health social workers had median annual earnings of $46,650. "The middle 50 percent [in this category]

earned between $35,550 and $57,690." Social workers not falling into any of these categories had median annual incomes of $46,220. "The middle 50 percent [of this remaining unlabeled category] earned between $34,420 and $60,850."

Prior research has established a number of other facts (Practitioners Surveyed, 2003; Survey Data, 2004). Social workers in private practice (which requires an MSW) earn higher salaries than workers in organizational contexts. Practicing for longer periods of time as a social worker also is related to higher earnings. One 2009 survey found that the median base pay for NASW members (the vast majority of whom are MSWs) was "$55,000 a year, with 12 percent earning $90,000 a year or more and 12 percent earning under $30,000" (Pace, 2010, p. 8). Assessment data gathered nationally in 2009 found that two years after graduation, the mean social work income for BSWs was $27,044 and the median $28,000. The implication of these studies is that MSWs earn significantly higher wages than BSWs.

Another influential variable involves gender (Brandwein, 2008; Pace, 2010). Employment in professions characterized by a majority of women, such as social work, pays less than occupations where men prevail (Brandwein, 2008). In 2004,

---

[14]The *median* is the midpoint where one half of all social workers earn more than the median and one half earn less.

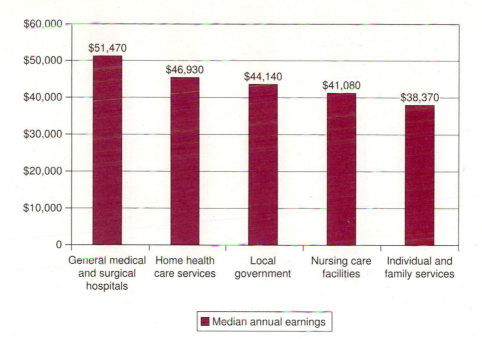

Figure 5.7 Median Annual Earnings for Medical and Public Health Social Workers, May 2008

SOURCE: U.S. Department of Labor. (2009). *Occupational outlook handbook 2010–2011: Social workers.* Retrieved May 7, 2011, from http://www.bls.gov/oco/ocos060.htm

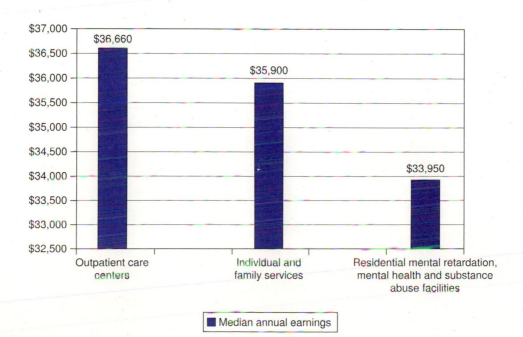

Figure 5.8 Median Annual Earnings for Mental Health and Substance Abuse Social Workers, May 2008

SOURCE: U.S. Department of Labor. (2009). *Occupational outlook handbook 2010–2011: Social workers.* Retrieved May 7, 2011, from http://www.bls.gov/oco/ocos060.htm

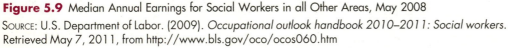

Figure 5.9 Median Annual Earnings for Social Workers in all Other Areas, May 2008

SOURCE: U.S. Department of Labor. (2009). *Occupational outlook handbook 2010–2011: Social workers.* Retrieved May 7, 2011, from http://www.bls.gov/oco/ocos060.htm

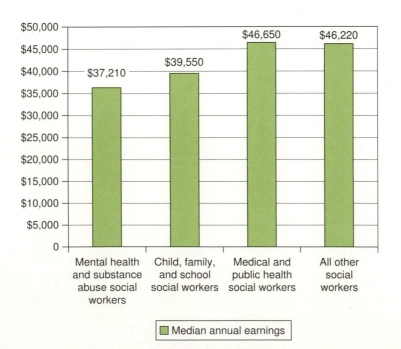

Figure 5.10 Median Annual Earnings for Social Workers in the Four Major Dimensions of Practice, May 2006

SOURCE: U.S. Department of Labor. (2009). *Occupational outlook handbook 2010–2011: Social workers.* Retrieved May 7, 2011, from http://www.bls.gov/oco/ocos060.htm

male social workers earned 14% more than their female counterparts, even when other variables such as educational level, field of practice, and practice experience were controlled (Brandwein, 2008). The 2009 NASW survey indicated that male social workers' salaries surpassed females' by over 17% (Pace, 2010).

The Future Employment Outlook for Social Work

According to the Bureau of Labor Statistics (2009):

Job prospects are expected to be favorable. Many job openings will stem from growth and the need to replace social workers who leave the occupation. However, competition for social worker jobs is expected in cities where training programs for social workers are prevalent. Opportunities should be good in rural areas, which often find it difficult to attract and retain qualified staff. By specialty, job prospects may be best for those social workers with a background in gerontology [as the older adult population is growing and will continue to increase as the "baby boomers" retire and eventually require more services] and substance abuse treatment.

Chapter Summary

The following summarizes this chapter's content as it relates to the chapter's learning objectives presented at the beginning of the chapter. Learning objectives include the following statements:

A Identify the context of social work practice today in organizations and communities.

Social services include the tasks that social work practitioners and other helping professionals perform with the goal of improving people's health, enhancing their quality of life, increasing autonomy and independence, supporting families, and helping people and larger systems improve their functioning in the social environment. A community is "a number of people who have something in common with one another that connects them in some way and that distinguishes them from others" (Homan, 2011, p. 8). From a social work perspective, communities are entities in which citizens can organize or be organized to address mutual concerns and improve their overall quality of life.

B Explain the core treatment approaches in practice with individuals, families, groups, organizations, and communities.

Micro practice is intervention involving an individual client (a micro system). Working with families combines micro and mezzo practice because it involves a small group (i.e., the family) linked by ties of an intimate nature. Social support systems can provide various types of support to family members. Mezzo practice is social work intervention with groups. Treatment groups include therapy, support, educational, growth, and socialization groups. Task groups include teams, treatment conferences, staff-development groups, committees, cabinets, boards of directors, social action groups, coalitions, and delegate councils. Macro practice is intervention involving organizations and communities (macro systems). Traditional macro practice or community organization may involve three approaches—social planning, locality development, and social action. Contemporary macro-practice approaches include "social advocacy," "policy practice," and "community capacity development" (Rothman, 2007, p. 12). Macro practice can address agency or public policy change, project initiation, and program development. The point of generalist social work practice is to seek change at any levels of practice, depending on what the client system needs.

C Explore the special contexts of social work in rural and urban communities.

Rural communities involve those having low population density, being located far from urban hubs, and concentrating activities in some specialized area such as farming or lumbering. Social workers practicing in rural communities must be true generalists, providing a wide range of services. They must work in close cooperation with other agencies. They must strive to understand the community and its values, developing relationships with community residents. Dual or multiple relationships must be addressed carefully. It's important to emphasize the strengths inherent in a rural community.

Urban social work is practiced within the context of large cities, with their vast array of social problems, exceptional diversity, and potential resources. Urban communities are characterized by their own special conditions. Problems characterizing urban communities include multiple problems resulting from dense population, widespread occurrence of discriminatory behavior, migration of people unprepared for the stress of urban living, financial shortfalls or unavailability of resources for a large population, and higher stress levels. Urban social workers should pay close attention to human diversity, understand their agency environment, seek resources in the external urban environment, and use advocacy when necessary.

D Identify some of the major professional associations in social work.

Professional organizations in social work include the National Association of Social Workers and the Council on Social Work Education.

E Describe social work licensure.

All states have laws that define and regulate social work practice, involving some form of licensure or certification. Typical categories of licensure include bachelors, masters, advanced generalist, and clinical. NASW provides a range of advanced and specialized credentials.

F Propose questions to stimulate critical thinking about participation in various systems.

Critical thinking questions addressed community involvement, support from social support systems, and group participation.

G Discuss employment settings for social workers in terms of fields of practice and compare earnings.

There is a wide range of fields of practice in social work. Many students earning a bachelor's degree in social work are most likely to get jobs in corrections and, secondly, in child welfare. Two years after graduation, BSWs are most likely to work in child welfare, mental health, aging, family services, and health care, in descending order. The largest proportion of MSWs work in mental health.

Most social workers at both the BSW and MSW level are employed in private social service agencies, with the rest (more than a third) working in public agencies. When identifying practice roles, BSWs tended to identify case management, advocacy, and counseling, in that order. Most MSWs identify counseling as a major role, then information and referral, screening and assessment, and case management.

Median annual earnings differ across fields of practice. The lowest earnings are in mental health and substance abuse, with increasing median earnings first by child, family, and school social workers, then by medical and public health social workers. MSWs tend to earn appreciably more than BSWs.

LOOKING AHEAD

Building on the process of social work practice discussed in the last chapter, this chapter described various settings in which social work takes place. Part 3 of this book includes three chapters focusing on social welfare policy. Policy establishes the parameters for what social workers can do, including how they practice and in what contexts. The next chapter lays the groundwork for understanding policy by reviewing the history of social welfare and social work.

COMPETENCY NOTES

The following identifies where Educational Policy (EP) competencies and practice behaviors are discussed in the chapter.

EP 2.1.1 Identify as a professional social worker and conduct oneself accordingly. *(p. 150):* Joining NASW and other professional organizations provides a means of establishing and reinforcing a professional identity. *(p. 151):* Obtaining social work licensure and professional credentials is part of establishing a professional identity.

EP 2.1.1b Practice personal reflection and self-correction to assure continual professional development. *(p. 139):* Personal reflection about your own community enhances your understanding of community functioning. This is an early step in preparation for working in and with communities. *(p. 143):* Self-reflection about your own family and social support systems can help one to understand other people's family functioning and social support systems. *(p. 149):* Self-reflection about your own participation in groups enhances your understanding of group functioning.

EP 2.1.1c Attend to professional roles and boundaries. *(p. 137):* Social work roles when working with individuals are discussed. *(p. 151):* Social work licensure and other credentials help to define professional practice and roles.

EP 2.1.1e Engage in career-long learning. *(p. 133):* Attending to changing rural issues and conditions requires career-long learning. *(p. 138):* Keeping abreast of the issues involved in urban social work and the skills needed is part of a career-long learning process.

EP 2.1.2c Tolerate ambiguity in resolving ethical conflicts. *(p. 135):* A case example involving a dual relationship is presented. Questions are posed that encourage tolerance of ambiguity.

EP 2.1.2d Apply strategies of ethical reasoning to arrive at principled decision. *(p. 135):* A case example is presented and strategic questions posed to evaluate what should have been done in this case situation.

EP 2.1.3 Apply critical thinking to inform and communicate professional judgments. *(p. 139):* Critical thinking about your community is encouraged. *(p. 143):* Critical thinking about your family and social networks is suggested. *(p. 149):* Critical thinking about your participation in groups is encouraged. *(p. 165):* A case example is presented and critical thinking questions are posed.

EP 2.1.3a Distinguish, appraise, and integrate multiple sources of knowledge, including research-based knowledge, and practice wisdom. *(p. 165):* A case example is presented and questions are asked to appraise and integrate multiple sources of knowledge in order to come to conclusions.

EP 2.1.3c Demonstrate effective oral and written communication in working with individuals, families, groups, organizations, communities, and colleagues. *(p. 165):* Questions are posed to encourage the articulation and communication of practice decisions.

EP 2.1.4a Recognize the extent to which culture's structures and values may oppress, marginalize, alienate, or create or enhance privilege and power. *(p. 165):* Questions are posed to help assess potential ageism and sexism on the part of the client in the case example.

EP 2.1.4c Recognize and communicate their understanding of the importance of difference in shaping life experiences. *(p. 138):* Social workers must pay close attention to the wide range of human diversity when working in urban settings. *(p. 165):* Questions are posed to help assess the extent to which aspects of diversity shape the client's life experiences.

EP 2.1.4d View themselves as learners and engage those with whom they work as informants. *(p. 138):* Social workers should view themselves as learners and engage their urban clients as informants.

EP 2.1.5c Engage in practices that advance social and economic justice. *(p. 148):* Social workers should engage in practices that advance social and economic justice through policy practice and policy advocacy for oppressed groups.

EP 2.1.7 Apply knowledge of human behavior and the social environment. *(p. 132):* Social workers must understand practice within the contexts of organizations and communities. *(p. 140):* Social workers should be knowledgeable about systems of all sizes, including families. *(p. 143):* Practitioners should be knowledgeable about the range of systems in which people live, including groups. *(p. 146):* Social workers should understand how they function in organizations and communities in order to practice effectively.

EP 2.1.7a Utilize conceptual frameworks to guide the processes of assessment, intervention, and evaluation. *(p. 146):* Conceptual frameworks for undertaking practice with organizations and communities are discussed.

EP 2.1.7b Critique and apply knowledge to understand person and environment. *(p. 132):* Practitioners must understand social services and social agencies in order to assess how clients function within their environment and help clients get necessary services. *(p. 133):* Social workers must critique and apply knowledge about communities to understand how communities affect people's behavior and conditions.

EP 2.1.8a Analyze, formulate, and advocate for policies that advance social well-being. *(p. 138):* Social workers should strive to establish policies, programs, and resources that meet the needs of urban clients. *(p. 146):* Social work with organizations and communities includes analyzing policies and advocating for improvements. *(p. 148):* NASW advocates for policies that meet clients' needs. *(p. 150):* Policy practice involves formulating and advocating for policies that advance social well-being.

EP 2.1.8b Collaborate with colleagues and clients for effective policy action. *(p. 146):* Social workers can collaborate with colleagues and clients to improve policies, conditions, and service provision in organizations and communities. *(p. 150):* NASW membership provides a mechanism for collaborating with colleagues to undertake effective policy action.

EP 2.1.9a Continuously discover, appraise, and attend to changing locales, populations, scientific and technological developments, and emerging societal trends to provide relevant services. *(p. 133):* Practitioners should continuously respond to the changing issues and conditions affecting people and practice in rural communities. *(p. 136):* It's important for social workers to appraise continuously the conditions and issues affecting people in urban environments in order to practice effectively.

EP 2.1.10a Substantively and affectively prepare for action with individuals, families, groups, organizations, and communities. *(p. 137):* One way social workers should prepare for intervention with individuals involves understanding their appropriate roles.

EP 2.1.10b Use empathy and other interpersonal skills. *(p. 137):* Interpersonal skills involved in interviewing are discussed. *(p. 140):* Social workers should use empathy and other interpersonal skills to work effectively with families. *(p. 143):* The treatment group leader uses empathy and other interpersonal skills with group members and models such skills for them.

EP 2.1.10c Develop a mutually agreed-on focus of work and desired outcomes. *(p. 143):* The treatment group leader helps group members develop a mutually agreed-on focus of work and desired outcomes.

EP2.1.10d Collect, organize, and interpret client data. *(p. 165):* Critical thinking questions are posed to help collect, organize, and interpret client data.

EP 2.1.10g Select appropriate intervention strategies. *(p. 140):* Social workers should select the appropriate intervention strategies when working with families. *(p. 143):* The treatment group leader should use the appropriate intervention strategies, including those discussed here. *(p. 146):* Practitioners should choose the appropriate strategy for working in and with organizations and communities. *(p. 150):* Social workers can choose from a range of intervention strategies when working with individuals, families, groups, organizations, and communities.

EP 2.1.20i Implement prevention interventions that enhance client capacities. *(p. 143):* Treatment group leaders may help group members develop skills and behaviors that will prevent problems for them in the future.

EP 2.1.10k Negotiate, mediate, and advocate for clients. *(p. 138):* Social workers should advocate for the services and resources that urban clients need. *(p. 148):* Social advocacy is discussed.

FOR FURTHER EXPLORATION ON THE INTERNET

See this text's Social Work CourseMate website at *www.cengagebrain.com* for learning tools such as chapter quizzing, videos, glossary flashcards, and more.

SOCIAL WELFARE POLICY

Part 3 of this book includes three chapters that introduce social welfare policy as the groundwork for social service provision. Policy dictates how social welfare programs may be implemented. It also structures the context in which practitioners can do their work.

Chapter 6 provides a brief overview of social welfare and social work history. History provides the necessary background to understand how people think about social welfare and develop social welfare policy.

Chapter 7 describes social welfare policy development and the structural components of policy. Because policy drives what programs can do, it must be clearly understood. The chapter explores value perspectives on social responsibility and social welfare program development. Additionally, it formulates an approach to policy analysis to evaluate how social welfare policy affects and serves clients. Finally, it defines policy practice and policy advocacy as basic responsibilities of generalist practitioners.

Chapter 8 describes the policies and programs that are designed to combat poverty in the United States. The concept of poverty is defined, and explanations for its existence are discussed. Social insurance and public assistance are defined and discussed, along with specific programs under the umbrella of each.

CHAPTER **6**

An Overview of Social Welfare and Social Work History

AP Photo/Khampha Bouaphanh

**EP 2.1.1,
2.1.7b,
2.1.9a**

You might feel that history is boring and irrelevant in view of alarming contemporary issues, rapidly accelerating technological advances, and global political, economic, and social concerns. However, events in history have shaped our current ways of thinking. To comprehend how and why social welfare programs are the way they are today, it is critical to understand social welfare history.

Current social welfare policy and programs didn't simply appear out of nowhere. Rather, a long history of ideas, values, and events has shaped the present—and paves the way for the future. Figure 6.1, which introduces this chapter, identifies major events in the history of social work.

The profession's history is intertwined with the history of social welfare. Social work grew and matured in response to significant social trends, events, and needs as they occurred over time. What social workers could do in the past and what they can do now are governed by social welfare policies and programs.

A Time Line of Major Events in Social Work

1898	First training course offered for "charity workers" by New York Charity Association
1918	Formation of American Association of Medical Social Workers
1919	Formation of Association of Training Schools for Professional Social Work (later becoming the American Association of Schools of Social Work [AASSW])
	Formation of National Association of School Social Workers
1920	Formation of American Association of Social Workers
1926	Formation of American Association of Psychiatric Social Workers
1927	AASSW development of educational requirements for its membership that quickly evolved into accreditation standards for MSW programs
1929	Beginning of Great Depression that opened doors for social workers in the public sector
1936	Formation of American Association of Group Workers
1942	Formation of National Association of Schools of Social Administration (NASSA)
1943	Recognition of NASSA as official accrediting body for baccalaureate programs
1946	Formation of National Council on Social Worker Education (NCSWE) to coordinate AASSW and NASSA activities
	Formation of Association for Study of Community Organization
1949	Formation of Social Worker Research Group
1952	Formation of Council on Social Work Accreditation (CSWE) reflecting the merger of AASSW and NASSA
	Writing of first CSWE Curriculum Policy Statement and Accreditation Standards
1955	Formation of National Association of Social Workers (NASW)
	Formation of National Association of Puerto Rican Hispanic Social Workers
1956	Publication of profession's primary journal, *Social Work*
1960	NASW approval of *Code of Ethics*
1960s	War on Poverty that focused attention on social change versus individual pathology
1962	CSWE development of criteria for accrediting BSW programs
1968	Formation of National Association of Black Social Workers (NABSW)
	Formation of National Association of Puerto Rican Social Service Workers (NAPRSSW)
1969	Formation of Association of American Indian Social Workers (later called NationalIndian Social Workers Association)
	Formation of Asian American Social Workers organization
1974	CSWE accreditation of BSW programs
1976	NASW establishes Political Action for Candidate Election (PACE)
1977	Formation of Group for Advancement of Doctoral Education in social work (GADE)
1979	Incorporation of American Association of State Social Work Boards (AASSWB) to synchronize state licensing procedures
1982	Formation of Association for Advancement of Social Work with Groups (AASWG)
1984	CSWE declares common generalist practice foundation for both BSW and MSW programs
1987	NASW initiates Center for Social Policy and Practice to disseminate information about social welfare policy
1991	Formation of Academy of Certified Baccalaureate Social Workers (ACBSW)
1996	NASW approval of revisions of *Code of Ethics*
1998	U.S. social workers commemorate over 100 years of social work

Figure 6.1 Major Events in the History of the Social Work Profession in the United States

It is beyond the scope of this book to provide a detailed history of social welfare and social work.[1] *Therefore, our focus will be on the key trends, events, and figures. The time line depicted in Figure 6.3 at the end of this chapter summarizes some of these events.*

Note that when we talk about ideas, trends, and social movements over time, it is impossible to quantify them as abruptly halting one year and being replaced by something else the next year. Ideas and concepts change gradually, and transitions between them are indistinct. Therefore, this chapter will periodically reflect some overlap from one section or historical period to another.

Because Europe, especially England, provided the primary model for the development of current social welfare strategies in North America, we will initially focus on what occurred there. We will then concentrate on events and developments in the United States from the early years to the present.

Learning Objectives

A Describe some of the early European approaches to social welfare.

B Review some of the main events characterizing the history of social welfare in the United States.

C Describe some of the issues and events affecting American Indians, Hispanics, African Americans, and Asian Americans over U.S. history.

D Focus on some of the historical issues concerning mental health, children and families, people with disabilities, and older adults.

E Propose questions to stimulate critical thinking about various historical trends and events.

F Discuss major events involved in the history of the social work profession.

G Provide a foundation for understanding social welfare policy and policy development.

Early European Approaches to Social Welfare

Some of our current basic ideas about how people should or should not be treated can be traced back a millennium to medieval times. Until the mid-1300s, *feudalism* reigned in Europe as the principal type of political organization. In this system, wealthy landed gentry oversaw the labor of landless serfs who made a living by working their overseer's lands. In return, serfs received general protection and care during sickness and old age.

EP 2.1.4a

---

[1]Many thorough books have been written about social welfare and social work history. This chapter can provide only a brief overview of and introduction to major concepts. For futher, more extensive information, you might refer to *From Poor Law to Welfare State* by W. I. Trattner (New York: Free Press, 1999); *A New History of Social Welfare* by P. J. Day (Boston: Allyn & Bacon, 2009); *The Faces of Social Policy: A Strengths Perspective* by C. J. Tice and K. Perkins (Pacific Grove, CA: Brooks/Cole, 2002); *Social Welfare: A History of the American Response to Need* (7th ed.) by J. Axinn and M. J. Stern (Boston: Allyn & Bacon, 2008); *Milestones* by R. L. Barker (Washington, DC: NASW Press, 1999), or to topics such as "Social Welfare History," "Social Welfare Policy," "Social Work Professon: History," "National Association of Social Workers," and "Council on Social Work Education" in T. Mizrahi & L. E. Davis (Editors-in-Chief), *Encyclopedia of Social Work* (New York: Oxford, 2008).

Other sources of aid included medieval hospitals that provided refuge and care for older adults, the impoverished, orphans, and people with serious illnesses and disabilities, as well as charitable help from the church. These times reflected a rigid social structure with little mobility, free choice, or potential for personal growth and change. Grounded in Judeo-Christian thought, a common theme was that those who were better off should provide help to those who were poor. That some people were poor and others were rich was perceived as an unalterable fact of life. The church played a primary role in redistributing resources from the rich to the poor. It emphasized "good deeds, love of one's enemies, and entry into heaven through mercy and charity" (Trattner, 1999, p. 3).

England After Feudalism's Demise

As time passed, trade increased, technology bloomed, and the feudal system with its rigid hierarchy of power and social expectations underwent a gradual demise. With the development of urban factories, rural people were drawn to the cities looking for work and, they hoped, better wages. Centralized government became stronger, and the church lost both political and financial power. With these changes, people gained mobility and independence but lost much of the safety and security the old feudal system had provided. Many wandered in search of work, with pain, suffering, and poverty the norm.

Political leaders decided that something must be done to control the mobile population and provide some relief for the poor. In 1348 the Black Death (bubonic plague) began its destruction of almost a third of the English population, causing a serious labor shortage. As people migrated in search of competitive wages, political leaders passed legislation to regain social control. For example, the Statute of Laborers, passed in 1349, restricted the unemployed from moving about and established maximum wages allowable. The intent was to make people stay put and take whatever work was available there instead of seeking better options.

In 1531 another statute was passed forbidding able-bodied people from begging, with violations punishable by bloody public whippings while naked. However, this legislation also provided for designated government figures to help people unable to work (referred to as the "impotent poor") by assigning them legitimate areas where they could beg.

Subsequent laws addressed who should receive aid, from whom, and under what conditions, as well as what punishments should befall those who did not obey the rules.

The English Elizabethan Poor Law of 1601

The 1601 Elizabethan Poor Law is often considered the first piece of legislation establishing coherent, consistent public support for needy people through local taxes. It also was the first to establish categories of eligible recipients by identifying the following three:

1. *Dependent children* without relatives capable of supporting them were placed in service under whatever citizen placed the lowest bid for public reimbursement to provide the child's care. Boys served as apprentices, theoretically being taught a trade, until their 24th birthday, and girls provided domestic help until they were either 21 or married.

2. The *impotent poor* included those who were physically or mentally unable to work. They were given either "indoor relief" (i.e., placed *inside* institutions providing food and shelter called *almshouses* or *poorhouses*) or "outdoor relief" (i.e., offered the opportunity to live *outside* of the institution but receive material help in the form of food, clothing, and fuel).

3. The *able-bodied poor* were provided any substandard employment available and forced to work or suffer jail or other punishment, even death. Some people were forced into *workhouses*, special facilities in which poor people were forced to work and live. Unlike the impotent poor, these people were considered undeserving of help because they should be able to take care of themselves.

One later change in the poor laws, the 1662 Law of Settlement, established a notable new principle of social welfare service provision, the *residency requirement*. Potential aid recipients were required to establish that they had dwelled in some location for some designated time before they could receive assistance or benefits from the political body governing that location. People who had moved and needed help were required to return to their former parish (a portion of a county coinciding with the original religious parish and serving as a unit of local government) to receive help.

The Speenhamland System

In 1795 what became known as the Speenhamland system (because it was developed in Speenhamland, England) reflected a new approach to the problems of working poor people. Bread had became so expensive that many poor people could not afford it. Speenhamland government leaders responded by initiating the policy of supplementing the income of all poor people so that everyone would have what was deemed the minimum income necessary for survival.

Unfortunately, the result was an unexpected flop for two reasons (Garvin & Tropman, 1998; Reid, 1995). First, wages fell. Why would employers pay higher wages when the government would supplement workers' wages to the minimum necessary for survival? Why shouldn't employers let the government pay the difference to have wages reach the minimum level, rather than taking it out of their own pockets? Second, unemployment soared because people didn't have to work. They would get the same amount whether they worked or not. And even if they did work, they had little chance of getting ahead. In other words, there were no *work incentives*—logical rewards or benefits that encourage people to work.

The English Poor Law Reforms of 1834

As time passed, people began to resent the Speenhamland system for two reasons (Garvin & Tropman, 1998): (1) It cost a fortune to support *everyone*, and (2) people felt it created a dependent population of people who would never get out of poverty. The Poor Law Reforms of 1834 significantly reduced all outdoor relief and brought back workhouses as the only place where able-bodied people could receive benefits.

Three important ideological trends resulted from these reforms (Garvin & Tropman, 1998). First, public attitudes toward the poor became hostile and resentful. Second, the public came to blame the poor for their poverty. Why couldn't those people pull themselves up by their bootstraps and make it on their own? Today we would refer to this as a form of *blaming the victim*—that is, ascribing fault to the people who are hurt, have problems beyond their control, have few resources, or have been victimized by some crime or unexpected circumstance. This reflects the attitude that if only poor people would expend a little more effort and put in a full day's work every day, they wouldn't be poor

(Barker, 2003). The third result of these reforms was the concept of being *less eligible* (Garvin & Tropman, 1998; Reid, 1995). This is the idea that benefits should be lower than what the poorest working people could earn. People who received public assistance, then, would always be poorer than the poorest people who worked.

U.S. Social Welfare History: Early Colonization to the Mid-1800s

Early poor laws in the American colonies closely resembled, and in some cases were identical to, those in England, although each colony remained unique in its specific legislation. The colonists maintained a strong sense of individualism and commitment to personal freedom; however, they also expressed concern for the well-being of others and respect for a sense of community (Reid, 1995). The result was an interesting and uneven blend of programs and services, such that the beneficiaries of some programs received substantial help and others received very little.

The colonists viewed the poor as a natural part of the social order and the community. In many ways, this reflected an *institutional* view of social welfare—namely, it's simply society's ongoing responsibility to provide its citizens with needed benefits and resources.

Services often reflected a mix of public and private collaboration, with services being provided in a relatively informal manner (Reid, 1995). Local government units assumed responsibility of administering aid but often called upon local churches for help (Dolgoff & Feldstein, 2009).

Early residency requirements for assistance were established. Communities tended to provide aid for their own residents, shunning strangers. Communities also made decisions about who was worthy to receive benefits and who was not. This demonstrated the concept of the *worthy* versus the *unworthy poor*; the former deserved help and the latter did not (the implication being that they were doing something wrong).

The worthy poor were pitied, and the community found ways to care for them. One of the easiest was for families to take turns housing the poor during the year. A second way to help the poor was to reduce their taxes. Still another way involved providing free medical attention to them, with physicians

EP 2.1.3b

HIGHLIGHT 6.1

Early Philosophical Views About Children

Trattner (1999) presents some of the early philosophical perspectives on children. From colonial times to the 1870s, children were viewed as similar entities with little individuality—they were all thought to be innately evil and lazy. Therefore, they required supervision to keep them busy and out of trouble so that they might grow up to be "industrious, upright, godly" adults (Trattner, 1999, p. 110). By the mid-18th century, however, philosophical thinking was changing. John Locke's *tabula rasa* (clean slate) approach suggested that children were inherently pure and good. It was society and its negative influences that corrupted children as they grew up.

Effects of the environment became increasingly important from a number of perspectives. Social Darwinism, espoused by 19th-century English sociologist Herbert Spencer, highlighted the importance of genetically inherited attributes, but also stressed the ability of the environment to influence these traits over time. Sigmund Freud emphasized the importance of early nurturing within the family and its effect on child development.

In general, trends in thinking reflected an increasing focus on children's welfare (Kadushin & Martin, 1988). People began to believe that children's environment and the treatment they received affected what kinds of adults they grew up to be.

either donating such care or receiving inducements such as tax breaks.

Dependent children were frequently placed in apprenticeships. This was viewed positively for a number of reasons (Trattner, 1999). First, apprenticeships afforded them some connection with a family and the related stability. Second, it provided a context in which they might be disciplined and taught to become good citizens. Third, it saved the community the cost of caring for children. Finally, it trained children to develop a useful skill and become productive community members. Because labor was scarce in colonial America, people who had learned trades were highly valued. Highlight 6.1 discusses some of the early philosophical views about children.

By the 1820s and 1830s, ideas were changing, and people were beginning to view poverty as a "social problem" and "a potential source of crime, social unrest, and long-term dependence" (Reid, 1995, p. 2209). Therefore, interest began to turn to reform. People now believed that outdoor relief had spoiled poor people and that it resulted only in dependence (Reid, 1995). Therefore, great almshouses were built in which the poor could be housed and converted into industrious, functional citizens.

Focus on Mental Health and Mental Illness

In colonial America, people who had mental illness, often referred to as "lunatics," typically were cared for by their own families or boarded out to other families, with communities paying these families to provide care (Dembling, 1995; Fellin, 1996, p. 56). As time passed, people with mental illness increasingly were placed in almshouses, clustered together with the poor and people with other disabilities.

By the early 19th century, the *moral treatment* movement, the first of three focusing on mental health policy, had been initiated by Philippe Pinel, a French physician who worked in a Parisian hospital for the "insane." The idea was that people with mental illness "should be treated with humane, sympathetic, and personal care in a hospital or asylum setting" (Fellin, 1996, p. 57; Lin, 1995; U.S. Department of Health and Human Services [USDHHS], 1999). (Figure 6.2 summarizes the three major mental health

Movement	Time Frame	Emphasis
Moral treatment	1770s–1900	Humane treatment in structured institutional settings
Mental hygiene	1900–1945	Specialized psychiatric units and psychotherapy
Deinstitutionalization	Early 1950s to present	Provision of care in people's own communities

© Cengage Learning 2013

Figure 6.2 Major Mental Health Movements in the United States

---

HIGHLIGHT 6.2

Dorothea Dix: Mental Health Advocate

EP 2.1.5b, 2.1.8a

A notable early advocate during the 1840s for people with mental illness was Dorothea Dix (Barker, 1999; Fellin, 1996; Trattner, 1999). A volunteer Sunday school teacher in a Massachusetts women's prison, she was appalled by the treatment of people with mental illness who were placed there. She waged a dynamic publicity campaign condemning the deplorable conditions in which these people were forced to live.

Trattner (1999) explains how Dix "described vividly how many of the unfortunate crazed were impounded in cabins, cages, closets, stalls, and other pens of one kind of another, often chained and then abandoned to filth and neglect, or else brutally beaten—a horrifying picture" (p. 65).

Beginning in Massachusetts and then focusing on other states, she insisted that it was the public's responsibility to establish hospitals providing more humane treatment and medical care for persons with mental illness.

As a result of Dix's and her followers' efforts, over 30 state mental hospitals were established (Fellin, 1996). Unfortunately, "although well intentioned, her selling and marketing of state-run institutions were based on two dubious premises: first, that such asylums were the most cost-effective means of treatment, and second, that insanity was a highly curable phenomenon" (Gomory, 1997, p. 165).

---

movements occurring in the United States during the 19th and 20th centuries. The last two will be described in greater detail later in the chapter.)

In the United States, the movement assumed "more of a moralistic flavor related to the idea that bad habits lead to tendencies toward mental disorders" (Fellin, 1996, p. 57; Rochefort, 1993). Structured, "corrective" settings providing a remedial environment were thought to help cure mental illness (Lin, 1995, p. 1705). Highlight 6.2 focuses on Dorothea Dix, an early advocate for the humane treatment of people with mental illness.

Focus on American Indian (First Nations Peoples) History: Treaties and Federal Control[2]

EP 2.1.5a

Most of social welfare history in the United States, including that discussed thus far, is written from a very white perspective (Lewis, 1995). In reality, American history did not begin in 1492 when Columbus "discovered" America. Rather, North America had been populated for 25,000 years or more (Day, 2009; Lewis, 1995). During initial European colonization, there were hundreds of different nations with a wide range of well-developed, self-sufficient societies (Weaver, 2003, 2008).

Residents of a conquered society generally remain on their own land and at least retain hope of regaining control. European victory over American Indian nations, however, usually resulted in their permanent removal from their lands, pressures to surrender their values and culture, and imposed submission to external laws and regulations.

Treaties

As whites pushed westward in exploding numbers and with an insatiable desire for land, the United States, newly formed and in its infancy, decided to deal with First Nations Peoples by developing treaties. The United States viewed treaties as ways of delineating the legal and political relationships between the federal government and various nations (Lewis, 1995). The first treaty to be established (of more than 600 over the next century) was with the Delaware nation in 1778. Congress finally ceased making treaties with nations in 1981 when other type of agreements and legislation formally replaced the treaty process (Lewis, 1995).

Other Early Policies

A significant early piece of legislation was the 1781 Articles of Confederation. This was related to

---

[2]For greater detail and good introductory content on American Indians, see Lewis (1995, pp. 216–231), which provides an excellent beginning source for understanding some of the crucial issues experienced by First Nations Peoples.

treaties because it gave the federal government singular and complete authority over Indian affairs, reinforcing the government's right to make treaties in any way it saw fit (Lewis, 1995). Thus the federal government could develop treaties regardless of First Nations Peoples' locations in North America. The implication is that, as the government broke treaties, First Nations Peoples could be moved from place to place, usually further west.

Other significant pieces of legislation, the Trade and Intercourse Acts passed between 1770 and 1834, reinforced two more ideas (Canby, 1981; Lewis, 1995). One was that American Indians and non–American Indians should be separated. The other was that the federal government should control all relations between American Indians and whites. The federal Bureau of Indian Affairs, established in 1824, reflected an attempt to address issues with American Indians.

The theme during this period was the conviction that American Indians had an inferior culture and that the federal government was responsible for civilizing them and making them Christians (Lewis, 1995). White people believed that the federal government should interfere not only in political matters but also in social, economic, religious, and cultural practices.

Removal Policy

Tensions continued to mount as whites pushed westward into American Indian territory. The Indian Removal Act, passed in 1830, resulted in thousands of American Indians being removed from their own lands and relocated to distant "reservations" that were generally smaller than their homelands and had clearly defined boundaries. There they experienced the spread of disease and numerous restrictions such as being forbidden to participate in spiritual ceremonies.

The Cherokee Nation poses a heartrending example of the cruel removal practice. By the early 1800s, the Cherokee had called western Georgia home for almost 1,000 years (Cherokee Messenger, 1995). By this time the nation had adopted many European customs, including women wearing gowns, and had developed a system of "roads, schools, and churches" (Cherokee Messenger, 1995). Their literacy rate in their own tongue was 90%, they published a bilingual newspaper and a range of textbooks, and they established a written constitution as an independent nation (Lewis, 1995). Most of them worked as farmers and ranchers (Golden Ink, 1997).

After gold was discovered in Georgia in 1828, the tension increased between the Cherokee and their non-Native counterparts. Although the Cherokee challenged the legality of the 1830 Indian Removal Act in the Supreme Court and at first appeared to be successful, it was determined that they could be removed if they signed a treaty to that effect (Golden Ink, 1997). Against the majority's will, in 1835 a small faction (less than 3%) of the Cherokee Nation signed such a treaty relinquishing all land east of the Mississippi in return for promised new western lands, cash, equipment, and supplies (Cherokee Messenger, 1995; Golden Ink, 1997). Three years later, 17,000 Cherokee men, women, and children were torn from their land and made to endure squalid conditions on a 1,200-mile trip to Indian Territory in the West (Cherokee Messenger, 1995). On that journey 4,000 perished "from hunger, exposure, and disease" (Cherokee Messenger, 1995). This infamous journey is aptly and sadly called "The Trail of Tears."

In all, during the 1830s between 70,000 and 100,000 American Indians were uprooted from their homes and herded to Oklahoma (Lewis, 1995).

Focus on Chicano/Chicana History: The Treaty of Guadalupe Hidalgo

The history of the Southwest and its early inhabitants merits attention, especially in view of the large and growing U.S. Chicano/Chicana population. Beginning in 1519 the Spanish conquistadors, along with their

EP 2.1.5a

Native allies, conquered the Aztec Empire in Central Mexico; from there expansion took place in all directions, overtaking areas including Arizona, New Mexico, Texas, and California (National Park Service, undated). Colonization of these regions continued, with many of the residents having a mixed heritage including Spanish and Native American ancestry (National Park Service, undated).

In view of a growing population, increasing infiltration by Anglos (whites), and budding trade with other areas, the struggle for control of land escalated. Texas declared itself an independent republic in 1836, but continued grappling with Mexico over its southern boundary (Library of Congress, 2004). When the United States decided to annex Texas in 1845, the boundary struggle with Mexico continued.

Conflict intensified and war was declared in 1846, initiating the Mexican-American War. Subsequently, the United States attacked Mexico on numerous fronts, eventually capturing Mexico City in mid-1847 (Library of Congress, 2004). The result was the February 2, 1848, signing of the Treaty of Guadalupe Hidalgo, in which Mexico ceded more than half of its territory to the United States, including contemporary Arizona, New Mexico, and upper California, in addition to portions of Colorado, Nevada, and Utah in exchange for $15,000,000; additionally, Mexico recognized U.S. retention of Texas with its southern boundary at the Rio Grande (U.S. National Archives and Records Administration, undated). (The remaining portions of present-day states were ceded under the 1853 Gadsden Purchase [Curiel, 1995].)

The Treaty of Guadalupe Hidalgo did address the rights of Mexicans living in the ceded regions. It provided the options of retaining their land and becoming U.S. citizens, which the vast majority chose, or moving south into Mexico (Curiel, 1995). Although the treaty guaranteed land, personal, and religious rights, Anglos generally opted to ignore these guarantees (Day, 2009). Many Anglos took Chicano landowners to court over land rights, usually winning because many Chicanos had lost proof of land titles during the conflict and could not afford to hire attorneys to defend themselves adequately (Day, 2009). As a result, Chicanos were generally disenfranchised from their property and their rights, becoming strangers in their own land (Curiel, 1995). Many were forced into hard agricultural labor that Anglos preferred not to do. Anglos commonly viewed Chicanos as a "minority" group with its own culture; although Chicanos outnumbered Anglos and were living in their own homelands, they were marginalized, discriminated against, and commonly treated as second-class citizens (Curiel, 1995). This set the stage for the discrimination and many of the issues Chicanos must deal with today.

The Civil War Era

The Civil War (1861–1865) had a huge impact on the social structure of the United States. Day (2009) explains that it "affirmed federal responsibility over states' rights and laid the groundwork for the United States to become a welfare state" (p. 206).

Jansson (2012) describes how, despite the fact that the main conflict concerned "the legal status

of slaves," President Abraham Lincoln (whose administration lasted from 1861 until his 1865 assassination) did not initially propose an immediate end to slavery (p. 126). Although his decisions were apparently made in the context of political concerns, such an omission might raise questions regarding the strength of Lincoln's opposition to slavery.[3] It was not until 1863 that he issued the Emancipation Proclamation, declaring freedom for all slaves in Confederate states at war with the Union. Note that this sidestepped the issue of freedom for slaves in border slave states, including Delaware, Kentucky, Maryland, Missouri, and West Virginia (Tice & Perkins, 2002).

Focus on African Americans: The Freedmen's Bureau

EP 2.1.5a

A major problem during this era involved the newly freed, dislocated former slaves, who had no property and few resources. Although charity groups in the North sent supplies and volunteers to help displaced people, this only scratched the surface in terms of meeting people's needs. National concern about the issues and needs resulted in Congress establishing the Bureau of Refugees, Freedmen, and Abandoned Land (more commonly known as the Freedmen's Bureau) in 1865. (Note that its formal name emphasizes how legislators sought to avoid giving African Americans preferential treatment [Jansson, 2012].) This bureau, the "first federal welfare agency" (Reid, 1995, p. 2210), established "a precedent for federal participation in social welfare during emergency periods" (Axinn & Stern, 2008, p. 96).

The Freedmen's Bureau was placed under the auspices of the War Department. This emphasized its temporary, crisis-related (postwar) purpose, as opposed to status as an institutional program designed to meet ongoing needs. Eligibility for resources was based purely on need. In its initial three years, the bureau distributed rations to 18.3 million people, over 28% of whom were white (Day, 2009; Tice & Perkins, 2002). Additionally, it

---

[3]Possible reasons for Lincoln's hesitation in eradicating slavery include having as a top priority keeping the Union together, believing that the Constitution gave him no authority to free slaves, being concerned that the Confederacy would only "fight harder" and the war would last longer if slaves were freed, and fearing alienation of the border slave states (Tice & Perkins, 2002, p. 74).

provided transportation home for refugees, distributed medical supplies, built 46 hospitals, and established over 4,300 schools for African American children (Axinn & Stern, 2008). The Freedmen's Bureau was disbanded in 1872.

One of the Freedmen's Bureau's initial goals was to distribute 40 acres of abandoned or confiscated land to each male refugee. This could be accomplished only if the government took possession of such property and legally distributed it. The results of this program were modest: Only a little over 1% of eligible African Americans were allocated property (Jansson, 2012). President Andrew Johnson (whose administration lasted from 1865 to 1869) subsequently proclaimed that the African Americans had no legal right to these properties and forced recipients to return land to its former owners (Jansson, 2012).

The 1870s to 1900

Economic growth skyrocketed between the Civil War and the early 20th century (Axinn & Stern, 2008). Three broad trends emerged in the United States both economically and socially (Garvin & Cox, 1995). The first was *industrialization.* Mammoth growth in manufacturing and technology brought with it a "wide range of social problems" including "problems of working hours and conditions, safety, and child labor" (Garvin & Cox, 1995, p. 65).

The second trend was *urbanization.* Concurrent with the centralization of industry within urban settings was the tremendous growth of urban populations. Masses of people moved from rural to urban areas in search of work and prosperity. Unfortunately, most were forced to move into the oldest, most crowded, and least sanitary portions of the cities.

The third trend was explosive *immigration*, primarily from northwestern Europe. Immigrants brought with them their own problems. Many came from poor rural environments and had little to start their lives with in this country, and many became ill during the immigration process. Immigrants usually were forced to live in some of the worst conditions and accept whatever work they could find.

Focus on Children: Early Policies

The 1870s saw the origins of child welfare policy as it has evolved today (Karger & Stoesz, 2010). Prior to this time, abandoned, unwanted, or orphaned children had been placed in almshouses along with

adults suffering from poverty and disabilities. By this time, however, people were beginning to view children as special beings requiring treatment qualitatively different from that provided adults and people with disabilities. Orphanages intended solely for children began to multiply, replacing almshouses as places to house children. This practice was, however, still institutional placement.

The Reverend Charles Loring Brace, founder of New York's Children's Aid Society, became the first proponent of placing children in homes other than their own instead of in institutions. Brace gathered up thousands of juvenile paupers from the New York City streets and sent them to live with farm families in the Midwest. He believed that farmers were the ideal citizens and that farming was the ideal occupation. A staunch believer in the importance of the environment, as stressed by Social Darwinism, Brace felt that placing children in such positive environments would make them better, more productive citizens.

By the early 20th century, most large cities had their own children's aid societies that placed or "farmed out" children to families instead of putting them in institutions. This movement reflected the beginnings of foster care and adoption in the United States. Highlight 6.3 discusses the early development of protective services.

Settlement Houses, Charity Organization Societies, and Generalist Social Work

In response to the rapidly growing social problems, two social and ideological movements became the foundation for social work practice in the 1880s and continued into the early 1900s (Lewis & Suarez, 1995). They were the settlement house movement and charity organization societies.

Settlement Houses

Settlement houses were neighborhood-based centers where humanitarians, interested students, and others "settled" (hence the name) to help people living in poverty improve their communities and their lives; goals included meeting residents' needs, such as providing education and training, and advocating for human rights and improved community conditions (Day, 2008).

Day (2009) elaborates:

Settlement houses were run in part by client groups, and they emphasized social reform rather

HIGHLIGHT 6.3

The Early Development of Protective Services

The concept of *protective services* was born under some unusual circumstances in 1874. Etta Wheeler, a New York City relief worker for the poor, discovered that Mary Ellen Wilson, age 9, who had been an indentured servant since age 18 months, "was being tied to a bed, whipped, and stabbed with scissors" (Karger & Stoesz, 2010, p. 386). It was subsequently determined that Mary Ellen was the illegitimate child of her tormentor, Mary Connelly's first husband.

Wheeler "sought help from the police, benevolent societies, and charitable gentlemen," but to no avail (Watkins, 1990, p. 501). Finally, in desperation, she appealed to the president of the New York Society for the Prevention of Cruelty to Animals. Interested in the case, he helped Wheeler get "a special warrant" from a New York Supreme Court judge to remove Mary Ellen from the abusive home (Watkins, 1990, p. 502).

Historical and current myths often imply that children living in the 1870s had to be categorized as ani-

mals before they could receive legal protection (Watkins, 1990). In reality, the court never treated Mary Ellen as if the same laws applied to her as to animals. However, the case received extensive publicity focusing on how Mary Ellen had been treated worse than what was legally allowed for animals. It brought to people's attention how children were sometimes in need of protective treatment.

What happened to Mary Ellen? Wheeler's own mother, and later her sister, took Mary Ellen in; Mary Ellen "was married at age 24 and had two daughters" (Watkins, 1990, p. 502). "As a punishment to herself, but more as a warning to others," Mary Connelly was sentenced to "one year in the Penitentiary at hard labor," the maximum sentence possible ("Mary Ellen Wilson," 1874, p. 8; Watkins, 1990, p. 502). As a result of Mary Ellen's case, societies for the prevention of cruelty to children were established all over the country in the late 1800s and early 1900s.

---

than relief or assistance. Three-fourths of settlement workers were women, and most were well-educated and dedicated to working on problems of urban poverty. Early sources of funding were wealthy individuals or clubs such as the Junior League, and at first their founders tried to provide "culture" to members, such as art, music, and lectures. When they found a need, they added new features such as playgrounds, day care, kindergartens, baths, and classes in English literacy. Other services included art exhibits, lectures, and classes in homemaking, cooking, sewing, and shopping, especially for immigrant women who were not used to the facilities available in the United States such as grocery stores and the products they offered (fresh bread, milk, and canned goods). Settlement workers tried to improve housing conditions, organized protests, offered job training and labor searches, supported organized labor, worked against child labor, and fought against corrupt politicians. Over time settlement houses became centers of social reform, and clubs, societies, and political groups such as the Socialist party used them as bases of operation. (p. 229)

Settlement houses formed a strong foundation for generalist social work practice within communities in at least three ways (Smith, 1995). First, the settlement house approach addressed the problems of people in an environmental context instead of focusing on individual pathology. Environmental problems created difficulties for individuals, who were not viewed as the targets of blame, punishment, and change. Settlement houses thus focused on addressing social issues and improving living conditions, especially for the poorest and least fortunate people.

Second, an environmental focus led naturally to an emphasis on advocacy and social reform. (We have established that *Advocacy* is the act of standing up for and defending the cause of another.) This is appropriate when the macro social environment requires change to meet people's needs.

Third, settlement houses emphasized the empowerment of people. At its most basic level, *empowerment* involves providing people with authority or power. According to the settlement house perspective, people had strengths and capabilities to effect their own change. Families and neighborhoods were seen as potential vehicles for positive change. The concepts of community organization and group work (both described in Chapter 5) developed within the settlement house context. Jane Addams and Ellen Gates Starr opened perhaps the most famous settlement house, Hull House, in Chicago in 1889. Highlight 6.4 focuses on Jane Addams, an immensely important figure in the development of social work and advocacy for social change.

Charity Organization Societies

The settlement perspective contrasted strikingly with *charity organization societies* (COS). According to Lewis and Suarez (1995), the "emphasis was not on lay communal expertise but on scientific practice and expert knowledge" (p. 1769). They continue that "the underlying assumption was that individual need was a result of moral turpitude and that moral

---

HIGHLIGHT 6.4

Jane Addams

EP 2.1.9b

Jane Addams "built her reputation as the country's most prominent woman through her writing, her settlement work, and her international efforts for world peace" (Jane Addams Hull-House Museum, 1997). She attained "worldwide recognition in the first third of the 20th century as a pioneer social worker in America, as a feminist, and as an internationalist" (Haberman, 1972).

Born in Cedarville, Illinois, on September 6, 1860, Jane was the youngest of six children in a well-to-do family. Her mother died when Jane was 2. Six years later, her father remarried and she gained two stepbrothers. Jane deeply respected her father, John Addams, a miller, who was "a shrewd and careful investor" and one of Cedarville's "leading citizens" (Stroup, 1986, p. 2). John "was a local political leader who served for 16 years as a state senator and fought as an officer in the Civil War; he was a friend of Abraham Lincoln, whose letters to him began 'My Dear Double D-'ed Addams' " (Haberman, 1972).

"Because of a congenital spinal defect, Jane was not physically vigorous when young nor truly robust even later in life," although the defect was corrected later by surgery (Haberman, 1972).

After graduating from the local school, Jane sought a college education at the Rockford Female Seminary (later called Rockford College) and graduated in 1881 as class valedictorian. Shortly afterward, her father died, which distressed her greatly as "she lost one of the most powerful influences in her life" (Stroup, 1986, p. 6).

Jane subsequently pursued further study in the field of medicine. "For seven months she worked at her medical studies with considerable zeal and secured high marks for her efforts. But the strain was too much, and her health broke down, forcing her to return

to Cedarville" (Stroup, 1986, p. 6). Over the next few years, Jane "was hospitalized intermittently, traveled and studied in Europe for 21 months, and then spent almost two years in reading and writing and in considering what her future objectives should be" (Haberman, 1972). Jane "wanted more in life" than marriage; if "her brothers could have careers in medicine and science, why couldn't she? Besides, she disliked household duties and the prospect of raising children held no appeal" (Women in History, 2005).

Stroup (1986) describes Jane's initial thoughts about the settlement house movement:

[In the spring of 1887 at age 27], Jane went to Madrid along with four friends [including Ellen Starr]. Their tour included a bullfight, and when her friends left the arena because of the brutality, Jane stayed to see five bulls killed. She was drawn to the activity because of its callousness and at the same time repelled because of her idealism. This seems to have been a significant experience in her life because the very next morning she approached Ellen Starr with the idea of establishing a "big house" right in the middle of "horrid little houses" as a means of bringing help to the poor. Ellen was enthusiastic about the idea, and from this experience, Hull House was conceived. Its birth had to wait until Jane and Ellen discovered the work of Cannon Samuel Barnett in the East Side of London.

Toynbee Hall had come into existence only four years prior to Jane Addams's visit. Barnett was its first warden, or "head resident," and it was the first settlement house. Its staff was composed of university men, mainly from Oxford, who lived in the slums of London . . . to learn conditions firsthand and to contribute to the improvement of life there with their own personal and financial resources. . . . It was this idea of the settlement house that Jane Addams also finally used. She believed that what Barnett had been able to do for the poor people of London she might attempt for the poor people

(continued)

of Chicago. She had found her mission, the purpose that she had struggled to find for so many years. (p. 9)

In 1889 with Ellen Gates Starr, an art teacher, Jane rented a house from "Charles J. Hull, an early resident of Chicago" who "had built his house when the neighborhood was young. It was a two-story brick house, set back from the street, and it seemed perfect as a settlement house" (Stroup, 1986, p. 10). A wide range of ranging programs were developed at Hull House that served as models for other settlement houses around the country. These included nurseries, children's clubs, a gymnasium, a library, an art gallery, a music school, an auditorium, a cafeteria, an employment bureau, a cooperative residence for women who worked, and a curriculum offering a range of classes including music, art, language, and mathematics (Johnson, 2005; Quam, 1995). Jane and other Hull House staff fought for improved conditions involving workplaces, housing, and sanitation; they advocated for improved policies concerning child labor laws, workplace safety, compulsory education, and women's rights (Johnson, 2005). Jane herself was appointed a neighborhood sanitation inspector to improve conditions and get more resources for people who needed them (Quam, 1995).

"Hull House was a refuge for individuals who had no other place to turn in time of trouble. One child, for example, was lodged at the House until he could return to live with his parents. His mother didn't want him because he had been born with a cleft palate. On another occasion, a new bride took shelter in Hull House because her husband beat her during the first week of marriage" (Stroup, 1986, p. 12).

Jane "directed her efforts at the root causes of poverty" and continued living and working at Hull House until her death (Women in History, 2005). However, she was also actively involved in many other organizations and causes. She and her colleagues "forged a powerful reform movement" that initiated projects including "the Immigrants' Protective League, the

Juvenile Protective Association, the first juvenile court in the nation, and a Juvenile Psychopathic Clinic (later called the Institute for Juvenile Research)" (Jane Addams Hull House Museum, 1997). Hull House workers advocated for and helped pass laws involving child labor and mandatory education, which eventually spread to the national level. "They worked for legislation to protect immigrants from exploitation, limit the working hours of women, ... recognize labor unions, and provide for industrial safety" (Women in History, 2005).

Jane, an exceptional speaker, often spoke publicly on the behalf of human welfare. She also wrote 11 books and published many articles. Her national efforts involving advocacy to improve social conditions included being the first female president of the National Conference of Charities and Corrections (an organization of social welfare agencies that changed its name to the National Conference of Social Work in 1917). Jane was involved in establishing the Chicago Federation of Settlements in 1894, and later helped found the National Federation of Settlements and Neighborhood Centers in 1911. Additionally, she was a member of national associations and committees too numerous to name here that were aimed at improving a wide range of social conditions and policies. She was a robust supporter of women's right to vote.

Jane was also a strong advocate for international peace. She initially helped form and later became president of the Women's Peace Party in 1915. She served as a delegate for a wide range of peace conferences around the world. Against opposition, she advocated for the United States to denounce war and join with other countries to form global organizations striving for international harmony. Because of her efforts, she was awarded the Nobel Peace Prize in 1931. Jane died in 1935 "three days after an operation revealed unsuspected cancer" (Haberman, 1972). She is remembered and revered as one of the most important advocates for human rights and well-being ever living in this country.

teaching, combined with minimal assistance, would support people in taking care of themselves" (p. 1769). Initially, the societies used "friendly visitors" who tried to help people figure out how to solve their problems (Brieland, 1995, p. 2247).

As time passed, charity organization societies sought to establish a base of scientific knowledge and apply it to the helping process. The scientific

emphasis in fields such as medicine and engineering inspired this orientation. The societies "wanted to study the problem of dependence, gather data, test theories, systematize administration, and develop techniques that would lead to a cure" (Popple, 1995, p. 2283). The impetus to obtain social work professionalism began when the societies recognized the fact that friendly visitors needed more education and training to perform their tasks effectively (Brieland, 1995; Popple, 1995).

Charity organization societies focused on curing individuals, not on empowering communities. Traditional social casework developed from the former approach. Additionally, because expert knowledge was emphasized, the significance of administration and supervised practice was incorporated in the casework concept. This emphasis on expertise contrasted sharply with the settlement approach, which stressed the empowerment and self-sufficiency of all. Highlight 6.5 focuses on the life and contributions of Mary Richmond, a primary proponent of the charity organization movement

and a significant force in the early definition of social work.

Focus on American Indians: Attempts at Assimilation

Earlier we discussed how treaty formulation and tribal relocation characterized the early treatment of American Indians. From the 1870s to 1900, a new trend, *assimilation,* emerged, perhaps because the federal government was "developing a conscience" (Lewis, 1995, p. 219). In this context, *assimilation* is the process of incorporating another culture into the

EP 2.1.5a

HIGHLIGHT 6.5

Mary Richmond

EP 2.1.10d

Born on August 5, 1861, in Belleville, Illinois, Mary Ellen Richmond, "a frail woman who spent most of her life overcoming chronic invalidism in order to help others" (Trattner, 1999, p. 255), "was the only surviving child of Henry and Lavinia Richmond" (Webster.edu, 2005). Tragedy struck Mary at the age of 3 when her mother became sick and died. She was then sent "to live with her grandmother and two aunts in Baltimore" (Webster.edu, 2005). "Frequently ill, she spent a lonely, unhappy childhood in Baltimore" (Trattner, 1999, p. 255). There she attended high school, graduating in 1878. At that time one of her aunts became ill, so Mary assumed responsibility for her care until the aunt died 10 years later. Soon after her aunt's death Mary began working for the Baltimore Charity Organization as an assistant treasurer in 1989, becoming its general secretary two years later.

As early as 1897, Mary began to advocate for the development of professional schools of social casework (which emphasizes helping individuals and families) and structured social work education programming. In 1899 she wrote the first book that provided a thorough description of practical techniques used in doing charitable work with poor people called *Friendly Visiting Among the Poor*. Topics included suggestions for exploring health, child care, religious involvement, and financial management (Webster.edu, 2005). Her basic belief was that the poor could be helped and reformed by using structured, planned methods.

In 1900 Mary became general secretary of the Philadelphia Society for Organizing Charity, where she stressed the use of volunteers (Longres, 1995). In 1909 she became the director of the Charity Organizational Department of the Russell Sage Foundation, where she conducted major social work research. The New York School of Philanthropy provided another setting where she taught and conducted research over the following years. One of Mary's major achievements was the development and wide dissemination of educational materials training workers in the process and techniques of social casework.

Mary "wrote *Social Diagnosis,* the first book to address professional social work practice, in 1917. A guide for the beginning caseworker, the book outlined ways to diagnose and assess need, and it greatly influenced the new profession" (Segal, Gerdes, & Steiner, 2004, p. 50). Mary focused on defining typical tasks performed by early charity workers, especially those related to assessing the causes of families' poverty and dependence (Popple & Leighninger, 2005). She steadfastly investigated the process used by charity organization workers and established a process involving "diagnosis, prognosis, and treatment as entities in a chainlike series; the treatment of individuals, then, was an extended, logical process, the techniques of which could be ordered, described, analyzed, and transmitted from one generation of social workers to another" (Trattner, 1999, p. 255). Mary's work established social casework as a cornerstone of social work by emphasizing individual functioning within the

(continued)

HIGHLIGHT 6.5 (continued)

person's and family's environment. Although her primary focus was the individual and family, she did not disapprove of social reform involving larger systems; she simply felt that such reform efforts were generally unsuccessful and that work with individuals would always be necessary (Trattner, 1999). In essence, Mary provided the first articulate formulation of social work theories and techniques upon which the profession could be based.

Mary was a self-taught woman with no college background who read extensively and applied her knowledge in various avenues of social work research. It is interesting that despite her lack of formal training, she strongly advocated for professional social work education and the formal provision of necessary knowledge and techniques. Mary died in 1928 after a flourishing career in which she served as one of the founders of professional social work.

---

mainstream culture. The assimilated culture (i.e., that of First Nations Peoples) was thus expected to assume the dominant culture's values and practices while relinquishing its own. The most destructive legislation relating to American Indians in the United States was the Indian General Allotment Act of 1887 (also known as the Dawes Act) (Lewis, 1995). Its intent was to assimilate American Indians by giving them land and potential citizenship in return for their turning their backs on their culture and becoming "productive" citizens (Lewis, 1995, p. 219).

One problem was that the European orientation of white Americans emphasized the importance of individuals owning their own property. The concept of sharing communal land, so integral to American Indians, was neither understood nor respected. Over the ensuing 35 years, the Dawes Act resulted in the loss of 75% of all American Indian lands, much of it being sold to non-American Indians or reverting back to federal control (Lewis, 1995).

At least three other thrusts were involved in assimilation (Lewis, 1995). First, the Bureau of Indian Affairs assumed responsibility for American Indian children's education, forcing them to abandon their own language, religion, and customs and to dress, speak, and act like whites. Second, government officials ignored the authority of tribal leaders when addressing legal and political issues. Third, missionaries were sent to reservations to "civilize" American Indians and purge them of their traditional spiritual beliefs and practices (Lewis, 1995, p. 220).

Assimilation attempts were finally mildly obstructed in 1934 with the Indian Reorganization Act. This legislation banned the practice of allocating tribal lands to individuals, established a credit fund to provide tribes with loans, and gave American Indians

preference for being hired in the Bureau of Indian Affairs (Lewis, 1995).

Even this restructuring met with resistance from many First Nations Peoples. As was typical, the act did not include any American Indian notions about how leadership should be structured or people governed (Lewis, 1995). Focus on Critical Thinking 6.1 raises some questions regarding the effects national policy can have on people's self-determination and human rights.

The Progressive Period: 1900 to 1930

The years from 1900 to 1930 were characterized by a progressive movement (Axinn & Stern, 2008; Karger & Stoesz, 2010), although settlement houses and charity organization societies continued to characterize the early 20th century. Historical overlap and gradual transitions among trends occur as people's ideas change slowly over time.

The progressive period was an era "when educated and socially conscious men and women sought to create structures that would advance social justice in the United States" (Karger & Stoesz, 2010, p. 229). This period emphasized a government that would assume active responsibility for the welfare of its citizens. Regulations were established that addressed political corruption and business practices (Reid, 1995). Many people tackled major issues such as child labor, women's working hours, women's suffrage, income security, and family welfare (Axinn & Stern, 2008).

The following are some of the major events characterizing this era:

- The National Association for the Advancement of Colored People (NAACP), "the largest and

FOCUS ON CRITICAL THINKING 6.1

Government Policy and Self-Determination for First Nations Peoples

EP 2.1.3, 2.1.5a, 2.1.5b, 2.1.8a

Critical thinking involves *asking* questions, *assessing* facts, and *asserting* a conclusion. What are your answers to the following?

Critical Thinking Questions

- To what extent did U.S. policy concerning American Indians reflect a racist orientation rather than appreciation for and nurturance of cultural differences?
- What types of policies might have been more sensitive to and supportive of American Indians' cultural differences and strengths?
- What policies do you think should have been instituted during this era?

---

oldest of the U.S. civil rights organizations," was created in 1909 (Barker, 2003, p. 286). Initially formed in outrage over the lynching of African Americans, and currently having over 1,500 chapters in all 50 states, the NAACP protects the rights of African Americans through legal proceedings, enforcement of civil rights laws, and provision of information to the public (Barker, 2003).

- The National Urban League was established in 1911 to help African Americans, especially those moving to New York City from the rural South, to find suitable employment and adjust to urban life; the organization soon expanded its influence to other cities (Nittle, 2011).
- Between 1911 and 1919, most states initiated pension programs that provided assistance to single mothers (Barker, 1999; Jansson, 2012). These were the first financial assistance programs for mothers with dependent children.
- A major step forward in the development of protective services was the first White House Conference on Dependent Children in 1909. The "resulting strong recommendation in favor of family care strengthened the movement for home rather than institutional care for dependent and delinquent children" (Trattner, 1999, p. 216). The conference was such a success that it has been held every 10 years since, except for 1981 when the Reagan administration canceled it (Karger & Stoesz, 2010). Another important result of the initial conference was the formation of the U.S. Children's Bureau in 1912. One of its

purposes was to collect systematic information on children. This marked the first time that children's welfare had been considered significant enough to spur creation of a permanent federal agency to oversee it (Trattner, 1999).

- In 1920 the 19th Amendment to the U.S. Constitution granted women the right to vote.

Focus on Mental Health Policy

Mental health policy in the beginning of the 20th century reflected the *mental hygiene* movement, replacing the earlier focus on moral treatment. The mental hygiene movement, which lasted from about 1900 to about 1945, was characterized by three main ideas (Fellin, 1996; Lin, 1995; USDHHS, 1999). First, people were becoming disillusioned with mental hospitals and the substandard conditions in many. Second, although institutionalization was not abandoned, alternative types of care such as specialized psychiatric units in hospitals were being developed. This paved the way for the next mental health movement (community mental health), which focused on treatment within the community context. Finally, the concept of "mental illness" began to replace "insanity," and psychotherapy as a treatment method gained in popularity. Chapter 13 discusses psychotherapy and mental health issues generally in greater detail.

Focus on Asian Immigration

The "progressive period" label notwithstanding, this era was not so progressive for Asians and Hispanics trying to enter the United States. The first Asian people to immigrate to the United States during the mid-19th century were Chinese, who came to the United States like many others seeking a better life (Jansson, 2012). They often performed "manual labor for farmers, manufacturers, miners, and the railroads" (Jansson, 2012, p. 122). Chinese immigrants were easy to exploit. "They could be paid minimal wages (coercive tactics were used when they threatened to strike for higher wages) and used to depress the wages of white workers, and they did not constitute a political threat because as 'aliens' and people of color they were denied legal rights. (The California Supreme Court ruled in 1854 that Chinese people could not testify in court against whites, even if one of their number had been murdered by a white citizen.) They were disallowed from owning mines by tax levies, could not become citizens, were required to attend segregated schools, and could not vote" (Jansson, 2012, p. 122). Blatant racism and apprehension that Chinese immigrants were stealing jobs away from their white counterparts resulted in the Chinese Exclusion Act of 1882, which denied them further access to the country (Jansson, 2012; Lu, 2008).

Japanese immigrants soon began to replace the Chinese in the U.S. labor market (Jansson, 2012). Like the Chinese, they were the victims of stereotypes and discrimination; for example, their children, too, attended segregated schools, they were prohibited from marrying interracially, laws banned the ownership of land, unions prohibited their entry into certain skilled trades, and instead they were diverted into manual labor jobs less appealing to white employees (Murase, 1995). Japanese immigration soon began to be politically discouraged, and finally the Immigration Acts of 1924 halted Asian immigration almost altogether, a state of affairs lasting until 1968 (Day, 2009). This act limited the number of immigrants allowed from any particular nationality to 2% of that nationality's population living in the United States in 1890. The effect was a greater percentage of people of Northern European heritage being admitted because a greater percentage already lived in the United States; because few Japanese lived in the United States during 1890, few were subsequently allowed admission (Jansson, 2012).

Focus on Chicano/Chicana and Puerto Rican Immigration

Initiated by the Mexican Revolution of 1910, large numbers of Chicano/Chicana professionals and businessmen in addition to laborers entered the United States as refugees (Curiel, 1995). As many as a million Chicanos/Chicanas migrated to the United States between 1910 and 1930 (Curiel, 1995; Meier, 1990). Substantial immigration continued across a 2,000-mile, relatively open boundary until 1924 when the U.S. Border Patrol was born; even then people continued to cross over to work on farms, orchards, and ranches and in food-processing plants (Jansson, 2012). White farmers and businessmen promoted Chicano/Chicana immigration. Hiring migrant labor was much cheaper than employing other citizens at minimum wage. No legal consequences existed for employers who hired people without documentation even if these employers were fully aware of their status. Employers did not concern themselves with the workers' conditions and could readily discourage protests.

When the Great Depression (described next) shook the economy in the 1930s, many Americans, including Chicanos, lost their jobs and found themselves desperately competing for survival (Curiel, 1995). To decrease the economic pressure, entire Chicano families were abruptly deported; shockingly, it is estimated that half of the deportees were U.S. citizens (Curiel, 1995).

Puerto Ricans migrated to the United States throughout the 20th century. (Highlight 6.6 provides a brief history of Puerto Rico.) Upon obtaining U.S. citizenship in 1917, Puerto Ricans gained the ability to readily travel back and forth without constraints.

The Great Depression and the 1930s

The Great Depression was initiated by the shocking stock market crash of 1929. The general trend over the next decade was an increasing reliance on the federal government to control and provide social services (Leiby, 1987). The Great Depression of the 1930s had a global impact, obliterating the idea that individuals control their own destiny. It became clear that the world contained various macro systems that worked together to profoundly affect

HIGHLIGHT 6.6

A Brief History of Puerto Rico

Campos (1995) presents a thumbnail sketch of Puerto Rico's history. The Taino Indians were the original inhabitants of Puerto Rico, which became a Spanish possession after Christopher Columbus "discovered" it in 1493. (Note how condescending the word *discovered* is when the island had probably been occupied for many centuries.) The Spanish conquerors believed that gold was plentiful on the island and coerced the Indians into working the mines. Poor treatment resulted in many Indian deaths, while others escaped the island entirely. When the available gold supply was exhausted, the Spaniards turned to agriculture, bringing in African slaves to work in the fields. Slavery was finally abolished in 1875.

The 19th century saw increased immigration to Puerto Rico from China, Spain, and other European countries, which together with the existing Spanish, Indian, and African residents resulted in a significantly diverse population (Campos, 1995). In 1898, after the Spanish-American War ended, Spain gave Puerto Rico to the United States under the Treaty of Paris of 1899.

No Puerto Rican representatives were allowed to participate in this process or to influence what was to happen to their country. Puerto Rico then came under U.S. military rule until the U.S. president appointed an American governor two years later.

Many Puerto Ricans, who attained U.S. citizenship in 1917 under the Jones Act, expressed ambivalence about that new status. One faction felt it was an asset, while another preferred that Puerto Rico pursue independence. It wasn't until 1950 that Puerto Ricans were allowed to write their own constitution; in 1952 they could first elect their own governor and legislature.

Currently, a close relationship exists between Puerto Rico and the United States where both are committed to a common citizenship, legal tender, protection, and the value of democracy. Practically speaking, the United States retains control over specified arenas including federal and military operations and foreign affairs (e.g., the U.S. Post Office) (Campos, 1995). Puerto Rico has primary control over its educational system, budget, governing laws, and correctional system.

---

individual lives. The United States was plagued by huge decreases in manufacturing productivity and wages, on the one hand, and skyrocketing unemployment, on the other. Banks closed, farmers lost everything, and urban poverty spread (Garvin & Tropman, 1998). Highlight 6.7 focuses on more of the Depression's consequences.

President Franklin Delano Roosevelt (holding office from 1933 to 1945) aggressively addressed the crisis. In 1933 he initiated the *New Deal,* a vigorous plan that created a wide range of social programs and significantly extended federal control in social welfare matters. Reid (1995) contends that the New Deal established a new perspective on how a welfare state operates that still is in effect today.

Early Initiatives of the New Deal

In view of the social and economic crisis, Roosevelt initiated a range of programs to address people's dire needs. The New Deal's basic philosophy was "relief for the unemployed through provision of jobs. Direct relief was to be a temporary, necessary expedient until those who were employable could be employed"

(Axinn & Stern, 2008, p. 185). Roosevelt pursued a three-pronged approach involving "cash relief, short-term work relief, and the expansion of employment" by hiring unemployed workers to undertake public works (Axinn & Stern, 2008, p. 189). The programs developed provide examples of what a government can do for its citizens during a national economic emergency.

The Federal Emergency Relief Act

In 1933 Roosevelt signed the Federal Emergency Relief Act (FERA), which provided federal grants to the states that would be administered by government units at the state and local levels to people in need. Although FERA's intent was to aid the unemployed, many working poor who could not earn enough to support their families also received aid. Additionally, it established camps for displaced persons, provided loans to college students, and purchased and sold 4 million acres of land to tenant farmers.

The Civilian Works Administration

Shortly after FERA was signed into law, Roosevelt assumed his presidential prerogative and created the Civilian Works Administration (CWA) in 1933.

HIGHLIGHT 6.7

Human Conditions During the Great Depression

Jansson (2012) lists some of the immediate consequences of the Depression:

- People from all levels of socioeconomic status were affected.
- Some families were forced to leave their homes and live in tents, and some had to share a small apartment with at least two other families.
- Single women clustered together in a single residence and often were compelled to depend on a single wage earner for sustenance.
- People raised crops in home gardens when they couldn't afford to buy food.

- Teenagers were booted from their homes to fend for themselves when families couldn't afford to support them.
- Middle-class citizens "feared foreclosure or evictions" and "had to pawn family possessions" to keep afloat.
- Starvation and malnutrition were rampant.
- Health care was often unavailable because people were denied care when they couldn't pay for it.
- Serious disturbances in family life and suicides were common occurrences. (pp. 199–200)

The CWA channeled funds to finance various public works such as building roads, cataloging resources in libraries, digging drainage ditches, and renovating parks. The intent, of course, was to create jobs.

The Civilian Conservation Corps

Another program developed as part of the New Deal was the Civilian Conservation Corps (CCC), also created in 1933. This program initially recruited males between 18 and 25 who were receiving public assistance, and transported them to revitalize parks in the West and participate in reforestation, flood prevention, and fire control projects. Once again, the intent was to provide employment to a population that had an exceptionally high unemployment rate. Similarly, the National Youth Administration (NYA) provided part-time work for high school and college students to encourage them to remain in school.

The Public Works Administration

In 1935 Roosevelt established the Public Works Administration (PWA). The PWA's intent was to "stimulate depressed industries" by contracting with private businesses to build public facilities, thereby increasing the number of available jobs (Barker, 2003, p. 351). Projects tended to be extensive and complex, such as "bridges, airports, dams, and school buildings" (Jansson, 2012, p. 211).

The Works Progress Administration

Similarly, in 1935 Roosevelt established the Works Progress Administration (WPA) (renamed the Works

Projects Administration in 1939). This was yet another program designed to provide work for unemployed people with various skills. One thrust was to support the "work of artists, musicians, writers, and scholars" (Barker, 2003, p. 468). WPA also provided jobs in a wide range of activities, from "heavy construction [of dams, bridges, parks, roads, and airports] to the painting of murals in local libraries and orchestral performances in the schools" (Axinn & Stern, 2008, p. 191; Jansson, 2012).

An End to the Programs

FERA, along with CWA, was terminated when the Social Security Act of 1935 was passed; CCC, NYA, PWA, and WPA saw their demise in the early 1940s at the beginning of World War II. Much of the legislation passed during the Depression was not intended to be permanent; rather, its purpose was to provide temporary jobs so people could support themselves during those hard times instead of being forced to accept charity (Day, 2009).

The Social Security Act of 1935

The most notable piece of legislation shaping social welfare policy during this period was the Social Security Act of 1935. Consisting of 11 titles (or major parts, each of which addresses a specified issue and program), this legislation totally reconfigured the social welfare system and placed the burden on the federal government to provide a coordinated system of resources. It established a structure of benefits in three major categories: (1) social insurance, (2) public assistance, and (3) health services ("federal monies for state and local public health works") (Tice & Perkins, 2002, p. 156). (Note that, because of their significance, Chapter 8 elaborates upon current policies and programs in greater detail. Although the Social Security Act of 1935 forms the basis for current policies and programs, numerous modifications and additions to the social welfare system have been made since that time.)

Federal legislation affects service provision in two basic ways. First, it provides federal funding to states to help them pay for programs and services. Without federal help, states often wouldn't have the money for many resources and services. Second, federal legislation imposes rules on the states that receive funding. If a state wants federal money, it must abide by the rules or forfeit the funding. All states want money. Therefore, federal legislation has set the stage for the types of programs that states must provide by making rules and establishing requirements to receive funding.

Social Insurance

Social insurance and public assistance both provide *financial benefits*—benefits in the form of cash or coupons that can be used in place of cash. *Social insurance* is a government program providing benefits related to certain designated risks working people assume; these include "old age, disability, death of a breadwinner, unemployment, and work-related injury and sickness" (Barker, 2003, p. 404). It's a type of insurance because workers and their employers pay premiums while they're working. They then receive benefits when encountering the specified conditions permitting benefits. The idea is that benefits are people's *right*: They worked and paid the premiums, and so deserve the benefits.

The Social Security Act established old age insurance (pensions) for older adults, in addition to unemployment insurance and worker's compensation for the unemployed (Tice & Perkins, 2002). *Unemployment insurance* provides cash benefits to employees who lose their jobs. *Workers' compensation* gives cash benefits to employees who suffer work-related injuries or illness.

Public Assistance

In contrast to social insurance, *public assistance* programs are based on *need*. Public assistance is a government program providing financial resources to people who can't support themselves. The Social Security Act established public assistance for older adults (Old Age Assistance), dependent children in single-parent families and children with disabilities (Aid to Dependent Children), and people who are blind (Aid to the Blind) (Tice & Perkins, 2002).

Often there is much greater stigma attached to people receiving public assistance than to those receiving social insurance. Many feel that it's their own fault that they're needy and that they should do something about it. Unlike people receiving social insurance, the argument goes, they never paid premiums for public assistance and so don't really deserve benefits. (Note that people receiving public assistance may also be eligible for social insurance benefits, depending on their work history and status.)

In reality, through no fault of their own, many people are in serious need of help—including many children. Although they are treated as a scourge primarily because of the costs, public assistance programs currently pay about 10% of all government payments to individuals (including retirement, disability, medical, unemployment, veterans', and federal education benefits) (U.S. Census Bureau, 2010). Highlight 6.8 focuses on public assistance for children and families.

War and Wealth: The 1940s

The U.S. involvement in World War II (1941–1945) brought an end to the Depression as unemployment plummeted and incomes rose significantly (Axinn & Stern, 2008). Many people felt optimistic about the future and believed that the Social Security Act had adequately solved most of the problems related to poverty.

A significant piece of 1940s legislation was the Serviceman's Readjustment Act of 1944, commonly referred to as the G.I. Bill. Its purpose was to give veterans opportunities for "education and training, home and business loans, and employment services" to help them return to civilian life (Segal & Brzuzy, 1998, p. 33).

It is beyond the scope of this chapter to discuss the intricacies of World War II. However, the history of social welfare includes not only policies providing services that enhance people's welfare but also those depriving people of resources and even causing them harm. Unfair, racist treatment is of special concern to social workers. Highlight 6.9

HIGHLIGHT 6.8

Public Assistance for Children and Families

The Social Security Act of 1935 expanded the government's responsibility for the well-being of children and their families. Title IV, Aid to Dependent Children (ADC) (later changed to Aid to Families with Dependent Children [AFDC] in 1962 to emphasize the importance of the family), "provided public relief to needy children through cash grants to their families"; another provision, Title V, broadened the role of the Children's Bureau to provide greater protection for children at risk of poverty, maltreatment, or delinquency (Karger & Stoesz, 2010, p. 387). The current public assistance program, which replaced AFDC in 1996, is Temporary Assistance for Needy Families (TANF), discussed further along with other public assistance programs in Chapter 8.

---

addresses the atrocious and unjust treatment of Japanese Americans during World War II.

Peace and Complacency: The 1950s

During the 1950s, the population exploded, resulting in the current huge bloc of aging baby boomers. (Chapter 10 addresses issues related to older adults more thoroughly.) Many people think of the 1950s as a period of domestic complacency and relative conservatism. Criticisms of social welfare policy at the time focused on restricting eligibility for benefits and making it difficult to continue getting them (Axinn & Stern, 2008).

For example, one social worker employed in a county public assistance program during those years reflects on how policies urged workers to literally look under beds and in closets to determine if "there was a man in the house." Two somewhat conflicting assumptions were at work (Axinn & Stern, 2008). First, it was assumed that a legally unattached man living in the home of a family receiving benefits made the home morally unsuitable for raising children. Second, such a man should be able to provide support for the family so it would no longer require

---

HIGHLIGHT 6.9

Japanese American Internment During World War II

EP 2.1.5a

On December 7, 1941, Japan bombed Pearl Harbor, and the United States entered the war the following day. Within days, Japanese Americans were placed under close and hostile public scrutiny. A few weeks later, California declared that Japanese Americans could no longer assume any civil service positions, including holding public office. Japanese American citizens were fired from their jobs, forced to close their businesses, unlawfully confined, and even viciously assaulted (Day, 2009).

Although Roosevelt declared that all German, Italian, and Japanese aliens should leave the West Coast, only Japanese Americans were pressured to remain away more permanently (Day, 2009). Japanese American soldiers were identified and discharged or assigned menial labor such as kitchen work.

By the fall of 1942, permanent detention (concentration) camps called "relocation centers" were established throughout the West, especially in California. With no trial or due process, over 112,000 Japanese Americans, two-thirds of whom were citizens, were forced to leave their homes and live in guarded camps until their release in 1944.

The secretary of the treasury charged the Federal Reserve Bank of San Francisco to look after Japanese American property, and the Farm Security Administration was supposed to do the same for Japanese farms and equipment. However, little, if anything, was done. The detainees lost $400 million worth of property, of which less than 10% was ever returned (Day, 2009).

benefits. (Focus on Critical Thinking 6.2 poses some questions regarding the appropriateness of these policies.) A California Supreme Court decision in 1967 effectively ended such policies when the court determined that workers could not be fired for failing to comply with such rules (Axinn & Stern, 2008; *Benny Max Parrish v. the Civil Service Commission of the County of Alameda*, 1967). Later court decisions eliminated man-in-the-house rules altogether (*King v. King*, 1968; *Shapiro v. Thompson*, 1969).

Amendments to the Social Security Act

A major 1950 piece of social welfare legislation involved amendments to the Social Security Act. Public assistance coverage was broadened to include people who had temporary and permanent disabilities through a program entitled Aid to the Disabled (later called Aid to the Permanently and Totally Disabled) (Tice & Perkins, 2002). Additionally, the ADC program was expanded to provide benefits to primary caregivers of dependent children (Axinn & Stern, 2008).

The End of School Segregation

In a landmark ruling in 1954 in *Brown v. Board of Education,* the Supreme Court overturned the "separate but equal" doctrine and declared that racial segregation in public schools was unconstitutional— even when separate schools provided the same quality of education. Although this decision paved the way for stopping blatant racial discrimination in various other public settings such as train and bus stations, restaurants, and recreational facilities, it took many years of struggle to effectively put this principle into practice (Pollard, 1995).

Focus on Mental Health: The Deinstitutionalization Movement

After World War II, the third mental health movement of the last century gained momentum, and it continues to characterize mental health service provision to this day (Fellin, 1996). The *deinstitutionalization* movement (following the mental hygiene movement) focuses on providing services and care for people within their own communities rather than in institutional settings (Fellin, 1996; Lin, 1995; USDHHS, 1999). It stresses placing people back in the community and providing mental health treatment and services to them there. The deinstitutionalization movement resulted from the increasing belief that, with outpatient psychotherapeutic treatment and psychotropic drugs (i.e., drugs intended to affect mental or emotional functioning), people with mental illness could function in the community environment (Fellin, 1996; USDHHS, 1999). This effort has also been referred to as the *community mental health movement.*

The 1960s and the War on Poverty

Any sense of optimism or complacency in the 1950s began to weaken as the 1960s began and poverty remained a large problem. Three dynamics shaped this view (Axinn & Stern, 2008). First, large pockets of poverty characterized various regions of the country, and attention was focused on what could be done to ameliorate this poverty. For example, "if the people of Appalachia suffered from the decrease of jobs in coal mining, then the expansion of factory employment seemed appropriate" (Axinn & Stern, 2008, p. 247). Questions might be raised regarding what could be done to stimulate employment and industrial growth in that area.

A second dynamic shaping the nation's perspective on poverty involved the fact that the risk of poverty for people of color was significantly greater than that for whites. People of color clearly experienced regular discrimination in employment throughout the country.

The third dynamic concerning poverty involved the fact that public assistance rolls were escalating even as unemployment decreased. Prior to the 1960s, the two had a correlated relationship. That is, when unemployment was low, public assistance rolls declined because more people were working. But now this was no longer the case. Public assistance rolls were escalating regardless of whether employment was available.

The Public Welfare Amendments of 1962

Under the administration of President John F. Kennedy (serving from 1961 until his assassination in 1963), significant new amendments to the Social Security Act were passed. The Public Welfare Amendments of 1962 were rooted in the idea that supportive social services would enhance welfare recipients' ability to get back on their feet and eventually become self-supporting. Services included job training, job placement, and counseling, among others (Trattner, 1999).

The act directed the federal government to assume 75% of the cost of providing social services to people receiving public assistance. This was a tremendous incentive for states to provide services because they had to assume only 25% of the financial burden for doing so. The idea was to reduce welfare rolls. Unfortunately, this did not work, and welfare rolls continued to escalate.

The "Great Society"

During the 1960s, President Lyndon B. Johnson (whose administration lasted from 1963 to 1969) initiated the "War on Poverty" in an effort to fashion a

"Great Society." The intent was to eliminate poverty and provide a high quality of life for all. The War on Poverty was founded on the idea that what poor families really needed was encouragement and training to acquire needed job skills, allowing them to achieve economic independence (Leiby, 1987). However, the poor faced not only economic hardship, but also psychological and sociological barriers (e.g., prejudice and discrimination) to living effective, successful lives (Leiby, 1987). Some theorists referred to the poor as living in a *culture of poverty*—the pattern of values, norms, and expectations conveyed from one generation to another that limits people to a life of poverty and discourages them from taking advantage of economic and social opportunities (Barker, 2003; Karger & Stoesz, 2010). The War on Poverty intended for poor families to be offered and have greater access to the resources and services they needed to pursue economic independence and a better quality of life.

As a result, numerous new programs were developed at the federal level, as the War on Poverty was entirely a federal initiative (Leiby, 1987). The Economic Opportunity Act of 1964 established a range of programs, including Volunteers in Service to America and Operation Head Start, among many others. Highlight 6.10 describes some of these programs. Primary efforts were concentrated on fighting poverty in poor neighborhoods and communities by increasing jobs, resources, and opportunities for residents (Karger & Stoesz, 2010). Such programs encouraged citizen participation. This was a time of activism for professional social workers on behalf of various populations in need, reflecting a renewed optimism that poverty could be eliminated and a good quality of life enjoyed by all.

Many other initiatives were undertaken during the War on Poverty. For instance, the Food Stamp Act of 1964 initiated a program in which eligible needy families could receive coupons that could be exchanged for food. Another initiative involved greatly expanded coverage by the Social Security Act in 1965 to include Medicare (a social insurance program of health care for older adults) and Medicaid (a public assistance program of health care for needy children and families). The Housing and Urban Development (HUD) Act of 1968 provided new low-income housing opportunities for eligible families. Chapter 8 describes all four of these programs in greater detail.

HIGHLIGHT 6.10

The Economic Opportunity Act of 1964

The following programs were established when the Economic Opportunity Act, also referred to as the "antipoverty bill," was passed in 1964 (Trattner, 1999, p. 322):

- *Volunteers in Service to America (VISTA):* A program designed to recruit volunteers to work in urban and rural neighborhoods experiencing economic and cultural problems, and to assist residents in enhancing their communities.
- *Job Corps:* A program that recruited impoverished youths ages 16–24 from disadvantaged urban and rural communities, and provided them with "residential training, employment, and work skills" (Barker, 2003, p. 232).

- *Upward Bound:* A program targeting school-age children and presenting them with special educational resources and incentives to prevent them from dropping out of school.
- *Neighborhood Youth Corps:* A program employing teenagers in local organizations.
- *Operation Head Start:* A program giving preschoolers resources designed to meet educational, health, and recreational needs throughout the year.
- *Community Action Program (CAP):* A program that developed and coordinated efforts by neighborhood organizations to fight poverty and improve social and economic conditions for community residents. (Operation Head Start was initially funded and coordinated under CAP.)

Amendments to the Social Security Act in 1967 reorganized resource and service distribution. These changes

divorced income maintenance functions from social services functions and split public welfare departments into two sections: social services, whose workers provide counseling services and services to neglected, abused, or dependent children and older people; and assistance payments, whose workers determine eligibility and set amounts of grants based on state levels of need, number in family, and their own discretion.

(Day, 2009, p. 346–347)

The driving force behind this change was the idea that "services to the poor should not be connected to whether they receive financial aid" (Day, 2009, p. 347).

Focus on Mental Health: The Community Mental Health Centers Act

In 1963 the Community Mental Health Centers Act was passed, providing federal funding for community "mental health centers, training programs, and outpatient treatment programs" (Barker, 1999, p. 19). This, of course, was a manifestation of the deinstitutionalization movement. However, problems arose for three reasons (Lin, 1995). First, treating people in the community was much more complicated and

difficult than anticipated. Second, many professionals preferred not to work with this population with its long-term problems. Third, communities either did not have or would not commit the resources necessary to sustain community care. As a result, many people with mental illness ended up on the streets or in jail, for lack of better placement and services. These problems continue to this day.

Note that during the 1960s a trend toward legal advocacy developed (Lin, 1995). As a consequence of the civil rights movement, it focused on emphasizing and clarifying the rights of mental patients. Two court cases are particularly significant (Lin, 1995). In *Wyatt v. Stickney* (1971), a federal court ruled that mental patients should not be exposed to extreme or possibly damaging types of treatment. In *O'Connor v. Donaldson* (1975), the Supreme Court determined that mental illness and treatment needs are insufficient grounds for confining a person involuntarily (Lin, 1995).

Focus on Older Adults: The Older Americans Act of 1965

Unlike the Social Security Act, the Older Americans Act (OAA) of 1965 is not a policy to provide programming and resources directly to people. Rather, it establishes an "administrative structure" for the

EP 2.1.8a

coordination and delivery of social services to older people (Barusch, 2012, p. 390). The OAA created an Administration on Aging (AOA) under the auspices of the Department of Health, Education, and Welfare to oversee state and area offices throughout the country.

Benefits coordinated by AOA offices include transportation; provision of hot meals delivered to people's homes or provided at senior centers ("focus points" where seniors can gather for a variety of purposes); preventive health care such as inoculations or health education; recreation; home care (in which various services involving health, daily living support, or other social services are provided in people's own homes); information; and resource referral (Barusch, 2009; Dobelstein, 2003, p. 258). Anyone age 60 or over is eligible for services, regardless of their economic status. Because the focus is on coordination of services, not prescriptions about what should be provided, services vary dramatically from one location to the next (Dobelstein, 2003). Chapter 10 discusses service provision to older adults in detail.

Civil Rights in the 1960s

EP 2.1.5a, 2.1.5b, 2.1.8a

The concept of *civil rights* "refers primarily to claims by African Americans and other minorities of color, women, and people of different sexual orientations to be free to do the same kinds of things and have the same kinds of civil entitlements that everyone else in the society enjoyed" (Garvin & Tropman, 1998, p. 255).

During the early 1960s, "poverty was widespread in America, and nonwhite people were systematically discriminated against in all facets of American life" (Day, 2009, p. 333). It might be said that the civil rights movement actually began in 1955 when organizers selected a young African American minister named Martin Luther King, Jr., to spearhead a bus boycott in Montgomery, Alabama (Jansson, 2012). The protesters refused to comply with the public policy whereby African Americans were relegated to the backs of buses while whites got to sit in the front. After a long period of controversy and conflict, including violent acts of retribution against African Americans, the policy was withdrawn.

The Civil Rights Act of 1964 was the most important piece of civil rights legislation since the Civil War. Chapin (2011) describes it as a "landmark law [that] attempted to decrease discrimination by:

- *barring unequal application of voter registration requirements;*
- *outlawing segregation in hotels, restaurants, theaters, and other public accommodations;*
- *encouraging school desegregation and authorizing the U.S. attorney general to file lawsuits against schools that resisted integration;*
- *empowering federal agencies to withhold funds from programs that practiced segregation; and,*
- *creating the Equal Employment Opportunity Commission (EEOC) to oversee antidiscrimination efforts in employment. (p. 236)*

Jimenez (2010) reports that after the act passed:

A movement of college students from across the country known as Freedom Summer sponsored a voter registration drive in the South. Three students working in the effort, two Whites and one African American, were murdered, and almost 100 others were beaten by Southerners who objected to their efforts to register African Americans to vote. Congress responded by passing the Voting Rights Act of 1965, which put federal registrars in districts where local officials were obstructing registration of African American voters. As a result of the effort to enfranchise African Americans in the South, the number of Black elected officials there tripled (from 1,000 to 3,000 from 1969 to 1975), and more than 930,000 new African American voters were added to registration rolls in the South. (pp. 197–198)

Focus on Critical Thinking 6.3 raises some key questions concerning these acts and the issues they address.

Focus on Mexican Americans: The Chicano/Chicana Movement

EP 2.1.4a, 2.1.4c, 2.1.5a

No clearly defined dates exist for the "Chicano movement" (Curiel, 1995). During the 1960s, various Chicano/Chicana groups came together to address their social and economic plight. Common goals included celebration of their ethnic and cultural identity and traditions, in addition to enhanced socioeconomic status (Curiel, 1995). A key issue involved how Chicano/Chicana income levels continued to lag significantly behind those of their white counterparts.

Because Chicano/Chicana agricultural laborers were prevented from joining labor unions, they lacked power and were deprived of economic opportunities to get ahead (Day, 2009). A leading political figure and vigorous advocate for the rights of farmworkers was Cesar E. Chavez. Born in 1927 in Yuma, Arizona, on a farm homesteaded by his grandfather in the 1880s, he was to become one of the most famous activists of the 20th century.

Chavez's family became migrant agricultural workers when they lost their farm during the Great Depression. At age 25, Chavez was picking apricots on a farm near San Jose, California, when a community organizer for a Hispanic-based self-help group, the Community Service Organization, recruited him to work for the grassroots (i.e., sponsored directly by citizens) organization. He began working part-time, went on to work full-time, and eventually became the organization's director.

In 1962, when the Community Service Organization ignored his pleas to advocate more intensively on the behalf of farmworkers, Chavez quit and founded the National Farm Workers Association (NFWA). He then traveled from farm to farm and camp to camp, recruiting members and urging workers to strive for fair wages and improved health conditions. In addition to better wages, issues included providing rest breaks, making clean drinking water available, prohibiting dangerous pesticide use, and providing protection from agricultural hazards. In 1965 the NFWA initiated a successful five-year strike and boycott against grape growers. In 1966

it became affiliated with the American Federation of Labor–Congress of Industrial Organizations (AFL–CIO), the oldest and most extensive labor union in the United States.

Chavez continued leading vital advocacy efforts on the behalf of farmworkers until his death in 1993 at the age of 66. Jimenez (2010) reflects:

> *Coming from a humble background, Cesar Chavez rose to a position of leadership because of his determination in the face of major opposition, his courage to keep fighting for the rights of workers, and his unwavering belief that social justice should be extended to everyone. His legacy of courage and leadership improved the lives of generations of farm workers, and he will be particularly remembered for his efforts on behalf of the millions of people who quietly toil in the agricultural fields of California. (p. 205)*

Focus on American Indians: Striving for Self-Determination

As with other population groups, the 1960s reflected the beginning of a more progressive era for Native Americans in their quest for self-determination. Despite the fact that policies enacted in the 1950s aimed at *terminating the* special status of and benefits for certain tribes, and even breaking up reservations, these were eventually abandoned during the 1960s. The 1960s began a period of activism in which "Native American protest groups formed to assert their rights" (Tice & Perkins, 2002, p. 212).

EP 2.1.4a,
2.1.4c,
2.1.5a

Historically, First Nations Peoples were often discouraged from practicing their customs. Here, women celebrate their culture by performing traditional dances in Gallup, New Mexico.

Tice and Perkins (2002) indicate

The most famous of these groups, the American Indian Movement (AIM), staged protests at Alcatraz in 1969, by then an unoccupied prison island, and in 1973 at Wounded Knee on Pine Ridge Reservation. In the former instance, AIM was trying to exercise its claimed treaty rights to unused federal lands. The protesters were removed in 1971. At Wounded Knee, they were armed and protesting the domination of the tribal government by whites. This action ended in violence as federal civilian and military forces took control of the reservation. Two Native Americans were killed and two federal officials wounded. (p. 212)

The struggle for self-determination continues today (Lewis, 1995). At least two critical social policy issues emerge (Weaver, 2008). First, American Indians must have rights to govern themselves and make their own decisions instead of being the victims of coercion by the federal government. Second, ongoing economic development must be pursued.

A Return to Conservatism in the 1970s

As the 1960s ended, so did the War on Poverty. The public was sick of the seemingly endless spending and questionable results. Johnson also had been battered by intense opposition to the Vietnam War and was increasingly unpopular in the polls. As a result, he withdrew from the presidential race, which was then won by Richard M. Nixon (who served from 1969 until his resignation in 1974). Nixon and subsequent presidents Gerald Ford (serving from 1974 to 1977) and Jimmy Carter (serving from 1977 to 1981) "were relatively conservative presidents who had little outward interest in major social reforms. Yet, social spending rose dramatically during this . . . [supposedly] conservative period" (Jansson, 2012, p. 292).

Old Age, Survivors, Disability, and Health Insurance

One notable change in social welfare benefit provision occurred in 1971 when it was proposed that the public assistance programs Old Age Assistance, Aid to the Blind, and Aid to the Permanently and Totally Disabled became social insurance programs. In 1972 these programs were replaced by the Supplementary Security Income (SSI) program. Because social insurance programs provide benefits to workers and their families based on their *right* to them rather than their *need*, recipient rolls soared. The changes obviously reflected a shift in public opinion regarding who was considered needy and who had the right to receive benefits without question. Older adults and people with disabilities automatically received benefits without having to prove they were poor enough to need such resources.

Focus on Social Welfare Policies Concerning Child and Family Welfare

Despite conservative times, one emerging concern involved child abuse and neglect. LeVine and Sallee (1999) describe conditions from the 1950s to 1970s: "The majority of services to children were financial in nature and not treatment oriented. Furthermore, what services and counseling children received were inconsistent and unorganized. Thus child abuse and neglect were 'rediscovered' in the late 1960s and early 1970s" (p. 31).

In 1974 the Child Abuse Prevention and Treatment Act was passed in response to increasing public concern about child maltreatment. To receive funding, states must establish a centralized reporting agency, collect systematic data about child maltreatment, and pass laws to protect children under age 18 from maltreatment (Liederman, 1995).

In 1975 Title XX of the Social Security Act was passed; (Liederman, 1995). It makes grants available "to states to provide social services to welfare recipients as well as to people above the poverty line" (Chapin, 2011, p. 75). One of its major goals was to prevent institutionalization of children (Barker, 2003; LeVine & Sallee, 1999).

The Indian Child Welfare Act of 1978 addressed the importance of maintaining children's racial and cultural identity. It reflected a response to concerns that American Indian children were being removed from their homes and placed in non–American Indian foster family and adoptive homes. The concern was that the linkage with their heritage, customs, and cultural identity was being severed. The act thus required that American Indian children be placed in homes that nurture the distinctive values, customs, and heritage of American Indian culture (Liederman, 1995).

The 1980 Adoption Assistance and Child Welfare Act had an impact on programs for children and families in two significant ways (Liederman, 1995). First, federal funding helped states assess, treat, and prevent child maltreatment. Second, funding was made available to states to help them pay for out-of-home care for children when necessary. This legislation also stressed the importance of *permanency planning* for children—that is, finding them a permanent home as soon as possible when return to their birth parents is not viable.

Conservative Extremes in the 1980s and Early 1990s

President Ronald Reagan (serving from 1981 to 1989) launched an overt return to conservative social welfare policies. Reagan "discounted the importance of racism and discrimination" and maintained that, "if they tried," African Americans, Hispanics, and American Indians could become just as successful as whites (Jansson, 2012, p. 330). He viewed American males as

rugged individualists who could accomplish almost anything if they tried. Similarly, he ascribed to women "primarily domestic functions" and failed to appoint many women to significant positions of power during his presidency (or his California governorship in the 1960s and 1970s) (Barrett, 1983; Jansson, 2012, p. 330). His primary accomplishments were (1) reducing taxes, (2) significantly increasing the defense budget, and (3) slashing social welfare spending (Haynes, 1991).

Reagan's frugal social welfare policies continued during President George H. W. Bush's term (from 1989 to 1993). Results included significant increases in the numbers of people living in poverty, in homelessness, in the numbers of oppression of vulnerable populations, and in racial tension leading to various confrontations (Jansson, 2012; Karger & Stoesz, 2006).

Focus on People with Disabilities: 1990s Legislation

Two positive pieces of legislation passed in the 1990s are of special significance for people with developmental or other disabilities in terms of improving access to resources (De-Weaver, 1995). The Americans with Disabilities Act (ADA) of 1990 requires that public buildings, areas, and workplaces provide ready access to people with physical or mental disabilities. The intent is to let them actively involve themselves in everyday life as readily as possible.

EP 2.1.5b

The second important piece of legislation is the Developmental Disabilities Assistance and Bill of Rights Act of 1990. This law accomplishes several things—including establishing grant programs for, promoting advocacy on behalf of, and requiring adequate services for people with developmental disabilities (DeWeaver, 1995). Chapter 11 discusses both pieces of legislation more thoroughly.

Welfare Reform in the Clinton Era

When Bill Clinton was elected president in 1992 (his service ending in 2001), liberals hoped for positive changes in social welfare policy. However, he faced a Senate and House of Representatives dominated by Republicans as early as 1994, so most of his proposals were squelched. Clinton should be recognized, however, for decreasing some proposed reductions in spending on social programs and reducing proposed tax cuts, in addition to ending annual budget deficits; note that had surpluses been applied to strengthening Social Security and Medicare, the nation might not now be in such dire financial straits in terms of its deficit and future support of these programs (Jansson, 2012).

A major conservative policy established during his presidency is the Personal Responsibility and Work Opportunities Act (PRWOA) of 1996, which affects public assistance, SSI, immigrants' ability to receive benefits, child care, and nutritional and food programs. One of its facets, Temporary Assistance for Needy Families (TANF), described more thoroughly in Chapter 8, greatly restricts benefits compared to the program preceding it (Aid to Families with Dependent Children [AFDC]). TANF essentially changed "welfare as we know it" by placing time limits on benefits, allowing states great discretion in benefit distribution, and establishing stringent work requirements.

Additional significant pieces of legislation implemented during the Clinton era were the Family and Medical Leave Act of 1993 and the Crime Bill of 1994 (Axinn & Stern, 2008; Jansson, 2012; Marx, 2004). The Family and Medical Leave Act requires that both public and private employers with 50 or more employees provide each employee up to 12 weeks of unpaid annual leave after a birth or child adoption, while caring for an ill family member, or during recuperation from illness (Axinn & Stern, 2008). Although health benefits must continue, the fact that the time is unpaid discourages many people from using this option. Leave only applies to caring for a spouse, child, or parent; others such as mother-in-law or a partner don't qualify (Axinn & Stern, 2008). The 1994 Crime Bill increased funding for hiring more police officers and building more prisons, in addition to enacting federal penalties and developing social services to decrease domestic violence.

The Conservatism of George W. Bush

The election of George W. Bush in 2000 and his reelection in 2004 marks an era of what he terms "compassionate conservatism." This is the philosophy that although government should not interfere directly with people's lives, it should help people to help themselves. The compassionate part involves the fact that people should be helped. The conservative part concerns the idea that people should be responsible for their own actions and lives. Bush's presidency was characterized by at least three major themes (Blau, 2010; Jansson, 2012).

First was the emphasis on homeland security. Domestic and foreign policy were critically intertwined during his terms because of the costs involved. With a finite amount of money available, spending in one area limits funding available to finance other areas. After two airplanes slammed into the World Trade Center towers on September 11, 2001, Bush initiated a "war on terrorism" and established a Homeland Security Agency. Despite no solid evidence, Bush maintained that Iraqi leaders were concealing weapons of mass destruction and that there were relationships between Iraq and the Afghanistan terrorist organization Al Qaeda (which took responsibility for the September 11 attack) (Jansson, 2012). Bush demanded information about the alleged weapons, failed to get enough for his satisfaction, and declared war on Iraq in spring 2003, despite little international support. Although Bush declared victory on May 1, the costs involved to maintain control and to rebuild the social and political infrastructures have skyrocketed far beyond initial projections (Jansson, 2012). Money spent on the war and security issues takes potential funding away from many social programs in addition to escalating the national debt. Bush initiated huge increases in defense spending while concurrently slashing spending on domestic programs (Jansson, 2012). Questions have also been raised regarding "the administration's policy of monitoring of communications in this country without a court order" (Blau, 2010, p. 121).

A second theme characterizing Bush's presidency was the push to trim the federal government and give more decision-making capabilities to the states. Critics of this trend caution that this results in inconsistent access to resources and programs, in addition to greater inequities between the "haves" and "have nots."

A third theme involved shifting service provision from the public to the private sector. Bush maintained that private organizations and businesses are generally more efficient than government agencies and give people a wider range of choices (Jansson, 2012). Bush also supported "faith-based initiatives" in which public funding would go to religious organizations, a plan that Congress did not support (Jansson, 2012). Although many religious organizations have a long history of providing effective social services, those receiving public funding have always carefully separated service provision from religious activities (Jansson, 2012). Bush proposed allowing such organizations greater freedom in terms of how they spend funding and combine these two facets. Critics of this view question the validity of using public funds to sponsor religious activities and wonder how such activities could be monitored for fairness and objectivity. A problem with financing religious activities with public funding involves a basic right to religious freedom. Which religious services should be supported? Those sponsored by Christians, Muslims, Roman Catholics, Jews, Buddhists, Unitarians? To what extent should public taxes finance religious doctrines and projects in which not everyone believes?

When Bush first took office he initiated and succeeded in getting a huge tax cut. The rationale was that giving money back to people would stimulate the economy because they would spend that money, which would in turn benefit business and the economy. However, critics maintained that the cut would have little effect on the economy because it primarily benefited the wealthy, who wouldn't spend the

money anyway; in reality, 1% of the population received 40% of the tax benefits (Jansson, 2012). Giving money to the rich and taking programs and benefits away from the poor increases inequity and the chasm between the rich and the poor.

Focus on Critical Thinking 6.4 raises some issues to consider for the future of social welfare.

The Great Recession

A severe recession began in December of 2007 and by the spring of 2009 was pronounced as the most devastating one since the Great Depression; Jansson (2012) refers to it as "the Great Recession" (p. 452). A *recession* is an economic downturn where businesses make less money, unemployment mounts, people's access to usable capital plummets, and their capacity to make purchases shrinks (Barker, 2003). The Great Recession characterized the end of the Bush administration and the beginning of the Obama presidency.

Jansson (2012) describes the progression of the crisis. The calamity was initially triggered beginning

---

FOCUS ON CRITICAL THINKING 6.4

What Are Future Issues in Social Welfare?

EP 2.1.3, 2.1.9a

Since the September 11, 2001, destruction of the World Trade Center, attention has been focused on the "war on terrorism," the aftermath of the war in Iraq, and the strong American military presence in many Middle Eastern nations. Many resources are being diverted to national and international security and to supporting troops. What effects will this have on domestic social welfare programs? Specific issues include the following.

Critical Thinking Questions

- "Without Social Security, almost half of all [older adults] . . . would be in poverty" (Segal, 2010, p. 320). "New congressional projections show Social Security running deficits every year until its trust funds are eventually drained in about 2037" (CBSNews.com, 2011c). What do you think should be done about Social Security? For example, should the minimum age to receive benefits be raised?

Should benefits be reduced? Should worker contributions be raised?

- What is the future of Medicare in view of the increasing proportion of older adults compared with working people, who support Medicare through taxes? What will happen when more people receive benefits from a much smaller contributing pool?

- What will happen to children and families currently receiving public assistance when their time-limited benefits end?

- To what extent should we continue to build new prisons to house an ever-increasing number of inmates at enormous public expense instead of focusing on treatment and rehabilitation?

- What should be done about the scarcity of low-cost housing and the large population of homeless people roaming the streets?

- Where should spending priorities be placed? On the "war on terrorism"? Supporting troops on an international level? Cutting the national deficit? Expanding social programs?

in the 1980s by the elimination of federal regulations governing banking lending (originally instituted during the Great Depression). Some of the abolished regulations had required banks to hold significant funds in reserve in the event that large numbers of loans and mortgages went delinquent, a common occurrence during recessions. Other eliminated regulations required that people who purchased homes submit significant down payments. This, in effect, would hold down monthly interest payments on the house and keep people from overextending themselves financially.

However, large American banks went on a "speculative spree," lending to people with low incomes who would not have qualified financially for loans in the past; as a result banks were making escalating profits (Jansson, 2012, p. 453). People who were required to make very low or no down payments on mortgages thought they could afford such purchases because house prices were skyrocketing at unrivaled levels. These people felt that if they had trouble making house payments, they could always sell their real estate at a great profit. They failed to realize that this was a "housing bubble" that was unsustainable and unrealistic. So, when the price of housing took a nose-dive, many people were left owing much more on the mortgage for their house than the house was worth. Because these people had put little or no money down on the house in the first place, it was to their advantage simply to walk away. Foreclosures were the result. Because of the avalanche of foreclosures, banks began to fail. Government assistance kept many of them solvent.

Double-digit unemployment did not help the situation. When people are unemployed, they have little money to pour into the economy. Unemployment is common during recessions. Shrinking profits and resources result in layoffs and business closures.

The "Fringe Economy"

EP 2.1.4a

Another facet contributing to economic problems involves people living in poverty and their problems with credit. Karger and Stoesz (2010) discuss the "fringe economy" and the credit options that maintain it. The *fringe economy* is an "alternative financial services sector" based on "[w]elfare [cutback of resources and services,] . . . deep federal and state budget cuts, the growth of the working poor, under- and

unemployment, dual labor markets, and a frozen minimum wage" (p. 127). It serves people who have no or almost no resources, must live day to day and paycheck to paycheck (if they have a paycheck), and are desperate to survive.

"Credit is a bridge between real household earnings and consumption decisions, offering relief during periods of economic distress and uncertainty" (Karger and Stoesz; p. 129). People with "good" credit can borrow and pay back with no collateral required. However, people with "questionable" or "compromised" credit must usually provide some collateral before receiving credit in addition to paying exorbitant interest rates. Limited credit cards, pawn shops, and payday loans are among credit options for people who are poor

Limited credit cards are for people considered greater credit risks after assessing "the cardholder's creditworthiness, past use of credit, and ability to repay debt" (Karger and Stoesz; p. 129–130). Most often, the amount of credit available is quite limited and the interest rates are excessive. There may be monthly participation fees in addition to fees for cash advances. Rates skyrocket with missed payments. Often there is a high origination fee. For example, one bank "charged $281 for a credit card with a limit of $300, leaving only $19 when the card arrived. This is predatory lending, especially when compared to mainstream credit cards that charge no setup or monthly fees, charge nothing to increase credit limits, and have free electronic access for account management" (p. 130).

Pawn shops provide fixed-term loans in return for holding collateral. "The customer is given a pawn ticket that includes his or her name and address, a description of the pledged good, the amount lent, the maturity date, and the amount that must be repaid to reclaim the property" (Karger and Stoesz, p. 132). At or before the date of maturity, the customer may repay the loan and regain his or her property. If the customer does not repay the loan on time, the pawn shop retains whatever the item is that served as collateral. Many pawn shops have an established maximum that they will loan regardless of the collateral's value. For instance, if the pawn shop's loan limit is $1,000, that is all it will loan even if an item is worth $3,000. Some pawn shops allow customers to borrow indefinitely to maintain access to the collateral, but usually at excessive interest rates (e.g., 15% per *month*).

Payday loan outlets have increased in number from 2,000 in 1995 to 24,000 in 2007. Customers must have a valid checking account to qualify to cover the loan's interest and the loan itself. Loans usually are for a maximum of $300 and are borrowed for 14 to 18 days. Interest usually is about 20% for the loan period, but can be as high as 37%. After paying the interest, the customer may extend the loan for a few additional periods, but must pay the interest for each extension period. Whereas pawn shops have collateral they keep upon loan default, payday loan outlets can be more aggressive. They can ruin your credit rating or press criminal charges for writing a bad check.

The Presidency of Barack Obama

Jansson (2012) reflects on the candidacy of Barack Obama, the nation's first multiracial president:

Relatively progressive voters saw Obama as an agent for change. He voiced liberal concerns. He spoke about positive functions of government. He lauded free markets, but wanted regulations to protect citizens from their excesses, such as higher minimum wages, reversal of some anti-union regulations, and crackdowns on private health insurance companies that often withdrew coverage when enrollees became ill. Independents and moderates often viewed him as a prudent reformer. He appealed to non-partisan voters who had tired of gridlocked government. (p. 452)

The Stimulus Plan

As indicated earlier, Obama entered the national scene in the midst of the Great Recession. One of the first things he did as president was enact a Stimulus Plan to address the dire economic situation. Jansson (2012) calls it a "*disguised* social welfare" plan because it included such a wide range of social programs (p. 455). Goals included:

- Protecting and generating jobs to encourage economic revitalization.
- Helping people most devastated by the recession.
- Investing in technology in health and science to enhance economic viability and growth.
- Supporting projects aimed at long-term benefits such as improving transportation systems, protecting the environment, and strengthening infrastructure.

- Stabilizing budgets at the state and local levels to prevent cutbacks in vital services and arbitrary increases in state and local taxes. (Jansson, 2012)

By September 2009, $12.5 trillion had been spent to help the economy; spending focused on saving banks and mortgage companies, battling against foreclosures to help mortgage holders, bailing out the floundering General Motors and Chrysler Corporation, and funding other aspects of the Stimulus Plan (Jansson, 2012).

Health Care Reform

Obama's health care reform plan entitled the Patient Protection and Affordable Care Act of 2010 was passed as amended by Congress. The plan's intent is to "hold insurance companies accountable, lower health care costs, guarantee more choice, and enhance the quality of care for all Americans" (WhiteHouse.gov, 2011b). Five advantages are emphasized (WhiteHouse.gov, 2011b). First, insurers are required to pay the full cost of recommended preventive services. Second, insurance companies are prohibited from denying coverage for pre-existing conditions. Third, many people on Medicare are helped with their prescription drug coverage. Fourth, it is predicted that billions will be saved on Medicare spending. Fifth, young adults may remain on their parents' insurance plan until age 26 instead of about age 19 (except for full-time students in some instances).

Jansson (2012) explains another aspect of the plan:

The legislation proposed that in 2014 states establish "insurance exchanges" to allow uninsured consumers, as well as business, to purchase insurance coverage that provided basic coverage. (Individuals and businesses would be mandated to insure themselves and their employees—or they would have to pay penalties to states that would use the funds to insure them.) (p. 464)

At the time of this writing, two lawsuits are being considered by the 4th U.S. Circuit Court of Appeals in Virginia; arguments are that it's unconstitutional to force uninsured people to pay for insurance and that such legislation interferes with business (CBSNews.com, 2011b). Thirty-one lawsuits have been filed to date; it is anticipated that the debate will eventually be settled by the Supreme Court (CBSNews.com, 2011b).

Foreign Policy

Obama's foreign policy has concentrated on a number of issues; these include refocusing on the al Qaeda threat in Afghanistan and Pakistan, ending the war in Iraq, keeping nuclear weapons out of terrorists' possession, and encouraging peace in Israel and the Middle East (WhiteHouse.gov, 2011a). Obama indicated that "Justice has been done" after the death on May 1, 2011, of Osama bin Laden, mastermind of the 9/11 attacks (CBSNews, 2011a).

The Development of the Social Work Profession

EP 2.1.1

Despite the different paths taken by the Settlement house and charity organization movements, social work pioneers were always dedicated to helping people victimized by the worst depths of poverty and oppression (Hernandez, 2008). Social work education actually began in 1898 when the New York Charity Organization Society offered a summer course to train charity workers (Beless, 1995). In the early 20th century, social workers continued to seek a professional identity regarding what social work practice involved. The emphasis on scientific advances and the enticing new therapeutic approaches introduced during the first half of the century (e.g., psychodynamic and social learning theories) strengthened the profession's commitment to social casework (Landon, 1995). Social casework stressed therapeutically helping individuals and families solve their problems. Thus the target of change was the individual or family.

The divergence between the settlement orientation, emphasizing group and community work, and the individually oriented charity organization approach remained strong. Therefore, three method tracks—casework, group work, and community organization—characterized social work through the 1950s. Casework was further fortified by developing fields of practice or specializations that were generally incorporated under its umbrella. These included medical social work, psychiatric social work, child welfare, and school social work (Brieland, 1995).

Early Development of Social Work Education

Beless (1995, p. 635) describes the initial development of formal social work education in the United States. In 1919, 17 U.S. and Canadian schools of social work joined together to form the Association of Training Schools for Professional Social Work. This organization soon changed its name to the American Association of Schools of Social Work (AASSW) and by 1927 had established membership requirements based on education. The AASSW also began developing criteria for what was considered adequate preparation for professional social work practice. These formed the foundation for the initial accreditation standards for master's degrees in social work education (Stuart, 2008).

Accreditation is the recognition and confirmation that an organization such as nursing home, mental health center, university, or other social service provider meets specific standards developed to make certain that the services provided are appropriate and effective. Accreditation with respect to social work education means that accredited programs must comply with a range of standards. These address curricular content and structure, staffing, adherence to nondiscrimination policies, adequate financial support from the college or university, and other variables.

Social Work During the Great Depression

During the Great Depression, the Social Security Act switched many aspects of service provision from the private to the public sector. Thus the type of social work jobs available and the characteristics of people getting them shifted (Popple, 1995). Prior to the Depression, social work was close to becoming a profession of graduate degrees only. The field was oriented to providing casework with a theoretical foundation in psychotherapy. Many clients were not poor but suffered from other problems such as mental health issues. Efforts to change communities and social policies were most often overlooked.

The Depression changed all this, however. The Social Security Act spurred a massive increase in the number of social work jobs, the majority of which involved problems for stable people caused by unemployment (Popple, 1995). Essentially, these jobs required different skills than the ability to perform therapy, as many master's degree social workers (MSWs) were doing. The need became evident for practitioners to work in the public sector assisting people in solving their problems, meeting their needs, and obtaining necessary resources—tasks unrelated to providing "therapy." Thus numerous bachelor's degree social workers (BSWs) were being employed in these jobs. However, MSWs refused to accept BSWs as professional colleagues, and AASSW would not acknowledge baccalaureate social work programs (Stuart, 2008). Highlight 6.11 explores how accreditation for social work programs was established.

Social Work in the 1950s

We have established that the economy grew rapidly during and after World War II with the increased demand for production of goods. Despite CSWE's call for social work to assume a broader role in seeking social justice (via its Curriculum Policy Statement and Accreditation Standards), the relative affluence of the 1950s once again encouraged social workers to turn to psychotherapy and casework (Popple, 1995). During this decade, 85% of social work students selected casework as their orientation of choice (Popple, 1995). MSWs dominated the scene, and BSW programs were not yet being accredited.

Formation of the National Association of Social Workers

In 1955 seven separate professional organizations came together to form the National Association of Social Workers (NASW) (Brieland, 1995; Clark,

2008). The intent was to provide a unified force to move the profession ahead and pursue broad goals far beyond what any more limited specialty organization might accomplish (Brieland, 1995). The following organizations participated in the merger (Brieland, 1995; Goldstein & Beebe, 1995):

- The American Association of Group Workers (founded in 1936)
- The American Association of Medical Social Workers (founded in 1918)
- The American Association of Psychiatric Social Workers (founded in 1926)
- The American Association of Social Workers (founded in 1921)
- The Association for the Study of Community Organization (founded in 1946)
- The National Association of School Social Workers (founded in 1919)
- The Social Work Research Group (founded in 1949)

The need for a unifying generalist approach was inherent in this merger. Many social work leaders and educators became increasingly concerned about the profession's commitment to rectifying social injustice and advocating on behalf of positive social change.

HIGHLIGHT 6.11

Social Work Accreditation at the Baccalaureate and Master's Levels

By 1942 several undergraduate social work programs had formed their own separate organization, the National Association of Schools of Social Administration (NASSA). By 1943 NASSA was officially acknowledged as the accrediting organization for baccalaureate programs that developed and oversaw their curricular and program standards (Beless, 1995).

Having two accrediting bodies for social work education was awkward and confusing. Therefore, in 1946 a coordinating body, the National Council on Social Work Education (NCSWE), was created to research the situation and make suggestions for achieving better coordination and consistency. The subsequent report and recommendations resulted in the birth of the Council on Social Work Education (CSWE) in 1952, representing the merger of the American Association

of Schools of Social Work (AASSW) and NASSA (Beless, 1995; Hoffman, 2008; Watkins & Holmes, 2008). At this time, the first Curriculum Policy Statement and Accreditation Standards were issued that reflected new guidelines for master's education concerning curricular content and structure (Brieland, 1995). Additionally, students were required to develop a philosophical approach to practice that emphasized human dignity (Brieland, 1995). Such a broad goal inferred that social work should be more than merely casework. Rather, social work should seek to benefit society in general and oppressed populations in particular. Although CSWE's objective was to oversee social work education, at this time it viewed undergraduate education as "preprofessional" and declined to offer these programs accreditation.

Social Work in the 1960s to the Early 1980s

The 1960s and the War on Poverty produced a new focus on social change versus individual pathology. Many came to realize that poverty and other vast social problems still existed in the United States. A series of federal administrations began implementing antipoverty programs. At first, these programs generally disregarded social workers because the intent was to empower the poor themselves (Popple, 1995). However, it soon became clear that expertise was needed in a range of fields, including community organization, administration, and direct practice, for programs to run effectively (Popple, 1995). As a result, most social work schools added social policy, social planning, and administration areas of specialization to their curricula (Stuart, 2008). This probably reflected the growing awareness of the importance of working with and within organizations as a major facet of generalist practice.

At this point, the social work profession faced a serious problem—namely, fewer than a quarter of all people holding social work jobs were identified as professional social workers because only they had MSW degrees (Popple, 1995). Needless to say, it did not enhance the profession's reputation or accountability that the vast majority of the people doing social work were not considered social workers. Thus a logical move was to emphasize the BSW as the viable entry-level qualification to the social work profession—people performing social work jobs should be social workers. CSWE began developing criteria for accrediting BSW programs in 1962 and finally offered accreditation to programs in 1974.

The prolific development of BSW programs in the late 1960s and early 1970s emphasized the need for a generalist foundation in social work practice (Landon, 1995). Many social work leaders began calling for a unified foundation for all social work practice (Bartlett, 1970; Boehm, 1959) and referring to social work practice as occurring among various-sized systems (Pincus & Minahan, 1973; Schwartz, 1961; Siporin, 1975). Social workers needed a broad base of skills to work with individuals, families, groups, organizations, and communities. Baccalaureate and master's programs required differentiation regarding purpose. The fact that CSWE made accreditation available to BSW programs in 1974 and required a generalist practice foundation for the BSW level of practice was a big forward step. Another important step occurred in 1984 when CSWE affirmed that the foundation for both undergraduate and graduate educational levels should include the knowledge, skills, and values inherent in generalist practice (Landon, 1995).

Other important developments, including the first NASW *Code of Ethics* in 1960, the establishment of Political Action for Candidate Election (PACE) in 1976, and increasing attention to BSW professionalism, are illustrated by the time line introducing this chapter.

Social Work Today

Currently, the social work professional assumes the stance that the BSW is the entry level into the profession, with the MSW reflecting advanced practice and specialization (CSWE, 2008b). The curriculum in an accredited program "achieves the program's competencies through an intentional design that includes the foundation offered at the baccalaureate and master's levels and the advanced curriculum offered at the master's level. The BSW curriculum prepares its graduates for generalist practice through mastery of the core competencies. The MSW curriculum prepares its graduates for advanced practice through mastery of the core competencies augmented by knowledge and practice behaviors specific to a concentration [e.g., administration, child welfare, mental health, substance abuse]" (CSWE, 2008b, EP 2.0). As later chapters will explain, BSWs can provide many services, such as crisis intervention, case management, community organization, and the linking of clients with services, while working with a wide range of populations. MSWs usually fulfill more specialized functions, such as providing psychotherapy, working in supervision and administration, or assuming higher levels of decision-making responsibility.

Chapter Summary

The following summarizes this chapter's content as it relates to the chapter's learning objectives presented at the beginning of the chapter. Learning objectives include the following statements:

A Describe some of the early European approaches to social welfare.

The 1601 English Elizabethan Poor Law is considered the first piece of legislation establishing coherent, consistent public support for needy people through taxes. The Speenhamland system initiated a policy of supplementing the income of all poor people so that everyone would have the necessary minimum income. The English Poor Law Reforms of 1834 significantly reduced all outdoor relief and brought back workhouses as the only place where able-bodied people could receive benefits.

B Review some of the main events characterizing the history of social welfare in the United States.

Early poor laws in the American colonies closely resembled, and in some cases were identical to, those in England, although each colony remained unique in its specific legislation. The poor were viewed as part of the natural social order in communities. Services often reflected a mix of public and private collaboration, frequently provided informally. Early residency requirements for assistance were established.

Economic growth skyrocketed between the Civil War and the early 20th century. In the early 1900s settlement houses and charity organization societies were founded. Settlement houses were neighborhood-based centers where humanitarians, interested students, and others "settled" to help people living in poverty improve their communities and their lives; goals included meeting residents' needs, such as providing education and training, and advocating for human rights and improved community conditions. Jane Addams, along with Ellen Gates Starr, started the first settlement house, Hull House, in Chicago. Charity organization societies used expert knowledge to support people in caring for themselves through the use of "friendly visitors." Mary Richmond was an early advocate for the development of professional schools of social casework.

During the progressive period from 1900 to 1930, people felt that government was responsible for people's welfare. Many issues were tackled, including child labor, women's working hours, women's suffrage, income security, and family welfare. Many advocacy groups were established, and steps were taken toward meeting human needs.

The Great Depression was initiated by the stock market crash of 1929. The general trend over the next decade was an increasing reliance on the federal government to control and provide social services.

President Franklin Delano Roosevelt initiated a range of programs, referred to as the New Deal, to address people's dire needs. Programs included the Federal Emergency Relief Act, the Civilian Works Administration, the Civilian Conservation Corps, the Public Works Administration, and the Works Progress Administration.

The Social Security Act of 1935 established current programs for social insurance, public assistance, and health services. A significant piece of 1940s legislation was the Serviceman's Readjustment Act of 1944, commonly referred to as the G.I. Bill.

The 1950s marked a time of relative peace and complacency. During this period the population exploded, resulting in the current large bloc of aging baby boomers. Aid to the Permanently and Totally Disabled became a later amendment to the Social Security Act. The year 1954 marked the end to school segregation in *Brown v. Board of Education*.

The 1960s was characterized by the War on Poverty in an effort to fashion a "Great Society." Poverty became a primary focus of public attention, and numerous new social welfare programs were developed. The Economic Opportunity Act of 1964 established programs including Volunteers in Service to America (VISTA) and Operation Head Start among many others.

The 1970s marked a return to conservatism, followed by increasing conservatism during the 1980s and early 1990s. The Clinton era from 1992 to 2001 was marked by the squelching of most of his proposals by the Republican Senate and House. Clinton did manage to diminish cuts in social programs and decrease tax cuts. The Personal Responsibility and Work Opportunities Act of 1996 was passed that replaced AFDC for public assistance for needy families.

George W. Bush's conservative regime in the first decade of the 21st century emphasized homeland security, transferring more decision-making power from the federal government to the states, and increased provision of services from the private sector, including faith-based organizations.

Barack Obama, the first multiracial president, ran on a platform that emphasized change. Entering his administration during the Great Recession, he focused on a Stimulus Plan, health care reform, and improving international relations, especially by combating terrorism.

C Describe some of the issues and events affecting American Indians, Hispanics, African Americans, and Asian Americans throughout U.S. history.

The U.S. government established treaties with American Indians that removed them from their native lands and relocated them on distant reservations. Anglos considered American Indians as culturally inferior. The federal government liberally interfered with Native American social, economic, religious, and cultural practices. The story of the Cherokee and their Trail of Tears is especially sad. From the 1870s to 1900 the federal government pursued the assimilation (the process of incorporating another culture into the mainstream culture) of First Nations Peoples. Native Americans' struggle for self-determination escalated during the 1960s.

In 1845 the United States annexed Texas, continuing to struggle over its boundary with Mexico, a situation greatly affecting Hispanics in the Southwest. In the 1848 Treaty of Guadalupe Hidalgo, Mexico ceded more than half of its territory to the United States, becoming the U.S. Southwest. Although Hispanics were often in the majority and were living in their native territory, Anglos often treated them as a "minority." After the Mexican Revolution of 1910, numerous Chicanos/Chicanas fled to the United States as refugees to find work. After the Great Depression when work was scarce, many, including U.S. citizens, were deported. Puerto Ricans obtained U.S. citizenship in 1917 and can travel to and from the mainland United States at will. During the 1960s the Chicano movement advocated for the appreciation of Chicano culture and improved socioeconomic status for Chicanos/Chicanas, especially agricultural laborers.

Lincoln issued the Emancipation Proclamation freeing the slaves in 1863. After the Civil War, the federal government established the Freedmen's Bureau to distribute rations and land to African Americans in need. Very few actually received any land, and those who did were forced to return it later.

The first Asian people to immigrate to the United States during the mid-19th century were Chinese. They experienced blatant racism and limited rights. After the Chinese Exclusion Act of 1882, Japanese immigrants soon began to replace the Chinese. They, too, experienced limited rights. The Immigration Acts of 1924 halted Asian immigration almost altogether.

Advocacy for civil rights for people of color characterized the 1960s. The Civil Rights Act of 1964 strengthened civil rights and established the Equal Employment Opportunity Commission.

D Focus on some of the historical issues concerning mental health, children and families, people with disabilities, and older adults.

In colonial times, people who had mental illness, often referred to as lunatics, were typically cared for by their own families or boarded out to other families, with communities paying these families to provide care. During the progressive period in the early 20th century, mental health policy reflected the mental hygiene movement. This emphasized, among other things, alternative types of care to institutionalization. The deinstitutionalization movement characterized the period following World War II. It stressed the provision of mental health care in the community instead of in institutions. The 1963 Community Mental Health Centers Act provided funding for a range of community mental health programs.

The 1870s saw the origins of child welfare policy as it has evolved today. Charles Loring Brace became the first proponent of placing children in homes other than their own instead of in institutions. The concept of Protective Services was born in 1874 with the case of Mary Ellen Wilson. The 1974 Child Abuse Prevention and Treatment Act established a centralized reporting agency and required states to pass laws protecting children under age 18. The Indian Child Welfare Act of 1978 addressed the importance of maintaining children's racial and cultural identity.

The Social Security Act of 1935 is a social insurance program that provided benefits to older adults and people with disabilities. It also established Title IV, Aid to Dependent Children (ADC), providing public assistance for children in need. In 1962 the name was changed to Aid to Families with Dependent Children (AFDC). The Personal Responsibility and Work Opportunities Act (PRWOA) of 1996 replaced AFDC and placed a range of limitations on public assistance benefits.

The Older Americans Act (OAA) of 1965 established an administrative structure for the coordination and delivery of social services to older people. OAA provides numerous benefits to people age 60 or over regardless of income. In 1972, Supplemental Security Income (SSI), a social insurance program, replaced earlier public assistance programs based on need.

Major legislation for people with disabilities includes the Americans with Disabilities Act of 1990 and the Developmental Disabilities Assistance and Bill of Rights Act of 1990.

E Propose questions to stimulate critical thinking about various historical trends and events.

To encourage critical thinking, questions were posed concerning government policy and the self-determination for First Nations Peoples, personal rights of public assistance recipients, civil rights, and future issues in social welfare.

F Discuss major events involved in the history of the social work profession.

Early social work was based in the settlement house and charity organization movements. As a result, casework, group work, and community organization were the three tracts characterizing social work through the 1950s. In 1919, the Association of Training Schools for Professional Social Work was formed by U.S. and Canadian schools of social work. The name was soon changed to the American Association of Schools of Social Work (AASSW). AASSW formed the foundation for initial accreditation standards for master's social work education.

During the Great Depression, social work switched many aspects of service provision from the private to the public sector. By 1942, different organizations formed to address BSW and MSW accreditation. In 1946 the National Council on Social Work Education (NCSWE) was formed to coordinate accreditation at both levels. NCSWE's findings resulted in the birth of the Council on Social Work

Education (CSWE), the current body that accredits both BSW and MSW programs.

The relative affluence of the 1950s encouraged social workers to focus on psychotherapy and casework instead of social justice issues. In 1955 seven social work organizations joined to form the National Association of Social Work (NASW).

The 1960s and the War on Poverty produced a new concentration on social change versus individual pathology. There was some debate regarding whether BSW programs should be accredited, but CSWE finally began accrediting them in 1974 along with MSW programs. The prolific development of BSW programs in the late 1960s and early 1970s emphasized the need for a generalist foundation for social work practice. Today, generalist practice, which characterizes the BSW foundation, has been established as the foundation of social work practice upon which specializations can be built (CSWE, 2008b).

G Provide a foundation for understanding social welfare policy and policy development.

The history of social welfare policy and policy development in the United States was examined.

LOOKING AHEAD

Social welfare and social work history pave the way for today's social welfare policy and programs. The time line in Figure 6.3 highlights some of the major events in social welfare history as discussed in this chapter. The next chapter will discuss policy development and the structural components of policies. It will also focus on theoretical perspectives regarding personal values and social welfare policy and program development, thereby setting the stage for policy and program analysis in various practice contexts.

English History

1300s	Feudalistic societies in Europe
1348	Europe devastated by Black Death
1349	Statute of Laborers
1531	Able-bodied people forbidden from begging
1601	Elizabethan Poor Law
1662	Law of Settlement
1795	Establishment of Speenhamland system
1834	Poor Law Reforms

U.S. History

1770s	Beginning of moral treatment movement in mental health
1778	First treaty between federal government and Native American Delaware tribe
1824	Establishment of Bureau of Indian Affairs
1830	Indian Removal Act
1838–1839	Trail of Tears
1840s	Dorothea Dix advocates for people with mental illness
1846	Beginning of the Mexican-American War
1848	The Treaty of Guadalupe Hidalgo (where Mexico ceded more than half of its territory to the United States)
1861–1865	Civil War
1865	Establishment of Freedmen's Bureau
1874	Etta Wheeler initiates child protective services
1882	Chinese Exclusion Act of 1882
1880s	Growth of settlement houses and charity organization societies
1870s	Federal attempts at assimilation for Native Americans
1899	Treaty of Paris of 1899 (where Spain ceded Puerto Rico to the United States)
1900s	Beginning of mental hygiene movement in mental health
1909	Establishment of National Association for the Advancement of Colored People (NAACP)
	First White House Conference on Dependent Children
1910	Establishment of National Urban League
	First major wave of Mexican immigration in response to the Mexican Revolution of 1910
1911	States begin to establish mothers' pensions
1917	Jones Act granting U.S. citizenship to all people born in Puerto Rico from then on
1924	Immigration Act of 1924 (which imposed stringent requirements on immigrants entering the United States, especially from Asia)
1929	Stock market crash initiates the Great Depression
1933	Federal Emergency Relief Act (FERA)
	Establishment of Civilian Works Administration (CSW)
	Establishment of Civilian Conservation Corps (CCC)
1935	Establishment of Public Works Administration (PWA)
	Establishment of Works Progress Administration (WPA)
	Social Security Act of 1935
1941	U.S. enters World War II
	Japanese American internment in response to bombing of Pearl Harbor
1942	Permanent relocation centers for Japanese American internment
1944	Serviceman's Readjustment Act of 1944 (G.I. Bill)
1945	World War II ends
1950	Amendments to Social Security Act adding Aid to Disabled

Figure 6.3 Major Events in the History of Social Welfare

Early 1950s	Beginning of deinstitutionalization movement in mental health
1954	*Brown v. Board of Education* ending school segregation
1962	Public Welfare Amendments of 1962
Early 1960s	Initiation of War on Poverty and Great Society
1962	Formation of National Farm Workers Association (NFWA) led by Cesar Chavez
1963	Community Mental Health Centers Act
1964	Economic Opportunity Act of 1964
	Food Stamp Act of 1964
	Civil Rights Act of 1964
1965	Older Americans Act of 1965
1967	Amendments to Social Security Act
1969	American Indian movement protests at Alcatraz
1971	*Wyatt v. Stickney*
	American Indian movement protests at Wounded Knee
	Establishment of Supplementary Security Income (SSI)
1974	Child Abuse Prevention and Treatment Act
1975	Passage of Title XX of Social Security Act
	O'Connor v. Donaldson
1978	Passage of Indian Child Welfare Act of 1978
1980	Passage of Adoption Assistance and Child Welfare Act
1990	Passage of Americans with Disabilities Act of 1990
	Passage of Developmental Disabilities Assistance and Bill of Rights Act of 1990
1993	Family and Medical Leave Act of 1993
1994	Crime Bill of 1994
1996	Personal Responsibility and Work Opportunities Act of 1996 (including Temporary Assistance for Needy Families [TANF])
2001	Terrorist attacks on the World Trade Center
2003	War on Iraq
	The Medicare Modernization Act of 2003
Late 2007	Beginning of "the Great Recession"
2009	The Obama Stimulus Plan
2010	Passage of the 2010 Patient Protection and Affordable Health Care Act

© Cengage Learning 2013

Figure 6.3 *(continued)*

COMPETENCY NOTES

The following identifies where Educational Policy (EP) competencies and practice behaviors are discussed in the chapter.

EP 2.1.1 Identify as a professional social worker and conduct oneself accordingly. *(p. 169):* Social workers should know the profession's history. *(p. 201):* Understanding the history of the profession is part of establishing a professional identity.

EP 2.1.1b Practice personal reflection and self-correction to assure continual professional development. *(p. 194):* Critical thinking questions encourage personal reflection about discrimination.

EP 2.1.3 Apply critical thinking to inform and communicate professional judgments. *(p. 184):* Critical thinking questions are posed concerning U.S. policy toward First Nations Peoples. *(p. 190):* Critical thinking questions are asked to examine the personal rights of assistance recipients. *(p. 194):* Critical thinking questions are posed concerning civil rights. *(p. 198):* Critical thinking questions are asked regarding future issues in social welfare.

EP 2.1.3b Analyze models of assessment, prevention, intervention, and evaluation. *(p. 174):* Philosophical approaches for assessing child development throughout history are reviewed.

EP 2.1.4a Recognize the extent to which culture's structures and values may oppress, marginalize, alienate, or create or enhance privilege and power. *(p. 171):* This and subsequent sections of this chapter review how culture's structures and values changing over time serve to oppress, marginalize, alienate, or create or enhance privilege and power. *(p. 190):* Critical thinking questions are raised to examine the extent to which public assistance policy might oppress recipients. *(p. 193):* The oppression of Chicanos/Chicanas is discussed. *(p. 194):* Critical thinking questions encourage exploration of the reasons for historical oppression and the lack of civil rights. *(p. 194):* The oppression of American Indians is discussed. *(p. 199):* Being members of a lower socioeconomic class can result in economic oppression with respect to receiving financial credit.

EP 2.1.4c Recognize and communicate their understanding of the importance of difference in shaping life experiences. *(p. 193):* Race and ethnicity, dimensions of diversity, can significantly shape life experiences for Chicanos/Chicanas. *(p. 194):* Race and ethnicity, dimensions of diversity, can significantly shape life experiences for American Indians.

EP 2.1.5a Understand the forms and mechanisms of oppression and discrimination. *(p. 175):* The forms and mechanisms of oppression against First Nations Peoples are discussed from a historical perspective. *(p. 176):* The forms and mechanisms of oppression against Latinos/Latinas are discussed from a historical perspective. *(p. 177):* The forms and mechanisms of oppression against African Americans are discussed from a historical perspective. *(p. 182):* The forms and mechanisms of oppression against American Indians from the 1870s to 1900 are discussed. *(p. 184):* Critical thinking questions are posed that relate to the oppression of American Indians. *(p. 185):* The oppression of and discrimination against Asian people in terms of immigration is discussed. *(p. 185):* The oppression of and discrimination against Chicanos/Chicanas in terms of immigration is discussed. *(p. 189):* The oppression of and discrimination against Japanese Americans during World War II is discussed. *(p. 193):* The oppression of and discrimination against people of color during the early 1960s is discussed. *(p. 193):* The oppression of Chicanos/

Chicanas is discussed. *(p. 194):* Critical thinking questions encourage exploration of the dynamics involved in racial oppression. *(p. 194):* The oppression of American Indians is discussed.

EP 2.1.5b Advocate for human rights and social and economic justice. *(p. 175):* Dorothea Dix provides an excellent example of an advocate for human rights. *(p. 184):* Critical thinking questions address the pursuit of self-determination, a basic human right. *(p. 193):* Legislation that advocated for social and economic justice is discussed. *(p. 193):* Cesar Chavez provides an excellent example of one who advocates for human rights and social and economic justice. *(p. 196):* Legislation is discussed that advocates for the rights of people with disabilities.

EP 2.1.7b Critique and apply knowledge to understand person and environment. *(p. 169):* Practitioners must critique and apply historical knowledge to understand how people function in their environments during different time periods.

EP 2.1.8a Analyze, formulate, and advocate for policies that advance social well-being. *(p. 175):* Dorothea Dix provides an excellent example of an advocate for policies that advance social well-being. *(p. 184):* Critical thinking questions encourage thinking about policies that would advance social well-being on the behalf of First Nations Peoples. *(p. 192):* The Older Americans Act of 1965 provides for the coordination of resources that advance the social well-being of older adults. *(p. 193):* Legislation establishing policies that advance social well-being is discussed. *(p. 194):* Critical thinking questions encourage consideration of policies that advance civil rights and, in effect, social well-being.

EP 2.1.9a Continuously discover, appraise, and attend to changing locales, populations, scientific and technological developments, and emerging societal trends to provide relevant services. *(p. 169):* Practitioners should continuously attend to the effects of historical events and changes upon people's lives. *(p. 198):* Social workers should continuously attend to and appraise the social welfare issues facing society.

EP 2.1.9b Provide leadership in promoting sustainable changes in service delivery and practice to improve the quality of social services.

(p. 180): Jane Addams provides an excellent example of a leader in promoting social service delivery.

EP 2.1.10d Collect, organize, and interpret client data. *(p. 182):* Mary Richmond stressed the importance of collecting, organizing, and interpreting client data.

FOR FURTHER EXPLORATION ON THE INTERNET

See this text's Social Work CourseMate website at *www.cengagebrain.com* for learning tools such as chapter quizzing, videos, glossary flashcards, and more.

CHAPTER 7

Policy, Policy Analysis, Policy Practice, and Policy Advocacy: Foundations for Service Provision

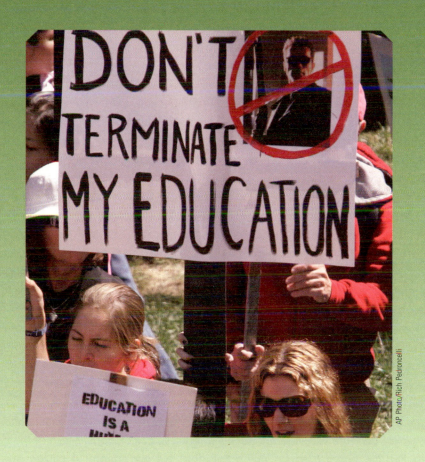

AP Photo/Rich Pedroncelli

Policies have huge effects on citizens—including you. The following newspaper headlines focus on controversial policies and their ramifications:[1]

"State Legislature May Slash Budget Across the Board: Local Officials Furious"
"County Executives Can Retire as Millionaires—A Retirement Policy Fluke?"
"Fetuses May Qualify for Federal Aid"[2]

---

[1]Note that the ideas for the first two headlines were based on real events, but details in the ensuing discussion have been altered significantly.

[2]This headline was taken from the *Milwaukee Journal Sentinel*, Feb. 1, 2002, page A1, from an article by M. Johnson.

**EP 2.1.3,
2.1.8a**

The first headline concerns a northern state legislature's serious consideration not to share state tax revenues with communities (cities, towns, and villages). The intent is to address a huge state budget crunch resulting from a lagging economy. This decision will result in a 10% decrease in one small community's total budget—hence the headline. Elected community officials are irate because such decisions by the state have a direct impact on local service provision such as garbage pickup, health care services, fire and rescue emergency services, and law enforcement. They indicate that such a slash focused on one budget item could wipe out the entire roads department budget (including road repair and snow removal) or the whole fire department budget and half of the rescue squad budget.

Critical thinking about policy: Policy—in this case, state public policy—has a direct effect on people's quality of life. How would you like it if you had to take your own garbage to the dump every Saturday because there was no pickup? What if your defective electric toaster started a fire in your kitchen, and no fire department was available to respond to your emergency? What if an older relative suddenly collapsed from a heart attack, and there was no rescue squad to call for help?

The second headline concerns a county board (the elected group that oversees county responsibilities and staff) that has approved a change in retirement policy that was not well publicized to the voting public. The policy's alleged intent is to retain good employees (including the board members themselves) by providing generous retirement benefits, thus rewarding long-term employees for staying with the county. However, an investigation by the local media reveals that the new policy actually will grant well over a million dollars in retirement benefits to some highly paid, high-level, long-term county employees if they choose to receive their benefits in one lump sum. The retirement formula is based on long-term employment and salary level. Therefore, only those in high-level positions who receive high salaries will be eligible for these extraordinary benefits.

Critical thinking about policy: Amazingly, potential recipients include the board chair, other long-term board members, and additional county government leaders. Most board members claim that they had no idea of the ramifications of this policy because they had not done the requisite calculations. Much of the public feels that the board tried to "pull a fast one" but got caught. A citizen group is collecting signatures on a petition calling for a recall election in which they can vote current board members out. County government is in turmoil. Such huge retirement allocations will hike up county taxes, and citizens will be forced to bear the burden. This retirement policy has direct implications for the county's citizens who are financially responsible.

Another negative implication involves the impact on other county employees' morale and reputation. The policy is not their fault; they had no input into the decision to enact it. Yet the public is scrutinizing all county employees as if they are to blame for the problem. County employees say they work long, hard hours and are committed to contributing to a strong community that fosters residents' health and well-being.

The vast majority of them will receive adequate, but certainly not exceptional, retirement benefits. It has already been established that the controversial retirement formula requires a high salary for the extraordinary benefits to kick in.

This example shows how policy—in this case, on the local level—has a major impact on various groups of citizens. Effects include county citizens' financial responsibility for huge outlays of cash, board members' potential receipt of large sums of money, and innocent county workers' diminished morale and reputation.

The third headline reflects a presidential policy decision "that developing human fetuses could be classified by states as unborn children so more low-income women would have access to prenatal care paid by the government" (Johnson, 2002, p. A1). The result is that states could choose to provide health care to the fetuses via their mothers in programs designed to provide health care to children, not women.

***Critical thinking about policy:** This policy decision resulted in a heated debate between right-to-choose and anti-abortion proponents. People supporting the right to choose maintain that pregnant women have the right to decide what happens to their own bodies, including the right to have an abortion. People backing the anti-abortion perspective feel that abortions are wrong and so should be illegal.*

Right-to-choose advocates "immediately labeled the move a blatant attempt to establish a fetus as a living person. They believe it lays the foundation . . . to make abortion a crime" (p. A1). Rather, these proponents recommended extending "health care coverage to more women than designating a fetus an unborn child" (p. A12). But anti-abortion advocates praised the decision, calling it a "compassionate" move to provide health care to pregnant women by expanding their access to prenatal care.

This policy has important potential implications for pregnant women. It paves the way for states to decide whether to pay for health care for unborn children— in essence, health care for pregnant women who were not eligible for services under child health-care programs. It may also have implications for future judicial decisions concerning women's right to choose whether to have an abortion.

Regardless of where you stand on issues like these, the point is that policies significantly affect people. Sometimes they primarily affect only some category of people or segment of the population, such as pregnant women. Other times they may affect virtually everyone to one extent or another. For example, policy changes may result in cutbacks of essential community services or skyrocketing taxes for all citizens.

If you do not have any experience as a recipient of a social welfare program, you may not understand how important such programs can be to people who depend on their benefits. The examples given here illustrate how policies implemented through public services and programs can directly impact someone like you or those close to you. Policies regulate a wide range of social programs to provide many types of services for various groups of people (e.g., children, older adults, people with disabilities, and those with health or mental health needs). Social welfare policies provide the basis for social welfare program implementation—what programs can and cannot do.

Learning Objectives

A Define social welfare policy and agency policy.

B Explore the process of policy development.

C Identify the primary structural components of social welfare programs.

D Explore the conservative–liberal–radical value continuum and examine how values affect policy development.

E Propose a model for analyzing a policy's appropriateness and adequacy.

F Describe policy practice and policy advocacy.

G Identify various methods social workers can use in policy practice, including involvement in politics.

H Encourage critical thinking about what kinds of policies should be formulated.

Social Welfare Policy

EP 2.1.8

In a very broad sense, we have defined *policy* as rules that govern people's lives and dictate expectations for behavior. Policy determines how governments, communities, and organizations run in a predictable, coordinated fashion. We have also defined *social welfare policy* as the laws and regulations that govern which social welfare programs exist, what categories of clients are served, and who qualifies for a given program. Social welfare policy involves "decisions of various levels of the government, especially the federal government, as expressed in budgetary expenditures, congressional appropriations, and approved programs" (Morris, 1987, p. 664). For example, social welfare policy determines who is eligible for public assistance. In addition, social welfare policy sets standards regarding the types of services to be provided and the qualifications of service providers. For instance, social welfare policy specifies what social workers can do for physically abused children, in addition to what qualifications they must have to work in this practice area.

Note that throughout the rest of this book, for brevity's sake, when we use the term *policy* we will be referring to social welfare policy. Obviously this is the policy arena most relevant to a book about social work and social welfare.

Social workers must be well versed in social welfare policies. They must know what is available for a client and how to get it. For example, Enrique, a social worker for a county social services department, has a young female client, Daniela, with three small children, who has just been evicted from her apartment. Although the rent was relatively low and the apartment small (one bedroom), Daniela had been unable to pay the rent for the past three months. All her money had gone to clothing and feeding her children.

Enrique needs to know what other resources, if any, are available for Daniela and whether she is eligible to receive these resources. Policies determine the answers to a variety of questions: Does Daniela qualify for some temporary additional public assistance to help her relocate? Is there a local shelter for the homeless available whose policies allow Daniela and her children admission? If so, what is the shelter's policy for how long she can stay? Is there any low-rent housing available? If so, what does its policy designate as the criteria and procedure for admittance? Such questions may continue endlessly.

Social welfare programs are simply the implementation (i.e., the putting into action) of social welfare policy. Sometimes the distinction between a social welfare policy and program is unclear. Some policies inherently provide detailed directions for how they should be implemented. In other words, they essentially *are* the program. Other policies are quite

HIGHLIGHT 7.1

How Policies Structure and Coordinate Life

**EP 2.1.5b,
2.1.8a,
2.1.10k**

Einbinder (1995) maintains that policies serve to synchronize three primary arenas of life: "(1) the government; (2) the economy; and (3) private life" (p. 1850). All three are integrally intertwined. For example, consider the first headline cited at the beginning of the chapter, concerning a state slashing its budget. First, the national economy suffers a decline. As a result, unemployment increases, people reduce their spending, and less money circulates in the economy. Thus the state government gets less money in taxes (e.g., from personal earnings and sales) and must cut its spending. The economy affects government.

Government also affects the economy. Various governmental units make decisions about economic policy. For instance, a state might decide to decrease taxes levied on businesses within the state to encourage more firms to relocate there. The intent is for more companies to employ more people, who, in turn, pay more taxes. Additionally, because a larger number of businesses are contributing to the tax pool, the pool should be larger as well, even with a lower tax rate.

People's private lives are directly affected by both the government and the economy. What tax rates does the government levy on their earnings? Is the economy healthy enough for them to keep their jobs? As a result of these and other factors, do they have sufficient resources to purchase bare necessities or luxuries? Within this complicated system of policies and controls, are they able to maintain a good quality of life?

All citizens should be aware of what policies exist because of policies' direct effects on many aspects of life. They should also be alert to *changes* in policies for similar reasons.

Social workers must pay special attention to social welfare policies for two reasons. First, these policies dictate how programs are administered and how services are provided. Second, some policies are unfair, ineffective, or inefficient, and social workers must advocate for them to be changed.

---

vague and require substantial elaboration regarding how they should be put into operation. In these instances, the social welfare program becomes more extensive than the policy on which it is based.

Consider the following fictitious policy: All publicly funded social service agencies have to provide child care for their employees. This policy simply mandates that agencies must provide this service; it does not elaborate upon details. A program must be developed that responds to the following questions, among others: Where will child care be provided (e.g., in the agency or in a separate day care center)? How will child care be funded? Who will run the child care center? What kind of environment will be available to the children (e.g., a stimulating, activity centered milieu or basic overseeing with little interaction)?

Highlight 7.1 expands on how policies structure and coordinate people's lives.

Agency Policy

Chapter 1 established that a second type of policy directly affecting social workers' ability to practice is *agency policy*. This entails standards adopted by organizations and programs that provide services (e.g., a treatment center for troubled youths, a department of social services, or a sheltered workshop[3] for people with cognitive disabilities).

The terms *social services agency, human services agency,* and *social welfare agency* can be used interchangeably to refer to agencies or organizations that provide social welfare services. Similarly, for our purposes, the words *agency* and *organization* mean the same thing. A *social services agency* is a coordinated system of staff units and processes providing social services. Such agencies typically employ social workers, other professionals providing various social services, paraprofessionals (people with specific knowledge and skills who, under close supervision, carry out various duties previously undertaken only by professionals), clerical staff, and sometimes

---

[3]A *sheltered workshop* is an organization that provides testing, counseling, social skills training, job training, sheltered employment, and job placement services for people with various disabilities or needs for rehabilitation (Barker, 2003).

volunteers (Barker, 2003). Services are provided according to a prescribed set of social welfare and agency policies.

Agency policy may specify the agency's structure, the qualifications of supervisors and workers, the rules governing what workers may or may not do, and the proper procedures to follow for completing an assessment.

Agency policy may address in greater detail how agencies can implement social welfare policy. It can iron out the wrinkles and specify rules regarding how agency staff should work within their individual agency setting. Agency policy can also address questions about how the agency runs on a daily basis. What hours do staff work? How are staff evaluated for job performance and raises? Who is responsible for supervising whom throughout the organizational structure? This involves everyone from the director or chief executive officer (CEO) running the entire agency down to practitioners working directly with clients.

Social Welfare Policy Development

EP 2.1.3c, 2.1.7a

How social welfare policies develop in government agencies is an extremely complex process due to the many opinions, people, and formal processes involved. However, to facilitate your basic understanding and emphasize the importance of policy for social work practice, Figure 7.1 depicts a basic six-phase process of how policy is developed and implemented. The process proposed here is quite simplistic, but it gives a general idea of how policies come into being.

An example that illustrates the policy development process is the development of and change in policy governing the provision of financial aid to needy children and families (Macarov, 1995). The value assumption upon which the policy was initially based was that it is most desirable for children to remain in their own homes, cared for by their own parents, rather than being institutionalized. Implications concern helping to keep a family together even when parents are poor and have trouble supporting children. This value is reflected in Aid to Families with Dependent Children (AFDC), a primary program that provided financial assistance to poor families with children until 1996, when new legislation was passed. (The next chapter discusses this and newer legislation more thoroughly.)

Phase 1

The *first phase* involves recognizing society's values about what is considered important or worthwhile. Absolute values are hard to pin down because of the tremendous number of people we're talking about.

Case Example For illustration, we will start with the value that children are generally best cared for within their own families. The task of identifying society's values becomes more complex because values also change over time. For instance, the value that children should remain in their own homes might be superseded by the value that all parents should work to support their families.

Phase 2

The *second phase* of the policy process concerns identifying problems and needs that require attention.

Case Example The problem related to our example is poverty and poor people's inability to provide adequate care for their families. Although the societal value is that children should remain in their own

Figure 7.1 Social Welfare Policy Development

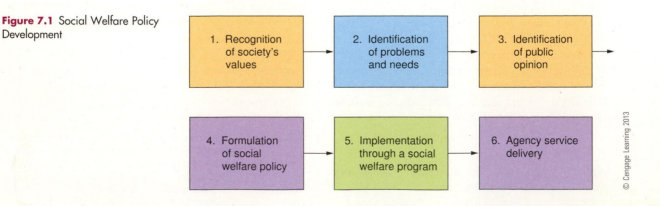

homes, a significant number of parents, mostly single mothers who are primary caregivers for children, lack resources to provide their children with adequate care. What should be done to address this problem?

Phase 3

The *third phase* of the policy process involves the identification of public opinion about an identified problem and people's related needs. Society's current values tend to guide public opinion concerning what should be done. Public opinion reflects values but involves more specific recommendations about what should be *done* to put these values into action. Values held by the majority sway public opinion in that direction. Dobelstein (2003) refers to such a prevailing public view as a *normative orientation* (p. 15). Highlight 7.2 discusses how the relationship between public opinion and policy development is often unclear.

Case Example For several decades prior to 1996, general public opinion maintained that poor families

should be given minimal assistance to keep children in their own homes.

Phase 4

In the *fourth phase* of the social policy process, legislators confronted with a problem or need and swamped with public opinion undertake the complicated formulation of social welfare policy to address the issue. It is beyond the scope of this text to elaborate on all the political processes involved. The following issues complicate the formulation of social policy (Barusch, 2012; Chapin 2011; DiNitto, 2011; Meenaghan, Kilty, & McNutt, 2004):

- *It is difficult to obtain a problem consensus because of the multiple perspectives and opinions involved. True public opinion is hard to pin down.*
- *Legislators' perceptions of the problem depend on the information and pressure they receive. Various factions and interest groups have varying degrees of access to legislators and wield varying degrees of influence.*

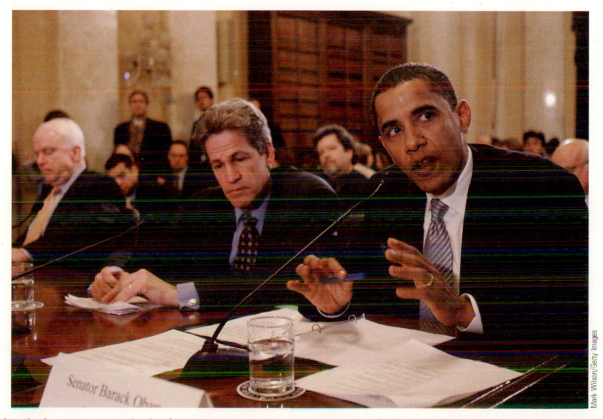

Policy development is a complex legislative process. Here, then U.S. Senator Barack Obama (D-Ill.) speaks as Senator John McCain (R-Ariz., left) and Senator Norm Coleman (R-Minn., center) listen during a committee hearing in Washington, D.C., as they discuss lobbying reform in 2006.

HIGHLIGHT 7.2

Public Opinion and Policy Development

Identification of public opinion is the third phase of the policy development process. Note, however, that the process may be more complicated than this. For one thing, majority public opinion is not always the deciding factor regarding what policy will be developed. Politicians usually pay attention to public opinion. Voters formulate public opinion, and they also vote politicians into or out of office. Thus it is usually in politicians' best interests to keep voters happy and to promote policies supported by voters.

However, many times such controversy exists over a policy issue that it is virtually impossible to satisfy the majority—or even to identify the majority. Sometimes many people will be dissatisfied no matter which side of the issue a politician supports. Consider the strong opposing opinions people hold over the death penalty or the right of women to get abortions.

Other times, it's difficult for legislators to get accurate information about public opinion on a particular issue. National Gallup polls aren't regularly done for every policy issue. Politicians must act on the basis of the information that is available. Sometimes this is biased because a small minority feels very strongly about an issue and regularly contacts politicians to voice their opinion. Consider people who have very strong feelings about the right to own guns. Hearing only from people supporting that side of the issue might leave legislators with the impression that most people hate gun control, when this may or may not be true.

Finally, even if legislators who formulate and vote on policy have fairly accurate data on public opinion, they may not pay much attention. Because the legislative decision-making process is so complex (as described in the fourth phase of the policy formulation process), public opinion about one issue may get lost. A politician may need to compromise significantly to get anything passed at all. Sometimes politicians will bargain by withdrawing support for one policy in order to pass another policy that is more important to them. Finally, politicians may receive extreme pressure from other party members or powerful leaders to support or not support a policy despite their own personal feelings to the contrary.

• *Because policy is formulated in such a political environment, the actual policy can change dramatically in focus while it is being debated. The policymaking process is characterized by an ongoing struggle of give and take, conflict resolution, and compromise.*

Consider a loosely analogous theoretical situation regarding how difficult it can be to come to a satisfactory consensus. Suppose during the first meeting of one of your classes your instructor indicates that it is the class's responsibility to determine how students will be graded. The only criterion given is that some configuration of exams and assignments must be specified and that they must not be too easy. Imagine the wide range of opinions students would probably voice. Some would want objective exams, and others would prefer essays. Some would want two exams, others four, and still others none. Some would prefer term papers, and others would opt for experiential assignments such as visits to relevant organizations or interviews with relevant people. Some would advocate for group projects, and others would express hatred for group projects and desire

individual ones instead. It is difficult to establish a consensus: Controversy and differences of opinion tend to characterize decision making even in a relatively small group. Imagine magnifying this many times over in the complex legislative process.

Case Example After much legislative debate and struggle, Aid to Dependent Children (ADC), renamed AFDC in 1962, was initially formulated as part of the Social Security Act of 1935.

Phase 5

Following the initial formulation of social policy, the *fifth phase* of the social welfare policy process is implementation through a social welfare program. Rocha (2007) comments:

EP 2.1.1d, 2.1.3c, 2.1.8b

Once a bill becomes law, policy practitioners may think that their task is done; it is only the beginning, however, because the law is then sent to the appropriate executive branch agency for interpretation and implementation into a program. Legislative policies are often broad and general in their language; it is then up to the various departments to interpret the broad language and make it specific enough so that programs can be created and implemented. Monitoring this implementation is extremely important and is the next target where intervention can occur. (p. 151)

Social workers may be called upon to work with administrators and agency staff to figure out what words mean when translated into actual behavior. People may cling to old beliefs and behaviors and resist change (Rocha, 2007). Worker input and communication may be necessary to help people who will actually be implementing the policy understand *how* they can implement it. This might involve lots of e-mails, reports, conversation, and time.

Case Example   The ensuing implementation process of ADC required substantial effort and specification of detail to make the program clear and functional.

Phase 6

In the *sixth phase* of social welfare policy development and implementation, social services are delivered by social workers and other staff in the context of social service agencies.

Case Example   Social service agency staff work directly with clients who apply for and receive benefits.

Highlight 7.3 explores how the six-phase process of policy development applies to this case example when society's values change.

Structural Components of Social Welfare Programs

Understanding a social welfare policy means investigating exactly what it says and what it does. There are five broad components to explore in order to understand any policy: (1) what people's needs and the program's goals are, (2) what kinds of benefits are provided, (3) what the eligibility criteria are to receive benefits, (4) how the program is financed, and (5) how the program is administered and run (Chapin, 2011, p. 158; Dolgoff & Feldstein, 2009, p. 138).

What Are People's Needs and Program Goals?

We have established that social welfare programs are the implementation of policies that are, in turn,

the results of public values and opinion and the political process. Programs exist to meet certain goals related to addressing problems, fulfilling needs, or improving people's lives (Dolgoff & Feldstein, 2009, p. 134; Gilbert & Terrell, 2010). Social welfare program goals address a wide range of problems including child maltreatment, "teen pregnancy, homelessness, and substance abuse." They attend to needs such as "economic security, child care, and health care." They enhance people's quality of life "through such means as education, socialization, and recreation" (p. 134).

Goals may be formal and clearly stated or implicit and unspoken. Dolgoff and Feldstein (2009) comment that "the food stamp program, for example, has a stated objective to alleviate hunger and malnutrition by enabling low-income households to purchase a nutritionally adequate diet"; another stated goal is to enhance the market for food grown and distributed internally within the country (p. 134). Low-income families using food stamps to "purchase" food results in profits for growers, producers, and distributors, thereby enhancing the economy. "But food stamps may not be used for the purchase of alcoholic beverages and tobacco, pet food, and cleaning and paper products, including toilet paper. Implicit in a portion of these restrictions is a moral objective to control the behavior of recipients" by regulating what they can and cannot buy (Dolgoff & Feldstein, 2009, p. 135).

What Kinds of Benefits Are Provided?

What does a particular social welfare program provide to recipients? Cash? Food? Housing? Counseling? In this context, a *benefit* is anything a client receives through a social welfare program. Because different programs serve people with different needs, the types of benefit also vary.

Benefits might be divided into two basic categories—cash and in-kind (Chambers & Wedel, 2005; Gilbert & Terrell, 2010; Marx, 2004). *Cash benefits* obviously involve providing eligible clients with prescribed amounts of money based on what the policies governing the program allow. *In-kind benefits* include virtually any benefit other than cash. Examples are food products (e.g., those available from agricultural surpluses), food stamps that can be exchanged for food, free school lunches, low-income housing, rent subsidies (e.g., whereby programs pay partial rent), day care, and personal social services.

HIGHLIGHT 7.3

When Values Change

EP 2.1.9a

Society's values—namely, that it is most desirable for children to remain in their own homes and be cared for by their parents (primarily the mother) rather than being institutionalized—have gradually changed. New values stress how parents, including mothers, should work to support their families. In light of more and more mothers working outside the home, Macarov (1995) explains how newer societal values came to characterize child care:

As programs that require ... parents [receiving financial assistance] to work became more popular, extensive child care facilities were needed. The desire of many mothers to take jobs outside the home also made such facilities a growth industry. As a result, providing child care outside the home has become not only accepted but prestigious. This social change led to a value change according to which contact with other children, even as early as age 2 or younger, is healthy, and professionally trained personnel provide better care than "amateur" mothers. This has reached the point to where working mothers are now postulated by some as more caring, and more capable of child care, than nonworking mothers. (p. 140)

This change in society's values led to a change in social policy, as illustrated by the following simplified process:

Phase 1—Recognition of society's (changing) values: Society's values changed from viewing parental child care as the optimum choice to viewing day care outside of the home as equally or even more valuable. (Note that you may or may not agree with Macarov's interpretation of how societal values have changed regarding this issue. That's not the point. The point is to provide an example of how policies can change in response to modifications in values.)

Phase 2—Identification of problems and needs: The problem remains generally the same: A significant number of parents, primarily single mothers who are primary caregivers for children, lack resources to provide their children with adequate care.

Phase 3—Recognition of public opinion: Society's new values were reflected in public opinion regarding this issue. Public opinion stressed the importance of parents, including single mothers, working to support themselves and their families. Requiring single parents, including mothers, to work outside the home means that someone must be responsible for caring for young children.

Phase 4—Development of social welfare policy: The Temporary Assistance to Needy Families (TANF) program was enacted in 1996 as part of significant legislation restructuring financial assistance eligibility and requirements. (Chapter 8 discusses this legislation more thoroughly.) This new legislation requires parents to receive job training and get jobs. It also places a five-year lifetime limit on recipients' ability to receive TANF payments; there had been no time limitation for the earlier AFDC.

Phase 5—Implementation through social welfare programs: The TANF program is being implemented throughout the United States. Because national policy gives states significant discretion in how to distribute benefits, each state has developed and is evaluating its own program.

Phase 6—Service provision by workers in agency settings: Social workers and other agency staff provide resources and services directly to clients according to the national policy and to state and local programs.

Personal social services are those intended to enhance people's quality of life by improving their ability to function within their environment. Such services (e.g., counseling) usually target specific groups (e.g., children or older adults) or particular problems (e.g., family planning or counseling). Subsequent chapters will describe programs implementing policies designed to provide various benefits to a range of populations in a variety of contexts. Focus

on Critical Thinking 7.1 raises some key issues related to cash versus in-kind benefits.

What Are the Eligibility Criteria for the Program?

Eligibility is the condition whereby people meet the designated criteria or requirements to receive benefits (Chambers & Wedel, 2005). For example, to be

FOCUS ON CRITICAL THINKING 7.1

Which Benefits Are Most Beneficial to People Living in Poverty?

EP 2.1.3

The next chapter discusses poverty and the programs implementing policies to help people who are poor. Some programs provide minimum cash benefits and allow people to determine for themselves how to budget the money and spend it. Other programs provide in-kind benefits, and the recipients have no choice in what they get.

Dobelstein (2003) questions the value of in-kind benefits versus cash. He indicates that "total federal government spending for all social programs, including cash and in-kind programs [including medical care], when added together is more than enough to raise the poor above the present poverty" line (p. 124). (The *poverty line* is the minimum amount of money the government believes a person needs to achieve the lowest acceptable standard of living [Orshansky, 1965].)

In other words, Dobelstein maintains that, if the government would divert the money it spends on in-kind benefits to providing cash directly, it would spend no more and possibly spend less. He continues that "the share of cash expenditures as a portion of all income-maintenance expenditures has been decreasing over the past 25 years, while the share of in-kind benefits has been increasing" (p. 125). (*Income maintenance programs* are all those that provide people with enough money, goods, and services to achieve an adequate standard of living and quality of life.)

Do you think it is better to provide people living in poverty with all cash, all in-kind, or some combination of both benefits? What are the pros and cons of each choice? Consider the following questions.

Critical Thinking Questions

- To what extent does provision of cash benefits allow for personal choice, thereby respecting an individual's right to self-determination and human dignity?
- To what extent does the provision of in-kind benefits ensure that individuals get their basic needs met?
- To what extent does the provision of in-kind benefits restrict individuals? For instance, people eligible for low-income housing (by having incomes under a designated level) must live in the housing provided; they have no choice about where to live. Similarly, people receiving food stamps must use them for food. Although such coupons allow people some choice in the food they obtain, recipients cannot choose to pay the electric or heating bill or to purchase toilet paper with them.
- What are the advantages and disadvantages of some mixture of cash and in-kind benefits?
- Where do your answers stand on the conservative–liberal continuum, and why?

eligible for a particular public assistance program, an individual must fulfill the required criteria. *Public assistance* is provision by the government of minimum monetary support to people who are unable to provide for themselves.

A common criterion used to determine eligibility is a *means test*—the evaluation of all the resources clients have at their disposal to determine if they have the *means* to pay for services or buy things for themselves. A means test might include assessment of people's "income, assets, debts and other obligations, number of dependents, and health factors" (Barker, 2003, p. 265). If people fail the means test, they are ineligible to receive benefits. Eligibility is an extremely important concept because it is the key to whether a person can obtain benefits.

Who Pays for the Program?

How the program is financed entails the fourth structural component for understanding a social welfare policy. There are several ways to finance social welfare programs (Dolgoff & Feldstein, 2007, pp. 136–137). National, state, and local taxes provide a primary avenue for getting funds. Sometimes funding is diverted from the general tax pool (referred to as *general revenues*); other times taxes are *earmarked* to provide specified services. For example, a county might increase its sales tax to help pay for a new stadium. Or funds from a state lottery might be earmarked to subsidize (partially pay for) citizens' property taxes. Finally, taxes might be collected specifically from employers and their employees to provide some benefit. Social Security, described more thoroughly in later chapters, is an example of such a program.

Sometimes benefits are not provided directly by government agencies. Rather, funds are collected by such agencies through taxes, and then specific services are purchased from another social service provider. Recall from Chapter 5 that this process is referred to as a *purchase-of-service agreement*. The purchasing agency and the provider agency agree in advance what types of services will be provided, for how long, and at what cost.

People who receive some benefit may also pay for it directly. Of course, many social welfare programs provide benefits to people with few resources. Therefore, a *sliding fee scale* might be used, with the amount paid based on the recipient's ability to pay rather than on fixed fees. The more income the person has, the more he or she is required to pay. Planned Parenthood, an agency providing family planning services and reproductive health care, including contraception, is an example of an agency that uses a sliding fee scale. Such family planning clinics are especially beneficial resources for teens and women with low incomes.

Finally, some programs are financed in a combination of ways. For example, a private agency providing mental health counseling may receive funding from various sources. This includes some funding through sliding-scale fees from clients, some through purchase of service by the state and county for clients unable to pay for the service themselves, some through grants furnished by private foundations, and some through charitable contributions from local citizens.

How Is the Program Administered and Run?

The fifth structural component involved in understanding a social welfare program is the level of government that actually oversees and runs the program. Is it national, state, or local? Many times this involves a combination. For example, consider Medicaid, a program that pays for medical and hospital services for eligible people in need. (Medicaid is discussed more thoroughly in the next chapter.) It is administered by state government but overseen at the federal level.

Another example involves TANF, mentioned earlier, a primary program providing financial assistance to needy families. (The next chapter also describes TANF in greater detail.) TANF policy dictates that the federal government grant sums of money to states. States then have much discretion regarding how to administer the program and spend the money. They may channel more into cash benefits or provide more in-kind benefits such as child care or nutritional programs for children.

A food bank located in a large city is an example of a locally administered program. Here food items such as canned goods and staples such as flour and rice are provided to eligible people living in poverty. This food bank may be financed by the city and county governments and by charitable contributions from private citizens.

There are other ways to look at how programs are administered and run. For example, you can explore program administration and service provision at the individual agency level. Chapter 5 reviewed the types of social agencies that implement social welfare programs, including public, private, nonprofit, for-profit, and proprietary.

Value Perspectives and Political Ideology: Effects on Social Responsibility and Social Welfare Program Development

Chapter 1 introduced some basic value differences about whether social welfare is the primary responsibility of individuals or of society in general. It also discussed some related perspectives concerning how social welfare policy and programs should be developed. The concepts will be reviewed here, and some questions posed for assessing the values that characterize a range of specific social welfare programs discussed in later chapters. An additional issue to be addressed is whether social welfare benefits should be available to everyone or to only a select few.

Note that the following discussion simplifies highly complex and controversial concepts. The purpose is not to provide an absolute decree for how to think about these issues, but rather to offer a foundation for thinking about how values affect social welfare policy and program development.

The Conservative–Liberal Continuum

Conservatism is the philosophy that individuals are responsible for themselves, that government should provide minimal interference in people's lives, and that change is generally unnecessary (Jansson, 2011). It involves the idea that if people fail or have problems, except in extreme circumstances, it is generally their own fault. It assumes that people who are weak or lazy deserve what they get, which is often little or nothing. If people have access to free benefits, they will readily take them and "milk" the system. And if they don't have to work, they won't. Therefore, government should not interfere in people's lives unless it is absolutely necessary (e.g., for people who are extremely "worthy" poor, as described in Chapter 6, or who need help in an emergency like a flood or hurricane). Thus these primary principles are involved in conservatism:

- It is each individual's responsibility to work and succeed.
- Failure to succeed is generally the individual's fault.
- The government should not interfere unless absolutely necessary.

Liberalism, in contrast, is the philosophy that supports government involvement in the social, political, and economic structure so that all people's rights and privileges are protected in the name of social justice (Jansson, 2011). Social welfare is the collective responsibility of society. It is society's obligation to assist people in adjusting to the turbulent and demanding contemporary environment. People will prosper only if given the chance to. Thus these major principles are involved in liberalism:

- It is society's responsibility to care for and support its members.
- Failure to succeed generally is due to complex, unfair stresses and problems in the environment.
- It is government's responsibility to support its citizens and help them cope with the stresses and problems in their environment.

The top portion of Figure 7.2 contrasts some of the basic principles of conservatism and liberalism. These include the view of responsibility, the conception of where problems and needs lie, and the divergent perspectives on government's responsibility.

Figure 7.2 Conservative versus Liberal Value Orientations

Value orientation	Conservative	Liberal
View of responsibility	Individual responsibility	Society's responsibility
Conception of where problems and needs lie	Pessimistic: people are basically lazy	Optimistic: people will thrive if given support
Perspective on governmental intervention	Government should not interfere	It's government's responsibility to help
Social welfare program orientation	Residual *reactive*	Institutional *supportive/ ongoing*
Benefit availability	Selective	Universal

© Cengage Learning 2013

Radicalism

Radicalism is the philosophy that the social and political system as it stands is not structurally capable of truly pursuing social justice (Marx, 2004). Rather, drastic, fundamental changes are necessary in the system to achieve true fair and equal treatment.

Radicalism involves extremes. It can reflect extreme conservatism or extreme liberalism. Essentially, the primary principle involved in radicalism is that the system requires a major overhaul to achieve more appropriate goals. Two questions may be asked:

- What goals should the system pursue?
- How should the system pursue these goals?

Chapter 1 established that a radical perspective requires the ability to propose a new social structure. It is beyond the scope of this introductory book to teach you how to plan new policies and promote major social changes. Therefore, critical thinking about social welfare policy in the remaining chapters will focus on the conservative–liberal continuum.

Residual and Institutional Perspectives on Social Welfare Policy and Program Development

We have established how policies and program implementation initially flow from society's values. Similarly, residual and institutional social welfare policy and program development, to some extent, are related to conservative and liberal values, respectively. Proposed here is one basic way to start thinking about social welfare policy and program development. The philosophical approaches and value systems involved are extremely complex.

The *residual* perspective conceives of social welfare as focusing on problems and gaps, with social welfare benefits and services supplied only when people fail to provide adequately for themselves and problems arise (Abramovitz, 2007; Dolgoff & Feldstein, 2009). The implication is that it's people's own fault if they require outside help. Basic concepts inherent in the residual view include these:

- Social welfare policies and programs should be *reactive*, solving problems only after they occur (McInnis-Dittrich, 1994, p. 7).
- Social welfare policies and programs generally respond to problems caused by individual personal failure.

The *institutional* perspective of social welfare, in contrast, views people's needs as a normal part of life (Abramovitz, 2007, Dolgoff & Feldstein, 2009). It is society's ongoing responsibility to support its members and provide needed benefits and services. It is not people's fault that they require such services, but rather an expected part of the human condition. Basic concepts inherent in the institutional view include these:

- Social welfare policies and programs should provide ongoing support to all people in need.
- Social welfare policies and programs relieve existing tensions and help solve problems distressing people in their environment.

The central portion of Figure 7.2 reflects how the residual perspective relates somewhat to the conservative value orientation and the institutional perspective to the liberal value orientation.

Universal Versus Selective Service Provision

One other perspective on social welfare policy and programming involves the concepts of universal versus selective benefits. *Universality* is the idea that social welfare benefits should be equally available "to all members of society, regardless of their income or means" (Segal & Brzuzy, 1998, p. 13). Public education through high school is a universal social welfare benefit available to all citizens regardless of status, class, or income level. This is despite the fact that the quality of education varies dramatically from one locale to another. Social Security is another universal program because it is available to all people who work (Dolgoff & Feldstein, 2009).

Universality contrasts sharply with *selectivity*— the idea that social welfare benefits should be "restricted to those who can demonstrate need through established eligibility criteria" (Segal & Brzuzy, 1998, p. 13). Any public assistance program requiring a means test that limits benefits to "the needy" reflects selective service provision. To some extent, the concept of universality coincides with the institutional perspective on social welfare, and the concept of selectivity with the residual (Dolgoff & Feldstein, 2009). Focus on Critical Thinking 7.2 raises some questions regarding the pros and cons of universal versus selective service provision.

Note that the bottom of Figure 7.2 shows how selective benefit availability coincides to some extent with a conservative value orientation and a residual

FOCUS ON CRITICAL THINKING 7.2

Universal Versus Selective Service Provision

Popple and Leighninger (2011) reflect:

EP 2.1.3

There are many arguments for and against each type of approach. The universal basis of allocation carries relatively little stigma and fits with democratic notions of equal treatment for all. Recipients can be seen as citizens or consumers. Proponents of selectivity herald its cost effectiveness; instead of resources being spread over a vast population, money or services can be used where they are most needed. This can help fill in the gaps between needy and non-needy groups. Debates over the future shape of Social Security in our society involve these issues, with some observers suggesting that we should stop paying Social Security to those who don't need it and instead target more money to the less-well-off [older adults] ...

Critics of selectivity argue, however, that it may be more cost effective to provide social welfare benefits across the board rather than to spend time and money sorting out those who are "truly disadvantaged." These critics add that selectivity leads to a two-track system; benefits for low-income groups don't seem as important to society as benefits for the majority and are thus allowed to be a lesser quality. This is a common argument today in discussions of health care; the system people can afford to pay for (on their own or through insurance) is often superior to publicly financed health care for the indigent. (p. 38)

When thinking about any social welfare policy, you might, then, ask two questions concerning the universality–selectivity issue.

Critical Thinking Questions

- Should benefits be available to everyone or only to a select group?
- What would be the relative costs for each option?

---

perspective on social welfare policy and programming. Similarly, the figure shows how universal benefit availability corresponds somewhat with a liberal value orientation and an institutional perspective toward social welfare.

This connection, however, is not perfect. Therefore, the arrows leading from the residual and institutional social welfare program orientations to selective and universal benefit availability, respectively, are broken instead of solid lines. Actual policies may reflect a combination of selective, universal, residual, and institutional aspects. For example, student loans are universally available in that anyone can apply for them (Dolgoff & Feldstein, 2009). However, they are selective in that students must meet a financial needs test to actually receive them.

Another example of the complex and intertwining nature of these concepts involves disaster relief after the horrifying earthquake and tsunami that devastated a large area in northern Japan on March 3, 2011. Relief initially was residual: Its main goal was to fulfill temporary needs in reaction to the catastrophe (although the earthquake causing the tsunami, of course, was no one's fault). However, institutional relief is also needed over a longer term to help rebuild Japan's economic infrastructures.

People who lost virtually everything require years of help in rebuilding their homes, work, communities, and lives. Disaster relief was also universal in that its availability was intended for everyone in need regardless of income level or social status. Universality was imperfect, however, because equitable distribution was initially difficult or impossible. Many areas were impenetrable because of destroyed roads, bridges, docks, and airstrips.

Policy Analysis

We have discussed different value perspectives that shape social welfare policy. Examining a policy from a values perspective is one way of understanding it. Another approach involves evaluating the appropriateness and effectiveness of a social welfare policy, a form of policy analysis. However, *policy analysis* is a broad term that can have many specific meanings. Some analyses are filled with complex flowcharts, graphs, and cost figures. Others are narratives that resemble a short story. Others reveal some combination of approaches.

EP 2.1.3a, 2.1.7a, 2.1.8a

Policy analysis can target how well a stated policy attains its goals, who should most likely benefit from the policy, whether the benefit type is appropriate, how efficiently the program that implements the policy is financed, or how the policy compares with alternative policies (Gilbert & Terrell, 2010; Haynes & Mickelson, 2003; Jansson, 2011). Policy analysis is conducted by specialists who carefully scrutinize policies and make recommendations to legislators for future policy changes. Policy analysis is undertaken by social workers who evaluate a policy's effectiveness with respect to clients. Finally, policy analysis can and should be undertaken by all citizens who are affected by a range of policies and who, as voters, are responsible to provide input into policymaking.

For our purposes, *policy analysis* is a systematic evaluation of how effectively a policy addresses the targeted problem or issue, meets people's needs, and achieves its goals. Most of the remaining chapters in this book focus on programs that implement social welfare policy. The model of policy analysis proposed here provides one framework from which you can evaluate for yourself how appropriate a policy is and how well its program implementation works.

The Five-E Approach to Policy Analysis

The proposed Five-E model of basic policy analysis for social welfare policy is as follows:

- How *effective* is the policy?
- How *efficient* is the policy?
- Is the policy *ethically* sound?
- What does *evaluation* of potential alternative policies reveal?
- What recommendations can be *established* for positive changes?

Figure 7.3 summarizes the Five-E approach. Policy analysis involves scrutiny of both the policy and the program implementation resulting from the policy.

How Effective Is the Policy?

Effectiveness involves the extent to which a policy accomplishes its goals. What are the outcomes of the policy? How well does the policy's program implementation achieve its stated goals?

It is important to use critical thinking and ask questions to seek information. What are the program's strengths, on the one hand, and weaknesses,

on the other (McInnis-Dittrich, 1994)? What empirical data are available to support program effectiveness? What do benefit recipients say about the policy and program implementation? Do workers administering the program support its effectiveness?

Case Example Popple and Leighninger (2011) describe and analyze a policy concerning mandatory drug testing (e.g., a urine test) for people receiving public assistance.[4] The basic idea is that people receiving public money should not be wasting it on illegal drugs but should spend it on nurturing and supporting their children. An assumption is that people receiving assistance are likely to be irresponsible and do "bad" things such as use drugs.

Several states have opted to require drug testing for welfare recipients. For example, Maryland became the first state to require such testing for all public assistance applicants. A state legislative committee approved a policy whereby anyone refusing the test would get no financial benefits. People testing positive for drug use would be forced to enter an expensive drug rehabilitation program. And failure to cooperate fully in the program would result in decreased benefits to the recipient's family.

How effective is the policy? What does *effectiveness* in this context mean? Does testing reduce drug use? Do welfare recipients who test positive and enter treatment stop using drugs? No clear evidence exists regarding the results of testing recipients for drugs.

Popple and Leighninger (2011) discuss drug testing in the general workplace:

It is estimated that around three percent of the workforce uses illicit drugs before coming to work or on the job. In an effort to maintain worker efficiency and productivity and to prevent safety hazards, public and private employers have set up a number of forms of drug testing for employees. These generally involve urine tests for traces of drugs in the body. They can be voluntary or required (usually the latter) and can be carried out at varying time intervals. In some cases, positive tests can lead to punitive measures such as firing

[4]The case example, the arguments posed, and many of the questions raised are adopted from a policy analysis of the issue discussed on pp. 230–231 from P. R. Popple and L. Leighninger, *The Policy-Based Profession: An Introduction to Social Welfare Policy Analysis for Social Workers*, 5th ed. (Boston: Allyn & Bacon, 2008).

Figure 7.3 The Five-E Approach to Policy Analysis for Social Welfare Policy

Effectiveness

Efficiency

Ethical considerations

Evaluation of alternatives

Establishment of recommendations for positive change

© Cengage Learning 2013

the employee. In other cases, employers may use the results of the test to refer employees for drug counseling and other treatment." (p. 230)

Proponents of drug testing for welfare recipients argue that forcing abusers to get treatment improves their ability to be productive citizens, as well as enhancing their own and their family's well-being. Critics counter that such drug testing violates recipients' privacy and forces them to endure a humiliating experience. Estimates of recipients who abuse drugs range from 10% to 16%, depending on the source (Popple & Leighninger, 2011). However, a study in Louisiana, a state that also initiated drug testing for recipients, found that only 2% tested positive. Therefore, no hard evidence exists that most welfare recipients abuse drugs.

How Efficient Is the Policy?

Efficiency concerns whether a policy and its implementation through a program are economical. To what extent does the policy address the problem or issue it intends to with the least expenditure of time, effort, and money?

Case Example   Drug testing is very expensive, especially when conducted on a large population such as people receiving public assistance. Maryland determined that testing welfare recipients for drugs for one year would cost at least $1.2 million. Additionally, the state would have to pour significant additional funds into providing treatment for recipients who tested positive. Needless to say, the Maryland legislature determined that the policy was too expensive and dropped it after two months.

Is the Policy Ethically Sound?

To what extent do the policy and the program implementing it respect people's rights to dignity, confidentiality, and self-determination? Is the policy honest and straightforward in its stated intent?

Do people who might be affected by the policy clearly understand it and its implications? Does it concur with current legal requirements?

EP 2.1.2b

Case Example   We have already raised numerous ethical concerns, including violating individual rights and forcing innocent people to subject themselves to the demeaning process of drug testing. Additionally, some questions have been raised regarding whether drug testing in this context is legal and constitutional. How would you like it if drug testing was required for you to go to school?

What Does Evaluation of Potential Alternative Policies Reveal?

To what extent does the policy under examination propose the best way to address the issue or solve the problem? Are there other more effective, efficient, and ethical policy approaches?

EP 2.1.6b

Case Example   What other alternative policy approaches to the problem of possible drug abuse by public assistance recipients might be proposed? One alternative is to limit the focus on the potential drug abuse of welfare recipients and to concentrate on drug abuse prevention with respect to the general population. Anti-drug programs could be conducted on a large-scale basis in the schools. Two other alternatives also involve the general population (Burke, 2008). First, legislative policies should emphasize the availability and use of evidence-based treatment approaches (in other words, treatment that really works). Second, insurance companies could be required to pay for substance abuse treatment to the same extent that they cover other chronic health problems such as diabetes or hypertension.

Burke (2008) raises questions concerning the current trend of spending money for enforcement, that is, reducing the supply of available drugs and arresting offenders. She indicates that there is no proof that supply has been reduced despite increased expenditures toward that end. She also explains that the 2005 cost to incarcerate a dealer or abuser for one year was approximately $22,000. She suggests that diverting money from incarceration to prevention and treatment might be more effective. The active debate on how to approach the drug problem continues to rage.

What Recommendations Can Be Established for Positive Changes?

How can the current policy be amended so that it becomes more effective, efficient, and ethically sound? Or should this policy be eradicated and a new one developed to take its place?

Case Example We established that Maryland legislators withdrew their policy on drug testing. Instead, they decided to require all public assistance applicants to undergo an extensive interview process by trained substance abuse counselors in order to discover ongoing drug addiction. Apparently, the legislators felt that this was a positive change. However, this policy approach still is founded on the degrading assumption that people receiving public assistance should somehow be subjected to scrutiny for drug abuse.

Policy Practice and Policy Advocacy

**EP 2.1.1c,
2.1.3c,
2.1.5b,
2.1.9b,
2.1.10k**

It is the responsibility of social workers not only to analyze social welfare policies but also to strive to make changes when clients are inadequately served, treated unfairly, or could be better served. Schneider and Lester (2001) define *advocacy* as "the exclusive and mutual representation of a client(s) or cause in a forum, attempting to systematically influence decision making in an unjust or unresponsive system" (p. 65). Hepworth and his colleagues (2010) elaborate a bit by defining *advocacy* as

a process of affecting or initiating change either with or on behalf of client groups to:

- *obtain services or resources that would not otherwise be provided*

- *modify or influence policies or practices that adversely affect groups or communities*
- *promote legislation or policies that will result in the provision of requisite resources or services.* (p. 430)

Social workers advocate on their clients' behalf to obtain or improve service provision. This may or may not involve changing a policy. Rather, advocacy is an umbrella concept that includes a wide range of scenarios. Advocacy might involve assisting a client in urging a landlord to make needed rental unit repairs. It can entail providing an argument to an agency administrator to make an exception to some rule on a client's behalf. It also might mean advocating to improve a public assistance policy to provide adequate benefits to clients or to expunge a policy that requires humiliating drug testing to receive benefits.

Advocacy in the policy arena, thus, is a more specific subset of advocacy. Jansson (2011) defines *policy practice* as "efforts to change policies in legislative, agency, and community settings, whether by establishing new policies, improving existing ones, or defeating the policy initiatives of other people" (p. 15). Policy practice may also involve advocacy on behalf of "relatively powerless groups, such as women, children, poor people, African Americans, Asian Americans, Latinos, Native Americans, gay men and lesbians, and people with disabilities, [to] improve their resources and opportunities" (Jansson, 2011, p. 15). This is also referred to as *policy advocacy.* Highlight 7.4 profiles several people who pursued advocacy through policy practice at various times in history.

There are many ways that social workers and others can pursue policy practice and advocacy. Segal and Brzuzy (1998) explain:

Policy practice is within the reach of all social workers. It can be as basic as registering to vote and voting, or as involved as running a political campaign or even running for office. The most important policy practice role is to become involved in one's community. Active participation in community affairs can open the way for involvement in local policy decision making, which may in turn lead to a national role. When greater numbers of social workers and social service agency clients become involved in the policymaking process, social welfare policies will become more responsive to people's needs. (p. 261)

Cummins, Byers, and Pedrick (2011) depict a rather creative means by which one social work faculty member has undertaken policy advocacy:

Ruth White describes herself as a "ranter." "I am always ranting about something," she says. She teaches social policy courses at Seattle University's BSW program. She already had several venues for her advocacy efforts, including a column in a parenting magazine and frequent commentaries in the Seattle papers with her op-ed pieces [citing opinions]. She had always wanted to have a radio talk show, particularly when she heard others on the radio expressing their views. She expressed the thought out loud and was overheard by the manager of the student radio station at Seattle University, KSUB, Seattle. The manager agreed it was a good idea and asked Dr. White to e-mail her ideas for the show. Before she had a chance to do so, the manager e-mailed her, stating the management team had discussed the idea and wanted her to proceed. And so she was off and running with her own radio show, Policy Brief, airing on Wednesdays at 9:00 a.m. Pacific Time, online at www.ksubseattle.org or FM96.

Ruth White's goal in hosting a radio show on social policy was to engage more young people in policy practice issues and get them involved. She structured the show around current policy issues, the first one being organized around the Farm Bill pending in Congress and issues of hunger. Another program was on the challenge of AIDS. She invited a panel for each hour-long show to address the particular issue from a variety of perspectives: service provider, client or consumer, activist, and policymaker. She always tried to include a student on each panel who was involved in the issue in some way, to help make the connections with her student audience. Her time slot saw an increase in the number of listeners despite the limitation of being available online only for some time.

Ruth's other goal was to educate the public in general about social policy issues and how they can help change policy and get involved in the policy-making process. (p. 138)

Approaches to Policy Practice and Policy Advocacy

Advocating for policy or program implementation change—whether at the national, state, local, or agency level—can involve a number of approaches. At least 10 methods exist that social workers can use to conduct policy practice and advocacy (Hepworth, Rooney, Rooney, Strom Gottfried, & Larsen 2011, Kirst-Ashman & Hull, 2012a, 2012b):

1. *Persuade:* In the policy practice context, *persuasion* is the process of attempting to influence decision makers by presenting an argument or rationale for another point of view. What information might a worker give decision makers so that they might view the issue or problem from a different perspective that coincides more with social work values?

2. *Use complaint or grievance processes:* These are "administrative procedures designed to ensure that clients or client groups who have been denied benefits or rights to which they are entitled get equitable treatment" (Kirst-Ashman & Hull, 2012a, p. 409). Usually this involves an outside objective person or group making a decision regarding whether rights or policies have been violated. Initiating a complaint or grievance process draws attention to an issue and forces an agency or governmental unit to publicly make a determination regarding the complaint's validity.

3. *Initiate legal action:* This involves filing a lawsuit. As with following a formal complaint or grievance process, pursuing this alternative brings an issue to public attention and forces a decision to be made. A downside of legal action, however, is that it's expensive.

4. *Form coalitions with other social workers and agencies:* These can enhance political pressure. Greater numbers working together can wield greater political clout.

   EP 2.1.8b

5. *Provide expert testimony in formal settings:* Doing this in courtrooms or community forums or before a legislature can help persuade decision makers. Social workers can significantly influence the development of policies and services by advocating forcefully on their clients' behalf.

6. *Gather information and supportive data to bolster claims about issues and recommendations for change*: Conducting surveys and researching facts can provide persuasive information.

7. *Educate pertinent community groups:* This can be helpful in initiating policy change. Various forms of media can be used to disseminate information and gain public support. These include

newspapers, television, public presentations, and panel discussions at professional conferences and public events. Relevant groups can also be educated by letter-writing and e-mail campaigns concerning issues.

8. *Provide decision makers with relevant information*: Sometimes collecting signatures on a petition can emphasize that substantial numbers of people feel as you do.

9. *Organize groups of clients affected by the policy:* This can help to convey to decision makers the strength of a policy change appeal.

10. *Practice legislative advocacy:* This is the process of influencing legislators to benefit some category of clients. Some of the approaches mentioned here (e.g., writing letters and working with other agencies and client groups) can be used to address issues in the political arena. The more people come together to raise issues and suggest policy changes, the greater the potential impact on politicians. NASW's PACE, described in Highlight 7.4, is an example of how an organization might undertake legislative advocacy. *Lobbying*—that is, hiring individuals (called *lobbyists*) who attempt to influence legislators' decisions and votes through direct communication—is another means of conducting legislative advocacy. Highlight 7.5 introduces one other potential policy practice role for social workers—becoming a politician.

HIGHLIGHT 7.4

Figures Pursuing Policy Practice and Advocacy in a Historical Context

EP 2.1.8b

Three cases reveal how social workers and other community advocates conducted policy practice and advocacy to improve social conditions and service provision. In 1966 George Wiley led various social workers, clients receiving public assistance, "civil rights workers," and assorted other welfare rights groups to take a stand against unfairness and inequity in public assistance policy and program implementation. Together, in 1967 they formed the National Welfare Rights Organization (NWRO), which planned and executed major welfare rights demonstrations (Day, 2009). Under Wiley's leadership, "the NWRO became an advocate for the poor in court, where it challenged welfare laws. The NWRO also appeared on behalf of the poor before congressional committees, again to promote welfare reform. The NWRO's efforts were augmented by the volunteered legal services of lawyers who shared the organization's convictions and supported the welfare reform movement. Many cases were argued and won before the Supreme Court, resulting in the expansion of the rights of those on welfare" (Jansson, 2012, p. 317). The organization "demanded publicity about welfare rights and benefits, information heretofore kept classified, and after extended struggles prepared and distributed handbooks on client rights to welfare mothers" (Day, 2009, p. 351).

Marian Wright Edelman provides another excellent example of policy practice and advocacy. She gave up other career aspirations to become a much-needed civil rights lawyer in the 1960s. She handled many civil rights cases, especially helping students get "out of jail" after involvement in civil rights efforts (Jansson, 2012, p. 302). Driven by her strong beliefs in positive change and hard work, she endured many hardships including being intimidated by dogs and even being thrown in jail herself. One of her greatest accomplishments was the establishment of the Children's Defense Fund (CDF) in 1973. This advocacy organization's purpose was "to provide systematic and long-term assistance to children and adolescents and to ensure that their needs are an important matter of public policy" (Jansson, 2012, p. 302). Work involved grant solicitation from a range of sources and lobbying legislators for positive change. Issues included teen pregnancy, mental health, family support, and child care. This paved the way for further attention to the necessity of providing adequate child care for the nation's children. In May 1996, over 3,000 organizations, along with the Children's Defense Fund, sponsored a "Stand for Children Rally" in Washington, D.C. Then, in 1997, President Bill Clinton and his wife, Hillary, sponsored another major event, the White House Conference on Child Care (Trattner, 1999, p. 133).

A final example of policy practice and advocacy involves the establishment of the Political Action Committee for Candidate Election (PACE) by the National Association of Social Workers (NASW) in 1976. PACE

(continued)

HIGHLIGHT 7.4 (continued)

solicits information from political candidates to establish their positions on social welfare issues and determine the extent to which their stances comply with social work values and goals. It organizes NASW members throughout the country to support appropriate candidates, encourage social workers to run for office, solicits funds, and provides significant campaign donations (Myers & Granstaff, 2008; Weismiller & Rome, 1995).

HIGHLIGHT 7.5

Focus on Another Policy Practice Role: Social Workers in Politics

Note that some social workers have also assumed political roles. Pace (2006, Sept.) highlights six social workers who ran and were subsequently reelected to national public office in the 2006 elections. These include one U.S. senator and five members of the U.S. House of Representatives.

Then NASW Government Relations Manager Dave Dempsey indicated that such people "have not forgotten their roots as social workers"; he continued that "social workers who become politicians can bring their principles, values, ethics, knowledge, and skills to bear on social problems in a larger context than individual practice. . . . Virtually all the social worker politicians that I've had a chance to talk to personally have made the point that social work skills fit the political process and environment beautifully" (Fred, 2004b, p. 11). Social workers have skills that are readily adoptable to work in public office. These include "interpersonal skills, like active listening and conflict management and resolution and technical skills, such as program development and grant writing. Social workers also have knowledge in group dynamics, social systems and social policy, as well as possessing analytical and interactional skills" (Stoesen, 2007b, p. 4).

Sen. Barbara Mikulski (D-Md.) provides an excellent example of a social worker who became a successful politician. First elected as a U.S. senator in 1986, she "is one of the highest-ranking social workers in the country's political system" (Stoesen, 2007b, p. 4). She has served as a long-term advocate for older adults, women, and people living in poverty; she has composed legislation protecting older adult couples from bankruptcy when one spouse has to enter a nursing home, pressed for "a prescription drug benefit under Medicare," written legislation requiring national "standards for mammograms," and advocated for "legislation that gives uninsured

women access to screenings and treatment for breast and cervical cancer" (Fred, 2004b, p. 11). She is currently a senior member of the Senate Appropriations Committee and the Health, Education, Labor, & Pensions Committee (HELP) (Mikulski, 2011).

Rep. Susan Davis (D-Ca.), one of the six social workers reelected in 2006, still holds office and provides another example of how a social worker can strive to affect national policy. She has "fought to regulate the dietary supplement industry and pushed for legislation requiring that health plans provide coverage for second medical opinions," in addition to advocating for increased benefits for veterans (Fred, 2004b, p. 11). Recently, she sponsored the Mentoring America's Children Act and the Women's Obstetrician and Gynecologist Medical Access Now Act (Davis, 2011).

Nancy Humphreys, Director of the Nancy A. Humphreys Institute for Political Social Work at the University of Connecticut School of Social Work, emphasizes that social workers can play a wide range of political roles; these include "observer, advocate, voter, lobbyist, campaigner, trainer, as well as elected official" (Stoesen, 2007b, Sept., p. 4). One doesn't necessarily have to start off by running for national office or the presidency. Political involvement can take many forms, although Humphreys emphasizes that social workers should keep their social work identity with its inherent value base (Stoesen, 2007b, Sept.). Policy practice and political advocacy does not necessarily mean devoting oneself to a new career. Even e-mailing or writing legislators or newspapers about important issues can help change or implement policy. There's also potential for involvement at local levels such as running for the local school board, city council, or town board. Actively supporting political candidates is still another avenue of political involvement.

Chapter Summary

The following summarizes this chapter's content as it relates to the chapter's learning objectives presented at the beginning of the chapter. Learning objectives include the following statements:

A Define social welfare policy and agency policy.

Social welfare concerns the laws and regulations that govern which social welfare programs exist, what categories of clients are served, and who qualifies for a given program. Social welfare programs are the implementation of social welfare policy. Agency policy involves standards adopted by organizations and programs that provide services and guide the provision of service.

B Explore the process of policy development.

Phases of policy development include recognition of society's values about what is considered important, identification of problems and needs that require attention, identification of public opinion about an identified problem and people's related needs, formulation of a policy by legislators, implementation of the policy through a social welfare program, and delivery of social services by social workers and other staff in the context of social service agencies.

C Identify the primary structural components of social welfare programs.

The five broad components to explore in order to understand any policy are (1) what people's needs and the program's goals are; (2) what kinds of benefits are provided; (3) what the eligibility criteria are to receive benefits; (4) how the program is financed; and (5) how the program is administered and run.

D Explore the conservative–liberal–radical value continuum and examine how values affect policy development.

Conservatism is the philosophy that individuals are responsible for themselves, that government should provide minimal interference in people's lives, and that change is generally unnecessary. Liberalism, in contrast, is the philosophy that supports government involvement in the social, political, and economic structure so that all people's rights and privileges are protected in the name of social justice. Radicalism

is the philosophy that the social and political system as it stands is not structurally capable of truly pursuing social justice. Each value philosophy shapes how policies are developed in terms of individual responsibility to take care of oneself versus governmental responsibility to oversee the population's overall well-being.

The residual perspective, related to conservative values, conceives of social welfare as focusing on problems and gaps, with social welfare benefits and services supplied only when people fail to provide adequately for themselves and problems arise. This is also related to the concept of selectivity, the idea that social welfare benefits should be "restricted to those who can demonstrate need through established eligibility criteria" (Segal & Brzuzy, 1998, p. 13). The institutional perspective of social welfare, related to liberal values, in contrast, views people's needs as a normal part of life. This is also related to the concept of universality, the idea that social welfare benefits should be equally available "to all members of society, regardless of their income or means" (Segal & Brzuzy, 1998, p. 13). Social policies, then, would be developed and services provided according to the value stance adopted.

E Propose a model for analyzing a policy's appropriateness and adequacy.

The Five-E approach to policy analysis is proposed involving the following questions: (1) How *effective* is the policy? (2) How *efficient* is the policy? (3) Is the policy *ethically* sound? (4) What does *evaluation* of potential alternative policies reveal? (5) What recommendations can be *established* for positive changes?

F Describe policy practice and policy advocacy.

Policy practice involves the "efforts to change policies in legislative, agency, and community settings, whether by establishing new policies, improving existing ones, or defeating the policy initiatives of other people" (Jansson, 2011, p. 15). Policy advocacy concerns the practice of advocating for improved "resources and opportunities" on the behalf of "relatively powerless groups, such as women, children, poor people, African Americans, Asian Americans, Latinos, Native Americans, gay men and lesbians, and people with disabilities" (Jansson, 2011, p. 15).

G Identify various methods social workers can use in policy practice, including involvement in politics.

Social workers can develop and join advocacy organizations such as the National Welfare Rights Organization or Children's Defense Fund. They can join political action committees such as NASW's Political Action Committee for Candidate Election (PACE). Additionally, social workers can use persuasion with decision makers, use grievance processes, initiate legal action, form coalitions with others, provide expert testimony in formal settings, gather information to support their causes, educate pertinent community groups, provide decision makers with relevant information, organize groups of clients affected by the targeted policy, practice legislative advocacy, support political candidates, or run for political office.

H Encourage critical thinking about what kinds of policies should be formulated.

Critical thinking questions were posed concerning whether cash or in-kind benefits are most beneficial to people living in poverty, and the value of universal versus selective service provision.

LOOKING AHEAD

This chapter provided a basic perspective on social welfare policy and the ways in which programs are implemented based on their policy foundation. The next chapter will discuss policies regulating the primary financial programs in the United States. Subsequent chapters will discuss various contexts in which workers practice, the populations with whom they work, and the policies and programs that govern what they do.

COMPETENCY NOTES

The following identifies where Educational Policy (EP) competencies and practice behaviors are discussed in the chapter.

EP 2.1.1c Attend to professional roles and boundaries. *(p. 228):* Policy practice and policy advocacy are among important professional roles.

EP 2.1.1d Demonstrate professional demeanor in behavior, appearance, and communication. *(p. 218):* When working with legislators, adminis-

trators, and others in the process of policy development, professional demeanor must be demonstrated through various types of communication and other behavior.

EP 2.1.2b Make ethical decisions by applying standards of the National Association of Social Workers (NASW) *Code of Ethics* and, as applicable, of the International Federation of Social Workers/International Association of Schools of Social Work *Ethics in Social Work, Statement of Principles.* *(p. 227):* Practitioners should evaluate the extent to which a policy reflects professional ethics.

EP 2.1.3 Apply critical thinking to inform and communicate professional judgments. *(p. 212):* Critical thinking is used to assess three different policies. *(p. 221):* Critical thinking questions are posed to explore which benefits are most beneficial to people living in poverty. *(p. 225):* Practitioners should critically appraise the extent to which social welfare policies concerning service provision should be universally or selectively applied.

EP 2.1.3a Distinguish, appraise, and integrate multiple sources of knowledge, including research-based knowledge, and practice wisdom. *(p. 225):* Multiple sources of knowledge must be taken into account when conducting a policy analysis.

EP 2.1.3c Demonstrate effective oral and written communication in working with individuals, families, groups, organizations, communities, and colleagues. *(p. 216):* Policy development requires clear oral and written articulation of the features involved. *(p. 218):* Initial formulation of policy requires clear, effective oral and written communication. *(p. 228):* Policy practice and policy advocacy require clear articulation of needs and recommendations.

EP 2.1.5b Advocate for human rights and social and economic justice. *(p. 215):* Practitioners should advocate for policies that are socially and economically just. *(p. 228):* Policy advocacy involves advocating for human rights and social and economic justice.

EP 2.1.6b Use research evidence to inform practice. *(p. 227):* Social workers should utilize research to determine the effectiveness of alternative policy approaches.

EP 2.1.7a Utilize conceptual frameworks to guide the processes of assessment, intervention, and evaluation. *(p. 216):* A conceptual framework is provided for policy development, an aspect of assessment and intervention in macro practice. *(p. 225):* A conceptual framework is presented to guide the policy analysis process, an aspect of macro assessment, intervention, and evaluation.

EP 2.1.8 Engage in policy practice to advance social and economic well-being and to deliver effective social work services. *(p. 214):* Policy and related concepts are defined and discussed.

EP 2.1.8a Analyze, formulate, and advocate for policies that advance social well-being. *(p. 212):* Three policies are analyzed. *(p. 215):* Practitioners should advocate for policies that advance social well-being. *(p. 225):* An approach for policy analysis is presented.

EP 2.1.8b Collaborate with colleagues and clients for effective policy action. *(p. 218):* Collaboration with colleagues and others is necessary to formulate policy. *(p. 229):* Forming coalitions and collaborating with colleagues is an important part of policy practice and policy advocacy. *(p. 230):* Examples are provided of how social workers and other community advocates work together for effective policy action.

EP 2.1.9a Continuously discover, appraise, and attend to changing locales, populations, scientific and technological developments, and emerging societal trends to provide relevant services. *(p. 220):* Practitioners should continuously attend to changing issues and conditions in order to understand changing social values, the resulting changes in policies, and the effects of policies on clients.

EP 2.1.9b Provide leadership in promoting sustainable changes in service delivery and practice to improve the quality of social services. *(p. 228):* Social workers provide leadership in promoting positive change as they undertake policy practice and policy advocacy.

EP 2.1.10k Negotiate, mediate, and advocate for clients. *(p. 215):* Social workers should advocate for policies that are fair, effective, and efficient for clients. *(p. 228):* Policy advocacy is an important part of social work practice.

FOR FURTHER EXPLORATION ON THE INTERNET

See this text's Social Work CourseMate website at *www.cengagebrain.com* for learning tools such as chapter quizzing, videos, glossary flashcards, and more.

CHAPTER 8

Policies and Programs to Combat Poverty

Bruce Ayres/Stone/Getty Images

Think about these questions:

- *Do you know people who live in poverty?*
- *What does poverty mean to you?*
- *Where would you place yourself on the continuum ranging from poor to middle class to wealthy?*
- *Who is to blame for people living in poverty? Is it their own fault, or are they victims of unfair social conditions?*

Now consider the following facts:

- *In the United States, 11.2% of whites, 24.7% of African Americans, 24.2% of American Indians and Alaskan Natives, 11.8% of Asian Americans, and 23.2% of Hispanics live in families with incomes below the poverty line; 13.2% of the total population or over 39.8 million people are poor (U.S. Census Bureau, 2010). (The poverty line is the annual cash income level, according to family size, that the federal government determines is necessary to maintain each individual or family at a minimal subsistence level.)*

- *19% of all U.S. children under age 18 and 9.7% of people age 65 or older are poor (U.S. Census Bureau, 2010).*
- *When considering race as a factor, 34.7% of African American children and 30.6% of Hispanic children under age 18 live in poverty, whereas 15.8% of white children do (U.S. Census Bureau, 2010).*
- *The quality of living for the majority of Americans has been decreasing in recent years (Kornblum & Julian, 2009).*
- *The median (midpoint) household income in the United States is $50,303; 24.7% of all households have incomes of less than $25,000, and 20.5% have incomes of $100,000 or more (U.S. Census Bureau, 2010).*
- *The median income for African American households is 65.4% and for Hispanic households 72.5% of the median income for white households (U.S. Census Bureau, 2010).*
- *About 1% of all households in the United States have more than one-third of the wealth (Kornblum & Julian, 2009).*

A huge and widening chasm exists between the wealthy and the impoverished, the "haves" and the "have-nots" (Kornblum & Julian, 2009, p. 187). This is true not only in the United States but also around the world, as Highlight 8.1 explains. This chapter explores the policies and programs designed to combat poverty in the United States.

Interestingly, although this chapter addresses policies formulating programs to combat poverty, there are many questions about their effectiveness. Do they really combat poverty, or do they simply alleviate some of people's most desperate needs?

Learning Objectives

A   Recognize poverty as a global and national problem.

B   Address race, gender, and single parenthood as variables related to poverty and the feminization of poverty.

C   Describe special assessment issues concerning women and examine empowerment of women through consciousness-raising and a grass-roots approach.

D   Investigate proposed explanations for and the consequences of poverty.

E   Explore the dynamics of homelessness in the United States.

F   Emphasize the importance of empowerment for people living in poverty.

G   Describe major social insurance and public assistance programs in the United States and address relevant policy issues concerning them.

H   Appraise stereotypes about public assistance recipients.

I   Review some aspects of the Canadian Child Tax benefit program to reflect an international perspective.

J   Encourage critical thinking about resource and service provision to combat poverty.

HIGHLIGHT 8.1

International Perspectives: Poverty Is a Global Problem

EP 2.1.5

The gap between rich and poor is dramatically increasing not only in the United States but also all over the world. Kornblum and Julian (2009) report that 1.2 billion of the 6.4 billion people on Earth are so poverty-stricken that they must survive on $1 per day or less. They continue:

One-fifth of the world's people live in the richest nations (including the United States), and their average incomes are 15 times higher than those of the one-fifth who live in the poorest nations. In the world today there are about 160 billionaires and about 2 million millionaires, but there are approximately 100 million homeless people. (p. 186)

Johannesen (1997) emphasizes how individual nations are no longer isolated and able to function independently from each other:

Today we are more dependent on each other than ever before. Globalization is a consequence of increased human mobility, enhanced communications, greatly increased trade and capital flows, and technological developments. In turn it has created opportunities for growth and development and permitted countries to share experiences and learn from each other. It also promotes a cross-fertilization of ideals, cultural values, and aspirations. (p. 147)

Because of their growing interdependence, U.S. citizens can no longer remain isolated and "safe" from global crises (Khinduka, 2008). Bibus and Link (1999) explain:

With an international perspective, it becomes clear that the well-being, income distribution, and social security of people in one region are intimately related to worldwide economic, environmental, political, health, and other forces. No one government can enact social policies effectively without the cooperation of other governments. For example, both the United States and the United Kingdom have embarked on strategies for welfare reform.... However, neither country, despite their status as economically developed and recently prospering, can assure their citizens that jobs with living wages and decent benefits for health care, retirement, or disability compensation will be available. Job markets in both countries are predominantly dependent on global market forces such as the prevailing wages for skilled or unskilled labor, the availability of energy and fuel, and the movements of multinational corporations. (pp. 98–99)

Midgley (1997) emphasizes the importance of pursuing economic survival and social justice from an international perspective. Social justice, which involves equal treatment for all, is related to economic justice—the distribution of resources in a fair and equitable manner. He stresses "the urgent need" for the social work profession "to engage in political activism and to campaign more effectively on issues of social justice.... If social work is to fulfill its historic commitment to helping oppressed ethnic minorities, the poor, refugees, and the victims of HIV/AIDS, it must itself have the political potency to effect progressive social change" (p. 175).

Poverty in the United States

**EP 2.1.4a,
2.1.5a**

People living in poverty obviously have less access to resources and, therefore, greater need. We have proposed that *poverty* is the condition of having inadequate "money to buy things that are considered necessary and desirable" (Kornblum & Julian, 2009, p. 193). This concept is more complex than might be immediately apparent. What is considered "necessary and

desirable" in Vietnam, Jamaica, or Morocco may be very different from what fulfills these criteria in the United States. Many people also expand the definition of poverty to include a *culture of poverty* characterized not only by lack of economic resources but also by deprivation, low expectations for what life can give, lack of hope for the future, and despair (Mooney, Knox, & Schacht, 2011).

When the U.S. government refers to *poverty*, it uses a designated formula focusing on the number of persons living in a family or household and the amount of income that family receives. Note the difference between income and wealth. *Income* is the amount of money earned by family members in a year. *Wealth* is the accumulated amount of money and other assets that makes up a person's total worth; this includes cars, property, stocks, and anything else of value the individual or family owns. The U.S. government gauges poverty by focusing on income because total wealth is too difficult to measure. It has established a *poverty line* intended to "specify the minimum amount required to support an average family of given composition at the lowest level consistent with standards of living prevailing in this country" (Orshansky, 1965, p. 214).

According to this measure, over 39.1 million people live in poverty in the United States (U.S. Census Bureau, 2010). White people, who have proportionately greater numbers, make up most of the poor population in the United States. However, as the U.S. Census Bureau data presented earlier suggest, people of color are much more likely to be poor.

Gender, Family Structure, and Race

EP 2.1.4c

Over 59% of all women age 16 and over work outside the home (U.S. Census Bureau, 2010). In general, women earn 78.7% of what men earn (U.S. Census Bureau, 2010). Chapter 3 established a number of facts. For one thing, discrepancies between men's and women's incomes exist regardless of occupation. Women tend to be clustered in low-paying, supportive occupations such as clerical workers, teachers, and service workers, whereas men tend to be found in higher-paying occupations such as managers, skilled blue-collar workers, construction workers, and engineers. Men also dominate in occupations involving math and science. Women are less likely than men to become doctors, dentists, or lawyers. They are also less likely to reach the top of their professions, a barrier that has been labeled the *glass ceiling*.

The U.S. Census Bureau (2010) provides the following facts regarding family structure. Twenty-five percent of households with children under age 18 are headed by single women. The median income of female-headed families is about 41% of the median for families with two parents present. Female-headed families are over five times more likely to

be poor than their married-couple counterparts. Almost 68% of single women with children under age 6 and almost 79% of single women with children aged 6 to 17 work outside the home.

Race is another factor involved in poverty, which is reflected in the following statistics (U.S. Census Bureau, 2010). Among individuals, 9.3% of all white people who are not Hispanic are below the poverty line compared to 24.1% of African Americans, 24.2% of American Indians and Alaskan Natives, 21.3% of Hispanics, 16.3% of Native Hawaiians and other Pacific Islanders, and 10.5% of Asian Americans. We have already established that the median income for all African American families is 65.4% and for Hispanic families 72.5% of the median income for all white families. African American (26.3%) and Hispanic (25.5%) females are significantly more likely to be poor than white females (12.3%). Similarly, 34.4% of all African American and 30.3% of all Hispanic children are poor compared to 15.3% of white children. Over 25% of white female-headed families are poor, and over 37% of African American and over 39% of Hispanic female-headed households live below the poverty line. As a result, children living in single-parent families headed by women, especially women of color, are at greater risk of poverty. All three of these variables—race, single parenthood, and female family head—increase risk.

Is this disturbing news for you? What do you think are the reasons for such discrepancies?

The Feminization of Poverty

An important concept, the *feminization of poverty* refers to the fact that women as a group are more likely to be poor than are men (Brandwein, 2008; Burn, 2005; Figueira-McDonough, 2008).

Case Example Ginny, a divorced single mother of three, isn't making it. She doesn't earn enough at her waitress job, even with Saturday night tips, to pay the rent and put enough food on her table. Her babysitter has quit, and her sister-in-law says she can't help out anymore. Now what? Ginny surely has no money to pay a new babysitter even if she could find one. Ginny is frantic. Where will she go? What will she do?

Consider how the feminization of poverty may be involved here. We have established that women in general earn less than men, even with equivalent education and experience in the same field, although women tend to enter fields with lower pay. Additionally, single women with children are at increased risk of lower incomes and poverty. If Ginny is a non-Asian woman of color, her risk is even greater.

In what ways might Ginny be the victim of oppression? What aspects of her situation decrease her potential to maintain an adequate standard of living and provide for her family? What opportunities are unavailable to her? What support systems are lacking?

In addition to having a greater likelihood of being poor, women are more likely to be primary caregivers for children and older adults than men, which can detract from their focus on career and making money. And they are victimized by specific kinds of violence, including sexual assault and domestic violence, rarely experienced by men.

As with other populations-at-risk and oppressed groups, social workers assess women's problems and issues within the context of their macro environments. Often problems are identified and goals defined with empowerment in mind. Sometimes planned changes focus on the individual; other times the focus is on the macro environment. Gutierrez and Lewis (1998) identify at least three approaches that assist in this assessment process: (1) using "a gender lens," (2) using "empowerment through consciousness-raising," and (3) thinking about a "grassroots, bottom-up approach" to changing communities (pp. 100–101). These principles help guide social workers' analysis of women's position within the macro social environment and provide clues for their empowerment.

A Gender Lens

Using a gender lens to view the plight of women in the macro social environment assumes that sexism is relevant to the experiences of many women and is the basis for many of women's difficulties. Such a gender lens emphasizes that women not only are part of the larger community but themselves make up a community of women within that larger community. In essence, this establishes a new way of looking at the world, with women and their issues becoming the focus (Hyde, 2008).

Empowerment Through Consciousness-Raising and Critical Thinking

Consciousness-raising is the process of facilitating people's understanding of a social issue with personal implications when there was little grasp of that issue before. (Chapter 3 discussed consciousness-raising as a means of empowerment for women in groups.) In this case, it involves a serious examination by women of themselves and their feelings about a range of issues involving women. Using this approach, social workers can help women become aware of the issues engulfing them in their environment before these women take steps to address them.

Bricker-Jenkins and Lockett (1995) suggest that a basic approach for consciousness-raising entails helping women ask themselves a series of questions and think about potential answers. Such questions involve critical thinking and might include these:

"Who am I?" What are my needs, my desires, my visions of a life that is safe, healthy, and fulfilling?

"Who says?" What is the source of my self-definition and that of my reality? Does it conform to my experience of self and the world?

"Who benefits from this definition?" Does it conform to my needs, my "truths"? Is it possible for me to live by these definitions? If not, . . .

"What must change, and how?" (p. 2535)

A social worker can help a woman answer these questions by focusing on and helping her define her self-worth, her values, and her treatment by the world. If she determines that her treatment is unfair or inadequate because she is a woman, how can she make changes in her macro environment to receive better or fairer treatment? Consciousness-raising thus can become a foundation of empowerment. First, a woman explores herself. Next, she examines issues and appraises her status. Finally, she proposes plans to improve her life and her environment.

Case Example   Jazlyn is a single mother of two children, ages 2½ and 4. For the past few months, she's been receiving public assistance through Temporary Assistance to Needy Families (TANF). She is about to begin a job training program in food services. One of her problems is finding adequate and flexible day care. Another problem is receiving court-mandated child support payments from her ex-husband, who can't seem to hold down a job for very long. Still another problem is the high rent on her tiny apartment, given the shortage of adequate affordable housing. Other problems are lack of a social life and difficulties in obtaining credit to buy a sorely needed new car. Her "ex" ruined her credit rating while they were married.

Alone, Jazlyn feels stuck. She views her problems as personal and individual. She tends to blame herself after the fact for making the "wrong decisions." Jazlyn's social worker, Rochelle, in a *counselor* role, can help Jazlyn think through these issues, identify alternatives, evaluate their pros and cons, and develop a plan of action. Part of Jazlyn's consciousness-raising concerns her growing awareness that she is not alone, but rather shares the same plight with many other women. She can come to realize that many things in her world are not her fault, but rather result from basic social conditions working against her. As an *educator*, Rochelle can provide information about resources, services, and tactics for macro change.

Empowerment Through a Grassroots, Bottom-Up Approach

The final facet of empowerment involves proposing and working toward positive changes in the macro environment. A "grassroots, bottom-up approach" means that people at the bottom of the formal power structure, such as ordinary citizens, band together to establish a power base and pursue macro changes. Often the focus is on helping individual community residents strengthen relationships among themselves, develop shared goals, and establish coordinated plans to achieve these goals. The focus of change is usually an issue that directly affects the community residents involved.

The common theme of women's grassroots efforts is that women work together to initiate and implement change. Examples of established grassroots organizations include the National Organization for Women, the National Women's Political Caucus, the Women's Action Alliance, and the Older Women's League.

Another phrase often used for this approach is "the personal is political" (Gutierrez & Lewis, 1998, p. 101; Hyde, 2008). In other words, some problems and issues that tend to affect women on the basis of their gender go beyond the personal or the individual. Rather, such problems are structurally based, affecting many women. The implication, then, is the need for macro-level social change to improve conditions and provide services.

Consider Jazlyn's plight and the ways in which a social worker like Rochelle might help women directly affected by circumstances and a lack of resources pursue macro changes. As a *mobilizer*, Rochelle can discuss with Jazlyn and other clients

having similar concerns how to join together and confront community leaders and politicians about their various problems. Together they can raise issues and try to identify a plan of action to address them. Specific questions to ask involve critical thinking and include the following:

EP 2.1.1c, 2.1.3, 2.1.5c, 2.1.8b, 2.1.9b, 2.1.10g, 2.1.10i

- Should they form a social action group?
- Can community funds be directed to help subsidize child care centers? Can Jazlyn and other local women establish their own center, pooling resources to pay for staff and volunteering their free time to help cut costs?
- How can Jazlyn and other women not receiving child support from itinerant ex-husbands or partners obtain their fair share? Is there some community agency available to help them locate missing fathers and force payment? If not, why not? Can such a service be developed?
- What about the lack of adequate, reasonable housing? How can the community address this problem? Can community leaders help? Can private developers be encouraged or subsidized to build the housing community mothers need?
- Might community events be organized to fulfill the social needs of single mothers and decrease their isolation? Can interested women form clubs or socialization groups to help them "get out" regularly? In a *facilitator* role, could Rochelle assist in establishing and coordinating such a group?
- How can Jazlyn and other community women work together to find ways to establish credit? As a group, might they approach local banks and businesses to discuss the issue? Can processes be established to determine when credit problems are not their fault, but rather the fault of ex-spouses?

Poverty and Social Class

Sociologists, who study how societies are structured, tend to divide the population into categories of social position based on the extent to which people have access to the goods and services the society values. Another term for this categorization is *social*

EP 2.1.4, 2.1.7b

stratification. The population, then, is divided into *social classes*—"categories of people who have similar access to resources and opportunities" (Macionis, 2010, p. 483). People in the same social class share things in common such as educational and employment opportunities, access to health care, and ability to acquire material possessions.

Nineteenth-century philosophers did much to shape the way we think about people and social class. Karl Marx, for example, viewed social class primarily as an economic phenomenon related to a person's wealth. Max Weber expanded on this idea, claiming that a person's social class is determined by status and power in addition to wealth. *Status* is one's social standing and prestige in comparison to others. Chapter 3 introduced the related concepts of power, privilege, and acclaim. *Power* is the ability to move people on a chosen course to produce an effect or achieve some goal (Homan, 2011). Status and power are related to privilege and acclaim (CSWE, 2008b). *Privilege* entails special rights or benefits enjoyed because of elevated social, political, or economic status. *Acclaim* is "enthusiastic and public praise" (Lindberg, 2007, p. 7). People who experience acclaim such as high-level politicians, well-known professionals, and famous entertainers maintain broad influence over what other people think. Subsequently, people with much privilege and acclaim have greater power to influence and control their destinies and those of others.

As you know, people live in very different circumstances and experience dramatically diverse levels of status and power. Consider, for instance, a homeless man who has a mental illness and who lives under the basement-level steps in a six-story parking garage (that is, when police or custodial staff don't chase him away). His status, power, and life are radically different from those of a physician who is also the administrator of a large, prestigious research hospital next door and who parks his Porsche 911 in that same parking garage.

We might think of our society as having several basic classes (Kendall, 2007). *Upper-class* people include "investors, heirs, and executives" who have extensive wealth, power, and status; this includes the billionaire creators of a computer company, powerful politicians from wealthy families, "sports or entertainment celebrities," chief executive officers (CEOs) of big corporations, and "top-level professionals" earning millions of dollars a year (Kendall, 2010, p. 31).

Upper-middle-class people include "professionals (for example, physicians and attorneys), business analysts, owners of small businesses, stockbrokers, and corporate managers. These individuals generally do not own the means of production but have substantial control over production and other workers" (Kendall, 2011, p. 31).

Middle-class people include "white-collar office workers, middle-management personnel, and people in support positions (for example, medical technologists, nurses, and legal and medical secretaries), semiprofessionals, and nonretail salesworkers" (Kendall, 2007, p. 34).

Working-class people include blue-collar workers who perform manual and semiskilled jobs in industrial settings or occupy lower-level service positions "(for example, day care workers, checkout clerks, cashiers, and counter help in fast-food restaurants)" (Kendall, 2010, p. 31). On the whole, they receive less prestige and have less access to resources than the classes above them.

The *working poor* are those who assume unskilled positions that might be seasonal, such as migrant agricultural workers, or work in jobs that receive the lowest pay; despite the fact that they're employed, they often live paycheck to paycheck, just barely getting by (Kendall, 2010, p. 31).

Finally, the *chronically poor,* about 20% of the U.S. population who have only 3.6% of the total U.S. wealth, have very few resources and have difficulty finding adequate employment to support their families; these people live below the poverty level and often have more debts than assets (Kendall, 2010).

Reasons People Are Living in Poverty

At least two major explanations have been proposed to explain the existence of poverty. They include "structural forces" operating in the economic and political systems, and individual factors (Rank, 2008).

Structural Causes of Poverty

One explanation for the existence of poverty involves structural factors in society. These concern how the social structure, shaped by economics and politics, fails to provide viable opportunities for everyone to find work. Three structural aspects are involved. These include economic, political, and discrimination based on race and gender.

EP 2.1.5a, 2.1.7a

Economic explanations for poverty focus on the structure of the economy (Coleman & Kerbo, 2009). Poverty occurs when wages are too low and not enough adequately paying jobs exist for people to earn what they need to survive. Another structural concern related to poverty involves the escalating number of technical jobs requiring specialized training. People without such training can be left behind. Still another factor contributing to poverty is the increasing trend for industries to move from North America to other parts of the world where production costs are cheaper because people are willing to work for less. The result, of course, is decreased availability of jobs here. The plight of many U.S. farmers poses yet an additional structural worry. If farming costs soar here and imported food is cheaper, farmers are put out of business because they can't compete. Where, then, do they turn to make a living?

Political explanations for poverty emphasize that politicians shape social policies that, in turn, structure the existence of poverty. Such policies can decrease, maintain, or increase poverty (Coleman & Kerbo, 2009). For example, decreasing levels of financial assistance, resources, and services available to poor people will likely increase the number of poor and the depths of their poverty. Similarly, increasing the tax rate for people in the working and lower classes, while decreasing the rate for people in the middle and upper classes, will also increase the likelihood that people in lower classes will be poor.

The third structural feature that encourages poverty involves racial and gender discrimination. Considerable research has established that our society reflects significant "economic, social, and political discrimination" based on variables of gender and race, especially for the African American and Hispanic populations (Rank, 2008, p. 391). Racial segregation in communities often results in the concentration of people of color in poor urban environments with few resources (Rank, 2008).

Gans (1971) proposes that the wealthy find that having a social class of poor people is useful. First, poor people can do the "dirty work" for rich people that the latter don't want to do. Poor people are more willing to take service jobs, jobs requiring hard labor, or those posing danger than their richer counterparts. Second, having a poor social class emphasizes that the wealthy are higher in the social structure. It reinforces their higher status and allows them to look down on classes below them.

Individual Factors Causing Poverty

As earlier chapters pointed out, there has been a historical tendency of blaming the victim when talking about poverty (Rank, 2008). In other words, it's the idea that if a person is poor, it's his or her own fault. This line of thinking blames poor people. It implies that they must have the wrong attitude about work, must not be motivated, and must not be trying hard enough. Substantial research indicates that this is not true; poor people express attitudes, ideas, and motivation very similar to those of middle-class people (Rank, 2008). So, why are they poor? One major difference involves their background and available opportunities from the day they're born. *Human capital*, the "skills, education, and credentials" people bring with themselves as they seek employment has critical consequences for their ability to get a job and for their economic success (Rank, 2008, p. 391).

Several variables contribute to having more or less human capital (Rank, 2008; U.S. Census Bureau, 2010). First, the families of poor people simply have less money than the families of rich people. Therefore, the playing field is not equal. Poor people start out behind. Fewer resources means decreased access to quality education and more lucrative opportunities. A second variable affecting human capital involves how poor people are more likely to originate in a single-parent family. Single-parent families have fewer resources and generally earn less than families where both parents are present. Third, poor people's families are more likely to have greater numbers of children than richer families. This means that whatever resources are available must be spread around more thinly. Fourth, poor people are more likely to have some disability that affects their ability to work.

Regardless of the cause, when a person starts out with disadvantages including a poverty-stricken environment, it's tough "to get ahead." Financial resources, strong familial support, and positive role models all improve a person's chances to succeed in work and maintain a good quality of life.

When thinking about impoverished children, several home visits come to mind. At the time, I was working as a social work counselor in a day treatment center for children and adolescents experiencing emotional, behavioral, and academic problems. The center provided counseling and special education for young people requiring special treatment but living in their own homes or with some other family in the community. The following are three case examples of children ensnared in poverty.

Case Example   The first case involved a home visit with a 16-year-old client, Danielle, at the two-room apartment where she, her mother, and her little brother lived. I knocked, and Danielle invited me in. I noticed that the door into the apartment from the dark, dingy hallway didn't quite shut tightly. The walls inside the tiny apartment looked grimy, with peeling yellowed wallpaper. I stood there for a moment until Danielle asked me if I'd like to sit down. This was perplexing because the only furniture in the room was a shabby table and a twin bed. For lack of other options, I sat down on the bed, as did Danielle. There we discussed the business for which I had come, involving Danielle's progress and future plans. I noticed the only other items in the two rooms were an old 18-inch television on the table, two mattresses on the floor with some bedding on top in the other room, and eight brown paper bags filled with what looked like clothes or rags. They apparently shared a bathroom down the hall with some other tenants. Her mother and brother were nowhere to be seen; in fact, her mother, a cocaine addict, was rarely around.

Danielle had a dream of marrying one of the many men 10 to 20 years her senior with whom she was having sex. Her vision included living in a neatly painted white house surrounded by a white picket fence in a well-to-do neighborhood and living happily ever after. She balked when I gently questioned how realistic that picture was. I presented to her other potential alternatives such as finishing school and getting a job. (A higher level of education is clearly related to higher income later in life.) But Danielle was several years behind her grade in school and was not much motivated to achieve in that area. She didn't understand what purpose academic achievement had. No one in her family, or her neighborhood for that matter, had ever thought much of school. It hadn't seemed to do any of them any good. Instead, she was hoping to find some Prince Charming to save her and care for her. The adult boyfriends she described didn't sound much like Prince Charming to me.

It was much more difficult for Danielle to climb out of poverty than it had been for the students I had known in my middle-class high school, which boasted a strong academic program and active parental involvement, to survive and prosper. There,

the majority of students simply assumed they would go to college. The main concern for many was whether they would get into one of the exclusive eastern private schools.

Case Example   Another young person living in poverty was Mike, an exceptionally bright 14-year-old who attended the day treatment center. Mike found life depressing and tried to escape through drugs. He simply withdrew, caused virtually no problems—(except failure to perform in school), and hoped that those around him would forget he was there. Like Danielle, he lived with his mother, a single parent who busied herself with her own life and relationships, and so was rarely home. Mike treasured an old broken camera he said his father had given him long ago. Mike's dream was to travel from his Midwestern home to Utah, where he thought his father lived with a new family. However, he had not had any contact with his father for over seven years.

Mike grasped ideas quickly and had a perceptive sensitivity concerning others' feelings. I felt that Mike was clearly "college material." When I approached him about the possibility, he chuckled and then quickly apologized because he didn't want to offend me. He explained, "Are you kidding? Me? Go to college? How could I ever go to college? I'm so far behind. Who would ever pay for it?" I couldn't respond because I didn't know the answer. What options were realistically open to Mike? What real chances did he have to "get ahead"?

Case Example   One other example, from the same treatment center, was Rosalie, age 13 going on 23. Rosalie looked like an attractive grown woman. She wore lots of makeup and expensive clothes. Although she supposedly lived with her mother, who had an intellectual disability, she usually resided with other people. Rosalie's attendance at the treatment center was spotty at best. She was too busy at night in her job as a prostitute. At that she made very good money and could afford many more things than her peers. She returned one Monday with a noticeable increase in bust size. She said one of her friends had taken her to a special clinic for implants, but it probably was her pimp. Eventually, Rosalie quit the center and disappeared. The perceptions of the future her teachers and social workers offered her could not compete with the concrete rewards she was getting from her life on the streets.

The Importance of Empowerment

One way of looking at poverty involves understanding how difficult it can be for people with few resources and little support to break through into a higher social class. Few or no role models may exist. People who experience frequent failure and deprivation may quit trying to achieve in the system. Why try if there's no hope? This is the reason the concept of empowerment is so critical. People in poverty must be empowered to see that change is possible. They must be provided viable options and credible hope.

Focus on Critical Thinking 8.1 explores what it might be like to be poor.

Consequences of Poverty

The impacts of poverty are devastating and far-reaching, affecting virtually all areas of life. Among them are health care, education and jobs, housing,

and criminal justice issues (Henslin, 2011; Kornblum & Julian, 2009).

Health Care

It's no newsflash that health care is expensive. Most low-paying jobs don't provide health insurance or many other benefits. Escalating health care and health insurance costs prohibit many people from purchasing coverage themselves. About 15.4% of all U.S. citizens are not covered by health insurance; almost 9.9% of all U.S. children are without health care coverage (U.S. Census Bureau, 2010).

EP 2.1.4a, 2.1.4c, 2.1.9a

Included among people who have some form of health insurance coverage are recipients of Medicare (a form of social insurance) or Medicaid (a form of public assistance based on need), both described later in the chapter. Many other people may have only partial health insurance coverage that might

---

FOCUS ON CRITICAL THINKING 8.1

What Is It Like to Live in Poverty?[1]

EP 2.1.1b, 2.1.3, 2.1.4b, 2.1.10b

What kind of background do you come from? How would you[1] describe it in terms of having adequate resources to grow, develop, and thrive? Do you come from a middle- or upper-class family in which resources were plentiful and you had lots of "stuff"? Or did your family have difficulty scraping by and paying essential bills on time?

Poor people must make hard choices regarding what things they can possess or what activities they can pursue. There's little room for luxury.

Critical Thinking Questions

Of the following items, which do you feel are absolute necessities for your daily life? Which could you live without? How would you prioritize them in order of importance? What would it be like to be poor and forced to make hard choices? What would it be like to have to live without?

A home that you or your family own
A room of your own
A home or apartment that your family rents
A single room where you and your family can stay
A working kitchen along with a range of utensils

A plug-in electric frying pan
Electricity
Heat
Air conditioning
Three meals a day that are nutritionally well balanced
Three meals a day of macaroni and artificial cheese
A private shower with hot water
Running water
Access to a communal water supply
A washer and dryer
A good job that pays adequately or well
A minimum-wage job
Health insurance
Dental insurance
Nice clothes
Two changes of old clothes
A cell phone
A new car
An old broken-down car
A digital plasma surround-sound home theater system
An Apple iPad
A used desktop

[1]The idea for this is derived from Burger and Youkeles (2000, p. 313).

cover only catastrophic illnesses, exclude any number of conditions, or have exorbitantly high deductibles. Insurance premiums for such policies generally cost less than policies that provide more extensive benefits. Note that the highest rate of those with no health insurance (28.6%) involves people ages 18 to 24; the second highest rate (26.5%) concerns people ages 25 to 34 (U.S. Census Bureau, 2009). People whose resources fall below the poverty line are the least likely to have health insurance; 30.4% of them have no coverage (U.S. Census Bureau, 2010).

Kornblum and Julian (2009) explain:

By almost every standard, the poor are less healthy than the rest of the population. For example, the mortality rates for poor infants are far higher than those for infants in more affluent families, and poor women are much more likely to die in childbirth. Poor women are also far more likely to give birth to their children in a municipal hospital. Inadequately housed, fed, and clothed, the poor can expect to be ill more often and to receive less adequate treatment. (p. 204)

One noticeable health issue often affecting the poor involves dental health. People who can't afford health insurance that may involve life or death issues surely can't afford dental insurance or expensive uninsured trips to the dentist to maintain their teeth and gums.

Education and Jobs

"In every respect, poor children get less education than those born into more affluent families" (Kornblum & Julian, 2009, p. 205). Henslin (2011) reflects:

Although public schools hold the idea of giving all children an equal opportunity to succeed, the poor are at a disadvantage. Because our schools are supported by property taxes, and property in poorer areas produces fewer taxes, the schools that the poor attend have smaller budgets. This translates into outdated textbooks, inexperienced teachers, and lower test scores (Kozol, 1999). Lower test scores, in turn, affect students' chances of going to college. (p. 198)

Other facts regarding education that characterize poor people produce life-long effects on their quality of life. Poor people are more likely to drop out and not graduate from high school (Kornblum & Julian, 2009; Macionis, 2010). They are also then much less

likely to attend college (Kornblum & Julian, 2009; Macionis, 2010). Less-educated people get lower paying jobs, experience less job security, receive fewer employment benefits, and find it much more difficult to become economically successful (Kornblum & Julian, 2009; U.S. Census Bureau, 2010).

Henslin (2011) elaborates:

Unlike the career paths that are open to the children of the middle class and the rich, the low-paying jobs of the working poor lead to fewer opportunities. Because workers are often laid off from these dead-end jobs, their incomes, already low, are erratic. During unemployment, they have to cope with the complex bureaucracies of unemployment insurance, welfare, and other social programs. Such experiences add to the stresses already knitted into their daily lives. (p. 198)

Housing

Poor people experience poor housing conditions. Henslin (2011) explains:

Most of the poor live in substandard housing. Many rent from landlords who neglect their buildings. The plumbing may not work. The heating system may break down in winter. Roaches and rats may run riot. And, unlike mortgage payments, the monthly rent does not build up equity in a home. (p. 197)

Note that poor people also don't have the buffer of money necessary to get into good housing. Renting attractive housing not only requires a high monthly rental price but also one or more months' rent in advance for a security deposit.

Many people can't afford rent at all. Highlight 8.2 explores homelessness in the United States.

Criminal Justice Issues

Henslin (2011) explains the differential treatment experienced by people who are poor in the criminal justice system:

The life experiences of the poor also make them more likely to commit robberies and assaults, crimes that are especially visible and for which offenders are punished severely. Those most likely to be the victims of these crimes are other people in poverty. White-collar crime may be more pervasive and costly to society, but it is less visible and carries milder punishments. . . . [W]hen the poor are

HIGHLIGHT 8.2

Homelessness in the United States

EP 2.1.4a

A *homeless person* is defined as one who "lacks a fixed, regular, and adequate nighttime residence," or who sleeps in a temporary shelter for people without adequate residence or in a place (e.g., an abandoned building) not intended for the purpose of sleep (U.S. Department of Housing and Urban Development, 2011).

In other words, homeless people are those who must live mainly on the streets. Because many homeless are transient or, sometimes, temporarily homeless, it's difficult to determine the exact number of homeless people at any given point in time. However, it is estimated that over a million people are homeless in the United States; between 9% and 15% of the U.S. population becomes homeless at some time during their lives (Mooney et al., 2011). About 39% of people in the homeless population are children (National Coalition for the Homeless, 2009).

Who Are the Homeless?

Homeless people are "the poorest of the poor" (Karger & Stoesz, 2010, p. 434). Figueira-McDonough (2007) describes the homeless population according to the data from one study (Burt, 2002):

A third of the homeless have completed high school, and 44 percent have worked during the previous month. These characteristics suggest a modicum of stability among at least some of the homeless population.

Still, in another one-third of the cases, homelessness was attributable to the loss of work or the failure to pay rent. Access to health [care] and food was very poor, the frequency of spells of homelessness was high, and their duration was protracted. Education among the homeless with children was lower than for the whole sample, and so was their labor force participation while homeless.

There are clear differences between men and women with children. Men are four times more likely than women to be accompanied by their spouses or partners, and they are more than three times less likely to have access to health care.

The homeless with children have greater access to emergency housing and Food Stamps than others. Yet they report levels of hunger similar to those experienced by those without children. Finally, the causes of homelessness are different for males and females with children. Failure to meet rent payments

drove over one-third of the men into homelessness, while domestic abuse was a major cause for 18 percent of the women. (p. 70)

Karger and Stoesz (2010) raise concerns regarding the increasing number of homeless youth who may comprise as great as 3% of urban homeless people. Many come from turbulent or abusive home environments. Some research indicates that 7% of homeless children had been in foster or other institutional care. Many on the streets resort to exchanging sex for money in order to survive. Because of this, it is estimated that they may have a 2 to 10 times greater risk of contracting HIV/AIDS.

What Causes Homelessness

Because homeless people are poor, some of the causes of homelessness are related to causes of poverty. Structural causes of homelessness include unavailability of adequate low-rent housing, increased numbers of single-parent families, increased unemployment and inadequate numbers of jobs, decreased salary levels as industries move overseas and low-paying service jobs increase in number, and inadequate care of people with mental illness who have been released from institutions into the community (discussed further in Chapter 13) (Wong, 2008). Individual factors that increase the likelihood of homelessness include mental illness, alcohol and other drug addiction, "domestic violence, foster care experience, and other traumatic childhood incidents (Wong, 2008).

Solving the Homelessness Problem

EP 2.1.8a, 2.1.10i, 2.1.10j

How can we solve the homelessness problem? The 1987 McKinney-Vento Homeless Assistance Act at least began to address the problem by creating over 20 programs to address the issue. These included programs providing grants to establish emergency shelters, incentives to develop transitional housing and single-room occupancy (SRO) dwellings, and other supportive services. A 1990 amendment mandated that homeless children be able to attend school even when prior educational records and verification of residency are unavailable. However, considering the fact that homelessness is still an extensive problem, this legislation has not been enough.

(continued)

HIGHLIGHT 8.2 (continued)

Solving the problem would require major structural changes in addition to addressing individual needs. Affordable rental housing should be increased; housing development takes money at the outset, but research indicates that expansion of such resources is cost-effective in the long run (Wong, 2008). Hartman (1987) also recommends refurbishing abandoned housing in urban settings to provide low-cost housing, conserving SRO lodging, legally requiring local governments to provide shelter for their homeless populations, and establishing viable community alternatives for people suffering from mental illness. Issues of homeless people should also be addressed at the individual level by providing services people need to function independently. Services might include outreach to homeless people in the community, provision of brokers and case managers to link them with the services they need, and assistance in finding jobs (Wong, 2008). Funding needs to be diverted to help people get back on their feet, or keep from slipping in the first place.

Karger and Stoesz (2010) conclude:

Homelessness cannot be eradicated without basic changes in federal housing, income support, social services, health care, education, and employment policies. Benefit levels for these programs must be made adequate; the erosion of welfare benefits must be stopped; residency and other requirements that exclude homeless persons must be changed; and programs (including outreach) must be made freely available to the homeless and the potentially homeless. Moreover, a real solution to the homeless problem must involve the provision of permanent housing for those who are currently or potentially homeless. Federal programs and legislation should be coordinated and expanded to provide decent, affordable housing, coupled with needed services, for all poor families. Finally, both the states and the federal government should intervene directly in the housing market by controlling rents, increasing the overall housing stock, limiting speculation [e.g., converting SRO hotels into condos for wealthy urban residents], and providing income supports. (p. 438)

arrested, they lack the resources to hire good lawyers to defend themselves. Often, they cannot even post bail, and they remain in jail for months while they await trial. (p. 198)

Focus on Critical Thinking 8.2 addresses residual versus institutional perspectives on poverty and its related issues. It urges you to explore which views you hold.

Social Welfare Policies and Programs

EP 2.1.8a

Chapter 6 established that the Social Security Act of 1935 was one of the most significant pieces of legislation shaping social welfare policy during the last century. It established programs in three major categories:

1. *Health and welfare services:* Services provided to people including foster care, adoption, protective services, activities for older adults, "maternal and child health services,... public health

activities," and a range of other public programs (U.S. Census Bureau, 2010, p. 349).

2. *Social insurance:* Financial benefits provided to people to "provide protection against wage loss resulting from retirement, prolonged disability, death, or unemployment, and protection against the cost of medical care during old age and disability" (U.S. Census Bureau, 2010, p. 347).

3. *Public assistance:* Financial and in-kind (services or goods versus cash) benefits provided to people who can't support themselves.

Chapter 6 also introduced divergent principles governing social insurance and public assistance, the two categories of programs discussed in this chapter. (The third category, health and welfare services, will be covered in subsequent chapters that address various fields of social work practice.) Social insurance is considered people's *right* because workers and their employers pay premiums while they work. Insurance protects people in the event of harm or loss. For example, you buy car insurance so that if you crash your car the insurance pays for repairs and any legal costs. Like other types of

FOCUS ON CRITICAL THINKING 8.2

Residual Versus Institutional Perspectives on Poverty

**EP 2.1.1b,
2.1.3,
2.1.4b,
2.1.10b**

Earlier chapters established that the *residual* perspective on social welfare maintains that individuals are ultimately responsible for securing their own personal well-being. It's people's own fault if they're poor. Society should only step in to provide resources when major problems arise. Then such provision should only be temporary until individuals get themselves back on their feet and can take care of themselves.

The *institutional* view of social welfare, on the other hand, views people's needs as an ongoing part of life. Society has the responsibility to support its members and provide needed benefits and services. It's not people's fault that they require such services but rather an expected part of the human condition. In other words, people have the right to receive benefits and services on a continuous basis. It's society's responsibility to address the problems of poverty and take care of poor people living in poverty.

Critical Thinking Questions

- What do you think are the reasons for poverty in the United States?
- To what extent do you feel it is the government's responsibility to alleviate poverty?
- To what extent do you feel that it is the fault of poor people that they are poor?
- What resources and services do you feel the government should provide citizens? Under what circumstances should they be offered? Explain.
- Do your views coincide more with the residual or institutional perspective on social welfare and poverty? Explain.

---

insurance, social insurance covers risks assumed while working, such as unemployment, injury, or illness, and inevitable conditions such as old age or death. Financial benefits are provided when such conditions occur. People receiving social insurance benefits work and pay premiums, so the benefits for them and their families are considered their right.

Public assistance, in contrast, is based on *need*. When people are unable to support themselves, the government provides financial benefits to help them do so. People receiving public assistance benefits never paid premiums, as did people collecting social insurance benefits. Therefore, many people believe that public assistance is not people's right and resent the fact that people need and get it. Public assistance is often derogatorily referred to as "welfare"—for example, TANF, which replaced Aid to Families with Dependent Children (AFDC) in 1996.

Note that terms can be confusing because they are used in different ways. Chapter 1 defined *social welfare* broadly as the general well-being of all people in a society. This is quite different from what most people mean when they refer to people "on welfare." Common negative conceptions about public assistance and its recipients are examined later in the chapter.

Both social insurance and public assistance are considered *income maintenance* programs. Such programs theoretically provide people with enough money, goods, and services to preserve an adequate standard of living and quality of life.

Figure 8.1 identifies some of the social programs under the U.S. social welfare system's social insurance and public assistance umbrellas. These reflect only a few examples of the many programs in the huge social welfare system.

Social Work Roles

Social workers may or may not work in social service agencies implementing the programs this chapter discusses. However, they will most likely work with clients who are concerned about financial matters and who receive benefits from these programs. Therefore, brief overviews of major social insurance and public assistance programs are provided. Note that it's also important for you as an individual to understand these systems because, on a personal level, sooner

EP 2.1.1c

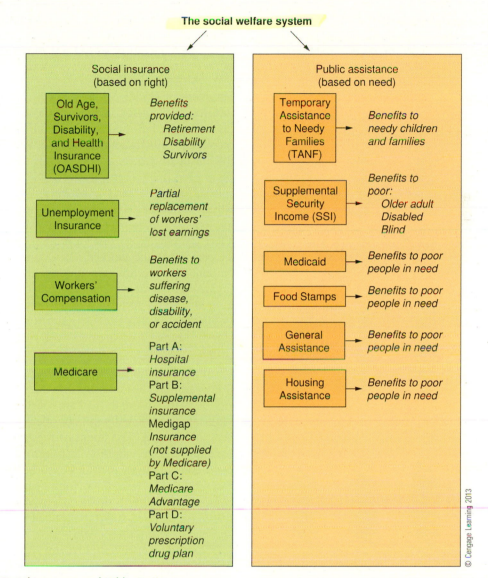

The social welfare system

Social insurance (based on right)	
Old Age, Survivors, Disability, and Health Insurance (OASDHI)	*Benefits provided:* Retirement Disability Survivors
Unemployment Insurance	*Partial replacement of workers' lost earnings*
Workers' Compensation	*Benefits to workers suffering disease, disability, or accident*
Medicare	Part A: *Hospital insurance* Part B: *Supplemental insurance* Medigap *Insurance (not supplied by Medicare)* Part C: *Medicare Advantage* Part D: *Voluntary prescription drug plan*

Public assistance (based on need)	
Temporary Assistance to Needy Families (TANF)	*Benefits to needy children and families*
Supplemental Security Income (SSI)	*Benefits to poor:* Older adult Disabled Blind
Medicaid	*Benefits to poor people in need*
Food Stamps	*Benefits to poor people in need*
General Assistance	*Benefits to poor people in need*
Housing Assistance	*Benefits to poor people in need*

© Cengage Learning 2013

Figure 8.1 Social Insurance and Public Assistance

or later they will probably impact you, your parents, and other older relatives.

Social Insurance Policy

The primary social insurance programs in the United States include Old Age, Survivors, Disability, and Health Insurance (OASDHI); unemployment insurance; workers' compensation; and Medicare.

Old Age, Survivors, Disability, and Health Insurance

The term *Social Security,* commonly used in the United States, is the program that provides financial benefits to workers who are retired or have a disability, their spouses or dependent children, and designated survivors of workers upon their death (Kingson, 2008). Social Security includes the financial benefits provided by Old Age, Survivors, Disability, and Health Insurance (OASDHI) and Medicare. Because these programs are types of social insurance, people are eligible to receive benefits only if they contributed an adequate part of their earnings according to established financial formulas. OASDHI, initially created by the Social Security Act of 1935, is the nation's most extensive social program, covering 93% of all workers; 52.5 million people receive Social Security checks each month

(Social Security Administration, 2010). Benefits are administered by the Social Security Administration (SSA). Each major facet of OASDHI and Medicare is described briefly.

Retirement Benefits

Workers contribute 6.2% of their income, with employers matching another 6.2%, to Old Age and Survivors Insurance and Disability Insurance. Workers pay these fees on income up to $106,800 in 2010 (SSA, 2010). The maximum ceiling of income changes each year. People are eligible to receive benefits if they are 62 or older, but they can receive full benefits only at age 66 or older. In the future, the minimum age to receive full benefits will increase to 67. In 2010 full retirement age was 66 years with a maximum benefit of $2,346 (National Academy of Social Insurance [NASI], 2011). "A complex set of factors including lifetime average earnings, age of retirement, and inflation factors determine the cash benefits that a person receives . . . . After a person begins receiving benefits, the Social Security Administration adjusts them each year to reflect changes in cost of living" (Whiteman, 2001 pp. 22–23). Because the eligibility requirements are highly complicated and complex, it's beyond the scope of this book to describe them in detail.

There has been much debate in recent years regarding the future of Social Security, especially with respect to retirement. Chapter 10 will review some of the issues as a major area of concern for people as they age.

Note that family members of retired or disabled Social Security beneficiaries may also receive benefits if they satisfy designated conditions. For example, a spouse or child may each receive some amount of benefits if they fulfill the required criteria (NASI, 2011).

Disability Benefits

Kingson (2008) explains eligibility for disability benefits. Workers are eligible for disability benefits five months after they become severely disabled. Widows or widowers (ages 50 to 64) of disabled people may also receive benefits. Severe disability is considered being unable to earn $900 a month ($1,500 for people who are blind) because of some physical or mental disability that has lasted or is expected to last for at least one year or is expected to result in death. After two years, disabled workers and adult disabled children may be eligible to receive Medicare

assistance, described in a later section (although other family members of the disabled person are not eligible until they satisfy age requirements).

Survivors Benefits

Survivors of Social Security beneficiaries may also receive some portion of that recipient's benefits after his or her death if these survivors fulfill designated requirements. For example, "widows and widowers of fully insured workers are eligible for unreduced benefits at FRA [full retirement age]. . . . Surviving divorced spouses can also receive benefits if married to the worker for at least 10 years and not remarried before age 60. . . . Children of deceased workers . . . under FRA are eligible to receive monthly benefits up to 75 percent of the worker's PIA [primary insurance amount—the monthly amount initially paid at full retirement age] if the worker dies either fully or currently insured" (Social Security Administration, 2010).

Unemployment Insurance and Workers' Compensation

Unemployment insurance and workers' compensation were also established by the Social Security Act of 1935. Although they are social insurance programs, they are usually not considered part of Social Security as such. The intent of these programs is to partially replace workers' lost earnings; unemployment compensation provides cash benefits to workers who have lost their jobs, whereas workers' compensation offers financial coverage to workers who have suffered some job-related injury or illness and can't work (Jones, 1995).

Financing for unemployment insurance comes from a tax employers must pay based on a complicated formula involving their employees' wages. There are general federal mandates for how this is done, yet states also can dictate many specifics such as who is eligible and how long benefits are provided. Eligibility criteria emphasize that workers may not receive unemployment insurance if they've lost their job through any fault of their own; the focus is on losing jobs for economic reasons such as industrial cutbacks or layoffs (Nackerud, 2008). Payments are based on some percentage of income over the past year and are time-limited, usually to 26 weeks (Nackerud, 2008).

Funding for workers' compensation is totally different and varies from state to state. Most states require employers to purchase insurance to cover injured workers (Terrell, 2008). As with other forms of social insurance, establishing eligibility for benefits is complex. A major issue involves whether injuries are really work-related, which is often difficult to prove; for example, some claim that *carpel tunnel syndrome* (characterized by weakness, numbness, or pain in the wrist and hand, its cause often blamed on doing repetitive tasks such as typing over a long period of time) is really a facet of normal aging, and, therefore, not to be compensated (Terrell, 2008).

Social workers have little to do with either of these programs, which concentrate on providing some minimum income and ignore all other social, emotional, and physical needs. In any case, both programs are inadequate to meet actual needs, and their eligibility standards place strict limitations on whom they cover (Jones, 1995; Nackerud, 2008; Terrell, 2008).

Medicare

The Health Insurance for the Aged Act, passed in 1965, created Medicare and Medicaid (the latter will be discussed later as a public assistance program). *Medicare* is a form of social insurance financed by both employer and employee contributions based on earnings and other federal tax revenues. People who are eligible for Medicare include those who are 65 or older, are disabled, or have kidney disease.

Medicare comprises four main facets—Parts A, B, C, and D. Part A, Hospital Insurance, pays for four basic types of services. First, it covers services provided in and by hospitals (which is probably pretty obvious from the title). Second, it pays for limited stays in skilled nursing facilities such as nursing homes. Third, it covers some services (e.g., nursing care and speech, physical, and occupational therapy[2]) for people under a physician's care who are confined to their homes. Fourth, it provides *hospice* care, which involves health, homemaker, and other social services provided either at home or in a supportive, homelike facility for people suffering from a terminal illness. The idea is to make people as comfortable as possible during their final hours.

Note that all these services have designated time limits. Benefits are restricted based on certain criteria and also are limited in duration. People first must meet the requirements to receive treatment. Then treatment is administered according to complicated rules. Like OASDHI, the program is complex. Social workers accustomed to the programs and rules governing them often can help people navigate through the miles of red tape required to establish eligibility for benefits.

Medicare's Part B, Supplementary Medical Insurance, is designed to do just as its name implies—supplement benefits provided by Part A. It is "a voluntary component that covers physician services, outpatient hospital services, certain home

Too many children live in poverty (U.S. Census Bureau, 2010); 18.5% of all children under age 18 in the United States live in poverty. When considering race as a factor, 34.4% of African American children and 30.3% of Hispanic children live in poverty here.

---

[2]*Physical therapy* is "the treatment or management of physical disability, malfunction, or pain by physical techniques, as exercise, massage, hydrotherapy, etc." (Nichols, 1999, p. 996). *Occupational therapy* is "therapy that utilizes useful and creative activities to facilitate psychological or physical rehabilitation" (Nichols, 1999, p. 914).

healthcare service, and durable medical equipment" (e.g., wheelchairs, hospital beds, or prosthetic devices [Tracy & Ozawa, 1995]) (DiNitto, 2011, p. 281).

However, there are many things it does not cover, including dental and vision care, routine physical examinations, and long-term nursing care (Whiteman, 2001). Medicare does provide some limited nursing home coverage, providing payment for some services received up to 90 days (Barusch, 2009).

Medicare Part B also is not free. Beneficiaries can enroll only during designated periods, have an initial deductible, and pay a monthly fee.

Launched in 2006, Medicare Part C, also referred to as Medicare Advantage, allows persons enrolled in Parts A and B to select receiving their health care via a number of ways, including managed care [where a third-party organization, beyond the attending physician, monitors health care provision to control for costs and determine that treatment is appropriate] and private fee-for-service plans [paying prescribed prices for the services received after you get them] (Rizzo, 2008). Those who select the Part C option receive coverage included in Parts A and B, but also "preventive care, dental care, and hearing aides" as specified in the plan selected (Rizzo, 2008, p. 201). The cost of Part C depends on the premiums and deductibles required in the chosen plan.

Medicare recipients may also opt to purchase "Medigap" insurance that covers services and treatment (gaps) not covered by other parts of Medicare (DiNitto, 2011). Like most other types of insurance, the amount and type of coverage vary according to how much people are willing to pay for it.

Medicare Part C and Medigap insurance do not cover all the health care and services a person may need. For example, "coverage for the costs of long-term care in nursing homes, adult family homes, assisted living, and adult day care must be covered by private means [such as additional personal insurance policies] or by welfare [public assistance] programs" (DiNitto, 2011; Whiteman, 2001, p. 36).

Medicare Part D involves a voluntary prescription drug plan initiated in 2006 in which 60% of Medicare beneficiaries have enrolled as of February 2010 (Kaiser Family Foundation, 2010). Participants can choose a prescription drug plan, for which they pay a monthly premium (that varies depending on the plan selected, and premiums increase based on income) (Centers for Medicare and Medicaid Services [CMS], 2011a). The national average is $32.34 (Medicare Rights Center, 2011). Highlight 8.3 summarizes the payment schedule based on the cost schedule as of January 2011. Participants must pay up to the first $310 (deductible) for prescriptions. A *deductible* is "the amount you must pay for health care or prescriptions, before Original Medicare [the traditional fee-for-service program offered directly through the federal government that includes Parts A and B], your prescription drug plan, or your other insurance begins to pay" (CMS, 2011a). As prescription drug costs add up, Part D participants and any insurance they have will pay a combined amount reaching $2,840 (CMS, 2011a). The gap between $2,840 and $4,550 was historically called the "donut hole" because the Part D recipient was responsible for paying it. As of 2011, recipients have to pay 50% of drug costs for brand name drugs and 93% for generic drugs while in the cost "donut hole" (Medical Rights Center, 2011). The reason for increased Part D payments is that the health care reform law

HIGHLIGHT 8.3

The Medicare Prescription Drug Plan

Participants Pay	Of Total Paid for Drugs	Total Amount Potentially Paid by Participants
100% Up to	$0–$310	$310
Copayments	$310–$2,840	Copayments
50–93%	$2,840–$4,550	$4,550
Small copayments	$4,550+	Small copayments

is phasing out the gap; by 2020 participants should not have to pay more than 25% for drugs at any time during the year (Medical Rights Center, 2011). After participants have paid $4,550 total they must only make small copayments ("5 percent of the cost of each drug, or $2.50 for generics and $6.30 for brand-name drugs [whichever is greater]") (emphasis omitted) (Medical Rights Center, 2011). Some assistance is provided to low-income participants (Kaiser Family Foundation, 2010).

Critics of the legislation emphasize how drugs are still quite expensive for participants. First, there's the monthly fee, an average of $32.34, which results in payments of $388.08 annually. Second, at this time participants must still pay a percentage of drug costs between expenditure totals of $2,840 to $4,550, and copayments after that.

Focus on Critical Thinking 8.3 raises some key unresolved policy issues concerning social insurance in general.

Public Assistance Policy

We have established that public assistance provides resources for people in *need* and that social insurance is based on people's *right* to receive benefits. Financing comes from general tax revenues—that is, taxes collected by federal, state, and local entities on personal income and property. Primary

categories of public assistance include Temporary Assistance to Needy Families (TANF); Supplemental Security Income (SSI), which includes Old Age Assistance (OAA), Aid to the Blind (AB), and Aid to the Permanently and Totally Disabled (APTD); Medicaid; food stamps; general assistance; and housing assistance.

EP 2.1.3a, 2.1.5b, 2.1.8a, 2.1.9a

Historical Perspectives on Public Assistance to Families

Prior to August 22, 1996, a primary program providing minimal financial assistance to individuals and families in the United States was Aid to Families with Dependent Children (AFDC) (Dickinson, 1997). It was originally established as Aid to Dependent Children (ADC) by the Social Security Act of 1935. AFDC was a program providing payments funded by federal and state governments to children deprived of parental support because a parent was absent from the home, had died, or was incapable of managing the household for physical or mental reasons (Abramovitz, 1995; Barker, 2003). Most families receiving benefits were single mothers whose partners were not in the home.

AFDC established eligibility standards based on the number and age of children in the family, the

---

FOCUS ON CRITICAL THINKING 8.3

Policy Issues in Social Insurance

EP 2.1.3

Meyer (2001) identifies two as yet unanswered issues concerning problems in the U.S. social insurance system as it now stands. People eligible for benefits are those who have had "substantial recent employment in the regular employment sector" (p. 40). The problem is this does not cover people who have been able to get only part-time or temporary work on a sporadic basis. Many people, especially those with low skill levels, are primary family breadwinners yet can't find adequate employment to qualify them for social insurance. Meyer (2001) asks, "How should the social insurance system be adapted to fit this new economy and integrated with other benefits for children?" (p. 41).

The second issue concerns how supplementary benefits (including "health coverage to employees and their families, sick leave, pensions, and 'family-friendly' policies like on-site child care and flexible hours") are rarely offered for workers in minimum-wage or low-paying jobs (p. 41). For these workers, many of whom have low skill levels, any crisis such as illness can result in devastation because, without sick leave, income can abruptly cease.

Critical Thinking Question

What programs or policies do you think can or should be developed to remedy this situation?

family's income, the applicant's motivation and readiness to work, and the applicant's willingness to work together with the welfare department to establish paternity and seek child support (Abramovitz, 1995, p. 184). Eligible families passed an *income test* (or *means test*)—that is, an eligibility guideline that established the maximum amount of income a family could earn without losing benefits. Those who made too much money were ineligible for benefits.

Eligible families could potentially receive financial assistance for many years in addition to Medicaid (provision of health care for qualified recipients), food stamps (coupons used like cash to purchase food), and partial financial support for housing; however, some states subtracted the monetary value of food stamps and housing allowances from AFDC payments (Abramovitz, 1995). (Medicaid and food stamps are described later in the chapter.) Note that the duration of public assistance benefits (i.e., how long families remain eligible to receive benefits) is a matter of strong debate. Numerous studies have determined that many families receive assistance for no more than two years, in stark contrast to the stereotype that once families get on welfare they never get off (Abramovitz, 1995).

Temporary Assistance to Needy Families

In 1996 Congress passed the Personal Responsibility and Work Opportunity Reconciliation Act (PRWORA) that set up a new grant program, Temporary Assistance to Needy Families (TANF). This "put a cap on federal funds provided to the states" and allowed states greater discretion in benefit distribution (Abramovitz, 1997, pp. 311–312).

As noted previously, TANF supplanted AFDC. Instead of providing cash payments directly to eligible poor families as AFDC did, TANF gives funds to states. These funds take the form of *block grants*—sums of money provided by the federal government that allow significant discretion in how the money should be spent. (This contrasts with *categorical grants* whereby specific amounts of funding are earmarked for specific objectives in designated programs.) These block grants replace "AFDC, food stamps, child care, child protection programs, school meals, and nutritional programs for low-income pregnant women and children" (Dickinson, 1997, p. 126). This also marks the first time that the federal government placed a limit on federal money

provided to states for public assistance (Abramovitz, 1997).

TANF's stated goals are as follows:

1. Assisting needy families so that children can be cared for in their own homes.
2. Reducing the dependence of needy parents on government benefits by promoting job preparation, work, and marriage.
3. Preventing incidence of out-of-wedlock pregnancies.
4. Encouraging the formation and maintenance of two-parent families (U.S. Administration for Children and Families [ACF], 2010b).

Note that among these there is no stated goal to decrease poverty (Chapin, 2011). Should not a major goal be to reduce poverty instead of decreasing welfare roles (Lens, 2002)? TANF participation rates have decreased by more than half during its first 10 years (Chapin, 2011; Hagen & Lawrence, 2008; Jimenez, 2010). Of those who left the roles, less than half were employed (Karger & Stoesz, 2010). Of course, a central theme endorsed by TANF is promotion of work. However, looking more carefully at what happens to the people involved raises serious concerns. "Most parents who left TANF for work had low earnings and were unable to increase their wages or earnings significantly over time" (Jimenez, 2010, p. 278). Generally speaking, people's standard of living declines when they leave TANF roles (Blau, 2010). Family incomes hover near the poverty line (Hagen & Lawrence, 2008). It is common for former TANF recipients to experience major problems, including hunger and difficulty finding adequate housing (Hagen & Lawrence, 2008).

Chapin (2011) affirms:

TANF did not change the reality of the social context that shapes these families. Affordable high-quality daycare for mothers on TANF continues to be in short supply, and when one person is working full-time and also doing all of the home chores, time for parental involvement is greatly reduced. These pressures have only been ratcheted up in the current economic downturn, as working mothers receiving TANF compete in the low-wage labor market with growing numbers of newly unemployed individuals, and as states and localities cut back further on necessary supports.

We know that poverty is a powerful predictor of all sorts of negative outcomes for children, from dropping out of school to teenage pregnancy to juvenile crime. Children in families receiving TANF are still living in poverty. (pp. 267–268)

Issues concerning TANF include time limits; work, child care, and transportation; equitable treatment by states; impositions on family structure; education and training for better jobs; and job quality and benefits.

Time Limits

TANF establishes time limits for how long recipients may receive benefits (ACF, 2010b). Clients must find work within two years of beginning the program (or sooner if the state so chooses) and can receive no more than five years of benefits in their lifetime. Beyond five years, states may opt to extend assistance to no more than 20% of their caseload or continue funding recipients through state funds alone. This is a huge change from AFDC, through which "people received assistance as long as they satisfied the program's eligibility rules, which were set by the individual states under federal guidelines" (Abramovitz, 1997, p. 312). Most states have adopted the five-year time frame, although some states have shorter time periods and some states have no lifetime limits (as they have developed alternative programs) (Hagen & Lawrence, 2008).

A problem with time limits involves people with multiple hardships that makes it difficult, if not impossible, for them to maintain adequate ongoing employment. Acs and Loprest (2007) explain:

Numerous studies have documented the prevalence of barriers to work among welfare recipients, both before and after welfare reform. Some of the barriers measured include physical health, mental health, domestic violence, substance abuse, criminal history, education levels, and work history. (p. 55)

Work, Child Care, and Transportation

TANF significantly increases the strictness of work requirements to make people eligible for financial assistance compared to AFDC. "With few exceptions, recipients must work as soon as they are job-ready or no later than two years after coming on assistance. To count toward a State's work participation rate, single parents must participate in work activities for an average of 30 hours per week, or an average of 20 hours per week if they have a child under age six. Two-parent families must participate in work activities for an average of 35 hours a week

or, if they receive Federal child care assistance, 55 hours a week. Failure to participate in work requirements can result in a reduction or termination of a family's benefits" (ACF, 2010b). This is increased from the 20 hours originally established in 1997 (Abramovitz, 1997). Questions concern how parents will cope with child care needs, work stress, homemaking responsibilities, and parenting. TANF will not allow mothers with children age 6 or older to cite lack of adequate child care as their rationale for not working outside the home (ACF, 2010b).

AFDC required states to provide child care, but TANF does not (DiNitto, 2011). States can provide child care if they so choose. Jimenez (2010) discusses TANF and child care:

Child care funds for TANF recipients are paid for out of block grants given to states for this purpose, as well as from a separate federal fund known as the Child Care and Development Fund. States have a great deal of flexibility as to how to meet child-care needs for TANF recipients. [This flexibility includes determination of eligibility requirements for receipt of child-care assistance, payment rates to child-care providers, and copayments TANF recipients must make (Hagen & Lawrence, 2008).] The funds are provided in the form of vouchers designed to meet 75% of child care costs in local communities, but the demand for child care has far outstripped the supply, both in terms of federal funding and in the availability of child care facilities. Many low-income families, including those on TANF, receive no help with child care, and the costs of licensed child care are often prohibitive. These families must settle for substandard child care arrangements, even though research suggests that good child care can have positive long-term consequences for children's cognitive, emotional, and social well-being. Child care support generally ends as soon as the TANF grants end or shortly thereafter. (p. 277)

Another issue involves how child care may not be readily available where the TANF recipient lives (Lens, 2002). Still another concern involves how many TANF recipients get service jobs where they must work odd shifts. Child care may not be available during these "off" times. Lens (2002) adds:

Many recipients need such specialized child care because they work in the services industry, which requires night and weekend hours. Still others need sick-child care or special needs care for children with disabilities. The need for such daycare varies, but in all instances the demand outstrips the supply of suitable facilities. (p. 284)

DiNitto (2011) indicates:

Only one in seven eligible children received child-care assistance through TANF in 2000. This proportion remained relatively constant through 2007. Only 6 percent of all children under age 6 and 15 percent of those under age 6 living in poverty received TANF childcare subsidies in 2003. The United States provides much less childcare assistance than other industrialized nations. (p. 260)

States may choose to divert some TANF money to help finance transportation. States are not required to spend TANF funding on transportation; however, "almost every state does, in one way or another, because the lack of transportation continues to be documented as one of the leading barriers to employment participation, especially among otherwise-unemployed single mothers" (National Resource Center, 2010). A big problem is that most TANF recipients live in urban or rural areas, whereas most jobs are in the suburbs (Lens, 2002). Public transportation is often sorely lacking. Cars, car insurance, and gas are exorbitantly expensive (as we so well know). Some states have used TANF funding to finance "a variety of transportation services, from paying for recipients' car repairs, to using volunteers to drive recipients to work, to organizing county-run van pools" (p. 285).

Lens (2002) summarizes the situation:

Although TANF has recognized that it must address the twin problems of daycare and transportation, it has not done so quickly, comprehensively, or effectively. Most telling is the fact that TANF requires welfare mothers to work whether or not daycare or transportation is available.

Focus on Critical Thinking 8.4 poses a number of questions regarding potential problems and issues.

Equitability Among States

TANF "eliminated the federal income test that previously determined eligibility for AFDC" (Abramovitz, 1997, p. 312). Instead, TANF lets states establish their own eligibility rules. However, with budget pressures, states could establish eligibility levels so low that only the very poorest of the poor would receive benefits.

Additionally, benefit levels vary appreciably from state to state, which raises questions regarding the program's fairness. DiNitto (2011) explains:

Most states have maintained cash benefits at the 1996 level. Some have increased TANF benefits,

---

FOCUS ON CRITICAL THINKING 8.4

Working Mothers, Child Care, and the Quality of Family Life

Many questions can be raised concerning potential effects of TANF's restrictions.

EP 2.1.3

Critical Thinking Questions

- Who will provide all the additional child care services for newly working mothers?
- Will funding be adequate in view of the potential influx of children requiring care?
- What if no adequate day care is available?
- Will centers accept infants or toddlers who are not yet toilet trained—children many current child care facilities reject?
- How will these services be monitored for adequacy, safety, and quality?
- Is it fair to force women into assuming responsibility for both household caregiving and outside work when the same pressures do not generally apply to men?
- How will mothers adjust to separation from their children?
- How will children be affected by limited access to their single parent?
- How does this policy affect children's welfare?

but six states and the District of Columbia actually reduced benefits below their 1996 level. In most states, the real value of cash TANF benefits has continued to decline. The greatest decline (nearly 35 percent) was in Hawaii. In 2008, the maximum benefit for a family of three ranged from a low of $170 per month (12 percent of the federal government's official poverty threshold) to a high of $923 (50 percent of the poverty threshold) in Alaska.... In 2006, 81 percent of TANF recipients also received food stamps ($322 per month on average), raising the monthly benefit package (cash plus food stamps) for a family of three to $558 (38 percent of the poverty threshold) in Mississippi to $1,191 (65 percent of the poverty threshold) in Alaska. (p. 257)

Benefits may also vary within a state, for example, by urban or rural area (Hagen & Lawrence, 2008).

Impositions on Family Structure

One of TANF's intents is to control family structure. Chapin (2011) indicates that "one stated goal of TANF is to reduce the number of out-of-wedlock pregnancies and births by promoting marriage (Office of Family Assistance, 2009). In 2005, TANF was reauthorized with a renewed focus on work and on strengthening families through the promotion of responsible fatherhood and healthy marriages. The TANF legislation gave states more flexibility to provide assistance to two-parent families" (p. 269). This, in effect, discourages the provision of resources for single-parent families.

Blau (2010) comments on people's reality:

For the Bush administration, marriage combined with work points the way out of poverty. In some respects, this position makes sense, because two married people can combine their incomes and share housing costs. Yet for poor women, the reality does not quite match the theory. Poor women are less likely to meet men who earn enough to raise the family out of poverty. They have little incentive to marry an adult for whom they are going to have to care, and no reason to do so if, as up to 30 percent of women on welfare report, that adult is abusive. (p. 311)

TANF also encourages limiting family size. States usually calculate benefit amounts according to the number of children present. TANF allows states to establish "a family cap that denies assistance to children born into families already receiving

public assistance" (Karger & Stoesz, 2010, p. 283). To date at least 19 states have such a family cap policy; additionally, two states have a flat-rate policy where a set amount is granted to recipients regardless of family size (National Conference of State Legislatures, 2011).

Education and Training for Better Jobs

EP 2.1.10i

States spend comparatively small amounts on providing education and training for participants; "less than 2% ($407 million) was used to 'enhance skills' in 2006" (DiNitto, 2011, p. 262). How can former TANF recipients seek better jobs and experience upward mobility with little or no education and training? In contrast, pregnancy prevention programs received over a sevenfold increase from 2000 ($102 million) to 2006 ($723 million), amounting to 2.5% of the total TANF budget (DiNitto, 2011).

Lens (2002) reflects:

Far from ensuring self-sufficiency, [the TANF] ... approach relegates welfare mothers to the low end of the labor market, a vulnerable place in good and bad economic times. It also ensures that the gap in wages based on educational level will persist and endure as poor women, forced to choose between losing their benefits or feeding their families, are trapped in low-paying jobs. (p. 284)

Job Quality and Benefits

A foundation principle of TANF focuses on work (Chapin, 2011; Gilbert & Terrell, 2010). Research sponsored by the Urban Institute resulted in a number of findings (Acs & Loprest, 2007; Urban Institute, 2010). Recipients just leaving TANF (or TANF leavers) in or before 2001 were more likely to find work than those just leaving TANF after 2001. Employment rates for recent TANF leavers continued to decline over time. In 2000, 54.5% of recent TANF leavers were employed, which dropped to 24.5% in 2005. After tracking TANF leavers over time, it was found that employment decreased for them over a five-year period, from 31% in 2000 to 24.5% in 2005. The average family income of all TANF leavers also declined from $25,528 in 2000 to $22,733 in 2005.

The percentage of TANF leavers having their own employer-provided health insurance dropped from 26.3% in 2000 to 21.8% in 2005 (Acs & Loprest, 2007). Additionally, about one-third get no paid sick leave (Acs & Loprest, 2007). The reason for this is that former TANF recipients are getting low-paying or minimum-wage jobs that have poor or no benefits. Realistically, how good are the benefits and potential for upward mobility offered by most low-paying jobs?

Some former TANF recipients and their families may be eligible for Medicaid (discussed more thoroughly later in the chapter). However, if you don't have "intimate knowledge of a state's Medicaid program, it would be difficult to say exactly who qualifies and who does not. Even in states with the most generous Medicaid programs, many poor people do not fit any of the eligibility categories and therefore have no claim to Medicaid" (DiNitto, 2011, p. 286).

Blau (2010) indicates that most research has established that TANF leavers basically fall into two different groups. The first group has fared much more poorly. People in this group are much more likely to be hungry and homeless, and to experience more severe hardships than people in the other group.

The second group of TANF leavers appears to be more successful. They "are employed, productive citizens," although their incomes are low and "they are still unquestionably poor" (Blau, 2010, p. 313). After leaving TANF and securing employment, their incomes rise somewhat. However, low-paid employment may actually diminish their standard of living. "[B]y the time they totaled up the cost associated with working—clothing, transportation, and child care—their standard of living had actually declined. ... [T]he issue is not whether welfare mothers work, but the terms of that work—in particular, whether the wages and benefits they receive actually improve their lives" (Blau, 2010, p. 313).

TANF recipients require obvious resources and conditions to escape poverty. They need "good jobs, health care, day care, job training, and education" (Blau, 2010, p. 314). Perhaps some TANF programs meet these needs, but clearly the majority do not (Blau, 2010). Although some say TANF is a success because "it cut the welfare rolls"; it has been a failure at getting families including children out of poverty (Blau, 2010, p. 314).

Focus on Critical Thinking 8.5 asks some questions concerning your views about public assistance

and where current policy stands on the conservative–liberal continuum.

Stereotypes About Public Assistance Recipients

Henley and Danziger (1997) reflect on the stereotypes often associated with public assistance recipients:

According to the commonly held stereotype, poor people are poor because of individual character faults. In particular, welfare recipients are presumed to be lazy, able yet unwilling to work, and lacking appropriate family values.... The dominant American values of individualism and self-sufficiency ... contribute to the unpopularity of welfare programs and support the popular opinion that welfare recipients are responsible for their impoverished condition and undeserving of assistance. (p. 125)

Who are the people receiving public assistance? To what extent is this portrayal accurate or false? Highlight 8.4 explores a number of these stereotypes.

Supplemental Security Income

Supplemental Security Income (SSI) is a federal public assistance program that provides a minimum income to poor people who are older adults, have a disability, or are blind. Most of it is administered by the federal government through the Social Security Administration. However, it is funded by general tax revenues, not employer and employee contributions as with social insurance. Older adults' eligibility is determined by a means test and proof of fitting into one of the three categories. Older adults must be at least 65, and people who are blind or disabled must have medical established proof of their disability (Meyer, 1995).

Maximum monthly SSI payments in 2011 were $674 for individuals (almost 62% of the poverty line) and $1,011 for couples (almost 69% of the poverty line) (U.S. Department of Health & Human Services [HHS], 2011; Social Security Online, 2010b). There were no cost-of-living increases for 2010 and 2011 (Social Security Online, 2010a) To be eligible, applicants must adhere to stringent, complex guidelines regarding income and assets. The program orients itself more to people who have physical versus mental disabilities

FOCUS ON CRITICAL THINKING 8.5

The Current State of Public Assistance

Where Do You Stand on the Conservative–Liberal Continuum?

EP 2.1.3, 2.1.5a, 2.1.7a

Remember that *conservatism* generally reflects the view that individuals should be responsible for themselves, that people will take advantage of the system if allowed to, and that government should not interfere in people's lives. Thus government should react and provide benefits only when it absolutely has to. *Liberalism*, in contrast, generally espouses the view that it is society's responsibility to care for its people and that people will rise to the occasion and care for themselves if provided the support they need. Thus the government should be integrally involved in improving people's lives.

Critical Thinking Questions

- Where do you stand on the conservative–liberal continuum with respect to what benefits should or should not be provided to needy families?
- Whose responsibility is it to provide for poor families and their young children—the responsibility of individual parents or society in general?

- Do you feel that people are basically lazy and are likely to abuse the system if they can? Or do you feel that people will function much better if they receive adequate resources?
- To what extent do you feel that government should involve itself in caring for people in need? Or should people be given the responsibility to care completely for themselves and their families?

Residual Versus Institutional Social Welfare Programming

Do you believe that financial assistance programs to families in need should be *residual* in nature, reacting only to problems and serious needs? Or should programs provide ongoing *institutional* support to them?

Where Does TANF Policy Stand on the Conservative–Liberal Continuum?

To what extent does TANF policy reflect a conservative or liberal perspective concerning consistency in benefit provision from one state to another? Time limits for receiving benefits? Provision of medical care to current and past recipients? Requirements that single parents (primarily mothers) work outside the home?

(e.g., people with mental illness who can work part-time are ineligible) and usually requires extensive documentation to verify medical conditions (Blau, 2010). As a result, it is estimated that only 55–60% of people eligible for SSI actually receive benefits (Blau, 2010).

Medicaid

Medicaid is a public assistance program funded by federal and state governments that pays for medical and hospital services for eligible people who are unable to pay for these services themselves and are determined to be in need. It was established in 1965 along with Medicare by the Health Insurance for the Aged Act.

The federal government disburses 57% of Medicaid payments, with the states paying the remaining 43% (DiNitto, 2011). Under federal guidelines, states administer the Medicaid program. A state agency must oversee Medicaid administration. Usually this is the state Department of Health and

Social Services, a designated state health agency, or some other state human services unit. The designated agency may process health claims itself or contract with other agencies such as health insuring organizations (e.g., a health maintenance organization [HMO]). Payments for services are made directly to health care providers.

States have wide discretion regarding who qualifies for benefits, what services are covered, and how much are paid for them (Barusch, 2012; Blau, 2010; CMS, 2011a). States vary so widely that a recipient who has an income that is 75% of the poverty line may be eligible for no benefits in one state, full benefits in another, and limited benefits in still another where he or she must struggle to find health care providers (Blau, 2010; Karger & Stoesz, 2010).

Criteria for Medicaid inclusion include income and resources, age, pregnancy, disability, blindness, and immigration status (CMS, 2011a). (Many immigrants who have been legally admitted to the

HIGHLIGHT 8.4

HIGHLIGHT 8.4

What Are the Stereotypes About People "on Welfare"— and to What Extent Are They Accurate?

EP 2.1.4a

A number of popular negative ideas about public assistance and stereotypes about people who receive it exist.

Stereotype 1: The Public Assistance Caseload Has Been Expanding Relentlessly

We have established that there has been a drop in TANF recipients by more than half from past years (Hagen & Lawrence, 2008). Over 80% of people receiving TANF assistance are children (Chapin, 2011; Hagen & Lawrence, 2008; Jimenez, 2010).

Stereotype 2: Public Assistance Costs the Nation a Fortune

In 2010, most of the federal budget paid for defense and security (20%), Social Security (20%), and health-care programs (21%) including Medicare, Medicaid, and the Children's Health Insurance Program (CHIP) (Medicare consumed almost two-thirds of the health care program amount.) (Center on Budget and Policy Priorities [CBPP], 2011). About 14% was spent on "safety net programs," including earned income and child tax credits, Supplemental Security Income (SSI), unemployment insurance, "food stamps, school meals, low-income housing assistance, child-care assistance," home energy assistance, and a wide range of other programs, including those directed at helping abused and neglected children (CBPP, 2011). Only a small fraction of the 14% for safety net programs went toward TANF.

Stereotype 3: People on Welfare Live "High on the Hog" (Abramovitz, 1997, p. 318)

Benefits for a family of three involved in TANF range from $170 a month (12% of the federal poverty threshold) to $923 a month (50% of the poverty threshold), depending on the state (DiNitto, 2011). Even including food stamps, which most TANF families receive, their benefits still range from 38% to 65% of the poverty threshold (DiNitto, 2011). TANF recipients usually can only gain employment in low- or minimum-wage jobs. This hardly reflects wealth.

Stereotype 4: Welfare Recipients Are Mainly African Americans

Almost two-thirds of TANF recipients are not African American; this includes 37.5% who are white, 20.7% who are Hispanic, 5.3% who have another ethnicity or are multiracial, and 0.9% who are of unknown ethnicity (Popple & Leighninger, 2011). The remaining 35.6%, then, are African American.

Stereotype 5: Families Receiving Welfare Are Huge

The average size for a family receiving TANF is 2.5 people (Hagen & Lawrence, 2008).

country are ineligible [DiNitto, 2011].) Widely ranging health and medical services are covered, "including inpatient hospital services, outpatient hospital services, rural health clinic services, laboratory and X-ray services, skilled nursing facility (nursing home) services, and physician services" (Barusch, 2012, p. 148).

In 2008, 50 million people (16% of the population) received Medicaid; this reflected an increase from over 40 million recipients in 1998 (Blau, 2010). Costs for 2008 were estimated at $339 billion (DiNitto, 2011). It is projected that costs will increase at the annual rate of 7.9% over the next several years to reach $674 billion by 2017 (HHS, 2010).

Despite high costs, estimates are that only 40% of people falling below the poverty line received Medicaid, although 55% of children in poverty received benefits (due to less restrictive eligibility rules) (Blau, 2010). Note that Medicaid is a major player in financing long-term nursing home care for older adults: 70% of nursing home residents rely at least partially on Medicaid to cover their care costs, which make up 44% of the total Medicaid budget (Blau, 2010). Medicaid covers some of the many gaps in Medicare for older adults in poverty.

"Medicaid is one of the most important governmental health programs in the United States" (Karger & Stoesz, 2010, p. 312). Major questions are being raised across the country concerning where the money will come from to finance future health care costs in general and Medicaid costs in particular.

The Children's Health Insurance Program

In 1997 Congress passed the State Children's Health Insurance Program (SCHIP) that extended health care coverage to children whose families were living under 200% of the poverty line (Jimenez, 2010). This helped to alleviate the major problem of children living in low-income families without insurance. Targeted families were not poor enough to receive Medicaid, but were still too poor to purchase health insurance. In 2009 President Obama signed into law the Children's Health Insurance Program Reauthorization Act (CHIPRA); CHIP (formerly SCHIP) expanded coverage to children in families earning up to 300% of the poverty line (Blau, 2010). This expanded the number of child beneficiaries from about 7 million to 11 million (Chapin, 2011).

"Like Medicaid, CHIP is a state–federal partnership. All states have a CHIP program, and they have considerable freedom in how they design their programs. They can be simple expansions of the Medicaid coverage already available to children in the state, an entirely separate program, or some combination of these. States' programs vary on a wide range of elements, including eligibility levels, whether or not to charge cost-sharing or premiums, and how the enrollment process works" (FamiliesUSA, 2011).

CHIP is a "block grant, which means it has a predetermined, fixed annual funding level"; this differs from Medicaid, where "federal funding increases automatically to compensate for increases in health care costs" (Jimenez, 2010, p. 378). When CHIP funding runs out, neither the federal government nor the state is required to continue financial support, and CHIP may simply run out of funds (Chapin, 2011). As Congress has not increased funding to keep up with uninsured children's health care needs, it is predicted that many technically eligible children will not receive benefits in future years (Jimenez, 2010). It is estimated that there were about 8.6 million children without health insurance in 2009 and that almost two-thirds of them were probably eligible either for Medicaid or CHIP (Chapin, 2010).

Food Stamps/Supplemental Nutrition Assistant Program

The Food Stamp Program involves vouchers distributed through a federal program to be used like cash to purchase primarily food, plants, and seeds (Barker, 2003). "Benefits may not be used for alcoholic beverages, tobacco, paper products, diapers, personal care products, or ready-to-eat foods" (Segal, 2010, p. 188). The program's intent is to fight hunger. It was renamed the Supplemental Nutrition and Assistance Program (SNAP) in 2008 to better reflect its intent of *supplementing* nutrition instead of providing all the food a family requires (Segal, 2010). Originally created in 1964, the Food Stamp Program, now SNAP, is administered through the U.S. Department of Agriculture and is paid for completely by the federal government, except for administrative costs, which are shared with the states (Barusch, 2012).

Blau (2010) further explains the current situation. Although originally benefits were distributed in the form of coupons, now states have replaced this system with an electronic benefit transfer that resembles a credit card. The card's maximum monthly benefit in 2009 was $463 for a household of three people (although the average payment each month per household was only $226.60) and $588 for a household of four (Blau, 2010). To be eligible, people must satisfy a means test, and benefits are determined by a formula involving income and assets. People who receive TANF, SSI, or general assistance (described next) routinely receive benefits (Blau, 2010).

Participation in SNAP has declined significantly in recent years (Barusch, 2012). It has become more and more difficult to get food stamps because of increasingly more complex and limiting eligibility requirements and confusing, tedious application processes (Barusch, 2012). Individual states make it progressively more difficult for people to negotiate the food stamp maze. Blau (2010) explains:

Food stamp applications within the 50 states now average 12 pages in length. California, New York, and 27 other states ask applicants if they own a burial plot. Nevada and Nebraska want to know if applicants have sold their blood and for how much. Hawaii demands garage sale receipts, South Dakota totals bingo winnings, and on page 20 of a 36-page application, Minnesota checks to see if anyone earns money from a paper route. Such a daunting application process surely gives pause to even the most eligible applicant. (p. 432)

General Assistance

General assistance (GA) includes programs run by state and local agencies that provide basic cash and in-kind benefits to people who satisfy whatever means test has been established and are ineligible for other types of public assistance. It's usually the last resort for people who are desperately in need but are not eligible for benefits provided by other programs. GA recipients are often childless or under age 65. Hence they're ineligible for TANF or SSI, respectively. Some GA recipients suffer from a disability but haven't had it long enough to qualify for SSI benefits.

GA is the only public assistance program that is financed completely by state, county, or local governments. Guidelines for who can receive GA vary from location to location and from state to state. Most states restrict benefits to those who are extremely poor, living far below the poverty level; states usually require able-bodied recipients to work if they want to receive benefits (Blau, 2010). Many states and localities have severely cut back on GA benefits in recent years, and the number of GA programs is decreasing (Blau, 2010).

Housing Assistance

Adequate housing is a problem for vast numbers of Americans. Many find it to be the single most expensive item in their monthly budget. There's often little left over for food and clothing, let alone luxury items, after the rent is paid. And it must be paid, or families will be out on the street.

One of the problems is a serious lack of affordable, low-income housing. One reason is the recent extensive renovation of downtown urban areas into higher-rent districts, so that poor people can no longer afford to live in their old neighborhoods. Another reason is the mass abandonment of other dilapidated, aging, urban properties. Building owners and landlords often find such buildings too expensive to keep up. Unable to find anyone who wants to buy the properties, they simply abandon them.

Some housing assistance is available, primarily from the U.S. Department of Housing and Urban Development (HUD) Dolgoff and Feldstein (2009) explain:

The primary purpose of housing assistance is to reduce housing costs and improve housing quality for low-income households by providing decent and safe rental housing for eligible low-income households, [older adults,] . . . and persons with disabilities. Other goals include promoting residential construction, expanding housing opportunities for disadvantaged groups and groups with special needs, promoting neighborhood preservation and revitalization, increasing home ownership, and empowering [people living in poverty] . . . to become self-sufficient. (p. 251)

Often, assistance assumes the form of rental subsidies or vouchers by which government programs assist with rent, mortgage payments, and low-rent public housing. Another form of assistance involves block grants given to state and local governments to encourage low-income housing (Jimenez, 2010). This might involve the acquisition of existing properties for refurbishment or construction of new housing. Tax incentives can also be made available to independent private businesses to develop "low-income rental units" (Jimenez, 2010, p. 422). Although the stereotype persists that public housing involves huge, often dilapidated complexes of apartments for dozens or hundreds of low-income families, current trends involve placing recipients in smaller neighborhood units; funding is administered locally through public housing authorities that primarily offer rental assistance (DiNitto, 2011). Recent housing development has involved construction of smaller housing units using available funding because HUD "has not provided new funding for public housing developments since 1994" (DiNitto, 2011).

Means tests are used to determine eligibility. However, housing assistance has been cut back significantly in recent years and is not automatically available to everyone in need. Usually people must apply for rent subsidies, low-rent housing, or other assistance (considered an in-kind benefit). Because demand greatly exceeds supply, they often remain on long waiting lists until benefits or residences become available, sometimes years later.

There are an infinite number of ways to provide financial assistance to families. Each country establishes its own priorities and policies. Highlight 8.5 discusses the "Cash for Kids" policy in Canada, where financial assistance is provided to all families without high incomes.

HIGHLIGHT 8.5

International Perspectives: "Cash for Kids" in Canada[3]

EP 2.1.3, 2.1.5

There are many ways to make financial benefits available to families other than those provided by public assistance in the United States. These include *family allowances* (programs in which all eligible families receive designated sums of money regardless of their financial need) and *children's benefits* (programs in which families are given monetary allocations based on the fact that they have children). Canada has initiated a program that provides such children's benefits to families (Institute for Research on Poverty, 2001, Spring). The program's goals are to "help prevent and reduce the depth of child poverty; promote attachment to the workforce by ensuring that families will always be better off as a result of parents working; and reduce overlap and duplication of government programs and services" (Canada Revenue Agency, 2008).

Initiated during the 1980s and brought to fruition in 1993 (Institute for Research on Poverty, 2001), the Child Tax Benefit pays a maximum basic benefit of about C$3,436 [C$ refers to Canadian dollars] per year for a child under age 18 (Canada Revenue Agency, 2010a). There are increments for each child in families who have more children. Families who have children with disabilities receive funding that is slightly higher than the maximum basic benefits. As income rises, benefits are reduced and eventually cease (Canada Revenue Agency, 2010).

All families without high incomes, therefore, receive cash benefits on the basis of how many children they have. The amount they receive decreases with the amount of income they earn until they surpass the upper limit, at which point benefits stop. Note that low-income families also receive financial support in addition to this basic benefit.

The Canadian Child Tax Benefit program contrasts sharply with the provision of financial benefits to families in the United States, which has the highest rate of child poverty among industrialized nations. Public assistance in the United States is limited to a maximum of five years regardless of the family's financial need and is subject to compliance with work requirements. Most families (with the exception of those considered well off) don't get financial benefits just because they have children. (Note that the United States does provide tax breaks such as deductions for families with children.)

How would you answer the following questions?

Critical Thinking Questions

- Should all families receive financial benefits to supplement the additional costs they experience simply by having children? Why or why not?
- If you believe families should receive financial benefits, should these benefits be based on the family's income—namely, poorer families receive higher benefits and wealthier families lower? Or should all families receive the same amount of benefits per child regardless of family income? What is the fair thing to do?

[3]The term *cash for kids* and other information in this highlight (unless otherwise indicated) are taken from the Institute for Research on Poverty (2001, Spring).

Chapter Summary

The following summarizes this chapter's content as it relates to the chapter's learning objectives presented at the beginning of the chapter. Learning objectives include the following statements:

A Recognize poverty as a global and national problem.

"One-fifth of the world's people live in the richest nations (including the United States), and their average incomes are 15 times higher than those of the one-fifth who live in the poorest nations" (Kornblum & Julian, 2009, p. 186). Poverty is the condition of having inadequate "money to buy things that are considered necessary and desirable" (Kornblum & Julian, 2009, p. 193). Almost 37 million people in the United States live in poverty.

B Address race, gender, and single parenthood as variables related to poverty and the feminization of poverty.

Variables related to an increased potential for poverty include being female, living in a female-headed family, and being a person of color. The feminization of poverty refers to the fact that women as a group are more likely to be poor than are men.

C Describe special assessment issues concerning women and examine empowerment of women through consciousness-raising and a grassroots approach.

Using a gender lens to view the plight of women in the macro social environment assumes that sexism is relevant to the experiences of many women and is the basis for many women's difficulties. Consciousness raising is the process of facilitating people's understanding of a social issue with personal implications when there was little grasp of that issue before. Using this approach, social workers can help women address issues engulfing them in their environment. A grassroots approach means that people at the bottom of the formal power structure, such as ordinary citizens, band together to establish a power base and pursue macro changes. The common theme of women's grassroots efforts is that women work together to initiate and implement change for the benefit of women.

D Investigate proposed explanations for and the consequences of poverty.

Poverty is related to social class. Structural reasons for poverty include economic, political, and discrimination based on race and gender. Individual factors increasing the potential for poverty include having little human capital, originating in a single-parent family or a family with more children, and having a disability. Consequences of poverty include poorer health care, lower levels of education, lower paying jobs, poorer housing, and negative consequences in the criminal justice system.

E Explore the dynamics of homelessness in the United States.

A homeless person is defined as one who "lacks a fixed, regular, and adequate nighttime residence" or who sleeps in a temporary shelter for people without adequate residence or in a place not intended for the purpose of sleep (U.S. Department of Housing and Urban Development, 2011). It is estimated that over one million people are homeless in the United States. Homeless people are the poorest people. Homelessness is often related to losing a job or failure to pay rent. Homeless youth present a major concern. Solutions to homelessness involve provision of adequate housing and helping individuals get services and jobs.

F Emphasize the importance of empowerment for people living in poverty.

People must be empowered and provided adequate resources to get out of poverty.

G Describe major social insurance and public assistance programs in the United States and address relevant policy issues concerning them.

Social insurance involves financial benefits provided to people to "provide protection against wage loss resulting from retirement, prolonged disability, death, or unemployment, and protection against the cost of medical care during old age and disability" (U.S. Census Bureau, 2010, p. 347). Public assistance includes financial and in-kind (services or goods versus cash) benefits provided to people who can't support themselves. Social insurance programs include Old Age, Survivors, Disability, and Health Insurance; Unemployment Insurance; Workers' Compensation; and Medicare.

Several concerns are raised about Temporary Assistance to Needy Families (TANF), a public assistance program. They include issues regarding time limits; work, child care, and transportation; equitability among states; impositions on family structure; education and training for better jobs; and job quality and benefits. Other public assistance programs include Supplemental Security Income, Medicaid, the Children's Health Insurance Program, Supplemental Nutrition Assistance Program (food stamps), general assistance, and housing assistance. Policy issues include adequacy of services and who should be responsible for financing services.

H Appraise stereotypes about public assistance recipients.

Untrue stereotypes about public assistance recipients include the idea that the welfare roles are expanding dramatically, that the program costs the nation a fortune, that people receiving assistance are living well, that recipients are usually African American, and that families receiving assistance are huge.

I Review some aspects of the Canadian Child Tax benefit program to reflect an international perspective.

The Canadian Child Tax Benefit pays cash to families whose incomes fall within guidelines to help support their children. The amount of the benefit decreases as income increases. Families with more children are given more funding.

J Encourage critical thinking about resource and service provision to combat poverty.

Critical thinking questions were raised concerning what it's like to be poor, residual versus institutional perspectives on poverty, potential practice goals when using a grassroots approach, the limitations of social insurance, TANF restrictions for working mothers, liberal versus conservative perspectives on public assistance, and the value of providing benefits to families with children.

LOOKING AHEAD

This chapter addressed the problem of poverty and discussed programs implementing policies to help poor families and children. Families obviously need adequate financial resources to provide a protective, nurturing environment for their children. In addition to financial resources, many families need other *supportive services* to remain intact and thrive. Sometimes, for many reasons, children must be removed from their homes of origin, either temporarily or permanently, and be provided with *substitute care*. The next chapter explores a number of such supportive and substitute services. Chapter 9 is the first of several chapters in Part 4 of this book that address various client populations and the contexts in which services are provided.

COMPETENCY NOTES

The following identifies where Educational Policy (EP) competencies and practice behaviors are discussed in the chapter.

EP 2.1.1b Practice personal reflection and self-correction to assure continual professional development. *(pp. 244, 248):* Practitioners should practice personal reflection concerning their feelings about poverty and people who are poor in order to better understand their clients.

EP 2.1.1c Attend to professional roles and boundaries. *(p. 240):* Social work roles to empower women are proposed. *(p. 248):* Social programs are examined because it's part of the professional role to make referrals to the appropriate services.

EP 2.1.3 Apply critical thinking to inform and communicate professional judgments. *(p. 240):* Critical thinking questions are posed concerning potential practice goals. *(p. 244):* Critical thinking questions are raised concerning what it's like to be poor. *(p. 248):* Questions are asked to encourage critical thinking about residual versus institutional perspectives on poverty and what should be done to eliminate it. *(p. 253):* A critical thinking question encourages thought about improving social insurance for people with low skill levels and part-time workers who have jobs with a poor benefit structure. *(p. 256):* Critical thinking questions are raised concerning the needs of TANF recipients and how well these needs are being met. *(p. 259):* Critical thinking questions address the current state of public assistance. *(p. 263):* Critical thinking questions are raised regarding what the goals of programs such as the Canadian Child Tax Benefit should be. *(p. 269):* Critical thinking questions are posed to assess the effectiveness of the WIC program.

EP 2.1.3a Distinguish, appraise, and integrate multiple sources of knowledge, including research-based knowledge, and practice wisdom. *(p. 253):* Social workers should distinguish, appraise, and integrate multiple sources of knowledge when assessing the effectiveness and fairness of public assistance programs.

EP 2.1.4 Engage diversity and difference in practice. *(p. 240):* Social class is a dimension of diversity.

EP 2.1.4a Recognize the extent to which culture's structures and values may oppress, marginalize, alienate, or create or enhance privilege and power. *(p. 237):* People in lower socioeconomic classes are oppressed, and denied privilege and power. *(p. 244):* People living in poverty are oppressed and marginalized. *(p. 246):* People who are homeless are marginalized and alienated. *(p. 260):* Stereotypes about people receiving public assistance oppress, marginalize, and alienate them.

EP 2.1.4b Gain sufficient self-awareness to eliminate the influence of personal biases and values in working with diverse groups. *(p. 244):* Practitioners must work hard at gaining self-awareness regarding any personal biases they might harbor concerning people living in poverty. *(p. 248):* Critical thinking questions encourage thought about personal values and biases.

EP 2.1.4c Recognize and communicate their understanding of the importance of difference in shaping life experiences. *(p. 238):* Gender, race, single parenthood, and having a female family head are factors shaping life experiences and increasing the risk of poverty. *(p. 244):* Practitioners should recognize the extent to which socioeconomic status shapes life experiences.

EP 2.1.5 Advance human rights social and economic justice. *(p. 237):* Social workers should recognize the global interconnections of poverty and oppression. *(p. 263):* Canada's Child Tax Benefit provides an international example of a strategy to promote the human rights of children in families.

EP 2.1.5a Understand the forms and mechanisms of oppression and discrimination. *(p. 237):* Extreme differences in income distribution result in the oppression of people in lower socioeconomic classes. *(p. 241):* Social workers should understand how the structural causes of poverty result in oppression and discrimination. *(p. 259):* Critical thinking questions encourage the examination of conservative, liberal, residual, and institutional perspectives toward public assistance and what perspectives might result in oppression.

EP 2.1.5b Advocate for human rights and social and economic justice. *(p. 253):* Practitioners should advocate on the behalf of people who need public assistance and promote programs that effectively meet their needs.

EP 2.1.5c Engage in practices that advance social and economic justice. *(p. 240):* Potential practices that advance social and economic justice for women are suggested.

EP 2.1.6b Use research evidence to inform practice. *(p. 269):* Critical thinking questions encourage the assessment of research evidence to assert an opinion involving WIC policy and policy practice.

EP 2.1.7a Utilize conceptual frameworks to guide the processes of assessment, intervention, and evaluation. *(p. 241):* Social workers can use conceptual frameworks such as the structural cause of poverty to conduct informed assessments. *(p. 259):* Critical thinking questions concerning conservative and liberal conceptual frameworks encourage thought about what effective service provi-

sion and intervention involves. *(p. 269):* The Five-E conceptual framework is used to assess policy within the context of policy practice.

EP 2.1.7b Critique and apply knowledge to understand person and environment. *(p. 240):* Practitioners must understand and apply knowledge about people's socioeconomic conditions to understand how they can function in their environments.

EP 2.1.8a Analyze, formulate, and advocate for policies that advance social well-being. *(p. 246):* Practitioners should advocate for policies and services that advance social well-being for people who are homeless or potentially homeless. *(p. 247):* Social workers analyze policies that address poverty and advocate for policies that advance social well-being. *(p. 253):* Social workers should analyze, formulate, and advocate for policies that advance social well-being for people in need. *(p. 269):* The WIC program and policies are analyzed in terms of effectiveness and advancement of social well-being.

EP 2.1.8b Collaborate with colleagues and clients for effective policy action. *(p. 240):* Questions are posed that suggest working with colleagues and clients to achieve improved policies and services for women.

EP 2.1.9a Continuously discover, appraise, and attend to changing locales, populations, scientific and technological developments, and emerging societal trends to provide relevant services. *(p. 244):* Practitioners should continuously respond to the changing issues and conditions affecting people, in this case involving socioeconomic status and the effects of poverty. *(p. 253):* It's important for social workers to appraise continuously emerging societal trends to determine the effectiveness of public assistance programs and advocate for improvements.

EP 2.1.9b Provide leadership in promoting sustainable changes in service delivery and practice to improve the quality of social services. *(p. 240):* Questions are posed suggesting that social workers can assume a leadership role in improving services and resources for women living in poverty.

EP 2.1.10b Use empathy and other interpersonal skills. *(pp. 244, 248):* Critical thinking questions are posed to help develop empathy toward clients living in poverty.

EP 2.1.10g Select appropriate intervention strategies. *(p. 240):* Questions posed suggest consideration of potential intervention strategies to address this case example.

EP 2.1.10i Implement prevention interventions that enhance client capacities. *(p. 240):* Questions posed suggest potential interventions that will prevent problems for clients in the future. *(p. 246):* Policies and programs can be put in place that prevent homelessness. *(p. 257):* Provision of education and training can help people prepare for better-paying jobs and prevent poverty.

EP 2.1.10j Help clients resolve problems. *(p. 246):* Suggestions are made for helping people who are homeless resolve their problems and find homes.

FOR FURTHER EXPLORATION ON THE INTERNET

See this text's Social Work CourseMate website at *www.cengagebrain.com* for learning tools such as chapter quizzing, videos, glossary flashcards, and more.

CASE STUDY FOR CRITICAL THINKING

The WIC Program

The case presented here is an example of a social welfare policy, the Special Supplemental Food Program for Women, Infants, and Children (WIC).

EP 2.1.3,
2.1.6b,
2.1.7a,
2.1.8a[4]

Case Study: WIC is a nutritional program designed to supplement the diets of low-income women and their young children up to age 5 who are determined by a health professional to be at nutritional risk according to federal guidelines (Food and Nutrition Service [FNS], 2011). Participants receive either food items or, more typically, coupons that can be exchanged for specific food that is high in important nutrients, including infant cereal, iron-fortified adult cereal, vitamin C–rich fruit or vegetable juice, eggs, milk, cheese, peanut butter, canned beans/peas, canned fish," "[s]oy-based beverages, tofu, fruits and vegetables, baby foods, whole-wheat bread, and other whole-grain options" (FNS, 2011). Physicians may also prescribe special infant formulas or medical foods when needed. Additionally, eligible women receive nutritional counseling to educate them about their own and their children's nutritional needs.

WIC is administered through the U.S. Department of Agriculture, with state agencies (e.g., a state health department) distributing benefits. Eligibility includes (1) being a pregnant woman, new mother, infant, or child up to age 5; (2) having an income level at or less than 185% of the poverty level (in November 2009, $40,793 for a family of four in the 48 continuous states, Washington, D.C., Guam, and Territories; $51,005 in Alaska; and $46,916 in Hawaii); (3) fulfilling state residency requirements; and (4) having been determined to be "at risk" by a health care professional (FNS, 2011). A person in a family participating in "certain other benefit programs, such as the Supplemental Nutrition Assistance Program, Medicaid, or Temporary Assistance for Needy Families, automatically meets the income eligibility requirement" (FNS, 2011). "Nutrition risk" factors involve medical conditions such as having anemia or being underweight, having a history of problem pregnancies, or inadequate diet and nutrition (FNS, 2011). Approximately 8.7 million people, the majority of whom are children, receive WIC benefits each month (FNS, 2011). Note that eligibility requirements are more lenient than those of TANF and other public assistance programs (Karger & Stoesz, 2010). The total WIC federal budget for 2010 was $7.252 billion (FNS, 2011).

Critical Thinking: You can apply critical thinking to evaluate the usefulness of this program by following the Five-E approach to policy analysis.

1. First, *ask* questions.
   a. How *effective* is the policy?
   b. How *efficient* is the policy?

---

[4]Competency Notes for this case study are located at the end of Chapter 8.

c. Is the policy *ethically* sound?

d. What does *evaluation* of potential alternative policies reveal?

e. What recommendations can be *established* for positive changes?

2. Second, *assess* the established facts and issues involved.

a. How *effective* is the WIC policy and its resulting program implementation? WIC advocates cite research that program participation results in improved conditions at birth, including higher birth weights and reductions in preterm births (Devaney, 2007; DiNitto, 2005; FNS, 2009). There also appear to be fewer infant deaths (FNS, 2009). Additionally, infants and young children generally prosper from good nutrition, which enhances normal development. More specifically, adequate iron in the diet has been found to reduce iron-deficiency anemia—a condition involving decreased hemoglobin levels in red blood cells that results in fatigue and lack of vitality (Devaney, 2007; DiNitto, 2005; FNS, 2009). Some research indicates that children involved with WIC demonstrate improved growth in weight and height (Devaney, 2007). Other research showed that such children experience improved cognitive development (FNS, 2009). Additional benefits not directly related to the program's stated goals include improved prenatal care and better immunization records (Devaney, 2007, DiNitto, 2005; FNS, 2009).

Critics caution that although results sound good superficially, it is difficult to find comparable groups to establish that WIC is really the cause of positive results (DiNitto, 2005).

Others have raised questions regarding the effectiveness of nutritional counseling (DiNitto, 2005). What does such counseling involve? Is it really useful and worth the expense? Would providing information about other topics such as cooking be more effective?

From this discussion, how effective do you feel the WIC policy and program are? What other information would help make your decision easier?

b. How *efficient* are the WIC policy and program? Participation in WIC is associated with significantly decreased Medicaid costs for newborns and new mothers during the first 60 days after birth; for every dollar spent on prenatal care, it is estimated that $1.77 to $3.13 is saved in Medicaid costs (Dolgoff & Feldstein, 2009; FNS, 2009). This implies that mothers and infants are generally healthier due to the WIC program, so they don't have to seek as much help from Medicaid.

Critics of the program, including the Institute of Medicine, report that because there really is no valid classification system for "risk," conducting expensive assessments is a waste of time and money (Food and Nutrition Board, 2002). If anything, the entire population of low-income mothers and young children is at risk of nutritional deprivation. Money could better be spent providing more food or getting it to more people.

It is estimated that 90% of people eligible to receive WIC benefits do actually receive them (DiNitto, 2005). However, that is not 100%. Additionally, due to funding limitations, people may be placed on prioritized waiting lists (Dolgoff & Feldstein, 2009). Besides those who didn't apply to begin with, many women, infants, and children did not receive benefits because of funding limitations (Dolgoff & Feldstein, 2009).

What does this mean to you in terms of efficiency? Do you think it's efficient because it saves public spending on Medicaid? Or do you think it's inefficient because it fails to reach a significant number of people who are eligible and sometimes makes potential recipients endure waiting lists?

c. To what extent is the policy *ethically* sound? We just established that some people who are eligible for WIC do not receive benefits. Is this fair? Or should nutritional support be provided to all pregnant women, new mothers, infants, and small children? What are our society's ethical values concerning the importance of healthy pregnancies, mothers, and children? What is society's responsibility for their care?

d. How does the *evaluation* of potential alternative policies compare with WIC? WIC's goals are to improve the nutritional intake of eligible mothers and children at risk of poor nutrition and to educate mothers about nutrition to prevent problems related to a poor diet. What other policies might be developed to achieve the same goals? Would they be able to better meet the established goals? Are there more efficient, less expensive ways to meet these goals?

e. What recommendations can be *established* for positive changes? How could the program be improved? How could benefits reach more eligible mothers? Would increased federal and state funding help? What changes in policy could facilitate program implementation?

3. The third step in critical thinking is to *assert* a concluding opinion. In summary, what do you think about WIC? Should it be continued, expanded, reduced, or discarded?

PART FOUR

CLIENT POPULATIONS AND CONTEXTS

Part 4 includes eight chapters that focus on various fields of practice in social work, the client populations served, the social welfare policies governing that service, and the context in which benefits are provided. They include social work and services:

1. For children and families.
2. For older adults.
3. For persons with disabilities.

4. In health care.
5. In mental health.
6. In substance use, abuse, and dependence.
7. In the schools.
8. In the criminal justice system.

CHAPTER 9

Social Work and Services for Children and Families

Steve Skjold/Alamy

Consider the following cases involving children and their families.

Case A: *Burgundy, age 23, is a single mother desperately seeking day care for her children Sean and Shane, ages 1½ and 3. She has just found a clerical job at a law office not far from her home. Her sister can baby-sit for her in the mornings but has her own job to go to in the afternoons. Some of the available day care costs as much as she will make in her new job. Other day care centers won't take children who aren't toilet trained, which Sean definitely is not. Burgundy is at her wit's end!*

Case B: *Clark and Lois aren't doing well. They have three children to support, and not nearly enough money is coming in to pay the rent and buy groceries. Clark was laid off eight months ago from his job at the airplane factory. The economy's depressed, and he's been unable to find anything else. And then there are medical bills for Lois's breast cancer. She's had surgery and is only now finishing up radiation and chemotherapy treatments. Clark feels as if he's losing his grip on things.*

The least bit of aggravation makes him blow his stack. He finds himself more frequently slapping the kids around when they don't behave. The other day, he caught himself right before he hit one of them with a baseball bat.

Case C: Corazon is exhausted. Her daughter Juanita, age 9, is bedridden with a rare skin disease that makes any movement difficult and painful. Juanita requires almost constant care and attention. Corazon, a single parent, has no relatives or friends in the area willing to give her a break and help out even for a few hours by caring for Juanita. Corazon feels as if she's going crazy.

Case D: Tom, 15, is clinically depressed. He attends a school that focuses on fulfilling special education needs, addressing school behavior problems, and providing family counseling. He had been in five foster homes since his parents were killed in a car accident. The multiple placements were not Tom's fault but were simple results of fate. Two foster families moved out of the state when breadwinners got better jobs. One foster mother became pregnant and decided that having a foster child in addition to her own was simply too much. One foster father had a heart attack and died. The other foster family began having problems with their own teenage children, and so Tom was removed from the home. Tom and his older brother and sister have been separated for the past 10 years. For various reasons, "the system" has been unable to keep the three siblings together. Tom is doing poorly in school partly due to multiple school changes and partly due to his despair at the misfortune and loneliness that has characterized his life.

Case E: Ginny, age 18 months, has a severe intellectual disability (previously referred to as mental retardation) and so can do little more than lie in a prone position, suck on a bottle, and cry. She was removed from her home because her mother, a crack addict, did not provide adequate care. Shortly after Ginny arrived at her foster home, Ginny's foster mother took her to a diagnostic and treatment center for children with multiple disabilities. During a physical examination, the physician noticed that Ginny had odd-looking bruises around her vaginal area. They wondered what and who had caused them.

Cases A through C depict families that need supportive help to stay intact. For whatever reasons, families can become stressed or weakened and have trouble making it on their own. Causes may be economic, health related, or emotional. Sometimes a family is hit with an unexpected crisis such as job loss or serious illness; other times, long-term problems wear a family down and undermine its ability to keep itself afloat.

Cases D and E portray children who can no longer stay with their families in their own homes. When families have such serious needs and problems that they can't care for their children, substitute services are necessary.

Because the family is the core of most people's lives, this chapter explores issues relevant to families. People who receive other types of social services (e.g., those concerning health, mental health, disabilities, or aging) are also members of families. Because of the complexity of people's needs and the services developed to meet them, the same individual or family may receive services or use resources from various fields of practice. Therefore, a thorough understanding of services for children and families is basic to understanding social welfare and social work.

Learning Objectives

A   Emphasize the wide diversity in families and their structure.

B   Explain the concept of child welfare and describe the continuum of supportive and substitute services in the United States.

C   Examine child maltreatment and child protective services.

D   Describe and examine family preservation, child day care, family life education, and respite care.

E   Address the ongoing macro need to advocate for resources for children and families.

F   Describe substitute placements for children.

G   Discuss adoption.

H   Propose questions to stimulate critical thinking about advocacy to combat child maltreatment and controversial issues in adoption.

The Diversity of Families

Before talking about the wide range of programs and services geared to helping children and families, it's important to emphasize the enormous diversity of families and their configurations or structure. A *family* is "a primary group whose members assume certain obligations for each other and generally share common residences" (Barker, 2003, p. 154). This definition shows how flexible the notion of family has become. First, a family is a *primary group*—that is, "people who are intimate and have frequent face-to-face contact with one another, have norms [that is, expectations regarding how members in the group should behave] in common, and share mutually enduring and extensive influences" (Barker, 2003, p. 338). Thus family members have significant influence on each other. The second concept in the definition of family involves having obligations for each other, which means a sense of mutual commitment to and responsibility for other family members. The third concept in the definition is common residences, such that, to some extent, family members live together.

Family structure is "the nuclear family as well as those nontraditional alternatives to nuclear family which are adopted by persons in committed relationships and the people they consider to be 'family'" (CSWE, 2002). The traditional family structure in the United States consisted of two married parents who had never been divorced living together in one household with their own birth children. Today, however, typical family structures are much more varied. *Single-parent families* are family units in which only one of the parents, usually the mother, is present in the household. *Stepfamilies* are family structures in which one or both members of a married couple bring a child or children from a prior marriage or relationship to the family unit. Children may be biologically a combination of his or hers from past relationships, and possibly theirs together. "A *blended family* is any nontraditional configuration of people who live together, are committed to each other, and perform functions traditionally assumed by families. Such relationships may not involve biological or legal linkages. The important thing is that such groups *function* as families" (Zastrow & Kirst-Ashman, 2010, p. 153). Stepfamilies are a type of blended family. *Intergenerational families* are those in which family members include persons spanning at least three generations (e.g., grandparents living under the same roof and caring for grandchildren while the parents work).

Social workers must be sensitive to the various configurations families may take and appreciate this aspect of diversity. Open-mindedness is essential when we assess the strengths of any family group, regardless of its structure. Workers should not make assumptions about how families *should be* but should work with the family group that *is.* Highlight 9.1 examines the special situation of gay, lesbian, and bisexual families.

HIGHLIGHT 9.1

Gay and Lesbian Families: A Population-at-Risk

At special risk of discrimination are families with lesbian, gay, or bisexual (LGB) parents. Patterson (1995) explains:

EP 2.1.4,
2.1.4a,
2.1.4b,
2.1.4c,
2.1.5a,
2.1.8a,
2.1.9a

The central heterosexist [the prejudiced attitude that gay and lesbian people are inferior or immoral, often resulting in discriminatory behavior toward them] assumption that everyone is or ought to be heterosexual is nowhere more prevalent than in the area of parent–child relationships. Not only are children usually assumed to be heterosexual in their orientation, but mothers and fathers are also generally expected to exemplify heterosexuality in their attitudes, values, and behaviors. (p. 255)

Matthews and Lease (2000) describe the exceptional circumstances of LGB families:

These special issues can include problems brought on by being members of a stigmatized group in which the relationships are disapproved of by the majority of society, lack of formal or legal recognition of lesbian and gay families, nonheterosexual lifestyles being seen as incompatible with child rearing, fear of losing custody, and the perceived need for secrecy. (p. 259)

Despite these additional stressors, children growing up in lesbian or gay homes do just as well as those raised in heterosexual homes (Mallon, 2008; Morrow, 2008). Most children in LGB families "want people to understand that there's lots of love in their household … it's the pressure from society that makes things hard for them…. Their lives are as traditional and boring as anyone else's" (Carton, 1994, p. 45). Their parents do what parents do—help with homework and school projects, drive them to soccer games, save up for college, and scold them for being naughty (Morales, 1995).

Marital Status

An issue that directly effects many LGB people and their families is the issue of gay marriage. The option of marriage provides many potential consequences for people. For heterosexual couples it involves access to health insurance benefits, social insurance benefits, property rights, child custody rights, and many other legal advantages.

The right of lesbian and gay people to marry legally in the United States is a hotly debated issue. Some progress has been made in recent years. As of this writing, Massachusetts, Iowa, Vermont, Connecticut, New Hampshire, and Washington, D.C., provide same-sex couples the right to marry (National Conference of State Legislatures [NCSL], 2011).

However, the complex controversy continues. "Congress enacted the Defense of Marriage Act (DOMA) in 1996, which bars federal recognition of same-sex marriages and allows states to do the same" (NCSL, 2011). Since then, 37 states have passed DOMA legislation (NCSL, 2011).

At any point, state laws to allow same-sex marriages may be overturned by changes in the state constitution (California Court Rules, 2008). Three states passed DOMA constitutional amendments in 2008 (NCSL, 2011).

Complicated battles also continue to rage in the courts. For example,

The California Supreme Court ruled on May 15, 2008, that same-sex couples have the right to marry in California. Proposition 8, which amended the California state constitution to define marriage as between one man and one woman, was passed on Nov. 4, 2008. On August 4, 2010, a federal district judge ruled that the same-sex marriage ban in Proposition 8 violated the equal protection provisions of the U.S. Constitution. Enforcement of that decision has been stayed pending appeal. California does not currently allow same-sex marriages to be performed.

(continued)

HIGHLIGHT 9.1 (continued)

Same-sex marriages performed before Proposition 8 was passed remain valid. (NCSL, 2011)

Some states have legalized civil unions or domestic partnerships. A *civil union* is a legally recognized union that is similar to marriage in some or many respects. Such rights include "child custody, probate court, workers' compensation, and family leave benefits" ([AASECT] American Association of Sex Educators Counselors and Therapist, 2000, p. 6). However, these civil union rights are not transferable to other states should a couple move. Factions criticizing the civil union legislation claim that it "undermine[s] traditional marriage," "goes against God's will," and reeks of "social rape" and "moral rot" (AASECT, American Association of Sex Educators Counselors and Therapist 2000, May, p. 9). As of this writing, three states have legalized civil unions; three other states formerly recognizing civil unions now have same-sex marriage laws (NCSL, 2011).

Civil unions are not marriages, however. Depending on how these laws are drafted, they may not allow a number of privileges inherent in marriages, including Social Security survivor and spousal benefits; unlimited exemptions from federal gift and estate taxes on transfers to a spouse; the right not to testify against one's spouse in court; and unpaid leave to care for an ill spouse (National Gay and Lesbian Task Force, 2005).

Another proposed alternative to marriage is a *domestic partnership*, a legal agreement where two people live together, establish a personal relationship intended to be permanent, and share a domestic life together without being in a marriage or civil union. States determine the extent to which same-sex partners have spousal rights, so rights may vary widely (NCSL, 2011). As of this writing, seven states and the District of Columbia currently have domestic partnership legislation.

How does the public feel about legalized same-sex relationships? A recent Gallup poll indicated that 53% oppose same-sex marriage and 44% support it; note that this reflects a much more positive view about the

issue than in 1996, when 68% opposed gay marriage and 27% supported it (Gallup.com, 2010). Also on a positive note, 66% are in favor of civil unions, whereas 31% are not (PollingReport.com, 2010).

Avery and her colleagues (2007) comment on this discrepancy:

It is interesting to speculate why Americans support civil unions for gay and lesbian couples but not legal marriages. Perhaps many Americans believe that marriage is a "holy union" that is not open to same-sex couples because many faiths do not sanction it. Others might oppose same-sex marriage because they believe that same-sex unions undermine the traditional marital bond between a man and a woman. (p. 77)

From an international perspective, the following nations have legalized gay marriage (as of July 2010); each is followed by the year of legalization:

EP 2.1.5

- The Netherlands (2000)
- Belgium (2003)
- Spain (2005)
- Canada (2005)
- South Africa (2006)
- Norway (2008)
- Sweden (2009)
- Portugal (2010)
- Iceland (2010)
- Argentina (2010) (Fastenburg, 2010)

This controversy over whether gay marriage is right or wrong continues in heated debate throughout the United States. The core of the dispute focuses on a person's constitutional right to find happiness in an intimate relationship with another person versus the religious approach about the sanctity of marriage between a man and a woman. What are your opinions regarding this issue? Do you feel LGB people have the right to marry? Do they have the right to establish legal civil unions or domestic partnerships? Why or why not?

Major Thrusts of Services for Children and Families

One way of classifying services for children and families is to place them on a continuum, as shown in Figure 9.1. At one end of the continuum, families

require basic financial and material resources to survive. Some families require additional supportive help (e.g., counseling) to continue functioning and remain intact. Some families need very little help to enhance their functioning and thrive. Others require comprehensive services and resources to solve

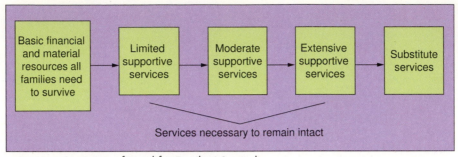

Figure 9.1 Continuum of Need for Families' Survival

problems and function as independent, healthy entities. The three middle boxes in Figure 9.1 reflect the continuum of need ranging from limited to moderate to extensive. Finally, at the other end of the continuum, some families are unable to function regardless of the resources and help they receive. In these cases, children must be removed from the home and substitute services provided.

Note that in the past, treatment and services involving children were referred to as "child welfare." The next section describes this field and the current status of practice with children and families.

Child Welfare: A Historical Social Work Field of Practice

EP 2.1.1

Child welfare is the traditional term for the network of policies and programs designed to empower families, promote a healthy environment, protect children, and meet children's needs. Basic goals of child welfare include:

- Meeting vulnerable children's unmet emotional, behavioral, and health needs.
- Providing adequate resources to address external conditions such as poverty and inadequate health care so children can develop and thrive in a healthy, nurturing social environment.
- Empowering families by building on strengths so parents can effectively provide for and protect their children.
- Improving internal family conditions involving interpersonal dynamics, communication, substance abuse, and conflict.
- Safeguarding children from various forms of neglect and abuse.

- When necessary, making permanent family living conditions available through adoption or transfer of guardianship.

Child welfare has always focused on children and families, with services traditionally provided by public agencies. Pecora and his colleagues (2010) comment:

Historical areas of service [include] foster care and adoptions, in-home family-centered services, child protective services, and residential services—where social work has a legitimate, long-standing, and important mission and role.... Readers also should be conscious of the many other fields of practice in which child and family services are provided or that involve substantial numbers of social work programs, such as services to adolescent parents, child mental health, health, education, special education, and juvenile justice agencies. (p. vii)

In recent years the emphasis concerning children and families has shifted from a focus on the child to one on the family and social environment. Children are now viewed in the context of their families and other people around them. The idea is that this environment must be strengthened to provide a nurturant, supportive setting in which children can grow and thrive. The next sections describe an array of services ranging from those supporting families to those providing options for substitute care outside of families.

Supportive Services

Supportive services "support, reinforce, and strengthen the ability of parents and children to meet the responsibilities of their respective statuses" (Kadushin & Martin, 1988, p. 83). The intent is simply to provide external support to enhance family functioning while children remain in the home. Services include basic financial and other resource assistance (discussed in Chapter 8); various types of mental health treatment such as family therapy, individual counseling, and group therapy (discussed more thoroughly in Chapter 13, which focuses on social work and mental health); child protective services; intensive family preservation services; day care; family life education; and respite care.

EP 2.1.10g, 2.1.10j

Case Example An example of supportive services involves Billy, a 13-year-old boy with moderate intellectual disabilities (Kadushin & Martin, 1988; Koch, 1979).[1] His parents, Norm and Norma Needing, had increasing difficulty controlling his behavior as he grew older and bigger. Billy was picking on his younger brother Benny and acting out uncontrollably in public settings such as grocery stores and restaurants. The Needings were at their wits' end and were considering placing Billy in an institutional setting.

Billy was referred by his school social worker to FACT (Family and Child Training), a program providing a range of services to persons with intellectual disabilities and their families. FACT assigned the case to Emma Getic, a social worker serving both as case coordinator and treatment provider. The first order of business was to assess the situation and develop a treatment plan. After spending substantial time observing Billy and his interactions both at school and at home, Emma worked with the Needings to develop goals and specify a plan for how to proceed.

Goals included improving Billy's interactions with peers and with Benny through supervised recreational activities, his ability to respond positively to parental guidance and directives, and his behavior in public places. The Needings attended parenting classes provided by FACT. Emma met weekly with the Needings to discuss what they had learned and help them apply the skills at home. Billy was enrolled in recreational activity groups sponsored and supervised by FACT staff. Initially, Billy was accompanied by a child care worker who modeled appropriate behavior for Billy and implemented the behavior modification program. Billy gradually

learned how to relate much more positively with Benny, his peers, and his parents. Billy enjoyed his new levels of interaction and acceptance, so his overall quality of life was significantly enhanced. Because family life had stabilized, the Needings no longer considered residential placement.

Further along the continuum of family needs are *substitute services* (described later), whereby another family or environment is substituted for the child's own family. Here "someone else takes over all aspects of the parental role on a temporary or permanent basis" (Kadushin & Martin, 1988, p. 344). Substitute services include foster care; residential placement in a group home, treatment center, or institution; independent living; and adoption.

An example of substitute care in an institutional setting could have involved the Needing family. For instance, suppose the family had not been referred to FACT or FACT had failed to help the family improve its functioning. The Needings might then have pursued Billy's placement in a residential institution.

Child Maltreatment and Child Protective Services

Jaron, age 3, and Tomas, age 2, attended a day care center while their mother, Joyita, worked during the day. Laura, the day care center social worker, and Sonja, Jaron's and Tomas's teacher, became increasingly concerned about the boys' health and hygiene. Their clothes were smeared with dirt, and their hair was filthy. They had an exceptionally strong, unappealing odor, apparently due to very infrequent bathing. Their teeth were dark with tartar. And they were ravenously hungry when they arrived at the center each day. The situation screamed neglect. Laura had the choice of sitting down with Joyita and talking with her about the problems or referring the case to child protective services.

Consider another case. Peter, age 6, had been placed in foster care with Becca for the past year. Peter's mother, Mary, had visitation rights every Saturday afternoon. During their lives, Peter and his four siblings had periodically been removed from the home because of neglect and placed in foster care. Mary had a long history of drug use and abuse. She had started treatment programs on numerous occasions but was never able to complete them. After one of the Saturday visits with Mary, Becca noticed that Peter had a series of small circular burns on his left arm that looked as if they might

---

[1]This case example is loosely based on one provided in the sources cited. Various situational variables such as referral source have been changed.

be from a lighted cigarette. Was Peter actually being tortured on Saturday afternoons? Becca called Peter's social worker.

Another case involved Juanita, age 13, who was referred to Cheung, the school social worker, by Agate, Juanita's English teacher. Agate had given Juanita and the rest of her class an assignment to write a poem on any subject they wished. Juanita had written 18 poems. (How many times have you done 18 times the work a teacher assigned you?) Each of Juanita's poems involved explicitly sexual language and imagery. Juanita lived with her mother, sisters, and a stepfather. There was some concern about potential sexual abuse by the latter. Upon further investigation after referral to child protective services, it was determined that a maternal uncle, not the stepfather, was guilty of sexual abuse.

These four children are victims of various types of child maltreatment. Before we discuss the types of supportive services and treatment provided for this grave family problem, it's important to understand some of the reasons why it occurs and the ways it affects children.

What Are Child Maltreatment, Abuse, and Neglect?

Child maltreatment is the umbrella term for physical abuse, sexual abuse, psychological abuse, neglect, and psychological maltreatment. Each term will be defined and discussed here. However, note that child maltreatment can be complex, with each case being unique in its own way. Therefore, sometimes terms will overlap, depending on the individual situation.

Physical abuse occurs when "a child younger than 18 years of age has experienced an injury . . . or risk of an injury . . . as a result of having been hit with a hand or other object or having been kicked, shaken, thrown, burned, stabbed, or choked by a parent or parent-surrogate" (Kolko, 2002, p. 22). Physical indicators include bruises, lacerations, fractures, burns, head injuries, and internal injuries. Often the injuries don't make sense. For example, they might occur in odd patterns or places. A doughnut-shaped burn will appear on the buttocks if a child has been immersed in very hot water, or she may have bruises on the soles of her feet from being hit there with a stick. Explanations for injuries may not be logical. Consider a child who says he broke his leg when he tripped on a crack in the sidewalk, but there are no sidewalks in his

neighborhood. Still another clue involves frequent or multiple injuries that are hard to explain.

Physically abused children can also exhibit behavioral indicators such as extreme passivity and submissiveness in order to avoid provoking an abusive parent or other caregiver. Other children will express themselves with marked aggression and hostility, modeling the behavior of a violent parent.

Sexual abuse is

any sexual activity with a child where consent is not or cannot be given.... This includes sexual contact that is accomplished by force or threat of force, regardless of the age of the participants, and all sexual contact between an adult and a child, regardless of whether there is deception or the child understands the sexual nature of the activity. Sexual contact between an older and a younger child also can be abusive if there is a significant disparity in age, development, or size, rendering the younger child incapable of giving informed consent. The sexually abusive acts may include sexual penetration, sexual touching, or non-contact sexual acts such as exposure or voyeurism.

(Berliner & Elliott, 2002, p. 55)

Incest, a form of sexual abuse, is "sexual intercourse between people too closely related to legally marry (usually interpreted to mean father–daughter, mother–son, or brother–sister combinations)" (Yarber, Sayad, & Strong, 2010, p. 596). Physical symptoms of sexual abuse include physical damage to or bleeding in the genital or anal areas. Emotional indicators are depression, low self-esteem, and thoughts of suicide. Other clues include compulsive masturbation and sexual behavior or knowledge inappropriate to a child's age.

Child neglect is "the failure of a parent, guardian, or other caregiver to provide for a child's basic needs. Neglect may be:

- Physical (e.g., failure to provide necessary food or shelter, or lack of appropriate supervision)
- Medical (e.g., failure to provide necessary medical or mental health treatment)
- Educational (e.g., failure to educate a child or attend to special education needs)
- Emotional (e.g., inattention to a child's emotional needs, failure to provide psychological care, or permitting the child to use alcohol or other drugs)" (Child Welfare Information Gateway, 2008).

For example, a child might lack appropriate winter clothing in a cold climate and, as a result, suffer frequent illness. Or a 6-year-old child might be left alone in charge of her two younger siblings. Constant hunger is yet another symptom.

Psychological maltreatment involves "a repeated pattern of behavior that conveys to a child that he or she is unwanted, worthless, valued only to the extent that he or she can meet others' needs, or is threatened with physical or psychological attack" (Downs, Moore, & McFadden, 2009, p. 213). Such maltreatment can involve withdrawal of support, attention, and encouragement. It may also entail active criticism, disapproval, and censure of children and their feelings and behavior.

EP 2.1.10d

The following categories reflect types of psychological maltreatment (Crosson-Tower, 2010; Downs et al., 2009; Hart & Brassard, 1991, 2001; Hart, Brassard, & Karlson, 1996; Hart et al., 2011; Miller-Perrin & Perrin, 2007):[2]

1. *Spurning* includes "belittling, degrading, shaming, ridiculing; singling out one child to do most of the household chores or to criticize and punish; and publicly humiliating" (Downs et al., 2009, p. 219). For example, "Jose's dad publicly humiliated him by coming to soccer games and screaming at him whenever he would fail to get in the correct position, fail to hold on to the ball, fail to kick it accurately to a fellow player, etc. 'You clumsy jerk! You poor excuse for a son! Can't you even pass!' he would bellow" (Hart et al., 2011, p. 128). Another example of spurning is refusing to help a child who asks for or needs help (Miller-Perrin & Perrin, 2007).

2. *Terrorizing* occurs when the caregiver "verbally assaults the child, creates a climate of fear, bullies and frightens the child, and makes the child believe that the world is hostile and unsafe" (Crosson-Tower, 2010, p. 212). Such actions cause "extreme fear and/or anxiety in a child" (Miller-Perrin & Perrin, 2007, p. 209). For instance, "Lamar's mother knew her son was in the apartment when she fired a shot through the front door in an attempt to kill his father" (Hart et al., 2011, p. 129). Other examples of terrorizing include threatening to harm the child him- or herself or threatening to commit suicide (Miller-Perrin & Perrin, 2007).

3. *Isolating* occurs when the caregiver cuts the child off from "normal social experiences, prevents the child from forming friendships, and makes the child believe that he or she is alone in the world" (Crosson-Tower, 2010, p. 212). For example, "Detian's family homeschooled her and would not allow her to play with neighborhood children. She could only leave the house with her parents or older sister, and she was strictly forbidden to converse with any adults or children who were not family members. She was told that other people didn't share the family's beliefs and were of the devil" (Hart et al., 2011, p. 129). Another example of isolating involves strapping a baby in a portable car seat all day to keep her from being underfoot (Hart et al., 2011). Still another illustration involves "locking a child in a closet or room" (Miller-Perrin & Perrin, 2007, p. 209).

4. *Exploiting/corrupting* includes "modeling, permitting, or encouraging such antisocial behavior as prostitution, performance in pornography, criminal activity, or substance abuse; [and] encouraging developmentally inappropriate behavior such as parentification [expecting the child to act like a parent] or infantilization [treating an older child like an infant]" (Downs et al., 2009, p. 213). For instance, "after Seth's father lost his job and the family home was lost to foreclosure, Seth's parents began a downhill slide into methamphetamine addiction. To help his parents obtain drugs, and to provide income for the family, Seth began selling drugs" (Hart et al., 2011, p. 129).

5. *Denying emotional responsiveness* includes "being detached and uninvolved, interacting only when absolutely necessary, and failing to express love and affection to the child" (Downs et al., 2009, p. 213). For example, "baby Jose was fed and changed on a regular schedule, but his parents rarely interacted with him. When they did, they changed him or bathed him but without any expression of affection. There was no cuddling, little talking, and no eye contact" (Hart et al., 2011, p. 129).

---

[2]These categories of psychological maltreatment are based on the "*1995 Guidelines for Psychosocial Evaluation of Suspected Psychological Maltreatment of Children and Adolescents*, published by the American Professional Society on the Abuse of Children (APSAC)" (Hart et al., 2011, p. 126).

Downs and her colleagues (2009) explain the complexity of psychological maltreatment:

Psychological maltreatment is related to other forms of maltreatment; it is the psychological dimension of abuse, neglect, and sexual abuse. Terrorizing may be embedded in physical abuse; denying emotional responsiveness may be the psychological aspect of physical neglect. However, psychological maltreatment may also exist by itself, without other forms of maltreatment. (p. 214)

We have established that child maltreatment in general is a complex issue. What's important is not that a particular case fits neatly into a clearly defined category, but rather that children are protected and their needs addressed. Highlight 9.2 provides an international perspective on child abuse—small children being sold as slaves in West Africa.

How Many Children Are Maltreated?

The actual number of child maltreatment cases is difficult to determine. Specific definitions for who is included in specific categories vary dramatically from one state or locale to another. One thing, however, is certain—any figures that are reported reflect a minimal number of actual cases. All indications are that vast numbers of cases go unreported.

In 2008 there were almost 2 million reported and investigated acts of child maltreatment in the United States, almost 774,000 of which were substantiated (U.S. Census Bureau, 2010). This, of course, doesn't reflect other cases not reported or investigated. "Recent findings suggest that the incidence of child

---

HIGHLIGHT 9.2

International Perspectives: The Child Slave Trade in West Africa

EP 2.1.5, 2.1.5a

Juliette Zinwue was thrilled! Although she lived in a small village in Benin, West Africa, she was actually going to travel somewhere in a car; some men said they would take her to work in Abidjan, a city in the Ivory Coast, and paid her parents to do so (Robinson & Palus, 2001). However, the journey soon turned into a horror story. Placed in a wealthy woman's home located in active, crowded Abidjan, Juliette "now rises at 6 AM to sweep the house and courtyard, wash dishes and clean out the garbage cans. She spends the rest of the day at a local market selling trinkets and hair accessories at her boss's stall" (Robinson & Palus, 2001, p. 40). She started three years ago. Today she's 10.

Chapter 2 established that human trafficking including the enslaving of children for the sex trade is a major global issue today (de Silva, 2007; Dixon, 2009). It is estimated that 200,000 West and Central African children are sold into slavery each year (Dixon, 2009). Robinson and Palus (2001) report on these children's experiences. The root of the problem is poverty. In the poorest countries, including Benin, where up to three-quarters of the population survives on less than $1 a day, children have no schools to attend and little hope for viable future employment. They are often sold, sometimes for the meager fee of $15, because impoverished parents feel the children might be better off in a richer country—even as slaves. Most girls find themselves working as domestic help or prostitutes. Boys end up as field hands on plantations or as workers on fishing boats. Generally, "Africa has the highest rate of child labor in the world: 41% of 5- to 14-year-olds work" (p. 40).

The practice is bolstered by tradition. Historically, young children resided with wealthier urban extended family members or were hired out as servants to newly married couples. However, the current practice of selling them to strangers in other countries is purely a matter of business. Somebody is making money in the process, and it surely is not the children. Although West African nations are attempting to halt the slavery process, it is difficult. Borders between nations are easily crossed, and police have few resources for enforcement.

Juliette resolutely states, "I don't care that I have not been to school ... but I would like to go to church" (p. 41). She can't though, because she doesn't get Sundays off.

maltreatment is increasing dramatically"; one study found that the incidence had doubled over a decade (Petr, 2004, p. 20). Of substantiated cases, 71% involved neglect, 16.3% physical abuse, 9.2% sexual abuse, 7.1% emotional maltreatment, and 2.2% medical neglect (U.S. Census Bureau, 2010).

What Causes Child Maltreatment?

EP 2.1.10d

People who physically abuse children tend to have the following needs (Crosson-Tower, 2009; Runyon & Urquiza, 2011):

- A need for personal support and nurturance.
- A need to overcome isolation and establish social contacts.
- A need to learn appropriate parenting skills.
- A need to improve self-esteem.

Crosson-Tower (2010) elaborates:

It is generally agreed that parents who abuse their children usually have a dearth of coping mechanisms. They may not have achieved the degree of social competence of nonabusive parents and lack their problem-solving abilities. Some authors see these parents as less flexible and more easily overwhelmed.... Although some studies do not find a history of abuse or dysfunctional childhoods, others suggest that they might be in evidence.... This may lead them to less appropriate disciplinary standards.... A number of abusive parents are inconsistent and approach child rearing with negativity....Their attitude leads them to feel less effective and overwhelmed, and as a result, they tend toward more aggressive models of discipline. (p. 101)

Parents who neglect their children appear to have characteristics similar to physically abusive parents, although poverty may add to the stresses that result in neglect (Crosson-Tower, 2009; Erickson & Egeland, 2011). Erickson and Egeland (2011) explain that neglectful parents tend to exhibit a number of characteristics. They display "a lack of understanding of the emotional complexity of human relationships, especially the parent-child relationship" and "have difficulty seeing things from the child's perspective" (p. 115). Such parents "often have unresolved issues of trust, dependency, and autonomy (reflecting their own childhood history) and may seek to meet their own needs through the parent-child relationship" (p. 115). There is evidence

that they are more likely to be depressed or have other mood disturbances. Other primary "risk factors include violence in the marital relationship, parental unemployment, other stressful life events, and the absence of a helpful, supportive social network" (p. 116). Neglectful parents may not have had their own needs met in their own childhoods.

Parents who physically abuse their children are actively lashing out. In contrast, neglectful parents are withdrawing and failing to provide adequately for their children.

Crooks and Baur (2011) describe people who sexually abuse children: No clear-cut description characterizes perpetrators of sexual abuse

other than that most are male and are known to the victim.... Child molesters cover the spectrum of social class, educational achievement, intelligence, occupation, religion, and ethnicity. Evidence suggests that many.... offenders, especially those who are prosecuted, are shy, lonely, poorly informed about sexuality, and moralistic or religious.... Many are likely to have poor interpersonal and sexual relations with other adults, and may feel socially inadequate and inferior.... However, it is not uncommon to encounter [offenders].... outside the legal system who are well educated, socially adept, civic-minded, and financially successful (p. 534).

Other possible characteristics include "alcoholism, severe marital problems, sexual difficulties, and poor emotional adjustment" (Crooks & Baur, 2011, p. 534).

Crosson-Tower (2010) adds that sexuality for a perpetrator "provides not only tension release but also enhances self-esteem and makes the individual feel more personally effective. Pornography may feed into this to normalize a distorted view of sexual relations. Sexuality and aggression also become fused in his mind" (p. 141).

Miller-Perrin and Perrin (2007) describe some of the characteristics of parents who emotionally maltreat their children:

Such parents, compared with nonabusive parents, appear to exhibit more difficulties with interpersonal and social interactions, problem solving, and psychiatric adjustment.... Emotionally abusive parents had more difficulty building relationships, exhibited poor coping skills, and displayed deficits in child management techniques. In addition, emotionally abusive mothers demonstrated a lack of support networks (both personal and community) as well as greater levels of perceived stress, marital discord, and alcohol and drug use. (p. 218)

Child Protective Services and the Social Work Role

EP 2.1.1c, 2.1.10i

Child protective services (CPS) are interventions aimed at protecting children at risk of maltreatment. CPS social workers are usually employed by state or county public agencies whose designated task is to protect children from harm. Miller-Perrin and Perrin (2007) describe agency functioning:

CPS agencies carry out their responsibility of protecting children in four ways: (a) by investigating reports of maltreatment, (b) by providing treatment services, (c) by coordinating the services offered by other agencies in the community to child victims and their families, and (d) by implementing preventive services. . . . Ideally, the goal of CPS

in all cases is to prevent child abuse and neglect in children's own homes through the provision of various services. (p. 280)

Interventions in child maltreatment cases follow the same sequential steps used in other areas of social work intervention. These include receipt of the initial referral; gathering information about the case through a social study; assessment of the situation; case planning including goal setting; provision of treatment; evaluation of the effects of treatment; and termination of the case (Depanfilis, 2011; Pecora et al., 2010). Note that the "treatment of families may be undertaken by the protective service agency but is more often handled by referrals to other appropriate agencies, in which case the worker plays a case management role" (Crosson-Tower, 2010, p. 312). (Chapter 4 established that *a case manager* is a practitioner who, on the behalf of a specific client system, coordinates needed services provided by any number of agencies, organizations, or facilities.) Highlight 9.3 focuses on the

---

HIGHLIGHT 9.3

The Assessment of Risk and Resiliency in Child Maltreatment Cases

EP 2.1.7a, 2.1.7b, 2.1.10d, 2.1.10e,

A key word in the assessment of child maltreatment is *risk* (Depanfilis, 2011; Shlonsky & Gambrill, 2005). After a case involving suspected maltreatment is reported, it's the social worker's job to *assess* the extent to which children are at risk of maltreatment. It is also vital that the family's strengths and resiliency be assessed (Crosson-Tower, 2010). Family strengths provide the basis for treatment planning to protect children from maltreatment and keep the family safely together if at all possible. Crosson-Tower (2010) urges that the following questions be answered during the assessment process:

- *Is the child at risk from abuse or neglect and to what degree?*
- *What is causing the problem?*
- *Could services be offered to alleviate the problem?*

- *Is the home a safe environment or must the child be placed elsewhere? (p. 229)*

Assessment focuses on many of the dynamics contributing to maltreatment discussed earlier. A numerous variables have been found to affect a worker's decision that a case assumes a high level of risk and merits intensive agency intervention (Crosson-Tower, 2010; Kadushin & Martin, 1988; Myers, 2002). These include:

- Clearly visible proof of abuse or environmental characteristics that obviously endanger a child.
- The degree of the child's helplessness and vulnerability (e.g., a child with a physical disability or an infant being extremely vulnerable).
- Self-destructive behavior on the part of the child.
- A history of severe abuse.
- Abusers who show no or little regret for their child's abuse and have difficulty accepting responsibility.

(continued)

HIGHLIGHT 9.3 (continued)

- Abusers who openly reject the child or blame the child for the problem.
- Serious emotional disturbances on the part of parents.
- Lack of cooperation by the parents.
- Families that are exposed to numerous and severe psychological and social pressures.
- Isolation of the family and lack of social support systems.

Protective elements potentially demonstrating *resiliency* (the ability to recover from adversity and resume functioning) should also be assessed as they relate to the child or children, the parents and family in general, and to the encompassing environment (Crosson-Tower, 2010). Factors associated with the child include the following:

- "Child is in good health and result of a normal pregnancy and birth *or*
- Mother receives and accepts support around any current or past problems with child
- Child has easy temperament, is well bonded with caretakers, and feels secure
- Child has healthy self-esteem, is able to problem solve (age appropriate), and shows age-appropriate degree of autonomy
- Child has good peer relationships
- Child has experienced relatively healthy development free from trauma
- Child has hobbies and interests" (Crosson-Tower, 2010, p. 233).

Protective elements associated with the parents or the family in general include the following:

- "Positive parent-child relationship with secure attachment
- Appropriate structure/family rules with fair, non-physical discipline
- Parents model healthy self-esteem and good problem-solving abilities
- Presence of concerned and caring extended family
- Higher parental educational level
- Family expects prosocial behavior" (Crosson-Tower, 2010, pp. 233–234).

Protective elements related to the family's relationship with its environment include the following:

- Access to health and educational resources
- Consistent parental employment
- Adequate housing
- Mid to high socioeconomic status
- Family is affiliated with religious faith community
- Presence of other positive and influential adult models" (Crosson-Tower, 2010, p. 234).

Assessment interviews involve both adults and children. Questions focus on the parents' history and current functioning; the way parents perceive their children; the way the family system functions as a whole; the condition of the home environment; the external support (e.g., friends or relatives) available to the family; and the children's condition, level of development, and overall functioning (Crosson-Tower, 2010).

---

importance of risk assessment in cases of child maltreatment.

Following assessment, a treatment *plan* is developed providing direction for how to proceed. According to Winton and Mara (2001), treatment goals for maltreatment victims "include increasing self-esteem, decreasing feelings of hopelessness and helplessness, decreasing aggressive behaviors, and decreasing negative behaviors such as lying, suicide attempts, running away, promiscuity, and drug or alcohol abuse" (p. 165). These can be achieved through individual counseling, group therapy, or family therapy.

Of course, basic aspects of treatment for physically abused children involve meeting their medical needs and keeping them safe. Sometimes removal

from a dangerous situation is necessary, at least temporarily.

Treatment goals for parents focus on strengthening their "coping skills, parenting skills, and child management techniques" (Winton & Mara, 2001, p. 171). Intervention may involve individual counseling or family therapy. Many believe that group therapy, including self-help groups such as Parents Anonymous, is often the most effective (Winton & Mara, 2001; Parents Anonymous 2007). Through such groups, parents learn that they are not alone and can discover how others are experiencing stress and frustration. They can share coping ideas with each other, suggest new child management techniques, provide mutual support, and improve their communication skills.

Treatment for families experiencing abuse or neglect varies radically depending on the resources and services available, the level of risk to the children's well-being, the family dynamics, and motivation of the abusive or neglectful caregivers. An intensive family preservation approach (described in detail later in the chapter) involves a social worker spending concentrated time with a family, identifying specific treatment goals, emphasizing family strengths, and teaching other skills as needed.

Working with and Referring to Other Agencies

EP 2.1.1c

During the intervention process, CPS staff often work with the courts to declare that children require protection and to determine appropriate safe placement for them. CPS workers are frequently called on to testify in court to report assessment information and make recommendations (Gibelman, 1995). In the event that family problems cannot be resolved, CPS workers may work with the courts to develop alternative long-term or permanent placements.

Additionally, social workers may refer to a number of social services (Alexander, 2004). *Respite care* is the temporary provision of care so that the regular caregivers, in this case parents, have some time away from child care responsibilities (Murphy, 2004). This can ease stress and allow parents to take a break. *Day care* is the regular provision of care for children or others dependent on help when regular caregivers must work or be away from the home. This is another way of providing alternative child care for children so parents can attend to their own needs, go to work, and practice newly learned skills. *Support services* involve a wide range of assistance in helping parents undertake their daily tasks and assume their responsibilities; examples include "parent educational services, employment counseling and training services, budget management, legal services, homemaker services, ... referrals to food banks, and transportation" (Alexander, 2004, p. 419). *Parental aides* are trained paraprofessionals, sometimes volunteers, who go into the home, serve as positive role models for behavior management and parent–child relationships, and provide someone for the parents to talk to. In effect, this is another way of taking the pressure off. Finally, *Big Brother/Big Sister* or *adopted grandparent programs* can let children

form a special relationship with a supportive adult role model or mentor. Volunteers are paired with a child and, under supervision, offer that child guidance and friendship.

Referral opportunities are endless. It's up to the social worker to accurately assess family members' needs and creatively link them to available services.

Case Example Cynthia, age 7, came to school one day with odd-looking bruises on her arm. Her teacher, Kari Meback, noticed them immediately and asked her where she got them. Cynthia, an aggressive, boisterous child who loved to get attention from her teachers, told Kari that she had tripped, fallen down the stairs, and hit her arm on some toys at the bottom. Kari thought that this seemed a bit peculiar but accepted Cynthia's answer and forgot about the incident.

Three days later, Kari again noticed some odd bruises on Cynthia's arm. She also observed that Cynthia was having difficulty writing, as if her fingers were sprained. Again she asked Cynthia what was wrong. The child answered that she had probably bumped her hand on something. But this time Kari did not leave the matter at that. That same day she talked to the school social worker, who, in turn, referred the matter to a protective services worker at the local social services agency.

The protective services worker assigned to the case, Brian Bornthumper, immediately began a case assessment. He interviewed both Cynthia and her parents. He focused on the elements indicating that abuse was taking place and on the probable risk that Cynthia would come to further harm. He also examined the needs of the family as a whole and of its individual members.

Brian assumed as nonthreatening an approach as possible and maintained a focus on the family's and the child's welfare. He discovered that Cynthia's family had moved to the area from another state only a year before. Cynthia's mother, Amelia, was a shy, withdrawn woman who found it difficult to make new friends. She had no relatives in the area. Additionally, Cynthia's baby sister, Julie, had been born only three months after the move. Julie was a colicky baby who rarely slept more than two hours at a time and cried almost incessantly. Cynthia's father, George, was a mop salesman who was frequently out of town. And when he was home, he spent his time watching football and other sports on television or sleeping.

Michael Austen/Alamy

Social workers work with abused children and their familes.

Amelia obviously was under severe stress. She felt lonely, isolated, and worthless. Even Julie didn't seem to love her. All the baby did was cry. George was hardly ever home, and when he was, he ignored the family. Amelia felt that her marital relationship was deteriorating. As a result of all these stresses, she found herself violently exploding at Cynthia. Whenever Cynthia did something the least bit wrong, Amelia found herself screaming at the girl and often physically assaulting her.

In fact, Amelia's relationship with her own family was quite poor. Her childhood memories were filled with her father beating her with little provocation.

Cynthia's family exemplified the types of needs that are common in abusive families. Loneliness, isolation, lack of emotional support, marital problems, life crises, and lack of effective parenting skills were all apparent. Brian conducted an assessment by gathering relevant information regarding family relationships, history, emotional status, and stress levels; child management approaches; and

available support systems. As a CPS worker, he sought to strengthen the family and enhance family members' interactions among themselves and with others in their environment.

Brian initially made several referrals to the appropriate services, after which he served as case manager, coordinating efforts and monitoring progress. He met with the family regularly to accomplish this. For instance, Brian referred Amelia to a Parents Anonymous group, in which she could experience mutual support, vent her frustrations, develop relationships, improve communication skills, and learn new coping methods. He referred both George and Amelia to a parent effectiveness training group to improve their ability to cope with and control their children's behavior. He also referred them to a local family services agency for marital counseling. The intent was to work on improving communication within the marriage and to address possible ways for George to spend more time with Amelia, provide her with greater support, and become more involved with the family.

In addition, Brian referred Cynthia to the family services agency for individual counseling. He also worked with her school social worker to involve her in a volleyball team and local Girl Scout troop.

Brian suggested that Amelia join a recreational group so she could develop some friendships and have some time to herself. Amelia decided to become a member of a bowling team and started attending an aerobics class. Finally, Brian helped Amelia find a day care center that would care for her children while she attended these activities.

In effect, Brian worked with this family to develop its members' strengths, improve communication and mutual support, utilize more effective behavior management techniques, stop abuse, maintain safety, and improve overall family functioning.

Sometimes it's necessary for social workers to do more than simply make referrals, as Brian's work with Cynthia and her family illustrates. Focus on Critical Thinking 9.1 addresses advocacy and child maltreatment in the macro arena.

Intensive Family Preservation: One Treatment Approach

Family preservation services are "short-term, family-based services designed to assist families in crisis by improving parenting and family

EP 2.1.10i

FOCUS ON CRITICAL THINKING 9.1

Advocacy and Child Maltreatment in the Macro Arena

**EP 2.1.3,
2.1.5b,
2.1.8a,
2.1.10k**

An ongoing part of the social worker's role is to evaluate the effectiveness of policy at the macro level and advocate for positive change where needed. Macro improvements are called for in at least five areas:

- More funding should be funneled to the *prevention* of child maltreatment (Chadwick, 2002; Daro & Donnelly, 2002). Until now "services and interventions have developed as *responses* to the problems of abuse as the problems have been recognized" (Chadwick, 2002, p. 509). Preventing children from suffering from maltreatment in the first place is certainly much better for them than reacting after it has already occurred (Wells, 2008).
- A more supportive system geared toward improving resources and services for families in general is essential to maintain family strengths. Families need tangible resources, including adequate shelter, food, clothing, and other necessities, to thrive (Alexander, 2004; Wells 2008).
- More community and neighborhood supports should be initiated and developed. Current availability of

resources and services is significantly inconsistent (Chadwick, 2002). For example, families in rural settings should have better access to child protective services (Chadwick, 2002).

- Public and private agencies should communicate and cooperate with each other more effectively concerning service provision (Chadwick, 2002). Sometimes "interventions are incompatible with others"; for example, an abusive parent may be imprisoned for a long period, conflicting with a treatment plan developed to reunite the family (Chadwick, 2002, p. 517).
- Organized continuing education plans should be developed to educate social workers and other social service providers about child maltreatment (Chadwick, 2002).

With the conservative–liberal and residual–institutional orientations in mind, answer these questions.

Critical Thinking Questions

- To what extent do these suggestions reflect conservative or liberal values, and why?
- To what extent do they reflect a residual or institutional orientation to social welfare policy, and why?

functioning while keeping children safe" (ACF, n.d.). Family preservation is based on the idea that children can be protected safely in their own homes when families are strengthened. This is done by giving parents the resources and services they need to function effectively. Family preservation stresses that it is in children's best interests to help them remain in their own homes. Removing them can traumatize them and result in permanent harmful consequences. The concept of family preservation has become a major thrust in agencies throughout the country. It involves doing everything possible to keep the child in the home and provide treatment for the family. Family preservation services are also referred to as family-based services, "home-based services, or in-home treatment" (Alexander, 2004; Berg, 1994, p. 4).

Six goals of family preservation services are "(1) to protect children, (2) to maintain and strengthen family bonds, (3) to stabilize the crisis

situation, (4) to increase the family's skills and competencies, (5) to facilitate the family's use of a variety of formal and informal helping resources, and (6) to prevent unnecessary out-of-home placement of children" (Berry, 2005; Downs et al., 2009; Piccola & Tracy 2008; Tracy, 1995; Tracy, Haapala, Kinney, & Pecora, 1991, p. 1).

In past decades, working with families usually involved focusing on protecting the child. This, in turn, often meant removing the child from the home. Services were then provided in a segmented manner by a variety of workers. For example, consider an alleged case of child abuse. One protective services intake worker would gather the intake data when the child was initially referred. Another outreach protective services worker would provide services to the family. Still another would work with the foster family if the child was placed there. And so it went.

Family preservation, in contrast, emphasizes service provision to the family unit in a more coordinated fashion. For instance, one worker might do the majority of the engagement, assessment, planning, intervention, evaluation, and termination. The child is likely to remain in the home during the entire process. All services are provided or coordinated by a designated worker with the intent of helping the intact family solve its range of problems. Service can be "provided by a treatment team" proceeding with a coordinated and unified effort, with the team "often made up of case manager, worker/therapist, and such support staff as the parent educator, homemaker, and so on" (Berg, 1994, p. 5).

Key Themes in Family Preservation

At least 11 themes tend to characterize family preservation programs (Berry, 2005; Downs et al., 2009; Maluccio, 1990, pp. 23–25; Piccola & Tracy, 2008). They include:

1. *Crisis orientation:* Family preservation is based on intervention when a crisis is taking place within the home. Workers can then take advantage of the family's motivation to alleviate the stress it's experiencing.
2. *Focus on family:* The family is all-important; it is considered the optimum place for children to remain. All intervention emphasis is directed toward keeping the family together and strengthening its members.
3. *Home-based services:* Services are provided in the home whenever possible. The ongoing thrust is improving the home environment.
4. *Time limits:* Because family preservation workers intervene during times of crisis, they work quickly. The intervention process in most models ranges from 4 to 12 weeks, although some extend longer than that. Setting time limits helps workers and their clients evaluate progress regularly.
5. *Limited, focused objectives:* All intervention objectives are clearly specified. The primary goal is to alleviate the crisis situation and strengthen the family unit so that a crisis is less likely to erupt again.
6. *Intensive, comprehensive services:* Workers' time and attention are concentrated on the families and their progress. Workers may spend as much as 20–25 hours each week arranging for resources and providing services (e.g., problem solving, counseling, and parenting skills education).
7. *Emphasis on education and skill building:* The family preservation approach is a positive one.

It assumes that people are capable of learning and can improve if they are given appropriate information and support.

8. *Coordination:* Because intervention is intensive and numerous resources may be involved, coordination is very important. Sometimes other service providers and specialists are involved with a case, requiring coordination of treatment efforts.
9. *Flexibility:* Each family is different, having varying problems and needs. Flexibility enables practitioners to match a wide range of services and resources with the individual family's needs.
10. *Accessibility:* Workers in family preservation must be readily accessible to families in crisis. Their work is intensive and time-limited. Workers' caseloads typically are small so they can concentrate their efforts.
11. *Accountability:* Accountability is the obligation of justifying one's work by accomplishing identified goals. The emphasis on focused objectives and time-limited interventions enhances workers' ability to evaluate their effectiveness.

The family preservation approach is expensive because workers have small caseloads; therefore, the ratio of worker salary to number of cases is high. For example, consider a worker being paid $36,000 per year who works with 12 families over the entire year. The cost of her salary is about $3,000 per family. Another worker serving in a more traditional child welfare capacity might have 90 cases in a year. The cost of her salary per case is only about $400. This is a bit oversimplified, but you probably get the idea.

Case Example   The following case illustrates how the themes just described might be employed in practice. (They are noted in italics.) Mary Jo, age 24, is the mother of three children—Ralphie, Sherry, and Jenna, ages 6, 4, and 3, respectively. Mary Jo has had a long, traumatic history of drug abuse and involvement with violent men. At her lowest point, high on crack, she was beaten bloody by her latest boyfriend and taken to the hospital emergency room. Her children, who had been removed from the home several times because of her neglect related to substance abuse, were taken from the home again. Mary Jo was told that unless she successfully underwent substance abuse treatment, she was not getting her children back.

It was a rough year, but she made it. She successfully completed a tough inpatient program and remained off crack. At the end of the year, she was desperate to get her children back. She was identified as a good potential recipient of family preservation services due to the *crisis* of trying to get her kids back and learning the skills she needed to do so. Edria was assigned as her social worker.

With a small caseload of two families, Edria was able to *focus on the family* and provide Mary Jo and her children with *intensive, comprehensive services.* Primary problems involved Mary Jo's homemaking abilities, child management skills, budgeting capability, and anger management. All three children were unruly and difficult to control, but only Ralphie was dangerous. He had set a number of fires and had threatened Mary Jo with a knife on three occasions.

Edria provided *home-based services* because she needed to help Mary Jo work out problems immediately when they occurred in her home environment. She also had to be *flexible* because of Mary Jo's unique set of needs. Edria focused on *education and skill building.* She helped Mary Jo work out a child behavior management program that identified negative behaviors requiring change and specified new, more appropriate behaviors to be established. Edria also worked with Mary Jo to teach her more effective responses to the children's behavior to enable her to regain control. One facet of this involved anger control, whereby Mary Jo developed a new awareness of her previously uncontrolled emotions and new, more appropriate responses to the children's behavior. For example, she replaced erratic physical punishment with a more methodical system involving positive and negative consequences. Edria also helped Mary Jo develop better household management and budgeting skills.

Edria established *limited, focused objectives* with Mary Jo concerning each area of skill development. The relatively high cost of treatment emphasized that Edria must be *accountable* for achieving these objectives. Because her time with Mary Jo was intensive, she also had to establish *time limits* within which objectives would be achieved. Edria's time was expensive, and she couldn't work with Mary Jo forever. But while she was working with Mary Jo, Edria had to be readily *accessible.* If a behavioral crisis occurred at 9:30 PM on a Saturday night, Edria needed to be available to help.

One other aspect of Edria's work with Mary Jo involved *coordination.* Remember that Ralphie had exhibited some fairly serious behavioral problems.

In addition to the child behavior management program being implemented at home, he was also receiving individual therapy provided by another social worker specializing in child counseling. Edria needed to coordinate objectives and progress between this therapist and the home program.

This turned out to be a successful intervention. Mary Jo regained substantial control over her children's behavior, although they never became perfect angels. Ralphie no longer threatened her or exhibited dangerous behavior. Mary Jo had immensely improved control of her temper. Finally, Mary Jo was running the household more effectively, including paying her bills and balancing her checkbook. She still hated to dust and hoped to win the lottery, but she was maintaining a status quo. The family was together and relatively happy. Edria went on to another case. That was a hard part of the job—leaving a family after becoming so involved. However, she wished Mary Jo the best and knew that tomorrow would be just as action packed when she started out with a new family preservation case.

Child Day Care

Child day care is an agency or program that provides supervision and care for children while parents or guardians are at work or otherwise unavailable. It is critical for many families because the majority of women work outside the home (U.S. Census Bureau, 2010). For instance, almost 59% of married mothers with infants under age 1 year are employed outside the home (U.S. Census Bureau, 2007). Almost 68% of single mothers and 61.6% of married mothers who have children under age 6 work outside the home (U.S. Census Bureau, 2010).

Although not all day care centers employ social workers, practitioners often work with clients requiring day care and must help them with referrals. This is especially true because Temporary Assistance for Needy Families (TANF) requires that parents receiving public assistance get training and find work. (TANF, described in Chapter 8, is the program replacing Aid to Families with Dependent Children that "provides cash assistance based on need, income, resources, and family sizes" [Dolgoff & Feldstein, 2009, p. 216]). Social workers may also have to help parents find high-quality day care.

Many types of day care are available. Downs and her colleagues (2009) describe the various forms of day care that are most common and the advantages and disadvantages of each. In about 67% of all working families with preschoolers, family members provide day care. Each parent takes turns caring for children while the other is working outside the home, or relatives such as grandparents or siblings provide supervision.

Outside the family, day care is provided in three basic ways. First, parents can hire someone such as a baby-sitter or a nanny to come into their home and provide care, which about 5% of working families with preschoolers do. Although most parents prefer this option, it's too expensive to be practical for many families. Second, parents can take their children to the care providers' homes for supervision. This is referred to as *family day care* and is used by 11% of families with preschoolers. Third, larger, organized day care centers in addition to preschool and Head Start programs can provide care. Over a third of all families use these larger settings. (Note that all of these numbers add up to over 100% because many families use multiple sources of day care.)

Almost two-thirds of preschoolers and almost 70% of school-aged children are in some type of day care arrangement; school-aged children are in care including that provided "by relatives, day care homes, enrichment activities, and school-based programs" (Downs et al., 2009, p. 55). Downs and her colleagues (2009) elaborate:

> The type of arrangement parents make varies with the age of the child.... Preschoolers are more apt to be cared for by relatives than nonrelatives. About a quarter of all preschoolers are cared for in day care centers, with smaller percentages cared for in day care homes or at home by babysitters. Preschool-aged children of working mothers spend long hours in day care, with an average of 32 hours per week.
>
> Once children reach school-age, the time spent in school accounts for much of their time while their parent is working. However, grade school-aged children also need supplementary care.... As children get older, self-care during nonschool hours becomes more likely. (p. 55)

Advantages of family day care include a small caregiver-to-child ratio, proximity to the home, and opportunities to develop a closer relationship with the caregiver.

A chief disadvantage of family day care is that the vast majority of such care is unregulated and the caregiver unsupervised; another disadvantage is that the caregiver probably lacks formal training in

how to provide educational opportunities for children.

Day care centers can serve from 15 to 300 children, although they average about 60. Advantages include being licensed under state supervision, usually having staff trained in child supervision and early education, and being able to provide a wider range of opportunities and activities than what's available in family day care. Disadvantages may include increased impersonality due to size, lack of parental knowledge of their children's individual caregivers, strict and inflexible hours, inconvenient locations, and restrictions regarding care for infants or sick children. Highlight 9.4 discusses variables involved generally in the quality of day care.

Other Supportive Services

Many other supportive services are clustered under the child welfare umbrella. They are not necessarily jobs assumed by social workers. However, because the broker role in social work is so important, practitioners must be aware of and knowledgeable about these services to be able to provide clients with appropriate referrals. Examples of other supportive services include family life education and respite care.

Family Life Education

Family life education (FLE) involves group learning experiences for the purpose of increasing people's knowledge, developing skills, or enhancing self-awareness concerning issues and crises relevant at some point during the life span (Harris, 2008; National Council on Family Relations, 2011; Riley, 1995). Several aspects of this definition are important. First, FLE is a group experience. The context usually involves a social worker or other professional providing information for 6 to 12 group members; weekly meetings last from one and a half to two hours and are held over a one- to eight-week period (Barker, 2003).

A second aspect of the definition involves the purpose of these meetings. Because they may address either normal developmental or specific crisis issues, they may be appropriate for almost anyone, depending on people's learning needs. Four categories of FLE groups are (1) normal development, (2) crisis, (3) personal growth, and (4) life adjustment groups (Riley, 1995).

Normal development groups provide information about various normal life stages. Examples include

HIGHLIGHT 9.4

What Makes for High-Quality Day Care?

EP 2.1.5b

The quality of day care varies dramatically among day care providers; the following variables are associated with high-quality day care (Clarke-Stewart, Gruber, & Fitzgerald, 1994; Downs et al., 2009; Papalia, Olds, & Feldman, 2009; Santrock, 2009):

- Well-trained caregivers who can provide educational experiences to enhance social, emotional, and intellectual development.
- A well-structured program that provides multiple growth opportunities unavailable at home.
- A low caregiver-to-child ratio that allows for greater interaction and attention.
- A safe, positively oriented environment where well-trained caregivers display positive characteristics "such as warmth, sensitivity, and responsiveness" and provide "stimulating interactions," which are

so "crucial to early cognitive, linguistic, and psychosocial development" (Papalia et al., 2009, p. 205).
- Sufficient chances to interact positively with other children.
- A physical environment that's interesting and thought-provoking.

In contrast, the worst day care provides no more than custodial care that gives children only the bare necessities of supervision and physical care. Crosson-Tower (2009) indicates that characteristics of good day care such as low caregiver-to-child ratios and stimulating environments have higher costs. She warns that "a two-tier system" may be developing, one for the middle-class and rich, and another for the poor (Crosson-Tower, 2009, p. 139; Scarr, 1998, p.105). The implication is that "more public support" should be provided "for child care so that quality services can be made available to any working family" (Crosson-Tower, 2009, p. 139).

---

sexuality, premarital and marital education, and parenting education programs (Harris, 2008). *Crisis groups* are oriented toward people facing a serious life turning point or upheaval. Often these people are unprepared for the crisis and require information and help to cope. Examples of such crises are serious illness, divorce, recent death of a loved one, and loss of a job. Group leaders usually must give members emotional support in addition to information.

Personal growth groups help people develop specified social skills. They are unlike crisis groups because there's no sudden upheaval involved, and they differ from life adjustment groups because members are not striving to cope with a chronic problem. Rather, group members have in common the interest of improving themselves in some way. Examples are groups focusing on assertiveness training, time management, and communication skills.

Life adjustment groups help people who are dealing with some ongoing problematic issue. Most often, group members are coping with a crisis of their own or of someone close to them. This differs from a crisis group because it focuses on long-term issues instead of temporary crises. Examples are parents of children with a chronic illness or developmental

disability, caregivers for older adults with Alzheimer's disease, and adults with Parkinson's disease.[3]

Respite Care

Respite care is supervision of a child by another caregiver, allowing the parent an interval of relief from the responsibilities of child care. In essence, it gives the individual a break, a brief time during which the caregiver is free from stressful responsibilities. It allows an opportunity for parents to run errands or simply to relax. Some agencies use volunteers to provide respite care; others have programs in which parents can drop children off and have them be supervised for a few hours (Mather lagera, & Harrisa, 2007). One of this chapter's opening vignettes, involving Corazon and Juanita, provides an example of a situation in which respite care would be appropriate.

Note that respite care can apply not only to parents but also to other caregivers with primary responsibility for a dependent. For example, respite

---

[3]*Parkinson's disease* is a neurological illness causing deterioration of brain cells and characterized by "tremors, especially of the fingers and hands, muscle rigidity, and a shuffling gait" (Nichols, 1999, p. 961).

care might be provided to a person caring for a spouse dying of a rapidly debilitating disease. It might also apply to an adult child caring for an aging parent who has limited mobility.

An Ongoing Macro Issue: Advocacy for Resources

EP 2.1.8a

Social workers live and struggle with many issues in providing supportive services to children and families. This book reflects only the tip of the iceberg. Children are indeed a population-at-risk, and social workers have a responsibility to advocate on their behalf. *Advocacy*, of course, involves taking an active, directive role on behalf of a client or client group in need of help. One important aspect of child advocacy is the acknowledgment and support of the basic rights of children. The concern for children's rights can be considered on a universal level; that is, every child should have certain specific rights such as the right to adequate food, clothing, shelter, and a decent home environment.

In an era of shrinking and competitive resources, ongoing advocacy is necessary for the following:

- Quality, accessible day care for children of working parents.
- Improved maternal and child health care in view of the high proportion of low-birth-weight babies (Law 2011).
- Better prevention and treatment programs to address child maltreatment.
- Welfare reform to raise families' income levels above the poverty line.

Substitute Services

Earlier we established that substitute services are those replacing

> *another family for the child's own family, so that someone else takes over all aspects of the parental role on a temporary or permanent basis. Such a change is necessary when the home presents deficiencies so serious that even intensive home-based preventive services cannot assist the family in providing the child with minimally adequate social, emotional, or physical care.*

(Kadushin & Martin, 1988, p. 344)

When the best attempts at providing supportive services to maintain children in a healthy family environment do not work, alternative living arrangements for the children become necessary. These substitute family environments then give children the supervision, shelter, food, and clothing required to meet their daily needs. Figure 9.1 portrayed the continuum of care from supportive to substitute services.

Children are removed from their parents' care for a number of reasons. Parents may be unable to care for children because of their own serious illness, physical disability, emotional immaturity, intellectual disability, or substance abuse. They may neglect, abandon, or abuse their children. Children may have such serious developmental, emotional, or physical disabilities that parents are incapable of caring for them. Finally, there may not be sufficient community resources to provide the necessary supportive services to keep children in their own homes.

Length of removal depends on the severity of problems in the home environment and the extent to which it can be strengthened to allow the children's safe return. Changing a child's living environment often involves a change in *legal custody*—formal assumption of caregiving responsibilities for a child, including meeting that child's daily needs.[4]

A guiding principle is to keep children in the *least restrictive* setting in which they can function with the greatest amount of independence. The overriding goal is to have children return to a normal family and community environment if at all possible.

EP 2.1.10g

Substitute care services can be placed on a continuum reflecting their intensity of supervision and restrictiveness. This continuum of care for children and adolescents ranges from supportive services for families with children remaining in their own homes to removal from the home and placement in a formal treatment setting. Pecora and his colleagues (2010) reflect:

> *It is useful to conceptualize child welfare as a comprehensive continuum of services with a strong preventive component. Each child welfare service tries*

---

[4]Note that legal custody may also involve granting responsibility to a caregiver for persons who are not children but who cannot function independently. Examples include people with severe intellectual disabilities and older adults with serious mental incapacities.

to prevent the use of a more intensive and intrusive service, and child welfare services in the aggregate endeavor to prevent the transition of children into more restrictive services like juvenile justice. (p. 68)

Proch and Taber (1987, pp. 9–10) rank children's placement from the least restrictive to most restrictive as follows (see Figure 9.2):

- Home of parent (rank 1).
- Home of relative (2).
- Foster family home (3).
- Specialized foster family home (4).
- Group home (5).
- Private child welfare institution (6).
- Shelter (7).
- Mental health facility (8).
- Correctional facility (9).

A theme characterizing substitute services is *permanency planning*—"a comprehensive care planning process directed toward the goal of a permanent, stable home for a child [placed in substitute care]" (Rycus, Hughes, & Ginther, 1988, p. 45). Children need a stable, healthy home environment. Being bounced from temporary home to temporary home does not contribute to emotional stability. Therefore, an ultimate goal of substitute care is to give children permanent homes.

Types of substitute services discussed here include kinship care, foster family care, residential placements, and adoption.

Kinship Care

One type of out-of-home placement involves relatives or part of the child's family's supportive network, in what is referred to as *kinship care*. There

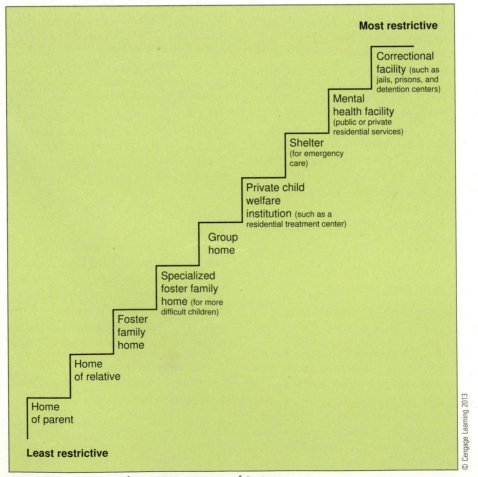

Figure 9.2 Continuum of Care: Restrictiveness of Setting

© Cengage Learning 2013

are positive reasons for placing children with people who are already close to them:

> *Family strengths often include a kinship network that functions as a support system. The kinship support system may be composed of nuclear family, extended family, blended family, foster family, or adoptive family members or members of tribes or clans. The involvement of kin may stabilize family situations, ensure the protection of children, and prevent the need to separate children from their families and place them in the formal child welfare system.*
>
> (Child Welfare League of America, 1994, p. 1)

Informal kinship care involves families taking children in without intervention by social service agencies. In *formal* kinship care, a social services agency gains legal custody of a child and places that child in a kinship home, which it licenses. The agency pays the caregivers and is expected to monitor the home's compliance with standards to oversee the child's well-being.

Foster Family Care

Foster family care is the provision of substitute care with a family for a planned temporary or extended period when parents or legal guardians are unable to care for a child. Foster care involves a serious placement decision when a family is in such crisis that adequate care for children in their own home is impossible.

At least four basic principles underlie foster care (Crosson-Tower, 2009; Downs et al., 2009; Everett, 2008; Pecora et al., 2010). First, the child's own family is important to the child, so that home environment should be maintained if at all possible. Therefore, supportive services should be provided to keep the child in the home. If the child still must be removed from the home, efforts should be made to maintain communication between children and parents to support and maintain the parent–child relationship. Second, when the child must be removed from the home, the foster care placement should provide a healthy, nurturing environment until the child is placed in a permanent family setting. Third, the child's own family should be viewed as the client system, with the child's return to a safe, healthy family environment a primary goal. In the event that a return to the family of origin is not viable, a plan for permanent placement should be developed either through adoption by a foster family

or for independent living if the child is old enough (Everett, 2008). Fourth, foster parents or child care staff in group homes are viewed as an important part of the treatment team working together toward the goal of permanent placement. Highlight 9.5 discusses some reasons children require foster family care.

Types of Foster Family Homes

Depending on their circumstances, children should be placed in the type of foster family care that best serves their needs. At least four types of foster family care reflect special circumstances for children needing more specific types of care—shelter homes, long-term foster homes, specialized foster homes, and treatment foster care (Downs et al., 2009, pp. 299–300). *Shelter homes* provide a transitory haven for children during assessment and placement. *Long-term foster homes* offer an ongoing residence for children unable to return to their parents' home and unadoptable for various reasons. One is that parents refuse to give up guardianship, as in Devin's case in Highlight 9.5. (*Guardianship* is the legal responsibility to care for another person and oversee that person's affairs. A child's guardian assumes decision-making responsibilities, such as giving consent for major surgery. This differs from custody, whereby the custodian is responsible only for daily care.) Other children aren't adopted because they have serious disabilities or health problems that adoptive parents couldn't afford. Additionally, there is often a shortage of people seeking to adopt children who are not infants.

Specialized foster homes serve children with special needs, such as intellectual disabilities or conditions such as fetal alcohol syndrome[5] or being infected with HIV. Other specialized homes prepare older children for living independently. Finally, *treatment foster care* provides specialized treatment for children with serious behavioral and emotional problems. The idea here is that a family setting offers a less restrictive environment than a group home or institution for children requiring more structured behavioral management. Parents in such homes need specialized training to provide children with a therapeutic experience.

---

[5]Fetal alcohol syndrome (FAS) is "a condition in a fetus characterized by abnormal growth, neurological damage, and facial distortion caused by the mother's heavy alcohol consumption" (Kelly, 2001, p. 567).

HIGHLIGHT 9.5

Reasons for Foster Family Care

Children need foster family care for various reasons (Crosson-Tower, 2009). The family might have an emergency such as a sudden illness or accident. Parents might be under such stress that they cannot care for their children adequately and desperately require relief. They may need time to address their problems and issues such as homelessness or substance abuse. Children may have to be temporarily removed from the home for their own safety because of abuse or neglect. Foster care may reflect a temporary placement to provide residence for the child before more permanent placement in an institution or adoption. The following are examples of reasons for placing children in foster care (Crosson-Tower, 2009):[6]

Example A: Cindy, a mother of five children, had heart disease. Although her physician told her to stop, she continued to have children because her religious beliefs prohibited her from using contraception. She had five more but died of a heart attack during the birth of her 10th child. Devin, her husband, was overwhelmed at being left alone with 10 children and began to drink. As an alcoholic, he relinquished his children to foster care but refused to give them up permanently for adoption.

Example B: Felicia, age 15, was a serious student who wanted to go to college. Unfortunately, her mother, Mystique, who was quite unstable and into drugs, was vacillating emotionally between two men—her current boyfriend and her ex-husband. As a result, Mystique moved from one man to the other every six months or so, dragging Felicia with her. Because this forced Felicia to keep switching schools and school districts, her grades began to fall. Seriously depressed, she longed for some stability. Finally, at her wit's end, she slit her wrists in the girls' locker room at school. Her school social worker called protective services, and Felicia was placed in a foster home. Much relieved, Felicia was happy in her new environment, finished school, and applied to college. She still maintained regular contact with Mystique.

Example C: Mariko, a single mother, was shocked to find out she had colon cancer. The prognosis was fair to good if she had surgery immediately and underwent the subsequent radiation and chemotherapy. But what would she do with her two children April, age 2, and Mac, age 4, during recovery? Mariko's family lived in a different state, and she had no friends able to care for her children. She decided to place them in foster care until she recovered.

_____

[6]These examples are loosely based on those provided by Crosson-Tower. Details and facts concerning the cases have been changed.

Social Work Roles in Foster Family Care

EP 2.1.1c

Social workers in foster care fulfill various functions. Before foster home placement, a worker must first carefully assess the risk in the child's own family to determine the necessity of removal from the home. The worker must conclude that supportive services will be unable to sustain the children and their family in the home environment.

Second, when a foster care placement is necessary, the worker must select the best available foster home. This should be "the least restrictive, most homelike environment possible," one that best meets the child's "particular physical, emotional and social needs" (Rycus et al., 1988, p. 55). For example, it's best to place children closer to their own homes to encourage involvement of the natural parents. Also, the fewer changes (e.g., a different school or lifestyle) the child is forced to experience, the better. The social worker also must assess the child's needs and "anticipated behavior problems" to place the child with a foster family that can best meet those needs (p. 55).

Throughout the foster care preplacement, placement, and postplacement process, the social worker fulfills a third function: case management. Coordinating services might require home visits, contacting schools regarding the child's performance, and dealing with crises such as children running away or natural and foster parents arguing.

The fourth function for foster care workers involves counseling and helping the children, natural parents, and foster parents prepare for changes, adjust to new circumstances, and work toward the children's return to the natural home. The worker should convey clear information about what's happening to all of them and encourage them to ask questions. The worker should also strive to develop "a supportive relationship" with children to help them deal with changes (Rycus et al., 1988, p. 58).

Children often are frightened of the unknown and worry about what will happen to them. They naturally experience a torrent of emotions including rejection, self-blame, anger, despair, depression, and apprehension. The worker may need to help a child verbalize such feelings to deal with them. For instance, a worker might say, "You look like you're about ready to cry. You probably feel really sad right now, and that's OK. You can cry if you like. I have lots of tissues," or, "I know how mad you are about having to move. It's a hard time, and it's OK to feel mad" (Rycus et al., 1988, p. 65). Regardless of how their parents treated them or what mistakes their parents made, children usually continue to care about their parents.

For example, one worker, Jannah, explained how difficult it was for her to work with Angel, a 9-year-old child in foster care (Crosson-Tower, 2009).[7] Before each of her mother's scheduled visits, Jannah would prepare Angel for her mother's visit by talking about how Angel felt toward her mother and what Angel might realistically expect during the visit. As the meeting time approached, Angel would eagerly await her mother by sitting at the front window, watching for her mother's car to pull in the driveway. Sometimes her mother would show up, but more frequently she wouldn't. Then Jannah had to watch Angel bite her lower lip and try to keep from crying in disappointment. Watching Angel's intense pain would infuriate Jannah. However, Jannah forced herself to remember that Angel deeply loved her mother and that their relationship was one of the most important things in Angel's life.

Foster care workers also counsel the birth parents. Sometimes goals involve teaching effective parenting skills and decreasing or controlling stressful life issues (e.g., poverty, substance abuse, social isolation, interpersonal conflict, mental illness). Other times, workers focus on maintaining the parent–child relationship, for several reasons (Crosson-Tower, 2009). It has been found that children adjust better to foster care when they maintain contact with their birth parents. They experience less trauma upon the initial separation. Ongoing involvement with their children may be part of the treatment process for the birth parents. Watching foster parents effectively interact with children may teach birth parents improved parenting and child management skills. Last, such ongoing contact may facilitate the transition of children returning home in the event that reunion occurs. When children do return home, foster care workers can provide counseling and careful supervision to the birth parents.

Additionally, foster care workers counsel foster parents. This might involve preparing foster parents for a new foster child by providing information or helping foster parents integrate the child into their own family system. Foster care workers help foster parents develop effective ways of handling foster children and attending to their individual needs. These workers also must help foster parents deal with the grief they experience when foster children to whom they're especially attached return home. Finally, foster care workers can act as mediators between birth parents and foster parents.

Case Example   Jamie, age 13, had lived with his foster parents, Millie and Mert Muffin, since he was 6 months old. The Muffins, who had two other adult children of their own, dearly loved Jamie and considered him an integral member of their family. He also had an ongoing relationship with his birth parents, Jack and Jill Smith, whom he visited every other Sunday. The Smiths had five other children, all older than Jamie.

During his first few months of life, Jamie suffered from a condition called *failure to thrive*, where an infant remains "below the third percentile for weight for a period of time" or demonstrates a significant decrease in the "rate of gaining weight from the time of birth" (Bukatko & Daehler, 2012, p. 181). Despite intensive medical attention, Jamie didn't improve. The Smiths had been involved with their county social services before because of neglect concerning their other children. After a child protective services assessment, the court placed Jamie in foster care with the Muffins.

Jack Smith, who had a 10th-grade education, was a janitor at a local grade school; Jill didn't work outside the home. Along with her twin sister, she

---

[7]This example is loosely based on one provided by Crosson-Tower. Details and facts concerning the case have been changed.

had been institutionalized throughout her childhood in a setting for persons with intellectual disabilities or mental illness. She had attended some high school classes but didn't graduate.

Over the years, the Smiths maintained an involvement with the social services system. All of their children had been in foster care at one time or another. Jamie's siblings all experienced difficulties in school, truancy, or skirmishes with the law. Because of the Smiths' limited ability to cope with raising their five other children, on the one hand, and the stability provided Jamie by the Muffins, on the other, Jamie remained in foster care. A pleasant, cooperative boy who loved both his families, Jamie had an intellectual disability, some congenital orthopedic problems, and poor coordination. He had always attended special education classes.

An ongoing problem was the huge discrepancy in lifestyle and values between the Smiths and the Muffins. Bill, Jamie's foster care worker, was constantly struggling to establish compromises that both families could live with. For example, Jack Smith and Millie Muffin could barely stand being in the same room with each other. Jack felt that Millie "mollycoddled" Jamie to the point of making him a "sissy." Millie thought Jack was a "macho man" who pushed Jamie into inappropriate, dangerous activities such as skateboarding and trampoline jumping—both difficult and dangerous for Jamie with his coordination problems.

Bill worked with the families to help them come to mutual agreements. One was that Jamie join a track team and a bowling league for children with intellectual disabilities. In the past, Millie wouldn't allow him to do so because she feared he'd hurt himself. Furthermore, she would not permit him to attend any activities with other children by himself, but rather stayed there with him. Reluctantly, she agreed to let him attend events alone. For his part, Jack agreed to stop encouraging Jamie to ride a skateboard and play on the trampoline. Instead, Jamie could play baseball or soccer with other children in the Smiths' neighborhood when he visited.

Another problem between the Smiths and the Muffins involved religious differences. The Muffins were Methodist, and the Smiths Roman Catholic. Each couple wanted Jamie to adopt their own faith. Bill helped both couples understand that constant bickering would do neither Jamie nor themselves any good. The reality was that, when Jamie was visiting the Smiths, he would attend the Catholic church with them regardless of what the Muffins requested.

Similarly, when he was with the Muffins, he would attend the Methodist church with them regardless of what the Smiths said. Bill helped the couples agree that this arrangement should continue, given that it was what they would do anyway. When Jamie grew older, he could choose his own faith.

The Smiths and the Muffins would never be best friends. However, Bill helped them realize that both families had Jamie's best interests at heart, despite their radical differences. Bill stressed this as a strength. He also worked with both families to help them focus on Jamie's future. As Jamie entered adolescence, he needed to realize his own capabilities and make his own decisions to the fullest extent possible. Bill discussed with both families the value of vocational aptitude testing—another means of emphasizing Jamie's strengths to best prepare him for his future.

An Important Trends in Foster Care: Permanency Planning and Family Preservation

Crosson-Tower (2009) comments on current trends in foster care that focus on permanency planning.

At one time the only apparent options for permanency for a child were family reunification or adoption. Today alternatives are considered. For example, there is now extensive exploration of the child's extended family as a potential placement alternative. Kinship care . . . is a viable plan for children whose parents cannot care for them but who can find a home with relatives, godparents, or close family friends. This trend may have gained strength from minority families who are connected with their own culture and extended families and who, in the past, have solved child care problems within their own familial circle. However, as increased stressors are placed on these families and they begin to look to the dominant culture to solve more of their problems, formalized kinship agreements may become more effective.

The nature of adoption has also changed. In contrast to the closed adoptions of the past, adoptions may now be arranged according to the child's needs. Open adoption, in which the child maintains contact with the birth parents and/or the foster parents, provides children with more consistency while still offering permanence. Subsidized adoptions [where additional funds are provided to adoptive parents for children who have special needs or characteristics that make it difficult for them to be adopted] by adoptive or foster parents help fund stable homes for children whose medical or emotional needs, and the financial obligation inherent in meeting these needs, may have formerly [interfered with or prohibited] . . . their ability to be adopted.

Finally, permanent foster homes or guardianship arrangements make it possible for many children to have more consistency in their lives. Such arrangement might not have been sanctioned in the past, but today there is greater emphasis on children's needs. (pp. 331–332)

Residential Settings: Group Homes, Treatment Centers, and Independent Living Arrangements

Residential settings reflect greater intensity and restrictiveness on the substitute care continuum than foster family care. They can be more beneficial for some troubled children than their own family environment in several ways. According to the Child Welfare League of America (2005, p. 1):

Residential care's primary purpose is to address the unique needs of children and youth who require more intensive services than a family setting can provide. Either on-site or through links with community programs, residential services provide educational, medical, psychiatric, and clinical/mental health services, as well as case management and recreation. . . . Within residential settings, children and their families are offered a variety of services, such as therapy, counseling, education, recreation, health, nutrition, daily living skills, pre-independent living skills, reunification services, aftercare, and advocacy.

Residential facilities may demonstrate advantages for some children in a number of ways (Crosson-Tower, 2009; Downs et al., 2009). First, they can provide a treatment *milieu* (an all-encompassing environmental setting), in which rules for how to behave are more clearly specified than in most families, thus providing greater structure. This, in turn, allows for more consistency and predictability in the children's living environment. Many residents feel safer in this more controlled setting.

Second, in most settings children interact with multiple caregivers instead of one or two parents. This allows children to experience less intensive interactions in a less concentrated emotional and interpersonal environment.

Third, the treatment milieu provides a "group living experience, where children and youths learn to develop responsibility to the group and to develop and improve relational skills and behavior and where peer pressure can have a positive impact" (Cohen, 1992, p. 59).

Fourth, children in residential settings often come with unique histories reflecting wide ranges of behavior. Stein (1995) explains:

They come with histories of lying, stealing, fighting, truancy, breaking things, hurting people, and running away. They come with tales of sexual abuse by parents, stepparents, relatives, and live-ins. They come with tales of beatings and confinements in closets and being tied up. They come from parents who yell at them constantly but never discipline them, from homes in which they could do no wrong, and from homes in which they were barely noticed.

There are those who fight the program every step of the way, those who have to be pushed or dragged through the program, and those who are so proud of their accomplishments you think they're going to burst. There are those who seem to do everything right, but you wonder what's really going on in their heads. (p. 17)

The residential milieu is oriented to addressing a wide range of emotional and behavioral issues. Therefore, it is designed to tolerate and deal with a wider range of negative behaviors, individualize treatment plans, and attend to children's diverse needs. Conversely, in families, similar rules and expectations often apply to everyone, and more extreme forms of troublesome behavior are unacceptable.

Highlight 9.6 describes scenarios in which children require placement in a residential setting.

Residential settings discussed here include group homes, residential treatment centers, and independent living services. Because most group homes and residential treatment centers are oriented toward mental health, their therapeutic aspects will be discussed in Chapter 13. Correctional facilities for youths that involve incarceration are, of course, the most restrictive on the service continuum. Chapter 16 discusses these further.

Group Homes

Group homes provide greater structure and more intensive therapeutic care than that found in foster family homes. A group home provides a substitute setting

HIGHLIGHT 9.6

Who Is Placed in Residential Settings?

Three examples reflect the types of behavior typically leading to placement in a residential setting.

Example A: Robert, age 13, already has a long record of criminal offenses, including theft, assault, and drug possession. He also has flunked several courses at school, having been truant most of the time. Robert lives with his parents, who are alcoholics and have a history of physically abusing him. Because he tends to fly into vicious rages at the least provocation, foster care is not a viable option. The juvenile court has ordered that Robert be placed in a residential facility.

Example B: Bree, age 15, constantly fights with her parents. She refuses to go to school, screaming that she hates it. When her parents try to force her to go by driving her there themselves, she leaves school anyway and runs away for several days. She smokes marijuana regularly and has started using crack cocaine. She likes to date men in their 20s and has been sexually active since age 12. Her parents are

at a loss as to what to do. The school social worker suggests residential placement.

Example C: Jaron, age 9, stabbed his 6-year-old sister to death. He has a long history of torturing and killing small animals. He has also set several fires in the home that, fortunately, were discovered before major damage was done. He frequently threatens to kill his parents and schoolmates. People around him including his parents fear that he means it. He is referred to a residential treatment center for young children with serious emotional disturbance and behavioral problems.

Each child is unique, so each placement decision must be made based on the problems and needs involved in that particular case. On one hand, children should be placed in the least restrictive setting. On the other, children require placement that can respond to the severity of their problems and the intensity of the supervision required.

---

and family environment for a group of children originating in different families. A small-group context allows residents to benefit from the group experience, yet still receive enough individual attention and treatment. The actual physical structure of a group home is usually a sizable single-family dwelling that blends into a residential neighborhood. Depending on the residents' needs, it can be staffed either by a live-in married couple or by counselors who work various shifts, "including overnight staff who are awake" (Stein, 1995, p. 357).

Group homes provide more structure than foster family homes but less than residential treatment centers. Thus they allow more "space" for adolescents seeking independence than for those living with their parents while providing consistent expectations and rules. Residents are expected to attend school, do assigned chores, and participate in counseling as specified in their treatment plans.

Residential Treatment Centers

Residential treatment centers are bigger agencies that are more structured and therefore more restrictive than smaller group home settings. They

typically consist of either larger dormitory settings or a series of smaller units or cottages forming one center. Each has its own supervising staff and assigns juvenile residents according to such variables as age and type of problem. Structured expectations usually revolve around a behavior management system based on behavior modification approaches. Highlight 9.7 describes the staff working in residential treatment centers.

Independent Living Services

An alternative available to older adolescents fast approaching adulthood is independent living services. These serve as a transitional residence between out-of-home placement and entrance into adulthood with its onerous responsibilities. Independent living services aim to prepare young people to function independently in society. Services focus on helping them develop skills they can use in their personal and work worlds. These include decision—making, budgeting, and planning skills to organize their lives; educational, vocational, and job search skills to establish a career; and interpersonal skills to develop and maintain relationships.

HIGHLIGHT 9.7

Who Works in Residential Treatment Centers?

Residential treatment centers have various responsibilities concerning residents' care and treatment (Crosson-Tower, 2009; Stein, 1995). Basic needs such as food and shelter must, of course, be met, so staff are employed to prepare food and to maintain the building and grounds. Supervisors and administrators oversee service provision, making certain that children are treated appropriately and that treatment plans are carried out. Designated medical staff must be available (although usually not on-site) to meet health and dental needs.

Residential staff attend to the children's daily care and supervise them when they're not in school. Sometimes referred to as counselors or child care workers, residential staff oversee daily living activities, implement treatment plans, and monitor behavior.

Residents' educational needs must also be met. Most children in residential treatment centers are lagging academically. Either their problems have consumed their energy, leaving little or none for academics, or they have long histories of truancy. And once they fall behind in school, there is little incentive to work hard because, compared with their peers, they look and feel like academic failures. Although some residents may attend public school, many remain on-site for their education. The center's

educational staff assess children's abilities and develop individualized educational plans designed to maximize each student's ability to succeed.

Treatment staff attend to the children's emotional and behavioral needs. Stein (1995) explains:

> The behavior of children is a major concern in residential treatment and likely to consume considerable time and effort, regardless of the philosophical or treatment orientation of the program. No matter what their other problems may be, it is problems with their behavior that most often bring children into residential treatment. (p. 107)

Social workers, psychologists, and other therapists assess problems and strengths, develop treatment plans, provide individual and group counseling, and work with the other staff components to coordinate services and monitor children's progress. They may also make home visits and do family counseling. Group treatment is very important in residential treatment centers because peer pressure is so significant for children and adolescents. Additionally, most treatment plans involve improving interpersonal relationships. Groups can focus on managing anger, eliminating substance abuse, improving communication and social relationships, or dealing with issues resulting from victimization.

Adoption

Adoption is the legal act of taking in a child born to other parents and formally making that child a full member of the family. Adoptive parents take on all the rights and responsibilities given to birth parents or other former legal guardians, who relinquish all rights concerning that child.

Types of Adoption

Adoptions are undertaken either by people related to a child by blood or by unrelated adoptive parents. Examples of *blood-related adoptions* include a stepparent married to a birth parent adopting the birth parent's child, grandparents adopting their daughter's child, and other relatives adopting a child born into some branch of their own family.

Unrelated adoptions occur when the adoptive parents have no prior blood link to the child being adopted. *Agency* (or *relinquishment*) *adoptions* are conducted through a public or private social service

organization, with the agency contracting with the adoptive parents, providing counseling, assessing the placement, and overseeing the entire adoption process. *Independent adoptions*, in contrast, are initiated and conducted independently by the adoptive and birth parents, without agency involvement. *International* or *intercountry adoptions* are those in which parents adopt children from other countries. Federal regulations that require the evaluation and acceptability of the adoptive home and proof of being orphaned govern these adoptions (Barth, 2008, p. 35).

Special needs adoptions involve children who have traditionally been more difficult to place in adoptive homes. These include children who have special characteristics or circumstances, including physical, intellectual, developmental, or emotional disabilities, racial background, or older age than is usually preferred, such that adoption is difficult without providing medical or other assistance (Barth, 2008). Sometimes such adoptions involving financial assistance are referred to as *subsidized adoptions*. Finally, *transracial adoptions* are those by parents of a different race than that of the child. For example, white parents might adopt an African American or Asian child. Highlight 9.8 stresses the importance of cultural competence for social workers in the adoption field or involved in any other aspect of practice with children and families.

The Adoption Process

Several steps are involved in the adoption process. In step 1, a child is identified as being in need of adoption. For example, children may have been removed from an extremely abusive environment, or the parents may have abandoned them or died.

In step 2, the child must be legally freed so that adoption can take place. Assistance should be given to children to ease the trauma of separation from birth parents or guardians. Similarly, they may require help in adjusting and becoming attached to the new adoptive parents. Guardianship rights of the birth parents must be formally terminated.

In step 3, adoptive parents are selected. Here the social worker conducts a home study in which potential adoptive parents are evaluated on a number of variables. These include "motivation," "stability of the relationship," "age," "physical and emotional health," and "financial stability" (Crosson-Tower, 2009, pp. 364–365).

Evaluation regarding motivation concerns the reasons why applicants want to adopt. Is it because they can't have their own children? Have they looked into the possibility of infertility treatment? Have they lost a child and are trying to replace it? Is it that they want to help some child have his or her own family? If so, to what extent will they be able to deal with this child's "baggage" in terms of the child's past problems? Investigation of the stability of the applicants' relationship is obviously important. Placing a child with people whose attachment and communication are deteriorating certainly is not in the child's best interest. The age variable concerns how "agencies usually consider applicants who are within normal child-rearing ages" (p. 365). However, the child's age is also an important aspect. For example, older children might be placed with older applicants. Because placement should be in the child's best interest, applicants should be healthy and capable of physically and emotionally caring for that child. Physical examinations are required. Additionally, "[s]ocial workers should look for

applicants who appear emotionally stable, are mature, have a good self-concept, and are able to meet a child's emotional needs" (p. 365). Applicants must also be financially stable in order to fulfill an adopted child's physical, educational, social, and other needs. "Despite these requirements [for applicants], agencies often find that they must be flexible, respectful of cultural diversity and increasingly different family values and lifestyles" (Crosson-Tower, 2009, p. 365).

In step 4, after the potential adoptive parents have been approved, the agency places the child with them. The agency social worker helps the adoptive family integrate the child into the family system.

In step 5, as Smith and Howard (1999) explain, "adoptive families undergo stresses and adjustments unique to the adoptive experience and lasting throughout the family life cycle whether the child is adopted in infancy or later" (p. 8). At least four types of agency services may be provided after placement. First, education on such issues as child behavior management can be helpful. Second, therapy may be necessary to deal with issues such as the child's grief at the loss of his or her family of origin or readjustment issues experienced by the entire adoptive family. Third, ongoing support groups may help both parents and adopted children handle emotional and relationship issues. Fourth, adoptive families may need help linking up with necessary resources (e.g., programs offering financial assistance, special education services, and therapy for children requiring special help).

Finally, in step 6, the adoption is formally legalized, and the birth parents' legal rights are terminated.

Social Work Roles in Adoption

EP 2.1.1c

Social workers assume various roles with respect to adoption. They always have the professional responsibility of advocating for children and serving children's best interests. They may help women with unwanted pregnancies evaluate their alternatives and determine the best course of action. Social workers may assess the readiness of a child for adoptive placement, especially if that child is older and has conflicting feelings about permanently leaving birth parents. Social workers may be in the position of helping children cope with their grief at bidding a final farewell to their birth family. One study revealed that adopted children often express strong

feelings of loss and abandonment…. One 6-year-old boy expressed his fear that someone would come and take him away, and talked about his nightmares,

HIGHLIGHT 9.8

Cultural Competence Issues

**EP 2.1.1e,
2.1.4a,
2.1.4b,
2.1.4c,
2.1.4d**

Children and adolescents of color are rapidly growing segments of the U.S. population (U.S. Census Bureau, 2010). Learning about clients' cultures and values is an ongoing process that social workers must continuously pursue. Henderson and Thompson (2011) explain (although they use the term "counselor," their points apply equally well to social workers):

Counselors [and social workers] will always have opportunities to work with children who have cultural practices and beliefs that the [social workers and] counselors do not know....Counselors may have communication difficulties and may misunderstand the culture and the impact of the culture on the process of counseling [and intervention]. Mental health professionals may hold mistaken assumptions about cultural assimilation [the incorporation of people from another culture into the mainstream culture] and acculturation [adapting the cultural values and expectations of the mainstream society]. The counselor and the client may have different social class values and orientations, and the counselor may be working from stereotypical generalizations. Counselors may make an assumption of cultural bias and may not be able to understand the [client's] worldview [a person's perceptions about how the world should function] (p. 41; Baruth & Manning, 2007)

Henderson and Thompson (2011) continue:

Children's lives reflect the culture in which they are raised. The rich, varied landscape of the United States includes a constellation of kinship systems, parenting practices, spiritual traditions, and many other ways of being in the world that influence child rearing. When young people enter school, they encounter other children who have family structures, housing arrangements, and other lifestyle differences. Sometimes as the awareness of these disparities increase, tension builds as children struggle to reconcile life at home with life at school.

Children who have ethnic or social class backgrounds different from those of the mainstream population may face challenges related to not being accepted, receiving unfair treatment, being ridiculed, and being subjected to lower expectations. The socioeconomic status of a family contributes sometimes favorably and sometimes unfavorably to the activities, friends, education attainment, lifestyle, occupational aspirations, and social roles of the family members. (p. 53)

Social workers must strive to learn about other cultures from their clients in order to understand their clients' life circumstances. Only then will practitioners be able to help these clients effectively. The following are questions social workers might ask to investigate the cultural perspectives of children and their families:

1. "What is the country of origin and cultural identity of the child and his or her family?
2. Which generation of family emigrated [from another country to the United States]?
3. What languages are spoken? Where are the languages spoken [e.g., at home or in the neighborhood]?
4. What English knowledge do the parents have? Can they understand the written word? Spoken word? How adequately can they express themselves in English?
5. What are the sleeping and eating patterns at home?
6. What are the expectations for children in the culture?
7. What is the level of acculturation?
8. Which holidays, celebrations, and cultural responsibilities are important?
9. What is the attitude of the family about play?
10. Who are the playmates of the child at home and in the community?
11. With what materials does the child play? What are the child's play activities?
12. What are the family members' attitudes toward discipline?
13. What are the patterns of discipline?
14. What responsibilities and expectations does the child have at home?" (Fascoli, 1999; Henderson & Thompson, 2011, p. 53; Kottman, 2001)

---

which reflected both strong anxiety and grief.... Although some children feared being kidnapped or abandoned again, others voiced their desire, expectation, or hope for a reunion with their birth family.

(Smith & Howard, 1999, p. 48)

Downs and colleagues (1996) describe one moving incident: "One worker recalled two preschool age brothers who clung together and sobbed over a picture of their mother, trying to stroke her long hair in the photograph" (p. 331).

Social workers conduct extensive home studies of the appropriateness of potential adoptive families. Finally, social workers may help birth parents, adopted children, and adoptive parents evaluate their situations and choices realistically, make decisions, and cope with issues.

Several other issues characterize adoptive families that social workers can help these families address (Crosson–Tower, 2009):

- *Lack of control*: Adoptive parents may experience feelings of inadequacy and lack of control because of their infertility. They may have been at the agency's mercy for years, patiently waiting for a child to become available. The integration of the child into the family system may be more difficult than they had anticipated.

For example, one adoptive family, the Humperdinks, consisted of two parents, two teenage sons, and a 20-year-old daughter. The Humperdinks wanted to provide a needy child with a good home. The mother was a special education teacher, and the father a newspaper reporter. They adopted Katrine, age 11, whose parents had been killed in a car accident. She was a pleasant child with no history of problematic behavior, so they were totally taken aback by a problem they had never anticipated. The Humperdinks were a family of readers. Typically, one would find all five of them reading various newspapers and magazines and an endless assortment of novels. Katrine, in contrast, was an average student who simply did not enjoy reading. She read only when she had to. The family required fairly extensive counseling to work on such goals as appreciating each family member's unique strengths, including Katrine's, and identifying activities other than reading they could all do together.

- *Something wrong with the kid*: Adoptive family members may worry that the adopted child has negative genetic traits or behavioral problems related to past treatment.
- *Strains on the adoptive mother and marriage*: Adopted children may manifest extreme needs that place pressure on the adoptive mother and, consequently, on the adoptive parents' marriage. Smith and Howard (1999) explain:

The mother is typically the primary focus of the child's anger, extreme dependence, or rejection. Mothers are more likely to be in the child's presence, to discipline the child, and to represent the family to school, neighbors, and others in the community. Mothers are subjected to more of the talking back, noncompliance, and control struggles than fathers.... One mother reported her frustration with her child's unfillable need for reassurance. This child, adopted at age 5, had experienced significant neglect. The child experienced panic when the mother was out of sight, even in the next room. When the mother would use the bathroom, the child would curl up against the door begging her to let him in. Consistent and very frequent reassurance and affection did nothing to alleviate his neediness. His incessant need to be near her, and her alone, left the mother feeling trapped and smothered.... The demanding child known by the mother is not the child known by the father. His wife's need to catalog the child's sins, her need for his sympathy, and her frustration and anger often appear exaggerated to the father. He sees a child pretty much being a child. She describes a monster. Tension in the marital pair emerges or is intensified by this very different understanding of the child. (pp. 61–62)

- *Quest for identity*: Adoptive children often ask themselves who they really are. Born to one set of parents and living with another, what does that make them? How should they think of themselves? How can they be positive about themselves and confident? Counseling is often needed to help them address these concerns.
- *Behavioral acting out (Downs et al., 2009)*: It's logical that children who have been uprooted from their birth families experience various degrees of insecurity, apprehension about the future, and pressure to establish their own identities. As a result, as many other children do, some adopted children act out. They may be seeking to establish some control over their lives. They may find that acting out gets them the attention they crave. Or they may use negative actions as a means of keeping themselves emotionally isolated from other people because they're terrified of getting close. They may believe that maintaining emotional distance keeps them from being vulnerable to rejection. Acting-out behaviors may include lying, stealing, committing acts of vandalism, engaging in sexual activity, wetting or soiling, and stockpiling food (Downs et al., 2009; Smith & Howard, 1999).

Focus on Critical Thinking 9.2 addresses several other controversial issues in adoption.

FOCUS ON CRITICAL THINKING 9.2

Controversial Issues in Adoption

**EP 2.1.2c,
2.1.3**

Numerous controversial issues characterize adoption today. First, in recent decades, the number of children available for adoption has decreased. Reasons for this include increased use of contraception, the possibility of abortion, and social acceptance of single-parent families. The greatest demand is for healthy, young, white children, who are in the least supply; children of color, older children, and those with special needs are in the greatest supply.

This leads us to a second issue—transracial adoption.

Critical Thinking Questions

To what extent is it appropriate for parents of one race to adopt children from another? On one hand, adoptive parents are needed for children of color. On the other, to what extent is it in a child of color's best interests to be placed with, for example, white parents? To what extent will these children be deprived of the rich fabric of cultural heritage manifested by their own race? How can they develop a strong, confident identity as a person of color in a white environment? To what extent will that child experience prejudice and discrimination in a social environment dominated by another race?

A third issue concerns special needs adoption. Unquestionably, children who have special needs are more difficult and often more expensive to care for.

Critical Thinking Questions

To what extent is it fair for agencies to encourage such adoptions when it's difficult for adoptive parents to fully comprehend the responsibilities involved in caring for a child with special needs? To what extent should financial burdens fall on such parents? To what degree should financial and medical assistance be provided to such adoptive parents?

A fourth issue involves open adoption. *Openness* is the extent to which, first, information about all parties involved (adopted child, adoptive parents, birth parents) is available, and second, the adoptive child and birth parents maintain contact with each other (Pecora et al., 2010).

Critical Thinking Questions

What can the adoptive parents know about the birth parents, and vice versa? What can the adopted child find out about the birth parents?

In the past, many people feared that openness concerning adoption might place children and parents in difficult or confusing positions. However, Grotevant and McRoy (1998) report that this really is not the case. In actuality, openness does not cause children to feel pulled between their family of origin and their adoptive family, or confused about which family is responsible for providing guidance and support.

Many questions can be raised about openness.

Critical Thinking Questions

Should children have ready access to their medical records and birth family history to identify hereditary diseases to which they might be prone? To what extent might adoptive parents feel threatened if their adopted children could readily contact the birth parents? Who should be allowed to make the decision about whether adoption records should be open? How open should they be—fully or only under some conditions and circumstances? This is a complex issue.

A fifth topic generating controversy involves independent versus agency adoptions. Although the independent adoption process may proceed more quickly than that in agency adoptions, Crosson-Tower (2009) raises three major concerns about independent adoptions. First, there is no guaranteed protection of the child's rights.

No extensive home study is conducted, and no evaluation of the appropriateness of the adoptive family is done. Second, once the child is placed, no follow-up is performed. No one monitors the extent to which the child is integrated into the family or whether the child is thriving. Third, there are no guarantees of confidentiality as there are in agency adoptions.

One other question about independent adoption involves the potential of black market adoptions, in which babies can be sold (Mather et al., 2007).

Critical Thinking Question

To what extent does the flexibility inherent in independent adoption make black market adoption possible?

Chapter Summary

The following summarizes this chapter's content as it relates to the chapter's learning objectives presented at the beginning of the chapter. Learning objectives include the following statements:

A Emphasize the wide diversity in families and their structure.

Families involve primary groups, mutual obligations, and common habitation. Family structure is "the nuclear family as well as those nontraditional alternatives to nuclear family which are adopted by persons in committed relationships and the people they consider to be 'family'" (CSWE, 2002). Variations in family structures include single-parent families, stepfamilies, blended families, and intergenerational families. Lesbian, gay, and bisexual families experience a special risk of discrimination.

B Explain the concept of child welfare and describe the continuum of supportive and substitute services in the United States.

Child welfare is the traditional term for the network of policies and programs designed to empower families, promote a healthy environment, protect children, and meet children's needs. Supportive services involve the provision of external support to enhance family functioning while children remain in the home. Substitute services assume all aspects of parental responsibilities on a temporary or permanent basis.

C Examine child maltreatment and child protective services.

Child maltreatment is the umbrella term for physical abuse, sexual abuse, and neglect, and psychological abuse. Physical abuse involves injury and results in physical and behavioral symptoms. Sexual abuse entails sexual activity with children. Incest involves sexual intercourse between family members. Child neglect concerns failure to provide for a child's needs. Psychological abuse entails belittlement, humiliation, and causing damage to self-esteem. Almost 2 million cases of child maltreatment are reported and investigated in the United States annually. Child protective services are interventions aimed at protecting children at risk of maltreatment.

The assessment of risk and protective factors is an important aspect of treatment planning.

D Describe and examine family preservation, child day care, family life education, and respite care.

Family preservation services are concentrated services provided to families in crisis in order to strengthen the family and prevent children's out-of-home placement. Child day care is an agency or program that provides supervision and care for children while parents or guardians are at work or otherwise unavailable. Family life education involves group learning experiences for the purpose of increasing people's knowledge, developing skills, or enhancing self-awareness concerning issues relevant at some point during the life span. Respite care is supervision of a child by another caregiver, allowing the parent an interval of relief from the responsibilities of child care.

E Address the ongoing macro need to advocate for resources for children and families.

Ongoing advocacy is needed to increase quality, accessible day care; improve maternal and child health; prevent and address child maltreatment; and help families get out of poverty.

F Describe substitute placements for children.

Kinship care involves informal or formal placement with a relative or part of the child's family's supportive network. Foster family care is the provision of substitute care with a family for a planned temporary or extended period when parents or legal guardians are unable to care for a child. Permanency planning is currently an important theme in foster care. A group home provides a substitute setting and family environment for a group of children originating from different families. Residential treatment centers are bigger agencies that are more structured and provide daily care, meet educational needs, and address emotional and behavioral issues. Independent living services provide out-of-home placement for youths approaching adulthood during their transition to adulthood.

G Discuss adoption.

Adoption is the legal act of taking in a child born to other parents and formally making that child a full member of the family. Types of adoptions include blood-related, unrelated, agency, independent, international, special needs (often subsidized), and transracial adoptions. Social workers can help adoptive families address issues involving lack of control, concerns about the adopted child, pressures on adoptive parents, and psychological and behavioral issues of the child.

H Propose questions to stimulate critical thinking about advocacy to combat child maltreatment and controversial issues in adoption.

Critical thinking questions regarding child maltreatment involve the conservative–liberal and residual–institutional orientations to addressing the issue. Questions concerning adoption include those examining transracial adoption, special needs adoption, openness about information, and independent adoptions.

COMPETENCY NOTES

The following identifies where Educational Policy (EP) competencies and practice behaviors are discussed in the chapter.

EP 2.1.1 Identify as a professional social worker and conduct oneself accordingly. *(p. 280):* Social workers should be knowledgeable about the history of the profession; child welfare reflects an important facet of that history.

EP 2.1.1c Attend to professional roles and boundaries. *(p. 286):* Social work roles in child protective services are discussed. *(p. 288):* The importance of the broker role is emphasized. The case example presented here illustrates the case manager role. *(p. 298):* Social work roles in foster family care are discussed. *(p. 304):* Social work roles in adoption are examined.

EP 2.1.1e Engage in career-long learning. *(p. 305):* Learning about clients' cultures and values is a career-long process.

EP 2.1.2c Tolerate ambiguity in resolving ethical conflicts. *(p. 307):* Practitioners must tolerate ambiguity when confronting controversial issues and making determinations about ethical practice and policy.

EP 2.1.3 Apply critical thinking to inform and communicate professional judgments. *(p. 290):* Critical thinking questions are posed concerning

the conservative-liberal and residual-institutional orientations. *(p. 307):* Critical thinking questions are raised concerning controversial issues in adoption.

EP 2.1.4 Engage diversity and difference in practice. *(p. 278):* Sexual orientation is a dimension of diversity.

EP 2.1.4a Recognize the extent to which culture's structures and values may oppress, marginalize, alienate, or create or enhance privilege and power. *(p. 278):* Social workers should recognize the extent to which gay and lesbian people are oppressed and alienated. *(p. 305):* People with cultural values and customs that differ from the mainstream ones may be oppressed and marginalized.

EP 2.1.4b Gain sufficient self-awareness to eliminate the influence of personal biases and values in working with diverse groups. *(p. 278):* Practitioners must work hard at self-awareness regarding any prejudices and stereotypes they may harbor toward people with nonheterosexual orientations. *(p. 305):* Social workers should strive to develop self-awareness concerning their own cultural values and biases in order to work effectively with people from diverse groups.

EP 2.1.4c Recognize and communicate their understanding of the importance of difference in shaping life experiences. *(p. 278):* Social workers must recognize how sexual orientation shapes life experiences. *(p. 305):* Practitioners should recognize the extent to which cultural values and customs shape life experiences.

EP 2.1.4d View themselves as learners and engage those with whom they work as informants. *(p. 305):* Social workers should view themselves as learners and seek knowledge about cultural values and customs from their clients.

EP 2.1.5 Advance human rights social and economic justice. *(p. 279):* Social workers should be knowledgeable about human rights issues such as gay rights and gay marriage from a global perspective. *(p. 284):* Social workers should recognize the global interconnections of oppression, in this case, regarding the child slave trade.

EP 2.1.5a Understand the forms and mechanisms of oppression and discrimination. *(p. 278):* Information is provided and questions are posed to assess the oppression and discrimination experienced by people with nonheterosexual orientations. *(p. 284):* Social workers should understand the oppression experienced by African children who are victims of the slave trade.

EP 2.1.5b Advocate for human rights and social and economic justice. *(p. 290):* Practitioners should advocate for children's human rights by supporting policies that stop and prevent child maltreatment. *(p. 294):* Social workers should advocate for policies and resources that make high-quality day care available to everyone who needs it, regardless of socioeconomic status.

EP 2.1.7a Utilize conceptual frameworks to guide the processes of assessment, intervention, and evaluation. *(p. 286):* Social workers can use the conceptual framework of risk and resiliency assessment to determine how to proceed in child maltreatment cases.

EP 2.1.7b Critique and apply knowledge to understand person and environment. *(p. 286):* Practitioners must understand and apply knowledge about factors contributing to and serving to prevent child maltreatment in order to develop effective treatment plans.

EP 2.1.8a Analyze, formulate, and advocate for policies that advance social well-being. *(p. 278):* Social workers should strive to establish policies and programs that advance the social well-being of people with nonheterosexual orientations. *(p. 290):* Practitioners should advocate for policies and services that advance children's well-being by stopping and preventing child maltreatment. *(p. 295):* Social workers should advocate for policies that advance the social well-being of children.

EP 2.1.9a Continuously discover, appraise, and attend to changing locales, populations, scientific and technological developments, and emerging societal trends to provide relevant services. *(p. 278):* Practitioners should continuously respond to the changing issues and conditions affecting people with nonheterosexual orientations.

EP 2.1.10d Collect, organize, and interpret client data. *(p. 283):* Categories of assessment concerning psychological maltreatment are identified to prepare workers for appropriately collecting, organizing, and interpreting client data. *(p. 285):* Causes of child maltreatment are discussed to prepare social workers for the assessment process. *(p. 286):* Data related to risk and resiliency should be collected and interpreted in dealing with child maltreatment.

EP 2.1.10e Assess clients' strengths and limitations. *(p. 286):* Limitations in the form of risk factors and strengths potentially demonstrating resiliency should be assessed in child maltreatment cases.

EP 2.1.10g Select appropriate intervention strategies. *(p. 281):* This case example discusses the selection of appropriate intervention strategies when providing supportive services. *(p. 295):* Intervention strategies for the treatment of children, when appropriate, should involve placement in the least restrictive setting.

EP 2.1.10i Implement prevention interventions that enhance client capacities. *(p. 286):* Child protective services implement interventions that seek to prevent future child maltreatment. *(p. 289):* Treatment approaches that emphasize family preservation seek to prevent the removal of children from their own homes.

EP 2.1.10j Help clients resolve problems. *(p. 281):* This case example depicts how a social worker helps clients resolve problems.

EP 2.1.10k Negotiate, mediate, and advocate for clients. *(p. 290):* Social workers should advocate on the behalf of clients for policies that stop and prevent child maltreatment.

LOOKING AHEAD

This chapter addressed the needs of families by focusing on children. Chapter 10 will shift the focus to the other end of the life span by talking about older adults—their needs and the policies and programs that serve them.

FOR FURTHER EXPLORATION ON THE INTERNET

See this text's Social Work CourseMate website at *www.cengagebrain.com* for learning tools such as chapter quizzing, videos, glossary flashcards, and more.

CHAPTER 10

Social Work and Services for Older Adults

David Grossman/Alamy

Consider the following facts:

- *In 2009, almost 12.9% of U.S. residents were 65 and older (U.S. Census Bureau, 2010).*
- *It is estimated that in 2050 that figure will increase to 20.2% (U.S. Census Bureau, 2010).*
- *From 2010 to 2030 the number of persons age 65 and older will increase by over 57% (White House, 2005a).*
- *"The great advances in health and well-being of the 20th century will lead to significant increases in the average life span in the 21st century" (White House, 2005b). For example, it is projected that people born in 2000 will live almost six years longer than those born in 1970 (White House, 2005b).*

People in the United States generally live longer than people in many other countries because of better nutrition and living conditions and significant advances in medicine and technology. On one hand, a higher proportion of older people means more people who are either retired or unable to work due to health reasons.

On the other, it means a smaller proportion of younger workers who pay taxes on current earnings and support social programs. Lower birth rates have also contributed to fewer people entering the workforce. This ratio of workers (paying taxes into Social Security) to recipients (of Social Security benefits) is referred to as the dependency ratio. Benefit recipients depend on workers to keep Social Security afloat. Potential issues resulting from this trend include an increasing burden on future workers to support older generations, significantly less money collected from taxes on earnings for social services and programs, deteriorating pension programs because of inadequate support, and struggles among members of different age groups for shrinking resources (Mooney, Knox, & Schacht, 2009). For whatever reason, most people think of 65 as the general retirement age (although, as we will discuss, the age for receiving full Social Security benefits is gradually creeping up).

Of course, this does not mean that all people work until age 65, their hair turns gray, and they abruptly retire. In reality, some people retire at age 65, others at 40, and still others at 80 or older. Consider the famous comedian and actor George Burns, who continued to tell stories and crack amazingly clever jokes until two years before his death at age 100. My own Aunt Mabel worked as a maid at a motel until age 82, when she no longer had the strength to drag the heavy service carts up the outside stairways in the summer heat and winter snow. There were no elevators available. (She was still active and driving at age 94.)

In view of this changing world, the increasing numbers of older adults, and dwindling resources, there are various implications for social work and social workers. (Note that Highlight 10.1 addresses a similar scenario on a global basis.) First, social workers will be called on to serve increasing numbers of older adults; indeed, social work with this population is a rapidly growing field. Second, social workers will be primary proponents of emphasizing and building on the strengths of older adults to maximize their self-determination and quality of life. Third, developing policies and services to meet future needs is an important priority in social welfare. Fourth, advocacy on behalf of older adults for essential resources and services will surely be necessary.

Learning Objectives

A Recognize an empowerment perspective for working with older adults that incorporates values and goals, and provide case examples of active aging.

B Introduce the issue of "global graying."

C Discuss problems older adults commonly face, including ageism, discrimination in employment, poverty, retirement, health care issues, abuse, living conditions and family variables, and transitional issues.

D Explain the concept of "gayging."

E Examine various contexts for social work practice with older adults, including home- and community-based services, discharge planning in hospital settings, and service provision in nursing homes.

HIGHLIGHT 10.1

International Perspectives: "Global Graying" and Empowerment of Older Adults

EP 2.1.5

George (1997) indicates that "global graying" is an international "phenomenon that affects the smallest Pacific islands as well as the most developed welfare states" (p. 57). Consider that throughout history, people age 65 or older never made up more than 2–3% of the total population; today they make up 14% of the population in "developed nations," which is expected to rise to 18% in 2023 and to as high as 25% of the total population in 30 years (Kornblum & Julian, 2009, p. 293).

Older adults are treated very differently depending on their culture. Mooney and colleagues (2009) provide the following facts:

- Some tribal societies simply let older adults die or actually kill them when these people are no longer "useful" and, instead, require care.
- Scandinavian nations pay for home care services for older adults who remain in their homes but require assistance in daily tasks such as food preparation and cleaning.
- "Eastern cultures such as Japan revere [older adults,] . . . in part, because of their presumed proximity to honored ancestors" (p. 482). It is anticipated that the world will face at least three key issues as greater numbers of people age (George, 1997). First, "it is expected that graying will bring greater dependence as a result of greater longevity accompanied by chronic ill health" (p. 59). Second, "there will be an inadequate supply of caregivers because of smaller family sizes (for example, China's one-child policy and a resulting family structure of four grandparents, two parents, and

one child), [and] women's increasing participation in paid employment outside the home" (p. 60). Third, "state finances will be inadequate to support the increasing dependence of older people" (p. 60).

What can social workers do about this from a global perspective? Social workers bring with them at least three strengths as they address the issues involved in aging. (George, 1997) First, they emphasize self-determination and the achievement of maximum autonomy. Second, they focus on changing not only the individual but also the environments encompassing the individual including the political milieu. Finally, they build plans that stress existing strengths.

Social workers can advocate on behalf of older adults around the world to establish policies and services that meet their vital needs for "health and autonomy" (George, 1997, p. 68). Initiatives can include:

- Educating the public to see older adults as a "resource" instead of as a burden (Torres-Gil & Puccinelli, 1995, p. 164).
- Expanding community-based care to maintain people in their own homes as long as possible.
- Providing supportive measures (e.g., financial assistance, tax incentives, respite care) to family members who care for aging relatives.
- Emphasizing the significance of older adults as having sufficient numbers to wield political clout and become important participants in the political process.
- Educating upcoming generations to prepare to care for an increasing proportion of older adults, on the one hand, and for themselves as they age, on the other.

F Explore general empowerment issues and those for diverse populations of older adults, including African American grandparents who are primary caregivers for grandchildren and the culturally competent treatment of older Navajo people residing in a nursing home.

G Encourage critical thinking about confronting myths about older adults, financing Social Security, determining whether Social Security discriminates against women, and proposing how older adults might be empowered through macro practice.

An Empowerment Perspective

EP 2.1.10e

An empowerment approach for working with older adults stresses at least five basic values (KPMG Consulting, 2002, p. 12). First, older adults should be treated with "dignity"; they should be "treated with respect regardless of the situation." Their self-esteem is essential. Second, older adults should be "in control" of their own lives, making their own choices and doing as much for themselves as possible. Third, active "participation" in family and community life and activities is vital. Older adults' views regarding social policies and practices should be encouraged and appreciated. Fourth, they should be treated fairly and have their rights treated equally with those of other citizens. Fifth, older adults have the right to "security" that includes "adequate income" and "access to a safe and supportive living environment."

The conceptual model for healthy aging in Alberta, Canada, includes four major goals to pursue on the behalf of older adults (KPMG, 2002):

- *Promoting health and preventing disease and injury—enabling people to increase control over and improve their health. Health promotion focuses on enhancing the capabilities and capacities of individuals, families and communities to make healthy choices and develop healthy and supportive environments.*
- *Optimizing mental and physical function—enabling people to remain as independent as possible in carrying out the routines of daily living.*
- *Managing chronic conditions—enabling people to effectively manage conditions caused by injuries or diseases, by facilitating self-care and independence and using collaborative approaches with professionals and caregivers.*
- *Engaging with life—enabling people to have meaningful relationships with others and be involved in activities that are satisfying and purposeful. (KPMG, 2002, p. 1)*

Rizzo and Seidman (2009) reflect:

This conceptual model incorporates the different levels of society and encompasses macro, mezzo,

and micro perspectives. It focuses on the health of the population, the health care systems, and the availability of partnerships that are capable of developing health strategies. Furthermore, it connects with the individual by incorporating some of social work's core values, including dignity, autonomy, participation, fairness, security, and recognizing and building on strengths and capacities (KPMG, 2002). The strategic framework ... takes into account health determinants, health strategies, and partnerships. ... [F]ive crucial methods of promoting health [include]: developing policy, building supportive environments, enriching community action, expanding individual skills, and enhancing awareness of the framework among health services (KPMG, 2002). (p. 6)

Generally speaking, an empowerment perspective for older adults involves giving them respect, appreciating difference, valuing their choices, and promoting health. This is so when interacting at the individual level. It is also so in terms of how older adults are treated in their communities and by social policies.

Active Aging

Rizzo and Seidman (2009) discuss the concept of *active aging*:

The [World Health Organization] WHO (2002) coined the term active aging based on the concept of healthy aging. However, active aging conveys a more inclusive definition that goes beyond the principles of health care to include the human rights of older adults and the United Nations' principles of independence, participation, dignity, care, and self-fulfillment. The term "active" represents one's participation in social, economic, cultural, spiritual, and civic affairs throughout life. The WHO (2002) conceptualization of active aging is based on three concepts: participation in life, meaning the family and community; health, meaning health promotion and activities to maintain an optimal health status; and security, including financial, community, and family security. (p. 4)

Hillier and Barrow (2011) provide a number of examples of older adults who are actively involved in life:

- Playing music can bring great joy to people of any age (Making Music, 2005). Music can decrease stress and lower blood pressure. It provides an excellent hobby for people who used to play and are now retired with more time to spend doing what they want. Joyce Gast, who lives in Miami, picked up her French horn after a lull of 15 years and joined a band in the community; one of her fellow band members is 90 years old (Making Music, 2005). Playing music even can be enjoyed by those who never played before. "For instance, Judy Murray of Winchester, Massachusetts, took up violin at age 51"; she laughs at how she is struggling to learn, but says she enjoys it each time she plays (Making Music, 2005).

- Frances Woofenden, 84, is a "competitive trick water skier who also bikes 10 miles a day" (Smith, 2009). She's proud of her strong and flexible knees on which she can elegantly maneuver "like a dancer"; she also takes pride in her appearance and prefers wearing "cotton-candy colored lipstick" (Smith, 2009). Woofenden has gained national attention and has starred in television commercials and magazine adds sponsoring V8, which stress a healthy lifestyle.

- Gloria Cox hasn't been able to walk for a long time without the assistance of a walker, but more recently has acquired a new skill (Karas, 2009, cited in Hillier & Barrow, 2011, pp. 227–228). Cox has arthritis, but used to love to bowl. Teen volunteers taught her how to play electronically on a Wii bowling video game. She says it's not quite the same, but she swings her arm using the same motion as she did when she was trying to knock down real bowling pins. However, now she can remain contentedly in her chair. She's having fun.

- Lorraine, 92, and Roland, 93, reunited and married after many decades of separation (Garvey & Houde, 2009). After going their own ways early on in their youth, both married others, had children, and subsequently lost their spouses when they died. Loraine's and Roland's siblings, who had kept in touch, eventually helped Loraine and Roland reconnect. "The look in their eyes just before they kissed for the first time as husband and wife echoed the innocent gazes in the picture on the altar"; the photo of them had been taken in the 1920s with Roland wearing old coveralls and Lorraine having bobbed hair and wearing a simple frock (Garvey & Houde, 2009).

- Former President Jimmy Carter provides a superb example of active aging and the pursuit of civic duty. After leaving presidential office following his 1980 "humiliating defeat," Jimmy Carter faced " 'an altogether new, unwanted, and potentially empty life' at the age of 56" (American Experience, 2010). Instead, in 1982 he used his determination and energy to open the Carter Center and become extensively involved in humanitarian efforts. The Center "has developed dozens of programs to alleviate suffering and improve lives around the world. Its efforts fall broadly under two categories, 'Waging Peace' and 'Fighting Disease.' The Carters' peace work includes conflict resolution, election monitoring, and the promotion of human rights and democracy. Health programs include agricultural initiatives to eliminate hunger in Africa, Rosalynn Carter's mental health task force, and programs to control or eradicate preventable diseases afflicting the world's poorest people" (American Experience, 2010). In addition, Jimmy Carter has also established a poignant role as an older adult statesperson; he has undertaken diplomatic missions under each president following Ronald Reagan, including peace missions to Ethiopia, North Korea, Haiti, and the former Yugoslavia (American Experience, 2010). "In May 2002 he became the highest American official to visit Cuba since Fidel Castro came to power, receiving front-page coverage which showed he had not exactly retired from the world stage, even at the age of 77" (American Experience, 2010).

The important thing for social workers is to focus on the strengths of older adults. Yes, increasing age does bring with it some developing problems over time. However, emphasizing the interests, talents, and assets of older adults focuses on the positives instead of dwelling on the negatives. Practitioners should establish a mind-set of listening well to their older adult clients, encouraging them to fulfill their dreams, and helping them accomplish their goals.

Because social workers are helpers, they typically have contact with older adult clients who are dealing with issues and problems. Therefore, much of this chapter focuses on common concerns and difficulties faced by older adults within the context of empowering them.

Demographic Characteristics of Older Adults: Race, Gender, and Social Class

EP 2.1.5a, 2.1.9a

Three important variables in discussing the older adult population are race, gender, and social class (Macionis, 2010; Mooney et al., 2009). People of color represented about 19% of U.S. older adults in 2008 (Macionis, 2010). Projections suggest this will increase to 25% in 2035; the population of older adults of color is expected to grow at a rate almost 2 1/2 times that of the white older adults between 2004 and 2030 (Mooney et al., 2009). This is partially due to higher fertility rates and increased immigration, especially on the part of Hispanics (Administration on Aging [AOA], 2000). The fact that people of color tend to experience higher rates of heart disease, diabetes, and arthritis than whites has direct implications for social workers and other professionals working in health care (Mooney et al., 2009; Newman, 2000).

Although the overall U.S. population is approximately 49% male and 51% female, the population of people age 65 and over is about 42.5% male and 57.5% female (U.S. Census Bureau, 2010). The average life expectancy for women is almost age 80, and for men just over age 75 (Kirk & Okazawa-Rey, 2010). People in this age group are most likely to die from heart disease, cancer, and stroke in that order (U.S. Census Bureau, 2010). Note, however, that women are more likely than men to suffer from "disabling diseases such as arthritis, Alzheimer's, diabetes, deafness, cataracts, broken bones, digestive conditions, and osteoporosis" (Kirk & Okazawa-Rey, 2010, p. 220).

In previous chapters we established how women are more likely to be poor and to earn less than men, even for comparable work. Living longer means savings must be stretched out further, which means women are more likely to run out of money toward the end of their lives. In addition, earning less or not working outside the home means they are likely to receive lower Social Security benefits. About 70% of the older adult poor in the United States are women

(Mooney et al., 2009). The social welfare system and social workers must, therefore, be prepared to address this population's needs.

Social class is the third important variable affecting older adults. People populating the lower social classes tend to have shorter life expectancies, to experience more severe incapacitating illnesses, and generally to have a lower quality of life (Mooney et al., 2009). One study revealed that 26% of people age 65 or older who have annual incomes of at least $35,000 label their health as "excellent"; in contrast, only 10% of older adults with incomes less than $10,000 could say the same thing (Mooney et al., 2009; Seeman & Adler, 1998). People of lower social classes generally are "chronically unemployed, underemployed, dependent on welfare, or working for a subsistence wage" (Longres, 2000, p. 239). Many barely survive, let alone have enough resources to save for old age.

Common Problems Facing Older Adults

I just told my father, age 73, who is a retired MSW social worker, that at this moment I'm writing about problems experienced by older adults. (He happens to be at my home planting daffodil bulbs for next spring.) He replied, "Older adults don't have problems. Why are you writing about that?" The point is that it's easy to focus on all the negatives about growing older instead of the positives.

This chapter emphasizes how social work with older adults is founded on clients' strengths and seeks to maximize their well-being. However, older people are more likely to experience some types of problems than are those who are younger. As people age, they eventually become weaker and more vulnerable to certain illnesses and diseases. *Primary aging* refers to the fact that physiological variables involving such decline will inevitably occur. However, there are huge variations among people concerning how fast this progresses. *Secondary aging,* then, concerns how the primary aging process can either be hastened or slowed by lifestyle and behavior. Factors that can slow aging include physical exercise, healthful diet, stress management, and ready access to adequate resources and medical treatment (Quadagno, 2005; Seeman & Adler, 1998).

The following section addresses some of the problematic issues affecting older adults. The intent is to establish the context for how social workers strive to focus on their strengths and meet their needs. Such matters include ageism, discrimination in employment, poverty, retirement, health care, older adult abuse, and living conditions, and transitional issues.

Ageism

**EP 2.1.4a,
2.1.5a**

Ageism involves harboring negative images of and attitudes toward people simply because they are older. Ageism is similar to sexism or racism in that it involves prejudice toward and discrimination against people who fit into a certain category. Ageism, like sexism and racism,

also fails to identify individual strengths as means of empowerment. Focus on Critical Thinking 10.1 reviews some of the typical myths and stereotypes about older people that are grounded in ageism.

One example of ageism involves how the media typically emphasize the importance of youth, beauty, strength, and physical prowess. For example, advertisers pitch expensive facial creams that minimize wrinkles and bring back youthful glow to aging skin. Still other reflections of ageism are discussed in the following sections.

Discrimination in Employment

One survey of 1,400 workers revealed that younger and older workers view the employment status of

---

FOCUS ON CRITICAL THINKING 10.1

Confronting Myths About Older Adults

**EP 2.1.3,
2.1.4a,
2.1.5a**

One dimension of critical thinking involves evaluating assumptions made by many people. Numerous stereotypes about older adults are cited here (Greene, 2000; Harrigan & Farmer, 2000; Hillier & Barrow 2011). Confronting stereotypes involves *asking* questions, *assessing* facts, and *asserting* a conclusion.

Critical Thinking Questions

What are your conclusions about each of the following myths?

Myth A: All older adults are burdened with multiple physical complaints and are riddled with disease.

Fact: Older adults do experience increasing weakness and illness as they age. Of people age 65 or over, 80% experience at least one form of chronic illness, such as arthritis, heart disease, or diabetes (Coleman & Kerbo, 2009). However, as with the younger population, huge variation exists concerning individual health status. Regardless of age, some people are simply healthier and stronger than others, for many reasons. A healthful lifestyle in terms of diet and exercise correlates with better health. Newman and Newman (2012) report:

The level of independent functioning among adults 80 years and older is high. . . . The area of greatest

limitation is walking. The percentage of adults needing assistance is small for those ages 65 to 74, increases slightly for those 75 to 84, and increases markedly for those 85 and older. However, even among this oldest group, fewer than half require help with walking, and fewer than 35% need help with other basic tasks of self-care [bathing/showering, dressing, eating, getting in and out of bed or a chair, walking, and using the toilet] (American Administration on Aging, 2010). (pp. 573–574)

Myth B: Old people are unattractive, have no teeth, and can barely see or hear.

Fact: Older adults, like their younger cohorts, pay varying degrees of attention to their personal appearance, hygiene, and conformity to current, popular styles. Many older people take great pride in their appearance and their strong social skills. They actively strive to put forth a pleasant, attractive persona. Physical changes such as the tendency of skin to wrinkle and body fat to redistribute do occur. However, these are facts of life having little to do with a person's overall appearance and personality.

Older adults who have not had "access to a lifetime of preventative dental care or fluorinated water" experience greater risk of losing their teeth as they age (McInnis-Dittrich, 2009, p. 35). The most common reason for tooth loss involves inflammation of the gums and bones surrounding the teeth, "usually caused by

(continued)

FOCUS ON CRITICAL THINKING 10.1 (continued)

dental plaque, which can be removed with regular brushing and routine cleaning" (McInnis-Dittrich, 2009, p. 35). Think about what times were like when many older adults were young. There was no preventive dental care or fluoride in the water supply (to combat cavities). They lived in an era in which they *expected* to lose their teeth and wear dentures. Everyone else did. My grandmother, born in 1890, told the story of how she never could stand pain very well. Whenever she got a toothache, she would get someone to pull the tooth out with the equivalent of pliers. Eventually she had no teeth left.

Sight and hearing tend to deteriorate with advancing age. However, having access to advanced medical services and techniques can slow the decline and even improve conditions. Hearing aids are now much more usable than in the past. Vision can be enhanced by glasses, contacts, laser surgery, and other new surgical techniques. One professor required cataract surgery at the relatively young age of 48. She had been nearsighted since her early teens and could barely find her glasses when she put them down somewhere. As the cataracts developed, her vision became increasingly cloudy, and she viewed the world as if through a dense fog. Reading and driving became almost impossible. Cataract surgery involves removing the natural lens in your eye and replacing it with an artificial one. After the 15-minute outpatient surgery, her distance vision was better than it had been at age 14. She marveled at medical advances as she recalled the effects of her own grandmother's cataract surgery years before. At that time, the natural lens could be removed but not replaced internally. Her grandmother had to wear glasses almost three-quarters of an inch thick to replace the lenses she lost in order to restore only a portion of her vision.

Myth C: "Old people sleep all the time" (Harrigan & Farmer, 2000, p. 33).
Fact: Older people don't necessarily sleep less than younger people, but their sleeping patterns are somewhat different. "Older adults need about the same amount of sleep as young adults—7 to 9 hours each night. But seniors tend to go to sleep earlier and get up earlier than when they were younger. Older people may nap more during the day, which can sometimes make it hard to fall asleep at night. . . . As people get older, they spend less time in deep sleep, which may be why older people are often light sleepers" (National Institute on Aging, 2009).

Myth D: You can't teach an old dog new tricks; "old people are set in their ways" (Harrigan & Farmer, 2000, p. 35).
Fact: Greene (2000) reflects:

Life span and life course theorists reject the view that growth ends with adulthood. They point out that, while there may be growth limits for attributes such as height, other qualities such as creativity and abstract reasoning do not fit this model. In this context, growth refers to differentiation, increased complexity, and greater organization, and can occur at every age. (p. 29)

Harrigan and Farmer (2000) add that

this growth and change vary from person to person and within each individual and are related to an individual's personality. . . . For example, a woman who is assertive, confident, and positive as she approaches new experiences will probably view old age as one more new and exciting adventure. Someone who approaches life from a pessimistic, complaining viewpoint no doubt will behave similarly as an aged person. (p. 36)

Myth E: All old people are senile.
Fact: Most older adults do not have dementia, and it is certainly not inevitable (Plassman et al., 2007). *Dementia* is a condition that involves various cognitive problems, such as impaired memory, poor judgment, and inability to control emotions. However, the likelihood of dementia does increase with advancing age; only 5% of people in their 70s, have dementia, 24% in their 80s, and 37.4% in their 90s, and older (Plassman et al., 2007).

older workers quite differently. Over half of the workers age 50 and older felt that people in their age group were valued by employers; however, only 25% of workers in younger age groups felt people age 50 and older were valued employees (Porter & Walsh, 2005).

It's true that people in general will eventually experience increased weakness and slowness as they age. However, this occurs at vastly different rates depending on the individual. Additionally, the younger old—those closer to age 65—are much more likely to enjoy good health than the older old—those age 85 and over.

Congress passed the Age Discrimination in Employment Act (ADEA) in 1967 that prohibited discrimination against people age 40–65. This means that employers can no longer do things like advertise for employees "who are under 30." However, employers can still state that a job is "entry level" or requires "2–3 years' experience," and then reject older people on the basis of being "overqualified" (Mooney et al., 2009, p. 502).

The ADEA also did little to help people age 65 and older. As the next section explains, many older adults require additional income to keep afloat, and many want to work.

Poverty

Whereas until the early part of the 20th century older adults were very likely poor, Social Security currently supports a large proportion of older people. Of the older adults living in the United States, almost half would fall below the poverty line if they were not receiving Social Security benefits (Karger & Stoesz, 2010). These benefits do not make people rich. In 2005, average monthly benefits for retired workers were $1,164 (U.S. Census Bureau, 2010). However, lumped together with personal savings, other assets, and occasionally pensions, these benefits allow many people to make it.

Poverty rates for older adults vary widely depending on age, gender, and race. Barusch (2012) explains:

The very old have lower incomes, primarily because at higher ages we see a disproportionately high number of single women. . . . Similarly, the very old are also more likely to live on incomes below poverty. Americans eighty years or older had a poverty rate of 11.5 percent in 2008, and 29.6 percent lived on incomes at or below 125 percent of the poverty level (U.S. Census Bureau, 2009).

Older women have a higher risk of poverty than older men. In 2003, older women over sixty-five had nearly twice the poverty rate of men in the same age bracket. The rate for women that year was 12.5 percent; for men, 7.3 percent. Further, nearly a quarter (23.6 percent) of women aged seventy-five and older had incomes at or below 125 percent of the poverty threshold (U.S. Census Bureau, 2005). Older women living alone in the United States are consistently the poorest group among the aged, faring worse than older couples.

Finally, people of color experience higher rates of poverty in their later years. African American [older adults] . . . overall have the highest rates of poverty. In 2003, the poverty rate for African Americans over *the age of sixty-five years was 23.6 percent compared to an overall rate of 10.2 percent for older adults of all races. The highest risk of poverty among [older adults] . . . was experienced by African American women, among whom more than a quarter (27.4 percent) had incomes below the poverty threshold (U.S. Census Bureau, 2005). Hispanic [older adults] . . . also experienced elevated risk of poverty, with an overall rate of 19.5 percent. (pp. 386–387)*

The poverty level for older adults age 75 and older is 23.2% for Africans American, 21.8% for Hispanics, 14.1% for Asian Americans, and 10% for whites (U.S. Census Bureau, 2010).

Saving Social Security

We have established that Social Security is a primary means of keeping older adults out of poverty. There has been much concern about the adequacy and ongoing solvency of the Social Security system. As Chapters 6 and 8 explained, workers automatically pay into Social Security, a type of social insurance, based on their earnings up to a specified annual maximum. It is tempting to think of Social Security as a savings account that automatically receives a percentage of each paycheck and lies there waiting for you to collect interest once you retire. But this is not the case. In reality, the money that workers contribute today is being spent to pay benefits to retired and other workers, as well as other government expenses. Tomorrow's beneficiaries—including you—must depend on tomorrow's workers.

The problem introduced at the beginning of the chapter is that the number of workers paying into the Social Security system is falling compared to the number of retirees and other beneficiaries receiving payments from it. As noted, this worker-to-beneficiary ratio is referred to as the *dependency ratio.* In 1945 there were 42 payers for each recipient (Sloan, 2000). "In 1960 the worker-to-beneficiary ratio was 5 to 1; by 2007 it had dropped to 3.4 to 1. By 2025 the dependency ratio is expected to be 2 to 1" (Karger & Stoesz, 2010, p. 269). So the disturbing question is, Who's going to pay for your Social Security when you retire?

It is predicted that Social Security will start going into the red as early as 2015, when baby boomers are retiring and the dependency ratio changes (Karger & Stoesz, 2010). At that point, workers' contributions will be less than the benefits that must be paid out, and any benefits paid must come from reserves.

By 2042, without changes the fund's "assets will be exhausted" (Karger & Stoesz, 2010, p. 268). Many indicate that it's much better to plan far ahead "so that individuals and families have time to adjust their retirement plans, and so that changes can be phased in slowly over time" (White House, 2005a).

Some indicate that fixing and saving the system will require cutting benefits and/or increasing payroll taxes. Benefits can be decreased in several ways, including

- Providing them at older ages (which has already been done to a limited degree).
- Decreasing the actual amount of benefits paid out to individuals.
- Increasing the maximum amount of income that can be taxed. In 2011, income was taxed up to a maximum of $106,800 (note that as of this writing, the maximum has gone up every year except for 2009 to 2011) (Social Security Online, 2010a).
- Cutting the increases in benefits regularly made to adjust for cost-of-living increases.
- More controversially, providing benefits only to those whose income or assets fall under some arbitrary line. This, of course, is quite radical because it violates the idea that all who pay into a social insurance system should benefit from returns.

Focus on Critical Thinking 10.2 urges you to think about how this problem should be solved.

Another controversial issue is whether Social Security discriminates against women. Focus on Critical Thinking 10.3 raises some key questions.

FOCUS ON CRITICAL THINKING 10.2

How Would You Fix Social Security?

What are your own thoughts and values concerning the Social Security crisis? How would you answer the following questions?

EP 2.1.3a, 2.1.5b, 2.1.8a

Critical Thinking Questions (concerning raising the retirement age)

- Because people tend to live longer, should the retirement age be raised?
- If so, to what age?
- When would you like to be able to retire? If you haven't thought much about this, when would your parents (or grandparents) like to retire?

Critical Thinking Questions (concerning decreasing benefits)

- Should benefits be decreased?
- If so, for whom—current recipients? Note that Social Security is a major source of income for most retired Americans. "Social Security comprises at least 90 percent of the income of 20 percent of older married couple beneficiaries and 41 percent for single beneficiaries. It comprises at least 50 percent of the income of 52 percent of older married couples and 72 percent of single beneficiaries" (DiNitto, 2011, p. 163).

- Should benefits for future recipients be reduced? If so, when should this start? How much should they be reduced?
- Do you want reduced benefits?
- Would your parents and grandparents want reduced benefits?

Critical Thinking Questions (concerning increasing the maximum amount of income that can be taxed)

- Should the maximum amount of income that can be taxed be increased more than it regularly is now?
- If so, by how much?
- Should all income regardless of the amount be taxed?
- Should people who pay significantly more into the fund receive proportionally more benefits?
- To what extent is it fair to pay significantly more into a social insurance program and get the same benefits as those paying significantly less?

(continued)

FOCUS ON CRITICAL THINKING 10.2 *(continued)*

- Should richer people help support poorer people by sharing their wealth through the Social Security system?
- What is fair?

Critical Thinking Questions (concerning cutting increases in benefits)

- Should cost-of-living increases in benefits be decreased?
- If so, by how much?
- How would a decreasing standard of living affect the many people depending on Social Security?
- How severe would these effects be on recipients living 20 years after first receiving Social Security benefits in terms of their quality of life?

Critical Thinking Questions (concerning offering Social Security benefits only to those less well off)

- Should benefits be given only to retirees who are less well off?
- If so, how well off?
- To what extent is this fair to workers who paid significant taxes into the fund for decades and then don't qualify for benefits?
- To what extent would this transform a social insurance system into a public assistance system? To what extent is this right or wrong?

FOCUS ON CRITICAL THINKING 10.3

Does Social Security Discriminate Against Women?

EP 2.1.3, 2.1.5a, 2.1.8a

One ongoing criticism of Social Security is that it discriminates against women. When a woman turns age 65, she is eligible to receive benefits equal to one-half of the benefits her husband receives. This is true whether she has ever worked outside the home or not. However, if she has worked outside the home, she may choose to take her own benefits instead. She cannot receive both.

How is this discriminatory? First, women who have been homemakers their entire lives are entitled to only half of what their husbands receive. Does this imply that their share of the marital partnership is worth only half of the husbands'? The system provides them with no way of making contributions based on their own labor within the home.

Many women work outside the home for years, build up their own benefits, but end up taking half of their husbands' anyway. Why? The husbands' benefits are worth more than twice as much as theirs, so they're better off taking half of the husbands'. We've established that men tend to enter higher-paid professions, earn significantly more than women in the same professions, and spend less time out of the workforce raising children and caring for a home. Thus women's contri-butions, as structured by the current system, are often significantly less than their husbands'.

Barusch (2000) explains:

Wives in dual-worker couples face a choice. They can receive benefits based on their earnings, or they can receive benefits as dependents. They cannot do both. Those who left the labor force to raise children or care for the sick, and those whose wages were lower than their spouses' receive more as dependents than on the basis of their own work histories. So they receive no benefit for the payroll taxes withheld from every one of their paychecks. (p. 570)

Note that a few positive changes have been made in the system. "For example, many divorced spouses may begin collecting Social Security benefits at age 62 if their former spouses are eligible even if the former spouse has not yet claimed benefits. In addition, payments to disabled widows and widowers aged 50–59 were increased" (DiNitto, 2011, p. 160).

Critical Thinking Questions

Should the system be further reformed to make it more equitable? If so, how should the contributions of homemakers be measured? What about those who take time off to bear and raise children?

Retirement

Previously we established the concept of age 65 as the magic number for retirement. A hundred years ago, the notion of retirement was essentially unknown. Most people didn't live that long. Few had enough savings to support them without working. No programs such as Social Security or pension plans existed to pick up the slack when their work careers ended. As we know, the Social Security Act of 1935 established 65 as the age when people stop working and begin receiving maximum benefits. Current policy indicates that by 2022, people won't be able to receive Social Security benefits until age 67 (Mooney et al., 2009; Whiteman, 2001).

One survey of nonretired workers indicated that the average age of planned retirement was 64; 15% planned on retirement before age 60, 22% between ages 60 and 64, 25% at age 65, and 31% after that (Carroll, 2008). Retirement might sound good to many, but it often requires quite an adjustment. Retirees must cope with a new way of life. How does a retiree respond when someone asks, "And what do you do?" Many people's careers or jobs become a substantial part of their personal identities. What happens when they give up that significant part of their lives? How might the loss affect their self-concept and self-respect?

Another potential problem in retirement involves reduced income. How much adjustment is involved when retirees can no longer spend money and buy things as they used to? Still another aspect of retirement concerns losing daily work routines. Retirees must discover new ways to spend their time.

Health Care

Medicare, established in 1966, is not the total answer to health care for older adults. Although it helps pay for medical expenses for an estimated 47 million people (Kaiser Family Foundation [KFF], 2011), it pays only half for a visit to a physician and nothing for long-term care, hearing aids, glasses, or dental work. Chapter 8 discussed the partial supplementary coverage available in Medicare Part B, Medigap insurance (to fill in Medicare's gaps), and the Medicare Modernization Act's prescription drug benefit. However, these also cost older adults more. And good coverage costs much more.

The older people get, the more likely they are to have long-term illnesses and to take more time to recuperate. Older adults spend two times as much on health care as younger population groups (Mooney et al., 2009).

Abuse of Older Adults

Physical and emotional abuse of older adults is receiving increasing public attention. It includes not only inflicting physical or emotional harm but also taking advantage of older adults financially or neglecting them (e.g., ignoring the fact that medical treatment is needed) (Hooyman & Kiyak, 1999). An estimated 1.5 million cases of physical abuse of older adults occur in the United States each year (Kornblum & Julian, 2009) in both private homes and residential facilities. Coleman and Kerbo, (2009) report shocking incidents of abuse involving family caregivers. One involved a man who sexually assaulted his 74-year-old mother-in-law. The victim's daughter refused to make a big deal of it or to allow her mother to report the incident to authorities. Another incident entailed an angry son chasing his 75-year-old father around with a hatchet.

In private homes, perpetrators of older adult abuse often are people who live with the victim, such as a spouse or adult child; frequently alcohol abuse is involved (McInnis-Dittrich, 2009). Older adults are also subject to abuse when living in residential settings. Abuse is more likely to occur when residents are isolated from family and friends who otherwise might look out for them.

Living Conditions and Family Variables

Many older adults prefer to live on their own or with other family members. However, many older people's homes are located in older, deteriorating, inner-city neighborhoods with high crime rates. This puts them at greater risk of harm and also makes it increasingly difficult to maintain their homes.

Relatively few older adults need the around-the-clock nursing and maintenance care of a nursing home. People are more likely to need this care when they suffer from debilitating chronic illnesses. Nursing homes vary markedly in cost and quality of service. Wealthy people can pay for private homes that have excellent facilities and attentive staff. People with fewer resources must often be satisfied with whatever care they can get.

Transitional Issues

As people get older, they are more likely to experience serious losses with which they must learn to cope. One issue already discussed concerns retirement and the accompanying drastic changes in productivity and routine. Other issues involve adjusting to more structured living situations. One spouse may die, leaving the other to adjust to a much more isolated life. Health may decline, requiring an older adult to accept and adjust to increasing levels of assistance and dependence. Losses in ability such as sight, hearing, and mobility may also require the ap-

plication of coping skills. There are many areas in which social workers can provide important assistance with respect to older adults' adjustment.

Note that lesbian, gay, and bisexual (LGB) people not only face the same issues and transitions that heterosexual people do but also continue to suffer the consequences of homophobia. Highlight 10.2 describes one dimension of homophobia—invisibility.

HIGHLIGHT 10.2

"Gayging" and Invisibility

**EP 2.1.1b,
2.1.3c,
2.1.4,
2.1.4a,
2.1.4c,
2.1.4d,
2.1.5a**

Older adults can experience *invisibility*—the condition that others fail to acknowledge, attend to, or even notice their existence (Hooyman, 2008; Hooyman & Kiyak, 1999; Tully, 2000). The myths discussed in Focus on Critical Thinking 10.1 tend to reinforce the views often held by younger people that older adults are inadequate, of lesser or little value, and unworthy of notice. Hence older adults become invisible. Obviously such unfair, discriminatory attitudes and treatment fail to uphold human dignity and appreciate human diversity.

Lesbian, gay, and bisexual (LGB) people experience an additional dimension of invisibility. Tully (2000) establishes that *gayging* (gay aging) results in additional stresses and scenarios not experienced by heterosexuals (p. 197). LGB people do not usually enjoy the legal and social support systems taken for granted by heterosexuals, such as being able to marry legally in the large majority of states. For example,

it is not uncommon for the surviving partner of a gay or lesbian couple to be the sole beneficiary of the partner's estate only to have the will legally challenged. Too often, family of origin members, children, or other legal relatives will be seen as the lawful heirs. Dividing household items between an unacknowledged partner and "legal" heirs can be particularly devastating to the gay or lesbian surviving partner. (Tully, 2001, p. 601)

Additionally, health insurance policies often do not include nonheterosexual partners Hospitals, nursing homes, and other health facilities may not acknowledge LGB relationships. Family members who deny

or fail to acknowledge a relationship may deny a long-time partner access to a dying partner.

LGB older adults of color are at risk of experiencing discrimination because of race in addition to risks associated with age and sexual orientation. Social workers are trained to be sensitive to all these factors in empowering clients and providing help. Tully (2000) provides an example:

Consider the older African-American gay man who, because of a stroke, has been confined to the hospital's intensive care unit. The hospital, long known for its racist practices, began treating African Americans in the 1970s and has few doctors or nurses who are minorities of color. Most of the hospital support staff are Hispanic or African American. The patient's Puerto Rican lover, a 70-year-old retired artist, is kept from visiting because he is not considered a family member. Because he believes the true nature of the relationship to be a private matter, he remains quiet. The hospital social worker, being sensitive to the perceived needs of the patient and his friend, arranges for visitation. There are times when empowering individuals requires institutional flexibility. (p. 217)

The following provides another example of how a social worker must be sensitive to sexual orientation to empower a client (Tully, 2001):

Cecilia, a 54-year-old lesbian who was the guardian of her 90-year-old hospitalized terminally ill mother, was referred to the hospital social worker to assess the mother's pending death and the impact it might have on Cecilia. Her sexual orientation was not germane to the immediate problem, but it would be important to know that Cecilia's partner of 30 years was the primary caretaker of Cecilia's mother and more likely to need the services. (pp. 608–609)

(continued)

HIGHLIGHT 10.2 *(continued)*

There are several ways social workers can address the issue of LGB people's invisibility for all clients including those who are older adults (Tully, 2001). First, practitioners can make their offices more "homosocial" or welcoming to people regardless of sexual orientation (p. 609). Including magazines and other reading material oriented to gay issues and interests can help. Second, using admissions or intake forms that feature more inclusive terms than *spouse* or *marital status* is constructive. When soliciting information,

phrasing questions by using terms such as *significant other, partner, mate,* and *special friend* reflects more flexibility toward and acceptance of nonheterosexual orientations (p. 609). Third, careful listening can provide clues to sexual orientation. For example, clients who mention involvement in lesbian/gay activities or events may, in fact, be lesbian or gay. However, they also may not be, so social workers must be careful not to succumb to stereotypes or jump to conclusions.

Contexts for Social Work Practice with Older Adults

EP 2.1.10e,
2.1.10g,
2.1.10i

As in services for children and families, there exists a continuum of care for older adults ranging from supplemental services for people in their own homes to intensive residential care. A primary value stressed when working with older adults is *autonomy*. Social workers strive to keep older adults as independent and autonomous as possible for as long as possible. Assessing and emphasizing strengths and capacities are essential to maximize autonomy.

Because older adults may have many needs, social workers practice in a wide range of agencies and settings. Three broader contexts for service provision are long-term care through home health and community services, discharge planning in hospitals, and service provision in nursing homes.

Long-Term Care Through Home-Based and Community Health Services

Long-term care is the provision of health, social, and personal services over an extended period of time to people who are unable to care for themselves in some, most, or almost all ways. The intent is to promote people's socio-emotional and physical well-being in the least restrictive environment possible. Long-term care implies that recipients need either ongoing or periodic help over an extended period. Nursing homes, discussed more thoroughly later, provide one type of long-term care. A second type

includes services provided to people living in their own homes. Finally, a third kind of long-term care includes services made readily available to people in their community.

Home-Based Services

As you know, social workers in the broker role link clients to services and in the case manager role oversee and coordinate service provision. *Home-based services* or *home care* are types of assistance provided to people in their own homes (Kaye, 2008). They may involve either assistance to family members caring for an older adult relative or provision of services by formal social service agencies.

An *informal support network* is a system of individuals who provide emotional, social, and economic support to a person in need. The family is "the primary and preferred source of support for older people in the United States" (Kropf, 2000, p. 171). Informal support networks also include friends, neighbors, and fellow worshipers. For example, members of an informal support network might periodically chauffeur an older adult who no longer can drive herself to the grocery store. Similarly, an older adult with vision problems might need help paying bills and balancing his checkbook. Investigating the adequacy of an older adult's informal support network is an important aspect of social work assessment.

"Because social workers are trained in understanding family dynamics, group processes, community organization, and volunteer management, they possess knowledge and skills to intervene in a variety of ways within an informal network" (Kropf, 2000, p. 175). For example, a social worker might help a family arrange for respite care while family members do other things such as "working, shopping, socializing, or relaxing" (Kropf, 2000, p. 177). *Respite care* is temporary care for an older adult or other person in need, giving the primary caregivers (often family members) some time free of responsibility. (Note that Chapter 9 introduced the concept of respite care with respect to child care.) Another example involves a social worker arranging for telephone reassurance services (i.e., calling older adults daily or periodically to make sure they're all right) when primary caregivers are unavailable.

In contrast, *formal support networks* include public and private agencies and their staffs, which provide services, including health care (e.g., nursing), social services, and housekeeping help, to older adults in need. Home-based services provided by formal support networks may be necessary for two reasons. First, they address needs directly involving the home itself, such as cleaning or repair. Second, they more efficiently serve recipients who have difficulty transporting themselves outside the home to receive services elsewhere. Home-based services include any provided to people directly in their homes and those intended to facilitate people's ability to remain in their homes. They include homemaker and chore services (to assist in daily living tasks such as cooking, cleaning, home maintenance, and laundry), home health care (e.g., physical *therapy*[1] or a visiting nurse), transportation, Meals-on-Wheels,[2] and respite care.

Community-Based Services

Community-based services—those provided outside the home in the community—form another dimension of the formal support network (Kaye, 2008). They can fulfill a wide range of functions, from providing health care to meeting psychological and social needs. The following are examples of community-based services (Kropf, 2000):

- *Adult daycare:* This service provides supervision outside the home for older adults who live at home but whose primary caregivers are unavailable during the day, usually because they must work. It differs from respite care in that it is provided

on a regular schedule and is generally provided in a daycare center outside the home (respite care can be provided either inside or outside the home).

- *Hospices:* These programs provide end-of-life care to terminally ill people. The intent is to make people as comfortable as possible during their final days. Services may be provided either in a comfortable setting outside the home or in the individual's home.
- *Senior centers:* Here seniors can gather for social, recreational, and educational reasons. Senior centers often offer a wide range of activities, including "drama, lectures, arts and crafts, physical fitness,... meal programs, health screenings, or day care" (Kropf, 2000, p. 179).
- *Congregate Meal Program:* Initially instituted by the 1973 Older Americans Act, this program provides hot meals for seniors at a variety of community locations. It offers seniors a source of good nutrition and an opportunity to socialize with their peers.
- *Senior home repair and maintenance programs:* These provide physical help in home upkeep. They may involve a handyperson service whereby volunteers make home repairs such as fixing pipes or repairing roofs as needed. They may also include seasonal services such as lawn mowing or snow removal.

Focus on Critical Thinking 10.4 gives you a framework to organize your thoughts as they relate to care for older adults.

Discharge Planning in Hospital Settings

"Hospitals provide much of the acute health care of [older adults] ... , and over a third of all nursing home admissions originate from hospitals" (Cummings & Jackson, 2000, p. 191). Social workers are integrally involved as leaders in interdisciplinary treatment planning[3] and in linking patients with necessary services. A common primary function of hospital social workers is *discharge planning*. This is the comprehensive assessment of a patient's abilities and needs, the development of a plan to facilitate that patient's transition out of the hospital and back into a community or agency setting, and the implementation of that plan. Discharge planning

---

[1]Physical therapy is "the treatment of disease, injury, or deformity by physical methods such as massage, heat treatment and exercise" (Lindberg, 2007, p. 1034).

[2]*Meals-on-Wheels* is a program in which meals are delivered directly to the homes of people who need them. This service can be sponsored or cosponsored by public agencies such as human service departments or private organizations such as senior centers.

[3]*Interdisciplinary treatment* involves teams composed of professionals from various disciplines, such as doctors, nurses, social workers, psychologists, physical therapists, and occupational therapists who, in collaboration, share findings, make recommendations, and implement treatment plans.

FOCUS ON CRITICAL THINKING 10.4

Macro Practice Empowerment for Older Adults

Social workers have the responsibility to become politically to become involved, and to "analyze, formulate, and advocate for policies that advance social well-being" on the behalf of older adults (CSWE, 2008b, EP 2.1.18a). Huber, Nelson, Netting, and Borders (2008) explain that such advocacy involves:

> *vigilant efforts by, with, or on behalf of older persons to influence decision makers in structures of imbalanced power and to promote justice in providing for, assisting with, or allowing needs to be met. Vigilant efforts implies a constant monitoring and attention devoted to the situation because it is too easy for people to fall through the cracks, particularly if they are highly vulnerable. By, with, or on behalf of older persons means that every effort will be made to empower older persons themselves to do what needs to be done, but sometimes it takes people working together to get things done. (pp. 4–5)*

EP 2.1.3, 2.1.5b, 2.1.8a, 2.1.8b, 2.1.10k

Keeping a careful eye on proposed legislation addressing older people's health care and social service needs is critical For example, increasing the age at which older people can first begin receiving Social Security benefits significantly and negatively impacts older adults' financial standing. Likewise, monitoring the availability of adequate health care for older adults is paramount. Legislative advocacy involves efforts to change legislation to benefit some category of clients—in this case, older adults. It includes such actions as contacting elected officials about some issue or policy under debate. It might also entail communicating with other professionals and clients, encouraging them to contact officials concerning their views and recommendations. Public officials usually listen to their constituents when they want to get reelected.

Working to improve and develop community services for older adults raises other important macro-practice possibilities (Greene, Cohen, Galamboss, & Kropf, 2007). For example, community-based adult daycare services can be expanded (Bellos & Ruffolo, 1995). Daycare programs can provide a wide range of "medical and social services . . . ; to older adults who commute from home" to attend the program; services include "medical and psychiatric treatment," recreational and social opportunities, meals, transportation,

and personal care (Hillier & Barrow, 2011, p. 274). Hillier and Barrow (2011) describe one example:

> The On Lok Health Center in San Francisco . . . provides day-care services to elders in Chinatown. A van with hydraulic lift transports [older adults] . . . to the center, where each day begins with exercise and reality orientation. People are introduced to one another in both English and Chinese. On Lok assumes responsibility for providing all services needed by the functionally dependent. If not for On Lok, the participants would need institutional care. (p. 275)

Another example of a community-based program is one directed at educating local clergy to enhance linkages "between organized and informal support systems" (Biegel et al., 1984, p. 99). A university school of social welfare provided training with the following goals: "to impart a foundation of knowledge of the aging process, to examine the specific needs and contributions of aged individuals, to impart knowledge of community resources available for the aged individuals, and to increase participants' awareness of creative ways to minister to the aged" (Biegel, Shore, & Gordon, 1984, p. 99).

With all this in mind, think about the following.

Critical Thinking Questions

- To what extent do the preceding suggestions for empowerment reflect *residual* versus *institutional* policies and programming? (Recall that residual policies focus on reactions to problems, generally providing as few benefits as possible. Institutional policies view social services as people's right, providing ongoing benefits to enhance people's lives and well-being.)
- To what extent does current service provision for older adults demonstrate *conservative* versus *liberal* values?

Now consider the three basic, divergent principles involved that relate to the following.

Critical Thinking Questions

- Who should assume responsibility? Should older adults be expected to provide for and take care of themselves? Or is it society's responsibility to help them when they need it?

(continued)

FOCUS ON CRITICAL THINKING 10.4 (*continued*)

- Who is to blame for older adults' problems and needs? To what extent will older adults take advantage of social welfare benefits when they really don't need them? Will providing ongoing services and benefits significantly enhance their health, welfare, and comfort?

- To what extent should the government interfere in people's lives? Is it the government's responsibility to improve older people's health and functioning?

also involves identifying the appropriate resources available to meet needs and working closely with the patient, family members, and other health care providers to implement the plan as effectively as possible. Advocacy on the patient's behalf to make certain needs are met is frequently required.

Social workers must be prepared to deal with multiple potential problems when conducting discharge planning (Naleppa & Reid, 2003). The patient may be confused, difficult to work with, or suffering from an unstable physical condition. Family members may be unavailable or may disagree with plans proposed by the patient or treatment team. Adequate financial resources for an appropriate placement or access to the placement itself may be unavailable.

Case Example[4]   Esra Tratnor, age 81, was admitted to the hospital after his two daughters, Vicki and Karen, suddenly noticed that he was having "spells" during which he would speak garbled nonsense or babble incessantly. This was quite unlike Esra, who was a quiet, withdrawn man of few words. Esra remained coherent the rest of the time.

The diagnosis was an inoperable brain tumor the size of a lemon. Upon hearing this, Esra insisted on returning to his farmhouse—the same house in which he was born. He wanted to live out his remaining days watching the birds and deer. He had been living alone since his wife of 53 years died 6 years ago.

Except for a liquid supplement, doctors prescribed no treatment except to make Esra as comfortable as possible. They anticipated ongoing mental and physical deterioration in the 6–12 months he had to live.

Esra gave Aiko, the hospital social worker, consent to contact Vicki and Karen regarding discharge plans. One or the other of them had visited him every day of his hospital stay. Aiko reviewed options

with them. Although they were very concerned about their father, both were adamant about being unable to take him into their own homes. Both had full-time jobs, husbands, and children, and no available room. Thus the only two alternatives for Esra were to return home and be provided with supportive home-based services or to enter a nursing home.

Aiko requested a psychiatric evaluation to assess Esra's mental competence. The psychiatrist's conclusion was that, although Esra manifested moderate depression, he was capable of making his own decisions. The psychiatrist prescribed an antidepressant.

Aiko consulted the hospital's attorney, who indicated that Esra had the right to return home because he had been pronounced mentally competent. Esra accepted Meals-on-Wheels (he confessed to being a pretty bad cook) but refused other home-based services, including a visiting nurse and homemaker help. He insisted on remaining independent. Aiko asked Esra if he could afford the prescribed antidepressants and nutritional supplements. Esra replied that although he had no medical insurance to cover them, Vicki and Karen would help him out. In reality, he had no intention of taking expensive drugs or of seeking financial help from his daughters.

Three weeks after his hospital discharge, Esra was readmitted with a broken hip. Apparently he had been climbing a stepladder to trim the branches of a tree in his front yard and had fallen. Luckily, neighbors noticed immediately and called an ambulance.

This time Esra was noticeably disoriented and confused. A psychiatric evaluation determined that he was mentally incompetent. Healing and rehabilitation for his hip would require extensive physical care for a long time, perhaps until his death. Vicki and Karen discussed with Aiko what they should do. Vicki couldn't bear the thought of placing her beloved dad in a nursing home, so she relented and said he could stay with her. Her own children would have to double up in a room. She would take an

[4]Vicki Vogel creatively developed the idea and substance for this case example.

extended leave of absence from work to care for him. The court appointed Vicki legal guardian, and Esra moved in.

Two months later, Vicki called Aiko in desperation, saying that she just couldn't take it anymore. The friction between her and her husband over Esra's residence in their home was escalating precipitously, financial pressure from her loss of income was contributing to the tension between them, and her 17-year-old son had been busted for dealing drugs. Aiko provided Vicki with information about potential nursing home or hospice placement.

Service Provision in Nursing Homes

Nursing homes are residential centers that provide extended maintenance and personal nursing care for people who can't adequately take care of themselves. Most of older adults do not reside in nursing homes. However, a person's likelihood of spending time in a nursing home is fairly good. At any point in time, only 5% of older adults reside in a nursing home facility; however, half of people over age 65 will spend time in a nursing home either temporarily or permanently (Zimmerman, 2008). Approximately 1.5 million people over age 65 reside in nursing homes (Newman & Newman, 2012).

The older you are, the more likely you are to have health problems that require extensive attention and help. You also become more likely to spend time in a structured environment that attends to such needs. Of the nursing home population, about 13% is age 65 to 74, 35% age 75 to 84, and 51% age 85 and over (Newman & Newman, 2012).

What are other characteristics of nursing home residents? Zimmerman (2008) cites several facts:

- The average age of nursing home residents at admission is 84.
- Almost three-quarters of residents are women (which isn't surprising, because the population is characterized increasingly by women as people age).
- About one-third of all admitted residents remain in the home for rehabilitation after hospitalization over a relatively short period of time.
- Approximately three-quarters of residents need help in at least three activities of daily living (ADLs), such as eating, dressing, getting up or moving from place to place, using the toilet, or washing up.
- The average length of stay is 2.5 years.

In terms of staffing, nursing homes consist of six categories (Stahlman & Kisor, 2000):

1. Dietary departments plan menus and focus on nutrition.
2. Activities departments plan and operate a range of activities for residents, such as outings, crafts, games, and celebrations.
3. Nursing services attend to the ongoing daily care of residents and oversee their health care needs.
4. Social services address the social and emotional needs of residents, work with their families, assist in financial planning, and link residents with services when necessary.
5. Housekeeping and laundry staff perform basic daily maintenance tasks.
6. Other medical staff, including a medical director and various medical specialists (e.g., physical therapists, dermatologists), attend to residents' varying special needs.

Highlight 10.3 focuses on the roles of social workers in nursing homes.

Regular physical activity and social interaction provide a means of empowerment for older adults.

Jon Feingersh/Blend Images/Getty Images

HIGHLIGHT 10.3

A Focus on Practice: Social Workers' Roles in Nursing Homes

EP 2.1.1c,
2.1.10f,
2.1.10g,
2.1.10j,
2.1.10k

Social workers help nursing home residents in many ways. First, they assess a resident's strengths and needs to develop and implement an appropriate treatment plan.

Second, they counsel residents when needed, helping them cope with illnesses and deteriorating functioning, deal with emotional problems, enhance social skills, and make decisions.

Third, social workers address issues concerning the residents' families. Sometimes communication difficulties must be ironed out. Other times social workers educate residents and their families about complicated medical conditions and treatments. Social workers also may assist residents and their families in making financial decisions such as applying for public assistance or a pension, contacting lawyers, or discussing end-of-life issues such as funeral arrangements.

Fourth, social workers link residents with outside services when needed. Perhaps a resident needs access to library holdings or wheelchair-capable transportation, or requires new glasses, a hearing aid, or a wheelchair.

Fifth, social workers assist other nursing home staff in understanding residents' needs and respecting their dignity. They can help residents maximize their autonomy by making their own choices whenever possible. This might involve how their room is decorated, what they wear, or what they can choose to eat. Because nursing homes are structured settings that provide such extensive care, maintaining residents' autonomy is an ongoing goal.

Finally, social workers advocate for clients. Sometimes they advocate for improved quality of care or individualized attention within the nursing home setting. Other times they advocate for agency or social policies that provide more resources or better services for clients.

Sahlins (2010) provides a case example where a nursing home social worker's plans, which were developed in conjunction with her client Millie Goldstein, are explained. Note that Millie's strengths, supports, and interests are emphasized:

The social worker will meet with Mrs. Goldstein to provide support and to encourage her to attend her care-plan meetings, discuss her medical condition with her doctor, and express her feelings about adjustment to her recent stroke and her progress toward her rehabilitation goal or returning to the community.

The social worker will assist Millie in contacting her local rabbi because she wishes him to visit.

The dietary department [after the social worker's advocacy efforts] will honor Millie's preference not to eat pork or shellfish.

The social worker will provide outreach to family and support . . . concerning major life changes in the family's situation due to the patient's illness and . . . encourage positive visits with the patient as they all adjust to their new family roles.

The social worker will encourage family members to bring in photo albums and will arrange brief visits with grandchildren. The daughter plans to arrange to bring the cat for a visit and has obtained a picture of the cat for the resident to put on her bulletin board, along with several pictures of her family and grandchildren.

The social worker will encourage Millie to maintain contact with her friends through phone calls.

The social worker will introduce the resident to several [other] . . . women living in the facility who play [the card game] canasta. (p. 138)

Empowerment for Diverse Populations of Older Adults

Zuniga (1995) describes practice with older adults as "complex and demanding, given the range of needs of this population, the various subgroups of at-risk [older adults,] . . . and the multiple roles social workers must undertake to address their needs" (p. 173). She adds that demographic trends indicate that practitioners will be working with increasing numbers of older people.

Cox and Parsons (1994) emphasize that an empowerment orientation to practice "can assist older people to utilize their strengths, abilities, and competencies in order to mobilize their resources toward problem solving and ultimately toward empowerment" (p. 19). They stress that empowerment rests on principles such as involving clients integrally in the problem definition and planned-change process, emphasizing and using clients' strengths, teaching needed skills, using support networks and collective action, and linking with necessary resources.

Older adults often must deal with decreased power on several levels. First, physical health tends to decline as people age, so older adults must rely increasingly on supportive help to survive. Second, although older adults generally maintain good mental health (Dunkle & Norgard, 1995), many experience "a modest impairment of short-term memory, a decrease in speed of learning, a slowing of reaction time, and some degree of mild forgetfulness" (Cox & Parsons, 1994, p. 23). Third, they often experience loss of support systems as their peers' health declines. Fourth, we have established that retirement may require adaptation on the part of older adults, requiring them to learn new ways to occupy their time. They may also experience feelings of uselessness when no longer employed. Fifth, older adults may encounter age discrimination by younger people based on prejudicial stereotypes, such as emphasis on physical, mental, and economic weakness.

Concepts and Strategies in Empowerment

EP 2.1.10e, 2.1.10g, 2.1.10j

Zuniga (1995) emphasizes four concepts essential to empowering older adults—adaptation, competence, relatedness, and autonomy. First, social workers should focus on *adaptation* to new experiences, issues, and even losses. An empowering approach emphasizes how people use their strengths to survive, adapt to new experiences, and learn to appreciate the positive aspects of these new experiences. A second concept is *competence*. Social workers can help older adults focus on and emphasize what they *can do* instead of what they *can't* do; each individual should appreciate her or his own level of competence. *Relatedness*, the third concept, involves the sense of belonging and relating to other people. Hence, practitioners should work to strengthen older adults' relationships with others, including friends, family members, and professional caregivers (e.g., visiting nurses, physical therapists). Support, activity, and educational groups are other mezzo options. Finally, *autonomy* involves helping people live as independently as possible. McInnis-Dittrich (2009) comments:

One of the most frequently stated goals older adults voice is their desire to maintain their independence as long as possible. This desire coincides with the social work profession's commitment to promote self-determination and preserve the dignity of the individual. On the surface, there appears to be no conflict. In reality, as older adults require more and more support services and experience increasing difficulties in maintaining independent living, tensions between older adults' desires and families' and social workers' perceptions of need are inevitable. A worker can appreciate the desperate efforts on the part of an older adult to stay in his or her own home. Yet when struggling with stairs or a deteriorating neighborhood, and difficulties in completing the simple activities of daily living challenge the feasibility of that effort, professional and personal dilemmas abound. Who ultimately must make a decision about an older adult's ability to stay in his or her own home? Who decides that an older adult is showing poor judgment about financial decisions? When does Protective Services step in to remove an older adult from a family member's home due to neglect or abuse despite the older adult's objections? When do the wishes of the family supersede the wishes of the older adult? These are difficult questions for which there are no simple answers. (p. 23)

Toseland (1995) suggests five strategies for social workers to increase their sensitivity to older adults and thus enhance their effectiveness:

1. *Identify and face any preconceived notions and stereotypes about older adults.* These must be identified before they can be eliminated or changed.

2. *Appreciate the different life situations experienced by people from different age groups within the older adult population.* For example, women seeking work in the 1930s will have experienced very different conditions from those employed in the 1940s (Toseland, 1995). Women in the 1930s probably had a very difficult time finding jobs during the Great Depression when unemployment was skyrocketing. However, women in the 1940s likely had a pick of many jobs when men were off fighting World War II and industry was begging women to come to work.

EP 2.1.4a, 2.1.4b, 2.1.4c, 2.1.4d, 2.1.5a

3. *Understand that older adults are individuals with unique characteristics, experiences, and personalities, just like anybody else.* Highlight 10.4 contrasts the personalities and life approaches of two women who were friends for many decades.

4. *Learn about how both gender and cultural background influence the aging experience.* Both older adult women and older adult people of color are much more likely to experience poor health, poverty, substandard housing conditions, and social isolation (Toseland, 1995). Long-term experiences with discrimination can affect attitudes and expectations. Worker sensitivity to cultural differences in terms of communication, family relationships, and gender roles is critical. (Chapter 12 discusses a range of cultural and ethnic differences more thoroughly.)

5. *Understand the developmental aspects of later life, including people's physical, mental, living, and socioeconomic conditions.*

There are at least six specific empowerment strategies for micro practice with older adults (Cox & Parsons, 1994). First, social workers can listen carefully to what clients are saying and work to understand what they mean. "Engaging and drawing out the emotions of [older adult] . . . clients and helping them frame their situations in view of past experiences and events are effective listening techniques" (Cox & Parsons, 1994, p. 112).

Second, social workers can help clients identify their coping skills and their abilities to implement planned change. Encouraging clients to talk about what's important to them, including their significant life experiences, is helpful. Exploring how they've coped with their difficulties in the past can also be valuable.

Third, social workers can show clients recordings of other older adults talking about how they've learned to cope with similar issues. As with support group involvement, this may help clients understand that they aren't isolated and alone in their concerns.

Fourth, workers can share newspaper articles, stories, and other informative materials with clients, especially those about older adults who have initiated service activities and political action. The Gray Panthers, an advocacy organization for the rights and socioeconomic needs of older adults, provides a good example of how people can work together for legislative and political change.

Fifth, practitioners can connect clients with other older people by forming support and educational

---

HIGHLIGHT 10.4

Diversity and Individual Differences Among Older Adults

Just like younger people, older people are unique individuals. Consider one woman, Myrtle, age 84, whose life was filled with difficulties, including a decade of tuberculosis, the abrupt death from a heart attack of her husband at age 51 as he slept beside her, her caregiving responsibilities for her own aging and mentally ill mother for 15 years, and the need to pinch pennies her entire life. Nonetheless, Myrtle remained cheerful, optimistic, and interested in the world around her throughout her life. One of her nieces took her to China, Disney World, New Orleans, and Europe after she turned 78 (not all in one trip, of course).

Contrast Myrtle with Paula, also age 84, Myrtle's maid of honor 65 years earlier. Paula had a long, good life with a husband who adored her. He cooked and cleaned for her in addition to holding a lucrative engineering job. He died when she was 78. At that time, Paula remained financially well off. Paula began experiencing health problems, including hearing loss and diabetes, at age 80. Complications from the diabetes forced her to enter a nursing home at age 83. Paula had always been persnickety. She demanded that she get her own way, and usually she did, thanks to her devoted spouse. She was never interested in the world around her, despite the many innovations developed during her lifetime (e.g., television, jetliners, computers). She was always a complainer; everything was always wrong.

Myrtle visited Paula faithfully every Sunday for years and endured her endless whining and complaining. There could hardly be two more different people.

groups. "Group interventions are an efficient, effective way to address residents' psychosocial and life-stage-related concerns, and they also effectively decrease depression, loneliness, and isolation" (Sahlins, 2010, pp. 37–38). Groups can focus on virtually any topic of interest to clients, including retirement issues, discussion about books or news, or specific health or mental health issues.

Sixth, social workers can encourage clients to help others. For example, one social services agency organized a number of older adult clients and helped them assess their special competencies. They were then organized as volunteers to help each other. Those who could drive chauffeured others who couldn't for grocery shopping and medical appointments. People with good eyesight read to those who could not see as well. People with exceptional organizational skills organized and oversaw the volunteer activities. Many people put their strengths to use and became productive members of the community.

Empowerment for People Facing Death

**EP 2.1.1c,
2.1.10l**

The prior section addressed empowering older adults by maximizing their social support, involvement in activities, and quality of life. Another important issue facing older adults, especially as they advance in age, is the idea of preparing for and coping with their eventual death. Social workers help people during their most difficult crises. Dealing with death—be it their own or that of a loved one—is certainly one of those times. It's hard because addressing death makes you face your own mortality. Yet, helping people get through their most trying times may be the most useful and rewarding service practitioners can offer. Social workers can empower clients by playing important roles that include counseling, offering emotional support, providing information, and assisting clients or their loved ones as they cope with ensuing death.

Phases of Emotion

Kubler-Ross (1969) developed a five-stage model of emotions that appear to be involved when people face death or extreme loss (James, 2008; Kanel, 2012). These stages include the following:

1. *Denial and isolation.* An initial response to bad news is refusal to believe the news is true. "That just can't be!" "There must be some mistake." "The case records were confused." "The test results must have been flawed."

2. *Anger.* Another emotional response is anger that "it had to happen to me!" "It's not fair." "It isn't right." "Why me?!!!"

3. *Bargaining.* Still another emotional response involves bargaining, trying to make deals to get a better outcome. "Maybe there's something I can do to make the problem stop or go away." "I'll pray really hard." "I'll take the right vitamins and go through all the experimental treatments. I'll do anything to make it go away."

4. *Depression.* Depression involves feelings of extreme sadness, fatigue, and hopelessness. "It's no use. It's over anyway." "Nothing will improve." "Poor me." "I might as well lie down and die right now."

5. *Acceptance.* A final stage involves accepting the inevitable and more objectively looking at the end. Acceptance involves people who "are in the process of disengaging from this life if they are dying or disengaging from a loved one if that person is dying or has died" (Kanel, 2012, p. 146; Kubler-Ross, 1969, pp. 35–77).

A significant aspect of Kubler-Ross's phases is that they focus on how normal it is to express strong emotions when you find out you're dying or that someone close to you is dying. Note that not all of these stages occur for everyone, however, nor do they occur in the same order they're presented here. Many people vacillate back and forth among emotional stages. Hopefully, these people finally experience acceptance.

McInnis-Dittrich (2009) describes the potential emotional turmoil involved when addressing death:

It is not uncommon for a relative of a dying person to become extremely angry at the dying person, blaming him or her for not seeking medical treatment earlier or for persisting in self-destructive behavior, such as heavy smoking or drinking. This intense anger may seem incongruous with the sadness and deep affection a family member really feels for a dying older adult. Older adults may also lash out at family caregivers, which may seem alarmingly ungrateful. The emotional roller coaster that accompanies the dying process is unpredictable and disconcerting to both an older adult and the family support system. (p. 289)

Empowerment of a Person Who Is Dying

EP 2.1.10g, 2.1.10l

There are several suggestions for empowering and helping a person who is dying cope with his or her own impending death. First, encourage the client to talk about his or her feelings, even the negative ones. People must let their feelings out before they can deal with them. Convey that you are willing to talk about even difficult matters. Don't discourage crying. This is just another means of coping with sadness. Sometimes, when talking about feelings and establishing a perspective, it's helpful to examine one's life. A life review of both positive and negative events can help a person find acceptance and set his or her mind at peace.

A second suggestion for helping a client who is dying involves focusing on spirituality, if that client has religious or spiritual beliefs. "The social worker's responsibility is to be especially responsive to and respectful of the client's unique religious and spiritual traditions"; such beliefs may help the client "prepare to leave this life and enter the transformation of death" (Derezotes, 2006, p. 252).

A third suggestion for empowering a dying person involves providing assistance in making any necessary decisions that may be of concern to the client. Does the client have opinions about his or her funeral or other treatment near or after death? Are there certain items that the person would like to give to loved ones? If so, encourage the client to indicate what they are and who should receive them. You might also provide the client with needed information such as that about medications, treatments, or pain relievers. Some clients might benefit from information about hospice care as a possible choice for them. A *hospice* is a homelike residence, emphasizing residents' comfort and peace, where a person can reside and interact with loved ones in the days or weeks preceding death.

Social workers can also help older adults complete documents to make decisions about their future in the event they lose mental competence. *Advance directives* are "written instructions by the individual [who is mentally competent] to health care providers and family members about end-of-life decisions" (McInnis-Dittrich, 2009, p. 302). Two types of advance directives include living wills and Durable Power of Attorney for Health Care (McInnis-Dittrich, 2005). "A *living will* is a written document that states what the patient does or does not want in medical treatment should he or she become incapacitated" (McInnis-Dittrich, 2009, p. 303). For instance, a living will could indicate whether or not an individual chooses to live on life support when brain functioning has ceased. The *Durable Power of Attorney for Health Care* "is a legal document that designates another person to make decisions about health care when a patient becomes incapacitated" (McInnis-Dittrich, 2009, p. 303).

Helping Loved Ones Cope

Kanel (2012) provides eight suggestions for helping survivors of a loved one after that person has died. This is another task of social workers who work in nursing homes and other settings such as hospitals where death is often experienced.

1. *Help survivors actualize the loss. Talk about the loss. What happened? Ask.*
2. *Help them identify and express feelings. If they are dealing with anger, be indirect (what do you miss the most/least?). Four common difficult emotions are anger, guilt, anxiety, and helplessness.*
3. *Help survivors in living without the deceased. The problem-solving approach works well for this. Discourage major life changes for a while.*
4. *Facilitate emotional withdrawal from the deceased. Encourage survivors to go on.*
5. *Provide time to grieve. Crucial times include 3 months and 1 year after the death, anniversaries of the death, and holidays. Help clients prepare in advance for these.*
6. *Educate clients about customary grieving reactions of other individuals to help normalize the experience.*
7. *Allow for individual differences [including cross-cultural differences]. Be sensitive to individual styles.*
8. *Provide for continuing support. Encourage clients to join support groups. (p. 151)*

Empowerment of African American Grandparents Who Become Primary Child Caregivers

Multiple examples exist of how social workers and social welfare programs can empower older adults. Various facets of the older adult

EP 2.1.4

population can be targeted and assisted in many creative ways.

Okazawa-Rey (1998) describes one approach to empowerment for African American grandparents who have become primary caregivers for their grandchildren. This reflects one type of programming social workers can initiate, develop, and provide. The problem addressed is one well established at the community and national levels. Many people have become addicted to crack cocaine or methamphetamine and are ignoring their responsibilities as parents and productive citizens to pursue drug use. "Grandparents have always played major roles in the lives of their grandchildren, but in recent years this role has magnified in intensity, as more and more grandparents have become the primary caregivers of grandchildren" (Cox, 2005, p. 128).

An example of a program responding to this problem is the Grandparents Who Care Support Network of San Francisco. Most members are "poor and working class, middle-aged and [older adult] ... African-American women" (Okazawa-Rey, 1998, p. 54). They have gained custody of their grandchildren because of their own children's neglect. This is due to drug abuse, incarceration because of drug convictions, and an unwillingness to relinquish their grandchildren to strangers in the public foster care system (McAdoo, 2007).

These grandparents have found themselves in the strange and unusual circumstance of suddenly having responsibility for small children at a stage in life when they thought they were done with all that. This situation is compounded by the health problems many of these children suffer due to poor prenatal care, parental drug use during pregnancy, and child neglect. These grandparents "desperately need day care, special education services, transportation, respite care, and money" (Okazawa-Rey, 1998, p. 54). To get services, they find themselves trying to negotiate the confusing maze of bureaucracies governing service provision.

Two health care workers, Doriane Miller and Sue Trupin, identified the problems and needs and established Grandparents Who Care (Okazawa-Rey, 1998). The program is based on four principles. First, individual health problems transcend any assignment of individual blame; rather, they are related to problems in the environment. Second, cultural, legal, and organizational barriers often hinder access to needed services. Third, even if people can obtain needed services, these may be inadequate to meet their needs. Fourth, empowerment at the micro, mezzo, and macro levels is necessary for maintaining optimal health and well-being. The grandparents require not only support as individuals (a facet of micro practice) but also the development of an organization (an aspect of macro practice) to provide support group services (a dimension of mezzo practice).

Mezzo-Practice Perspectives: Establishing Support Groups

Grandparents Who Care established a series of support groups to provide information, emotional support, and practical advice. "Support groups can play important roles in combating the isolation that is frequently experienced by grandparent caregivers" (Cox, 2005, p. 133). Groups consist of 2–25 grandparents, are co-led by professional health care personnel, including social workers and nurses, and meet weekly for 90 minutes. Grandparents Who Care has a board of directors made up of grandparents, citizens, and concerned health care professionals who advise the organization.

Group members support each other in addressing a range of issues. For example, "When one woman faces a particular problem with her grandchild in the school system, another one will describe her dealings with this system and offer suggestions concerning the most effective ways to intercede" (Okazawa-Rey, 1998, p. 58). In this way members can share their experiences and work through issues. The professional co-leaders can assist the group by providing technical information about service availability, eligibility, and accessibility.

Macro-Practice Perspectives: Expanding Influence

Grandparents Who Care expanded its work in several macro dimensions to further empower its members. First, grandparents were trained as group leaders to go out and form new groups, thereby extending support to grandparents elsewhere in the community.

Second, Grandparents Who Care undertook political advocacy and lobbying on its members' behalf. One problem that advocates addressed involved the legal difficulties grandparents experienced in receiving foster care payments. As relatives, they did not technically qualify as foster parents. Other financial support available to them was not nearly as good as that provided to unrelated foster parents. Grandparents Who Care advocates lobbied with a state legislator to pass a bill allowing grandparents to receive increased benefits.

Appreciation of Spirituality and Empowerment for Navajo Older Adults in a Nursing Home

The Navajo community traditionally has maintained a rich fabric of cultural traditions, values, and spiritual beliefs. It is a nongeographical community because of its intricate interpersonal relationships, sense of identity, and recognition of members' belongingness, regardless of where they reside. Members are tied to each other by much more than simple location. Of course, many Navajos live on the Navajo reservation, a large geographical community located in the south central Colorado Plateau, which includes parts of Arizona, New Mexico, and Utah. (*Geographical communities* have geographical boundaries and occupy a designated space.)

An ongoing theme in social work practice is the importance of responding to diverse ethnic and cultural values and needs. The following account portrays how the Navajo community and a nursing home it sponsors have responded to meet the needs of aging members in ways differing from commonly held Euro-American traditions.

A Focus on Traditional Navajo Values

Traditional Navajo older adults, referred to here as "Grandparents," adhere to cultural values that differ from Euro-American traditions. For one thing, Mercer (1996) explains that

> traditional Navajo religion deals with controlling the many supernatural powers in the Navajo world. Earth Surface People (living and dead humans) and Holy People (supernatural beings) interact.... Navajos abide by prescriptions and proscriptions (taboos) given by the Holy People to maintain harmony with others, nature, and supernatural forces.... The goal of traditional Navajo life is to live in harmony and die of old age. If one indulges in excesses, has improper contacts with dangerous powers, or deliberately or accidentally breaks other rules, then disharmony, conflict, evil, sickness of body and mind, misfortune, and disaster result. (pp. 182–183)[5]

Thus, when an imbalance occurs, a person may become sick, which can be attributed to "infection by animals, natural phenomena, or evil spirits such as ghosts (*chindi*) and witches" (p. 183). Preventive ceremonies can address the root of the illness, involve the appropriate Holy People, seek to restore harmony, and forestall ill fortune. "As major social and religious events involving entire communities, ceremonies are a major investment of time and resources for the afflicted person, extended family, and clan" (p. 183).

Another primary traditional value in Navajo life is the importance placed on the extended family. Referred to as a *clan,* such families include a much more extensive membership than that of grandparents, parents, and children. The Navajo community has "more than 60 clan-based kinship groups" (p. 183). A related concept is the importance of the *hogan,* or home, as the center of Navajo family life.

Culturally Competent Treatment of Older Adult Navajo People

EP 2.1.3c, 2.1.10h, 2.1.10l

Mercer (1996) explored the treatment of older adult Navajo people, the Grandparents, who reside in the Chinle Nursing Home, a nonprofit agency whose board of directors is composed solely of Navajos. She investigated how treatment for Grandparents in Chinle differs from typical treatment provided outside the reservation. She found that, essentially, Chinle emphasizes the importance of *cultural care*—"the learned and transmitted values and beliefs that enable people to maintain their well-being and health and to deal with illness, disability, and death" (Bearse, 2008; Leininger, 1990, 1992; Mercer, 1996, p. 186).

Mercer (1996) found that culturally competent care is applied in at least six major areas (pp. 186–188):

1. *Communication:* Few Navajo Grandparents are fluent in English, so translators are used. Such translation is done with great sensitivity, because the Navajo language often has no word that means exactly what an English word does. Additionally, sensitivity is important while listening because interrupting a speaker is considered extremely rude.

2. *Clan associations and social structure:* Clan associations are very important to Navajo people.

Upon introduction, Navajos traditionally announce their clan membership. Nursing home staff are sensitive to the fact that Grandparents often have many visitors from their clan who have traveled great distances at significant cost.

3. *Personal space, modesty, privacy, and cleanliness:* Grandparents value personal space. They often find it difficult and uncomfortable to sleep in the high nursing home beds, having been accustomed to mattresses or sheep skins on the floor. Staff comply with Grandparents' wishes to sleep where they want and usually find that Grandparents eventually adjust to sleeping in beds.

Grandparents also value modesty and privacy. Therefore, communal showering is a problem. Rather, Grandparents often prefer sweat baths, which they feel cleanse them both physically and spiritually. The nursing home provides saunas to simulate these sweat baths and offers showers to residents twice each week.

Finally, Grandparents often prefer sleeping in their daytime clothes rather than changing into nightgowns or pajamas. Staff allow Grandparents to sleep in whatever they want. In time most choose night clothes.

4. *Traditional food:* Grandparents prefer "grilled mutton [meat of a mature sheep], mutton stew, fry bread, corn, fried potatoes, and coffee" (p. 187). In response, nursing home staff serve lamb three times a month and usually bake fresh bread. Staff also encourage family members to bring foods Grandparents prefer, as long as these comply with health-related dietary constraints.

5. *Dying and death:* "Traditional Navajo people have many restrictions regarding contact with the dead. They do not talk about death, believing that discussing death may 'bring it to you'" (p. 187). Navajo families will usually move a dying person to a nearby brush shelter to avoid having death occur in the hogan. In the event of a home death, that hogan is usually deserted and even demolished.

Traditionally, people touching a dead body followed specific rituals to avoid taboos. Similarly, most Grandparents and staff seek to avoid touching a dead person or his or her clothing. Usually a dying Grandparent is transferred to a hospital so that death will not occur in the nursing home. If a death does occur there, cleansing rituals are performed before other residents inhabit the room.

Because of their aversion to talking about death, no Grandparents will discuss such issues as living wills or power of attorney. Staff respect this value and do not pressure residents to do so.

6. *Cultural rituals:* To hold cultural rituals, a hogan was constructed near Chinle and is made available for ceremonies and prayers that remain important aspects of Grandparents' lives.

Examples of how diverse communities and social agencies may respond to members' values and needs are countless. The important thing for social workers is to respect and appreciate cultural differences and strive to help social services meet diverse members' needs.

Chapter Summary

The following summarizes this chapter's content as it relates to the chapter's learning objectives presented at the beginning of the chapter. Learning objectives include the following:

A Recognize an empowerment perspective for working with older adults that incorporates values and goals, and provide case examples of active aging.

An empowerment perspective for working with older adults stresses values and goals involving respect, appreciating difference, valuing choice, and promoting health. Active aging emphasizes "participation in life," "health," and "security" (Rizzo & Seidman, 2009). Various examples of active aging are provided.

B Introduce the issue of "global graying."

Global graying is an international phenomenon where the proportion of older adults is increasing globally. When addressing this issue, social workers should emphasize self-determination, enhancement of the environment and political milieu on the behalf of older adults, and existing strengths of the older adult population.

C Discuss problems older adults commonly face, including ageism, discrimination in employment, poverty, retirement, health care issues, abuse, living conditions and family variables, and transitional issues.

Ageism involves harboring negative images of and attitudes toward people simply because they are older. Older adults experience discrimination in employment. Almost half of the older adults living in the United States would fall below the poverty line if they were not receiving Social Security benefits. Current debate focuses on how to save Social Security. Suggestions include changing benefit amounts, worker contribution amounts, time lines, and criteria for recipients. Factors that increase the potential for poverty include advanced age, female gender, and being a person of color. The average age of planned retirement is 64.

The older people get, the more likely they are to experience health problems. An estimated 1.5 million older adults are victims of physical or emotional abuse. Many older adults prefer to live on their own or with other family members. Transitional issues as people age include coping with health problems and increasing dependence.

D Explain the concept of "gayging."

"Gayging" is the invisibility, lack of attention, and unfair treatment many LGB people experience as they get older (Tully, 2000). Social workers must be sensitive to their needs and their increased risk of discrimination.

E Examine various contexts for social work practice with older adults, including home- and community-based services, discharge planning in hospital settings, and service provision in nursing homes.

Home-based services are types of assistance provided to people in their own homes, either formally or informally by informal support networks. Community-based services are those provided to meet psychological and social needs outside the home in the community. Discharge planning is the comprehensive assessment of a patient's abilities and needs, the development of a plan to facilitate that patient's transition out of the hospital and back into the community or agency setting, and the implementation of that plan. Nursing homes are residential centers that provide extended maintenance and personal nursing care for people who can't adequately take care of themselves.

F Explore general empowerment issues and those for diverse populations of older adults, including African American grandparents who are primary caregivers for grandchildren and the culturally competent treatment of older Navajo people residing in a nursing home.

In nursing homes, social workers can empower residents by developing plans based on strengths, helping residents make decisions, addressing issues of concern raised by family members, linking residents with outside services, assisting other staff in understanding residents' needs, and advocating for residents' rights. Empowerment strategies should focus on adaptation, competence, relatedness, and autonomy. Increasing sensitivity to older adults and their issues can enhance effective work with this population.

Grandparents Who Care is a program that provides support for African American grandparents who are the primary caregivers of their grandchildren. Support groups and political advocacy are emphasized. The Chinle nursing home in the central Colorado Plateau provides culturally sensitive care to older adult Navajo residents. Grandparents Who Care emphasizes traditional values including communication; clan associations and social structure; respect for personal space, modesty, privacy, and cleanliness; traditional food; rituals concerning dying and death; and other cultural rituals.

G Encourage critical thinking about confronting myths about older adults, financing Social Security, determining whether Social Security discriminates against women, and proposing how older adults might be empowered through macro practice.

Critical thinking questions are posed concerning untrue myths about older adults, including that they are riddled with disease, are unattractive, sleep all the time, can't learn new things, and are senile. Questions raised about Social Security concern raising the retirement age, decreasing benefits, increasing the maximum amount of income that can be taxed, cutting increases in benefits, and offering benefits only to those who are less well off (establishing a means test). Questions also concern whether Social Security is fair to women and, if so, whether it should be reformed. Finally, critical thinking questions are raised about how older adults might be treated, resources provided, and services developed from residual versus institutional and conservative versus liberal perspectives.

LOOKING AHEAD

This chapter addressed the needs of older adults, a population-at-risk in terms of poverty, discrimination, and other problems associated with aging, such as declines in health. It discussed service provision to older adults and approaches to empowerment. Chapter 18 focuses on another population-at-risk that has special needs for policies and services—people with disabilities.

COMPETENCY NOTES

The following identifies where Educational Policy (EP) competencies and practice behaviors are discussed in the chapter.

EP 2.1.1b Practice personal reflection and self-correction to assure continual professional development. *(p. 323):* Practitioners must practice personal reflection to be sensitive to the needs and situations of LGB older adults.

EP 2.1.1c Attend to professional roles and boundaries. *(p. 329):* Social work roles with respect to people living in nursing homes are explained. *(p. 332):* One of social workers' most important roles involves helping people deal with crises, including those address facing death.

EP 2.1.3 Apply critical thinking to inform and communicate professional judgments. *(p. 317):* Stereotypes about older adults are questioned. *(p. 321):* Critical thinking questions are posed concerning the extent to which Social Security discriminates against women. *(p. 326):* Critical thinking questions address the relationship between political orientation and policies that empower older adults.

EP 2.1.3a Distinguish, appraise, and integrate multiple sources of knowledge, including research-based knowledge, and practice wisdom. *(p. 320):* Critical thinking questions encourage thought about how to address the complex issues involved in Social Security.

EP 2.1.3c Demonstrate effective oral and written communication in working with individuals, families, groups, organizations, communities, and colleagues. *(p. 323):* Social workers should use language that is respectful of and sensitive to LGB relationships and situations. *(p. 335):* Communication with Navajo grandparents should be culturally sensitive.

EP 2.1.4 Engage diversity and difference in practice. *(p. 323):* Sexual orientation is a dimension of diversity. *(p. 333):* Race and culture, both aspects of diversity, are discussed in this and the next section concerning African Americans and Navajo people, respectively.

EP 2.1.4a Recognize the extent to which culture's structures and values may oppress, marginalize, alienate, or create or enhance privilege and power. *(p. 317):* Social workers should recognize the extent to which older adults can be oppressed, marginalized, and alienated because of negative false stereotypes. *(p. 317):* Stereotypes about older adults serve to oppress, marginalize, and alienate them. *(p. 323):* Social workers should recognize the extent to which society oppresses and marginalizes LGB older adults. *(p. 330):* Practitioners must understand how society potentially oppresses and alienates older adults.

EP 2.1.4b Gain sufficient self-awareness to eliminate the influence of personal biases and values in working with diverse groups. *(p. 330):* Practitioners must work hard at self-awareness regarding any prejudices and stereotypes they may harbor toward older adults.

EP 2.1.4c Recognize and communicate their understanding of the importance of difference in shaping life experiences. *(p. 323):* Social workers must recognize how sexual orientation shapes life experiences for LGB older adults. *(p. 330):* Practitioners should recognize the extent to which their age shapes life experiences for older adults.

EP 2.1.4d View themselves as learners and engage those with whom they work as informants. *(p. 323):* Social workers should view themselves as learners and engage LGB older adults as informants. *(p. 330):* Practitioners must learn about their clients' perspectives, including those involving gender and culture.

EP 2.1.5 Advance human rights social and economic justice. *(p. 313):* It's important for social workers to understand the global ramifications for older adults as a population-at-risk.

EP 2.1.5a Understand the forms and mechanisms of oppression and discrimination. *(p. 316):* Social workers should understand the variables related to race, gender, and social class that affect and oppress segments of the older adult population. *(p. 317):* Practitioners should understand that ageism and other forces such as job discrimination and poverty (described in subsequent sections) serve as mechanisms of oppression and discrimination. *(p. 317):* Stereotypes about older adults are blind to individual strengths and serve as mechanisms of oppression. *(p. 321):* Critical thinking questions stimulate thought about Social Security and discrimination against women. *(p. 323):* Social workers should understand the oppression and discrimination faced by LGB older adults. *(p. 330):* Practitioners should identify stereotypes that serve to oppress older adults.

EP 2.1.5b Advocate for human rights and social and economic justice. *(p. 320):* Critical thinking questions encourage thought about how social and economic justice might be achieved through Social Security. *(p. 326):* Critical thinking questions encourage thought about advocating for older adults' human rights and society's responsibility to respect and care for them.

EP 2.1.8a Analyze, formulate, and advocate for policies that advance social well-being. *(p. 320):* Critical thinking questions encourage thought about Social Security policies that advance social well-being. *(p. 321):* Critical thinking questions encourage thought about the extent to which Social Security policies advance the social well-being of women. *(p. 326):* Critical thinking questions encourage thought about policies that advance older adults' social well-being.

EP 2.1.8b Collaborate with colleagues and clients for effective policy action. *(p. 326):* Political advocacy involves collaboration with colleagues and clients.

EP 2.1.9a Continuously discover, appraise, and attend to changing locales, populations, scientific and technological developments, and emerging societal trends to provide relevant services. *(p. 316):* Practitioners should continuously respond to the changing issues and conditions characterizing the older adult population.

EP 2.1.10e Assess clients' strengths and limitations. *(p. 314):* Practitioners should assess and emphasize older adult clients' strengths to help them maintain the most autonomy possible in the least restrictive environment. *(p. 324):* Social workers should assess and emphasize strengths in addition to assessing limitations when working with older adults. *(p. 330):* An empowerment perspective emphasizes the assessment and appreciation of older adult clients' strengths.

EP 2.1.10f Develop mutually agreed-on intervention goals and objectives. *(p. 329):* The case example illustrates how a nursing home social worker developed mutually agreed-upon goals with the client.

EP 2.1.10g Select appropriate intervention strategies. *(p. 324):* Social workers should select the appropriate intervention strategies involving the least restrictive settings when working with older adults. *(p. 329):* The case example demonstrates how the social worker developed appropriate intervention strategies. *(p. 330):* Appropriate intervention strategies for working with older adults are discussed. *(p. 333):* Appropriate interventions are suggested for helping clients and their loved ones deal with death.

EP 2.1.10h Initiate actions to achieve organizational goals. *(p. 335):* Chinle Nursing Home staff initiated culturally sensitive policies to provide care to residents as a major organizational goal.

EP 2.1.10j Help clients resolve problems. *(p. 324):* Practitioners can help older adults resolve problems by helping them gain access to the services they need in the least restrictive setting. *(p. 329):* Nursing home social workers' roles include helping clients resolve problems. *(p. 330):* Social workers help older adult clients resolve problems by emphasizing the strategies presented here.

EP 2.1.10k Negotiate, mediate, and advocate for clients. *(p. 326):* Social workers should advocate for policies that empower their older adult clients.

(p. 329): Advocating for clients is part of the nursing home social worker's role.

EP 2.1.10l Facilitate transitions and endings. *(p. 332):* Social workers can help clients and their families prepare for and cope with death. *(p. 333):* Specific suggestions are proposed for helping clients and their families cope with death. *(p. 335):* Culturally sensitive communication and behavior should be used when addressing the concept of death in Navajo families.

FOR FURTHER EXPLORATION ON THE INTERNET

See this text's Social Work CourseMate website at *www.cengagebrain.com* for learning tools such as chapter quizzing, videos, glossary flashcards, and more.

CHAPTER 11

Social Work and Services for People with Disabilities

Tony Savino/Image Works

Jane, age 20, was on a motorcycle outing with her fiancé, age 21, when he crashed head-on into a tree while trying to evade an oncoming car.[1] He was killed instantly. Jane's leg was so mangled she ultimately had to have it removed. "One year later she was seen by a social worker during her rehabilitation of the amputation. She was demonstrating signs of complicated grief and traumatic stress: continuing to live in her fiancé's room, refusing to let anyone remove his possessions from the room, delaying rehabilitation of her severed limb, and developing increasing fears and phobias. With the social worker she began to confront her anger toward her fiancé for losing control of the bike and causing her amputation, an emotion that seemed unacceptable to her since she had survived and he had not. Expressing and working through these feelings empowered her to become active in making more realistic plans for her life, including moving out of her fiancé's room" (Christ, Sormanti, & Francoeur, 2001, p. 126).

---

[1]This vignette was cited in "Chronic Physical Illness & Disability," by Christ, G. H., Sormanti, M., & Francoeur, R. B., in A. Gitterman (Ed.), *Handbook of Social Work Practice with Vulnerable and Resilient Populations* (2nd ed., pp. 124–162), 2001, New York: Columbia University Press.

Jane provides an example of a person who has experienced a disability result-ing from an accident happening when she was an adult. Of course, people can also be born with disabilities or gradually acquire them as a result of chronic debili-tating illness. Regardless of the cause, social workers can fulfill at least the following roles when working with people who have disabilities:

- *As counselors, social workers help people explore their feelings, confront issues, and make life plans. They can work with individuals, families, or groups to ad-dress various aspects of life with disability. For example, social workers may help families of people with disabilities discuss interpersonal issues, focus on strengths, cope with difficulties, and address needs. Similarly, working with groups of people with disabilities may involve exploring feelings, coping me-chanisms, and potential resources in addition to providing mutual support.*

- *As educators, social workers provide information about disabilities and related issues.*

- *As brokers, social workers link people who have disabilities and their families with needed services.*

- *As rehabilitative team members, social workers consult with occupational thera-pists, physical therapists, speech therapists, psychologists, nurses, and other med-ical personnel to develop coordinated treatment plans for people with disabilities.*

- *As case coordinators, social workers synchronize and oversee service provision for people with disabilities who have multiple needs.*

- *As advocates, social workers seek to improve the treatment of people with dis-abilities through legislation and agency provision of service.*

EP 2.1.4

The U.S. Census Bureau indicates that almost 36 million people in the United States, or almost 12% of the population age 5 or older, have some type of disability; over 20.2 million people ages 16 to 64 have some condition that prevents them from working or limits the amount of work they can do (U.S. Census Bureau, 2010).

Who are people with disabilities? They are anyone who has a permanent "phys-ical or mental impairment [or ongoing health or mental health condition] that sub-stantially limits one or more major life activities"; these activities include "seeing, hearing, speaking, walking, breathing, performing manual tasks, learning, caring for oneself, and working" (Equal Employment Opportunity Commission, 1997, p. 1). Disabilities, which vary widely in severity and the extent to which they affect daily functioning, can commence at any point in life, from birth to old age.

To some extent, disabilities are related to both poverty and race. People who are poor are more likely to experience disability, and more severe disabilities, than people who are better off financially. And African Americans age 45–64 are over five times as likely to experience a work disability as white Americans in that same age group (U.S. Census Bureau, 2010).

How various people including experts categorize disabilities varies markedly, depending on what aspects of the disability they emphasize (Patchner & DeWeaver,

2008). For example, developmental disabilities *involve early onset and a lifelong time span. This umbrella concept can include difficulties in cognitive ability, such as intellectual disability (formerly mental retardation), and physical disabilities, such as orthopedic problems affecting bones and joints, and hearing problems.*

Mobility disabilities, in contrast, can occur at any time. Mobility disabilities reflect a lack of physical ability to get around and conduct life tasks.

However, different categories of disability may overlap. Some mobility disabilities can also be considered developmental. For instance, a person with cerebral palsy (a type of developmental disability involving problems in muscular control) who cannot walk without crutches also has a mobility disability.

Mobility disabilities are also a type of physical disability because they involve physical bodily performance, as opposed to cognitive or emotional functioning. Many developmental disabilities such as hearing loss or visual impairment are also physical disabilities because of their physical rather than mental nature. The matter is further complicated because many people have multiple disabilities.

The point of this discussion is not to confuse you but to clarify this chapter's overall approach to the wide range of disabilities. Arbitrary distinctions are made regarding how disabilities are sorted and discussed. It is far beyond the scope of this chapter to cover all disabilities. Thus the intent is to provide a general introduction to what disabilities might involve and how social work practitioners help empower people who have them.

On one hand, social workers practice directly with people who have disabilities and their families on the micro and mezzo levels. On the other, social workers have a responsibility to advocate on behalf of people with disabilities to make sure they get the resources and services they need.

A primary goal of social work education is "to promote human and community well-being. . . . [S]ocial work's purpose is actualized through its quest for social and economic justice, the prevention of conditions that limit human rights, the elimination of poverty, and the enhancement of the quality of life for all persons" (CSWE, 2008b, p. 1). Social workers strive to enhance people's living conditions in their social environment to make them as comfortable and supportive as possible. One way to accomplish this is to "analyze, formulate, and advocate for policies that advance social well-being" (CSWE, 2008b, EP 2.1.8a).

Learning Objectives

A Define mobility disabilities and developmental disabilities, and identify a range of specific disabilities clustered under each concept.

B Investigate the importance of self-determination for people with disabilities as an ethical aspect of social work practice.

C Examine the history of how people with developmental disabilities have been treated in the macro social environment.

D Describe generalist social work practice with people who have developmental disabilities.

E   Discuss avenues of legislative, community, and worker empowerment.

F   Examine the macro environment's potential for empowering people with visual impairment and intellectual disabilities.

G   Encourage critical thinking about residual versus institutional approaches to service provision for people with disabilities, empowerment through language, deinstitutionalization, and the Americans with Disabilities Act.

People with Mobility Disabilities

People who have mobility disabilities "are those whose physical differences require them to achieve physical activities in a variety of alternate ways" (Mackelprang & Salsgiver, 2009, p. 177). For example, a person with a spinal cord injury may require a wheelchair to move from place to place and achieve the mobility needed to conduct the business of life.

Mobility disorders may be *congenital*—that is, "acquired before, during, or immediately after birth"—or they may be *acquired* at some time later in life (Mackelprang & Salsgiver, 2009, p. 178). Many congenital mobility disabilities are also considered developmental disabilities (e.g., cerebral palsy, orthopedic problems) and will be discussed later in the chapter. A number of acquired mobility problems are described in Highlight 11.1.

Ethical Implications for Social Work Practice: The Importance of Self-Determination

EP 2.1.2a, 2.1.2c, 2.1.4a, 2.1.4b, 2.1.5a

It's easy to make false assumptions about people who have mobility and other physical disabilities. Myths about disabilities include the following:

Myth: The more severe a physical disability is, the less intelligent the person.

Fact: A person may have a severe physical disability and yet have a brilliant mind.

Myth: People with physical disabilities are unable to function normally in society.

Fact: People with physical disabilities can live productive, fruitful, happy lives when they receive the support they need.

Myth: People with one kind of disability also have other disabilities.

Fact: One disability may have nothing to do with other disabilities. A person with one disability can function as well as anyone else in other areas. This myth sometimes is referred to as the *spread of disability*.

For example, Steve, age 19, has quadriplegia—the paralysis of all four limbs. He broke his neck in a swimming accident three years ago. He tells the story of how he went out to eat with his parents at a local family restaurant several months after the accident. The waitress approached the table and began to take orders. When it was Steve's turn to order, the waitress turned to his father and asked, "What would he like to order?"

Steve's father replied, "I don't know. Why don't you ask him?"

The waitress turned to Steve and shouted verrrrrry slowly, "WHAT ... WOULD ... YOU ... LIKE ... TO ... ORDER?"

Steve, whose hearing was just fine, verrrrrry slowly shouted back, "A ... QUARTER POUND ... CHEESE-BURGER ... AND ... FRIES ... PLEASE!"

EP 2.1.2b, 2.1.4c, 2.1.5c

The waitress had made the assumption that because Steve couldn't walk and had limited use of his arms, he couldn't hear, either. She also took for granted that there was something wrong with his brain. She made the mistake of assuming a spread of disability–namely, that a person with one disability automatically has others. People with disabilities have

the right to participate fully and equitably in society. This participation includes the freedom, to the fullest extent possible, to live independently, to exercise self-determination, to make decisions about

HIGHLIGHT 11.1

Acquired Mobility Disabilities

The following are examples of *acquired* mobility disabilities (Mackelprang & Salsgiver, 1999). All may require the use of supportive equipment depending on the severity.

Stroke: "A blockage or hemorrhage of a blood vessel leading to the brain, causing an inadequate oxygen supply and often long-term impairment of sensation, movement, or functioning" (Nichols, 1999, p. 1295). Brain cells die when they don't receive adequate oxygen, causing damage to the nervous system. Strokes can result in a wide range of symptoms including partial or total paralysis, memory loss, speech or language deficits, and inability to think clearly.

Muscular dystrophy: "Any of a group of hereditary diseases characterized by a progressive wasting of the muscles" (Mish, 2008, p. 818). Some forms progress so quickly that people require the use of wheelchairs by the time they reach adolescence. Symptoms include increasingly weakened muscles, an awkward gait, and increasing lack of coordination.

Rheumatoid arthritis (RA): A chronic condition in which a person's immune system attacks the joints, causing pain, inflammation, stiffness, swelling, and deterioration. Joints tend to experience progressive deformity, often resulting in the need for increased support through

devices such as canes, crutches, or wheelchairs. About 1% of the adult population in the United States has this disease, three-quarters of whom are women (Mackelprang & Salsgiver, 1999, p. 88).

Multiple sclerosis (MS): A disease of the brain tissue in which the myelin sheath—the fatty material wrapped around and insulating the parts of nerve cells that conduct nerve impulses in the brain to other nerve cells—deteriorates, thereby causing varying degrees of muscular dysfunction, paralysis, and muscle tremors.

Myasthenia gravis (MG): A disease affecting voluntary muscles (those controlled by one's will) in which nerve impulses are impaired, resulting in fatigue, weakness, and difficulties controlling muscles. Virtually any muscles can be affected, and symptoms range from weakness in the arms and legs to difficulties in swallowing, controlling eye movements, or breathing.

Spinal cord injury: Damage to the spinal cord, often due to accidents or incidents of violence, resulting in the loss of muscular control and inability to experience sensation. Paraplegia is paralysis of the lower part of the body; quadriplegia is paralysis from the neck down. The severity of effects depends on the location and extent of damage to the spinal cord.

---

their living conditions and treatment plans, to obtain an education, to be employed, and to participate as citizens.

(NASW, 2009, p. 249)

The concept of self-determination has special ethical implications for adults with mobility and other physical disabilities. Major (2000) indicates that "client self-determination is closely linked with the concept of autonomy"—a person's ability to function independently (p. 9). Related to the type and degree of their disabilities, people with physical disabilities often experience greater difficulties maintaining autonomy than able-bodied people. For example, a person with a serious visual impairment may have great difficulty getting around in an unfamiliar neighborhood without assistance.

Gilson, Bricout, and Baskind (1998) interviewed six people with physical disabilities who felt that social workers tended to focus more on their health

status and limitations than on themselves as unique individuals. Ethical concerns included stereotyping people based on the disability label and clearly visible disabilities, ignoring strengths, accessing personal information without receiving client permission, and not consulting with clients as expert resources for information about their disabilities and issues. Despite the small sample size, this study, with its implications of paternalism by practitioners, raises serious ethical questions regarding social workers' efforts to maximize self-determination. Apparently it is easy for social workers to make assumptions about people with disabilities that emphasize weakness instead of strength.

Social workers should follow three recommendations to maximize service provision and client self-determination. These include adopting a consumer-centered approach, learning about services and resources, and advocating for clients with disabilities whenever possible.

Adopting a Consumer-Oriented Approach

**EP 2.1.1d,
2.1.4b,
2.1.4d,
2.1.10c,
2.1.10f**

First, social workers should adopt a *consumer-centered approach* (Tower, 1994, p. 191). Treating people as consumers means accepting that they know their own needs and can make intelligent decisions about services. The term *consumer* implies greater power and choice than does the term *client*. This approach contrasts sharply with that of making decisions about what's best for clients without their input, recommendations, and consent. Adopting a consumer-centered approach, of course, is important in working with any client. However, because of stereotypes and misconceptions about disability, social workers must be particularly vigilant about this when working with clients who have disabilities.

Four facets are especially important. First, social workers must listen carefully to what the client is saying instead of jumping to conclusions based on the disability label. Second, they must ask questions and seek clarification whenever they do not understand something. Third, they must scrutinize any possible assumptions they may be making about their client and his or her disability. In essence, they must confront their stereotypes and work to get rid of them. Fourth, they should obtain clients' *informed consent*. This is the condition in which clients grant permission for a social worker to undertake the intervention process after the worker clearly informs clients of all the facts, risks, and alternatives involved (NASW, 2008, 1.03).

Case Example Kachina is a case manager for people with severe physical disabilities. Earlier chapters established that case managers are practitioners who, on behalf of a specific client, assess needs; coordinate required services provided by any number of agencies, organizations, or facilities; and monitor service provision. Usually one individual is designated case manager for specific cases and coordinates a range of services, often provided by a variety of workers from different agencies. The intent is to make total service provision as effective and efficient as possible.

Kachina often coordinates services of group homes, in-home support services, Meals-on-Wheels, medical centers, physical therapists, speech therapists, occupational therapists, and others depending on individual client needs. Kachina always makes it a point to work the service plan out with individual clients, obtaining their permission to proceed. She reviews with clients the pros and cons of each prescribed service. She works hard to make certain clients understand what each service involves and what expectations they must fulfill. For example, physical therapy might involve a designated number of weekly sessions, physical work, and possible pain. Positive results may include significantly increased agility, flexibility, strength, and speed. Clients then can make informed decisions about whether to proceed with that service.

Learning About Services and Resources

A second way social workers can maximize service provision and self-determination for people with disabilities is to learn about services and resources (Major, 2000; NASW, 2009). People with physical disabilities have the same needs and wants as able-bodied people. They simply have more obstacles getting in the way of what they need. Services include those associated with rehabilitation, employment, health, place of residence, recreation, and personal care. Financial resources include various sources of public funding such as disability insurance, workers' compensation, Supplemental Security Income (SSI), and other forms of public assistance.

The Self-Determination Movement: Recommendations for Policy Change

Major (2000) urges that social workers familiarize themselves with various advocacy and resource groups. For example, the Self-Determination Movement, funded by grants from the Robert Wood Johnson Foundation, "is an attempt on the part of people with disabilities to guarantee client autonomy in their quest for services" (Major, 2000, p. 11). It provides an information network, advocacy, and a range of supportive services. Additionally, supporters encourage public policy changes that incorporate self-determination initiatives.

The Self-Determination Movement is founded on four primary principles (National Program Office on Self-Determination [NPOSD], 1998). First, *freedom* concerns people with disabilities having the same rights as other citizens. They should be able to choose where they want to live and how to spend their time just like anybody else.

The second principle, *authority*, involves people with disabilities having control over their own finances, prioritizing how their money should be spent, and developing their own budgets. Major (2000) cites the following example:

A married couple who had been previously receiving supports and services from two different agencies "frequently sought psychiatric hospitalizations to be together" (NPOSD, 1998). After implementing a self-determination program, the couple now lives together and is served by one agency. Because the couple can supply each other with many of the supports they need, they are much more comfortable and content with their situation. What is equally important to note here is that the overall cost of providing their services has decreased significantly. (p. 12)

Support, the third foundation principle for the Self-Determination Movement, involves having people with disabilities make decisions about where their support comes from. Instead of being given "supervision," people with disabilities should be able to seek their own support systems for companionship. Similarly, they should be able to determine what specific tasks necessitate formal assistance from paid staff and others.

The final principle, *responsibility*, involves the wise disbursement of public funding. Resources used by people with disabilities should be considered as investments in their quality of life, and not simply as lists specifying purchase of specific services. Just as all citizens should be responsible for the efficient and effective use of resources, so should they. Similarly, people with disabilities should be able to contribute to their communities' well-being in meaningful ways (e.g., volunteering, voting, running for public office).

The National Association of Social Workers' (2009) issue statement on people with disabilities stresses the importance of self-determination:

This approach encompasses a continuum that ranges from involving the client in the decision making about the treatment plan to having people with disabilities define the goals of such a plan. People with disabilities may define program objectives in organizations where they are themselves employed as decision makers. . . . People with disabilities may become . . . experts, assisting others as well. (p. 249)

Advocating for Clients with Disabilities Whenever Possible

A third suggestion for social workers to maximize service provision and client self-determination involves advocating for clients with disabilities when

necessary in collaboration with them (NASW, 2009). Clients may need expanded services or additional resources. Social work practitioners work with their clients to determine their needs. Workers also strive to change agency policy and laws governing resources to benefit people with physical disabilities. Subsequent sections of the chapter discuss advocacy in more detail.

Sometimes political advocacy is necessary. The Americans with Disabilities Act of 1990 (ADA), discussed more thoroughly later in the chapter, is a good example of positive legislation on behalf of people with disabilities. Focus on Critical Thinking 11.1 raises questions concerning value orientations to working with people who have disabilities and to social welfare policy perspectives.

Defining Developmental Disabilities

Five attributes characterize people with *developmental disabilities* (Centers for Disease Control [CDC], 2011b; Patchner & DeWeaver, 2008; P.L. 101-496, 104 Stat. 1191, 1990). First, the disability is both severe and chronic, resulting from some mental or physical impairment. Second, the disability occurs before age 22. Third, the conditions are likely to be permanent. Fourth, the disability "results in substantial functional limitations in three or more of the following areas of major life activity: (i) self-care, (ii) receptive and expressive language, (iii) learning, (iv) mobility, (v) self-direction, (vi) capacity for independent living, and (vii) economic self-sufficiency" (P.L. 101-496, 104 Stat. 1191, 1990). Fifth, a developmental disability demonstrates the need for lifelong supplementary help and services.

Examples of developmental disabilities are intellectual disabilities, cerebral palsy, epilepsy, orthopedic problems, hearing impairment or deafness, visual impairment or blindness, and autism (Barker, 2003; CDC, 2008b; DeWeaver, 1995). Each has serious implications for living in the macro social environment.

Intellectual Disabilities

Intellectual disabilities (also referred to as *mental retardation* and, sometimes, *cognitive disabilities*) involve a condition manifested before age 18 such that an individual scores significantly below average on standard intelligence tests and has deficits in adaptive functioning (i.e., the ability to conduct daily living

Residual Versus Institutional Approaches to Service Provision for People with Disabilities

Critical Thinking Questions

EP 2.1.3, 2.1.8a

- To what extent do the suggestions for empowerment through promoting self-determination for people with disabilities reflect *residual* versus *institutional* policies and programming? (Recall that residual policies focus on reactions to problems, generally providing as few benefits as possible. Institutional policies view social services as people's right and provide ongoing benefits to enhance people's lives and well-being.)
- To what extent does service provision for people with disabilities demonstrate *conservative* versus *liberal* values?

Now consider the three basic principles involved that relate to the following questions (these are similar to the questions posed concerning value orientations to service provision to older adults):

Critical Thinking Questions

- Who should assume responsibility? Should people with disabilities be expected to provide for and take care of themselves? Or is it society's responsibility to help them when they need it?
- Who is to blame for the problems and needs of people with disabilities? To what extent will people with disabilities take advantage of social welfare benefits when they really don't need them? Will providing ongoing services and benefits significantly enhance their health, welfare, and comfort?
- To what extent should the government interfere in people's lives? Is it the government's responsibility to improve the health and functioning of people with disabilities?

tasks) (American Psychiatric Association [APA], 2000; Friend, 2011; Smith & Tyler, 2010). It appears that 2.5% to 3% of schoolchildren ages 6 to 17 have intellectual disabilities; although government educational authorities cite a much smaller percentage, this underrepresentation apparently is due to the stigma of labeling a child as having "mental retardation" and the subsequent avoidance of using such a label (Friend, 2011; Smith & Tyler, 2010). *Mental retardation* (not *intellectual disabilities*) has been the term traditionally used in federal legislation governing the provision of special education. However, in fall 2010 President Barack Obama signed into law a bill that would change the term "mental retardation" to "intellectual disability" in many aspects of federal policy; in order to avert costs, the changes in specific pieces of legislation will occur over the next several years as they are periodically reviewed and revised (Diament, 2010). Focus on Critical Thinking 11.2 examines the language used to refer to people with such disabilities.

Cerebral Palsy

Cerebral palsy is a disability involving problems in muscular control and coordination resulting from damage to the brain before it has matured—that is, before or during birth. Problems include lack of balance, difficulty walking, weakness, and uncontrolled or restricted movements, depending on where in the brain the damage occurred. It should be emphasized that these people may experience only motor impairment, with intellectual ability being unaffected.

Epilepsy

Epilepsy (commonly referred to as *seizure disorder*) is an abrupt change in an individual's conscious state that may involve unconsciousness, convulsive motor activity, or sensory distortions. Seizures are caused by sudden bursts of electrical activity in some brain cells causing reactions in other brain cells. Epilepsy can result from virtually any type of injury to or condition in the brain including high fevers, chemical imbalances, infections, and physical damage; in up to 70% of all cases, the specific cause remains unidentified (Friend, 2011).

Orthopedic Problems

Orthopedic problems are "defects or diseases of the muscles and bones" (Hallahan, Kauffman, & Pullen, 2012,

FOCUS ON CRITICAL THINKING 11.2

Empowerment Through Language: People with Intellectual Disabilities

Critical Thinking Questions

EP 2.1.1d, 2.1.3c

How do the words you use to describe people affect your opinions about them and the way you view them? To what extent can labels place people in a negative—or positive—light?

The following brief discussion focuses on the significance of words with respect to people who have intellectual disabilities. After reading it, think about what terms might be best to use when talking about this population. Terms used to discuss these people have changed over time (Mackelprang, 2008; Mackelprang & Salsgiver, 2009). In the past, derogatory terms included "crippled," "handicapped," "retarded," and "disabled," among others. Using such terms to define people with the disability stated first (e.g., handicapped person) placed emphasis on the disability, not the fact that you are referring to a unique individual. Current terminology emphasizes placing the person first, and hence using terms like "person with a disability" (NASW, 2009).

The term *mental retardation* clearly has negative connotations. One of the nastiest things children call other children when they're angry or making fun of others is "Retard!" or "Mental!" Social workers and others working with people who have this type of disability are trying to use less negative terms.

Friend (2011) reflects that different states may use still other terms (e.g., "cognitive disability," "cognitive impairment," "mental impairment," "mental disability," or "mental handicap"). Much apparently depends on tradition and the terminology used in current legislation. The new change in federal law from using "mental retardation" to "intellectual disability" should gradually influence state legislation.

This book will use the term *people with intellectual disabilities* because it is more positive and thus most empowering, in addition to being the new legal term. It is interesting that Moreno (2001) suggests using the term *disAbility* (with a capital A) to replace *disability* (p. 205).

p. 405). Although there is no neurological impairment, orthopedic problems result in an inability to move about normally. Usually difficulties involve "the legs, arms, joints, or spine, making it difficult or impossible for the child to walk, stand, sit, or use his or her hands" (Hallahan et al., 2012, p. 405). These problems can have genetic origins or can result from injury, disease, accidents, or other developmental disorders (Hallahan et al., 2012).

Deafness and Hardness of Hearing

"The deaf and hard of hearing community is diverse. There are variations in the cause and degree of hearing loss, age at the onset, educational background, communication methods, and how individuals feel about their hearing loss" (The National Association of the Deaf [NAD], 2011a). Two opposing perceptions of people who are deaf exist, one based on the medical model and one a cultural model (Sheridan & White, 2008). The medical model views deafness as a medical problem and focuses on alleviating a person's "deficits" such as improvement of hearing,

if possible, and use of spoken language. The cultural perspective views the *Deaf* (with uppercase spelling) as a community with its own culture, a vibrant, expressive use of sign language, and a strong emphasis on its members' strengths.

It's very important for social workers to respect how people identify and feel about themselves (NAD, 2011a; Sheridan & White, 2008). Prioritizing needs and referrals to services and support systems clearly depends on clients' values and reference group. Social workers who work with people who are deaf should be culturally competent and preferably fluent in the use of sign language (Sheridan & White, 2008).

The degree to which people are unable to hear varies dramatically. The term *hardness of hearing* refers to people with mild to moderate hearing loss. People who are *deaf* experience a moderate to severe hearing loss that may include no hearing ability. Any of these people may or may not identify themselves with the Deaf community. Those who identify with the Deaf feel they are an integral part of the community with all its culture and customs and appreciate the richness of their sign language. On the other hand, people who are hard of hearing or deaf may have little contact with other Deaf people who use sign language and do not feel they are part of the Deaf community. One factor that may be involved is the time of life when the hearing loss occurs and how strongly group identification has already been established. Note that identification may change over the life span. "Individuals can choose an audiological or cultural [lifestyle] perspective. It's all about choices, comfort level, mode of communication, and acceptance [of hearing loss]" (NAD, 2011).

Note that the National Association of the Deaf (NAD) and the World Federation of the Deaf (WFD) strongly recommend the use of the terms *deaf* and *hard of hearing* over *hearing impaired* (NAD, 2011). NAD (2011) indicates that hearing people are comfortable with "hearing impaired" and feel that it's "politically correct." On the other hand, people who are deaf and hard of hearing feel that the terms "deaf" and "hard of hearing" are "not negative in any way at all" (NAD, 2011). They feel the term "hearing impaired" is negative for them because it sets up a standard of "hearing" that implies there's something wrong with them when there is not.

Visual Impairment

Visual impairment is difficulty in perception compared to the norm that is experienced through sight. Many people have a mild visual impairment correctable by glasses or contact lenses. People of special concern here are those whose vision cannot be corrected and so experience significant functional limitations. Rothman (2003) explains:

> *We are all familiar with the expression "20/20 vision." Having 20/20 vision means that one can see, at a distance of 20 feet, what a "normal" eye can see. As visual acuity decreases, the standard 20 that represent "20 feet" remains the same, but the second number changes. The higher the second number, the greater the visual impairment. To be legally blind [emphasis added] a person's vision must be 20/200, meaning that he or she can see at 20 feet what the "normal" eye can see at 200 feet. A measure of 20/80 in the best eye, with corrections, indicates a visual impairment. Using this model, there are about 500,000 people in the United States who are legally blind (Mackelprang & Salsgiver, 1999, p. 125) and a much larger number who are visually impaired. (p. 131)*

Autism Spectrum Disorders

Autism spectrum disorders (ASD) are conditions "that share similar characteristics in the areas of (a) social interaction, (b) verbal or nonverbal communication, and (c) repetitive behaviors or interests. Unusual responses to sensory stimuli are also often present. The key word in the term ASD is *spectrum,* which implies similar characteristics but great variance in the actual behavioral patterns exhibited" (Smith & Tyler, 2010, p. 406). Autism spectrum disorders involve three syndromes, although significant differences in characteristics and behavior exist within each syndrome. These syndromes, ranging from most severe to mildest on the spectrum, are: autism, Asperger syndrome, and pervasive developmental disorder—not otherwise specified (Smith & Tyler, 2010, p. 406).

Autism is an all-encompassing condition often characterized by the following six characteristics (Hallahan et al., 2012):

1. People with autism have an intense inner–directedness and problems such as inability to participate in "normal" social interaction and relationships.
2. They tend to experience communication difficulties. They might have difficulties acquiring language in the first place, effectively expressing their thoughts and feelings, or accurately reading the meaning of nonverbal behavior and facial expressions.
3. People with autism often demonstrate repetitive self-stimulating movements such as waving a hand in front of their eyes for a long time.
4. They may experience an intense obsession with objects, a limited range of interests that can capture their attention, and a compulsive need for predictability and sameness (e.g., they won't tolerate a piece of furniture being moved).
5. Autism is characterized by demonstration of "cognitive deficits similar to those of people with intellectual disabilities," but with some aspects "peculiar to autism" (Hallahan et al., 2012, p. 244). For example, people with autism may have difficulty organizing and understanding information. They might easily remember a series of words but have absolutely no idea about what the words mean (Friend, 2011).
6. People with autism often experience difficulties with sensory perception, being either overly sensitive to or extremely unresponsive to types of

sensory stimulation. They might not respond to sounds as if they were deaf, or they might be unresponsive to some sounds (e.g., a school bell signaling the beginning and end of classes), but very responsive to other sounds (e.g., whispering by peers). Examples of being hypersensitive include the inability to tolerate fluorescent lights or the touch of another person.

Asperger syndrome (AS) involves abnormalities including the same characteristics displayed in autism, but in a much milder form (Hallahan et al., 2012). For example, a person with AS might do reasonably well in school and be fairly adept at communication. However, that person might also find it difficult to establish "normal" interpersonal relationships and might feel the compulsive need to control his or her environment. Hallahan and his colleagues (2012) elaborate:

> *Many of the social interaction difficulties of those with Asperger syndrome are due to their inability to think about situations in a nuanced way. They are often overly literal in how they 'read' the behavior and language of others. And they often interpret situations using logic to the exclusion of emotion or sentiment. Stephen Shore (2003) provides an example of his struggles with being overly literal:*
>
> *A friend of mine ... said he felt "like a pizza." "What do you mean—'feel like a pizza'?" And it wasn't until college that I realized, "Oh, he meant he felt like EATING a pizza." At this time, idioms [unusual expressions in a language that mean something different from the precise individual words involved] usually go zipping past me but I am often able to "pull them back" for further examination before I say something ridiculous. But it takes some additional thinking on my part, to figure out "Well, what's the meaning? How do I interpret this?" (pp. 245–246)*

The third disorder in the autistic spectrum is *pervasive developmental disorder—not otherwise specified* (PDD-NOS). In this condition, not all "ASD characteristics (problems in communication, social interaction, and repetitive or manneristic behaviors) are present or they are mild" (Smith & Tyler, 2010, p. 413). "The PDD part of the diagnosis signifies characteristics very similar to those of autism and Asperger syndrome, but the characteristics are not as clearly expressed.

The NOS part refers to [not having] other specified disorders or syndromes" (Smith & Tyler, 2010, p. 413).

Multiple Disabilities

Any individual may experience several disabilities at the same time (DeWeaver, 1995; Freedman, 1995; Gargiulo, 2006). For instance, a person with intellectual disabilities may also have an orthopedic problem or epilepsy (Freedman, 1995). A developmental disability may originate in some genetic disorder or from a problem occurring before, during, or after birth (DeWeaver, 1995). It may also result from problems derived from some combination of these conditions.

Treatment over Time of People with Developmental Disabilities: The Quest for Social and Economic Justice

EP 2.1.4a, 2.1.5a, 2.1.9a

Because of the difficulties experienced by people with developmental disabilities, community support systems, and available agency resources are extremely important. How community residents and macro-level decision makers view people with developmental disabilities has tremendous implications for the latter's quality of life. To more fully understand the macro social environment's impacts, Mary (1998) describes how community attitudes and resulting social policies have changed in recent decades.

Prior to the Late 1960s: Individual Pathology

Until the late 1960s, community treatment and public policy emphasized individual pathology. The medical model formed the basis for conceptualizing developmental disabilities. People were considered "patients," with caregivers focusing on individual diagnoses and the resulting problems (Mary, 1998, p. 249; NASW, 2009). This "traditional model emphasized pathology, deficit, and malfunctioning ... inappropriately viewing ... [people with disabilities] as passive, dependent, and deficient" (NASW, 2000, p. 246). Many people with developmental disabilities were placed in large state or regional institutions, where they received custodial care and were kept clean and safe. These times obviously did not foster the current strong professional values of client self-determination and empowerment.

The 1970s and 1980s: A Community-Based Approach

The 1970s and early 1980s saw significant changes in how people with developmental disabilities were viewed. Principles becoming important, especially for people with intellectual disabilities, were "normalization," deinstitutionalization, "individual program planning," and "the developmental model" (Mary, 1998, p. 249).

Normalization

Normalization is the belief that every person, even those with the most severe disabilities, should have life conditions and behavioral patterns that are as close as possible to those ordinarily experienced by others in the social and physical environment. Previously, people with developmental disabilities had been placed "out of sight and mind" in obscurely located institutions. During the 1970s and 1980s, however, communities and organizations started viewing such people as clients who had a right to live as normally as possible. This approach "shifted much of the problem from the individual to the environment" (Mary, 1998, p. 250). Instead of focusing on people's negative diagnoses, emphasis was placed on the importance of the social environment for an individual's quality of life.

Deinstitutionalization

A parallel concept to normalization is *deinstitutionalization*—the practice of moving people who require supportive care for physical or mental conditions from institutional settings into the community (DeWeaver, 2008; Mary, 1998; Mish, 2008). Community facilities vary in size and complexity, and include larger transitional settings, group homes, family homes, and individual residences. Placement depends on client needs and facility availability. Sometimes these facilities are referred to as *community-based residential facilities* (CBRFs). As explained earlier, deinstitutionalization assumes that the more people with developmental disabilities can be assimilated into the community and lead "normal" lives, the better their quality of life will be. Focus on Critical Thinking 11.3 addresses some of the problems with this approach.

Individual Program Planning

Social workers, often functioning as case managers, developed *individual programs*, a third principle espoused in the 1970s and 1980s. Such programs emphasized people's environments and intervention results that would enhance their functioning within those environments. With intervention, the focus was on helping people with disabilities maximize independence and self-determination in the least restrictive environment possible (Garvin & Tropman, 1998; Mackelprang, 2008; Mary, 1998). The concept of *least restrictive environment* (discussed in Chapter 9) concerns the encouragement of clients to enjoy as much freedom and to make as many decisions for themselves as they can. This concept is related to normalization and deinstitutionalization. That is, people living in the community are more likely to lead normal lives and make their own decisions than those living under institutional care. Evaluating the effectiveness of entire programs was also stressed.

The Developmental Model

The fourth important concept during the 1970s and 1980s was that treatment should be guided by a *developmental model* based on a continuum of service. People received services depending on the type and intensity of their needs. People with developmental disabilities were *clients* whom professionals assessed in terms of their needs. These professionals then determined necessary services depending on where the clients fell on the developmental continuum of service. You might picture a ruler. If a client was assessed as functioning at the 6¼-inch point, then that client would receive the services appropriate for that exact point. Likewise, a client at the 10-inch point would receive services designated for that level of assessment. Emphasis was placed not on the individual as a unique personality but rather on the assessed level of need and the designated services available to address that need.

Often clients' needs change over time. One assumption was that many clients made progress toward greater independence in a step-by-step process. A client had to master one skill first before attempting a more difficult one. For example, a young woman with mild intellectual disabilities might start out living in a group home where she could learn basic housekeeping, cooking, and self-care skills including shopping and paying bills. She might then move to an apartment complex or boarding house for people with intellectual disabilities. Houseparents

FOCUS ON CRITICAL THINKING 11.3

Deinstitutionalization: An Attempt at Empowerment

Think about people with intellectual disabilities who need some degree of support and care.

Critical Thinking Questions

EP 2.1.3

Is it better to shelter and coddle them, to ensure that they're protected from life's perils—and many of its pleasures? Or is it worth the effort to encourage as much independence as possible? Consider the following issues concerning deinstitutionalization.

Although the proponents of deinstitutionalization had good intentions and many successes, there were also significant problems. For one thing, simply placing clients in the community did not necessarily mean integration or acceptance in that community (Mary, 1998). It did not mean automatic attitude readjustments on the part of community residents to alter their old stereotypes and unfounded fears about people with developmental disabilities.

Another problem with deinstitutionalization concerned inadequate community resources and services.

Institutions were expensive, but so were community-based services. People could get lost and be severed from service provision altogether. Frequently community-based services were furnished by a complicated mixture of state, local, public, and private agencies providing an unevenly distributed conglomeration of services (Freedman, 1995). Service provision could be confusing to clients and their families because some services were available to the general public and others only to those with specific disabilities (DeWeaver, 1995). (Try calling the Social Security Office to get some specific information about a case. See how well you understand what's going on—and you're in college, at that.) Other criticisms of deinstitutionalization included people being discharged too quickly and sometimes inappropriately (e.g., without adequate planning for continued community service provision).

Critical Thinking Questions

To what extent do you think the concept of deinstitutionalization is good or bad? What are your reasons? Under what circumstances might it be more likely to work?

---

or residential caregivers would not be living with her, but would be available in another apartment to help her with problems or questions. Eventually the woman might achieve enough self-care mastery to live on her own or with a roommate.

Another assumption was that clients' needs changed over time, but they required increasing levels of help and assistance. A person with a deteriorating orthopedic problem involving his knees might require increasingly more intensive help as he lost mobility. Depending on his assessed state of need at any time, in the 1970s and 1980s he would have received a designated level of service.

The 1990s and Beyond: Consumer Empowerment

The 1990s brought with them a significantly greater emphasis on individual choice and personalized planning for people with developmental disabilities (DePoy & Gilson, 2004; Freedman, 1995; Mary, 1998). Previously, people with developmental disabilities had been viewed as clients whom professionals

assessed and provided services to based on their level of functioning. There was relatively little variation of service provision at the assessed level. Today's perspective reflects four new important concepts—individualization, choices, innovation, and family support.

Individualization

Today practitioners should assume a much more *individualized* approach wherein that "services are driven by client needs, and clients are viewed as consumers with choices" (Mary, 1998, p. 253; Tower, 1994). We have established that the term *consumer* implies greater power and choice than does the term *client*. Each client has a unique set of needs. As consumers, clients should be able to choose their purchases or resource providers within a competitive market rather than having someone else do so for them.

Emphasis on Choice

A key word here is *choice*. The ruler concept explained earlier as characterizing the 1970s and 1980s no longer applies. Rather, clients are encouraged to make

EP 2.1.5c,
2.1.10c,
2.1.10f,
2.1.10g,
2.1.10j

choices and decide what supports they want and what goals they wish to pursue. Earlier we discussed the importance of self-determination for people with disabilities.

Consider Dimitri, 44, a quadriplegic whose condition is the result of a congenital spinal cord malformation. Instead of professionals assessing his capabilities and designating where it is best for him to live, he can make those decisions himself. With practitioners and other caregiving professionals' input regarding what resources and services are available, Dimitri can determine the environment that will give him what he perceives as the highest quality of life. Of course, his choices are influenced by his own capabilities and the resources available. It is impossible for Dimitri to live in an apartment alone with no supportive help. His viable choices might include living in a nursing home or in a group home for people with severe physical disabilities, staying in an apartment with the necessary supportive attendants, or living with his family whose members would serve as primary caregivers (assuming, of course, that they were willing to do so).

Another example is Juanita, who has cerebral palsy resulting in major difficulties controlling her arm movements. With professional help and practice, she has learned to dress herself if her clothes have zippers and no buttons. However, it takes her over an hour each time and leaves her physically exhausted. A personal care attendant can do the job in about four minutes. Juanita might choose to have the attendant help her dress even though this option reflects less independence. This choice might be in her best interest to save herself substantial time and energy (Renz-Beaulaurier, 1998).

The concept of choice is important. However, social workers must also carefully evaluate a client's ability to make choices, as Highlight 11.2 explains.

Innovation

A key concept in today's approach toward working with people with developmental disabilities is *innovation*—the initiation, development, and application of new ideas. Innovative service provision may involve a unique combination of services depending on what an individual wishes to accomplish. In other words, "consumers define their own vision of the future—where they want to live, learn, work, and recreate—in a community that they define" (Mary, 1998, p. 253).

For example, Larisa, age 7, has spina bifida, a condition in which the spinal column has not fused shut and so some nerves remain exposed. Although she had surgery immediately after birth to close her

---

HIGHLIGHT 11.2

A Word of Caution About Choice

Mackelprang and Salsgiver (1996) caution that practitioners "not be too quick to assume that consumers already have knowledge and abilities rather than recognizing that they may need assistance to develop their strengths" (p. 12). They present an example involving Jim, age 28, who had suffered traumatic brain injury. Although technically not a developmental disability because the injury occurred after age 22, it still illustrates concepts commonly addressed when working with people who have developmental disabilities.

While residing in an independent living center, Jim initially sought help with financial planning. As his counselor, an MSW student, helped him with budgeting issues, it became apparent that Jim was also experiencing difficulty in his marriage. However,

because Jim did not specifically seek help concerning his marriage, the student decided not to interfere with those issues. Because of his head injury, Jim lacked insight into the depths of his relationship problems. By the time he began to understand how far his marital situation had deteriorated, his wife had divorced him, retaining custody of their adolescent daughter.

Mackelprang and Salsgiver (1996) suggest,

This case illustrates the conflict between absolute self-determination and the need to sometimes impose professional intervention. Although some would argue against any change in Jim's intervention, a social work approach would have allowed for broader intervention and ultimately may have been more empowering to Jim and his family. (p. 13)

HIGHLIGHT 11.3

Discrimination Against People with Developmental Disabilities

EP 2.1.5a

People with developmental disabilities continue to suffer discrimination. Shapiro (1995) cites the example of Sandra, a 35-year-old woman with Down syndrome who was denied a heart–lung transplant even though insurance covered the $250,000 necessary for the operation. Down syndrome is a congenital type of intellectual disability "characterized by moderate to severe mental retardation, slanting eyes, a broad short skull, broad hands with short fingers, and trisomy of the human chromosome numbered 21" (Mish, 2008, p. 376). The two hospitals granted approval to conduct this type of surgery "made issue of her intelligence and rejected her" (Shapiro, 1995, p. 59). One hospital administrator allegedly said, "We do not feel that patients with

Down syndrome are appropriate candidates for heart–lung transplantation" (Shapiro, 1995, p. 59). Others at the hospitals indicated that they doubted she could maintain the rigorous medical requirements involved in taking medication and monitoring her health after the operations.

Sandra and her doctor strongly disagreed with these allegations. Sandra had bused tables in a public cafeteria, lived in her own apartment, and "testified eloquently before committees" on the behalf of people with developmental disabilities (Shapiro, 1995, p. 59). Sandra already had assumed responsibility for taking various medications and monitoring her blood pressure every day. Publicity compelled the hospitals to reconsider her plea. Without the surgery, Sandra had only a few years to live.

spinal column, damage to the unprotected nerves resulted in paralysis and difficulties with bladder and bowel control. Larisa has an individualized service plan designed to meet her unique needs. She can live at home with an innovative combination of supports. A motorized wheelchair maximizes her mobility. Family counseling gives her parents information and help in responding to her special needs. A wheelchair-accessible van transports her to and from school. A teacher's aid assists her as needed in completing school assignments. Designated medical staff help Larisa and her family meet her special health and surgical needs.

Family Support

One other important concept in current service provision for people with developmental disabilities is *family support* (Freedman, 1995; Mary, 1998). Families often need special resources and help to respond to the extraordinary needs of members with developmental disabilities. For example, parents with a young child who has a developmental disability may experience a range of stresses, including avoidance by others, exhaustion from the long-term burden of caregiving, lack of adequate information about the condition, and child behavior management problems (Freedman, 1995).

Family members' strengths must be identified and fortified. Examples of strengths include good communication skills, sincere caring and consideration for each other, effective organizational and planning skills, a strong support network of friends and relatives, spiritual involvement with clergy and religious groups, and adequate financial resources.

Social workers and other professionals working with people who have developmental disabilities continuously strive to individualize plans, emphasize choice, initiate innovative treatment approaches, and maximize family support. Nonetheless, discrimination against them persists, as Highlight 11.3 shows.

Social Work with People Who Have Developmental Disabilities

Social workers often must use brokering, case management, and advocacy skills to provide effective services. We've established that *brokering* is the linkage of clients (consumers) to needed resources. *Case management* is the process of organizing, coordinating, and maintaining "a network of formal and informal supports and

EP 2.1.1c, 2.1.5b, 2.1.5c, 2.1.10f, 2.1.10k

activities designed to optimize the functioning and well-being of people with multiple needs" (Moxley, 1989, p. 21). Obviously, many people with developmental disabilities require an innovative range of services to maximize self-determination and pursue an optimal quality of life. The key here is coordinating and monitoring services so clients with ongoing or changing needs get these needs met.

Advocacy is "the process of working with and/or on behalf of clients (1) to obtain services or resources for clients that would not otherwise be provided, (2) to modify or influence policies, procedures, or practices that adversely affect clients, or (3) to promote new legislation or policies that will result in the provision of [much-needed] ... resources or services" (Hepworth Rooney, Rooney, Strom-Gottfried, & Larsen, 2010, p. 430). There is usually no problem when adequate resources and services are available. However, in reality, this is often not the case. When clients are not getting their needs met, the practitioner is obliged to advocate on their behalf. Resources may require redistribution. Policies may require change and improvement. New services may need development.

Case Example One facet of advocacy is helping clients advocate for themselves when they can instead of doing it for them (Mackelprang & Salsgiver, 2009). This is another form of client empowerment. For example, it might be easy for Gamal, a social worker, to advocate for his client RyAnne, age 38, who has muscular dystrophy. We have established that this condition is "any of a group of hereditary diseases characterized by a progressive wasting of the muscles" (Mish, 2008, p. 818)

RyAnne was diagnosed with the disease at age 12. Although RyAnne can take a few steps by herself, it is difficult for her, and she usually uses a motorized wheelchair. Balance is difficult because she has lost eight of her toes to the disease. She has little strength in her arms and hands, and so accomplishes tasks such as writing and eating very slowly. As her muscles deteriorate, her voice is weakening, so she tries to do most of her necessary talking earlier in the day when she is stronger. RyAnne is a strong-willed, independent-minded person who prides herself in accomplishing her goals. For example, she has earned a bachelor's degree in accounting and is able to work part-time at her own pace.

RyAnne lives with other people who have physical disabilities in a group home where Gamal is the social worker. RyAnne has several issues to address, such as some funding glitches and the need for some new medical equipment, including a new wheelchair. Gamal talks to RyAnne about these needs and volunteers to make the calls, write the letters, and advocate on her behalf. He is taken aback when RyAnne responds with a dour look on her face and then avoids eye contact with him. He asks her what's wrong. She hesitantly responds that she would rather do it herself, although she admits she will probably need help negotiating the complicated bureaucratic maze. Gamal suddenly grasps the issue. He backs off and volunteers to help find out whom she needs to contact and what information she needs to present. Although it will be much slower for her to advocate for herself than for him to do it, the process will empower her. Gamal realizes that it's best to support her in her advocacy efforts instead of performing the primary advocacy role himself.

Empowerment Through Legislation: Seeking Social and Economic Justice

EP 2.1.5b

At least three positive pieces of legislation passed in the past few decades are of special significance for people with developmental or other disabilities in terms of improving access to resources in the macro social environment (DeWeaver, 1995; Makelprang, 2008).

The Americans with Disabilities Act of 1990

The Americans with Disabilities Act of 1990 (ADA) intends to provide the millions of American "people [who have physical or mental disabilities] with access to public areas and workplaces" and to blast away barriers keeping these people isolated from "the mainstream of public life" (Smolowe, 1995, p. 54). The ADA defines people with disabilities as those who have substantial physical or mental difficulties that significantly hinder at least one primary life activity, who have an established record of such hindrances, or who are regarded by other people as demonstrating such difficulties (Asch & Mudrick, 1995; Kopels, 1995).

The ADA reflects one attempt by a national macro system to affect and improve the lives of a population-at-risk and provide greater social and economic justice (Kopels, 1995). The ADA consists of five major provisions. Title I forbids job and employment discrimination against people with disabilities. This includes discrimination concerning "job application procedures, hiring, advancement, compensation, job training, and other conditions and privileges of employment *simply because they have disabilities*" (Kopels, 1995, p. 399; emphasis added). Title II forbids public facilities, organizations, and transportation providers to discriminate against people with disabilities. Title III "prohibits discrimination in public accommodations and services operated by private entities" (Kopels, 1995, p. 338). Title IV requires that state and national telecommunication relay services accommodate people who are hard of hearing and allow them communication access. Finally, Title V includes a number of miscellaneous provisions relating to more specific aspects of service provision and access.

The ADA "has legitimized the idea that the fundamental problems facing people are less medical than social and structural" (Renz-Beaulaurier, 1998, p. 81). It redefines problems as belonging to the *community*, and not to people with disabilities living in the community. For example, "the problem of how to get up the steps (problem within the individual) changes to how to get a ramp installed (problem outside the individual)" (Renz-Beaulaurier, 1998, p. 80).

This sounds wonderful in terms of providing people with fair access and service. The law requires "universal access to public buildings, transit systems, and communications networks" (Friend, 2011; Smolowe, 1995, p. 54). Significant gains have been made in terms of accessible curb ramps, wide bathroom stalls, and public vehicles with lifts for wheelchairs for persons with physical disabilities (Smolowe, 1995). Focus on Critical Thinking 11.4, however, poses some questions regarding the overall effectiveness of the ADA.

The Developmental Disabilities Assistance and Bill of Rights Act of 1990

The second major piece of 1990s legislation is the Developmental Disabilities Assistance and Bill of Rights Act of 1990, which accomplished several things (DeWeaver, 1995). First, it renewed funding for four major grant programs on behalf of people with developmental disabilities. Second, it increased the total estimated "number of people with developmental disabilities," thereby acknowledging that more resources are necessary. Third, it called for advocacy on behalf of people with developmental disabilities. It requires provision of adequate services so people can attain their optimum potential, quality of life, and independence as integral members of the community.

Individuals with Disabilities Education Improvement Act of 2004 (IDEA)

Major legislation has positively affected educational programming for children with learning and other disabilities in the past few decades (Mackelprang, 2008; Lightfoot, 2009). Mackelprang and Salsgiver (2009) explain:

> The All Handicapped Children Act of 1975 is one of the few pieces of legislation known to professionals in human services and education by its original number, Pub. L. No. 94-142. The All Handicapped Children Act of 1975 went through several levels of evolution and was renamed the Individuals with Disabilities Education Act (IDEA) in 1990, and most recently the Individuals with Disabilities Education Improvement Act [of 2004].... Individuals from birth up through the age of twenty-one years are covered under this historic act. IDEA stipulates that "free appropriate public education" be provided at public expense to all children, including children with disabilities from age three through twenty-one years. The education of children with disabilities should be provided in the most open and "normal" environment possible (the least restrictive environment). When children need to be diagnosed, be evaluated, and receive prescriptions, the diagnosis, evaluation, and prescription should not produce stigmatization and discrimination. Parents and the child need to be primary players in any remedial or pedagogical plan established for the child's education (Albrecht, 1992; Altschuler, 2007)....
>
> It is important ... to understand some of the unique qualities of IDEA as a disability law. First, it covers...youths [with disabilities] through age twenty-one or until high school graduation, whichever comes first. Second, it mandates public support of substantial services placing financial and service responsibility on states and schools. Third, it mandates substantial involvement of both ... individuals [with disabilities] and their families. Fourth, IDEA is entitling legislation: not only are people eligible for services, but schools and states are responsible for providing services. (pp. 144–145)

FOCUS ON CRITICAL THINKING 11.4

Does the Americans with Disabilities Act (ADA) Actually Help People with Disabilities Attain Social and Economic Justice?

EP 2.1.3

Although the ADA has helped people with disabilities in some areas, questions must be raised about its effectiveness in others. For one thing, employers and public agencies must make only "reasonable accommodation." In reality, they are not compelled to provide such access or encouragement if the ensuing costs would result in "undue hardship," often in the form of excessive financial burdens.

Because of the vagueness in terminology and lack of specification regarding how changes must be implemented, gains have been limited (Smolowe, 1995). For instance, what do the words *reasonable accommodation, undue hardship,* and *excessive financial burdens* mean? What kind of accommodation is reasonable? How much money is excessive? How can discrimination against capable people with intellectual or other developmental disabilities be prohibited? How can the law be enforced?

The 2008 Amendments to the Americans with Disabilities Act was signed into law in response to a range of Supreme Court decisions addressing some of the more nebulous concepts inherent in the ADA. Taking effect in January 2009, the Amendments attempted to clarify who is protected by the law and revised "the definition of 'disability' to more broadly encompass impairments that substantially limit a major life activity" (ADA Amendments Act of 2008). Clarification of terms and who is included appears to be an ongoing process.

The unemployment rate of people with disabilities far exceeds that of able-bodied people (U.S. Census Bureau, 2010). The incomes of people with disabilities are far less than those of their able-bodied counterparts (Mackelprang, 2008). Of people with a disability, 22.4% are employed; this contrasts with an almost 71% employment rate for people without a disability (U.S. Census Bureau, 2010). More people with a disability, about one-third, were employed in 1990 before the ADA was passed (Smolowe, 1995).

Therefore, the battle for equal access and opportunity for people with disabilities has not been won. Much of the public attention to the act has focused on people with physical disabilities, many of whom require wheelchairs for transportation. In what ways do people with intellectual and other developmental disabilities fit in? Kopels (1995) states that the ADA "will be successful only to the extent that these individuals [with disabilities] and those who advocate on their behalf learn about the ADA and use it as a means to ensure employment opportunities" (p. 345). Mackelprang and Salsgiver (1996) call for the social work profession to ally itself with the movement to enhance access for people with either physical or mental disabilities. They encourage social workers to "become more involved in disability advocacy work in agencies with activist philosophies" and to work with the disability movement to "better empower oppressed and devalued groups, and understand the needs of people with disabilities" (p. 134).

Critical Thinking Questions

To what extent do you think the ADA has been effective? What might be done to improve its effectiveness?

Social Work and Community Empowerment for People with Disabilities

EP 2.1.8a, 2.1.8b

Social workers are concerned with how organizations, communities, and the government can offer resources and supports to people with disabilities. This is possible in at least two ways. First, federal and state legislation can make programs available to community residents with disabilities. (We just reviewed three pieces of federal legislation passed on behalf of this population.) Second, social workers can work with community residents to establish their own resources within the community.

Some examples of how to make progress through legislation, direct community support, and social work advocacy are presented next. The populations-at-risk addressed include people with visual impairment and those with intellectual disabilities.

Legislative Empowerment for People with Visual Impairment

The Rehabilitation Act of 1973 and its 1992 amendments mandated reimbursement for some services provided by agencies specifically designated to help people with visual impairment (Asch & Mudrick, 2008). One difficulty, however, is that individual states define *blindness* differently, which means that some states may limit service provision to those people with severe impairment or total blindness (Asch, 1995).

Other examples of supportive legislation are two 1930s laws that provide certain employment opportunities for people who are blind. The Wagner-O'Day Act (P.L. 75-739) created a system of sheltered workshops, and the Randolph-Sheppard Act (P.L. 74-734) gave people who are blind "preference in getting jobs running vending operations on federal land" (Asch & Mudrik, 2008). Sheltered workshops offer a protective, supervised work environment for people who have trouble functioning more independently.

Additionally, people who are legally blind, who are unemployed, and who have assets falling below prescribed levels may receive Supplemental Security Income (SSI). We have established that SSI is a federal program that offers uniform assistance to people who are blind, are older adults, or have a disability. Maximum monthly federal payments to SSI recipients in 2011 were $674 for an individual and $1,011 for a couple (Social Security Online, 2010b). Benefits are provided on the basis of need instead of work history.

Several pieces of legislation make reading materials more accessible for people with visual impairment. For example, the 1931 Pratt-Smoot Act (P.L. 71-787) established a Library of Congress program that later formed the foundation for regional centers providing Braille and recorded materials to people with visual impairment.

Highlight 11.4 suggests how social workers can work with communities to further empower people with visual impairment.

Community Empowerment for People with Intellectual Disabilities

Considerable time will be spent here discussing people with intellectual disabilities for three reasons (Freedman, 1995). First, they constitute a large proportion of people with developmental disabilities. Second, they are likely to use services provided by state agencies. Third, social workers are an integral part of service provision to this population (DeWeaver, 1995).

HIGHLIGHT 11.4

Social Work and Community Empowerment for People with Visual Impairment

EP 2.1.10g, 2.1.10j

Laws and mandated programs make some resources available to people with visual impairment. However, social workers can serve as important advocates in their communities and agencies for additional needed services. One goal might be to disseminate information concerning the issues addressed by and strengths inherent in people with visual impairment. These people and their families require precise, relevant information about what services are available, what their legal rights are, and what alternative approaches can be used to undertake activities of daily living (Asch, 1995; Asch & Mudrick, 2008). For example, social workers can help people realize that the long cane ("a mobility aid used by individuals with visual impairment who sweep it in a wide arc in front of them"), guide dogs, human guides, recorded information, adapted computers, and other technological devices (e.g., reading machines that convert print into spoken words) can help people organize home, work, and social lives in an effective and efficient, although different, manner (Asch, 1995; Hallahan et al., 2012, p. 460).

Another goal social workers might pursue with communities is sponsorship of self-help groups in which people with visual impairment can discuss issues, suggest ideas to each other, and offer mutual support. A third goal might be to work with schools that have students with visual impairment to educate parents about services, resources, and aids. Schools can encourage students with visual impairment to participate in sports, recreation, and other extracurricular and educational activities just as children with normal vision do.

As for people with visual impairment, legislation provides support and programs for some people with intellectual disabilities. Funding for people with intellectual disabilities comes from a range of sources depending on whether individuals fulfill eligibility criteria, which often are related to their income level. For example, SSI may be available to people with intellectual disabilities who satisfy a means test (i.e., as Chapter 8 explained, a person or family must have an income less than a designated amount to be eligible for benefits).

EP 2.1.9b, 2.1.10g

Social workers can help communities and social service organizations develop resources and programs to integrate people with intellectual disabilities and enhance their quality of life. For instance, one state has a Community Options Program (COP), funded at the state level, that "provides assessments, case plans, and community services as an alternative to nursing home placements" (ARC Milwaukee, undated, b, p. 2).

ARCs and Related Resources

One excellent example of how a community can use a support system for people with intellectual disabilities is an organization called ARC. Historically known as the Association for Retarded Citizens, ARCs now are established in communities nationwide. The following discussion focuses specifically on ARCs. However, the types of services ARCs offer can certainly be sponsored by other organizations and community groups.

Typically funded through a variety of sources including donations by private citizens, corporations, local service clubs, and foundations, as well as government service contracts, ARCs provide a wide range of services that reflect a creative meld of public services, private contributions, and community resources. Social workers are often integrally involved with the provision of ARC services, which may include information and referral services, help lines, noninstitutional residential facilities, vocational and employment programs, support services, intervention advocacy, volunteer programs, and recreational activities.

Information and Referral Services and Help Lines

An information and referral service provides information about what services and resources are available in a community and assists people in accessing them. A help line is an information and referral system based on telephone contact. Persons requiring information about services, laws, or issues related to a specific problem or population—in this case, intellectual disabilities—call a trained professional (often a social worker), who connects them with the appropriate resource or gives them necessary information. Many ARCs develop an extensive computerized system that can quickly identify relevant linkages between questions, needs, information, and resources.

Noninstitutional Living Facilities

One type of resource that can help people with a disability maintain maximum independence and self-determination is a noninstitutional living facility. As discussed earlier in the context of deinstitutionalization, the intent is to place people in the least restrictive setting possible. Social workers often oversee or work in such settings. These include adult family care homes, where clients reside in the home of caregivers who supervise and care for them. Another setting is a group home or community-based residential facility (CBRF). Residents often are selected on the basis of having similar needs such as required levels of supervision and support. For example, one CBRF might have residents capable of taking care of personal needs and working at a sheltered workshop.

Other, even more independent, supported living options include living with a roommate or by oneself in an apartment. Some limited supervision and assistance, such as help with paying bills or arranging transportation to work, is usually needed in these cases.

Vocational and Employment Programs

ARCs are also quite creative regarding vocational and employment opportunities. They can help clients gain employment by preparing them for the expectations of the workplace, assisting in placement, helping employers restructure jobs to maximize clients' ability to complete job tasks, and providing job coaching in basic work skills (e.g., getting to work on time, following a supervisor's instructions).

Individuals may also gain employment in more structured settings such as sheltered workshops. One ARC agency developed an employment program whereby clients made ceramic gifts for special occasions such as weddings and graduations. Another ARC organization created a work setting in which clients manufactured pillows for a national airline.

People who are unable to function in more demanding settings may receive "day services"; these aim to "maximize an individual's independent functional level in self-care, physical and emotional growth, mobility and community transportation, socialization, recreation, leisure time, and educational and prevocational skills" (ARC Milwaukee, undated, a, p. 2).

Other Support Services

Social workers and other human service professionals offer multifaceted support services. Organizations can provide outreach support services to clients in their own homes that involve instruction in daily living skills, budgeting and financial management, transportation, parenting skills, and personal issues such as interpersonal interaction, leisure activities, self-esteem, and assertiveness.

Respite care programs help parents and other caregivers for persons with intellectual disabilities, giving them a break from their responsibilities. Highlight 11.5 focuses on the special needs of aging caregivers.

Support groups can focus on many different issues. For instance, parent support groups "provide parents with an opportunity to get together and share stories, concerns, and achievements with other parents who are experiencing similar circumstances" (ARC, undated, a, p. 2). Support groups for seniors with disabilities give them opportunities to share concerns, discuss suggestions for prospering, and talk about how to maximize their quality of life.

Advocacy

Intervention advocacy "is designed to respond to the needs of persons with disabilities and their families when serious problems arise affecting legal rights, safety and health, financial security, or access to

community resources" (ARC, undated, c, p. 2). The service system is complicated, and clients and their families may find it difficult to negotiate. As emphasized previously, social work advocacy is often necessary to get clients the resources and services they need.

EP 2.1.5b, 2.1.10k

Community Volunteers

Volunteers can help ARC programming in many ways. These include performing clerical duties and answering phones; caring for small children while parents attend support groups; serving as matched "friends" with persons who have disabilities to provide support and encouragement; giving support via telephone to persons needing intermittent help; participating in fund-raising activities; assisting in supervision at events such as group outings; and helping with household upkeep and maintenance (ARC, undated, c). Social workers often seek out, organize, and oversee volunteers performing such functions.

Recreational Activities

Recreational activities and functions represent still another means of enhancing the quality of life for people with disabilities. Examples include athletic programs, Special Olympics, and summer camps at which groups of clients of any age can interact socially, work on crafts, play games, learn appreciation for nature, increase leisure skills, and gain confidence in expressing themselves (ARC, undated, c).

The past few sections have suggested means by which social workers and communities can empower people with intellectual disabilities. The following case example examines various dimensions of how a community both pursues and falls short of empowerment for one of its citizens.

HIGHLIGHT 11.5

Empowerment of Older Adult Caregivers

Family services can support older adult caregivers who find it increasingly difficult to maintain the same level of care as in the past. For example, because of decreasing strength, an aging caregiver might find it much more difficult to assist a person with a severe disability in dressing himself. Family services for older adult caregivers can help during crises such as a caregiver

experiencing her own acute health problems. They can also assist caregivers in long-term planning for and with the person who has the disability. A common concern of aging caregivers is what will happen to the individual with a disability when the caregiver can no longer assume that function.

Case Example   Consider Frank and how his community both succeeds and fails in supporting him. Frank, age 58, lives in a midwestern town of about 8,000 people in a rural farming community. Frank has mild intellectual disabilities. He graduated from high school, but only because in those days students like him were passed on whether they could perform the work or not. He is very proud of the high school ring he purchased at graduation. However, his community, especially the school system, did not serve him well. Instead of receiving special services and training that might now be available, the system basically ignored him and passed him on through.

A major problem for Frank is his speech. He has difficulty forming words and takes considerable time to structure his sentences. His comprehension of verbal communication is good, and he has an excellent sense of humor. His speech often fools people who don't know him well into thinking he is much less competent than he really is. Speech therapy might have helped if it had been available when he was young.

Frank works at a sheltered workshop in addition to working six hours per week as a janitor at Hilda's Happy Hot Dog Haven. Frank has a solid work history. For almost 20 years he worked at a local tanning factory hauling deer hides from one area to another as they proceeded through the leather-making process. It was gruesome, backbreaking work, and when Frank got home, he was exhausted. At the time, he was living with his father, who cooked for him, did his laundry, and helped him with other daily living tasks.

Work at the tanning factory was not without problems. Frank told his relatives about another "guy at work" who liked to pick on him. Frank had lots of experience being picked on. The guy would draw a knife and tease Frank, pretending to cut him and

Special Olympics provide an excellent means of empowerment for people with intellectual disabilities. Begun in 1968 when Eunice Kennedy Shriver organized the first sports competition at Soldier Field in Chicago, Special Olympics is now an international program that provides year-round opportunities for sports participation. Here, a Special Olympics athlete competes in a race in California at UCLA.

Joe Sohm/Visions of America, LLC/Alamy

actually slitting his right hand one time. Frank also told how, one night after work, he slit all "the guy's tires. The guy, who was fired shortly thereafter, never did find out who did it.

Frank was a saver. He would wear the same pair of polyester pants for years until the threads in the hem seams gave way. Although Frank made little more than minimum wage, he put almost all of it in savings while he lived with his dad. When the plant closed and he was laid off, he had accumulated over $40,000. Investing with the help of his brother Sharif and a slick financial planner brought his assets to almost $200,000 by the time he turned 61. Unfortunately, this prevented him from receiving public assistance and resources because he did not meet various programs' means tests.

When his father died, Frank was able, with Sharif's help, to live in and pay rent for his own apartment. He preferred living alone to living with a roommate. One of Frank's strengths was his strong relationship with Sharif and his family, even though they lived 185 miles away. Frank didn't see his family as often as he liked since busing was deregulated and federal regulations no longer required companies to sponsor less popular runs. Sharif and his wife were periodically forced to endure a deadly dull four-hour trip through flat farmland to pick Frank up and spend another four hours to drive him home.

A major strength in Frank's life was his involvement with the local Center for People with Developmental Disabilities, an agency that did not have a means test. In its sheltered workshop, Frank felt productive and established many social contacts. As one of the highest-functioning clients, he achieved significant social status. At the center's periodic social dances, he was quite accomplished and admired. Frank also had a knack for taking pictures and videos, which he did regularly at the center's events. The center sponsored or cosponsored numerous events including Special Olympics, bowling tournaments, picnics, and outings to movies. Frank was extremely proud of a Volunteer's Award plaque he received from the center for all of the time he spent photographing and videotaping events.

At the center, he was assigned a social work case manager, Mandze, who helped to coordinate services and activities. To evaluate his daily living skills, she linked him with a trainer who tried to teach him how to cook. However, Frank didn't like to cook, so he ended up subsisting mostly on frozen dinners. (It might be noted that Sharif, who had superior intelligence, could barely boil water; he didn't like to cook, either.) Mandze also helped coordinate any other supportive services Frank might need with Sharif and his family.

Although Mandze and Sharif tried to encourage Frank to manage his own finances and checkbook, this was too difficult for him. Frank didn't like doing computations or writing checks because he was afraid of making mistakes. When mail-ordering gifts for family members, he would always send cash despite the risk of losing it. Sharif finally gave up and determined that it was easier simply to keep track of Frank's finances himself than to keep after Frank.

Another major community strength was the spiritual and emotional support Frank received from his church. He attended services regularly and was involved in a group called the Sunday Evening Club, consisting of adult church members who met every other Sunday for a potluck dinner and a chance to socialize or hear speakers.

Frank's work at Hilda's was helpful in terms of making him feel useful and conserving his savings. However, the six-hour weekly work allocation was minimal. The management could have given him many more hours if they had not viewed him as an inadequate, "retarded" person. And the town provided no public transportation, so Frank had to walk to get anywhere, including two miles to work.

In summary, community strengths for Frank include the Center for People with Developmental Disabilities, its sheltered workshop, his social worker Mandze, public recognition via the Volunteer's Award, his spiritual involvement at church, his job at Hilda's, and strong connections with his family. Community weaknesses for Frank include the history of inattention to his special needs, local residents who made fun of him in a demeaning manner whenever they had the chance, inadequate involvement in his paid work environment, and lack of public transportation. Thus, in some ways, Frank's community environment supported and integrated him, thereby enhancing his quality of life. In other ways, the lack of community support hindered his ability to live the most useful, productive, and happiest life possible.

Highlight 11.6 reviews three other examples of how social workers might help people with intellectual disabilities become more integrally involved in community life.

> **HIGHLIGHT 11.6**
>
> ## Empowerment for People with Intellectual Disabilities: Creating Linkages with Community Life
>
> Kretzmann and McKnight (1993) cite a number of situations in which adults with intellectual disabilities can be mainstreamed[2] and integrated as part of a large community. These are the types of scenarios social workers can actively seek out on their clients' behalf. The following three are adapted from Kretzmann and McKnight's ideas.
>
> *Example A:* Reggie, age 28, thrives at playing games, so Reggie's social worker linked him with the local Boys Club. He now volunteers there regularly, teaching children games and supervising their activities.
>
> *Example B:* Gina, age 22, spent most weekdays at a day program with other people who have intellectual disabilities. She passed much of her time coloring and watching other residents. She is an exceptionally warm person who lights up with a dazzling smile when spoken to or given any attention. Her social worker at the day program introduced her to a local day-care center to see if she could help out there.
>
> At first, her social worker or other day program staff always accompanied her to the day-care center and provided some supervision. Now she goes to the center by herself several times a week. The children love her and the attention she pays to them. She always has time to listen to what they have to say and bestow affection when needed. They realize she's different from their other teachers because sometimes they have to help her out in completing activities, but they don't care. They love her anyway.
>
> *Example C:* Hugh, age 68, lives in a group home. He loves to bowl. Danyelle, his group home social worker, found out that a local church had a Thursday night bowling league. She talked to the team members and asked if they would consider including Hugh on their team. They were a bit hesitant because they take bowling very seriously and play to win. They were even more hesitant when they discovered that Hugh was not a very good bowler. However, Hugh obviously was ecstatic about being on the team. Team members worked out a rotation system whereby Hugh could periodically bowl but his score was omitted from the final total. Hugh beamed proudly as he wore his Beaver's Bowling Buddies T-shirt.
>
> ---
>
> [2]*Mainstreaming* is "bringing people who have some exceptional characteristics into the living, working, or educational environments to which all others have access" (Barker, 1995, p. 221). Examples of such special groups include people with intellectual and other developmental disabilities.

Chapter Summary

The following summarizes this chapter's content as it relates to the chapter's learning objectives presented at the beginning of the chapter. Learning objectives include the following:

A Define mobility disabilities and developmental disabilities, and identify a range of specific disabilities clustered under each concept.

People with mobility disabilities "are those whose physical differences require them to achieve physical activities in a variety of alternate ways" (Mackelprang & Salsgiver, 2009, p. 177). Acquired mobility disabilities include stroke, muscular dystrophy, rheumatoid arthritis, multiple sclerosis, myasthenia gravis, and spinal cord injury.

Developmental disabilities are severe and chronic, occur before age 22, are likely to be permanent, and result in substantial functional limitations. Developmental disabilities include intellectual disabilities, cerebral palsy, epilepsy, orthopedic problems, deafness and hardness of hearing, visual impairment, and autistic spectrum disorders. Some people have multiple disabilities.

B Investigate the importance of self-determination for people with disabilities as an ethical aspect of social work practice.

To maximize self-determination, social workers should adopt three approaches. First, they should assume a consumer-centered approach, accepting people as knowing their own needs and as being capable of making intelligent decisions about services. Second, social workers should learn about services and resources so that they may convey this information to clients. Third, they should advocate for people with disabilities whenever possible.

C Examine the history of how people with developmental disabilities have been treated in the macro social environment.

Prior to the late 1960s, community treatment and legislation focused on individual pathology. During the 1970s and 1980s, people assumed a more community-based approach. Important concepts included normalization, deinstitutionalization, individual program planning, and the developmental model. During the 1990s and beyond, consumer empowerment has been emphasized. Major concepts include individualization, emphasis on choice, innovation, and family support.

D Describe generalist social work practice with people who have developmental disabilities.

Case management and advocacy are important when working with people who have developmental disabilities. Case management is the process of organizing, coordinating, and maintaining "a network of formal and informal supports and activities designed to optimize the functioning and well-being of people with multiple needs" (Moxley, 1989, p. 21). Advocacy is "the process of working with and/or on behalf of clients (1) to obtain services or resources for clients that would not otherwise be provided, (2) to modify or influence policies, procedures, or practices that adversely affect clients, or (3) to promote new legislation or policies that will result in the provision of [much-needed] … resources or services" (Hepworth et al., 2010, p. 430).

E Discuss avenues of legislative, community, and worker empowerment.

Legislation that has empowered people with disabilities includes the Americans with Disabilities Act (ADA) of 1990 that forbids discrimination and requires public accommodations in many circumstances. Another example of legislation is the Developmental Disabilities Assistance and Bill of Rights Act of 1990 that renewed grant programs and acknowledged that more resources were needed for people with disabilities. The Individuals with Disabilities Education Improvement Act of 2004 requires that a free appropriate public education be provided to all children (including children with disabilities) from ages 3 to 21 in the least restrictive environment possible. Ways social workers can work toward empowerment include advocating for federal and state legislation to make resources available to clients and working with community residents to establish resources.

F Examine the macro environment's potential for empowering people with visual impairment and intellectual disabilities.

Legislation empowering people with visual impairment includes the Rehabilitation Act of 1973, the Wagner-O'Day Act, the Randolph-Sheppard Act, and the 1931 Pratt-Smoot Act. SSI can provide benefits to people who are legally blind. Social workers can advocate for services, link people with needed resources, work with schools to empower children with visual impairment, and work to ensure that Braille is readily available.

Communities can empower people with intellectual disabilities by establishing and using ARCs, providing information and referral services and help lines, providing noninstitutional living facilities, offering vocational and employment programs, developing other support services, advocating for equal rights, soliciting community volunteers to help ARC programming, providing recreational activities, and initiating various creative linkages with community life.

G Encourage critical thinking about residual versus institutional approaches to service provision for people with disabilities, empowerment through language, deinstitutionalization, and the Americans with Disabilities Act.

Critical thinking questions were posed concerning who should be responsible for funding and providing services to people with disabilities, how words can affect how people with intellectual disabilities are viewed, the pros and cons of deinstitutionalization, and the extent to which the ADA is effective.

LOOKING AHEAD

Many people with disabilities require special health services. Another field of practice in which social practitioners serve clients is health care. Chapter 12 will explore social work roles, health care policy problems in the macro environment, and AIDS in an international context.

COMPETENCY NOTES

The following identifies where Educational Policy (EP) competencies and practice behaviors are discussed in the chapter.

EP 2.1.1c Attend to professional roles and boundaries. *(p. 355):* Social work roles including broker, case manager, and advocate are discussed in the context of people who have developmental disabilities.

EP 2.1.1d Demonstrate professional demeanor in behavior, appearance, and communication. *(p. 346):* A consumer-oriented approach emphasizes the importance of demonstrating a professional demeanor. *(p. 349):* Professional demeanor includes communicating appropriately and using the correct terminology.

EP 2.1.2a Recognize and manage personal values in a way that allows professional values to guide practice. *(p. 344):* Social workers should recognize and manage personal values and presumptions they harbor regarding people with disabilities.

EP 2.1.2b Make ethical decisions by applying standards of the National Association of Social Workers (NASW) *Code of Ethics* and, as applicable, of the International Federation of Social Workers/International Association of Schools of Social Work *Ethics* in Social Work, Statement of Principles. *(p. 344):* Self-determination is a major principle espoused by the NASW *Code of Ethics.*

EP 2.1.2c Tolerate ambiguity in resolving ethical conflicts. *(p. 344):* Practitioners must tolerate ambiguity in determining with a client what will meet that client's needs and yet maximize that client's self-determination.

EP 2.1.3 Apply critical thinking to inform and communicate professional judgments. *(p. 348):* Critical thinking questions are posed to encourage thought about residual versus institutional approaches to service provision for people with disabilities. *(p. 353):* Critical thinking questions address the effectiveness of deinstitutionalization. *(p. 358):* Discussion and ensuing critical thinking questions focus on the ADA and its effectiveness.

EP 2.1.3c Demonstrate effective oral and written communication in working with individuals, families, groups, organizations, communities, and colleagues. *(p. 349):* Social workers should communicate using correct language.

EP 2.1.4 Engage diversity and difference in practice. *(p. 342):* Disability is a dimension of diversity.

EP 2.1.4a Recognize the extent to which culture's structures and values may oppress, marginalize, alienate, or create or enhance privilege and power. *(p. 344):* Social workers should recognize the ways in which society oppresses people with disabilities. *(p. 351):* People with developmental disabilities have been subject to oppression and marginalization.

EP 2.1.4b Gain sufficient self-awareness to eliminate the influence of personal biases and values in working with diverse groups. *(p. 344):* Practitioners should gain self-awareness regarding their personal biases about people with mobility disabilities. *(p. 346):* Social workers must be especially vigilant regarding stereotypes they and others might harbor when working with people who have disabilities.

EP 2.1.4c Recognize and communicate their understanding of the importance of difference in shaping life experiences. *(p. 344):* Social workers should recognize and communicate their understanding of how disability shapes life experiences.

EP 2.1.4d View themselves as learners and engage those with whom they work as informants. *(p. 346):* A consumer-oriented approach stresses listening to and learning from clients.

EP 2.1.5a Understand the forms and mechanisms of oppression and discrimination. *(p. 344):* Social workers should understand how society oppresses and discriminates against people with disabilities. *(p. 351):* People with developmental disabilities have historically experienced oppression and discrimination. *(p. 355):* An example of discrimination against a person with disabilities is presented.

EP 2.1.5b Advocate for human rights and social and economic justice. *(p. 355):* Practitioners should advocate on the behalf of people who have developmental disabilities. *(p. 356):* Legislation that advocates on the behalf of people with disabilities is discussed. *(p. 361):* Practitioners should advocate for social and economic justice on the behalf of people with intellectual disabilities.

EP 2.1.5c Engage in practices that advance social and economic justice. *(p. 344):* Social workers should engage in practices and interventions that advance self-determination and social and economic justice for people with mobility disabilities. *(p. 354):* Practitioners should emphasize clients' right to self-determination, a practice that advances social justice. *(p. 355):* Social workers should engage in practices that advance social and economic justice for people with developmental disabilities.

EP 2.1.8a Analyze, formulate, and advocate for policies that advance social well-being. *(p. 348):* Critical thinking questions are posed to encourage thought about policies that advance social well-being. *(p. 358):* Practitioners should advocate for policies that advance the social well-being of people with disabilities.

EP 2.1.8b Collaborate with colleagues and clients for effective policy action. *(p. 358):* Social workers scan collaborate with colleagues and clients to develop policies that provide resources to people with disabilities.

EP 2.1.9a Continuously discover, appraise, and attend to changing locales, populations, scientific and technological developments, and emerging societal trends to provide relevant services. *(p. 351):* Practitioners should continuously respond to the changing issues, conditions, and legal developments affecting people with developmental disabilities.

EP 2.1.9b Provide leadership in promoting sustainable changes in service delivery and practice to improve the quality of social services. *(p. 360):* Social workers can serve as leaders in the development of policies and services for people with intellectual disabilities.

EP 2.1.10c Develop a mutually agreed-on focus of work and desired outcomes. *(p. 346):* A consumer-directed approach stresses the development of a mutually agreed-on focus of work and desired outcomes. *(p. 354):* Practitioners should emphasize client self-determination and develop with clients a mutually agreed-on focus of work.

EP 2.1.10f Develop mutually agreed-on intervention goals and objectives. *(p. 346):* A consumer-oriented approach emphasizes the development of mutually agreed-on goals and objectives. *(p. 354):* Social workers should emphasize clients' self-determination and work with clients to develop mutually agreed-on goals. *(p. 355):* A case example illustrates how a social worker develops mutually agreed-on intervention goals and objectives as a client engages in self-advocacy.

EP 2.1.10g Select appropriate intervention strategies. *(p. 354):* Social workers should work in conjunction with clients to select appropriate intervention strategies. *(p. 359):* Some intervention strategies for working with people who have visual impairment are discussed. *(p. 360):* Subsequent sections address appropriate intervention strategies at the community and organizational levels.

EP 2.1.10j Help clients resolve problems. *(p. 354):* Practitioners should emphasize client self-determination as they help clients resolve problems. *(p. 359):* Social workers can help people with visual impairment develop creative ways to solve problems.

EP 2.1.10k Negotiate, mediate, and advocate for clients. *(p. 355):* Social workers should advocate on the behalf of people with developmental disabilities. *(p. 361):* Practitioners should advocate for needed services and resources on the behalf of clients who have intellectual disabilities and their families.

FOR FURTHER EXPLORATION ON THE INTERNET

See this text's Social Work CourseMate website at *www.cengagebrain.com* for learning tools such as chapter quizzing, videos, glossary flashcards, and more.

CHAPTER 12

Social Work and Services in Health Care

Phil Degginger/Alamy

Consider the following headlines in the national news:

- *U.S. sick health system killing too many Americans*[1]
- *Judges sharply challenge healthcare law*[2]
- *Coalition speaks out against Medicaid cuts*[3]
- *Medicare Sellers Are After Me!*[4]

[1] Collins, W. A. (2011, June 9). U.S. sick health system killing too many Americans. Health Care News Headlines. 1st Headlines. Retrieved (June 9, 2011). from www.1stheadlines.com/healthcare.htm.

[2] Savage, D. G. (2011, June 8). Judges sharply challenge healthcare law. Health Care News Headlines. 1st Headlines. Retrieved (June 9, 2011). from http://www.1stheadlines.com/healthcare.htm.

[3] Levinsky, D. (2011, June 9). Coalition speaks out against Medicaid cuts. Health Care News Headlines. 1st Headlines. Retrieved (June 9, 2011). from http://www.1stheadlines.com/healthcare.htm.

[4] Lieberman, T. (2011, June 9). Medicare Sellers Are After Me! Health Care News Headlines. 1st Headlines. Retrieved (June 9, 2011). from http://www.1stheadlines.com/healthcare.htm.

- *Healthcare Will Take Up Nearly 20% of the US Economy by 2019*[5]
- *Health Care Costs New Threat to Military*[6]
- *As Cancer Treatments Advance, So Do Costs*[7]

These headlines reflect some of the critical issues in health-care provision in the United States today. The World Health Organization (WHO) defines health as "a state of complete physical, mental, and social well-being and not merely the absence of disease and infirmity" (Ahmed & Kolker, 1979, p. 113). This definition goes beyond the conception of health as simply the lack of illness. Rather, it stresses the importance of strengthening and maximizing health, and not merely curing what's wrong.

Good health and health care involve every one of us. No one is immune to all the health problems encountered in life. People suffer maladies ranging from influenza, to chronic back pain, to cancer. Consider that almost 34.4 million people, excluding newborns, were discharged from U.S. hospitals in one recent year (U.S. Census Bureau, 2010).

Social workers can play an important role in helping people live healthful lifestyles and seek the health services and resources they need. Practitioners can empower people by facilitating their pursuit of physical, mental, and social well-being.

Many social workers also practice in the arena of mental health. Note that sometimes health care is also used as an umbrella term to include mental health care. Although some of the issues involved in both mental health and physical health care are similar, this chapter will focus on the provision of physical health care and services. Chapter 13 will explore assessment issues and mental health services in greater detail.

Learning Objectives

A Identify the major types of health problems people encounter.

B Describe primary social work roles in health-care provision.

C Discuss major problems in the macro environment concerning health care, including escalating costs, unequal access, ethical dilemmas in managed care, and the need to enhance cultural competence in the health-care system.

D Explore some of the value discrepancies between Asian and Pacific Islander (API) cultures and the U.S. health-care system.

E Describe HIV/AIDS, social work roles, and empowerment for people living with AIDS.

---

[5]Mearian, L. Healthcare Will Take Up Nearly 20% of the US Economy by 2019. Health Care News Headlines. 1st Headlines. Retrieved (June 9, 2011). from http://www.1stheadlines.com/healthcare.htm.

[6]Keith, T. (2011, June 7). Health Care Costs New Threat to Military. Health care. NPR. Retrieved (June 9, 2011). from http://www.npr.org/sections/health-care/.

[7]Hensley, S. (2011, June 6). As Cancer Treatments Advance, So Do Costs. Health care. NPR. Retrieved (June 9, 2011). from http://www.npr.org/sections/health-care/.

F   Examine the severity of AIDS as an international problem, particularly in sub-Saharan Africa.

G   Encourage critical thinking about universal health-care coverage, overgeneralizations regarding various racial and ethnic groups, and ways to address the HIV/AIDS problem in sub-Saharan Africa.

Health Problems

Health problems include virtually any physical malfunction, injury, or disease you can imagine. They can affect anyone in the population, from an infant born two and half months prematurely, to a 97-year-old suffering from arthritis and heart disease, to a young adult badly burned during the devastating September 11, 2001, terrorist attack on the World Trade Center in Manhattan or the Pentagon in Washington, D.C.

Coleman and Kerbo (2009, pp. 134–140) cite five key factors causing or contributing to health problems. First, people who pursue unhealthful lifestyles are more likely to experience health problems and die at a younger age. These include:

- Lack of regular exercise.
- An unhealthful diet high in fat and cholesterol.
- Cigarette smoking.
- Being overweight.
- High levels of stress over long periods.

A second factor related to health problems is physical injuries. Sometimes these are related to mortality (i.e., death). For example, in 2007, of young people age 15–24 in the United States who died, almost 47% did so as a result of accidents, including motor vehicle accidents, over 16% from homicide, and over 12% from suicide (U.S. Census Bureau, 2010).

A third factor contributing to health problems involves environmental factors. Air pollution is a serious threat, especially in larger cities such as Los Angeles, Beijing, Bangkok, and Mexico City. During the 1990s, simply breathing the air in Mexico City during one day was the equivalent of smoking two packs of cigarettes (Weiner, 2001). Other environmental dangers include water pollution, use of pesticides, and exposure to buried nuclear and other industrial wastes.

Poverty is the fourth variable related to health problems. It is associated with malnutrition, poor indoor air quality, higher death rates, lack of access to medical care, unsafe water, and poor sanitation conditions (Mooney, Knox, & Schacht, 2011).

Contagious disease poses the fifth serious health concern. On a global level, such diseases as cholera and typhoid still plague people in nonindustrialized nations; the industrialized countries have virtually eliminated them with improved sanitation. However, respiratory and intestinal diseases still afflict people in the United States regularly. Sexually transmitted infections of various types also continue to infect millions of people annually (Yarber, Sayad, & Strong, 2010). Human immunodeficiency virus (HIV), which causes acquired immune deficiency syndrome (AIDS), poses another major problem, one that will be discussed later in the chapter.

Social Work Roles in Health Care

Social workers who work in the health-care field are often referred to as *medical social workers*. Social workers serve in both direct and macro-practice capacities concerning health care.

EP 2.1.1c

Social Work Roles in Direct Health-Care Practice

Dhooper (1997) explains social work's involvement in health-care practice:

Social work has been a part of the health care scene for more than 100 years. It has an impressive history of significant contributions to the field of health care in such settings as hospitals, clinics, rehabilitation centers, nursing homes, health departments, hospices, and home health agencies.

Social workers have been involved in health care at all levels: preventive care, primary care [ongoing care for patients prior to the onset of disease symptoms or care for those experiencing early symptoms], secondary care [treatment of full-blown illness], tertiary care [treatment of illness seriously endangering a person's health], restorative care [help during recovery from illness], and continuing care. Depending on the major purposes and functions of each health care setting, their roles have varied, requiring differential professional skills. (p. 1)

Health-care settings in which social workers practice include hospitals, medical clinics, diagnostic and treatment centers,[8] public health settings, and managed care companies.

Hospitals, Medical Clinics, and Diagnostic and Treatment Centers

EP 2.1.10b, 2.1.10g, 2.1.10i, 2.1.10j, 2.1.10l

Social workers can fulfill many functions in hospitals, medical clinics, and diagnostic and treatment centers, including the following:

1. *Help patients understand and interpret technical medical jargon.* Physicians often receive little training in interpersonal and communication skills. Social workers can help define technical terms, explain physical and health implications of illnesses and injuries, and communicate with patients to make certain they understand what's happening to them.

2. *Offer emotional support.* Receiving a medical diagnosis can be a scary thing. Most patients are not experts on most illnesses, injuries, and health issues. Social workers can help patients look more objectively at health conditions and understand realistic potential consequences of various treatments.

3. *Help terminally ill people deal with their feelings and make end-of-life plans.* (This is discussed more thoroughly later in the chapter.) Social workers can also help people requiring more intensive care than that provided at home make the transition to a more supportive setting, such as a group home, nursing home, or hospice.

4. *Help patients adjust their lives and lifestyles to accommodate to new conditions when they return home after medical treatment.* For example, persons diagnosed with heart disease or asthma, or those adjusting to an amputation or to blindness, may require help in adapting their behavior and habits to make life as healthy and efficient as possible.

5. *Help parents of children who have serious illnesses or disabilities cope with these conditions and respond to children's needs.*

6. *Serve as brokers who link patients with necessary supportive resources and services after leaving the medical facility.* **Discharge planning**, introduced in Chapter 10, is often involved. This is the comprehensive assessment of a patient's abilities and needs, the development of a plan to facilitate that patient's transition out of the hospital and back into a community or agency setting, and the implementation of that plan. Discharge planning focuses on the client's ability to function after a hospital or institutional stay (Springer & Casey, 2008). Placement is required that provides enough support, on the one hand, and allows for as much independence as possible, on the other. For example, a person recuperating from severe injuries suffered during a car accident might require a rehabilitative setting where time allows for rest, the appropriate therapy, and recovery. The discharge plan may also include ongoing medication, involvement with medical specialists, or significant supportive services.

7. *Help patients make financial arrangements to pay hospital and other medical bills.* Social workers often assist patients in contacting insurance companies or applying for financial assistance, guiding them through the complex maze of rules and policies.

8. *Provide health education aimed at establishing a healthful lifestyle and preventing illness.*

Case Example Donald, age 73, and Gerri, age 71, have been married for 50 years. At Donald's most recent annual physical examination, he was diagnosed with prostate cancer. (The *prostate* is "a gland surrounding the neck of the bladder" in men and "releasing a fluid component of semen" [Lindberg, 2007, p. 1096]). It is the second most common form of cancer in men, the first being lung cancer (Hyde & DeLamater, 2011). Prostate cancer is usually slow to spread and, when caught and treated early, generally has a good prognosis. Donald and Gerri, both retired, are avid health advocates who work out at

---

[8]*Diagnostic and treatment centers* are facilities to which persons such as children with multiple disabilities are brought for assessment, diagnosis of various conditions, treatment planning, and specialized treatment by a range of therapists (e.g., speech, occupational, or physical therapists).

their local health club four times a week and vigilantly eat food high in fiber and low in fat. They visibly tremble at the thought of not rinsing dishes thoroughly after washing because of the possibility of ingesting soap residue. When Donald and Gerri found out about the cancer they were terrified. They wouldn't even tell any of their friends, whom they thought would immediately start discussing Donald's imminent death.

Bethany, the hospital social worker involved, sat down with them and discussed realistic expectations for and consequences of treatment. Donald's physician had recommended chemotherapy and radiation treatments instead of surgically removing the prostate gland. Bethany encouraged Donald and Gerri to express their feelings and fears. She provided them with statistics about the high success rates of treatment and facts about its effects. Donald and Gerri's terror subsided, and they began to develop a more realistic view of what lay ahead. Bethany encouraged them to turn to their three children and their families for support, which they did.

It's interesting to note that prior to this experience, neither Donald nor Gerri had a positive word to say about social work and social workers. They had run a successful hardware store business that Donald had inherited from his father. They had believed that people who turned to social workers or other such helpers were weak and lazy and didn't have the wherewithal to make it on their own. Now they changed their minds. They had developed sincere respect for Bethany, who helped them through an emotionally turbulent time.

Public Health Departments and Other Health-Care Contexts

Public health is the complex system of health-care programs and policies that address the following on the public's behalf (Dhooper, 1997; Hanlon & Pickett, 1984; Winslow, 1920, pp. 183–191):

(1) Preventing diseases, (2) prolonging life, and (3) promoting health and efficiency through organized community effort for:

   a. *the sanitation of the environment.*
   b. *the control of communicable infections.*
   c. *the education of the individual in personal hygiene.*
   d. *the organization of medical and nursing services for the prevention and treatment of diseases.*
   e. *the development of social machinery to ensure everyone a standard of living adequate for the*

maintenance of health ... so organizing these benefits as to enable every citizen to realize his [or her] birthright of health and longevity.

Such broad goals relating to such a wide range of issues result in multiple facets of service provision. Facilities providing public health services include local, state, and federal health departments and agencies; private foundations and agencies focusing on specific health issues (e.g., the American Cancer Society, the March of Dimes); social service organizations; community health and mental health centers; family planning clinics; and virtually any other public agency providing services and benefits related to healthy living.

Specific services include any aiming to enhance health and mental health or prevent disease. These include crisis intervention, substance abuse treatment, health services for pregnant women, services to prevent and stop child maltreatment, health education, stress management training, and mental health counseling.

Veteran's Affairs Hospitals

The U.S. Department of Veterans Affairs (VA) manages the biggest health-care operation in the country, serving 5.6 million veterans at 1,300 locations (Manske, 2008). The VA requires that social workers function at the licensed independent practice level; it is the largest employer of MSWs in the country, with over 4,500 workers (Manske, 2008).

VA social workers assume

treatment responsibilities in all patient care areas, helping patients and families to achieve their highest level of adjustment/coping in society, promoting vocational and psychosocial rehabilitation. Social workers develop and implement treatment approaches which address individual social problems and work with acute/chronic medical conditions, dying patients, and bereaved families. VA social workers are responsible for ensuring continuity of care[9] through the admission, evaluation, treatment, and follow-up processes. This includes coordinating discharge planning and providing case management services based on the patients' clinical and community health and social services resources. Over the years, Social Work staff has addressed

---

[9]*Continuity of care* refers to the efficient ongoing provision of services by different or the same agencies to meet clients' needs as their circumstances and needs change.

the needs of distinct Veteran populations, i.e., the homeless, [older adults,] ... HIV/AIDS patients, [veterans with] spinal cord injury, Ex-POWs, ... Viet Nam and Persian Gulf Veterans and their families, etc. (VA, 2011c)

The VA provides a wide range of other services and programs for veterans, including blind rehabilitation services, cancer programs, centers for women veterans, diabetes programs, and homeless programs, among many others (VA, 2011c). It also provides education (through the GI bill), life insurance, vocational rehabilitation, pensions, and burial benefits in VA cemeteries, among a range of other services (VA, 2011b). In recent years, the VA has greatly expanded its outreach programs, providing supportive services to veterans in their communities (Manske, 2008).

Social workers serve many roles in the VA setting. Specific tasks include linking veterans with financial, housing, or other community assistance (e.g., Meals-on-Wheels); assisting with the application process for benefits; arranging for respite care for caregivers of veterans; providing counseling for relationship or mental health problems; addressing substance abuse issues; and assisting with child-care issues, on the one hand, or ailing parents, on the other (VA, 2011b).

Managed Care Settings

Increasing numbers of social workers are also practicing in various facets of managed care. Kornblum and Julian (2009) define *managed care* as

a wide range of health plans and practices that depart from the traditional model of private health insurance provided by one's employer. In the traditional model, insured patients chose their physician; physicians treated patients with absolute clinical autonomy; insurers generally paid physicians whatever they billed on a fee-for-service basis; and employers paid premiums for their workers to private insurers, regardless of the cost. Managed care has altered all these arrangements by setting limits on individual medical visits or treatments—that is, by managing care. (p. 61)

Social workers hold management positions in managed care. They also participate in assessment to determine whether patients are eligible for benefits and which are most appropriate. Managed care, discussed more thoroughly later in the chapter,

involves work in health insurance companies, hospitals, and health maintenance organizations (HMOs). *HMOs* are organizations that provide a wide range of health-care services for participants and employers, who typically pay an established monthly fee for services. These services generally must be provided by facilities and practitioners designated by the HMO.

Macro Practice in Health Care: Seeking Empowerment

As administrators and members of administrative committees in health-care facilities, social workers work to develop agency policies that promote effective health care available to people who need it. Additionally, social workers can advocate for more comprehensive health coverage. Social

EP 2.1.5b, 2.1.8a, 2.1.9a

workers and the National Association of Social Workers have historically served as significant forces in advocating for improved health-care legislation, policies, and resources.

Health-Care Policy and Problems in the Macro Environment

At least four main issues plague the U.S. health-care system today. First, expenses are escalating dramatically. Second, people have unequal access to adequate health care, with people living in poverty and people of color especially at risk of deprivation. Third, social workers and others working

EP 2.1.2c, 2.1.5a, 2.1.5b

under the health-care system's umbrella are plagued by a series of ethical dilemmas. Finally, many questions can be raised regarding the U.S. health-care system's cultural competence in responding to the needs of various ethnic, racial, and cultural groups.

The Escalating Cost of Health Care

The U.S. health-care system costs significantly more per capita than the health-care system in any other industrialized nation (Mooney et al., 2011). In 2009, the United States spent 17.6% of its gross domestic product on health care (Kaiser Family Foundation [KFF], 2011c). The expenditure for health care amounted to $7,538 per person in 2008 (KFF,

2011c). Mooney Knox, & Schacht (2009) argue that health-care costs are soaring for at least five reasons:

1. *The rapid acceleration of technological advances has increased the types of services, drugs, and testing available.*
2. *The population is aging.* Because of better medical treatment, more people are living longer. And the older people are, the more likely they are to suffer from more health problems that require more expensive treatment.
3. *Administrative overhead for running health-care organizations is huge.* Administrative expenses for health care are six times higher than in Western European countries (Mooney et al., 2011). Reinhardt (2008) indicates that much of this expense is excess spending used for "product design, underwriting, and marketing."

4. *The price of prescription drugs is skyrocketing.* Sixteen percent of Americans say that paying for prescription drugs is a "serious problem" financially, and another 25% say it's a "problem" (KFF, 2008a).
5. *Costs of public and private health insurance continue to rise.* In 1990 the national health expenditure per person was $2,810 (KFF, 2011c). We've already indicated that in 2008 it was $7,538.

Unequal Access to Health Care

Over 46.3 million, or over 15.2%, of Americans lack any health insurance (U.S. Census Bureau, 2010), and millions more have strikingly insufficient coverage (Macionis, 2010). What are the reasons for this? How can this occur in such a rich, industrialized, high-tech society? Highlight 12.1 describes how

---

HIGHLIGHT 12.1

Poverty, Social Class, Race, and Health Care

**EP 2.1.4,
2.1.4a,
2.1.5a**

People living in poverty are more likely to have poorer health (Kornblum & Julian, 2009). In 2008, although over 17.7 million people below the poverty level were enrolled in the Medicaid program, 30.4% of people living in poverty, or 12.1 million of them, had no insurance of any kind during the year (U.S. Census Bureau, 2010). For example, one study found that people with private insurance were twice as likely to get the surgery they needed as people receiving Medicaid (Coleman & Kerbo, 2009). Economic variables inevitably affect health; generally speaking, *"the poorer people are, the sicker they are"* (Henslin, 2011, p. 326).

Social class is another variable related to poorer health; Leon-Guerrero (2011) explains:

Although no factor has been singled out as the primary link between socioeconomic position and health, scholars have offered many factors—standard of living, work conditions, housing conditions, and the social and psychological connection with others at work, at home, or in the community—to explain the relationship . . .

The type of work available to poorly educated people can cause illness or death by exposing them to hazardous conditions. Poor and middle-class individuals who live in poor neighborhoods are exposed to air, noise, water, and chemical pollution that can increase rates of morbidity and mortality. Inadequate and unsafe housing increases the risk of injury, infections, and illnesses, including lead poisoning when children eat peeling paint. The diet of [people living in lower socioeconomic classes] . . . increases the risk of illness. [People with few resources] . . . have little time or opportunity to practice healthy activities such as exercise, and because of life stresses, they may also be encouraged to adopt behaviors that might further endanger their health. Finally, poverty limits individual access to preventative and therapeutic health care. (pp. 264–265)

People of color, who are more likely to live in poverty, also are more likely to lack adequate health care (Coleman & Kerbo, 2009; Kornblum & Julian, 2009). African American men are one-third less likely to undergo heart bypass surgery than their white counterparts (Coleman & Kerbo, 2009; Kornblum & Julian, 2009). Whites are twice as likely to get a kidney transplant as African Americans (Coleman & Kerbo, 2009). The life expectancy for white males is almost six years greater than that for African American males, and it is four years greater for white than African American females (U.S. Census Bureau, 2010).

people living in poverty, people with lower socioeconomic status, and people of color are at special risk of receiving inadequate or no health care.

For decades U.S. politicians have been debating the issue of *national health insurance*—a publicly funded program that would expand the current system of health-care provision to give some level of coverage to everyone, regardless of their ability to pay. All industrialized countries except for the United States have established some kind of national system so that all citizens have access to some type of health-care coverage (Coleman & Kerbo, 2009).

After a long and bitter debate, Congress passed the Patient Protection and Affordable Care Act in 2010, some of which Highlight 12.2 summarizes. Henslin (2011) reports:

The intention of this law is to reduce the inequalities in health care by requiring all U.S. citizens and legal residents to have medical insurance. Those who cannot afford health insurance will be provided it by raising taxes on those who have higher incomes ...

Only as the years pass will we see what impact this law has on inequalities in health care. In advance, however, we can be certain that the law will not eliminate the inequalities. These are built into our social structure. People with higher incomes will always be able to afford higher-quality medical care. And ... unless there is fundamental change—which there will not be—[people living in poverty] ... will continue to be exposed to more harmful conditions at work. In the absence of such fundamental change,

---

HIGHLIGHT 12.2

Health-Care Reform 2010

EP 2.1.1e, 2.1.9a

According to the Obama administration, the Patient Protection and Affordable Care Act of 2010 promotes a wide range of health-care advantages involved in improving quality while lowering costs (Healthcare.gov, 2011a). At the time of this writing, it has been passed, but is being challenged in the courts by many adversaries, including at least 26 states. The administration indicates that the act:

1. Allows states to cover more people on Medicaid.
2. Encourages access to preventive services without cost.
3. Permits young adults under age 26 to remain on their parents' health insurance policy.
4. Provides tax credits to help more Americans pay for insurance even if they lose or change jobs or in the event that they become ill.
5. Offers consumer protection by closer monitoring of insurance companies and their practices.
6. Ends lifetime maximums and most annual maximums imposed by insurance companies.
7. Cracks down on insurance fraud.
8. Extends health insurance coverage to people with preexisting health conditions.
9. Provides a 50% discount on brand-name prescription drugs for older adults on Medicare who enter the "donut-hole" where their drugs are not covered (described in Chapter 8).

10. Offers tax credits to small businesses for providing health insurance to their employees.

Adversaries of the act vehemently say that it is not possible to provide better service to more people without incurring more costs. Many of the court challenges hinge on the idea that it's unconstitutional to require citizens to purchase insurance from private insurance companies. The law requires "virtually all Americans to purchase health insurance or pay a fine" (Danner, 2010; Lewis, 2011). Many small business owners maintain they can't afford health insurance for all employees and that the Act involves "an onslaught of new taxes and burdensome paperwork"; it may be much more economical for them to forego the tax credit rather than purchase expensive insurance (Danner, 2011). The National Federation of Independent Business (NFIB), an organization of small business owners across the country, has joined in the lawsuit questioning the act's constitutionality (Danner, 2010).

At any rate, people are polarized concerning the pros and cons of the act. Health care is vital for everyone, including clients. The issues identified here reflect just a small sample of those being addressed. It is essential for social workers to keep abreast of developments and changing conditions regarding health care as part of a career-long learning process.

they will also continue to eat less healthy food, exercise less, and have a higher rate of obesity. The end result is that they will continue to suffer from more health problems and to die at a younger age. (p. 327)

Much of the debate in the United States about establishing a national system has historically focused on two issues—cost and freedom of choice. Covering health-care costs for everyone would require the government to expend huge amounts of money. Questions involve what types of coverage should be included and how coverage would be funded. Focus on Critical Thinking 12.1 addresses this policy issue.

The freedom-of-choice debate concerns the extent to which each citizen could choose his or her own health-care provider. The United States has a strongly ingrained commitment to freedom of choice. How much would a government-sponsored system restrict people's ability to choose the care they want? However, with the advent of managed care, this latter question may not be as relevant. Most people's choices for health care are already seriously restricted.

Problems in Managed Care

We've established that *managed care* is "a wide range of health plans and practices that depart from the traditional model of private health insurance provided by one's employer" (Kornblum & Julian, 2009, p. 61). It is "a healthcare system under which the insurer controls the person's health care, and health care providers agree to accept a set fee per treatment or a flat rate per patient" (Chapin, 2011, p. I-14). Managed care is a primary context in which social workers practice. Even social workers who don't practice in health-care or nursing home settings will still work with clients for whom health care is a major concern.

Although there are various definitions of managed care, a major concept characterizing any form of it is *capitation* or *cost containment* (Vandiver, 2008, p. 145). Chambers and Wedel (2005) explain: "*Capitation* is a term used to indicate a specified amount paid periodically to the provider for a group of specified services, regardless of quantity rendered. With capitation, a reimbursement system involves paying providers a fixed amount to service a client/consumer over a given period" (p. 201). In other words, a rate is established that the managed care organization is given for each insured worker. An identified group or range of health and mental health care providers contract with the managed care organization to provide health care at a negotiated rate. Instead of paying for each visit or treatment received on a *fee-for-service* basis, the contracted health-care providers are supposed to provide whatever services the insured employees (in individual insurance plans) in addition to their families (in family insurance plans) require. Managed care programs often provide services beyond those typically paid for by health insurance (e.g., prevention services).

FOCUS ON CRITICAL THINKING 12.1

Health-Care Costs and Policy

Critical Thinking Questions

EP 2.1.3

- How do you think health care should be handled in the United States? Should coverage be universal, that is, available to all? To what extent does the Patient Protection and Affordable Care Act accomplish this? To what extent should individual choice in terms of selecting benefits be sustained?

- Do your views reflect a *conservative* or *liberal* perspective regarding this issue?

These value orientations involve the following variables:

- Is it individuals' responsibility to take care of themselves and their families with minimal governmental interference? Or is it the government's responsibility to provide health-care services because they are so critically important to survival?
- Because health care is increasingly expensive, who should bear the burden of paying for it? Workers? Employers? All citizens through increased taxes and subsequent government funding?
- People who are rich?

One intent of capitation is to control medical costs (Vandiver, 2008). Providers are paid one sum per worker regardless of how many services providers supply. However, medical costs have continued to escalate. It has been difficult to establish whether managed care is less expensive than the old approach that was based on fee-for-services because of the complexity of the managed care environment and other variables that are difficult to control and measure (Vandiver, 2008).

Another potential goal of managed care was to improve health-care outcomes. That is, health and mental health services should be of high quality and readily accessible to clients. Yet they should also be cost-effective. However, research has indicated that improved quality of care has not necessarily been achieved in a range of areas (Vandiver, 2008). Managed care "fundamentally transformed" traditional relationships between clients and workers (Lohmann, 1997, p. 201). Historically, social workers in agency settings established treatment plans in conjunction with clients, in addition to stressing informed consent and confidentiality to comply with ethical standards. Managed care takes these decisions out of workers' and clients' hands and puts them into the hands of third-party decision makers. A managed care representative, often a utilization reviewer or case manager, then reviews documentation and regulates "the services that clients receive, especially what specific services will be provided and at what cost" (Corcoran, 1997, p. 194). To Lohmann (1997), managed care "represents the complete (and seemingly sudden) triumph of financial management concerns over virtually all other professional considerations" (p. 202).

Ethical Dilemmas in Managed Care

EP 2.1.2b, 2.1.2c

Spragins (1998) comments on the potential of managed care:

Done right, managed care is not just a cheap imitation of fee-for-service medicine. It can work better. Its simplest contribution is to link hospitals, doctors and specialists so that they can administer care more efficiently. Besides saving money, shared electronic records and preset treatment protocols can improve the care that individual patients receive. (p. 62)

However, cost cutting and inappropriate decisions often hamper this potential effectiveness. The following are sad occurrences involving managed care that illustrate some of its potential problems:

- "A Medicare HMO threatened to take a 94-year-old's wheelchair" (Vallianatos, 2001, p. 7).
- A woman experiencing a "life-threatening asthma attack" was taken to a more distant HMO-sponsored hospital instead of being rushed to the nearest medical facility (Vallianatos, 2001, January, p. 7).
- "A person with AIDS was denied approval by his managed care organization . . . of medications he had previously been on" (Vallianatos, 2001, January, p. 7).
- A man "suffered a stroke . . . after his HMO failed to treat his blood disorder. Clots have since cost him both legs. 'They treated my stroke like the flu,' he says" (Spragins, 1998, p. 62).
- A 62-year-old woman "lost a kidney after her primary care doctor . . . [working under the auspices of a managed care system] refused her repeated requests to see a specialist for her constant abdominal pain." She noted that he prescribed "range-of-motion exercises" when she really "had an infected kidney" (Spragins, 1998).

Social workers must work within their agency settings. However, they are also responsible for maintaining ethical practices and for making sure clients' needs are met. Several ethical issues may be raised concerning managed care.

The first involves the potential conflict between "the gatekeeping role of some managed care organizations and client self-determination" (Corcoran, 1997, p. 196). With managed care, clients often no longer have the right to the service provider of their choice. Rather, clients are offered a limited range of providers or the managed care utilization reviewer makes this determination.

Similarly, managed care may conflict with the ethical principle of informed consent. Corcoran (1997) remarks,

Informed consent requires that the client know in advance the clinical procedures, the risk of those procedures, and the available alternative procedures. Managed care may destroy informed consent by restricting the available procedures to a limited number. For example, a managed care company may determine the preferred practice and the preferred providers, with little consideration or disclosure of alternative procedures. (p. 196)

Responding to Ethical Dilemmas: Improving Health-Care Provision on the Macro Level

**EP 2.1.5b,
2.1.8a,
2.1.8b,
2.1.9a,
2.1.9b**

Managed care is here whether we like it or not. Social workers must respond to any ethical dilemmas it poses. There are at least five suggestions for how social workers might shape the future managed care environment (Barusch, 2012; Vandiver, 2008). First, social workers can participate in the formation and scrutiny of contracts with health providers to make sure they're fair. Second, practitioners can advocate for managed care organizations to pay attention and respond to consumers' rights and needs. Third, social workers can stand up and speak out on the behalf of

Medicaid recipients to make sure these clients are receiving the effective services they need. Fourth, workers can encourage Medicaid participants' greater participation in the planning and implementation of managed care programs. For example, social workers can initiate surveys evaluating recipients' opinions of treatment and treatment effectiveness, make certain that grievance procedures are in place and used when appropriate, and advocate for recipient representation on advisory groups to maximize consumer input. Fifth, social workers can also lobby legislators for improvements in the effectiveness of health-care provision (Edinburg & Cottler, 1995).

Managed care also has the potential to violate client confidentiality (Corcoran, 1997). Social workers are bound by the National Association of Social Workers (NASW) *Code of Ethics*, which emphasizes how "social workers should respect clients' right to privacy" and "protect the confidentiality of all information obtained in the course of professional service" (NASW, 2008, 1.07a, 1.07c). (Chapter 2 reviewed major tenets of the NASW *Code*.) Additionally, it specifies that social workers "may disclose confidential information when appropriate with valid consent from a client" (NASW, 2008, 1.07b). However, the *Code* also provides an exception. It indicates that social workers should maintain confidentiality "except for compelling reasons. The general expectation that social workers will keep information confidential does not apply when disclosure is necessary to prevent serious, foreseeable, and imminent harm to a client or other identifiable person" (NASW, 2008, 1.07c). If a managed care organization demands information before providing services, what should the worker do? What if the worker does not agree with the organization's expressed need for information and believes that the regulations violate clients' right to privacy? Workers may be required to report confidential information whether or not they feel it's ethical in order for

clients to receive necessary health care. Highlight 12.3 suggests what social workers can do to address some of these issues.

Cultural Competence and the U.S. Health-Care System

**EP 2.1.1d,
2.1.4,
2.1.4a,
2.1.4c,
2.1.10g,
2.1.10j**

Another important issue involves the U.S. health-care system's responsiveness to the needs and values of the nation's various racial, ethnic, and cultural groups. Social workers have the ethical responsibility to examine, attend to, and advocate for positive change concerning these groups' health and welfare. It is beyond the scope of this book to examine the treatment of every cultural group, so we will explore one case example—the U.S. health-care system's treatment of Americans with Asian and Pacific Islander roots in the context of their cultural values.

The U.S. health-care system is a huge bureaucracy, with many of the characteristics of traditional bureaucracies. Although management approaches vary within its many organizational structures, strict regulations and decision-making hierarchies for health-care provision tend to dominate. A problem commonly faced by such bureaucracies is the lack of cultural sensitivity. Rigid rules do not provide flexibility for adapting to culturally diverse values and needs. A major goal in social work is to enhance service provision for clients. Lack of responsiveness to clients' cultural values and belief systems can represent a major barrier to the provision of effective services.

The following discussion describes six general dimensions important in understanding Asian and Pacific Islander (API) cultures with respect to involvement in the health-care system. (Note, however, that we should not overgeneralize. For example, we should not assume that all members of API groups adhere to traditional API values to the same extent. Focus on Critical Thinking 12.2 addresses this issue.) Subsequent content addresses five topics concerning in U.S. health-care policy—informed consent, advance directives, decisions about nursing home placement, disclosure of terminal illness, and making end-of-life decisions—and examines implications for improved health-care provision.

Value Dimensions in API Cultures Relating to Health-Care Provision

At least five concepts inherent in API cultures relate directly to U.S. health-care provision. These include filial piety, collective versus individual decision making, emphasis on harmony versus conflict, nonverbal communication, fatalism, and a sense of shame at asking for help.

FOCUS ON CRITICAL THINKING 12.2

The Hazards of Overgeneralizing

EP 2.1.3

Note that when we speak about any racial, ethnic, or cultural group, it is important not to overgeneralize. Here we talk about general value dimensions evident in API cultures. However, individuals or families from any ethnic or racial group may embrace traditional cultural norms to various degrees. They may also experience *acculturation*, which we have established as "the adaptation of language, identity, behavior patterns, and preferences to those of the host/majority society" (Lum, 2004, p. 229). In other words, members of a diverse group may gradually blend into the larger society and adopt its values and customs.

Braun and Browne (2000) comment on other influential dynamics:

> Some of the factors, besides timing of immigration, that influence culturally linked health behaviors include socioeconomic status, language spoken at home, extent to which the community (and family) is ethnically homogeneous, educational attainment, and expectations about returning to one's ancestral home. (p. 186)

Therefore, when we think about a racial, ethnic, or cultural group, it's important not to assume that all members comply with all cultural values or conform to the same extent. Being of Chinese ethnic heritage does not automatically mean a person loves pan-fried dumplings, Szechuan shrimp, roast pork lo mein, kung pao chicken, or mushroom egg foo young simply because these might be traditional ethnic foods. The trick is to view each person as a unique personality, yet be sensitive to the possible cultural values and beliefs that person may hold.

Another word of caution concerns differences among the many cultures included under the API umbrella. For example, a common theme in many API cultures is the importance of extended family and the subordination of individual family members. However, in Cambodian culture, the family group is not necessarily more significant than any individual; if anything, the relationship of a couple is the significant facet in a family's structure (DuongTran & Matsuoka, 1995). Another example concerns the Filipino culture. Whereas many API cultures are patriarchal, "[a]mong Filipinos, sex roles are egalitarian rather than patriarchal. Filipinos place a high value on family, but they are also encouraged to be independent and competitive" (Weaver, 2005, p. 170).

Consider the following questions regarding your own ethnic and cultural heritage.

Critical Thinking Questions

- What traditions and values characterize your heritage?
- To what extent do your own values comply with traditional ideas?
- What are the reasons for these discrepancies?

Filial Piety

An important value dimension in API cultures is *filial piety*—"the expression of respect for and showing affection toward parents, as well as sacrificing for them in times of need" (Baskin, 2012, p. 172). For example, "*Oya-KoKo*, a Japanese version of filial piety to parents, requires a child's sensitivity, obligation, and unquestionable loyalty to lineage and parents" (Ho, 1992, p. 37). Especially significant is the obligation of younger people to care for parents as they age.

Collective Versus Individual Decision Making

In contrast to the individualist orientation emphasized in U.S. health care, API values center on reliance on the family or larger group to make ultimate decisions about any individual member's care (Mokuau, 2008; Sue & Sue, 2008; Yeo & Hikoyeda, 2000). In the U.S. health-care system the focus is on individuals making decisions about their own medical care.

Emphasis on Harmony Versus Conflict

API cultures emphasize the importance of members getting along and not causing trouble for the family, a concept that characterizes collectivist societies. The implication, then, is that individuals must "endure hardship and pain," especially if addressing issues that might disturb or cause discomfort for other family or group members (McLaughlin & Braun, 1999, p. 325). For example, in Vietnamese culture, getting along harmoniously is done through civility, gracious politeness, and courtesy; at times this occurs at the expense of being honest and direct (DuongTran & Matsuoka, 1995). Many values in Hawaiian culture reflect the importance of harmony and affiliation, including sharing resources, being congenial, fulfilling promises, and using one's intellect (Mokuau, 1995, 2008).

There also tends to be respect for clearly defined family structures and hierarchies of authority, which clarifies expectations and encourages predictability of behavior. For instance, Samoan culture stresses "hierarchical systems with clearly defined roles. The highly structured organization of the family defines an individual's roles and responsibilities and guides the individual in interactions with others" (Ewalt & Mokuau, 1996, p. 261).

Nonverbal Communication

A fourth value inherent in API cultures involves silent or nonverbal communication. Yamashiro and Matsuoka (1997) explain that "in Asian and Pacific

[Islander] cultures, language may not accommodate all that individuals think and feel—especially for those who are not socialized to use language as a primary means for expressing feelings" (Fong, 2008; Leong, Lee, & Chang, 2008; Yamashiro & Matsuoka, 1997, p. 180). Diller (2011) remarks:

EP 2.1.3c

> *Asians also tend to have a very different nonverbal communication system. Providers need to be aware of this, because unlike the Western therapeutic focus on speaking, much of the communication in Asian cultures is nonverbal. The meanings of facial expressions, gestures, eye contact, and various cultural symbols or metaphors are usually completely different from Western ones. Research has found Asians to have a "low-contact" culture—[where people are] . . . more comfortable with little physical contact and larger interpersonal distances. (p. 285)*

Much can be learned by carefully observing people's silent responses and subtle nonverbal gestures. For example, it is "improper" for children "to discuss issues of death and dying with parents, yet concern by either party may be expressed by nonverbal cues such as bowing of the head or eye contact" (McLaughlin & Braun, 1999, p. 324).

API cultures value both self-control and inconspicuousness, both of which discourage the sharing of information, especially about personal issues (Kitano & Maki, 1996). For example, conventional Japanese tradition stresses the value of personal self-control and discourages the expression of annoyance, dissatisfaction, or distress (Murase, 1995). Laotian culture emphasizes the avoidance of embarrassment by exhibiting concentrated emotional control; direct criticism of another's mistakes is considered rude and degrading (DuongTran & Matsuoka, 1995).

Shame at Asking for Help

API values include an emphasis on family, cooperation, and harmony, and an aversion to causing trouble. All these contribute to avoidance of the U.S. health-care system. For Asian Americans and Pacific Islanders, "there is stigma about and shame in experiencing mental and emotional distress" (Balgopal, 1995, p. 236; Fong, 2008; Leong, et al., 2008 McLaughlin & Braun, 1999). Thus family and group members strongly prefer to deal with issues and illnesses within the family, rather than expose problems to outsiders. For example, Chinese Americans generally feel that revealing family problems outside of the family dishonors the family name; even issues such as intellectual disability, losing a job, inferior performance at school, or tangling with the law are considered shameful and kept within the family (Lum, 1995).

When it becomes obvious to family members that the family is incapable of resolving health problems, they hesitantly turn to health-care providers as a last resort. For example, Japanese Americans will seek mental health help only when faced with an extremely severe and unmanageable problem (Murase, 1995).

For physical illness, API families tend to pursue external health-care services "only if emergency care is needed" (McLaughlin & Braun, 1999, p. 325). Once that step is taken, health-care professionals are expected to make collectivist decisions—that is, those "in the best interest of the greatest number of people involved with the patient" (McLaughlin & Braun, 1999, p. 325).

Conflicts Between API Cultural Values and the U.S. Health-Care System

Conflicts between API cultures and U.S. health-care system policies and practice revolve around at least five areas: informed consent, advance directives, decisions about nursing home placement (McLaughlin & Braun, 1999), disclosure of terminal illness, and end-of-life decisions (Yeo & Hikoyeda, 2000). Given these conflicts, the U.S. health-care system can either detract from the health and well-being of Asian Americans and Pacific Islanders or empower them.

Informed Consent

In the U.S. health-care system, individual patients are subject to *informed consent*, which involves a person's right to receive adequate information about "the consequences and risks of a medical procedure" or treatment process, evaluate alternatives, and give permission for a procedure before it's begun (Pietsch & Braun, 2000, p. 38). In many API cultures, this presumed right does not comply with prevailing values and norms (McLaughlin & Braun, 1999). For instance, "unlike the custom among white people, for whom the individual patient is the decision maker, many Japanese and Chinese families assign decision-making duties to the eldest son. In Pacific Islander families, it may be less obvious who the decision maker is" (McLaughlin & Braun, 1999, pp. 323–324). The entire family may share duties and assume designated responsibilities such as

getting food. Because of the collective nature of decision making in API cultures, it is customary for "all family members" to "receive the same level of detail about the patient's diagnosis, prognosis, and treatment options" (Braun, Mokuau, & Tsark, 1997; McLaughlin & Braun, 1999, p. 324).

Three problematic issues relate to informed consent (McLaughlin & Braun, 1999). First, consider Asian Americans' and Pacific Islanders' emphasis on harmony and conformity to group wishes. Given the API cultural orientation toward cooperation, patients may feel obligated to sign consent papers presented to them when they don't really want to. Second, cultural norms emphasizing silence and inconspicuousness may prevent patients from voicing contrary opinions, asking questions about illnesses, and declining to sign papers. Third, health-care personnel are often unaware of how API cultural values can affect the consent process and interfere with its integrity.

Advance Directives

A second problematic issue concerning API cultures and the health-care system involves *advance directives*. Introduced in Chapter 10, these are written, witnessed, signed instructions regarding what individuals wish to have done in the event that they are unable to make decisions (McLaughlin & Braun, 1999; Yeo & Hikoyeda, 2000). They can either describe what should be done under certain medical circumstances or identify some other individual to make these decisions. For example, what should be done for a person who is brain-dead and living on a respirator? Should that person be kept alive as long as possible, or should someone "pull the plug"?

Two issues tend to surface here with respect to API cultures (McLaughlin & Braun, 1999). First, health-care practitioners are legally required to "approach patients for copies of advance directives" (McLaughlin & Braun, 1999, p. 331). However, in Chinese, Japanese, and Hawaiian cultures, people avoid discussing death for fear of inviting it or suffering negative consequences (Corr, Nabe, & Corr, 2009). Second, it is pointless for Asian Americans and Pacific Islanders to discuss such issues because of their collectivist approach. They assume that family members will address those issues when the appropriate time comes.

Decisions About Nursing Home Placement

Many Asian Americans and Pacific Islanders embrace the concept of filial piety and believe that children should care for aging parents (Balgopal, 1995; DuongTran & Matsuoka, 1995; Lum, 1995; McLaughlin & Braun, 1999; Murase, 1995). For them, nursing home placements are to be avoided at all costs. Thus API families tend to wait until situations reach crisis proportions before investigating possible nursing home placement (McLaughlin & Braun, 1999; Murase, 1995). Stress may escalate due to pressure to maintain two incomes, care for both children and aging parents, and deal with the physical and cognitive health problems experienced by aging parents.

Interestingly, in contrast to Western culture, "many traditional API cultures expect death to occur at home and have mourning traditions that involve keeping the body at home for a number of days before burial" (McLaughlin & Braun, 1999, p. 331; Nichols & Braun, 1996). Thus imminent death may not spur API families to remove the dying member to a nursing or hospital facility.

Disclosure of Terminal Illness

EP 2.1.10l

Although physicians generally tell family members about a terminal illness, informing the patient about ensuing death is taboo in many API cultures (Yeo & Hikoyeda, 2000). It may be "that the family does not want the patient to become disheartened and give up on living, that the family feels it is disrespectful to speak of such things to an elder, or that talking about death is 'polluting' or will cause bad luck" (McLaughlin & Braun, 1999, p. 330). People in Japan, for example, believe that "a patient should not be informed of a terminal illness because he or she would lose the strength and hope needed to cope with the illness" (Yeo & Hikoyeda, 2000, p. 114).

Health-care personnel thus face an ethical dilemma. Policy and professional ethics may require that a patient be informed of a terminal diagnosis so that practitioner and patient can discuss and weigh treatment options. However, culturally, the patient may not want to know and may well choose ignorance if given that option.

End-of-Life Decisions

A related issue to disclosure of terminal illness is whether to continue life support for individuals who cannot make decisions and have no hope of recovery (e.g., those who are brain-dead) (Yeo &

Hikoyeda, 2000). We have established that traditional API cultures tend to rebuff advance directives. Yeo and Hikoyeda (2000) explain:

> *Cultural values might emphasize longevity over quality of life, especially for one's parent. Some families do not want to make decisions that would preclude the possibility of a miracle from either God or the American medical system, of which they might have unrealistically high expectations. (p. 104)*

Highlight 12.4 proposes five recommendations to address the five value conflicts discussed here—informed consent, advance directives, placement decisions, disclosure of terminal illness, and end-of-life decisions.

International Perspectives: AIDS—A Global Crisis

Consider these international scenarios.

EP 2.1.5, 2.1.7b

In sub-Saharan Africa, 22.5 million people are HIV positive; in 2009 about 1.3 million people died from AIDS-related conditions (AVERT, 2011a). Although the region has 14% of the world's population, it has 68% of the world's AIDS-related deaths (Macionis, 2010). "Unscrupulous entrepreneurs" are "hustling for corpses" as thousands die from AIDS and funeral parlors are swamped with bodies; picture this scene:

> *So fast are AIDS victims piling up that ... morgues and cemeteries are out of space. A lively black market has grown up in stolen burial equipment. Crooked morgue workers sell corpses to favored undertakers, or to the highest bidder, sometimes even before bereaved families arrive to claim a body—leaving the relatives no choice but to pay the undertaker who collected the remains. (Masland, 2001, p. 45)*

In China AIDS has become an "epidemic that races across the country" following a "route [from Burma] of drug smugglers, of truck drivers, of migrant workers and the prostitutes that wait for them." Consider this picture:

> *Chen Ah-Yan usually gets up after midnight. She lounges on an L-shaped couch with three other girls in a tiny room open to the sticky air of the street,*

HIGHLIGHT 12.4

Recommendations for a More Culturally Competent Health-Care System

**EP 2.1.8a,
2.1.8b,
2.1.9b,
2.1.10g,
2.1.10j**

Large service provision systems are never perfect. There are always quirks and problems because such broadly ranging people are involved. Bureaucracies have established rules to assist in their functioning. A large health-care system cannot adapt itself perfectly to all its beneficiaries' needs. However, an ongoing concern for social workers is the need to assess large systems' functioning, recommend improvements, and work to achieve positive changes. This is especially true in view of the U.S. population's cultural diversity.

How can the U.S. health-care system become more sensitive to API (and other) cultures? And how can social workers address this issue? Five recommendations are proposed here:

1. Provide training for health-care personnel that sensitizes them to API cultural values and issues (Braun & Browne, 2000; McLaughlin & Braun, 1999; Yamashiro & Matsuoka, 1997). Staff should be taught to carefully observe periods of silence, nonverbal behavior, and family or group interaction for clues to understanding such behavior. They should pay careful attention to "the language used to discuss the patient's disease, . . . whether decisions are made by the patient or by the larger family unit, . . . the relevance of religious beliefs, . . . [and] the patient's and family's degree of fatalism versus an active desire for control of events" (Braun & Browne, 2000, p. 186).

2. Encourage personnel in the health-care system to "begin addressing end-of-life planning issues with whole families (not just individual patients) earlier in the life course (rather than waiting until the end) and in nonhospital venues" (McLaughlin & Braun, 1999, p. 333). Agency policy should encourage staff to tune in to cultural values regarding collectivist versus individual perspectives on decision making and to work with families accordingly.

3. Urge the health-care system to begin investigating the adoption of family-centered rather than individual-centered decision making models for virtually all health-related decisions (Fong, 2008; McLaughlin & Braun, 1999; Mokuau, 1995). Health-care personnel should seek to understand individuals' and families' values and to work within those value systems to the greatest extent possible. The health-care system should respect both the individual's and the family's right to self-determination (Ewalt & Mokuau, 1996).

4. Establish "parallel services" whereby attention and treatment are tailored to meet the cultural needs and expectations of API people. For example, some "successful programs in San Francisco and Los Angeles" use "language, signs, food and drinks, and [service] providers" representing "the culture being served" (Braun & Browne, 2000, p. 186). The downside of this approach, of course, is that it's expensive to duplicate services. In the event that it's financially unfeasible to develop parallel services, programs could at least employ bilingual staff to assist in the assessment and treatment process (Braun & Browne, 2000).

5. Encourage social workers to advocate for policy and practice changes in the health-care system. The system should respect and appreciate cultural diversity and self-determination, not pretend they don't exist.

---

watching music videos halfheartedly and calling out to passers-by. Occasionally . . . [she] catches the attention of a man in one of the fancy cars with blackened windows cruising the streets —"drug smuggler," she comments casually—and brings him upstairs to the makeshift room not much larger than a twin mattress. The slim 18-year-old wearing dark-red lipstick . . . came to this town [from the country] a few months ago [seeking excitement]. . . . "Sure, we know about AIDS,"

Chen giggles. "But we're just here to have fun." (Fang, 2001, pp. 22–23)

In 2009, 1.8 million people died from AIDS around the globe, and there were 2.6 million new HIV infections (KFF, 2010a). A total of 33.3 million people in the world were living with HIV at the end of 2009 (KFF, 2010a).

In the United States, it is estimated that 1.1 million people are HIV infected (KFF, 2011b). In 2008, approximately 56,300 new cases of HIV-positive people were diagnosed (CDC, 2011b).

Race and gender are variables involved in HIV transmission. Whereas African Americans embody 12.9% of the U.S. population (U.S. Census Bureau, 2010), they accounted for almost 49% of the diagnoses (CDC, 2011b). Hispanics, who make up about 15.8% of the population, made up 19.6% of new diagnoses (CDC, 2011b).

Women accounted for 27% of new transmissions in the United States (KFF, 2011b). This increased from 8% in 1985 and 13% in 1990 (KFF, 2008a). African American women account for 61% of HIV infections among women, a rate almost 15 times that of white women (KFF, 2011a). Latinas account for 16% of new HIV infections, a rate nearly four times that of white women (KFF, 2011e).

Because of its significance on a national and global level, this section will devote considerable attention to AIDS and health care.

HIV and AIDS

Acquired immune deficiency syndrome (AIDS), caused by human immunodeficiency virus (HIV), is a disease that destroys the body's immune system. Infected people thus gradually become increasingly vulnerable to *opportunistic diseases*—conditions and infections that themselves are usually not life threatening but that take advantage of a weakened immune system and use this opportunity to invade it.

HIV is a type of virus called a *retrovirus*. A *virus* is a submicroscopic, infectious parcel of genetic material, resembling in some ways a tiny living organism and in other ways inert (lifeless) material, that can grow and multiply only within the living cells of bacteria, plants, and animals. There is no cure for a virus. Note that viruses also cause the common cold and influenza; available medications may alleviate symptoms but will not cure the virus.

A *retrovirus is* a special kind of virus that invades normal cells and causes them to reproduce more of the virus rather than reproduce themselves like other normal cells. HIV attacks normal white blood cells (called *T-cells*) that fight off diseases invading the body (Yarber et al., 2010). The specific type of T-cell that's vulnerable has *CD4 molecules* on its surface that help coordinate the body's resistance "to certain microorganisms such as viruses" (About.com, 2011). Hereafter, we will refer to these cells as *CD4 T-cells*.

After invading the CD4 T-cell, HIV immediately begins destroying this host cell and injecting its own genetic material into the cell. The transformed CD4 T-cell then begins producing more HIV instead of reproducing its former self. As the invaded CD4 T-cells produce more of the virus and fewer disease attacking white blood cells, the body's immune system deteriorates. As a result, the body is left defenseless and becomes easy prey to other infections. In short, HIV destroys the body's immune or defense system so that other diseases invade and eventually cause death. HIV is a frightening agent that has continued to mutate into various strains, making it difficult to find a cure.

People may have contracted HIV and be HIV-positive but not yet be diagnosed with AIDS. HIV gradually destroys the immune system, so it may take a while to develop the serious conditions characterizing AIDS. According to the CDC, full-blown AIDS diagnosis applies when a person has a positive HIV blood test and a CD4 T-cell count below 200 per microliter of blood (normal people have between 600 and 1200) (Crooks & Baur, 2011). Among the numerous illnesses that may develop as the immune system plummets are blood and other serious viral infections; brain infections and deterioration; *Pneumocystis carinii* pneumonia (a rare form of pneumonia from which people with normal immune systems are protected); yeast infection of the esophagus, mouth, or genitals; cancer of the lymph glands; tuberculosis;[10] and exacerbated herpes simplex conditions (resulting in ulcers in the mouth or on the genitals that occur more frequently and severely than usual) (AllRefer.com, 2005; Yarber et al., 2010). People who have not contracted HIV are generally immune to these ailments.

HIV affects each individual differently. Some people go for years before experiencing negative effects; others exhibit symptoms much earlier. Initial indications include a dry cough, abdominal discomfort, headaches, oral thrush, loss of appetite, fever, night sweats, weight loss, diarrhea, skin rashes, fatigue, swollen lymph nodes, and lack of resistance to infection. Unfortunately, other illnesses have similar symptoms, so it's easy for people to overlook the possibility that they are HIV-positive. As AIDS progresses, the immune system becomes less capable of fighting off opportunistic diseases, making the

---

[10]*Tuberculosis* is a disease usually affecting the lungs that is characterized by the development of tubercules ("small, firm, rounded nodule[s] or swelling[s]") (Nichols, 1999, p. 1402).

infected person vulnerable to a variety of cancers, nervous system degeneration, and infections caused by other viruses, bacteria, parasites, and fungi. AIDS is "one of the world's most serious health and development challenges" (KFF, 2010a). It is "among the leading causes of death worldwide and the leading cause of death in sub-Saharan Africa" (KFF, 2008a). Highlight 12.5 reviews methods of HIV transmission.

Measurement of the CD4 T-Cell Count

Several tests have been developed to determine if a person has been exposed to the AIDS virus. These tests directly detect not the virus but the antibodies a person's immune system develops to fight the virus. Two of the most widely used tests are the ELISA (short for enzyme-linked immunosorbent assay) and the Western blot. The ELISA can be used in

---

HIGHLIGHT 12.5

How Is HIV Transmitted?

Transmission of HIV has been clearly documented through the exchange of bodily fluids from one person to another. "Semen, blood, and vaginal secretions are the fluids most often implicated in transmission of HIV" (Kelly, 2008, p. 499).

Kelly (2008) describes various means of transmitting HIV:

Several routes of HIV infection have been clearly documented:

1. Anal or vaginal intercourse.
2. Oral-genital activity.
3. Contact with semen or vaginal fluids from an infected person.
4. Organs transplanted from infected persons.
5. Contact with infected blood, through use of contaminated needles and syringes shared by drug users or used for tattooing, ear piercing, or injection of steroids.
6. Transfer from mother to child [during pregnancy or birth] . . .

Sharing anal intercourse is especially risky behavior, because the virus from the semen enters the bloodstream through the many small tears in the colon. [The colon is not lined with a mucus membrane like the vagina, so it is much more likely to experience tears.] . . .

The risks associated with oral-genital sex have been difficult to quantify, partly because this behavior usually is practiced in conjunction with other sexual activities that may be highly risky. However, there have been cases in which HIV was transmitted from a man's semen during fellatio (oral sex performed on a male). [For example, any cuts or sores in the mouth might allow for tainted semen to enter the bloodstream.]

Although ordinary kissing appears to pose only a minor threat, the CDC [Centers for Disease Control] has reported a case of HIV transmission through kissing. Both parties had gum disease, confirming the earlier suspicion that viruses carried in saliva could enter the body through tiny breaks or sores within the mouth or enter the lymphatic cells in the tonsils. Experts therefore continue to caution against prolonged, wet deep kissing (French kissing). . . .

Casual contacts with infected persons—even in crowded households, social settings, schools, or the workplace—are not dangerous. There are no documented cases of HIV being transmitted through food, water, toilets, swimming pools or hot tubs, shared drinking or eating utensils, telephones, or used clothing. Several research studies have demonstrated that the virus is not transmitted by insects. (pp. 499–500)

One group with a high likelihood of HIV transmission includes IV drug users who share needles, as this may involve direct injection of minute quantities of HIV infected blood. People, heterosexual and gay, who engage in unprotected anal intercourse increase risk of transmission. Of course, many types of sexual interaction that includes unprotected transmission of bodily fluids enhance the risk of contracting HIV.

Yarber and his colleagues (2010) explain transmission during pregnancy and birth:

About one quarter to one third of all untreated pregnancy women infected with HIV will pass the infection to their babies. HIV can also be transmitted to babies through the breast milk of mothers infected with the virus. If an HIV-infected woman is treated with certain drugs during pregnancy, she can greatly reduce the chances that her baby will get infected with HIV. If she is treated and her baby is delivered by cesarean section, the chances of the baby being infected can be reduced to a rate of 1%. HIV infection of newborns has been almost eradicated in the United States because of voluntary prenatal HIV testing and medical treatment. (p. 541) two important ways. First, donated blood can be screened to prevent the AIDS virus from being transmitted by blood transfusions. Second, individuals who fear they may be carriers of the virus can have their blood tested. For a person who has been infected with HIV, it generally takes two to three months before enough antibodies are produced to be detected by the test.

The ELISA is an extremely sensitive test and therefore is highly accurate in detecting the presence of antibodies. It rarely gives a negative result when antibodies are present. However, it has a much higher rate of false positive results; that is, it indicates that antibodies are present when in reality they are not. Therefore, it is recommended that positive results on the ELISA be confirmed by another test called the Western blot or immunoblot. This test is much more specific and less likely to give a false positive. Because the Western blot is expensive and difficult to administer, it can't be used for mass blood screening as can the ELISA. It may take up to two weeks to receive the results of these tests (Welch, 2011).

Welch (2011) describes other types of tests available for HIV:

- "Urine Test": "ELISA and Western blot type tests have been developed to test for HIV in urine. This result may take a few days to two weeks)."
- "Oral Fluid Test": "This test checks for HIV antibodies in the oral fluids—a test pad is placed between the cheeks and the gums; the pad absorbs fluids in the mouth. Results may take up to two weeks."
- "Quick Test": "Since 2002, the FDA has approved quick tests (blood and oral swab) that yield results within 10 to 20 minutes. If the result is negative, no further testing is needed; if it is positive, a Western blot test is done (final results are received within two weeks)."
- "Home Testing": "As of 2009, the FDA has approved only one HIV home test kit, *Home Access* (although many others are on the market). After using a simple finger-prick process to collect a blood sample, the sample is smeared on a special paper in the kit; the paper with the sample is mailed to a lab, along with a personal identification number (PIN). To get results, the person calls the lab and gives them their PIN." (p. 304)

Treatment for AIDS

Welsh (2011) comments on the current state of treatment for HIV/AIDS:

There is no cure for HIV or AIDS. Today, the main type of treatment, antiretroviral drugs (ARV), is not a cure, but it does stop the virus from advancing to AIDS for many years. There are three broad classes of antiviral drugs (Marieb & Hoehn, 2010):

- *Reverse transcriptase inhibitors: This class includes AZT and DDC, the first-generation HIV treatments, which inhibit the virus after it gains entry into the T-helper cells.*
- *Protease inhibitors: This includes saquinavir and ritonavir. These also inhibit the virus once it enters the T-helper cells.*
- *Fusion inhibitors: This new class of drugs, which includes enfuvirtide, prevent HIV from entering the T-helper cell in the first place.*

Today, the most common type of treatment is combination therapy, where two or more drugs are taken at the same time. When a person takes a combination of three or more anti-HIV drugs, it is referred to as highly active antiretroviral therapy (HAART). [Mixtures of such drugs are also referred to as "cocktail drugs."]

Once an HIV-infected person begins ARV treatment, its effectiveness is tracked through a viral load blood test. Viral load refers to the amount of HIV found in the bloodstream. If the viral load is high, it signifies that the T-helper cells are being quickly destroyed and that the ARV treatment is not effective. It takes as long as three to six months for the ARV to become effective in keeping down the viral load. In some people, the treatment is so effective, the viral load drops to [being] undetectable. (pp. 306–307)

Unfortunately, HIV can mutate and become resistant to drugs. As a result ARV becomes ineffective for some people. As ARV stops working, the viral load increases, people lose their immunity to illnesses, and they get sick. It does help ARV effectiveness to follow the drug regimen precisely as directed.

HAART has cut the death rate from conditions resulting from HIV/AIDS by 75% since the 1990s; however, 10,000 people in the United States still die from HIV/AIDS-related causes annually (Rathus et al., 2011).

Clinical research on vaccines is currently being conducted, although clinical trials take years to complete (AVERT, 2011b). Two avenues of research are being pursued. *Preventive vaccines* are being investigated to prevent HIV infection in HIV-negative people. *Therapeutic vaccines* are being explored to help improve the immune system in HIV-positive individuals.

Empowerment for People Living with AIDS

Empowerment is a key concept for social workers helping persons with AIDS. Empowerment involves feeling good about ourselves and feeling that we have some control and direction over our lives. Empowerment is clearly related to hope.

Because of the prevalence of AIDS in the United States, social workers will likely work directly or indirectly with persons having the disease. The essence of social work practice with people who are HIV-positive involves providing support, focusing on strengths, and seeking empowerment. People need to develop positive feelings about themselves and maximize the control they have over their lives. Social workers can help HIV-positive people seriously consider alternatives and make their best choices. It's important to remain as active in normal life activities as possible.

EP 2.1.3c, 2.1.10e

With the advent of cocktail drugs and significantly longer life expectancies for people with AIDS, the concept of empowerment becomes especially important. Persons with AIDS should never be referred to as *victims*. Rather, they should be referred to as *people living with AIDS*, with an emphasis on *living*. The word *victim* implies helplessness, powerlessness, and lack of control. People living with AIDS need to be viewed as individuals capable of empowerment, not as helpless victims. Hope should be maintained because many people living with AIDS have years of fruitful living ahead of them. Much research and effort are being directed at combating the disease. Highlight 12.6 explores the importance of critically evaluating both the positive and negative sides of life experiences.

Haney (1988) emphasizes that positives can come from any negative experience. Working through difficulties makes people stronger and wiser. He cites some of the positives that he has experienced since contracting AIDS, which include

learning to accept [my] limitations; learning to cope by getting in touch with [my] strengths; experiencing a clarity of purpose; learning to live one day at a time; learning to focus on the good in [my] life here and now; and the incredibly moving experience of having complete support from [my] family, friends, lover, people [I] hardly know, and sometimes even complete strangers. (p. 252)

Social Work Roles and Empowerment for People Living with AIDS

Social workers assume many roles when working with people living with AIDS. First, a social worker can provide counseling, in which a client's issues are addressed, feelings and emotions are expressed and discussed, and plans are made. A social worker may help a client work out issues and objectively evaluate life situations. The worker may also assist the client in focusing on positives, even when the client is coping with the negative aspects of HIV/AIDS.

EP 2.1.1c, 2.1.5b, 2.1.10k

Social workers may help HIV-positive people deal with feelings of fear, guilt, anger, depression, hopelessness, abandonment, and any other emotions they may experience. Regardless of how clients feel, it is crucial to bring these feelings out in the open so clients can deal with them. Emotional repression and isolation should be avoided. If health significantly deteriorates, social workers may also help people with AIDS cope with disfigurement and loss of function. Highlight 12.7 discusses the importance of dealing with all life issues, including death.

As an educator, a social worker can provide information about the progression of the disease, drug treatments, stress management, positive lifestyle choices, and safe sex practices. Social workers may also provide *crisis intervention*, a brief and time limited therapeutic intervention through which a social worker helps a client learn to cope with or adjust to extreme external pressures. Examples of crises experienced by people with AIDS include sudden bouts of illness, job loss due to illness, and escalating expenses for medical treatments.

Empowerment can come from reconnections (Haney, 1988). Having AIDS often makes people feel isolated from family, friends, and others, and disconnected from their old lives. Social workers can help people with AIDS reconnect with other

HIGHLIGHT 12.6

Evaluating the Consequences of Life Experiences

EP 2.1.10e

Maintaining a meaningful quality of life involves focusing on the positive instead of the negative aspects of life. Each moment of each day, we can choose how to look at the exact same situation in either a positive or a negative light. For example, many of us dream of winning the lottery. When one man won $21 million, he was thrilled. He had spent many happy hours over the years with his pals at a local bar, watching the televised announcements of lottery winners and hoping that he would be one of them. Finally, it happened. Ecstatic, he said he would "take care of" all of his bar buddies. Although envious, they were also happy that he had won and were enthusiastically looking forward to their "cut."

However, the story does not have the happiest of endings. It seems the man forgot to give his friends the share they felt they had coming. Hard feelings emerged as former friends bandied about threats of lawsuits for unfair treatment. The winning man found that he no longer had friends at the bar. For that matter, he no longer had friends in his neighborhood, so he decided to move to a "better" neighborhood where he knew no one. He had lost most of his friends.

Additionally, he had to get an unlisted telephone number because he and his wife couldn't stand the barrage of solicitations. The man was approached by almost everyone he knew, including relatives. They either not so subtly hinted that they could use a few extra bucks or asked him point-blank for loans they felt they would never have to repay. Taxes eradicated a third of his winnings almost immediately. Still wealthy, he bought a red Porsche. But the man's life had changed. He no longer experienced the same sense of belongingness, peace, and happiness that he had in his poorer days.

There are numerous other examples of positive and negative sides to any event. The birth of a long awaited baby may mark a couple's most joyous occasion. However, the hospital and other medical costs not covered by insurance may place a heavy financial burden on them. Finding reasonable yet high-quality day care so that the mother can return to work may be difficult. A colicky baby may keep them both up much of the night, making the thought of getting up the next day a nightmare.

The moral of this story is the importance of focusing on the positive aspects of any particular situation. People with AIDS need to work hard at identifying, concentrating on, and enjoying the positive elements in their daily lives.

---

people. Support systems are essential and can include family members, friends, intimate others, and coworkers. Lines of communication need to be maintained. Significant others must also express and face their feelings in order to deal with them and support people living with AIDS. Otherwise they might shun negative feelings by avoiding and withdrawing from people with AIDS.

Social workers may also provide *family counseling*, in which they help the person with AIDS discuss issues with other family members. Just as clients themselves must learn to cope, so must significant others and family members. Their feelings and fears must also be elicited so that they can be addressed.

Social workers, as brokers, may help link clients to needed resources and services. People with AIDS may need services concerning health, income maintenance, housing, mental health care, and legal assistance.

Social workers may refer clients with AIDS to support groups, in which they can talk with others who also have AIDS and are experiencing similar problems and issues. HIV-positive people need not feel isolated and alone. They can see that there are other people who understand their issues and feelings. Additionally, such groups provide excellent channels for gaining information on how others have worked out similar problems. Social workers can also facilitate support or educational groups by serving as leader and keeping the group on track.

In addition, social workers can provide case management services to people living with AIDS. Earlier chapters established that case management involves assessing a client's needs, developing plans to meet these needs, linking the client with the appropriate services, monitoring service delivery, and advocating for the client when necessary (Taylor-Brown, 1995).

HIGHLIGHT 12.7

Empowerment by Dealing with Life and Death

EP 2.1.10l

It is important for people with AIDS to deal not only with life but also with death. Social workers can help people with AIDS address any spiritual issues that may concern them. Helping people with AIDS discuss plans for what will happen after their death can be useful. In a way, this may help them gain greater control. They may need to write a will or make funeral arrangements. They may want to finish unsettled business or resolve disputes with significant others. A useful concept in working with people who are facing their own death is the idea of making them "the star of their own death." In other words, instead of avoiding issues concerning death because this can make people feel uncomfortable, emphasize that people approaching death have the right to make decisions and settle their affairs.

Note that part of case management involves *advocacy*—the act of stepping forward and speaking out on the behalf of clients to promote fair and equitable treatment or gain needed resources. Social workers may advocate for clients with AIDS whether those workers are case managers or not.

Advocacy may be necessary for several reasons. Advocacy can target unfair treatment when HIV-positive people are discriminated against, denied services, fired from jobs, or evicted from housing. Advocacy can also be used to seek necessary resources such as health care or financial assistance when it's not readily available.

International Perspectives: AIDS in Sub-Saharan Africa

EP 2.1.5

Sub-Saharan Africa is the region on the globe most severely ravaged by AIDS. We've established that 22.5 million people are HIV-positive in sub-Saharan Africa. About 14.8 million children have lost one or both parents (AVERT, 2011a). "The social and economic consequences of the AIDS epidemic are widely felt, not only in the health sector but also in education, industry, agriculture, transport, human resources and the economy in general. The AIDS epidemic in sub-Saharan Africa continues to devastate communities, rolling back decades of development progress" (AVERT, 2011a).

Although HIV/AIDS is a major problem throughout the region, percentages of infection vary greatly from one country to another (AVERT, 2011a). For example, less than 1% of people in Namibia are infected, whereas the infection rate in South Africa is 17.8% and in Swaziland 25.9%. The better news is that the epidemic appears to have peaked in the late 1990s, although it still remains a huge problem (AVERT, 2011a; KFF, 2009).

A woman with AIDS rests in a hospital bed in Togo.

Paul Kelly/PhotoLibrary

HIGHLIGHT 12.8

What Would Your Life Be Like If You Had AIDS and Lived in Sub-Saharan Africa?

EP 2.1.10b

McGeary (2001) suggests that you consider what your life would be like if you lived in sub-Saharan Africa. She describes several scenarios.

Scenario A: Fundisi Khumao, age 22, has AIDS and tuberculosis (TB). He knows he has TB but does not acknowledge that he has AIDS. AIDS is something not to be talked about. Breathing is tremendously difficult for him and often characterized by violent coughing spasms. He lives in abject poverty. He is cold and alone. Vomiting, constipation, and extreme weakness are common occurrences. Before he got sick, he worked as a hairdresser in a large city. There he had several girlfriends, from one of whom he likely caught HIV. When he couldn't work anymore, he retreated to his rural village. No medicine is available for AIDS, and he has no money anyway. Fundisi won't go to a hospital because he feels people go there only to die.

Scenario B: Laetitia Hambahlane, age 51, has AIDS and admits it. She worked as a domestic servant for wealthy people in a large city before she became too sick. It was very difficult for her to accept the fact that she had AIDS. She told her four children, who were "ashamed and frightened" (p. 38). The worst part for her is the total rejection by her mother. Having AIDS is shameful, and having almost anything else would be better. Laetitia's children are sick of hearing about her problems and will no longer help her (e.g., by bringing her food when she's too weak to get it herself). "One day local youths barged into her room, cursed her as a witch and a whore,

and beat her. When she told the police, the youths returned, threatening to burn down the house" (p. 40).

Scenario C: Louis Chikoka, age 39, is a married truck driver with three children. Because work close to home is rarely available, it is common in Africa to have to work elsewhere and spend the majority of time away from home. When Louis is away from home for long periods, he has sex with other women. He knows this places him at great risk of contracting HIV, but he says he has needs and sees no other way to meet them. His life situation reflects a typical picture. The region is economically dependent on migrant laborers who often find themselves far from home, so having multiple sexual partners is common practice. Unfortunately, this frequently results in bringing the disease home to wives and girlfriends.

Scenario D: A tiny 3-year-old child whom we will arbitrarily call Adwowa lies dying of AIDS in the hospital. "Now her skin wrinkles around her body like an oversize suit, and her twig size bones can barely hold her vertical as nurses search for a vein to take blood. In the frail arms hooked up to transfusion tubes, her veins have collapsed. . . . She mews like a wounded animal" while the nurses struggle to raise a vein to obtain a minuscule sample of her blood (p. 44). Her mother, age 25, does not know the little girl has AIDS. She has heard of AIDS but knows little else about it. For example, she does not know that it can be contracted through sexual intercourse or passed on to an infant at birth. She doesn't even know if she or her husband has it. Adwowa's father works far away in a large city and can return home only a couple of times each year. He probably often seeks sexual solace from strangers.

Life expectancy in sub-Saharan Africa is age 52 and less than age 51 in those countries most severely affected by HIV/AIDS (AVERT, 2011a). Women are hardest hit, as they account for 59% of adults living with HIV/AIDS in the region (KFF, 2009). Young people age 15 to 24, especially young women, are at exceptional risk of contracting the virus (KFF, 2009).

Highlight 12.8 provides several scenarios describing what it might be like to have AIDS and live in sub-Saharan Africa.

HIV infection rates present a devastating problem. (This is true especially among women, who are significantly more likely to catch HIV through sexual intercourse [Macionis, 2010; Masland, 2000; UNAIDS, 2008].) Because of the stigma associated with AIDS, people cling to denial, often resulting in lack of

treatment and death. The migrant worker lifestyle contributes to the commonplace acceptance of casual sex. Women are taught early on that men "rule the roost" and they should be obeyed sexually and in many other ways (Macionis, 2010). It's not uncommon for women who deny their partners sex or request that they use condoms to suffer severe beatings or even desertion. Men typically loathe condoms (Macionis, 2010). The following myths about condoms might prevail.

- Condoms inhibit erections and detract from pleasurable sensations.
- One is not a real man if he has to use a condom.
- When condoms fill up with semen, they spread HIV.

FOCUS ON CRITICAL THINKING 12.3

What Should Be Done About HIV/AIDS in Sub-Saharan Africa?

EP 2.1.3, 2.1.5c

The following are suggested approaches to address the problem of HIV/AIDS in sub-Saharan Africa:

1. Launch serious and extensive preventive programs to educate people about HIV/AIDS and its transmission. The stigma associated with HIV/AIDS should be eliminated (AVERT, 2011a; Cowley, 2000, p. 38).

2. Publicize the potential consequences of unprotected casual sex with programs stressing safer sex (Cowley, 2000, p. 38). Some sub-Saharan African countries have carried out major prevention campaigns resulting in lower infection rates (AVERT, 2011a). For instance, in Senegal political leaders initiated an intense campaign and significantly decreased the prevalence of HIV (AVERT, 2011a). Senegal developed educational programming in addition to having "cut taxes on condoms and got[ten] religious leaders to participate in AIDS education" (Cowley, 2000; Lemonick, 2000, p. 39). Similarly, Uganda's prevention initiative decreased the prevalence of HIV among pregnant women (AVERT, 2011a). Early on, the nation took steps to promote sex education; "[p]rimary schools and health centers tout the ABCs (**a**bstinence, **b**e faithful, and use **c**ondoms). The taboos [about discussing HIV] have eroded so much that personal ads in [one] . . . steamy *Red Pepper* tabloid list HIV status along with age, height, and interests. Correspondingly, infection rates among the most vulnerable age groups dropped"

considerably (Whitelaw, 2003, p. 19; emphasis added). South Africa, on the other hand, did little in terms of prevention, which led to "an unprecedented number of people living with HIV" (AVERT, 2011a).

3. Empower women to have greater control over their sex lives. One option is the development of low-cost contraception over which they have more influence (Cowley, 2000).

4. Very importantly, have developed countries provide significant financial contributions and aid in the form of subsidized drug costs so that African nations can better afford to provide drug treatment. Everyone who needs antiretroviral drugs should have them; today only about 40% of Africans requiring treatment are receiving it (AVERT, 2011a). "Millions are not even receiving treatment for opportunistic infections [e.g., bacterial diseases such as tuberculosis, fungal diseases, viral diseases, and HIV-associated cancers], which affect individuals whose immune systems have been weakened by HIV infection" (AVERT, 2011a).

5. Develop a vaccine to prevent AIDS (Cowley, 2000).

Critical Thinking Questions

- Which of the above suggestions do you think is (are) the most feasible to address the problem of HIV/AIDS in sub-Saharan Africa?
- Who might fund such a plan? How might a person go about getting such funding?
- What could you do as an individual do to address a problem such as this?

- Condoms manufactured by foreigners come to Africa already infected with HIV.

Focus on Critical Thinking 12.3 addresses issues and raises questions about what could be done to contend with the HIV problem in sub-Saharan Africa.

Chapter Summary

The following summarizes this chapter's content as it relates to the chapter's learning objectives presented at the beginning of the chapter. Learning objectives include the following:

A Identify the major types of health problems people encounter.

Health problems include those related to unhealthy lifestyles, physical injuries, environmental factors, poverty, and contagious diseases.

B Describe primary social work roles in health-care provision.

Social workers have been involved in preventive, primary, tertiary, restorative, and continuing care in health-care practice. Settings include hospitals, medical clinics, and diagnostic and treatment centers; public health departments and other health-care contexts; Veteran's Affairs hospitals; and managed care settings.

C Discuss major problems in the macro environment concerning health care, including escalating costs, unequal access, ethical dilemmas in managed care, and the need to enhance cultural competence in the health-care system.

The U.S. health-care system costs significantly more per capita than the health-care system in any other industrialized nation. People living in poverty, people with lower socioeconomic status, and people of color are at special risk of having poorer and unequal access to adequate health care. The Patient Protection and Affordable Care Act of 2010 is summarized and discussed.

Problems in managed care include questions regarding the efficiency and effectiveness of capitation. Ethical dilemmas include the gate-keeping role of managed care organizations, potential issues with informed consent, and possible violations of confidentiality when patients seek treatment. Suggestions for improving health-care provision on the macro level are proposed. Questions are raised concerning the U.S. health-care system's responsiveness to the needs and values of the nation's various racial, ethnic, and cultural groups. Social workers have the ethical responsibility to examine, attend to, and advocate for positive change concerning these groups' health and welfare.

D Explore some of the value discrepancies between Asian and Pacific Islander (API) cultures and the U.S. health-care system.

Five concepts directly related to API cultures that affect health-care provision include filial piety, collective versus individual decision making, emphasis on harmony versus conflict, nonverbal communication, and a sense of shame at asking for help. Potential conflicts between API cultures and the U.S. health-care system include informed consent, advance directives, decisions about nursing home placement, disclosure of terminal illness, and end-of-life decisions.

Suggestions include training health-care personnel to sensitize them to API cultural values, addressing end-of-life decisions with whole families instead of just individuals, assuming a family-centered

decision-making model, establishing parallel services to traditional services that better meet the needs of API culture, and encouraging social workers to advocate for improved policies and practice strategies.

E Describe HIV/AIDS, social work roles, and empowerment for people living with AIDS.

HIV is caused by a retrovirus that attacks the immune system. People gradually become less resistant and more vulnerable to opportunistic diseases. Extremely low CD4 T-cell counts result in AIDS. HIV is transmitted by the exchange of bodily fluids, especially by semen, blood, and vaginal secretions. Tests for HIV/AIDS include ELISA and the Western blot, in addition to other tests. HIV/AIDS cannot be cured, but cocktail drugs (a mixture of different drugs) referred to as HAART (highly active antiretroviral therapy) have been used effectively to inhibit progression of the disease in many people. A problem is the drugs' high cost.

Social workers can provide support and focus on strengths for people living with HIV/AIDS. They can provide counseling, crisis intervention, linkage with support systems, family counseling, support group referral, and advocacy.

F Examine the severity of AIDS as an international problem, particularly in sub-Saharan Africa.

In 2009, 1.8 million people died from AIDS around the globe, and there were 2.6 million new HIV infections. Currently, 22.5 million people are HIV-positive in sub-Saharan Africa. HIV infection is especially a problem for African women. Approaches to addressing the problem include providing education about HIV/AIDS, providing safe sex programming, empowering women to gain greater control over their lives, providing funding for treatment, and developing a cure.

G Encourage critical thinking about universal health-care coverage, overgeneralizations regarding various racial and ethnic groups, and ways to address the HIV/AIDS problem in sub-Saharan Africa.

Critical thinking questions were posed regarding the provision of national health insurance and the adoption of a liberal or conservative perspective. Other questions were raised concerning personal values and the extent to which those values coincided with the host/majority culture. Finally, questions were posed about how to address the HIV/AIDS problem in sub-Saharan Africa.

LOOKING AHEAD

Health care and mental health care are related. Each has important issues involving managed care, health-care access, and culturally competent service provision. Chapter 13 explores employment settings in mental health for social workers, as well as social work roles, policy issues, and cultural competence in mental health settings.

COMPETENCY NOTES

The following identifies where Educational Policy (EP) competencies and practice behaviors are discussed in the chapter.

EP 2.1.1c Attend to professional roles and boundaries. *(p. 371):* Social work roles in health care are discussed. *(p. 388):* Social work roles involved in working with people living with HIV/AIDS are discussed.

EP 2.1.1d Demonstrate professional demeanor in behavior, appearance, and communication. *(p. 379):* Behavior and communication respectful of cultural differences is part of professional demeanor.

EP 2.1.1e Engage in career-long learning. *(p. 376):* Social workers should engage in career-long learning about health care, as it involves an ever-changing array of conditions and issues.

EP 2.1.2b Make ethical decisions by applying standards of the National Association of Social Workers (NASW) *Code of Ethics* and, as applicable, of the International Federation of Social Workers/International Association of Schools of Social Work *Ethics in Social Work, Statement of Principles.* *(p. 378):* Managed care is discussed and questions are raised concerning the extent to which such care complies with professional ethics.

EP 2.1.2c Tolerate ambiguity in resolving ethical conflicts. *(p. 374):* Social workers must tolerate ambiguity when addressing ethical conflicts that concern health-care policy and problems in the macro environment. *(p. 378):* Ethical conflicts regarding managed care are discussed; by nature, such dilemmas require tolerating ambiguity.

EP 2.1.3 Apply critical thinking to inform and communicate professional judgments. *(p. 377):* Critical thinking questions promote thought about health-care costs and policy. *(p. 380):* Critical thinking questions encourage thought about cultural heritage, values, and acculturation. *(p. 392):* Critical thinking questions invite thought about addressing the HIV/AIDS problems in sub-Saharan Africa.

EP 2.1.3c Demonstrate effective oral and written communication in working with individuals, families, groups, organizations, communities, and colleagues. *(p. 381):* Social workers should demonstrate culturally sensitive communication skills when working with people from API cultures. *(p. 388):* Practitioners should use the appropriate, empowering terminology when referring to people living with HIV/AIDS.

EP 2.1.4 Engage diversity and difference in practice. *(p. 375):* Class and race are dimensions of diversity. *(p. 379):* Culture, ethnicity, and race are aspects of diversity.

EP 2.1.4a Recognize the extent to which culture's structures and values may oppress, marginalize, alienate, or create or enhance privilege and power. *(p. 375):* Social workers should recognize the extent to which society oppresses groups based on socioeconomic status, class, and race with respect to health-care provision. *(p. 379):* Social workers should recognize the extent to which the U.S. health-care system may marginalize or alienate people from API cultures.

EP 2.1.4c Recognize and communicate their understanding of the importance of difference in shaping life experiences. *(p. 379):* Social workers should recognize how cultural values and expectations shape life experiences.

EP 2.1.5 Advance human rights social and economic justice. *(p. 383):* Social workers should recognize the global interconnections of oppression, in this case, the lack of resources to address HIV/AIDS in sub-Saharan Africa. *(p. 390):* Social workers should be knowledgeable about the global ramifications of HIV/AIDS in order to advance human rights.

EP 2.1.5a Understand the forms and mechanisms of oppression and discrimination. *(p. 374):* Unequal access to adequate health care is a form of oppression. *(p. 375):* Oppression for people having a lower socioeconomic status, including those living in poverty, and people of color involves not having equal access to high-quality health care.

EP 2.1.5b Advocate for human rights and social and economic justice. *(p. 374):* Practitioners can advocate for improved health-care provision in the pursuit of social and economic justice. *(p. 379):* Social workers can advocate for improved health-care provision in the managed care environment. *(p. 388):* Practitioners should advocate on the behalf of people living with HIV/AIDS to promote fair and equitable treatment.

2.1.5c Engage in practices that advance social and economic justice. *(p. 379):* Social workers should engage in practices that advance social and economic justice in health-care provision. *(p. 392):* Practices are recommended that would help people living with HIV/AIDS and advance social and economic justice on their behalf.

EP 2.1.7b Critique and apply knowledge to understand person and environment. *(p. 383):* Practitioners must understand and apply knowledge about HIV/AIDS in order to understand person and environment in sub-Saharan Africa.

EP 2.1.8a Analyze, formulate, and advocate for policies that advance social well-being. *(p. 374):* Social workers should strive to establish policies that promote high-quality, available health care. *(p. 379):* Practitioners should advocate for health policies and services that advance social well-being. *(p. 384):* Social workers should advocate for policies that make the health-care system more culturally competent.

EP 2.1.8b Collaborate with colleagues and clients for effective policy action. *(p. 379):* Social workers scan collaborate with colleagues and clients to improve the managed care environment and encourage Medicaid recipients to provide input. *(p. 384):* Practitioners can collaborate with colleagues and clients to establish policies that make the health-care system more culturally competent.

EP 2.1.9a Continuously discover, appraise, and attend to changing locales, populations, scientific and technological developments, and emerging societal trends to provide relevant services. *(pp. 374, 376):* Practitioners should continuously respond to the ever-changing issues and conditions evident in health-care provision. *(p. 379):* It's important for social workers to attend continuously to the conditions and societal trends evident in health-care provision in order to provide relevant services.

EP 2.1.9b Provide leadership in promoting sustainable changes in service delivery and practice to improve the quality of social services. *(p. 379):* Social workers can provide leadership in improving the quality of health-care services. *(p. 384):* Practitioners can provide leadership in establishing culturally competent policies that improve the quality of health-care provision.

EP 2.1.10b Use empathy and other interpersonal skills. *(p. 372):* Social workers must use empathy and other interpersonal skills when helping clients who are dealing with health issues. *(p. 391):* Case examples are presented to encourage empathy for people living with HIV/AIDS in sub-Saharan Africa.

EP 2.1.10e Assess clients' strengths and limitations. *(pp. 388, 389):* Practitioners should assess and emphasize the strengths of people living with HIV/AIDS.

EP 2.1.10g Select appropriate intervention strategies. *(p. 372):* Social workers should select the appropriate intervention strategies when working in health care. *(p. 379):* Practitioners should select culturally sensitive intervention strategies (as described in the following sections) when working with API peoples. *(p. 384):* Appropriate intervention strategies in health care for working with people from API cultures are discussed.

EP 2.1.10i Implement prevention interventions that enhance client capacities. *(p. 372):* Social workers can provide health education to clients to prevent health problems in the future.

EP 2.1.10j Help clients resolve problems. *(p. 372):* Practitioners can help clients address and resolve their health problems. *(p. 379):* Social workers should help clients resolve problems within the context of their cultural values. *(p. 384):* Practitioners can use culturally sensitive approaches to help people from API cultures resolve problems.

EP 2.1.10k Negotiate, mediate, and advocate for clients. *(p. 388):* Social workers should advocate on the behalf of people living with HIV/AIDS.

EP 2.1.10l Facilitate transitions and endings. *(p. 372):* Social workers can help clients address end-of-life issues. *(p. 383):* Practitioners can assist with disclosure of terminal illness and end-of-life decisions for people from API cultures. *(p. 390):* Social workers can help people address and deal with the issue of their death.

FOR FURTHER EXPLORATION ON THE INTERNET

See this text's Social Work CourseMate website at *www.cengagebrain.com* for learning tools such as chapter quizzing, videos, glossary flashcards, and more.

CHAPTER 13

Social Work and Services in Mental Health

iStockphoto/Stockphoto4u

Jennifer, age 18, is an extremely tall, thin young woman with olive skin and waist-length black hair. She is receiving psychotherapy for anorexia nervosa[1] and depression. She regularly found herself drinking a few shots of cheap whiskey prior to any social event she attended. Actually, she felt compelled to do so to avoid the inevitable panic attack she would abruptly experience. Each attack was characterized by extreme anxiety, dread, shortness of breath, sweaty palms, racing heart, and fears of going crazy. (Note that panic attacks had never been part of her diagnosis.) She

---

[1]*Anorexia nervosa*, mainly afflicting girls and young women, is a condition whereby a person refuses to maintain a normal minimal body weight and has an extreme dread of gaining weight.

always knew she'd get an attack at a party or a dance if she didn't come "prepared," but she never could predict exactly when it would happen. She was terrified of behaving "like a crazy woman" in front of everybody. She has even started to avoid social situations altogether if she can't figure out a way to drink discreetly first.[2]

Larry, a college sophomore, can't seem to get out of bed in the morning. He hasn't been to class in a week and a half. Nothing seems to matter to him anymore. Everything seems dark and murky. He feels his grades are terrible, his parents are disappointed in him, and people don't really like him. No one seems to care whether he lives or dies. Life is futile. What does anything matter? Larry is depressed.

Aquinnah, age 38, has murdered her 71-year-old mother. She responded to voices in her head commanding her to take the large kitchen knife and do so. Diagnosed with schizophrenia at age 18, she had a history of hearing voices and of getting into fights. She also compulsively collected hundreds of empty shampoo bottles and the shoelaces from discarded running shoes, which she kept in her mother's basement. Sometimes, when the voices told her to leave her mother's home, where she usually stayed, she would camp out behind dumpsters in parking lots of discount department stores. She was arrested for murder when found roaming around aimlessly in her mother's yard carrying the bloodied knife. At the time, she had her 11-year-old son with her; he was wearing girls' clothing and brilliantly colored makeup.

Roger, age 51, served two terms in Afghanistan. Since he left the military, "he has worked erratically in construction, a pattern that has contributed to marital problems. Roger reports having flashbacks of his war experiences, difficulty sleeping, and angry outbursts against others. Occasionally he has gotten into fistfights with men at work, and on a few occasions he has beaten his wife. He has been going to the VA [Veterans Affairs][3] clinic on and off for 10 years, has been on medication, but has never been hospitalized. The mental health staff at the VA clinic suspect that he has minimal brain dysfunction, an organic condition, which is not war related, as well as posttraumatic stress disorder, which is war related. He has been turned down for disability. (Sands, 1991, pp. 186–187)

These vignettes illustrate various facets of emotional, psychological, and behavioral problems, also referred to as mental illness, a serious social problem. The first reflects a panic attack (a type of anxiety disorder), the second a case of depression, the third schizophrenia, and the fourth posttraumatic stress disorder. These represent the types of problems and issues social workers confront every day in mental health practice.

[2]This vignette is loosely adapted from one described in Hayward and Collier (1996).

[3]The U.S. Department of Veterans' Affairs, formerly the Veterans' Administration, provides a wide range of services to veterans including health and mental health care, long-term care such as nursing homes, educational benefits, and housing (Becerra & Damron-Rodriquez, 1995).

Note the following facts:

- *More than a quarter of all people will develop some form of mental illness during their lifetime (Greeno, 2008; Kendall, 2010).*
- *At least 40% of people with mental illness receive no treatment for their condition (Coleman & Kerbo, 2009).*
- *Approximately 6%, or 1 in 17, people experience extreme forms of mental illness such as schizophrenia and manic-depressive disorder every year (Kendall, 2010).*

Half of NASW members, most of whom have MSWs, indicate that mental health is "a major practice area" for them (O'Neill, 2003, p. 8). "Professional social workers are the largest group of mental health providers in the United States, comprising as much as 60 percent of the core mental health professionals" (including psychiatrists, psychologists, and psychiatric nurses) (Gibelman, 2005, pp. 43–44). The Encyclopedia of Social Work affirms that many social workers will indeed work in mental health contexts, but all social workers will come into contact with clients or clients' family members who are experiencing mental illness (Greeno, 2008). Therefore, significant time will be spent discussing what social workers do in mental health and where.

Learning Objectives

A   Review the wide range of mental health settings in which social workers practice.

B   Identify and discuss the range of psychiatric diagnoses for mental health problems.

C   Discuss some of the functions social workers perform in mental health settings.

D   Recognize some trends in evidence-based practice in mental health.

E   Examine managed care within the mental health context.

F   Address the issue of cultural competence in mental health settings, identify barriers many people of color face in accessing services, and suggest ways of improving cultural competence.

G   Encourage critical thinking about various issues related to mental health.

Mental Health, Mental Illness, and Social Work Roles

The concept of mental health has many dimensions. *Mental health* is the state of relative psychological and emotional well-being in which an individual can make acceptably rational decisions, cope adequately with personal and external stresses, and maintain satisfactory adjustment to society. *Mental illness* is any of a wide range of psychological, emotional, or cognitive disorders that impair a person's ability to function effectively. Causes may be "biological, chemical, physiological, genetic, psychological, or social"; mental illness is "extremely variable in duration, severity, and prognosis" (Barker, 2003, p. 269). Primary symptoms of mental illness include extreme anxiety, disturbed thinking processes, perceptual distortions, extreme mood variations, and other difficulties in thinking (USDHHS, 1999). Another common term for mental illness is *mental disorder*. A later section of this chapter will describe some of the conditions clients face when they have a mental illness.

Employment Settings in Mental Health for Social Workers

Social workers practice in a broad range of settings and can assume many roles. Just as in other practice areas, advocacy for rights and services is a vital social work function here. Rising costs for mental health care and increasing numbers of people requiring treatment and resources will challenge social workers in the coming years. Mental health programs compete for limited funds just like other forms of social services. There is a constant struggle in the political environment to empower people by getting them the services they need.

Social workers are employed, along with professionals in other related fields, in a wide range of mental health facilities. These include inpatient mental and psychiatric hospitals, psychiatric units in general hospitals, residential treatment centers for children and adolescents, outpatient treatment agencies, employee assistance programs, and community mental health centers. Highlight 13.1 addresses the differences between social workers with a BSW and those with an MSW.

HIGHLIGHT 13.1

Differences Between BSW and MSW Positions and Responsibilities

Both BSWs and MSWs can find employment in a wide range of mental health settings. Likewise, both can have field internships in mental health agencies. However, there are some differences in the types of jobs for which each is qualified. MSWs are considered more specialized than BSWs. The implication is that MSWs are competent to address more difficult psychological problems than BSWs and have the potential to assume greater responsibility. However, both can and do work in mental health settings.

Generalist social work practice can involve many facets of mental health. BSWs can provide both individual and group counseling to help clients make plans and solve problems. They can work with families, encouraging them to use their strengths to deal with issues. BSWs can also teach parents effective techniques for managing their children's behavior. BSWs often provide crisis intervention when clients face difficult or traumatic situations. They can link people in need to mental health resources within the community. They can also educate other professionals and community citizens about mental health issues.

A major difference between BSWs and MSWs is that providing psychotherapy is solely the domain of MSWs. *Psychotherapy* is a skilled treatment process whereby a therapist works with an individual, couple, family, or group to address a mental disorder or alleviate other problems the client(s) may be having in the social environment. Sometimes the term *therapy* is used, especially in reference to various psychotherapeutic approaches such as behavioral therapy, psychodynamic therapy, or cognitive therapy. The term *therapy*, however, can also refer to treatment of problems other than mental health and adjustment problems. Examples are speech therapy, occupational therapy, and physical therapy.

Often, as Chapter 1 noted, higher-level supervisory and administrative positions require an MSW or other master's level degree. Such positions usually offer higher salaries. Finally, MSWs generally earn significantly more than BSWs, although years of experience enhance salaries for both groups.

The Least Restrictive Setting on a Continuum of Care: Empowering Clients

A critical concept in mental health treatment is client treatment in the *least restrictive setting* possible. Earlier chapters defined this as the setting that allows the client maximum self-determination while providing the intensity of treatment needed to be effective. This involves the idea that clients should be empowered to have maximum control over their own lives while having access to the treatment level needed. The restrictiveness of the treatment setting is related to the concept of the *continuum of care*. The continuum of available services should provide a range of treatment alternatives ranging from the least restrictive to the most. Chapter 9 discussed similar concepts with respect to substitute placements for children in out-of-home care.

One of the most restrictive settings is placement in a locked ward of a mental hospital. Clients placed here have minimal control over their lives and, theoretically, maximum access to treatment 24 hours a day. One of the least restrictive settings involves individuals receiving treatment in an outpatient facility for an hour or two each week while residing in their own homes and going about their regular daily activities.

One problem with the idea of minimal restrictiveness of setting is that adequate, effective services must be readily available in less restrictive parts of the continuum. For example, if a client released from an institution into the community requires some level of service, that service must be readily available to that client. The process of providing services and care for people within their own communities rather than in institutional settings is called *deinstitutionalization*.

Mental health settings that employ social workers include inpatient mental and psychiatric hospitals; residential treatment centers for children and adolescents; group homes; psychiatric units in general hospitals; outpatient treatment agencies; employee assistance programs; and community mental health centers, which provide a wide range of services.

Inpatient Mental and Psychiatric Hospitals

Inpatient treatment facilities such as publicly funded state and county mental hospitals and private psychiatric clinics provide one employment setting for social workers. *Inpatient* means that clients reside in the facility for some period. They are among the most restrictive treatment settings available. Depending on the problem, this period might be as short as days or as long as a lifetime. Medicare or Medicaid usually pays for treatment in public institutions. Private psychiatric facilities, which are usually quite expensive, most frequently are funded directly by clients or by their private insurance. Both types fulfill the functions of assessment, planning, provision of medications, and therapeutic treatment for various severe mental disorders.

Note that other long-term care facilities are also used when people with deteriorating or acute mental conditions can no longer remain in their own homes; examples are nursing homes and foster care homes (Ginsberg, 2001).

Residential Treatment Centers for Children and Adolescents

An area in which child welfare and mental health overlap is *residential treatment centers* (RTCs) and group homes for children. An RTC is an agency that provides children who have serious emotional and behavioral problems with residential round-the-clock care, education (often with an emphasis on special education), interpersonal skills training, and individual, group, and sometimes family therapy. Although all RTCs, by definition, provide residential care, other aspects of their orientation and programming vary substantially. Treatment may involve any of a wide range of psychotherapeutic approaches (e.g., behavioral, cognitive, psychoanalytic). Some RTCs have a school right on the premises, and others use public schools. Some RTCs are located in rural settings; others are in urban metropolises. Some have only male residents, others have only females, and still others have both.

Residents spend most of their time with the residential staff (typically called something like child care workers or unit counselors) caring for them. Therefore, such staff can have a huge impact on the treatment process. Residents usually spend relatively little time with psychotherapists, who may be MSWs, psychiatrists, psychologists, or some combination of these.

Many settings emphasize behavioral programming and provide structured guidelines for how counselors should respond to various types of

EP 2.1.10b

behavior on the part of residents. Techniques such as using positive reinforcement (e.g., praising), employing empathy, and giving feedback about behavior can be useful in changing behavior for the better (Stein, 1995; Thompson & Henderson, 2007). *Positive reinforcement* is a procedure or consequence that increases the frequency of the behavior immediately preceding it. For example, a staff member might say to a resident, "Hey, Billy, you really did a nice job completing your chores this week. Way to go!" This is positive reinforcement if the result is that Billy continues doing his assigned chores on time. *Empathy* is the act of not only understanding how another person feels but also conveying to that person an awareness of how he or she feels. For example, a staff member might say to a client, "I can see how frustrated you are with your homework. I know how difficult it is for you." *Feedback* is the process of giving people information, positive or negative, about their performance or behavior.

Often RTCs use token or point systems in which tokens (i.e., symbolic objects such as poker chips or artificial coins that reflect units of value) or points on a chart are used in a coordinated system to control poor behavior, develop good behavior, and monitor progress. Appropriate and inappropriate behaviors are clearly defined, as are expectations and consequences for various behaviors. Residents earn tokens or points for good behavior and lose them for bad conduct. Highlight 13.2 gives an example of how positive reinforcement (usually in the form of praise), empathy, and feedback are used by a staff member in an RTC (Stein, 1995, pp. 205–206).

Group Homes

As Chapter 9 explained, group homes are considered less extreme on the continuum of care in terms of restrictiveness of setting. Children and adolescents placed in group homes don't need the more extreme institutional placement in an RTC. However, group homes also vary dramatically in terms of restrictiveness and intensity. Some are run by married couples; others have staff available around the clock. Some provide intensive individual, group, and family psychotherapy; others provide little, if any, such treatment. Group homes are smaller than RTCs, usually limited by law to a maximum number of residents, such as eight.

The reasons children are placed in group homes also vary. The courts determine that they cannot remain in their own homes for reasons ranging from abusive situations to their own emotional and behavioral problems. Some simply need a protective environment with emotional support, consistent treatment, and exposure to positive role models. Others demonstrate extremely aggressive, deviant, or uncontrollable behavior and require a treatment setting almost as structured as an RTC, but smaller and more personal.

Why, then, are some children and adolescents placed in RTCs and others in group homes when their behavior is similar? Placement decisions involve complex issues. The value system of the person determining the placement (e.g., a judge or a social worker making recommendations to a judge), types of RTCs and group homes available, openings within these settings, and cost can all contribute to decisions about where a young client is ultimately placed.

Psychiatric Units in General Hospitals

Psychiatric units in general hospitals offer emergency psychiatric care on a temporary inpatient basis for people in crisis. They usually work closely with other, longer-term inpatient and outpatient facilities to provide care at whatever level on the continuum of care a client needs.

Outpatient Treatment Agencies

Not all people, of course, need inpatient treatment. *Outpatient treatment* agencies and clinics provide individual, group, and family counseling for a wide range of mental health and substance abuse problems. Clients come in for their treatment and then leave when they're done.

Sometimes private practitioners, including social workers, psychologists, and psychiatrists, establish their own practice and serve their own clientele, working as individuals or with a small group of colleagues. Social workers who do this often call themselves *clinical social workers* (previously *psychiatric social workers*). This means that they provide psychotherapy to clients to address mental health issues and other life problems. Clinical social workers may also work for other types of mental health agencies.

A *family service association* is a type of outpatient treatment agency that offers various types of counseling, often in addition to child welfare services such as adoption and foster care. These agencies usually have multiple funding sources and are governed by a board of directors. Many are part of a

HIGHLIGHT 13.2

Using Positive Reinforcement, Empathy, and Feedback to Change Behavior

EP 2.1.10b

The scene: Pete, age 12, is a resident of the Earl E. Bird Residential Treatment Center for Boys. He is quite unhappy. He needs to earn a certain number of points to go on a field trip to a big basketball game, which he *really* wants to do. But he lost points for poking another guy in the ear on Monday. Then, on Wednesday, Jethro, another kid in his unit, picked a fight with him. Although Pete ended up with a bloody nose, he gave Jethro a black eye, which cost him more points. He was so angry the entire week that he refused to make his bed, which resulted in still more points lost. By Thursday, it was impossible for Pete to earn enough points to go to the game. Furious, he stomps out of the unit and down the long driveway, contemplating running away. Rashaun, one of the residential staff on Pete's unit, catches up to Pete and starts to talk with him. (Note that in the following dialogue nonverbal behavior is indicated by regular roman type within brackets, and positive reinforcement [usually in the form of praise], empathy, and feedback are indicated by boldface type within brackets.)

Rashaun: Pete, it's time to get back to the unit.
Pete: [Continues walking, trying to ignore Rashaun]
Rashaun: Pete, did you hear me?
Pete: F____ you, buzzard breath. I ain't goin' back and you can't make me!
Rashaun: You sound like you're upset about something **[expression of empathy]**. You'll only lose points if you don't get back **[feedback]**.
Pete: Shove your f____ing points up your a____!

Rashaun: Come on. Let's walk over to the basketball court and talk. [Turns and walks toward the basketball court, which is empty right now]
Pete: [Pretends to ignore Rashaun at first, but eventually follows him, his eyes downcast]
Rashaun: It's been a bad week for you, hasn't it? **[empathy]**
Pete: Yeah . . . [Said gloomily and without eye contact]
Rashaun: You haven't earned enough points to go to the game this weekend, have you?
Pete: Nope. Life's a b_____. I'll never get to go anywhere.
Rashaun: Well, you know, getting points for the game next weekend starts tomorrow **[feedback]**. How about starting fresh? You usually do a good job of keeping yourself together and getting enough points to go along **[praise]**.
Pete: [Finally looking up] Maybe. But it's such a long time till then.
Rashaun: I know, it's really tough living up to all the rules around here **[empathy]**. But, come on now, you can do it. You need to start getting those points back so you can get to the game next weekend **[feedback]**.
Pete: [Saying nothing, starts walking toward the unit, while Rashaun walks along with him]
Rashaun: I give you a lot of credit for getting yourself under control **[praise]**. I know it was hard for you **[empathy]**. I think you deserve 10 extra points for going back to the unit so quickly **[positive reinforcement]**. That should help you toward next week's goal so you can go to the game **[feedback]**.
Pete: [Finally looking up at Rashaun and smiling just a little] OK, thanks.

national organization, such as Family Service America (FSA), Catholic Social Services, and Lutheran Social Services.

Employee Assistance Programs

Employee assistance programs (EAPs) are services provided by organizations that focus on workers' mental health and on adjustment problems that interfere with their work performance. An underlying

principle is that impaired worker performance due to factors such as absenteeism and stress costs companies money and that EAPs can significantly reduce such costs (Akabas, 2008; Gibelman, 2005). Problems addressed include substance abuse, family conflicts, financial problems, job stress, difficulties with day care for children or dependent parents, and other personal issues interfering with workers' psychological ability to do their jobs.

Occupational social work is the provision of mental health treatment by social workers in the workplace under the auspices of employers. Services can be either delivered by an internal office or purchased by employers from external contractors. EAPs have experienced "enormous" growth in recent years (NASW, 2009, p. 113). It is estimated that 63% of employees in organizations with 100 or more workers are served by EAPs (Akabas, 2008). Social workers comprise a substantial proportion of people providing EAP services (Akabas, 2008; NASW, 2009).

There is a vast range of services an EAP social worker can provide. Core services can include "assessment and referral" and "brief counseling" (NASW, 2009, p. 111). EAPs vary dramatically in terms of their scope (Akabas, 2008). For example, some are very limited in purpose and address a narrow range of identified problems such as substance abuse. Others target a wide range of difficulties including almost any personal issue. These may include grief counseling, stress and time management, marital problems, child care needs, financial issues, retirement planning, and crisis intervention. EAP social workers may provide individual or group counseling. For example, they might run a support group focused on some concern such as organizational downsizing to help employees cope with the organization's loss of staff (Gibelman, 2005). EAP social workers also may make referrals to more specialized community agencies to meet employees' specific needs. EAP services might also include consultation to management regarding supervision of employees, employee training (e.g., about sexual harassment), or assistance with administrative tasks such as rewriting an agency policy manual (Gibelman, 2005; NASW, 2009).

There are two issues that EAP social workers must carefully address (Akabas, 2008; Gibelman, 2005). First, they must be very careful about confidentiality. This might involve potential conflicts of interest because EAP social workers are employed by the organization and yet are there to help individual employees. The question involves the extent to which EAP social workers can ethically share information about employees with management. A breach of confidentiality could have serious effects on an employee such as losing a job or becoming victimized by discriminatory behavior (Gibelman, 2005).

This leads to the second issue, namely, where the EAP social worker's loyalty should lie. Is it with the

organization or with the individual employees the social worker serves? EAP social workers should turn to the NASW *Code of Ethics* for guidance; it's critical for social workers to be honest with all involved, including management and employees, about their responsibilities and obligations (Akabas, 2008; Gibelman, 2005). It should be very clear regarding what an EAP social worker can and cannot reveal even before any problem develops.

Community Mental Health Centers: A Macro Response to Individual Needs

Community mental health centers are versatile local organizations that provide a range of services, from mental health treatment to education about and prevention of mental illness. They fulfill a range of functions for which social workers may be employed. Ginsberg (2001, pp. 124–127) identifies and describes at least six functions community mental health centers perform:

1. *Case management:* This is the process of assessing clients' needs, linking clients to appropriate services, coordinating service provision, and monitoring its effectiveness. Whereas the broker role involves linking clients to resources, key concepts in the case manager role are coordinating and monitoring service provision. Kanter (1985) describes how case management can be used with clients having a serious mental illness:

   [Such people] require a wide range of treatment and rehabilitation approaches that include medication, psychotherapy, family involvement, day treatment, crisis intervention, and brief and extended hospitalizations. Simultaneously, they often need a variety of social services that include housing, financial assistance, vocational training and placement, and medical care. Although obtaining needed services is not easy for "healthy persons," these . . . [clients] have particular difficulty in locating and negotiating such assistance. (p. 78)

   Case management is described more thoroughly in the discussion of what social workers do in the mental health context.

2. *Child and adolescent services:* These are aimed at enhancing the overall functioning of child and adolescent clients. Activities may include counseling, working with the schools on behalf

of these young people, making referrals for services such as prescription drugs or family therapy, and involving clients in recreational activities.

3. *Information and education programs:* Staff including social workers educate community residents, family members of people with mental illness, and other professionals in the community about prevention, the problems involved, and the treatment of mental illness.

4. *Long-term community care programs:* These serve people with mental illness on an ongoing basis. Often case managers help such people remain in the community by regularly visiting their homes, monitoring medication, and coordinating other needed services.

5. *Day treatment programs:* These provide daily activities for people with mental illness, including recreational pursuits such as games or crafts, health services, and educational programs.

6. *Alcohol and other drug treatment programs:* These provide treatment, including individual and group counseling. Often staff in such units work cooperatively with other inpatient facilities to give clients the type of care they need.

Highlight 13.3 addresses the fact that the titles of professionals working in community mental health settings can be confusing.

Clients with Mental Health Problems

Because of their significance to social work practice and to practitioners in the mental health field, a number of conditions affecting people's mental health will be described here. The most commonly used classification system for defining and diagnosing

EP 2.1.7a, 2.1.7b

mental illness is the *Diagnostic and Statistical Manual of Mental Disorders Text Revision (DSM–IV–TR)* (2000), written by work groups composed of professional clinicians and published by the American Psychiatric Association. (Note that the "IV" indicates that this is the fourth edition, and "TR" refers to *Text Revision.*)

The *DSM–IV–TR* includes 17 major diagnostic categories and dozens of more specific diagnostic classifications. It describes each diagnosis in detail, providing a description of symptoms and diagnostic criteria to determine whether a person falls within that category.

Despite some serious concerns raised in Focus on Critical Thinking 13.1, the *DSM–IV–TR* serves as the primary guideline for classifying various types of mental illness. This, in turn, qualifies people to receive treatment paid for by the government (e.g., Medicaid or Medicare) or private health

---

HIGHLIGHT 13.3

What's in a Title?

Mental health settings are often characterized by professionals from a variety of disciplines working together for the benefit of clients. Such groups are referred to as *interdisciplinary or multidisciplinary teams.* Each professional brings to the team his or her professional perspective and area of expertise.

As you know, social workers can assume many roles. *Clinical social workers* provide psychotherapy in mental health settings. *Psychiatrists* are medical doctors with additional training in psychiatry, which, of course, focuses on mental health treatment. They are the only professionals who can prescribe psychotropic drugs. Other professionals rely on psychiatrists to fulfill

this function. *Psychologists* have a doctorate or master's degree in psychology. Depending on their area of expertise, they may do psychotherapy and/or psychological testing. *Psychiatric nurses* who work in mental health settings have a bachelor's or master's degree in nursing. They bring their medical background and patient care expertise to the mental health setting.

Teams also may include *paraprofessionals*—persons with specialized training in some area—who are supervised by a professional and assume some of the professional's tasks. For example, a *case aid* might assist a social worker by helping clients fill out necessary forms or transporting clients to a treatment center.

FOCUS ON CRITICAL THINKING 13.1

Potential Shortcomings of the *DSM–IV–TR*

**EP 2.1.2c,
2.1.3,
2.1.4c**

Critical thinking involves asking questions, assessing facts, and asserting a logical conclusion. The *DSM–IV–TR* serves as the primary guide in the United States for assessing mental health problems and placing labels on people so they can receive treatment. Just because the manual exists doesn't mean it provides the best way or even the right way to approach dealing with people who have mental illness. In fact, many social workers have questioned the importance placed upon this manual and its reliability (Sheafor & Horejsi, 2012; Williams, 2008). For one thing, it focuses on people's pathologies and virtually ignores their strengths. Additionally, it places little value on the importance of the environment. Rather, it reflects the medical model that focuses on how to *cure* individuals. It does not stress how individuals are integrally involved with other people and systems in their environment, which provides the crucial context for mental health problems.

Another problem involves labeling. Critics maintain that labeling according to specified criteria is arbitrary and based on cultural expectations. What is considered normal for one culture or class might be viewed very differently by another. For example, Popple and Leighninger (2002) note that "a wealthy older woman who sometimes thinks she is the reincarnation of Cleopatra may simply be regarded as 'eccentric.' A bag lady who talks to herself as she roams the streets of New York may well be called 'crazy'" (p. 458). A later section of the chapter stresses the importance of enhancing cultural competence through understanding the values and expectations of other cultural groups.

Critical Thinking Questions

To what extent do you feel that the *DSM–IV–TR's* assessment and labeling system is fair and adequate? What are the reasons for your answer? What do you see as the *DSM–IV–TR's* strengths and weaknesses?

---

insurance. In other words, to be eligible for services and payment for these services, a person must first have the appropriate diagnosis. The *DSM–IV–TR* includes not only mental disorders but also other conditions that may be the focus of clinical treatment. Note that psychiatrists usually must make the official diagnosis for clients to qualify for benefits.

To provide some insight into what mental illness is like, a number of conditions will be briefly described here. These include dementia, schizophrenia and other psychotic disorders, mood disorders, anxiety disorders, dissociative disorders, eating disorders, sexual disorders, impulse control disorders, and personality disorders.

Dementia

Dementia is a state in which people develop numerous cognitive problems due to some medical problem. *Alzheimer's disease* is a common type of dementia of unknown origin, characterized by mental decline and usually occurring in late middle age.

Case Example Jose, age 59, has Alzheimer's disease, having been diagnosed five years ago. His wife Maria, age 56, first started noticing Jose gradually withdrawing from her and spending more time to himself. He began having more and more trouble accomplishing at first more complex and, later, simpler tasks. He had been a professional trumpet player. Now when he picks up his trumpet, he doesn't know what to do with it. Sometimes he bangs it against the clothes dryer. Other times he picks up his razor and tries to make music with it. He constantly asks Maria questions. By the time she answers, he forgets what he asked and why. He has difficulty completing a simple task like drying the dishes because he forgets what he's doing even as he does it. He might put the dish down and walk away or else notice it in his hand and start washing it again.

While administering psychological testing to determine the extent of Jose's cognitive deterioration, a psychologist placed a pencil, a piece of paper, and fluorescent orange plastic scissors in front of him on a table. He then asked Jose to place the pen on the piece of paper. In response, Jose ignored the pen and paper, picking up the scissors and placing it back on the table upside down. His personality, what made Jose a special and unique individual, was gradually being drained from him. It was difficult for his family to cope.

Schizophrenia and Other Psychotic Disorders

Schizophrenia is a severe mental disturbance characterized by delusions; hallucinations; confused, incoherent speech; bizarre behavior; flattened emotional responses; short, empty verbal responses that lack attentiveness; and inability to participate in goal-directed activities.

Schizophrenia is one of the most common forms of *psychosis*—any of a number of serious mental disorders characterized by disturbed, inappropriate behavior and loss of contact with reality. Psychosis is often contrasted with *neurosis*, a mental disorder characterized by "feelings of anxiety, obsessional thoughts, compulsive acts, and physical complaints without objective evidence of disease" that occur "in various degrees and patterns" (Nichols, 1999, p. 888). Psychosis is sometimes thought of as more severe than neurosis because psychotic people lose contact with reality. The key concepts involved in neurosis are anxiety and the behaviors resulting from its extreme forms.

Case Example   Frances, age 61, has been diagnosed with schizophrenia. She lives in a tiny 75-year-old house in a rural midwestern town 80 miles from the nearest city. Even in the heat of summer, she wears multiple layers of clothing to "keep the evil spirits away." She never turns her lights on at night because, she believes, hands reach out from the ceiling light fixtures and try to grab her. Although most of her neighbors shy away from her, she seeks them out whenever she sees them outdoors. A typical comment she makes to them is, "Sometimes Sylvester Stallone appears and I take over his body and fight the spirits. But they can't tell who it is and sometimes we're the same. The dark makes the squash purple." Needless to say, this makes no sense. She also puts her garbage in small lunch bags, sometimes as many as 40, and lines them up in a perfect row along the curb for pickup. Frances periodically is hospitalized, in which event medication helps to curb her bizarre thought processes and behaviors. However, when she returns home she ceases taking her medication and her symptoms subsequently resume.

Mood Disorders

Although *mood* is a difficult word to define, most of us have a general idea of what it means. *Mood disorders* are mental disorders involving extreme disturbances in a person's mood—that is, his or her emotional state and attitude. As with many other mental disorders, those concerning mood involve extremes beyond what people normally experience. Such extremes, involving intensity, duration, or fluctuation of mood, cause problems in a person's ability to function normally. Specific diagnostic classifications include depressive disorders and bipolar disorders.

Depressive disorders (often referred to as *depression* in common conversation) are characterized by low spirits, unhappiness, lack of interest in daily activities, inability to experience pleasure, pessimism, significant weight loss not related to dieting (or significant weight gain), insomnia, extremely low energy levels, feelings of hopelessness and worthlessness, decreased capacity to focus and make decisions, and preoccupation with thoughts of suicide and death. It's depressing even reading that list of symptoms.

Case Example   Sharissa, age 31, is an example of a depressed person. She has been married for eight years to Jarell, age 34, who labors full-time as a welder in addition to working overtime whenever he can. Sharissa does not work outside the home. The couple has two sons, ages 3 and 5, both of whom have intellectual disabilities.

Sharissa consistently dwells on the negative aspects of her life, usually speaking to others in a high-pitched, whining tone. She complains that Jarell "never pays any attention" to her or the boys and doesn't "know the meaning of housework." When together, she criticizes him nonstop, to the point at which he simply "tunes her out." This only escalates her whining. In addition to complaining about Jarell, she grumbles about how difficult it is caring for the two boys with their special needs. She complains that all she does is work, and she gets no joy out of her life. She has no time for friends, and she and Jarell never go out anywhere together. Each night, she lies awake dwelling on all the supposedly horrible things that happened to her that day. She frequently says she is much too fat (although she is

5 feet 5 inches and weighs 125 pounds), but she has no time or money to go to a health club. She also claims that she is really "ugly" (although she is really quite attractive) and that she has a "shy, bad personality." A common lament is, "What is the point of living anymore when everything is so terrible?" Sharissa spews forth one negative statement after another whenever given the opportunity to talk to someone else, so it's difficult to get a word in edgewise. It's depressing and draining talking to Sharissa.

Bipolar Disorders

Bipolar disorders (formerly referred to as *manic-depressive illness*) involve extreme mood swings. With some bipolar disorders, people experience primarily *manic* episodes characterized by abnormally elevated levels of emotion, feelings of euphoria, a grandiose sense of self, excessive movement or talkativeness, and poor judgment. With other bipolar disorders, people experience primarily periods of depression and at least one *hypomanic* episode

Vincent Oliver/Riser/Getty Images

Depression has negative effects on one's emotional state.

(i.e., being extremely irritable). Finally, bipolar disorders may involve mixed mood swings resulting in abrupt changes from manic to depressive episodes.

Anxiety Disorders

Anxiety disorders are persistent or periodic states of extreme anxiety characterized by excessive fear, worry, apprehensiveness, and dread of the future. Physical symptoms include a rapid pulse, dizziness, perspiration, cold hands or feet, and rapid breathing (National Mental Health Association [NMHA], 2008). Examples of anxiety disorders are panic attacks and posttraumatic stress disorder.

Panic attacks are distinct episodes of extreme anxiety and excessive dread of the future. They are often accompanied by physical symptoms such as shortness of breath, sweaty palms, chest pains, racing heart, and fears of going crazy or dying.

Posttraumatic stress disorder (PTSD) is a condition in which a person continues to reexperience some traumatic event such as a bloody battle or a sexual assault. James (2008) explains that, regardless of the cause, the basis of PTSD "is maladaptive adjustment to a traumatic event. The disorder is both acute and chronic. In its chronic form it is insidious and may take months or years to appear. Its symptoms include, but are not limited to anxiety, depression, substance abuse, hypervigilance [excessive, heightened watchfulness], eating disorders, intrusive-repetitive thoughts, sleep disturbance, somatic [physical] problems, poor social relationships, suicidal ideation, and denial and affective numbing of the traumatic event" (pp. 169–170).

James (2008) elaborates on how some people try to elude facing trauma through self-medication:

Accompanying emotions of guilt, sadness, anger, and rage occur as the thoughts continue to intrude into awareness. To keep these disturbing thoughts out of awareness, the individual may resort to self-medication in the form of alcohol or drugs. Self-medication may temporarily relieve depressive, hostile, anxious, and fearful mood states (Horowitz & Solomon, 1975), but what usually occurs is a vicious cycle that alternates between being anesthetized to reality by the narcotic and experiencing elevated intrusion of the trauma with every return to sobriety. The ultimate outcome is increased dependence on the addictive substance as a method of keeping the intrusive thoughts submerged (LaCoursiere, Bodfrey, & Ruby, 1980). (p. 135)

War Veterans and Posttraumatic Stress Disorder (PTSD)

Just as in previous wars, veterans returning from Iraq, Afghanistan, and the Gulf War often experience PTSD (James, 2008; Kanel, 2012). Imagine seeing one of your best friends being blown up before your eyes. Or picture, because you were commanded to do so, mowing down a civilian who refuses to get out of your way with the convoy vehicle you're driving. That civilian may well be carrying deadly explosives that are much more likely to kill you and your fellow soldiers if that civilian has time to aim or detonate. What if that civilian is a child or a woman with a baby?

Many soldiers function and survive during deployment but begin to break down when they get home. Kanel (2012) explains:

When soldiers are engaged in combat and see the trauma of war, some do experience acute stress disorder. They are often treated by doctors and given time to recuperate. However, the military does such a good job of training soldiers to numb themselves to war trauma that the majority are able to deal with combat as it is happening. It is when they return home that they show signs of PTSD. The disorder has been delayed, almost by training. Once soldiers return home, many have difficulty adjusting to civilian life. They report being preoccupied with the troops that are still fighting. They often feel guilty for leaving the other soldiers and think they should return to help fight. (p. 164)

Variables increasing the risk of PTSD as veterans reintegrate into society include having experiences while deployed that involved dangerous military action, risk of exposure to deadly chemical weapons, and watching other soldiers being hurt or killed; other variables increasing PTSD risk include variables encountered upon return home, such as job loss, overwhelming financial obligations, feeling overloaded with new responsibilities, facing altered interpersonal relationships (as family members and others had adapted their behavior to cope with the veteran's absence), and disrupted everyday habits and regimens that had been established before deployment (Whealin, DeCarvalho, & Vega, 2008a).

Whealin and her colleagues (2008b) explain four types of reactions often experienced by returning veterans—reexperiencing, hyperarousal, avoidance, and emotional numbing:

[Reexperiencing] includes "different ways that combat events may seem to repeat in our mind or body. Reexperiencing can include upsetting memories, thoughts, and images that come into your mind even when you are not trying to think about them, as well as dreams or nightmares about stressful events. The reminder—sometimes called triggers or cues—can be many different things. Following war, a trigger may occur when veterans see people who remind them of the enemy, when they are in places that are similar to the war zone, or when they hear sounds or smell odors that remind them of their deployment. Although reexperiencing often includes thoughts, memories, and images in the mind, it also causes reactions in the body. For example, a person might experience a physical stress reaction (heart beating faster, sweating more, muscles tensing up, etc.) when something reminds them of a severely stressful event. . . .

[Hyperarousal is] "the experience of being amped-up . . . Arousal is just energy or activation in the body. We all need some level of arousal or we could not get up and move around. Hyperarousal just means more arousal than we need, or more than is healthy or makes sense. Some veterans may feel like they have to be on guard all the time. They may startle following sudden noises and they may feel "jacked up" or "amped" a lot of the time. Some may feel very anxious or panicky. Some veterans find it hard to concentrate. They might be more irritable or angry than they used to. Also, veterans may have trouble falling asleep or staying asleep due to hyperarousal. . . .

[Avoidance] refers to going out of our way not to think about or to stay away from something. Because the other reactions—reexperiencing and hyperarousal—feel bad, some veterans try to avoid reminders of their deployment or anything that might trigger these other stress reactions. If a veteran feels uncomfortable in a shopping mall, he or she might begin avoiding going to the mall. . . . Veterans might try to avoid thinking about the war zone, or talking to people about it. Some people start to keep to themselves or avoid watching TV or reading the news. . . .

Related to avoidance, some people may experience emotional numbing, or may feel depressed.

This can include having a hard time relating to other people or having a hard time trusting others. Veterans with emotional numbing may feel fewer positive feelings, like happiness. Often after stressful events people have a harder time enjoying things they used to, such as hobbies or going out with other people. Sometimes veterans lose their interest in food or sex, or may not be able to function sexually.... After combat deployment, many people feel that they just don't have as much energy as they used to, or that their memory is not as good as it used to be. (pp. 19–20)

Currey (2007) describes former Army National Guard Captain Jullian Goodrum's experiences upon returning from Iraq: "I was coming apart at the seams. There were the dreams, the edginess, the constant sense that I had something to fear—as if something or somebody that meant me harm was just around the corner. My mind was no longer my mind. I was going over a cliff" (p. 14).

Imagine what it would be like to be stationed in a place where almost anyone might be a suicide bomber or some other attacker who could kill you. Hypervigilance is required at all times for basic survival. You always carry a big weapon. Now envision returning home to Smalltown, USA. Think about what it might be like to switch gears suddenly from being in a war zone to being at home. How difficult might it be to make yourself stop worrying that the checker at Pick 'n' Shop or the man standing at the stoplight waiting for the red light to change are potential martyrs ready to take you out with them?

Philpott and Hill (2009) advise us to keep in mind that "[m]ost service members do not develop PTSD. It is also important to remember that [a service member] ... can experience some PTSD symptoms without having a diagnosis of PTSD. PTSD cases often resolve on their own in the first three months, but even without a full diagnosis, if [a service member has] ... symptoms, [he or she] ... can benefit from counseling or therapy" (p. 20).

EP 2.1.10g, 2.1.10i, 2.1.10j

Treatment for Veterans with PTSD PTSD is a complex condition that involves an "intricate interplay between traumatic events and the brain's physiological responses to the trauma. Contemporary treatment includes both group and individual intervention that is multimodal and considers psychological, biological,

and social bases as equally important" (James, 2008, p. 170). Kanel (2012) indicates:

The first phase of treatment with PTSD survivors and their families includes educating them about how people get PTSD and how it affects survivors and their loved ones, and other problems that are commonly associated with PTSD symptoms. It is helpful to inform people that PTSD is a medically recognized anxiety disorder that occurs in normal individuals under extremely stressful conditions. (pp. 178–179)

Treatment for PTSD then may involve a number of therapeutic approaches. These include: cognitive-behavioral therapy; medication; and individual, group, and family contexts for therapy (Kanel, 2012; U.S. VA, 2010; Whealin et al., 2008a). Note that here the focus is on social work therapists' work with veterans, although therapists from other disciplines, including psychologists, counselors, and psychiatrists also can provide therapy.

Cognitive-behavioral therapy involves commonly used and effective approaches that address changes in both thinking and behavior (Kanel, 2012; U.S. VA, 2010). One aspect of cognitive-behavioral therapy involves cognitive processing; "[t]his approach helps veterans learn about the relationship between thoughts, events and emotions and the negative beliefs held by veterans regarding their war zone experiences. The most useful aspect is that it helps veterans develop alternative interpretations about their thoughts which then influence their feelings" (Exum, Coll, & Weiss, 2011, p. 97). Thus, the social work therapist can help veterans understand how they think about their traumatic experiences and the psychological, emotional, and behavioral effects of these incidents. The intent is to help the veteran recognize how thinking patterns can trigger stress.

One aspect of this therapy involves helping the veteran identify "extreme views" that are causing stress and replacing them with "a more reasonable perspective" that is more accurate and less upsetting (Armstrong, Best, & Domenici, 2006, p. 145). After war, a veteran's views can change because of vivid and disturbing experiences. Armstrong and his colleagues (2006, p. 145) provide an example. A veteran's views on "safety and trust" may change and become extreme, meaning "not rational, reasonable, or understandable." The veteran may think "I can't trust anybody anymore." A social worker or other therapist can help the veteran reevaluate this extreme perspective in terms of how true and rational it really is. Is there really no one anywhere that the veteran can trust? "Extreme views" like this "are sometimes called 'distorted thinking.' This type of thinking is not helpful because it can lead to further negative thoughts and feelings" such as "anxiety of depression."

A social work therapist can help the veteran identify distorted thinking, which often falls within the following areas:

- *Black-or-White Thinking:* Viewing your military experience in extremes and not seeing anything in between; seeing situations as either good or bad, black or white, all or none, perfect or imperfect. Example: "I completely failed all the men and women in my unit when I left Iraq."
- *Doomsday Thinking:* Viewing [the] … future as hopeless from every angle. Thinking that bad outcomes are your destiny no matter what you do. Example: "I will never be able to relate to civilians after serving in war no matter how much I try."
- *Mind-Reading Thinking:* Thinking that other people have negative views about you or negative intentions toward you without any real reason or evidence to support this belief. Example: "Everybody thinks I'm incompetent since I came home from the war."
- *If-Only Thinking:* Thinking about the past with regret and disappointment by wondering "If only I had …" over and over again. Example: "If only I had waited five more minutes, the convoy wouldn't have been hit by an IED [improvised explosive device such as those terrorists might use]." (Armstrong et al., 2006, pp. 145–146)

After distorted thinking has been identified and targeted, the social work therapist can help the veteran restore more realistic thinking (Armstrong et al., 2006). For instance, the belief "I can't trust anybody anymore" can be replaced with "It's hard to trust people after going to war, but I do have a few friends I can rely on" (p. 146). This new perspective can be reinforced and repeated until it begins to replace the extreme, unrealistic view. It's also important for the social work therapist to reinforce any positive perspectives the veteran might have. For example, the fact that he or she is finally reunited with a significant other, family, and friends might be stressed. The perspective that "certain material things aren't as important anymore or that it's important to live each day fully" might also be emphasized

(p. 146). An important goal is to identify and focus on the positive aspects of life and stop dwelling on the negative ones. Positive activities might include: caregiving for children, other family members, or sick friends; volunteering for a religious or social services organization; or even taking up a hobby, interest, or activity participated in prior to deployment.

Whealin and her colleagues (2008a) discuss three other issues that might be addressed with veterans as they reintegrate into society after returning home—control, hypervigilance, and coping with civilians. A returning veteran, having had little control over his life or what he did in his wartime experience, may still feel out of *control*. However, a social work therapist may help such veterans think through and distinguish more realistically what they can control and what they can't. For example, they can't control military decisions about their deployment, other people's behavior, or the weather. However, they can control how they spend their time, who they spend it with, their communication with and behavior toward others, and their decisions about what to do in the future.

Hypervigilance means "being overly alert for possible dangers" (Whealin et al., 2008a, p. 98). "Over time … people in a war zone often get used to feeling threatened—in their environment or with other people—and they may continue to feel that way when they return home" (Whealin et al., 2008a, p. 98). However, hypervigilance is not constructive in a safe home environment. It may cause sleeplessness, stress, or anger. It may make others around the veteran tense and uncomfortable. A social work therapist can help veterans think through these feelings and evaluate the actual safety of any particular environment. Instead of avoiding places that make them anxious ("such as being in a crowd or going to the mall"), they can gradually make themselves enter such environments and use stress management techniques to help them cope (e.g., deep breathing exercises or progressive muscle relaxation) (Whealin et al., 2008a, p. 99). Thus, they can retrain their thinking and "adjust back to the fact" that they "are no longer in danger" (Whealin et al., 2008a, p. 99).

Coping with civilians can be another problem for returning veterans. People can make stupid, thoughtless, and offensive comments. Veterans may have experienced losses in terms of significant others or friends, or missed important events back home such as weddings or highlights in their children's lives. A social work therapist can help veterans prepare for the inevitable "culture shock" they experience as they try to reintegrate into civilian society (Whealin et al., 2008a, p. 99). They can work out decisions in advance regarding how to handle relationships and issues. A social work therapist can help veterans cope by thinking ahead about what problematic events they might encounter with civilians. Together, worker and veteran can discuss in advance how the veteran will handle the situations. For example, how might the veteran respond to a critical antiwar comment?

There are almost endless other approaches and techniques under the cognitive-behavioral therapy umbrella (Neukrug, 2011). For instance, other useful cognitive-behavioral techniques include "teaching clients how to engage in deep breathing and relaxation exercises, manage anger, prepare for future stress reactions, . . . and communicate and relate effectively with people" (Kanel, 2012, p. 179; Whealin et al., 2008a). It is beyond the scope of this text to go into a great deal of detail. The intent here is to give you a sample of what social workers can do.

Medications that are a type of antidepressant, can help many veterans (U.S. VA, 2010). "Medication may be necessary for some trauma survivors. It can reduce the anxiety, depression, and insomnia often experienced. It is useful for relieving symptoms so that the survivor is able to participate in psychological treatment" (Kanel, 2012, p. 179).

Highlight 13.4 addresses the contexts for treatment of veterans with PTSD within groups and families.

Relevance for Social Workers   Social workers don't have to work for the Department of Veterans Affairs in order to come into contact with returning veterans experiencing PTSD. Veterans or their family members may be involved in virtually any social work practice context. It is very important that, regardless of people's views about the war, veterans must not be abandoned (Currey, 2007). They must receive support and treatment or be referred to services where they can get what they need.

Other Injuries   Note that PTSD is only one of the many conditions faced by veterans returning from Afghanistan and other war-torn areas. A "signature injury" of the war is traumatic brain injury (TBI) where soldiers experience severe concussions such as those resulting from explosions; often TBI survivors "must relearn walking, speaking, and simple motor skills" (Armstrong et al., 2008; Currey, 2007, p. 15).

Because of today's heavily armored vehicles and body armor, many soldiers survive experiences and injuries that would have killed them in the past; as a result, many veterans are living with lost limbs and severe burns (Stoesen, 2007a). Social workers must prepare themselves to address any of these issues.

Dissociative Disorders

Dissociative disorders involve "a disruption in the usually integrated functions of consciousness, memory, identity, or perception" (American Psychiatric Association [APA], 2000, p. 519). An example of a dissociative disorder is *dissociative identity disorder* (formerly referred to as *multiple personality disorder*). This occurs when parts of a person's personality "split off" from the rest of that person's personality, resulting in at least two totally different identities existing within the same person.

I once had a student who confided in me that she had this disorder. She said that through therapy she was now down from several personalities to only two. The one who was speaking to me at that moment was 35 years old; there was also Joey, age 7. She said Joey might come out at any time during class, so I should be prepared. I thought, "Prepared for what?" Luckily, Joey never emerged in class.

Highlight 13.5 describes the world's most famous anonymous person with a multiple personality, who was finally identified right before she died.

Sexual Disorders

A *sexual disorder,* also often referred to as a *sexual dysfunction,* is "a problem with a sexual response that causes a person mental distress" (Hyde & DeLamater, 2011, p. 408). Examples are sexual arousal disorders, orgasmic disorders, and paraphilias (Rathus et al., 2011, p. 463).

Sexual arousal disorders are "[s]exual dysfunctions in which people persistently or recurrently fail to become adequately sexually aroused to engage in or sustain sexual intercourse" (Rathus et al., 2011, p. 463). For example, a *male erectile disorder* is the "persistent difficulty in achieving or maintaining an erection sufficient to allow the man to engage in or complete sexual intercourse" or other "sexual activity" (Rathus et al., 2011, pp. 465–466).

Orgasmic disorders are sexual dysfunctions where "[m]en or women may have difficulty reaching

HIGHLIGHT 13.4

Contexts for PTSD Treatment—Veterans' Groups and Families

EP 2.1.10

A social work therapist can work with an individual veteran, with groups of veterans, or with the veteran and his or her family. Individual therapy can address any of the issues discussed earlier. Group therapy provides an alternative arena that allows veterans to talk about their trauma with others who understand because they've had similar experiences. It provides a forum where "[t]rauma survivors can share traumatic material within an atmosphere of safety, cohesion, and empathy provided by other survivors. By sharing their feelings of shame, fear, anger, and self-condemnation, survivors are enabled to resolve many issues related to their trauma" (Kanel, 2012, p. 179). Group therapy "can help ... build self-confidence and trust" in addition to providing a "focus on [one's] ... present life, rather than feeling overwhelmed by the past" (U.S. VA, 2010).

A social work therapist can also work with a veteran and his or her family to address whatever issues they are dealing with. Whealin and colleagues (2008a) explain potential reasons for family involvement:

> For veterans who get sent back home after being in a war zone, there may be some very mixed feelings about being reunited with their families and other loved ones. Most of them feel relieved to be getting into a safer living zone. Still, many veterans may also feel conflicted because they feel like the people they deployed with are the only ones who can understand them. . . .

> [I]t is common for those returning from a war to get irritated more easily and to isolate from others due to feelings of discomfort. [We have already established that it] . . . is possible that the veteran may experience numbing of affect, and he or she may find it hard to have feelings such as love, happiness, empathy, and sadness.
> Veterans may also be experiencing some underlying anger or resentment from the spouse or partner, as well as the children in the family, for leaving them. . . .
> All of these issues can present some problems in communication between the veterans and their significant others. (p. 105)

A social work therapist can help the family articulate their feelings so that they can understand each other's emotions and address them. Family members should be encouraged to express honestly their "fears and concerns" and "to listen to others"; a therapist can help develop improved communication skills and establish positive, supportive relationships (U.S. VA, 2010). A therapist can help the family understand how the veteran feels about the war experience, his or her "PTSD symptoms and what triggers them," and the "important parts of treatment and recovery" (U.S. VA, 2010). "The major task for the service member is to accept the changes that have occurred in the family routine and family members during his or her absence and to re-establish his or her relationships with family members" (Exum et al., 2011, p. 110).

---

orgasm or reaching orgasm more quickly than they would like. Women are more likely to encounter difficulties reaching orgasm. Men are more likely to reach orgasm too quickly (have premature ejaculation)" (Rathus et al., 2011, p. 463). A *female orgasmic disorder* is "a recurrent problem with reaching orgasm despite adequate erotic stimulation" (Carroll, 2010; McAnulty & Burnette, 2001, p. 612).

Paraphilias are "types of sexual expressions that are seen as unusual and potentially problematic" (Carroll, 2010, p. 451). "Literally meaning 'beyond usual or typical love,' this term stresses that such behaviors are usually not based on an affectionate or loving relationship but rather are expressions of behavior in

which sexual arousal and/or response depends on some unusual, extraordinary, or even bizarre activity" (American Psychiatric Association, 2000; Crooks & Baur, 2011, p. 496). One type of paraphilia, *exhibitionism,* is the act of achieving "sexual excitement/arousal through the compulsion to show one's genitals to an unsuspecting stranger," on occasion while masturbating (Welch, 2011, p. 322).

Eating Disorders

Eating disorders involve extreme difficulties with eating behavior. They include anorexia nervosa and bulimia nervosa.

Who Was Sybil? The Most Famous Case of Multiple Personalities

The condition of dissociative identity disorder gained the public's attention in 1973 when Flora Rheta Schreiber wrote her best-seller *Sybil*. The book concerned an anonymous woman identified as "Sybil" who suffered from having 16 different personalities as a result of severe childhood abuse. The book suggested that, with each major trauma Sybil experienced, a new personality split off from her initial identity.

Sybil has been identified as Shirley Ardell Mason.[4] (To avoid confusion, we will continue referring to Shirley as Sybil.) Sybil, a retired teacher and artist, died on February 26, 1998, in Lexington, Kentucky, only a few weeks after confessing that she was indeed the real Sybil. Before *Sybil*'s publication, only about 75 cases of dissociative identity disorder had been diagnosed (Miller & Kantrowitz, 1999).

It's very difficult to determine how many cases have been identified since then. Many mental health professionals are quite skeptical about the validity of the disorder, its relationship with other psychological problems, and the potential for people to fake the disorder (Nairne, 2011). One source indicates the condition characterizes .01% to 1% of the population (International Society for the Study of Trauma and Dissociation, 2011).

Many people who knew Sybil, as well as psychiatrists and others, have questioned whether she was diagnosed correctly. Sybil remained a patient of Cornelia Wilbur, the psychiatrist who provided the book's story, beginning in 1954 and continuing for 11 years, during which time she participated in over 2,300 psychotherapy sessions. Sybil, described as "a very fragile and sensitive person," began treatment as an undergraduate at Mankato State Teacher's College after she "was questioned by an English teacher as to the originality of one of her poems"; this, in conjunction with financial pressures from home, caused Sybil to experience "anxiety attacks and even blackouts in the middle of class" (Romsdahl, 1997).

Sybil stayed in close contact with Wilbur in the years after her therapy. In 1991, when Wilbur developed Parkinson's disease, Sybil acted as her nurse and companion until Wilbur's death in 1992 (Miller & Kantrowitz, 1999).

Another psychiatrist who treated Sybil described her as "a brilliant hysteric" who was "highly hypnotizable" and subject to suggestion (Miller & Kantrowitz, 1999, p. 67). He indicated that Wilbur may well have helped create various characters during the therapeutic process, which involved frequent hypnosis and doses of sodium pentothal ("truth serum").

Sybil's parents were Mattie and Walter Mason, whom Miller and Kantrowitz (1999) describe as "strictly observant Seventh-Day Adventists" (p. 67). People from Sybil's hometown of Dodge Center, Minnesota, described Mattie, the supposed perpetrator of the abuse, as "bizarre" and having a "witchlike laugh" the few times she did see humor in things; some remember Mattie "as walking around after dark, looking in neighbors' windows" and at one time "apparently being diagnosed as schizophrenic" (Miller & Kantrowitz, 1999, p. 67). According to the book, alleged "tortures primarily featured enemas that she [Sybil] was forced to hold while her mother played piano concertos, but the sadistic parent also enjoyed pushing spoons and other items up her child's vagina, making Sybil watch sexual intercourse, and hoisting her up to hang helplessly from a pulley." Some neighbors report Mattie as being exceptionally strict with Sybil. However, no one seems to remember any physical or sexual abuse taking place, especially any resembling the horrors described in the book.

No one questions that Sybil had a serious mental illness, but the truth of her story and her diagnosis remains in doubt. In any case, Sybil never married or had children. During the last years of her life, apparently "happy," she primarily cared for her pets, gardened, and painted until arthritis prevented her from doing so (Miller & Kantrowitz, 1999, p. 68; Van Arsdale, 2002).

Among the 16 personalities attributed to Sybil in the book were the following (Van Arsdale, 2002):

- Peggy Lou, "an assertive, enthusiastic, and often angry pixie with a pug nose."

---

[4]Facts presented here were retrieved from the following sources: Aestraea's Web (1998), Borch-Jacobsen (1997), Hewlett (1998), Quiet's Corner (2002a, 2002b), Romsdahl (1997), and Van Arsdale (2002).

(continued)

- Marcia, "a writer and painter" who was "extremely emotional" and had a British accent (Miller & Kantrowitz, 1999).
- Mike, a self-important, olive-skinned carpenter who hoped to get a woman pregnant (Miller & Kantrowitz, 1999).
- Sybil Ann, a pale, shy, fearful person with almost no energy.

- Mary, a heavyset, "thoughtful, contemplative, maternal, home-loving person."
- Vanessa, a tall, slim, attractive redhead.
- Ruthie, a toddler with an undeveloped and childlike personality.
- The Blonde, a playful, high-spirited, happy-go-lucky teenager.

Both conditions involve a fixation on food and how much (or little) one eats. Common psychological features include low self-esteem, extreme responsiveness to cultural expectations for thinness, the use of food as a means of coping with uncomfortable emotions, and rigid expectations for themselves (Mental Health America [MHA], 2011a). Most people with eating disorders are female; only an estimated 5% to 15% are male (NMHA, 2011) Anorexics and bulimics tend to have a distorted perception of their physical appearance. A young woman within a normal or low weight range might look into the mirror and "see" a fat person with a double chin and bulging stomach. People with either condition are obsessed with body image. Our culture places a high value on thinness and its clear-cut positive correlation with attractiveness. Two of the "Thin Commandments" include "If you aren't thin you aren't attractive" and "You can never be too thin" (Costin, 2008).

Anorexia Nervosa

Anorexia nervosa, usually afflicting girls and young women, is a condition in which a person refuses to maintain a weight level of at least 85% of normal minimal body weight and dreads gaining weight (APA, 2000). Essentially, the person starves herself because she never sees herself as "thin enough." An anorexic frequently will skip meals, develop rationales for why she doesn't want to eat, eat only extremely low-calorie foods, exercise "excessively and compulsively," view herself and others as having to live up to "rigid, perfectionist standards," experience hair loss, wear large or baggy clothes to disguise her low weight, and withdraw into herself, becoming socially isolated (MHA, 2011a). It is estimated that in Western countries this condition characterizes 0.3% to 0.5% of adolescent girls and young women and a smaller, but increasing proportion of boys and young men (Papalia, Olds, & Feldman, 2009).

Bulimia Nervosa

Bulimia nervosa, also primarily involving females, is characterized by experiencing a severe lack of control over eating behavior, binging (i.e., consuming huge amounts of food, often "junk food"), and using methods to get rid of calories (e.g., forcing oneself to vomit [purging], using laxatives or enemas, and undergoing extreme exercising). Several other factors characterize people suffering from bulimia nervosa (MHA, 2011a). First, like anorexics, they are obsessed with being thin. Second, bulimics experience poor impulse control that may affect decisions about money, relationships, and other aspects of life in addition to their consumption of food (MHA, 2011a). Third, bulimics tend to experience depression (Papalia et al., 2009). However, it is unclear whether depression, along with its accompanying shame and loss of control, is a result of or a trigger for bulimia nervosa. Bulimia nervosa afflicts an estimated 1.1% to 4.2% of females in the United States and one-tenth as many males (MHA, 2011a).

Bulimia's Pattern A pattern typically characterizes people developing bulimia nervosa. First, a person concerned with being thin and attractive begins dieting. Second, dieting and the resulting deprivation become extremely difficult to maintain. Third, the craving for food results in overeating; this phase is usually initiated by some crisis or stress, and eating provides comfort that leads to contentment. Fourth, the person gains weight because of the overeating and so feels guilty, ashamed, and out of control. Fifth, the person discovers that weight can be somewhat controlled through methods such as purging, using laxatives or enemas, and exercising excessively. Sixth, the binge/purge cycle becomes an established way of coping with life's stresses, and the person comes to depend upon it. Seventh, as guilt and shame continue to build, the person expends increasingly greater energy to conceal the binge/purge behavior from those around her (or him).

Case Example   Elena, age 17, was an active high school junior—she was an attractive, popular cross-country runner and cheerleader. She also did some professional modeling on the side. Her cross-country coach and her modeling supervisor stressed the need for her to remain thin, and indicated that losing a few pounds couldn't hurt. (This demonstrates phase 1 of the bulimia nervosa pattern.)

Elena dieted to lose those few extra pounds and began to crave carbohydrates and sweets (phase 2). She had always adored Little Debbie snack cakes, doughnut holes, and potato chips. Finally, struggling to find time for cheerleading, running, modeling, and studying for exams, she broke down and ate two dozen snack cakes and two large bags of potato chips (phase 3). This happened more than once. A few days later, she discovered that she had gained a couple of pounds. She was ashamed of her gluttonous behavior and horrified at getting "fat" (phase 4). When she looked in the mirror, she saw every ounce of the added weight. She even thought she could see cellulite on her thighs that had never been there before.

Elena remembered hearing that girls could "get rid of" the food they've eaten by throwing up. She tried it after a binge (phase 5). She also discovered that laxatives and enemas helped. She continued to find comfort in binging and strove for control by purging, popping pills, and taking enemas. The binge/purge cycle was established (phase 6).

Elena continued to feel ashamed and guilty about her compulsive behavior. She expended great amounts of energy to hide it from her parents, siblings, and friends (phase 7). Usually she threw up in jars, which she hid in small brown paper bags in the back of her closet until she could get rid of them. She would also borrow her parents' car, tell them she was going out with friends, find a solitary place to park, and binge on junk food. The cycle continued.

Treatment Approaches for Anorexia and Bulimia

Anorexia and bulimia are very difficult to treat because so many variables are involved including emotional needs, established behavioral patterns, and external social stresses. Papalia and her colleagues (2009) explain:

> The immediate goal of treatment for anorexia is to get patients to eat and gain weight—goals that are often difficult to achieve given the strength of patients' beliefs about their bodies. One widely used treatment is a type of family therapy in which parents take control of their child's eating patterns. When the child begins to comply with parental directives, she (or he) may be given more age-appropriate autonomy (Wilson et al., 2007). Cognitive behavioral therapy, which seeks to change a distorted body image and rewards eating with such privileges as being allowed to get out of bed and leave the room, may be part of the treatment (Beumont et al., 1993). [Cognitive behavioral therapy includes therapeutic approaches that "seek to change negative thoughts through gradual exposure, modeling, rewards, or talking to oneself" (Papalia et al., 2009, p. 345)]. Patients who show signs of severe malnutrition, are resistant to treatment, or do not make progress on an outpatient basis may be admitted to a hospital, where they can be given 24-hour nursing. Once their weight is stabilized, patients may enter less intensive daytime care (McCallum & Bruton, 2003).
>
> Bulimia, too, may be treated with cognitive behavioral therapy (Wilson et al., 2007). Patients keep daily diaries of their eating patterns and are taught ways to avoid the temptation to binge. Individual, group, or family psychotherapy can help both anorexia and bulimia patients, usually after initial behavior therapy has brought symptoms under control. Because these patients are at risk for depression and suicide, antidepressant drugs may be combined with psychotherapy (McCallum & Bruton, 2003), but evidence of their long-term effectiveness on either anorexia or bulimia is lacking (Wilson et al., 2007). (pp. 365–366)

Medical attention is often necessary to treat any physical symptoms for people with an eating disorder resulting from nutritional deficits. For anorexics, "[b]esides interfering with reproductive functions, the condition is associated with low blood pressure, loss of bone density, and gastrointestinal problems, and it may lead to death"; "between 5% and 8% of those with the disorder will eventually die as a result, either from medical problems or from suicide" (Nairne, 2011, p. 356). "Bulimia is often associated with serious medical problems, although the condition tends not to be life threatening. . . . Yet repeated vomiting can damage the intestines, lead to nutritional problems, and even promote tooth decay" (Nairne, 2011, p. 357).

Papalia and her colleagues (2009) summarize treatment effectiveness:

> *Nearly half of anorexia patients eventually make a full recovery (Steinhausen, 2002), but up to one-third drop out of treatment before achieving an appropriate weight (McCallum & Bruton, 2003). Recovery rates from bulimia average 30-50 percent after cognitive behavioral therapy, and many other patients show improvement (Wilson et al., 2007). (p. 366)*

Impulse Control Disorders

Impulse control disorders are conditions in which people are unable to resist the temptation to participate in some activity that causes them or others harm or regret. Usually people with such disorders follow a cycle of succumbing to extreme temptation, participating in the activity, getting a real "high" during the activity, and suffering extreme remorse and guilt afterward.

Examples of impulse control disorders include kleptomania, pathological gambling, and trichotillomania. *Kleptomania* is characterized by a compulsive desire to steal things, not for personal need or gain, but simply for the sake of stealing them. *Pathological gambling* involves being driven irresistibly to gamble despite suffering extremely negative effects such as huge debt, considerable difficulties with significant others, and other life disruptions. *Trichotillomania* involves compulsively pulling out one's own hair, primarily from "the scalp, eyebrows, and eyelashes," to the extent that the loss is readily apparent to others (Barker, 2003, p. 442).

Personality Disorders

Personality disorders reflect long-term patterns of behavior, emotions, and views of self and the world that strikingly diverge from cultural expectations, cause considerable stress, and result in problematic social interactions. The following are the most common personality disorders and the persistent patterns characterizing each:

- *Schizoid:* Disconnection from interpersonal relationships and an extremely limited ability to express emotions.
- *Paranoid:* Extreme distrust of others, in addition to expectations that others have evil motives and, essentially, "are out to get you."
- *Schizotypal:* Social deficits characterized by difficulties forming close relationships and distorted views of appropriate behavior.
- *Antisocial:* Disrespect for and infringement on other people's rights.
- *Borderline:* Instability in interpersonal relationships, view of self, and emotional makeup, in addition to striking impulsivity.
- *Histrionic:* Excessive emotional expression and attention-seeking behavior.
- *Narcissistic:* Pompous and pretentious behavior, constant search for admiration, and lack of empathy.
- *Avoidant:* Uncomfortableness in social situations, feelings of inadequacy, and oversensitivity to negative feedback.
- *Dependent:* Needy, clinging, submissive behavior resulting from the "pervasive need to be taken care of" (APA, 2000, p. 725).
- *Obsessive–compulsive:* Preoccupation with organization and neatness, perfectionism, and control.

One major study of American adults age 18 and older found a 9.1% prevalence rate for personality disorders according to *DSM–IV–TR* criteria (National Institute of Mental Health [NIMH], 2007b). The study estimated rates of borderline personality rates at 1.4% and antisocial personality disorder at 0.6%. Of study respondents, 39% had received treatment within the past year an average of two times, usually from general medical providers instead of mental health therapists. The study also discovered that people with personality disorders often had more than one disorder at the same time. The co-occurring disorders included "anxiety disorders (e.g., panic disorder, post-traumatic stress disorder), mood disorders (e.g., depression, bipolar disorder), impulse control disorders (e.g., attention deficit hyperactivity disorder), and substance abuse or dependence."

What Social Workers Do in Mental Health

EP 2.1.1c, 2.1.9b, 2.1.10

Generalist social workers can address mental illness at all three practice levels. At the micro level, social workers provide case management, counseling (e.g., crisis intervention or substance abuse counseling), and intensive psychotherapy for chronically (long-term) mentally ill people. At the mezzo level, they conduct group therapy and provide various kinds of family treatment. Finally, at the macro level, they initiate changes in organizational and public policy to improve service provision to large groups of clients. Social workers may also assume administrative or supervisory responsibilities in agencies providing any level of service.

Case Management in Micro Practice

We have established that case management is a micro-level method of service provision whereby a social worker coordinates ongoing multiple services for a client. Specific tasks include assessing client needs and strengths, linking clients to services, planning treatment strategies, monitoring the appropriateness and effectiveness of these services, and advocating for improved service provision when necessary. Earlier we established that coordination and monitoring of services are key concepts. Case management is the treatment of choice for clients with chronic mental illness who have many ongoing needs that can be met only through services from a range of sources. The idea is that somebody has to take responsibility for making sure service provision makes sense and is effective.

Case managers may also provide direct services to clients that are related to the need for coordinated service provision. These include "crisis intervention (e.g., locating temporary housing for desperate, homeless people), supporting clients making difficult decisions, helping to modify clients' environments (e.g., arranging for transportation within the community), and helping clients overcome emotional reactions to their crisis situations" (Kirst-Ashman & Hull, 2012b, pp. 556–557). Case management is an important role for social workers in mental health at both the BSW and the MSW levels.

EP 2.1.10d, 2.1.10e, 2.1.10g, 2.1.10j, 2.1.10m

Case Example Amos, a case manager at a community mental health center, provides an example of what a case manager does. One of his clients, Beth, age 28, has schizophrenia. When taking her medication, she can function in the community, living in an efficiency apartment. Amos conducted her original assessment and developed a plan with her. After helping link her to the appropriate resources, he now coordinates and monitors a number of services she

receives. Amos regularly talks to Beth about how she's doing and what new goals she wants to set.

Amos keeps in touch with Beth's psychiatrist, making certain she keeps her appointments and continues taking her psychotropic medication. He also makes sure she keeps appointments with her general physician (she has diabetes). Amos helped her get a part-time job at Betty's Best Butter Burger Bistro, and he maintains contact with Betty, Beth's boss, to monitor Beth's performance at work.

Amos referred her to a support group at the community health center for people who have schizophrenia and are coping with independent life in the community. He periodically contacts the group's facilitator to monitor her progress and participation there.

Beth has a sister living within a couple miles of her apartment who helps Beth with shopping and getting to the doctor. Amos checks with her regularly to make sure no problems are surfacing. Several times, Beth has stopped taking her medication when she felt she had recovered and didn't need it. Each time, she relapsed and was eventually found wandering half-naked through a park in her neighborhood. Once Amos advocated fervently on Beth's behalf when her benefits were mistakenly slashed. In summary, Amos watches over Beth, monitors the resources she receives, and helps her get new ones when she needs them.

Micro Practice: Psychotherapy

EP 2.1.7a, 2.1.7b, 2.1.10, 2.1.10g, 2.1.10j

Chapter 4 discussed the process of generalist social work practice that reflects the foundation of social work skills. Building on this foundation, there is an infinite array of specific approaches to social work intervention.

Specialized psychotherapy is often used to treat people with mental illness. The purpose of this book is not to teach you how to practice psychotherapy. But its intent is to introduce you to the range of interventions and perspectives that social work practice can involve. Because some MSWs enter the mental health field and become psychotherapists, the philosophies of a few psychotherapeutic approaches, arbitrarily chosen, will be summarized briefly here. Two broad categories among the many specific theoretical approaches include humanistic theories and cognitive-behavioral theories. (Note that the terms *psychotherapy* and *therapy* are used interchangeably as the discussion focuses only on mental health, not other types of therapy not involving mental health.)

Humanistic theories emphasize the importance of the individual's perception of reality and experience, a focus on strengths, and an optimistic approach to human character (Grogan & Richardson, 2008). Such theories emphasize "an individual's dignity and worth and capacity for self-realization through reason" (Mish, 2008, p. 604). "These approaches tend to focus on the 'here and now' and gently challenge clients to make new choices in their lives" (Neukrug, 2011, p. 143). The two humanistic theories discussed in subsequent sections include existential therapy and person-centered therapy.

Note that earlier in the chapter cognitive-behavioral therapy was discussed in the context of treatment for veterans with PTSD. "Cognitive-behavioral therapy [or cognitive behavioral therapy or cognitive behavior therapy, depending on the source] does *not* exist as a distinct therapeutic technique. The term 'cognitive-behavioral therapy (CBT)' is a very general term for a classification of therapies with similarities. There are several approaches to cognitive-behavioral therapy, including Rational Emotive Behavior Therapy, Rational Behavior Therapy, Rational Living Therapy, Cognitive Therapy, and Dialectic Behavior Therapy" (National Association of Cognitive-Behavioral Therapy [NACBT], 2010, emphasis omitted). (It is beyond the scope of this text to explain every therapy.) All of these more specific approaches under the cognitive-behavioral umbrella are based on the idea that thinking and behavior are intimately intertwined. However, each therapy has differences in its philosophy and what it emphasizes. They all have in common the concept that changing thinking will ultimately affect behavior and emotion even though the surrounding circumstances don't change (e.g., other people and the general environment) (NACBT, 2010). Corey (2009) elaborates:

All of the cognitive behavioral therapies are based on a structured psychoeducational model [stressing the importance of learning], emphasize the role of homework, place responsibility on the client to assume an active role both during and outside of the therapy sessions, and draw from a variety of cognitive and behavioral strategies to bring about change.

To a large degree, cognitive behavior therapy is based on the assumption that a reorganization of one's self-statements will result in a corresponding reorganization of one's behavior. (p. 275)

The two cognitive-behavioral therapies subsequently discussed here include behavior therapy, which, of course, emphasizes behavior, and cognitive therapy, which stresses changing thought processes.

Existential Therapy

Sharf describes existential therapy (2008):

Existential psychotherapy deals with important life themes. Rather than prescribing techniques and methods, existential psychotherapy is an attitudinal approach to issues of living. Themes include living and dying, freedom, responsibility to self and others, finding meaning in life, and dealing with a sense of meaninglessness. More than other therapies, existential psychotherapy examines individuals' awareness of themselves and their ability to look beyond their immediate problems and daily events to problems of human existence. Because individuals do not exist in isolation from others, developing honest and intimate relationships with others is a theme throughout existential therapy. (p. 146)

In existential therapy, the therapist can:

- *Assist clients in recognizing that they are not fully present in the therapy process itself and in seeing how this pattern may limit them outside of therapy.*
- *Support clients in confronting the anxieties that they have so long sought to avoid.*
- *Help clients redefine themselves and their world in ways that foster greater genuineness of contact with life.*

(*Bugental, 1990; Corey, 2009, p. 148*)

"Increased awareness is the central goal of existential therapy, which allows clients to discover that alternative possibilities exist where none were recognized before. Clients come to realize that they are able to make changes in their way of being in the world" (Corey, 2009, p. 148).

Person-Centered Therapy

According to Sharf (2008):

Person-centered therapy ... developed by Carl Rogers, takes a positive view of individuals, believing that they tend to move toward becoming fully functioning. Rogers's work represents a way of being rather than a set of techniques for doing therapy. Emphasizing understanding and caring rather than diagnosis, advice, and persuasion, Rogers believed that therapeutic change could take place if only a few conditions were met. The client must be anxious or incongruent and in contact with the therapist. Therapists must be genuine, in that their words, nonverbal behavior, and feelings agree with each other. They must also accept the client and care unconditionally for the client. Furthermore, they must understand the client's thoughts, ideas, experiences, and feelings and communicate this empathic understanding to the client. If clients are able to perceive these conditions as offered by the therapist, Rogers believed that therapeutic change will take place. (p. 187)

Corey (2009) continues:

The person-centered therapist focuses on the constructive side of human nature, on what is right with the person, and on the assets the individual brings to therapy. The emphasis is on how clients act in their world with others, how they can move forward in constructive directions, and how they can successfully encounter obstacles (both from within themselves and outside of themselves) that are blocking their growth. Practitioners with a humanistic orientation encourage their clients to make changes that will lead to living fully and authentically, with the realization that this kind of existence demands a continuing struggle. People never arrive at a final state of being self-actualized; rather, they are continually involved in the process of actualizing themselves. (pp. 169–170)

Behavior Therapy

Good and Beitman (2006) introduce behavior (or behavioral) therapy:

Behavioral theory focuses on ... how theories of learning apply to observable behaviors.... In general, learning principles and procedures derived from scientific investigation are employed. Behavioral therapy exercises usually progress from easier to harder, from simple to complex, and from less threatening to more threatening behaviors.... Traditional behavior therapists focus only upon the observable, considering the mind to be an unknowable 'black box.' (pp. 19–20)

Corey (2009) elaborates:

A cornerstone of behavior therapy is identifying specific goals at the outset of the therapeutic process. In helping clients achieve their goals, behavior therapists typically assume an active and directive role. Although the client generally determines what behavior will be changed, the therapist typically determines how their behavior can best be modified. In designing a treatment plan, behavior therapists employ techniques and procedures from a wide variety of therapeutic systems and apply them to the unique needs of each client. (p. 262)

"Basic principles of behavior derived from classical conditioning, operant conditioning, and modeling directly affect the development of behavioral therapeutic approaches" (Sharf, 2008, p. 295). *Classical conditioning* is a view of understanding behavior that focuses on a stimulus and the response resulting from that stimulus. (A *stimulus* is a thing or happening perceived by a person that may subsequently influence that person's response or behavior.) *Operant conditioning* is a view of understanding behavior that focuses on how behavior is affected by its consequences. *Modeling* involves learning of behavior by observing someone else demonstrating that behavior.

Sharf (2008) continues:

One of the first methods used to help individuals was Wolpe's systematic desensitization procedure, a gradual process of introducing relaxation to reduce fear and anxiety. Other methods use intense and prolonged exposure to the feared stimulus and may use in vivo procedures, in which the client deals with anxiety in the natural environment. Modeling techniques using role-playing and other methods have been derived from observational learning. (p. 295)

Cognitive Therapy

Cognitive therapy was originated by Aaron T. Beck as an outcome of his work with people affected by depression (Corey, 2009). It "stresses the importance of belief systems and thinking in determining behavior and feelings" (Sharf, 2008, p. 334). Corey (2009) continues:

Cognitive therapy perceives psychological problems as stemming from commonplace processes such as faulty thinking, making incorrect inferences on the basis of inadequate or incorrect information, and failing to distinguish between fantasy and reality.... [It] is an insight-focused therapy that emphasizes recognizing and changing negative thoughts and maladaptive beliefs.... Cognitive therapy is based on the theoretical rationale that the way people feel and behave is determined by how they perceive and structure their experience. (pp. 287–288)

Cognitive schemas involve how clients "think about their world and their important beliefs and assumptions about people, events, and the environment" (Sharf, 2008, p. 339). Beck and Weishaar (2011) elaborate:

Cognitive schemas contain people's perceptions of themselves and others and of their goals and expectations, memories, fantasies, and previous learning. These greatly influence, if not control, the processing of information.

In various psychopathological conditions such as anxiety disorder, depressive disorders, mania, paranoid states, obsessive-compulsive neuroses, and others, a specific bias affects how the person incorporates new information. Thus, a depressed person has a negative bias, including a negative view of self, world, and future....

Contributing to these shifts are certain specific attitudes or core beliefs that predispose people under the influence of certain life situations to interpret their experiences in a biased way. These are known as cognitive vulnerabilities. For example, a person who has the belief that any minor loss represents a major deprivation may react catastrophically to even the smallest loss. (p. 277)

Cognitive distortion occurs when a person experiences consistently flawed and inaccurate perceptions of reality (Beck & Weishaar, 2011; Sharf, 2008). One type of cognitive distortion involves "labeling and mislabeling" (Corey, 2009, p. 289). Sharf (2008) explains:

A negative view of oneself is created by self-labeling based on some errors or mistakes. A person who has had some awkward incidents with acquaintances might conclude, "I'm unpopular. I'm a loser" rather than "I felt awkward talking to Harriet." In labeling and mislabeling in this way, individuals can create an inaccurate sense of themselves or their identity. (p. 342)

The aim of cognitive therapy is to help clients identify their unproductive and negative thoughts (cognitions), evaluate their thought patterns (cognitive schema), and alleviate inaccurate perceptions about self, others, or circumstances (cognitive distortions). For example, therapists using cognitive therapy can help depressed clients evaluate their thinking and eventually change their perceptions and behavior by using the following process (Beck, Rush, Shaw, & Emery, 1979; Beck & Weishaar, 2012). First, under a psychotherapist's direction, clients identify and monitor negative thoughts about themselves. Second, clients examine their schema—that is, their typical reactions to their negative thoughts. Third, clients assess the extent to which such negative thoughts are valid and realistic. To what extent have they been exaggerating or even fabricating all the negative things they've been thinking about themselves? To what extent are they experiencing cognitive distortion? Fourth, clients begin to develop more realistic ways of viewing themselves and the world. What are their actual weaknesses, and, more important, what are their genuine strengths? Fifth, clients develop new beliefs and ways of thinking about themselves that are more realistic and productive.

The following section portrays a case example in which a psychotherapist who has an MSW practices cognitive therapy with an adult male who has depression. This does not imply that cognitive therapy is necessarily any better or worse than other psychotherapeutic approaches. It merely represents an example of one type of therapy applied to one type of problem. Practitioners must evaluate or conduct research to find the evidence regarding what psychotherapeutic approaches are most effective with what mental disorders and other problems.

EP 2.1.6b

Case Example: Cognitive Therapy for Depression

In the following case a therapist successfully uses cognitive therapy with Ed, a divorced 38-year-old male (Geary, 1992). Ed was a soft-spoken, composed man of medium height, with a pale complexion and slightly receding light brown hair. He came to Juana Dance, a psychotherapist with an MSW, for help with his depression. Ed had been unemployed for over a year and, because he had nowhere else to go, was living with his parents.

He described his childhood as stable, living with both parents and two older brothers. He mentioned that his family was neither very demonstrative in showing affection nor very talkative with each other. Ed did well in school and graduated from college with a business degree. He married Anna, his college sweetheart, got a managerial job in sales, and had three daughters.

Everything seemed to be going fine until he turned 30. Suddenly his world started to crumble. His job was going nowhere—with no promotions or significant raises in sight. Ed told Juana that Anna, bored with the marriage, "dumped" him for Hank, a singer in a country-western band. She ran off with Hank, taking Ed's three daughters and moving to another state 1,000 miles away. This devastated Ed.

Ed subsequently quit his job and started several new ones, trying to make something go right in his life. Failing miserably, he had been forced to accept his parents' invitation to live with them.

Ed was at an all-time low. He felt listless, useless, and inadequate. Whenever he talked about anything, self-degrading comments peppered his conversation. For example, he'd say things like "It seems as if I can't do anything right," "I don't have a future so I don't have much to live for," and "What a flop I turned out to be."

EP 2.1.10d, 2.1.10e, 2.1.10g, 2.1.10j

During the first several sessions, Juana spent time easing Ed into the therapeutic relationship and learning about his history and current status. Ed described his typical day as sitting around a lot, watching Home Shopping Network, and bothering his parents. He rarely went out and had virtually no social life. He broke off relationships with old friends, who he felt were getting sick of all his misery and whining. He told Juana that he felt like he was carrying a picket sign that read "I'm a useless, no good piece of crap." In better, happier days, he might have said that people generally treated him as if he'd just eaten a clove of garlic and forgotten his breath mints.

Juana administered test instruments that measured Ed's level of depression and the type and incidence of his negative self-statements. Results indicated moderate to severe depression and a significant frequency of negative thoughts about himself.

With Juana's help, Ed began identifying and monitoring his negative self-thoughts. Whenever he criticized himself, Juana would discuss with him the implications of what he said and what he really meant. Juana continued to explore with Ed his schema—how he automatically experienced self-critical thoughts and how they were directly related to feeling badly about himself. Periodically Juana administered the instruments measuring depression and incidence of negative self-statements to monitor progress.

Additionally, Juana assigned Ed graded homework assignments that he completed between sessions and subsequently discussed with her. *Graded assignments* refer to tasks of increasing difficulty and complexity that expand a client's repertoire of behavior. For example, at first Ed was to talk with a friend for 10 minutes each day to start opening his social world. Later he started attending a weekly support group for divorced men. Still later, he began a job search.

When reporting his progress, Ed continued to demean himself with comments like "Aw, that's nothin' " or "Anybody could do that." Juana praised his accomplishments and emphasized how so many small steps, taken together, eventually added up to real progress. She discussed with him the extent to which his perception of himself was realistic. Where was he being exceptionally and unfairly critical about himself? What strengths was he trying to ignore instead of giving himself realistic credit for solid accomplishments?

One way Ed began to demonstrate increased awareness of self-criticism was to verbalize more frequently how Juana would respond before she said it (Geary, 1992). In other words, he would give himself the same kind of feedback she had given him many times before. For example, he'd say, "I know what you're thinking—I should appreciate how I am improving. I guess it beats being poked in the eye with a sharp stick."

Juana initiated a treatment method during therapy called the "triple column technique" to help Ed recognize cognitive distortion concerning his self-concept (Burns, 1980, p. 60; Geary, 1992). In the first column he would identify his automatic negative self-thought (e.g., "I never do anything right"). In the second column he'd identify his cognitive distortion (e.g., "Of course, I do some things right, although certainly not everything"). In the third column he'd write logical, more realistic reactions to the automatic negative self-thought (e.g., "Although I sometimes feel that my progress is as lively as a turtle's, I know that I am gradually doing better").

Although Ed suffered several setbacks when he panicked when thinking about returning to work, he generally made steady progress. His activity level markedly increased, although he experienced a few ups and downs. His scores on the instruments measuring depression and incidence of negative self-statements also continued to improve.

Treatment began to focus on additional behavioral means Ed could use to validate his self-worth and improve how he thought about himself. Homework assignments included talking to other people such as family members about his insights in therapy and seeking their perspective (Geary, 1992). He even contacted old friends he hadn't seen in years. What he found out was that a lot of people really cared about him. They appreciated him for being the pleasant, thoughtful, kind person with a good sense of humor that he was. This bolstered his self-confidence.

He got a dog, found a full-time job, and even started dating. Life still wasn't perfect, and dating was a lot harder than he remembered it in college. However, he was generally much happier and more self-confident, and emotionally stronger than he had been prior to therapy.

During his last session, Ed reverted to some imagery he had used during an earlier meeting, which can be a useful therapeutic technique (Geary, 1992). He indicated his new picket sign read, "I'm okay and proud of it." He said he was amazed at how much better other people responded to him now. He added that he responded to himself a lot better, too. He also told Juana that he felt he could look at himself, the world, and others more realistically now. Jokingly, he added, "And Hank really can't sing."

The Use of Psychotropic Drugs to Treat Mental Disorders

We have established that psychotropic drugs are employed by psychiatrists and other physicians to alter thinking, mood, and behavior. Classes of psychotropic medication include antipsychotic, antidepressant, mood-stabilizing, anti-anxiety, and psychostimulant (Bentley & Kogut, 2008; Walsh & Bentley, 2002, pp. 646–649). These are frequently used to treat various mental disorders, often very effectively. Their uses, in addition to examples of generic drugs in each category and their brand names (in parentheses), are given here (Bentley & Kogut, 2008; National Alliance on mental Illness, 2011; Walsh & Bentley, 2002):

- Antipsychotic drugs are used to treat schizophrenia. Examples are thioridazine (Mellaril) and chlorpromizine (Thorazine).
- Antidepressant drugs are employed in the treatment of major depression and anxiety disorders, particularly panic disorders. Examples are amitriptyline (Elavil) and fluoxetine (Prozac).
- Mood-stabilizing drugs are used to treat bipolar disorder. An example is lithium (Lithobid).
- Anti-anxiety drugs are used to control anxiety disorders and insomnia. Examples are alprazolam (Xanax) and diazepam (Valium).
- Psychostimulant drugs are used to treat attention deficit hyperactivity disorder (ADHD). (ADHD is a syndrome of learning and behavioral problems beginning in childhood that is characterized by a persistent pattern of inattention, excessive physical movement, and impulsivity that appear in at least two settings [including home, school, work, or social contexts].) An example is methylphenidate (Ritalin).

There has been significant controversy over the use of many psychotropic drugs (Bentley & Kogut, 2008; Bentley & Walsh, 1998). Are they used too frequently when other means of treatment would suffice? Are drugs prescribed too freely for children with ADHD? Why does the "dramatic increase" in their use "have some claiming that such use hides the 'true' origins of problems and leads to stunted growth and underuse of effective psychosocial interventions"? Do some antidepressants "change or modify personality" so that people are no longer really themselves?

These issues notwithstanding, psychotropic drugs have become a mainstay in mental health treatment. Thus it's critical for mental health professionals to review current research carefully and use such medications carefully.

Note that psychotropic drugs are not used for all disorders and that many other methods of treatment exist and are being developed. Focus on Critical Thinking 13.3 examines the comeback of electroshock therapy.

Mezzo Practice: Running Treatment Groups

As discussed in Chapter 5, *treatment groups* help individuals solve personal problems, change unwanted behaviors, cope with stress, and improve their quality of life. Types of treatment groups include therapy, support, education, growth, and socialization; here are some examples:

- *Therapy:* A group of people diagnosed with schizophrenia who live in the community and meet at a local community health center.
- *Support:* A group of adults caring for their parents who have Alzheimer's disease.
- *Education:* A group of parents learning about effective child management techniques.
- *Growth:* A group of gay men focusing on gay pride issues (Toseland & Rivas, 2012).
- *Socialization:* A current events group at a nursing home that gets together to discuss their opinions.

FOCUS ON CRITICAL THINKING 13.3

Electroshock Therapy Is Back[5]

EP 2.1.3, 2.1.10m

What do you picture when you think about electroshock therapy (now referred to as *electroconvulsive therapy*)? Is it a group of physicians and nurses gathered around a patient lying on a gurney with electrodes protruding from his head? Do you picture his body convulsing violently and then him drooling like an imbecile? Perhaps you remember the scene from the movie *One Flew over the Cuckoo's Nest* in which the formerly spunky and rebellious mental patient Randle Patrick McMurphy (played by Jack Nicholson) lies mindlessly on his hospital bed, bereft of any remaining personality after receiving electroconvulsive therapy. (If you're going to be a social work major, this is a good movie to see because it portrays some of the dimensions of institutional life [Downey & Jackson, 2000].)

Electroconvulsive therapy (ECT) is the most controversial technique in modern psychiatry (Mental Health

America [MHA], 2011b; National Mental Health Association [NMHA], 2008). It is used to treat mental health problems such as depression or schizophrenia, usually when drug therapies fail or patients are acutely suicidal (Mayo Foundation for Medical Education and Research, 2010; NMHA, 2008). Apparently at least 100,000 Americans are treated with electroconvulsive therapy each year, although the actual number is hard to pinpoint because reporting is not formally required (MHA, 2011b; NMHA, 2008). The controversy focuses on the fact that for some it works wonderfully to temporarily control depressive and bipolar disorders. For others it represents a nightmare of memory loss, brain malfunction, and continued mood disorder. Cloud (2001) suggests that "it works a little bit like banging the side of a fuzzy TV—it just works, except when it doesn't" (p. 60).

So how does ECT work? No one really knows. Electrodes are placed on a patient's head, and an electrical burst powerful enough to light a 40-watt bulb is sent through the patient's brain for 30–60 seconds. Currently, prior to the procedure, patients are given a muscle relaxant and anesthesia to eliminate pain and prevent the violent flailing of limbs that caused broken bones in the past. During ECT, a mouth guard is inserted to protect the tongue and teeth, and an oxygen mask is put in place to sustain breathing. ECT usually

---

[5]Facts for this highlight are from Electroshock Therapy (2000); Familydoctor.org (2003); Griner (2002); Henderson (2002); Marcotty (1999); MayoS Foundation for Medical Education and Research 2010; Mental Health Amercia,2011b; National Mental Health Association, 2005a, 2008; Paplos (2002); Sabbatini (2002); Sackheim, Devanand, and Nobler (2002); and U.S. Office of the Surgeon General (2001).

(continued)

involves 6–12 sessions administered three times per week. Theories about how ECT works focus on chemical interactions in the brain. It is thought that the electrical current either enhances the transmission of neurological impulses or releases hormones that influence (and thus improve) mood.

ECT technically dates back to the 16th century when torpedo fish (also known as electric rays), which transmit electrical impulses, were used to treat headaches. During the 1930s, insulin and camphor were used to induce seizures and temporarily improve some mental health conditions. "In the Oscar-winning film *A Beautiful Mind,* math scholar John Nash undergoes such insulin shock treatment for schizophrenia" (Griner, 2002). In 1938 two Italians, Ugo Cerletti and Lucio Bini, were the first to actually use an electrical current to treat a schizophrenic man experiencing severe hallucinations.

Curtis Hartmann, age 47, a lawyer in Westfield, Massachusetts, who indicates that he's had 100 treatments altogether, remains an avid advocate of ECT (Cloud, 2001). He says it's the only treatment that's been consistently able to control his bipolar disorder since 1976. He feels infinitely better after a treatment, stating that "depression is like being a corpse with a pulse" (Cloud, 2001, p. 62).

Similarly, Diane (no last name) notes that "after numerous hospital visits over a two-year period, ECT treatments were presented as my last chance at controlling depression. Medications were unable to control the illness." Although she did experience some temporary memory loss, she concludes, "In retrospect, the ECT treatments allowed the depression to improve significantly to be treatable by medications alone" (Voices of Experience, 2002).

Opponents of the approach vehemently protest its use. For example, Liz McGillicuddy, "once a decorated Marine Lt. Colonel with several college degrees to her name," underwent ECT when suffering from severe depression (The Horror, 2000). McGillicuddy claims that the "results were devastating." She can't remember her childhood or "anything" about her past; she also lost "her future" as she is "unable to form new memories" (The Horror, 2000).

Juli Lawrence provides another example of a negative experience. Prior to her undergoing ECT, her attending physician told her family that "it was an absolute cure for depression." However, he did not caution her and her family about the potential side effects such as memory loss, "which can range from forgetting where you parked your car to forgetting that you own a car at all" (Cloud, 2001, p. 60). She attempted suicide a week later and now claims that she can't remember a thing from two years prior to the treatment to several months following it.

In 2000 the U.S. surgeon general issued a report stating the following:

- Of persons receiving ECT, 60–70% improve. These rates resemble those for psychotropic drugs, but remember that most people receiving ECT have not responded to drug treatments.
- ECT is not considered long-term protection against suicide, but rather a short-term treatment for acute illness.
- The major risk of ECT involves anesthesia, the same risk occurring any time anesthesia is administered.
- "The most common adverse effects of this treatment are confusion and memory loss for events surrounding the period of ECT treatment. The confusion and disorientation seen upon awakening after ECT typically clear within an hour. More persistent memory problems are variable."
- "Although most patients return to full functioning following successful ECT, the degree of posttreatment memory impairment and resulting impact on functioning are highly variable across individuals. . . . Fears that ECT causes gross structural brain pathology have not been supported by decades of methodologically sound research in both humans and animals."
- "The decision to use ECT must be evaluated for each individual, weighing the potential benefits and known risks of all available and appropriate treatments in the context of informed consent."

Despite the furor over ECT, its use probably will continue. It does provide short-term relief for some people experiencing some types of severe mental disorders who don't respond to other treatment modalities or who are acutely suicidal. But ECT is not a cure-all. Its effects are usually only temporary; effects can vary radically from one recipient to the next; and it may cause brain damage. In any event, apparently ECT, for better or worse, is back.

Critical Thinking Questions

What are your opinions about ECT? Do you think the advantages outweigh the disadvantages, or vice versa? Would you ever consider ECT for yourself or for someone close to you? What are the reasons for your answer?

Mezzo Practice: Treating Families

Collins, Jordan, and Coleman (1999) state that the major purpose of social work with families is "to help families learn to function more competently while meeting the developmental and emotional needs of *all* members" (p. 2). They continue that it "targets the following objectives: (1) reinforce family strengths to get families ready for change (or intervention); (2) provide additional support following family therapy so families maintain effective family functioning; [and] (3) create concrete changes in family functioning to sustain effective and satisfying daily routines" (p. 2).

Family counseling can involve virtually any aspect of family communication and dynamics. Chapter 9 discussed family preservation and social work with families at high risk of child maltreatment. Other issues for which families may need treatment include members' inability to get along, parental inability to control children's behavior, divorce, stepfamily issues, or crises (e.g., a death in the family, an unwanted pregnancy, unemployment, a natural disaster).

At this point, are you considering a career in mental health? Highlight 13.6 poses some suggestions for helping you think about a possible career in mental health.

HIGHLIGHT 13.6

Are You Thinking About Working in the Mental Health Field?

EP 2.1.1, 2.1.1b

If you're considering a social work major, choosing a field of practice is not necessarily easy. A number of issues, problem areas, or populations may sound interesting to you. Kelly (2002) provides at least eight suggestions for exploring the mental health field before you commit to a professional job. Any of these suggestions can offer excellent opportunities for networking with mental health professionals. They may be effective ways of talking with practitioners about what they do and how they do it, in addition to finding out what jobs are available.

1. Check out job possibilities and mental health issues through Mental Health America (MHA) at http://www.nmha.org./go/we-serve It addresses "the full spectrum of mental and substance use conditions and their effects nationwide, [and] works to inform, advocate and enable access to quality behavioral health services for all Americans" (MHA, 2011c).

2. Become a member of the U.S. Psychiatric Rehabilitation Association (USPRA) (formerly the International Association of Psychosocial Rehabilitation Services [IAPSRS]) at http://www.iapsrs.org/mental-health.html. This is "an organization of psychosocial rehabilitation agencies, practitioners, and interested organizations and individuals dedicated to promoting, supporting and strengthening community-oriented rehabilitation services and resources for persons with psychiatric disabilities" (USPRA, 2004).

3. Become a member of the National Association of Social Workers (NASW), an organization with chapters in all 50 states, Washington, D.C., Puerto Rico, the Virgin Islands, and Guam, that has almost 145,000 members (NASW, 2011a) (http://www.naswdc.org/). NASW also provides an excellent resource for networking with social workers practicing in mental health. Members receive 10 issues annually of *NASW News*, containing updates on both issues and jobs in mental health and other social work fields of practice, in addition to the quarterly professional journal *Social Work*. "NASW membership connects you with cutting-edge ideas, current information, practice expertise, and quality resources" (NASW, 2005). Numerous continuing education programs are offered in specific aspects of mental health and other areas in which social workers practice.

4. Volunteer at a local crisis intervention program. Such programs usually offer excellent training to prepare volunteers for answering crisis hotlines. This may offer experience in addressing a wide range of crises (for example, suicide threats, drug overdoses, loneliness, and depression). You never know what the next phone call may bring.

5. Work as a paraprofessional or volunteer in an inpatient mental health clinic or in other facilities with clients who are dealing with mental health issues. If inpatient hospitals are unavailable due to deinstitutionalization, seek out opportunities "in community-based mental health centers, group homes for . . . [people with mental health issues], or

(continued)

HIGHLIGHT 13.6 *(continued)*

day treatment programs" for people with chronic problems (Kelly, 2002, p. 5).

6. Work or volunteer at a homeless shelter. Although being homeless by no means indicates that a person has a mental disorder, many people who were living in inpatient facilities have been discharged into the community. Sometimes the community lacks funding and an adequate support network to sustain these people. The result may be that they stop taking their medication and suffer a significantly decreased ability to function—involving work, socializing with others, and maintaining a place to live. One result may be homelessness. Homeless shelters may let you learn about community resources and link people with supportive services and benefits so they can maintain themselves in the community.

7. "Attend open meetings of support groups related to mental health" (Kelly, 2002, p. 5). Groups may be available for people with specific types of disorders (for example, schizophrenia, anxiety disorders, or eating disorders) or for family members of people with disorders. Support groups can teach you about the mental health issues people must address and provide suggestions for how to cope. However,

make sure the meetings are "open" (i.e., anyone who is interested may attend). Always honestly identify your purpose for being there.

8. Use continuing education opportunities to explore your interests. NASW is only one of the numerous organizations addressing mental health issues that provide chances to learn about specific mental health disorders and treatment approaches. The following are examples of continuing education topics from one brochure: "Eating Disorders"; "Sex Matters for Women"; "Master Your Panic"; "The Ethics of Professional Practice"; "Anxiety and Depression"; "Child and Adolescent Counseling"; "Overcoming Binge Eating"; and "Anger Management" (Homestead Schools, 2004).

   Note that after graduation your state might have certification or licensing requirements for a designated number of continuing education hours (CEHs) or units (CEUs). You can take these classes before you graduate, too, if there's an area in which you're exceptionally interested and are willing to pay the fee to attend.

EP 2.1.1e

Macro Practice and Policy Practice in Mental Health

EP 2.1.5b, 2.1.5c, 2.1.8a, 2.1.8b, 2.1.9a, 2.1.9b

Social workers practice in the mental health macro arena in at least three ways. First, they can advocate for positive change on behalf of large groups of clients. (The following section on managed care discusses some issues of concern and calls for advocacy to address these issues.) Second, social workers who function as managers and administrators in mental health agencies can strive to improve policies and service provision in collaboration with colleagues and clients. (A later section discusses the need to improve cultural competence in the mental health macro system.) Third, social workers can strive to develop innovative programs to meet mental health needs.

For example, Johnson, Noe, Collins, Strader, and Bucholtz (2000) describe a project in which members of local church communities were recruited "to implement and evaluate alcohol and other drug (AOD) abuse prevention programs" (p. 1). "Community advocate teams" were created, made up of significant church leaders, usually pastors (p. 7). These teams subsequently recruited families with children at high risk of AOD abuse. Families and children were then given "comprehensive training" consisting of 25 weeks of 2½-hour sessions along with case management services (pp. 10–11). Incentives were offered to keep families in the program, including "the provision of food for participants, day care assistance, family portraits, transportation provisions, social activities, and nominal payments for the research interviews" (p. 12). Evaluation research revealed that the program was "highly successful in white American rural and suburban church communities" although "only partially successful in urban African American church communities" (p. 21).

Evidence-Based Practice in Mental Health

EP 2.1.6b

Evidence-based practice in social work relies on the knowledge and established proof, the best evidence available, to determine what works. This, in turn, informs social workers how to proceed in planning and implementing interventions. Solomon (2008) identifies five trends in mental health practice that have been found to be evidence-based and effective. They include comprehensive community support, family education and support, work encouragement and assistance, coordinated treatment for concurrent substance abuse issues, and educational and coping skill development groups. These should be emphasized and pursued in future mental health program and practice skill development to increase effective treatment. Note that they involve various aspects of micro, mezzo, and macro practice.

Comprehensive Community Support

EP 2.1.10g, 2.1.10j

Comprehensive community support and treatment involves establishing teams of professionals who are available in the community to work with people on a 24/7 basis. Development of such teams and involvement of people with mental illness in the community would require assertive and resourceful action. Intervention would involve finding and linking people who have psychiatric conditions with resources, providing treatment, and monitoring progress. This approach would focus on the 10–20% of people with mental illness who have the most relentless, extreme conditions that require continued monitoring (Solomon, 2008). Many of these people are currently homeless and adrift outside of support systems. Community teams would address whatever the clients' needs might involve, including securing housing, enrolling in vocational training, finding employment, getting and taking psychotropic medication, or establishing and monitoring support systems. The idea is to keep people with severe forms of mental illness actively involved in a productive life as part of the community.

Family Education and Support

Family education and support targets the families of people with severe mental illness. Evidence proves that educating the family about mental illness and teaching family members problem-solving and coping skills have positive results for the person with the psychiatric disorder. Family members become better able to provide social support for the client to help him or her maintain a healthier existence in the community. Usually, a case manager oversees service provision and helps family members make certain the client takes prescribed medication.

Work Encouragement and Assistance

Work encouragement and assistance involves ongoing provision of support to a client with a psychiatric disorder as he or she prepares for, seeks, obtains, and continues to work. This is another program that should provide ongoing support instead of limited treatment. Evidence indicates that this results in the enhanced ability of a person with a mental illness to maintain and support him- or herself in the community through employment.

Coordinated Treatment for Concurrent Substance Abuse Issues

EP 2.1.5b, 2.1.10k

The current health-care environment emphasizes designated treatments for specific diagnoses. Therefore, in that context a person with a psychiatric disorder would receive a diagnosis and be treated by a professional according to the health-care organization's criteria. If that same person also was diagnosed with a substance abuse disorder, in typical managed care environments, for example, that problem would be treated elsewhere by a different provider using the criteria established for that condition. Evidence concerning effective mental health practice indicates that this uncoordinated approach is not as effective as treatment of the two diagnoses together by the same provider. The multiple problems experienced by any individual are intertwined and interrelated. Therefore, to treat them as separate conditions is much less effective and really doesn't make much sense. Advocacy is needed to change the health-care provision system so that it will allow for and support treatments that are effective—namely, more coordinated, comprehensive approaches to mental illness and substance abuse.

Educational and Coping Skill Development Groups

The fifth evidence-based best practice approach for people with mental health problems involves forming groups of clients. Goals are to help group members better understand their psychiatric conditions and develop methods to cope with them. Teaching people with psychiatric disorders how to manage their conditions and symptoms has been proven effective. Groups have the advantages of providing members with mutual support and the sharing of ideas about how to monitor medication and cope with situations related to the illness. The recommended protocol involves weekly sessions for a period of three to six months (Solomon, 2008). Family members and other members of a client's support system can also attend and learn. An alternative to group work is provision of education and the development of skills on an individual basis. Evidence has shown that this decreases relapses, increases adherence to medication schedules, and enhances the development and use of coping skills to control problematic behaviors.

At this point we have discussed various aspects of what social workers do in mental health and some of the approaches proven to be effective. Issues addressed next involve other dimensions of working in the mental health system. These include managed care, which is the context for service provision, and the importance of cultural competence when working with clients.

Managed Care Policies and Programs in Mental Health

Most of the same issues apply to managed care in mental health as in other health-care settings, as discussed in Chapter 12. There *managed care* was defined as "a wide range of health plans and practices that depart from the traditional model of private health insurance provided by one's employer" (Kornblum & Julian, 2009, p. 61). It is "a healthcare system under which the insurer [the managed care organization] controls the person's health care" (Chapin, 2011, p. I-14). An identified group or range of providers of health and mental health care contracts with managed care agencies to provide health care at a negotiated rate. Two primary principles promoted by managed care involve retaining quality and access while controlling costs. In other words, care should be readily accessible and of high quality, and yet be as inexpensive as possible. This is a hard row to hoe.

There is much pressure on physicians and clinicians to find the least expensive treatment modalities possible for any particular client in order to minimize costs. For example, because psychiatric

hospitalization is very expensive, there is pressure to keep clients in that setting for as brief a time as possible. This pressure exists even when the client needs that kind of intensive treatment for a longer period. Less intensive settings, of course, include group homes and outpatient treatment facilities. Focus on Critical Thinking 13.4 questions the real intent of managed care.

Social workers are responsible for advocating for their clients. Vandivort-Warren (1998) urges social workers to advocate on the behalf of people with mental illness. She maintains that "advocacy forms the root of this profession and is needed now more than ever to infuse social work values into insurance-dominated interests" (p. 263). She makes three specific suggestions. First, social workers can fight for more adequate funding for mental health services. Second, states should "be actively involved in evaluating the services provided under managed care rather than delegating quality concerns to managed care firms" (p. 264). The latter resembles asking you to decide what grade you deserve for this course. Third, social workers can advocate for services that go beyond mere "medical necessity" and help empower people to improve their psychosocial functioning and quality of life.

EP 2.1.8a, 2.1.10k

Focus on Critical Thinking 13.5 addresses issues about mental health policy and programming.

Cultural Competence in Mental Health Settings

Cultural competence has been defined as "mastery of a particular set of knowledge, skills, policies, and programs used by the social worker that address the cultural needs of individuals, families, groups, and communities" (Lum, 2005, p. 4). People of color underutilize the U.S. mental health system (Greeno, 2008; NIMH, 2007a, 2010; USDHHS, 1999). These groups include (1) African American, (2) Asian and Pacific Islander [API], (3) Hispanic/Latino, and (4) Native American/Alaskan Native/Hawaiian Native.

EP 2.1.4a, 2.1.4c, 2.1.7b

Several characteristics of these groups differentiate them to various degrees from the white mainstream (USDHHS, 1999). First, their cultural orientation in terms of values, traditions, and beliefs often conflicts with the existing mental health system. Second, for

FOCUS ON CRITICAL THINKING 13.4

What Is the Real Intent of Managed Care?

**EP 2.1.3,
2.1.3a,
2.1.5b**

Mechanic (2008) cites at least three concepts important in understanding the impact of managed care on mental health service provision: "capitation," "gatekeeping," and "utilization management" (pp. 167–169). *Capitation*, discussed in Chapter 12, is

a form of payment involving a fixed, predetermined payment per person for a specified range of services for a fixed period of time.... The capitation received by a provider organization is the same regardless of how many services the person actually uses or what they cost. Some provision can be made to adjust capitation to take account of differences in age, sex, illness history, or other characteristics, but the basic idea in any case is that such prospective payment induces providers to carefully consider how they use expensive resources. Use of too many expensive services can lead to financial losses, and efficient practices can result in higher earnings.

(Mechanic, 2008, p. 168)

A difference between mental health and other health care often involves the intensity of services needed (Dulmus & Roberts, 2008; Mechanic, 2008). With general health problems, managed care providers assume that patient claims will vary greatly in any one year, with some people getting very sick unpredictably. However, they also assume that most people will not get sick, so costs are spread out over a large number of people (Mechanic, 2008). Thus insurance premiums from the many who don't get that sick and their employers support health-care services for the few who do. People with mental illness, however, often require much more intensive care over long periods, and sometimes forever. This can be very expensive for managed care organizations. Hence managed care programs usually distinguish between mental health and general health benefits, placing more stringent limitations on those available for mental health (Dulmus & Roberts, 2008; Mechanic, 2008).

Note that many people with mental illness don't have their own insurance, but receive benefits through government programs such as Medicare or Medicaid. Most states are assertively moving to have these benefits administered through managed care organizations (Essock & Goldman, 1995; Mechanic, 2008). Figuring out how to fund treatment for the mentally ill population with its intensive need for service is a complex process.

A second issue concerning managed care and mental health involves the *gatekeeping* function of a person's primary care physician. Generally, patients in a managed care program pick their own doctor from a limited list. They then must go through this doctor to get referrals to any specialists they may need (e.g., psychotherapists, neurologists, ophthalmologists, proctologists). The main purpose of gatekeeping is to make certain patients see specialists only when necessary, essentially to cut down on costs. One problem is that a primary care physician may not be highly knowledgeable about a particular client's type of mental health problem—especially more severe, more chronic, or rarer disorders. One study reports three interesting findings regarding primary care physicians (Mechanic, 2008; Wells et al., 1989). First, primary care physicians fail to identify even such common problems as depression about half the time. Second, even when they accurately recognize the problem, they often prescribe inappropriate drugs or administer the wrong dosage. Third, primary care physicians in managed care organizations fare worse in identifying depression than their counterparts working outside such organizations.

Utilization management means that certain medical and mental health services must be authorized ahead of time; otherwise the managed care organization won't pay for them. This involves a clinician or physician contacting the managed care organization and explaining the problem in sufficient detail to get permission for the service or procedure. A managed care representative, often a utilization reviewer or case manager, then reviews the documentation and, using a structured set of rules and steps, determines whether the symptoms and diagnosis warrant the requested procedure (Corcoran, 1997; Mechanic, 2008). "Clinical decisions are now routinely challenged" (Matorin, 1998, p. 161). In this process, clinicians have lost a huge amount of decision-making power regarding what should and can be done to help clients.

Most mental health professionals have little trust in managed care and generally don't like it (Matorin, 1998; Mechanic, 1999, 2008; Popple & Leighninger, 2011). Matorin (1998) highlights several concerns. First, clinicians must often defensively justify their treatment recommendations to a managed care staff member who may or may not be familiar with the client's type of condition. Second, clinicians are often pressured "to discharge clients from the hospital prematurely, knowing

(continued)

FOCUS ON CRITICAL THINKING 13.4 (continued)

full well the limited availability of adequate aftercare resources" (Matorin, 1998, p. 161). Third, "fragile patients are often shifted to lesser levels of care over the course of a week. Such 'treatment' plans subject them to multiple separations and changes in treatment team at the point when they most need continuity" (Matorin, 1998, p. 161).

Managed care in mental health practice is in place. Its proponents maintain that it's an effective way to

provide mental health care, which is very expensive, while controlling costs.

Critical Thinking Questions

What do you think are the strengths and weaknesses of managed care in mental health? To what extent do you support or fail to support it? What are your reasons?

FOCUS ON CRITICAL THINKING 13.5

Mental Health Care and Policy

EP 2.1.3

Some mental health policy issues resemble those in other types of health-care provision. Who is covered and who has access are major concerns.

Critical Thinking Questions

Should U.S. policy in mental health care be overhauled to establish a national health insurance program providing *universal* mental health coverage? Should the government fund a program made

available to all citizens, making private health insurance with its *selective* mental health benefits obsolete?

Consider other, more specific questions:

- Should limits be placed on the type of treatment and number of sessions with a professional?
- Should all people who need them have ready access to expensive psychotropic drugs?
- As with other types of health care, who should pay for it? Workers? Employers? The government?

---

many reasons, these groups generally have lower income levels and higher levels of poverty. Third, their generally lower socioeconomic status (as measured by such variables as income, education, and occupation) is clearly related to mental illness.

Barriers to Receiving Mental Health Services

Many people of color find the mental health system to be threatening, unresponsive, and noncompliant with many of their beliefs. Five barriers to these groups' access to services are lack of help-seeking behavior, mistrust, stigma, cost, and clinician bias (USDHHS, 1999).

Lack of Help-Seeking Behavior

To receive services, people must acknowledge that a problem exists and seek help to address it. We have established that for various reasons people of color

don't seek out and receive mental health services to the extent that white people do.

Yamashiro and Matsuoka (1997) explain some of the reasons people of Asian and Pacific Islander (API) cultural heritage fail to utilize the mental health system adequately. They resemble some of the reasons API people fail to seek formal services for other health problems, as discussed in Chapter 12. Reasons include an emphasis on "collective identities," "fatalism," use of language, and the fear of transmission to offspring (Yamashiro & Matsuoka, 1997, p. 458).

As earlier chapters explained, the worldview of Asian Americans and Pacific Islanders involves a greater sense of collective identity than dominant Euro-American culture, which stresses the importance of individualism. Dependence on the family, extended family, and cultural community are emphasized. The implication is that API people will first turn to their families and others in their cultural community to address problems, including mental health issues, before turning to strangers, whether professionals or not.

A second reason for API underutilization of mental health services involves a sense of *fatalism*. This is the idea that everything happens as a result of predetermined fate, with individuals having little control over their general life course.

A third reason for underutilization of mental health services involves language. Not only might API people speak a different language or at least use a different language as their primary one, they also might use language differently in general. The Western world emphasizes the importance of people talking about emotions and feelings to improve how they feel. A clear connection between emotions and language is assumed. In Eastern psychology, no such clear connection exists. Yamashiro and Matsuoka (1997) explain that in API cultures "language may not accommodate all that individuals think and feel—especially for those who are not socialized to use language as a primary means for expressing feelings" (p. 463). Participating in some form of therapy that emphasizes talking about feelings and behavior may make no sense in the context of traditional API culture.

A fourth reason involves the fact that

an ancient tradition in Asian and Pacific Islander cultures is arranging marriages to ensure that one's offspring is united with an appropriate partner for the primary purpose of procreation. . . . Because mental illness is believed to be genetically inherited, evidence of mental illness in a family's lineage could render their offspring unsuitable for marriage.

(Yamashiro & Matsuoka, 1997, p. 465)

In other words, if the word got out that mental illness ran in the family, potential marriage partners would run in the opposite direction.

Herring (1999) reflects on reasons Native American people often fail to seek and receive formal mental health services. They tend to use such services only when help is unavailable in their own cultural communities (Weinbach & Kuehner, 1985). First, older Native Americans avoid services because of past bad experiences with the system. Second, many think that "mental illness is a justifiable outcome of human weakness or the result of avoiding the discipline necessary to maintain cultural values and community respect" (Harras, 1987; Herring, 1999, p. 52). Thus they believe that they do not

need the system, that they should be able to take care of such problems themselves. Other Native Americans who have had experiences with the mental health system note how biased it is concerning Western beliefs, which often clash with traditional cultural values (LaFromboise & Bigfoot, 1988).

Mistrust

Mistrust is a second barrier to people of color receiving mental health treatment (USDHHS, 1999). For example, African Americans' reasons for avoiding the system include not having enough time and being apprehensive about what treatment involves (Sussman, Robins, & Earls, 1987). Many have also experienced racism and discrimination (Primm, Lima, & Rowe, 1996).

Central and South American immigrants and many from Southeast Asia who have experienced oppression and imprisonment, and have even had family members murdered in their countries of origin, fear involvement with any system, including that of mental health services (USDHHS, 1999). Illegal immigrants from Mexico also fear involvement because they dread being deported.

Native Americans have a long history of negative experiences with white mainstream culture. These include facing recurring attempts to squelch their traditional culture and absorb them into the mainstream; being denied U.S. citizenship until 1924; and not having a constitutional right to pursue traditional religious practices until the American Indian Religious Freedom Act of 1978 was passed (Herring, 1999).

Stigma

A *stigma* is a smear of shame and reproach upon one's reputation. People of color often don't want to suffer the stigma of being labeled mentally ill (USDHHS, 1999). Uba (1994) found this to be true of Asian Americans; Sussman and colleagues (1987) did the same for both whites and African Americans. African Americans generally make every effort to combat mental illness themselves, without having to rely on external formal resources (USDHHS, 1999).

Yamashiro and Matsuoka (1997) report that there is a strong tradition of shame regarding mental illness in many API families; because of their collective identity, what one family member does "reflects on the entire family" (p. 466). The mental illness of one family member makes the others feel ashamed, so it makes sense to keep it a secret instead of seeking help.

Cost

Cost is yet another barrier to people of color using mental health services (Dulmus & Roberts, 2008; USDHHS, 1999). We have established that people of color generally have lower incomes than their white counterparts. Not only are they more unlikely than whites to be covered by private health insurance, but even those who have such benefits underutilize services (USDHHS, 1999).

Clinician Bias

EP 2.1.1b

Clinician bias is the fifth barrier to people of color utilizing mental health services (Dulmus & Roberts, 2008; USDHHS, 1999). How the assessing clinician perceives a person's emotional state and behavioral symptoms directly relates to the diagnosis. Clinicians who are unfamiliar with the cultural customs of people having different beliefs, values, and behaviors may well misdiagnose the problem. Behaviors considered appropriate for other cultures might be considered quite inappropriate in Western eyes. For example,

Latino families seem to be more tolerant of unusual behavior, such as hearing voices or having delusions of grandeur, because of the way Latino cultures view religion.... In the Latino culture, people often talk to Jesus and the saints and feel close to spirits, so family members are not as concerned about a patient hearing voices as they are by disruptive or disrespectful behavior.

(*Schram & Mandell, 2000, pp. 176–177*)

Similarly, Earle (1999) indicates that for Seneca Indians "such attributes as having visions and guiding one's life according to spirits may incorrectly appear to be symptoms of a serious mental disorder such as schizophrenia" when they are really expressions of traditional religious practices (p. 434).

Several studies report significant bias on the part of clinicians diagnosing African Americans for schizophrenia and depression; African Americans are much more likely than whites to be diagnosed with schizophrenia and less likely to be diagnosed with depression (Hu, Snowden, Jerrell, & Nguyen, 1991; Lawson, Hepler, Holladay, & Cuffel, 1994; Snowden & Cheung, 1990; USDHHS, 1999).

Highlight 13.7 focuses on what can be done to improve mental health services to people of color.

Macro Perspectives on Cultural Competence

From a macro perspective, say Sue and colleagues (1998), not only do mental health agencies need to "employ individuals with multicultural counseling skills, but the agency itself needs to have a 'multicultural culture'" (p. 103). This involves establishing an organizational environment that celebrates diversity. Administrators should empower staff members by helping them develop and employ culturally

---

HIGHLIGHT 13.7

What Can Be Done to Improve Mental Health Services to People of Color?

EP 2.1.1e, 2.1.4d

An obvious suggestion for improving services for people of color involves all social workers continuously striving to enhance their own cultural competence. Developing guidelines to assist individual social workers in their practice is also helpful (Snowden, 2000). Lum (2003), for example, describes a cultural competence framework for social work that emphasizes four primary dimensions of competence. The first is *cultural awareness*—consciousness of one's own cultural values and "of ethnicity and racism and its impact on professional attitude, perception, and behavior" (p. 31). Second, *knowledge acquisition* is the process of gaining and organizing knowledge to critically think about ethnicity and to better understand its significance. Third, *skill development* involves learning effective ways to communicate with people of other cultures and applying culturally sensitive techniques to improve interventions. Finally, *inductive learning* is the creative quest for new information and the sharing of new ideas with others to enhance practice effectiveness.

competent skills. Agencies should be sensitive to the cultural perspectives of their clients and responsive to their needs.

EP 2.1.6a, 2.1.6b, 2.1.8a, 2.1.10h

Cross, Bazron, Dennis, and Isaacs (1989) describe culturally competent and culturally proficient organizations. *Culturally competent* mental health organizations display "continuing self-assessment regarding culture, careful attention to the dynamics of difference, continuous expansion of cultural knowledge and resources, and a variety of adaptations to service models to better meet the needs of culturally diverse populations" (p. 17). Such agencies have a diverse staff reflecting a range of racial and cultural backgrounds. Administrators and staff have clear ideas about what cultural competence involves. Staff members have frequent opportunities to enhance their level of cultural competence. Any services delivered to specific cultural groups are viewed as a vital part of an agency's total package of programs.

Culturally proficient agencies strive to expand knowledge about cultural competence by "conducting research, developing new therapeutic approaches based on culture, and disseminating the results of demonstration projects" (Cross et al., 1989, p. 17). Few organizations ever reach this level of proficiency. Such organizations serve as dynamic models for creative program development focusing on cultural competence in other programs.

Chapter Summary

The following summarizes this chapter's content as it relates to the chapter's learning objectives presented at the beginning of the chapter. Learning objectives include the following:

A Review the wide range of mental health settings in which social workers practice.

Half of NASW members indicate that mental health is a major context for their practice. A critical concept in mental health treatment is client treatment in the least restrictive setting possible. Mental health settings that employ social workers include inpatient mental and psychiatric hospitals, residential treatment centers for children and adolescents, group homes, psychiatric units in general hospitals, outpatient treatment agencies, employee assistance programs, and community mental health centers, which provide a wide range of services.

B Identify and discuss the range of psychiatric diagnoses for mental health problems.

Diagnoses for psychiatric disorders include dementia, schizophrenia and other psychotic disorders, mood disorders, bipolar disorders, anxiety disorders, dissociative disorders, sexual disorders, eating disorders (including anorexia nervosa and bulimia nervosa), impulse control disorders, and personality disorders. Understanding of and practice with veterans who have posttraumatic stress disorder, an anxiety disorder, is explored.

C Discuss some of the functions social workers perform in mental health settings.

In micro practice social workers can be case managers. They can also provide counseling and crisis intervention, in addition to linking clients with needed resources and providing community education about mental health. MSWs can be psychotherapists. Four examples of therapeutic approaches—existential, person-centered, behavior, and cognitive therapies—are explained. In mezzo practice social workers can run treatment groups and treat families. In macro practice social workers can be advocates for change, function as managers and administrators who can improve policies and service provision, and develop innovative programs to meet mental health needs.

D Recognize some trends in evidence-based practice in mental health.

Trends in evidence-based practice include comprehensive community support, family education and support, work encouragement and assistance, coordinated treatment for concurrent substance abuse issues, and educational and coping skill development groups.

E Examine managed care within the mental health context.

Most of the same issues apply to managed care in mental health as in other health-care settings. Three important concepts are capitation, gatekeeping, and utilization management. There is much pressure on physicians and clinicians to find the least expensive treatment modalities possible for any particular client to minimize cost. Often, this is not in the best interests of the client. It is therefore social workers' responsibility to advocate on their clients' behalf.

F Address the issue of cultural competence in mental health settings, identify barriers many people of color face in accessing services, and suggest ways of improving cultural competence.

Cultural competence, defined as "mastery of a particular set of knowledge, skills, policies, and programs used by the social worker that address the cultural needs of individuals, families, groups, and communities," is just as important in mental health as in other social work settings (Lum, 2005, p. 4). Barriers people of color often face in receiving mental health services include lack of help-seeking behavior, mistrust, stigma, cost, and clinician bias. Cultural competence can be enhanced by developing individual practitioners' skills. It can also be enhanced by culturally competent organizations that celebrate diversity and constantly strive to develop cultural competence throughout the agency.

G Encourage critical thinking about various issues related to mental health.

Critical thinking questions were posed regarding the extent to which the *DSM–IV–TR*'s assessment and labeling system is fair and adequate. Questions were raised about the suitability of several approaches to psychotherapy, the advantages and disadvantages of electroconvulsive therapy, and the advantages, and disadvantages of managed care. Finally, critical thinking questions were proposed regarding whether a national mental health insurance program providing universal coverage should be established.

LOOKING AHEAD

Mental health issues and concerns overlap with many other areas of social work practice. For example, social workers frequently take part in the prevention and treatment of alcohol and other drug abuse. Chapter 14 explores some of the dynamics and treatment approaches involved in that area. Another example of overlap with mental health issues concerns social work in schools and with youths, addressed in Chapter 15. Such practice might focus on group work to address specific issues, the prevention

of school violence, teenage sexual activity, pregnancy, and parenting issues.

COMPETENCY NOTES

The following identifies where Educational Policy (EP) competencies and practice behaviors are discussed in the chapter.

EP 2.1.1 Identify as a professional social worker and conduct oneself accordingly. *(p. 426):* Belonging to professional organizations such as the National Association of Social Workers is part of establishing a professional identity.

EP 2.1.1b Practice personal reflection and self-correction to assure continual professional development. *(p. 426):* Choosing a career involves personal reflection regarding how to pursue the appropriate routes of professional development. *(p. 433):* Practitioners should practice personal reflection and self-correction to address personal bias and provide culturally competent treatment.

EP 2.1.1c Attend to professional roles and boundaries. *(p. 417):* Professional roles involved in mental health practice, including those of case manager, counselor, treatment group leader, and macro practitioner are identified.

EP 2.1.1e Engage in career-long learning. *(p. 427):* Continued education provides a means of career-long learning. *(p. 433):* Developing cultural competence concerning mental health service provision is a career-long learning process.

EP 2.1.2c Tolerate ambiguity in resolving ethical conflicts. *(p. 406):* Questions raised regarding potential shortcomings of the *DSM–IV–TR* require tolerating possible ambiguity when using the manual as a diagnostic tool.

EP 2.1.3 Apply critical thinking to inform and communicate professional judgments. *(p. 406):* Critical thinking questions address the potential shortcomings of the *DSM–IV–TR*. (p. 422): Critical thinking questions encourage thought about the usefulness and relevance of the psychotherapeutic theories discussed here. *(p. 424):* Critical thinking questions are raised regarding the consequences and effectiveness of electroconvulsive therapy. *(p. 430):* Critical thinking questions are posed regarding the intent and effectiveness of managed care. *(p. 431):* Critical thinking questions are raised regarding mental health care and policy.

EP 2.1.3a Distinguish, appraise, and integrate multiple sources of knowledge, including research-based knowledge, and practice wisdom. *(p. 430):* Social workers should appraise and integrate multiple sources of knowledge when evaluating approaches to mental health policy such as managed care.

EP 2.1.4a Recognize the extent to which culture's structures and values may oppress, marginalize, alienate, or create or enhance privilege and power. *(p. 429):* Social workers should recognize how societal structures, policies, and barriers concerning mental health policies and services may oppress or alienate people from various cultures.

EP 2.1.4c Recognize and communicate their understanding of the importance of difference in shaping life experiences. *(p. 406):* The example given in this Highlight portrays how social class shapes life experiences. *(p. 429):* Practitioners should recognize how cultural differences shape life experiences for people regarding their access to and use of mental health services.

EP 2.1.4d View themselves as learners and engage those with whom they work as informants. *(p. 433):* Social workers should view themselves as ongoing learners about cultural differences.

EP 2.1.5b Advocate for human rights and social and economic justice. *(p. 427):* Social workers should advocate for human rights in mental health. *(p. 428):* Practitioners should advocate for improved treatment policies on the behalf of people who have mental disorders. *(p. 430):* Social workers should advocate for managed care practices that respect human rights.

EP 2.1.5c Engage in practices that advance social and economic justice. *(p. 427):* Practitioners should engage in practices that advance social and economic justice in mental health service provision.

EP 2.1.6a Use practice experience to inform scientific inquiry. *(p. 434):* Culturally competent mental health organizations should conduct research based on practice experience with clients.

EP 2.1.6b Use research evidence to inform practice. *(p. 421):* Social workers should utilize research on the effectiveness of various therapeutic approaches with specific problems to inform practice. *(p. 428):* Social workers should employ evidence-based interventions in their mental health practice. *(p. 434):* Social workers should utilize research on the effectiveness of culturally sensitive mental health treatment approaches to improve their practice effectiveness.

EP 2.1.7a Utilize conceptual frameworks to guide the processes of assessment, intervention, and evaluation. *(p. 405):* Social workers and other mental health professionals use the *DSM–IV–TR* as a conceptual framework for assessing and understanding mental health problems. *(p. 418):* Conceptual frameworks are described that can guide the processes of assessment, intervention, and evaluation in mental health treatment.

EP 2.1.7b Critique and apply knowledge to understand person and environment. *(p. 405):* The *DSM–IV–TR* assists social workers and other professionals to understand people's ability to function in their social environment. *(p. 418):* Practitioners should critique and apply knowledge involving psychotherapeutic conceptual frameworks to understand mental health and how people function in their social environment. *(p. 429):* Social workers should critique and apply knowledge about cultural differences to understand how people receive services and care in the mental health service provision environment.

EP 2.1.8a Analyze, formulate, and advocate for policies that advance social well-being. *(p. 427):* Social workers should analyze, formulate, and advocate for policies addressing mental health issues that advance social well-being. *(p. 429):* Social workers should analyze and advocate for policies that advance social well-being. *(p. 434):* Social workers and agencies should advocate for mental health policies that advance social well-being.

EP 2.1.8b Collaborate with colleagues and clients for effective policy action. *(p. 427):* Practitioners can collaborate with colleagues and clients for effective mental health policy action.

EP 2.1.9a Continuously discover, appraise, and attend to changing locales, populations, scientific and technological developments, and emerging societal trends to provide relevant services. *(p. 427):* Practitioners should continuously appraise and attend to changing developments and trends in mental health service provision to provide effective services.

EP 2.1.9b Provide leadership in promoting sustainable changes in service delivery and practice to improve the quality of social services. *(p. 417):* Social workers can serve as leaders in providing and improving mental health service provision. *(p. 427):* Practitioners can serve as leaders in promoting changes to improve the quality of mental health service provision.

EP 2.1.10 Engage, assess, intervene, and evaluate with individuals, families, groups, organizations, and communities. *(p. 413):* Social workers practice with individuals, families and groups. *(p. 417):* Social workers in mental health practice can work with individuals, groups, families, organizations, and communities. *(p. 418):* This and subsequent sections address how social workers intervene with individuals, families, groups, organizations, and communities in mental health practice.

EP 2.1.10b Use empathy and other interpersonal skills. *(p. 401):* Using empathy and other skills when working with clients in a residential treatment center is discussed. *(p. 403):* A case example illustrates the use of empathy and other interpersonal skills.

EP 2.1.10d Collect, organize, and interpret client data. *(p. 418):* Case management includes collecting, organizing, and interpreting client data. *(p. 422):* This case example demonstrates the importance of collecting, organizing, and interpreting client data.

EP 2.1.10e Assess clients' strengths and limitations. *(p. 418):* Facets of case management include assessing client strengths and limitations. *(p. 422):* The worker in the case example assesses the client's strengths and limitations.

EP 2.1.10g Select appropriate intervention strategies. *(p. 410):* Appropriate intervention strategies are discussed for working with veterans with PTSD. *(p. 418):* Case management involves selecting and coordinating appropriate intervention strategies. *(p. 418):* Social workers should select appropriate intervention strategies in micro, mezzo, and macro practice. *(p. 422):* The case example demonstrates

an appropriate intervention strategy using cognitive therapy with a person who has depression. *(p. 428):* This and subsequent sections discuss various macro approaches to intervention in mental health. Practitioners should use research evidence to select appropriate intervention strategies.

EP 2.1.10h Initiate actions to achieve organizational goals. *(p. 434):* Practitioners should strive to achieve the organizational goals of culturally competent agencies.

EP 2.1.10i Implement prevention interventions that enhance client capacities. *(p. 410):* Therapeutic approaches are discussed to help veterans prevent symptoms of PTSD.

EP 2.1.10j Help clients resolve problems. *(p. 410):* Interventions are proposed to help veterans with PTSD and their families resolve problems. *(p. 418):* Social workers serving as case managers help clients resolve problems. *(p. 418):* Social workers use micro, mezzo, and macro approaches to help clients address and resolve mental health problems. *(p. 422):* The case example illustrates how the social worker helped her client resolve problems. *(p. 428):* Various macro approaches are identified in this and subsequent sections regarding how to help clients resolve mental health problems.

EP 2.1.10k Negotiate, mediate, and advocate for clients. *(p. 428):* Social workers should advocate on the behalf of clients who have mental disorders. *(p. 429):* Social workers should advocate for effective mental health services for clients.

EP 2.1.10m Critically analyze, monitor, and evaluate interventions. *(p. 418):* A major aspect of case management entails ongoing analysis, monitoring, and evaluation of intervention. *(p. 424):* The effectiveness of electroconvulsive therapy is discussed and evaluated.

FOR FURTHER EXPLORATION ON THE INTERNET

See this text's Social Work CourseMate website at *www.cengagebrain.com* for learning tools such as chapter quizzing, videos, glossary, flashcards, and more.

CHAPTER 14

Social Work and Substance Use, Abuse, and Dependence

Janine Wiedel/Photo Library/Alamy

Jeremy has been using crystal meth for almost 10 years now. At first, he used it because it made him feel hyper-energized. Having been a shy, insecure teenager, meth changed his social life as it made him popular with other users. It made him feel heroic and important. Gradually, he found himself running out of money. Drugs are expensive when you use them a lot. At first, he couldn't pay the phone bill; then it was the rent. Then he lost his car. His wife left him and won't let him see his two kids at all anymore. The rest of his family is sick of him. Now he's homeless unless he can find somewhere to crash. He's barely got more than the clothes on his back. He's surviving by eating free meals for homeless people and transients at places like the Salvation Army's soup kitchen. He steals whatever he can to sell and rips people off whenever he has the chance because he has to buy his meth. His body is emaciated and his teeth are rotting. He doesn't think he's going to make it much longer.

Eva is a 42-year-old air traffic controller who likes to fly in her spare time. The problem is that she likes to fly without a plane. Eva's substance of choice is cocaine, which she freebases. Her mottoes since high school are 'Party hearty' and 'Life is too short to be sober.' How she became an air traffic controller with this attitude and lifestyle choice remains a mystery. Somehow, she has been able to do her job and keep her drug use separate from her career.

Eva started to use illicit drugs when she was 14. Although her parents raised her with strong Mormon values in a small-town Utah home environment, Eva rebelled hard when she became a teenager. When her parents first discovered her drug use they threatened to ground her for life. Eva took off and moved in with a hippie cousin [who amazingly still existed as a 'hippie'] in the big town, Salt Lake City (Barsky, 2006, p. 28).

Stephanie is a college junior who majors in education and loves to "party." She has been known to label herself a "party animal." She goes out drinking almost every night (after some studying, of course). She drank occasionally at parties during high school and even got drunk a dozen or two times. When she first got to college, she limited herself to going out and "getting plastered" only on Friday and Saturday nights. However, as time goes by, she's found herself wanting to go out every night.

She has fun, all right. But twice last month she found herself waking up in bed with some guy she didn't remember ever seeing before. Those guys were pretty "sleazy-looking," too. How embarrassing! Each time she surely got out of there in a hurry. She hopes she remembered to use condoms.

After all, she's doing okay in school. Sure, her grades have slumped a little bit. She's dropped from a B+ to a straight C average. But that's because the older she gets, the more difficult her courses get. For example, that stats course is pure misery. She often tells herself she's doing fine.

She's not crazy about the headaches she has most mornings. It takes her a while to get going. But she's only missed six or seven mornings of class since the semester started. She's doing okay. She surely isn't an alcoholic or anything like that.

The problem is that as she was driving from one bar to another the other night, a cop (who must've come out of the Twilight Zone because she surely didn't see him) busted her for drunk driving. Rats. What a bummer. What a fine. She also has to take a series of drug education courses, which surely is not fun either.

The preceding vignettes depict illustrations of people who use alcohol or other drugs. It is estimated that 9.1% of the U.S. population, or 22.2 million people, abuse or are dependent on some mind-altering substance; of these, over 69% involve alcohol use, over 16% illicit drug use, and the remaining almost 15% use of both (Straussner & Isralowitz, 2008). Clearly, alcohol and other drug use poses a big problem for many people and their families.

**EP 2.1.1c,
2.1.7b**

Social workers need knowledge and understanding about substance abuse, also referred to as alcohol and other drug abuse *(AODA) or* alcohol and other drug *(AOD) problems, for two basic reasons. First, social workers are "involved in the prevention and treatment of substance abuse work in a variety of settings, including health facilities, inpatient and outpatient substance abuse treatment centers, mental health centers, schools, and in the workplace ... [They are also] involved in many aspects of substance abuse treatment, including planning and program development, diagnosis and assessment, information and referral, counseling, and program evaluation" (Gibelman, 2005, pp. 243–244). Many social workers specialize in AODA treatment and provide AODA counseling to clients and their families.*

A second reason for needing some background in AODA involves social workers' role as referral agents. Even if they don't work in such a specialized AODA setting, they will still probably have clients or family members of clients with alcohol and drug problems. Thus, they must be capable of making appropriate referrals to relevant occupational, health, employment, and social services in addition to helping clients navigate these complex systems.

Alcohol and other drug abuse is often masked by and interrelated to many other problems:

> The addicted person may seek help in a medical setting, a crisis clinic, a mental health agency, a family service agency, or from a private practitioner or a public assistance agency. In the medical setting, the presenting problem may be pancreatitis, liver disease, traumatic injury, or broken bones. In the mental health setting, the person may present depression, suicidal feelings, self-destructive behavior, anxiety, psychotic symptoms, or problems associated with an organic brain syndrome. Each of these problems may be the result of alcoholism or drug addiction. (Raskin & Daley, 1991, p. 25)

Thus, in almost any practice setting, a social worker may need to address AODA problems.

Learning Objectives

A   Review common definitions used in the AODA field.

B   Describe the substances involved in abuse and dependence and their methods of administration.

C   Explore common defense mechanisms and family relationships of substance abusers.

D   Explain major aspects of the treatment process for substance abuse and dependence.

E   Identify community resources for people who abuse substances.
F   Compare two treatment models for substance abusers.
G   Pose critical thinking questions that address the dynamics of substance abuse and compare treatment models.

Definitions in Alcohol and Other Drug Abuse

Language commonly used in substance abuse intervention tends to revolve around the terms *alcohol*, *drug*, and *substance* (often referred to as *psychoactive substance*). In everyday usage the term *alcohol* refers to any type of fermented or distilled liquor containing alcohol, such as whiskey or beer. *Drug* refers to a wide range of materials that alter mood or consciousness when ingested, including amphetamines, cannabis, cocaine, and hallucinogens. *Substance* is commonly used to refer to mind-altering drugs, including alcohol (hence the term *alcohol and other substance abuse*). In the context of abuse described here, the terms *substance* and *drug* are often used interchangeably (Straussner & Isrolowitz, 2008). Several other terms used in conjunction with alcohol, drugs, and substances are *dependence*, *tolerance*, *withdrawal*, *abuse*, *intoxication*, *alcoholism*, *alcoholic*, and *addiction*.

EP 2.1.7a

The *Diagnostic and Statistical Manual of Mental Disorders (DSM–IV–TR)*, published by the American Psychiatric Association (APA, 2000), defines *substance dependence* as "a cluster of cognitive, behavioral, and physiological symptoms" resulting from continued use of a substance despite significant resulting problems (p. 192). (Sometimes substance dependence is referred to as *chemical dependence.*) It occurs when three or more of the following happen within one year:

1. Tolerance of the substance increases. *Tolerance* is "resistance to the drug's effects developed over time as the body adapts to the repeated administration of a chemical compound" (Doweiko, 2009, p. 467). As a result, the user requires increasing doses of the substance to reach the same level of mood alteration initially achieved.

2. Withdrawal occurs. *Withdrawal* is the array of symptoms that develop as a result of discontinued use of the substance or the compulsion to absorb the substance to avert these symptoms. Despite discontinued use, the user still craves the substance. Withdrawal symptoms may include severe abdominal pain, convulsions, anxiety attacks, depression, and uncontrollable trembling.

3. The user takes greater amounts of the substance over a longer period than he or she meant to.

4. The user expresses an ongoing desire or failed attempts to decrease or control substance use.

5. The user spends large amounts of time participating in activities aimed at obtaining or using the substance and recuperating from its aftermath.

6. The user curtails or avoids significant social, work, or recreational involvement due to substance use.

7. The user continues to use the substance despite being aware that the substance is causing or intensifying physical or psychological difficulties.

The *DSM–IV–TR* defines *substance abuse* as "a maladaptive pattern of substance use manifested by recurrent and significant adverse consequences related to the repeated use of substances" (APA, 2000, pp. 198–199). This is reflected by one or more of the following criteria in any 12-month period:

1. Repeated failure to accomplish major work, educational, or social responsibilities due to substance use.

2. Repeated use of the substance at times when it could cause physical harm (such as when driving).

3. Repeated use of the substance that results in legal problems (such as tickets for driving under the substance's influence or arrests for disorderly conduct).

4. Continued use of the substance despite the fact that it causes frequent interpersonal problems.

The *DSM–IV–TR* adds one other criterion for abuse—namely, it involves people who have never been diagnosed with substance dependence. Substance *abuse* might be regarded as "less problematic" than substance *dependence* because many of the physical and psychological symptoms associated with *dependence* are not yet evident (Barker, 2003, p. 422).

Intoxication, linked to drug abuse and dependence, is the development of a series of symptoms, often involving psychological or behavioral changes, directly related to intake of the substance and its influence on the central nervous system. Specific symptoms may include inability to think clearly, distorted perception, temporary euphoria, and impaired motor functioning.

Alcoholism is "a chronic disorder characterized by repeated excessive use of alcoholic beverages and decreased ability to function socially and vocationally" (Nichols, 1999, p. 31). *Alcoholics* are people who suffer from alcoholism. *Addiction* is a term referring to dependence on some substance, having the same consequences as those already described; the term *substance dependence* is now commonly replacing *addiction* (Barker, 2003).

Professionals working with alcohol and other substance abusers may be referred to as *substance abuse, AODA,* or *chemical dependence counselors.* Practitioners counseling people who abuse or are dependent on alcohol may be called *alcoholism* or *alcohol abuse counselors.*

With respect to substance use problems, in everyday usage the term *abuse* often is used to include symptoms evident in the technical definitions of both abuse and dependence. Similarly, the line between abuse and dependence is often not clearly distinct. Many of the dynamics are similar or identical. Therefore, in our ensuing discussion we will use the terms *abuse* and *dependence* interchangeably.

Note that people often have a substance of choice. That is, they prefer the type of mood alterations produced by one drug over that produced by another. For instance, one person may prefer beer over cocaine. Another person may feel just the opposite. Note that there are many similarities between alcohol abuse and dependence and other drug abuse and dependence in terms of the psychological and interpersonal dynamics (APA, 2000).

The following section addresses *pharmacology,* "the effects of the various drugs on the human body" (Johnson, 2004, p. 28). It's important to understand this to comprehend the dynamics and driving forces involved in AOD abuse and dependence.

AOD Substances Causing Abuse and Dependence

A wide range of mind-altering substances can lead to abuse and dependence. These include central nervous system (CNS) stimulants, CNS depressants, and other mind-altering substances. Before describing the specific drugs, we will discuss the ways in which they may be ingested.

EP 2.1.7b

Methods of Administration

There are four major means of administering mind-altering substances; oral consumption, inhalation or smoking, injection, or ingestion via mucous membranes (Johnson, 2004). Except for alcohol, all drugs can be administered in more than one way. Sometimes, the means of ingestion can give you clues regarding the scope of the problem; for example, if a person "uses needles to inject cocaine, this can be a reliable indicator that he or she has, or is about to develop, serious problems" (Johnson, 2004, p. 33).

Oral Ingestion

Oral consumption of a drug involves drinking or swallowing it. Such ingestion takes the most time because the stomach and intestine must absorb the drug into the bloodstream before it can affect the brain (Abadinsky, 2011). Subsequently, unlike other types of ingestion, user attributes may influence the drug's effects (Johnson, 2004). For example, if the drug is taken on a full stomach, it will take longer to produce effects than when consumed on an empty stomach.

Inhalation or Smoking

Another common method of drug ingestion is inhalation or smoking. This is an efficient and fast means of getting an effect because the lungs are filled with tiny blood vessels that absorb the drug rapidly. The blood then quickly delivers the drug directly to the brain, which experiences its effects within a few seconds. "Most drugs of abuse can be smoked (cocaine, heroin, or marijuana) or inhaled (common household chemicals, gasoline, or model glue). The drug that is most commonly used in this manner is nicotine" (Johnson, 2004, p. 34).

Injection

Another common means of drug ingestion involves injecting the drug directly into the bloodstream, usually via a vein (Johnson, 2004). This method also allows the substance to sidestep the digestive process and proceed directly to the brain, thereby producing nearly immediate, concentrated effects.

Johnson (2004) suggests that you can observe people's behavior to determine if they're injecting drugs. For example, people who wear long-sleeved shirts on a hot summer day "may be trying to hide needle tracks" (p. 34).

Mucous Membranes

Johnson (2004) explains how drugs can be ingested using mucous membranes and how the method of ingestion provides clues concerning related physical problems:

Another route of administration is saturation of mucous membranes, allowing a drug to dissolve into the bloodstream....

Most commonly known as "snorting," this route of administration is quicker than drinking/swallowing, but slower than either inhalation or injection. Users chop a drug into fine power and quickly inhale it into the nose. Powder cocaine is commonly used this way; however, most drugs can be snorted. Any drug that can be crushed into powder can be snorted. Many people choose to snort heroin instead of injecting it. People also use the mucous membranes in the eye (LSD), genital areas, and the rectum via suppositories.

A client's chosen route of administration is important assessment information. Not only does it provide clues about the potential seriousness of the drug use, but also about medical issues that may require attention. For example, people who drink heavily often irritate the inside of the mouth, esophagus, and stomach lining. People who smoke or inhale drugs often develop lung infections, oral infections, or impaired breathing. IV drug users can develop a number of dangerous health problems, and those who regularly snort drugs can severely damage their nasal passages and sinuses. [Nosebleeds provide a clue concerning this practice.] (p. 35)

Types of Mind-Altering Substances

One way of dividing up mind-altering substances is to categorize them as CNS stimulants, CNS depressants, and other addictive substances (Dziegielewski, 2005; Johnson, 2004). Dziegielewski (2005) explains:

A psychoactive substance is any substance that directly affects the normal functioning of the central nervous system. Stimulants are psychoactive substances that boost the functioning of the central nervous system. Taking these substances usually causes excessive stimulation to the central nervous system that can result in medical problems such as increased heart rate, increased blood pressure, insomnia, decreased need for sleep, and decreased appetite....

Amphetamines and their more potent amphetamine derivatives, methamphetamines (aka meth, ice, speed, and crank) and cocaine (aka freebase and crack).... are often considered "top shelf" or "top of the line" stimulants. Although individuals addicted to these strong substances often experience dilated pupils and easily become angry and aggressive, reactions to use are unpredictable. Sometimes the individual may feel more confident, eager, and outgoing. At other times, particularly as the dosages increase, these feelings may change to paranoia, anxiety, an inability to experience pleasure (anhedonea), and confusion....

Caffeine and nicotine ... are known as "bottom shelf" stimulants. Although these stimulants are considered weaker and less dangerous, [they may still have significant effects] ... For example, repeated and excessive use of caffeine can lead to problems similar to those created by the stronger stimulants....

Furthermore, use of tobacco, the source of nicotine, is responsible for more than 400,000 deaths in the United States each year (p. 53)....[Nicotine is] highly addictive. (p. 105)

One of the so-called club drugs, ecstasy is also a stimulant (National Institute on Drug Abuse [NIDA], 2010b). Ecstasy, which has "psychedelic" properties, produces mental stimulation, enhanced energy and sensory perception, and, potentially, nausea and muscle cramping (NIDA, 2010b).

FOCUS ON CRITICAL THINKING 14.1

The Dynamics of Substance Use and Abuse

EP 2.1.3

The use of alcohol and other drugs is running rampant. Many issues and questions are involved. Current government policy regarding alcohol and drug problems emphasizes and funds three strategies—"Prevention, Treatment, and Enforcement" (Burke, 2008, p. 132).

Critical Thinking Questions

- What do you think are the reasons so many people use mind-altering substances—escape from a hectic, high-pressured reality, peer pressure, fun?
- Are you familiar with people who use alcohol and/or other drugs frequently? What do you think are their reasons for use?
- What, if anything, do you think should be done about substance abuse and dependence? New stricter laws and penalties? Prohibition? Legalization of currently illegal substances? Prevention through education?
- Where should public funding be focused—on prevention, treatment, or enforcement?

Dziegielewski (2005) describes depressants:

Depressants *are psychoactive substances that suppress, slow, or relax the central nervous system. The most commonly used major depressants are alcohol ... and the sedatives and hypnotics such as prescription painkillers. [Other examples of depressants are barbiturates, Xanax, Valium, and Quaaludes (NIDA, 2008).] Some of these substances, when used to the advantage of the individual, can have great social or therapeutic value....*

When depressants are misused or abused, the outcome can be disastrous.... Medical problems that often occur when the central nervous system becomes depressed range from mild sedation to breathing cessation to coma and possible death. (p. 123) *[emphasis added]*

The club drugs GHB and Rohypnol (also known as "roofies") are depressants (NIDA, 2010a). GHB (Xyrem) was approved in 2002 for treatment of a sleep disorder, but with severely restricted use; Rohypnol (flunitrazepam) is similar to sedatives such as Valium or Xanax, but is not legally approved for use in the United States (NIDA, 2010a). Both have been known as "date rape drugs" because they "can sedate and incapacitate unsuspecting victims, preventing them from resisting sexual assault" (NIDA, 2010a).

Other commonly used addictive drugs that don't fit into the stimulant or depressant categories include the following (NIDA, 2008):

- *Cannabinoids*, including hashish and marijuana, produce euphoria, slowed thinking, impaired coordination, confusion, and sometimes anxiety.
- *Dissociative anesthetics*, including ketamine (Special K) and PCP, can cause increased heart rate and blood pressure, slowed motor functioning, memory loss, and, potentially, nausea. PCP can cause aggression and depression.
- *Hallucinogens*, including LSD, mescaline (peyote), and psyilocybin (magic mushroom), result in unpredictably altered mental states, distorted perception, hallucinations, and, sometimes, flashbacks.
- *Opioids and morphine derivatives*, including heroin, morphine, and opium, cause euphoria, pain relief, drowsiness, and, potentially, coma and death.

Focus on Critical Thinking 14.1 raises some questions about why people use any of the wide range of drugs described here.

People Who Use Alcohol and Other Drugs

Historically, the concept of drug abuse and dependence was based on the medical model (i.e., it was considered a disease with the cure being abstinence). However, more current thought views drug abuse and dependence as a more complex problem that can be analyzed from a range of theoretical perspectives having their respective treatment approaches (Doweiko, 2012; Johnson, 2004; Velleman, 2001; Wood & Dunn, 2000).

People who use and abuse substances can't be categorized at fixed

points on a substance use continuum. . . . Only the end points—total abstinence and active physical addiction to a chemical(s), remain relatively fixed. One very real advantage of a drug use continuum is that it allows for the classification of various intensities and patterns of substance use. Drug use/abuse/addiction thus becomes a behavior with a number of possible intermediate steps between the two extreme points of total abstinence and physical addiction, not a "condition" that either is or is not present.

(Doweiko, 2009, p. 8)

Velleman (2001) suggests that a better term for substance abuse and dependence is a *substance problem*, defined as follows—"if someone's [consumption of a substance] . . . causes problems for him or her, or for someone else, in any area of their lives, then that [consumption] . . . is problematic"; this includes problems with "health, finances, the law, work, friends, or relationships" (p. 3).

Figure 14.1 reflects how people may fall anywhere on a continuum involving how much of the substance they ingest and how many problems it causes them. Of course, the legal issues involved in consuming illegal substances must also be considered and addressed.

Most people who use alcohol and other drugs do so on a social basis and consume socially acceptable amounts that do not result in drunkenness or total loss of control (Dunn, 2000). Problems arise for people who lose control of their consumption and become increasingly dependent on the substance's effects. Kingery-McCabe and Frances (1991) stress that each individual responds differently to alcohol and other substance dependence in terms of severity of physical and psychological effects and the length of time it takes to become dependent. Highlight 14.1 discusses common defense mechanisms employed by people who are substance dependent.

AOD Abuse and Dependence Affects Family Relationships

AOD abuse and dependence are family system problems (Doweiko, 2012; Johnson, 2004; Paulus, 2000). That is, the problem affects the entire family; what happens to one family member affects all others.

People living in such families "live in a whirlwind" of stress and crisis (Perkinson, 2008, p. 242). Their lives focus on the abuser's substance-related behavior, whether it's coming home drunk or stoned, throwing up or hitting them, losing jobs and money, failing to carry through with any range of responsibilities, breaking promises, or embarrassing them in front of friends and neighbors.

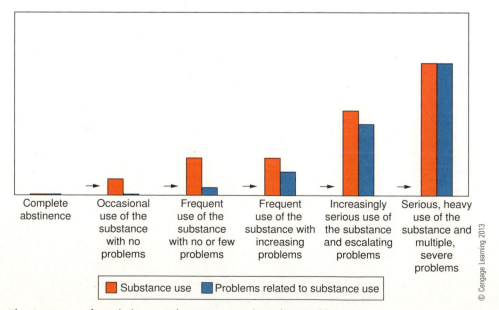

© Cengage Learning 2013

Figure 14.1 The Continuum of Mind-altering Substance Use and Resulting Problems

HIGHLIGHT 14.1

Common Defense Mechanisms

People who abuse alcohol or other drugs typically adopt a series of defense mechanisms to protect themselves from having to deal with the problems caused by substance dependence. These include "minimization," "denial," and "rationalization" (Perkinson, 2008, p. 99). Each mechanism helps the person avoid taking responsibility for his or her behavior.

Minimization means assigning little importance to drug use or its consequences. The individual "distorts reality and makes it smaller than it actually is" (Perkinson, 2008, p. 99). The user will minimize the amount of the substance actually consumed by referring to it as being a smaller amount than it actually is. Minimization may also involve indicating that substance consumption actually had a lesser impact on behavior, a situation, or life in general than it actually did. Here the addicted person acknowledges that consumption is occurring but admits to very little and tries to make it unimportant. For example, an alcoholic might fill a 10-ounce glass halfway with whiskey instead of pouring it into a much smaller shot glass. This becomes "just one drink." Or an alcoholic might say, "I really don't drink that much," even though he drinks three six-packs of beer a night. Or, "I just have a snort or two of blow [cocaine] a day" when she really snorts up to a dozen times daily.

Rationalization involves making excuses for the problems caused by the dependence on the substance. For example, an alcoholic might say to herself, "I really didn't flunk that exam because I had a hangover; the professor made the questions much harder than she said she would," or "It's been a rotten day. I deserve a drink or two," or, perhaps, "a couple of joints."

Denial, the most prevalent defense used by people who are substance dependent, involves insisting to oneself that nothing's wrong. There's no problem. Denial distorts reality so you just don't see the truth. An alcoholic who drinks a fifth of cheap vodka or 12 cans of beer a day might say to himself, "I don't really have to drink." Or a substance user might ignore his wife's complaints about spending money on booze or drugs or being verbally abusive to her when drunk or high. If you don't think about a problem, it doesn't exist: out of sight, out of mind.

Numerous social and relationship problems result from alcohol and other substance abuse. They include marital and family difficulties, disruptions in friendships, trouble in work and school performance, accidents when operating vehicles, and being arrested for crimes committed while under the influence.

Alcohol or another substance of choice (i.e., the preferred substance) becomes the abuser's "best friend." It is something the abuser can always depend on. The effects are pleasantly predictable, and the abuser can escape from life's stresses whenever he or she wants. People can disappoint or place pressure on you, but a drug always acts the same.

Themes Characterizing Families of Substance Abusers

At least eight themes characterize the families of people who are substance dependent. First, the abuser's use of his or her substance of choice becomes the "most important thing in the family's life" (Johnson, 2004; Wegscheider, 1981, p. 81). Because the abuser's top goal is getting enough of the substance, other family members must structure their own behavior around this.

Second, family members strive to keep the family together even when conditions are deteriorating due to the abuser's behavior (Johnson, 2004; Wegscheider, 1981). The unknown is scary. At least they know what the current conditions are, regardless of how bad.

Third, family members often act as *enablers* for the abuser's substance use (Perkinson, 2008; Wegscheider, 1981). Enablers assume increasing responsibility for maintaining family functioning and making excuses on the abuser's behalf (e.g., calling in sick for the abuser at work when the real problem is a terrible hangover). In essence, this role enables the dependent person to continue consuming the substance, yet assume less and less responsibility for the consequences of that behavior.

Fourth, "family members often feel tremendous guilt. They think that they are at fault. The addicted person keeps denying responsibility, and someone must be held accountable, so the family members often take the blame" (Perkinson, 2008, p. 243).

Fifth, family members often "do not know what they want. Their lives are centered around the addicted individual. They only know what the addict wants. That is the focus of attention. Most family members are trying to hold onto their sanity and to keep themselves, and the family, from going under" (Perkinson, 2008, p. 244).

Sixth, "family members feel worthless. They feel as though no one cares for how they feel or for what they want. They feel profoundly inadequate and unlovable ... and somehow they feel as though ... it is all their fault anyway. This would not be happening to them if they were better persons. This is all they deserve. This is the best they can get" (Perkinson, 2008, p. 245).

Seventh, family members don't trust others (Perkinson, 2008). They have been disappointed so many times by the dependent person's behavior that they can't afford to dream about things getting better. They avoid discussing the problem with others inside or outside the family. They don't want to rock the boat.

Eighth, family members "have poor communication skills. They learned a long time ago the credo of the addicted family: 'Don't talk, don't trust, and don't feel.' These individuals do not talk to their friends or other family members. They are cut off from everyone. They feel afraid of open communication. If they talked openly, then the truth might come out and the family would be destroyed" (Perkinson, 2008, p. 245).

The Treatment Process

**EP 2.1.10a,
2.1.10b,
2.1.10c**

There are numerous theoretical treatment approaches to chemical dependence (Connors, Donovan, & DiClemente, 2001). However, at least five principles are important regardless of the treatment approach or program (Johnson, 2004).

Engagement

First, engagement with the social worker in a positive and supportive relationship is essential for successful treatment. Boyle (2000) elaborates:

Engagement is the process of building and maintaining a productive relationship with the client. It is the interaction between the client and clinician that results in both being motivated to work collaboratively to achieve mutually agreed upon goals. ... It should be emphasized that engagement involves both the client and clinician. It is not the sole responsibility of the client to become engaged; it is also the responsibility of the clinician to motivate the client to become engaged.

It is important to remember that an engaged client is more than one who is punctual and attends all scheduled sessions. An engaged client is one who actively participates in both the selection of therapeutic goals and in each therapeutic activity. In other words, an engaged client is one who is invested in the entire treatment process. (p. 144)

Assessment

A second principle important in treatment involves a thorough assessment of the problem. Taylor (2005) states that the initial assessment interview should have two goals in addition to engaging the client. One is to "assess and evaluate the presenting complaints," and the other to "determine the best course of treatment." Miller (2005) describes the assessment process:

**EP 2.1.10d,
2.1.10e**

One way to approach an assessment process fairly is to tell the client that information will be drawn from numerous sources and that a pattern of behaviors will be looked for throughout the assessment process. The client will have an awareness from the beginning, then, that not only will his or her story be a source of information but also other avenues of information will be sought. ...

In the interview process, the counselor needs to ask the client what the client sees as the presenting problem. Although this answer may be different from the answer of the referral source (if the referral source is different from the client [for example, a spouse or an employer]) it may assist the counselor in determining the client's level of concern with his or her alcohol/drug use. In addition, gathering information about the client's family of origin, particularly around history of addiction, may be beneficial to the assessment process. Finally, knowledge of the client's living situation may underscore some environmental factors (e.g., roommate's usage) that are influencing client use and may be possible sources for relapse if it is determined that the client has an alcohol/drug problem. As to the chemical use history, a counselor should find out the date of the client's last use, drug of choice, drugs that have been used, prior treatments for abuse and addiction problems, and any consequences for using drugs (legal; family, significant others, friends; job, school, military; medical; financial; etc.).... The reported date of last use can provide the counselor with helpful baseline information for possible confrontation later in the interview. For example, the client may say he drinks only a couple of beers once a week on Fridays, yet he may say he had four mixed drinks on Tuesday....

When taking drug history information, the counselor should note the age of the client's first use and the age of last use for each drug reported. Then, for each drug, the counselor should examine the typical use pattern and the most recent typical use pattern (including how much, how often, use setting, and administration route). For example, a woman may have increased her marijuana usage to daily at the time of a divorce for about 2 years, even though she had been smoking marijuana once a week for 10 years, and in the past year (3 years since her divorce) she has smoked it only once a month. This provides an indication that she probably used the marijuana as a way to cope with the stress of her divorce. (pp. 33–35)

Note that many assessment mechanisms are available to administer to assist in the assessment process. Highlight 14.2 provides some examples of questions that may be asked during an assessment interview.

Multiple-System Approach to Individualized Treatment

EP 2.1.10, 2.1.10b, 2.1.10g

A third principle involved in the treatment of substance dependence is that a multiple-system approach should be used. That is, an individualized treatment plan should be developed to address the "client's unique needs, issues, and strengths"; the practitioner might "provide individual, group, or family treatment, engage the client's local community if needed, and provide access to specialty services such as vocational, recreational,

or spiritual counseling when appropriate" (Johnson, 2004, pp. 291–292).

Burman (2000) comments on individualized and group treatment modalities:

Individual counseling, although provided less frequently than group sessions in most agencies, provides an intimate and personal forum for self-disclosure. Often it is used as a preliminary introduction to and preparation for the group setting. The skills of reflective listening [an interviewing technique where social workers or counselors translate what they think the client is feeling into words], making inquiries and giving feedback to encourage self-expression and exploration, reframing [helping the client view a problem or issue with a different outlook or understand it in a different way] and restructuring the client's statements to provide new meaning or interpretations, summarizing key points, and affirming and supporting self-efficacy [a person's confidence in his or her ability to address issues and cope with problems] through the process can increase motivation toward problem solving and productive change....

[Regarding intervention with groups,] traditional strategies in substance abuse groups often have had a confrontational focus for the purpose of targeting denial and rationalization processes (Milkman & Sederer, 1990). This technique can be beneficial to some clients, but may have a detrimental effect on others, particularly if their self-esteem is fragile and vulnerable in reaction to what may be overly harsh and ego-deflating tactics. Yet, the curative dimensions of groups can have a powerful effect on instilling hope, optimism, and increased motivation for individuals struggling with addictive behaviors and their consequences. The recovery process is advanced through the group dynamics of sharing similar experiences and traumas, gaining constructive feedback and support for problem solving and change, feeling that one is not alone with his or her dilemmas, securing a sense of belonging and camaraderie, and the encouragement and inspiration to "make it" from others with longer-term sobriety (serving as role models). (p. 209)

We have established that family relationships and functioning are critically important parts of a substance-dependent person's life. Work with the

HIGHLIGHT 14.2

Potential Questions During an Assessment Interview

Taylor (2005) proposes potential questions to ask about a client during a substance abuse or dependence assessment. They focus on the following seven basic areas.

EP 2.1.3c

Denial

- What is getting in the way of the client accepting that there is a drug/alcohol abuse problem?
- What are the client's mood and feelings? . . .
- In what methods does the client engage to blame others concerning his/her problems? . . .
- How is the client affecting the lives of others? . . .

Esteem

- How does the client view himself/herself?
- What is the client's self-image? . . .
- What happens when the client experiences feelings of worthlessness? . . .
- What are the client's best assets? . . .

Confusion

- What happens when the client recognizes that his/her life is out of control?
- What happens when the client loses self-control over his/her drinking/drugging?
- How often has the client experienced a loss of memory resulting from the abuse of drugs and/or alcohol? . . .
- What experiences did the client have as a result of his/her first arrest and confinement [e.g., for drunk driving, disorderly conduct, injury]? . . .

Loss of Significant Resources

- What is the client's state of health?
- Does the client experience any difficulties in his/her sex life?
- Does the client have any difficulties in the workplace resulting from drug/alcohol abuse? . . .
- What values does the client cherish the most? . . .

Acceptance . . .

- Does the client admit to having a problem with drugs/alcohol?
- What caused the client to seek treatment? . . .
- What, if any, plans does the client have for the future? . . .
- What expectations does the client have about treatment? . . .

Resolution . . .

- What level of commitment is the client willing to give?
- Does the client believe that there is any hope for him/her? . . .
- How will the client live without the use of drugs and/or alcohol?
- What goals, if any, has the client established?

Entry [into treatment] . . .

- Who, if anyone, is supportive of the client? . . .
- What plans has the client considered making in an effort to change his/her lifestyle?
- What problems does the client foresee? . . .
- How will the client monitor himself/herself? (pp. 41–43)

abuser's family can be a major focus of treatment. Green, Dziegielewski, & Turnage (2005) explain:

According to the family system perspective, successful treatment of alcoholism [or other drug dependence] requires a multidimensional approach involving the abuser, his or her family, and the environment. The . . . addicted individual is viewed as a human system that requires more than one intervention approach, often in combination. The family

is viewed as a set of interconnected individuals acting together to maintain a homeostatic balance. The basic premise of this model is to allow each member of the family to achieve a higher level of functioning and emotional security (Curtis, 1999). The view of the family as a system is essential to accomplishing the intended outcome. The . . . addicted individual does not exist in a vacuum. Rather, he or she is a living, breathing, interacting element of his or her environment and the environment of his or her family. An exclusionary observation of the person, without consideration of these other factors, is impossible. (p. 141)

Therefore, "family treatment interventions...can elicit resilience and healing in family members" (Van Wormer & Davis, 2008, p. 383).

Follow-Up

EP 2.1.10m

The fourth principle involved in the treatment of substance abuse and dependence is follow-up care after the primary treatment has ceased. This is critical to maintain progress and avoid relapse.

The Importance of a Social Support Network

The fifth treatment principle is that "clients need help in developing a social network" of "people or groups to call upon for support, guidance, and recreation" (Johnson, 2004, p. 292). These might include "12-step meetings, church groups, sober friends, family members, and other sources" (p. 292). Such a network helps them maintain control of their gains by providing "social and recreational outlets that replace key elements" in a lifestyle sustaining abuse or dependence (p. 292). The next section identifies a range of community resources that are available for addicts and their families.

Resources for the Treatment of Addiction to Alcohol and Other Substances

EP 2.1.10g

The following are some of the resources that are available for alcohol and other drug abusers (Doweiko, 2012; Johnson, 2004; Lewis, Dana, & Blevins, 2011):

1. *Detoxification* "is short-term treatment designed to oversee the client's safe withdrawal from the substance to which he or she is addicted" (Lewis et al., 2011, p. 21). Clients may participate in an inpatient or outpatient program (both described here) overseen by medical personnel and professional counselors (Doweiko, 2012; Lewis et al., 2011). The severity of withdrawal symptoms is one factor to consider when choosing the appropriate program.

2. *Outpatient treatment* is received by clients who participate in a program without staying overnight at a treatment facility. "The outpatient substance abuse rehabilitation program might best be defined as (a) a formal treatment program involving one or more professionals, (b) designed to help clients address their SUD [substance use disorder] and maintain a recovery program, (c) which will utilize a variety of treatment approaches (psycho-educational, family and marital therapies, individual and group therapy formats), which is (d) designed to do so on an outpatient basis" (Doweiko, 2012, p. 388). This means that people who are drug dependent can remain in their own homes and still have services available to them. Programs vary greatly regarding types of treatment involved and the extent of daily or weekly involvement.

3. *Inpatient treatment* offers "a more intensive approach than outpatient treatment programs.... Such programs thus usually work with the resistant client, suicidal or homicidal clients, or clients who are unable to abstain in the less restrictive outpatient treatment programs... Many residential treatment programs have a strong 12-step [described in Highlight 14.3] group orientation, with clients being expected to attend multiple 12-step meetings during the week. They utilize a large number of group therapy meetings within each week, supplemented by individual therapy sessions with specialized treatment professionals as indicated. The client will meet with the case manager at least once a week, and usually more often than this as treatment issues are identified. Barriers to recovery are identified, including an assessment of the client's support system, client's level of motivation, and past treatment history" (Doweiko, 2012, p. 391). Thus, inpatient treatment provides a comprehensive, structured environment that maximizes control of the treatment process.

4. *Therapeutic communities* are residential programs where clients remain for one to three years, although some require only a six-month stay. Their intent is to immerse clients in an environment aimed at "a global change in lifestyle: abstinence from illicit substances, elimination of antisocial activity, development of employability, and prosocial attitudes" (Abadinsky, 2011; DeLeon, 1994, p. 392).

Many social workers specialize in AODA treatment and provide AODA counseling to clients and their families.

5. *Halfway houses* are temporary residences to assist in the transition from an inpatient program to the real-life community. They provide support and supervision that is less extensive than that given on a 24-hour institutional basis. Emphasis is on gradually increasing each resident's ability to handle responsibility at his or her own pace.

6. *Pharmacological adjuncts* are prescribed medications that help addicts begin the recovery process. For example, Antabuse combats alcoholism as, when ingested, "drinking produces a severe physical reaction: nausea, flushing, and shortness of breath" (Van Wormer & Davis, 2008, p. 150). Such medication, of course, must be carefully monitored by medical staff.

7. *Self-help groups* are composed of "members who share the problem experienced by the other members of the group"; they are led by a group member who may be either a layperson or a professional, but who faces the same problem (Toseland & Rivas, 2012, p. 27). Group members voluntarily gather to provide mutual support and share information aimed at improving their lives. Specific programs include Alcoholics Anonymous (AA), Narcotics Anonymous (NA), and Cocaine Anonymous (CA). These groups provide exceptionally relevant treatment approaches in view of their established success. Support from peers in the process of recovery is especially critical. Highlight 14.3 discusses AA.

HIGHLIGHT 14.3

Alcoholics Anonymous (AA)

Because of its prevalence, we will focus on AA here. This large nationwide group provides support, information, and guidance necessary for many recovering alcoholics to maintain their recovery process. The organization's success seems to rest on several principles. First, other people who "really understand" are available to give the recovering dependent person friendship and warmth. Each new member is given a "sponsor" who can be called for support at any time during the day or night. Whenever the dependent person feels depressed or tempted, he or she can always turn to the sponsor.

Additionally, AA provides the recovering alcoholic a new social group with whom to talk and enjoy activities. Old friends with established drinking patterns usually become difficult to associate with. The recovering alcoholic can no longer participate in the drinking activity, and social pressure is often applied to drink again. AA provides a respite from such pressure and the opportunity to meet new people.

AA also helps the recovering person to view alcoholism as a disease. This means that the alcoholic cannot cure himself or herself. He or she no longer needs to feel guilty about being an alcoholic. All that is required is to stop drinking.

Doweiko (2012) summarizes the AA 12-step program:

At the core of AA are the 12 steps. These steps are not required for members but are suggested as a way that a person might achieve lasting recovery ... A central tenet of both the 12 steps and AA as a whole is that individuals' resources alone are inadequate to help them abstain from alcohol. It is only through a commitment to a support group that people are able to draw upon the strength of the entire group in their battle to abstain from alcohol....

The first 12 steps fall into three groups, the first of which includes Steps 1–3. These steps focus on helping individuals make a profound choice: that

(continued)

HIGHLIGHT 14.3 (continued)

of surrender and turning their life over to a "Higher Power" of their choice....

Steps 4–9 are a series of change-oriented procedures designed to help individuals (a) identify, (b) confront, and (c) ultimately overcome the personal character shortcomings that are thought to support their addiction....

Steps 10–12 challenge the individual to continue to build on the foundation established in earlier steps. Part of the process includes a continued search to identify additional personal shortcomings, which are then addressed by that person. (pp. 462–463)

AA thus encourages introspection. Members are encouraged to look deeply inside themselves and face whatever they see. They are urged to acknowledge the fact that they have flaws and will never be perfect. This perspective often helps people to stop fleeing from the pain of reality and hiding in alcohol or drugs. It helps them to redefine expectations for themselves and to gain control. Within the context of this honesty, people often can also acknowledge their strengths. They learn that they have some control over their own behavior and can accomplish things for themselves and for others.

Organizations are also available to provide support for other family members and to give them information and suggestions. For example, Al-Anon is an organization for the families of alcoholics, and Alateen is specifically for teenagers within these families.

Treatment Models

EP 2.1.3b

Two contrasting treatment models are briefly described here. One is based on the traditional abstinence approach to recovery, and the other is a strengths-based model focused on achieving greater control of substance consumption (which may not include total abstinence).

A Four-Stage Recovery Model

One approach to substance dependence treatment maintains that dependence involves an entire lifestyle; therefore, to recover, one must abstain from consuming the substance entirely to establish a healthier, substance-free way of life. The following four steps are involved (Johnson, 2004, pp. 286–290):

Stage 1—Abstinence: During this stage, which can persist for as long as two years, clients strive to maintain sobriety. A major focus is on avoidance of mind-altering substances. In essence, "the individual learns to get through most days without experiencing or giving in to overwhelming cravings or urges to use" (p. 286). Relapses are common.

Stage 2—Confrontation: Lasting up to five years, this stage sees "clients begin confronting and changing the personal, family, and social issues that contributed to their chemically dependent lifestyle.... They learn how to conduct adult relationships, assume responsibility for their actions, and explore lifestyles that do not include drugs and the people associated with their chemically dependent past" (p. 287). Clients are often "obsessed" with their abstinence and recovery, confronting people and experiences in their past daily, often with shame and guilt about what happened. For example, a recovering client was with new friends who knew little about her past. She abruptly ran into old friends who unabashedly talked about the "good old days" when they got "really high" together and would do "wild and crazy things" like running through the city streets naked. The client felt extremely ashamed.

Stage 3—Growth: Usually occurring after at least five years of abstinence, this phase reflects beginning a new lifestyle not involving substance use. New social support networks are established, and "daily life does not involve constant attention to maintaining abstinence and recovery" (p. 289).

Stage 4—Transformation: This stage marks a true change in life orientation from the former substance-using days. The client has established "social networks and personal skills" to live and thrive. The mind-altering substance no longer has a place in this new existence.

Note that although these stages are presented as if they occur in a "smooth and recognizable manner," in many (perhaps most) cases they don't (p. 290). People can move back and forth between stages, and sometimes relapses occur. A relapse "signals the need to discover which parts of the client's recovery foundation need work" (p. 290).

The Strengths Perspective on Alcohol Abuse and Dependence Treatment

McCollum and Trepper (2001) stress that practitioners "should find ways to recognize the strengths and abilities that clients bring with them to treatment and not just focus on their liabilities" (p. 40). Identification of strengths provides clues to how clients can make positive changes occur.

Van Wormer and Davis (2008) propose a strengths-based approach to treating alcohol and other substance abuse and dependence based on *harm reduction*, a treatment approach emphasizing means "to reduce the harm to users" caused by the addiction (p. 25). They explain that the idea is to

help people help themselves by moving from safer use, to managed use, to abstinence, if so desired. The labeling of clients, as is the custom in mental health circles ("He has an antisocial personality," "She is borderline") or in treatment circles ("He's an alcoholic," "She has an eating disorder") is avoided; clients provide the definition of the situation as they see it. Clients who wish it are given advice on how to reduce the harm in drug use such as, "Don't drink on an empty stomach," or "Always make sure to use a clean needle." Most of the advice, however, is provided in a less direct fashion, such as, "Here are some options you might want to consider." Consistent with the strengths perspective, the counselor and client collaborate to consider a broad range of solutions to the client-defined problem; resources are gathered or located to meet the

individual needs of the client. Above all, clients are viewed as amenable to change. (p. 25)

Van Wormer and Davis (2008) state that a more traditional disease model espoused by AA and described previously may experience success with "extroverted, severely addicted, structure seeking" people (p. 26). However, a harm reduction approach provides more flexibility in terms of treatment planning and goals. It also stresses how clients have the strength to assume responsibility for changing their behavior. The emphasis is on what people can *do*, not the problems they have. This approach emphasizes "healing" instead of "punishment" (p. 26).

A key component of this approach is *choice* "about goals of the helping relationship (harm reduction, including abstinence); informed choice about a variety of treatment contexts (same gender, group, individual, day treatment, outpatient, inpatient, mutual-help groups); and informed choice about treatment methods" (p. 86).

"Harm reduction strategies for alcohol [or other drug] misuse are based on the premise that alcohol [or other drug] use ranges across a continuum, starting with no consequences for use and ending with devastating consequences for use, with lots of states in between" (Van Wormer & Davis, 2008, p. 96). A client may choose to establish a state of controlled consumption (e.g., limiting the amount drunk or times when drinking occurs) instead of seeking total abstinence. A plan might entail drinking only during weekends or special occasions and then limiting it to some designated amount. Drinking less is not as harmful as heavy, continuous, uncontrolled drinking.

FOCUS ON CRITICAL THINKING 14.2

Comparing Treatment Models

EP 2.1.3

We have talked about two very different approaches to treating a person who is abusing or dependent upon a mind-altering substance. The four-stage recovery model demands total abstinence, whereas the harm reduction approach allows greater flexibility in pursuing control over the substance.

Critical Thinking Questions

- What are the strengths and weaknesses of each model?
- Which do you believe is more effective, and why?

HIGHLIGHT 14.4

A Case Example of an Alcoholic in Treatment

**EP 2.1.10f,
2.1.10g,
2.1.10j**

Velleman (2001) describes his therapeutic work with a client named Harry who changed his goal from attaining abstinence to gaining greater control over his drinking without stopping it altogether:

Harry developed the goal that he wanted to abstain from drinking altogether. The two of us worked out a plan of action for the forthcoming week to enable him to do this, with the major thrust coming from Harry rather than from me: We identified possible at-risk situations, and we clarified the strategies and tactics he was going to employ so as to successfully overcome these.

The next week, Harry returned saying he had failed: He had drunk four units of alcohol. He was out with one of his adult daughters, they went for a country walk, and ended up in a ... [tavern] for lunch. He had two ... [bottles of beer] with his meal, then continued with his walk, and had drunk nothing else throughout the week.

This information was used in a variety of ways. It added more material which was useful for exploration—Harry can successfully control his intake under some circumstances, drinking four units did not precipitate a full-scale relapse, and so on. It also provided the possibility for reassessing the goal—perhaps some drinking, under controlled and monitored conditions, with certain people and in certain contexts might be a desired goal? This new material altered the plan of campaign for the next and subsequent weeks.

If abstinence was still the goal, new at-risk situations had been identified, and new strategies had to be developed to overcome them, that is, do not go for walks, ... or stop in a village with a café,...[but do] get his daughter to buy the (nonalcoholic) drinks, or get her to hold the money.

Alternatively, if occasional controlled drinking was now the goal, the details of when, how much, with whom, where, and so on needed to be clarified; risky situations relating to these actions needed to be identified; and strategies to overcome them needed to be thought through—with, as always, the major thrust coming from Harry rather than me. (pp. 48–49)

The practitioner does not force clients to place labels on themselves. Rather, the practitioner helps clients understand the costs of drinking and explore what options they have to gain greater control of their lives if that is what they desire. In essence, the practitioner focuses on the client's motivation to make positive changes.

Focus on Critical Thinking 14.2 urges you to compare the effectiveness of the two treatment models discussed here. Highlight 14.4 cites a case example where a practitioner works with a client who changes his goal from total abstinence to decreased use of alcohol.

Chapter Summary

The following summarizes this chapter's content as it relates to the chapter's learning objectives presented at the beginning of the chapter. Learning objectives include the following:

A Review common definitions used in the AODA field.

Language commonly used in substance abuse intervention tends to revolve around the terms *alcohol*, *drug*, and *substance* (often referred to as *psychoactive*

substance). In everyday usage the term *alcohol* refers to any type of fermented or distilled liquor containing alcohol such as whiskey or beer. *Drug* refers to a wide range of materials that alter mood or consciousness when ingested, including amphetamines, cannabis, cocaine, and hallucinogens. *Substance* is commonly used to refer to mind-altering drugs, including alcohol (hence the term *alcohol and other substance abuse*). In the context of abuse described here, the terms *substance* and *drug* are often used interchangeably. Several other terms used in conjunction with alcohol, drugs, and substances are *dependence*, *tolerance*, *withdrawal*, *abuse*, *intoxication*, *alcoholism*, *alcoholic*, and *addiction*.

B Describe the substances involved in abuse and dependence and their methods of administration.

Types of mind-altering substances include CNS stimulants, CNS depressants, and other addictive substances. "Stimulants are psychoactive substances that boost the functioning of the central nervous system"; "depressants are psychoactive substances that suppress, slow, or relax the central nervous system" (Dziegielewski, 2005, pp. 53, 123). Other substance categories include cannabinoids, dissociative anesthetics, hallucinogens, and opioids and morphine derivatives.

Methods of substance administration include oral consumption, inhalation or smoking, injection, or ingestion via mucous membranes.

C Explore common defense mechanisms and family relationships of substance abusers.

Common defense mechanisms employed by substance abusers include minimization, rationalization, and denial. Eight themes characterize the families of substance abusers that focus on the substance becoming the most important center of the family's life.

D Explain major aspects of the treatment process for substance abuse and dependence.

The treatment process for substance abusers involves engagement; assessment; a multiple-system approach to individualized treatment including individual, group, and family treatment; follow-up; and the importance of developing social support networks.

E Identify community resources for people who abuse substances.

Community resources for substance abusers include detoxification, outpatient treatment, inpatient treatment, therapeutic communities, halfway houses, pharmacological adjuncts, and self-help groups. Alcoholics Anonymous (AA) provides an example of a self-help organization.

F Compare two treatment models for substance abusers.

Two contrasting treatment models are described. One is based on the traditional abstinence approach to recovery, and the other is a strengths-based model that emphasizes a least harm approach and focuses on achieving greater control of substance consumption (which may not include total abstinence).

G Pose critical thinking questions that address the dynamics of substance abuse and compare treatment models.

Critical thinking questions are posed concerning the rationale for using and abusing substances. Other questions address the comparison of a traditional four-phase abstinence model of treatment with a treatment model focusing on strengths and the concept of least harm.

LOOKING AHEAD

This chapter addressed an important field of social work practice, alcohol and other drug abuse, that is often an issue for the client populations targeted in the next two chapters. Chapter 15 focuses on social work and services for youths and in the schools. Chapter 16 explores social work and services in the criminal justice system.

COMPETENCY NOTES

The following identifies where Educational Policy (EP) competencies and practice behaviors are discussed in the chapter.

EP 2.1.1c Attend to professional roles and boundaries. *(p. 441):* Social work roles with respect to AODA treatment are discussed.

EP 2.1.3 Apply critical thinking to inform and communicate professional judgments. *(p. 445):* Critical thinking questions are posed to promote understanding of the dynamics of substance abuse and its treatment. *(p. 454):* Critical thinking questions are raised to encourage the comparison and assessment of the two treatment models that have been discussed.

EP 2.1.3b Analyze models of assessment, prevention, intervention, and evaluation. *(p. 453):* Two models involving AODA treatment are discussed and analyzed.

EP 2.1.3c Demonstrate effective oral and written communication in working with individuals, families, groups, organizations, communities, and colleagues. *(p. 450):* Social workers should use effective communication techniques such as these questions when providing AODA treatment.

EP 2.1.7a Utilize conceptual frameworks to guide the processes of assessment, intervention, and evaluation. *(p. 442):* The *DSM–IV–TR* provides a conceptual framework for AODA assessment to guide the processes of treament, intervention, and evaluation.

EP 2.1.7b Critique and apply knowledge to understand person and environment. *(p. 441):* Practitioners require knowledge about AODA to understand how people involved function within their environments, provide treatment, and make appropriate referrals. *(p. 443):* Social workers require knowledge about drugs, drug use, and drug abuse in order to understand the dynamics involved in AODA and what treatment is needed.

EP 2.1.10 Engage, assess, intervene, and evaluate with individuals, families, groups, organizations, and communities. *(p. 449):* Social workers practice in AODA treatment by working with systems of all sizes, including families and groups.

EP 2.1.10a Substantively and affectively prepare for action with individuals, families, groups, organizations, and communities. *(p. 448):* During the engagement process, a practitioner prepares for action with individuals and families in AODA treatment.

EP 2.1.10b Use empathy and other interpersonal skills. *(p. 448):* Practitioners use interpersonal skills during the engagement process in AODA treatment. *(p. 449):* Practitioners should use interpersonal skills and carefully chosen techniques when providing AODA treatment.

EP 2.1.10c Develop a mutually agreed-on focus of work and desired outcomes. *(p. 448):* Collaboration with the client to establish mutually agreed-on goals is critical in AODA treatment.

EP 2.1.10d Collect, organize, and interpret client data. *(p. 448):* Social workers must collect, organize, and interpret appropriate client data in order to prepare for AODA treatment provision.

EP 2.1.10e Assess clients' strengths and limitations. *(p. 448):* Practitioners should assess a client's strengths and limitations as part of AODA treatment.

EP 2.1.10f Develop mutually agreed-on intervention goals and objectives. *(p. 455):* The case example demonstrates how the practitioner and client develop mutually agreed-on goals.

EP 2.1.10g Select appropriate intervention strategies. *(p. 449):* Social workers should select appropriate intervention strategies when providing AODA treatment. *(p. 451):* Practitioners should select appropriate intervention strategies, potentially including one or more of the various AODA treatment approaches presented here. *(p. 455):* In this case example, the practitioner and client choose appropriate intervention strategies.

EP 2.1.10j Help clients resolve problems. *(p. 455):* In this case example, the practitioner helps the client resolve problems.

EP 2.1.10m Critically analyze, monitor, and evaluate interventions. *(p. 451):* Follow-up provides one means of monitoring interventions in AODA treatment.

FOR FURTHER EXPLORATION ON THE INTERNET

See this text's Social Work CourseMate website at *www.cengagebrain.com* for learning tools such as chapter quizzing, videos, glossary, flashcards, and more.

CHAPTER 15

Social Work and Services for Youths and in the Schools

Laurence Mouton/PhotoAlto Agency RF Collections/Getty Images

Penny, a ninth-grader, tells Ms. Bijou, the school social worker, that Levina, her best friend, has been awfully moody lately. Levina has even said that she doesn't care much about living anymore, that every day gets gloomier, and that it just isn't worth it. Penny is worried that Levina might do something to hurt herself.

Jorge and Jeremy, both juniors in a multiracial high school, are concerned about the racial tensions and even fights in school. They're glad when Mr. Reinheich, the school social worker, announces that he's organizing some encounter discussion groups in which students can talk about racial issues, share things about their own cultures, and try to work out their conflicts.

Marinda, age 15, is terrified that she's pregnant. She hasn't had her period for almost two and a half months now. She hasn't told her boyfriend Teddy, age 16, the bad news yet, because she's afraid he'll break up with her. And she hasn't told her parents, either. What is she going to do?

These examples reflect slices carved from adolescent life. Emotions run high, and a social crisis can erupt at any moment. Things are critically important *right now*—not tomorrow, next week, or next year.

Social work practitioners work with youths in a wide range of settings and fields of practice—school social work, corrections, mental health, child welfare, runaway shelters, and family planning clinics. This chapter will focus on three dimensions of social work with youths: (1) school social work, (2) macro programs servicing youths, and (3) teenage sexual activity, pregnancy, and parenting.

Learning Objectives

A   Describe school social work and define the various roles of school social workers.

B   Identify the types of groups school social workers run.

C   Suggest ways multiculturalism can be enhanced and racism reduced in schools.

D   Discuss lesbian, gay, bisexual, and transgender (LGBT) youths as populations-at-risk, focusing on issues involved in the "coming-out" process.

E   Identify and refute various myths about LGBT people.

F   Describe two community programs for youths—one that empowers Latino/Latina youths through a community assets assessment and one that explores how an African American spiritual community empowers its youths.

G   Review social workers' potential role in the prevention of school violence.

H   Examine the issues of teenage sexual activity, pregnancy, and parenting issues, and describe social work roles concerning them.

I   Encourage critical thinking about the reasons for teen pregnancy, what should be done about it, and the provision of sex education.

School Social Work

School social work takes place in school settings, where practitioners work with students, families, other school personnel, and communities to provide the best education possible for today's youths. Constable (2009) explains:

The educational process is dynamic and wide ranging. Involving children, their families, and an institution called school, it is the context for school social work. School is no longer viewed as a building, or a collection of classrooms in which teachers and pupils work together. The school community, no longer simply bounded by geography, comprises all those who engage in the educational process. (p. 23)

School social workers, then, strive to improve the overall functioning of students, teachers, school systems, and communities. They address "conditions that interfere with the pupil's ability to connect with the educational system" (Allen-Meares, 2008; Constable, 1999, p. 209). School social workers must be skilled and flexible because they assume a wide range of roles

EP 2.1.1c

and usually must define their key functions within their own school setting (Constable, 2009). School social work involves not only providing clinical services such as counseling for students who have behavioral problems, are depressed, or are experiencing family difficulties. It also entails working with the multiple systems with which students are involved to strengthen them and make it easier for students to perform in the school environment.

As students in colleges and universities, you know it takes substantial concentration, work, and stamina to succeed in a school environment. This is also true for students in earlier phases of the educational process. One of the first things to suffer when a child experiences social and emotional problems is school performance and attendance. Such children simply do not have the strength and endurance to expend the emotional energy required to cope with serious personal problems and still have enough energy left over to perform well in school. School becomes a lower priority.

School social workers, then, may become major players in helping such children, along with their families, teachers, school administration, and social service agencies within the community, develop a plan to empower them. The following case example illustrates how a school social worker collaborated with various systems in a child's environment to improve it and empower her.

EP 2.1.10d, 2.1.10e, 2.1.10f, 2.1.10g, 2.1.10h, 2.1.10j, 2.1.10k

Case Example   Minnie Series, age 8, started having problems in school shortly after she entered third grade. She had transferred during the middle of the year when her family moved to the area. By that time the other third-graders had already formed friendships and cliques, so Minnie had a hard time fitting in. A shy, withdrawn child, she usually found herself on the fringes of class and recess activities. She also was having a hard time with her reading, spelling, and writing, in addition to having a terrible time concentrating on her lessons.

Minnie's teacher, Sybil Servant, noticed these difficulties and referred Minnie to the school's multidisciplinary Individualized Education Program (IEP) team for evaluation and planning. (An IEP "describes the goals the team [made up of various involved persons including relevant professionals] sets

for a child during the school year, as well as any special support needed to help achieve them" (Nemours Foundation, 2011). In this case, part of the evaluation process involved the school social worker, Alan Aladdin, making a home visit and conducting a family assessment. Alan called Minnie's mother, Sue Series, and requested permission to make a home visit, during which he gathered the following information.

Minnie had two siblings, Buffy and Brutus, both preschoolers, who also lived in the home. Minnie's father had abruptly left the family one years earlier and had not been heard from since. Sue appeared to be depressed: She expressed little emotion and emphasized how overwhelmed and alone she felt. She worked full time as a dental assistant and was having difficulty finding adequate day care for her preschool children.

At school, Alan met with Minnie, who seemed to lack self-confidence and made a number of derogatory remarks about herself. She also mentioned how she really missed her "Daddy" and wondered if he was OK. Sybil had told Alan that during their class art time, Minnie had drawn pictures of black daggers dripping red blood. Alan was concerned that Minnie was depressed.

Specialized testing revealed that Minnie had a mild learning disability, a disorder whereby a child has marked difficulty learning in some particular area (e.g., reading or working with numbers) while learning and functioning in other areas are normal or above average. Among other recommendations, the IEP team recommended unanimously that Minnie required special education. Although there was a special learning disabilities class at the school, it was currently jam-packed. Alan advocated with the school principal to open up another section of the class. The principal said that was not possible because of cost. However, the school was legally responsible for providing needed services. After doing his homework, Alan proposed that a special education teacher from another school would be willing to help. The school could purchase services from her for Minnie. Minnie could spent the rest of her school time with her regular third-grade class.

At a subsequent meeting with Sue, Alan discussed resources in the community that could potentially meet the family's needs. He suggested that Minnie become involved with recreational programming at a nearby community center and that she be signed up for the Big Sister program, which would pair

Minnie with a young adult who would spend time regularly with her, provide support, and serve as a positive role model. Alan also helped Sue look into some day-care options for Buffy and Brutus. He suggested that Sue attend a Parents Without Partners meeting for companionship, support, and social activities.

Alan also recommended that Sue consider individual counseling for herself to address her feelings of being overwhelmed and isolated, and for Minnie to deal with personal issues, lack of self-confidence, feelings about her father, and social skills development. Although Sue was responsive to Alan's other suggestions, she was not at all interested in counseling. She maintained that she and Minnie were not "mentally ill" and so did not need it.

At school, Alan decided to provide Minnie with weekly counseling, which he had time to do with a select few students. Alan also urged Minnie to join a support group he ran for children of single parents. Minnie did so and began to develop a circle of friends she met there and in her learning disabilities class. As she became more outgoing, her relationships with children in her regular classes continued to improve.

Alan worked with Sybil to structure activities within the educational context so that Minnie could feel important and gain confidence. For example, at Alan's suggestion, Sybil gave Minnie the "special" responsibility of pinning up student artwork on the bulletin board and assigned Minnie to work in peer groups made up of children who were the most receptive to her.

This is not the end of Minnie's story. Alan, Minnie's teachers, and the Pupil Services team continued to monitor her progress and provide special services and attention. She persisted in making academic progress, developing social skills, and joining various social groups. As a sixth-grader, she was a socially and emotionally well-adjusted girl who could keep up with her classmates academically.

This case example illustrates how a school social worker can work with various individuals and aspects of systems to help students and their families get what they need. Alan worked with Minnie (providing individual and group counseling) and her family (linking her mother with needed services). He also provided consultation to Sybil and, in subsequent years, to other teachers to maximize Minnie's adjustment. He served as case manager to coordinate and oversee all aspects of service

provision for Minnie. Additionally, he advocated with the school system's decision maker (i.e., the school principal) and helped to figure out a way to get Minnie the special education services she needed.

School Social Work Roles

EP 2.1.1c

Franklin Harris, and Lagana-Riordan (2009) cite at least nine roles that school social workers may assume. These include consultant, counselor, facilitator, educator, advocate, broker, case manager, community intervention collaborator, and policy initiator and developer.

Consultant

First, a school social worker may be a *consultant*—a person with specialized knowledge and expertise to whom others turn for information, help, and advice. Consultation may entail providing information about behavior management techniques or emotional problems to teachers as Alan did in the case example involving Minnie, or helping a school administration develop a new program.

Counselor

A second school social work role is that of *counselor*—a person who provides clinical intervention concerning social, emotional, or behavioral issues to individuals, families, groups, and communities. Clinical activities might include recognizing feelings, identifying issues and alternatives, offering information, and providing assistance to establish a plan of action. Problems that bring students to school social workers' attention may include behavioral difficulties in the classroom, controlled substance use and abuse, fighting and other acts of violence, truancy, and threats of suicide. In the earlier example, Alan counseled Minnie regarding her lack of self-confidence, depression, feelings about her father, and relationships with peers.

Facilitator

A third role for school social workers is *facilitator*—a person who "suggests, guides, eases, or expedites the way for others during a group experience" (Kirst-Ashman & Hull, 2012b, p. 101). This role can involve groups of students, parents, teachers, administrators, and community leaders. Highlight 15.1 reviews 10 types of groups school social workers run.

HIGHLIGHT 15.1

Focus on Mezzo Practice: Types of Groups School Social Workers Run

**EP 2.1.10g,
2.1.10i,
2.1.10j**

Bye and Alvarez (2007) cite some of the advantages of using group work in a school setting:

- Groups enable children and adolescents to form bonds with peers and to discuss feelings and ideas openly.
- Groups enable children and adolescents to understand that their concerns are not unique and that there is nothing wrong with them.
- Groups allow participants to articulate personal feelings and obtain feedback from their peers.
- Groups with children and adolescents enable social workers to serve more young people [more quickly] . . .
- Groups often use play and art, which are a child's first language. (p. 158)

Pawlak, Wozniak, and McGowen (1999) reviewed a decade's worth of articles published in the journal *Social Work in Education*. They identified the following 10 types of groups that school social workers run:

1. *Groups for parents of students:* School social workers may run such groups for any number of reasons, including dealing with children who have behavioral problems or eating disorders, helping parents who are recent immigrants cope with differences in language or customs, or discussing neighborhood issues such as crime.

2. *Groups for students who are parents:* Young single parents can face difficult issues including maintaining good health during pregnancy, balancing school and parenthood, caring for infants, and obtaining support from fathers.

3. *Groups for students whose families are experiencing divorce:* Divorce can have serious consequences for children's emotional well-being. Children might tackle many questions. (Was I to blame for my parents' breakup? How could Mom and Dad do this to me? What will happen to me now? Will I ever see Daddy [or Mommy] again? Why doesn't Dad [or Mom] talk to me much anymore? Will Daddy [or Mommy] like their new family better

than me?) Groups for children of divorce can "address children's feelings of isolation, loss, anger, guilt, and helplessness" (Pawlak et al., 1999, pp. 357–358).

4. *Groups for students dealing with substance abuse issues:* Such groups might deal with students' own or parental substance abuse, providing coping strategies in potentially abusive situations or peer support for abstinence. Groups can also be used to focus on substance abuse prevention (Franklin et al., 2010).

5. *Groups for students with attention deficit hyperactivity disorder:* Recall that attention deficit hyperactivity disorder (ADHD) is a syndrome of learning and behavioral problems beginning in childhood that is characterized by a persistent pattern of inattention, excessive physical movement, and impulsivity that appears in at least two settings (including home, school, work, and social contexts). Such groups can focus on "self-esteem, feelings, behavior change, communication, conflict, friendship, anger, and problem solving" (Pawlak et al., 1999, p. 358).

6. *Groups for trauma-related recovery:* These groups can provide crisis intervention for students recovering from virtually any trauma, from a school bus accident, to a tornado in a small rural town, to a murderous assault by fellow students, as Dylan Klebold, age 17, and Eric Harris, age 18, carried out at Columbine High in Littleton, Colorado, in 1999. Traumas can result in posttraumatic stress disorder (described in Chapter 13). Groups can help students confront their fears, deal with anxiety, and provide mutual support.

7. *Groups for students at risk of dropping out:* Groups for these students may address how to handle their personal or behavioral problems, confront their anger at "the system," improve study habits, deal with family problems, and plan positively for the future.

8. *Groups addressing stress, grief, and loss issues:* These groups can focus on any type of grief or loss issues, including the death of a loved one, the closing of a manufacturing plant that was a town's primary employer, or a recent miscarriage. School social workers can also run stress management

(continued)

families. Refugees are often away from school for various reasons, such as initial medical checkups. Likewise, the A family children were often needed as interpreters during food stamp interviews, medical appointments, and immigration and documentation procedures. Not fully understanding the requirement of written parental permission, both students encountered difficulties with unexcused absences. Subsequently, Mrs. A missed parent-teacher conferences because of miscommunications and the language barrier. One child was also suspended for fighting with another student who insulted Mrs. A. The student explained that in his country of origin, these sorts of verbal attacks are incredibly hostile and provoking. The student did not understand why he was punished for defending his mother. (pp. 806–807)

Fong and her colleagues (2006) suggest a school social worker engage in five steps concerning this case. The school social worker first should assess the situation and needs. The boys required an accurate appraisal of both grade level and language ability. Since they couldn't speak a word of Spanish, placement in Spanish-oriented ESL courses was totally inappropriate. The boys' perspective concerning their "strengths and interests" also required assessment to place them in classes that were relevant to them (Fong et al., 2006 p. 807). The social worker also should conduct a family assessment regarding its needs. The parents obviously had difficulties understanding the school system and its expectations, so they required information and clarification of these expectations.

The second step in handling this case involved identifying appropriate resources and services. An interpreter for their Eastern European language, instead of Spanish, was essential. The interpreter could assist the social worker in arranging for "assessments for the boys in the areas of language ability, strengths and vocational interests, and appropriate course selections" (Fong et al., p. 807). After assessing what the family required, the social worker should link the family with a refugee resettlement organization, if available, to determine what services the family could receive there. Connection with interpreters is especially important so that the family can conduct its daily business more effectively.

The third step the social worker should pursue involves establishing a thorough plan that addresses the broader picture for the boys and the family. For example, the boys happened to be exceptional soccer and basketball players and love to play. However, their poor grades made them ineligible for the teams. An IEP (Individualized Education Program) that incorporates sports team involvement as an incentive to learn English and improve their grades could be appropriate.

Step four entails advocating for necessary services. "School social workers should lobby their principals to develop services for the growing immigrant and refugee student populations. Minimally, every educational institution should have on hand a list of relevant interpreters to be available to the school social workers" (Fong et al., 2006 p. 807).

Step five concerns continued advocacy and monitoring of the intervention process. The school social worker can advocate with the school administration in addition to medical and other service providers including refugee assistance agencies, so that the A family receives needed services. In addition to interpreters, organizations offering resettlement assistance to refugees can provide financial assistance, counseling, assistance with the migration process, and referrals to educational, vocational, and medical resources (Jewish Child & Family Services, n.d.). The social worker can also educate other school staff regarding the refugee experience and the obstacles such families encounter. Finally, the social worker can continue to help the family coordinate activities such as medical appointments, administration of medication, transportation arrangements, understanding involving language, and fulfillment of school-related expectations.

Broker

A sixth role for school social workers is that of *broker*—a person who helps link clients with community resources and services. In Alan's case, he attempted to link Minnie and her mother with a therapist in an outside social services agency. Linkages or referrals might involve any type of resource (e.g., recreational programs, financial resources).

Case Manager

Related to the role of broker is that of *case manager*—a person who coordinates services from a variety of sources. Alan also functioned as case manager in Minnie's case, coordinating services provided by Minnie's teachers, other school personnel, and outside resources.

Community Intervention Collaborator

Another role assumed by school social workers is that of *community intervention collaborator*—a person who works with others in the community to initiate change or develop needed programs. Social workers can use their communication and organizational skills to educate and mobilize community groups. Potential goals include developing a shelter for runaways, crisis hot lines, bilingual education programs, or preschool day-care programs for student parents.

Policy Initiator and Developer

EP 2.1.8a, 2.1.8b, 2.1.9b

The final role that school social workers might assume is that of *policy initiator and developer*—a person who works to "influence, initiate, and develop policy, which affects the social and emotional development of children and youth within the school and community. Through participating in policymaking committees, writing grants, and as members of professional organizations, they are active in creating programs that benefit the education process" (Franklin, 2004, p. 308). An example is writing letters to or e-mailing legislators to support social welfare policies that benefit students and their families.

The importance of advocating for cultural competence in schools has already been introduced. Highlight 15.2 broadens the discussion of multiculturalism's importance in education. It suggests how social workers might enhance appreciation of cultural differences while assuming educator, advocate, community intervention collaborator, and policy initiator and developer roles.

Gay and Lesbian Youths: A Population-at-Risk

EP 2.1.4a, 2.1.4c

Social workers must respond to the special issues and needs of all children with whom they work. This is the case for not only school social workers but any practitioners serving children and families. Just as social workers must attend to a child's cultural heritage and racial identity, so must they be competent to deal with the issues of an adolescent's sexual orientation.

Generally, lesbian, gay, bisexual, and transgender (LGBT) people have some "personal awareness of

same-sex erotic feelings before puberty and that awareness becomes crystallized at puberty" (Hershberger & D'Augelli, 2000, p. 226). Morrow (2006b) explains:

Adolescent development for GLBT [gay, lesbian, bisexual, and transgender] youth can be a perilous journey. Peer pressure to fit in socially is tremendous during the adolescent years. The stress of feeling different from the majority of their peers— whether with regard to sexual orientation or gender expression—can be daunting (Morrow, 1993). Thus, a primary task in identity development for GLBT adolescents is that of adjusting to a socially stigmatized role (Hetrick & Martin, 1987). GLBT adolescents must cope with developing a sexual minority identity in the midst of negative comments, jokes, and often the threat of violence because of their sexual orientation and/or transgender identity. To develop an overall positive identity in the midst of such negative social stigma requires courage and resilience. (p. 178)

When LGBT youth experience problems typical during adolescence, they must deal not only with these problems but also with their own sexual identity and related issues. Individual and group counseling in which they are offered support and provided an arena to address feelings and discuss issues can help LGBT youths through this difficult period.

Social Workers Can Assist in the Coming-Out Process

One such issue is *coming out*—the process of a person acknowledging that he or she is lesbian, gay, bisexual, or transgender. Becoming aware of one's identity as a gay or lesbian person takes time. It's not like a 250-watt lightbulb suddenly being turned on in a pitch-dark room. Rather, it's

EP 2.1.10g, 2.1.10j, 2.1.10l

a gradual, frequently difficult process in view of the homophobia[1] and stereotypes saturating our society (Swigonski, 1995).

Note that although we are discussing coming out in the context of adolescence, this process can occur during various stages of life (Tully, 2000). We examine it here because of sexual orientation's significance beginning very early in life and extending across the life span.

---

[1]We have established that *homophobia* is irrational, obsessive fear and hatred of LGBT people.

HIGHLIGHT 15.2

Enhancing Multiculturalism and Reducing Racism in Schools

**EP 2.1.4a,
2.1.4c,
2.1.10g,
2.1.10i**

School populations are becoming more diverse. Now "public schools are faced with the challenge of educating a population of students who are more racially and ethnically diverse, as well as disadvantaged, than at any other time in our nation's history" (Dupper, 2003, p. 156). It is time to broaden children's perspectives and appreciation of multiple cultures.

Spencer (1999) explains the nature of multicultural education:

Multicultural education incorporates the study of racial and ethnic differences, as well as issues related to gender, age, socioeconomic status, and physical disabilities.... [Its aims] are to foster a sense of understanding and respect for differences, to overcome prejudice and discrimination and provide an understanding of the dynamics of racism, to replace historical and cultural misnomers [using wrong names] with accurate information, and to ensure that all students receive equitable benefits from the education system. (p. 155)

Note that an "outgrowth" of the multicultural education movement is "global education" (Drum & Howard, 1989; Spencer, 1999, p. 158). Spencer (1999) explains:

Global education deals with diversity at the global level and focuses on the interrelated systems that affect the entire planet. The primary goal is to build understanding and respect for peoples and nations outside the United States. A global effort goes beyond the "Western-centric" curriculum pervasive in schools by providing an understanding of the dynamics of imperialism [nations extending their own power and authority over other nations and areas] and oppression and creating an awareness of the earth as an interrelated holistic system. (p. 158)

Social workers can pursue at least five approaches to enhancing the appreciation of multiculturalism and reducing racism in schools:

1. Initiate and encourage open discussions and dialogues among various ethnic, racial, and cultural groups (Dupper, 2000; Spencer, 1999). Sciarra

(2001) explains: "Both small group counseling and classroom guidance units are excellent modalities for developing multicultural awareness. Small groups that are racially and culturally diverse give students the opportunity to share their heritage with the other members" (p. 721). Such interaction gives students a forum for discovering commonalities, appreciating differences, and working out conflicts.

2. Seek and adopt curricula that emphasize multiculturalism (and non-Western perspectives) (Dupper, 2000; Spencer, 1999).

3. Empower children by focusing on and appreciating their racial, ethnic, and cultural identities, and by teaching them strategies to stop racism (Dupper, 2000; Spencer, 1999).

4. Give teachers and other school staff training and consultation regarding multiculturalism (Franklin et al., 2009; Kiselica, Changizi, Cureton, & Gridley, 1995; Spencer, 1999).

5. Involve parents in efforts to promote multiculturalism by encouraging their participation in and understanding of their children's education (Kiselica et al., 1995). Factors discouraging the parental involvement of people of color include "cultural value conflicts," "racism and alienation," and "poverty" (Kiselica et al., 1995, pp. 519–520). Social workers can

work toward preventing and mediating cultural values conflicts and misunderstanding, taking measures to reduce feelings of alienation, and assisting parents in overcoming socioeconomic hardships.... Ethnic minority parents benefit from community awareness workshops and parent training programs designed to familiarize them with school policies, procedures, and goals.... Sending letters to parents ... and making home visits ... are other tactics that have been recommended for keeping racial/ethnic minority parents informed about school activities and for promoting parental participation in those activities.... Other strategies for reducing alienation from the school system include genuinely showing an interest in how the parents feel about the educational system and working to empower parents. (Kiselica et al., 1995, pp. 521–522)

Coming out involves both "coming out to oneself (recognizing one's sexual orientation) and coming out to others (declaring one's orientation to the world)" (Rathus, Navid, & Fichner-Rathus, 2011, p. 306). Often, it occurs in four stages (Boston Women's Health Book Collective, 1984): (1) coming out to oneself, (2) getting to know other people within the gay and lesbian community, (3) sharing with family and friends that one is lesbian or gay, and (4) coming out of the closet—that is, openly and publicly acknowledging one's sexual orientation.

Step 1, coming out to oneself, is difficult because of the negativity associated with being gay. The logic might go something like this: "Society says gay and lesbian people are bad. I am gay. Therefore, I am bad."

Morrow (2006a) explains how social workers "can play a key role" in assisting adolescents and others as they work through the coming—out process:

> *Social workers . . . can explore with clients the costs and benefits of coming out, and they can help clients make decisions about disclosure across a variety of social contexts. In addition, they can help clients gain necessary knowledge and interpersonal relationship skills that will facilitate their decisions and actions on disclosure. (p. 140)*

Practitioners must avoid minimizing or denying the young person's developing identity and sexual orientation. Rather, they can empower gay and lesbian adolescents by taking their expressed thoughts and feelings seriously and providing them with the information and support they need. Hershberger and D'Augelli (2000) maintain that "the fundamental approach" of professionals working with youths "who are questioning and exploring their sexual identity should be one of acceptance" (p. 237).

EP 2.1.4b, 2.1.4d

Step 2 in the coming-out process involves the LGBT adolescent seeking out other LGBT people and learning about what it means to be gay. Social workers should strive to increase their own awareness, and that of their agency, regarding how to provide accessible services to gay and lesbian youths (Woodman, 1995). Such services may include establishing peer support groups and recreational activities for LGBT young people (Laird, 1995). Many participants have indicated that support groups help to decrease isolation and encourage positive identity

development (Elze, 2006). Integrating LGBT content into the curriculum and establishing anti-harassment policies are also helpful (Elze, 2006).

Morrow (2006a) explains the importance of the person coming out being knowledgeable about gay issues and concerns:

> *Social workers can help clients brainstorm questions and concerns that they would likely encounter in coming out in various social contexts. Workers can assist clients in developing an accurate knowledge base of information to address identified questions and concerns. Common issues of concern that might be raised by people unfamiliar with accurate information on GLBT issues can include the following: HIV/AIDS risk, sexual orientation versus sexual "preference" [people don't choose to be gay], misinformation and stereotypes regarding sexual perversion and child molestation, religious rhetoric commonly used to oppress gay and lesbian people, and the value of loving, committed GLBT relationships versus stereotypes of sexual promiscuity. (pp. 141–142)*

Step 3 concerns youths taking the risk of sharing this self-identity with people who are close to them. This is scary because they might be rejected purely on the basis of being gay or lesbian. Hershberger and D'Augelli (2000) suggest that practitioners help adolescents "proceed with caution" and "discuss the risks involved"; they continue that "unless youths are certain of support from family members who matter, they should not be encouraged to disclose" (p. 239). Morrow (2006a) suggests that a social worker "can help clients identify those who they expect will respond to their coming out in an accepting manner. Having at least one successful experience before disclosure to families can be a vital confidence builder for clients" (p. 142).

The next issues involve decisions about how and when the revelation should be made (Morrow, 2006a). Morrow (2006a) suggests:

> *Clients preparing for disclosure must select the method through which the news will be communicated. Typical options include person-to-person sharing, phone communication, letters, and e-mail correspondence. Workers can help clients explore these communication options. . . . Social workers can utilize role play and rehearsal exercises to help clients prepare their method of information delivery. . . .*

availability of contact people, the social services provided (if a social services agency), and their "willingness to collaborate with schools and agencies on community projects" (Delgado, 1998, p. 205). Goals were to "provide youths with an appreciation of community strengths, raise school and human services agency awareness of community assets, and develop an assets directory" (Delgado, 1998, p. 205).

Results and Recommendations

Results indicate that "the use of Latino adolescents in community asset assessments offers much promise" for social work (Delgado, 1998, p. 210). Although this assessment was conducted via a grant-created community agency, Delgado (1998) offers a number of suggestions for implementation of community assets assessments. This is accomplished mainly through the schools because they give easy access to youths, including those at risk.

First, school social workers can recruit youths to identify "potential student leaders, candidates for peer education programs, and possible projects involving natural support systems" (Delgado, 1998, p. 209). For example, the young people involved in the New Bridges project decided that they wanted to go on a trip and financed it by holding a car wash. They asked Latino/Latina businesses to contribute a small amount of money (e.g., a nickel or a quarter) for each car washed. In return, the youths listed the sponsors' names on a billboard to provide publicity for them. This is a good example of how community members can work together to enhance relationships among various facets (i.e., this group of young people and local businesses) to reach mutually positive goals (i.e., financial backing for the youths' trip and publicity for the businesses).

A second idea for using the community assets assessment is for schools to invite business owners from the community in to talk about how they started their businesses. In this way owners can provide positive role models for young people and sow some seeds related to career possibilities and goals.

A third idea is to use the information gathered in special school projects. Students might earn extra credit in a social studies course by investigating community strengths. They could videotape interviews with interested residents or community service representatives. They might then share these tapes with other students or even social service agencies to provide education about social issues and information about cultural strengths.

Helping a Spiritual Community Empower Its African American Youths[3]

EP 2.1.7b

The following is an example of how social workers helped to empower African American youths by mobilizing a spiritual community in Utah. First, a study was conducted to identify the values and opinions of community members. Subsequently, a program was implemented that demonstrates how social workers can creatively work with a spiritual community to help meet the needs of its youths.

The Study

Haight (1998) conducted an *ethnographic study*—that is, the scientific description of a culture—targeting African American youths belonging to the First Baptist Church in Salt Lake City, Utah. The church was established over a hundred years ago by "'a Baptist Prayer Band,' a group of African Americans who, excluded from worshipping in the white churches, met in one another's homes" (p. 215). Haight (1998) notes that "African American Utahns, like African Americans in other parts of the country, experience racial discrimination in employment, housing, education, and everyday social interactions" (p. 216). African Americans are a tiny minority in Utah. Additionally, most of the Utah population belongs to the Church of Jesus Christ of Latter-Day Saints, a tightly knit spiritual community that sponsors an array of social and cultural activities for its members.

Extensive interviews with First Baptist Church members revealed an environmental context for children that was "negligent at best and virulently racist at worst" (p. 216). Of special concern were the perceived "negative expectations" of white educators in the public school system (p. 216). First Baptist Church members felt that the church's spiritual community provided a safe, supportive environment in which children could learn about their cultural heritage. Emphasis was placed on "helping children understand the relevance of, and then apply, biblical concepts to their own lives" (p. 218). Additionally, children were strongly encouraged to participate in ongoing learning activities and were

[3]This study is from "'Gathering the Spirit' at First Baptist Church: Spirituality as a Protective Factor in the Lives of African American Children," by W. L. Haight, *Social Work*, 43 (3), 123–221. May 1998, National Association of Social Workers.

expected to respond to a series of "call-and-response sequences. For example, when the teacher said that they would no longer be fishermen, but that they would be fishers of _____?, the class responded that they would be fishers of men" (p. 217). The nurturing spiritual community gave children an environment in which they could develop the resilience to cope with any rejection, isolation, or discrimination they experienced in the outside world. Church members also placed great importance on positive, supportive relationships between adults and children.

The Intervention

Along with First Baptist Church leaders, social workers initiated and developed "an intervention, informed by knowledge generated through the ethnographic study, to support the development of children's resilience" (Haight, 1998, p. 219). This intervention strategy was the establishment of a "Computer Club" (p. 219). First Baptist Church members "both prioritized educational achievement and identified school as problematic for African American children" (p. 219). Furthermore, children's computer literacy was identified as "a specific area of need, and learning more about computers as an opportunity that children and families would embrace" (p. 219). Thus members viewed enhancing children's competence with computers as a valuable goal. Although the Computer Club's primary focus was educational computer games, student volunteers from a local university also participated with children in a range of activities, including field trips, parties, picnics, "several computer-generated art shows," African dance groups, and a gospel choir (p. 219). The activities enabled students and children to enjoy mutual experiences, share ideas, and develop positive relationships.

The workers portrayed in this example first explored the values and strengths of the community, and then worked with community members toward a mutually desirable goal. Haight (1998) concludes that

> the ability of social workers to develop knowledge of cultural beliefs and practices relevant both to African American communities in general and to the unique African American communities in which they are practicing is critical to the development of ethnic-sensitive social work interventions such as the Computer Club. (p. 220)

School Social Workers' Role in the Prevention of School Violence

EP 2.1.1c, 2.1.9a, 2.1.9b, 2.1.10h, 2.1.10i

It was a phone call that will stay with Denver Police Officer John Lietz for the rest of his life. Shortly after 11 ... [on a] Tuesday morning, he picked up the line to hear the voice of Matthew Depew, the son of a fellow cop: Depew and 17 other Columbine High School students were trapped in a storage room off the school cafeteria, hiding from kids with guns. Lietz himself had a daughter in the school, and he could hear bursts of gunfire in the background. Lietz told the kids to barricade the door with chairs and sacks of food, and to be ready to attack the gunmen if they got in. Several times Lietz heard the shooters trying to break into the room; they were so close that he could hear them reloading cartridges. At one point, as they pounded on the door, Depew calmly told Lietz that he was sure he was going to die. "Please tell my father I love him," he said.

(Mai, 1999, p. 25)

Several hours later on April 20, 1999, 12 students, two gunmen, and a teacher at Columbine High in Littleton, Colorado, were dead; 23 more students were wounded (Mai, 1999). The shooters were high school students Eric Harris, 18, and Dennis Klebold, 17. Isolated and filled with hatred, they shot themselves as part of the carnage. Harris allegedly explained his actions in an unnerving note: "Your children who have ridiculed me, who have chosen not to accept me, who have treated me like I am not worth their time are dead. THEY ARE (expletive) DEAD" (Williams, 1999, p. 18A). The two teens couldn't "manage their emotions. They feel rejected, enraged, jealous. They are kids who never learned how to solve problems. Combine that with easy access to guns, parents who may have too little time, as well as movies, video games, and music that toast violence, and the result can be lethal" (Cannon, Streisand, & McGraw, 1999, p. 19).

The tragedy in Colorado shook the nation and brought the issue of school violence to the forefront. Years later the Columbine incident remains a painful issue for those close to the ones who died

(Markels, 2007). However, this was not an isolated incident. Consider the following:

- Luke Woodham, 16, who "first killed his mother, [and] then . . . went to his high school and opened fire, killing three and wounding seven."
- Michael Carneal, 14, who "shot three students to death at an early-morning high school prayer meeting."
- Mitchell Johnson, 13, and Andrew Golden, 11, who "set off a fire alarm to draw their schoolmates outside and then started shooting, killing four students and a teacher."
- Kip Kinkel, 15, who "after killing his parents, . . . shot 24 students at school. Two died. Wrestled to the ground, he yelled, 'Shoot me!' " (Begley, 1999, pp. 32–33)
- More recently, Seung-Hui Cho, 23, killed two people in a dorm room and then 30 more in four classrooms on the other side of the Virginia Tech campus on April 16, 2007; then he shot himself in the head (Potter, Schoetz, Esposito, & Thomas, 2007).

Violence among young people and in schools is amazingly common. One major study by the Centers for Disease Control (CDC, 2009) surveyed students from grades 9 to 12 in public and private schools around the country. Findings indicated that 27.1% of males and 7.1% of females said they had carried a weapon at least one day within the 30 days prior to the survey; 9.8% of males and 1.7% of females indicated they had carried a gun. When asked about being involved in a physical fight at least once within the prior 12 months, 39.3% of males and 22.9% of females said they had.

Fiske (2002, September 16) reports on a violence assessment tool developed by Donald. A. Shulman, a crisis specialist at Crestwood Children's Center in Rochester, New Jersey, and explains the dynamics of youth violence:

> *Children most likely to explode in violence are those who feel that nobody cares about them, who believe they have no support, and who feel truly alienated, according to Shulman. Therefore, what can be done to help potential perpetrators of violence and their possible victims? The answer, he states, is simple, inexpensive, and can be done by anyone, regardless of training or background. "When you, myself, or anyone—whether you are a social worker, teacher, or friend—look a child in the eye and say, 'You count. I care about you.*

> *You are important,' you can prevent a murder,"* Shulman offers. *"It is when we feel meaningless and purposeless that we prey on others through violence." (p. 15)*

Other research indicates that the following risk factors may predict youth violence:

- *Hyperactivity or attention deficits.*
- *Parent criminality.*
- *Poor family management practice.*
- *Low bonding to school [which is related to disinterest in school, truancy, and academic failure].*
- *Having delinquent friends.*
- *Gang membership.*

(Sciarra, 2004, p. 346)

Similarly, the following provide early warning signs for violence potential:

- *Social withdrawal.*
- *Excessive feelings of isolation and loneliness.*
- *Excessive feelings of rejection.*
- *Being a victim of violence.*
- *A feeling of being picked on or persecuted.*
- *Low interest in school and poor academic performance.*
- *Expressions of violence in writings and drawings.*
- *Uncontrolled anger.*
- *Patterns of impulsive and chronic hitting, intimidating, and bullying.*
- *A history of discipline problems.*
- *A history of violence and aggressive behaviors.*
- *Intolerance and prejudice.*
- *Drug and alcohol use.*
- *Gang membership.*
- *Inappropriate access to, possession of, and use of firearms.*
- *Serious threats of violence.*

(Sciarra, 2004, p. 347)

On the other hand, the following are protective factors that decrease the risk of violence:

- *Intolerant attitude toward deviance*
- *High IQ*
- *High grade point average*
- *Positive social orientation*
- *Religiosity*
- *Connectedness to family or adults outside the family*
- *Ability to discuss problems with parents*

- *Perceived parental expectations about school performance are high*
- *Frequent shared activities with parents*
- *Consistent presence of parent during at least one of the following: when awakening, when arriving home from school, at evening mealtime or going to bed*
- *Involvement in social activities . . .*
- *Commitment to school*
- *Involvement in social activities (CDC, 2009)*

Bullying

Bullying is a dimension of violence that can occur in school settings. Consider the following scenarios:

- Billy, a fourth-grader, was bigger than most of the other kids in his class. He always went to the head of any line—for recess, the cafeteria, the school bus. If the other kids didn't step aside, he swatted them as hard as he could. Then they stepped aside, all right.
- Shelia, a seventh-grader, was pretty and popular. She couldn't stand Eva, who was withdrawn, had a big nose, and was overweight. She called Eva "Fatty" or "Miss Hippo" or worse whenever she had the chance.
- Dylan, a high school junior, loved to show off in front of his peers. He particularly liked to step in the way of smaller male students, especially those in special ed., and prevent them from using the restroom. He liked to watch them squirm. Twice a kid urinated right there in the hallway.

Steinberg, Bornstein, Vandell, and Rook (2011a) describe bullying:

Bullying refers to aggression by an individual that is repeatedly directed toward particular peers (victims).... It may be physical (hitting, kicking, shoving, tripping), verbal (teasing, harassing, name-calling), or social (public humiliation or exclusion). Bullying differs from other forms of aggression in that it is characterized by specificity (bullies direct their acts to certain peers) and by an imbalance of power between the bully and the victim.... An older child bullies a younger one; a large child picks on a small, weaker one; a verbally assertive child torments a shy, quiet child. It is not bullying when equals have an occasional fight or disagreement. Bullies are more likely to use force unemotionally and outside of the flow of an ongoing conflict. (pp. 318–319)

Although boys are more likely to bully, girls can also participate in such aggressive behavior (Perren & Alsaker, 2006). "In a national survey of more than 15,000 sixth- through tenth-grade students, nearly one of every three students said that they had experienced occasional or frequent involvement as a victim or perpetrator in bullying (Nansel & others, 2001)" (Santrock, 2010a, p. 362). Therefore, it is a significant problem in children's social environment. Santrock (2010a) explains:

Social contexts also influence bullying (Bowes et al., 2009; Bradshaw, Sawyer, & O'Brennan, 2009). Recent research indicates that 70 to 80 percent of victims and their bullies are in the same school classroom (Salmivalli & Peets, 2009). Classmates are often aware of bullying incidents and in many cases witness bullying. The larger social context of the peer group plays an important role in bullying (Salmivalli & Peets, 2009). In many cases, bullies torment victims to gain higher status in the peer group, and bullies need others to witness their power displays. (p. 363)

Victims tend to fall into two categories (Rubin, Bukowski, & Parker, 2006). "The first are children who are shy, anxious, and socially withdrawn, which makes them easy prey. Often they do not have friends to protect them. But other victims are high in aggression themselves and engage in irritating behavior that elicits aggression. Other children see them as 'asking for it.'" (Steinberg et al., 2011a, p. 319).

What results from bullying? Some recent research indicates that when bullies and bully-victims become adolescents, they are more likely to become depressed, think about committing suicide, and actually commit suicide (Brunstein, Klomek, Marrocco, Kleinman, Schofeld, & Gould, 2007). Other research indicates that adolescents who had been either bullies or bully-victims "had more health problems (such as headaches, dizziness, sleep problems, and anxiety) than their counterparts who were not involved in bullying" (Santrock, 2010a, p. 363; Srabstein, McCarter, Shao, & Huang, 2006).

So what can be done about bullying? Santrock (2010a) suggests that school staff can implement the following approaches:

- *Get older peers to serve as monitors for bullying and intervene when they see it taking place.*
- *Develop school-wide rules and sanctions against bullying and post them throughout the school.*

- *Form friendship groups for [children and] adolescents who are regularly bullied by peers.*
- *Incorporate the message of the antibullying program into places of worship, school, and other community activities where [children and] adolescents are involved.*
- *Encourage parents to reinforce their [children's and] adolescent's positive behaviors and model appropriate interpersonal interactions.*
- *Identify bullies and victims early and use social-skills training [including teaching about empathy, communication, and self-control] to improve their behavior.*
- *Encourage parents to contact the school's psychologist, counselor, or social worker and ask for help with their adolescent's bullying or victimization concerns. (p. 364)*

Highlight 15.4 explores a dimension of bullying—cyberbullying.

What Social Workers Can Do

What can school social workers do to prevent school violence? "Violence prevention in schools is becoming a major focus of practice for school social workers"; "school social workers play an increasingly important role in shaping and implementing policy, interventions, and procedures that make U.S. schools safer" (Astor, Benbenishty, & Marachi, 2010, p. 125). Regardless of how they proceed, school social workers must work closely with teachers, school administration, students, their families, and the community to effectively address school violence. Practitioners can assist "in the formulation of school policies and development of programs. Centrally involved in the school community, they are often the first to know about a problem. They have been trained to interpret the meanings of interpersonal behavior and to work with others to find respectful solutions. In so doing they draw on their skills of collaboration; consultation; individual, group, and family intervention; social skills education; crisis intervention; conflict resolution; and the development of mediation systems" (McDonald, Constable, and Moriarty, 2009, p. 729). Other specific suggestions practitioners might follow to prevent school violence include conducting needs assessments, establishing conflict resolution strategies and teams, and developing violence prevention programs.

Needs Assessments

Social workers can work with teachers and school administrators to conduct *needs assessments*—systematic analyses of client problems and issues to determine clients' needs and develop problem-solving strategies. A needs

EP 2.1.6b

assessment can be as easy as reviewing available data, or as complicated as conducting a multifaceted study over several years. Another way of gaining such information is through the use of *focus groups*, where members gather to discuss and explore designated subjects; such groups generate ideas, describe issues, and potentially propose recommendations to address problems (Toseland & Rivas, 2012). In the context of school violence, students representing various social factions might be selected for group membership and asked to describe their perceptions of student hostility and the potential for violence. Regardless of how a needs assessment is done, the important thing is to gain an understanding of the school climate and to identify potential hot spots where violence might be brewing.

Conflict Resolution

Conflict resolution programs provide another means of addressing school violence (McDonald, Fineran, Constable, & Moriarty, 2002). *Conflict resolution* is the process of resolving disputes to come to some sort of

EP 2.1.10j

agreement or compromise between opposing parties. McDonald and Moriarty (2002) explain:

> *Students become increasingly vulnerable to a variety of problems, such as anxiety, stress, a sense of personal inadequacy, and low self-esteem when they are blocked from developing autonomy and self-determination. Such alienated students are at risk of becoming involved in conflict and can be disruptive to the educational process. Social workers can counter this alienation with strategies that reconnect and empower students in a positive manner. Conflict resolution skills are such a tool. (pp. 501–502)*

"The actual process of conflict resolution has several components: (1) identification of the problem in specific language, (2) brainstorming possible solutions, (3) agreeing on a solution, and (4) confirming intent to make the resolution work" (McDonald,

HIGHLIGHT 15.4

Cyberbullying

EP 2.1.9a

Cyberbullying is the use of communication technology (including cell phones, the Internet, and other newly developed technology) to intentionally annoy or harm emotionally another person through repeated hostile or disturbing communication. Some of the ways cyberbullying occurs include when perpetrators:

- Pretend they are other people online to trick others
- Spread lies and rumors about victims
- Trick people into revealing personal information
- Send or forward mean text messages
- Post pictures of victims without their consent (National Crime Prevention Association [NCPA], 2011)

Almost half of American teenagers have experienced cyberbullying (NCPA, 2011). This behavior is difficult to control because it can take place in school or anywhere outside of school. "Often it is difficult to separate between violence that overflows from school grounds to after-school time and vice versa. The consequences of such victimization are felt at school, through mental health and academic problems and engagement in retaliatory violence" (Astor et al., 2010, p. 146).

The California School Boards Association (2007) makes a number of recommendations regarding how school districts can combat cyberbullying; strategies involve:

- *Education of students, parents, and staff.* People should be educated regarding what cyberbullying is, what the warning signs are, and what the legal and school consequences entail. Students should be taught what is appropriate and what is inappropriate electronic communication. Parents and school staff should be taught prevention and intervention tactics.
- *Acceptable use of the district's technological resources.* Policy regarding the use of technology and equipment should be clarified. Cyberbullying should be prohibited and its consequences clearly stated.
- *Use of filters to block Internet sites.* Although this cannot block all potential cyberbullying, it can serve to curb it by blocking access to some social networking sites where cyberbullying easily occurs.
- *Supervision and monitoring of students' online activity.* Students' online activity should be supervised. Staff doing such monitoring should be taught about the district's policy and what is considered the appropriate use of equipment.
- *Mechanisms for reporting cyberbullying.* Students should be encouraged to report any incidents of cyberbullying. Because the victim often fears retaliation by the perpetrator, when possible, confidential or anonymous means of reporting should be established.
- *Assessment of imminent threat.* The district should develop procedures for assessing the legitimacy of the threat and the potential for ensuing violence. Protection from harm should be a top priority.
- *Investigation of reported incidents.* Procedures for other types of harassment should also be followed in incidents of cyberbullying. Students should be discouraged from responding to any cyberbullying that occurs and to save or print out any messages for evidence.
- *Appropriate response to incidents of cyberbullying.* School disciplinary procedures should be followed. "Depending on the seriousness of the harassment, responses might include notifying the parents of both the victim and perpetrator, filing a complaint with the Internet service provider or social networking site to have the content removed and/or the student's user privileges revoked, using conflict resolution procedures, suspending or expelling the perpetrator, and/or contacting law enforcement if the behavior involves a threat of violence to a person, a threat of damage to property, extortion, obscene or harassing phone calls or text messages, stalking, a hate crime, invading someone's privacy by taking a photo where there should be a reasonable expectation of privacy, or sending sexually explicit images of children or teens" (pp. 4–5).

et al., 2009, p. 739). Whereas the process of conflict resolution is usually the same, the way programs are implemented can differ. McDonald and her colleagues (2009) elaborate:

Some school districts have instituted system-wide training in conflict resolution skills. Some have a formal program, such as specially trained teams of student-mediators or conflict resolvers. [Mediators are neutral referees or peacemakers who help resolve disputes between opposing parties.] These specially trained students are often identified as a team and have regular meetings. In schools that have such teams, there is likely to be a set policy regarding which types of problems are appropriate for referral to mediation. Other districts do some training with all students, but also train a [core group] . . . of students who are available for more difficult situations. When emotions are running high, or when there seems to be an imbalance in power, the team would ensure that each party to the dispute is respectful to the other. Younger students may wear special vests on playgrounds and in lunchrooms or during special functions where students are not being closely supervised, to identify them as mediators. Some schools have students identified in each classroom as the designated conflict resolvers. They may hold dispute-resolution sessions in the classroom, ideally in an area somewhat removed from the rest of the class. In all cases, the school must have a way to oversee the referral process and mediation session so that conflict resolvers and mediators are at all times protected from serious problems or risks. (p. 739)

Violence Prevention Programs

Astor and colleagues (2010) maintain that successful violence prevention programs must be organized endeavors with the following characteristics:

- *They raise the awareness and responsibility of students, teachers, and parents regarding the types of violence in their schools (e.g., sexual harassment, fighting, weapon use).*
- *They create clear guidelines and rules for the entire school [that reinforce appropriate positive behavior and stress penalties for aggressive behavior].*
- *They target the various social systems in the school and clearly communicate to the entire school community what procedures should be followed before, during, and after violent events.*

- *They focus on getting the school staff, students, and parents involved in the program.*
- *The interventions often fit easily into the normal flow and mission of the school setting.*
- *They utilize faculty, staff, and parents in the school setting in order to plan, implement, and sustain the program.*
- *They increase monitoring and supervision in non-classroom areas.*
- *They are culturally sensitive, culturally competent, and immersed within the community/culture of the students. (p. 136)*

An example is the Positive Adolescents Choices Training (PACT) program "designed to teach African-American youth social skills to aid in prevention of violence (Hammond & Yung, 1991, 1993; Yung & Hammond, 1998)" (Astor et al., 2010, p. 146).

A unique aspect of PACT is that it is culturally relevant and aimed at reducing aggression and victimization in high-risk youth. The program components include anger management, prosocial skills training, and violence risk education. The sessions are built around [DVDs] . . . that demonstrate culturally sensitive social situations. Participants learn specific skills needed to solve the situation peacefully. Participants in the programs [improved their behavior] . . . in the areas of giving feedback, problem-solving, and resisting peer pressure [in addition to demonstrating a significant decrease in] physical aggression at school.

(Astor et al., 2010, p. 174)

Teenage Sexual Activity, Pregnancy, and Parenting Issues

Sexual activity and teenage pregnancy are important issues for young people today. Any social worker working with youths will likely address the decisions concerning and the consequences of early sexual activity. **EP 2.1.9a** Social work settings overlap. Work with youths occurs in various settings and fields of practice, including school social work, corrections, mental health, child welfare, runaway shelters, and Planned Parenthood clinics.[4]

[4]Planned Parenthood is a national organization created in 1921 to promote research and disseminate information about contraception and family planning.

Of all births in the United States, 10.5% are to teenage mothers (U.S. Census Bureau, 2010). Although there was a slight decline in the pregnancy rate for this group over the past decade, there still are about 750,000 such pregnancies annually (Crooks & Baur, 2011). Papalia, Olds, and Feldman (2009) elaborate:

More than 4 in 10 adolescent girls in the United States have been pregnant at least once before age 20. More than half (51 percent) of pregnant teenagers in the United States have their babies, and 35 percent choose to abort. Fourteen percent of teen pregnancies end in miscarriage or stillbirth....

Although declines in teenage pregnancy and childbearing have occurred among all population groups, birthrates have fallen most sharply among black teenagers—by 46 percent. Still, black and Hispanic girls are more likely to have babies than white, American Indian, or Asian American girls....

More than 90 percent of pregnant teenagers describe their pregnancies as unintended, and 50 percent of teen pregnancies occur within six months of sexual initiation. (p. 402)

Santrock (2010b) reflects on the international picture:

The United States continues to have one of the highest rates of adolescent pregnancy and childbearing in the developed world, despite a considerable decline in the 1990s.... The U.S. adolescent pregnancy rate is eight times as high as in the Netherlands. Although U.S. adolescents are no more sexually active than their counterparts in the Netherlands, their adolescent pregnancy rate is dramatically higher. (p. 454)

Focus on Critical Thinking 15.1 raises questions regarding the reasons for the high rates of adolescent pregnancy in the United States.

Reasons for Concern

What happens to these babies after birth? Teenage pregnancy is a serious social welfare concern for at least four reasons.

Children Begetting Children

First, teen mothers are children themselves. Most babies born to single teens remain at home with their young mothers. "Among U.S. adolescents who do not abort their pregnancy, the vast majority—over 90 percent—keep and raise the infant, whereas only 1 in 10 chooses to have the child adopted" (Steinberg, et al., 2011a, p. 344).

Keeping their babies places these young women in a situation very different from that of most of their peers. Adolescence and young adulthood are the usual times of life for finding a mate, obtaining an education, and making a career choice. The additional responsibility of motherhood places serious restrictions on the amount of freedom and time available for these activities. Additionally, such young women are often ill prepared for motherhood. They are usually in the midst of establishing their own identities and learning to care for themselves.

Negative Physical Consequences

A second reason teenage pregnancy is a social welfare concern involves the likely negative physical consequences for mother and baby. Young mothers are more likely than more mature women to experience difficulties (Kail & Cavanaugh, 2010; Papalia, et al., 2009; Santrock, 2010b). Young mothers' problems include prolonged labor, hemorrhaging, and miscarriage. The infant is more likely to have a low birth weight, to be born prematurely, and to have neurological and developmental difficulties than infants born to adult mothers (Papalia et al., 2009; Sansrock 2010b). Many of these problems are due to poor or nonexistent prenatal care and to poor nutrition.

Long-Term Negative Effects for Mothers

Research indicates that negative effects on the young mother continue long after the baby's birth. Teenage mothers often drop out of school (Newman & Newman, 2012; Papalia et al., 2009; Santrock, 2010b). They are also more likely to be poor and have subsequent pregnancies (Papalia et al., 2009). Many have less ambition to pursue higher levels of education in the future (Mooney et al., 2009).

They may not have "the maturity, skills, and social support" to be effective parents (Papalia et al., 2009, p. 403). The stress and responsibility of motherhood tend to take a heavy toll on teen mothers. Raising a child demands time, energy, and attention. Time taken to care for a baby must be subtracted from the time available for school and recreational activities.

All this sounds quite negative. Santrock (2010b) cautions that "not every adolescent female who bears a child lives a life of poverty and low achievement. Thus, although adolescent pregnancy is a high-risk circumstance, and adolescents who do not become pregnant generally fare better than those

FOCUS ON CRITICAL THINKING 15.1

The Pregnancy Rate for Adolescents in the United States

EP 2.1.3, 2.1.9a

Santrock (2007) indicates that "U.S. adolescents are no more sexually active than their counterparts in countries such as France and Sweden. Why, then, are U.S. adolescent pregnancy rates so high?" (p. 464). He suggests three possible reasons (Boonstra, 2002, pp. 9–10, cited in Santrock, 2007, pp. 464–465). First, in other countries, "'*childbearing is considered an adult activity*'" (Boonstra, 2002, pp. 9–10, cited in Santrock, 2007, p. 464). Adolescents are given clear messages that pregnancy is part of adulthood, not childhood. Employed, responsible adults are ready to assume caregiving responsibilities for children.

Second, adolescents in the United States don't receive

'clear messages about sexual behavior. While adults in other countries strongly encourage teens to wait until they have established themselves before having children, they are generally more accepting than American adults of teens having sex. In France and Sweden, in particular, teen sexual expression is seen as normal and positive, but there is also widespread expectation that sexual intercourse will take place within committed relationships. (In fact, relationships among U.S. teens tend to be more sporadic and of shorter duration.) Equally strong is the expectation that young people who are having sex will take actions to protect themselves and their partners from pregnancy and sexually transmitted infections' which is much stronger in Europe than in the United States. 'In keeping with this view, schools in Great Britain, France, Sweden, and most of Canada' have sex education programs that provide more comprehensive information about prevention than U.S. schools. In addition, these countries use the media more often in

'government-sponsored campaigns for promoting responsible sexual behavior.'

> (Boonstra, 2002, pp. 9–10,
> cited in Santrock, 2007, pp. 464–465)

A third reason for the differences in teen pregnancy rates between the United States and other Western countries involves

access to family planning services. In countries that are more accepting of teenage sexual relationships, teenagers also have easier access to reproductive health services. In Canada, France, Great Britain, and Sweden, contraceptive services are integrated into other types of primary health care and are available free or at low cost for all teenagers. Generally, teens (in these countries) know where to obtain information and services and receive confidential and nonjudgmental care. In the United States, where attitudes about teenage sexual relationships are more conflicted, teens have a harder time obtaining contraceptive services. Many do not have health insurance or cannot get birth control as part of their basic health care.

> (Boonstra, 2002, pp. 9–10,
> cited in Santrock, 2007, pp. 464–465)

Critical Thinking Questions

- What do you think are the reasons why so many teenagers in the United States get pregnant? What are their motivating factors?
- Are U.S. teenagers getting the wrong messages about sexuality and pregnancy? If so, what are they? What messages should U.S. teenagers be getting?
- Should sexual expression by U.S. adolescents be more accepted? Why or why not? If so, how should society convey ideas about appropriate behavior?
- Should contraception be made more readily available to U.S. adolescents? Why or why not?

who do, some adolescent mothers do well in school and have positive outcomes" (p. 455). Adolescent motherhood puts adolescents at risk of hardship. It does not necessarily doom them to a bad life.

Long-Term Negative Effects for Children

Studies also reveal negative effects on the children of teen pregnancies themselves. As the children of teenage mothers mature, they tend to have more

difficulties in school (Kail & Cavenaugh, 2010). Many of them "face a life of challenges that accompany poverty, including poor nutrition, violence in the local neighborhood, little schooling, and inadequate health care"; they also "grow up at high risk of becoming single parents themselves" (Macionis, 2010, p. 192).

What does all this mean for social workers? It means that children having children is a serious issue. Social work practitioners working with youths may need to provide these young people with information about contraception, sexually transmitted infections, and the responsibilities of parenthood. Social workers may also be in the position to help adolescents undertake a decision-making process whereby they make educated, responsible choices.

Reasons Teens Get Pregnant

To determine what resources and services are needed, we must understand the dynamics behind a problem. Why does the problem exist? What are teenagers' needs? What can social services and social workers do to meet them?

Although female adolescents are more likely to use contraception than they've been in past decades, many fail to use it every time or in some situations. Consider the following facts (Guttmacher Institute, 2011):

- *Although only 13% of teens have ever had vaginal sex by age 15, sexual activity is common by the late teen years.... [Seventy percent have had sexual intercourse by age 19.]*
- *On average, young people have sex for the first time at about age 17,... but they do not marry until their mid-20s.... [This long time frame increases the risk of pregnancy and sexually transmitted infections (STIs).]*
- *A sexually active teen who does not use a contraceptive has a 90% chance of becoming pregnant within a year....*
- *The majority of sexually experienced teens (79% of females and 87% of males) used contraceptives the first time they had sex....*
- *Contraceptive use at first premarital sex has been increasing. Fifty-six percent of women whose first premarital sex occurred before 1985 used a method, compared with 76% in 2000–2004 and 84% in 2005–2008....*
- *In 2006–2008, some 84% of female teens and 93% of male teens reported using contraceptives at last sex. These proportions represent a marked improvement since 1995, when only 71% of female teens and 82% of male teens had reported using a method at last sex. However, the proportions were unchanged between 2002 and 2006–2008....*
- *Nearly one in five female teens at risk of unintended pregnancy (19%) were not using any contraceptive method at last intercourse.*

Teens who are not in stable relationships, have sexual intercourse only infrequently, have a significantly older partner, or begin having intercourse at an early age are less likely to use contraception (Crooks & Baur, 2011). Factors related to increased likelihood of contraceptive use include a close relationship with parents, including good communication channels, success in school, family values that stress responsible behavior, and having accurate information about contraception (Crooks & Baur, 2011).

Failure to Use Birth Control

There are a number of reasons for imperfect contraceptive use. Adolescents often have a deep sense of privacy about sexual behavior and feel embarrassed discussing it with partners, friends, or parents (Crooks & Baur, 2011; Hyde & DeLamater, 2008). Thus a young woman may feel extremely uncomfortable talking to a partner about such intimate issues as putting a condom on his penis or placing a diaphragm in her vagina.

Many adolescents may have inadequate knowledge about birth control methods and inadequate access to contraception (Crooks & Baur, 2011; Hyde & DeLamater, 2008). Other adolescents adhere to myths about sex (Crooks & Baur, 2008). For instance, many teens inaccurately believe that they are not old enough to conceive, that "the first time" doesn't count, that they must have intercourse much more frequently than they do in order to conceive, that it is perfectly safe to have sex during certain times of the month, and that withdrawal before ejaculation is an effective birth control method.

Focus on Critical Thinking 15.2 discusses conservative and liberal views concerning whose responsibility it is to provide young people with adequate sex education and information.

Case Example Once I gave a one-time sex education program (as an invited guest social work professor) to about 200 teenagers in which I responded to their questions, written anonymously. After the program, two teenagers sheepishly approached me. Apparently they had been too embarrassed to ask their questions even anonymously. The first young woman, age 16, said that she had had sex with her boyfriend and used vaginal foam as a contraceptive. Unfortunately, afterward she had noticed that the container had an expiration date of six months before. She asked if I thought that she would be all

---

FOCUS ON CRITICAL THINKING 15.2

Conservative and Liberal Views on Policy Regarding the Provision of Sex Education

EP 2.1.3, 2.1.7a

A *conservative* value orientation might emphasize that it is parents' responsibility to provide information about sex to their children and that schools should not interfere with parental prerogative. A *liberal* perspective, in contrast, might stress that children need information about sex regardless of who provides it. The important thing is that they get information so they can make responsible decisions.

Critical Thinking Questions

• Should parents have primary responsibility for providing sex education to their children?

• Should schools ask parents permission to provide sex information to their children?
• In the event that parents refuse permission, should their children be denied information about sex?
• What type of content about sex should be provided to young people? Information about contraception? Moral values? Abortion?
• Do your answers to these questions reflect more of a conservative or a liberal perspective?

---

right, that she would not be pregnant. This was a difficult situation, and there was not much I could do. Even when they have not expired, spermicides (sperm killers) such as contraceptive foam used without other forms of contraception such as a condom have a failure rate as high as 25% (Hyde & DeLamater, 2011). I responded by encouraging the young woman to get a home pregnancy test or go to a Planned Parenthood clinic for one. Even if she chose the home test, I suggested going to Planned Parenthood anyway. In the event that she was pregnant, a counselor could help her make a decision about what to do. And if she was not pregnant, a counselor could assist her in determining what type of contraception would be most effective for her in the future. I made certain she knew the nearest Planned Parenthood clinic's location and that she had a means of getting there.

The second teen, a thin, gangly young woman with braces who looked like she was 12, hesitantly approached me. She bluntly asked, "If someone gives a guy oral sex and swallows it, can she get pregnant?" I had to keep myself from smiling and explained to her that someone could not get pregnant under those circumstances. I did caution her, however, about the potential for contracting sexually transmitted infections, including HIV.

Other Psychological Reasons

Other reasons for not using birth control involve psychologically wanting to have a baby. Strong, Devault, Sayad, and Yarber (2005) comment, "The idea of having someone to love them exclusively and unconditionally is a strong incentive for some teenage girls" (pp. 402–403). In essence, they feel a baby will fulfill their own emotional needs. Unfortunately, they don't understand that it's supposed to be the other way around. The last person you should expect to meet all of your needs for nurturance is a helpless infant. Strong and colleagues (2008) comment:

> Others see having a baby as a way to escape from an oppressive home environment. Both teen males and females may see parenthood as a way to enhance their status, to give them an aura of maturity, or to enhance their masculinity or femininity. Some believe a baby will cement a shaky relationship. (p. 180)

There are yet other reasons teens may not use birth control. They might not want to bother with contraception. They might believe that sexual activity is more pleasurable without it. They may worry that their parents will find out. Finally, they may feel invulnerable to pregnancy, viewing it as something that happens only to other people.

Social Work Roles

EP 2.1.1c

No consistent national policy exists for addressing teen pregnancies and parenting services; however, federal funding is available to develop programs through "block grants to states for direct services" (Mather & Lager, 2000, p. 204). Social workers may assume many roles and pursue various goals when providing services to adolescents concerning pregnancy and parenting. Goals include prevention of pregnancy, identification of pregnancy, counseling concerning alternatives, help during pregnancy, help for teenage fathers, and help after the pregnancy.

Prevention of Pregnancy

EP 2.1.10i

Primary prevention of pregnancy involves preventing the problem altogether, assuming that the pregnancy is a problem (Weatherley & Cartoof, 1988). Adolescents need both information and ready access to contraception so they can make responsible decisions.

Some people may wonder whether sex education programs in schools teach youths everything they need to know. The answer is, not necessarily. Program content and methods vary radically (Hyde & DeLamater, 2011; Rathus et al., 2011). They range from showing a couple of DVDs and handing out brochures to offering "well-developed curricula which include lectures, books, DVDs ... and classroom discussion" (Hyde & DeLamater, 2003, p. 618). Rathus and colleagues (2008) comment:

> Nearly all states mandate or recommend sex education, although its content varies widely. Most programs emphasize biological aspects of puberty, reproduction, and sexually transmitted infections (STIs). Few deal with controversial, topics such as abortion, masturbation, sexual orientation, or even sexual pleasure. (p. 409–410)

Research strongly indicates that "comprehensive sex education programs that stress safer sex and provide accurate information about various contraceptive methods actually increase the use of birth control, reduce teenage pregnancies, reduce high-risk sexual behavior, do not hasten the onset of intercourse (and in some cases actually delay onset), do not increase the frequency of intercourse, and do not increase the number of an adolescent's sexual partners (in some cases they reduce partner

number)" (Crooks & Baur, 2011, p. 369). Effective sex education programs:

- *focus on reducing risk-taking behavior ...*
- *are based on theories of social learning ...*
- *teach through experiential activities that personalize the messages ...*
- *address media and other social influences that encourage sexual risk-taking behaviors ...*
- *reinforce clear and appropriate values ...*
- *enhance communication skills. (Hyde & DeLamater, 2011, pp. 514–515)*

Social workers working in social service agencies or schools may see the need to advocate for and develop sex education programs for adolescent clients. They may also provide information during counseling to individuals or groups. Highlight 15.5 offers some suggestions about how to provide straightforward information about sex.

Access to methods of birth control also is important in preventing pregnancy. Components that seem to increase adolescents' use of clinics include "free services, an absence of parental notification, convenient hours for students, walk-in service, a diversity of locations, and warm and caring staff" (Weatherley & Cartoof, 1988, p. 39).

Identification of Pregnancy

It's important for social workers to help young clients identify a pregnancy as early as possible for two basic reasons. First, good nutrition, prenatal medical care, and avoidance of harmful substances are essential for healthy fetal development. A fetus is at greatest risk of harm early in the pregnancy. Second, adolescents have more options potentially available to them early in the pregnancy (e.g., a first-trimester abortion).

Social workers who work with teenagers should encourage them to confront the fact that pregnancy might result from sexual activities. As discussed previously, workers can give adolescent information about potential consequences of their behavior so they can make more responsible decisions. Workers can also help adolescents face the fact that they might be pregnant instead of ignoring the possibility as long as possible. Many pregnant teenagers adopt an "out of sight, out of mind" attitude: If they don't think about the pregnancy, it doesn't exist. Unfortunately, their options decrease as time goes on. Unless there's a miscarriage, pregnancy usually doesn't go away by itself.

HIGHLIGHT 15.5

Providing Straightforward Information About Sex

Effectively conveying sensitive information about sexuality can be difficult. Social workers and other professionals in the position of supplying sexual information to teenagers (and adults, for that matter) ideally should do the following (Hyde & DeLamater, 2011):

1. *Have accurate information about sexuality.* To convey information about sex and answer explicit questions, accurate information is essential. Workers don't need a degree in sexology to convey such information. Rather, they can learn via taking courses, attending seminars, or reading sexuality textbooks. No one knows the answer to every question. Instead of being defensive about gaps in their knowledge, workers should feel comfortable enough to admit ignorance and simply look up the answer.

2. *Feel comfortable talking about sexuality.* Providing accurate information is only one part of teaching about sex. Teenagers should feel as comfortable as possible approaching a worker and asking questions. They should not fear that the worker will criticize them or make fun of them.

3. *Be a good listener.* No matter how much knowledge workers have or how warm and caring they are, if they don't connect with the teenager, they won't convey the information needed. Listening means striving to understand what the person making a statement or asking a question really means. What does she or he really want and need to know?

The following are actual questions asked anonymously by teenagers age 13–18. They are straightforward and may be considered vulgar by some. However, they reflect the serious need for specific, practical information concerning topics usually not addressed in school. They are cited as they were written, spelling errors and all (actually, these are some of the tamer questions asked).

As you read the questions, think about how you might answer them.

- What is the average age a woman has an organism?
- What happens if a girl is too tight?
- When a girl gives a guy "head" can she get any STDs?

- How big is the average penis?
- What are the girls erotic zones?
- Do women always bleed when the hymen is broken?
- What are the risks of having an abortion?
- How does it feel when you get devirginized?
- What can you do if your boyfriends is too big and it hurts every time you have sex?
- What can you do if the guy tries something and you say no but he keep going?
- Should you have sex if you're ashamed of your body?
- What is the percentage of boys that masturbate? Girls?
- When you're making love with a guy, does he honestly think of the emotional aspect or does he just want a piece?
- What is group sex?
- Why do males and females hide their feelings about each other?
- How do you have better orgasm?
- How do you know if you've had an orgasm? For female, what does it feel like inside?
- What is the next best contraceptive other than the pill for girls and guys?
- Can a man sperm and urine at the same time?

Note that professionals must be aware of the controversial nature of talk about sex. They must also be attuned to the attitudes and expectations of agencies, administrators, communities, and parents. This can pose a dilemma for workers. On the one hand, they may know what information teens require to make responsible decisions. On the other, they may face negative reactions by parents and others.[5]

---

[5]SIECUS (Sexuality Information and Education Council of the United States) is an excellent source of information concerning sex education programming, and how to work with agencies and communities to provide young people with information concerning sexuality. The New York office is located at 90 John St., Suite 402, New York, NY 10038. Phone: 212/819-9970. Fax: 212/819-9776. The Washington, D.C., office is located at 1706 R Street, NW, Washington, DC 20009. Phone: 202/265-2405. Fax: 202/462-2340. E-mail: http://www.siecus.org/.

Counseling Concerning Alternatives

**EP 2.1.10g,
2.1.10j**

Once the pregnancy has been established as fact, decisions must be made. Social workers apply the basic approach of helping the adolescent identify her alternatives, and then evaluate the pros and cons of each. Options include having an abortion, going through with the pregnancy and keeping the baby, or continuing with the pregnancy and giving the baby up for adoption.

For each individual, options will have different pros and cons. One individual may have strong religious beliefs that affect her decision; another will not have such convictions. States also have large variations regarding the legal circumstances under which abortions may be obtained. It's a social worker's job to help the client evaluate the situation from her unique perspective and make the choice that's best for her.

Mather and Lager (2000) also suggest that the father "needs to be given every opportunity to take part in this decision, if possible, and his legal rights need to be clearly laid out for him" (p. 205).

Help During Pregnancy

Social workers can provide important help and support during pregnancy (Weatherley & Cartoof, 1988). It's easy for teenagers to become depressed and isolated during that time. Physical changes may have an impact, especially in view of the great emphasis placed on physical appearance, attractiveness, and popularity during adolescence. One junior high teacher once said that talking about the responsibility of pregnancy and teen parenthood had absolutely no effect on her students. However, the young women sat up with serious faces and widened eyes when told that once they have a baby women often have stretch marks on their abdomens for the rest of their lives. To these young women, stretch marks were serious consequences.

Pregnant adolescents may also need help relating to friends and family members. This involves maintaining good communication with and receiving emotional support from others around them. Many times a social worker may need to do active outreach to the pregnant teen. Home visits may be especially useful. Counseling can be provided either individually or on a group basis.

Pregnant teens most often need counseling about good nutrition and the effects of lifestyle on the fetus. For instance, they need to be well informed about the results of alcohol and drug use during pregnancy. Teens also may need help in determining what to do about the pregnancy and making other plans involving living conditions, day care, education, and employment.

Case Example   Prenatal care is critically important for mothers and infants. Some good news is that the use of prenatal care during the first three months of pregnancy has increased since 1990 from 75.8% of pregnant women to 83.9% (Papalia et al., 2009). However, "3.5 percent of expectant mothers received no care until the last trimester or no care at all" (Papalia et al., 2009, p. 90). Prenatal care is not available to everyone who needs it. It makes sense that women who are "young, poor, unmarried, relatively uneducated, uninsured, or living in inner cities or rural areas" are likely to receive the poorest prenatal care (Balsanek, 1998, p. 411). These women are thus at risk of problems and complications. Women who receive less than adequate prenatal care are significantly more likely to have infants with low birth weights and other problems at birth (Papalia et al., 2009).

Shared Beginnings, a Denver program, provides a good example of how various facets of a community came together to address the issue of at-risk young pregnant women and provide resources (Balsanek, 1998).[6] Initial consciousness-raising occurred through extensive media coverage of the problem, alerting the public to the fact that increasing numbers of poor, single, and young mothers were failing to seek or receive prenatal care. Although the program was spearheaded by a concerned volunteer philanthropist, it illustrates how social workers can start up a program to meet clients' needs. The initiator brought citizens, social services representatives, health care personnel, and potential financial backers together to launch the project. Fund-raising efforts included a luncheon program supported by influential community members and solicitation of financial donations.

---

[6]From "Addressing At-Risk Pregnant Women's Issues Through Community, Individual, and Corporate Grassroots Efforts," by J. Balsanek. In P. L. Ewalt, E. M. Freeman, and D. L. Poole (Eds.), Community Building: Renewal, Well-Being, and Shared Responsibility, pp. 411–419, 1998, National Association of Social Workers, Inc.

Participants involved in the project established five basic program goals. The first was to educate the community concerning the importance of prenatal health care and to alter attitudes on health care's behalf. The second goal was the initiation of a "Sharing Partners" program that sent volunteer paraprofessionals out into the community to educate residents about prenatal care and to encourage them to use services. The third goal was to establish an agency complete with director, administrative assistant, and volunteer coordinator to monitor progress. The fourth was the creation of a "Baby Store" located in a local hospital where "coupons could be redeemed for new baby care items to reinforce health care appointment attendance before the baby is born and immunizations after the baby is born" (Balsanek, 1998, p. 414). The final goal was to integrate a research component to evaluate the program's effectiveness and provide suggestions for improvement. In summary, "Shared Beginnings represents a grassroots [developed and supported by citizens at lower levels of the power structure] approach to providing the community support that poor and at-risk families need to raise healthy children" (p. 418).

Helping Adolescent Fathers

It's important not to forget that babies born to adolescent mothers also have fathers (Weatherley & Cartoof, 1988). Despite myths to the contrary, most teen fathers are significantly affected by their child's birth and are involved to various degrees in the child's early life (Strong et al., 2008; Weatherley & Cartoof, 1988).

An adolescent father may need help in expressing his feelings, defining his role, and contributing where he can in caring for his child. Many adolescent fathers have psychological repercussions as a result of the pregnancy (Carroll & Wolpe, 1996; Strong et al., 2008). Additionally, they may need help and encouragement in pursuing educational and vocational goals.

Helping Mothers After the Pregnancy

EP 2.1.10l

It's important to keep in mind the continuum of service that social workers may provide. The young mother's needs do not suddenly stop after the baby is born; the case is not automatically closed. Weatherley and Cartoof (1988) cite three major areas where adolescent mothers may need ongoing help.

First, they may need help in learning about positive parenting and child management skills. Several features have been found to enhance this training. For one thing, training should be "flexible, informal, and individualized" (Weatherley & Cartoof, 1988, p. 49). For another, training is more beneficial when provided after the baby is born rather than during the pregnancy (McGee, 1982). Finally, all involved family members and caregivers, including the child's father, should be included in the training (Furstenberg & Crawford, 1978).

Second, adolescent mothers often need help in avoiding more pregnancies. Pregnancy is no guarantee that they have an adequate knowledge of conception or of birth control methodology. Both information and ready access to contraception are necessary.

Third, young mothers often need assistance in life planning. Issues include continuing their education, gaining employment, finding day care for their children, and determining where and how they will live.

Chapter Summary

The following summarizes this chapter's content as it relates to the chapter objectives presented at the beginning of the chapter. Objectives include the following:

A Describe school social work and define the various roles of school social workers.

School social workers strive to improve the overall functioning of students, teachers, school systems, and communities. Their roles include consultant, counselor, facilitator, educator, advocate, broker, case manager, community intervention collaborator, and policy initiator and developer. Advocacy for cultural competence and on the behalf of refugee and immigrant students is discussed.

B Identify the types of groups school social workers run.

Groups social workers run include groups for parents of students; for students who are parents; for students whose families are experiencing divorce; for students who are addressing substance abuse issues; for students with attention deficit hyperactivity disorder; for trauma-related recovery; for students at risk of dropping out; for students addressing stress, grief, and loss issues; for socialization and peer interaction skill development; and for addressing racial and cultural issues.

C Suggest ways multiculturalism can be enhanced and racism reduced in schools.

Social workers can fight racism and encourage multiculturalism by running open discussion, infusing such content in curricula, focusing on the appreciation of difference, providing school staff with multicultural training, and involving parents in efforts to promote multiculturalism.

D Discuss lesbian, gay, bisexual, and transgender (LGBT) youths as populations-at-risk, focusing on issues involved in the "coming out" process.

Social workers can help LGBT people explore their sexual identities and come out to others. Coming out involves both coming out to oneself and also to others. Careful thought should be given to whom to trust and how to come out.

E Identify and refute various myths about LGBT people.

Untrue myths about LGBT people include that people's outward appearance looks "gay" or "lesbian," that gay men are child molesters, that lesbian and gay couples assume traditional gender-role stereotypes, that all LGBT people are promiscuous, and that children growing up in LGBT families become psychologically damaged.

F Describe two community programs for youths— one that empowers Latino/Latina youths through a community assets assessment and one that explores how an African American spiritual community empowers its youths.

New Bridges targeted a group of Latino/Latina youths who were at risk and hired them to conduct a community assets assessment. Results included the identification of student leaders to sponsor community projects, the provision of invitations to local business leaders to come in to speak to students, and special school projects emphasizing community strengths.

An ethnographic study in Utah resulted in a church-sponsored support program for African American youth and the development of a computer literacy program.

G Review social workers' potential role in the prevention of school violence.

To assist in the prevention of school violence, social workers can conduct needs assessments, provide conflict resolution, and develop violence prevention programs. Bullying and cyberbullying are also discussed.

H Examine the issues of teenage sexual activity, pregnancy, and parenting issues, and describe social work roles concerning them.

Of all births in the United States, 10.5% are to teenage mothers. More than half have their babies and most keep them. The U.S. pregnancy rate is significantly higher than that of other Western countries. Possible reasons include that society is not clearly conveying to teens that childbearing is an adult activity, they are not receiving clear messages about the normalcy of sexual behavior, and family planning information and contraception are not readily available. The importance of comprehensive sex education and the provision of straightforward information about sexuality is stressed.

I Encourage critical thinking about reasons for teen pregnancy, what should be done about it, and the provision of sex education.

Critical thinking questions were raised concerning the reasons for teen pregnancy and how the issue could be addressed. Other questions were raised concerning conservative and liberal views on policies regarding the provision of sex education and the programmatic content that should be included.

LOOKING AHEAD

Chapter 16 explores the final field of social work practice in this book—social work and services in criminal justice. As with health care and mental health, there is some overlap between social work with youths and criminal justice—specifically, juvenile corrections and young people's involvement with gangs. Chapter 16 will introduce crime and criminal justice, describe social work roles, and explore primary criminal justice settings.

COMPETENCY NOTES

The following identifies where Educational Policy (EP) competencies and practice behaviors are discussed in the chapter.

EP 2.1.1c Attend to professional roles and boundaries. *(p. 460):* The wide range of professional roles assumed by social workers within school settings is introduced. *(p. 462):* Nine specific roles in school social work are identified and explained. *(p. 473):* Professional social workers' role in the prevention of school violence is discussed. *(p. 483):* Social workers' role with respect to the prevention of teen pregnancy is addressed.

EP 2.1.3 Apply critical thinking to inform and communicate professional judgments. *(p. 480):* Critical thinking questions are posed regarding adolescent pregnancy, the dynamics involved, and how it should be addressed. *(p. 482):* Critical thinking questions are asked concerning conservative and liberal perspectives on sex education.

EP 2.1.4 Engage diversity and difference in practice. *(p. 465):* Immigration status is a dimension of diversity.

EP 2.1.4a Recognize the extent to which culture's structures and values may oppress, marginalize, alienate, or create or enhance privilege and power. *(p. 465):* School social workers should recognize the extent to which societal structures in education may oppress and alienate people from diverse cultures. *(p. 467):* Social workers should recognize the extent to which people with nonheterosexual orientations may be oppressed, marginalized, and alienated. *(p. 468):* Social workers should recognize the extent to which people from diverse cultures may be marginalized and alienated.

EP 2.1.4b Gain sufficient self-awareness to eliminate the influence of personal biases and values in working with diverse groups. *(p. 469):* Social workers should increase their own self-awareness about personal biases concerning LGBT people.

EP 2.1.4c Recognize and communicate their understanding of the importance of difference in shaping life experiences. *(p. 465):* Social workers should recognize how cultural differences shape life experiences in school settings. *(p. 467):* Social workers should recognize that sexual orientation is important in shaping life experiences. *(p. 468):*

Practitioners should recognize the extent to which cultural differences shape life experiences.

EP 2.1.4d View themselves as learners and engage those with whom they work as informants. *(p. 469):* Social workers should view themselves as learners about LGBT issues and engage lesbian and gay adolescents as informants.

EP 2.1.5a Understand the forms and mechanisms of oppression and discrimination. *(p. 471):* Stereotypes and myths about LGBT people serve as forms of oppression and discrimination.

EP 2.1.5b Advocate for human rights and social and economic justice. *(p. 464):* School social workers should advocate for human rights and social and economic justice on the behalf of their students.

EP 2.1.6b Use research evidence to inform practice. *(p. 471):* The New Bridges program involved a community assets assessment that could be used to inform service delivery and practice. *(p. 476):* A needs assessment gathers information to inform practice.

EP 2.1.7a Utilize conceptual frameworks to guide the processes of assessment, intervention, and evaluation. *(p. 482):* Critical thinking questions encourage thought about assessing sex education from conservative and liberal conceptual frameworks.

EP 2.1.7b Critique and apply knowledge to understand person and environment. *(p. 472):* An ethnographic study such as that employed here can be used to assess the environment.

EP 2.1.8a Analyze, formulate, and advocate for policies that advance social well-being. *(p. 467):* Social workers should strive to establish policies and programs that advance the social well-being of students and enhance the educational system.

EP 2.1.8b Collaborate with colleagues and clients for effective policy action. *(p. 467):* Social workers can collaborate with colleagues and clients to initiate and develop effective educational policies.

EP 2.1.9a Continuously discover, appraise, and attend to changing locales, populations, scientific and technological developments, and emerging societal trends to provide relevant services. *(p. 473):* School social workers should continuously respond to the changing issues and conditions affecting the potential for violence in the school environment. *(p. 477):* School social workers should continuously respond to the changing issues and conditions in the world of electronic communication in order to provide relevant services. *(p. 478):* It's important for social workers to appraise continuously technological developments and societal trends to provide relevant services to adolescents who are beginning to engage in sexual activity. *(p. 480):* School social workers should attend to the changing conditions regarding adolescents, pregnancy rates, and sexual behavior in order to provide relevant services.

EP 2.1.9b Provide leadership in promoting sustainable changes in service delivery and practice to improve the quality of social services. *(p. 467):* School social workers can provide leadership in promoting changes to improve the quality and effectiveness of education. *(p. 473):* School social workers can provide leadership in addressing and preventing school violence.

EP 2.1.10 Engage, assess, intervene, and evaluate with individuals, families, groups, organizations, and communities. *(p. 470):* Social work intervention involves change and improvement at the organizational and community levels.

EP 2.1.10d Collect, organize, and interpret client data. *(p. 461):* The case example illustrates how school social workers collect, organize, and interpret client data.

EP 2.1.10e Assess clients' strengths and limitations. *(p. 461):* The case example reflects how a school social worker assesses individual and family strengths and limitations.

EP 2.1.10f Develop mutually agreed-on intervention goals and objectives. *(p. 461):* The case example demonstrates how the school social worker works with the mother to develop mutually agreed-on intervention goals.

EP 2.1.10g Select appropriate intervention strategies. *(p. 461):* The case example demonstrates how the school social worker selects appropriate intervention strategies. *(p. 463):* Examples of groups in school settings are explained that a school social worker may select as appropriate intervention strategies. *(p. 467):* Appropriate intervention strategies are discussed for helping LGBT adolescents in the coming-out process. *(p. 468):* Appropriate intervention strategies for enhancing multiculturalism in schools are discussed. *(p. 485):* Social workers can help pregnant adolescents select appropriate intervention strategies.

EP 2.1.10h Initiate actions to achieve organizational goals. *(p. 461):* The case example illustrates how the school social worker helps initiate actions to achieve the school's organizational goal of helping a child with special needs. *(p. 473):* Discussion focuses on how to address and prevent school violence so that the organizational goal of providing education can be pursued.

EP 2.1.10i Implement prevention interventions that enhance client capacities. *(p. 463):* Some types of groups (such as groups for students at risk of dropping out) are prevention interventions. *(p. 468):* Strategies are discussed that promote multicultural understanding and aim to prevent conflict based on cultural and racial backgrounds. *(p. 473):* Strategies are discussed that implement interventions intended to prevent school violence and enhance students' capacities. *(p. 483):* Implementation of interventions that prevent pregnancy (such as comprehensive sex education) is discussed.

EP 2.1.10j Help clients resolve problems. *(p. 461):* The case example portrays how a school social worker helps clients resolve problems. *(p. 463):* Groups can help students solve problems. *(p. 467):* Social workers can help LGBT students resolve problems in the coming-out process. *(p. 476):* Using conflict resolution approaches helps students resolve problems. *(p. 485):* Social workers can help pregnant adolescents resolve their problems.

EP 2.1.10k Negotiate, mediate, and advocate for clients. *(p. 461):* The case example illustrates how a school social worker can advocate for clients. *(p. 464):* School social workers should advocate on the behalf of their students to improve conditions and services.

EP 2.1.10l Facilitate transitions and endings. *(p. 467):* Social workers can help LGBT students make the transition of coming out. *(p. 486):* Social workers can help to facilitate adolescents' transition to motherhood.

FOR FURTHER EXPLORATION ON THE INTERNET

See this text's Social Work CourseMate website at *www.cengagebrain.com* for learning tools such as chapter quizzing, videos, glossary, flashcards, and more.

CHAPTER 16

Social Work and Services in the Criminal Justice System

Ted S. Warren/AP Photo

Consider the following facts about crime and the criminal justice system:

Over 1.6 million people were jailed, imprisoned, or on probation or parole in 2008 (U.S. Census Bureau, 2010).

Every year 11 million serious crimes are committed in the United States; it's likely that every one of us will be victim of crime sometime in our lives (Macionis, 2010).

Although men are by far more likely to commit crimes, "the number of women arrested and incarcerated is growing faster than that for men" (Eitzen, Zinn, & Smith, 2009, p. 351).

African Americans, who represent about 14% of the population in the United States, commit 38% of all violent crimes and almost 28.6% of all property crimes (Mooney Knox, & Schucht, 2009).

In 2007 in the United States, a murder occurred every 31 minutes, a forcible rape every 6 minutes, a robbery every minute, a burglary every 15 seconds, and a motor vehicle theft every 29 seconds (Macionis, 2010).

As these figures suggest, crime is a serious social problem in the United States. Social workers practice in a range of settings characterized by people who have committed or are accused of committing crimes.

Learning Objectives

A Introduce the criminal justice system and define some of the key concepts involved.

B Describe the types of crime.

C Examine who commits crime.

D Explore whether crime rates are rising or falling.

E Review the wide range of criminal justice settings in which social workers practice.

F Describe the cycle of domestic violence, its dynamics, and treatment.

G Describe a program focusing on the empowerment of African American youths involved in the juvenile justice system.

H Discuss youth membership in gangs, types of gangs, and gang prevention and treatment.

I Examine and encourage critical thinking about the ethical dilemma of punishment versus empowerment and the issue of providing expensive health care for prisoners.

Introducing Crime and Criminal Justice

Social workers are among the many people who work in the *criminal justice system*—the complex, integrated system of programs, policies, laws, and agencies devoted to preventing and controlling crime. The system's functions include *adjudication* (passing legal judgment), *incarceration* (confining by putting in prison or jail), and *rehabilitation* (restoring to a state of productive, noncriminal functioning in society).

Crime is the commission of a harmful offense or act that is legally prohibited. *Criminals* include anyone whom the courts convict of a crime. *Law* is the body of formal principles and decisions established by government that determine what behavior is appropriate and allowed and what is not. Laws essentially guide social behavior. Highlight 16.1 describes the main types of crime committed in the United States.

HIGHLIGHT 16.1

Main Types of Crime

EP 2.1.9a

Crimes are either felonies or misdemeanors. *Felonies* are grave offenses punishable by at least a year in prison and possibly even death; *misdemeanors* are less severe offenses, with punishments ranging from incarceration of less than a year to monetary fines (Macionis, 2010).

Crimes fall within three categories. *Violent crime* (or crime against persons) is the act of using "force or the threat of force against others"; *property crime* (or crime against property) is "the taking of money or property from another without force, the threat of force, or the destruction of property"(emphasis omitted) (Kendall, 2010, pp. 178, 183). These two categories involve eight more specific crimes identified by the *Uniform Crime Reports* (compiled by the FBI) that are "most likely to be reported to the police by victims, that occur frequently, and that are serious by nature or as a result of their frequency of occurrence" (Abadinsky, 2000, p. 5).

Violent crimes include

- *Homicide*: The act of "causing the death of another person without legal justification or excuse" (Abadinsky, 2000, p. 5).
- *Aggravated assault*: The act of attacking another person with the intent to inflict serious harm or kill that person.
- *Rape:* "Sexual penetration against a person's will through the use or threat of force" (Yarber et al., 2010, p. G-10). (Note that *statutory rape* is "a legal term used to indicate sexual activity when one partner is under the age of consent; in most states that age is 18" [Kelly, 2008, p. G-9].)
- *Robbery*: The act of stealing property in the hands of another person by using force or the threat of force. (Note that because of the force involved this is considered a violent crime even though it involves property.)

Property crimes include

- *Larceny (simple theft):* The act of stealing property.
- *Burglary*: The act of breaking into a house or other building with the intent to steal.
- *Motor vehicle theft:* The act of stealing a "self-propelled road vehicle" from another person with

the goal of keeping it "permanently or temporarily" (Abadinsky, 2000, p. 6)
- *Arson:* The "malicious burning of another's property or, sometimes, one's own property, as in an attempt to collect insurance" (Nichols, 1999, p. 75).

A third umbrella category of crime involves those offenses not considered violent or property crimes. Examples include the following:

- *White-collar crime:* Offenses "committed by middle-class and upper-middle-class people in their business and social activities, (such as theft of company goods; embezzlement; bankruptcy fraud; swindles; tax evasion; forgery; theft of property by computer; passing bad checks; illicit copying of computer software, movies, and music; and fraudulent use of credit cards, automatic teller machines, and telephones)" (Eitzen et al., 2009, p. 359).
- *Corporate crime:* Illegal acts committed by large organizations to enhance profits. For example, consider the utility conglomerate Enron's fall into bankruptcy, of the largest in U.S. history (CNN.com, 2001). Corporate leaders were accused of "fraudulent trading schemes" and devious "financial moves to hide debt and inflate profits that fueled Enron's downfall in 2001" (FindLaw, 2005). The bankruptcy resulted in thousands of Enron "employees losing their life savings in 401(k) plans" linked with Enron stock (CNN.com, 2001). Another example involves Halliburton, one of the world's largest oilfield services providers. It had "been found guilty repeatedly of overcharging the government for fuel, services (food and housing of troops), and construction during and following Iraqi combat. Moreover, contrary to federal laws prohibiting companies from doing business with countries supporting terror—Iraq, Iran, and Libya—Halliburton circumvented these restrictions by setting up subsidiaries in foreign countries (Herbert, 2003)" (Eitzen et al., 2009, p. 362).
- *Victimless (vice) crimes*: Illegal acts that technically have no victim or complainant (e.g., prostitution, selling illegal drugs, unlawful gambling). These are also referred to as "crimes against the moral order"

(continued)

HIGHLIGHT 16.1 (*continued*)

(Eitzen et al., 2009, p. 356) or "public-order crimes" (Kornblum & Julian, 2009, p. 148).

- *Organized (syndicated) crime*: Illegal acts committed by an organized, hierarchical network of professional criminals working together to make money . Such crime organizations "tend to be large and diversified regional or national units. They may organize initially to carry on a particular crime, such as drug trafficking, extortion, prostitution, or gambling. Later they may seek to control this activity in a given city or neighborhood, destroying or absorbing the competition. Eventually, they may expand into other types of crime, protecting their members from arrest through intimidation or bribery of public officials" (Eitzen et al., 2009, p. 149).

- *Hate crime:* The "violence of intolerance and bigotry, intended to hurt and intimidate someone because of their race, ethnicity, national origin, religion, sexual orientation, or disability. The purveyors of hate use explosives, arson, weapons, vandalism, physical violence, and verbal threats of violence to instill fear in their victims, leaving them vulnerable to more attacks and feeling alienated, helpless, suspicious, and fearful" (U.S. Department of Justice, 2001).

Who Commits Crimes? Race, Social Class, and Gender Issues

EP 2.1.4a, 2.1.4c

Although people with virtually any characteristics can commit crimes, some people are simply more likely than others to do so. Crime is related to the variables of gender, age, race, and social class (Eitzen et al., 2009; Mooney et al., 2009).

Gender and Crime

Eitzen and colleagues (2009) comment on the variable of gender and its relationship to crime:

> *The arrest rates by types of crimes committed vary by sex. Slightly more than one in five of all arrests are of women, with juvenile females arrested nearly twice as often as adult females. Women are about twice as likely to be arrested for property crimes as for violent crimes. Men commit murder at almost ten times the rate of women. (p. 350)*

In view of these findings, Eitzen and colleagues (2009) "raise two questions: (1) Why is there such an apparent difference in criminal behavior by gender? (2) Why are women committing more property crimes now?" (p. 351). Some reflect that the women's movement has opened up more opportunities for women, not only in the legal realm, but also the illegal (Eitzen et al., 2009). Others "attribute the rise in female crime rates more to the growing poverty among young, unattached mothers and the new ways society treats women than to the wider opportunities they have. More men are abandoning their families, leaving women with the burdens of children and with the temptations to commit crimes to care for them" (Eitzen et al., 2009, p. 351).

Age and Crime

Age is another factor related to crime. Younger people are more likely to commit crimes and commit more violent crimes (Eitzen et al., 2009; Mooney et al., 2009). Mooney and his colleagues (2009) explain:

> *The highest arrest rates are for individuals younger than age 25. In 2005, 44.3 percent of all arrests in the United States were of people younger than age 25 (FBI, 2006). Although those younger than age 25 made up over half of all arrests in the United States for crimes such as robbery, burglary, motor vehicle theft, and arson, those younger than age 25 were significantly less likely to be arrested for crimes such as fraud and forgery and counterfeiting. Those older than age 65 made up less than 1.0 percent of total arrests for the same year (FBI, 2006). (p. 141)*

These high rates for young people may be attributed to the facts that penalties are not as severe for youths and that young people have trouble getting good jobs and adequate incomes (Mooney et al., 2009).

Race, Social Class, and Crime

Mooney and his colleagues (2009) report concerning the variables of race and social class, both also related to crime:

> Race is a factor in who gets arrested. Minorities are disproportionately represented in official statistics. [We have established that] ... although African Americans represent about 14% of the population, they account for more than 38% of all violent index offenses and 28.6% of all property index offenses (FBI, 2006). In addition, an estimated 12% of all black males in their late 20s are in prison or jail compared with 1.7% of all white males in their late 20s ...
>
> Nevertheless, it is inaccurate to conclude that race and crime are causally related. First, official statistics reflect the behaviors and policies of criminal justice actors. Thus the high rate of arrests, conviction, and incarceration of minorities may be a consequence of individual and institutional bias against minorities. For example, investigating race and ethnicity in sentencing outcomes, Steffensmeier and Demuth (2000) concluded that both race and ethnicity continue to be factors in the organizational decision-making process of the criminal justice system.
>
> Furthermore, blacks are sent to prison for drug offenses at a rate 8.2 times higher than the rate for whites. If current trends continue, by 2020 two of every three black men between the ages of 18 and 34 will be in prison.... These disturbing statistics have led to concerns about racial profiling—the practice or targeting suspects on the basis of race ... Opponents hold that racial profiling is little more than discrimination and should therefore be abolished....
>
> Race and social class are closely related in that nonwhites are over-represented in the lower classes. Because lower-class members lack legitimate means to acquire material goods, they may turn to instrumental, or economically motivated, crimes. In addition, although the "haves" typically earn social respect through their socioeconomic status, education achievement, and occupational role, the "have-nots" more often live in communities where respect is based on physical strength and violence. (pp. 142–143)

Macionis (2010) proposes other rationales for racial differences:

> [Another reason] is closely related to the first: More police patrols are found in poor neighborhoods, which have a high African American population. Prejudice based on race and class can prompt people to suspect blacks of criminal behavior simply on the basis of skin color ... Research suggests that such biases lead police to be quicker to arrest African Americans than whites ...
>
> [An added] factor involves family patterns. Two-thirds of black children are born to single mothers, compared with one-third of white children. Single mothers and single fathers have less time to supervise children, and single mothers especially earn less money, which adds to family pressures. For these reasons, children who "grow up in poor families without fathers are at higher risk for criminality. (p. 150)

Note that Asian Americans are less likely to be arrested for crimes; making up 4.4% of the population, they account for only 0.8% of arrests (Macionis, 2010). "This lower criminality is due to higher income levels and also a strong cultural emphasis on family, discipline, and honor, all of which tend to discourage criminal behavior" (Macionis, 2010, p. 150).

Are Crime Rates Rising or Falling?

Crime rates are recorded in three basic ways: official statistics of crimes reported to police (i.e., the *Uniform Crime Reports),* surveys administered to population samples regarding victimization rates, and offenders' self-reports (Mooney et al., 2009).

According to the Uniform Crime Reports of the Federal Bureau of Investigation (FBI) (2010), there was a 5.3% decrease in violent crime from 2008 to 2009. The largest decreases were in robbery (–8%), and homicide (–7.1%). The decrease in all violent crimes between 2000 and 2009 was 7.5%.

Property crime is also on the decline (FBI, 2010). There was a 4.6% decrease from 2008 to 2009, and an 8.5% decrease from 2000 to 2009. Motor vehicle theft decreased by 31.5% and larceny by 16.8% between 2000 and 2009.

Macionis (2010) elaborates:

> Violent crimes, that is, crimes against persons, account for only 12 percent of all serious offenses; crimes against property account for the remaining 88 percent. Put differently, the crime rate for property offenses is about seven times higher than that

for violent crimes against persons (Federal Bureau of Investigation, 2008)....

From 1960 until the early 1990s, the rate of violent crime rose quickly. After that, the trend turned downward. (The property offenses also went up after 1960, with a downturn in the early 1980s and further decline through 2009.) What accounts for the drop in crime rates? Analysts point to a number of factors, including a strong economy during the 1990s, a drop in the use of crack cocaine, the hiring of more police, and tougher sentences for criminal convictions. (p. 143)

In any event, crime statistics may be misleading. For one thing, victimization surveys indicate that many crimes are not reported. Some surveys suggest less than half of serious crimes are actually reported to the police (Macionis, 2008). Why do victims fail to report crimes? People may believe that nothing can be done about the crime anyway or that the crime was too insignificant to report. They might also fear negative repercussions.

For example, Florence, age 78, was sideswiped by a young man as he was trying to pass her car. She had been driving along a familiar neighborhood road, being careful not to exceed the speed limit. The man, who looked to be about 20, stopped to see if she was all right but then jumped in his car and sped away. The accident was his fault. However, Florence's insurance agent suggested that filing a formal police report of the incident would almost certainly *not* result in the man's apprehension. But it *would* result in a significant increase in her own car insurance simply because the accident happened to a person of her age. Needless to say, Florence did not report the incident and paid for the repairs herself.

Focus on Critical Thinking 16.1 addresses a controversial issue concerning the purposes of imprisonment.

FOCUS ON CRITICAL THINKING 16.1

An Ethical Dilemma: Punishment Versus Empowerment

Disparity in Goals

EP 2.1.2a,
2.1.2c,
2.1.4a,
2.1.4b,
2.1.5b,
2.1.5c,
2.1.8a

A great debate rages regarding the purpose of imprisonment (or incarceration). Prisons exist to achieve four primary purposes (Coleman & Kerbo, 2009; Kendall, 2010; Macionia, 2010). First, prisons punish people who commit crimes by denying them freedom for some designated period. Second, prisons discourage people who have committed crimes from committing them again and deter others from committing them in the first place—at least theoretically. Third, prisons protect potential victims from dangerous offenders by putting them behind bars. These first three goals basically focus on the rights of society. They might be clustered under the umbrella of *incapacitation*—namely, using various means to inhibit offenders from committing more crimes, thereby protecting other members of society.

The fourth goal, established much more recently in the 1940s and 1950s, involves inmate *rehabilitation* through programs involving therapy, education, and job training. The intent is to help criminals become productive members of society who do not commit crimes. The concept of *corrections* implies that people who break the law should be treated in ways that attempt to make them correct their inappropriate behavior and stop breaking the law. Rehabilitation ideally involves empowering offenders so they have viable alternatives to pursue other than a life of crime.

The wide disparity in goals poses a serious question for social workers: To what extent can offenders be empowered at the same time that they are incapacitated as a means of control and punishment? Prison life allows for few choices, and most prisoners definitely do not want to be there.

To make it worse, the public has increasingly supported stricter, more incapacitating policies. Tactics include longer mandatory sentences, less use of probation and parole, policies requiring lifetime imprisonment after committing three serious crimes (sometimes referred to as the *three strikes and you're out* approach), mandated sentences that reflect the seriousness of the crime, accelerated prison construction, and increased use of the death penalty (Karger & Stoesz, 2010).

(continued)

FOCUS ON CRITICAL THINKING 16.1 (continued)

Kenyon (1999) reflects:

Finding a compromise between what seems ethically appropriate and what is legally mandated can be a source of professional burnout. Feeling forced to make decisions and to take actions that cause internal conflict leads to feelings of helplessness and hopelessness and a belief that one is ineffective. (p. 162)

Issues and Potential Solutions

The following are examples of potential issues:

- Mandatory sentencing results in prisons accommodating over double the number of prisoners for which they were built. Cells built to house two inmates now must house four. Prison conditions are almost unbearable.
- A prisoner made a mistake at age 19 and accidentally killed another teenager in a fight. The court sentenced him to several decades of time with no possibility of parole. Now, at age 21, he has expressed serious remorse for his crime and a willingness to shape up his life. A prison social worker sees great potential for rehabilitation. But what can be done when there is no hope of freedom for many years?
- A 25-year-old inmate has been sentenced to life imprisonment in a state requiring such punishment after the commission of three serious crimes—in his case, armed robberies. What kind of treatment and rehabilitation can help him?

To what extent does incapacitation as a means of control and punishment conflict with the basic social work values of self-determination and empowerment? How can social workers who are empowerment oriented function in such a constricted and controlled setting? Should offenders be forced to participate in treatment activities against their will?

Garvin and Tropman (1998) make five suggestions for working with offenders:

1. When possible, help offenders identify alternative behaviors to solve problems and address their needs.

This is especially useful for inmates returning to their communities.

2. Advocate for inmates when prison conditions work against their best interests. In the community, social workers can advocate for prisoner's rights as they try to reintegrate themselves. For example, neighborhood residents might resent a former inmate living in their neighborhood. Or a parolee might be fired from her job when her employer finds out about her prison history.

3. Provide opportunities for individual and group treatment for inmates to work on personal issues (e.g., substance abuse treatment groups).

4. Seek positions in prison administration so as to improve prison policies concerning humane rehabilitation approaches.

5. Advocate in the macro arena for less punitive legislation that provides greater opportunity for rehabilitation.

Conservative Versus Liberal Value Orientations Toward Crime and Criminals

Critical Thinking Questions

- What are your personal values concerning the issues just described? To what extent do your values reflect a *conservative* perspective that emphasizes individuals' responsibility for their own behavior and that people who do bad things deserve to be punished?

EP 2.1.3, 2.1.7a

- To what extent do you support a *liberal* approach that focuses on rehabilitating offenders and emphasizes the idea that people will thrive and do well when given enough support?
- To what extent should resources be used to build more prisons and keep offenders in prison longer? Or to what extent should resources be diverted to rehabilitation and the goal of reintegrating offenders into communities?

Criminal Justice Settings and Forensic Social Work

Forensic social work is "the application of social work to questions and issues relating to the law and legal systems" (Walker, 2002, p. 19). It involves social workers' practice and dealings with criminal and civil (concerning personal rights such as child custody) legal systems. Forensic social work tasks include conducting assessments regarding suspects' mental

EP 2.1.1c

competence to understand their behavior and stand trial; making recommendations concerning child custody, divorce, and the placement of emotionally disturbed or delinquent juveniles; preparing for court presentations as expert witnesses; and advocating for welfare rights.

Ginsberg (2001) cites six broad criminal justice settings in which social workers can serve important functions. These include adult correctional institutions, administrative planning centers, probation and parole services, victim assistance programs, domestic violence services, and juvenile corrections.

What provides greater hope—punishment or empowerment?

Adult Correctional Institutions

Social workers in adult correctional institutions perform at least five functions (Ginsberg, 2001). First, they can provide either individual or group counseling to inmates when needed or requested. Treatment might focus on such issues as anger management, preparation for release, and coping with substance abuse.

The second social work function involves helping prison administrators make determinations regarding job placement within the institution. Inmates often seek prison jobs to combat the boredom of prison life, to earn extra privileges, or to establish credit for good behavior thereby increasing the possibility of parole (McNeece, 1995).

The third function for social workers in correctional facilities involves assisting prison personnel in determining how individual inmates are treated. Fourth, social workers can help develop and organize prison activities. Finally, practitioners can "assist in planning modifications in prison procedures"

and advocate for improved conditions (Ginsberg, 2001, p. 148).

Focus on Critical Thinking 16.2 addresses the question of providing expensive health care for prison inmates.

Administrative Planning Centers

As in other fields of practice, social workers can take on administrative and planning roles for correctional systems. These might involve planning new programs and procedures, developing more humane policies, and supervising lower-level administrators and other employees.

Community-Based Corrections: Probation and Parole Services

The criminal justice system may give people who have been convicted of crimes alternatives to serving a full sentence of incarceration. Two primary options are probation and parole. These are considered *community-based corrections*—programs that supervise or monitor offenders' behavior while they reside in the community.

EP 2.1.10i

Probation

Morgan (2000) describes *probation:*

> *Probation takes place when a person is convicted but the judge determines that confinement is not warranted. Instead, that person is placed on probation and is allowed to live in society but under the court's supervision. Terms of probation often include psychological or chemical-dependence treatment and mandatory community service. People who receive probation are generally considered low risk, and the goal of probation officers is to involve them in community service and steer them away from criminal behavior. (pp. 142–143)*

Probation officers conduct assessments prior to when clients begin probation in order to provide recommendations to the court. They help clients establish work and other living plans and subsequently see them regularly, overseeing their activities and often making home and work visits. Probation officers also link clients with needed resources.

To avoid incarceration, probationers must abide by whatever restrictions and terms the judge establishes. Typically these include obeying the law,

FOCUS ON CRITICAL THINKING 16.2

Should Prisoners Get Expensive Health Care?

The costs of keeping more people in prison longer are huge. The average annual cost for supervising a person on probation is over $3800 (Holden, 2010), and in prison it's approximately $30,000 (Macionis, 2010), although spending varies widely from state to state (Kendall, 2010).

Health care for aging and ill prisoners is also an expensive issue. Coggins and Frezquez (2007) explain:

EP 2.1.2a, 2.1.3

According to U.S. Census Bureau reports, the fastest growing segment of the criminal offender and correctional facility population is comprised of individuals over the age of 65 ... By the year 2010, 33% of inmates in U.S. correctional facilities will be fifty years of age and older (Fresquez, [Khalsa, & Bell,] 1998). Given the trend toward mandatory longer sentences and the growing number of inmates age fifty and over, the year 2025 could witness a substantial number of correctional facilities having to face difficult decisions regarding the allocation of resources for the concerns of the aged." (p. 100)

One estimate for the annual care of an older adult inmate is $70,000 (Kendall, 2010). Money spent on prison populations detracts from the total financial pool available for other benefits and services including schools, police, the environment, and domestic security. A number of ethical questions can be raised: "Should a killer in a Minnesota prison have received a life-saving, $900,000 bone marrow transplant? Should a California robber have received a new heart" costing approximately $1 million? Both states provided these treatments because they determined it would be "cruel and unusual punishment" not to (Levine, 2002, p. 44).

Critical Thinking Questions

- To what health care standards should prisons adhere in providing treatment to prisoners?
- Should prisoners receive extremely expensive health care treatment?
- How would you define "extremely expensive"?
- To what extent is it fair that prisoners are "the only people in America guaranteed medical treatment" when many other U.S. residents may have no health insurance?
- Should all U.S. residents receive the same health care benefits as prisoners? If so, who should pay for these benefits?
- Should more time, money, and effort be expended to rehabilitate prisoners instead of imprisoning them so they will become responsible for their own health care needs "on the outside"?

getting and keeping a job, staying within a prescribed geographical location, avoiding relationships with other identified felons, and shunning firearms (Morgan, 2000). Individualized restrictions may also apply, such as getting substance abuse treatment or attending anger management groups.

Parole

Parole is the early release of inmates from prison based on the "promise and likelihood of good behavior" (Morgan, 2000, p. 139). Parole officers must initially assess the amount of supervision necessary. Some parolees require extensive supervision to stay out of trouble; others require very little. Parolees must abide by the general restrictions and requirements established by their parole officer. These include avoiding illegal activity, possession of firearms, involvement with identified felons, and use of alcohol or other drugs. They must also remain gainfully employed and attend regularly scheduled meetings with their parole officer.

Both probation and parole officer positions usually require a bachelor's degree in social work, psychology, criminal justice, or a related field in addition to "strong interpersonal skills" (Morgan, 2000, pp. 142, 144).

There are other community-based corrections programs in addition to probation and parole. For example, *victim/offender mediation programs* are face-to-face confrontations between victims and offenders in which an impartial third party serves as a mediator. The intent is to give victims an opportunity to confront offenders with the emotional and other consequences of their behavior, address emotional issues, and arrange compensation for losses. Similarly, *restitution programs* involve arranging cash reimbursement from offenders to victims (typically of property crimes) to compensate for losses.

Victim Assistance Programs

Included under the victim assistance umbrella are both victim/witness assistance programs and crisis intervention programs. *Victim/witness assistance programs* include various facets intended to assist victims and witnesses in the stressful and potentially traumatic process of testifying in court against offenders, thereby enhancing their ability to testify effectively. Specific services include ongoing notification to witnesses of the case's legal status as it progresses through the courts; provision of separate, comfortable waiting rooms for witnesses; transportation to court; and support staff who accompany witnesses throughout the court process, helping them understand what's happening.

Crisis intervention programs, although not as common, provide wide-ranging services for crime victims, frequently within the first 24 hours after the crime occurs. Services can include crisis counseling, provision of transportation, assistance in making a legal complaint, linkage to needed resources such as support groups for survivors of violence, and temporary financial help. Agencies providing services include rape crisis centers and domestic violence shelters.

Jobs include counselor/advocate and administrator. Volunteers are also often used. Most counselor/advocates have a bachelor's degree, and most program directors have a master's degree in social work or a related discipline (Roberts, 1995).

Domestic Violence Services

Domestic violence services and shelters for battered women have sprung up across the country. Often they have been initiated and are staffed and run by social workers. Women who have been battered by their male partners frequently need temporary shelter for themselves and their children, usually having nowhere else to go. Additional services include providing counseling and linking women with necessary resources. Battered women eventually need a permanent place to stay. They might require additional education or job training so they can support themselves and their families. They may need help finding employment and getting legal assistance.

Of course, females can batter their male partners, or one partner may batter the other of the same gender. However, as Shaw and Lee (2009) indicate:

Although women are much less likely to be victims of violent crime overall, women are 5 to 8 times more likely [than men] to be victimized by an intimate partner. Intimate partner violence is primarily a crime against women and all races are equally vulnerable. In 2007, the Bureau of Justice reported that 96 percent of women experiencing nonfatal partner violence were victimized by a male and about 85 percent of all victims were female. According to FBI statistics, every day about four women (approximately 1,400 a year) die in the United States as a result of domestic violence. Although about half a million reports of physical assault by intimates officially reach federal officials each year, it is estimated that 2 to 4 million women are battered each year; about one every 20 seconds or so. Women of all races and classes are battered, although rates are 5 times higher among families below poverty levels, and severe spouse abuse is twice as likely to be committed by unemployed men as by those working full time. These differences reflect economic vulnerability and lack of resources, as well as the ways these families have more contact with authorities like social services that increases opportunities for reporting. Women who are pregnant are especially at risk of violence....

Women who are physically abused are also always emotionally abused because they experience emotional abuse by virtue of being physically terrorized. Emotional abuse, however, does not always involve physical abuse. A man, for example, who constantly tells his partner that she is worthless, stupid, or ugly can emotionally abuse without being physically abusive. Sometimes the scars of emotional abuse take longer to heal than physical abuse and help explain why women might stay with abusive partners. (pp. 568–569)

Therefore, Highlight 16.2 focuses on domestic violence as a women's issue.

Juvenile Corrections

Juvenile corrections is the broad concept reflecting the many interventions for young people who are brought to the attention of police or the courts because of their behavior or alleged behavior (Barton, 1995). Juveniles—people under age 18—are generally treated differently than adults who commit

The Cycle of Domestic Violence: Empowering Women as Survivors

**EP 2.1.4a,
2.1.7a,
2.1.7b**

The dynamics of domestic violence usually revolve around the male partner's need to control the victim. Over time, the perpetrator gradually cuts off his female partner from her family, friends, church, workplace, and other sources of support. He typically criticizes her on as many grounds as possible. Without support and validation from others, the victim often comes to believe what the perpetrator is saying—to see herself as no good, stupid, and worthless, as a whore and a tramp. In some ways this process resembles brainwashing. Prior rational thinking is gradually erased and replaced with a barrage of criticism.

Phase 1: Buildup of Tension

The cycle of violence typically occurs in three phases. First, tension builds as the perpetrator becomes increasingly controlling, demanding, and annoyed with the victim. He might place impossible demands on her such as ordering her to have dinner ready at 5:30 sharp when he arrives home. Then he might show up at 7:00 and blame her for the food being cold and dried up. Or he might chastise her for making the wrong kind of food or not cooking it the way he likes it. He often plays a game with her, making demands and then changing them after she complies with his original instructions.

Phase 2: The Explosion

The second phase in the cycle involves the explosion—the abusive incident in which he beats her to teach her a lesson. He then usually tells her it's all her fault. If she had cooked better or not yelled back or done what she was told, he wouldn't have *had* to hit her. She *made* him try to keep her in line.

Phase 3: The Honeymoon

The third phase is the honeymoon period. The perpetrator has released his tension. The victim is frightened,

hurt, emotionally beaten, downtrodden, and depressed. She might be so damaged that she considers leaving him, but he will never allow her to do this. He makes up with her, says loving things, and perhaps brings her flowers or candy. He often tells her that he loves her and that he can't live without her. For that matter, he might also tell her that she could never survive without him. The pain is gone—temporarily—so she stays. And the cycle begins all over again.

Reasons Women Stay

Women continue to stay with abusive partners for a number of reasons (Zastrow & Kirst-Ashman, 2010). These include economic dependence, lack of self-confidence, lack of power, fear of the abuser, guilt about what they did wrong or how they failed to nurture their relationship with the abuser, fear of isolation, fear for their children's safety, hope that things will somehow improve, and the fact they still feel they love their partners despite it all.

Treatment Strategies

Social work treatment strategies involve empowering the victim and helping her survive. She changes from a victim to a survivor. Strategies include the following:

**EP 2.1.10f,
2.1.10g,
2.1.10j,
2.1.10k**

1. Offer support.
2. Identify and focus on her strengths.
3. Provide information regarding resources and services.
4. Help her establish a plan of action.
5. Advocate on her behalf with legal, medical, and social services when necessary.

The goal is to help the domestic violence survivor gain confidence and get back on her feet. It takes a brave and strong person to break the cycle of violence.

---

crimes. *Juvenile delinquent offenses* are acts that are considered crimes if committed by adults. (Highlight 16.1 reviewed common crimes.) *Status offenses* are acts that are considered inappropriate when done by juveniles but are not crimes if committed by

adults. These include running away, being truant, being out of parental control, having sexual intercourse, and drinking alcohol. Considered together, juvenile delinquent and status offenses are regarded as *antisocial behavior*—acts that are hostile, detrimental to others, and contrary to social expectations. *Juvenile courts* are those having jurisdiction over proceedings involving delinquent, dependent, or maltreated children and their parents or guardians.

We have already established that young people (particularly males of African American and, to a lesser extent, Hispanic heritage) are more likely than older people to commit crimes (Macionis, 2010; Mooney et al., 2011). Remember, however, that juveniles from virtually any racial, ethnic, and socioeconomic background can and do participate in antisocial behavior.

A Special Perspective on Juveniles

EP 2.1.10d

Juveniles require a special perspective because they are minors whose parents (or guardians) are supposed to care for, supervise, and protect them. One ongoing question concerns the extent to which juveniles, on the one hand, and their parents, on the other, are responsible for juveniles' antisocial behavior. It is beyond the scope of this book to review all the potential causes of such behavior. However, the following are a few of the family, environmental, and individual factors that research suggests may contribute to violent behavior (Kail & Cavenaugh, 2010; McWhirter, McWhirter, McWhirter, & McWhirter, 2007; Sigelman & Rider, 2009; Smith & Darman, 2008).

- *Coercive Family Environments:* Sigelman and Rider (2009) explain the dynamics involved in coercive family environments as suggested by Patterson, DeBaryshe, and Ramsey (1989):

  Adolescents who are antisocial "often experience coercive family environments in which family members are locked in power struggles, each trying to control the others through negative, coercive tactics (Kiesner, Dishion, & Poulin, 2001; Patterson, DeBaryshe, and Ramsey, 1989). Parents learn ... that they can stop their children's misbehavior, temporarily at least, by threatening, yelling, and hitting. Meanwhile, children learn ... that they can get their parents to lay off them by ignoring requests, whining, throwing full-blown temper tantrums, and otherwise being as difficult as possible. As both parents and children learn to rely on coercive tactics, parents increasingly lose control over their children's behavior until even

the loudest lectures and hardest spankings have little effect and the child's conduct problems spiral out of control. [Thus, coercive family environments are marked by conflict, in addition to harsh and inconsistent discipline.] It is easy to see how a child who has grown up in a coercive family environment might attribute hostile intent to other people and rely on aggressive tactics to resolve disputes.

Growing up in a coercive family environment sets in motion the next steps in the making of an antisocial adolescent.... The child, already aggressive and unpleasant to be around, ends up performing poorly in school and being rejected by other children. Having no better options, he becomes involved in a peer group made up of other low-achieving, antisocial, and unpopular youths, who positively reinforce one another's delinquency (Dodge, Dishion, & Lansford, 2006; Kiesner et al., 2001). Rejection by peers may further reinforce a tendency to attribute hostile intent to others and in the process strengthen aggressive tendencies (Dodge et al., 2006). Overall, there is much support for the view that ineffective parenting in childhood contributes to behavior problems, peer rejection, involvement with antisocial peers, and, in turn, antisocial behavior in adolescence. (pp. 395–396)

- *Poverty and Economic Deprivation:* An environment marked by deprivation can contribute to the potential for delinquency (Kail and Cavanaugh, 2010). Children who live in poverty exhibit more violent and antisocial behavior than those who live in more prosperous surroundings (Keiley, Bates, Dodge, & Pettit, 2000). Poverty imposes stress on families that often must struggle just to survive and "often leads to the very parental behaviors that promote aggression—harsh discipline and lax monitoring (Tolan, Gorman-Smith, & Henry, 2003).... In addition, violent crime is far more common in poverty-stricken neighborhoods. Older children and adolescents exposed to such violence are, as they get older, more likely to be aggressive and violent themselves (Binghenheimer, Brennan, & Earls, 2005)" (Kail & Cavanaugh, 2010, p. 350)

Children whose families have a long history of continuous poverty are more apt to become "more antisocial" with time (Papalia et al., 2009, p. 416). In families that get out of poverty early on in a child's life, that child is no more likely to demonstrate subsequent problematic behavior than a child living in a family that never experienced poverty (Macmillan, McMorris, & Kruttschnitt, 2004; Papalia et al., 2009).

- *Individual Factors*: Although personality variables do not directly produce a delinquent, they do increase the probability of delinquency. For example, having poor impulse control and an easily provoked temper can make delinquent behavior more likely (Sigelman & Rider, 2009; Smith & Darman, 2008). Kail and Cavanaugh (2010) explain:

Adolescent boys often respond aggressively because they are not skilled at interpreting other people's intentions. Without a clear interpretation in mind, they respond aggressively by default. That is, aggressive boys far too often think, "I don't know what you're up to, and when in doubt, attack" (Crick & Dodge, 1994; Crizier et al., 2008). Antisocial adolescents are often inclined to act impulsively, and they often are unable or unwilling to postpone pleasure (Fontaine, 2007). Seeing a fancy new CD player or a car, delinquent youth are tempted to steal it, simply so that they can have it right now. When others inadvertently get in their way, delinquent adolescents often respond without regard to the nature of the other person's acts or intentions." (pp. 349–350)

McWhirter and his colleagues (2007) note that levels of aggression often follow a pattern where "less serious problem behaviors precede more serious delinquency"; the authors continue that "disruptive and delinquent behavior generally progresses in an orderly, sequential fashion from authority conflict (e.g., defiance and disobedience), to covert actions (e.g., lying and stealing), to overt actions (e.g., fighting, delinquency, and violent behavior" (p. 181).

As with adult offenders, the current trend in the juvenile justice system is an emphasis on punishment rather than treatment and rehabilitation for delinquent youth (Smith & Darman, 2008). One development involves passing laws that require more juvenile offenders who commit serious violent crimes to be treated as adults. Another concerns the imposition of stricter sentences on juvenile offenders who in the past might have been given a warning or probation.

We have established that social work values generally comply more directly with rehabilitation and treatment approaches than with punishment. The problem of juvenile delinquency can be tackled in many

EP 2.1.10g

ways. None are accomplished easily and all require resources. Kail and Cavanaugh (2010) suggest the following tactics:

- *Delinquent adolescents can be taught more effective social skills and better methods of self-control.*
- *Parents of delinquent youth can be taught the importance of supervising and monitoring their children's behavior and the necessity for consistent discipline.*
- *Families of delinquents can learn to function more effectively as a unit, with special emphasis on better means of resolving conflict.*
- *Schools can develop programs that motivate delinquent youth to become invested in their school performance.*
- *Communities can improve economic conditions in neighborhoods where delinquency reigns. (p. 350)*

Kail and Cavanaugh (2010) continue by describing a preventive program at the Oregon Social Learning Center entitled Linking the Interests of Families and Teachers (LIFT) that attempts to implement most of these suggestions:

EP 2.1.10i

The aim of the LIFT program is to nip aggressive behavior in the bud during the elementary-school years. This program includes a 10-week intervention that attacks aggressive behavior on many fronts. Parents receive training on discipline, resolving disputes with their children, and monitoring their children's schoolwork. Children receive training designed to improve their social skills, with a particular emphasis on effective problem solving and nonaggressive play. At school, teachers are taught effective ways of dealing with off-task and disruptive behaviors, and playground and cafeteria monitors are trained to reward children for positive social interactions and to prevent children from bullying peers. Finally, each classroom has a dedicated phone line with an answering machine so that teachers can record daily homework assignments and parents can leave messages for teachers. (p. 350)

Early results of LIFT have been promising (Eddy, Reid, Stoolmiller, & Fetrow, 2003; Stoolmiller, Eddy, & Reid, 2000). In the classroom children's aggressive behavior decreased and cooperative behavior increased. Family interactions improved with decreased conflict concerning behavior and discipline. Better behavior at school and a decreased likelihood to consume alcohol were evident three years after LIFT involvement. Of course, the ulti-mate evidence of whether LIFT is successful will be the rates of children's antisocial and delinquent behavior in the future.

Highlight 16.3 describes another more positive, empowerment-oriented approach to help youth already involved in the juvenile justice system. It emphasizes empowerment through responsibility, group cohesiveness, and the appreciation of cultural identity.

HIGHLIGHT 16.3

Mezzo Practice and Empowerment for African American Youths in the Juvenile Justice System

EP 2.1.4c, 2.1.10g

Harvey (1997) describes the development and implementation of a program for groups of African American juvenile offenders that uses an Afrocentric approach. The groups' purpose is to enhance members' self-respect, establish a stronger identity with African heritage and culture, create ties with a positive peer group, develop vocational aspirations, and strengthen members' ability to make socially responsible decisions. Although in some ways these might be considered treatment groups, they address and help members cope with broader social issues.

Common Themes

Young African American offenders are viewed within their macro context. Poverty, marital and family dissolution, white oppression and discrimination, the strong antisocial pressure of peer groups and gangs, and a lack of career prospects all contribute to an environment in which crime becomes a logical means of survival. These young men typically express a number of themes (Harvey, 1997):

- Adults around here do it, so why shouldn't I?
- Violence is a way of life. If you don't stand up for yourself, you're history.
- How can I be moral and still survive the horrendous peer pressure to be bad?
- You have to be "cool" (i.e., strong and not expressing emotion) to get any respect and protect yourself (p. 166).
- Women should be treated as inferior and handled with violent behavior.

- Police are the bad guys.
- How can I deal with whites' racist treatment?
- I don't know that much about African culture.

An Afrocentric Approach

An Afrocentric approach emphasizes both spirituality and connectedness with others in the environment, including family members and community residents. The goal is to engender self-understanding, self-respect, and "a strong sense of responsibility for the well-being and harmonious interconnection between self and others" (Harvey, 1997, p. 163; Nobles, 1976). The Afrocentric approach rests on seven basic principles called the *Nguzo Saba*, described in Chapter 3 (Karenga, 1965; Karenga, 2000, pp. 58–59). These include (1) "unity among families, neighborhoods, and nations," (2) "self-determination," (3) "collective work and responsibility," (4) "cooperation economics" to establish a strong economic base, (5) "purpose" to gain respect as a world community, (6) "creativity," and (7) "faith" in themselves and their capabilities.

Group Formation and Progress

The group, then, is designed to provide members with "a positive perspective on African and African American culture, assist them in developing their own African American group identity, and provide them with tools to deal with the oppressiveness of white supremacy" (Harvey, 1997, p. 164). The group is viewed as part of a program rather than a treatment group. To many potential group members, treatment implies mental illness and turns them off. The final group consists of 15 boys ages 14–18 who are on probation.

(continued)

HIGHLIGHT 16.3 (continued)

Offenses include drug dealing, sexual assault, car theft, armed robbery, and burglary.

Group coleaders include social workers and people with other types of expertise, such as in African studies, music, or theater. Group process involves the acquisition of positive interpersonal, relationship-building, communication, and introspective skills. The group stresses enhancing members' self-concepts, developing "constructive lifestyles and positive solutions to life problems," and appreciating their cultural heritage and personal strengths (Harvey, 1997, p. 167).

The initial large group phase involving potential group initiate stakes eight weeks, during which time coleaders teach participants about the group process, the Afrocentric perspective, and the important formalized rites of passage involved in group membership. Group participants then partake in a weekend retreat in which coleaders and older adult men decide which 15 young men will be included in the final group. Chosen members then undergo an initiation ritual in which they pledge to uphold the Nguzo Saba's principles, are given an African name, and are presented a "special identifying symbol" they are expected to wear at all group meetings. No new members are admitted after this point (Harvey, 1997, p. 167)

The group then meets weekly for 90 minutes as members develop their group identity and learn skills. Group activities may include DVDs and music depending on the topics addressed. Guests are invited to speak on various topics, called "modules," that stress the importance of African and African American culture (Harvey, 1997, p. 168). Modules, which last from four to six group sessions, address any number of topics ranging from African American culture, to relationships between men and women, to racism.

Upon completion of all modules, group members participate in another weekend retreat in which they demonstrate their newly learned skills and prepare for the final recognition ceremony. This ceremony is the culmination of the group experience as members demonstrate before their families and community what they have achieved. They proclaim their sacred name and "receive a symbol and a certificate of sacred transformation" (Harvey, 1997, p. 168).

Intent and Results

We have established that this process seeks to enhance group members' self-respect, sense of African American identity, and sense of responsibility for and belonging to the African American community. Other anticipated effects include crime reduction, improved school attendance, better grades, and increased employment. Initial results are promising (Harvey, 1997). Family members report improved behavior at home, and group members express enhanced self-respect and appreciation of their African heritage.

EP 2.1.10m

Overlaps Among Juvenile Corrections, Mental Health Services, and Child Welfare

Note that substantial overlap exists among juvenile corrections, mental health services, and, to some extent, child welfare. Chapters 9 and 13 address issues concerning child welfare and mental health. Decisions about the needs and placement of each individual depend on a number of conditions. Statutes, policies, and agency practices may vary from state to state and from locality to locality. Available resources for placement also differ dramatically. Finally, juvenile court judges often have great discretion regarding the appropriate placement of juveniles.

Youth Gangs

An additional concern related to violent behavior by youths involves escalating gang membership. It is estimated that over 732,000 gang members belong to almost 21,500 gangs throughout the United States (McWhirter et al., 2007). Most gang members are male, although female membership appears to be increasing, as is their participation in violent crimes (Jenson & Howard, 1999; Potter, 1999).

EP 2.1.10d

McWhirter and his colleagues (2007) provide a further overview of gang activity and composition:

Youth[s] in these gangs were responsible for a wide variety of offenses including street crime, drug trafficking, and witness intimidation, and they are highly likely to use firearms in an assault crime (Esbensen, 2000). A high percentage of gang activity occurs in high schools (95%) or intermediate schools (91%), and involvement with gangs remains one of the most powerful predictors of violence (Office of the Surgeon General, 2001).

When one gang gains power and control in an area, rival gangs sometimes relocate to other areas of the city or even to other cities. These divisions of power and region are frequently related to ethnicity, although there is some evidence to suggest that a new type of gang, hybrid gangs, *is emerging. Hybrid gang culture is characterized by mixed racial and ethnic participation within a single gang (Starbuck, Howell, & Linquist, 2001). Economic opportunities, such as the availability of new markets for drug profits, may also play a part in a gang's decision to relocate. Many communities and neighborhoods once untouched by organized violence now find themselves threatened by gang activity. The proliferation of youth gangs in recent decades is of concern, and of particular concern is the spread of homegrown youth gangs to rural communities (Esbensen, 2000). (p. 183)*

Defining Gangs

There is no consensus regarding an accurate definition for the concept of gang. Morales and Sheafor (2002) reflect on how a "popular criterion [for identifying a gang member] is 'if it looks like a duck, walks like a duck, and quacks like a duck, it is a duck'" (p. 174; Morales, Sheafor, & Scott, 2007). However, they continue by noting that

not all ducks are the same, and even among ducks, some are more passive and some are more aggressive than others. Even with many years of experience in working with gang members,... [it is difficult to] tell if an 8- to 25-year-old person 10 feet in front of ... [you] is in fact a gang member with a violent criminal past or simply one who has knowingly or unknowingly adopted some of the gang culture (e.g., clothing, hairstyle, or speech). (p. 174)

Williams and Van Dorn (1999) identify some common themes evident in gangs:

Some consensus about the nature of juvenile gangs has emerged in recent literature. First, gangs cannot be stereotyped. Some gangs are simply a source of social support and entertainment for members, others serve as drug distribution organizations, and still others do both. Gang members may commit a significant number of crimes, but crime is often not their primary, and certainly not their only, focus. Second, youths often join gangs to achieve goals that they perceive as difficult or impossible to achieve without gang support. However, members differ in their motivations for joining and their degree of commitment to gang life. Third, it is rare for entire gangs to organize their activities exclusively around the sale of drugs. Finally, communities with gangs differ in some respects, but generally all are struggling with social problems such as poverty, racism, ..., and demographic changes. (p. 200)

McWhirter and his colleagues (2007) arbitrarily define a *youth gang* as "a group consisting primarily of adolescents and young adults who interact frequently with one another, share a common identity expressed through a gang name and common symbols, claim control over a certain geographical area, and are deliberately involved in illegal activities" (p. 183). Highlight 16.4 offers a global perspective on gangs.

HIGHLIGHT 16.4

International Perspectives: Gangs Around the World

Huff (1993) emphasizes that gangs as a group experience are a typically occurring pattern often characterizing the "adolescent subculture" that "represent an extreme manifestation of that age-typical emphasis on being together and belonging to something." He continues,

Gangs are certainly not unique to the United States. In fact, most societies seem to have a term that corresponds, at least loosely, to our own term gang. Whether it is the *chimpira* of Japan, the *raggare* of Sweden, the Dutch *nozem*, the Italian *vitelloni*, the *stilyagi* of the USSR, the Yugoslavian *tapkaroschi*, or their counterparts in many other nations, there is usually some way of designating youth gangs. (p. 6)

Types of Gangs

Morales and his colleagues (2012, pp. 179–180) categorize juvenile gangs into four basic types. First, *criminal gangs* have as their "primary goal material gain through criminal activities" that include "theft of property from premises or persons, extortion, fencing, and obtaining and selling illegal substances such as drugs." Second, *conflict gangs* are extremely "turf oriented and will engage in violent battle with individuals or rival groups that invade their neighborhood or commit acts they consider insulting or degrading. Respect is highly valued or defended." *Retreatist gangs*' primary aim is to get "loaded" or "high" on various mind-altering substances and thereby withdraw from the stresses of real life. Retreatist gangs differ from criminal gangs despite the fact that they both may be involved in illegal drug activity. Retreatist gangs emphasize escape from reality, whereas criminal gangs focus on financial gain. *Cult/occult gangs* have appeared to emerge in more recent years. The term *cult* refers to devil worship or participation in evil practices, whereas the concept *occult* implies secretiveness or involvement in supernatural activities (Morales et al., 2012). Cult/occult gangs may focus their interests on hating some group such as gay people or nonwhites.

Prevention and Intervention Involving Gangs

EP 2.1.10g, 2.1.10i

Young people often become gang members to meet personal needs and gain power. In a way, gang membership is a means for youths to empower themselves. Young people should be empowered in other ways so they don't have to turn to gangs for support, belongingness, financial gain, or social status.

Combating gangs can assume three primary thrusts: prevention, intervention, and suppression (Regulus, 1995; Williams & Van Dorn, 1999). *Prevention* involves providing enough resources and services to communities and individuals that young people don't need to seek out gang membership in the first place. Prevention requires communities to offer adequate social programs for reducing poverty, educating parents about children's needs and child management, enhancing policing resources, developing high-quality educational systems that respond to young people's needs, and diminishing accessibility to handguns (Williams & Van Dorn, 1999).

Prevention can also be geared to individual youths' needs. For example, the Peace Power program in New York City was developed by several social work graduate students in conjunction with some "local social service agencies and high schools." This empowerment approach emphasizes

four essential steps: recognizing contributions and successes [e.g., even simple things such as offering feedback notes recognizing specific positive actions on the part of young people]; acting with respect [e.g., initiating a "respect day" during which young people interview each other and share their own definitions of respect]; sharing power to build community [e.g., "working collectively and sharing responsibility"]; and making peace [e.g., teaching conflict resolution strategies].

(Vallianatos, 2001, July, p. 3)

Morales, Sheafor, and Scott (2012) comment on *intervention* with gangs in micro social work practice:

Many traditional forms of social work intervention are thought to be effective in helping individuals have their needs met in ways other than through participation in gangs. For example, the efforts of school social workers to engage teachers and parents in supporting a child's academic development helps the child find school more rewarding and satisfying. Hospital social workers are often among the first to interact with victims or family members of victims experiencing gang violence. They provide services involving acquisition of tangible resources, as well as counseling about the terrorizing event that helps to minimize psychological damage and lower the likelihood of escalating the situation into one of retaliatory violence. In mental health centers, residential treatment facilities, probation departments, and many other human services agencies, it is not uncommon for social workers to help gang members or the victims of gang violence address issues resulting from gang activities.

What about the role of the family? [Many parents find it necessary to work even if they have children under age 6. This makes it hard to provide all the support and supervision children need. As a result, social programs are developed to provide alternative care.] ... [F]amily counseling, family therapy, and other social work services to families can help to minimize family breakdown. Social programs such as Boys and Girls Clubs, Partners, and various recreation programs are examples of how social workers can assist youth in identifying with positive adult role models, as opposed to the role models represented by gang members. (p. 181)

A *suppression* approach to gangs involves focusing on controlling them through law enforcement and prosecution. The focus, of course, is on punishment, not rehabilitation and treatment. Suppression generally involves "the local community, schools, public housing projects, or prison" (Spergel & Grossman, 1997, p. 457).

A Case Example of a Macro Approach to Addressing Gangs: The Little Village Project

The Little Village Project in Chicago combines aspects of prevention, intervention, and suppression in a macro approach to dealing with gangs. It is founded on six major concepts (Morales et al., 2012; Spergel & Grossman, 1997, pp. 458–459):

1. *Community Mobilization.* To address the problems of gang conflict, violence, and illegal behavior, a wide range of people in the community are mobilized to communicate with, work together with, and support each other (National Crime Prevention Council [NCPC], 2011). Those involved include "local residents and groups, youth agencies, police and probation officers, and former gang youths" (Spergel & Grossman 1997, p. 458).

2. *Opportunities Provision.* This involves the idea that people need opportunities other than gang membership as means of preventing such involvement (NCPC, 2011). Opportunities can include "more and better jobs, special education programs, and training programs" (Spergel & Grossman, 1997, p. 458). Opportunities can also entail "recreation at safe locations," linkage of at-risk young people with community-based services, support for nonviolent neighborhood activities, and involvement of parents in actions aimed at preventing gang activities (NCPC, 2011).

3. *Social Intervention.* This essentially refers to "outreach to gang youths in the streets" (Morales et al., 2012, p. 182). Community youth workers can seek out gang members, get to know them, and help link them and other at-risk youths with "services and resources such as drug treatment, jobs, training, educational programs, and some recreation"

(NCPC, 2011; Spergel & Grossman, 1997, p. 458). Youth workers can also help "gang youths avoid probation violations by getting them to report to their probation officers on time" and "avoid harassment from the police" (Spergel & Grossman, 1997, p. 462).

4. *Suppression.* "Suppression for purposes of gang control requires the application of a variety of informal as well as formal controls on the behavior of individual youths and the structure and process of their gangs. Not only supervision and surveillance, arrest, probation, and imprisonment, but also positive communication with youths, information sharing with other agency service and control providers, and joint decision making among agency and community group representatives are essential elements of social control" (Spergel & Grossman 1997, p. 458).

5. *Organizational Change and Development.* This emphasizes the need for social agencies, police, citizens, and others to work together to control crime. "Mutual trust, interdependence, and high levels of morale" need to be generated in a climate of collaboration (Spergel & Grossman 1997, p. 459). For example, regular channels of communication can be established among residents involved in neighborhood organizations, police and probation administrators, staff in social service agencies, and job training program personnel (NCPC, 2011).

6. *Targeting.* Not all gang members are equally involved in the gang (Morales et al., 2012). Some hover at the fringes of gang involvement, either uncertain of what to do or not yet having gained the respect of other gang members. Other members experience various levels of intensity of criminal behavior (including homicide) and imprisonment. Targeting involves identifying the most deeply committed gang leaders as objects of attention.

Chapter Summary

The following summarizes this chapter's content as it relates to the chapter objectives presented at the beginning of the chapter. Objectives include the following:

A Introduce the criminal justice system and define some of the key concepts involved.

The criminal justice system is the complex, integrated system of programs, policies, laws, and agencies devoted to preventing and controlling crime. The system's functions include adjudication (passing legal judgment), incarceration (confining by putting in prison or jail), and rehabilitation (restoring to a state of productive, noncriminal functioning in society).

B Describe the types of crime.

Felonies are grave offenses punishable by at least a year in prison and possibly even death. Misdemeanors are less severe offenses, with punishments ranging from incarceration of less than a year to monetary fines. Categories of crime include violent, property, and offenses not fitting in these two categories. Such offenses involve white-collar, corporate, victimless, organized, and hate crimes.

C Examine who commits crime.

Variables related to crime include gender, age, race, and social class. Men are much more likely to commit crimes, although the arrest rate for women is increasing, especially for female adolescents. People younger than age 25 are the most likely to commit crimes and commit the most violent crimes. Crime is also related to race in that African Americans have a much higher crime rate. However, the crime rate is also related to social class that involves poverty, increased police surveillance and potential racial profiling, and single-parent family structure. Asian Americans have a markedly lower crime rate than their representation in the population.

D Explore whether crime rates are rising or falling.

The crime rate has experienced a decrease over the past decade. The crime rate appears to be related to the state of the economy, decreased crack cocaine use, a larger police force, and more severe sentences for criminals.

E Review the wide range of criminal justice settings in which social workers practice.

Criminal justice settings include forensic social work, adult correctional institutions, administrative planning centers, community-based corrections involving probation and parole, victim assistance programs, domestic violence services, and juvenile corrections. Some settings reflect an overlap among juvenile corrections, mental health services, and child welfare.

F Describe the cycle of domestic violence, its dynamics, and treatment.

The cycle involves buildup of tension, the explosion, and a honeymoon period. There are many reasons why women stay in abusive relationships. Treatment strategies emphasize providing support and emphasizing empowerment.

G Describe a program focusing on the empowerment of African American youth involved in the juvenile justice system.

A program for African American juvenile offenders uses a group format to enhance self, respect, establish a stronger identity with African heritage and culture, create ties with a positive peer group, develop vocational aspirations, and strengthen members' ability to make socially responsible decisions.

H Discuss youth membership in gangs, types of gangs, and gang prevention and treatment.

It is estimated that 21,500 gangs exist throughout the United States. Gangs provide members with social support, assist members in achieving goals they can't attain by themselves, and participate in selling drugs. Types of gangs include criminal, conflict, retreatist, and cult/occult. Prevention, intervention, and suppression are three means of combating gangs.

I Examine and encourage critical thinking about the ethical dilemma of punishment versus empowerment and the issue of providing expensive health care for prisoners.

Critical thinking questions were raised regarding conservative and liberal approaches to providing punishment versus empowerment to prisoners. Questions were also posed concerning the practice of providing prisoners with expensive health care.

LOOKING AHEAD

This book concludes by stressing the importance of critical thinking in evaluating social welfare policy issues in various fields of practice. It also encourages you to explore your personal values and ideas about your future career.

COMPETENCY NOTES

The following identifies where Educational Policy (EP) competencies and practice behaviors are discussed in the chapter.

EP 2.1.1c Attend to professional roles and boundaries. *(p. 497):* Social workers' role in forensic social work is discussed.

EP 2.1.2 Apply social work ethical principles to guide professional practice. *(p. 513):* A case scenario requires the application of ethical principles.

EP 2.1.2a Recognize and manage personal values in a way that allows professional values to guide practice. *(p. 496):* Reflection about personal values concerning punishment versus empowerment allows practitioners to manage these values so that they don't interfere with professional values and ethics. *(p. 499):* Critical thinking questions encourage consideration of personal values concerning the provision of expensive health care to people in prison.

EP 2.1.2c Tolerate ambiguity in resolving ethical conflicts. *(p. 496):* The controversial issues involved in the treatment of criminals may be ambiguous in terms of the best solution. Social workers must learn to tolerate such ambiguity as they seek to resolve ethical conflicts. *(p. 513):* Difficult ethical questions are posed that require toleration of ambiguity in order to arrive at ethical decisions.

EP 2.1.2d Apply strategies of ethical reasoning to arrive at principled decisions. *(p. 513):* The Triple-A strategy to arrive at ethical decisions is applied.

EP 2.1.3 Apply critical thinking to inform and communicate professional judgments. *(p. 497):* Critical thinking questions are posed regarding the treatment of people in prison. *(p. 499):* Critical thinking questions encourage thought about prisoners receiving expensive health care. *(p. 513):* Critical thinking questions are posed.

EP 2.1.3a Distinguish, appraise, and integrate multiple sources of knowledge, including research-based knowledge, and practice wisdom. *(p. 513):* The case and critical thinking questions posed require the appraisal and integration of multiple sources of knowledge.

EP 2.1.4a Recognize the extent to which culture's structures and values may oppress, marginalize, alienate, or create or enhance privilege and power. *(p. 494):* The dimensions of diversity—race, culture, and class—operate to marginalize people and make it more likely that they turn to crime. *(p. 496):* The concept of punishment can be assessed to determine when it becomes oppressive. *(p. 501):* The dynamics involved in domestic violence oppress women.

EP 2.1.4b Gain sufficient self-awareness to eliminate the influence of personal biases and values in working with diverse groups. *(p. 496):* Practitioners must develop self-awareness regarding any prejudices and stereotypes they may harbor toward people in prison.

EP 2.1.4c Recognize and communicate their understanding of the importance of difference in shaping life experiences. *(p. 494):* Social workers must recognize how race, class, and gender shape life experiences concerning participation in criminal behavior. *(p. 504):* Practitioners should recognize the extent to which race and cultural background shape life experiences. The program discussed stresses racial and cultural appreciation and pride.

EP 2.1.5b Advocate for human rights and social and economic justice. *(p. 496):* Practitioners should advocate on the behalf of prisoners' human rights.

EP 2.1.5c Engage in practices that advance social and economic justice. *(p. 496):* Social workers should engage in practices that advance social and economic justice for prisoners.

EP 2.1.7a Utilize conceptual frameworks to guide the processes of assessment, intervention, and evaluation. *(p. 497):* Critical thinking questions encourage thought concerning the application of conservative and liberal conceptual frameworks to imprisonment and its purposes. *(p. 501):* The cycle of violence provides a useful conceptual framework for assessing domestic violence and proceeding with intervention.

EP 2.1.7b Critique and apply knowledge to understand person and environment. *(p. 501):* Practitioners should apply knowledge about factors contributing to domestic violence to understand the dynamics involved.

EP 2.1.8a Analyze, formulate, and advocate for policies that advance social well-being. *(p. 496):* Social workers should strive to establish policies and programs that help prisoners in the rehabilitation process.

EP 2.1.9a Continuously discover, appraise, and attend to changing locales, populations, scientific and technological developments, and emerging societal trends to provide relevant services. *(p. 493):* Practitioners should continuously appraise the changing trends in crime in order to provide relevant services.

EP 2.1.10d Collect, organize, and interpret client data. *(p. 502):* This section discusses the dynamics and variables related to delinquent behavior, which social workers must understand to effectively collect, organize, and interpret client data. *(p. 505):* The dynamics of gangs are discussed to prepare practitioners who work with gang members for the collection, organization, and interpretation of client data.

EP 2.1.10f Develop mutually agreed-on intervention goals and objectives. *(p. 501):* Practitioners can work with a domestic violence survivor to develop mutually agreed-on intervention goals based on what the survivor wants to do.

EP 2.1.10g Select appropriate intervention strategies. *(p. 501):* Social workers should select the appropriate intervention strategies as suggested here when working with survivors of domestic violence. *(p. 503):* Potential appropriate intervention strategies for working with delinquent adolescents are

described. *(p. 504):* An intervention strategy that focuses on cultural appreciation and enhanced self-esteem is selected in this case example. *(p. 507):* Intervention strategies for working with gang members at the micro and macro levels are discussed.

EP 2.1.10i Implement prevention interventions that enhance client capacities. *(p. 498):* Being on probation or parole prevents people from serving that time in prison. *(p. 503):* A program aimed at the prevention of juvenile delinquency is described. *(p. 507):* Interventions to prevent gang involvement are proposed.

EP 2.1.10j Help clients resolve problems. *(p. 501):* Practitioners can help survivors of domestic violence resolve problems.

EP 2.1.10k Negotiate, mediate, and advocate for clients. *(p. 501):* Social workers should advocate on the behalf of survivors of domestic violence.

EP 2.1.10m Critically analyze, monitor, and evaluate interventions. *(p. 505):* Evaluation of program effectiveness is an important aspect of the planned-change process.

FOR FURTHER EXPLORATION ON THE INTERNET

See this text's Social Work CourseMate website at *www.cengagebrain.com* for learning tools such as chapter quizzing, videos, glossary flashcards, and more.

CASE STUDY FOR CRITICAL THINKING

A Client with a Serious Hereditary Disease

**EP 2.1.2,
2.1.2c,
2.1.2d,
2.1.3,
2.1.3a[2]**

The case presented here represents an application of this entire section of the book on client populations and contexts, not specifically on criminal justice. This case involves a hospital social worker talking with a client who just discovered she has a serious hereditary disease involving mental and physical deterioration and eventual death.[1] Subsequent questions are posed to promote critical thinking.

Case Study: A hospital social worker is counseling Myla, age 24, a patient who has just been informed that she has a genetic marker for Huntington's chorea, a hereditary disease commencing in middle age that causes gradual deterioration of the brain and voluntary muscular movement. No cure currently exists for the disease. Myla greatly desires to have children, but they could all potentially be infected with the disease.

Myla states she does not want her husband, Richard, or her family to know about this. Myla fears that if Richard finds out he will refuse to have children with her and possibly leave her because he, too, desires children. Myla is reeling over the shocking news.

Critical Thinking: The first step in the critical thinking process involves *asking* questions about problems, needs, and issues. A number of basic ethical questions can be raised:

- What are the issues involving confidentiality in this case? Does Richard have the right to know that Myla has the disease and that their future children might also have it? Does he have the right to know that within the next 20 or 30 years Myla will likely begin experiencing serious mental and physical deterioration?
- "What is the best interest of the as-yet-unborn child?"
- "Who is the person or are the persons entitled to make such decisions?"
- "What are the religious implications for all concerned (if any) of playing God?"
- "Who speaks for the fetus?"
- "What are statistical relationships between a genetic marker and the actual occurrence of the genetic defect, and what bearing do they have on making a decision?"
- "What is society's best interest in this situation?" (Loewenberg, Dolgoff, & Harrington, 2000, p. 218).

Additionally, what specific questions might be asked concerning Myla's responsibility to herself and others in addition to planning for the future?

---

[1]This case study is based on one presented in Loewenberg, Dolgoff, and Harrington (2000, p. 218).
[2]Competency notes for this case study are located at the end of Chaper 16.

Consider the following:

- If Myla does not tell Richard, how will he react when he inevitably does find out about her condition? If she doesn't tell him beforehand, how will he feel toward her after having children who potentially harbor the disease?
- Might Myla consider the alternative of not having children or of adopting them?
- How can Myla plan her life over the next few decades to maximize her appreciation and enjoyment of it?
- How might she plan for the more distant future when she begins to experience symptoms of the disease?

Note that these latter questions are very solemn and would not be ones a social worker would pose to Myla flippantly. Rather, the practitioner would help Myla address them over time when she was emotionally ready. First Myla would have to work through her grief concerning the diagnosis and begin coping with her reality. Only then could she begin to make more objective decisions about and plans for her future.

The second step in critical thinking entails *assessing* the established facts and issues involved. What are the answers to the questions posed? Some require facts such as more information about Huntington's chorea. Others involve serious thinking about values and ethics.

The final step in critical thinking is the *assertion* of a concluding opinion. The social worker would assist Myla in *asking* questions about her situation and options and then in *assessing* her answers. The worker would also be forced to address the ethical questions posed and determine what was the right thing to do. For example, should Richard be told? There are no easy answers. If you were Myla, what would you do?

Your Values and Your Future: Applying Critical Thinking Skills

Jeremy Woodhouse/Getty Images

This book has discussed a wide range of social welfare policy and programming issues. The emphasis has been on critical thinking about these issues using the Triple-A approach:

1. *Ask* questions.
2. *Assess* the established facts and issues involved.
3. *Assert* a concluding opinion.

At this point, what are your opinions and values concerning the following issues?

- What policies should the government adopt concerning the treatment of poor children and families?

- Can poverty be eliminated? If so, how? What policies and programs need to be developed? To what extent do you feel this is possible?
- What supportive and supplementary services best serve children and families? What are the most important concepts involved in developing policies and services?
- To what extent should society support older adults by providing services and benefits? What services and benefits are most critical? What new policies could improve their quality of life?
- To what extent should society promote self-determination on the part of people with disabilities by providing services and benefits? What policies could improve this population's quality of life? What important concepts are involved in policy development and service provision?
- What are the major issues involved in the provision of health care in the United States? What are the pros and cons of managed care? Should changes in health care policy be pursued? If so, what changes? Should a universal national health insurance policy initiative be advanced? If so, who would pay for it?
- What are the primary issues involved in mental health policy and service provision? What policy initiatives might be advanced to address these concerns?
- What are the principal issues and concerns in providing services to youths and in the schools? What methods of empowerment can be proposed?
- What are the main issues and concerns involved in criminal justice and service provision? To what extent does criminal justice policy reflect a punitive versus rehabilitative perspective? Can policy be improved, and if so, how?

Do these values and opinions tend to reflect a conservative or a liberal perspective? Do you tend to support a residual or an institutional orientation to service provision?

The Importance of Values in Career Decision Making

This book has stressed the significance of professional values in social work practice. It has also emphasized the importance of social workers pursuing policy practice when advocacy is called for to improve social welfare policies and programming. It is important that professional values be acceptable to people who choose to become social workers. Of course, we all have personal opinions about an extensive range of topics. However, social workers' personal values must be in adequate compliance with professional values for individuals to be comfortable and productive professionals.

Assessing Your Own Capabilities and Interests

The following sections encourage you to think about your personal capabilities, potential job preferences, and initial career goals. They are intended to give you some insight into whether social work might be the field for you.

What Are Your Competencies?

Competencies involve your skills and abilities. In social work practice, *competencies* are "measureable practice behaviors that are comprised of knowledge, values, and skills" (CSWE, 2008b, EP 2.1). What are you good at? What skills have you mastered that would enhance your performance in a professional social work

Box A ▶ Assessing Your Capabilities

The following are areas that may reflect your professional knowledge, skills, and values. Place a check mark next to each item that you consider a strength:

_____ Assessment of individual, family, group, community, and organizational problems and functioning

_____ Communication

_____ Understanding people

_____ Problem solving

_____ Decision making

_____ Planning

_____ Organizing

_____ Recording

_____ Clear thinking

_____ Acceptance of responsibility

_____ Dependability

_____ Pacing efforts

_____ Coordination

_____ Case management

_____ Conducting meetings

_____ Use of critical thinking

_____ Application of ethical principles

_____ Understanding of diverse racial and ethnic groups

_____ Advocacy

_____ Creativity

_____ Initiating ideas

_____ Undertaking action

These concepts simply reflect the beginning of your capability assessment. The potential list is unlimited. These are merely intended to give you some initial ideas.

After giving your capabilities serious thought, write out several paragraphs summarizing and prioritizing your greatest strengths. This can help you articulate for yourself (and later for potential employers) the reasons you are or will be a capable professional.

setting? Think about the social work knowledge and values that you have acquired and the skills that you have mastered. Box A identifies some potential competencies.

What Are Your Employment Goals?

This question concerns the context of employment. What aspects of work are important to you other than the type of social work skills you use or population you serve? In other words, what aspects of your working environment motivate you to perform and encourage you to like your job? Box B portrays a range of work dimensions that may be of varying importance to you. To what extent do you think that these would characterize a career as a social worker?

What Are Your Job Preferences?

If you are considering a career in social work, what would the ideal job be? Think in terms of four areas: (1) the types of professional activities you would most like to pursue, (2) your preferred client population, (3) the problems you are interested in addressing, and (4) the type of agency setting in which you would like to work. The questions posed in Box C illustrate examples in each area.

Note that simple identification of your preferred job characteristics does not mean that you will get that exact job or even one very similar. The intent here is to help you seriously consider your own goals and career objectives. The better you know yourself, the more capable you will be of both presenting yourself to others (such as potential employers) and making decisions about what job to pursue and accept.

Box B Employment Goals and Work Context

What aspects of the work environment are the most important to you? Prioritize the following:

_____ Salary
_____ Sick leave
_____ Hours of work
_____ Effective supervision
_____ Geographic location
_____ Potential for advancement
_____ Substantial discretion in decision making
_____ Vacation time
_____ Health-care benefits
_____ Not being "on call"
_____ In-service training opportunities
_____ Clear job description
_____ Opportunity to function independently
_____ Challenging environment
_____ Low stress levels
_____ Realistic record-keeping requirements
_____ Being rewarded for achievement
_____ Little travel
_____ Potential for new skill development
_____ Competent colleagues
_____ Good office
_____ Good relationships with colleagues
_____ Working as part of a team
_____ Potential for travel
_____ Respect from other staff members
_____ Clear rules and regulations
_____ Responsive administration
_____ Time flexibility

Is there anything else that would be motivating to you? If so, specify.

_____ _____
_____ _____

Box C Job Preferences

1. What types of professional activities are you most interested in pursuing? Prioritize the following:

_____ Counseling
_____ Brokering resources
_____ Supervising volunteers
_____ Writing grants
_____ Running groups
_____ Management
_____ Community organizing
_____ Program evaluation
_____ Public relations
_____ Running meetings
_____ Budgeting
_____ Administrative activities in general
_____ Case management
_____ Supervising staff
_____ Lobbying
_____ Research
_____ Fund-raising
_____ Training staff
_____ Policy development
_____ Advocacy

What else? _____
_____ _____
_____ _____

2. Ideally, what client population would you prefer to work with? Prioritize the following:

_____ Children
_____ Young adults
_____ Older adults
_____ Women
_____ Intact families
_____ Teenagers
_____ Middle-aged adults
_____ Married couples
_____ Men
_____ Single parents
_____ Minority groups (If so, specify which) _____
_____ Other client populations (If so, specify which) _____

3. What problems and issues are you interested in addressing? Prioritize the following:
_____ Community development
_____ Alcohol and other drugs
_____ Child maltreatment
_____ Battered women
_____ Probation and parole
_____ Mental illness
_____ Family problems

(continued)

Box C   Job Preferences *(continued)*

———— Crime in communities
———— Teen pregnancy
———— School problems (e.g., truancy)
———— Financial resources acquisition
———— Prison
———— Couples conflict
———— Unemployment
———— Vocational rehabilitation
———— Developmental disability
———— Health
———— Eating disorders
———— Suicide prevention
———— Physical challenges
———— HIV/AIDS
———— Homelessness

What else? _____
———— _____
———— _____

4. In what type of agency setting would you prefer to work? Prioritize the following:

———— Private *or*
———— Public
———— Large bureaucracy *or*
———— Smaller agency
———— County social services
———— Institution
———— Group home
———— Primary social work setting
———— Primary medical setting
———— Primary educational setting
———— Serving clients with a wide range of problems *or*
———— Focusing on specialized problems
———— Close, directive supervision *or*
———— Supervision primarily on a consultation basis
———— Hospital
———— School
———— Community organization
———— Prison
———— Family planning agency
———— Mental health center or counseling agency
———— Hospice
———— Shelter (e.g., for homeless people or survivors of domestic violence)

Looking Ahead

These exercises and this book only scratch the surface of what social work is all about. It's just the beginning if you're thinking about some area of social work as the career for you.

References

Abadinsky, H. (2000). *Probation and parole* (7th ed.). Upper Saddle River, NJ: Prentice-Hall.

Abadinsky, H. (2011). *Drug use and abuse: A comprehensive introduction* (7th ed.). Belmont, CA: Brooks/Cole.

Abdelkarim, R. Z. (2002, September–October). American Muslims and 9/11: A community looks back . . . and to the future. *Washington Report on Middle East Affairs, 21*(7), 82–85. Retrieved July 9, 2004 from http://infotrac-college. thomsonlearning.com.

About.com. (2011). What are CD4 cells? Retrieved on June 13, 2011 from http://aids.about.com/od/newlydiagnosed/qt/cd4.htm.

Abramovitz, M. (1995). Aid to families with dependent children. In R. L. Edwards (Ed.), *Encyclopedia of social work* (19th ed., Vol. 1, pp. 183–194). Washington, DC: NASW Press.

Abramovitz, M. (1997). Temporary assistance to needy families. In R. L. Edwards (Ed.), *Encyclopedia of social work supplement* (pp. 311–330). Washington, DC: NASW Press.

Abramovitz, M. (2007). Ideological perspectives and conflicts. In J. Blau (Ed., with M. Abramovitz), *The dynamics of social welfare policy* (2nd ed., pp. 126–183). New York: Oxford.

Abramovitz, M. (2008). Political ideology and social welfare. In T. Mizrahi & L. E. Davis (Editors-in-Chief), *Encyclopedia of Social Work* (Vol. 3, pp. 368–374). Washington, DC: NASW Press.

Abramovitz, M. (2010). Ideological perspectives and conflicts. In J. Blau (Ed., with M. Abramovitz), *The dynamics of social welfare policy* (3rd ed., pp. 131–188). New York: Oxford.

Acs, G., & Lopres, P. (2007). Final report: TANF caseload composition and leavers synthesis report. Retrieved on May 21, 2011 from http://www.urban.org/UploadedPDF/411553_tanf_caseload.pdf.

ADA Amendments Act of 2008. (2008). P.L. 110-125. Retrieved from http://www.access-board.gov/about/laws/ada-amendments. htm.

Administration for Children and Families (ACF). (n.d.). Family preservation services. Retrieved on May 30, 2011 from http://www.childwelfare.gov/supporting/preservation/.

Administration for Children and Families (ACF). (2010a). Child care and development fund fact sheet, September 2010. Retrieved on May 19, 2011 from http://www.acf.hhs.gov/programs/ccb/ccdf/factsheet.htm.

Administration for Children and Families (ACF). (2010b). Office of family assistance (OFA). Retrieved on May 19, 2011 from http://www.acf.hhs.gov/opa/fact_sheets/tanf_factsheet.html

Aestraea's Web. (1998). Was "Sybil" really a multiple personality? Retrieved April 27, 2002 from http://www.aestraeaweb. net/plural/sybilbogus.html.

Ahluwalia, M. K., & Zaman, N. K. (2010). Counseling Muslims and Sikhs in a post-9/11 world. In J. G. Ponterotto, J. M. Cases, L. A. Suzuki, & C. M. Alexander (Eds.), *Handbook of multicultural counseling* (3rd ed., pp. 467–478). Thousand Oaks, CA: Sage.

Ahmed, P. I., & Kolker, A. (1979). The role of indigenous medicine in WHO's definition of health. In P. I. Ahmed & G. V. Coelhi (Eds.), *Toward a new definition of health.* New York: Plenum.

Ajrouch, K. J. (2008). Arab Americans. In T. Mizrahi & L. E. Davis (Editors-in-Chief), *Encyclopedia of Social Work* (Vol. 1, pp. 151–153). Washington, DC: NASW Press.

Akabas, S. H. (2008). Employee assistance programs. In T. Mizrahi & L. E. Davis (Editors-in-Chief), *Encyclopedia of Social Work* (Vol. 2, pp. 115–118). Washington, DC: NASW Press.

Alavi, K. (2001, October). At risk of prejudice: Teaching tolerance about Muslim Americans. *Social Education, 65*(6), 344–349. Retrieved July 13, 2004 from http://infotrac-college. thomsonlearning.com/itw/infomark/145/808/51630275w5/22!ar_fmt.

Albrecht, G. (1992). *The disability business: Rehabilitation in America.* Newbury Park, CA: Sage.

Alexander, S. (2004). Intervention with families. In C. R. Brittain & D. E. Hunt (Eds.), *Helping in child protective services: A competency-based casework handbook* (pp. 393–446). New York: Oxford.

Allen, J. A. (1995). African Americans: Caribbean. In R. L. Edwards (Ed.), *Encyclopedia of social work* (19th ed., Vol. 1, pp. 121–129). Washington, DC: NASW Press.

Allen-Meares, P. (2008). School social work. In T. Mizrahi & L. E. Davis (Editors-in-Chief), *Encyclopedia of Social Work* (Vol. 4, pp. 3–7). Washington, DC: NASW Press.

AllRefer.com. (2005). AIDS. Retrieved January 29, 2005 from http://health.allrefer.com/health/aids-diagnosis-tests.html.

Altshuler, S. J. (2007). Everything you never wanted to know about special education . . . and were afraid to ask (I.D.E.A.). *Journal of Social Work in Disability and Rehabilitation, 6*(1/2), 23–34.

American Administration on Aging. (2010). *Profile of older Americans, 2009.* Washington, DC: U.S. Government Printing Office.

American Association of Sex Educators, Counselors, and Therapists (AASECT). (2000, April). Quick hits: Sex in the news. *Contemporary Sexuality, 34*(4), 6–9.

American Experience. (2010). Jimmy Carter's post-presidency. Retrieved on June 4, 2011 from http://www.pbs.org/wgbh/americanExperience/features/general-article/carter-post-presidency/.

American Psychiatric Association (APA). (2000). *Diagnostic and statistical manual of mental disorders text revision* (4th ed.). Washington, DC: Author.

American Psychological Association. (2010). *Publication manual of the American psychological association* (6th ed.). Washington, DC: Author.

ARC Milwaukee. (Undated, a). Employment programs. Milwaukee, WI: Author.

ARC Milwaukee. (Undated, b). Figuring out funding. Milwaukee, WI: Author.

ARC Milwaukee. (Undated, c). Services profile. Milwaukee, WI: Author.

Armstrong, K., Best, S., & Domenici, P. (2006). *Courage after fire.* Berkeley, CA: Ulysses Press.

Aronowitz, A. A. (2004). Victimization of trafficked persons and illegal migrants. *International Review of Victimology, 11,* 11–32.

Arredondo, P., et al. (1996). *Operationalization of the multicultural counseling competencies.* Washington, DC: Association for Multicultural Counseling and Development.

Asch, A. (1995). Visual impairment and blindness. In R. L. Edwards (Ed.), *Encyclopedia of social work* (19th ed., Vol. 3, pp. 2461–2468). Washington, DC: NASW Press.

Asch, A., & Mudrick, N. R. (1995). Disability. In R. L. Edwards (Ed.), *Encyclopedia of social work* (19th ed., Vol. 1, pp. 752–761). Washington, DC: NASW Press.

Asch, A., & Mudrick, N. R. (2008). Blindness and visual impairment. In T. Mizrahi & L. E. Davis (Editors-in-Chief), *Encyclopedia of Social Work* (Vol. 1, pp. 206–214). Washington, DC: NASW Press.

Association of Baccalaureate Program Directors (BPD). (2008). Definition of generalist practice. Retrieved July 5, 2008 from http://www.bpdonline.org.

Association of Social Work Boards (ASWB). (2008). ASWB: Summer 2008. Retrieved July 6, 2008 from http://www.aswb.org/.

Association of Social Work Boards (ASWB). (2011). Association of social work boards. Retrieved on May 6, 2011 from http://www.bls.gov/oco/ocos060.htm.

Astor, R. A., Benbenishty, R., & Marachi, R. (2010). Violence in schools. In P. Allen-Meares (Ed.), *Social work services in schools* (6th ed., pp. 125–156). Boston: Allyn & Bacon.

Atkins-Burnett, S. (2010). Children with disabilities. In P. Allen-Meares (Ed.), *Social work in schools* (6th ed., pp. 157–190). Boston: Allyn & Bacon.

AVERT. (2011a). HIV and AIDS in Africa. Retrieved on June 13, 2011 from http://www.avert.org/hiv-aids-africa.htm.

AVERT. (2011b). HIV and AIDS vaccine. Retrieved on June 13, 2011 from http://www.avert.org/aids-vaccine.htm.

Avery, A., Chase, J., Johansson, L., Litvak, S., Montero, D., & Wydra, M. (2007). America's changing attitudes toward homosexuality, civil unions, and same-gender marriage: 1977–2004. *Social Work, 52*(1), 71–79.

Axinn, J., & Stern, M. J. (2008). *Social welfare: A history of the American response to need* (7th ed.). Boston: Allyn & Bacon.

Balgopal, P. R. (1995). Asian Americans overview. In R. L. Edwards (Ed.), *Encyclopedia of social work* (19th ed., Vol. 1, pp. 231–238). Washington, DC: NASW Press.

Balgopal, P. R. (2008). Asian Americans: Overview. In T. Mizrahi & L. E. Davis (Editors-in-Chief), *Encyclopedia of Social Work* (Vol. 1, pp. 153–160). Washington, DC: NASW Press.

Balsanek, J. (1998). Addressing at-risk pregnant women's issues through community, individual, and corporate grassroots efforts. In P. L. Ewalt, E. M. Freeman, & D. L. Poole (Eds.), *Community building: Renewal, well-being, and shared responsibility* (pp. 411–419). Washington, DC: NASW Press.

Barker, R. L. (1995). *The social work dictionary* (3rd ed.). Washington, DC: NASW Press.

Barker, R. L. (1999). *Milestones.* Washington, DC: NASW Press.

Barker, R. L. (2003). *The social work dictionary* (5th ed.). Washington, DC: NASW Press.

Barnett, O. W., Miller-Perrin, C. L., & Perrin, R. D. (2011). *Family violence across the lifespan: An introduction* (3rd ed.). Thousand Oaks, CA: Sage.

Barrett, L. (1983). *Gambling with history: Reagan in the White House.* New York: Penguin Books.

Barsky, A. E. (2006). *Alcohol, other drugs, and addictions: A professional development manual for social workers and the human services.* Belmont, CA: Brooks/Cole.

Barth, R. P. (2008). Adoption. In T. Mizrahi & L. E. Davis (Editors-in-Chief), *Encyclopedia of Social Work* (Vol. 1, pp. 33–44). Washington, DC: NASW Press.

Bartlett, H. (1970). *The common base of social work practice.* New York: National Association of Social Workers.

Barton, W. H. (1995). Juvenile corrections. In R. L. Edwards (Ed.), *Encyclopedia of social work* (19th ed., Vol. 2, pp. 1563–1577). Washington, DC: NASW Press.

Barusch, A. S. (2000). Social Security is not for babies: Trends and policies affecting older women in the United States. *Families in Society, 81*(6), 568–575.

Barusch, A. S. (2009). *Foundations of social policy: Social justice in human perspective* (3rd ed.). Belmont, CA: Brooks/Cole.

Barusch, A. S. (2012). *Foundations of social policy: Social justice in human perspective* (4th ed.). Belmont, CA: Brooks/Cole.

Baruth, L. G., & Manning, M. L. (1999). *Multicultural counseling and psychotherapy: A lifespan perspective* (2nd ed.). Upper Saddle River, NJ: Prentice-Hall.

Baruth, L. G., & Manning, M. L. (2007). *Multicultural counseling and psychotherapy: A lifespan perspective* (4th ed.). Upper Saddle River, NJ: Merrill.

Baskin, T. (2012). Age. In D. D. Choudhuri, A. L. Santiago-Rivera, & M. T. Garrett, *Counseling & diversity* (pp. 153–178). Belmont, CA: Brooks/Cole.

Bearse, M. L. (2008). Native Americans: Practice interventions. In T. Mizrahi & L. E. Davis (Editors-in-Chief), *Encyclopedia of Social Work* (Vol. 3, pp. 299–308). Washington, DC: NASW Press.

Becerra, R. M., & Damron-Rodriguez, J. (1995). Veterans and veterans services. In R. L. Edwards (Ed.), *Encyclopedia of social work* (19th ed., Vol. 3, pp. 2431–2439). Washington, DC: NASW Press.

Beck, A. T., Rush, A. J., Shaw, B. F., & Emery, G. (1979). *Cognitive therapy of depression.* New York: Guilford Press.

Beck, A. T., & Weishaar, M. E. (2011). Cognitive therapy. In R. J. Corsini & D. Wedding (Eds.), *Current psychotherapies* (9th ed., pp. 276–309). Belmont, CA: Brooks/Cole.

Beckett, J. O., & Johnson, H. C. (1995). Human development. In R. L. Edwards (Ed.), *Encyclopedia of social work* (19th ed., Vol. 2, pp. 1385–1405). Washington, DC: NASW Press.

Begley, S. (1999, May 3). Why the young kill. *Newsweek,* 32–35.

Beless, D. W. (1995). Council on Social Work Education. In R. L. Edwards (Ed.), *Encyclopedia of social work* (19th ed., Vol. 1, pp. 632–637). Washington, DC: NASW Press.

Bellos, N. S., & Ruffolo, M. C. (1995). Aging: Services. In R. L. Edwards (Ed.), *Encyclopedia of social work* (19th ed., Vol. 1, pp. 165–173). Washington, DC: NASW Press.

Bennett, B. (2006, April 23). Stolen away. Retrieved June 29, 2008 from http://www.time.com/time/printout/0,8816,1186558,00.html.

Bentley, K. J., & Kogut, C. P. (2008). Psychotropic medications. In T. Mizrahi & L. E. Davis (Editors-in-Chief), *Encyclopedia of Social Work* (Vol. 3, pp. 467–476). Washington, DC: NASW Press.

Bentley, K. J., & Walsh, J. (1998). Advances in psychopharmacology and psychosocial aspects of medication management: A review for social workers. In J. B. W. Williams & K. Ell (Eds.), *Advances in mental health research: Implications for practice* (pp. 309–342). Washington, DC: NASW Press.

Berg, I. K. (1994). *Family based services: A solution-focused approach.* New York: Norton.

Berg, I. K., & Jaya, K. P. (1993). Different and same: Family therapy with Asian-American families. *Journal of Marital and Family Therapy, 19*(1), 31–38.

Berg-Cross, L., Craig, K., & Wessel, T. (2001). Multiculturalism at historically black colleges and universities: A case study of Howard University. In J. G. Ponterotto, J. M. Casas, L. A. Suzuki, & C. M. Alexander (Eds.), *Handbook of multicultural counseling* (2nd ed., pp. 849–870). Thousand Oaks, CA: Sage.

Berger, R. M., & Kelly, J. J. (1995). Gay men overview. In R. L. Edwards (Ed.), *Encyclopedia of social work* (19th ed., Vol. 2, pp. 1064–1075). Washington, DC: NASW Press.

Berliner, L. (2011). Child sexual abuse. In J. E. B. Myers (Ed.), *The APSAC handbook on child maltreatment* (3rd ed., pp. 215–252). Thousand Oaks, CA: Sage.

Berliner, L., & Elliott, D. M. (2002). Sexual abuse of children. In J. E. B. Myers, L. Berliner, J. Briere, C. T. Hendrix, C. Jenny, & T. A. Reid (Eds.), *The APSAC handbook on child maltreatment* (2nd ed., pp. 55–78). Thousand Oaks, CA: Sage.

Berry, M. (2005). Overview of family preservation. In G. P. Mallon & P. M. Hess (Eds.), *Child welfare for the 21st century: A handbook of practices, policies, and programs* (pp. 319–334). New York: Columbia.

Beumont, P. J. V., Russell, J. E., & Touyz, S. W. (1993). Treatment of anorexia nervosa. *Lancet, 341,* 1635–1640.

Bibus, A., & Link, R. J. (1999). Global approaches to learning social welfare policy. In C. S. Ramanathan & R. J. Link (Eds.), *All our futures: Principles and resources for social work practice in a global era.* Pacific Grove, CA: Brooks/Cole.

Biegel, D. E., Shore, B. K., & Gordon, E. (1984). *Building support networks for the elderly: Theory and application.* Thousand Oaks, CA: Sage.

Binghenheimer, J. B., Brennan, R. T., & Earls, F. J. (2005). Firearm violence exposure and serious violent behavior. *Science, 308,* 1323–1326.

Black, L. (1996). Families of African origin: An overview. In M. McGoldrick, J. Giordan, & J. K. Pearce (Eds.), *Ethnicity and family therapy* (2nd ed., pp. 57–65). New York: Guilford.

Blau, J., with Abramovitz, M. (2010). *The dynamics of social welfare policy* (3rd ed.). New York: Oxford.

Bleyer, L. R., & Joiner, K. (2009). Needs assessment: A tool of policy practice in school social work. In C. R. Massat, R. Constable, S. McDonald, & J. P. Flynn (Eds.), *School social work: Practice, policy, and research* (7th ed., pp. 217–232). Chicago: Lyceum.

Bradshaw, C. P., Sawyer, A. L., & O'Brennan, L. M. (2009). A social disorganization perspective on bulling-related attitudes and bvehaviors: The influence of school context. *American Journal of Community Psychology, 43,* 204–220.

Blundo, R. (2008). Men: Practice interventions. In T. Mizrahi & L. E. Davis (Editors-in-Chief), *Encyclopedia of Social Work* (Vol. 3, pp. 217–221). Washington, DC: NASW Press.

Blythe, B., & Reithoffer, A. (2000). Assessment and measurement issues in direct practice in social work. In P. Allen-Meares & C. Garvin (Eds.), *The handbook of social work practice* (pp. 551–564). Thousand Oaks, CA: Sage.

Boehm, W. W. (1959). *Objectives of the social work curriculum of the future.* New York: Council on Social Work Education.

Boonstra, H. (2002, February). Teen pregnancy: Trends and lessons learned. *The Guttmacher Report on Public Policy,* pp. 9–10.

Borch-Jacobsen, M. (1997, April 24). Sybil: The making of a disease? *New York Review of Books.* Retrieved April 28, 2002 from http://www.aestraeasweb.net/plural/spiegel.html.

Boston Women's Health Book Collective. (1984). *The new our bodies, ourselves.* New York: Simon & Schuster.

Bowes, D., Marquis, M., Young, W., Holowaty, P., & Isaac, W. (2009, July). Process evaluation of a school-based intervention to increase physical activity and reduce bullying. *Health Promotion Practice, 10*(3), 394–401.

Boyle, C. (2000). Engagement: An ongoing process. In A. A. Abbott (Ed.), *Alcohol, tobacco, and other drugs: Challenging myths, assessing theories, individualizing interventions* (pp. 144–158). Washington, DC: NASW Press.

Brammer, R. (2012). *Diversity in counseling* (2nd ed.). Belmont, CA: Brooks/Cole.

Brandwein, R. A. (2008). Women: Overview. In T. Mizrahi & L. E. Davis (Editors-in-Chief), *Encyclopedia of Social Work* (Vol. 4, pp. 281–290). Washington, DC: NASW Press.

Braun, K. L., & Browne, C. V. (2000). Perceptions of dementia, caregiving, and help seeking among Asian and Pacific Islander Americans. In S. M. Keigher, A. E. Fortune, & S. L. Witkin (Eds.), *Aging and social work: The changing landscapes* (pp. 175–191). Washington, DC: NASW Press.

Braun, K. L., Mokuau, N., & Tsark, J. (1997). Cultural themes in health, illness, and rehabilitation for Native Hawaiians: Observations of rehabilitation staff and physicians. *Topics in Geriatric Rehabilitation, 12,* 19–37.

Brave Heart, M. Y. H., & Chase, J. (2005). Social work practice with First Nations Peoples. In D. Lum (Ed.), *Cultural competence, practice stages, and client systems: A case study approach* (pp. 32–58). Pacific Grove, CA: Brooks/Cole.

Breton, M., & Nosko, A. (1997). Group work with women who have experienced abuse. In G. L. Greif & P. H. Ephross (Eds.), *Group work with populations at risk* (pp. 134–146). New York: Oxford University Press.

Bricker-Jenkins, M., & Lockett, P. W. (1995). Women: Direct practice. In R. L. Edwards (Ed.), *Encyclopedia of social work* (19th ed., Vol. 3, pp. 2529–2539). Washington, DC: NASW Press.

Brieland, D. (1995). Social work practice: History and evolution. In R. L. Edwards (Ed.), *Encyclopedia of social work* (19th ed., Vol. 3, pp. 2247–2258). Washington, DC: NASW Press.

Brody, R. (2005). *Effectively managing human service organizations* (3rd ed.). Thousand Oaks, CA: Sage.

Brunstein Klomek, A., Marrocco, F., Kleinman, M., Schofeld, I. S., & Gould, M. S. (2007). Bullying, depression, and suicidality in adolescents. *Journal of the American Academy of Child and Adolescent Psychiatry, 46,* 40-49.

Buchan, V., Hull, G., Rogers, J., Rodenhiser, R., & Smith, M. (2004, November). BEAP use and outcome trend summary. Paper presented at the meeting of the Baccalaureate Association of (Social Work) Program Directors, Detroit, MI.

Bugental, J. F. T. (1990). Existential-humanistic psychotherapy. In J. K. Zeig & W. M. Munion (Eds.), *What is psychotherapy? Contemporary perspectives* (pp. 189–193). San Francisco: Jossey-Bass.

Bukatko, D., & Daehler, M. W. (2012). *Child development: A thematic approach* (6th ed.). Belmont, CA: Wadsworth.

Burke, A. C. (2008). Alcohol and drug problems: Law enforcement and legal policy. In T. Mizrahi & L. E. Davis (Editors-in-Chief), *Encyclopedia of Social Work* (Vol. 1, pp. 131–136). Washington, DC: NASW Press.

Burman, S. (2000). Strategies for intervention with individuals. In A. A. Abbott (Ed.), *Alcohol, tobacco, and other drugs: Challenging myths, assessing theories, individualizing interventions* (pp. 204–246). Washington, DC: NASW Press.

Burn, S. M. (2005). *Women across cultures: A global perspective* (2nd ed.). New York: McGraw-Hill.

Butterfield, A. K. J., & Chisanga, B. (2008). Community development. In T. Mizrahi & L. E. Davis (Editors-in-Chief), *Encyclopedia of Social Work* (Vol. 1, pp. 375–381). Washington, DC: NASW Press.

Bye, L., & Alvarez, M. (2007). *School social work: Theory to practice.* Belmont, CA: Brooks/Cole.

California School Boards Association (CSBA). (2007). Cyberbullying: Policy considerations for boards. Retrieved on June 26, 2011 from http://www.csba.org/Services/Services/PolicyServices/~/media/Files/Services/PolicyServices/SamplePolicies/Cyberbullying.ashx.

Campos, A. P. (1995). Hispanics: Puerto Ricans. In R. L. Edwards (Ed.), *Encyclopedia of social work* (19th ed., Vol. 2, pp. 1245–1252). Washington, DC: NASW Press.

Canada Revenue Agency. (2010). CCTB/NCBS guideline table effective July 2010–June 2011 (2009 tax year). Retrieved on May 24, 2011 from http://www.cra-arc.gc.ca/bnfts/cctb/cctb_pymnt09-eng.html.

Canby, W. (1981). *American Indian law in a nutshell.* St. Paul, MN: West.

Canda, E. R., & Furman, L. D. (2010). *Spiritual diversity in social work practice: The heart of helping* (2nd ed.). New York: Oxford.

Cannon, A., Streisand, B., & McGraw, D. (1999, May 3). Why? There were plenty of warnings, but no one stopped two twisted teens. *U.S. News & World Report,* 16–19.

Caple, F. S., & Salcido, R. M. (2009). A framework for cross-cultural practice in school settings. In C. R. Massat, R. Constable, S. McDonald, & J. P. Flynn (Eds.), *School social work: Practice, policy, and research* (7th ed., pp. 339–361). Chicago: Lyceum.

Carlton-LaNey, B., Edwards, R. L., & Reid, P. N. (1999). Small towns and rural communities: From romantic notions to harsh realities. In I. B. Carlton-LaNey, R. L. Edwards, & P. N. Reid (Eds.), *Preserving and strengthening small towns and rural communities* (pp. 5–12). Washington, DC: NASW Press.

Carroll, J. (2008). Retirement age expectations and realities. Retrieved July 17, 2008 from http://www.gallup.com/poll/16375/Retirement-Age-Expectations-Realities.aspx.

Carroll, J. L. (2007). *Sexuality now* (2nd ed.). Belmont, CA: Wadsworth.

Carroll, J. L. (2010). *Sexuality now: Embracing diversity* (3rd ed.). Belmont, CA: Wadsworth.

Carroll, J. L., & Wolpe, P. R. (1996). *Sexuality and gender in society.* New York: HarperCollins.

Carton, B. (1994, January 27). Growing up in a gay household. *Boston Globe,* 45.

CBSNew.com. (2011a, May, 1). Osama bin Laden is dead. Retrieved on May 11, 2011 from http://www.cbsnews.com/stories/2011/05/01/national/main20058777.shtml.

CBSNews.com. (2011b, May 11). Should a court kill Obama's health care plan? Retrieved on May 11, 2011 from http://www.cbsnews.com/8301-504763_162-20061857-10391704.html.

CBSNews.com. (2011c, January 27). Social security on pace to be drained by 2037. Retrieved on May 11, 2011 from http://www.cbsnews.com/stories/2011/01/26/politics/main7286861.shtml.

Center for Workforce Studies. (2006). *Licensed social workers in the United States, 2004.* Washington, DC: National Association of Social Workers.

Center on Budget and Policy Priorities (CBPP). (2011). Policy basics: Where do our federal tax dollars go? Retrieved on May 22, 2011 from http://www.cbpp.org/cms/index.cfm?fa=view&id=1258.

Centers for Disease Control and Prevention (CDC). (2008a). HIV/AIDS in the United States. Retrieved July 21, 2008 from http://www.cdc.gov.

Centers for Disease Control and Prevention (CDC). (2008b). Developmental disabilities: Topic home. Retrieved November 3, 2008 from http://www.cdc.gov/ncbddd/dd/.

Centers for Disease Control and Prevention (CDC). (2009). Youth risk behavior surveillance system (YRBSS) 2009 national youth risk behavior survey overview. Retrieved June 26, 2011 from http://www.cdc.gov/healthyyouth/yrbs/pdf/us_overview_yrbs.pdf.

Centers for Disease Control and Prevention (CDC). (2011a). About school violence. Retrieved on June 26, 2011 from http://www.cdc.gov/ViolencePrevention/youthviolence/schoolviolence/index.html.

Centers for Disease Control and Prevention (CDC). (2011b). Developmental disabilities: Topic home. Retrieved on June 8, 2011 from http://www.cdc.gov/ncbddd/dd/default.htm.

Centers for Disease Control and Prevention (CDC). (2011c). HIV/AIDS statistics and surveillance. Retrieved on June 13, 2011 from http://www.cdc.gov/hiv/topics/surveillance/basic.htm#hivest.

Centers for Medicare and Medicaid Services (CMS). (2011a). Medicaid. Retrieved on May 23, 2011 from https://www.cms.gov/home/medicaid.asp.

Centers for Medicare and Medicaid Services (CMS). (2011b). Medicare & you. Retrieved on May 19, 2011 from http://www.medicare.gov/publications/pubs/pdf/10050.pdf.

Chadwick, D. L. (2002). Community organization of services to deal with and end child abuse. In J. E. B. Myers, L. Berliner, J. Briere, C. T. Hendrix, C. Jenny, & T. A. Reid (Eds.), *The APSAC handbook on child maltreatment* (2nd ed., pp. 509–523). Thousand Oaks, CA: Sage.

Chambers, D. E., & Wedel, K. R. (2005). *Social policy and social programs: A method for the practical public policy analyst* (4th ed.). Boston: Allyn & Bacon.

Chan, S., & Lee, E. (2004). Families with Asian roots. In E. W. Lynch & M. J. Hanson (Eds.), *Developing, cross-cultural competence: A guide for working with children and their families* (3rd ed., pp. 219–298). Baltimore, MD: Brookes.

Chapin, R. K. (2011). *Social policy for effective practice: A strengths approach* (2nd ed.). New York: Routledge.

Cherokee Messenger (1995). Brief history of the trail of tears. Retrieved November 20, 2004 from http://www.powersource.com/cherokee/history.html.

Childress, S. (2006, March 6). Invasion of the body snatchers. *Newsweek, 46.*

Child Welfare Information Gateway. (2008). What is child abuse and neglect? Retrieved on June 1, 2011 from http://www.childwelfare.gov/pubs/factsheets/whatiscan.cfm.

Child Welfare League of America (CWLA). (1994). *Kinship care: A natural bridge.* Washington, DC: Author.

Child Welfare League of America (CWLA). (2005). Position statement on residential services. Retrieved on May 31, 2011 from http://www.cwla.org/programs/groupcare/rgcpositionstatement.pdf.

Chilman, C. S. (1993). Hispanic families in the United States: Research perspectives. In H. P. McAdoo (Ed.), *Family ethnicity: Strength in diversity.* Newbury Park, CA: Sage.

Christ, G. H., Sormanti, M., & Francoer, R. B. (2001). Chronic physical illness & disability. In A Gitterman (Ed.), *Handbook of social work practice with vulnerable and resilient populations* (2nd ed., pp. 124–162). New York: Columbia University Press.

Clark, E. J. (2008). National association of social workers. In T. Mizrahi & L. E. Davis (Editors-in-Chief), *Encyclopedia of Social Work* (Vol. 3, pp. 292–295). Washington, DC: NASW Press.

Clarke-Stewart, K. A., Gruber, C. P., & Fitzgerald, L. M. (1994). *Children at home and in day care.* Hillsdale, NJ: Erlbaum.

Cloud, J. (2001, Feb. 26). New sparks over electroshock. *Time,* 60–62.

Clute, M. A. (2008). Disability: Physical disabilities. In T. Mizrahi & L. E. Davis (Editors-in-Chief), *Encyclopedia of Social Work* (Vol. 2, pp. 49–55). Washington, DC: NASW Press.

CNN.com. (2001). The end of Enron? Retrieved February 5, 2005 from http://cnn.com/SPECIALS/2002/enron/.

Coggins, K., & Fresquez, J. E. (2007). *Working with clients in correctional settings: A guide for social workers and corrections professional* (Rev. ed.). Peosta, IA: Eddie Bowers.

Cohen, N. A. (1992). The continuum of child welfare services. In N. A. Cohen (Ed.), *Child welfare: A multicultural approach* (pp. 39–83). Needham Heights, MA: Allyn & Bacon.

Coleman, J. W., & Kerbo, H. R. (2009). *Social problems* (10th ed.). New York: Vango.

Collins, D., Jordan, C., & Coleman, H. (1999). *An introduction to family social work.* Itasca, IL: Peacock.

Collins, D., Jordan, C., & Coleman, H. (2010). *An introduction to family social work* (3rd ed.). Belmont, CA: Brooks/Cole.

Connaway, R. S., & Gentry, M. E. (1988). *Social work practice.* Englewood Cliffs, NJ: Prentice-Hall.

Connors, G. J., Donovan, D. M., & DiClemente, C. C. (2001). *Selecting and planning interventions: Substance abuse treatment and the stages of change.* New York: Guilford Press.

Constable, R. (1999). Developing and defining the school social worker's role. In R. Constable, S. McDonald, & J. P. Flynn (Eds.), *School social work: Practice, policy, and research perspectives* (4th ed., pp. 207–225). Chicago: Lyceum.

Constable, R. (2009). The role of the school social worker. In C. R. Massat, R. Constable, S. McDonald, & J. P. Flynn (Eds.), *School social work: Practice, policy, and research* (7th ed., pp. 3–29). Chicago: Lyceum.

Corcoran, K. (1997). Managed care: Implications for social work practice. In *Encyclopedia of social work 1997 supplement.* Washington, DC: NASW Press.

Corey, G. (2009). *Theory and practice of counseling and psychotherapy* (8th ed.). Belmont, CA: Brooks/Cole.

Corey, G. (2012). *Theory & practice of group counseling* (8th ed.). Belmont, CA: Brooks/Cole.

Corey, G., Corey, M. S., & Callanan, P. (2011). *Issues and ethics in the helping professions* (8th ed.). Belmont, CA: Brooks/Cole.

Corey, M. S., & Corey, G. (2011). *Becoming a helper* (6th ed.). Belmont, CA: Brooks/Cole.

Corey, M. S., Corey, G., & Corey, C. (2010). *Groups: Process and practice* (8th ed.). Belmont, CA: Brooks/Cole.

Corr, C. A., Nabe, C. M., & Corr, D. M. (2009). *Death & dying, life & living* (6th ed.). Belmont, CA: Wadsworth.

Costin, C. (2008). The thin commandments. Retrieved July 22, 2008 from http://www.edreferral.com/thin_commandments.htm.

Council on Social Work Education (CSWE). (2002). *Glossary to Educational Policy and Accreditation Standards developed by commission of the Council on Social Work Education.* Alexandria, VA: Author.

Council on Social Work Education (CSWE). (2008a). Accreditation news, reports and archives. Retrieved July 6, 2008 from http://www.cswe.org/CSWE/accreditation/Accreditation+News+Reports+And+Archives/.

Council on Social Work Education (CSWE). (2008b). *Educational Policy and Accreditation Standards.* Alexandria, VA: Author.

Council on Social Work Education. (2011). Accreditation. Retrieved on September 17, 2011 from http://www.cswe.org/Accreditation.aspx.

Cournoyer, B. R. (2011). *The social work skills workbook* (6th ed.). Belmont, CA: Brooks/Cole.

Courtenay, W. H. (2003). Key determinants of the health and well-being of men and boys. *International Journal of Men's Health, 2*(1), 1–30.

Cowger, C. D. (1994). Assessing client strengths: Clinical assessment for client empowerment. *Social Work, 39*(3), 262–268.

Cowley, G. (2000, January 17). Fighting the disease: What can be done. *Newsweek,* 38.

Cox, C. B. (2005). Grandparents raising grandchildren from a multicultural perspective. In E. P. Congress & M. J. Gonzalez (Eds.), *Multicultural perspectives in working with families* (2nd ed., 128–141). New York: Springer.

Cox, E. O., & Parsons, R. J. (1994). *Empowerment-oriented social work practice with the elderly.* Pacific Grove, CA: Brooks/Cole.

Crick, N. R., & Dodge, K. A. (1994). A review and reformulation of social information-processing mechanisms in children's social adjustment. *Psychological Bulletin, 115,* 74–101.

Crooks, R., & Baur, K. (2008). *Our sexuality* (10th ed.). Belmont, CA: Wadsworth.

Crooks, R., & Baur, K. (2011). *Our sexuality* (11th ed.). Belmont, CA: Wadsworth.

Cross, T. L., Bazron, B. J., Dennis, K. W., & Isaacs, M. R. (1989). *Toward a culturally competent system of care.* Washington, DC: Child and Adolescent Service System Program Technical Assistance Center.

Crosson-Tower, C. (2009). *Exploring child welfare: A practice perspective* (5th ed.). Boston: Allyn & Bacon.

Crosson-Tower, C. (2010). *Understanding child abuse and neglect* (8th ed.). Boston: Allyn & Bacon.

Cummerton, J. M. (1986). A feminist perspective on research: What does it help us see? In N. Van Den Bergh & L. B. Cooper (Eds.), *Feminist visions for social work* (pp. 80–100). Washington, DC: NASW Press.

Cummings, S. M., & Jackson, D. R. (2000). Hospital discharge planning. In R. L. Schneider, N. P. Kropf, & A. J. Kisor (Eds.), *Gerontological social work: Knowledge, service settings, and special populations* (2nd ed., pp. 191–224). Pacific Grove, CA: Brooks/Cole.

Cummins, L. K., Byers, K. V., & Pedrick, L. (2011). *Policy practice for social workers: New strategies for a new era.* Boston: Allyn & Bacon.

Curiel, H. (1995). Hispanics: Mexican Americans. In R. L. Edwards (Ed.), *Encyclopedia of social work* (19th ed., Vol. 2, pp. 1233–1244). Washington, DC: NASW Press.

Currey, R. (2007, July/August). PTSD in today's war veterans: The road to recovery. *Social Work Today,* 12–16.

Curtis, O. (1999). *Chemical dependency: A family affair.* Pacific Grove, CA: Brooks/Cole.

Daft, R. L. (2012). *Management* (10th ed.). Mason, OH: South-Western.

Daley, M. R., & Avant, F. L. (2004). Rural social work: Reconceptualizing the framework for practice. In T. L. Scales & C. L. Streeter (Eds.), *Rural social work: Building and sustaining community assets* (pp. 34–41). Belmont, CA: Brooks/Cole.

Daley, M. R., & Hickman, S. (2011). Dual relations and beyond: Understanding and addressing ethical challenges for rural social work. *Journal of Social Work Values & Ethics, 8* (1). Retrieved from http://www.socialworker.com/jswve.

Danner, D. (2010, May 27). ObamaCare vs. small business. *The Wall Street Journal.* Retrieved on June 11, 2011 from http://online.wsj.com/article/SB10001424052748704113504575264802756326086.html.

Daro, D., & Donnelly, A. C. (2002). Child abuse prevention: Accomplishments and challenges. In J. E. B. Myers, L. Berliner, J. Briere, C. T. Hendrix, C. Jenny, & T. A. Reid (Eds.), *The APSAC handbook on child maltreatment* (2nd ed., pp. 431–448). Thousand Oaks, CA: Sage.

Davenport, J. A., & Davenport, J., III. (2008). Rural practice. In T. Mizrahi & L. E. Davis (Editors-in-Chief), *Encyclopedia of Social Work* (Vol. 3, pp. 536–541). Washington, DC: NASW Press.

Davis, S. (2011). Congresswoman Susan Davis. Retrieved on May 15, 2011 from http://www.house.gov/susandavis/.

Day, P. (2008). Social policy: History (colonial times to 1900). In T. Mizrahi & L. E. Davis (Editors-in-Chief), *Encyclopedia of Social Work* (Vol. 4, pp. 66–70). Washington, DC: NASW Press.

Day, P. J. (2009). *A new history of social welfare* (6th ed.). Boston: Allyn & Bacon.

de Silva, E. C. (2007, October). Slavery persists in modern day. *NASW News,* 3.

DeCesare, D. (1993, March). El Salvador: War, poverty and migration: A photo essay. *Fellowship, 59,* 3.

DeLeon, G. (1994). Therapeutic communities. In M. Galanter & H. D. Kleber (Eds.), *Textbook of substance abuse treatment.* Washington, DC: American Psychiatric Press.

Delgado, M. (1998). Community asset assessments by Latino youth. In P. L. Ewalt, E. M. Freeman, & D. L. Poole (Eds.), *Community building: Renewal, well-being, and shared responsibility* (pp. 202–212). Washington, DC: NASW Press.

Delgado, M., & Barton, K. (1999). Murals in Latino communities: Social indicators of community strengths. In P. L. Ewalt, E. M. Freeman, A. E. Fortune, D. L. Poole, & S. L. Witkin (Eds.), *Multicultural issues in social work: Practice and research* (pp. 229–244). Washington, DC: NASW Press.

Delgado, M., & Staples, L. (2008). *You-led community organizing: Theory and action.* New York: Oxford.

Dembling, B. (1995). Colonial family care. *Psychiatric Services, 46* (2).

DePanfilis, D. (2011). Child protection system. In J. E. B. Myers (Ed.), *The APSAC handbook on child maltreatment* (3rd ed., pp. 39–52). Thousand Oaks, CA: Sage.

DePoy, E., & Gilson, S. F. (2004). *Rethinking disability: Principles for professional and social change.* Belmont, CA: Brooks/Cole.

Derezotes, D. S. (2006). *Spiritually oriented social work practice.* Boston: Allyn & Bacon.

Devaney, B. (2007). WIC turns 35: Program effectiveness and future directions. Retrieved on May 25, 2011 from http://www.earlychildhoodrc.org/events/presentations/devaney.pdf.

Devore, W. (2001). "Whence came these people?": An exploration of the values and ethics of African American individuals, families, and communities. In R. Fong & S. Furuto (Eds.), *Culturally competent practice: Skills, interventions, and evaluations* (pp. 33–46). Boston: Allyn & Bacon.

DeWeaver, K. L. (1995). Developmental disabilities: Definitions and policies. In R. L. Edwards (Ed.), *Encyclopedia of social work* (19th ed., Vol. 1, pp. 712–720). Washington, DC: NASW Press.

Dey, J. G., & Hill, C. (2007). *Behind the pay gap.* Washington, DC: American Association of University Women.

Dhooper, S. S. (1997). *Social work in health care in the 21st century.* Thousand Oaks, CA: Sage.

Dhooper, S. S., & Moore, S. E. (2001). *Social work practice with culturally diverse people.* Thousand Oaks, CA: Sage.

Diament, M. (2010). Obama signs bill replacing "mental retardation" with "intellectual disability." Retrieved on June 6, 2011 from http://www.disabilityscoop.com/2010/10/05/obama-signs-rosas-law/10547/.

Dickinson, N. S. (1997). Federal social legislation from 1994–1997. In R. L. Edwards (Ed.), *Encyclopedia of social work: Supplement 1997* (19th ed., pp. 125–131). Washington, DC: NASW Press.

Diller, J. V. (2011). *Cultural diversity: A primer for the human services* (4th ed.). Belmont, CA: Brooks/Cole.

DiNitto, D. M. (2005). *Social welfare: Politics and public policy* (6th ed.). Boston: Allyn & Bacon.

DiNitto, D. M. (2011). *Social welfare: Politics and public policy* (7th ed.). Boston: Allyn & Bacon.

Dixn, R. (2009). Africa's bitter cycle of child slavery. Retrieved on May 30, 2011 from http://articles.latimes.com/2009/jul/12/world/fg-ghana-slavery12.

Dobelstein, A. W. (2003). *Social welfare policy and analysis* (3rd ed.). Pacific Grove, CA: Brooks/Cole.

Dodge, K. A., Dishion, T. J., & Lansford, J. E. (Eds.). (2006). *Deviant peer influences in programs for youth: Problems and solutions.* New York: Guilford.

Dolgoff, R., & Feldstein, D. (2007). *Understanding social welfare: A search for social justice* (7th ed.). Boston: Allyn & Bacon.

Dolgoff, R., & Feldstein, D. (2009). *Understanding social welfare: A search for social justice* (8th ed.). Boston: Allyn & Bacon.

Dolgoff, R., Harrington, D., & Loewenberg, F. M. (2012). *Ethical decisions for social work practice* (9th ed.). Belmont, CA: Brooks/Cole.

Dolgoff, R., Loewenberg, F. M., & Harrington, D. (2005). *Ethical decisions for social work practice* (7th ed.). Pacific Grove, CA: Brooks/Cole.

Doweiko, H. E. (2009). *Concepts of chemical dependency* (7th ed.). Belmont, CA: Brooks/Cole.

Doweiko, H. E. (2012). *Concepts of chemical dependency* (8th ed.). Belmont, CA: Brooks/Cole.

Downey, E. P., & Jackson, R. L. (2000). Contemporary film applications in social work education: Bridging classroom and practice. Paper presented at the Meeting of the Association of Baccalaureate Program Directors, Dallas, TX.

Downs, S. W., Costin, L. B., & McFadden, E. J. (1996). *Child welfare and family services: Policies and practice* (5th ed.). White Plains, NY: Longman.

Downs, S. W., Moore, E., & McFadden, E. J. (2009). *Child welfare and family services: Policies and practice* (8th ed.). Boston: Allyn & Bacon.

Drum, J., & Howard, G. (1989, January). Multicultural and global education: Seeking common ground (Summary). Paper presented at a conference cosponsored by Las Palomas de Taos, REACH Center for Multicultural and Global Education, and the Stanley Foundation, Taos, NM.

Dulmus, C. N., & Roberts, A. R. (2008). Mental illness: Adults. In T. Mizrahi & L. E. Davis (Editors-in-Chief), *Encyclopedia of Social Work* (Vol. 3, pp. 237–242). Washington, DC: NASW Press.

Dunkle, R. E., & Norgard, T. (1995). Aging overview. In R. L. Edwards (Ed.), *Encyclopedia of social work* (19th ed., Vol. 1, pp. 142–153). Washington, DC: NASW Press.

Dunn, P. C. (2000). In A. A. Abbott (Ed.), *Alcohol, tobacco, and other drugs: Challenging myths, assessing theories, individualizing interventions* (pp. 74–110). Washington, DC: NASW Press.

DuongTran, Q., & Matsuoka, J. K. (1995). Asian-Americans: Southeast Asians. In R. L. Edwards (Ed.), *Encyclopedia of social work* (19th ed., Vol. 1, pp. 249–255). Washington, DC: NASW Press.

Dupper, D. R. (2000). The design of social work services. In P. Allen-Meares, R. O. Washington, & B. L. Welsh (Eds.), *Social work services in schools* (3rd ed., pp. 243–272). Boston: Allyn & Bacon.

Dworkin, S. H. (2000). Individual therapy with lesbian, gay, and bisexual clients. In R. M. Perez, K. A. DeBord, & K. J. Bieschke (Eds.), *Handbook of counseling and psychotherapy with lesbian, gay, and bisexual clients* (pp. 157–181). Washington, DC: American Psychological Association.

Dziegielewski, S. F. (2005). *Understanding substance addictions: Assessment and intervention.* Chicago: Lyceum.

Earle, K. A. (1999). Cultural diversity and mental health: The Haudenosaunee of New York State. In P. L. Ewalt, E. M. Freeman, A. E. Fortune, D. L. Poole, & S. L. Witkin (Eds.), *Multicultural issues in social work: Practice and research* (pp. 423–438). Washington, DC: NASW Press.

Earth Charter Initiative. (2011). Earth Charter. Retrieved on April 16, 2011 from http://www.earthcharterinaction.org/content/pages/Read-the-Charter.html#top.

Eddy, J. M., Reid, J. B., Stoolmiller, M., & Fetrow, R. A. (2003). Outcomes during middle school for an elementary school-based preventive intervention for conduct problems: Follow-up results from a randomized trial. *Behavior Therapy, 34,* 535–552.

Edinburg, G. M., & Cottler, J. M. (1995). Managed care. In R. L. Edwards (Ed.), *Encyclopedia of social work* (19th ed., Vol. 2, pp. 1635–1642). Washington, DC: NASW Press.

Edwards, E. D., & Edwards, M. E. (2002). Social work practice with American Indians and Alaskan Natives. In A. T. Morales & B. W. Sheafor (Eds.), *The many faces of social work clients* (pp. 239–265). Boston: Allyn & Bacon.

Einbinder, S. D. (1995). Policy analysis. In R. L. Edwards (Ed.), *Encyclopedia of social work* (19th ed., Vol. 3, pp. 1849–1855). Washington, DC: NASW Press.

Eitzen, D. S., Zinn, M. B., & Smith, K. E. (2009). *Social problems* (11th ed.). Boston: Allyn & Bacon.

Electroshock therapy slowly gains greater use in the treatment of mental illness. (2000, March–April). *American Scientist.* Retrieved April 27, 2002 from http://www.signaI.org/news&events/ArchivesAmsci/0003summary.htm.

Ellis, L., Robb, B., & Burke, D. (2005). Sexual orientation in the United States and Canadian college students. *Archives of Sexual Behavior, 34*(5), 569–581.

Elze, D. E. (2006). Working with gay, lesbian, bisexual, and transgender students. In C. Franklin, M. B. Harris, & P. Allen-Meares (Eds.), *The school services sourcebook: A guide for school-based professionals* (pp. 861–870). New York: Oxford.

Epstein, L. (1981). Advocates on advocacy: An exploratory study. *Social work research and abstracts, 17*(2), 5–12.

Equal Employment Opportunity Commission, U.S. Department of Justice Civil Rights Division. (1997, May). *The Americans with Disabilities Act: Questions and answers.* Washington, DC: Author.

Erickson, M. F., & Egeland, B. (2011). Child neglect. In J. E. B. Myers (Ed.), *The APSAC handbook on child maltreatment* (3rd ed., pp. 103–124). Thousand Oaks, CA: Sage.

Esbensen, F. (2000). *Preventing adolescent gang involvement.* Youth Gang Series Bulletin. Bulletin of the Office of Justice Programs. Washington, DC: U.S. Department of Justice, Office of Juvenile Justice and Delinquency Prevention.

Essock, S. M., & Goldman, H. H. (1995). Embrace of managed mental health care. *Health Affairs, 14,* 34–44.

Everett, J. E. (2008). Foster care. In T. Mizrahi & L. E. Davis (Editors-in-Chief), *Encyclopedia of Social Work* (Vol. 2, pp. 223–236). Washington, DC: NASW Press.

Ewalt, P. L., & Mokuau, N. (1996). Self-determination from a Pacific perspective. In P. L. Ewalt, M. Freeman, A. E. Fortune, D. L. Poole, & S. L. Witkin (Eds.), *Multicultural issues in social work: Practice and research* (pp. 225–268). Washington, DC: NASW Press.

Exum, H. A., Coll, J. E., & Weiss, E. L. (2011). A civilian counselor's primer for counseling veterans (2nd ed.). Deer Park, NY: Linus.

FamiliesUSA. (2011). Children's health: About CHIP. Retrieved on May 23, 2011 from http://www.familiesusa.org/issues/childrens-health/about-chip/.

Familydoctor.org. (2003, March). Depression: Electroconvulsive therapy. Retrieved January 30, 2005 from http://familydoctor.org/058.sml?printMl.

Fang, B. (2001, September 3). On the trail of a killer. *U.S. News & World Report,* 22–26.

Fascoli, L. (1999). Developmentally appropriate play and turtle hunting. In E. Dau (Ed.), *Child's play: Revisiting play in early childhood* (pp. 53–59). Sydney, Australia: Maqclennan & Petty.

Fastenburg, D. (2010). International gay marriage. Retrieved on May 26, 2001 from http://www.time.com/time/world/article/0,8599,2005678,00.html.

Fatout, M., & Rose, S. R. (1995). *Task groups in the social services.* Thousand Oaks, CA: Sage.

Federal Bureau of Investigation (FBI). (2006). *Crime in the United States: Uniform Crime Reports.* Washington, DC: U.S. Government Printing Office.

Federal Bureau of Investigation (FBI). (2008). Human trafficking. Retrieved on April 20, 2011 from http://www.fbi.gov/news/stories/2008/may/humantrafficking_050908.

Federal Bureau of Investigation (FBI). (2010). Crime in the United States, 2009. Retrieved on June 28, 2011 from http://www2.fbi.gov/ucr/cius2009/index.html.

Fellin, P. (1996). *Mental health and mental illness: Policies, programs, and services.* Itasca, IL: Peacock.

Figueira-McDonough, J. (2008). Women: Practice interventions. In T. Mizrahi & L. E. Davis (Editors-in-Chief), *Encyclopedia of Social Work* (Vol. 4, pp. 290–298). Washington, DC: NASW Press.

FindLaw Legal News and Commentary. (2005). Evidence shows longstanding Enron scams. Retrieved February 5, 2005 from http://news.findlaw.com/ap_stories/f/1310/2-3-2005/20050203151127_17.html.

Fiske, H. (2002, September 16). A youth violence assessment tool: Can we predict problems? *Social Work Today,* 13–15.

Fiske, H. (2002, November 11). Adolescent group therapy: Not just hearing, listening, too. *Social Work Today, 2*(23), 16–18.

Fong, R. (2008). Asian Americans: Practice interventions. In T. Mizrahi & L. E. Davis (Editors-in-Chief), *Encyclopedia of Social Work* (Vol. 1, pp. 161–163). Washington, DC: NASW Press.

Fong, R., Armour, M., Busch, N., Heffron, L. C., McClendon, A. (2006). Case management intervention with immigrant and refugee students and families. In C. Franklin, M. B. Harris, & P. Allen-Meares (Eds.), *The school services sourcebook: A guide for school-based professionals* (pp. 803–809). New York: Oxford.

Fontaine, R. G. (2007). On-line social decision making and antisocial behavior: Some essential but neglected issues. *Clinical Psychology Review, 28,* 17–35.

Food and Nutrition Service (FNS). (2009). About WIC: How WIC helps. Retrieved on May 25, 2011 from http://www.fns.usda.gov/wic/aboutwic/howwichelps.htm.

Food and Nutrition Service (FNS). (2011). Nutrition assistance programs. Retrieved on May 25, 2008 from http://www.fns.usda.gov/fns/.

Frame, M. W. (2003). *Integrating religion and spirituality into counseling: A comprehensive approach.* Pacific Grove, CA: Brooks/Cole.

Franklin, C. (2004). The delivery of school social work services. In P. Allen-Meares (Ed.), *Social work services in schools* (4th ed., pp. 295–325). Boston: Allyn & Bacon.

Franklin, C., Harris, M. B., & Lagana-Riordan, C. (2010). The delivery of school social work services. In P. Allen-Meares (Ed.), *Social work services in schools* (6th ed., pp. 278–321). Boston: Allyn & Bacon.

Fred, S. (2004a, September). Human trafficking: Snaring the spirit. *NASW News,* 4.

Fred, S. (2004b, October 24). Social workers vie for federal office. *NASW News,* 11.

Freedman, R. I. (1995). Developmental disabilities: Direct practice. In R. L. Edwards (Ed.), *Encyclopedia of social work* (19th ed., Vol. 1, pp. 721–729). Washington, DC: NASW Press.

Fresquez, J. E., Khalsa, S. S., & Bell, C. (1998, February). Application of social work methods in corrections. Paper presented at the National Association of Social Workers Conference, Albuquerque, New Mexico.

Friend, M. (2011). *Special education: Contemporary perspectives for school professionals* (3rd ed.). Boston: Pearson.

Furstenberg, F., & Crawford, A. (1978). Family support: Helping teenage mothers to cope. *Family Planning Perspectives, 10,* 322–333.

Gallup.com (2010, May 24). Americans' opposition to gay marriage eases slightly. Retrieved from http://www.gallup.com/poll/128291/americans-opposition-gay-marriage-eases-slightly.aspx.

Gamble, D. N., & Weil, M. (2008). Community: Practice interventions. In T. Mizrahi & L. E. Davis (Editors-in-Chief), *Encyclopedia of Social Work* (Vol. 1, pp. 355–368). Washington, DC: NASW Press.

Gambrill, E. (2000). The role of critical thinking in evidence-based social work. In P. Allen-Meares & C. Garvin (Eds.), *The handbook of social work direct practice* (pp. 43–64). Thousand Oaks, CA: Sage.

Gambrill, E. (2005). *Critical thinking in clinical practice: Improving the quality of judgments and decisions.* Hoboken, NJ: Wiley.

Gambrill, E., & Gibbs, L. (2009). *Critical thinking for helping professionals: A skills-based workbook* (3rd ed.). New York: Oxford.

Gans, H. J. (1971). The uses of poverty: The poor pay all. *Social Policy, 2,* 21–23.

Garcia, B. (2009). Theory and social work practice with immigrant populations. In F. Chang-Muy & E. P. Congress (Eds.), *Social work with immigrants and refugees: Legal issues, clinical skills, and advocacy* (pp. 79–101). New York: Springer.

Gargiulo, R. M. (2006). *Special education in contemporary society* (2nd ed.). Belmont, CA: Wadsworth.

Garrett, M. T., & Pitchette, E. F. (2000). Red as an apple: Native American acculturation and counseling with or without reservation. *Journal of Counseling and Development, 78,* 3–13.

Garvey, G. & Houde, G. (2009, July 26). Childhood sweethearts reconnect after 85 years. *Chicago Tribune.* Retrieved on Jun 3, 2011 from http://articles.chicagotribune.com/2009-07-26/news/0907250224_1_sweethearts-family-friend-separate-ways.

Garvin, C. D., & Cox, F. M. (1995). A history of community organizing since the Civil War with special reference to oppressed communities. In J. Rothman, J. L. Erlich, & J. E. Tropman (Eds.), *Strategies of community intervention* (pp. 64–69). Itasca, IL: Peacock.

Garvin, C. D., & Tropman, J. E. (1998). *Social work in contemporary society* (2nd ed.). Boston: Allyn & Bacon.

Geary, B. B. (1992). Individual treatment of depression using cognitive therapy. In C. W. Lecroy (Ed.), *Case studies in social work practice.* Belmont, CA: Wadsworth.

George, J. (1997). Global graying. In M. C. Hokenstad & J. Midgley (Eds.), *Issues in international social work: Global challenges in a new century* (pp. 57–73). Washington, DC: NASW Press.

Gibbs, L., Gambrill, E., Blakemore, J., Begun, A., Keniston, A., Peden, B., & Lefcowitz, J. (1994). A measure of critical thinking about practice. Unpublished paper presented at the Fall Conference of the Wisconsin Council on Social Work Education, Stevens Point, WI.

Gibelman, M. (1995). *What social workers do.* Washington, DC: NASW Press.

Gibelman, M. (2003). So how far have we come? Pestilent and persistent gender gap in pay. *Social Work, 48*(1), 22–32.

Gibelman, M. (2005). *What social workers do* (2nd ed.). Washington, DC: NASW Press.

Gibelman, M., & Furman, R. (2008). *Navigating human service organizations* (2nd ed.). Chicago: Lyceum.

Gibelman, M., & Schervish, P. (1997). *Who we are: A second look.* Washington, DC: NASW Press.

Gilbert, M. J. (2008). Transgender people. In T. Mizrahi & L. E. Davis (Editors-in-Chief), *Encyclopedia of Social Work* (Vol. 4, pp. 238–241). Washington, DC: NASW Press.

Gilbert, N., & Terrell, P. (2010). *Dimensions of social welfare policy* (7th ed.). Boston: Allyn & Bacon.

Gilson, S. F., Bricout, J. C., & Baskind, F. R. (1998). Listening to the voices of people with disabilities. *Families in Society: The Journal of Contemporary Human Services, 79*(2), 188–202.

Ginsberg, L. H. (2001). *Careers in social work* (2nd ed.). Boston: Allyn & Bacon.

Golden Ink. (1997). The trail of tears. Retrieved from http://ngeorgia.com/history/nghisttt.html.

Goldenberg, H., & Goldenberg, I. (2002). *Counseling today's families* (4th ed.). Pacific Grove, CA: Brooks/Cole.

Goldman, L. (2008). *Coming out, coming in: Nurturing the well-being and inclusion of gay youth in mainstream society.* New York: Routledge.

Goldstein, S. R., & Beebe, L. (1995). National Association of Social Workers. In R. L. Edwards (Editor-in-Chief), *Encyclopedia of social work* (19th ed., Vol. 1, pp. 1747–1764). Washington, DC: NASW Press.

Gomory, T. (1997). Mental health services. In M. Reisch & E. Gambrill (Eds.), *Social work in the 21st century* (pp. 163–174). Thousand Oaks, CA: Pine Forge.

Good, G. E., & Beitman, B. D. (2006). *Counseling and psychotherapy essentials: Integrating theories, skills, and practices.* New York: Norton.

Gotterer, R. (2001). The spiritual dimension in clinical social work practice: A client perspective. *Families in Society, 82* (20), 187–193.

Graybeal, C. (2001). Strengths-based social work assessment: Transforming the dominant paradigm. *Families in Society, 82* (3), 233–242.

Green, C., Dziegielewski, S. F., & Turnage, B. F. (2005). Alcohol. In S. F. Dziegielewski (Ed.), *Understanding substance addictions: Assessment and treatment* (pp. 125–129). Chicago: Lyceum.

Green, J. W. (1999). *Cultural awareness in the human services: A multi-ethnic approach* (3rd ed.). Boston: Allyn & Bacon.

Greene, R. R. (2000). *Social work with the aged and their families* (2nd ed.). New York: Aldine de Gruyter.

Greene, R. R. (2007). *Social work practice: A risk and resilience perspective.* Belmont, CA: Brooks/Cole.

Greene, R. R., Cohen, H. G., Galambos, C. M., & Kropf, N. P. (2007). *Foundations of social work practice in the field of aging: A competency-based approach.* Washington, DC: NASW Press.

Greene, R. R., & Livingston, N. C. (2002). A social construct. In R. R. Green (Ed.), *Resiliency: An integrated approach to practice, policy, and research* (pp. 63–93). Washington, DC: NASW Press.

Greeno, C. G. (2008). Mental health: Overview. In T. Mizrahi & L. E. Davis (Editors-in-Chief), *Encyclopedia of Social Work* (Vol. 3, pp. 221–232). Washington, DC: NASW Press.

Griner, D. (2002, April 7). Electroshock therapy emerges from disrepute. *The Journal Gazette.* Retrieved April 27, 2002 from http://www.fortwayne.com/mld/journalgazette/3017094.htm.

Grogan, J., & Richardson, F. (2008). Humanistic therapies. In T. Mizrahi & L. E. Davis (Editors-in-Chief), *Encyclopedia of Social Work* (Vol. 2, pp. 395–398). Washington, DC: NASW Press.

Guffy, M. E. (2010). *Essentials of business communication* (8th ed.). Mason, OH: South-Western.

Gushue, G. V., & Sciarra, D. T. (1995). Culture and families: A multidimensional approach. In J. G. Ponterotto, J. M. Casas, L. A. Suzuki, & C. M. Alexander (Eds.), *Handbook of multicultural counseling* (2nd ed., pp. 586–606). Thousand Oaks, CA: Sage.

Gutierrez, L. M. (2001). Working with women of color: An empowerment perspective. In J. Rothman, J. L. Erlich, & J. E. Tropman (Eds.), *Strategies of community intervention* (6th ed., pp. 209–217). Itasca, IL: Peacock.

Gutierrez, L. M., & Lewis, E. A. (1998). A feminist perspective on organizing women of color. In F. G. Rivera & J. L. Erlich (Eds.), *Community organizing in a diverse society* (3rd ed., pp. 97–116). Needham Heights, MA: Allyn & Bacon.

Guttmacher Institute. (2011). Facts on American teens' sexual and reproductive health. Retrieved on June 27, 2011 from http://www.guttmacher.org/pubs/FB-ATSRH.html.

Haberman, F. W. (Ed.). (1972). Jane Addams—Biography. In F. W. Haberman (Ed.), *Nobel Lecture, Peace 1926–1950.* Amsterdam: Elsevier. Retrieved June 14, 2005 from http://nobelprize.org/peace/laureates/1931/addams-bio.html.

Hagen, J. L., & Lawrence, C. K. (2008). Temporary assistance for needy families. In T. Mizrahi & L. E. Davis (Editors-in-Chief), *Encyclopedia of Social Work* (Vol. 4, pp. 225–229). Washington, DC: NASW Press.

Haight, W. L. (1998, May). "Gathering the spirit" at First Baptist Church: Spirituality as a protective factor in the lives of African American children. *Social Work, 43*(3), 123–221.

Hallahan, D. P., Kauffman, J. M., & Pullen, P. C. (2012). *Exceptional learners: An introduction to special education* (12th ed.). Boston: Pearson.

Halley, A. A., Kopp, J., & Austin, M. J. (1998). *Delivering human services: A learning approach to practice* (5th ed.). New York: Longman.

Hammond, W., & Yung, B. (1993). Preventing violence in at-risk African American youth. *Journal of Health Care for the Poor and Underserved, 2,* 358–372.

Haney, P. (1988, May–June). Comments on currents: Providing empowerment to persons with AIDS. *Social Work, 33*(3), 251–253.

Hanlon, J., & Pickett, G. (1984). *Public health administration and practice.* St. Louis, MO: Times Mirror/Mosby.

Harjo, S. S. (1993). The American Indian Experience. In H. P. McAdoo (Ed.), *Family ethnicity: Strength in diversity.* Newbury Park, CA: Sage.

Harkness, D. (2008). Consultation. In T. Mizrahi & L. E. Davis (Editors-in-Chief), *Encyclopedia of Social Work* (Vol. 3, pp. 295–299). Washington, DC: NASW Press.

Harras, A. (1987). *Issues in adolescent Indian health: Suicide* (Division of Medical Systems Research and Development Monograph Series). Washington, DC: U.S. Department of Health and Human Services.

Harrigan, M. P., & Farmer, R. L. (2000). The myths and facts about aging. In R. L. Schneider, N. P. Kropf, & A. J. Kisor (Eds.), *Gerontological social work: Knowledge, service settings, and special populations* (2nd ed., pp. 26–64). Pacific Grove CA: Brooks/Cole.

Harris, J. J., & Pehrson, K. L. (2008). Military social work. In T. Mizrahi & L. E. Davis (Editors-in-Chief), *Encyclopedia of Social Work* (Vol. 1, pp. 420–423). Washington, DC: NASW Press.

Harris, M. B. (2008). Family life education. In T. Mizrahi & L. E. Davis (Editors-in-Chief), *Encyclopedia of Social Work* (Vol. 2, pp. 197–200). Washington, DC: NASW Press.

Harrison, W. D. (1995). Community development. In R. L. Edwards (Ed.), *Encyclopedia of social work* (19th ed., Vol. 1, pp. 555–562). Washington, DC: NASW Press.

Hart, S. N., & Brassard, M. R. (1991, 2001). *Definition of psychological maltreatment.* Indianapolis: Office for the Study of the Psychological Rights of the Child, Indiana University School of Education.

Hart, S. N., Brassard, M. R., Davidson, H. A., Rivelis, E., Diaz, V., & Binggeli, N. J. (2011). Psychological maltreatment. In J. E. B. Myers (Ed.), *The APSAC handbook on child maltreatment* (3rd ed., pp. 125–144). Thousand Oaks, CA: Sage.

Hart, S. N., Brassard, M. R., & Karlson, H. C. (1996). Psychological maltreatment. In J. Briere, L. Berliner, J. A. Bulkley, C. Jenny, & T. Reid, *The APSAC handbook on child maltreatment* (pp. 72–89). Thousand Oaks, CA: Sage.

Hartman, C. (1987). The housing part of the homeless problem. In Boston Foundation (Ed.), *Homelessness: Critical issues for policy and practice* (pp. 17–19). Boston: Boston Foundation.

Harvey, A. R. (1997). Group work with African American youth in the criminal justice system: A culturally competent model. In G. L. Greif & P. H. Ephross (Eds.), *Group work with populations at risk* (pp. 160–174). New York: Oxford University Press.

Haynes, K. S., & Mickelson, J. S. (2003). *Affecting change: Social workers in the political arena* (5th ed.). Boston: Allyn & Bacon.

Hayward, C., & Collier, J. A. (1996). Anxiety disorders. In H. Steiner (Ed.), *Treating adolescents* (pp. 187–221). San Francisco: Jossey-Bass.

Healthcare.gov. (2011a). Strengthening Medicare. Retrieved on May 19, 2011 from http://www.healthcare.gov/law/provisions/rebate/index.html.

Healthcare.gov. (2011b). Understanding the Affordable Care Act: Introduction. Retrieved on June 11, 2011 from http://www.healthcare.gov/law/introduction/index.html.

Healy, L. M. (2008). *International social work: Professional action in an independent world* (2nd ed.). New York: Oxford.

Hellenbrand, S. (1987). Termination in direct practice. In A. Minahan (Ed.), *Encyclopedia of social work* (Vol. 2, pp. 765–770). Silver Spring, MD: NASW Press.

Hellriegel, D., Jackson, S. E., & Slocum, J. W., Jr. (2002). *Management: A competency-based approach* (9th ed.). Cincinnati, OH: South-Western.

Henderson, C. (2002). What is electroshock therapy? Retrieved April 27, 2002 from http://ky.essortment.com/whatiselectroc_riek.htm.

Henderson, D. A., & Thompson, C. L. (2011). *Counseling children* (8th ed.). Belmont, CA: Brooks/Cole.

Henley, J. R., & Danziger, S. K. (1997). Confronting welfare stereotypes: Characteristics of general assistance recipients and postassistance employment. In P. W. Ewalt, E. M. Freeman, S. A. Kirk, & D. L. Poole (Eds.), *Social policy reform research and practice* (pp. 124–139). Washington, DC: NASW Press.

Henslin, J. M. (2011). *Social problems: A down-to-earth approach* (10th ed.). Boston: Allyn & Bacon.

Hepworth, D. H., Rooney, R. H., Rooney, G. D., Strom-Gottfried, K., & Larsen, J. (2010). *Direct social work practice: Theory and skills* (8th ed.). Belmont, CA: Brooks/Cole.

Herbert, B. (2003, May 22). Dancing with the devil. Retrieved October 22, 2008 from http://www.nytimes.com/2003/05/22/opinion/22HERB.html.

Hernandez, V. R. (2008). Generalist and advanced generalist practice. In T. Mizrahi & L. E. Davis (Editors-in-Chief), *Encyclopedia of Social Work* (Vol. 2, pp. 260–268). Washington, DC: NASW Press.

Herrick, J. M. (2008). Social policy: Overview. In T. Mizrahi & L. E. Davis (Editors-in-Chief), *Encyclopedia of Social Work* (Vol. 4, pp. 61–66). Washington, DC: NASW Press.

Herring, R. D. (1999). *Counseling with Native American Indians and Alaska natives: Strategies for helping professionals.* Thousand Oaks, CA: Sage.

Hershberger, S. L., & D'Augelli, A. R. (2000). Issues in counseling lesbian, gay, and bisexual adolescents. In R. M. Perez, K. A. DeBord, & K. J. Bieschke (Eds.), *Handbook of counseling and psychotherapy with lesbian, gay, and bisexual clients* (pp. 225–247). Washington, DC: American Psychological Association.

Hetrick, E. S., & Martin, A. D. (1987). Developmental issues and their resolution for gay and lesbian adolescents. *Journal of Homosexuality, 14*(1/2), 25–42.

Hewlett, J. (1998, December 23). Kentucky art teacher was "Sybil," scholar confirms. *Detroit Free Press.* Retrieved April 27, 2002 from http://www.asarian.org/~quiet/sybildfp.html.

Hill, C., Corbett, C., St. Rose, A. (2010). *Why so few? Women in science, technology, engineering, and mathematics.* Washington, DC: American Association of University Women (AAUW).

Hillier, S. M., & Barrow, G. M. (2011). *Aging, the individual, and society.* Belmont, CA: Wadsworth.

Ho, M. K. (1987). *Family therapy with ethnic minorities.* Newbury Park, CA: Sage.

Ho, M. K. (1992). *Minority children and adolescents in therapy.* Thousand Oaks, CA: Sage.

Hodge, D. R. (2008). Sexual trafficking in the United States: A domestic problem with transnational dimensions. *Social Work, 53*(2), 143–152.

Hodge, J. L., Struckmann, D. K., & Trost, L. D. (1975). *Cultural bases of racism and group oppression.* Berkeley, CA: Two Riders Press.

Hoffman, K. S. (2008). Social work education: Overview. In T. Mizrahi & L. E. Davis (Editors-in-Chief), *Encyclopedia of Social Work* (Vol. 4, pp. 107–114). Washington, DC: NASW Press.

Hokenstad, M. C., & Midgley, J. (1997). Realities of global interdependence: Challenges for social work in a new century. In M. B. Hokenstad & J. Midgley (Eds.), *Issues in international social work: Global challenges for a new century* (pp. 1–10). Washington, DC: NASW Press.

Holden, J. (2010). Big probation: O'Keefe's crime to cost more than $34,000 in probation expenses. Retrieved on June 28, 2011 from http://mediamatters.org/blog/201006010031.

Homan, M. S. (2011). *Promoting community change: Making it happen in the real world* (4th ed.). Belmont, CA: Brooks/Cole.

Homestead Schools, Inc. (2004, September). *Continuing education courses for social workers, counselors, and marriage family therapists.* Torrance, CA: Author.

Hooyman, N. R. (2008). Aging: Overview. In T. Mizrahi & L. E. Davis (Editors-in-Chief), *Encyclopedia of Social Work* (Vol. 4, pp. 144–156). Washington, DC: NASW Press.

Hooyman, N. R., & Kiyak, H. A. (1999). *Social gerontology: A multidisciplinary perspective* (2nd ed.). Boston: Allyn & Bacon.

Hopps, J. G., & Lowe, T. B. (2008). Social work profession: Overview. In T. Mizrahi & L. E. Davis (Editors-in-Chief), *Encyclopedia of Social Work* (Vol. 1, pp. 88–96). Washington, DC: NASW Press.

Horowitz, M. J., & Solomon, G. F. (1975). A prediction of delayed stress response syndromes in Vietnam veterans. *Journal of Social Issues, 31,* 67–80.

Hu, T. W., Snowden, L. R., Jerrell, J. M., & Nguyen, T. D. (1991). Ethnic populations in public mental health: Services choice and level of use. *American Journal of Public Health, 81,* 1429–1434.

Huber, R., Nelson, H. W., Netting, F. E., & Borders, K. W. (2008). *Elder advocacy: Essential knowledge & skills across settings.* Belmont, CA: Brooks/Cole.

Huff, C. R. (1993). Gangs in the United States. In A. P. Goldstein & C. R. Huff (Eds.), *The gang intervention handbook* (pp. 3–20). Champaign, IL: Research Press.

Hyde, C. (2008). Feminist social work practice. In T. Mizrahi & L. E. Davis (Editors-in-Chief), *Encyclopedia of Social Work* (Vol. 2, pp. 216–221). Washington, DC: NASW Press.

Hyde, J. S., & DeLamater, J. D. (2008). *Understanding human sexuality* (10th ed.). Boston: McGraw-Hill.

Hyde, J. S., & DeLamater, J. D. (2011). *Understanding human sexuality* (11th ed.). New York: McGraw-Hill.

Institute for Research on Poverty. (2001, Spring). Cash for kids in four countries: Child benefits in Australia, Canada, the United Kingdom, and the United States. *Focus, 21*(3), 44-49.

International Association of Schools of Social Work (IASSW). (2011). *Welcome to IASSW.* Retrieved on April 20, 2011 from http://www.iassw-aiets.org/.

International Federation of Social Workers (IFSW). (2011). Welcome to IFSW. Retrieved on April 20, 2011 from http://www.ifsw.org/.

International Society for the Study of Trauma and Dissociation. (2011). Frequently asked questions: Dissociation and dissociative disorders. Retrieved on June 17, 2011 from http://www.isst-d.org/education/faq-dissociation.htm#prev.

Intersex Society of North America (ISNA). (2008a). How common is intersex? Retrieved from http://www.isna.org/faq/frequency.

Intersex Society of North America (ISNA). (2008b). What do doctors do now when they encounter a patient with intersex? Retrieved from http://www.isna.org/faq/standard_of_care.

Intersex Society of North America (ISNA). (2008c). What does ISNA recommend for children with intersex? Retrieved from http://www.isna.org/faq/patient-centered.

Ivey, A. E., & Ivey, M. B. (2008). *Essentials of intentional interviewing: Counseling in a multicultural world.* Belmont, CA: Brooks/Cole.

Ivey, A. E., Ivey, M. B., & Zalaquett, C. P. (2010). *Intentional interviewing & counseling* (7th ed.). Belmont, CA: Brooks/Cole.

Jacobs, E. E., Masson, R. L., & Harvil, L. H. (2009). *Group counseling: Strategies and skills* (6th ed.). Belmont, CA: Brooks/Cole.

James, R. K. (2008). *Crisis intervention strategies* (6th ed.). Belmont, CA: Brooks/Cole.

Jane Addams Hull House Museum. (1997, February). Biographical sketch of Jane Addams. Retrieved June 14, 2005 from http://www.uic.edu/jaddams/hull/ja_bio.html.

Jansson, B. S. (2008). *Becoming an effective policy advocate: From policy practice to social justice* (5th ed.). Belmont, CA: Brooks/Cole.

Jansson, B. S. (2009). *The reluctant welfare state: American social welfare policies: Past, present, and future* (6th ed.). Belmont, CA: Brooks/Cole.

Jansson, B. S. (2011). *Becoming an effective policy advocate: From policy practice to social justice* (6th ed.). Belmont, CA: Brooks/Cole.

Jansson, B. S. (2012). *The reluctant welfare state: Engaging history to advance social work practice in contemporary society* (6th ed.). Belmont, CA: Brooks/Cole.

Jenson, J. M., & Howard, M. O. (1999). Prevalence and patterns of youth violence. In J. M. Jenson & M. O. Howard (Eds.), *Youth violence: Current research and recent practice innovations* (pp. 3–18). Washington, DC: NASW Press.

Jewish Child & Family Services. (n.d.). *Refugee resettlement services.* Retrieved on June 24, 2011 from http://www.jcfs.org/p_program.cfm?cat=cs&id=6.

Jimenez, J. (2010). *Social policy and social change: Toward the creation of social and economic justice.* Thousand Oaks, CA: Sage.

Johannesen, T. (1997). Social work as an international profession. In M. C. Hokenstad & J. Midgley (Eds.), *Issues in international social work: Global challenges for a new century.* Washington, DC: NASW Press.

Johnson, J. L. (2004). *Fundamentals of substance abuse practice.* Belmont, CA: Brooks/Cole.

Johnson, K., Noe, T., Collins, D., Strader, T., & Bucholtz, G. (2000). Mobilizing church communities to prevent alcohol and other drug abuse: A model strategy and its evaluation. *Journal of Community Practice, 7*(2), 1–27.

Johnson, M. (2002, February 1). Fetuses may qualify for federal aid. *Milwaukee Journal Sentinel,* A1.

Johnson, M. A. (2005). *Hull House.* Retrieved on May 9, 2011 from http://www.encyclopedia.chicagohistory.org/pages/615.html.

Jones, L. R. W. (1995). Unemployment compensation and workers' compensation. In R. L. Edwards (Ed.), *Encyclopedia of social work* (19th ed., Vol. 3, pp. 2413–2417). Washington, DC: NASW Press.

Kadushin, A., & Harkness, D. (2002). *Supervision in social work* (4th ed.). New York: Columbia University Press.

Kadushin, A., & Martin, J. A. (1988). *Child welfare services* (4th ed.). New York: Macmillan.

Kail, R. V., & Cavanaugh, J. C. (2010). *Human development: A life-span view* (5th ed.). Belmont, CA: Wadsworth.

Kaiser Family Foundation (KFF). (2008a). HIV/AIDS. Retrieved July 20, 2008 from http://kff.org.

Kaiser Family Foundation (KFF). (2008b). Kaiser slides. Retrieved July 20, 2008 from http://facts.kff.org/results.aspx?view=slides&topic=3.

Kaiser Family Foundation (KFF). (2009). The HIV/AIDS epidemic in sub-Saharan Africa. Retrieved on June 13, 2011 from http://www.kff.org/hivaids/upload/7391-08.pdf.

Kaiser Family Foundation (KFF). (2010a). The global HIV/AIDS epidemic. Retrieved on June 13, 2011 from http://www.kff.org/hivaids/upload/3030-15.pdf.

Kaiser Family Foundation (KFF). (2010b). The Medicare prescription drug benefit. Retrieved on May 18, 2011 from http://www.kff.org/medicare/upload/7044-11.pdf.

Kaiser Family Foundation (KFF). (2011a). Black Americans and HIV/AIDS. Retrieved on June 13, 2011 from http://www.kff.org/hivaids/upload/6089-09.pdf.

Kaiser Family Foundation (KFF). (2011b). HIV/AIDS epidemic in the United States. Retrieved on June 13, 2011 from http://www.kff.org/hivaids/upload/3029-12.pdf.

Kaiser Family Foundation (KFF). (2011c). Kaiser slides: Costs/insurance. Retrieved June 9, 2011 from http://facts.kff.org/results.aspx?view=slides&topic=3.

Kaiser Family Foundation (KFF). (2011d). Kaiser slides: Medicare. Retrieved September 20, 2011 from http://facts.kff.org/results.aspx?view=slides&topic=2.

Kaiser Family Foundation (KFF). (2011e). Latinos and HIV/AIDS. Retrieved June 13, 2011 from http://www.kff.org/hivaids/upload/6007-09.pdf.

Kamya, H. A. (1999). African immigrants in the United States: The challenge for research and practice. In P. L. Ewalt, E. M. Freeman, A. E. Fortune, D. L. Poole, & S. L. Witkin (Eds.), *Multicultural issues in social work: Practice and research* (pp. 605–621). Washington, DC: NASW Press.

Kanel, K. (2012). *A guide to crisis intervention* (4th ed.). Belmont, CA: Brooks/Cole.

Kanter, J. S. (1985). Case management of the young adult chronic patient: A clinical perspective. In J. S. Kanter (Ed.), *Clinical issues in treating the chronic mentally ill.* San Francisco: Jossey-Bass.

Karas, T. (2009, September 15). Teens give their elders some video gaming tips. *AARP: The Magazine.* Retrieved on June 3, 2011 from http://www.highbeam.com/doc/1N1-129BFE62B3E30908.html.

Karenga, M. (1965). *Kwanzaa: Origin, concepts and practice.* Los Angeles: Kawaida Publications.

Karenga, M. (2000). Making the past meaningful: Kwanzaa and the concept of sankofa. In S. L. Abels (Ed.), *Spirituality in social work practice: Narratives for professional helping* (pp. 51–67). Denver, CO: Love.

Karger, H. J., & Stoesz, D. (2006). *American social welfare policy: A pluralist approach* (5th ed.). Boston: Allyn & Bacon.

Karger, H. J., & Stoesz, D. (2010). *American social welfare policy: A pluralist approach* (6th ed.). Boston: Allyn & Bacon.

Kasee, C. R. (1995). Identity, recovery and religious imperialism: Native American women and the New Age. In J. Ochshorn & Cole (Eds.), *Women's spirituality, women's lives* (pp. 83–93). Binghamton, NY: Haworth.

Kaye, L. W. (2008). Aging: Practice interventions. In T. Mizrahi & L. E. Davis (Editors-in-Chief), *Encyclopedia of Social Work* (Vol. 1, pp. 96–100). Washington, DC: NASW Press.

Keiley, M. K., Bates, J. F., Dodge, K. A., & Pettit, G. (2000). A cross-domain growth analysis: Externalizing and internalizing behaviors during 8 years of childhood. *Journal of Abnormal Child Psychology, 28,* 161–179.

Kelly, G. F. (2001). *Sexuality today: The human perspective* (7th ed.). Boston: McGraw-Hill.

Kelly, G. F. (2008). *Sexuality today* (9th ed.). Boston: McGraw-Hill.

Kelly, L. W. (2002, Summer). So you want to practice in mental health! *The New Social Worker,* 4–6.

Kelly, M. S., Raines, J. C., Stone, S., & Frey, A. (2010). *School social work: An evidence-informed framework for practice.* New York: Oxford.

Kendall, D. (2007). *Social problems in a diverse society* (4th ed.). Boston: Allyn & Bacon.

Kendall, D. (2010). *Social problems in a diverse society* (5th ed.). Boston: Allyn & Bacon.

Kenyon, P. (1999). *What would you do? An ethical case workbook for human service professionals.* Pacific Grove, CA: Brooks/Cole.

Khinduka, S. K. (2008). Globalization. In T. Mizrahi & L. E. Davis (Editors-in-Chief), *Encyclopedia of Social Work* (Vol. 2, pp. 275–279). Washington, DC: NASW Press.

Kiesner, J., Dishion, T. J., & Poulin, F. (2001). A reinforcement model of conduct problems in children and adolescents: Advances in theory and intervention. In J. Hill & B. Maughan (Eds.), *Conduct disorders in childhood and adolescence.* New York: Cambridge University Press.

King v. King, 392 U.S. 309 (1968).

Kingery-McCabe, L. B., & Frances, A. C. (1991). Effects of addiction on the addict. In D. C. Daley & M. S. Raskin (Eds.), *Treating the chemically dependent and their families* (pp. 57–78). Newbury Park, CA: Sage.

Kingson, E. R. (2008). Social security program. In T. Mizrahi & L. E. Davis (Editors-in-Chief), *Encyclopedia of Social Work* (Vol. 4, pp. 89–97). Washington, DC: NASW Press.

Kirk, G. & Okazawa-Rey, M. (2010). *Women's lives: Multicultural perspectives* (5th ed.). Boston: McGraw-Hill.

Kirst-Ashman, K. K. (1992, Summer). Feminist values and social work: A model for educating nonfeminists. *Arete, 17*(1), 13–25.

Kirst-Ashman, K. K. (2011). *Human behavior in the macro social environment: An empowerment approach to understanding communities, organizations, and groups* (3rd ed.). Belmont, CA: Brooks/Cole.

Kirst-Ashman, K. K., & Hull, G. H., Jr. (2006). *Understanding generalist practice* (4th ed.). Pacific Grove, CA: Brooks/Cole.

Kirst-Ashman, K. K., & Hull, G. H., Jr. (2009). *Understanding generalist practice* (5th ed.). Belmont, CA: Brooks/Cole.

Kirst-Ashman, K. K., & Hull, G. H., Jr. (2012a). *Generalist practice with organizations and communities* (5th ed.). Belmont, CA: Brooks/Cole.

Kirst-Ashman, K. K., & Hull, G. H., Jr. (2012b). *Understanding generalist practice* (6th ed.). Belmont, CA: Brooks/Cole.

Kiselica, M. S., Changizi, J. C., Cureton, V. L. L., & Gridley, B. E. (1995). Counseling children and adolescents in schools: Salient multicultural issues. In J. G. Ponterotto, J. M. Cases, L. A. Suzuki, & C. M. Alexander (Eds.), *Handbook of multicultural counseling* (pp. 516–532). Thousand Oaks, CA: Sage.

Kitano, H. H. L., & Maki, M. T. (1996). Continuity, change, and diversity: Counseling Asian Americans. In P. B. Pederson, J. G. Draguns, W. J. Lonner, & J. E. Trimble (Eds.), *Counseling across cultures* (4th ed., pp. 124–125). Thousand Oaks, CA: Sage.

Koch, G. (1979). Home-based support services: An alternative to residential placement for the developmentally disabled. In S. Maybanks & M. Bruce (Eds.), *Home-based services for children and families: Policy, practice, and research* (pp. 157–164). Springfield, IL: Thomas.

Kolb, P. J. (1999). A stage of migration approach to understanding nursing home placement in Latino families. *Journal of Multicultural Social Work, 7*(3/4), 95–112.

Kolko, D. J. (2002). Child physical abuse. In J. E. B. Myers, L. Berliner, J. Briere, C. T. Hendrix, C. Jenny, & T. A. Reid (Eds.), *The APSAC handbook on child maltreatment* (2nd ed., pp. 21–54). Thousand Oaks, CA: Sage.

Kopels, S. (1995). The Americans with Disabilities Act: A tool to combat poverty. *Journal of Social Work Education, 31*(3), 337–346.

Kornblum, W., & Julian, J. (2009). *Social problems* (13th ed.). Upper Saddle River, NJ: Prentice-Hall.

Kosberg, J. I., & Adams, J. I. (2008). Men: Overview. In T. Mizrahi & L. E. Davis (Editors-in-Chief), *Encyclopedia of Social Work* (Vol. 3, pp. 205–214). Washington, DC: NASW Press.

Kottman, T. (2001). *Play therapy: Basics and beyond.* Alexandria, VA: American Counseling Association.

Kozol, J. (1999). Savage inequalities. In J. M. Henslin (Ed.), *In down-to-earth sociology: Introductory readings* (10th ed., pp. 343–351). New York: Free Press.

KPMG Consulting. (2002). *Alberta's health gaining & seniors wellness strategic framework 2002–2012.* Edmonton, AB: Alberta Health and Wellness. Retrieved on June 2, 2011 from http://www.gov.ab.ca/acn/images/2002/702/12861.pdf.

Kretzmann, J. P., & McKnight, J. L. (1993). *Building communities from the inside out: A path toward finding and mobilizing a community's assets.* Chicago: ACTA Publications.

Kropf, N. P. (2000). Home health and community services. In R. L. Schneider, N. P. Kropf, & A. J. Kisor (Eds.), *Gerontological social work: Knowledge, service settings, and special populations* (pp. 167–190). Pacific Grove, CA: Brooks/Cole.

Kropf, N. P., & Hutchinson, E. D. (2000). Effective practice with elderly clients. In R. L. Schneider, N. P. Kropf, & A. J. Kisor (Eds.), *Gerontological social work: Knowledge, service settings, and special populations* (pp. 3–25). Pacific Grove, CA: Brooks/Cole.

Krout, J. (1994). Community size differences in senior center resources, programming, and participation. *Research on Aging, 16*, 440–462.

Kubler-Ross, E. (1969). *On death and dying.* New York: Macmillan.

Kurland, R., & Salmon, R. (1992). When problems seem overwhelming: Emphases in teaching, supervision, and consultation. *Social Work. 37*(3), 240–244.

Kurtz, L. F. (2004). Support and self-help groups. In C. D. Garvin, L. M. Gutierrez, & M. J. Galinsky (Eds.), *Handbook of social work with groups* (pp. 139–159). New York: Guilford.

LaCoursiere, R. B., Bodfrey, K. E., & Ruby, L. M. (1980). Traumatic neurosis in the etiology of alcoholism: Vietnam and other trauma. *American Journal of Psychiatry, 137*, 966–968.

LaFromboise, T. D., & Bigfoot, D. (1988). Cultural and cognitive considerations in the prevention of American Indian adolescent suicide. *Journal of Adolescence, 11*, 139–153.

Land, H. (1995). Feminist clinical social work in the 21st century. In N. Van Den Bergh (Ed.), *Feminist practice in the 21st century* (pp. 3–19). Washington, DC: NASW Press.

Landon, P. S. (1995). Generalist and advanced generalist practice. In R. L. Edwards (Ed.), *Encyclopedia of social work* (19th ed., Vol. 2, pp. 1101–1108). Washington, DC: NASW Press.

Lawson, W. B., Hepler, N., Holladay, J., & Cuffel, B. (1994). Race as a factor in inpatient and outpatient admissions and diagnosis. *Hospital and Community Psychiatry, 45*, 72–74.

LeCroy, C. W. (2006). Designing and facilitating groups with children. In C. Franklin, M. B. Harris, & P. Allen-Meares (Eds.), *The school services sourcebook: A guide for school-based professionals* (pp. 595–602). New York: Oxford.

Lee, Y. S., Cheng, A. W., Ahmed, S. F., Shaw, N., J., & Hughes, I. A. (2007). Genital anomalies in Klinefelter's syndrome. *Hormonal Research, 68*, 150–153.

Leiby, J. (1987). History of social welfare. In A. Minahan (Ed.), *Encyclopedia of social work* (Vol. 1, pp. 755–777). Silver Spring, MD: National Association of Social Workers.

Leininger, M. M. (1990). Historic and epistemologic dimensions of care and caring with future directions. In J. Stevenson (Ed.), *American academy of nursing* (pp. 19–31). Kansas City, MO: American Nurses Association Press.

Leininger, M. M. (1992). *Cultural care diversity and universality: A theory of nursing* (Pub. No. 15–2401). New York: National League for Nursing Press.

Lemonick, M. D. (2000, July 24). Little hope, less help. *Time,* 38–39.

Lens, V. (2002). TANF: What went wrong and what to do next. *Social Work, 47*(3), 279–290.

Leong, F. T. L., Lee, S-H, & Chang, D. (2008). Counseling Asian Americans. In P. B. Pedersen, J. G. Draguns, W. J. Lonner, & J. E. Trimble (Eds.), *Counseling across cultures* (6th ed., pp. 113–128. Thousand Oaks, CA: Sage.

Leon-Guerrero, A. (2009). *Social problems: Community, policy, and social action* (2nd ed.). Thousand Oaks, CA: Pine Forge.

Leon-Guerrero, A. (2011). *Social problems: Community, policy, and social action* (3rd ed.). Thousand Oaks, CA: Sage.

LeVine, E. S., & Sallee, A. L. (1999). *Child welfare: Clinical theory and practice.* Dubuque, IA: Eddie Bowers.

Levine, S. (2002, August 5). Criminal care at a high price. *U.S. News & World Report,* 44–45.

Lewis, E. A., & Suarez, Z. E. (1995). Natural helping networks. In R. L. Edwards (Ed.), *Encyclopedia of social work* (19th ed., Vol. 2, pp. 1765–1772). Washington, DC: NASW Press.

Lewis, J. (2011). Obama's health care plan is snagged by courts. *StarTribune.* Retrieved on June 12, 2011 from http://www.startribune.com/opinion/otherviews/123661264.html.

Lewis, J. A., Dana, R. Q., & Blevins, G. A. (2011). *Substance abuse counseling* (4th ed.). Belmont, CA: Brooks/Cole.

Lewis, J. A., Lewis, M. D., Packard, T., & Souflee, F., Jr. (2001). *Management of human service programs* (3rd ed.). Pacific Grove, CA: Brooks/Cole.

Lewis, R. G. (1995). American Indians. In R. L. Edwards (Ed.), *Encyclopedia of social work* (19th ed., Vol. 1, pp. 216–225). Washington, DC: NASW Press.

Library of Congress. (2004, May 14). *The treaty of Guadalupe Hidalgo.* Retrieved November 20, 2004 from http://www.loc.gov/eHibits/ghtreaty/.

Licensure boosts profession, protects public. (2004, October). *NASW News,* p. 12.

Liederman, D. S. (1995). Child welfare overview. In R. L. Edwards (Ed.), *Encyclopedia of social work* (19th ed., Vol. 1, pp. 424–433). Washington, DC: NASW Press.

Lightfoot, E. (2009). Social policies for people with disabilities. In J. Midgley & M. Livermore (Eds.), *The handbook of social policy* (2nd ed., pp. 445–462). Thousand Oaks, CA: Sage.

Lin, A. M. P. (1995). Mental health overview. In R. L. Edwards (Ed.), *Encyclopedia of social work* (19th ed., Vol. 2, pp. 1705–1711). Washington, DC: NASW Press.

Lindberg, C. A. (Managing Editor). (2007). *The Oxford College Dictionary.* New York: Spark.

Link, R. J., Ramanathan, C. S., & Asamoah, Y. (1999). Understanding the human condition and human behavior in a global era. In C. S. Ramanathan & R. J. Link (Eds.), *All our futures: Principles and resources for social work practice in a global era* (pp. 30–51). Pacific Grove, CA: Brooks/Cole.

Locke, D. C. (1998). *Increasing multicultural understanding: A comprehensive model* (2nd ed.). Thousand Oaks, CA: Sage.

Loewenberg, F. M., Dolgoff, R., & Harrington, D. (2000). *Ethical decisions for social work practice* (6th ed.). Itasca, IL: Peacock.

Lohmann, N. (2005). Social work education for rural practice. In N. Lohmann & R. A. Lohmann (Eds.), *Rural social work practice* (pp. 293–311). New York: Columbia University Press.

Lohmann, R. A. (1997). Managed care: A review of recent research. In R. L. Edwards (Ed.), *Encyclopedia of social work: Supplement 1997* (19th ed., pp. 200–213). Washington, DC: NASW Press.

Longres, J. F. (1995). Biographies: Richmond, Mary Ellen (1861–1928). In R. L. Edwards (Ed.), *Encyclopedia of social work* (19th ed., Vol. 3, p. 2605). Washington, DC: NASW Press.

Longres, J. F. (2000). *Human behavior in the social environment* (3rd ed.). Itasca, IL: Peacock.

Longres, J. F., & Aisenberg, E. (2008). Latinos and Latinas: Overview. In T. Mizrahi & L. E. Davis (Editors-in-Chief), *Encyclopedia of Social Work* (Vol. 3, pp. 31–41). Washington, DC: NASW Press.

Lorber, J. (2010). Gender inequality: *Feminist theories and politics* (4th ed.). New York: Oxford.

Loue, W. (1998). Defining the immigrant. In S. Loue (Ed.), *Handbook of immigrant health* (pp. 19–36). New York: Plenum Press.

Lowe, G. R. (1995). Social development. In R. L. Edwards (Ed.), *Encyclopedia of social work* (19th ed., Vol. 3, pp. 2168–2173). Washington, DC: NASW Press.

Lowe, S. M., & Mascher, J. (2001). The role of sexual orientation in multicultural counseling: Integrating bodies of knowledge. In J. G. Ponterotto, J. M. Casas, L. A. Suzuki, & C. M. Alexander (Eds.), *Handbook of multicultural counseling* (2nd ed., pp. 755–778). Thousand Oaks, CA: Sage.

Lu, Y. E. (2008). Asian Americans: Chinese. In T. Mizrahi & L. E. Davis (Editors-in-Chief), *Encyclopedia of Social Work* (Vol. 1, pp. 164–166). Washington, DC: NASW Press.

Lum, D. (1995). Asian Americans: Chinese. In R. L. Edwards (Ed.), *Encyclopedia of social work* (19th ed., Vol. 1, pp. 238–241). Washington, DC: NASW Press.

Lum, D. (2003). *Culturally competent practice: A framework for understanding diverse groups and justice issues* (2nd ed.). Pacific Grove, CA: Brooks/Cole.

Lum, D. (2004). *Social work practice with people of color: A process-stage approach* (5th ed.). Belmont, CA: Brooks/Cole.

Lum, D. (2005). *Cultural competence, practice stages, and client systems: A case study approach.* Belmont, CA: Brooks/Cole.

Lum, D. (2007). *Culturally competent practice: A framework for understanding diverse groups and justice issues* (3rd ed.). Belmont, CA: Brooks/Cole.

Lum, D. (2011). *Culturally competent practice: A framework for understanding diverse groups and justice issues* (4th ed.). Belmont, CA: Brooks/Cole.

Macarov, D. (1995). *Social welfare structure and practice.* Thousand Oaks, CA: Sage.

Macionis, J. J. (2008). *Social problems* (3rd ed.). Upper Saddle River, NJ: Pearson.

Macionis, J. J. (2010). *Social problems* (4th ed.). Upper Saddle River, NJ: Pearson.

Mackelprang, R. (2008). Disability: Overview. In T. Mizrahi & L. E. Davis (Editors-in-Chief), *Encyclopedia of Social Work* (Vol. 2, pp. 36–43). Washington, DC: NASW Press.

Mackelprang, R., & Salsgiver, R. (1996). People with disabilities and social work: Historical and contemporary issues. *Social Work, 41*(1), 7–14.

Mackelprang, R., & Salsgiver, R. (1999). *Disability: A diversity model approach in human service practice.* Pacific Grove, CA: Brooks/Cole.

Mackelprang, R. W., & Salsgiver, R. O. (2009). *Disability: A diversity model approach in human service practice* (2nd ed.). Chicago: Lyceum.

Macmillan, R., McMorris, B. J., & Kruttschnitt, C. (2004). Linked lives: Stability and change in maternal circumstances and trajectories of antisocial behavior in children. *Child Development, 75,* 205–220.

Mai, M. (1999, May 3). Anatomy of a massacre. *Newsweek,* 25–31.

Major, E. (2000, Winter). Self-determination and the disabled adult. *The New Social Worker, 7*(1), 9–16.

Making Music: The key to healthy aging. (2005, September 19). *The Norman Transcript.* Retrieved on June 3, 2011 from http://normantranscript.com/features/x518929115/Making-music-The-key-to-healthy-aging.

Mallon, G. P. (2008). Gay parents and parenting. In T. Mizrahi & L. E. Davis (Editors-in-Chief), *Encyclopedia of Social Work* (Vol. 2, pp. 241–247). Washington, DC: NASW Press.

Maluccio, A. N. (1990). Family preservation: An overview. In A. L. Sallee & J. C. Lloyd (Eds.), *Family preservation: Papers from the Institute for Social Work Educators 1990.* Riverdale, IL: National Association for Family-Based Services.

Maluccio, A. N., Pine, B. A., & Tracy, E. M. (2002). *Social work practice with families and children.* New York: Columbia.

Manske, J. (2008). Veteran services. In T. Mizrahi & L. E. Davis (Editors-in-Chief), *Encyclopedia of Social Work* (Vol. 4, pp. 257–259). Washington, DC: NASW Press.

Mapp, S. (2008). *Human rights and social justice in a global perspective: An introduction to international social work.* Washington, DC: NASW Press.

Marcotty, J. (1999, November 11). Electroshock therapy revised. *Minnesota Star Tribune.* Retrieved April 27, 2002 from http://www.ect.org/news/revised.htm.

Markels, A. (2007, April 30). Recovery's long road. *U.S. News & World Report,* 54–55.

Marsella, A. J. (1998, June). Urbanization, mental health, and social deviancy. *American Psychologist, 53*(6), 624–634.

Marson, S. M. (1998). Major uses of the Internet for social workers: A brief report for new users. *Arete, 22*(2), 21–28.

Marson, S. M. (2000). Internet ethics for social workers. *The New Social Worker, 7*(3), 29–30.

Martinez-Brawley, E. E. (1995). Community. In R. L. Edwards (Ed.), *Encyclopedia of social work* (19th ed., Vol. 1, pp. 539–548). Washington, DC: NASW Press.

Marx, J. D. (2004). *Social welfare: The American partnership.* Boston: Allyn & Bacon.

Mary, N. L. (1998). Social work and the support model of services for people with developmental disabilities. *Journal of Social Work Education, 34*(2), 247–260.

Mary, N. L. (2008). *Social work in a sustainable world.* Chicago: Lyceum.

Mary Ellen Wilson. (1874, April 22). *New York Times,* p. 8.

Masland, T. (2000, July 17). Breaking the silence. *Newsweek,* 30–31.

Mather, J., Lager, P. B., & Harris, N. J. (2007). *Child welfare: Policies and best practices* (2nd ed.) Belmont, CA: Brooks/Cole.

Mather, J. H., & Lager, P. B. (2000). *Child welfare: A unifying model of practice.* Belmont, CA: Wadsworth.

Matorin, S. (1998). The corporatization of mental health services: The impact on service, training, and values. In G. Schamess & A. Lightburn (Eds.), *Human managed care?* (pp. 159–170). Washington, DC: NASW Press.

Matthews, C. R., & Lease, S. H. (2000). Focus on lesbian, gay, and bisexual families. In R. M. Perez, K. A. DeBord, & K. J. Bieschke (Eds.), *Handbook of counseling and psychotherapy with lesbian, gay, and bisexual clients* (pp. 225–273). Washington, DC: American Psychological Association.

Mayo Foundation for Medical Education and Research (MFMER). (2010). Electroconvulsive therapy (ECT). Retrieved on June 21, 2011 from http://www.mayoclinic.com/health/electroconvulsive-therapy/MY00129.

McAdoo, H. P. (2007). *Black families* (4th ed.). Thousand Oaks, CA: Sage.

McAnulty, R. D., & Burnette, M. M. (2001). *Exploring human sexuality: Making healthy decisions.* Boston: Allyn & Bacon.

McCammon, S., & Knox, D. (2007). *Choices in sexuality* (3rd ed.). Mason, OH: Thomson.

McCollum, E. E., & Trepper, T. S. (2001). *Family solutions for substance abuse.* Binghamton, NY: Haworth.

McCallum, K. E., & Bruton, J. R. (2003). The continuum of care in the treatment of eating disorders. *Primary Psychiatry, 10*(6), 48–54.

McDonald, S., Constable, R., & Moriarty, A. (2009). *Developing safe, responsive, and respectful school communities: Pathways to intervention.* In C. R. Massat, R. Constable, S. McDonald, & J. P. Flynn (Eds.), *School social work: Practice, policy, and research* (7th ed., pp. 728–752). Chicago: Lyceum.

McDonald, S., Fineran, S., Constable, R., & Moriarty, A. (2002). Creating safe and responsive schools: Bullying and peer sexual harassment. In R. Constable, S. McDonald, & J. P. Flynn (Eds.), *School social work: Practice, policy, and research perspectives* (5th ed., pp. 458–480). Chicago: Lyceum.

McDonald, S., & Moriarty, A. (2002). Mediation as a form of peer-based conflict resolution. In R. Constable, S. McDonald, & J. P. Flynn (Eds.), *School social work: Practice, policy, and research perspectives* (5th ed., pp. 501–514). Chicago: Lyceum.

McGeary, J. (2001, February 12). Death stalks a continent. *Time,* 36–45.

McGee, E. (1982). *Too little, too late: Services for teenage parents.* New York: Ford Foundation.

McInnis-Dittrich, K. (1994). *Integrating social welfare policy and social work practice.* Pacific Grove, CA: Brooks/Cole.

McInnis-Dittrich, K. (2005). *Social work with elders: A biopsychosocial approach to assessment and intervention* (2nd ed.). Boston: Allyn & Bacon.

McInnis-Dittrich, K. (2009). *Social work with older adults* (3rd ed.). Boston: Allyn & Bacon.

McLaughlin, L. A., & Braun, K. L. (1999). Asian and Pacific Islander cultural values: Considerations for health care decision-making. In P. L. Ewalt, E. M. Freeman, A. E. Fortune, D. L. Poole, & S. L. Witkin (Eds.), *Multicultural issues in social work: Practice and research* (pp. 321–336). Washington, DC: NASW Press.

McNeece, C. A. (1995). Adult corrections. In R. L. Edwards (Ed.), *Encyclopedia of social work* (19th ed., Vol. 1, pp. 60–68). Washington, DC: NASW Press.

McNutt, J. (2008). Social work practice: History and evolution. In T. Mizrahi & L. E. Davis (Editors-in-Chief), *Encyclopedia of Social Work* (Vol. 4, pp. 138–141). Washington, DC: NASW Press.

McRoy, R. G., & Lombe, M. (2011). Cultural competence with African Americans. In D. Lum, *Culturally competent practice* (4th ed., pp. 273–301). Belmont, CA: Brooks/Cole.

McWhirter, J. J., McWhirter, B. T., McWhirter, E. H., & McWhirter, R. J. (2007). *At risk youth: A comprehensive response for counselors, teachers, psychologists, and human services professionals* (4th ed.). Belmont, CA: Brooks/Cole.

Mechanic, D. (2008). *Mental health and social policy: Beyond managed care* (5th ed.). Boston: Allyn & Bacon.

Medicare Rights Center. (2011). *Medicare drug benefit (Part D) costs.* Retrieved on May 19, 2011 from http://www.medicareinteractive.org/page2.php?topic=counselor&page=script&slide_id=1479.

Meenaghan, T. M., Kilty, K. M., & McNutt, J. G. (2004). *Social policy analysis and practice.* Chicago, IL: Lyceum.

Meier, M. S. (1990). Politics, educations, and culture. In C. McWilliams (Ed.), *North from Mexico* (rev. ed., pp. 285–308). Westport, CT: Greenwood Press.

Menefee, D. (2000). What managers do and why they do it. In R. J. Patti (Ed.), *The handbook of social welfare management* (pp. 247–266). Thousand Oaks, CA: Sage.

Mental Health America (MHA). (2011a). Eating disorders. Retrieved on June 17, 2011 from http://www.nmha.org/go/eating-disorders.

Mental Health America (MHA). (2011b). Electroconvulsive therapy (ECT). Retrieved on June 21, 2011 from http://www.nmha.org/go/information/get-info/treatment/electroconvulsive-therapy-ect.

Mental Health America (MHA). (2011c). Mission, vision, statement of purpose, and guiding principles. Retrieved on June 21, 2011 from http://www.nmha.org/go/mission-vision.

Mercer, S. O. (1996, March). Navajo elderly people in a reservation nursing home: Admission predictors and culture care practices. *Social Work, 41*(2), 181–189.

Meyer, D. R. (1995). Supplemental Security Income. In R. L. Edwards (Ed.), *Encyclopedia of social work* (19th ed., Vol. 3, pp. 2379–2385). Washington, DC: NASW Press.

Meyer, D. R. (2001, Spring). Income support for children in the United States. *Focus, 21*(3), 38–41.

Midgley, J. (1997). *Social welfare in global context.* Thousand Oaks, CA: Sage.

Midgley, J., & Livermore, M. (1997). The developmental perspective in social work: Educational implications for a new century. *Social Work, 33*(3), 573–585.

Mikulski, B. A. (2011). *Barbara A. Mikulski.* Retrieved on May 15, 2011 from http://mikulski.senate.gov/.

Milkman, H. B., & Sederer, L. I. (1990). *Treatment choices for alcoholism and substance abuse.* New York: Lexington Books.

Miller, D. W. (2001, May 18). Programs in social work embrace the teaching of spirituality. *The Chronicle of Higher Education,* A12.

Miller, G. (2005). *Learning the language of addiction counseling* (2nd ed.). Hoboken, NJ: Wiley.

Miller, M., & Kantrowitz, B. (1999, January 25). Unmasking Sybil: A re-examination of the most famous psychiatric patient in history. *Newsweek,* 66–68.

Miller, R. L., Jr. (2008). Gay men: Overview. In T. Mizrahi & L. E. Davis (Editors-in-Chief), *Encyclopedia of Social Work* (Vol. 2, pp. 256–260). Washington, DC: NASW Press.

Miller-Perrin, C. L., & Perrin, R. D. (2007). *Child maltreatment: An introduction* (2nd ed.). Thousand Oaks, CA: Sage.

Mish, F. C. (Ed.). (1995). *Merriam Webster's collegiate dictionary* (10th ed.). Springfield, MA: Merriam-Webster.

Mish, F. C. (Editor-in-Chief). (2008). *Merriam-Webster's collegiate dictionary* (11th ed.). Springfield, MA: Merriam-Webster, Inc.

Mitchell, E. P., & Mitchell, H. H. (1989). Black spirituality: The values in that ol'time religion. *Journal of the Interdenominational Theological Center, 17*(1/2), 98–109.

Mokuau, N. (1995). Pacific Islanders. In R. L. Edwards (Ed.), *Encyclopedia of social work* (19th ed., Vol. 3, pp. 1795–1801). Washington, DC: NASW Press.

Mokuau, N. (2008). Native Hawaiians and Pacific Islanders. In T. Mizrahi & L. E. Davis (Editors-in-Chief), *Encyclopedia of Social Work* (Vol. 3, pp. 308–310). Washington, DC: NASW Press.

Money, J. (1987). Sin, sickness, or status: Homosexual gender identify and psychoneuroendocrinology. *American Psychologist, 42,* 384–399.

Monzini, P. (2004). Trafficking in women and girls and the involvement of organized crime in Western and Central Europe. *International Review of Victimology, 11,* 73–88.

Mooney, L. A., Knox, D., & Schacht, C. (2009). *Understanding social problems* (6th ed.). Belmont, CA: Wadsworth.

Mooney, L. A., Knox, D., & Schacht, C. (2011). *Understanding social problems* (7th ed.). Belmont, CA: Wadsworth.

Moore, S. E. (2008). African Americans: Practice interventions. In T. Mizrahi & L. E. Davis (Editors-in-Chief), *Encyclopedia of Social Work* (Vol. 1, pp. 81–85). Washington, DC: NASW Press.

Morales, A. T., & Sheafor, B. W. (2002). *The many faces of social work clients.* Boston: Allyn & Bacon.

Morales, A. T., Sheafor, B. W., & Scott, M. E. (2007). *Social work: A profession of many faces* (11th ed.). Boston: Allyn & Bacon.

Morales, A. T., Sheafor, B. W., & Scott, M. E. (2012). *Social work: A profession of many faces* (12th ed.). Boston: Allyn & Bacon.

Morales, J. (1995). Gay men: Parenting. In R. L. Edwards (Ed.), *Encyclopedia of social work* (19th ed., Vol. 2, pp. 1085–1095). Washington, DC: NASW Press.

Moreno, C. L. (2001). Developmental disabilities. In A. Gitterman (Ed.), *Handbook of social work practice with vulnerable and resilient populations* (2nd ed., pp. 205–223). New York: Columbia University Press.

Morgan, M. (2000). *Careers in criminology.* Los Angeles: RoBury Park.

Morris, R. (1987). Social welfare policy: Trends and issues. In A. Monahan (Ed.), *Encyclopedia of social work* (Vol. 2, pp. 664–681). Silver Spring, MD: NASW Press.

Morrow, D. F. (1993). Social work with gay and lesbian adolescents. *Social Work, 38*(6), 655–660.

Morrow, D. F. (2006a). Coming out as a gay, lesbian, bisexual, and transgender. In D. F. Morrow & L. Messinger (Eds.), *Sexual orientation & gender expression in social work practice: Working with gay, lesbian, bisexual, & transgender people* (pp. 129–152). New York: Columbia.

Morrow, D. F. (2006b). Gay, lesbian, bisexual, and transgender adolescents. In D. F. Morrow & L. Messinger (Eds.), *Sexual orientation & gender expression in social work practice: Working with gay, lesbian, bisexual, & transgender people* (pp. 177–195). New York: Columbia.

Morrow, D. F. (2008). Lesbians: Practice interventions. In T. Mizrahi & L. E. Davis (Editors-in-Chief), *Encyclopedia of Social Work* (Vol. 3, pp. 79-87). Washington, DC: NASW Press.

Moxley, D. P. (1989). *The practice of case management.* Newbury Park, CA: Sage.

Murase, K. (1995). Asian Americans: Japanese. In R. L. Edwards (Ed.), *Encyclopedia of social work* (19th ed., Vol. 1, pp. 241–249). Washington, DC: NASW Press.

Murphy, B. C., & Dillon, C. (2011). *Interviewing in action in a multicultural world* (4th ed.). Belmont, CA: Brooks/Cole.

Murphy, K. C. (2004). Child development. In C. R. Brittain & D. E. Hunt (Eds.), *Helping in child protective services: A competency-based casework handbook* (pp. 249–306). Washington, DC: NASW Press.

Murphy, Y, Hunt, V., Zajicek, A. M., Norris, A. N., & Hamilton, L. (2009). *Incorporating intersectionality in social work practice, research, policy, and education.* Washington, DC: NASW Press.

Myers, J. E. B. (2002). Risk management for professionals working with maltreated children and adult survivors. In J. E. B. Myers, L. Berliner, J. Briere, C. T. Hendrix, C. Jenny, & T. A. Reid (Eds.), *The APSAC handbook on child maltreatment* (2nd ed., pp. 403–427). Thousand Oaks, CA: Sage.

Myers, R., & Granstaff, C. (2008). Political social work. In T. Mizrahi & L. E. Davis (Editors-in-Chief), *Encyclopedia of Social Work* (Vol. 3, pp. 383–387). Washington, DC: NASW Press.

Nackerud, L. (2008). Unemployment insurance. In T. Mizrahi & L. E. Davis (Editors-in-Chief), *Encyclopedia of Social Work* (Vol. 4, pp. 247–249). Washington, DC: NASW Press.

Nadir, A., & Dziegielewski, S. F. (2001). Islam. In M. Van Hook, B. Hugen, & M. Aguilar (Eds.), *Spirituality within religious traditions in social work practice* (pp. 146–166). Belmont, CA: Brooks/Cole.

Nadir, P. A. (2008). Muslim social services. In T. Mizrahi & L. E. Davis (Editors-in-Chief), *Encyclopedia of Social Work* (Vol. 3, pp. 282–286). Washington, DC: NASW Press.

Nairne, J. S. (2011). Psychology (5th ed.). Belmont, CA: Wadsworth.

Naleppa, M. J., & Reid, W. J. (2003). *Gerontological social work: A task-centered approach.* New York: Columbia.

Nansel, T. R., Overpeck, M., Pilla, R., Ruan, W., Simons-Morton, B., & Scheidt, P. (2001). Bullying behaviors among U.S. youth. *Journal of the American Medical Association, 285,* 2094–2100.

National Alliance on Mental Illness (NAMI). (2011). Commonly prescribed psychotropic medications. Retrieved on June 18, 2011 from http://www.nami.org/Template.cfm?Section= Policymakers_Toolkit&Template=/ContentManagement/ HTMLDisplay.cfm&ContentID=18971.

National Association of Cognitive-Behavioral Therapy (NACBT). (2010). Cognitive-behavioral therapy. Retrieved on June 18, 2011 from http://www.nacbt.org/whatiscbt.htm.

National Association of the Deaf (NAD). (2011). Community and culture—frequently asked questions. Retrieved on June 8, 2011 from http://www.nad.org/issues/american-sign-language/ community-and-culture-faq.

National Association of Social Workers (NASW). (1973). *Standards for social service manpower.* New York: Author.

National Association of Social Workers (NASW). (1999). *NASW Code of Ethics* (amended). Washington, DC: Author.

National Association of Social Workers (NASW). (2005). The power of social work. Retrieved February 12, 2005 from http://www.socialworkers.org/.

National Association of Social Workers (NASW). (2006). *Social work speaks* (7th ed.). Washington, DC: Author.

National Association of Social Workers (NASW). (2008). *Code of Ethics.* Washington, DC: Author.

National Association of Social Workers (NASW). (2009). *Social work speaks: National; Association of Social Workers policy statements 2009–2012* (8th ed.). Washington, DC: Author.

National Association of Social Workers (NASW). (2011a). NASW chapters. Retrieved on June 21, 2011 from http:// www.naswdc.org/chapters/default.asp.

National Association of Social Workers (NASW). (2011b). NASW professional social work credentials and advanced practice specialty credentials. Retrieved on May 6, 2011 from http://www.naswdc.org/credentials/default.asp.

National Coalition for the Homeless. (2009). Fact sheets. Retrieved on May 17, 2011 from http://www.nationalhomeless. org/factsheets/.

National Conference of State Legislatures (NCSL). (2011). Same-sex marriage, civil unions and domestic partnerships. Retrieved on April 11, 2001 from http://www.ncsl.org/default. aspx?tabid=16430.

National Council on Family Relations (NCFR). (2011). What is family life education? Retrieved on May 30, 2011 from http:// www.ncfr.org/cfle-certification/what-family-life-education.

National Crime Prevention Association (NCPA). (2011). Cyber-bullying. Retrieved on June 26, 2011 from http://www.ncpc. org/cyberbullying.

National Crime Prevention Council (NCPC). (2011). Strategy: Gang prevention through community intervention with high-risk youth. Retrieved on June 26, 2011 from http://www.ncpc. org/topics/violent-crime-and-personal-safety/strategies/ strategy-gang-prevention-through-community-intervention-with-high-risk-youth.

National Gay and Lesbian Task Force. (2005). Why civil unions are not enough. Retrieved May 26, 2008 from http://www. thetaskforce.org/node/945/print.

National Institute on Aging. (2009). A good night's sleep. Retrieved on June 3, 2011 from http://www.nia.nih.gov/ healthinformation/publications/sleep.htm.

National Institute on Drug Abuse (NIDA). (2008). Prescription drug abuse chart. Retrieved November 12, 2008 from http:// www.drugabuse.gov/DrugPages/PrescripDrugsChart.html.

National Institute on Drug Abuse (NIDA). (2010a). NIDA InfoFacts: Club drugs (GHB, Ketamine, and Rohypnol. Retrieved on June 22, 2011 from http://www.drugabuse. gov/infofacts/clubdrugs.html.

National Institute on Drug Abuse (NIDA). (2010b). NIDA Info-Facts: MDNA (Ecstasy). Retrieved on June 22, 2011 from http://www.drugabuse.gov/infofacts/ecstasy.html.

National Institute on Drug Abuse (NIDA). (2011). Prescription drug abuse chart. Retrieved on June 22, 2011 from http://www.drugabuse.gov/DrugPages/PrescripDrugsChart.html.

National Institute of Mental Health (NIMH). (2007a). African Americans, Black Caribbeans, and Whites differ in depression risk and treatment. Retrieved on June 21, 2011 from http://www.nimh.nih.gov/science-news/2007/african-americans-black-caribbeans-and-whites-differ-in-depression-risk-treatment.shtml.

National Institute of Mental Health (NIMH). (2007b). National survey tracks prevalence of personality disorders in U.S. population. Retrieved on June 18, 2011 from http://www.nimh.nih.gov/science-news/2007/national-survey-tracks-prevalence-of-personality-disorders-in-us-population.shtml.

National Institute of Mental Health (NIMH). (2010). Just over half of Americans diagnosed with major depression receive care. Retrieved on June 21, 2011 from http://www.nimh.nih.gov/science-news/2010/just-over-half-of-americans-diagnosed-with-major-depression-receive-care.shtml.

National Mental Health Association. (2005a). Electroconvulsive therapy (ECT). Retrieved January 30, 2005 from http://www.nmha.org/infoctr/factsheets/ect.cfm.

National Mental Health Association (NMHA). (2008). Mental health America. Retrieved July 22, 2008 from http://www.nmha.org.

National Program Office on Self-Determination (NPOSD). (1998). *The Robert Wood Johnson Foundation initiative in self-determination for persons with developmental disabilities* [online]. Princeton, NJ: The Robert Wood Johnson Foundation. Retrieved from http://www.selfdetermination.org.

National Resource Center (NRC). (2010). On TANF & transportation. Retrieved on May 19, 2010 from http://nrccapitolclips.blogspot.com/2010/06/on-tanf-transportation.html.

Negroni-Rodriguez, L. K., & Morales, J. (2001). Individual and family assessment skills with Latino/Hispanic Americans. In R. Fong & S. Furuto (Eds.), *Culturally competent practice: Skills, interventions, and evaluations* (pp. 132–146). Boston: Allyn & Bacon.

Nemours Foundation. (2011). Individualized education programs (IEPs). Retrieved on June 24, 2011 from http://kidshealth.org/parent/growth/learning/iep.html.

Neukrug, E. (2008). *Theory, practice, and trends in human services: An introduction* (4th ed.). Belmont, CA: Brooks/Cole.

Neukrug, E. S. (2011). *Counseling theory and practice.* Belmont, CA: Brooks/Cole.

Newman, B. E., & Newman, P. R. (2012). *Development through life: A psychosocial approach* (11th ed.). Belmont, CA: Wadsworth.

Newman, C. (2000, August 10). Older, healthier and wealthier. *Washington Post*, A3.

Nichols, R., & Braun, K. L. (1996). *Death and dying in five Asian and Pacific Islander cultures: A preliminary study.* Honolulu: University of Hawaii, School of Public Health, Center on Aging.

Nichols, W. R. (Ed.). (1999). *Random House Webster's college dictionary* (2nd ed.). New York: Random House.

Nittle, N. K. (2011). *The national urban league: An overview.* Retrieved on May 10, 2011 from http://racerelations.about.com/od/organizations/a/NationalUrbanLeagueOverview.htm.

Nobles, W. W. (1976). African consciousness and black research: The consciousness of self. In L. M. King, V. DiOn, & W. Nobles (Eds.), *African philosophy: Assumptions and paradigms for research on black persons* (pp. 163–174). Los Angeles: Fanon Center.

Norman, E. (2000). Introduction: The strengths perspective and resiliency enhancement—A natural partnership. In E. Norman (Ed.), *Resiliency enhancement: Putting the strengths perspective into social work practice* (pp. 1–16). New York: Columbia.

O'Connor v. Donaldson, 422 U.S. 563 (1975).

Office of Family Assistance. (2009). *Fact sheet.* Washington, DC: Author. Retrieved on August 25, 2011 from www.acf.hhs.gov/opa/fact_sheets/tanf_factsheet.html.

Office of the Surgeon General. (2001). Youth violence: A report of the surgeon general. Retrieved February 6, 2005 from http://www.surgeongeneral.gov/library/youthviolence/.

Okazawa-Rey, M. (1998). Empowering poor communities of color: A self-help model. In L. M. Gutierrez, R. J. Parsons, & E. O. Cox (Eds.), *Empowerment in social work practice: A sourcebook.* Pacific Grove, CA: Brooks/Cole.

O'Neill, J. V. (1999, September). Social work turns back to the spiritual. *NASW News,* 3.

O'Neill, J. V. (2003, February). Private sector employs most members. *NASW News,* 8.

Orshansky, M. (1965). Measuring poverty. In *The social welfare forum: Proceedings of the 92nd annual forum of the national conference on social welfare.* New York: Columbia University Press.

Pace, P. R. (2006, September). Social workers vie for House, Senate seats. *NASW News, 51*(8), 1, 8.

Pace, P. R. (2010, June). Salary survey released. *NASW News, 55*(6), 8.

Pace, P. R. (2011, January). CSWE meeting addresses profession's sustainability. *NASW News,* 10.

Padavic, I., & Reskin, B. (2004). Moving up and taking charge. In L. Richardson, V. Taylor, & N. Whittier (Eds.), *Feminist frontiers* (6th ed., pp. 209–225). Boston: McGraw-Hill.

Paniagua, F. A. (2005). *Assessing and treating culturally diverse clients: A practical guide* (3rd ed.). Thousand Oaks, CA: Sage.

Papalia, D. E., Olds, S. W., & Feldman, R. D. (2009). *Human development* (11th ed.). Boston: McGraw-Hill.

Paplos, D. (2002). *About ECT—Electroconvulsive therapy.* Retrieved April 27, 2002 from http://www.medhelp.org/lib/ect.htm.

Parents Anonymous. (2007). Parents Anonymous prevents child abuse & neglect: New research demonstrates evidence-based program. Retrieved on May 30, 2001 from http://www.parentsanonymous.org/pahtml/eviBased1a.html.

Parsons, R. D. (2001). *The ethics of professional practice.* Boston: Allyn & Bacon.

Patchner, L. S., & DeWeaver, K. L. (2008). Disability: Neuro-cognitive disabilities. In T. Mizrahi & L. E. Davis (Editors-in-Chief), *Encyclopedia of Social Work* (Vol. 2, pp. 43–49). Washington, DC: NASW Press.

Patterson, C. J. (1995). Lesbian and gay parenthood. In M. H. Bornstein (Ed.), *Handbook of parenting: Vol. 4. Status and social conditions of parenting* (pp. 255–274). Mahwah, NJ: Erlbaum.

Patterson, G. R., DeBaryshe, B. D., & Ramsey, E. (1989). A developmental perspective on antisocial behavior. *American Psychologist, 44,* 329–335.

Patterson, L. E., & Welfel, E. R. (2000). *The counseling process* (5th ed.). Pacific Grove, CA: Brooks/Cole.

Paulus, M. D. (2000). Intervention with families. In A. A. Abbott (Ed.), *Alcohol, tobacco, and other drugs: Challenging myths, assessing theories, individualizing interventions* (pp. 305–340). Washington, DC: NASW Press.

Pawlak, E. J., Wozniak, D., & McGowen, M. (1999). Perspectives on groups for school social workers. In R. Constable, S. McDonald, & J. P. Flynn (Eds.), *School social work: Practice, policy, and research perspectives* (4th ed., pp. 356–375). Chicago: Lyceum.

Pecora, P. J., Whittaker, J. K., Maluccio, A. N., Barth, R. P., DePanfilis, D., with Plotnick, R. D. (2010). *The child welfare challenge: Policy, practice, and research* (3rd ed.). New Brunswick, NJ: Transaction.

Perkinson, R. R. (2008). *Chemical dependency counseling: A practical guide* (3rd ed.). Thousand Oaks, CA: Sage.

Perren, S., & Alsaker, F. D. (2006). Social behavior and peer relationships of victims, bullyvictims, and bullies in kindergarten. *Journal of Child Psychology and psychiatry, 47*(1), 45–57.

Phillips, N. K., & Straussner, S. L. (2002). *Urban social work: An introduction to policy and practice in cities.* Boston: Allyn & Bacon.

Philpott, D., & Hill, J. (2009). *The wounded warrior handbook: A resource guide for returning veterans.* Lanham, MD: Government Institutes.

Piccola, T. D., & Tracy, E. M. (2008). Family preservation and home-based services. In T. Mizrahi & L. E. Davis (Editors-in-Chief), *Encyclopedia of Social Work* (Vol. 2, pp. 200–206). Washington, DC: NASW Press.

Pickett, J. P. (Ed.). (2002). *The American Heritage college dictionary* (4th ed.). Boston: Houghton Mifflin.

Pietsch, J. H., & Braun, K. L. (2000). Autonomy, advance directives, and the patient self-determination act. In K. L. Braun, J. H. Pietsch, & P. L. Blanchette (Eds.), *Cultural issues in end-of-life decision making* (pp. 37–54). Thousand Oaks, CA: Sage.

Pincus, A., & Minahan, A. (1973). *Social work practice: Model and method.* Itasca, IL: Peacock.

Pinderhughes, E. (1995). Direct practice overview. In R. L. Edwards (Ed.), *Encyclopedia of social work* (19th ed., Vol. 1, pp. 2282–2292). Washington, DC: NASW Press.

Plassman, B. L. Langa, K. M., Fisher, G. G., Heeringa, S.G., Weir, D. R. Ofstedal, M. B., . . . Wallace, R. B. (2007). Prevalence of dementia in the United States: The aging, demographics, and memory study. *Neuroepidemiology, 29,* 125–132.

Pollard, W. L. (1995). Civil rights. In R. L. Edwards (Ed.), *Encyclopedia of social work* (19th ed., Vol. 1, pp. 740–751). Washington, DC: NASW Press.

PollingReport.com. (2010). Same sex marriage, gay rights. Retrieved on April 11, 2011 from http://www.pollingreport.com/civil.htm.

Popple, P. R. (1995). The social work profession: History. In R. L. Edwards (Ed.), *Encyclopedia of social work* (19th ed., Vol. 3, pp. 2282–2292). Washington, DC: NASW Press.

Popple, P. R., & Leighninger, L. (2002). *Social work, social welfare, and American society* (5th ed.). Boston: Allyn & Bacon.

Popple, P. R., & Leighninger, L. (2005). *Social work, social welfare, and American society* (6th ed.). Boston: Allyn & Bacon.

Popple, P. R., & Leighninger, L. (2011). *The policy-based profession: An introduction to social welfare policy analysis for social workers* (5th ed.). Boston: Allyn & Bacon.

Porter, E., & Walsh, M. (2005, February 9). Retirement turns into a rest stop as benefits dwindle. *New York Times.* Retrieved November 3, 2008 from http://www.nytimes.com/2005/02/09/business/09retire.html?_r=1&scp=1&sq=\retirement%20turns%20into%20a%20rest%20stop&st=cse&oref=slogin.

Potocky, M. (2008). Immigrants and refugees. In T. Mizrahi & L. E. Davis (Editors-in-Chief), *Encyclopedia of Social Work* (Vol. 2, pp. 441–445). Washington, DC: NASW Press.

Potocky-Tripodi, M. (2002). *Best practices for social work with refugees & immigrants.* New York: Columbia.

Potter, C. C. (1999). Violence and aggression in girls. In J. M. Jenson & M. O. Howard (Eds.), *Youth violence: Current research and recent practice innovations* (pp. 113–138). Washington, DC: NASW Press.

Potter, N., Schoetz, D., Esposito, R., & Thomas, P. (2007, April 17). Killer's note: "You caused me to do this." Retrieved on June 26, 2011 from http://abcnews.go.com/US/story?id=3048108&page=1.

Practitioners surveyed: Incomes increase. (2003, February). *NASW News,* pp. 1, 8.

Primm, A. B., Lima, B. R., & Rowe, C. L. (1996). Cultural and ethnic sensitivity. In W. R. Breakey (Ed.), *Integrated mental health services: Modern community psychiatry* (pp. 146–159). New York: Oxford University Press.

Proch, K., & Taber. M. A. (1987). Alienated adolescents in foster care. *Social Work Research & Abstracts, 23* (2), 9–13.

Quadagno, J. (2005). *Aging and the life course.* Boston: McGraw-Hill.

Quam, J. K. (1995). Biographies: Addams, Jane (1860–1935). In R. L. Edwards (Ed.), *Encyclopedia of social work* (19th ed., Vol. 3, pp. 2571–2572). Washington, DC: NASW Press.

Quiet's Corner. (2002a). Shirley Ardell Mason's (Sybil's) obituary. Retrieved April 27, 2002 from http://www.asarian.org/~quiet/sybilobit.html.

Quiet's Corner. (2002b). *Where multiple personal(ity) bodies are considered normal.* Retrieved April 27, 2002 from http://www.pooh.asarian.org/~quiet/.

Race, P. R. (2008, January). Evidence-based practice moves ahead. *NASW News,* 4.

Ragg, D. M. (2006). *Building family practice skills: Methods, strategies, and tools.* Belmont, CA: Brooks/Cole.

Rank, M. R. (2008). Poverty. In T. Mizrahi & L. E. Davis (Editors-in Chief), *Encyclopedia of Social Work* (Vol. 3, pp. 387–395). Washington, DC: NASW Press.

Rasheed, M. N., & Rasheed, J. M. (2008). Family: Practice interventions. In T. Mizrahi & L. E. Davis (Editors-in-Chief), *Encyclopedia of Social Work* (Vol. 2, pp. 182–191). Washington, DC: NASW Press.

Raskin, M. S., & Daley, D. C. (1991). Assessment of addiction problems. In M. S. Raskin & D. C. Daley (Eds.), *Treating the chemically dependent and their families* (pp. 22–56). Newbury Park, CA: Sage.

Rathus, S. A., Nevid, J. S., & Fichner-Rathus, L. (2011). *Human sexuality in a world of diversity* (8th ed.). Boston: Allyn & Bacon.

Rautkis, M. E., & Koeske, G. R. (1994). Maintaining social work morale: When supportive supervision is not enough. *Administration in Social Work, 18*(1), 39–60.

Reamer, F. G. (1998). *Ethical standards in social work.* Washington, DC: NASW Press.

Reamer, F. G. (2001). *Tangled relationships: Managing boundary issues in the human services.* New York: Columbia.

Reamer, F. G. (2006). *Ethical standards in social work: A review of the NASW Code of Ethics* (2nd ed.). Washington, DC: NASW Press.

Regulus, T. A. (1995). Gang violence. In R. L. Edwards (Ed.), *Encyclopedia of social work* (19th ed., Vol. 2, pp. 1045–1055). Washington, DC: NASW Press.

Reid, P. M. (1995). Social welfare history. In R. L. Edwards (Ed.), *Encyclopedia of social work* (19th ed., Vol. 3, pp. 2206–2225). Washington, DC: NASW Press.

Reinhardt, U. E. (2008, November 21). Why does U.S. health care cost so much? (Part II: Indefensible administrative costs). Retrieved on June 10, 2011 from http://economix.blogs. nytimes.com/2008/11/21/why-does-us-health-care-cost-so-much-part-ii-indefensible-administrative-costs/.

Renz-Beaulaurier, R. (1998). Empowering people with disabilities: The role of choice. In L. M. Gutierrez, R. J. Parsons, & E. O. Cox (Eds.), *Empowerment in social work practice: A sourcebook* (pp. 73–84). Pacific Grove, CA: Brooks/Cole.

Resnick, H. (1980a). Effecting internal change in human service organizations. In H. Resnick & R. J. Patti (Eds.), *Change from within: Humanizing social welfare organizations* (pp. 187–199). Philadelphia: Temple University Press.

Resnick, H. (1980b). Tasks in changing the organization from within. In H. Resnick & R. J. Patti (Eds.), *Change from within: Humanizing social welfare organizations* (pp. 200–216). Philadelphia: Temple University Press.

Riley, D. P. (1995). Family life education. In R. L. Edwards (Ed.), *Encyclopedia of social work* (19th ed., Vol. 2, pp. 960–965). Washington, DC: NASW Press.

Rizzo, V. M. (2008). Medicaid and Medicare. In T. Mizrahi & L. E. Davis (Editors-in-Chief), *Encyclopedia of Social Work* (Vol. 3, pp. 198–202). Washington, DC: NASW Press.

Rizzo, V. M., & Seidman, J. (2009). Section 2: A framework for health promotion in aging. Gero-Ed Center *Health Resource Review.* Retrieved on June 2, 2011 from http://www.cswe.org/ CentersInitiatives/GeroEdCenter/Programs/MAC/Reviews/ Health.aspx.

Roberts, A. R. (1995). Victim services and victim/witness assistance programs. In R. L. Edwards (Ed.), *Encyclopedia of social work* (19th ed., Vol. 3, pp. 2440–2444). Washington, DC: NASW Press.

Robinson, S., & Palus, N. (2001, April 30). An awful human trade. *Time,* 40–41.

Robison, W., & Reeser, L. C. (2000). *Ethical decision making in social work.* Boston: Allyn & Bacon.

Rocha, C. J. (2007). *Essentials of social work policy practice.* Hoboken, NJ: Wiley.

Rochefort, D. A. (1993). *From poor houses to homelessness: Policy analysis and mental health care.* Westport, CT: Auburn House.

Romsdahl, I. (1997, April 27). Sybil: Multiple personalities manufactured. Retrieved April 27, 2002 from http://www.mankato. msus.edu/dept/reporter/reparchive/04_27_97/news3.html.

Rothman, J. (2001). Approaches to community intervention. In J. Rothman, J. L. Erlich, & J. E. Tropman (Eds.), *Strategies of community intervention* (6th ed., pp. 27–64). Pacific Grove, CA: Brooks/Cole.

Rothman, J. (2007). Multi modes of intervention at the macro level. *Journal of Community Practice, 15*(4), 11–40.

Rothman, J. C. (2003). *Social work practice across disability.* Boston: Allyn & Bacon.

Rubin, A. (2008). *Practitioner's guide to using research for evidence-based practice.* Hoboken, NJ: Wiley.

Rubin, A., & Babbie, E. (2011). *Research methods for social work* (7th ed.). Belmont, CA: Brooks/Cole.

Rubin, K. H., Bukowski, W., & Parker, J. G. (2006). Peer interactions, relationships, and groups. In W. Damon & R. M. Lerner (Series Eds.), & N. Eisenberg (Vol. Ed.), *Handbook of child psychology: Vol. 3. Social, emotional, and personality development* (6th ed., pp. 571–645). New York: Wiley.

Runyon, M. D., & Urquiza, A. J. (2011). Child physical abuse. In J. E. B. Myers (Ed.), *The APSAC handbook on child maltreatment* (3rd ed., pp. 195–212). Thousand Oaks, CA: Sage.

Rycus, J. S., Hughes R. C., & Ginther, N. (1988). *Separation and placement in child protective services: A training curriculum.* Washington, DC: Child Welfare League of America.

Sabbatini, R. M. E. (2002). The history of shock therapy in psychiatry. Retrieved April 28, 2002 from http://www.epub.org. br/cm/n04/historia/shock_i/htm.

Sackheim, H. A., Devanand, D. P., & Nobler, M. S. (2002). Electroconvulsive therapy. Retrieved April 28, 2002 from http://www.acrip.org/g4/GN401000108/CH106.html.

Sahlins, J. (2010). *Social work practice in nursing homes: Creativity, leadership, and program development.* Chicago: Lyceum.

Saleebey, D. (2006a). Introduction: Power in the people. In D. Saleebey (Ed.), *The strengths perspective in social work practice* (4th ed., pp. 77–92). Boston: Allyn & Bacon.

Saleebey, D. (2006b). The strengths approach to practice. In D. Saleebey (Ed.), *The strengths perspective in social work practice* (4th ed., pp. 1–24). Boston: Allyn & Bacon.

Saleebey, D. (2009). *The strengths perspective in social work practice* (5th ed.). Boston: Allyn & Bacon.

Salmivalli, C., & Peets, K. (2009). Bullies, victims, and bully-victim relationships in middle childhood and adolescence. In K. H. Rubin, W. M. Bukowski, & B. Laursen (Eds.), *Handbook of peer interactions, relationships, and groups.* New York: Guilford.

Santiago-Rivera, A. L., Arredondo, P., & Gallardo-Cooper, M. (2002). *Counseling Latinos and la familia: A practical guide.* Thousand Oaks, CA: Sage.

Santrock, J. W. (2007). *A topical approach to life-span development* (3rd ed.). Boston: McGraw-Hill.

Santrock, J. W. (2009). *Child development* (12th ed.). Boston: McGraw-Hill.

Santrock, J. W. (2010a). *Adolescence* (13th ed.). New York: McGraw-Hill.

Santrock, J. W. (2010b). *A topical approach to life-span development* (5th ed.). New York: McGraw-Hill.

Scarr, S. (1998). American child care today. *American Psychologist, 53*(2), 95–108.

Schaefer, R. T. (2011). *Racial and ethnic groups* (12th ed.). Upper Saddle River, NJ: Prentice-Hall.

Schneider, R. L., & Lester, L. (2001). *Social work advocacy*. Pacific Grove, CA: Brooks/Cole.

Schram, B., & Mandell, B. R. (2000). *An introduction to human services* (4th ed.). Boston: Allyn & Bacon.

Schwartz, W. (1961). The social worker in the group. In W. Schwartz (Ed.), *New perspectives on services to groups: Theory, organization, practice* (pp. 104–111). New York: National Association of Social Workers.

Sciarra, D. T. (2001). School counseling in a multicultural society. In J. G. Ponterotto, J. M. Casas, L. A. Suzuki, & C. M. Alexander (Eds.), *Handbook of multicultural counseling* (2nd ed., pp. 701–728). Thousand Oaks, CA: Sage.

Sciarra, D. T. (2004). *School counseling: Foundations and contemporary issues*. Belmont, CA: Brooks/Cole.

Seeman, T. E., & Adler, N. (1998, Spring). Older Americans: Who will they be? *National Forum*, 22–25.

Segal, E., & Brzuzy, S. (1998). *Social welfare, policy, programs, and practice*. Itasca, IL: Peacock.

Segal, E. A. (2010). *Social welfare policy and social programs: A values perspective* (2nd ed.). Belmont, CA: Brooks/Cole.

Segal, E. A., Gerdes, K. E., & Steiner, S. (2004). *Social work: An introduction to the profession*. Belmont, CA: Brooks/Cole.

Segal, U. A. (2010). United States: The changing face of the United States of America. In U. A. Segal, D. Elliott, & N. S. Mayadas (Eds.), *Immigration worldwide: Policies, practices, and trends* (pp. 29–46). New York: Oxford.

Shapiro, J. P. (1995, September 11). Who cares how high her IQ really is? *U.S. News & World Report*, 59.

Shapiro v. Thompson, 364 U.S. 618 (1969).

Sharf, R. S. (2008). *Theories of psychotherapy and counseling: Concepts and cases* (4th ed.). Belmont, CA: Brooks/Cole.

Shaw, S. M., & Lee, J. (2009). *Women's voices: Feminist visions* (4th ed.). Boston: McGraw-Hill.

Sheafor, B. W., & Horejsi, C. R. (2008). *Techniques and guidelines for social work practice* (8th ed.). Boston: Allyn & Bacon.

Sheafor, B. W., & Horejsi, C. R. (2012). *Techniques and guidelines for social work practice* (9th ed.). Boston: Allyn & Bacon.

Sheridan, M. A., & White, B. J. (2008). Deafness and hardness of hearing. In T. Mizrahi & L. E. Davis (Editors-in-Chief), *Encyclopedia of Social Work* (Vol. 2, pp. 1–10). Washington, DC: NASW Press.

Shernoff, M. (1995). Gay men: Direct practice. In R. L. Edwards (Ed.), *Encyclopedia of social work* (19th ed., Vol. 3, pp. 1075–1085). Washington, DC: NASW Press.

Shlonsky, A., & Gambrill, E. D. (2005). Risk assessment in child welfare. In G. P. Mallon & P. M. Hess (Eds.), *Child welfare for the 21st century: A handbook of practices, policies, and programs* (pp. 302–318). New York: Columbia.

Shore, S. (2003). My life with Asperger syndrome. In R. W. Du Charme & T. P. Gullotta (Eds.), *Asperger syndrome: A guide for professionals and families* (pp. 189–209). New York: Kluwer Academic/Plenum.

Sigelman, C. K., & Rider, E. A. (2009). *Life-span development* (6th ed.). Belmont, CA: Wadsworth.

Simmons, C. A., & Rycraft, J. R. (2010). Ethical challenges of military social workers serving in a combat zone. *Social Work, 55*(1), 9–18.

Siporin, M. (1975). *Introduction to social work practice*. New York: Macmillan.

Slattery, J. M. (2004). *Counseling diverse clients: Bringing context into therapy*. Pacific Grove, CA: Brooks/Cole.

Sloan, A. (2000, July 3). The social security crackup. *Newsweek*, pp. 18–23.

Smith, C., & Darman, J. (2008). Juvenile delinquency. In T. Mizrahi & L. E. Davis (Editors-in-Chief), *Encyclopedia of Social Work* (Vol. 3, pp. 9–12). Washington, DC: NASW Press.

Smith, D. (2009, June 28). Frances Woofenden started skiing when she was 50. *The Palm Beach Post*. Retrieved on June 3, 2011 from http://www.theledger.com/article/20090628/news/906285058.

Smith, D. D., & Tyler, N. C. (2010). *Introduction to special education: Making a difference* (7th ed.). Upper Saddle River, NJ: Merrill.

Social Security Administration. (2010). Annual statistical supplement. Retrieved May 17, 2011 from http://www.ssa.gov/policy/docs/statcomps/supplement/.

Social Security Online. (2010a). Automatic increases. Retrieved on June 3, 2011 from http://www.ssa.gov/oact/cola/cbb.html.

Social Security Online. (2010b). SSI federal payment amounts. Retrieved on May 21, 2011 from http://www.ssa.gov/oact/cola/SSIamts.html.

Smith, R. F. (1995). Settlements and neighborhood centers. In R. L. Edwards (Ed.), *Encyclopedia of social work* (19th ed., Vol. 3, pp. 2129–2135). Washington, DC: NASW Press.

Smith, S. L., & Howard, J. A. (1999). *Promoting successful adoptions: Practice with troubled families*. Thousand Oaks, CA: Sage.

Smolowe, J. (1995, July 31). Noble aims, mixed results. *Time*, 54–55.

Snowden, L. R. (2000). The new world of practice in physical and mental health: Comorbidity, cultural competence, and managed care. In P. Allen-Meares & C. Garvin (Eds.), *The handbook of social work direct practice* (pp. 437–450). Thousand Oaks, CA: Sage.

Snowden, L. R., & Cheung, F. K. (1990). Use of inpatient mental health services by members of ethnic minority groups. *American Psychologist, 45*, 347–355.

Solomon, B. B. (2002). Social work practice with African Americans. In A. T. Morales & B. W. Sheafor (Eds.), *The many faces of social work clients* (pp. 295–315). Boston: Allyn & Bacon.

Solomon, P. (2008). Mental illness: Practice interventions. In T. Mizrahi & L. E. Davis (Editors-in-Chief), *Encyclopedia of Social Work* (Vol. 3, pp. 232–237). Washington, DC: NASW Press.

Spencer, M. S. (1999). Reducing racism in schools: Moving beyond the rhetoric. In P. L. Ewalt, E. M. Freeman, A. E. Fortune, D. L. Poole, & S. L. Witkin (Eds.), *Multicultural issues in social work: Practice and research* (pp. 151–163). Washington, DC: NASW Press.

Spergel, I. A., & Grossman, S. F. (2007). The Little Village Project: A community approach to the gang problem. *Social Work, 42*(5), 456–470.

Spraggins, E. E. (1998, September 28). Does managed care work? *Newsweek*, 61–66.

Springer, D. W., & Casey, K. A. (2008). Rehabilitation. In T. Mizrahi & L. E. Davis (Editors-in-Chief), *Encyclopedia of Social Work* (Vol. 3, pp. 499–505). Washington, DC: NASW Press.

Srabstein, J. C., McCarter, R. J., Shao, C., & Huang, Z. J. (2006). Morbidities associated with bullying behaviors in adolescents: School based study of American adolescents. *International Journal of Adolescent Medicine and Health, 18,* 587–596.

Stahlman, S. D., & Kisor, A. J. (2000). Nursing homes. In R. L. Schneider, N. P. Kropf, & A. J. Kisor (Eds.), *Gerontological social work: Knowledge, service settings, and special populations* (2nd ed., pp. 225–254). Pacific Grove, CA: Brooks/Cole.

Staples, L. H. (2004). In C. D. Garvin, L. M. Gutierrez, & M. J. Galinsky (Eds.)., *Handbook of social work with groups* (pp. 344–359). New York: Guilford.

Starbuck, D., Howell, J. C., & Lindquist, D. (2001, December). Hybrid and other modern gangs. *Bulletin of the Office of Juvenile Justice and Delinquency Prevention.* Washington, DC: U.S. Department of Justice, Office of Justice Programs.

Steffensmeier, D., & Demuth, S. (2000). Ethnicity and sentencing outcomes in U.S. federal courts: Who is punished more harshly? *American Sociological Review, 65,* 705–729.

Stein, J. A. (1995). *Residential treatment of adolescents & children: Issues, principles, and techniques.* Chicago: Nelson-Hall.

Steinberg, L., Bornstein, M. H., Vandell, D. L., & Rook, K. S. (2011a). *Lifespan development: Infancy through adulthood.* Belmont, CA: Wadsworth.

Steinberg, L., Vandell, D. L., & Bornstein, M. H. (2011b). *Development: Infancy through adolescence.* Belmont, CA: Wadsworth.

Steinhausen, H. C. (2002). The outcome of anorexia nervosa in the 20th century. *American Journal of Psychiatry, 159,* 1284–1293.

Stewart, P., & Goldfarb, K. P. (2007). Historical trends in the study of diverse families. In B. S. Trask & R. R. Hamon (Eds.), *Cultural diversity and families: Expanding perspectives* (pp. 3–19). Thousand Oaks, CA: Sage.

Stoesen, L. (2007a, February). Veterans aided with transition struggle. *NASW News,* 4.

Stoesen, L. (2007b, September). Putting the profession in public office. *NASW News,* 4.

Stoesen, L. (2007c, November). New Internet tools changing practice. *NASW News,* 4.

Stoolmiller, M., Eddy, J. M., & Reid, J. B. (2000). Detecting and describing preventive intervention effects in a universal school-based randomized trial targeting delinquent and violent behavior. *Journal of Consulting and Clinical Psychology, 68,* 296–306.

Straussner, S. L. A., & Isralowitz, R. (2008). Alcohol and drug problems: Overview. In T. Mizrahi & L. E. Davis (Editors-in-Chief), *Encyclopedia of Social Work* (Vol. 1, pp. 121–130). Washington, DC: NASW Press.

Strom-Gottfried, K. (2007). *Straight talk about professional ethics.* Chicago: Lyceum.

Strong, B., DeVault, C., Sayad, B. W., & Yarber, W. L. (2005). *Human sexuality: Diversity in contemporary America* (5th ed.). Boston: McGraw-Hill.

Stroup, H. (1986). *Social welfare pioneers.* Chicago: Nelson-Hall.

Stuart, P. H. (2008). Social welfare: History. In T. Mizrahi & L. E. Davis (Editors-in-Chief), *Encyclopedia of Social Work* (Vol. 4, pp. 156–164). Washington, DC: NASW Press.

Sue, D. W. (1992). The challenge of multiculturalism: The road less traveled. *American Counselor, 1*(1), 6–15.

Sue, D. W. (2006). *Multicultural social work practice.* Hoboken, NJ: Wiley.

Sue, D. W., Carter, R. T., Casas, J. M., Fouad, N. A., Ivey, A. E., Jensen, M., LaFromboise, T., Manese, J. E., Ponterotto, J. G., & Vazquez-Nutall, E. (1998). *Multicultural counseling competencies: Individual and organizational development.* Thousand Oaks, CA: Sage.

Sue, D. W., & Sue, D. (2008). *Counseling the culturally diverse: Theory and practice* (5th ed.). Hoboken, NJ: Wiley.

Sullivan, W. P. (2008). Disability: Psychiatric disabilities. In T. Mizrahi & L. E. Davis (Editors-in-Chief), *Encyclopedia of Social Work* (Vol. 2, pp. 55–60). Washington, DC: NASW Press.

Survey data show earnings increased. (2004, October). *NASW News,* pp. 1, 8.

Sussman, L. K., Robins, L. N., & Earls, F. (1987). Treatment-seeking for depression by black and white Americans. *Social Science and Medicine, 24,* 187–196.

Swigonski, M. E. (1995, Winter). Claiming a lesbian identity as an act of empowerment. *Affilia, 10*(4).

Syme, G. (2003). *Dual relationships in counseling & psychotherapy.* Thousand Oaks, CA: Sage.

Taylor, P. (2005). *Diagnosis & treatment of substance-related disorders: The DECLARE model.* Boston: Pearson.

Taylor-Brown, S. (1995). HIV/AIDS: Direct practice. In R. L. Edwards (Ed.), *Encyclopedia of social work* (19th ed., Vol. 2, pp. 1291–1305). Washington, DC: NASW Press.

Terrell, P. (2008). Workers' compensation. In T. Mizrahi & L. E. Davis (Editors-in-Chief), *Encyclopedia of Social Work* (Vol. 4, pp. 304–306). Washington, DC: NASW Press.

The horror of electroshock therapy. (2000, March 1). *Extra: Daily News.* Retrieved April 27, 2002 from http://extratv. warnerbros.com.cmp/spotlight/2000/03_01b.htm.

Thompson, C. L., & Henderson, D. A. (2007). *Counseling children* (7th ed.). Belmont, CA: Brooks/Cole.

Tice, C. J. (2005). Celebrating rural communities: A strengths assessment. In L. H. Ginsberg (Ed.), *Social work in rural communities* (4th ed., pp. 95–108). Alexandria, VA: CSWE Press.

Tice, C. J., & Perkins, K. (2002). *The faces of social policy: A strengths perspective.* Pacific Grove, CA: Brooks/Cole.

Tolan, P. H., Gorman-Smith, D., & Henry, D. B. (2003). The developmental ecology of urban males' youth violence. *Developmental Psychology 39,* 274–291.

Torres-Gil, F. M., & Puccinelli, M. A. (1995). Aging: Public policy issues and trends. In R. L. Edwards (Ed.), *Encyclopedia of social work* (19th ed., Vol. 1, pp. 159–164). Washington, DC: NASW Press.

Toseland, R. W. (1995). Aging: Direct practice. In R. L. Edwards (Eds.), *Encyclopedia of social work* (19th ed., Vol. 1, pp. 153–159). Washington, DC: NASW Press.

Toseland, R. W., & Horton, H. (2008). Group work. In T. Mizrahi & L. E. Davis (Editors-in-Chief), *Encyclopedia of Social Work* (Vol. 2, pp. 298–308). Washington, DC: NASW Press.

Toseland, R. W., & Rivas, R. F. (2012). *An introduction to group work practice* (7th ed.). Boston: Allyn & Bacon.

Tower, K. D. (1994, March). Consumer-centered social work practice: Restoring client self-determination. *Social Work, 39*(2), 191–196.

Tracy, E. M. (1995). Family preservation and home-based services. In R. L. Edwards (Ed.), *Encyclopedia of social work* (19th ed., Vol. 2, pp. 973–983). Washington, DC: NASW Press.

Tracy, E. M. (2002). Working with and strengthening social networks. In A. R. Roberts & G. J. Greene (Eds.), *Social workers' desk reference* (pp. 402–405). Washington, DC: NASW Press.

Tracy, E. M., Haapala, D. A., Kinney, J. M., & Pecora, P. J. (1991). Intensive family preservation services: A strategic response to families in crisis. In E. M. Tracy, D. A. Haapala, J. M. Kinney, & P. J. Pecora (Eds.), *Intensive family preservation services: An instructional sourcebook*. Cleveland, OH: Case Western Reserve University.

Tracy, M. B., & Ozawa, M. N. (1995). Social Security. In R. L. Edwards (Ed.), *Encyclopedia of social work* (19th ed., Vol. 3, pp. 2186–2195). Washington, DC: NASW Press.

Trattner, W. I. (1999). *From poor law to welfare state: A history of social welfare in America* (6th ed.). New York: Free Press.

Treguer, A. (1992). The Chicanos—Muralists with a message. *UNESCO Courier, 45*, 22–24.

Tripodi, T., & Lalayants, M. (2008). Research: Overview. In T. Mizrahi & L. E. Davis (Editors-in-Chief), *Encyclopedia of Social Work* (Vol. 3, pp. 512–520). Washington, DC: NASW Press.

Tully, C. T. (2000). *Lesbians, gays, and the empowerment perspective*. New York: Columbia University Press.

Tully, C. T. (2001). Gay and lesbian persons. In A. Gitterman (Ed.), *Handbook of social work practice with vulnerable and resilient populations* (2nd ed., pp. 582–627). New York: Columbia University Press.

Uba, L. (1994). *Asian Americans: Personality patterns, identity, and mental health*. New York: Guilford Press.

United Nations (UN). (1948). Universal Declaration of Human Rights. Retrieved June 28, 2008 from http://www.un.org/Overview/rights.html.

Urban Institute. (2010). TANF: Temporary assistance for needy families. Retrieved on May 21, 2011 from http://www.urban.org/welfare/tanf.cfm.

U.S. Census Bureau. (2005). 65+ in the United States: 2005. Retrieved on June 3, 2011 from http://www.census.gov/prod/2006pubs/p23-209.pdf.

U.S. Census Bureau. (2009). *Statistical abstract of the United States: 2010.* (129th ed.). Washington, DC: Author.

U.S. Census Bureau. (2010). *Statistical abstract of the United States: 2011* (130th ed.). Washington, DC: Author.

U.S. Department of Health & Human Services (UHHS). (1999). *Mental health: A report of the Surgeon General—-Executive summary*. Rockville, MD: Author. Retrived from http://www.nimh.nih.gov.

U.S. Department of Health & Human Services (HHS). (2010). Fiscal year 2010 budget in brief. Retrieved on May 23, 2011 from http://dhhs.gov/asfr/ob/docbudget/2010budgetinbriefm.html.

U.S. Department of Health & Human Services (HHS). (2011). The 2011 HHS poverty guidelines. Retrieved on May 21, 2011 from http://aspe.hhs.gov/poverty/11poverty.shtml.

U.S. Department of Housing and Urban Development. (2011). Federal definition of homelessness. Retrieved on August 25, 2011 from http://portal.hud.gov/hudportal/HUD?src=/topics/homelessness/definition.

U.S. Department of Justice Community Relations Service. (2001, December). Hate crime: The violence of intolerance. Retrieved February 5, 2005 from http://www.usdoj.gov/crs/pubs/crs_pub_hate_crime_bulletin_1201.htm.

U.S. Department of Labor. (2009). Occupational outlook handbook 2010–2011: Social workers. Retrieved on May 7, 2011 from http://www.bls.gov/oco/ocos060.htm.

U.S. Department of Veterans Affairs (VA). (2010). Treatment for PTSD. Retrieved on June 16, 2011 from http://www.ptsd.va.gov/public/pages/treatment-ptsd.asp.

U.S. Department of Veterans Affairs (VA). (2011a). *About VHA*. Retrieved on May 5, 2011 from http://www.va.gov/health/aboutVHA.asp.

U.S. Department of Veterans Affairs (VA). (2011b). Cognitive processing therapy. Retrieved on June 16, 2011 from http://www.ptsd.va.gov/public/pages/cognitive_processing_therapy.asp.

U.S. Department of Veterans Affairs (VA). (2011c). VA home. Retrieved on June 9, 2011 from http://www.va.gov/.

U.S. Department of Veterans Affairs (VA). (2011d). VA social work. Retrieved on June 9, 2011 from http://www.socialwork.va.gov/index.asp.

U.S. Office of the Surgeon General, Report on Mental Health. (2001). Adults and mental health treatment of mood disorders. Retrieved April 28, 2002 from http://www.loren.bennett.org/osgtreat.htm.

U.S. Psychiatric Rehabilitation Association (USPRA). (2004). Who we are. Retrieved February 12, 2005 from http://www.iapsrs.org/.

Usita, P. M. (2007). Parent-child ties of culturally diverse aging families. In B. S. Trask & R. R. Hamon (Eds.), *Cultural diversity and families: Expanding perspectives* (pp. 154–169). Thousand Oaks, CA: Sage.

Vallianatos, C. (2001, January). Managed care is faulted. *NASW News, 46*(1), 7.

Vallianatos, C. (2001, May). Profession extolled on Hill. *NASW News, 46*(5), 1.

Van Arsdale, S. (2002, January 8). Sybil: Famous multiple-personality case was stranger in our midst. *Ace Weekly*. Retrieved from http://www.aceweekly.com/Backissues_ACE-Weekly/010802/cover_story010802.html.

Van Den Bergh, N., & Cooper, L. B. (1986). *Feminist visions for social work*. Washington, DC: NASW Press.

Van Wormer, K., & Davis, D. R. (2003). *Addiction treatment: A strengths perspective*. Pacific Grove, CA: Brooks/Cole.

Van Wormer, K., & Davis, D. R. (2008). *Addiction treatment: A strengths perspective* (2nd ed.). Belmont, CA: Brooks/Cole.

Vandiver, V. L. (2008). Managed care. In T. Mizrahi & L. E. Davis (Editors-in-Chief), *Encyclopedia of Social Work* (Vol. 3, pp. 144–148). Washington, DC: NASW Press.

Vandivort-Warren, R. (1998). How social workers can manage managed care. In G. Schamess & A. Lightburn (Eds.), *Human managed care?* (pp. 255–267). Washington, DC: NASW Press.

Velleman, R. (2001). *Counseling for alcohol problems* (2nd ed.). Thousand Oaks, CA: Sage.

Voices of Experience. (2002). *Electroshock therapy: First-person stories from our community*. Retrieved April 27, 2002 from http://bipolar.about.com/library/uc/uc-shock1.htm.

Walker, D. (2002). Forensic social work: A developing field of practice. *The New Social Worker, 9*(3), 18–20.

Walsh, J., & Bentley, K. J. (2002). Psychopharmacology basics. In A. R. Roberts & G. J. Greene (Eds.), *Social workers' desk reference* (pp. 646–651). New York: Oxford.

Walsh, J. A. (1990). From clinician to supervisor: Essential ingredients for training. *Families in Society, 71*(2), 82–87.

Watkins, J. M., & Holmes, J. (2008). Council on Social Work Education. In T. Mizrahi & L. E. Davis (Editors-in-Chief), *Encyclopedia of Social Work* (Vol. 1, pp. 457–460). Washington, DC: NASW Press.

Watkins, M. L. (2002). Listening to girls: A study in resilience. In R. R. Greene (Ed.), *Resiliency: An integrated approach to practice, policy, and research* (pp. 115–131). Washington, DC: NASW Press.

Watkins, S. A. (1990). The Mary Ellen myth: Correcting child welfare history. *Social Work, 35*(6), 500–503.

Watkins, T. R. (2004). Natural helping networks: Assets for rural communities. In T. L. Scales & C. L. Streeter (Eds.), *Rural social work: Building and sustaining community assets* (pp. 65–76). Belmont, CA: Brooks/Cole.

Weatherley, R. A., & Cartoof, V. G. (1988). Helping single adolescent parents. In C. Chilman, E. Nunnally, & F. Cox (Eds.), *Variant family forms*. Newbury Park, CA: Sage.

Weaver, H. N. (2003). Cultural competence with First Nations Peoples. In D. Lum (Ed.), *Culturally competent practice: A framework for understanding diverse groups and justice issues* (2nd ed., pp. 197–216). Pacific Grove, CA: Brooks/Cole.

Weaver, H. N. (2005). *Explorations in cultural competence: Journeys to the four directions*. Pacific Grove, CA: Brooks/Cole.

Weaver, H. N. (2007). Cultural competence with First Nations Peoples. In D. Lum (Ed.), *Culturally competent practice: A framework for understanding diverse groups and justice issues* (3rd ed., pp. 254–275). Belmont, CA: Brooks/Cole.

Weaver, H. N. (2008). Native Americans: Overview. In T. Mizrahi & L. E. Davis (Editors-in-Chief), *Encyclopedia of Social Work* (Vol. 3, pp. 295–299). Washington, DC: NASW Press.

Webster.edu. (2005). Mary Ellen Richmond. Retrieved June 14, 2005 from http://www.webster.edu/~woolflm/richmond.html.

Wegscheider, S. (1981). *Another chance: Hope and health for the alcoholic family*. Palo Alto, CA: Science Behavior Books.

Weinbach, R. W., & Kuehner, K. M. (1985). Selecting the provider of continuing education for child welfare agencies. *Child Welfare, 64*, 477–488.

Weiner, T. (2001, January 5). Terrific news in Mexico City: Air is sometimes breathable. *The New York Times*. Retrieved from http://www.nytimes.com/2001/01/05/world/05MEI.html.

Weismiller, T., & Rome, S. H. (1995). Social workers in politics. In R. L. Edwards (Editor-in-Chief), *Encyclopedia of social work* (19th ed., Vol. 3, pp. 2305–2313).

Welch, K. (2011). *THINK human sexuality*. Boston: Allyn & Bacon.

Wells, K., et al. (1989). Detection of depressive disorder for patients receiving prepaid or fee-for-service care: Results from the medical outcomes study. *Journal of the American Medical Association, 262*, 3298–3302.

Wells, S. J. (2008). Child abuse and neglect. In T. Mizrahi & L. E. Davis (Editors-in-Chief), *Encyclopedia of Social Work* (Vol. 1, pp. 236–240). Washington, DC: NASW Press.

Whealin, J. M., DeCarvalho, L. R., & Vega, E. M. (2008a). *Clinician's guide to treating stress after war*. Hoboken, NJ: John Wiley.

Whealin, J. M., DeCarvalho, L. R., & Vega, E. M. (2008b). *Strategies for managing stress after war: Veteran's workbook and guide to wellness*. Hoboken, NJ: John Wiley.

Wheeler, J., Newring, K., & Draper, C. (2008). Transvestic fetishism: Psychopathology and theory. In D. Laws & W. O'Donohue (Eds.), Sexual deviance: Theory, assessment and treatment (2nd ed., pp. 272–285). New York: Guilford Press.

White House. (2005a). 4. Modernize and reform Social Security. Retrieved January 8, 2005 from http://www.whitehouse.gov/news/usbudget/blueprint/bud04.html.

White House. (2005b). 5. Modernize and reform Medicare. Retrieved January 8, 2005 from http://www.whitehouse.gov/news/usbudget/blueprint/bud04.html.

WhiteHouse.gov. (2011a). Foreign policy. Retrieved on May 12, 2011 from http://www.whitehouse.gov/issues/foreign-policy.

WhiteHouse.gov. (2011b). Health care reform in action. Retrieved on May 11, 2011 from http://www.whitehouse.gov/healthreform.

Whitelaw, K. (2003, July 21). In death's shadow. *U.S. News & World Report*, 17–20.

Whiteman, V. L. (2001). *Social Security: What every human services professional should know*. Boston: Allyn & Bacon.

Wilensky, H. L., & Lebeaux, C. N. (1965). *Industrial society and social welfare*. New York: Free Press.

Williams, J. B. W. (2008). Diagnostic and statistical manual of mental disorders. In T. Mizrahi & L. E. Davis (Editors-in-Chief), *Encyclopedia of Social Work* (Vol. 2, pp. 26–31). Washington, DC: NASW Press.

Williams, J. H., & Van Dorn, R. A. (1999). Delinquency, gangs, and youth violence. In J. M. Jenson & M. O. Howard (Eds.), *Youth violence: Current research and recent practice innovations* (pp. 199–225). Washington, DC: NASW Press.

Williams, M. (1999, April 25). Diary reveals school attack "timeline." *Milwaukee Journal Sentinel*, 1A, 18A.

Wilson, G. T., Grilo, C. M., & Vitousek, K. M. (2007, April). Psychological treatment of eating disorders. *American Psychologist, 62*(3), 199–216.

Wimberly, E. P. (1991). *African American pastoral care*. Nashville, TN: Abingdon Press.

Winslow, C. E. A. (1920, March). The untilled field of public health. *Modern Medicine, 2*, 183–191.

Winton, M. A., & Mara, B. A. (2001). *Child abuse and neglect: Multidisciplinary approaches*. Boston: Allyn & Bacon.

Wirth, L. (1945). The problem of minority groups. In R. Linton (Ed.), *The science of man in the world crisis* (pp. 347–372). New York: Columbia University Press.

Women in History. (2005, June 14). Jane Addams biography. Lakewood Public Library. Retrieved June 14, 2005 from http://www.lkwdpl.org/wihohio/adda-jan.htm.

Wong, I. (2008). Homelessness. In T. Mizrahi & L. E. Davis (Editors-in-Chief), *Encyclopedia of Social Work* (Vol. 2, pp. 377–383). Washington, DC: NASW Press.

Wood, K. M., & Dunn, P. C. (2000). Criteria for selecting theories and models for ATOD practice. In A. A. Abbott (Ed.), *Alcohol, tobacco, and other drugs: Challenging myths, assessing theories, individualizing interventions* (pp. 20–43). Washington, DC: NASW Press.

Woodman, N. J. (1995). Lesbians: Direct practice. In R. L. Edwards (Ed.), *Encyclopedia of social work* (19th ed., Vol. 2, pp. 1597–1604). Washington, DC: NASW Press.

Woodward, K. L., & Johnson, P. (1995, December 11). The advent of Kwanzaa: Will success spoil an African-American fest? *Newsweek*, 88.

World Health Organization (WHO). (2002). *Active ageing: A policy framework*. Geneva, Switzerland: Author. Retrieved on June3, 2011 from http://whqlibdoc.who.int/hq/2002/who_nmh_nph_02.8.pdf.

Wyatt v. Stickney, 324 F. Supp. 781 (1971).

Yamashiro, G., & Matsuoka, J. K. (1997). Help-seeking among Asian and Pacific Americans: A multiperspective analysis. *Social Work*, 42(2), 176–186.

Yarber, W. L., Sayad, B. W., & Strong, B. (2010). *Human sexuality: Diversity in contemporary America* (7th ed.). Boston: McGraw-Hill.

Yeo, G., & Hikoyeda, N. (2000). Cultural issues in end-of-life decision making among Asians and Pacific Islanders in the United States. In K. L. Braun, J. H. Pietsch, & P. L. Blanchette (Eds.), *Cultural issues in end-of-life decision making* (pp. 101–125). Thousand Oaks, CA: Sage.

Yessian, M. R., & Broskowski, A. (1983). Generalists in human service systems: Their problems and prospects. In R. M. Kramer & H. Specht (Eds.), *Readings in community organization practice* (pp. 180–197). Englewood Cliffs, NJ: Prentice-Hall.

Yung, B., & Hammond, R. (1998). Breaking the cycle: A culturally sensitive violence prevention program for African-American children. In L. Lutzker (Ed.), *Handbook of child abuse research and treatments*. New York: Plenum Press.

Zastrow, C., & Kirst-Ashman, K. K. (2010). *Understanding human behavior and the social environment* (8th ed.). Belmont, CA: Brooks/Cole.

Zhang, W. (2010). Use with care—Culturally incorrect attending can be rude. In A. E. Ivey, M. B. Ivey, & C. P. Zalaquett (Eds.), *Intentional interviewing & counseling* (7th ed., p. 76). Belmont, CA: Brooks/Cole.

Zimmerman, S. (2008). Adults: Group care. In T. Mizrahi & L. E. Davis (Editors-in-Chief), *Encyclopedia of Social Work* (Vol. 1, pp. 56–59). Washington, DC: NASW Press.

Zuniga, M. E. (1995). Aging: Social work practice. In R. L. Edwards (Ed.), *Encyclopedia of social work* (19th ed., Vol. 1, pp. 173–183). Washington, DC: NASW Press.

Name Index

Subject Index